HOLT
ELEMENTS OF
LITERATURE

Fourth Course

HOLT, RINEHART AND WINSTON

A Harcourt Education Company

Orlando • Austin • New York • San Diego • Toronto • London

EDITORIAL
Editorial Vice President: Laura Wood
Project Directors: Kathleen Daniel, Mescal Evler
Executive Book Editors: Kristine E. Marshall, Laura Mongello, Katie Vignery
Senior Book Editors: Amy Fleming, Julie Barnett Hoover, Karen Peterfreund, Kathryn Rogers
Senior Product Manager: Don Wulbrecht
Managing Editor: Marie Price
Editorial Staff: Susan Kent Cakars, Gail Coupland, Randy Dickson, Ann Michelle Gison, Sean W. Henry, Kerry Johnson, Karen Kolar, Jennifer Schwan, Crystal Wirth
Copyediting Manager: Michael Neibergall
Copyediting Supervisors: Kristen Azzara, Mary Malone
Copyeditors: Christine Altgelt, Elizabeth Dickson, Emily Force, Leora Harris, Anne Heausler, Julia Thomas Hu, Kathleen Scheiner, Nancy Shore
Associate Managing Editor: Elizabeth LaManna
Editorial Support: Christine Degollado, Betty Gabriel, Danielle Greer, Mark Koenig, Erik Netcher, Janet Jenkins, Gloria Shahan, Emily Stern
Editorial Permissions: Ann Farrar, Susan Lowrance

Index: Robert Zolnerzak

ART, DESIGN, AND PRODUCTION
Director: Athena Blackorby
Senior Design Director: Betty Mintz
Series Design: Kirchoff/Wohlberg, Inc.
Design and Electronic Files: MorganCain & Associates; Preface, Inc.
Photo Research: MorganCain & Associates; Photosearch, Inc.
Production Manager: Carol Trammel
Sr. Production Coordinators: Belinda Lopez, Michael Roche
Prepress: Progressive Information Technologies
Manufacturing: R. R. Donnelley & Sons Company, Willard, Ohio

COVER
Photo Credits: (Inset) *Valley Farms* (ca. 1933–1934) by Ross Dickinson. Oil on canvas. Copyright Smithsonian American Art Museum, Washington, D.C./Art Resource, NY. (Background) Farmland. © Adam Jones/Getty Images.

Language Arts Standards

The following chart lists Pennsylvania's **Academic Standards for Reading, Writing, and Speaking and Listening,** which you will be required to master by the end of the eleventh grade. As a tenth grader, you need to continue working to achieve these standards.

The standards are divided into eight categories. Each standard appears in a yellow box. Below each standard, you will find either an explanation or a more detailed list of the standard's content. To the right of each standard, you will find a specific example of how *Elements of Literature* helps you master the standard.

1.1.   LEARNING TO READ INDEPENDENTLY

1.1.11.A. Locate various texts, media and traditional resources for assigned and independent projects before reading.

This textbook presents information on locating various kinds of texts in a library, on the Internet, or through community resources. You'll find strategies for identifying appropriate texts for a specific school purpose or for your own enjoyment and information. You'll get practice in locating traditional resources by using the card catalog and the *Readers' Guide to Periodical Literature,* as well as practice using almanacs, media sources, and electronic resources, such as the Internet.

EXAMPLE: Locating Texts for Different Purposes

You will find suggestions for independent reading of fiction and nonfiction at the end of each collection.

Page 206 discusses library and Internet resources. The informational text that follows, "An Ancient Enemy Gets Tougher" (pages 207–209), shows you how to use a Web site with multimedia and interactive features.

The Writing Workshop "Writing a Research Paper" (pages 690–709) contains a list of library and community resources that you can use for assigned and independent projects.

1.1.11.B. Analyze the structure of informational materials explaining how authors used these to achieve their purposes.

To master this standard, you'll learn about the ways authors help you locate and comprehend information. You'll practice identifying organizational structures such as logical order and order of importance. You'll analyze features of print material (titles, subtitles, headings, tables of contents, indices) and graphic organizers, such as charts and diagrams.

EXAMPLE: Analyzing Structure

The Handbook of Reading and Informational Terms, pages 993–1007, defines and explains the various kinds of organizational structures. Each Handbook entry includes page numbers on which examples can be found. For a quick summary, see the entry for "Text Structures," pages 1006–1007.

Collection 11 (pages 907–939) focuses on the structure of consumer, workplace, and technical documents.

1.1.11.C. Use knowledge of root words and words from literary works to recognize and understand the meaning of new words during reading. Use these words accurately in speaking and writing.

You'll find clues to the meaning of a word by studying its **root,** the part that establishes its core meaning. The **context** of a new word can also give you clues to its meaning.

EXAMPLE: Learning New Words

Root: The root *–ortho–* [Greek] means "straight." You can find this root in *orthopedics* and *orthodontics.* For a chart of Greek and Latin roots, see page 1046 and pages 1003–1004.

Context: Many exercises in this textbook give you practice in determining the meaning of a new word from its context, the text surrounding the word. See, for example, the Vocabulary Development on page 432, "Context Clues: Filling in the Blanks."

1.1.11.D. Identify, describe, evaluate and synthesize the essential ideas in text. Assess those reading strategies that were most effective in learning from a variety of texts.

Finding and evaluating essential ideas uses reading skills such as predicting, questioning, visualizing, retelling, and finding implicitly stated main ideas.

EXAMPLE: Focusing on What's Important

In Reading Matters (pages 941–953) you'll find tips to help you understand essential ideas in text that is difficult to read.

The Skills Review pages at the end of collections emphasize using reading strategies. See, for instance, page 69, which compares essential ideas in two articles on the same subject.

1.1.11.E. Establish a reading vocabulary by identifying and correctly using new words acquired through the study of their relationships to other words. Use a dictionary or related reference.

You can expand your vocabulary by finding words, such as synonyms, homographs, and homophones, that are related in various ways to other words.

EXAMPLE: Building Vocabulary

Several exercises in every chapter help you develop your reading vocabulary. You'll also find practice activities that show you how to map unfamiliar words. See "Word Mapping: How to Own a New Word" on page 192 and "Word Mapping: Pinning Down Meaning" on page 417.

1.1.11.F. Understand the meaning of and apply key vocabulary across the various subject areas.

Many subjects have their own key words, such as *herbivore* in science. Applying a knowledge of word derivations is one way to figure out what words mean.

EXAMPLE: Learning Key Vocabulary

"Jargon: Legalese—Words That Lawyers Use" on page 292 and "Technical Vocabulary—Widgets, Whatsits, Thingamajigs" on page 365 provide practice recognizing and understanding technical vocabulary.

See the Vocabulary Development lesson on page 42 for an introduction to **etymology,** tracing the derivation, or origin, of a word to find its meaning.

1.1.11.G. Demonstrate after reading understanding and interpretation of both fiction and nonfiction text, including public documents.

This standard asks you to (1) Make, and support with evidence, assertions about texts. (2) Compare and contrast texts using themes, settings, characters and ideas. (3) Make extensions to related ideas, topics or information. (4) Assess the validity of the document based on context. (5) Analyze the positions, arguments and evidence in public documents. (6) Evaluate the author's strategies. (7) Critique public documents to identify strategies common in public discourse.

EXAMPLE: Demonstrating Understanding

Collection 4, pages 229–311, contains several lessons that deal with comparing themes in fiction and nonfiction texts. This collection also focuses on analyzing and evaluating arguments.

On page 283, you are asked to compare and contrast themes in a short story and a newspaper article.

For help in critiquing public discourse strategies, see "Analyzing and Evaluating Speeches" and the Skills Review that follows it, pages 898–903.

1.1.11.H. Demonstrate fluency and comprehension in reading.

This standard includes (1) Read familiar materials aloud with accuracy. (2) Self-correct mistakes. (3) Use appropriate rhythm, flow, meter and pronunciation. (4) Read a variety of genres and types of text. (5) Demonstrate comprehension.

EXAMPLE: Reading Fluently

In Reading Matters (pages 941–953), you'll find many ideas for ways to improve—and vary—your reading methods and your reading speed. See, especially, "Improving Your Reading Rate," on pages 951–953.

1.2. READING CRITICALLY IN ALL CONTENT AREAS

1.2.11.A. Read and understand essential content of informational texts and documents in all academic areas.

This standard includes (1) Differentiate fact from opinion across a variety of texts using accurate information, coherent arguments and points of view. (2) Distinguish between essential and nonessential information, identifying the use of proper references or authorities and propaganda techniques. (3) Use teacher and student established criteria for making decisions and drawing conclusions. (4) Evaluate text organization and content to determine the author's purpose and effectiveness.

EXAMPLE: Separating Fact from Opinion

The following examples are from a persuasive text, "Call of the Wild—Save Us!" (pages 579–582):

Fact: "Each day we lose roughly fifty to one hundred wildlife species." (page 579)

Opinion: "If wildlife can pay its way in the marketplace, they will listen; if not, then they won't." (page 580)

For more about facts and opinions, see pages 577 and 1000–1001.

For help evaluating an argument, see "Evaluating Arguments: Pro and Con" on pages 284–285.

1.2.11.B. Use and understand a variety of media and evaluate the quality of material produced.

This standard asks you to (1) Select appropriate electronic media for research and evaluate the quality of the information received. (2) Explain how the techniques used in electronic media modify traditional forms of discourse for different purposes. (3) Use, design and develop a media project to demonstrate understanding (e.g., a major writer or literary period or movement).

EXAMPLE: Using and Understanding Media

For information on using a Web site, turn to "An Ancient Enemy Gets Tougher" (pages 206–210).

For help in comparing and evaluating media, see the Writing Workshop "Comparing Media Genres" (pages 382–389), especially the chart on page 383, which lists points of comparison for analyzing media.

Another Writing Workshop, "Comparing a Play and a Film" (pages 890–897), gives you tips for understanding both genres.

1.2.11.C. Produce work in at least one literary genre that follows the conventions of the genre.

This standard requires you to create a short story, poem, play, or essay that follows the rules of that particular type of writing.

EXAMPLE: Producing Your Own Work

The Writing Workshop "Writing a Short Story" (pages 602–609) gives step-by-step instruction for writing a story that follows the conventions of the genre.

1.3. READING, ANALYZING AND INTERPRETING LITERATURE

1.3.11.A. Read and understand works of literature.

In addition to reading the literature in this textbook, you will be asked questions that will help you understand and evaluate the literature, as well as connect it to your own life.

EXAMPLE: Reading and Understanding

Authors introduce related works of literature with essays on literature. See "Irony and Ambiguity: Surprises and Uncertainties" (pages 314–315) by the novelist, biographer, and former teacher John Leggett. Response and Analysis pages throughout the textbook help you understand what you've read.

1.3.11.B. Analyze the relationships, uses and effectiveness of literary elements used by one or more authors in similar genres including characterization, setting, plot, theme, point of view, tone and style.

You will evaluate **characterization**, analyze **setting**, recognize the building blocks of **plot**, and look at how authors use **theme, point of view, tone**, and **style** to evoke emotions and create meaning.

EXAMPLE: Analyzing Literary Elements

The selections in Collection 2 focus on characterization, the literary element introduced in the essay "Characters: The Actors in a Story" (pages 74–75) by John Leggett. Throughout the textbook, connections are made between genres. For example, you will infer character traits in Alice Walker's story "Everyday Use" (pages 76–83) and then connect the characters in that story to the speaker in Edgar Lee Masters's dramatic monologue "Lucinda Matlock" (page 85).

1.3.11.C. Analyze the effectiveness, in terms of literary quality, of the author's use of literary devices.

This standard includes (1) Sound techniques (e.g., rhyme, rhythm, meter, alliteration). (2) Figurative language (e.g., personification, simile, metaphor, hyperbole, irony, satire). (3) Literary structures.

EXAMPLE: Analyzing Literary Devices

A feature called Literary Focus introduces a literary device with most of the selections. Questions after reading selections then ask you to analyze and evaluate the author's use of the literary device. See "Two Kinds of Irony," the Literary Focus on page 316 before Roald Dahl's story "Lamb to the Slaughter," and the four questions about irony that follow.

1.3.11.D. Analyze and evaluate in poetry the appropriateness of diction and figurative language (e.g., irony, understatement, overstatement, paradox).

Collection 7 presents more than twenty-five poems for you to analyze and evaluate. Many of these poems focus on **diction** (word choice) and figurative language.

EXAMPLE: Analyzing Diction and Figurative Language

Poets choose words carefully for their connotations and their effect on the reader. Think, for example, of the different connotations of the word *cover* (line 44) in the poem "The Legend" (pages 472–473) by Garrett Hongo.

1.3.11.E. Analyze how a scriptwriter's use of words creates tone and mood, and how choice of words advances the theme or purpose of the work.

This standard emphasizes the influence of word choice on **tone** (the writer's attitude toward a subject, a character, or the audience) and **mood** (the atmosphere or feeling that a work evokes). Diction may also influence the play's theme or purpose.

EXAMPLE: Paraphrasing Shakespeare

To help you understand the importance of diction, on page 833 you are asked to paraphrase speeches from *The Tragedy of Julius Caesar*. Here is an example from Act III, Scene 1, lines 254–255:

Antony: O pardon me, thou bleeding piece of earth, That I am meek and gentle with these butchers!

Paraphrase: Forgive me, dead body, when I'm kind to these murderers!

1.3.11.F. Read and respond to nonfiction and fiction including poetry and drama.

To address this standard, the textbook asks you to read and respond in discussion and writing to many types of nonfiction (autobiography, biography, interviews, letters, articles, essays) and fiction (myths, legends, short stories, poems, and plays).

EXAMPLE: Responding to Texts

Tim O'Brien's story "Where Have You Gone, Charming Billy?" (pages 621–627) focuses on a soldier's feelings during the Vietnam War. Following this story, you'll read and respond to fictional and non-fictional texts that explore similar topics and themes.

1.4. TYPES OF WRITING

1.4.11.A. Write short stories, poems and plays.

This standard asks you to (1) Apply varying organizational methods. (2) Use relevant illustrations. (3) Utilize dialogue. (4) Apply literary conflict. (5) Include varying characteristics (e.g., from limerick to epic, from whimsical to dramatic). (6) Include literary elements. (7) Use literary devices.

EXAMPLE: Writing Stories, Poems, and Plays

The Writing Workshop on pages 602–609 guides you through the process of writing a short story. Several writing assignments suggest that you write poems and plays. On page 534, for example, you are asked to write a poem with sound effects. On page 738, you are asked to invent dialogue for a new act of Anton Chekhov's *The Brute*.

1.4.11.B. Write complex informational pieces (e.g., research papers, analyses, evaluations, essays).

This standard requires you to (1) Include a variety of methods to develop the main idea. (2) Use precise language and specific detail. (3) Include cause and effect. (4) Use relevant graphics (e.g., maps, charts, graphs, tables, illustrations, photographs). (5) Use primary and secondary sources.

EXAMPLE: Writing for a Variety of Purposes

The Writing Workshops walk you through writing various kinds of informational pieces. For one example, see "Analyzing a Short Story" (pages 440–447). Throughout the textbook you'll be asked to write analyses, evaluations, and essays. The Writer's Handbook (pages 963–966) shows you how to use graphics to communicate information.

1.4.11.C. Write persuasive pieces.

For mastery, you will need to (1) Include a clearly stated position or opinion. (2) Include convincing, elaborated and properly cited evidence. (3) Develop reader interest. (4) Anticipate and counter reader concerns and arguments. (5) Include a variety of methods to advance the argument or position.

EXAMPLE: Writing Persuasive Essays

Two Writing Workshops take you step by step through the process of writing a good persuasive essay: "Analyzing Problems and Solutions" on pages 212–219 and "Writing a Persuasive Essay" on pages 294–301. Both workshops explain types of evidence as well as methods to advance the argument.

1.4.11.D. Maintain a written record of activities, course work, experience, honors and interests.

This standard requires you to keep a record of your schoolwork, life experiences, awards, and hobbies.

EXAMPLE: Keeping a Record of Your Life

The Writing Workshop "Writing an Autobiographical Narrative" (pages 56–63) will help you create a written record of an important or memorable personal experience.

1.4.11.E. Write a personal resume.

You will need to learn how to create a résumé.

EXAMPLE: Writing a Résumé

In Collection 11, you will learn to create and evaluate workplace documents.

1.5. QUALITY OF WRITING

1.5.11.A. Write with a sharp, distinct focus.

The following are included in this standard: (1) Identify topic, task and audience. (2) Establish and maintain a single point of view. Your PSSA writing will be scored on **focus,** one of the five **domains** (elements) of effective writing.

EXAMPLE: Writing with a Focus

Many of the Writing Workshops deal with aspects of focus in the prewriting stage of the writing process. See, for example, "Consider Purpose and Audience" on page 56 and "Develop a Thesis" on page 384. See also pages 955–956 of the Writer's Handbook.

1.5.11.B. Write using well-developed content appropriate for the topic.

For this standard, you'll be required to (1) Gather, determine validity and reliability of, analyze and organize information. (2) Employ the most effective format for purpose and audience. (3) Write fully developed paragraphs that have details and information specific to the topic and relevant to the focus. **Content** is also a PSSA writing domain.

EXAMPLE: Developing Content

Pages 955–962 of the Writer's Handbook review and give examples of a paragraph's main idea as well as types of support (sensory details, facts and statistics, examples, and so on). See pages 963–964 of the Writer's Handbook, "Designing Your Writing," for ideas on format and design. Note especially the lists of design elements and font categories.

1.5.11.C. Write with controlled and/or subtle organization.

For mastery of this standard, you must (1) Sustain a logical order throughout the piece. (2) Include an effective introduction and conclusion. Your PSSA writing tests will be evaluated for **organization.**

EXAMPLE: Keeping Order

Every Writer's Workshop includes a Writer's Framework, which gives suggestions for the introduction, body, and conclusion. For a list of organizational patterns, see the "Text Structures" entry on pages 1006–1007.

1.5.11.D. Write with a command of the stylistic aspects of composition.

This standard includes the following: (1) Use different types and lengths of sentences. (2) Use precise language. Your PSSA writing will be scored for **style.**

EXAMPLE: Improving Your Style

See "Writing Effective Sentences" on pages 1030–1034. Several Grammar Links give you practice in improving style and using clear language. See "Say It Straight: Eliminating Wordiness," page 282, and "Using Transitions to Connect Related Ideas," page 740.

1.5.11.E. Revise writing to improve style, word choice, sentence variety and subtlety of meaning after rethinking how questions of purpose, audience and genre have been addressed.

There are many ways to express the same idea. When you pay attention to **subtleties,** fine distinctions in language, you look for the best way.

EXAMPLE: Improving Words and Sentences

See "Give It Flair!" on pages 961–962 of the Writer's Handbook for techniques to improve style.

Every Writing Workshop includes an annotated Writer's Model and a rubric with evaluation questions, tips, and revision techniques to help you improve your first draft. There is also a feature called Style Guidelines in every Writing Workshop.

1.5.11.F. Edit writing using the conventions of language.

This standard asks you to (1) Spell all words correctly. (2) Use capital letters correctly. (3) Punctuate correctly (periods, exclamation points, question marks, commas, quotation marks, apostrophes, colons, semicolons, parentheses, hyphens, brackets, ellipses). (4) Use nouns, pronouns, verbs, adjectives, adverbs, conjunctions, prepositions and interjections properly. (5) Use complete sentences (simple, compound, complex, declarative, interrogative, exclamatory and imperative). The fifth scorable domain on PSSA writing tests is **conventions.**

EXAMPLE: Obeying Language Rules

The Language Handbook on pages 1009–1052 serves as a reference for all aspects of spelling, capitalization, punctuation, grammar, and sentence structure. There you'll find plenty of instruction, examples, and practice exercises. Be sure to consult the Handbook for help in writing your essays, especially when you're at the revising stage. In addition, see the two charts on page 956: "Guidelines for Proofreading" and "Symbols for Revising and Proofreading."

1.5.11.G. Present and/or defend written work for publication when appropriate.

You may want to keep some of your writing just for your own eyes, but there will be times when you'll show your work to a wider audience.

EXAMPLE: Publishing Your Work

All of the Writing Workshops contain suggestions of where and how to share, present, or publish various kinds of writing. See "May I Introduce You?" on page 129, for example, which gives you ideas for sharing a biographical narrative that you've written.

1.6. SPEAKING AND LISTENING

1.6.11.A. Listen to others.

This standard includes the following: (1) Ask clarifying questions. (2) Synthesize information, ideas and opinions to determine relevancy. (3) Take notes.

EXAMPLE: Analyzing What People Say

The Listening and Speaking Workshop "Analyzing and Evaluating Speeches" (pages 898–901) shows you how to analyze rhetorical devices as well as how to evaluate delivery.

1.6.11.B. Listen to selections of literature (fiction and/or nonfiction).

For this standard, you must (1) Relate them to previous knowledge. (2) Predict solutions to identified problems. (3) Summarize and reflect on what has been heard. (4) Identify and define new words and concepts. (5) Analyze and synthesize the selections relating them to other selections heard or read.

EXAMPLE: Listening to Literature

You can listen to many of the textbook's nonfiction and fiction selections on audio recordings.

One feature of the *Elements of Literature* Internet site gives you video and sound clips of famous speeches with tips for analyzing the elements that make speeches great.

1.6.11.C. Speak using skills appropriate to formal speech situations.

This standard covers the following: (1) Use a variety of sentence structures to add interest to a presentation. (2) Pace the presentation according to audience and purpose. (3) Adjust stress, volume and inflection to provide emphasis to ideas or to influence the audience.

EXAMPLE: Speaking Skillfully

The Listening and Speaking Workshops identify and give you practice in using speaking skills. See, for example, suggestions for delivering a speech in "Giving a Persuasive Speech" (pages 220–221) and "Presenting a Literary Response" (pages 448–449).

1.6.11.D. Contribute to discussions.

This standard requires you to (1) Ask relevant, clarifying questions. (2) Respond with relevant information or opinions to questions asked. (3) Listen to and acknowledge the contributions of others. (4) Adjust tone and involvement to encourage equitable participation. (5) Facilitate total group participation. (6) Introduce relevant, facilitating information, ideas and opinions to enrich the discussion. (7) Paraphrase and summarize as needed.

EXAMPLE: Classroom Discussion

All of the Thinking Critically and Extending and Evaluating questions on the Response and Analysis pages give you practice in class discussion. See, for example, the questions on page 270 about "And of Clay Are We Created" by Isabel Allende.

For an explanation of paraphrasing, see page 411. Summarizing is defined on page 651.

1.6.11.E. Participate in small and large group discussions and presentations.

To master this standard, you'll need to (1) Initiate everyday conversation. (2) Select and present an oral reading on an assigned topic. (3) Conduct interviews. (4) Participate in a formal interview (e.g., for a job, college). (5) Organize and participate in informal debate around a specific topic. (6) Use evaluation guides (e.g., National Issues Forum, Toastmasters) to evaluate group discussion (e.g., of peers, on television).

EXAMPLE: Speaking with Others

There are several Listening and Speaking assignments for oral readings of various kinds. See, for instance, page 780. It suggests that you and a partner present an oral interpretation of the dialogue between Cassius and Brutus in *The Tragedy of Julius Caesar*. See pages 220–221 for "Guidelines for Conducting Interviews." The Listening and Speaking Workshop "Participating in a Debate" (pages 302–305) gives you information about holding and judging debates. Also, see "Analyzing and Evaluating Speeches" (pages 898–901).

1.6.11.F. Use media for learning purposes.

For this standard you will (1) Use various forms of media to elicit information, to make a student presentation and to complete class assignments and projects. (2) Evaluate the role of media in focusing attention and forming opinions. (3) Create a multimedia (e.g., film, music, computer-graphic) presentation for display or transmission that demonstrates an understanding of a specific topic or issue or teaches others about it.

EXAMPLE: Using Media

You will find help using film and video in the Writing Workshop "Comparing a Play and a Film" (pages 890–897). See the two charts "Identifying Narrative Techniques" and "Analyzing Film Techniques." To evaluate and compare the role of media, see the Writing Workshop "Comparing Media Genres," especially pages 383–386 (including the Writer's Model). Media tutorials are available on the *Elements of Literature* Internet site.

1.7.   CHARACTERISTICS AND FUNCTIONS OF THE ENGLISH LANGUAGE

1.7.11.A. Describe the influence of historical events on the English language.

Knowing the origins and meanings of commonly used English words as well as prefixes, suffixes, and roots that came from other languages will help broaden your vocabulary.

EXAMPLE: History of English

"A Changing Language: English Word Origins" overviews the history of English. See page 659. Many Vocabulary Development pages deal with words from other languages. See, for instance, page 688, "Words from Old Norse and Anglo-Saxon."

1.7.11.B. Analyze when differences in language are a source of negative or positive stereotypes among groups.

Dialect, slang, and jargon are varieties of informal speech that may identify a person either positively or negatively as a member of a group. When you know the variations of standard American English, you choose language appropriate to your audience.

EXAMPLE: Distinguishing Among Formal, Informal, Standard, and Nonstandard English

The "Glossary of Usage," pages 1049–1052 in the Language Handbook, lists, defines, and explains words and expressions that are standard, nonstandard, formal, or informal usage. See the Grammar Link "Dialect: Nonstandard but Authentic" (page 95) for practice in analyzing dialect, one kind of language difference.

1.7.11.C. Explain and evaluate the role and influence of the English language within and across countries.

Many words come into English from other parts of the world, and English words find their way into other languages.

EXAMPLE: Understanding the Role and Influence of the English Language

The Vocabulary Development lesson on page 271, "Mapping a Word's Origin," shows you how to find word origins and words related by their Greek and Latin roots. Also, see "Words from Spanish" on page 563 and "Understanding Elizabethan English" on page 805.

1.8. RESEARCH

1.8.11.A. Select and refine a topic for research.

First, you need to find a subject that interests you and might interest others. Then, you ask questions and track down a few answers to narrow your research topic.

EXAMPLE: Selecting a Research Topic

Questions following the informational texts in Collection 3 give you practice in generating questions for a research topic. For example, see pages 187–191 for hints on research questions. See page 213 for information on how to use the *5W-How?* questions.

The Writing Workshop "Writing a Research Paper" provides instruction in choosing and narrowing a topic (pages 690–692).

1.8.11.B. Locate information using appropriate sources and strategies.

You'll need to (1) Determine valid resources for researching the topic, including primary and secondary sources. (2) Evaluate the importance and quality of the sources. (3) Select sources appropriate to the breadth and depth of the research (e.g., dictionaries, thesauruses, other reference materials, interviews, observations, computer databases). (4) Use tables of contents, indices, key words, cross references and appendices. (5) Use traditional and electronic search tools.

EXAMPLE: Locating Information

See page 206 for ways to find reliable sources in a library and on the Internet. The article "An Ancient Enemy Gets Tougher" (pages 207–210) shows you how to use audio links and links to related Web pages. For practice in generating research questions and evaluating sources, see "Explorers Say There's Still Lots to Look For" (pages 366–372). The Informational Text selections on pages 88–95 and 632–643 include extensive instruction on using and evaluating primary and secondary sources.

1.8.11.C. Organize, summarize and present the main ideas from research.

This standard covers the following: (1) Take notes relevant to the research topic. (2) Develop a thesis statement based on research. (3) Anticipate readers' problems or misunderstandings. (4) Give precise, formal credit for others' ideas, images or information using a standard method of documentation. (5) Use formatting techniques (e.g., headings, graphics) to aid reader understanding.

EXAMPLE: Researching and Writing

See the Writing Workshop "Writing a Research Paper" on pages 690–709. You will be guided to take notes, prepare source cards, develop a thesis statement, organize information, and give credit by means of footnotes and *Works Cited* pages.

See "Designing Your Writing" on pages 963–966 of the Writer's Handbook for tips on how to use the design elements (fonts, headings, graphics) available on a computer to make your paper visually appealing.

Taking the PSSA

You have probably been taking national and statewide **standardized tests** throughout your school career. These tests become increasingly important as you approach graduation and think about applying to college.

Next year, you will take the **PSSA** tests in reading and writing. These tests, as part of the **Pennsylvania System of School Assessment** program, measure your mastery of Pennsylvania's **Academic Standards for Reading and Writing.**

The PSSA test in reading consists of two parts. The first part contains a **reading passage** and **multiple-choice questions.** The second part contains a **performance task,** which is a written response to a question related to the passage. The PSSA test in writing consists of **prompts** for a narrative essay, an informational essay, and a persuasive essay.

The following pages provide hints for doing well on the PSSA in reading and writing as well as on other tests, such as the PSAT, SAT, and ACT. The items on these pages are similar in format but not identical to the ones that you will see on the PSSA.

TIPS FOR TAKING SELECTED-RESPONSE TESTS

Multiple-choice, or selected-response, questions are the most common type of assessment on standardized tests. Teachers suggest the following tips for success.

TIP 1   **Keep track of the time.** Before you start, quickly skim the test to see how many questions you will have to answer. Figure out about how much time you can afford to spend on each question. Check the time often to see whether you need to work faster.

TIP 2   **Read everything carefully.** Stay focused and alert as you read, and don't skip anything. Pay special attention to *all* of these:
- the **reading passage**
- the **directions**
- the **entire question,** including all four answer choices

TIP Stay calm. If you feel nervous, take some deep breaths. Don't get discouraged when you come across questions that you can't answer right away. Questions are not arranged by difficulty. Keep going. You may find easier questions later in the test.

TIP 3 **There are no trick questions.** The test is designed to find out how much you know, not to trap you into guessing wrong answers. Don't waste time wondering what a question *really* means. *Do* look closely for words that limit the choices that could be correct. Look for words such as *not* and *except,* which require you to choose an answer that is opposite or false in some way. Remember that *never* and *always* signal a choice that applies in no or all situations.

TIP 4 **Trust yourself.** Read the entire question, and see whether you can predict what the answer will be. Then, read the choices. Eliminate choices that you know are wrong. Always have a good reason for changing an answer.

TIP 5 **Go back to those hard questions.** The right answer didn't jump out at you? Read the entire question with each different answer choice, as if the other choices didn't exist. Also, look for phrases that you can recall seeing in the text or hearing your teacher say.

TIP 6 **Mark each answer carefully.** After you have answered each question, double-check to make sure you've selected the letter that goes with that answer. If you have an answer sheet, match every question's number to the same number on the form.

TIP 7 **Review the test.** If you have time, go back to make sure you haven't skipped any questions. Erase any stray pencil marks.

Taking the Reading Test

The PSSA test in reading measures your ability to think critically about narrative and informational passages. During the test, you will answer **multiple-choice** questions about the ideas in the passage. You will also produce a written response to a **performance task,** which is an open-ended question related to the passage. All multiple-choice questions and performance tasks are aligned with Pennsylvania's grade 11 **Academic Standards** for reading, which describe what you should know about reading by the end of the year.

In the section that follows, you will find a sample informational passage followed by questions like those on the PSSA reading test. After each question, you will find tips that help you understand the correct answer. These questions have been labeled and grouped into five categories, each of which corresponds to one of Pennsylvania's Academic Standards for reading. On the actual test, you will not see labels, questions may not be grouped by category, and some categories may have more questions than others.

The following article is about adventurers and explorers. Below are two items of background information to prepare you for the article.

• **Millions of people enjoy exciting or dangerous experiences.**

• **Explorers risk their lives going where no one has gone before.**

Adventurers crave the struggle for survival. Explorers, though, want more than that. Read the following article to find out how adventurers are different from explorers—and to see into which category you might fit. After reading the article, answer the questions that follow.

Explorers Say There's Still Lots to Look For
by Helen O'Neill

NEW YORK—The crickets were roasted to perfection. Baby scorpions adorned points of savory toast. And the saddle of beaver simmered gently in a decorative silver tureen.

Oceanographer Sylvia Earle glided across the room in a shimmering red gown and golden shawl. She'd rather have been in her wet suit. She'd rather have been diving to the darkest corners of the abyss. Instead, "Her Deepness," as Earle is known, was busy in her role as honorary president of the Explorers Club, charming the cocktail crowd with her latest exploit: dancing a solitary dance with a giant octopus at the bottom of the Pacific.

Across the room, tuxedoed archaeologist Johan Reinhard clutched his wineglass and chatted about his latest find—a 500-year-old Inca mummy unearthed atop a remote Andean peak. Next to him, Bertrand Piccard, first man to circumnavigate earth in a balloon, engaged in intense debate about the future of solar-powered planes.

All around were people who have bush-whacked through jungles, trekked across deserts, floated in space. Dripping medals and jewels and tales from afar, they gathered in the ballroom of the Waldorf Astoria hotel for the annual Explorers Club banquet. Once a year they come here, to mingle with sponsors and troll for support, to nibble on loin of kangaroo and explain to the world that there are still places to be discovered.

A Great Era of Exploration

"There is a popular illusion that all corners of the earth have been explored," Earle says. "The greatest mountain ranges on the planet are underwater, where there is a whole continent waiting to be explored."

In the past two years alone, Ian Baker reported discovering the fabled Shangri-La waterfall on Tibet's mighty Tsangpo River; Reinhard recovered three frozen Inca mummies from an Andean volcano; the body of English climber George Mallory, who disappeared in 1924, was discovered on Mount Everest; and Robert Ballard located the world's oldest shipwrecks— two Phoenician cargo vessels in the Mediterranean. The same trip led him to uncover evidence of a giant flood about 7,000 years ago—perhaps the biblical flood of Noah.

Explorers still scale peaks that never have been climbed, crawl through caves to the insides of earth, hurtle into space to walk among the stars. They find ancient tribes and ancient cities. They dig up dinosaurs. They journey to places where no one has reported being before: the jungles of central Congo, the Amazon and Peru, the deserts of Tibet and China, vast underwater caves in Mexico and Belize. They are only beginning to probe the oceans; 5 percent has been explored, though water covers 71 percent of the planet.

All of which makes Earle say, "I think the great era of exploration has just begun. . . ."

What Sets Them Apart

"Men wanted for hazardous journey. Small wages, bitter cold, long months of complete darkness, constant danger, safe return doubtful. Honor and recognition in case of success."—Ernest Shackleton's 1914 advertisement for crew members for *Endurance*.

The ship was aptly named. Although Shackleton failed in his quest to cross the Antarctic, his journey became one of the great epics of survival. Marooned for months on an ice floe, his ship crushed by pack ice, Shackleton managed to sail a lifeboat 800 miles, scale an unmapped mountain range, reach a Norwegian whaling station, and return to rescue all of his men.

Seventy-five years later, Robert Ballard wants to dig through the ice and find his hero's ship.

Ballard is one of the most famous living explorers, and not just because he discovered the world's most famous shipwreck. Long before the lights of his little roaming robot lit up *Titanic*'s ghostly bow in 1985, the former naval officer and oceanographer dedicated his life to exploration. *Bismarck*. U.S.S. *Yorktown*. *Lusitania*. Ballard has explored them all.

"When I die," Ballard says, "I want one word on my tombstone: *Explorer*."

He is standing in his Institute of Exploration in Mystic, Connecticut, in a replica of the control room from which he discovered *Titanic*. The institute, which opened last year, is packed with videos and displays from Ballard's finds. On one wall, a large chart details his plans: searching for ancient wrecks in the Black Sea, the lost ships of the Franklin expedition in the Canadian Arctic, Shackleton's *Endurance.*

"A lot of people do adventure," Ballard says. "They retrace Hannibal's route in a Winnebago. They take a helicopter to the North Pole and have cocktails. That is not exploration."

True exploration, he says, is about having a vision and following it, about going where no one has dared go before, about bringing back scientific information and publishing it in journals.

"It's about having the heart to push on when you want to turn back," he says. "That is what sets explorers apart."

Seeking Knowledge

"Explorers are foragers," says Anna Roosevelt, curator of archaeology at the Field Museum of Natural History in Chicago and professor of anthropology at the University of Illinois. "They will seek until they find."

The great-granddaughter of Theodore Roosevelt spends much of her time foraging in the Amazon River basin, challenging conventional wisdom about early settlements there. She also challenges any notion that she is following in the footsteps of her famous ancestor, whose faded expedition photographs decorate the walls of the Explorers Club. Teddy Roosevelt, she says, was a great adventurer and a great president, but he wasn't an explorer in the true sense.

"People and animals died on his expeditions," she said of his legendary African safaris and canoe trips down the Amazon's River of Doubt. "They don't die on mine."

Roosevelt was one of the first women inducted into the Explorers Club after it opened its doors to women in 1981. Another was astronaut Kathryn Sullivan, first American woman to walk in space.

Sullivan didn't particularly feel like an explorer when she nudged her spaceship out of the way so she could get a better view of earth. She was more amused by the whimsy of it all: having trained for this moment so long, it actually felt normal. It wasn't until she got back to earth that she pondered its meaning.

"I think sometimes we learn more about ourselves and our place in society and in the universe than the places we thought we were going to explore. . . ."

1.1. LEARNING TO READ INDEPENDENTLY

Questions in this reading category measure your ability to **comprehend** passages. Some of the questions may test your understanding of how and why authors use certain **text structures.** Other questions may test your ability to identify and evaluate **key words** or **ideas.** You may re-read the passage.

1.1.11.B. ANALYZING STRUCTURE

1. **A major purpose of the section "What Sets Them Apart" is to**

   A contrast Robert Ballard and Ernest Shackleton.

   B liken the thrill of helicopter rides to exploration.

   C distinguish between explorers and adventure seekers.

   D compare the *Endurance* and the *Titanic.*

EXPLANATION: A look at the choices reveals that the answer concerns similarities or differences. Return to the article, looking for key words listed in the answer choices. B and D are inconsistent with passage details and with the contrast implied in its heading ("What Sets Them Apart"). A involves contrast, but it, too, is inconsistent with the details. **The correct answer is C.**

1.1.11.D. IDENTIFYING ESSENTIAL IDEAS

2. **An important idea in this article is the explorer's belief that**

   E long life is less important than the thrill of exploring.

   F discoveries should be kept secret from the public.

   G many places have still not been explored.

   H exotic foods are exciting to eat.

EXPLANATION: You can eliminate E, since it is not discussed. F contradicts another important idea in the article. H may be true, but it is not an important idea in the article. G is the only choice discussed as an important idea. **The correct answer is G.**

1.1.11.E. EXPANDING READING VOCABULARY

3. **In "Explorers still scale peaks that never have been climbed . . . ," the best meaning for the word *scale* is**

   A to measure.

   B to weigh.

   C to remove material with a sharp instrument.

   D to go up or over.

EXPLANATION: A, B, C, and D are all meanings of the word *scale.* However, only one choice makes sense in the context in which the word is used. The word *peaks* following *scale* is the first clue. The second clue is *climbed,* which is a synonym for *scale* in the sentence. The only meaning that fits the context is D, so **D is the correct answer.**

1.1.11.G. UNDERSTANDING NONFICTION TEXT

4. **Anna Roosevelt is primarily interested in exploring**

   E mummies in the Andean mountains.

   F planes lost in the ocean.

   G the Canadian Arctic.

   H the Amazon River basin.

EXPLANATION: This question tests your ability to recall or to locate details. If you do not recall the detail about Anna Roosevelt, go back to the article. You will see that E, F, and G are interests of other explorers. The particular interest of Roosevelt is the Amazon River basin. **H is the correct answer.**

1.2. READING CRITICALLY IN ALL CONTENT AREAS

Questions in this standards category test your ability to **think critically** about what you read. Some questions require you to distinguish **facts** from **opinions** or **essential** from **nonessential information.** Other questions require you to **make inferences,** to **draw conclusions,** or to **analyze an author's writing.**

1.2.11.A.1. SEPARATING FACTS FROM OPINIONS

5. Which of the following is a fact?

  A Explorers are braver than adventurers.

  B The *Endurance* is the world's most famous shipwreck.

  C Kathryn Sullivan was the first American woman to walk in space.

  D Explorers seek until they find.

EXPLANATION: A fact can be proved true or false. An opinion is a personal belief or feeling that cannot be proved. A, B, and D are opinions. Answer C is a fact that can be verified or checked in an authoritative source, such as an encyclopedia. **The correct answer is C.**

1.2.11.A.2. DISTINGUISHING ESSENTIAL FROM NONESSENTIAL INFORMATION

6. Earle indicates that explorers attend the annual Explorers Club banquet because they

  E need money for their projects.

  F get recognition and medals there.

  G want to meet other explorers.

  H are invited.

EXPLANATION: F, G, and H may be true, but E is the only choice that reflects important information stated in the article. The explorers attend "to mingle with sponsors and troll for support." **The correct answer is E.**

1.2.11.A.3. DRAWING CONCLUSIONS

7. From the information given throughout this article, you can conclude that explorers are most interested in seeking

  A knowledge.

  B danger.

  C adventure.

  D fame.

EXPLANATION: A conclusion should be based on information in the reading passage. Ballard, Roosevelt, and Sullivan all state the same idea but in different words: *Explorers bring back information. They seek until they find. They learn about themselves as well as about the places they explore.* **A is the correct answer.**

1.2.11.A.4. DETERMINING THE AUTHOR'S PURPOSE

8. The author's primary purpose is to

  E persuade the reader to become an explorer.

  F tell about some of today's explorers.

  G create an entertaining narrative about explorers.

  H convince the reader to give donations to explorers.

EXPLANATION: You can eliminate E and H, since the author does not try to persuade or convince. The author is not telling a story, so you can eliminate G. Most of the details provide information about explorers and their recent finds. **The correct answer is F.**

1.3. READING, ANALYZING AND INTERPRETING LITERATURE

Questions in this standards category test your understanding of **literature,** both fiction and nonfiction. Some questions may ask you about **literary elements,** such as characterization, setting, plot, theme, point of view, and tone. Other questions may ask you about **literary devices,** such as sound techniques (rhythm, alliteration), figurative language (metaphor, hyperbole, irony), and literary structures (foreshadowing, flashbacks).

1.3.11.A. UNDERSTANDING LITERATURE

9. **Based on comments in the article, Sylvia Earle used the banquet as an opportunity to promote the idea that**
   A present-day explorers are just as brave as earlier ones.
   B this century will be a time of underwater exploration.
   C the era of exploration has just begun.
   D women can and should be explorers.

EXPLANATION: Although Sylvia Earle might agree with A, B, and D, statements in the article itself do not lead to these conclusions as motivation for the comments. **C is the correct answer.**

1.3.11.B. UNDERSTANDING LITERARY ELEMENTS

10. **Three words that characterize most explorers, as described in this article, would be**
    E humble, hardworking, self-sacrificing.
    F brave, self-confident, determined.
    G proud, greedy, lonely.
    H lucky, intelligent, kind.

EXPLANATION: To answer this question, you need to look at all three words in each choice. All of the words must describe the character of explorers as revealed in this article. E, G, and H each contain at least one word that does not fit the characterization. **The correct answer is F.**

1.3.11.C.1. ANALYZING LITERARY DEVICES

11. **"Marooned for months" is an example of**
    A setting.
    B rhyme.
    C alliteration.
    D metaphor.

EXPLANATION: Multiple-choice tests sometimes include questions that require you to know the definitions of literary elements and devices, so you should try to learn as many as you can. **Alliteration** is the repetition of the same or similar consonant sounds at beginnings of words close together. **The correct answer is C.**

1.3.11.C.2. ANALYZING LITERARY DEVICES

12. **The phrase "dancing a solitary dance with a giant octopus at the bottom of the Pacific" is an example of**
    E theme.
    F simile.
    G personification.
    H irony.

EXPLANATION: Personification is the giving of human qualities to something non-human, such as a rock or an animal. In this case, Earle personifies the octopus by describing it as her partner in an underwater dance. **G is the correct answer.**

1.7. CHARACTERISTICS AND FUNCTIONS OF THE ENGLISH LANGUAGE

Questions in this standards category involve the **nature of the English language.** Some questions test your knowledge of **word origins** and **meanings.** Other questions test your understanding of the power of language and of the forces that have shaped it.

1.7.11.A. UNDERSTANDING HISTORY'S INFLUENCE ON ENGLISH

13. **The word *abyss* comes from the Greek *abyssos* and means**
    A against the light.
    B with hope.
    C without bottom.
    D no safety.

EXPLANATION: The word is made up of the prefix *a–*, meaning "without," combined with the word *byssos,* meaning "bottom." You can also figure out the meaning of the word by studying the context for clues: "She'd rather have been diving to the darkest corners of the abyss." From the context, you know that she is talking about the ocean ("diving") and that it is very deep ("darkest corners"). **The correct answer is C.**

1.7.11.A. UNDERSTANDING HISTORY'S INFLUENCE ON ENGLISH

14. **The word *astronaut* is made up of two roots, *–astro–* and *–naut–*, which together mean**
    E sky traveler.
    F planet pilot.
    G sun hunter.
    H star sailor.

EXPLANATION: The word *astronaut* comes from the Greek roots *–astro–*, meaning "star," and *–naut–*, meaning "sailor." **The correct answer is H.**

1.711.B. ANALYZING LANGUAGE AS A SOURCE OF STEREOTYPES

15. **In their own group, some explorers consider it an insult to be called**
    A adventurers.
    B philosophers.
    C heroes.
    D foragers.

EXPLANATION: B, C, and D can be eliminated— explorers might even be flattered to be called philosophers, heroes, or foragers (people who search for what is needed or wanted). The explorers seem to be more interested in seeking knowledge than in seeking adventure. In fact, Ballard and Roosevelt look down on adventurers. **A is the correct answer.**

1.7.11.A. UNDERSTANDING HISTORY'S INFLUENCE ON ENGLISH

16. **The best definition of the word *whimsy* as used in this article is**
    E quaint saying.
    F unusual art object.
    G odd humor.
    H nervous feeling.

EXPLANATION: The origin of the word *whimsy* is unknown. Words related to *whimsy* are *whim* and *whimsical.* In the context of the passage, the word *whimsy* means "odd humor." **The correct answer is G.**

1.8. RESEARCH

Questions in this category test your understanding of the **research process.** You may be asked questions dealing with selecting and locating resources and information, taking and organizing notes, developing a thesis statement, crediting the ideas of other writers, and using formatting techniques.

1.8.11.B.5. USING TRADITIONAL AND ELECTRONIC SEARCH TOOLS

17. **To find information about Kathryn Sullivan on the Internet, the *key words* that would probably get the best results are**

  A Kathryn Sullivan.
  B female astronauts.
  C Sullivan astronaut.
  D space explorers.

EXPLANATION: It is best to begin with key words that limit your topic. Choice A is a fairly common name. B and D are more specific, but you would still have to sift through sources that have nothing to do with your topic. **The correct answer is C.**

1.8.11.B.3. SELECTING APPROPRIATE SOURCES

18. **Which of the following sources would have been *least* useful to the author in research that she did before writing this article?**

  E the Internet
  F magazine articles
  G interviews
  H government agencies

EXPLANATION: The article contains quotations, so you know that the author consulted or conducted interviews (G). To find up-to-date information on each explorer, she may have used the Internet (E) and magazine articles (F). She would have been least likely to consult government agencies (H), since it is unlikely that those agencies would have had the kind of information she wanted. **H is the correct answer.**

1.8.11.B.2. EVALUATING SOURCES

19. **Based on his or her comments, which explorer seems to be most biased against adventurers?**

  A Sylvia Earle
  B Bertrand Piccard
  C Robert Ballard
  D Kathryn Sullivan

EXPLANATION: Only two explorers, Robert Ballard and Anna Roosevelt, make negative comments about adventurers. Since Roosevelt is not one of the choices, **C is the correct answer.**

1.8.11.C.4. GIVING FORMAL CREDIT

20. **If you use this article as a source in a research report, which of these requires a formal citation?**

  E Ernest Shackleton's quest to cross the Antarctic was unsuccessful.
  F Anna Roosevelt is an archaeologist, an anthropologist, and an explorer.
  G Only a small part of the ocean has been explored.
  H According to Robert Ballard, true exploration is "about having a vision and following it. . . ."

EXPLANATION: You do not need to cite statements containing information that is common knowledge, but you need to put them in your own words. You do need to cite any direct quotation you use. **The correct answer is H.**

RESPONDING TO A PERFORMANCE TASK

The second part of the PSSA in reading requires you to respond to a **performance task** (also known as an open-ended or a constructed-response question). The performance task tests your ability to analyze and evaluate what you read. It asks you to make connections between the text and what you know. It also gives you a chance to express your own ideas. You may re-read the article.

HOW PERFORMANCE TASKS ARE SCORED

Your response will receive a score ranging from 0 to 4. Level 4 is the highest score; level 0 applies to nonsense answers or blank answers. The people who score your response will evaluate it according to a **rubric,** an outline that lists the characteristics of a typical response at each level of scoring. The performance standard for Pennsylvania students is level 3 or higher. Here is a summary of Pennsylvania's scoring rubric:

- A **level 4** response shows a thorough understanding of the text; includes no factual errors; shows a level of understanding that goes beyond the literal; cites evidence from the text and makes connections to other experiences, ideas, and reading material.
- A **level 3** response shows a clear, adequate understanding of the text; includes no major factual errors; shows a level of understanding that is more literal and personal than a level 4 response; draws upon background information and personal experience.

- A **level 2** response shows a limited understanding of the text; may include factual errors; shows a mostly literal level of understanding; makes limited, unclear connections between outside experiences and the text.
- A **level 1** response shows a very limited understanding of the text; may include factual errors; includes responses that are unclear or irrelevant; makes only vague connections to the text.
- A **level 0** essay is blank or consists of responses that have no relationship to the text and performance task.

Here is a sample performance task and response. An explanation of how it would be scored follows the response.

In this article, the explorer Robert Ballard seems convinced that explorers are quite different from adventurers. Tell why you agree or disagree with him. Use information from the article to support your answer. As you write, be sure to:

- ■ **Explain whether you agree or disagree with Ballard.**
- ■ **Use information from the article.**
- ■ **Include your own ideas.**
- ■ **Write clearly and neatly.**
- ■ **Use only the space provided.**

statement of agreement/ disagreement —

connects personal experience to information from the article —

quotes article —

personal insight —

Robert Ballard indicates that adventurers and explorers are not alike. In distinguishing the two, he characterizes adventurers as pleasure seekers who might occasionally "take a helicopter to the North Pole and have cocktails" or "retrace Hannibal's route in a Winnebago." I agree that there are differences between explorers and adventurers. However, they do have some characteristics in common that I think make them more alike than different.

Adventurers clearly crave excitement. I have two friends, Craig and Debby, who would call themselves adventurers. Craig gets a rush from biking; Debby loves white-water rafting. Explorers probably experience the same kind of excitement as those two do. It must be a rush to find an important fossil or dive to "the darkest corners of the abyss." Adventurers also enjoy a good challenge. Craig and Debby constantly look for ways to push the limits. Like explorers, they, too, seek mountain "peaks that never have been climbed."

However, I think explorers and adventurers are different in some ways. Explorers have more on their minds than excitement. For explorers, danger is not something they face on vacation. They dedicate their lives to go, as Ballard says, "where no one has dared go before." Like Sylvia Earle, they explore places deep in the ocean. Like Kathryn Sullivan, they risk their lives high above the earth. They do so not only for the thrill but also for the pursuit of knowledge.

I am grateful that there are brave explorers in the world. I also appreciate adventure seekers who push the limits. I believe that their goals are different but that they share a very distinctive characteristic: a passion for experience and challenges. It is this characteristic that sets them apart from the rest of us.

Score 4—This writer shows a good understanding of the text, does not include mistakes regarding the facts presented in the text, and makes some connections to personal experiences and background knowledge.

Taking the PSSA Writing Test

The PSSA writing test for grade 11 is given in three sessions. In each session, you will be required to respond to a writing **prompt** that will direct you to write an informational, narrative, or persuasive essay. Each essay should be at least five paragraphs long.

A method called **domain scoring** will be used to evaluate your writing. The domains are the five characteristics of good writing: **focus, content, organization, style,** and **conventions.** Each domain is scored on a four-point scale. A score of 3 or 4 is considered acceptable; a score of 1 or 2 is considered unacceptable. A paper may be acceptable in some of the five domains but unacceptable in others.

To help you focus your essay-writing practice, first take a look at the characteristics of a paper that would receive a score of 3 or 4 in each writing domain. Note that the types of writing and the five domains are aligned with Pennsylvania's **Academic Standards for Writing 1.4. and 1.5.**

CHARACTERISTICS OF AN EXCELLENT ESSAY

Focus. The paper has a strong, single controlling point made with a clear awareness of the task: to write an informational, narrative, or persuasive essay about a specific topic. The paper establishes and maintains a clear purpose and a single point of view.

Content. The essay presents specific, important ideas that are related to the topic and focus. The ideas are fully developed through examples, details, facts, anecdotes, opinions, statistics, reasons, and/or explanations.

Organization. The content is arranged in a logical order or sequence that is well suited to the purpose of the paper. Order is developed between and within paragraphs using transitions. The essay should have an interesting introduction and a conclusion.

Style. The writer chooses and arranges words and sentence structures that create a consistent voice and tone. The voice and tone are appropriate to the audience while expressing the writer's personality. The language is precise and the word choice effective. The overall impression should be that the writer was fully aware of both "what" needed to be said and "how" to say it.

Conventions. The writer shows knowledge and control of the conventions of written language: grammar, mechanics, spelling, usage, and sentence formation. The essay contains consistently clear, complete sentences with correct end punctuation. Sentences are connected effectively, and competence is shown in subordination and coordination.

STEPS FOR TAKING THE PSSA WRITING TEST

Here are some steps that contain tips and a suggested timetable for writing your essay.

STEP 1   **Read the writing prompt carefully.** Look for key verbs (such as *analyze, summarize, identify, persuade*) that define your writing task. Identify your audience and purpose.

STEP 2   **Plan what you will write.** You have a total of sixty minutes to plan, write, and proofread your paper, so take about ten minutes for prewriting. Make notes on scratch paper. To help you organize your ideas, make a rough outline, map, or chart. You can use a cluster diagram or other graphic organizer to gather main ideas and supporting details. Number your major points in the order you think you will use them.

Watch Your Time

Prewriting	10 min.
Drafting	30 min.
Editing and Revising	15 min.
Proofreading	5 min.

STEP 3   **Draft your essay.** Allow about thirty minutes to draft your essay. Use your best handwriting (in case you don't have time to copy your work before the sixty minutes is up). Try to present your ideas clearly and in an order that will make them easy to follow. Pay special attention to creating a strong opening paragraph and a definite closing. Make every effort to express your ideas as clearly as you can while making your essay interesting to read. Vary the kinds of sentences (long, short, simple, compound, complex, compound-complex) you use.

STEP 4   **Edit and revise your draft.** Allow about fifteen minutes to re-read and improve your draft. Make sure your essay is readable! If it isn't, decide whether you have time to copy it over, revising as you go. Look for places where you can add transitions or combine sentences. Be sure to eliminate unnecessary repetition and wordiness. Check your essay by referring to the copy of the domain scoring guide on the back of the prompt.

STEP 5   **Proofread.** Take at least five minutes to search for and correct errors in grammar, spelling, usage, and mechanics. You will not be allowed to use a dictionary, thesaurus, or electronic spell checker, but don't panic. If you don't know how to spell a word, consider using a different word that has the same meaning.

A SAMPLE WRITING PROMPT

On-demand writing prompts ask you to write an informational, narrative, or persuasive essay in a limited time. Here is a sample prompt for a persuasive essay. A set of five guideline statements follows the prompt. Each statement refers to one of the five domains of writing described on page PA27.

> Your school board is considering a policy that would require all students to wear a uniform (white shirt with navy blue pants for both boys and girls). — **Background information**
>
> What do you think of this policy? Write an essay to persuade the school board to accept your position. — **Task and audience**

As you write your paper, remember to

★ Clearly state what the issue is and what position you support.

★ Use specific reasons, examples, facts, and details to persuade the school board to accept your opinion.

★ Present your ideas clearly and in a logical order, including an introduction, body, and conclusion.

★ Use well-constructed sentences and a variety of words.

★ Correct any errors in spelling, grammar, usage, mechanics, and sentence formation.

PREWRITING: ORGANIZING YOUR IDEAS

Form your opinion. The writing prompt presents an issue that you can respond to without doing research or knowing a great deal about the topic.

Gather your ideas. Here's a cluster diagram by a writer who does not support the policy. Before drafting, the writer will **evaluate** support, choosing the **reasons** and **evidence** most likely to convince the school board.

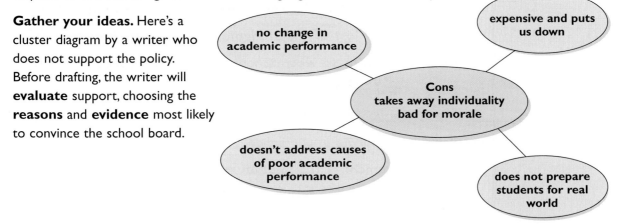

no change in academic performance

expensive and puts us down

Cons
takes away individuality
bad for morale

doesn't address causes of poor academic performance

does not prepare students for real world

DRAFTING: GETTING IT DOWN ON PAPER

Time to write. You have a big head start because you know what you are going to say and roughly how you're going to organize your ideas. Keep in mind your **purpose** and **audience,** and use appropriate language.

Keep your focus in mind. Early in your introductory paragraph, include a clear statement of your opinion. This sentence is sometimes called your **controlling point, opinion statement,** or **thesis statement.**

Add the details. As you draft, concentrate on **elaborating** (supporting) each paragraph's **main idea.** Use **transitions** to connect ideas and details.

Find your own voice. Do not use slang, but try to write the way you would sound if you were speaking naturally.

REVISING AND PROOFREADING: POLISHING YOUR DRAFT

Time's almost up. Allow enough time to re-read your paper. Read it once for sense and clarity; read it a second time for style and sentence variety. Then, proofread it to catch mistakes in grammar, usage, mechanics, and spelling.

A SAMPLE ESSAY

Here is one writer's essay in response to the writing prompt on page PA29.

statement of issue and position —

    Men and women in the armed services are proud to wear uniforms. Other adults choose jobs that require them to wear uniforms. However, I see no reason high school students should be forced to do so. Most of the students at Lincoln High agree with me that requiring us to wear school uniforms is a policy that would harm our school, not benefit it.

reason —

    The school board has good intentions in wanting to address problems with morale in our school. The idea, however, that a uniform requirement is the solution might be misguided. I believe that wearing look-alike clothes would most likely damage student morale, not raise it. At a time in our lives when we want to feel that we are individuals—unique—to be forced to wear uniforms is to be forced into chains of conformity.

When I was in kindergarten through fifth grade, I had to wear — **example**
a school uniform. My friends and I never stopped wanting to wear other kinds of clothes. On rare free-dress days, we could wear whatever we wanted. When we were out of uniform, our conduct and academic performance were no different than on days when we had to dress alike. If anything, we were more alert and — **reason**
energized when we were allowed to dress "as ourselves."

Another reason the high school uniform policy is a bad idea is that wearing a uniform would do nothing to help us prepare for — **reason**
the real world. For example, in most jobs, you are expected to make good decisions about the appropriate kind of clothes to wear. The problem is, school uniforms, in effect, make the decisions for us.

Additionally, wearing a uniform in high school is both expensive — **reason**
and demeaning. When I wore a uniform as a child, my parents spent a lot of money on school clothes and on clothes that I could wear after school and on weekends. More harmful than this double expense, however, is the suggestion that students who are almost adults cannot be trusted to make responsible choices about what to wear.

Like the school board, I do believe that we should address low morale and poor academic performance. However, I also believe that the answers are not as easy as a white shirt and navy pants. I ask — **conclusion**
that school board members and students take a close look at our school's problems and look for practical answers together. Meanwhile, please do not restrict our ability to express ourselves as individuals.

Academic Standards

REVIEWING YOUR WRITING

Test readers will evaluate your PSSA essays to see how well you have mastered the five **domains** of effective writing. The checklist below shows the academic standard that aligns with each checklisted item. At the end of the checklist for each domain, you will see the score that the preceding essay might have received.

CHECKLIST FOR WRITING

Domain 1: Focus

Has a clear, distinct focus been maintained from the beginning of the essay to the end?

✓ The paper identifies a single topic, task, and audience. The ideas are appropriate for the topic and audience. **1.5.11.A**

✓ The writer makes a single, controlling point. **1.5.11.A**

Focus: 4—The essay approaches its task and audience with clear focus.

Domain 2: Content

Are the information, ideas, and details well developed? Are they related to the topic?

✓ The ideas are clear, specific, and substantial (important) to the topic. **1.5.11.B**

✓ An informational essay includes developed paragraphs with specific details. **1.4.11.B, 1.5.11.B**

✓ A persuasive essay includes evidence that advances an opinion. **1.4.11.C**

Content: 4—The ideas are fully elaborated and related to the topic and focus.

Domain 3: Organization

Are the ideas and details within and across paragraphs clearly arranged?

✓ Time sequence or logical order is maintained. **1.5.11.C**

✓ Each paragraph has one main idea. **1.5.11.B**

✓ Transitions make the order easy to follow. **1.5.11.C**

✓ The introduction and conclusion unify the ideas in the paper. **1.5.11.C**

Organization: 4—The essay's introduction, conclusion, and transitions are effective.

Domain 4: Style

Are words and sentences carefully chosen?

✓ Voice and tone are consistent and appropriate to the audience. **1.5.11.D, E**

✓ Sentences are of different lengths and types. **1.5.11.D, F**

✓ Word choice is precise. **1.5.11.D**

✓ The paper expresses the writer's personality. **1.5.11.D**

Style: 4—The word choice and sentence structure are varied and interesting.

Domain 5: Conventions

Does the writer obey the rules of written language?

✓ The mechanics (capitalization, spelling, and punctuation) are correct. **1.5.11.F**

✓ Usage is correct for subject-verb agreement and pronoun references. **1.5.11.F**

✓ Every sentence has a subject and verb. **1.5.11.F**

Conventions: 4—No errors.

HOLT
ELEMENTS OF LITERATURE

Fourth Course

HOLT
ELEMENTS OF
LITERATURE

Fourth Course

HOLT, RINEHART AND WINSTON

A Harcourt Education Company

Orlando • **Austin** • New York • San Diego • Toronto • London

EDITORIAL
Editorial Vice President: Laura Wood
Project Directors: Kathleen Daniel, Mescal Evler
Executive Editors: Kristine E. Marshall, Laura Mongello
Senior Book Editors: Amy Fleming, Julie Barnett Hoover
Senior Product Manager: Don Wulbrecht
Managing Editor: Marie Price
Editorial Staff: Jane Archer-Feinstein, Susan Kent Cakars, Ann Michelle Gibson, Christine Han, Sean W. Henry, Errol Smith, Crystal Wirth
Copyediting Manager: Michael Neibergall
Copyediting Supervisor: Mary Malone
Copyeditors: Christine Altgelt, Elizabeth Dickson, Emily Force, Leora Harris, Anne Heausler, Julia Thomas Hu, Kathleen Scheiner, Nancy Shore
Associate Managing Editors: Lori De La Garza, Elizabeth LaManna
Editorial Support: Christine Degollado, Betty Gabriel, Danielle Greer, Mark Koenig, Erik Netcher, Janet Riley, Gloria Shahan
Editorial Permissions: Ann Farrar, Susan Lowrance, Erik Netcher

Index: Robert Zolnerzak

ART, DESIGN, AND PRODUCTION
Director: Athena Blackorby
Senior Design Director: Betty Mintz
Series Design: Kirchoff/Wohlberg, Inc.
Design and Electronic Files: MorganCain & Associates; Preface, Inc.
Photo Research: MorganCain & Associates; Photosearch, Inc.
Production Manager: Carol Trammel
Sr. Production Coordinators: Belinda Lopez, Michael Roche
Prepress: Progressive Information Technologies
Manufacturing: R. R. Donnelley & Sons Company, Willard, Ohio

COVER
Photo Credits: (Inset) *Valley Farms* (ca. 1933–1934) by Ross Dickinson. Oil on canvas. Copyright Smithsonian American Art Museum, Washington, D.C./Art Resource, NY. (Background) Farmland. © Adam Jones/Getty Images.

Program Authors

Kylene Beers established the reading pedagogy for *Elements of Literature*. A former middle-school teacher, Dr. Beers has turned her commitment to helping readers having difficulty into the major focus of her research, writing, speaking, and teaching. Dr. Beers is currently Senior Reading Researcher at the Child Study Center of the School Development Program at Yale University and was formerly a Research Associate Professor at the University of Houston. Dr. Beers is also currently the editor of the National Council of Teachers of English journal *Voices from the Middle*. She is the author of *When Kids Can't Read: What Teachers Can Do* and the co-editor of *Into Focus: Understanding and Creating Middle School Readers*. Dr. Beers is the 2001 recipient of the Richard Halle Award from the NCTE for outstanding contributions to middle-level literacy education. She has served on the review boards of the *English Journal* and *The Alan Review*. Dr. Beers currently serves on the board of directors of the International Reading Association's Special Interest Group on Adolescent Literature.

Lee Odell helped establish the pedagogical framework for writing, listening, and speaking for *Elements of Literature*. Dr. Odell is Professor of Composition Theory and Research and, since 1996, Director of the Writing Program at Rensselaer Polytechnic Institute. He began his career teaching English in middle and high schools. More recently he has worked with teachers in grades K–12 to establish a program that involves students from all disciplines in writing across the curriculum and for communities outside their classrooms. Dr. Odell's most recent book (with Charles R. Cooper) is *Evaluating Writing: The Role of Teachers' Knowledge About Text, Learning, and Culture*. He is past chair of the Conference on College Composition and Communication and of NCTE's Assembly for Research. Dr. Odell is currently working on a college-level writing textbook.

Writers

Robert Anderson is a playwright, novelist, screenwriter, and teacher. His plays include *Tea and Sympathy; Silent Night, Lonely Night; You Know I Can't Hear You When the Water's Running;* and *I Never Sang for My Father*. His screenplays include *The Nun's Story* and *The Sand Pebbles*. Mr. Anderson has taught at the Writers' Workshop at the University of Iowa, the American Theater Wing Professional Training Program, and the Salzburg Seminar in American Studies. He is a past president of the Dramatists Guild of America, a past vice president of the Authors League of America, and a member of the Theater Hall of Fame.

John Malcolm Brinnin, author of six volumes of poetry that have received many prizes and awards, was a member of the American Academy and Institute of Arts and Letters. He was a critic of poetry, a biographer of poets, and for a number of years the director of New York's famous Poetry Center. His teaching career included terms at Vassar College, the University of Connecticut, and Boston University, where he succeeded Robert Lowell as Professor of Creative Writing and Contemporary Letters. Mr. Brinnin wrote *Dylan Thomas in America: An Intimate Journal* and *Sextet: T. S. Eliot & Truman Capote & Others*.

Flo Ota De Lange and **Sheri Henderson**

Flo Ota De Lange is a former teacher with a thirty-year second career in psychotherapy, during which she studied learning processes in children and adults. Those careers led to her third career, as a writer.

Sheri Henderson brings to the program twenty years of experience as a California middle-school research practitioner and full-time reading and language arts teacher at La Paz International School in Saddleback Valley Unified School District. She regularly speaks at statewide and national conferences.

Since 1991, DeLangeHenderson LLC has published forty-three titles designed to integrate the teaching of literature with standards requirements and state and national tests.

Phyllis Goldenberg graduated from the University of Chicago and did graduate work in literature at Columbia University. She has more than thirty years' experience as an educational writer and editor specializing in literature, grammar, and composition materials for secondary-school students. She is the author of a student guide to writing a research paper and the author and series editor of a grammar and composition program for middle- and high school students.

Madeline Travers Hovland, who taught language arts for several years, is a writer of educational materials. She studied English at Bates College and received a master's degree in education from Harvard University.

John Leggett is a novelist, biographer, and former teacher. He went to the Writers' Workshop at the University of Iowa in the spring of 1969. In 1970, he assumed temporary charge of the program, and for the next seventeen years he was its director. Mr. Leggett's novels include *Wilder Stone, The Gloucester Branch, Who Took the Gold Away?, Gulliver House,* and *Making Believe.* He is also the author of the highly acclaimed biography *Ross and Tom: Two American Tragedies* and of a biography of William Saroyan, *A Daring Young Man.* Mr. Leggett lives in Napa Valley, California.

Mara Rockliff is a writer and editor with a degree in American civilization from Brown University. She has written dramatizations of classic stories, collected in a book called *Stories for Performance.* She has also published feature stories in national newspapers and is currently writing a novel for young adults.

Diane Tasca, a graduate of Temple University, earned a doctorate in English from the University of Illinois. Over the past thirty years, Dr. Tasca has taught various college courses in composition, literature, and performance and has developed, written, and edited instructional materials for high school and college language arts textbooks. A member of the San Francisco Bay Area theater community, she has performed in numerous plays and assisted playwrights with the development of new dramatic works. She currently teaches drama at Foothill College in Los Altos Hills, California.

Senior Program Consultant

Carol Jago is the editor of CATE's quarterly journal, *California English*. She teaches English at Santa Monica High School, in Santa Monica, and directs the California Reading and Literature Project at UCLA. She writes a weekly education column for the *Los Angeles Times*. She is the author of several books, including three in a series on contemporary writers in the classroom: *Alice Walker in the Classroom; Nikki Giovanni in the Classroom;* and *Sandra Cisneros in the Classroom*. She is also the author of *With Rigor for All: Teaching the Classics to Contemporary Students; Beyond Standards: Excellence in the High School English Classroom;* and *Cohesive Writing: Why Concept Is Not Enough.*

ADVISORS

Cynthia A. Arceneaux
Administrative Coordinator
Office of Deputy Super-
    intendent, Instructional
    Services
Los Angeles Unified School District
Los Angeles, California

Dr. Julie M. T. Chan
Director of Literacy Instruction
Newport-Mesa Unified School
    District
Costa Mesa, California

Al Desmarais
English Department Chair
    and Curriculum Specialist in
    Language Arts
El Toro High School
Saddleback Valley Unified School
    District
Lake Forest, California

José M. Ibarra-Tiznado
ELL Program Coordinator
Bassett Unified School District
La Puente, California

Dr. Ronald Klemp
Instructor
California State University,
    Northridge
Northridge, California

Fern M. Sheldon
K–12 Curriculum and Instruction
    Specialist
Rowland Unified School District
Rowland Heights, California

Jim Shields
Instructor
El Toro High School
Saddleback Valley Unified School
    District
Lake Forest, California

CRITICAL REVIEWERS

Oscar Browne
Lincoln High School
San Diego, California

Paulette Dewey
Toledo Public School
Toledo, Ohio

R. E. Fisher
Westlake High School
Atlanta, Georgia

Janice Gauthier
Everett High School
Everett, Massachusetts

Victor Jaccarino
Herricks High School
New Hyde Park, New York

Barbara Kimbrough
Kane Area High School
Kane, Pennsylvania

Dr. Louisa Kramer-Vida
Oyster Bay-East Norwich School
    District
Oyster Bay, New York

Dara Mosher
Ramona High School
Riverside, California

Toni Lee Olson
Nogales High School
La Puente, California

Mary Ellen Snodgrass
Hickory High School
Hickory, North Carolina

David Trimble
Norwin High School
N. Huntingdon, Pennsylvania

Donna Walthour
Greensburg Salem High School
Greensburg, Pennsylvania

John R. Williamson
Highlands High School
Fort Thomas, Kentucky

Rod Warren
Martin Luther King High School
Riverside, California

FIELD-TEST PARTICIPANTS

Sandra J. Gilligan
Passaic High School
Passaic, New Jersey

Lee Lowery
Highlands High School
Fort Thomas, Kentucky

Pamela Rockich
Barberton High School
Barberton, Ohio

Ellen Schunks
North County High School
Bonne Terre, Missouri

Casey Williams
Highlands High School
Fort Thomas, Kentucky

CONTENTS IN BRIEF

COLLECTION 1

Plot and Setting 1
Writing Workshop Writing an Autobiographical Narrative 56
Listening and Speaking Workshop Presenting a Narrative 64

COLLECTION 2

Character 73
Writing Workshop Writing a Biographical Narrative 122

COLLECTION 3

Narrator and Voice 137
Writing Workshop Analyzing Problems and Solutions 212
Listening and Speaking Workshop Giving a Persuasive Speech 220

COLLECTION 4

Comparing Themes 229
Writing Workshop Writing a Persuasive Essay 294
Listening and Speaking Workshop Participating in a Debate 302

COLLECTION 5

Irony and Ambiguity 313
Writing Workshop Comparing Media Genres 382

COLLECTION 6

Symbolism and Allegory 397
Writing Workshop Analyzing a Short Story 440
Listening and Speaking Workshop Presenting a
Literary Response 448

COLLECTION 7

Poetry 455
Writing Workshop Describing a Person 540
Listening and Speaking Workshop Presenting a Description 548

COLLECTION 8

Literary Criticism: Evaluating Style 555

Writing Workshop Writing a Short Story 602

COLLECTION 9

Literary Criticism: Biographical and Historical Approach 617

Writing Workshop Writing a Research Paper 690

Listening and Speaking Workshop Presenting Research 710

COLLECTION 10

Drama 719

Writing Workshop Comparing a Play and a Film 890

Listening and Speaking Workshop Analyzing and Evaluating Speeches 898

COLLECTION 11

Consumer and Workplace Documents 907

RESOURCE CENTER

Reading Matters 941

Writer's Handbook 955

Test Smarts 967

Handbook of Literary Terms 979

Handbook of Reading and Informational Terms 993

Language Handbook 1009

Glossary 1053

Spanish Glossary 1059

INFORMATIONAL READING FOCUS

COLLECTION 1
Synthesizing Sources   21

COLLECTION 2
Using Primary and
Secondary Sources   88

COLLECTION 3
Generating Research
Questions   187, 206

COLLECTION 4
Evaluating Arguments:
Pro and Con   284

COLLECTION 5
Generating Research
Questions and
Evaluating Sources   366

COLLECTION 6
Synthesizing Sources   411

COLLECTION 8
Evaluating an
Argument   577

COLLECTION 9
Using Primary and
Secondary Sources   632

COLLECTION 10
Evaluating an
Argument   881

Collection 1

PLOT AND SETTING

INFORMATIONAL READING FOCUS

SYNTHESIZING SOURCES

Elements of Literature
■ **Plot: A Sequence of Events** John Leggett 2

Jack Finney **Contents of the Dead Man's Pocket** .... SHORT STORY 4
Kenneth Koch CONNECTION / **You want a social life, with friends** .... POEM 18

Informational Text Link to Literature
Double Daddy Penny Parker .... NEWSPAPER ARTICLE 21
Diary of a Mad Blender
Sue Shellenbarger .... NEWSPAPER ARTICLE 24
The Child's View of Working Parents
Cora Daniels .... MAGAZINE ARTICLE 26

Louise Erdrich **The Leap** .... SHORT STORY 31
R. J. Brown CONNECTION / **The Day the Clowns Cried** .... INTERNET ARTICLE 40

Elements of Literature
■ **Setting: Putting Us There** John Leggett 44

Ray Bradbury **The Pedestrian** .... SHORT STORY 46

Read On FOR INDEPENDENT READING 55

Writing Workshop Writing an Autobiographical Narrative 56

Listening and Speaking Workshop Presenting a Narrative 64

Vocabulary Development

Word Analysis:
Prefixes 20

Analogies 29

Etymologies 42

Vocabulary
Resource File 54

The Power of
Connotations 54

COLLECTION 1: SKILLS REVIEW

Informational Reading Skills
What Price Glory? *by* Len Lewis .... MAGAZINE ARTICLE   66
Deprived of Parent Time? *by* Kim Campbell ... NEWSPAPER ARTICLE   67

Vocabulary Skills 70

Writing Skills 71

Collection 2

CHARACTER

INFORMATIONAL READING FOCUS

USING PRIMARY AND
SECONDARY SOURCES

Elements of Literature

■ **Characters: The Actors in a Story** John Leggett 74

| | | |
Alice Walker **Everyday Use** .... SHORT STORY 76
Nikki Giovanni CONNECTION / *from* **Hands: For Mother's Day** ..... PROSE POEM 84
Edgar Lee Masters CONNECTION / **Lucinda Matlock** .... DRAMATIC MONOLOGUE 85

Informational Text Link to Literature

Interview with Alice Walker Roland L. Freeman ... INTERVIEW 88

Interview with Nikki Giovanni
Roland L. Freeman .... INTERVIEW 91

"Thinkin' on Marryin'" Patricia Cooper *and*
Norma Bradley Allen .... ORAL HISTORY 91

A Baby's Quilt to Sew Up the Generations
Felicia R. Lee .... NEWSPAPER ARTICLE 93

Elements of Literature

■ **Character Interactions: Relationships and
Conflicts** John Leggett 96

Amy Tan **Two Kinds** .... SHORT STORY 98

Santha Rama Rau **By Any Other Name** .... AUTOBIOGRAPHY 112

Read On FOR INDEPENDENT READING 121

Writing Workshop Writing a Biographical Narrative 122

COLLECTION 2: SKILLS REVIEW

Literary Skills
Powder *by* Tobias Wolff .... SHORT STORY 130

Vocabulary Skills 134

Writing Skills 135

Vocabulary Development

Clarifying Word Meanings: Look at the Context 87

Clarifying Word Meanings: Comparison and Contrast 110

Putting Words in Context: Cluster Diagrams 120

Collection 3

Narrator and Voice

INFORMATIONAL READING FOCUS

GENERATING RESEARCH
QUESTIONS

Elements of Literature

■ **Point of View: The Story's Voice** John Leggett 138

Stephen Vincent Benét **By the Waters of Babylon** .... SHORT STORY 140

Saki **The Storyteller** .... SHORT STORY 154

Tom Godwin **The Cold Equations** .... SHORT STORY 163
Richard Brautigan CONNECTION / **All Watched Over by Machines
of Loving Grace** .... POEM 184

Informational Text Link to Literature
Taste—The Final Frontier Esther Addley .... NEWSPAPER ARTICLE 187

Frank McCourt **Typhoid Fever** *from* **Angela's Ashes** ...... AUTOBIOGRAPHY 193
Barbara Sande Dimmitt CONNECTION / **The Education of
Frank McCourt** .... MAGAZINE ARTICLE 201

Informational Text Link to Literature
An Ancient Enemy Gets Tougher Karen Watson .... WEB SITE 206

Read On FOR INDEPENDENT READING 211

Writing Workshop Analyzing Problems and Solutions 212

Listening and Speaking Workshop Giving a
Persuasive Speech 220

Vocabulary Development

Suffixes 153

Using Context Clues . . . 162

Using a Thesaurus to
Find Synonyms 186

Word Mapping 192

Antonyms 205

COLLECTION **3**: SKILLS REVIEW

Informational Reading Skills
Local Hands on a New Space Project
by Seema Mehta . . . . NEWSPAPER ARTICLE 222

Vocabulary Skills 226

Writing Skills 227

Collection 4

Comparing Themes

INFORMATIONAL READING FOCUS
EVALUATING ARGUMENTS: PRO AND CON

Elements of Literature
■ **Theme: What Does It Mean?** John Leggett 230

Elements of Literature
Comparing Universal Themes 232

Judith Ortiz Cofer   **Catch the Moon** . . . . SHORT STORY   233

W. D. Wetherell   **The Bass, the River, and Sheila Mant** . . . . . . SHORT STORY   243
Richard Brautigan   CONNECTION / **It's Raining in Love** . . . . POEM   251

Writing a Comparison-Contrast Essay:
Comparing Universal Themes 254

Elements of Literature
Comparing a Theme Across Genres 255

Isabel Allende   **And of Clay Are We Created**
translated by Margaret Sayers Peden .... SHORT STORY 256

Bradley Graham   CONNECTION / **Ill-Equipped Rescuers**
Dig Out Volcano Victims .... NEWSPAPER ARTICLE 267

Roger Rosenblatt   **The Man in the Water** .... ESSAY 272
King James Bible   CONNECTION / **The Parable of the**
Good Samaritan .... BIBLE PARABLE 278

John Christian Hoyle   CONNECTION / **A State Championship Versus**
Runner's Conscience .... OP-ED ARTICLE 279

Writing a Comparison-Contrast Essay:
Comparing a Theme Across Genres 283

Informational Text Link to Literature

**If Decency Doesn't, Law Should Make Us
Samaritans** Gloria Allred *and* Lisa Bloom .... OP-ED ARTICLE 284

Good Samaritans U.S.A. Are Afraid to Act
Ann Sjoerdsma .... OP-ED ARTICLE 288

Read On FOR INDEPENDENT READING 293

Writing Workshop Writing a Persuasive Essay 294

Listening and Speaking Workshop
Participating in a Debate 302

Vocabulary Development

Word Meanings 242

Figurative Language 242

Synonyms and
Antonyms 253

Mapping a Word's
Origins 271

Word Roots 271

Synonyms and
Connotations 282

Jargon: Legalese 292

Use a Word, and
"Own" It 292

COLLECTION 4: SKILLS REVIEW

Literary Skills
What Happened During the Ice Storm
by Jim Heynen . . . . SHORT STORY 306
Gracious Goodness by Marge Piercy . . . . POEM 308

Vocabulary Skills 310

Writing Skills 311

Collection 5

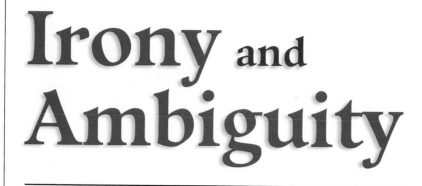

Irony and Ambiguity

INFORMATIONAL READING FOCUS

GENERATING RESEARCH
QUESTIONS AND
EVALUATING SOURCES

Elements of Literature

■ **Irony and Ambiguity: Surprises and Uncertainties**
John Leggett 314

Roald Dahl   **Lamb to the Slaughter** .... SHORT STORY   316

Hanson W. Baldwin   **R.M.S. Titanic** .... HISTORICAL ARTICLE   328
Harry Senior   CONNECTION / **A Fireman's Story** .... EYEWITNESS ACCOUNT   345
Mrs. D. H. Bishop   CONNECTION / **From a Lifeboat** .... EYEWITNESS ACCOUNT   346

Jon Krakauer   *from* **Into Thin Air** .... MAGAZINE ARTICLE   349
Informational Text Link to Literature
Explorers Say There's Still Lots to Look For
Helen O'Neill .... NEWSPAPER ARTICLE   366

James Stevenson   **Notes from a Bottle** .... SHORT STORY   374

Read On FOR INDEPENDENT READING 381

Writing Workshop Comparing Media Genres 382

Vocabulary Development

Using Context Clues ... 327

Word Maps 348

Words from
Mythology 348

Analogies 365

Technical Vocabulary 365

Words in Context 373

Word Clues: Greek
and Latin Roots and
Relations 373

Word Roots and
Their Families 380

COLLECTION 5: SKILLS REVIEW

Reading Skills

The Last Frontier *by* Michael D. Lemonick ..... MAGAZINE ARTICLE 390

Vocabulary Skills 394

Writing Skills 395

Collection 6

SYMBOLISM AND ALLEGORY

INFORMATIONAL READING FOCUS

SYNTHESIZING SOURCES

Elements of Literature

■ **Symbolism and Allegory: Signs of Something More**
John Leggett 398

Doris Lessing   **Through the Tunnel** .... SHORT STORY   400

Informational Text   Link to Literature

Coming of Age, Latino Style: Special Rite Ushers
Girls into Adulthood   Cindy Rodriguez ..... NEWSPAPER ARTICLE   411

Vision Quest .... ENCYCLOPEDIA ARTICLE   413

Crossing a Threshold to Adulthood
Jessica Barnes .... OP-ED ARTICLE   414

Edgar Allan Poe   **The Masque of the Red Death** .... SHORT STORY   418

James Cross Giblin   CONNECTION / **The Black Death**
from **When Plague Strikes** .... HISTORY   429

Robert Frost   **Stopping by Woods on a Snowy Evening** .... POEM   433
After Apple-Picking .... POEM   435

Read On FOR INDEPENDENT READING 439

Writing Workshop Analyzing a Short Story 440

Listening and Speaking Workshop Presenting a
Literary Response 448

Vocabulary Development

Analogies 410
Word Mapping 417
Context Clues 432

COLLECTION 6: SKILLS REVIEW

Literary Skills
The Blue Stones by Isak Dinesen .... SHORT STORY 450

Vocabulary Skills 452

Writing Skills 453

Collection 7

Poetry

IMAGERY

Elements of Literature

■ **Imagery: Seeing with Our Minds**

John Malcolm Brinnin 456

John Haines   **Moons** .... POEM   456

Emily Dickinson   **The Moon was but a Chin of Gold** .... POEM   457

Aleksandr Solzhenitsyn   **A Storm in the Mountains**
translated by Michael Glenny .... PROSE POEM   458

Pat Mora   **Same Song** .... POEM   461

Li-Young Lee   **Eating Together** .... POEM   465

Rita Dove   **Grape Sherbet** .... POEM   468

Garrett Hongo   **The Legend** .... ELEGY   471

Garrett Hongo   CONNECTION / **Hongo Reflects
on "The Legend"** .... REFLECTION   474

FIGURATIVE LANGUAGE

Elements of Literature

■ **Figurative Language: Language of the Imagination**
John Malcolm Brinnin 477

N. Scott Momaday   **Simile** . . . . POEM   479

Amy Lowell   **The Taxi** . . . . POEM   481

Jimmy Santiago Baca   **I Am Offering This Poem** . . . . POEM   482

E. E. Cummings   **since feeling is first** . . . . POEM   484

Emily Dickinson   **Heart! We will forget him!** . . . . POEM   487

Ono Komachi   **Three Japanese Tankas**
translated by Jane Hirshfield *with* Mariko Aratani . . . . TANKAS   489

William Shakespeare   **Shall I Compare Thee to a Summer's Day?** . . . . SONNET   493

Pablo Neruda   **Ode to My Socks** *translated by* Robert Bly . . . . ODE   497
Pablo Neruda   CONNECTION / **The Word** . . . . MEMOIR   501

THE SOUNDS OF POETRY

Elements of Literature

■ **The Sounds of Poetry: Rhythm, Rhyme, and Other Sound Effects** John Malcolm Brinnin

.... 503

Emily Dickinson **This is the land the Sunset washes** .... POEM 505

John Masefield **Sea Fever** .... POEM 506

Anonymous **Bonny Barbara Allan** .... BALLAD 509

Naomi Shihab Nye **The Flying Cat** .... POEM 513
Bill Moyers CONNECTION / **Interview with Naomi Shihab Nye** ... INTERVIEW 516

John Updike **Ex–Basketball Player** .... POEM 518

Lucille Clifton **miss rosie** .... POEM 521

Joy Harjo **Remember** .... POEM 527

Gwendolyn Brooks **We Real Cool** .... POEM 531

Carl Sandburg **Jazz Fantasia** .... POEM 535

Read On FOR INDEPENDENT READING 539

Writing Workshop Describing a Person 540

Listening and Speaking Workshop
Presenting a Description 548

Vocabulary Development

Archaic Words 496

Idioms 525

Jargon: Job-Related
Vocabulary 526

COLLECTION 7: SKILLS REVIEW

Literary Skills

Fireworks *by* Amy Lowell . . . . POEM 550

Writing Skills 552

Collection 8

LITERARY CRITICISM
Evaluating Style

INFORMATIONAL READING FOCUS
EVALUATING AN ARGUMENT

Elements of Literature
■ **Evaluating Style:** *How* **It's Said** Mara Rockliff 556

Sandra Cisneros   **Geraldo No Last Name** . . . . SHORT STORY   558

Lisa Fugard   **Night Calls** . . . . SHORT STORY   564
Linda Pastan   CONNECTION / **Waiting for E. gularis** . . . . POEM   573
Informational Text   Link to Literature
Call of the Wild—Save Us! Norman Myers . . . MAGAZINE ARTICLE   577

Gabriel García Márquez   **A Very Old Man with Enormous Wings**
translated by Gregory Rabassa . . . . SHORT STORY   586
Jack Agüeros   CONNECTION / **Sonnet for Heaven Below** . . . . POEM   597

Vocabulary Development

Words from Spanish 563

Verifying Meanings
by Examples 576

Using Contexts 585

Literal and Figurative
Use of Words 585

Roots and Relations 599

Literal and Figurative
Language: Imagery 599

Read On FOR INDEPENDENT READING 601

Writing Workshop Writing a Short Story 602

COLLECTION 8: SKILLS REVIEW

Literary Skills
My Lucy Friend Who Smells Like Corn
by Sandra Cisneros ....SHORT STORY 610

Vocabulary Skills 613

Writing Skills 614

Collection 9

LITERARY CRITICISM

Biographical and Historical Approach

INFORMATIONAL READING FOCUS

USING PRIMARY AND SECONDARY SOURCES

Elements of Literature

■ **Biography and History: How the Two Affect Literary Criticism** Kylene Beers 618

Langston Hughes   **I, Too** .... POEM 618

Tim O'Brien   **Where Have You Gone, Charming Billy?** .... SHORT STORY 620
Lily Lee Adams   CONNECTION / **The Friendship Only Lasted a Few Seconds** .... POEM 629

Informational Text Link to Literature

The War Escalates *from* **The American Nation**
Paul Boyer .... TEXTBOOK 632

Dear Folks Kenneth W. Bagby .... LETTER 637

from **Declaration of Independence from the War in Vietnam** Martin Luther King, Jr. .... SPEECH 639

Sir Thomas Malory   **The Sword in the Stone** *retold by* Keith Baines ..... LEGEND   **644**

John Steinbeck   CONNECTION / **"The Magic Happened"** .... REFLECTION   **648**

Sir Thomas Malory   **The Tale of Sir Launcelot du Lake**
retold by Keith Baines .... LEGEND   **651**

David Adams Leeming   CONNECTION / **The Romance: Where Good**
Always Triumphs .... ESSAY   **657**

retold by Edith Hamilton   **Theseus** .... GREEK MYTH   **660**

Bill Moyers *with* Joseph Campbell   CONNECTION / **"All We Need Is That Piece**
of String" .... INTERVIEW   **669**

retold by
Olivia E. Coolidge   **Sigurd, the Dragon Slayer** .... NORSE MYTH   **673**

Read On FOR INDEPENDENT READING **689**

Writing Workshop Writing a Research Paper **690**

Listening and Speaking Workshop Presenting Research **710**

Vocabulary Development

Meaning Maps 631

Synonyms and
Connotations 631

Clarifying Word
Meanings 643

Analogies 650

Demonstrating Word
Knowledge 659

English Word
Origins 659

Words Derived
from Greek and
Roman Myths 672

Words from Old Norse
and Anglo-Saxon 688

COLLECTION 9: SKILLS REVIEW

Informational Reading Skills

The Media and the War *from* The American Nation
by Paul Boyer . . . . TEXTBOOK 712

from The Vietnam War: An Eyewitness History
edited by Sanford Wexler

"Thanks a lot" *by* Pfc. John M. G. Brown . . . . LETTER 713

"As I fell" *by* Dickey Chappelle . . . . EYEWITNESS ACCOUNT 713

"For the third time" *by* Du Luc . . . . DIARY 714

from Born on the Fourth of July *by* Ron Kovic . . . . AUTOBIOGRAPHY 714

Vocabulary Skills 716

Writing Skills 717

Collection 10

DRAMA

INFORMATIONAL READING FOCUS

EVALUATING AN ARGUMENT

Elements of Literature
■ **Drama: Forms and Stagecraft** Diane Tasca 720

Anton Chekhov   **The Brute: A Joke in One Act**
translated by Eric Bentley .... COMEDY 724

William Shakespeare's Life: A Biographical Sketch
Robert Anderson 741
The Elizabethan Stage Robert Anderson 745
The Play: The Results of Violence 750
How to Read Shakespeare 752

William Shakespeare   **The Tragedy of Julius Caesar** .... TRAGEDY 754
Act I 758
Act II 782
Act III 806
Act IV 834
Act V 854

Aristotle   CONNECTION / **What Is a Tragic Hero?**
translated by S. H. Butcher .... THEORY 872

Jimmy Breslin   CONNECTION / **The Fear and the Flames** ...... FEATURE ARTICLE 874

Informational Text Link to Literature
Julius Caesar **in an Absorbing Production**
John Mason Brown .... PLAY REVIEW 881

Read On FOR INDEPENDENT READING 889

Writing Workshop Comparing a Play and a Film 890

Listening and Speaking Workshop Analyzing and
Evaluating Speeches 898

Vocabulary Development

Word Analogies 739

Word Connotations 739

Multiple Meanings:
Recognizing Puns 781

Understanding
Elizabethan English 805

Clarifying Meanings:
Words in Context 888

COLLECTION 10: SKILLS REVIEW

Informational Reading Skills

Brutus's Funeral Speech *by* Phyllis Goldenberg .... ESSAY 902

Vocabulary Skills 904

Writing Skills 905

Collection 11

CONSUMER AND WORKPLACE DOCUMENTS

Music on the E-frontier

by Flo Ota De Lange *and*
Sheri Henderson

Introduction: Music on the E-frontier 908

Evaluating the Logic of Functional Documents 909

Following Technical Directions 913

Analyzing Functional Workplace Documents 916

Citing Internet Sources 921

Reading Consumer Documents 927

Writing Technical Documents 932

Writing Business Letters 934

COLLECTION 11: SKILLS REVIEW

Informational Reading Skills
Consumer and Workplace Documents 938

Resource Center

Reading Matters *by* Kylene Beers 941
Why Reading Matters 941
When the Text Is Tough 942
Improving Your Comprehension 943
Improving Your Reading Rate 951

Writer's Handbook 955
The Writing Process 955
Paragraphs 957
The Writer's Language 961
Designing Your Writing 963

Test Smarts *by* Flo Ota De Lange *and* Sheri Henderson 967
Strategies for Taking Multiple-Choice Tests 967
Strategies for Taking Writing Tests 974

Handbook of Literary Terms 979

Handbook of Reading and Informational Terms 993

Language Handbook 1009
The Parts of Speech 1009
Agreement 1010
Using Verbs 1014
Using Pronouns 1017
Using Modifiers 1019
Phrases 1022
Clauses 1024
Sentence Structure 1026
Writing Complete Sentences 1029
Writing Effective Sentences 1030
Capitalization 1034
Punctuation 1038, 1041, 1044
Spelling 1046
Glossary of Usage 1049

Glossary 1053

Spanish Glossary 1059

Acknowledgments 1066

Picture Credits 1070

Index of Skills
Literary Skills 1073
Informational Reading Skills 1075
Vocabulary Skills 1077
Reading Skills 1078
Writing Skills 1078
Language (Grammar, Usage, and Mechanics) Skills 1083
Listening and Speaking Skills 1086
Independent Reading 1088

Index of Art 1089

Index of Authors and Titles 1091

SKILLS, WORKSHOPS, AND FEATURES

SKILLS

ELEMENTS OF LITERATURE ESSAYS

Plot: A Sequence of Events
John Leggett 2

Setting: Putting Us There
John Leggett 44

Characters: The Actors in a Story
John Leggett 74

Character Interactions:
Relationships and Conflicts
John Leggett 96

Point of View: The Story's Voice
John Leggett 138

Theme: What Does It Mean?
John Leggett 230

Irony and Ambiguity:
Surprises and Uncertainties
John Leggett 314

Symbolism and Allegory:
Signs of Something More
John Leggett 398

Imagery: Seeing with Our Minds
John Malcolm Brinnin 456

Figurative Language:
Language of the Imagination
John Malcolm Brinnin 477

The Sounds of Poetry: Rhythm,
Rhyme, and Other Sound Effects
John Malcolm Brinnin 503

Evaluating Style: *How* It's Said
Mara Rockliff 556

Biography and History:
How the Two Affect Literary Criticism
Kylene Beers 618

Drama: Forms and Stagecraft
Diane Tasca 720

The Elizabethan Stage
Robert Anderson 745

LITERARY SKILLS

Time and Sequence 4

Flashback and Foreshadowing 31

Setting 46, 140

Mood 46, 564

Character Traits 76

Conflict and Motivation 98

Character and Autobiography 112

First-Person Point of View 140

Omniscient Point of View 154

Satire 154

Third-Person-Limited Point of View 163

Voice 193

Comparing Universal Themes 232

Theme 233, 243, 256

Comparing a Theme Across Genres 255

Fact Versus Fiction 256

Essays 272

Irony 316, 328, 349

Objective and Subjective Writing 328

Contradictions 349

Ambiguities and Subtleties 374

Symbols 400, 433

Allegory 418

Prose Poems 458

Imagery 461

Speaker 465

Tone 471, 558

Simile 479

Lyric Poetry 482

Metaphors 484

Personification 487

Tanka Structure 489

Sonnet 493

Ode 497

Meter 506

Rhyme 506

Ballad 509

Free Verse 513

Sound Effects 518

Idioms 521

Repetition and Refrain 527

Alliteration 531

Onomatopoeia 535

Style 558

Diction 558

Magic Realism 586

Understanding Historical Context 620

Seeing an Author in His Work 620

Arthurian Legend 644

Literature of Romance 651

Greek Myths 660

Norse Myths 673

Comedy 724

Farce 724

Tragedy 754

READING SKILLS FOR LITERARY TEXTS

Cause and Effect 4, 349

Making Predictions 31, 316, 724

Author's Purpose 46, 154, 256

Making Inferences 98, 243, 374

Comparison and Contrast 112, 232, 255

Drawing Conclusions 140

Monitoring
Your Reading 163, 400, 418, 433, 558, 564

Evaluating Credibility 193

Making a Generalization 233

Summarizing 272, 651

Understanding Text Structures 328

Appreciating a Writer's Style 586

How to Read Shakespeare 752

Paraphrasing 833

Recognizing Anachronisms 853

Memorizing Famous Passages 880

READING MATTERS

Why Reading Matters 941

When the Text Is Tough 942

Improving Your Comprehension 943

Improving Your Reading Rate 951

READING SKILLS FOR INFORMATIONAL TEXTS

Synthesizing Sources 21, 411

Main Idea 21, 88, 411, 577, 632

Paraphrase 21, 411

Compare and Contrast 21, 411

Using Primary and Secondary Sources 88, 632

Evaluating Sources 88, 366, 411, 578, 633

Facts and Opinions 88, 284, 366, 411, 577, 633

Generating Research Questions 187, 206, 366

Researching Information 206

Evaluating an Argument 284, 577, 881

Evidence 284, 577, 881

Credibility 284, 411, 577, 578, 633, 881

Generalization 284, 577, 881

Logical Appeals 284, 577

Emotional Appeals 284, 577

Evaluating Internet Sources 366

Author's Purpose or Intent ... 411, 577, 578, 632, 881

Author's Claim or Opinion 577

Text Structure 577, 919

Tone 578, 633, 881

Audience 633, 881

Evaluating the Logic of
Functional Documents 909

Following Technical Directions 913

Analyzing Functional
Workplace Documents 916

Citing Internet Sources 921

Reading Consumer Documents 927

VOCABULARY SKILLS

Prefixes 20

Analogies 29, 365, 410, 650, 739

Word Derivations 42, 271, 373, 563, 599, 659, 688

Vocabulary Resource File 54

Connotations 54, 282, 631, 739

Context Clues ... 87, 120, 162, 327, 373, 432, 576, 585

Word Knowledge 110, 242, 292, 576, 643, 659

Suffixes 153

Using a Thesaurus 186

Semantic (Word) Maps 192, 271, 348, 417, 631

Antonyms 205, 253

Figurative Language 242, 585, 599

Synonyms 253, 282, 631

Jargon 292, 526

Words from Mythology 348, 672

Technical Vocabulary 365

Idioms 525

A Changing Language:
English Word Origins 659

Multiple Meanings 781

WORKSHOPS

WRITING WORKSHOPS

Writing an Autobiographical Narrative 56

Writing a Biographical Narrative 122

Analyzing Problems and Solutions 212

Writing a Persuasive Essay 294

Comparing Media Genres 382

Analyzing a Short Story 440

Describing a Person 540

Writing a Short Story 602

Writing a Research Paper 690

Comparing a Play and a Film 890

LISTENING AND SPEAKING WORKSHOPS

Presenting a Narrative 64

Giving a Persuasive Speech 220

Participating in a Debate 302

Presenting a Literary Response 448

Presenting a Description 548

Presenting Research 710

Analyzing and Evaluating Speeches 898

FEATURES

A CLOSER LOOK

Black Box: Air Florida Flight 90 275

Initiation Rights 407

Poetry in the Golden Age of Japan 489

Database: Vietnam 624

Roman Superstitions 778

Roman Government: Rule by the Rich 831

GRAMMAR LINK

Using Personal Pronouns 43

Dialect 95

Main or Subordinate Clause 111

Making Pronouns Clear 120

Inverted Order 162, 496

Subject and Verb Agreement 186

Usage and Style: Creating Voice 205

Run-on Sentences 253

Eliminating Wordiness 282

Active or Passive Voice 327

Using Modifiers Correctly 380

Participles 410

Revising Sentence Fragments 563

Varying Sentence Length and Structure 600

Misplaced Modifiers 650

Using Transitions 740

SKILLS, WORKSHOPS, AND FEATURES

LANGUAGE HANDBOOK

The Parts of Speech 1009

Agreement 1010

Using Verbs 1014

Using Pronouns 1017

Using Modifiers 1019

Phrases.......................................1022

Clauses 1024

Sentence Structure 1026

Writing Complete Sentences 1029

Writing Effective Sentences 1030

Capitalization 1034

Punctuation 1038, 1041, 1044

Spelling.......................................1046

Glossary of Usage 1049

SKILLS REVIEW

Literary Skills 130, 306, 450, 550, 610

Informational
Reading Skills 66, 222, 390, 712, 902, 938

Vocabulary Skills 70, 134, 226, 310, 394,
452, 613, 716, 904

Writing Skills 71, 135, 227, 311, 395, 453,
552, 614, 717, 905

TEST SMARTS

Strategies for Taking Multiple-Choice Tests 967

Strategies for Taking Writing Tests 974

WRITER'S HANDBOOK

The Writing Process 955

Paragraphs 957

The Writer's Language 961

Designing Your Writing 963

SELECTIONS BY GENRE

FICTION

LEGEND

The Sword in the Stone
Sir Thomas Malory 644

The Tale of Sir Launcelot du Lake
Sir Thomas Malory 651

MYTH

Theseus
retold by Edith Hamilton 660

Sigurd, the Dragon Slayer
retold by Olivia E. Coolidge 673

SHORT STORY

Contents of the Dead Man's Pocket
Jack Finney 4

The Leap
Louise Erdrich 31

The Pedestrian
Ray Bradbury 46

Everyday Use
Alice Walker 76

Two Kinds
Amy Tan 98

Powder
Tobias Wolff 130

By the Waters of Babylon
Stephen Vincent Benét 140

The Storyteller
Saki 154

The Cold Equations
Tom Godwin 163

Catch the Moon
Judith Ortiz Cofer 233

The Bass, the River, and Sheila Mant
W. D. Wetherell 243

And of Clay Are We Created
Isabel Allende 256

What Happened During the Ice Storm
Jim Heynen 306

Lamb to the Slaughter
Roald Dahl 316

Notes from a Bottle
James Stevenson 374

Through the Tunnel
Doris Lessing 400

The Masque of the Red Death
Edgar Allan Poe 418

The Blue Stones
Isak Dinesen 450

Geraldo No Last Name
Sandra Cisneros 558

Night Calls
Lisa Fugard 564

A Very Old Man with Enormous Wings
Gabriel García Márquez 586

My Lucy Friend Who Smells Like Corn
Sandra Cisneros 610

Where Have You Gone, Charming Billy?
Tim O'Brien 620

DRAMA

COMEDY

The Brute: A Joke in One Act
Anton Chekhov 724

TRAGEDY

The Tragedy of Julius Caesar
William Shakespeare 754

POETRY

You want a social life, with friends
Kenneth Koch 18

from **Hands: For Mother's Day**
Nikki Giovanni 84

Lucinda Matlock
Edgar Lee Masters 85

**All Watched Over by Machines
of Loving Grace**
Richard Brautigan 184

It's Raining in Love
Richard Brautigan 251

Gracious Goodness
Marge Piercy 308

Stopping by Woods on a Snowy Evening
Robert Frost 433

After Apple-Picking
Robert Frost 435

Moons
John Haines 456

The Moon was but a Chin of Gold
Emily Dickinson 457

A Storm in the Mountains
Aleksandr Solzhenitsyn 458

Same Song
Pat Mora 461

Eating Together
Li-Young Lee 465

Grape Sherbet
Rita Dove 468

The Legend
Garrett Hongo 471

Simile
N. Scott Momaday 479

The Taxi
Amy Lowell 481

I Am Offering This Poem
Jimmy Santiago Baca 482

since feeling is first
E. E. Cummings 484

Heart! We will forget him!
Emily Dickinson 487

Three Japanese Tankas
Ono Komachi 489

Shall I Compare Thee to a Summer's Day?
William Shakespeare 493

Ode to My Socks
Pablo Neruda 497

This is the land the Sunset washes
Emily Dickinson 505

Sea Fever
John Masefield 506

Bonny Barbara Allan
Anonymous 509

The Flying Cat
Naomi Shihab Nye 513

Ex–Basketball Player
John Updike 518

miss rosie
Lucille Clifton 521

Remember
Joy Harjo 527

We Real Cool
Gwendolyn Brooks 531

Jazz Fantasia
Carl Sandburg 535

Fireworks
Amy Lowell 550

Waiting for *E. gularis*
Linda Pastan 573

Sonnet for Heaven Below
Jack Agüeros 597

I, Too
Langston Hughes 618

**The Friendship Only Lasted
a Few Seconds**
Lily Lee Adams 629

BIBLE

The Parable of the Good Samaritan
King James Bible 278

NONFICTION AND INFORMATIONAL TEXT

AUTOBIOGRAPHY

By Any Other Name
Santha Rama Rau 112

Typhoid Fever *from* **Angela's Ashes**
Frank McCourt 193

from **Born on the Fourth of July**
Ron Kovic 714

BIOGRAPHY

**William Shakespeare's Life:
A Biographical Sketch**
Robert Anderson 741

DIARY

"For the third time" *from* **The Vietnam
War: An Eyewitness History**
Du Luc 714

ENCYCLOPEDIA ARTICLE

Vision Quest 413

ESSAY

The Man in the Water
Roger Rosenblatt 272

Brutus's Funeral Speech
Phyllis Goldenberg 902

EYEWITNESS ACCOUNT

A Fireman's Story
Harry Senior 345

From a Lifeboat
Mrs. D. H. Bishop 346

"As I fell" *from* **The Vietnam War:
An Eyewitness History**
Dickey Chappelle 713

FEATURE ARTICLE

The Fear and the Flames
Jimmy Breslin 874

HISTORICAL ARTICLE

R.M.S. Titanic
Hanson W. Baldwin 328

The Black Death
from **When Plague Strikes**
James Cross Giblin 429

INTERNET ARTICLE

The Day the Clowns Cried
R. J. Brown 40

INTERVIEW

Interview with Alice Walker
Roland L. Freeman 88

Interview with Nikki Giovanni
Roland L. Freeman 91

Interview with Naomi Shihab Nye
Bill Moyers 516

"All We Need Is That Piece of String"
(interview with Joseph Campbell)
Bill Moyers 669

LETTER

Dear Folks
Kenneth W. Bagby 637

"Thanks a lot" *from* **The Vietnam War:
An Eyewitness History**
Pfc. John M. G. Brown 713

MAGAZINE ARTICLE

The Child's View of Working Parents
Cora Daniels 26

What Price Glory?
Len Lewis 66

The Education of Frank McCourt
Barbara Sande Dimmitt 201

from **Into Thin Air**
Jon Krakauer 349

The Last Frontier
Michael D. Lemonick 390

Call of the Wild—Save Us!
Norman Myers 577

MEMOIR

The Word
Pablo Neruda 501

NEWSPAPER ARTICLE

Double Daddy
Penny Parker 21

Diary of a Mad Blender
Sue Shellenbarger 24

Deprived of Parent Time?
Kim Campbell 67

A Baby's Quilt to Sew Up the Generations
Felicia R. Lee 93

Taste—The Final Frontier
Esther Addley 187

Local Hands on a New Space Project
Seema Mehta 222

**Ill-Equipped Rescuers Dig Out
Volcano Victims**
Bradley Graham 267

**Explorers Say There's Still Lots
to Look For**
Helen O'Neill 366

**Coming of Age, Latino Style:
Special Rite Ushers Girls into Adulthood**
Cindy Rodriguez 411

OP-ED ARTICLE

**A State Championship Versus
Runner's Conscience**
John Christian Hoyle 279

**If Decency Doesn't, Law Should
Make Us Samaritans**
Gloria Allred *and* Lisa Bloom 284

**Good Samaritans U.S.A. Are
Afraid to Act**
Ann Sjoerdsma 288

Crossing a Threshold to Adulthood
Jessica Barnes 414

SELECTIONS BY GENRE

ORAL HISTORY

"Thinkin' on Marryin'"
Patricia Cooper *and* Norma Bradley Allen 91

PLAY REVIEW

***Julius Caesar* in an Absorbing Production**
John Mason Brown 881

REFLECTION

Hongo Reflects on "The Legend"
Garrett Hongo 474

"The Magic Happened"
John Steinbeck 648

SPEECH

from **Declaration of Independence**
from the War in Vietnam
Martin Luther King, Jr. 639

TEXTBOOK

The War Escalates
from **The American Nation**
Paul Boyer 632

The Media and the War
from **The American Nation**
Paul Boyer 712

THEORY

What Is a Tragic Hero?
Aristotle 872

WEB SITE

An Ancient Enemy Gets Tougher
Karen Watson 206

WORKPLACE AND CONSUMER DOCUMENTS

Multimedia Sound Card and Speakers:
Buying Guide and Reviews 910

Installing a Computer Sound Card 914

Music Lead Sheet 916

Collaboration Agreement 918

Aulsound Extended Service Contract 928

Troubleshooting Guide 929

FCC Information (USA) 930

Six Rules for Conflict Resolution 932

Business Letters 936, 937

Elements of Literature on the Internet

TO THE STUDENT

At the *Elements of Literature* Internet site, you can read texts by professional writers and learn the inside stories behind your favorite authors. You can also build your word power and analyze messages in the media. As you move through *Elements of Literature*, you will find the best online resources at **go.hrw.com.**

Here's how to log on:

1. Start your Web browser, and enter **go.hrw.com** in the Address or Location field.

2. Note the keyword in your textbook.

INTERNET

More About Plot

Keyword: LE5 10-1

3. Enter the keyword and click "go."

FEATURES OF THE SITE

More About the Writer
Author biographies provide the inside stories behind the lives and works of great writers.

More About the Literary Element
Graphic organizers present visual representations of literary concepts.

Interactive Reading Model
Interactive Reading Workshops guide you through high-interest informational articles and allow you to share your opinions through pop-up questions and polls.

More Writer's Models
Interactive Writer's Models use annotations and reading tips to help you with your own writing. Printable Professional Models and Student Models provide you with quality writing by real writers and students across the country.

Vocabulary Practice
Interactive vocabulary-building activities help you build your word power.

Projects and Activities
Projects and activities help you extend your study of literature through writing, research, art, and public speaking.

Speeches
Video clips from historical speeches provide you with the tools you need to analyze elements of great speechmaking.

Media Tutorials
Media tutorials help you dissect messages in the media and learn to create your own multimedia presentations.

PLOT AND SETTING

INFORMATIONAL READING FOCUS

SYNTHESIZING SOURCES

If you're a writer, a real writer, you're a descendant of those medieval storytellers who used to go into the square of a town and spread a little mat on the ground and sit on it and beat a bowl and say, "If you give me a copper coin, I will tell you a golden tale."

—Robertson Davies

INTERNET

Collection Resources

Keyword: LE5 10-1

Men exist for the sake of one another. Teach them then or bear with them.—Marcus Antoninus, *Meditations* VIII:59 (1958) by Jacob Lawrence. Egg tempera on hardboard (20¾″ × 16¾″).

Elements of Literature

Plot *by* John Leggett
A SEQUENCE OF EVENTS

go.
hrw
.com

INTERNET
More About Plot
Keyword: LE5 10-1

SKILLS FOCUS

Literary Skills
Understand plot structure and development of time and sequence.

How to Tell a Tale—In Sequence

This cartoon is funny—and it shows the nuts-and-bolts plot elements of any story. **Plot** is the sequence of related events that make a story hang together—it's what happens between "once upon a time" and "happily ever after." A plot will include characters who experience some problem or conflict (maybe facing a dragon), which is resolved in some way (maybe by a superhero). A complete story, of course, fills in the interesting details. It also takes place within a specific span of time.

The Building Blocks of Plot

1 A typical plot has four parts. The first part is the **basic situation** (sometimes called the **exposition**). The basic situation presents a main character who wants something very much and who encounters a conflict while trying to get it.

A young girl is cruelly treated by her jealous stepmother and stepsisters. She longs to go to the prince's ball, but all she has to wear is rags.

At this point the writer might develop the element of conflict further. Cinderella's stepmother might lock her in the cellar to keep her from going to the ball. That would be an **external conflict,** because it pits Cinderella against an *outside* force. If, however, Cinderella could go to the ball and hesitated out of shyness, she would experience an **internal conflict,** a struggle *inside* her own heart or mind.

2 In the next part of the plot, a series of **complications** arises, which causes new problems:

Cinderella's fairy godmother gets her an invitation to the ball, as well as a fashion makeover. There's a catch, however: If she isn't home by midnight, her gown will turn to rags and her coachmen into mice. At the ball the prince dances with Cinderella all night. At midnight she flees, losing her tiny glass slipper on the palace steps.

3 The high point of the plot is the **climax,** the story's most exciting or suspenseful moment, when something happens that decides the outcome of the conflict. The climax of this tale takes place when the prince discovers that the glass slipper fits Cinderella's dainty foot.

4 The last part of the plot is the **resolution,** or **denouement** (dā′ nōō·mä*n*′), when the problems are resolved and the story ends. In Cinderella's case she marries the prince in a fancy wedding, to which her wicked family is not invited. A more modern resolution to our story would suggest "they lived happily ever after, sort of" and would hint at what's behind the "sort of."

Timing Is Everything

The sequence of events described in Cinderella's tale is common to almost all stories. However, another important plot element remains to be considered: how the writer reveals the story's events within a span of time.

The usual way is to begin at the beginning and then tell about each event in the order in which it happens. This is called **chronological order.** However, writers also choose other techniques to manipulate time and control our feelings. To create **suspense,** for example, and to dramatize a moment of danger, they might slow time down—agonizingly. (You'll find this technique used in the following story, "Contents of the Dead Man's Pocket.")

Playing with Time

Writers also play with time by using **flashbacks,** in which the present action in a story is interrupted with a scene or scenes from the past. Flashbacks can reveal the past life of a character, explaining why someone is in a current situation. Some flashbacks cover a mere moment in time; others span many years. Sometimes writers also use **flash-forwards,** in which you visit a character's future.

With **foreshadowing**—another method for manipulating time—a writer plants clues that hint at something that will happen later in the plot. When you notice such a clue, you're drawn into the story: A clue that foreshadows danger, for example, will keep you on edge.

So whether writers have you looking back or thinking ahead, by playing with time, they hook you and draw you into their stories.

Practice

You can chart the **plot** of a story by using a diagram like the one below. Fill in a **plot diagram** for a fairy tale or a TV drama you know well. Television and movies make frequent use of **flashbacks** and **foreshadowing.** Insert those time tricks on your plot diagram as well.

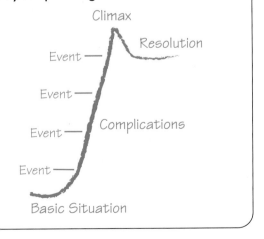

Climax

Resolution

Event —

Event —

Event — Complications

Event —

Basic Situation

Before You Read

Contents of the Dead Man's Pocket

Make the Connection

Quickwrite ✏️

In the story you're about to read, the main character finds himself in a hair-raising situation. Think of a time when you or someone you know felt almost paralyzed by fear. Where were you or the other person, and what happened? In your notebook, jot down some details about the tense situation.

Literary Focus

Time and Sequence: Ticktock . . .

Imagine a TV camera focused for eight hours on a sleeping teenager. TV producers have tried something like this, and the ratings for the experimental show were disappointing. The reason is simple: TV viewers, moviegoers, and story readers all want action. *Something* has to happen to the characters.

The series of related events that we all expect to find in a story is called the **plot.** Usually these events are told in **chronological order,** beginning with the first event and moving in sequence through a whole series of events until the story ends.

In "Contents of the Dead Man's Pocket," each event intensifies the reader's tension. To make the tension even stronger, the writer does something very interesting with time: He slows down the action so that you can almost feel the seconds ticking away. In fact, the time it takes to read the story probably matches the timing of the character's ordeal.

Reading Skills 📖

Understanding Cause and Effect

A **cause** is the reason *why* something happens. An **effect** is the result of some event or action. Most causes and effects happen in chains, with cause leading to effect leading to another cause, and so on. As this story unfolds, you'll be caught up in just such a chain of causes and effects. Indeed, many suspense-filled stories rely on edge-of-your-seat causes and effects that keep readers guessing.

Vocabulary Development

projection (prō·jek′shən) *n.*: something that juts out from a surface.

discarding (dis·kärd′iŋ) *v.* used as *adj.*: abandoning; getting rid of.

confirmation (kän′fər·mā′shən) *n.*: proof.

exhalation (eks′hə·lā′shən) *n.*: something breathed out; breath.

imperceptibly (im′pər·sep′tə·blē) *adv.*: in such a slight way as to be almost unnoticeable.

rebounded (ri·bound′id) *v.*: bounced back.

interminable (in·tur′mi·nə·bəl) *adj.*: endless.

irrelevantly (i·rel′ə·vənt·lē) *adv.*: in a way not relating to the point or situation.

incomprehensible (in·käm′prē·hen′sə·bəl) *adj.*: not understandable.

unimpeded (un′im·pēd′id) *adj.*: not blocked; unobstructed.

---

go.hrw.com

INTERNET

Vocabulary Practice

Keyword: LE5 10-1

SKILLS FOCUS

Literary Skills
Understand time and sequence.

Reading Skills
Understand cause and effect.

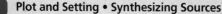

Contents of the Dead Man's Pocket

Jack Finney

He understood fully
that he might actually
be going to die . . .

At the little living-room desk Tom Benecke rolled two sheets of flimsy[1] and a heavier top sheet, carbon paper sandwiched between them, into his portable. *Interoffice Memo,* the top sheet was headed, and he typed tomorrow's date just below this; then he glanced at a creased yellow sheet, covered with his own handwriting, beside the typewriter. "Hot in here," he muttered to himself. Then, from the short hallway at his back, he heard the muffled clang of wire coat hangers in the bedroom closet, and at this reminder of what his wife was doing he thought: hot—guilty conscience.

He got up, shoving his hands into the back pockets of his gray wash slacks, stepped to the living-room window beside the desk and stood breathing on the glass, watching the expanding circlet of mist, staring down through the autumn night at Lexington Avenue,[2] eleven stories below. He was a tall, lean, dark-haired young man in a pullover sweater, who looked as though he had played not football, probably, but basketball in college. Now he placed the heels of his hands against the top edge of the lower window frame and shoved upward. But as usual the window didn't budge, and he had to lower his hands and then shoot them hard upward to jolt the window open a few inches. He dusted his hands, muttering.

But still he didn't begin his work. He crossed the room to the hallway entrance and, leaning against the doorjamb, hands shoved into his back pockets again, he called, "Clare?" When his wife answered, he said, "Sure you don't mind going alone?"

"No." Her voice was muffled, and he knew her head and shoulders were in the bedroom closet. Then the tap of her high heels sounded on the wood floor, and she appeared at the end of the little hallway, wearing a slip, both hands raised to one ear, clipping on an earring. She smiled at him—a slender, very pretty girl with light brown, almost blond, hair—her prettiness emphasized by the pleasant nature that showed in her face. "It's just that I hate you to miss this movie; you wanted to see it, too."

"Yeah, I know." He ran his fingers through his hair. "Got to get this done, though."

She nodded, accepting this. Then, glancing at the desk across the living room, she said, "You work too much, though, Tom—and too hard."

He smiled. "You won't mind, though, will you, when the money comes rolling in and I'm known as the Boy Wizard of Wholesale Groceries?"

"I guess not." She smiled and turned back toward the bedroom.

At his desk again, Tom lighted a cigarette; then a few moments later, as Clare appeared, dressed and ready to leave, he set it on the rim of the ashtray. "Just after seven," she said. "I can make the beginning of the first feature."

He walked to the front-door closet to help her on with her coat. He kissed her then and, for an instant, holding her close, smelling the perfume she had used, he was tempted to go with her; it was not actually true that he had to work tonight, though he very much wanted to. This was his own project, unannounced as yet in his office, and it could be postponed. But then they won't see it till Monday, he thought once again, and if I give it to the boss tomorrow he might read it over the weekend . . . "Have a good time," he said aloud. He gave his wife a little swat and opened the door for her, feeling the air from the building hallway, smelling faintly of floor wax, stream gently past his face.

He watched her walk down the hall, flicked a hand in response as she waved, and then he started to close the door, but it resisted for a

1. **flimsy** *n.*: thin paper used for typing carbon copies. Before computers and copying machines, copies of business communications were made with carbon paper.
2. **Lexington Avenue:** one of the main streets in New York City.

moment. As the door opening narrowed, the current of warm air from the hallway, channeled through this smaller opening now, suddenly rushed past him with accelerated force. Behind him he heard the slap of the window curtains against the wall and the sound of paper fluttering from his desk, and he had to push to close the door.

Turning, he saw a sheet of white paper drifting to the floor in a series of arcs, and another sheet, yellow, moving toward the window, caught in the dying current flowing through the narrow opening. As he watched, the paper struck the bottom edge of the window and hung there for an instant, plastered against the glass and wood. Then as the moving air stilled completely, the curtains swinging back from the wall to hang free again, he saw the yellow sheet drop to the window ledge and slide over out of sight.

He ran across the room, grasped the bottom of the window and tugged, staring through the glass. He saw the yellow sheet, dimly now in the darkness outside, lying on the ornamental ledge a yard below the window. Even as he watched, it was moving, scraping slowly along the ledge, pushed by the breeze that pressed steadily against the building wall. He heaved on the window with all his strength, and it shot open with a bang, the window weight rattling in the casing. But the paper was past his reach and, leaning out into the night, he watched it scud[3] steadily along the ledge to the south, half plastered against the building wall. Above the muffled sound of the street traffic far below, he could hear the dry scrape of its movement, like a leaf on the pavement.

The living room of the next apartment to the south projected a yard or more further out toward the street than this one; because of this the Beneckes paid seven and a half dollars less rent than their neighbors. And now the yellow sheet, sliding along the stone ledge, nearly invisible in the night, was stopped by the projecting blank wall of the next apartment. It lay motionless, then, in the corner formed by the two walls—a good five yards away, pressed firmly against the ornate corner ornament of the ledge by the breeze that moved past Tom Benecke's face.

He knelt at the window and stared at the yellow paper for a full minute or more, waiting for it to move, to slide off the ledge and fall, hoping he could follow its course to the street, and then hurry down in the elevator and retrieve it. But it didn't move, and then he saw that the paper was caught firmly between a projection of the convoluted[4] corner ornament and the ledge. He thought about the poker from the fireplace, then the broom, then the mop—discarding each thought as it occurred to him. There was nothing in the apartment long enough to reach that paper.

It was hard for him to understand that he actually had to abandon it—it was ridiculous—and he began to curse. Of all the papers on his desk, why did it have to be this one in particular! On four long Saturday afternoons he had stood in supermarkets, counting the people who passed certain displays, and the results were scribbled on that yellow sheet. From stacks of trade publications, gone over page by page in snatched half hours at work and during evenings at home, he had copied facts, quotations, and figures onto that sheet. And he had carried it with him to the Public Library on Fifth Avenue, where he'd spent a dozen lunch hours and early evenings adding more. All were needed to support and lend authority to his idea for a new grocery-store display method; without them his

---

4. **convoluted** (kän′və·l o͞ot′id) *adj.:* intricate; coiled.

Vocabulary

projection (prō·jek′shən) *n.:* something that juts out from a surface.

discarding (dis·kärd′iŋ) *v.* used as *adj.:* abandoning; getting rid of.

---

3. **scud** *v.:* glide or move swiftly.

idea was a mere opinion. And there they all lay, in his own improvised shorthand—countless hours of work—out there on the ledge.

For many seconds he believed he was going to abandon the yellow sheet, that there was nothing else to do. The work could be duplicated. But it would take two months, and the time to present this idea was *now,* for use in the spring displays. He struck his fist on the window ledge. Then he shrugged. Even though his plan was adopted, he told himself, it wouldn't bring him a raise in pay—not immediately, anyway, or as a direct result. It won't bring me a promotion either, he argued—not of itself.

But just the same—and he couldn't escape the thought—this and other independent projects, some already done and others planned for the future, would gradually mark him out from the score of other young men in his company. They were the way to change from a name on the payroll to a name in the minds of the company officials. They were the beginning of the long, long climb to where he was determined to be—at the very top. And he knew he was going out there in the darkness, after the yellow sheet fifteen feet beyond his reach.

By a kind of instinct, he instantly began making his intention acceptable to himself by laughing at it. The mental picture of himself sidling along the ledge outside was absurd—it was actually comical—and he smiled. He imagined himself describing it; it would make a good story at the office and, it occurred to him, would add a special interest and importance to his memorandum, which would do it no harm at all.

To simply go out and get his paper was an easy task—he could be back here with it in less than two minutes—and he knew he wasn't deceiving himself. The ledge, he saw, measuring it with his eye, was about as wide as the length of his shoe, and perfectly flat. And every fifth row of brick in the face of the building, he remembered—

leaning out, he verified this—was indented half an inch, enough for the tips of his fingers, enough to maintain balance easily. It occurred to him that if this ledge and wall were only a yard aboveground—as he knelt at the window staring out, this thought was the final confirmation of his intention—he could move along the ledge indefinitely.

On a sudden impulse, he got to his feet, walked to the front closet, and took out an old tweed jacket; it would be cold outside. He put it on and buttoned it as he crossed the room rapidly toward the open window. In the back of his mind he knew he'd better hurry and get this over with before he thought too much, and at the window he didn't allow himself to hesitate.

He swung a leg over the sill, then felt for and found the ledge a yard below the window with his foot. Gripping the bottom of the window frame very tightly and carefully, he slowly ducked his head under it, feeling on his face the sudden change from the warm air of the room to the chill outside. With infinite care he brought out his other leg, his mind concentrating on what he was doing. Then he slowly stood erect. Most of the putty, dried out and brittle, had dropped off the bottom edging of the window frame, he found, and the flat wooden edging provided a good gripping surface, a half inch or more deep, for the tips of his fingers.

Now, balanced easily and firmly, he stood on the ledge outside in the slight, chill breeze, eleven stories above the street, staring into his own lighted apartment, odd and different-seeming now.

First his right hand, then his left, he carefully shifted his fingertip grip from the puttyless window edging to an indented row of bricks directly to his right. It was hard to take the first shuffling

Vocabulary
confirmation (kän′fər·mā′shən) *n.*: proof.

sideways step then—to make himself move—and the fear stirred in his stomach, but he did it, again by not allowing himself time to think. And now—with his chest, stomach, and the left side of his face pressed against the rough cold brick—his lighted apartment was suddenly gone, and it was much darker out here than he had thought.

Without pause he continued—right foot, left foot, right foot, left—his shoe soles shuffling and scraping along the rough stone, never lifting from it, fingers sliding along the exposed edging of brick. He moved on the balls of his feet, heels lifted slightly; the ledge was not quite as wide as he'd expected. But leaning slightly inward toward the face of the building and pressed against it, he could feel his balance firm and secure, and moving along the ledge was quite as easy as he had thought it would be. He could hear the buttons of his jacket scraping steadily along the rough bricks and feel them catch momentarily, tugging a little, at each mortared crack. He simply did not permit himself to look down, though the compulsion[5] to do so never left him; nor did he allow himself actually to think. Mechanically—right foot, left foot, over and again—he shuffled along crabwise, watching the projecting wall ahead loom steadily closer. . . .

---

5. compulsion *n.:* driving force.

Then he reached it, and at the corner—he'd decided how he was going to pick up the paper—he lifted his right foot and placed it carefully on the ledge that ran along the projecting wall at a right angle to the ledge on which his other foot rested. And now, facing the building, he stood in the corner formed by the two walls, one foot on the ledging of each, a hand on the shoulder-high indentation of each wall. His forehead was pressed directly into the corner against the cold bricks, and now he carefully lowered first one hand, then the other, perhaps a foot farther down, to the next indentation in the rows of bricks.

Very slowly, sliding his forehead down the trough of the brick corner and bending his knees, he lowered his body toward the paper lying between his outstretched feet. Again he lowered his fingerholds another foot and bent his knees still more, thigh muscles taut, his forehead sliding and bumping down the brick V. Half squatting now, he dropped his left hand to the next indentation and then slowly reached with his right hand toward the paper between his feet.

He couldn't quite touch it, and his knees now were pressed against the wall; he could bend them no farther. But by ducking his head another inch lower, the top of his head now pressed against the bricks, he lowered his right shoulder and his fingers had the paper by a corner, pulling it loose. At the same instant he saw, between his legs and far below, Lexington Avenue stretched out for miles ahead.

He saw, in that instant, the Loew's theater sign, blocks ahead past Fiftieth Street; the miles of traffic signals, all green now; the lights of cars and street lamps; countless neon signs; and the moving black dots of people. And a violent, instantaneous explosion of absolute terror roared through him. For a motionless instant he saw himself externally—bent practically double, balanced on this narrow ledge, nearly half his body projecting out above the street far below—and he began to tremble violently, panic flaring through his mind and muscles, and he felt the blood rush from the surface of his skin.

In the fractional moment before horror paralyzed him, as he stared between his legs at that terrible length of street far beneath him, a fragment of his mind raised his body in a spasmodic jerk to an upright position again, but so violently that his head scraped hard against the wall, bouncing off it, and his body swayed outward to the knife-edge of balance, and he very nearly plunged backward and fell. Then he was leaning far into the corner again, squeezing and pushing into it, not only his face but his chest and stomach, his back arching; and his fingertips clung with all the pressure of his pulling arms to the shoulder-high half-inch indentation in the bricks.

He was more than trembling now; his whole body was racked with a violent shuddering beyond control, his eyes squeezed so tightly shut it was painful, though he was past awareness of that. His teeth were exposed in a frozen grimace, the strength draining like water from his knees and calves. It was extremely likely, he knew, that he would faint, slump down along the wall, his face scraping, and then drop backward, a limp weight, out into nothing. And to save his life he concentrated on holding on to consciousness, drawing deliberate deep breaths of cold air into his lungs, fighting to keep his senses aware.

Then he knew that he would not faint, but he could not stop shaking nor open his eyes. He stood where he was, breathing deeply, trying to hold back the terror of the glimpse he had had of what lay below him; and he knew he had made a mistake in not making himself stare down at the street, getting used to it and accepting it, when he had first stepped out onto the ledge.

It was impossible to walk back. He simply could not do it. He couldn't bring himself to make the slightest movement. The strength was gone from his legs; his shivering hands—numb, cold, and desperately rigid—had lost all deftness;[6] his easy ability to move and balance was gone. Within a step or two, if he tried to move, he knew that he would stumble clumsily and fall.

Seconds passed, with the chill faint wind pressing the side of his face, and he could hear the toned-down volume of the street traffic far beneath him. Again and again it slowed and then stopped, almost to silence; then presently, even this high, he would hear the click of the traffic signals and the subdued roar of the cars starting up again. During a lull in the street sounds, he called out. Then he was shouting *"Help!"* so loudly it rasped his throat. But he felt the steady pressure of the wind, moving between his face and the blank wall, snatch up his cries as he uttered them, and he knew they must sound directionless and distant. And he remembered how habitually, here in New York, he himself heard and ignored shouts in the night. If anyone heard him, there was no sign of it, and presently

6. **deftness** *n.:* skillfulness; coordination.

Tom Benecke knew he had to try moving; there was nothing else he could do.

Eyes squeezed shut, he watched scenes in his mind like scraps of motion-picture film—he could not stop them. He saw himself stumbling suddenly sideways as he crept along the ledge and saw his upper body arc outward, arms flailing. He saw a dangling shoestring caught between the ledge and the sole of his other shoe, saw a foot start to move, to be stopped with a jerk, and felt his balance leaving him. He saw himself falling with a terrible speed as his body revolved in the air, knees clutched tight to his chest, eyes squeezed shut, moaning softly.

Out of utter necessity, knowing that any of these thoughts might be reality in the very next seconds, he was slowly able to shut his mind against every thought but what he now began to do. With fear-soaked slowness, he slid his left foot an inch or two toward his own impossibly distant window. Then he slid the fingers of his shivering left hand a corresponding distance. For a moment he could not bring himself to lift his right foot from one ledge to the other; then he did it, and became aware of the harsh exhalation of air from his throat and realized that he was panting. As his right hand, then, began to slide along the brick edging, he was astonished to feel the yellow paper pressed to the bricks underneath his stiff fingers, and he uttered a terrible, abrupt bark that might have been a laugh or a moan. He opened his mouth and took the paper in his teeth, pulling it out from under his fingers.

By a kind of trick—by concentrating his entire mind on first his left foot, then his left hand, then the other foot, then the other hand—he was able to move, almost imperceptibly, trembling steadily, very nearly without thought. But he could feel the terrible strength of the pent-up horror on just the other side of the flimsy barrier he had erected in his mind; and he knew that if it broke through he would lose this thin artificial control of his body.

During one slow step he tried keeping his eyes closed; it made him feel safer, shutting him off a little from the fearful reality of where he was. Then a sudden rush of giddiness swept over him and he had to open his eyes wide, staring sideways at the cold rough brick and angled lines of mortar, his cheek tight against the building. He kept his eyes open then, knowing that if he once let them flick outward, to stare for an instant at the lighted windows across the street, he would be past help.

He didn't know how many dozens of tiny sidling steps he had taken, his chest, belly, and face pressed to the wall; but he knew the slender hold he was keeping on his mind and body was going to break. He had a sudden mental picture of his apartment on just the other side of this wall—warm, cheerful, incredibly spacious. And he saw himself striding through it, lying down on the floor on his back, arms spread wide, reveling[7] in its unbelievable security. The impossible remoteness of this utter safety, the contrast between it and where he now stood, was more than he could bear. And the barrier broke then, and the fear of the awful height he stood on coursed through his nerves and muscles.

A fraction of his mind knew he was going to fall, and he began taking rapid blind steps with no feeling of what he was doing, sidling with a clumsy desperate swiftness, fingers scrabbling along the brick, almost hopelessly resigned to the sudden backward pull and swift motion outward and down. Then his moving left hand slid onto not brick but sheer emptiness, an impossible gap in the face of the wall, and he stumbled.

---

7. **reveling** (rev′əl·iŋ) v. used as adj.: taking great pleasure or delight.

Vocabulary

exhalation (eks′hə·lā′shən) n.: something breathed out; breath.

imperceptibly (im′pər·sep′tə·blē) adv.: in such a slight way as to be almost unnoticeable.

His right foot smashed into his left anklebone; he staggered sideways, began falling, and the claw of his hand cracked against glass and wood, slid down it, and his fingertips were pressed hard on the puttyless edging of his window. His right hand smacked gropingly beside it as he fell to his knees; and, under the full weight and direct downward pull of his sagging body, the open window dropped shudderingly in its frame till it closed and his wrists struck the sill and were jarred off.

For a single moment he knelt, knee bones against stone on the very edge of the ledge, body swaying and touching nowhere else, fighting for balance. Then he lost it, his shoulders plunging backward, and he flung his arms forward, his hands smashing against the window casing on either side; and—his body moving backward—his fingers clutched the narrow wood stripping of the upper pane.

For an instant he hung suspended between balance and falling, his fingertips pressed onto the quarter-inch wood strips. Then, with utmost delicacy, with a focused concentration of all his senses, he increased even further the strain on his fingertips hooked to these slim edgings of wood. Elbows slowly bending, he began to draw the full weight of his upper body forward, knowing that the instant his fingers slipped off these quarter-inch strips he'd plunge backward and be falling. Elbows imperceptibly bending, body shaking with the strain, the sweat starting from his forehead in great sudden drops, he pulled, his entire being and thought concentrated in his fingertips. Then suddenly, the strain slackened and ended, his chest touching the windowsill, and he was kneeling on the ledge, his forehead pressed to the glass of the closed window.

Dropping his palms to the sill, he stared into his living room—at the red-brown davenport[8] across the room, and a magazine he had left there; at the pictures on the walls and the gray rug; the entrance to the hallway; and at his papers, typewriter, and desk, not two feet from his nose. A movement from his desk caught his eye and he saw that it was a thin curl of blue smoke; his cigarette, the ash long, was still burning in the ashtray where he'd left it—this was past all belief—only a few minutes before.

His head moved, and in faint reflection from the glass before him he saw the yellow paper clenched in his front teeth. Lifting a hand from the sill he took it from his mouth; the moistened corner parted from the paper, and he spat it out.

For a moment, in the light from the living room, he stared wonderingly at the yellow sheet in his hand and then crushed it into the side pocket of his jacket.

He couldn't open the window. It had been pulled not completely closed, but its lower edge was below the level of the outside sill; there was no room to get his fingers underneath it. Between the upper sash and the lower was a gap not wide enough—reaching up, he tried—to get his fingers into; he couldn't push it open. The upper window panel, he knew from long experience, was impossible to move, frozen tight with dried paint.

Very carefully observing his balance, the fingertips of his left hand again hooked to the narrow stripping of the window casing, he drew back his right hand, palm facing the glass, and then struck the glass with the heel of his hand.

His arm rebounded from the pane, his body tottering, and he knew he didn't dare strike a harder blow.

But in the security and relief of his new position, he simply smiled; with only a sheet of glass between him and the room just before him, it was not possible that there wasn't a way past it. Eyes narrowing, he thought for a few moments about what to do. Then his eyes widened, for

---

8. **davenport** (dav′ən·pôrt′) *n.:* large sofa or couch.

Vocabulary
rebounded (ri·bound′id) *v.:* bounced back.

nothing occurred to him. But still he felt calm; the trembling, he realized, had stopped. At the back of his mind there still lay the thought that once he was again in his home, he could give release to his feelings. He actually *would* lie on the floor, rolling, clenching tufts of the rug in his hands. He would literally run across the room, free to move as he liked, jumping on the floor, testing and reveling in its absolute security, letting the relief flood through him, draining the fear from his mind and body. His yearning for this was astonishingly intense, and somehow he understood that he had better keep this feeling at bay.

He took a half dollar from his pocket and struck it against the pane, but without any hope that the glass would break and with very little disappointment when it did not. After a few moments of thought he drew his leg up onto the ledge and picked loose the knot of his shoelace. He slipped off the shoe and, holding it across the instep, drew back his arm as far as he dared and struck the leather heel against the glass. The pane rattled, but he knew he'd been a long way from breaking it. His foot was cold and he slipped the shoe back on. He shouted again, experimentally, and then once more, but there was no answer.

The realization suddenly struck him that he might have to wait here till Clare came home, and for a moment the thought was funny. He could see Clare opening the front door, withdrawing her key from the lock, closing the door behind her, and then glancing up to see him crouched on the other side of the window. He could see her rush across the room, face astounded and frightened, and hear himself shouting instructions: "Never mind how I got here! Just open the wind—" She couldn't open it, he remembered, she'd never been able to; she'd always had to call him. She'd have to get the building superintendent or a neighbor, and he pictured himself smiling and answering their questions as he climbed in. "I just wanted to get a breath of fresh air, so—"

He couldn't possibly wait here till Clare came home. It was the second feature she'd wanted to see, and she'd left in time to see the first. She'd be another three hours or— He glanced at his watch; Clare had been gone eight minutes. It wasn't possible, but only eight minutes ago he had kissed his wife goodbye. She wasn't even at the theater yet!

It would be four hours before she could possibly be home, and he tried to picture himself kneeling out here, fingertips hooked to these narrow strippings, while first one movie, preceded by a slow listing of credits, began, developed, reached its climax, and then finally ended. There'd be a newsreel next, maybe, and then an animated cartoon, and then interminable scenes from coming pictures. And then, once more, the beginning of a full-length picture—while all the time he hung out here in the night.

Vocabulary
interminable (in·tʉr′mi·nə·bəl) *adj.*: endless.

paper turned a page and then continued his reading. A figure passed another of the windows and was immediately gone.

In the inside pocket of his jacket he found a little sheaf of papers, and he pulled one out and looked at it in the light from the living room. It was an old letter, an advertisement of some sort; his name and address, in purple ink, were on a label pasted to the envelope. Gripping one end of the envelope in his teeth, he twisted it into a tight curl. From his shirt pocket he brought out a book of matches. He didn't dare let go the casing with both hands but, with the twist of paper in his teeth, he opened the matchbook with his free hand; then he bent one of the matches in two without tearing it from the folder, its red-tipped end now touching the striking surface. With his thumb, he rubbed the red tip across the striking area.

He did it again, then again, and still again, pressing harder each time, and the match suddenly flared, burning his thumb. But he kept it alight, cupping the matchbook in his hand and shielding it with his body. He held the flame to the paper in his mouth till it caught. Then he snuffed out the match flame with his thumb and forefinger, careless of the burn, and replaced the book in his pocket. Taking the paper twist in his hand, he held it flame down, watching the flame crawl up the paper, till it flared bright. Then he held it behind him over the street, moving it from side to side, watching it over his shoulder, the flame flickering and guttering in the wind.

There were three letters in his pocket and he lighted each of them, holding each till the flame touched his hand and then dropping it to the street below. At one point, watching over his shoulder while the last of the letters burned, he

He might possibly get to his feet, but he was afraid to try. Already his legs were cramped, his thigh muscles tired; his knees hurt, his feet felt numb, and his hands were stiff. He couldn't possibly stay out here for four hours or anywhere near it. Long before that his legs and arms would give out; he would be forced to try changing his position often—stiffly, clumsily, his coordination and strength gone—and he would fall. Quite realistically, he knew that he would fall; no one could stay out here on this ledge for four hours.

A dozen windows in the apartment building across the street were lighted. Looking over his shoulder, he could see the top of a man's head behind the newspaper he was reading; in another window he saw the blue-gray flicker of a television screen. No more than twenty-odd yards from his back were scores of people, and if just one of them would walk idly to his window and glance out. . . . For some moments he stared over his shoulder at the lighted rectangles, waiting. But no one appeared. The man reading his

saw the man across the street put down his paper and stand—even seeming, to Tom, to glance toward his window. But when he moved, it was only to walk across the room and disappear from sight.

There were a dozen coins in Tom Benecke's pocket and he dropped them, three or four at a time. But if they struck anyone, or if anyone noticed their falling, no one connected them with their source, and no one glanced upward.

His arms had begun to tremble from the steady strain of clinging to this narrow perch, and he did not know what to do now and was terribly frightened. Clinging to the window stripping with one hand, he again searched his pockets. But now—he had left his wallet on his dresser when he'd changed clothes—there was nothing left but the yellow sheet. It occurred to him irrelevantly that his death on the sidewalk below would be an eternal mystery; the window closed—why, how, and from where could he have fallen? No one would be able to identify his body for a time, either—the thought was somehow unbearable and increased his fear. All they'd find in his pockets would be the yellow sheet. *Contents of the dead man's pockets,* he thought, *one sheet of paper bearing penciled notations— incomprehensible.*

He understood fully that he might actually be going to die; his arms, maintaining his balance on the ledge, were trembling steadily now. And it occurred to him then with all the force of a revelation that, if he fell, all he was ever going to have out of life he would then, abruptly, have had. Nothing, then, could ever be changed; and nothing more—no least experience or pleasure— could ever be added to his life. He wished, then, that he had not allowed his wife to go off by herself tonight—and on similar nights. He thought of all the evenings he had spent away from her, working; and he regretted them. He thought wonderingly of his fierce ambition and of the direction his life had taken; he thought of the hours he'd spent by himself, filling the yellow sheet that had brought him out here. *Contents of the dead man's pockets,* he thought with sudden fierce anger, *a wasted life.*

He was simply not going to cling here till he slipped and fell; he told himself that now. There was one last thing he could try; he had been aware of it for some moments, refusing to think about it, but now he faced it. Kneeling here on the ledge, the fingertips of one hand pressed to the narrow strip of wood, he could, he knew, draw his other hand back a yard perhaps, fist clenched tight, doing it very slowly till he sensed the outer limit of balance, then, as hard as he was able from the distance, he could drive his fist forward against the glass. If it broke, his fist smashing through, he was safe; he might cut himself badly, and probably would, but with his arm inside the room, he would be secure. But if the glass did not break, the rebound, flinging his arm back, would topple him off the ledge. He was certain of that.

He tested his plan. The fingers of his left hand clawlike on the little stripping, he drew back his other fist until his body began teetering backward. But he had no leverage now—he could feel that there would be no force to his swing— and he moved his fist slowly forward till he rocked forward on his knees again and could sense that his swing would carry its greatest force. Glancing down, however, measuring the distance from his fist to the glass, he saw that it was less than two feet.

It occurred to him that he could raise his arm over his head, to bring it down against the glass. But, experimentally in slow motion, he knew it

Vocabulary

irrelevantly (i·rel′ə·vənt·lē) *adv.*: in a way not relating to the point or situation.

incomprehensible (in·käm′prē·hen′sə·bəl) *adj.*: not understandable.

would be an awkward blow without the force of a driving punch, and not nearly enough to break the glass.

Facing the window, he had to drive a blow from the shoulder, he knew now, at a distance of less than two feet; and he did not know whether it would break through the heavy glass. It might; he could picture it happening, he could feel it in the nerves of his arm. And it might not; he could feel that too—feel his fist striking this glass and being instantaneously flung back by the unbreaking pane, feel the fingers of his other hand breaking loose, nails scraping along the casing as he fell.

He waited, arm drawn back, fist balled, but in no hurry to strike; this pause, he knew, might be an extension of his life. And to live even a few seconds longer, he felt, even out here on this ledge in the night, was infinitely better than to die a moment earlier than he had to. His arm grew tired, and he brought it down and rested it.

Then he knew that it was time to make the attempt. He could not kneel here hesitating indefinitely till he lost all courage to act, waiting till he slipped off the ledge. Again he drew back his arm, knowing this time that he would not bring it down till he struck. His elbow protruding over Lexington Avenue far below, the fingers of his other hand pressed down bloodlessly tight against the narrow stripping, he waited, feeling the sick tenseness and terrible excitement building. It grew and swelled toward the moment of action, his nerves tautening. He thought of Clare—just a wordless, yearning thought— and then drew his arm back just a bit more, fist so tight his fingers pained him, and knowing he was going to do it. Then with full power, with every last scrap of strength he could bring to bear, he shot his arm forward toward the glass, and he said "Clare!"

He heard the sound, felt the blow, felt himself falling forward, and his hand closed on the living-room curtains, the shards and fragments of glass showering onto the floor. And then, kneeling there on the ledge, an arm thrust into the room up to the shoulder, he began picking away the protruding slivers and great wedges of glass from the window frame, tossing them in onto the rug. And, as he grasped the edges of the empty window frame and climbed into his home, he was grinning in triumph.

He did not lie down on the floor or run through the apartment, as he had promised himself; even in the first few moments it seemed to him natural and normal that he should be where he was. He simply turned to his desk, pulled the crumpled yellow sheet from his pocket, and laid it down where it had been, smoothing it out; then he absently laid a pencil across it to weight it down. He shook his head wonderingly, and turned to walk toward the closet.

There he got out his topcoat and hat and, without waiting to put them on, opened the front door and stepped out, to go find his wife. He turned to pull the door closed and warm air from the hall rushed through the narrow opening again. As he saw the yellow paper, the pencil flying, scooped off the desk and, unimpeded by the glassless window, sail out into the night and out of his life, Tom Benecke burst into laughter and then closed the door behind him. ■

Vocabulary

unimpeded (un'im·pēd'id) *adj.*: not blocked; unobstructed.

Meet the Writer

Jack Finney

Space Aliens and Time Travel

Menacing alien plants hatch from pods, take human form, and gradually replace everyone—or almost everyone—in a small California town. Jack Finney (1911–1995) created this science fiction scenario in his second novel, *The Body Snatchers* (1955). The novel was turned into a horror-movie classic, *The Invasion of the Body Snatchers,* in 1956. For years, critics debated the secret meaning of the story—was it a protest against communism or a criticism of anti-Communist hysteria? Finney, a reclusive author who gave few interviews, had his own terse explanation: "I wrote the story purely as a good read."

Jack Finney, born Walter Braden Finney, was originally an advertising copywriter in New York City in the 1940s. Bored with his job, he began to write short stories in his spare time. When his stories began appearing regularly in popular magazines, such as *The Saturday Evening Post* and *Collier's,* Finney quit his advertising job to write full time. He published several collections of short stories and eight novels, five of which were made into movies.

Finney's second bestseller, *Time and Again* (1970), combines science fiction, mystery, and romance in a suspenseful time-travel adventure. In this tale a top-secret government project drafts Simon Morley, a young advertising illustrator in New York City, for an important mission that sends him back in time from 1970 to 1882. Finney's accurate, detailed picture of late-nineteenth-century Manhattan makes this novel a cult favorite, especially among those who love New York.

In commenting on the research needed to paint his meticulously realistic settings, Finney said,

> **❝** I find a good thing to do is to get newspapers. . . . I look at anything that was going on. . . . I'm doing my best to give a feeling of what it was like. . . . That kind of stuff is fun, but that's also why it takes a long, long time. **❞**

For Independent Reading

You might want to read Finney's sequel to *Time and Again,* titled *From Time to Time* (1995). In the sequel, Morley is sent on another time-travel mission. This time he journeys back to 1912 to prevent the outbreak of World War I (in order to save the life of his young son) and to stop the sailing of the doomed R.M.S. *Titanic.*

You want a social life, with friends

Kenneth Koch

You want a social life, with friends,
A passionate love life and as well
To work hard every day. What's true
Is of these three you may have two
5 And two can pay you dividends
But never may have three.

There isn't enough time, my friends—
Though dawn begins, yet midnight ends—
To find the time to have love, work, and friends.
10 Michelangelo had feeling
For Vittoria and the Ceiling°
But did he go to parties at day's end?

Homer° nightly went to banquets
Wrote all day but had no lockets
15 Bright with pictures of his Girl.
I know one who loves and parties
And has done so since his thirties
But writes hardly anything at all.

---

11. **Michelangelo . . . Ceiling:** Michelangelo Buonarroti (1475–1564) was an Italian Renaissance painter, sculptor, and architect. He sculpted *La Vittoria* (or *Victory*) for the tomb of Pope Julius II and painted the famous ceiling of the Sistine Chapel at the Vatican in Rome.
13. **Homer:** ancient Greek epic poet (eighth or ninth century B.C.) credited with composing the *Iliad* and the *Odyssey*.

Response and Analysis

Reading Check

1. **Summarize** the key events of the plot, being careful to identify **causes** and their **effects.** To indicate causes and effects, use words and phrases like *as a result, because of, then, thus, therefore.*

Thinking Critically

2. Like many stories, this one is built on choices made by the main character. What choice has Tom already made when the story opens? Why does he choose to risk his life to retrieve the paper?

3. Stories are also built on conflict. Does Tom experience **internal conflict, external conflict,** or both? Which is more compelling to you as a reader? Explain.

4. The story's events are told in **chronological order,** yet on page 13, Tom—and the reader also—is shocked to discover that only eight minutes have passed. How does Finney make time move slowly?

5. The two **settings**—ledge and apartment—are important in this story. How are they contrasted? How are you supposed to feel about each setting?

6. Name at least three ways in which Finney creates intense, hold-your-breath **suspense.** Consider the effects of the **setting** and the story's title. In your opinion, at what moment of the plot is the suspense greatest?

7. Based on Tom's actions at the very end of the story, what can you infer is the story's **theme** (its revelation about life)? How does the theme compare with that of Kenneth Koch's poem (see the **Connection** on page 18)?

Extending and Evaluating

8. Was the **resolution** of the story credible to you? Did you find Tom's actions believable?

9. What is your opinion of the premise of Koch's poem (See the **Connection** on page 18)? Can a person have all three—a social life with friends, a love life, and a successful career—or can you have only two? Be sure to give reasons for your opinion.

WRITING

Just Add the Details

Look back at your Quickwrite notes, and replay the events in your mind's eye, as if you were watching yourself or the other person on a video. Take notes as you think about the sensory aspects of the scene—what could be seen, heard, touched, smelled. Then, write a **narrative** about the experience. Relate the events, and add enough sensory details to make readers feel they are there. You could draw out the suspense by imitating Finney: Describe each action and reaction of your character in exact detail, second by second.

▶ **Use "Writing an Autobiographical Narrative," pages 56–63, for help with this assignment.**

SKILLS FOCUS

Literary Skills
Analyze time and sequence.

Reading Skills
Identify causes and effects.

Writing Skills
Write an autobiographical narrative.

Vocabulary Development

Word Analysis: Prefixes

Just by adding a few letters upfront, you can turn *appear* into *disappear*, *locate* into *relocate*, and *legible* into *illegible*. *Dis–*, *re–*, and *il–* are **prefixes,** word parts that attach to the front of a word or word root to change its meaning. The diagram on the lower right shows seven prefixes that attach to the root *–ject–* (from the Latin word *jacere*, "to throw") to create new English words. Learning the meanings of common prefixes can help you figure out the meanings of some unfamiliar words.

Spelling hint: When a prefix is added to a word, the spelling of the original word usually remains the same: *dis–* + *similar* = *dissimilar; extra–* + *ordinary* = *extraordinary.*

Latin Prefix	Meaning	Example
com–, con–	together; with	conjunction
in–, il–, im–, ir–	no, not; in, into, on	inoperable
inter–	between, among; together	international
pre–	before	prefabricate
pro–	forward; defending	prolabor
re–	again	reexamine
sub–	under; below	subnormal
Greek Prefix	**Meaning**	**Example**
hyper–	above; more than normal	hyperactive
micro–	small	microorganism
mono–	one	monologue
ex–	away from; out	expand
Anglo-Saxon Prefix	**Meaning**	**Example**
a–	out; up	arise
with–	away; back; against	withstand
un–	not; opposite of	unable

re
in
sub
pro
e
inter
ob
ject

PRACTICE

1. Working with a partner, use a dictionary to find the **etymology**—word history—of the Word Bank words. Be sure to identify each prefix and its meaning. Remember that for some words that have prefixes, only the root word will be defined in the dictionary.

2. Work with a partner or team to think of as many other example words as you can for each of the prefixes in the chart.

3. Combine the root *–vert–* (from the Latin *vertere*, "to turn") with prefixes from the prefix chart to form new words.

SKILLS FOCUS

Vocabulary Skills
Understand and use prefixes.

Double Daddy ◆ Diary of a Mad Blender ◆ The Child's View of Working Parents

Synthesizing: Putting It All Together

When you are doing research or reading several articles on a topic, you want to **synthesize** the material—that is, put it all together so that you can better understand the subject.

What's the best way to do that? Examine each source, and then compare the sources. Try following these steps:

- **Determine the message.** Look for each writer's **main ideas,** and take notes. For a difficult text or passage, try **paraphrasing,** or restating the sentences in your own words.

- **Look for supporting evidence.** As you read, be aware of how the writer supports each main idea. Does the writer offer facts, statistics, examples, anecdotes (brief stories about real people), or quotations?

- **Compare and contrast.** Note where each source agrees with or differs from the others on a topic or idea.

- **Make connections.** Relate each writer's message to other works you've read. Is the writer expressing the same ideas you found in other articles or books or even in a story or poem?

- **Put it all together.** When you have completed the above steps, you are ready to put everything together in a discussion about the topic. To practice **synthesizing,** you might write a research report, an editorial, a speech, or a letter. Be sure to acknowledge the source of the information or ideas that you cite.

Vocabulary Development

phenomenon (fə·näm′ə·nən) *n.:* observable event, fact, or circumstance.

chronic (krän′ik) *adj.:* constant; habitual.

trekked (trekt) *v.:* journeyed.

splicing (splīs′iŋ) *v.* used as *n.:* joining by inserting and binding together.

integrate (in′tə·grāt′) *v.:* combine; unify.

colleague (käl′ēg′) *n.:* fellow worker.

conviction (kən·vik′shən) *n.:* strong belief.

maximizes (mak′sə·mīz′iz) *v.:* increases as much as possible.

autonomy (ô·tän′ə·mē) *n.:* independence.

poignant (poin′yənt) *adj.:* emotionally moving; touching.

Connecting to the Literature

At the end of "Contents of the Dead Man's Pocket," Tom has decided to spend more time with his wife instead of overworking. In the articles that follow, different people comment on the difficulties of balancing time at work with time at home in today's busy world.

INTERNET

Interactive Reading Model

Keyword: LE5 10-1

SKILLS FOCUS

Reading Skills
Synthesize information from several sources on a single topic.

Double Daddy

from *The Denver Post*, September 5, 1999

Penny Parker

They struggle between the responsibilities of work and the needs of their families.

They have demanding jobs; they have children.

In some cases, they go to work before dawn, or take work home.

They race home to make it in time for their child's game, or play, or concert.

They worry that a business trip might take them away on their son's or daughter's birthday.

And surprise: They're men.

The Super Mom syndrome has jumped genders. Now it's working men who also want to be great fathers.

What has changed to make the working dad's life more stressful?

More is expected of fathers at home these days—and they expect more of themselves—but the demands of the workplace have, if anything, increased in recent years.

The phenomenon of "daddy stress"—as *Forbes* magazine dubbed it in a recent cover story—affects men from the executive office to the rank and file, and while a growing number of single dads may feel it most, married fathers are hardly immune.

"It's a familiar theme to women and not to men, and not to men's employers," said Linda Dunlap, chairwoman of the psychology department at Marist College in Poughkeepsie, N.Y., and an expert on families. "These men are saying, 'I'm working my tail off to get ahead, for the most part for my family, but I'm not spending time with my family. This doesn't make sense.'"

Ryan Streeter, a research fellow in the Welfare Policy Center at Hudson Institute in Indianapolis, calls the growing trend of men examining their roles as fathers "a national movement."

"There's been an increasing amount of literature, events, commercials, and public service announcements around the country in the last five years that have targeted the need for fathers to be engaged in their children's lives," Streeter said. "A group of largely men said it's time to take responsibility for their children not only economically, but emotionally and spiritually. There's a national consciousness around this matter."

The next step has to be a shift in the workplace mentality that says it's OK for a woman to take time off to stay home with a sick child or attend a child's football game, but it's not OK for a dad to do the same thing.

"It's popular to say there needs to be workplace flexibility for men," Streeter said, "but in general, corporations have the expectation for men to put business over family."

Brian Wills never set out to become a stay-at-home dad. It just worked out that way.

When he left his job in the marketing department of the *Denver Rocky Mountain News*

Vocabulary

phenomenon (fə·näm′ə·nən) *n.*: observable event, fact, or circumstance.

two and a half years ago, Wills says, he thought he'd pick up work as a freelance[1] copywriter for a while until a "regular job" came his way.

But because he was at home, Wills started "plugging into" more parts of his three children's lives. Now he's so engaged with their schedules and activities that he says he'd never go back to the corporate world.

On a typical recent day, Wills' focus was ferrets.[2]

His 11-year-old daughter Ashley wanted to take her ferrets to school for show and tell, and Wills' job was to ferry the ferrets back and forth.

A single dad who has remarried, Wills shares parental time and responsibilities with his ex-wife, who lives two miles away.

Three mornings a week, Wills and his oldest son, Eric, 15, work out at a health club together.

1. **freelance** *adj.:* not under contract for regular work but providing services independently.
2. **ferrets** *n.:* mammals about the size of a cat that are sometimes domesticated or used in hunting.

"That started to become a real important time of dialogue between us and has remained that," Wills said.

Once a week, Wills picks up Ashley at school and takes her out to lunch.

After school, Wills watches his sons, Eric and Ben, 12, practice in their rock band.

"They call me their band manager," Wills said, with more than a hint of pride.

Wills said he did time in the corporate rat race.

"In my 20s I really wanted to succeed in my job," he said. "I had a company car by the time I was 30. I was traveling a lot and never seeing my kids. Now it's become really precious for me in the sense that I know it's going to be somewhat short-lived."

Wills said he's gotten over his fear of being a freelancer, where he can't count on a regular income.

"I have a much greater fear about going into a stable income environment and losing time with my kids," he says. "That scares me way more."

Diary of a Mad Blender

A Week of Managing Every Spare Minute

from *The Wall Street Journal*, March 22, 2000

Sue Shellenbarger

It's one of the hottest work-life trends: integrating work and personal roles with the help of technology and flexible work setups.

I work from home, but there's certainly more I could do to integrate my work and my personal life. And as a chronic stretcher of deadlines whose home office looks like a landfill, I could use some help. So I trekked to a bookstore for an armload of time-management and life-balance books and tried some of their tips for a week. A few notes on the results follow.

Thursday. Heeding author Kathy Peel's advice to "never underestimate the potential of small snippets of time" (in *Be Your Best: The Family Manager's Guide to Personal Success*), I begin splicing work into unoccupied moments. I take my laptop to my son's dentist appointment and work in the waiting room. I edit a story on a treadmill at the gym, where I find it easy to slash the fat out of my copy.

Friday. To integrate some play with my work, I quit my office a couple of hours early, pack my cell phone and laptop, and drive my kids to a nearby ski area for a little night snowboarding. As I help my son with his bindings, a colleague calls on my cell phone to ask for sources for a story. Though I know the subject, I draw a blank. Somehow, the grandeur of my environment has idled the needed part of my brain.

After a stint on the slopes, I head to the lodge to work. My son bursts in. "Did you see me? I was bombing it!" he cries, thrilled by a rocket-fast run. Disappointed that I wasn't watching out the window, he leaves. At this moment, I realize, my presence is a pretense of little value to him. I'm actually consumed by work.

Monday. The experts suggest a laundry list of things to do while my computer is booting up. I love one bit of advice from *Family Education Today,* a newsletter: Write a postcard to a friend. But when I try taking a "minivacation," closing my eyes and breathing deep, I can't seem to relax.

I try another tip: Meow loudly like a cat to firm your facial muscles. While I enjoy acting like an animal, our family Labrador, cat, and kitten gather in a puzzled circle around my chair. Then the kitten bites me in the ankle and runs away. I wonder what human co-workers would do.

Revved up to twitch speed, I pick up voice mail on my cell phone while driving my kids

---

Vocabulary

chronic (krän′ik) *adj.:* constant; habitual.

trekked (trekt) *v.:* journeyed.

splicing (splīs′iŋ) *v.* used as *n.:* joining by inserting and binding together.

integrate (in′tə·grāt′) *v.:* combine; unify.

colleague (käl′ēg′) *n.:* fellow worker.

home from school and listen to a time-management book on tape. Though I get it all done, my brain feels like Los Angeles after an earthquake.

Later, I discover that amid the self-imposed pressure, I forgot an editor's request that I review some copy that evening. I apologize, but the damage is done.

Tuesday. In *Take Back Your Time*, Jan Jasper advises getting little tasks done while watching television. I try opening mail and sorting work papers into stacks. I make a big dent in my office piles. But my daughter, who usually looks forward to watching TV with me, leaves the room.

Wednesday. By week's end, I am an also-ran in the X-Games of Extreme Integration. My experiment has indeed made me more efficient. My office is neater, and I'm embracing some of the integration tips permanently, such as writing some postcards during free moments and taking work with me to do while waiting in doctors' offices and other appointments.

But jugglers beware. It was far easier for me to splice more work into my week than to add time for rest and relationships. For me, at least, extreme integration is a rigged game—in favor of work.

And as I review my work, I agree, as James Gleick suggests in his 1999 book *Faster*, that the more I cram into my days, the stupider I get. My jampacked week has produced not one fresh idea or novel insight. Only after family needs force me to take a complete break does my mind kick back into a creative mode.

Maybe, as some management gurus suggest, my brain just needs a little cross-training. But in its current condition, it clearly needs a good long rest.

The Child's View of Working Parents

from *Fortune*, November 8, 1999

Cora Daniels

The image of working parents as jugglers long ago entered the gallery of cultural clichés. We know that balancing work and family life produces stress and guilt, not to mention the uncomfortable <u>conviction</u> that one day your child will cry to a therapist about how the baby sitter nursed her through the chickenpox. But what do children really feel about all this? That was the question that Ellen Galinsky, cofounder and president of the Families and Work Institute, set out to answer in her new book, *Ask the Children: What America's Children Really Think About Working Parents*. Galinsky surveyed 1,023 children in the third through twelfth grades, as well as 605 employed parents. She had help designing the questions from her own daughter, Lara, who did one-on-one interviews with children of various backgrounds to find out what issues were important to them. Galinsky made some surprising discoveries. For one thing, children don't seem to mind that their parents work. But they do wish that when their parents were around, they were less tired and stressed. Galinsky found that the amount of time parents (both mothers and fathers) spend with their children does matter, but so does the kind of time. Children who reported that their parents can focus on them when they're together were more likely to feel that their parents were good jugglers. And as Galinsky told *Fortune*'s Cora Daniels in a recent interview, when children have the chickenpox—or any illness—they really do want their parents around.

What did you find when you looked at spillover from family life to work life?

We asked parents, "How often have you been in a good mood at work because of your children?" Seventy-one percent said that they'd been in a good mood either often or very often at work because of their children. If you look at the people who say that they've been in a good mood at home because of their work, it's 37 percent. In fact, kids really energize us for work.

Do companies need to adopt new policies to help out?

People who work more tend to feel more stressed. But the real thing that's powerful is job pressure. You have deadlines that are difficult to meet; you have such a large amount of work, you can never get everything done. So the message to employers is to think about creating a work environment that <u>maximizes</u> people's productivity. We've tended to think of the main thing to do with children as helping to provide child care. That's important, but I think that for real return on investment, you need to think about creating an environment that helps people work in a more constructive way.

You also recommend that working parents be home when their child is sick.

Vocabulary

conviction (kən·vik′shən) *n.*: strong belief.

maximizes (mak′sə·mīz′iz) *v.*: increases as much as possible.

In the early days when I was doing research on this subject, the conventional wisdom was that if you provide flexibility, employees will take a mile. We followed Johnson & Johnson through a process where it provided more flexibility, and it found that absenteeism went down. If you give people an inch, they give you an inch. If people have the flexibility to take care of family issues, they tend to be there for you when you need them as an employer. Give and take.

What can you tell about the next generation of workers?

A lot of business leaders I talk to think people aren't going to be willing to just get involved in the kind of frantic overwork that so many people do today. Children who have seen their parents struggle aren't going to be willing to do that. Not many people want to work harder than their parents. They might want to work as hard, but they don't want to work harder. People who are managing Generation X already feel there are some differences. Generation Xers want more autonomy; they're less willing to settle for less say in their jobs.

What is the bottom line of what kids are trying to tell us?

They're telling us that there is a problem, but it's not *that* we work, it's *how* we work. They worry about us. Two thirds of the kids worried about their parents at least some of the time, and mostly if we were tired and stressed. They often worried about our safety. Will we get to work safely? Will there be an accident? Will something go wrong? They are telling us to be there for them. And they're telling us—and I think this is perhaps one of the most poignant findings of the study—"If we act as if we don't want to talk, we may not know just how to tell you that we want to talk, but we really do. Don't set up the moment for the perfect quality time. Hang out with us, and then we'll warm up to it. And hang in there."

Vocabulary

autonomy (ô·tän′ə·mē) *n.*: independence.

poignant (pɔin′yənt) *adj.*: emotionally moving; touching.

Analyzing Informational Text

Reading Check

1. What conflict does "Double Daddy" deal with?
2. Explain the title "Diary of a Mad Blender."
3. In "The Child's View of Working Parents," what does Ellen Galinsky predict will be the next generation's attitude toward overwork?
4. According to Galinsky, why do kids worry about their working parents?

Test Practice

1. Which statement *best* summarizes the **main idea** of "Double Daddy"?
   A Fathers need to work hard.
   B Mothers don't need help.
   C Kids should help parents more.
   D Fathers are helping out more than before.

2. After experiencing the events of "Contents of the Dead Man's Pocket," what would Tom probably say about Linda Dunlap's quotation in "Double Daddy"?
   F "I agree."
   G "I disagree."
   H "I have no opinion."
   J "I always knew that."

3. What proof does Galinsky give to **support** her statements?
   A Personal anecdotes
   B Statistics from interviews
   C Quotations from experts
   D Examples from other countries

4. In what important way does "Diary of a Mad Blender" *differ* from "The Child's View of Working Parents"?
   F It describes the stresses of parenting.

   G It is based on the writer's own experiences.
   H It supports the goals of working parents.
   J It discusses other family members' points of view on working parents.

5. What is the **tone** of "Diary of a Mad Blender"? That is, what attitude does the writer take toward her subject?
   A Sad   C Bitter
   B Humorous   D Angry

6. Which phrase *best* describes the **topic** of all three articles?
   F Daddy stress
   G Mommy stress
   H Flexible work setups
   J Career-family conflict

7. The writers of all three articles imply that balancing work and family life is —
   A unimportant
   B impossible
   C very easy
   D not easy

SKILLS FOCUS

Reading Skills
Synthesize information from several sources on a single topic.

8. Which of the following opinions is *not* expressed in any of the three articles?

  F Life will soon be easier for working parents.

  G Children are worried about their working parents.

  H Corporations still expect men to put business before family.

  J In the future, people will probably refuse to work as hard as their parents do now.

Constructed Response

Synthesize the three articles you have read by writing your own one-page article or editorial about the problems of balancing work and family life. Support your opinions or ideas by **paraphrasing** the articles, and make sure to acknowledge the source. Draw on other sources (such as Finney's story and Koch's poem) and on your own experiences. You might also want to interview your parents for their point of view and synthesize this information, including it in your article.

Vocabulary Development

Analogies: Two Word Pairs with the Same Relationship

In an **analogy** question, the words in one pair relate to each other in the same way as the words in a second pair. The words in the pairs may be synonyms (words with the same meaning) or antonyms (words with opposite meanings), or they may share some other relationship. Follow the steps below when you complete an analogy question:

    DARK : LIGHT :: _____ : expensive
    a. dear   **b.** cheap   **c.** costly   **d.** bright

1. Identify the relationship between the words in the first pair. (In the example above, *dark* and *light* are opposites, or antonyms.)

2. Express the analogy in sentence or question form. ("*Dark* is the opposite of *light*, just as _____ is the opposite of *expensive*.")

3. From the choices available, choose the word that makes the second relationship the same as the first. (Look for a word that means the opposite of *expensive*. Choice b, *cheap*, is correct.)

(continued on next page)

SKILLS FOCUS

Vocabulary Skills
Understand and complete word analogies.

Analogies (continued)

The following chart shows some of the relationships you'll find in analogy test items and gives an example for each:

Type of Relationship	Example
Synonyms	QUICK : FAST :: loud : noisy
Antonyms	ENTER : DEPART :: build : destroy
Part of something to the whole	TOE : FOOT :: roof : house
Thing/object to a category it belongs to	ROBIN : BIRD :: maple : tree
Thing to the characteristic of the thing	BASEBALL : ROUND :: silk : smooth
Degree of intensity	GOOD : GREAT :: thin : emaciated
Worker to the tool the worker uses	PAINTER : BRUSH :: plumber : wrench

PRACTICE 1

Complete each analogy below with the word from the Word Bank that fits best. The first analogy has been done for you.

Word Bank

phenomenon
chronic
trekked
splicing
integrate
colleague
conviction
maximizes
autonomy
poignant

1. REWARD : PUNISH :: integrate : separate
2. STRONG : STURDY :: _____ : habitual
3. VIGOR : WEAKNESS :: _____ : disbelief
4. HOPE : DESPAIR :: _____ : slavery
5. FRIEND : PAL :: _____ : co-worker
6. SUPPORT : OPPOSE :: _____ : minimizes
7. CREEP : CRAWL :: _____ : journeyed
8. RARE : UNUSUAL :: _____ : touching
9. REPAIR : FIX :: _____ : joining
10. GHOST : INVISIBLE :: _____ : observable

PRACTICE 2

Using the chart above as a reference, identify the type of relationship in each of the following word pairs:

1. keyboard : laptop
2. Labrador : dog
3. children : young
4. writer : computer
5. earthquake : shaking
6. busy : frantic
7. ferret : mammal
8. fear : terror

The Leap

Make the Connection

Quickwrite ✏

Has anyone ever acted courageously to help you? Maybe you yourself have acted bravely to help someone else. Why do you think people take risks to do what they think is the right thing? What is the reward? Jot down your thoughts on these complex questions about motivation and selfless behavior.

Literary Focus

Flashback: Back to the Past

You're watching an exciting chase scene in a movie when suddenly the screen darkens and the main character becomes twenty years younger. What's happening? You're watching a **flashback,** a literary device that interrupts the present action in a story to show events that happened at an earlier time.

Flashbacks are effective for several reasons. They often add an emotional impact by showing the lasting effect of memory, and they can help you understand a character, especially a character's past. Flashbacks can also introduce an element of surprise or change the pace in a story.

In "The Leap" the narrator returns to the past more than once. As you read, be on the lookout for those time shifts.

Foreshadowing: Clues to the Future

Writers use another literary device, **foreshadowing,** to plant hints about events that will occur later in the plot. Look for words, images, or events in "The Leap" that seem to be clues to what lies ahead.

Reading Skills

Making Predictions

Part of the pleasure of reading a story is in **making predictions,** guessing what will happen to the characters as the plot moves ahead. You base your predictions on what you already know about the characters and their situation, along with what you know about how people behave in real life. Foreshadowing helps, too, if you're clever enough to recognize the writer's clues.

When you spot foreshadowing as you read "The Leap," use it to make a prediction about the characters and future events. The questions at the open-book signs should help you.

Vocabulary Development

encroaching (en·krōch′iŋ) v. used as *adj.*: advancing.

commemorates (kə·mem′ə·rāts′) *v.*: serves as a reminder of.

generate (jen′ər·āt′) *v.*: arise; come into being.

radiance (rā′dē·əns) *n.*: brightness; light.

extricating (eks′tri·kāt′iŋ) *v.* used as *n.*: releasing; disentangling.

illiterate (i·lit′ər·it) *adj.*: uneducated; unable to read or write.

constricting (kən·strikt′iŋ) *v.* used as *adj.*: limiting; confining.

tentative (ten′tə·tiv) *adj.*: timid; hesitant.

INTERNET

Vocabulary Practice
•
More About Louise Erdrich

Keyword: LE5 10-1

SKILLS FOCUS

Literary Skills
Understand flashback and foreshadowing.

Reading Skills
Make predictions.

The Leap **31**

The Leap

Louise Erdrich

As you fall, there is time to think.

My mother is the surviving half of a blindfold trapeze act, not a fact I think about much even now that she is sightless, the result of <u>encroaching</u> and stubborn cataracts.[1] She walks slowly through her house here in New Hampshire, lightly touching her way along walls and running her hands over knickknacks, books, the drift of a grown child's belongings and castoffs. She has never upset an object or as much as brushed a magazine onto the floor. She has never lost her balance or bumped into a closet door left carelessly open.

It has occurred to me that the catlike precision of her movements in old age might be the result of her early training, but she shows so little of the drama or flair one might expect from a performer that I tend to forget the Flying Avalons. She has kept no sequined costume, no photographs, no fliers or posters from that part of her youth. I would, in fact, tend to think that all memory of double somersaults and heart-stopping catches had left her arms and legs were it not for the fact that sometimes, as I sit sewing in the room of the rebuilt house in which I slept as a child, I hear the crackle, catch a whiff of smoke from the stove downstairs, and suddenly the room goes dark, the stitches burn beneath my fingers, and I am sewing with a needle of hot silver, a thread of fire.

MAKING PREDICTIONS

1. What clues in the last sentence hint at something to come? What might that event be?

I owe her my existence three times. The first was when she saved herself. In the town square a replica[2] tent pole, cracked and splintered, now stands cast in concrete. It <u>commemorates</u> the disaster that put our town smack on the front page of the Boston and New York tabloids.[3] It is from those old newspapers, now historical records, that I get my information. Not from my mother, Anna of the Flying Avalons, nor from any of her in-laws, nor certainly from the other half of her particular act, Harold Avalon, her first husband. In one news account it says, "The day was mildly overcast, but nothing in the air or temperature gave any hint of the sudden force with which the deadly gale would strike."

MAKING PREDICTIONS

2. The newspaper quotation creates suspense. What do you **predict** will happen? What effects might there be?

I have lived in the West, where you can see the weather coming for miles, and it is true that out here we are at something of a disadvantage. When extremes of temperature collide, a hot and cold front, winds <u>generate</u> instantaneously behind a hill and crash upon you without warning. That, I think, was the likely situation on that day in June. People probably commented on the pleasant air, grateful that no hot sun beat upon the striped tent that stretched over the entire center green. They bought their tickets and surrendered them in anticipation. They sat. They ate caramelized popcorn and roasted peanuts. There was time, before the storm, for three acts. The White Arabians of Ali-Khazar rose on their hind legs and waltzed. The Mysterious Bernie folded himself into a painted cracker tin, and the Lady of the Mists made herself appear and disappear in surprising places. As the clouds gathered outside, unnoticed, the ringmaster cracked his whip, shouted his introduction, and pointed to the ceiling of the tent, where the Flying Avalons were perched.

---

1. **cataracts** (kat′ə·rakts′) *n.*: clouded areas on the lens of the eye that can cause partial or total blindness.
2. **replica** (rep′li·kə) *n.*: exact copy or reproduction.
3. **tabloids** (tab′loidz′) *n.*: newspapers that often feature sensational, exciting news stories.

Vocabulary

encroaching (en·krōch′iŋ) *v.* used as *adj.*: advancing.

commemorates (kə·mem′ə·rāts′) *v.*: serves as a reminder of.

generate (jen′ər·āt′) *v.*: arise; come into being.

They loved to drop gracefully from nowhere, like two sparkling birds, and blow kisses as they threw off their plumed helmets and high-collared capes. They laughed and flirted openly as they beat their way up again on the trapeze bars. In the final vignette[4] of their act, they actually would kiss in midair, pausing, almost hovering as they swooped past one another. On the ground, between bows, Harry Avalon would skip quickly to the front rows and point out the smear of my mother's lipstick, just off the edge of his mouth. They made a romantic pair all right, especially in the blindfold sequence.

That afternoon, as the anticipation increased, as Mr. and Mrs. Avalon tied sparkling strips of cloth onto each other's face and as they puckered their lips in mock kisses—lips destined "never again to meet," as one long breathless

article put it—the wind rose, miles off, wrapped itself into a cone, and howled. There came a rumble of electrical energy, drowned out by the sudden roll of drums. One detail not mentioned by the press, perhaps unknown—Anna was pregnant at the time, seven months and hardly showing, her stomach muscles were that strong. It seems incredible that she would work high above the ground when any fall could be so dangerous, but the explanation—I know from watching her go blind—is that my mother lives comfortably in extreme elements. She is one with the constant dark now, just as the air was her home, familiar to her, safe, before the storm that afternoon.

From opposite ends of the tent they waved, blind and smiling, to the crowd below. The ringmaster removed his hat and called for silence, so that the two above could concentrate. They rubbed their hands in chalky powder, then Harry launched himself and swung, once, twice, in huge calibrated[5] beats across space. He hung from his knees and on the third swing stretched wide his arms, held his hands out to receive his pregnant wife as she dove from her shining bar.

It was while the two were in midair, their hands about to meet, that lightning struck the main pole and sizzled down the guy wires, filling the air with a blue radiance that Harry Avalon must certainly have seen through the cloth of his blindfold as the tent buckled and the edifice[6] toppled him forward, the swing continuing and not returning in its sweep, and Harry going down, down into the crowd with his last thought, perhaps, just a prickle of surprise at his empty hands.

My mother once said that I'd be amazed at how many things a person can do within the act

---

5. **calibrated** (kal′ə·brāt′id) *v.* used as *adj.:* measured.
6. **edifice** (ed′i·fis) *n.:* structure.

Vocabulary
radiance (rā′dē·əns) *n.:* brightness; light.

---

4. **vignette** (vin·yet′) *n.:* short, memorable scene.

of falling. Perhaps, at the time, she was teaching me to dive off a board at the town pool, for I associated the idea with midair somersaults. But I also think she meant that even in that awful doomed second one could think, for she certainly did. When her hands did not meet her husband's, my mother tore her blindfold away. As he swept past her on the wrong side, she could have grasped his ankle, the toe end of his tights, and gone down clutching him. Instead, she changed direction. Her body twisted toward a heavy wire and she managed to hang on to the braided metal, still hot from the lightning strike. Her palms were burned so terribly that once healed they bore no lines, only the blank scar tissue of a quieter future. She was lowered, gently, to the sawdust ring just underneath the dome of the canvas roof, which did not entirely settle but was held up on one end and jabbed through, torn, and still on fire in places from the giant spark, though rain and men's jackets soon put that out.

Three people died, but except for her hands my mother was not seriously harmed until an overeager rescuer broke her arm in <u>extricating</u> her and also, in the process, collapsed a portion of the tent bearing a huge buckle that knocked her unconscious. She was taken to the town hospital, and there she must have hemorrhaged,[7] for they kept her, confined to her bed, a month and a half before her baby was born without life.

Harry Avalon had wanted to be buried in the circus cemetery next to the original Avalon, his uncle, so she sent him back with his brothers. The child, however, is buried around the corner, beyond this house and just down the highway. Sometimes I used to walk there just to sit. She was a girl, but I rarely thought of her as a sister or even as a separate person really. I suppose you

> **Even in that awful doomed second one could think.**

could call it the egocentrism[8] of a child, of all young children, but I considered her a less finished version of myself.

When the snow falls, throwing shadows among the stones, I can easily pick her out from the road, for it is bigger than the others and in the shape of a lamb at rest, its legs curled beneath. The carved lamb looms larger as the years pass, though it is probably only my eyes, the vision shifting, as what is close to me blurs and distances sharpen. In odd moments, I think it is the edge drawing near, the edge of everything, the unseen horizon we do not really speak of in the eastern woods. And it also seems to me, although this is probably an idle fantasy, that the statue is growing more sharply etched, as if, instead of weathering itself into a porous mass, it is hardening on the hillside with each snowfall, perfecting itself.

MAKING INFERENCES

3. Notice what the narrator says about her sister and her sister's grave. How do you think the narrator feels about her sister?

*I*t was during her confinement in the hospital that my mother met my father. He was called in to look at the set of her arm, which was complicated. He stayed, sitting at her bedside, for he was something of an armchair traveler and had spent his war quietly, at an air force training grounds, where he became a specialist in arms and legs broken during parachute training exercises. Anna Avalon had been to many of the places he longed to visit—Venice, Rome, Mexico, all through France and Spain. She had no family of

---

7. **hemorrhaged** (hem′ər·ijd′) *v.*: lost a great deal of blood.

8. **egocentrism** (ē′gō·sen′triz′əm) *n.*: self-centeredness.

Vocabulary

extricating (eks′tri·kāt′iŋ) *v.* used as *n.*: releasing; disentangling.

her own and was taken in by the Avalons, trained to perform from a very young age. They toured Europe before the war, then based themselves in New York. She was <u>illiterate</u>.

It was in the hospital that she finally learned to read and write, as a way of overcoming the boredom and depression of those weeks, and it was my father who insisted on teaching her. In return for stories of her adventures, he graded her first exercises. He bought her her first book, and over her bold letters, which the pale guides of the penmanship pads could not contain, they fell in love.

I wonder if my father calculated the exchange he offered: one form of flight for another. For after that, and for as long as I can remember, my mother has never been without a book. Until now, that is, and it remains the greatest difficulty of her blindness. Since my father's recent death, there is no one to read to her, which is why I returned, in fact, from my failed life where the land is flat. I came home to read to my mother, to read out loud, to read long into the dark if I must, to read all night.

Vocabulary

illiterate (i·lit′ər·it) *adj.:* uneducated; unable to read or write.

I owe my existence, the second time then, to the two of them and the hospital that brought them together. That is the debt we take for granted since none of us asks for life. It is only once we have it that we hang on so dearly.

I was seven the year the house caught fire, probably from standing ash. It can rekindle, and my father, forgetful around the house and perpetually[9] exhausted from night hours on call, often emptied what he thought were ashes from cold stoves into wooden or cardboard containers. The fire could have started from a flaming box, or perhaps a buildup of creosote[10] inside the chimney was the culprit. It started right around the stove, and the heart of the house was gutted. The baby sitter, fallen asleep in my father's den on the first floor, woke to find the stairway to my upstairs room cut off by flames. She used the phone, then ran outside to stand beneath my window.

When my parents arrived, the town volunteers had drawn water from the fire pond and were spraying the outside of the house, preparing to go inside after me, not knowing at the time that there was only one staircase and that it was lost. On the other side of the house, the superannuated[11] extension ladder broke in half. Perhaps the clatter of it falling against the walls woke me, for I'd been asleep up to that point.

As soon as I awakened, in the small room that I now use for sewing, I smelled the smoke. I followed things by the letter then, was good at memorizing instructions, and so I did exactly what was taught in the second-grade home fire drill. I got up, I touched the back of my door before opening it. Finding it hot, I left it closed and stuffed my rolled-up rug beneath the crack.

---

9. perpetually (pər·pech′o͞o·əl·ē) *adv.*: constantly.
10. creosote (krē′ə·sōt′) *n.*: oily deposit of tar, a byproduct of burning wood.
11. superannuated (so͞o′pər·an′yo͞o·āt′id) *adj.*: too old or worn-out to be of service.

Vocabulary
constricting (kən·strikt′iŋ) *v.* used as *adj.*: limiting; confining.

Once my father and mother married, they moved onto the old farm he had inherited but didn't care much for. Though he'd been thinking of moving to a larger city, he settled down and broadened his practice in this valley. It still seems odd to me, when they could have gone anywhere else, that they chose to stay in the town where the disaster had occurred, and which my father in the first place had found so constricting. It was my mother who insisted upon it, after her child did not survive. And then, too, she loved the sagging farmhouse with its scrap of what was left of a vast acreage of woods and hidden hayfields that stretched to the game park.

I did not hide under my bed or crawl into my closet. I put on my flannel robe, and then I sat down to wait.

Outside, my mother stood below my dark window and saw clearly that there was no rescue. Flames had pierced one side wall, and the glare of the fire lighted the massive limbs and trunk of the vigorous old elm that had probably been planted the year the house was built, a hundred years ago at least. No leaf touched the wall, and just one thin branch scraped the roof. From below, it looked as though even a squirrel would have had trouble jumping from the tree onto the house, for the breadth of that small branch was no bigger than my mother's wrist.

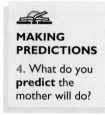

MAKING PREDICTIONS

4. What do you **predict** the mother will do?

Standing there, beside Father, who was preparing to rush back around to the front of the house, my mother asked him to unzip her dress. When he wouldn't be bothered, she made him understand. He couldn't make his hands work, so she finally tore it off and stood there in her pearls and stockings. She directed one of the men to lean the broken half of the extension ladder up against the trunk of the tree. In surprise, he complied. She ascended. She vanished. Then she could be seen among the leafless branches of late November as she made her way up and, along her stomach, inched the length of a bough that curved above the branch that brushed the roof.

Once there, swaying, she stood and balanced. There were plenty of people in the crowd and many who still remember, or think they do, my mother's leap through the ice-dark air toward that thinnest extension, and how she broke the branch falling so that it cracked in her hands, cracked louder than the flames as she vaulted with it toward the edge of the roof, and how it

hurtled down end over end without her, and their eyes went up, again, to see where she had flown.

I didn't see her leap through air, only heard the sudden thump and looked out my window. She was hanging by the backs of her heels from the new gutter we had put in that year, and she was smiling. I was not surprised to see her, she was so matter-of-fact. She tapped on the window. I remember how she did it, too. It was the friendliest tap, a bit tentative, as if she was afraid she had arrived too early at a friend's house. Then she gestured at the latch, and when I opened the window she told me to raise it wider and prop it up with the stick so it wouldn't crush her fingers. She swung down, caught the ledge, and crawled through the opening. Once she was in my room, I realized she had on only underclothing, a bra of the heavy stitched cotton women used to wear and step-in, lace-trimmed drawers. I remember feeling lightheaded, of course, terribly relieved, and then embarrassed for her to be seen by the crowd undressed.

I was still embarrassed as we flew out the window, toward earth, me in her lap, her toes pointed as we skimmed toward the painted target of the firefighter's net.

I know that she's right. I knew it even then. As you fall, there is time to think. Curled as I was, against her stomach, I was not startled by the cries of the crowd or the looming faces. The wind roared and beat its hot breath at our back, and flames whistled. I slowly wondered what would happen if we missed the circle or bounced out of it. Then I wrapped my hands around my mother's hands. I felt the brush of her lips and heard the beat of her heart in my ears, loud as thunder, long as the roll of drums. ∎

Vocabulary
tentative (ten'tə·tiv) *adj.:* timid; hesitant.

Meet the Writer

Louise Erdrich

A Storytelling Tradition

When Louise Erdrich (1954–   ) was very young, her father paid her a nickel for every story she wrote, and her mother "published" the stories with construction-paper covers. "I had that kind of childhood where I didn't feel art was something strange," she recalls. "I felt that it was good for you to do it."

Erdrich, the oldest of seven children, grew up in a storytelling family in North Dakota. Both her German American father and her French Chippewa mother worked at an Indian boarding school. She described once in an interview how everyone in her family would tell stories.

66 When I think what's a story, I can hear somebody in my family, my dad or my mom or my grandma, telling it. There's something particularly strong about a *told story*. You know your listener's right there, you've got to keep him hooked—or her. So you use all those little lures: 'And then . . . ,' 'So the next day. . . ,' etc. There are some very nuts-and-bolts things about storytelling. It also is something you can't really put your finger on. . . . The story starts to take over if it is good. . . . If it's good, you let the story tell itself. You don't control the story. 99

Erdrich, who started out as a poet, finished her first novel, *Love Medicine,* when she was twenty-eight. Although she had great difficulty finding a publisher for the book, it became a runaway bestseller and won the National Book Critics Circle Award in 1984. That story and many of her subsequent novels are set in the landscape of her childhood, in and around Turtle Mountain Reservation, North Dakota, where her grandfather was tribal chairman.

Although Erdrich continues to publish novels and short stories, she has branched out into nonfiction as well. In *The Blue Jay's Dance: A Birth Year* (1995), Erdrich writes about motherhood, marriage, family, writing, nature, and food during a year in which she awaits the birth of her daughter and then cares for her.

The Day the Clowns Cried

R. J. Brown

The worst tragedy in the annals of circus history occurred during the afternoon show of the Ringling Brothers Circus on July 6, 1944, at Hartford, Connecticut. With nearly 7,000 people enjoying the performance, the big tent suddenly became engulfed in flames. As fire spread up the side walls and raced across the top of the tent, the bandmaster, Merle Evans, swung his band into the song "Stars and Stripes Forever"—the circus disaster tune. The sound of this tune moved all employees into high gear. The horses, elephants, the lions and tigers, were quickly led out of the tent out of danger.

People stampeded toward the exit they had entered from. Unfortunately, this was the end on fire. Fire had not spread to the other end yet and employees tried directing them to that exit. In the panic, crowds still stampeded the end on fire. Three minutes later, the tent poles started collapsing and the roof—what was left—caved in. In six minutes total, almost all of the tent was burned completely and the entire area was nothing more than smoldering ashes. One hundred sixty-eight men, women, and children died as a result. Hundreds more were badly injured.

An important footnote to this fire story is the fact that the circus had tried unsuccessfully to obtain the necessary quantity of a new canvas flameproofing compound that was developed by the armed services. It was pointed out by the army that no civilian concern was allowed the use of the compound. Soon after the fire, however, the army approached Ringling's and granted them the necessary priority to obtain enough compound to fireproof their tents. From 1945 on, the circus tents were treated with a flame-retardant compound.

—from "The History Buff" on Discovery.com, October 31, 2000

Crowds flee the Ringling Brothers tent when it caught fire one summer day in 1944.

Response and Analysis

Reading Check

1. Why has the narrator returned to her childhood home?

2. In a sentence or two, **summarize** the event that causes the end of the Flying Avalons' act.

3. How do the narrator's parents meet?

4. The narrator says she owes her mother her existence "three times." What are those three times?

Thinking Critically

5. Why is "The Leap" a good **title** for this story? Name all the leaps—both literal and figurative—that occur in the story.

6. Analyze the author's use of **flashbacks** by tracing the point where the story shifts from present to past and back again. Then, put the story's main events in **chronological order** on a time line. Begin with the day at the circus.

7. How are the different **flashback** episodes related to one another? What does the author's use of flashback add to the story that a strict chronological telling would not accomplish?

8. Find three examples of **foreshadowing** in the story. Did the clues help you make predictions about the story's outcome? Explain your answer.

9. What are the many ways in which the narrator's mother displays courage? What do her actions imply about her **character**?

Extending and Evaluating

10. Look back at your Quickwrite notes about people who behave courageously. Based on what you know about brave, selfless people, are the mother's actions **credible**? Explain your answer.

11. Compare the disaster in the story with the true-life disaster described in "The Day the Clowns Cried" (see the **Connection** on page 40). Do you think the real-life event would make a good topic for a story? Why?

WRITING

Wild Woman?

Erdrich is known for her strong female characters. She has said of women,

> We are taught to present a demure face to the world, and yet there is a kind of wild energy behind it in many women that is transformational energy, and not only transforming to them but to other people.

Do you think the mother in "The Leap" fits the description above? Write a few paragraphs in which you support your **opinion.** Be sure to address each of the points in the statement: Does the mother seem outwardly demure and reserved? Does she have a hidden, wild energy? Is she able to transform, or change, herself and others? Include examples from the story to support your opinion.

SKILLS FOCUS

Literary Skills
Analyze flashback and foreshadowing.

Reading Skills
Analyze predictions.

Writing Skills
Write an essay supporting an opinion.

Vocabulary Development

Etymologies: Words Tell Their Stories

An **etymology** (et′ə·mäl′ə·jē) traces a word's **derivation,** or origin. You can use a dictionary to find a derivation: It usually appears in brackets after the entry word's pronunciation and part-of-speech designation. The oldest form of the word will appear last. The dictionary should contain a section that explains the organization, abbreviations, and symbols used in its etymologies. Let's look at the beginning of a dictionary entry for the Word Bank word *commemorates.*

Word Bank

encroaching
commemorates
generate
radiance
extricating
illiterate
constricting
tentative

> **com·mem·o·rate** (kə·mem′ə·rāt′) *vt.* [< L *commemoratus,* pp. of *commemorare,* to call to mind < *com–,* intens. + *memorare,* to remind]

The entry tells us that *commemorate* derives from ("<") the Latin ("L") word *commemoratus,* which is a past participle ("pp.") of *commemorare,* Latin for "to call to mind." The entry further shows that *commemorare* is derived from *com–,* an intensive ("intens.")—a word that emphasizes a meaning—plus ("+") *memorare,* Latin for "to remind."

Some etymologies refer to a prefix and root word that combine to form the entry word, as in the entry below for the Word Bank word *illiterate:*

> **il·lit·er·ate** (i·lit′ər·it) *adj.* [L *illiteratus,* unlettered: see IN– & LITERATE]

The above entry tells us that the English word *illiterate* comes from the Latin ("L") word *illiteratus,* meaning "unlettered." The etymology also refers us to the prefix *in–* and the English word *literate.* When we look up *in–,* we find out that it is a prefix meaning "no, not, or without" and that it is spelled *il–* before the letter *l.*

A dictionary entry for *literate* reveals that the word derives from a Middle English word (*litterate*), which derives from a Latin word (*litteratus*), which derives from the Latin word for *letter:*

> [ME *litterate* < L *litteratus* < *littera,* LETTER]

SKILLS FOCUS

PRACTICE

Vocabulary Skills
Understand etymology.

Use a dictionary to research the **derivation,** or origin, of the other Word Bank words. Write the oldest form of the word and the language from which it originally derived.

Grammar Link

Using Personal Pronouns— In the Right Places

The narrator of "The Leap" uses the first-person pronouns *I* and *me* to refer to herself. Using **personal pronouns** correctly in your writing can be tricky because there are two forms, or **cases,** and you need to choose the right form to fit each situation.

> **Nominative Case:** I, you, he, she, it, we, they
>
> **Objective Case:** me, you, him, her, it, us, them

Use a **nominative-case pronoun** if the pronoun functions as a subject or predicate nominative in a sentence.

He and I read "The Leap." [Pronouns are subjects: *He* and *I* carry out the action.]

The main characters are she and the mother. [Pronoun is a predicate nominative: *She* identifies the subject after a linking verb.]

Use an **objective-case pronoun** if the pronoun functions as a direct object, an indirect object, or the object of a preposition.

The firefighters saved the mother and her. [Pronoun is a direct object.]

The narrator tells us her mother's story. [Pronoun is an indirect object.]

The rescue seems unreal to him and me. [Pronouns are objects of preposition.]

PRACTICE

Edit and rewrite the following paragraph, correcting the personal pronouns. Hint: Not every pronoun needs to be corrected.

Julio told Carrie and I about a fabulous trapeze act he saw at the circus. Mara and him went to the circus last night and were astonished by what they saw. They described to the teacher and we the trapeze artists' daring tricks. Then him and Mara gave Carrie and I two discount tickets to the circus.

▶ **For more help, see Case, 4a–e, in the Language Handbook.**

Grammar Skills
Use personal pronouns correctly.

Elements of Literature

Setting *by* John Leggett
PUTTING US THERE

Where and When?

Is it possible for an interesting story to have no **setting** at all—that is, no indication of where or when the action takes place? Yes—if the characters and their situation are strong enough, they will hold our attention in empty space, just as a play presented on a bare stage can hold our interest.

In real life all events occur somewhere, so fiction specifies a setting most of the time. Think of how crucial setting would be in a story about a prisoner, in a story about castaways adrift on the Pacific, or in a story about a colony on Mars.

Setting puts us there—it gives us a feeling of being *in* the situation with the characters. Setting even includes people's customs—how they live, dress, eat, and behave.

Imagine a story that takes place in a town square in Honduras. The details of the setting should make us feel hot, sweaty, and thirsty. We should see the townspeople taking their afternoon siesta to escape the heat while the sun bakes the back of a little burro tethered beside the church. We should smell the *zozo,* the local delicacy of fish heads and banana skins, as it sizzles over charcoal.

Setting tells us not only *where* we are but also *when.* Setting can reveal a **time frame.** If the passing traffic is horse drawn, we can guess that we have gone back in time. An inch of new-fallen snow on a porch rail tells us it's winter. If the sun is just up over a pine ridge or if the *Ledger* is being tossed onto the front steps, it's early morning.

Details of setting give a story a kind of truth or believability. It is this realistic sense of place in fiction that gives us the joy of armchair travel—the chance to visit faraway places and times without ever leaving home.

Setting, Mood, and Tone

A more important function of setting, however, is to contribute to a story's emotional effect—its **mood,** or **atmosphere.** We all know that some settings can make us feel gloomy and others can make us feel cheerful. An autumnal setting can increase the sense of loss about a doomed love in a story. A spring setting can give a note of hope to a story of a girl's coming of age.

Details of setting can also help express **tone**—the writer's attitude toward a subject or character. Like a tone of voice, the writer's tone can be, for example, mocking or tender, joyful or nostalgic.

Here is a description of a rice paddy in Vietnam. How does it make you feel? How would you describe its **mood** and **tone?**

His boots sank into the thick paddy water, and he smelled it all around him. He would tell his mother how it smelled: mud and algae and cattle manure and chlorophyll; decay, breeding mosquitoes and leeches as big as mice; the fecund warmth of the paddy waters rising up to his cut knee.

—Tim O'Brien, from "Where Have You Gone, Charming Billy?" (page 621)

go.hrw.com

INTERNET
More About Setting
Keyword: LE5 10-1

SKILLS FOCUS

Literary Skills
Understand setting.

Elsewhere in the story this Vietnam jungle setting contrasts starkly with the young soldier's comforting memories of another setting, his home in Iowa. The mood and tone are different, and the emotional effect of that contrast is shattering.

> He was pretending he was a boy again, camping with his father in the midnight summer along the Des Moines River. In the dark, with his eyes pinched shut, he pretended. He pretended that when he opened his eyes, his father would be there by the campfire and they would talk softly about whatever came to mind and then roll into their sleeping bags. . . .

Setting and Character

Setting also helps reveal **character.** We all affect our environment in one way or another, so a writer wishing to portray an untidy Alice will show us the mess in her bedroom: pajamas, hangers, and sneakers in a snarl on the floor of her closet; CDs and magazines strewn on the unmade bed. Even before we meet Alice, we know something about her.

Now consider Jim's room: a set of weights in one corner; a copy of the *Guinness Book of World Records* on the bedside table; school pennants, photographs of the basketball team, and a set of antlers on the wall; and a pair of boxing gloves hanging from a hook on the closet door. What do we know about Jim before he even steps into the story?

Setting and Conflict

Though in some stories, setting hardly matters, in others it provides the main **conflict** and can directly affect a story's meaning. In such a story, members of a polar expedition might fight the harshness of the arctic tundra and survive (or, alternatively, perish). In "Contents of the Dead Man's Pocket" (page 5), Tom's near-fatal struggle on the window ledge leads him to reevaluate the priorities in his life.

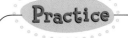

Practice

Work alone or with a partner to plan a story in which setting will play a major role. Use the chart shown here for your notes. It includes an example to help you.

Setting

Time: Late one winter night, early 1950s
Place: Run-down mansion in rural Scotland
Details of setting that affect mood or tone: Outside—dense fog; howling dog   Inside—ticking clock; cold, damp rooms
Details of setting that reveal character: Bare rooms with few chairs; no rugs; dim light; hundreds of books in piles and bookcases
Details of setting that affect conflict and meaning: Isolated mansion; doors locked and barred

Before You Read

The Pedestrian

Make the Connection

Quickwrite

Ray Bradbury's portrayal of a twenty-first-century world may raise as many questions as it provides answers.

What questions and ideas do you have about what life will be like in 2053, when the story takes place? Write down your questions and ideas, and save your notes.

Literary Focus

Setting and Mood

The **setting** of a story establishes the time and place of the action. Writers can also use setting to create a **mood,** or **atmosphere**—a subtle emotional overtone that can strongly affect our feelings. For example, settings can be used to suggest freedom, community, and peace. Settings can also be used to suggest control, isolation, and anxiety.

See what mood you sense in Bradbury's first paragraph. How does he use setting in the rest of the story to suggest his particular worldview?

Reading Skills

Does the Writer Have a Purpose?

Many fiction writers, poets, and dramatists have no **purpose** when they sit down to write other than to share a feeling or an experience, to re-create a world of their own making.

Ray Bradbury, however, is the kind of fiction writer who often writes for another purpose. Like many nonfiction writers, Bradbury tries to persuade us to accept his views on some issue.

To discover a writer's purpose, you must read closely. Take notes as you read.

Look for **key passages** that directly express opinions. Watch for **loaded words.** Bradbury's comparison of the city to a graveyard in the second paragraph should immediately send you signals. In this story the **setting** relates closely to Bradbury's purpose and the story's meaning.

Background

In the early 1950s, Ray Bradbury was a young man living in southern California. He did not know how to drive, and he liked walking around his suburban neighborhood at night. Even back then such behavior was so rare that he was once stopped and questioned by the police. If an innocent walk was so suspicious in mid-twentieth-century America, Bradbury wondered how it might be viewed in the future. Then he wrote this story.

Vocabulary Development

manifest (man′ə·fest′) *v.*: appear; become evident. *Manifest* also means "show; reveal."

intermittent (in′tər·mit′′nt) *adj.*: appearing or occurring from time to time.

ebbing (eb′iŋ) *v.*: lessening or weakening. The ebb is the flow of water away from the land as the tide falls.

antiseptic (an′tə·sep′tik) *n.*: substance used to sterilize or to prevent infection.

regressive (ri·gres′iv) *adj.*: moving backward or returning to an earlier or less advanced condition.

The Pedestrian

Ray Bradbury

A metallic voice called to him: "Stand still. Stay where you are!"

To enter out into that silence that was the city at eight o'clock of a misty evening in November, to put your feet upon that buckling concrete walk, to step over grassy seams and make your way, hands in pockets, through the silences, that was what Mr. Leonard Mead most dearly loved to do. He would stand upon the corner of an intersection and peer down long moonlit avenues of sidewalk in four directions, deciding which way to go, but it really made no difference; he was alone in this world of A.D. 2053, or as good as alone, and with a final decision made, a path selected, he would stride off, sending patterns of frosty air before him like the smoke of a cigar.

Sometimes he would walk for hours and miles and return only at midnight to his house. And on his way he would see the cottages and homes with their dark windows, and it was not unequal to walking through a graveyard where only the faintest glimmers of firefly light appeared in flickers behind the windows. Sudden gray phantoms[1] seemed to <u>manifest</u> upon inner room walls where a curtain was still undrawn against the night, or there were whisperings and murmurs where a window in a tomblike building was still open.

---

1. **phantoms** (fan′təmz) *n.*: ghosts; illusions.

Vocabulary
manifest (man′ə·fest′) *v.*: appear; become evident. *Manifest* also means "show; reveal."

Freeway Interchange (1982) by Wayne Thiebaud. Oil on canvas.

Mr. Leonard Mead would pause, cock his head, listen, look, and march on, his feet making no noise on the lumpy walk. For long ago he had wisely changed to sneakers when strolling at night, because the dogs in intermittent squads would parallel his journey with barkings if he wore hard heels, and lights might click on and faces appear and an entire street be startled by the passing of a lone figure, himself, in the early November evening.

On this particular evening he began his journey in a westerly direction, toward the hidden sea. There was a good crystal frost in the air; it cut the nose and made the lungs blaze like a Christmas tree inside; you could feel the cold light going on and off, all the branches filled with invisible snow. He listened to the faint push of his soft shoes through autumn leaves with satisfaction and whistled a cold, quiet whistle between his teeth, occasionally picking up a leaf as he passed, examining its skeletal pattern in the infrequent lamplights as he went on, smelling its rusty smell.

"Hello, in there," he whispered to every house on every side as he moved. "What's up tonight on Channel 4, Channel 7, Channel 9? Where are the cowboys rushing, and do I see the United States Cavalry over the next hill to the rescue?"

The street was silent and long and empty, with only his shadow moving like the shadow of a hawk in midcountry. If he closed his eyes and stood very still, frozen, he could imagine himself upon the center of a plain, a wintry, windless Arizona desert with no house in a thousand miles, and only dry riverbeds, the streets, for company.

"What is it now?" he asked the houses, noticing his wristwatch. "Eight-thirty p.m.? Time for a dozen assorted murders? A quiz? A revue? A comedian falling off the stage?"

Was that a murmur of laughter from within a moon-white house? He hesitated but went on when nothing more happened. He stumbled over a particularly uneven section of sidewalk.

The cement was vanishing under flowers and grass. In ten years of walking by night or day, for thousands of miles, he had never met another person walking, not one in all that time.

He came to a cloverleaf intersection which stood silent where two main highways crossed the town. During the day it was a thunderous surge of cars, the gas stations open, a great insect rustling, and a ceaseless jockeying for position as the scarab beetles,[2] a faint incense[3] puttering from their exhausts, skimmed homeward to the far directions. But now these highways, too, were like streams in a dry season, all stone and bed and moon radiance.

He turned back on a side street, circling around toward his home. He was within a block of his destination when the lone car turned a corner quite suddenly and flashed a fierce white cone of light upon him. He stood entranced, not unlike a night moth, stunned by the illumination and then drawn toward it.

A metallic voice called to him:

"Stand still. Stay where you are! Don't move!"

He halted.

"Put up your hands!"

"But—" he said.

"Your hands up! Or we'll shoot!"

The police, of course, but what a rare, incredible thing; in a city of three million, there was only *one* police car left, wasn't that correct? Ever since a year ago, 2052, the election year, the force had been cut down from three cars to one. Crime was ebbing; there was no need now for

---

2. **scarab beetles:** stout-bodied, brilliantly colored beetles. Bradbury is using the term as a metaphor for automobiles.
3. **incense** (in′sens′) *n.:* here, smoke.

Vocabulary

intermittent (in′tər·mit′′nt) *adj.:* appearing or occurring from time to time.

ebbing (eb′iŋ) *v.:* lessening or weakening. The ebb is the flow of water away from the land as the tide falls.

the police, save for this one lone car wandering and wandering the empty streets.

"Your name?" said the police car in a metallic whisper. He couldn't see the men in it for the bright light in his eyes.

"Leonard Mead," he said.

"Speak up!"

"Leonard Mead!"

"Business or profession?"

"I guess you'd call me a writer."

"No profession," said the police car, as if talking to itself. The light held him fixed, like a museum specimen, needle thrust through chest.

"You might say that," said Mr. Mead. He hadn't written in years. Magazines and books didn't sell anymore. Everything went on in the tomblike houses at night now, he thought, continuing his fancy. The tombs, ill-lit by television light, where the people sat like the dead, the gray or multicolored lights touching their faces, but never really touching them.

"No profession," said the phonograph voice, hissing. "What are you doing out?"

"Walking," said Leonard Mead.

"Walking!"

"Just walking," he said simply, but his face felt cold.

"Walking, just walking, walking?"

"Yes, sir."

"Walking where? For what?"

Highway Patrol (1986) by James Doolin. Oil on canvas.

Courtesy of Koplin Gallery, Los Angeles, CA.

"Walking for air. Walking to *see*."

"Your address!"

"Eleven South Saint James Street."

"And there is air *in* your house, you have an air *conditioner*, Mr. Mead?"

"Yes."

"And you have a viewing screen in your house to see with?"

"No."

"No?" There was a crackling quiet that in itself was an accusation.

"Are you married, Mr. Mead?"

"No."

"Not married," said the police voice behind the fiery beam. The moon was high and clear among the stars and the houses were gray and silent.

"Nobody wanted me," said Leonard Mead with a smile.

"Don't speak unless you're spoken to!"

Leonard Mead waited in the cold night.

"Just *walking*, Mr. Mead?"

"Yes."

"But you haven't explained for what purpose."

"I explained: for air, and to see, and just to walk."

"Have you done this often?"

"Every night for years."

The police car sat in the center of the street with its radio throat faintly humming.

"Well, Mr. Mead," it said.

"Is that all?" he asked politely.

"Yes," said the voice. "Here." There was a sigh, a pop. The back door of the police car sprang wide. "Get in."

"Wait a minute, I haven't done anything!"

"Get in."

"I protest!"

"Mr. Mead."

He walked like a man suddenly drunk. As he passed the front window of the car, he looked in.

> **"Wait a minute, I haven't done anything!"**

As he had expected, there was no one in the front seat, no one in the car at all.

"Get in."

He put his hand to the door and peered into the back seat, which was a little cell, a little black jail with bars. It smelled of riveted[4] steel. It smelled of harsh antiseptic; it smelled too clean and hard and metallic. There was nothing soft there.

"Now, if you had a wife to give you an alibi," said the iron voice. "But—"

"Where are you taking me?"

The car hesitated, or rather gave a faint, whirring click, as if information, somewhere, was dropping card by punch-slotted card under electric eyes. "To the Psychiatric Center for Research on Regressive Tendencies."

He got in. The door shut with a soft thud. The police car rolled through the night avenues, flashing its dim lights ahead.

They passed one house on one street a moment later, one house in an entire city of houses that were dark, but this one particular house had all of its electric lights brightly lit, every window a loud yellow illumination, square and warm in the cool darkness.

"That's *my* house," said Leonard Mead.

No one answered him.

The car moved down the empty riverbed streets and off away, leaving the empty streets with the empty sidewalks and no sound and no motion all the rest of the chill November night. ■

---

4. **riveted** (riv′it·id) *v.* used as *adj.*: held together by rivets (metal bolts or pins).

Vocabulary

antiseptic (an′tə·sep′tik) *n.*: substance used to sterilize or to prevent infection.

regressive (ri·gres′iv) *adj.*: moving backward or returning to an earlier or less advanced condition.

Meet the Writer

Ray Bradbury

The Man with the Child Inside

Ray Bradbury (1920–   ) calls himself "that special freak—the man with the child inside who remembers all." Bradbury was born in Waukegan, Illinois, and began writing when he was seven.

Bradbury sees himself as a magic realist (see page 586) and a disciple of Edgar Allan Poe (see page 428). He says that his lifelong hatred of thought control grows out of his sympathy for his ancestor Mary Bradbury, who was tried as a witch in seventeenth-century Salem, Massachusetts. Here is how his imagination grew:

66 When I was three my mother snuck me in and out of movies two or three times a week. My first film was Lon Chaney in *The Hunchback of Notre Dame*. I suffered

permanent curvature of the spine and of my imagination that day a long time ago in 1923. From that hour on, I knew a kindred and wonderfully grotesque compatriot of the dark when I saw one. . . .

I was in love, then, with monsters and skeletons and circuses and carnivals and dinosaurs and at last, the red planet, Mars.

From these primitive bricks I have built a life and a career. By my staying in love with all of these amazing things, all of the good things in my existence have come about.

In other words, I was *not* embarrassed at circuses. Some people are. Circuses are loud, vulgar, and smell in the sun. By the time many people are fourteen or fifteen, they have been divested of their loves, their ancient and intuitive tastes, one by one, until when they reach maturity there is no fun left, no zest, no gusto, no flavor. Others have criticized, and they have criticized themselves, into embarrassment. When the circus pulls in at five of a dark cold summer morn, and the calliope sounds, they do not rise and run, they turn in their sleep, and life passes by.

I did rise and run. . . . 99

For Independent Reading

If you enjoyed "The Pedestrian," you might enjoy reading some of Bradbury's well-known novels. *The Martian Chronicles* describes the adventures of a colony of pioneers on Mars. *Dandelion Wine* paints a fantasy of a boy with special mental powers.

Response and Analysis

Reading Check

1. What ominous fact about this future society is **foreshadowed,** or hinted at, by the "buckling concrete walk" in the first paragraph? As the story develops, what else are you told about the **setting** of "The Pedestrian"?

2. Find the sentences and phrases that at first suggest that Leonard Mead is the only person living in this **setting** in A.D. 2053. Find the passage that reveals that there are other people living in this setting.

3. Explain Leonard Mead's "regressive tendencies."

4. Describe the police automaton's response when Mead says he is a writer.

Thinking Critically

5. Leonard Mead is the only human character in the story. Who—or what—appears to be in charge of this future world?

6. List several details that describe the houses Leonard passes and the evening streets. What **mood** do these details create?

7. What do you think Bradbury's **purpose** was in writing this story? How does the setting he chose help him achieve his purpose? Cite details from the story to support your answers.

8. Which of today's problems seem to have been eliminated from Leonard Mead's society? What does Leonard miss that we still enjoy today?

9. How is technology used to control Leonard's world? What point about technology and its power do you think Bradbury is making in this story? Find some key words, phrases, or events in the story to support your interpretation.

Extending and Evaluating

10. Do you think Bradbury is too pessimistic about technology? Support your opinion with details from the text and from the real world.

WRITING

Picture the Setting

Use your imagination to help you describe the Psychiatric Center for Research on Regressive Tendencies that Leonard is sent to. Consider whether the researchers are human or robots, what they look like (including how they are dressed), and how the building is furnished. Be sure your **setting** creates a **mood** that fits with Bradbury's story.

LISTENING AND SPEAKING

Debating the Future

Form a panel, and discuss what you think society will be like in 2053. Will technology isolate us from one another, as "The Pedestrian" suggests, or will technology be a force for good? Will individuals be more free or less free? Check your Quickwrite notes for other questions. Before you begin, assign a moderator, and establish rules for the panel. At the end of the discussion, audience members should prepare a **summary** of the panel's views and an **evaluation** of the participants' performances.

SKILLS FOCUS

Literary Skills
Analyze setting and mood.

Reading Skills
Analyze the writer's purpose.

Writing Skills
Write a description of a setting that creates a specific mood.

Listening and Speaking Skills
Participate in or evaluate the effectiveness of a panel discussion.

Vocabulary Development

Vocabulary Resource File

PRACTICE 1

Begin a vocabulary resource file, starting with the words in the Word Bank. Put each word on an index card (or create a file on your computer). Use the example below as a model. Include a note to yourself to help you remember the word.

Word Bank

manifest
intermittent
ebbing
antiseptic
regressive

> **Word:** antiseptic (noun)
> **Definition:** substance used on the skin to prevent infection
> **Sentences:** Before giving me the shot, the nurse swabbed my arm with an antiseptic.
> After washing the cut, Dave applied iodine as an antiseptic.
> **Note:** An antiseptic is used to kill bacteria on the outside of the body—on the skin. An antibiotic destroys bacteria inside the body.

The Power of Connotations

Certain words have emotional overtones, or **connotations,** that go beyond their literal meanings, or **denotations.** Consider the difference between the two words in the following pairs:

unusual/odd	young/immature	proud/smug
assertive/pushy	frugal/stingy	

In each pair the first word has more positive connotations than the second word. We might use the first word to describe ourselves but the second word to describe someone else. In fact, the British philosopher Bertrand Russell once gave a classic example of the different connotations of words: "I am firm. You are obstinate. He is a pig-headed fool."

The following passages from "The Pedestrian" use words with strong **connotations:**

1. "And on his way he would see the cottages and homes with their dark windows, and it was not unequal to walking through a graveyard. . . ."

2. "Sudden gray phantoms seemed to manifest upon inner room walls . . . , or there were whisperings and murmurs where a window in a tomblike building was still open."

PRACTICE 2

1. Write down what you think is the strongest word or phrase in each of the numbered passages on the left. Then, describe briefly what the word or phrase suggests to you or how it makes you feel.

2. Rewrite each passage with words that have more positive connotations. The graveyard, for example, could become a sleepy village.

SKILLS FOCUS

Vocabulary Skills
Create a vocabulary resource file. Understand connotations and denotations.

FICTION

The Good Old Days

Jack Finney's flair for fast-paced time-travel stories with a comic edge is beautifully realized in his short story collection *About Time.* In these twelve tales you'll enter places where odd neighbors, magical coin collections, X-ray-vision eyeglasses, disappearing dogs, and candy bars made from unusual ingredients are your passports to the world of the past.

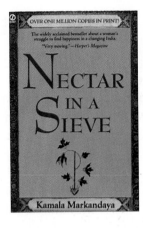

FICTION

Woman of Strength

Life in rural India is difficult for Rukmani and her family. Drought, disease, death, and desperate poverty threaten them at every turn. Yet Kamala Markandaya's *Nectar in a Sieve* is ultimately a story of hope—a beautiful tale of how a mother's strength, faith, and endurance manage to unite her loved ones in the worst of times.

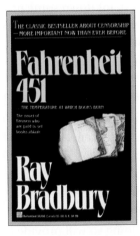

FICTION

Burning Books

A little knowledge is a dangerous thing in Ray Bradbury's futuristic world of *Fahrenheit 451.* People are forbidden to read, and any books that are found are immediately burned by "firemen." Then one day a fireman named Guy Montag begins to question the wisdom of what he's doing and soon discovers a secret and beautiful world he'd never dreamed of.

NONFICTION

A Very Close Call . . .

For a suspenseful and completely true story that even Stephen King found frightening, get *The Hot Zone* by Richard Preston. This nonfiction thriller focuses on a deadly virus that almost escaped from a research laboratory in Reston, Virginia. Find out how this tropical threat was brought under control—barely.

Writing an Autobiographical Narrative

Writing Assignment
Write a narrative about a significant autobiographical experience.

Somewhere, sometime, you've picked up a writer's account of a personal experience—something like, say, Sir Edmund Hillary's account of climbing Mt. Everest, your younger sister's account of the first day of first grade, or Sue Shellenbarger's account of her attempts to balance her personal and professional lives in "Diary of a Mad Blender"—and thought, "I've felt that way, too." People write **autobiographical narratives** to share their experiences and life lessons with others. What kind of experience do *you* have to share?

Prewriting

Choose an Experience

Who Are You? To find an experience to use as the topic for an autobiographical narrative, begin by exploring the defining moments of your life—the experiences that have shaped who you are. Brainstorm a list of experiences you remember vividly. Then, jot down some notes about each one. Finally, look over your notes and choose the experience that stirs up the most vivid memories or feelings. Be sure to choose an experience you feel comfortable sharing with an audience.

Consider Purpose and Audience

Basic Considerations A basic principle of good writing requires you to keep two considerations—**purpose** and **audience**—in mind as you write, no matter what you're writing. Your purpose is to describe an experience that had a significant effect on your life. Provide your readers with the background information they will need to understand the significance of your experience fully. For example, introduce yourself as you were before the experience. Doing so will provide a hint about the effect the experience had on you.

Gather Details

Putting the Pieces Together The details of your experience are like the brightly colored pieces of a jigsaw puzzle. Put them together and they will create a vivid and coherent picture for your readers.

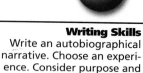

SKILLS FOCUS

Writing Skills
Write an autobiographical narrative. Choose an experience. Consider purpose and audience.

Events First, brainstorm the **sequence of events** that is central to your narrative. Make sure that you **focus** the narrative by choosing only those events that are relevant to the experience. Then, list the events in a rough outline like the one below.

DO THIS

> ### Events
> 1. I watched others practicing tae kwon do, the Korean martial art I had always wanted to learn, and imagined that I could do it, too.
> 2. I met an instructor who taught me techniques and encouraged me to practice hard.
> 3. I entered a competition.
> 4. My mom and dad saw me compete.

People and Places Close your eyes and walk yourself through the events you listed. Try to remember as specifically as possible the people and **specific places** involved in your experience. Jot down **factual details,** such as names, dates, and numbers; concrete **sensory details,** which have to do with the senses of touch, smell, hearing, sight, and taste; and the **specific appearances, gestures, actions,** and **dialogue** of the people involved, including yourself. Keep in mind that dialogue should be recorded as informally as it was spoken. For example, it can include slang and sentence fragments.

As you list details, jot down any **figurative language** (**similes, metaphors,** or **personification**) that will help you describe your experience more clearly and create more effective images. Also try to use precise **action verbs**—*paced* or *lurched* instead of *walked,* for example—to note events and actions. Take a look at part of the list that one student prepared about learning tae kwon do.

Reference Note

For more on **figurative language,** see pages 477–478.

> ### Details about People and Places
> Me—Shy, not very confident, age 13, physically scrawny and awkward
> Gwen—College student, strong and swift, encouraging—"Hey, wallflower! Why don't you come help me practice some of my blocks?"

Thoughts and Feelings Your narrative should reveal what you thought and felt during your experience. In your rough outline, make some notes about your thoughts and feelings at each point. In your final draft, consider showing thoughts and feelings through **interior monologue,** or what you say to yourself in your head as the events of your narrative unfold. You may also want to **shift perspectives** by imagining the thoughts and feelings of other people in the narrative.

SKILLS FOCUS

Writing Skills
Gather details.

Reflect on Your Experience

That Was Then, This Is Now An autobiographical narrative should convey the **significance,** or meaning, of the experience you describe. At the end, your readers should clearly understand the difference between who you were before the experience and who you became after it was over. To reflect on the meaning of your experience, think about what you were like before the experience, how you changed, and what you learned about yourself and about life in general. Start reflecting on your experience by filling in a couple of simple sentences:

DO THIS

At first I _____, but afterward I _____.
I realized _____.

The student writing about tae kwon do jotted the following sentences to express the meaning of her experience.

TIP Remember to signal the passage of time with **transitional expressions** such as *next, then, eventually, soon, the next day,* and so on.

At first I <u>was shy and lacked confidence</u>, but afterward I <u>was more self-assured</u>. I realized <u>that I had felt myself to be only a shadow of my older brother and sister, but now I had an accomplishment of my own to prove I was my own person</u>.

Don't include these sentences in your narrative's introduction. Instead, use them to help you choose those details that contribute to a **controlling impression,** or central idea, about your experience. For example, the student writing about tae kwon do chose details to create the controlling impression that the sport gave her self-confidence and a sense of identity. Save any direct statement of the significance of your experience for the conclusion of your narrative—after your readers have had a chance to determine for themselves how the experience changed your life.

Organize Your Details

Following the Leader **Chronological order** is usually the easiest for readers to follow. However, a **flashback** is another effective way to organize a narrative: The narrative starts at the end and then "flashes back" to the earlier events that led up to that point.

Pace is also important to consider as you plan your essay. For example, quicken the pace of your narrative by using a series of short, to-the-point sentences to describe events that occurred rapidly. Slow your pace by using longer sentences to describe events that occurred slowly.

SKILLS FOCUS

Writing Skills
Reflect on the experience.
Organize details.

PRACTICE & APPLY 1 Choose a significant experience from your life as the subject of your autobiographical narrative. Then, plan the details of the narrative.

Writing

Writing an Autobiographical Narrative

A Writer's Framework

Introduction

- Start with an interesting opener.
- Provide necessary background information.
- Hint at the significance of the experience.

Body

- Organize events so that they are easy to follow.
- Include details about people, places, thoughts, and feelings.
- Use figurative language and precise action verbs.

Conclusion

- Reflect on what the experience meant to you.
- End with a direct statement of the significance of the experience.

A Writer's Model

Kicking Shyness

My whole way of looking at the world began to change around the time I turned thirteen. That May, my parents began taking the family to a local YMCA. At the time, although I didn't admit it to myself, I always seemed to live in the shadows of my older brother and sister. However, beginning with those hot summer days at the center, I started to lose track of what my brother and sister were doing—because for the first time in my life I was too busy doing my own thing.

After about a month, I found a tae kwon do class at the YMCA and was mesmerized as I watched men and women, boys and girls practice moves and spar with each other. The room was filled with swishing, white uniforms and roaring *ki-hop* yells. I imagined I was one of these people, timing my strokes perfectly, blocking so gracefully, delivering the winning point at the last moment. In reality I spent weeks blending into the wall farthest from the class, shadowboxing at home behind locked doors, too afraid to join the others.

Then, after weeks of watching, one day it happened. The *sabom-nim* (instructor), a college student named Gwen who moved as if the law of gravity did not apply to her, called to me just as I was about to sneak out the door. "Hey, wallflower! Why don't you come help me practice some of my blocks?" she asked. I told her that I was not part of the class, but she insisted, saying, "I promise I'll only block your moves. No countermoves until you're ready—and I can teach you some other techniques, too."

(continued)

INTRODUCTION
Interesting opener
Background information
Hint at significance

BODY
Event 1
Sensory details
Thoughts

Slow pace
Details about actions/Feelings

Event 2
Details about appearance

Dialogue

(continued)

Figurative language
Rapid pace

If Gwen had not been so friendly, I might have tried to escape. Instead, I found myself on the mats, outfitted in all the cushioned protective gear. My knees were mashed potatoes. My heartbeat thundered in my head. My breath came in gasps. There was no escape. I tucked my head safely behind my pads. Now I was barely able to see. I moved haltingly forward, fearful and fascinated. After a few minutes, though, I started to relax and enjoy myself. "See?" Gwen said afterward. "Once you've loosened up, you're a natural." That was the right thing to say then, because I needed praise.

Event 3
Factual details

That night, I convinced my parents to let me enroll in the class. I memorized all the moves: *ahre maggi*, "down block"; *guligi cha-gi*, "hook kick"; *poom sogi*, "tiger stance"; and so on. Believe me, this "natural" never worked so hard in her life. There is no doubt about it—tae kwon do is a tough, aerobic workout. Sometimes my muscles felt like limp noodles by the end of the day. My friends thought I was crazy. "Here comes Jackie Chan," they would tease. Eventually, though, I was not just graceful but good enough to earn a yellow, then an orange, and later, a green belt.

Figurative language
Dialogue

Event 4
Factual details

My mother still likes to tell the next part of this story. The following March, I had invited her, Dad, and my brother and sister to the center one Saturday for the spring tournaments—not telling them that I was competing. While they were looking for me on the bench, they were surprised to hear my name blared over a loudspeaker. Their shock was compounded when they finally noticed their younger daughter, poised confidently in the ring, waiting to spar in her first competition match. "I can't believe I'm here!" I remember thinking. I didn't win, but I did get my picture in the newspaper (a close-up of my determined face) and have the reward of my parents' amazed and proud faces.

Shifting perspective

Interior monologue

CONCLUSION

Significance of experience

Looking back, I realize now that my parents did not need proof that I was worth something—*I* did. I needed an accomplishment all my own, and tae kwon do was it. I learned confidence and greater respect for myself, not from winning, but from trying. From then on, I felt like a real person, not just a shadow.

go.
hrw
.com

INTERNET
More Writer's
Models
Keyword: LE5 10-1

PRACTICE & APPLY 2 Use the framework on page 59 and the Writer's Model above to guide you as you write a first draft of your autobiographical narrative. Return to the Prewriting section to refresh your understanding of basic concepts.

Revising

Evaluate and Revise Your Draft

Taking a Second Look Your task as a writer doesn't end once you've written your first draft. Now, with your readers in mind, evaluate and revise what you have written. Will they be able to follow the organization? Are your details vivid enough to set the scene? Re-read your narrative at least twice—first to improve the organization and content of your draft and second to focus on style.

PEER REVIEW

Before you revise, ask a classmate to read your paper and suggest ways you might improve your content, organization, or style. You might ask, for example, if the meaning of your experience is clear.

▶ **First Reading: Content and Organization** Use the following guidelines to evaluate and revise your autobiographical narrative. Because an autobiographical narrative is usually informal, check that you have consistently used first-person pronouns: *I, me, our,* and *we.* Also check on the **focus** of your narrative to make sure that each event you describe is relevant to the experience.

Rubric: Writing an Autobiographical Narrative

Evaluation Questions	▶ Tips	▶ Revision Techniques
❶ Does the introduction grab the reader's attention, provide background information, and hint at the meaning of the experience?	▶ **Circle** the sentences in the intro-duction that capture the reader's attention. **Put parentheses around** background information. **Bracket** the hint at the meaning of the experience.	▶ **Replace** the opening sentences with sentences that grab the reader's attention. **Add** back-ground or a hint of the mean-ing of the experience.
❷ Does the narrative include sensory and factual details that support the control-ling impression?	▶ **Underline** each sentence that begins a description of a sepa-rate event, person, or place. **Double underline** concrete details that support the control-ling impression.	▶ **Add** concrete sensory and factual details that support the controlling impression or **elaborate** on existing details.
❸ Do the body paragraphs include descriptions of thoughts and feelings?	▶ **Mark with a star** any sentences that describe thoughts and feelings.	▶ **Add** or **elaborate** on details about thoughts and feelings.
❹ Is the sequence of events in the narrative organized logically? Are all the events relevant to the experience?	▶ **Number** the events in the narra-tive, looking for gaps or a con-fusing order. **Put an X** next to any irrelevant event.	▶ **Reorder** the events in a way that will be clearer for the reader. **Cut** any events marked with an X.
❺ Does the conclusion end with a statement of the sig-nificance of the experience?	▶ **Highlight** any sentences that state why the experience was important to the writer.	▶ **Add** sentences that clearly state the significance of the experience.

Second Reading: **Style** A writer's style can be so dull that it lulls readers to sleep, or it can be so lively and engaging that readers regret coming to the end of the piece. During your second reading, focus on style—the way you express yourself. One common style problem in autobiographical narratives is **vague modifiers**—adjectives or adverbs that are ineffective because they don't create a precise mental image in readers' minds. For example, *firetruck red car* is more precise than merely *red car*.

Style Guidelines

Evaluation Question	▶ Tip	▶ Revision Technique
● Are the modifiers specific enough to make the words they modify clearer or more vivid to readers?	▶ **Put a jagged line** beneath each modifier and draw an arrow to the word it modifies.	▶ **Replace** vague or ineffective modifiers with more specific or appropriate ones.

ANALYZING THE REVISION PROCESS
Study these revisions, and answer the questions that follow.

The room was filled with swishing, white uniforms and

roaring

replace ~~loud~~ ki-hop yells. I imagined I was one of these people, timing

my strokes perfectly, blocking so gracefully, delivering the

winning point at the last moment. In reality I spent weeks

blending into the wall farthest from the class, shadowboxing at

add home behind locked doors, *, too afraid to join the others.*

Responding to the Revision Process
1. Why does the writer replace *loud* in the first sentence?
2. What is the effect of the writer's addition to the last sentence?

SKILLS FOCUS

Writing Skills
Revise for content and style.

PRACTICE & APPLY ❸ First, use the content and organization guidelines in this section to evaluate and revise those aspects of your narrative. Then, use the style guidelines to evaluate and revise the style of your narrative.

Publishing

Proofread and Publish Your Essay

A Smooth Finish Think about it: When you run across errors in spelling, punctuation, or grammar in something you're reading, you become distracted—you focus on the errors instead of what the essay or article means. To pave a clear path for your own readers, proofread your narrative carefully. It often helps to work with a partner.

It's a Small World, After All Writing an autobiographical narrative can give you insight into yourself you might never have achieved otherwise. Now, share that insight with others. Here are some ways to encourage others to read and respond to your narrative.

- Ask your teacher to arrange a "cultural exchange" of autobiographical narratives with a class in another part of the country or world. Look for the ways your experiences are similar—and different.

- Create a family memento by pasting or scanning old photos of your experience onto your narrative.

- Give or send a copy of your narrative to one of the people involved in the experience you narrated. Then, ask how he or she remembers the same experience.

- Turn your autobiographical narrative into a narrative poem told from the third-person point of view. Submit your poem to a literary magazine.

Reflect on Your Essay

Looking Back, Looking Forward Answering the following questions will help you think about what you have learned while writing your narrative and what you might do differently the next time you write one.

- Which prewriting step did you find most difficult? Do you think it will be easier for you the next time you write an autobiographical piece? Why or why not?

- While writing your narrative, what new insights did you have into the experience you chose as a topic?

- How was writing an autobiographical narrative different from the other kinds of writing you do in school? How was it similar?

PRACTICE & APPLY   Proofread your narrative for errors in the conventions of standard American grammar, usage, and mechanics before publishing it for an audience. Finally, answer the reflection questions above.

 TIP A thorough proofreading will help you catch any problems in the **conventions** of standard American usage. Be especially sure to correct errors in **verb tense,** which often crop up when you are narrating a sequence of events. For more on **verb tense,** see Tense, 3d–f, in the Language Handbook.

SKILLS FOCUS

Writing Skills
Proofread, especially for correct use of verb tense.

Presenting a Narrative

Speaking Assignment
Adapt your autobiographical narrative for an oral presentation to an audience.

A good storyteller is an artist who has a sense of pace, an eye for detail, and an ear for dialogue. It doesn't matter whether you are reading or hearing a story by such an artist. Your attention is riveted upon the story. There are differences between a written and an oral narrative, but they result from the difference between a reading and a listening audience. As you adapt your written autobiographical narrative for an oral presentation, keep your new audience in mind.

Adapt Your Written Narrative

The Big Picture Readers can always re-read a word, a passage, or an entire story until they understand it. Listeners can't. They must understand what a speaker says immediately. When you adapt your written narrative for an oral presentation, keep this simple fact in mind. Here are some things you can do throughout your adaptation to make it immediately understandable for your audience.

- **Simplify the vocabulary.** Substitute familiar words for words that might be unfamiliar to your audience.

- **Simplify sentence structure.** Find long, complex sentences in your written narrative and break them up into shorter sentences that get more directly to the point.

- **Use strict chronological order.** Readers can follow flashbacks and flash-forwards in a written narrative. Strict chronological order—a simple sequence of events—is easier for listeners to follow.

The Sands of Time If time limitations force you to adapt your written narrative by cutting it, be careful to retain the most important events. For example, if your written narrative includes transitional events—minor events that bridge the gaps between major events— keep the transitional events but cut the details used to describe them. If your written narrative includes an event that was part of the experience but had no role in making the experience significant, cut it.

The Indispensable Certain parts of your narrative are vital. Retain or strengthen the concrete sensory details that bring characters and action to life and that locate scenes and events in specific places, a strategy that allows your listener to visualize those characters, scenes, and events. Also retain the details necessary to create and maintain a controlling impression and those parts of your narrative that communicate the significance of your experience.

SKILLS FOCUS

Listening and Speaking Skills
Present an autobiographical narrative.

Hello and Goodbye Your oral presentation should be organized in the same introduction, body, and conclusion arrangement you used for your written narrative. The introduction and conclusion of an oral presentation are especially important.

- In the **introduction,** try to get the audience to identify with you—to think that they share common feelings and experiences with you. Make the introduction as intriguing and personal as possible.

- In the **conclusion,** try to make the significance of your subject clear and to make your listeners identify with your experience by thinking of similar significant experiences of their own.

Here are examples of techniques you can use to adapt the introduction and conclusion of your written narrative. If you use one of the techniques in the introduction, use another in the conclusion.

- Use an appropriate well-known quotation: "They say 'Every dog has its day.' I found out how true that is one Saturday three summers ago."

- Make an observation about life that hints at the importance of your experience: "I had always thought it was normal for the youngest child in a family to be completely without talent or skill."

Deliver Your Narrative

Prepare to Be Natural Once you've finished your adaptation, deliver it **extemporaneously** rather than from memory. Extemporaneous speakers rehearse their presentations thoroughly and refer briefly to a few written notes from time to time during their presentations.

To prepare to deliver your presentation extemporaneously, first write down the main events of your narrative and a few of the major details on note cards. If a particular piece of dialogue is important, write it down in its entirety. Then, arrange the note cards in the order in which you will use them.

Use All the Tools Speakers have verbal and nonverbal tools that a writer doesn't have. Speakers can use **gestures, facial expressions,** and **eye contact** to enhance their words. They can use their voices to **pace** the action in the narrative, slowing down or speeding up to mimic the action and accommodate changes in mood or time. They can use the **volume** of their voices to emphasize a point. A word or phrase said quietly can be as emphatic as a word or phrase said very loudly. Just be sure you always speak loudly enough to be heard.

SKILLS FOCUS

PRACTICE & APPLY 5 Use the instructions in this section to adapt your written autobiographical narrative for an oral presentation. Rehearse your presentation until your delivery feels natural. Then, present your narrative to an audience.

Listening and Speaking Skills
Adapt and deliver your presentation.

Test Practice

Synthesizing Sources

DIRECTIONS: Read the following two articles. Then, read and respond to the questions that follow.

What Price Glory?
Len Lewis

Your flight is delayed for the third time this week, you have 22 e-mails and 10 voice messages since you checked one hour ago, and another late night will turn into another lost weekend of just trying to catch up—let alone getting ahead of the power curve.

If this seems like a familiar scenario,[1] it's one being played out every day in the industry by a cast of thousands. When playwright Arthur Miller created the character of Willy Loman,[2] the quintessential[3] road warrior, one character uttered the now famous line: "Attention must be paid." But attention to business and career at what price?

Clearly, success in an increasingly competitive and complex industry carries a stiff price. The question is, how much is too much?

Will the legacy of the late twentieth century be a generation of managers whose commitment and passion for career and company lead to emotional distress or boardroom burnout? When does an executive's total attention to business become his or her downfall? How many boards, committees, synergy or share groups can you sit on? And what is the point of diminishing returns when building a career makes you a better candidate for antidepressants, psychotherapy, and family counseling than a promotion?

An overstatement? Perhaps! But the road to success for a new generation of managers is a bumpy one in terms of personal growth. Adding richness to daily life by striking a balance between home and office is the essence of a successful businessperson. Yet emotional connections to home and family and even oneself can be easily lost in a maze of meetings, workshops, committee work, or just the frustrating business of clearing the morning's e-mails.

---

1. **scenario** (sə·ner′ē·ō′) *n.*: outline of a play or movie or of any planned series of events.
2. **Willy Loman:** traveling salesman and the main character in Arthur Miller's 1949 play *Death of a Salesman.*
3. **quintessential** (kwin′te·sen′shəl) *adj.*: serving as a perfect example.

SKILLS FOCUS

Pages 66–69 cover **Reading Skills** Synthesize information from several sources on a single topic.

Life outside the office is not a weakness. It's what makes people stronger. Taking the time to attend a school function or have dinner with a spouse or friend will not burst the new economic bubble. A child's hug after a bad day won't suffocate, but invigorate. And taking the time to decompress alone or with family—even if it means missing a conference or another meeting—won't derail years of hard work and dedication.

The solution to this dilemma won't be found in the hallowed halls of academia[4] or in the next workshop. It lies in a self-analysis of what we want to be. Maybe it is this self-analysis that has led so many food executives to walk away from 30-year careers into the arms of the new economy—for better or worse.

—**from** *Progressive Grocer*, **May 2000**

---

4. **academia** (ak′ə · dē′mē · ə) *n.:* academic world; colleges and universities.

Deprived of Parent Time?

Kim Campbell

Houses may be messier and parents may be sleepier, but that's a good sign for kids.

Across America, time spent in the company of children has become the holy grail[1] of working parents—and it appears to be well within their grasp. By curtailing everything from shut-eye to volunteer work to vacuuming, most moms and dads today are finding ways to put kids first, perhaps more consciously than in earlier eras.

"Anytime I'm not working, I'm with my kids," says Pamela Alexander, a manager at Ford Motor Company in Deerborn, Mich. To have more hours with their two girls, she and her husband hire out the housecleaning, and instead of giving time to charities, "I write big checks," she says.

With dual-income families now the norm, spending time with children requires more creativity than it did during the days of *Ozzie and Harriet*.[2] Solutions vary—from staggered job schedules, to one parent quitting work for a time, to dads picking up more of the child-rearing responsibility.

"We're in the midst of an evolution, not a revolution," says James Levine, director

---

1. **holy grail** (grāl): ultimate, hard-to-attain goal. According to medieval legend, the grail was a magical cup that Jesus drank from at the Last Supper.

2. *Ozzie and Harriet: The Adventures of Ozzie and Harriet* was a very popular TV show from the early 1950s to the mid-1960s.

of the Fatherhood Project at the Families and Work Institute in New York.

Changes in technology and lifestyle patterns have certainly helped parents eke out more family time. Fast food and microwaves, for example, offer shortcuts for meal preparation. Children are also home less often than they used to be, being pulled out for activities like preschool, summer camp, and swimming lessons. Couples today also have fewer children than did their counterparts of recent decades, allowing for more parental "face time" per child.

Thanks to such changes, mothers today spend about the same amount of time with their children as mothers did in the 1960s, according to new findings by Suzanne Bianchi, a sociologist at the University of Maryland in College Park. In 1998, women spent 5.8 waking hours with their children each day, versus 5.6 hours for mothers in 1965. Fathers did even better—increasing their time from 2.7 hours per day in 1965 to 4 hours in 1998.

Indeed, dads are the resource parents are drawing on most often to make up for the time women are spending at the office. Perhaps as a result, attitudes about men's role in the family are gradually changing.

"When fathers define success today, it's no longer just in terms of being a breadwinner. It means being involved with the kids as well," says Dr. Levine, author of *Working Fathers.*

Many mothers say their husbands help with everything from folding laundry to picking up kids after school. Fathers' share of housework has increased in recent years, too, with men taking over some of the duties (although not half of them) from moms—both working and nonworking.

Luvie Myers, a stay-at-home mom in Winnetka, Illinois, says her husband can more easily leave work for a family event than a father could have in her parents' era. "Spending time with family is an excuse at work that people are willing to accept," she says.

—from *The Christian Science Monitor,*
April 5, 2000

1. The **main idea** of "What Price Glory?" is that busy executives —
   A need more time at the office
   B need to work more efficiently
   C need to balance their home and office lives
   D should change careers

2. In "What Price Glory?" the author's **attitude** toward the topic can *best* be described as —
   F hesitant
   G impassioned
   H bitter
   J indifferent

3. One of the **main ideas** of "Deprived of Parent Time?" is that fathers today —
   A spend less time with their children than in the past
   B spend more time with their children than in the past
   C cannot juggle jobs and family life
   D are conflicted over family roles

4. "Deprived of Parent Time?" includes all of the following types of **supporting evidence** *except* —
   F quotations
   G examples
   H statistics
   J opinion polls

5. Which article would you cite in a research report on boardroom burnout?
   A "Deprived of Parent Time?"
   B "What Price Glory?"

   C Both articles
   D Neither article

6. "What Price Glory?" *differs* from "Deprived of Parent Time?" because the former is based on —
   F the author's opinion
   G statistical research
   H extensive interviews
   J opinion polls

7. *Both* articles discuss the importance of —
   A more efficient work schedules
   B better child-care programs
   C a shorter work week
   D more quality time for families

8. Which of the following ideas is *not* discussed in *both* articles?
   F Many working people are redefining the meaning of success.
   G Spending time with children brings parents many rewards.
   H Modern technology can help solve our time-crunch problems.
   J Career success alone is not enough for a rich life.

Constructed Response

9. Compare and contrast the main ideas of the two articles. Use details from the texts to support your answer.

Collection 1: Skills Review

Vocabulary Skills

Multiple-Meaning Words

DIRECTIONS: Choose the answer in which the underlined word is used in the same way as it is used in these sentences from "The Leap."

1. "She has never upset an object or as much as brushed a magazine onto the floor."

   A In that sentence, *him* is the object of the preposition *to*.

   B What is the object of this plan?

   C That tiny carved statue is an object she treasures.

   D Does anyone object to my suggestion?

2. "In the town square a replica tent pole, cracked and splintered, now stands cast in concrete."

   F He ate three square meals a day.

   G The park benches in the square are new.

   H Rachel drew an uneven-looking square.

   J Two is the square root of four.

3. "I wonder if my father calculated the exchange he offered: one form of flight for another."

   A Please fill out this form.

   B In ceramics class we form clay into bowls.

   C The runner was in great form.

   D Which is your favorite form of travel—cars, trains, or planes?

4. "Though he'd been thinking of moving . . . , he settled down and broadened his practice in this valley."

   F It is her practice to walk every morning.

   G Dara looks forward to band practice.

   H Good musicians practice every day.

   J His law practice covers two counties.

5. "It started right around the stove, and the heart of the house was gutted."

   A The tallest buildings were in the heart of downtown.

   B My heart skipped a beat.

   C In this game a heart beats a diamond, spade, or club.

   D At heart I think Len's very shy.

6. "There came a rumble of electrical energy, drowned out by the sudden roll of drums."

   F The bad weather made the ship roll with the waves.

   G She was frightened by the roll of thunder.

   H He made sure to roll the dough on a flat, smooth surface.

   J Sue ate a roll at breakfast.

7. "My mother once said that I'd be amazed at how many things a person can do within the act of falling."

   A The play had only one act.

   B Maria tried to act like an adult.

   C He had to act as the committee chairman.

   D Tony considered the gift an act of kindness.

Collection 1: Skills Review

Writing Skills

Test Practice

DIRECTIONS: Read the following paragraph from a draft of a student's autobiographical narrative. Then, read the questions below it. Choose the best answer for each question.

(1) Even though I had a traumatic first experience, I still love riding horses. (2) I rode a trail horse named Potato who refused to follow the horse in front of him. (3) It was during a family vacation in Ruidoso, New Mexico, that I rode my first horse. (4) He kept stopping to eat the leaves and bushes on the side of the path through the forest, and we got separated from the group. (5) When I tried to go faster to catch up with everybody, Potato ran through some thick branches, and I was knocked off the saddle. (6) Luckily, I was more mad than hurt, so I grabbed the reins determinedly and got back on the horse. (7) By the end of the ride, Potato had begun to follow my directions, and I had learned how to control him.

1. Which of the following sentences could be added at the end to relate the significance of the experience?
    A On the next family vacation, I was careful to pick a better horse.
    B Young children shouldn't ride horses.
    C Learning to ride a horse wasn't easy, but it was worth it.
    D Horses are the most obedient and trainable of animals.

2. Which sentences should be switched to better reflect chronological order?
    F 1 and 7   **H** 4 and 5
    G 2 and 3   **J** 6 and 7

3. To add sensory details, which sentence could the writer include?
    A Being separated from the group on my first trail ride was scary.
    B The forest was dense with fragrant evergreens that muffled the *clop clop* of the horses.

    C Ruidoso is a small town nestled in the heart of New Mexico's southern Rocky Mountains.
    D Potato was a stubborn seven-year-old quarter horse.

4. Which action verb would best replace the word *eat* in sentence 4?
    F nibble   **H** consume
    G drink   **J** smell

5. If you were presenting this passage as an oral narrative, how would your tone change over the course of the presentation?
    A from embarrassment to sadness
    B from happiness to disappointment
    C from fear to relief
    D from concern to triumph

SKILLS FOCUS

Writing Skills
Write an autobiographical narrative.

CHARACTER

INFORMATIONAL READING FOCUS

USING PRIMARY AND SECONDARY SOURCES

One cannot "make" characters. . . .
They are *found*.

—Elizabeth Bowen

INTERNET

Collection
Resources

Keyword: LE5 10-2

Portrait of Dr. Gachet (1890) by Vincent van Gogh.
Oil on canvas (66 cm × 57 cm).

© Private Collection/Superstock.

Elements of Literature

Characters *by* John Leggett
THE ACTORS IN A STORY

What They Tell Us

Good fiction can tell us more about ourselves—about how human beings feel and behave in any imaginable situation—than just about any other form of art or science. Through fiction we can imagine how it feels to be a woman who has lived all her life on the prairie or glimpse how it feels to be a soldier lying wounded on a battlefield.

The revelations fiction offers lie largely in the element called **character**—that is, the story's actors. When the characters in a story behave in convincing ways, then we believe in them and maybe even love or hate them.

Creating Characters: How Do They Do It?

Writers reveal their characters' **traits,** or special qualities, either directly or indirectly. In **direct characterization** a writer simply tells us directly what the character is like.

Esmeralda was the most serious person in the school. She longed for fun but was afraid of disappointing her very serious aunt.

We would learn about Esmeralda in more subtle ways, however, if the writer were to use **indirect characterization.** With this technique a writer reveals characters' traits in the following five ways:

1 A character's **appearance** is a natural place for a writer to begin an indirect characterization.

Esmeralda, tall and thin, wore her mouse-brown hair pulled tightly back into a ponytail. She always dressed in a gray skirt and blouse and never wore jewelry.

This description says a lot about Esmeralda—we imagine a quiet, serious, perhaps shy person.

2 We can learn even more about Esmeralda when we hear her speak to other characters—through **dialogue.**

"Hey, Esmeralda, want to come with us to the movies tonight?" Ginger asked.

"Ooh, no," Esmeralda sighed. "My aunt would never allow it. She says I have to work on my research paper all weekend."

3 The writer can also take us into a character's mind to reveal his or her **private thoughts.** This is especially important when the **narrator** (the storytelling "I") is the main character. We eavesdrop on the narrator's thoughts—something we can never do in real life—and discover what that character wants or fears or worries about. If Esmeralda were the narrator, we might discover the following information:

"Why can't I be like other kids?" Esmeralda moped. She pressed her nose against the window. "I'd like to be out there with everybody else—laughing and skating and going to movies and just belonging."

4 In fiction as in real life, we learn a great deal about people by observing their **actions.**

That afternoon, Leon ran to catch up to Esmeralda as she walked home. "Hey," he called excitedly and tapped her on the shoulder. She flinched—then looked away, blushing.

5 In one way or another most writers will reveal their characters through what they actually do and the **effects** those actions have on other characters.

Leon, puzzled, wondered why Esmeralda was so upset by his friendly gesture.

Dramatic Monologue and Soliloquy

Narrators who talk about themselves are found mostly in fiction, but they also appear in poetry and in plays. A form of poetry called **dramatic monologue** features a single character who addresses one or more silent listeners. From what this character says and the way it is said, we can infer his or her personality **traits.**

In plays we usually learn about character through dialogue and action. In a **soliloquy,** however, a character speaks his or her thoughts directly to the audience. Shakespeare's plays have many memorable soliloquies, such as Hamlet's famous "To Be or Not to Be" speech.

Flat, Round, and Stock Characters

Critics often use these terms to refer to fictional characters. A **flat character,** like a paper doll, is two-dimensional, with only one or two key personality traits: "Amy is extremely stubborn."

A **round character** has the three-dimensional qualities of real-life people, with many traits and complexities. In good fiction, writers include flat characters for a reason: Too many round characters would be distracting. Nonetheless, some flat characters are needed to get the story told.

Finally, a **stock character** is one who fits our preconceived notions about a "type" (for example, the mad scientist or the cruel-looking villain twirling his waxed moustache).

Stock characters are so familiar that as soon as we encounter any of their well-known traits, we can imagine the rest of their personalities. Of course, real people aren't like this—they are complex and unpredictable. What fascinates us in fiction are the characters who manage to confound our expectations yet still seem true to life.

Practice

Pick a character in a short story you have read. Review the story, and take notes in a chart like the one below. Identify two or three of the character's traits, and list the details in the story that illustrate those traits. Then, identify which literary device (such as narration, dialogue, or description) helped you identify each trait.

Character Traits	Supporting Details	Literary Device Used

Everyday Use

Make the Connection

Quickwrite ✏️

"Everyday Use" takes place in the rural South during the 1960s, when values and ways of life were changing rapidly. The story concerns traditions and, in particular, some family heirlooms.

Many families have traditions or heirlooms that are handed down to the younger generation. Do you have any in your family? Jot down your feelings about maintaining family traditions.

Literary Focus

Determining Characters' Traits: What They Say and Do

What would the world be like if we could read one another's minds? It can't happen in real life, but in fiction we step easily into characters' minds. When characters **narrate,** or tell their stories, we know their thoughts and feelings, and we get an idea of their **character traits**—their values, likes, dislikes, even their quirks.

We also learn about characters by noticing what they say to other characters in the story's **dialogue.** As in real life, we also notice what they do, how they look, and what other people say about them.

You'll find these methods of character development in the next story. As you read, pay attention to what you learn about Mama and the other characters.

Reading Skills 📖

Making Inferences About Characters

An **inference** is an intelligent guess based on evidence in the story and on what you already know. You'll base many of your inferences about characters on what they say and do. For example, here's what you can infer from just the first sentence of "Everyday Use": The narrator and someone named Maggie are expecting a female visitor. They've cleaned the yard especially for the visit, so it's obviously important to them. The phrase "made so clean and wavy" suggests that the narrator takes pride in a job well done. From just that one sentence you've made some inferences about character. Keep track of the other inferences you make as you read.

Background

Quilting is an American folk art. In the South, quilts have a rich tradition influenced by African textile designs and historic American patterns. Quilts are often passed down in families for generations.

Vocabulary Development

sidle (sīd'l) *v.*: move sideways, especially in a shy or sneaky manner.

furtive (fur'tiv) *adj.*: acting as if trying not to be seen. *Furtive* also means "done secretly."

cowering (kou'ər·iŋ) *v.* used as *adj.*: drawing back or huddling in fear.

oppress (ə·pres') *v.*: persecute; keep down by unjust use of power.

doctrines (däk'trinz) *n.*: principles; teachings; beliefs.

rifling (rī'fliŋ) *v.* used as *n.*: searching thoroughly or in a rough manner.

INTERNET

Vocabulary Practice
•
More About Alice Walker

Keyword: LE5 10-2

SKILLS FOCUS

Literary Skills
Understand character traits.

Reading Skills
Make inferences about characters.

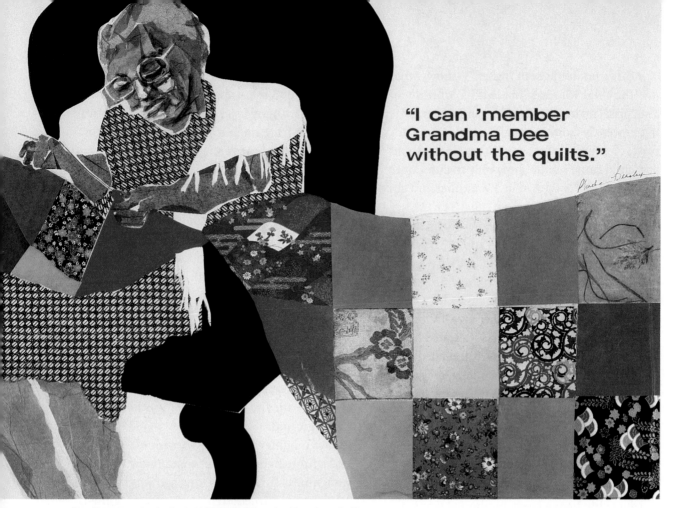

"I can 'member
Grandma Dee
without the quilts."

His Grandmother's Quilt (1988) by Phoebe Beasley. Collage.
Courtesy of the artist.

Everyday Use

For Your Grandmama

Alice Walker

I will wait for her in the yard that Maggie and I made so clean and wavy yesterday
afternoon. A yard like this is more comfortable than most people know. It is not
just a yard. It is like an extended living room. When the hard clay is swept clean as
a floor and the fine sand around the edges lined with tiny, irregular grooves, anyone can come and sit and look up into the elm tree and wait for the breezes that
never come inside the house.

Maggie will be nervous until after her sister goes: She will stand hopelessly in
corners, homely and ashamed of the burn scars down her arms and legs, eyeing
her sister with a mixture of envy and awe. She thinks her sister had held life always
in the palm of one hand, that "no" is a word the world never learned to say to her.

You've no doubt seen those TV shows where the child who has "made it" is confronted, as a surprise, by her own mother and father, tottering in weakly from backstage. (A pleasant surprise, of course: What would they do if parent and child came on the show only to curse out and insult each other?) On TV mother and child embrace and smile into each other's faces. Sometimes the mother and father weep; the child wraps them in her arms and leans across the table to tell how she would not have made it without their help. I have seen these programs.

Sometimes I dream a dream in which Dee and I are suddenly brought together on a TV program of this sort. Out of a dark and soft-seated limousine I am ushered into a bright room filled with many people. There I meet a smiling, gray, sporty man like Johnny Carson who shakes my hand and tells me what a fine girl I have. Then we are on the stage, and Dee is embracing me with tears in her eyes. She pins on my dress a large orchid, even though she had told me once that she thinks orchids are tacky flowers.

In real life I am a large, big-boned woman with rough, man-working hands. In the winter I wear flannel nightgowns to bed and overalls during the day. I can kill and clean a hog as mercilessly as a man. My fat keeps me hot in zero weather. I can work outside all day, breaking ice to get water for washing; I can eat pork liver cooked over the open fire minutes after it comes steaming from the hog. One winter I knocked a bull calf straight in the brain between the eyes with a sledgehammer and had the meat hung up to chill before nightfall. But of course all this does not show on television. I am the way my daughter would want me to be: a hundred pounds lighter, my skin like an uncooked barley pancake. My hair glistens in the hot bright lights. Johnny Carson has much to do to keep up with my quick and witty tongue.

But that is a mistake. I know even before I wake up. Who ever knew a Johnson with a quick tongue? Who can even imagine me looking a strange white man in the eye? It seems to me I have talked to them always with one foot raised in flight, with my head turned in whichever way is farthest from them. Dee, though. She would always look anyone in the eye. Hesitation was no part of her nature.

"How do I look, Mama?" Maggie says, showing just enough of her thin body enveloped in pink skirt and red blouse for me to know she's there, almost hidden by the door.

"Come out into the yard," I say.

Have you ever seen a lame animal, perhaps a dog run over by some careless person rich enough to own a car, sidle up to someone who is ignorant enough to be kind to him? That is the way my Maggie walks. She has been like this, chin on chest, eyes on ground, feet in shuffle, ever since the fire that burned the other house to the ground.

Dee is lighter than Maggie, with nicer hair and a fuller figure. She's a woman now, though sometimes I forget. How long ago was it that the other house burned? Ten, twelve years? Sometimes I can still hear the flames and feel Maggie's arms sticking to me, her hair smoking and her dress falling off her in little black papery flakes. Her eyes seemed stretched open, blazed open by the flames reflected in them. And Dee. I see her standing off under the sweet gum tree she used to dig gum out of, a look of concentration on her face as she watched the last dingy gray board of the house fall in toward the red-hot brick chimney. Why don't you do a dance around the ashes? I'd wanted to ask her. She had hated the house that much.

I used to think she hated Maggie, too. But that was before we raised the money, the church and me, to send her to Augusta[1] to school. She

---

1. **Augusta:** city in Georgia.

Vocabulary

sidle (sīd′'l) v.: move sideways, especially in a shy or sneaky manner.

used to read to us without pity, forcing words, lies, other folks' habits, whole lives upon us two, sitting trapped and ignorant underneath her voice. She washed us in a river of make-believe, burned us with a lot of knowledge we didn't necessarily need to know. Pressed us to her with the serious ways she read, to shove us away at just the moment, like dimwits, we seemed about to understand.

Dee wanted nice things. A yellow organdy dress to wear to her graduation from high school; black pumps to match a green suit she'd made from an old suit somebody gave me. She was determined to stare down any disaster in her efforts. Her eyelids would not flicker for minutes at a time. Often I fought off the temptation to shake her. At sixteen she had a style of her own: and knew what style was.

I never had an education myself. After second grade the school closed down. Don't ask me why: In 1927 colored asked fewer questions than they do now. Sometimes Maggie reads to me. She stumbles along good-naturedly but can't see well. She knows she is not bright. Like good looks and money, quickness passed her by. She will marry John Thomas (who has mossy teeth in an earnest face), and then I'll be free to sit here and I guess just sing church songs to myself. Although I never was a good singer. Never could carry a tune. I was always better at a man's job. I used to love to milk till I was hooked in the side in '49. Cows are soothing and slow and don't bother you, unless you try to milk them the wrong way.

I have deliberately turned my back on the house. It is three rooms, just like the one that burned, except the roof is tin; they don't make shingle roofs anymore. There are no real windows, just some holes cut in the sides, like the portholes in a ship, but not round and not square, with rawhide holding the shutters up on the outside. This house is in a pasture, too, like the other one. No doubt when Dee sees it she will want to tear it down. She wrote me once

that no matter where we "choose" to live, she will manage to come see us. But she will never bring her friends. Maggie and I thought about this and Maggie asked me, "Mama, when did Dee ever *have* any friends?"

She had a few. Furtive boys in pink shirts hanging about on washday after school. Nervous girls who never laughed. Impressed with her, they worshiped the well-turned phrase, the cute shape, the scalding[2] humor that erupted like bubbles in lye. She read to them.

When she was courting Jimmy T, she didn't have much time to pay to us but turned all her faultfinding power on him. He *flew* to marry a cheap city girl from a family of ignorant, flashy people. She hardly had time to recompose herself.

When she comes, I will meet—but there they are!

Maggie attempts to make a dash for the house, in her shuffling way, but I stay her with my hand. "Come back here," I say. And she stops and tries to dig a well in the sand with her toe.

It is hard to see them clearly through the strong sun. But even the first glimpse of leg out of the car tells me it is Dee. Her feet were always neat looking, as if God himself shaped them with a certain style. From the other side of the car comes a short, stocky man. Hair is all over his head a foot long and hanging from his chin like a kinky mule tail. I hear Maggie suck in her breath. "Uhnnnh" is what it sounds like. Like when you see the wriggling end of a snake just in front of your foot on the road. "Uhnnnh."

Dee next. A dress down to the ground, in this hot weather. A dress so loud it hurts my eyes. There are yellows and oranges enough to throw back the light of the sun. I feel my whole face warming from the heat waves it throws out.

---

2. **scalding** (skôld′iŋ) *v.* used as *adj.*: burning hot; here, biting or stinging.

Vocabulary
furtive (fur′tiv) *adj.*: acting as if trying not to be seen. *Furtive* also means "done secretly."

Earrings gold, too, and hanging down to her shoulders. Bracelets dangling and making noises when she moves her arm up to shake the folds of the dress out of her armpits. The dress is loose and flows, and as she walks closer, I like it. I hear Maggie go "Uhnnnh" again. It is her sister's hair. It stands straight up like the wool on a sheep. It is black as night and around the edges are two long pigtails that rope about like small lizards disappearing behind her ears.

"Wa-su-zo-Tean-o!" she says, coming on in that gliding way the dress makes her move. The short, stocky fellow with the hair to his navel is all grinning, and he follows up with "Asalamalakim,[3] my mother and sister!" He moves to hug Maggie but she falls back, right up against the back of my chair. I feel her trembling there, and when I look up I see the perspiration falling off her chin.

"Don't get up," says Dee. Since I am stout, it takes something of a push. You can see me trying to move a second or two before I make it. She turns, showing white heels through her sandals, and goes back to the car. Out she peeks next with a Polaroid. She stoops down quickly and lines up picture after picture of me sitting there in front of the house with Maggie cowering behind me. She never takes a shot without making sure the house is included. When a cow comes nibbling around in the edge of the yard, she snaps it and me and Maggie *and* the house. Then she puts the Polaroid in the back seat of the car and comes up and kisses me on the forehead.

Meanwhile, Asalamalakim is going through motions with Maggie's hand. Maggie's hand is as limp as a fish, and probably as cold, despite the sweat, and she keeps trying to pull it back. It looks like Asalamalakim wants to shake hands but wants to do it fancy. Or maybe he don't know how people shake hands. Anyhow, he soon gives up on Maggie.

---

3. **Asalamalakim:** Asalaam aleikum (ä·sə·läm′ ä·lä′koom′), greeting used by Muslims, meaning "peace to you."

"Well," I say. "Dee."

"No, Mama," she says. "Not 'Dee,' Wangero Leewanika Kemanjo!"

"What happened to 'Dee'?" I wanted to know.

"She's dead," Wangero said. "I couldn't bear it any longer, being named after the people who oppress me."

"You know as well as me you was named after your aunt Dicie," I said. Dicie is my sister. She named Dee. We called her "Big Dee" after Dee was born.

"But who was *she* named after?" asked Wangero.

"I guess after Grandma Dee," I said.

"And who was she named after?" asked Wangero.

"Her mother," I said, and saw Wangero was getting tired. "That's about as far back as I can trace it," I said. Though, in fact, I probably could have carried it back beyond the Civil War through the branches.

"Well," said Asalamalakim, "there you are."

"Uhnnnh," I heard Maggie say.

"There I was not," I said, "before 'Dicie' cropped up in our family, so why should I try to trace it that far back?"

He just stood there grinning, looking down on me like somebody inspecting a Model A car. Every once in a while he and Wangero sent eye signals over my head.

"How do you pronounce this name?" I asked.

"You don't have to call me by it if you don't want to," said Wangero.

"Why shouldn't I?" I asked. "If that's what you want us to call you, we'll call you."

"I know it might sound awkward at first," said Wangero.

"I'll get used to it," I said. "Ream it out again."

Vocabulary

cowering (kou′ər·iŋ) v. used as *adj.*: drawing back or huddling in fear.

oppress (ə·pres′) v.: persecute; keep down by unjust use of power.

Well, soon we got the name out of the way. Asalamalakim had a name twice as long and three times as hard. After I tripped over it two or three times, he told me to just call him Hakim-a-barber. I wanted to ask him was he a barber, but I didn't really think he was, so I didn't ask.

"You must belong to those beef-cattle peoples down the road," I said. They said "Asalam-alakim" when they met you, too, but they didn't shake hands. Always too busy: feeding the cattle, fixing the fences, putting up salt-lick shelters, throwing down hay. When the white folks poisoned some of the herd, the men stayed up all night with rifles in their hands. I walked a mile and a half just to see the sight.

Hakim-a-barber said, "I accept some of their doctrines, but farming and raising cattle is not my style." (They didn't tell me, and I didn't ask, whether Wangero—Dee—had really gone and married him.)

We sat down to eat and right away he said he didn't eat collards, and pork was unclean. Wangero, though, went on through the chitlins and corn bread, the greens, and everything else. She talked a blue streak over the sweet potatoes. Everything delighted her. Even the fact that we still used the benches her daddy made for the table when we couldn't afford to buy chairs.

"Oh, Mama!" she cried. Then turned to Hakim-a-barber. "I never knew how lovely these benches are. You can feel the rump prints," she said, running her hands underneath her and along the bench. Then she gave a sigh, and her hand closed over Grandma Dee's butter dish. "That's it!" she said. "I knew there was something I wanted to ask you if I could have." She jumped up from the table and went over in the corner where the churn stood, the milk in it clabber[4] by now. She looked at the churn and looked at it.

"This churn top is what I need," she said.

"Didn't Uncle Buddy whittle it out of a tree you all used to have?"

"Yes," I said.

"Uh huh," she said happily. "And I want the dasher,[5] too."

"Uncle Buddy whittle that, too?" asked the barber.

Dee (Wangero) looked up at me.

"Aunt Dee's first husband whittled the dash," said Maggie so low you almost couldn't hear her. "His name was Henry, but they called him Stash."

"Maggie's brain is like an elephant's," Wangero said, laughing. "I can use the churn top as a centerpiece for the alcove table," she said, sliding a plate over the churn, "and I'll think of something artistic to do with the dasher."

When she finished wrapping the dasher, the handle stuck out. I took it for a moment in my hands. You didn't even have to look close to see where hands pushing the dasher up and down to make butter had left a kind of sink in the wood. In fact, there were a lot of small sinks; you could see where thumbs and fingers had sunk into the wood. It was beautiful light-yellow wood, from a tree that grew in the yard where Big Dee and Stash had lived.

After dinner Dee (Wangero) went to the trunk at the foot of my bed and started rifling through it. Maggie hung back in the kitchen over the dishpan. Out came Wangero with two quilts. They had been pieced by Grandma Dee, and then Big Dee and me had hung them on the quilt frames on the front porch and quilted them. One was in the Lone Star pattern. The other was Walk Around the Mountain. In both of them were scraps of dresses Grandma Dee had worn fifty and more years ago. Bits and pieces of Grandpa Jarrell's paisley shirts. And

---

4. **clabber** (klab′ər) n: thickened or curdled sour milk.

5. **dasher** n: pole that stirs the milk in a churn.

Vocabulary

doctrines (däk′trinz) n.: principles; teachings; beliefs.

rifling (rī′fliŋ) v. used as n.: searching thoroughly or in a rough manner.

one teeny faded blue piece, about the size of a penny matchbox, that was from Great Grandpa Ezra's uniform that he wore in the Civil War.

"Mama," Wangero said sweet as a bird. "Can I have these old quilts?"

I heard something fall in the kitchen, and a minute later the kitchen door slammed.

"Why don't you take one or two of the others?" I asked. "These old things was just done by me and Big Dee from some tops your grandma pieced before she died."

"No," said Wangero. "I don't want those. They are stitched around the borders by machine."

"That'll make them last better," I said.

"That's not the point," said Wangero. "These are all pieces of dresses Grandma used to wear. She did all this stitching by hand. Imagine!" She held the quilts securely in her arms, stroking them.

"Some of the pieces, like those lavender ones, come from old clothes her mother handed down to her," I said, moving up to touch the quilts. Dee (Wangero) moved back just enough so that I couldn't reach the quilts. They already belonged to her.

"Imagine!" she breathed again, clutching them closely to her bosom.

"The truth is," I said, "I promised to give them quilts to Maggie, for when she marries John Thomas."

She gasped like a bee had stung her.

"Maggie can't appreciate these quilts!" she said. "She'd probably be backward enough to put them to everyday use."

"I reckon she would," I said. "God knows I been saving 'em for long enough with nobody using 'em. I hope she will!" I didn't want to bring up how I had offered Dee (Wangero) a quilt when she went away to college. Then she had told me they were old-fashioned, out of style.

"But they're *priceless!*" she was saying now, furiously; for she has a temper. "Maggie would put them on the bed and in five years they'd be in rags. Less than that!"

"She can always make some more," I said. "Maggie knows how to quilt."

Dee (Wangero) looked at me with hatred. "You just will not understand. The point is *these* quilts, these quilts!"

"Well," I said, stumped. "What would *you* do with them?"

"Hang them," she said. As if that was the only thing you *could* do with quilts.

Maggie by now was standing in the door. I could almost hear the sound her feet made as they scraped over each other.

"She can have them, Mama," she said, like somebody used to never winning anything or having anything reserved for her. "I can 'member Grandma Dee without the quilts."

I looked at her hard. She had filled her bottom lip with checkerberry snuff, and it gave her face a kind of dopey, hangdog look. It was Grandma Dee and Big Dee who taught her how to quilt herself. She stood there with her scarred hands hidden in the folds of her skirt. She looked at her sister with something like fear, but she wasn't mad at her. This was Maggie's portion. This was the way she knew God to work.

When I looked at her like that, something hit me in the top of my head and ran down to the soles of my feet. Just like when I'm in church and the spirit of God touches me and I get happy and shout. I did something I never had done before: hugged Maggie to me, then dragged her on into the room, snatched the quilts out of Miss Wangero's hands, and dumped them into Maggie's lap. Maggie just sat there on my bed with her mouth open.

"Take one or two of the others," I said to Dee.

But she turned without a word and went out to Hakim-a-barber.

"You just don't understand," she said, as Maggie and I came out to the car.

"What don't I understand?" I wanted to know.

"Your heritage," she said. And then she turned

to Maggie, kissed her, and said, "You ought to try to make something of yourself, too, Maggie. It's really a new day for us. But from the way you and Mama still live, you'd never know it."

She put on some sunglasses that hid everything above the tip of her nose and her chin.

Maggie smiled, maybe at the sunglasses. But a real smile, not scared. After we watched the car dust settle, I asked Maggie to bring me a dip of snuff. And then the two of us sat there just enjoying, until it was time to go in the house and go to bed. ■

Meet the Writer

Alice Walker

Writing All the While

Alice Walker (1944–   ), shown here with her daughter, Rebecca, was born in the small town of Eatonton, Georgia, the youngest of eight children. Her father was a sharecropper, and her mother worked as a maid. When she was eight years old, Walker was blinded in one eye by a shot from a BB gun. The resulting scar tissue made her painfully shy and self-conscious, and she spent her free time alone outdoors, reading and writing stories. With the aid of a scholarship for handicapped students, she attended Spelman College, a college for African American women in Atlanta. After two years, she transferred to Sarah Lawrence College in New York.

Women have always played an important role in Walker's life. She has said that she grew up believing there was absolutely nothing her mother couldn't do once she set her mind to it. So when the women's movement came along, she said that she was delighted because she felt it was trying to go where her mother was and where she had always assumed she would go.

Walker's third novel, *The Color Purple*, won the Pulitzer Prize for fiction in 1983 and was made into a popular movie. Walker has

Alice Walker and her daughter, Rebecca.

been a contributing editor of *Ms.* magazine and has been active in both the women's movement and the civil rights movement.

Walker has published short stories, poems, essays, and novels, so it comes as a surprise to learn that she never intended to be a writer.

❝I just kind of found myself doing it. I remember wanting to be a scientist, wanting to be a pianist, wanting to be a painter. But all the while I was wanting to be these other things, I was writing. We were really poor, and writing was about the cheapest thing to do. You know, I feel amazed that I have been able to do exactly what I wanted to do.❞

For Independent Reading

In Search of Our Mothers' Gardens, a book of Walker's essays, has influenced many writers and many American women.

from Hands: For Mother's Day

Nikki Giovanni

Some people think a quilt is a blanket stretched across a Lincoln bed . . .[1] or from frames on a wall . . . a quaint museum piece to be purchased on Bloomingdale's[2] 30-day same-as-cash plan . . . Quilts are our mosaics . . . **Michelle-Angelo's**[3] contribution to beauty . . . We weave a quilt with dry, rough hands . . . Quilts are the way our lives are lived . . . We survive on patches . . . scraps . . . the leftovers from a materially richer culture . . . the throwaways from those with emotional options . . . We do the far more difficult job of taking that which nobody wants and not only loving it . . . not only seeing its worth . . . but making it lovable . . . and intrinsically worthwhile . . .

---

1. **Lincoln bed:** probably a reference to a large, elaborately carved bed similar to one in the White House that is associated with President Abraham Lincoln (1809–1865).
2. **Bloomingdale's:** department-store chain.
3. **Michelle-Angelo:** tongue-in-cheek comparison to the famous Italian Renaissance artist Michelangelo Buonarroti (1475–1564).

Quilting Time (1986) by Romare Bearden.

Founders Society Purchase with funds from the Detroit Edison Company. © Romare Bearden Foundation/Licensed by VAGA, New York, NY.

© 1996 The Detroit Institute of Art.

Edgar Lee Masters's "Lucinda Matlock" is a famous **dramatic monologue,** *a type of poem in which a speaker (who is not the poet) addresses one or more silent listeners. Typically the speaker expresses deep thoughts or feelings. In this case the speaker is the spirit of Lucinda Matlock, who tells what she has learned about life's struggles during her many years as a wife and mother.*

© Hulton Archive.

Lucinda Matlock

Edgar Lee Masters

I went to the dances at Chandlerville,
And played snap-out° at Winchester.
One time we changed partners,
Driving home in the moonlight of middle June,
5   And then I found Davis.
We were married and lived together for seventy years,
Enjoying, working, raising the twelve children,
Eight of whom we lost
Ere I had reached the age of sixty.
10   I spun, I wove, I kept the house, I nursed the sick,
I made the garden, and for holiday
Rambled over the fields where sang the larks,
And by Spoon River gathering many a shell,
And many a flower and medicinal weed—
15   Shouting to the wooded hills, singing to the green valleys.
At ninety-six I had lived enough, that is all,
And passed to a sweet repose.
What is this I hear of sorrow and weariness,
Anger, discontent and drooping hopes?
20   Degenerate° sons and daughters,
Life is too strong for you—
It takes life to love Life.

---

2. **snap-out** *n.:* game in which a line of players holding hands makes sudden twists and turns, so that those players at the ends of the line are flung off.
20. **degenerate** (dē·jen′ər·it) *adj:* weak; in decline.

Response and Analysis

Reading Check

1. According to Mama, how is Dee different from her and from Maggie?

2. What different uses would Maggie and Dee have for the quilts?

3. What terrible thing happened to Maggie when she was a child?

4. How does Mama choose to resolve the **conflict** over the quilts?

5. Find the passage in the text that explains the **title.**

Thinking Critically

6. Find passages in the story where Mama tells the reader about herself. Also, find passages of **dialogue** in which Mama reveals her character. On the basis of these passages, how would you describe Mama's **character traits?** Be sure to cite details in the story that support the traits you mention.

7. **Compare and contrast** Dee and Maggie. Find passages of **dialogue** about these characters, and make inferences about their **character traits.** What is the most significant thing they have in common? What's their most compelling difference?

8. Dee is referred to as the child who has "made it." What does that mean, and what signs tell you that she has made it?

9. Near the end of the story, Dee accuses Mama of not understanding their African American heritage. Do you agree or disagree with Dee? Why?

10. Has any character changed by the end of the story? Go back to the text, and find details to support your answer.

11. Do you think Dee would agree with the speaker in Nikki Giovanni's poem (see the **Connection** on page 84)? Why or why not?

Extending and Evaluating

12. Which character did you side with in the conflict over the quilts? Why?

13. This story occurs in a specific time, place, and culture. Could the conflict over traditions faced by this family be experienced by any family anywhere? What role do your heritage and family traditions play in your life today? (Look back at your Quickwrite notes.) ✏

WRITING

Two Strong Women

In a paragraph or two, **compare and contrast** Mama in this story with Lucinda Matlock in the **dramatic monologue** (see the **Connection** on page 85). Use a diagram like the one shown below to identify both characters' traits. Include what they say about themselves and what they say to others.

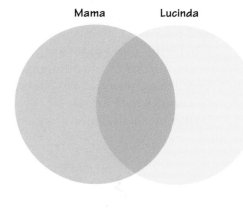

Mama   Lucinda

go.hrw.com

INTERNET

Projects and Activities

Keyword: LE5 10-2

SKILLS FOCUS

Literary Skills
Analyze character traits.

Reading Skills
Make inferences about characters.

Writing Skills
Write an essay, comparing and contrasting two characters from different selections.

Vocabulary Development

Clarifying Word Meanings: Look at the Context

When you come across an unfamiliar word, don't focus on the word alone. Look at the big picture—the **context,** or the words and sentences surrounding the unfamiliar word. Writers often help you out by providing a built-in **definition,** a **restatement,** or an **example.**

DEFINITION   Dee complains that Mama doesn't understand her heritage, **the traditions and culture of her ancestors.**

RESTATEMENT   When Dee's old boyfriend Jimmy T marries another girl, Dee has to recompose herself, and it takes quite an effort before she can **get herself calmed down again.**

EXAMPLE   Mama compares Maggie to a lame animal, **"perhaps a dog run over by some careless person,"** that sidles up to someone who is kind to it.

The diagram below shows how one reader figured out the meaning of *sidle* by using various kinds of **context clues.**

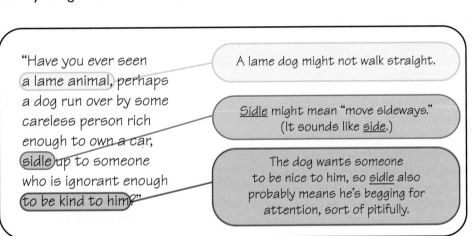

"Have you ever seen a lame animal, perhaps a dog run over by some careless person rich enough to own a car, sidle up to someone who is ignorant enough to be kind to him?"

A lame dog might not walk straight.

Sidle might mean "move sideways." (It sounds like side.)

The dog wants someone to be nice to him, so sidle also probably means he's begging for attention, sort of pitifully.

PRACTICE

1. Find the context for each of the other Word Bank words—the passage where each word appears in the story. Re-read the passage that the underlined word is in. Then, make a context diagram for each word.

2. For each of the words in the Word Bank, write one sentence with a definition, restatement, or example context clue that clarifies the word's meaning.

SKILLS FOCUS

Vocabulary Skills
Use context clues.

Interview with Alice Walker ◆ Interview with Nikki Giovanni ◆ "Thinkin' on Marryin'" ◆ A Baby's Quilt to Sew Up the Generations

Primary and Secondary Sources

Primary Versus Secondary: What's the Difference?

The materials you find when researching historical information can generally be classified into two categories: primary sources and secondary sources.

- A **primary source** is original material, a firsthand account of information that has not been interpreted or edited by other writers. It may give us eyewitness testimony to an event or tell us the writer's own opinions and ideas on a subject. Oral histories, interviews, autobiographies, letters, speeches, editorials, eyewitness news reports, and literary works are examples of primary sources.

- A **secondary source,** on the other hand, is based on other sources. It contains information that is at least one step removed from an event and is usually retold, interpreted, or summarized by the writer. Secondary sources are often based on a variety of primary sources. Encyclopedia articles and most magazine articles are secondary sources; so are biographies, textbooks, reference books, and literary criticism. Most newspaper articles are secondary sources, unless they are firsthand accounts written at the time of an event, editorials, or opinion pieces.

Using the Sources

The following steps can help you use the information in a primary or secondary source to learn about a topic:

- **Analyze.** Read the material carefully to figure out what's being said. Who is the speaker or writer, and who is the intended audience? What is the message, or **main idea**? What details support the main idea?

- **Evaluate.** How accurate or credible is the message? Do you agree with the writer's message? Look for clues that tell you if you are reading **opinions** or **facts.** Using a primary source, try to confirm the information in other primary sources or in secondary sources.

- **Elaborate.** When doing research, you'll want to elaborate on the information you find in your primary and secondary sources. When you **elaborate,** you add something, usually more details. You might offer your own ideas on the topic, or you might do further research. If you are using a secondary source, you can check to see whether it has a **bibliography** or a list of **works cited.** This will help you find out where to look for more information.

INTERNET
Interactive Reading Model
Keyword: LE5 10-2

Reading Skills
Understand the uses of primary and secondary sources.

Connecting to the Literature

The central conflict in "Everyday Use" concerns some treasured family quilts. Quilting has long been an important folk art and cultural tradition in America. In the following primary and secondary sources you'll learn more about quilting. One source features Alice Walker, author of "Everyday Use," who is herself a quilter.

Here are three **primary sources** and one **secondary source** on quilting. The first two selections are interviews, one with Alice Walker (the author of "Everyday Use") and one with Nikki Giovanni (the author of "Hands: For Mother's Day"). The next selection is an **oral history** of a quilter that was tape-recorded in the Southwest in 1975. She speaks a distinctive regional dialect that differs in many ways from standard English. The last selection, the secondary source, is a newspaper article about one family's modern version of the family-quilt tradition.

PRIMARY SOURCE

INTERVIEW

Interview with Alice Walker

from *A Communion of the Spirits: African American Quilters, Preservers, and Their Stories*

Roland L. Freeman

Alice Walker at home with her quilts.

I asked Alice to talk first about the tradition of quilting in her family.

Well, my mother was a quilter, and I remember many, many afternoons of my mother and the neighborhood women sitting on the porch around the quilting frame, quilting and talking, you know; getting up to stir something on the stove and coming back and sitting down.

The first quilt I worked on was the *In Love and Trouble* quilt. And I did that one when I was living in Mississippi. It was during a period when we were wearing African-inspired dresses. So all of the pieces are from dresses that I actually wore. This yellow and black fabric I bought when I was in Uganda,[1] and I

---

1. **Uganda:** country in central Africa.

had a beautiful dress made of it that I wore and wore and wore and eventually I couldn't wear it anymore; partly I had worn it out and also I was pregnant, so it didn't fit, and I used that and I used the red and white and black, which was a long, floor-length dress that I had when I was pregnant with my daughter, Rebecca, who is now twenty-three. I took these things apart or I used scraps. I put them together in this quilt, because it just seemed perfect. Mississippi was full of political and social struggle, and regular quilts were all African American with emphasis on being here in the United States. But because of the African consciousness that was being raised[2] and the way that we were all wearing our hair in naturals[3] and wearing all of these African dresses, I felt the need to blend these two traditions. So it's a quilt of great memory and importance to me. I use it a lot and that's why it's so worn.

I asked her what happens when she sleeps under that quilt.

Oh . . . I am warm and I am secure and I am safe. I feel that I know how to create my own environment, and I know how to protect it. And I know how to choose it. I realize that my quilts are really simple, and yet, they give me so much pleasure, because even in their extreme simplicity they are just as useful as the most complex. And in their own way, they are beautiful because they do express what I was feeling and they clearly mark a particular time for me.

---

2. **the African . . . raised:** reference to the increased pride that many African Americans were taking in their African ethnic heritage in the early 1970s.
3. **naturals** *n.:* African American hairstyles that don't involve chemical straightening.

I asked her if she had made a quilt for her daughter.

No. I'm sure that she will make her own quilt. I'll be happy to leave her these if they are not worn out, which they will probably be, but I hope that she will make quilts for her own grounding and her own connection to me and to her grandmother and to her great-grandmother. I've seen quilts that my grandmother made. They tended to be very serviceable, very heavy and really for warmth, and, well of course, beautiful. My daughter has a quilt that she travels with. It's just a beautiful simple quilt that she loves. I gave it to her because she just feels like you can't sleep under just any old thing. It's got to be something that is congenial[4] with your dreams—your dream sense, your dream-time. I'm trying to think of where I got it. I think that I just bought it somewhere. I believe it is from Texas.

I asked Alice what she'd like to say to people in general about quilting.

That they should learn to do it. That they should think less about collecting quilts and give more thought to making them. Because, really, that is the power. It may do all kinds of good things, too, to collect what others have made, but I think that it is essential that we know how to express, you know, our own sense of connection. And there is no better sense of understanding our own creation than to create, and so we should do that.●

> ● **EVALUATE**
> Do you agree with Walker's **opinion** that there is power in making and creating? Explain.

---

4. **congenial** *adj.:* agreeable; in accord.

Interview with Nikki Giovanni

from *A Communion of the Spirits: African American Quilters, Preservers, and Their Stories*

Roland L. Freeman

I asked Nikki whether she had ever written about quilts.

I have used quilts as a metaphor. That's because I have a line in a poem called "Hands," which is a poem I wrote for Mother's Day. It says, "Quilts are the way our lives are lived. We survive on the scraps, the leftovers from a materially richer society." Quilts are such a—what's the word I'm looking for—banner to black women. Because what they ended up taking was that which nobody wanted, and making something totally beautiful out of it. Making something in fact quite valuable. At least to this day. But that's like the spirituals.° We took a bad situation and found a way to make a song. So it's a definite part of the heritage.●

> ● **EVALUATE**
>
> Explain Giovanni's use of quilts as a metaphor. Do you think the metaphor is effective? Explain why or why not.

°**spirituals:** folk hymns created by African Americans in the South in the eighteenth and nineteenth centuries.

"Thinkin' on Marryin'"

from *The Quilters: Women and Domestic Art*

Patricia Cooper *and* Norma Bradley Allen

Back when I was a girl, quilts was something that a family had to have. It takes a whole lot of cover to keep warm in one of them old open houses on the plains.

When a girl was thinkin' on marryin', and we all done a lot of that, she had to start thinkin' on gettin' her quilts pieced. The way I done mine was real nice, I think. Papa had laid up a beautiful arbor[1] with the brush he had cleared from the land. It was set up a ways back of the house. Well, I jest went out under that arbor, set up my frame, and went to quiltin' outdoors. Now some thought that was real funny, but I sure thought it was nice.

Mama gave me one real beautiful quilt, a Lone Star[2] that she had done herself. I made

---

1. arbor *n.:* shady covering, usually made of plants.

2. Lone Star: traditional American quilt pattern, also known as the Star of Bethlehem. The pattern features an eight-pointed star made up of contrasting dark and light diamonds.

Star of Bethlehem or *Lone Star* (1832) by Hannah Huxley.
Cottons, pieced and appliquéd (112″ × 108″).

Collection of Rowland and Eleanor Bingham Miller; photograph courtesy of Shelly Zegart.

three by myself that I don't reckon were much to look at, but I was awful proud of them then. And that's what I set out with when I married my sweetheart. Now that's a story. You won't believe it to look at me now, but I married me the finest-looking young man for three counties around when I was eighteen. And I didn't meet him at no dance neither. I don't reckon I would have stood a chance there. These big size tens were never so graceful. They're just good strong platforms for standin' on.

Anyways, what I was doin' was settin' there under that quiltin' arbor one spring afternoon, April fourteenth, just quiltin' and dreamin' a dream on ever' stitch and just plannin' who might share 'em with me.

And this deep, fine voice says, "Pardon me, ma'am, but I've been seein' you out here ever' day for weeks and I jest got up my nerve to come over and speak to you and see what you were workin' on with such care."

Lordy, girl, I married him and, as I recall it now, that was the longest speech he ever said at one time to this day.●

● **ANALYZE**

What can you **infer** about women's lives in this speaker's community when she was young?

A Baby's Quilt to Sew Up the Generations

from *The New York Times*, July 9, 2000

Felicia R. Lee

The stepgrandparents on the mother's side sent a photo of themselves in Pisa, Italy. Cousin Barbara sent a paraphrased quotation from *The Little Prince*[1] that said, "What is essential is invisible to the eye." From a maternal great-great-grandmother came a piece of her apron, on which was inscribed a cookie recipe.

Each contribution was attached to a fabric square and each is part of a quilt that Marilyn Webb, a writer who lives on the Upper West Side, is making for her first grandchild. The boy will be born to her daughter, Jennifer Kiefer, and her son-in-law, Jason Kiefer, in Manhattan Beach, California.

The people behind the 40 squares represent the modern version of an extended family tree that includes half siblings,[2] step-parents, and step-siblings, as well as the usual branches.

The quilt, with a blue border of little dogs, is draped over a couch in Ms. Webb's dining room, an old-fashioned gift for a new kind of family. It is a family story literally stitched together at a time when so many families drift apart, connecting mostly by e-mail and telephone through marriages, remarriages, births, and deaths.

In January, Ms. Webb sent a letter to dozens of family members that read, in part: "Following a women's tradition that apparently dates back to the 1800s, if not way before, I'd like to make this new baby a welcome quilt in which he or she can be wrapped in the very fabric of our families' lives. A true family quilt and maybe a new family tradition."

In addition to a seven-inch square, the letter also asked family members to write a letter introducing themselves to the new child and telling him (they later found out it would be a boy) what was special about the fabric and design they were contributing.

And so the pieces of lives came by mail from all over the country. Scraps of table-cloths, shirts, baby blankets, bibs. Some of the pieces came from people connected to the baby by blood, some from people linked by marriage.

Ms. Webb used books to teach herself to make a quilt and turned her dining room into a sewing room.

She believes quilting is an idea for these times, as many people seek ways to have more family time and preserve family history.

"We lose track of where we came from. We lose track of the fabrics we wore, the cookie recipes, the fabric that covered the sofa in our parents' living room."

> **● EVALUATE**
>
> Evaluate what the writer says about modern families. Do you agree or disagree?

---

1. *The Little Prince:* classic children's book by Antoine de Saint-Exupéry (1900–1944).
2. **half siblings** *n.:* half sisters or half brothers.

Analyzing Informational Text

Reading Check

1. What was the name of Alice Walker's first quilt, and what was it made from?

2. In "'Thinkin' on Marryin','" how did the speaker meet the man she would later marry?

3. In "A Baby's Quilt to Sew Up the Generations," why is Marilyn Webb making her quilt?

Test Practice

1. Which statement best summarizes Nikki Giovanni's **main idea**?
   A Quilts are beautiful.
   B Quilts remind us of family and our heritage.
   C African Americans created beauty with quilts and spirituals despite their bad circumstances.
   D African Americans created quilts as a form of political and moral protest.

2. All of the quilters in these excerpts agree that quilting is —
   F tedious
   G difficult
   H rewarding
   J expensive

3. If you were writing a report on quilting and needed a **secondary source,** which would you choose?
   A An autobiography of a quilter
   B A collection of quilters' letters
   C An encyclopedia article about quilting
   D A speech about quilting

4. How can you **evaluate** whether the speaker in an oral history is telling the truth?
   F By asking the interviewer
   G By reading the text aloud
   H By reading the text carefully
   J By checking other sources

5. The **oral history** included here is most similar to which of the following kinds of sources?
   A Interview
   B Newspaper article
   C Editorial
   D Encyclopedia article

6. Which of the following *best* describes the **main idea** in "A Baby's Quilt to Sew Up the Generations"?
   F A quilt can tie together an extended family living in many different places.
   G Family quilts don't suit our modern styles.
   H It's time to come up with new family traditions to replace older ones, like quilting.
   J Many people own treasured family quilts.

SKILLS FOCUS

Reading Skills
Analyze primary and secondary sources.

Grammar Skills
Understand dialect.

7. In a secondary source such as a newspaper article, you can identify a speaker's exact words by observing the —

   A italic type

   B title and author of the source

   C paragraph breaks

   D quotation marks

8. If you were trying to find out what it might feel like to sew your own quilt, which kind of source would be *least* helpful?

   F An oral history

   G An interview

   H An encyclopedia article

   J A short story

Constructed Response

Plan a quilt that will show real-life events in your own life. Then, create some actual quilt squares (seven inches by seven inches) on white cotton fabric, on an old T-shirt, or even on a piece of paper. You can use permanent markers, fabric paint, or crayons to decorate your quilt squares. Your class can then assemble everyone's squares into a class quilt.

Grammar Link

Dialect: Nonstandard but Authentic

Language is a living thing—it changes over time and in different environments. The spoken form of a language can also differ in some cases from its standard written form.

The oral history " 'Thinkin' on Marryin' ' " contains regional **dialect,** which is a way of speaking that is characteristic of a particular region or group of people. In this case the dialect can be heard in parts of the rural Southwest, where speakers typically don't pronounce the *g* in words ending in *–ing,* so that *morning* becomes *mornin'.* These speakers also use **colloquialisms,** or local expressions, like *reckon* (for *think*). **Nonstandard grammar** is also common, such as *they was* (instead of the standard *they were*).

In fiction a writer often includes regional dialect in dialogue to give a fuller, more precisely descriptive portrait of the characters or to give a more realistic sense of setting. In the oral history you have read here, the exact reproduction of the woman's speech patterns gives an authentic quality to the material.

PRACTICE 1

Look through the oral history, and find at least six examples of regional dialect. On a separate sheet of paper, write the standard-English equivalent next to each example. See the models below:

DIALECT	reckon
STANDARD ENGLISH	think

DIALECT	they was
STANDARD ENGLISH	they were

PRACTICE 2

Try this experiment: Take a paragraph from the oral history, and rewrite it in standard English, without the dialect. What is lost?

▶ **For more help, see the Glossary of Usage in the Language Handbook.**

Elements of Literature

Character Interactions *by* John Leggett
RELATIONSHIPS AND CONFLICTS

The Protagonist

A story that puts its emphasis on revealing character is likely to be a story of higher quality than a simple narrative with an action-packed plot. Of course, we all enjoy these plots: We are gripped by the adventures of the rancher who faces an army of flesh-eating ants, and we fear for the spy caught as a double agent. Yet the main concern of literature is more often the portrayal of character rather than action itself.

Most stories have a main character, called the **protagonist,** who is the focus of our attention. In a good story the protagonist is a realistic, complicated human being with just enough strengths, weaknesses, and contradictions to remind us of ourselves.

Conflict: It Drives the Plot

As a rule, a story's plot gets under way when the protagonist wants something and sets out to get it. The **antagonist** in a story is the character or force that blocks the protagonist from achieving his or her goal.

The **conflict** between the protagonist and the antagonist is what hooks our interest, creates suspense, and drives the plot of most stories. This struggle is an example of **external conflict,** since it involves a conflict between the protagonist and some outside force. This outside force might be another character or group, society as a whole, or even something in nature. In an **internal conflict** the protagonist wrestles with his or her own fear or worry or the need to make a decision.

Protagonists and antagonists rarely inhabit a story alone. We also meet friends, neighbors, family members, even passing strangers. These **subordinate characters** may not seem as important as the protagonist, but they're in the story for a reason. The main character's relationship with a subordinate character helps to reveal the protagonist's character and may also help develop the story's conflict. (A young man refuses to fight with a bully despite his classmates' jeers. He is in conflict with the bully—his antagonist—as well as with his classmates—subordinate characters.)

Dynamic Characters and Static Characters

The protagonist of a story is almost always a **dynamic character**—someone who changes in an important way during the course of the story. By the end of the story, a dynamic character has gained a new understanding, made an important decision, or taken a crucial action. Dynamic characters are capable of growing, learning, and changing.

In contrast, subordinate characters are almost always **static characters,** exactly the same at the end of the story as they are at the beginning. Static characters do not necessarily represent failures of the writer's art. In good fiction static characters are supposed to be static. Too many characters undergoing important changes would be distracting, especially in a short story, where we want to focus on what is happening to the main character.

The change that a dynamic character

INTERNET

More About Character Interactions

Keyword: LE5 10-2

SKILLS FOCUS

Literary Skills Understand character interactions.

undergoes (he learns not to be so arrogant; she learns not to be so jealous of her younger sister) must be **believable.** It should not be some miraculous, magic-wand transformation that neatly wraps up the plot. When that change is believable, it provides the key to understanding the character and also the best clue to the story's **meaning.**

Motivation: What Makes Characters Tick

One of the ways writers make characters believable is by showing what **motivates** them to act as they do. Unless we understand *why* an otherwise dutiful daughter suddenly lashes out at her mother, her behavior will strike us as inconsistent and unbelievable. However, once we recognize the need the daughter is trying to satisfy (say, to punish someone—anyone she can get her hands on—for the way her boyfriend has been ignoring her), her behavior begins to make sense. She is no longer the two-dimensional "dutiful daughter" but seems more like a real person—

someone who is usually kind but who is also capable of cruelty.

Writers seldom state a character's motives directly. (She screams at her mother because Bill, her boyfriend, has been flirting with Jana, her best friend.) Instead, writers imply what those motives are—maybe even scattering clues throughout the story—and trust their readers to make inferences about why their characters act the way they do.

Trying to understand the motivation of characters in literature can be as puzzling and as satisfying as trying to understand people's motives in real life. While we know that real people often surprise us with their behavior, we also know that there are probably reasons for what they do and say. In real life we may never find out what those reasons are. In fiction we do.

"O.K., so I dig a hole and put the bone in the hole. But what's my motivation for burying it?"

© The New Yorker Collection 1998 Michael Maslin from cartoonbank.com.

Practice

Work with a partner to analyze a short story you have read recently. Use this data bank:

Data Bank
Main character:
What main character wants (motivation):
Relationship with subordinate character(s):
Conflict:
Resolution:
How main character changes:

Before You Read

Two Kinds

Make the Connection
Quickwrite ✏️

Disagreements sometimes arise when what we want to do differs from what others want us to do. Has anyone ever expected you to do something you really didn't want to do? Write about your experience and how you felt before, during, and after it.

Literary Focus

Conflict and Motivation: Blocked Desires

Conflict is struggle. In a story a conflict can be **internal**—inside a character's mind—or **external**—in the outside world. The deepest conflicts are both internal and external. You may, for example, have difficulty making an important decision yet argue with a parent who wants to make the decision for you.

Conflict and motivation are closely tied. When actors study their parts, they ask, "Why do I do this?" to discover their **motivation,** or the reasons for a character's behavior. When a character is motivated to fulfill a certain desire and is prevented from doing so, conflict occurs. Conflicts often arise when people are strongly motivated to influence each other—in relationships like the one between the mother and daughter in this story.

Reading Skills 📖

Making Inferences About Motivation

Understanding motivation is important for anyone who wants to create a convincing character, and it's important for readers

too. To understand a character's motivation, you must make **inferences,** or intelligent guesses, based on clues from the text. You think about the character's actions and words, and you observe how others react to the character. Using these clues—and your own life experiences with people—think about what motivates both Jing-mei and her mother in this story.

Vocabulary Development

prodigy (präd′ə·jē) *n.:* child of highly unusual talent or genius.

lamented (lə·ment′id) *v.:* said with regret or sorrow. *Lamented* also means "mourned for; regretted intensely."

listlessly (list′lis·lē) *adv.:* without energy or interest.

mesmerizing (mez′mər·īz′iŋ) *v.* used as *adj.:* spellbinding; fascinating.

discordant (dis·kôrd′′nt) *adj.:* clashing; not in harmony.

dawdled (dôd′′ld) *v.:* wasted time; lingered.

stricken (strik′ən) *adj.:* heartbroken; affected by or suffering from something painful or distressing.

fiasco (fē·as′kō) *n.:* total failure.

nonchalantly (nän′shə·länt′lē) *adv.:* without interest or concern; indifferently.

betrayal (bē·trā′əl) *n.:* failure to fulfill another's hopes. *Betrayal* also means "act of disloyalty; deception."

Two Kinds

Amy Tan

"I'll never be the kind of daughter you want me to be!"

My mother believed you could be anything you wanted to be in America. You could open a restaurant. You could work for the government and get good retirement. You could buy a house with almost no money down. You could become rich. You could become instantly famous.

"Of course you can be prodigy, too," my mother told me when I was nine. "You can be best anything. What does Auntie Lindo know? Her daughter, she is only best tricky."

America was where all my mother's hopes lay. She had come here in 1949 after losing everything in China: her mother and father, her family home, her first husband, and two daughters, twin baby girls. But she never looked back with regret. There were so many ways for things to get better.

We didn't immediately pick the right kind of prodigy. At first my mother thought I could be a Chinese Shirley Temple.[1] We'd watch Shirley's old movies on TV as though they were training films. My mother would poke my arm and say, "*Ni kan*"—You watch. And I would see Shirley tapping her feet, or singing a sailor song, or pursing her lips into a very round O while saying, "Oh my goodness."

"*Ni kan*," said my mother as Shirley's eyes flooded with tears. "You already know how. Don't need talent for crying!"

---

1. **Shirley Temple** (1928–   ): child movie star who was popular during the 1930s. Mothers all across the United States tried to set their daughters' hair to look like Shirley Temple's sausage curls.

Vocabulary
prodigy (präd′ə·jē) *n*.: child of highly unusual talent or genius.

Soon after my mother got this idea about Shirley Temple, she took me to a beauty training school in the Mission district and put me in the hands of a student who could barely hold the scissors without shaking. Instead of getting big fat curls, I emerged with an uneven mass of crinkly black fuzz. My mother dragged me off to the bathroom and tried to wet down my hair.

"You look like Negro Chinese," she <u>lamented</u>, as if I had done this on purpose.

The instructor of the beauty training school had to lop off these soggy clumps to make my hair even again. "Peter Pan is very popular these days," the instructor assured my mother. I now had hair the length of a boy's, with straight-across bangs that hung at a slant two inches above my eyebrows. I liked the haircut and it made me actually look forward to my future fame.

In fact, in the beginning, I was just as excited as my mother, maybe even more so. I pictured this prodigy part of me as many different images, trying each one on for size. I was a dainty ballerina girl standing by the curtains, waiting to hear the right music that would send me floating on my tiptoes. I was like the Christ child lifted out of the straw manger, crying with holy indignity.[2] I was Cinderella stepping from her pumpkin carriage with sparkly cartoon music filling the air.

In all of my imaginings, I was filled with a sense that I would soon become *perfect*. My mother and father would adore me. I would be beyond reproach. I would never feel the need to sulk for anything.

But sometimes the prodigy in me became impatient. "If you don't hurry up and get me out of here, I'm disappearing for good," it warned. "And then you'll always be nothing."

Every night after dinner, my mother and I would sit at the Formica kitchen table. She would present new tests, taking her examples from stories of amazing children she had read in *Ripley's Believe It or Not,* or *Good Housekeeping, Reader's Digest,* and a dozen other magazines she kept in a pile in our bathroom. My mother got these magazines from people whose houses she cleaned. And since she cleaned many houses each week, we had a great assortment. She would look through them all, searching for stories about remarkable children.

The first night she brought out a story about a three-year-old boy who knew the capitals of all the states and even most of the European countries. A teacher was quoted as saying the little boy could also pronounce the names of the foreign cities correctly.

"What's the capital of Finland?" my mother asked me, looking at the magazine story.

All I knew was the capital of California, because Sacramento was the name of the street we lived on in Chinatown. "Nairobi!"[3] I guessed, saying the most foreign word I could think of. She checked to see if that was possibly one way to pronounce "Helsinki" before showing me the answer.

The tests got harder—multiplying numbers in my head, finding the queen of hearts in a deck of cards, trying to stand on my head without using my hands, predicting the daily temperatures in Los Angeles, New York, and London.

One night I had to look at a page from the Bible for three minutes and then report everything I could remember. "Now Jehoshaphat had riches and honor in abundance and . . . that's all I remember, Ma," I said.

And after seeing my mother's disappointed face once again, something inside of me began to die. I hated the tests, the raised hopes and failed expectations. Before going to bed that night, I

---

2. **indignity** (in·dig′nə·tē) *n.*: loss of dignity or honor.

3. **Nairobi** (nī·rō′bē): capital of Kenya, a nation in Africa.

Vocabulary

lamented (lə·ment′id) *v.*: said with regret or sorrow. *Lamented* also means "mourned for; regretted intensely."

looked in the mirror above the bathroom sink and when I saw only my face staring back—and that it would always be this ordinary face—I began to cry. Such a sad, ugly girl! I made high-pitched noises like a crazed animal, trying to scratch out the face in the mirror.

And then I saw what seemed to be the prodigy side of me—because I had never seen that face before. I looked at my reflection, blinking so I could see more clearly. The girl staring back at me was angry, powerful. This girl and I were the same. I had new thoughts, willful thoughts, or rather thoughts filled with lots of won'ts. I won't let her change me, I promised myself. I won't be what I'm not.

So now, on nights when my mother presented her tests, I performed listlessly, my head propped on one arm. I pretended to be bored. And I was. I got so bored I started counting the bellows of the foghorns out on the bay while my mother drilled me in other areas. The sound was comforting and reminded me of the cow jumping over the moon. And the next day, I played a game with myself, seeing if my mother would give up on me before eight bellows. After a while I usually counted only one, maybe two bellows at most. At last she was beginning to give up hope.

Two or three months had gone by without any mention of my being a prodigy again. And then one day my mother was watching *The Ed Sullivan Show* on TV. The TV was old and the sound kept shorting out. Every time my mother got halfway up from the sofa to adjust the set, the sound would go back on and Ed would be talking. As soon as she sat down, Ed would go silent again. She got up, the TV broke into loud piano music. She sat down. Silence. Up and

Chinatown, San Francisco, at night.

Vocabulary
listlessly (list′lis·lē) *adv.*: without energy or interest.

down, back and forth, quiet and loud. It was like a stiff embraceless dance between her and the TV set. Finally she stood by the set with her hand on the sound dial.

She seemed entranced by the music, a little frenzied piano piece with this <u>mesmerizing</u> quality, sort of quick passages and then teasing, lilting[4] ones before it returned to the quick, playful parts.

"*Ni kan*," my mother said, calling me over with hurried hand gestures. "Look here."

I could see why my mother was fascinated by the music. It was being pounded out by a little Chinese girl, about nine years old, with a Peter Pan haircut. The girl had the sauciness[5] of a Shirley Temple. She was proudly modest like a proper Chinese child. And she also did this fancy sweep of a curtsy, so that the fluffy skirt of her white dress cascaded slowly to the floor like the petals of a large carnation.

In spite of these warning signs, I wasn't worried. Our family had no piano and we couldn't afford to buy one, let alone reams[6] of sheet music and piano lessons. So I could be generous in my comments when my mother bad-mouthed the little girl on TV.

"Play note right, but doesn't sound good! No singing sound," complained my mother.

"What are you picking on her for?" I said carelessly. "She's pretty good. Maybe she's not the best, but she's trying hard." I knew almost immediately I would be sorry I said that.

"Just like you," she said. "Not the best. Because you not trying." She gave a little huff as she let go of the sound dial and sat down on the sofa.

The little Chinese girl sat down also to play an

> "I'm not a genius! I can't play the piano."

encore of "Anitra's Dance" by Grieg.[7] I remember the song, because later on I had to learn how to play it.

Three days after watching *The Ed Sullivan Show*, my mother told me what my schedule would be for piano lessons and piano practice. She had talked to Mr. Chong, who lived on the first floor of our apartment building. Mr. Chong was a retired piano teacher, and my mother had traded housecleaning services for weekly lessons and a piano for me to practice on every day, two hours a day, from four until six.

When my mother told me this, I felt as though I had been sent to hell. I whined and then kicked my foot a little when I couldn't stand it anymore.

"Why don't you like me the way I am? I'm *not* a genius! I can't play the piano. And even if I could, I wouldn't go on TV if you paid me a million dollars!" I cried.

My mother slapped me. "Who ask you be genius?" she shouted. "Only ask you be your best. For you sake. You think I want you be genius? Hnnh! What for! Who ask you!"

"So ungrateful," I heard her mutter in Chinese. "If she had as much talent as she has temper, she would be famous now."

Mr. Chong, whom I secretly nicknamed Old Chong, was very strange, always tapping his fingers to the silent music of an invisible orchestra. He looked ancient in my eyes. He had lost most of the hair on top of his head and he wore thick glasses and had eyes that always looked tired and sleepy. But he must have been younger than I

---

7. **Grieg** (grēg): Edvard Grieg (1843–1907), Norwegian composer. "Anitra's Dance" is from his *Peer Gynt Suite*.

4. **lilting** *adj.*: with a light, graceful rhythm.
5. **sauciness** (sô′sē·nis) *n.*: liveliness.
6. **reams** *n.*: here, great amount. A ream of paper is about five hundred sheets.

Vocabulary
mesmerizing (mez′mər·īz′iŋ) *v.* used as *adj.*: spellbinding; fascinating.

thought, since he lived with his mother and was not yet married.

I met Old Lady Chong once and that was enough. She had this peculiar smell like a baby that had done something in its pants. And her fingers felt like a dead person's, like an old peach I once found in the back of the refrigerator; the skin just slid off the meat when I picked it up.

I soon found out why Old Chong had retired from teaching piano. He was deaf. "Like Beethoven!" he shouted to me. "We're both listening only in our head!" And he would start to conduct his frantic silent sonatas.[8]

Our lessons went like this. He would open the book and point to different things, explaining their purpose: "Key! Treble! Bass! No sharps or flats! So this is C major! Listen now and play after me!"

And then he would play the C scale a few times, a simple chord, and then, as if inspired by an old, unreachable itch, he gradually added more notes and running trills and a pounding bass until the music was really something quite grand.

I would play after him, the simple scale, the simple chord, and then I just played some nonsense that sounded like a cat running up and down on top of garbage cans. Old Chong smiled and applauded and then said, "Very good! But now you must learn to keep time!"

So that's how I discovered that Old Chong's eyes were too slow to keep up with the wrong notes I was playing. He went through the motions in half-time. To help me keep rhythm, he stood behind me, pushing down on my right shoulder for every beat. He balanced pennies on top of my wrists so I would keep them still as I slowly played scales and arpeggios.[9] He had me curve my hand around an apple and keep that

shape when playing chords. He marched stiffly to show me how to make each finger dance up and down, staccato,[10] like an obedient little soldier.

He taught me all these things, and that was how I also learned I could be lazy and get away with mistakes, lots of mistakes. If I hit the wrong notes because I hadn't practiced enough, I never corrected myself. I just kept playing in rhythm. And Old Chong kept conducting his own private reverie.[11]

So maybe I never really gave myself a fair chance. I did pick up the basics pretty quickly, and I might have become a good pianist at that young age. But I was so determined not to try, not to be anybody different, that I learned to play only the most earsplitting preludes, the most discordant hymns.

Over the next year, I practiced like this, dutifully in my own way. And then one day I heard my mother and her friend Lindo Jong both talking in a loud bragging tone of voice so others could hear. It was after church, and I was leaning against the brick wall, wearing a dress with stiff white petticoats. Auntie Lindo's daughter, Waverly, who was about my age, was standing farther down the wall, about five feet away. We had grown up together and shared all the closeness of two sisters squabbling over crayons and dolls. In other words, for the most part, we hated each other. I thought she was snotty. Waverly Jong had gained a certain amount of fame as "Chinatown's Littlest Chinese Chess Champion."

"She bring home too many trophy," lamented Auntie Lindo that Sunday. "All day she play chess. All day I have no time do nothing but dust off her winnings." She threw a scolding look at Waverly, who pretended not to see her.

---

8. **sonatas** (sə·nät′əz) *n.*: musical compositions, usually for one or two instruments.
9. **arpeggios** (är·pej′ōz) *n.*: chords whose notes are played quickly one after another, rather than at the same time.
10. **staccato** (stə·kät′ō) *adv.*: with clear-cut breaks between notes.
11. **reverie** (rev′ə·rē) *n.*: daydream.

Vocabulary
discordant (dis·kôrd″nt) *adj.*: clashing; not in harmony.

"You lucky you don't have this problem," said Auntie Lindo with a sigh to my mother.

And my mother squared her shoulders and bragged: "Our problem worser than yours. If we ask Jing-mei wash dish, she hear nothing but music. It's like you can't stop this natural talent."

And right then, I was determined to put a stop to her foolish pride.

A few weeks later, Old Chong and my mother conspired to have me play in a talent show which would be held in the church hall. By then, my parents had saved up enough to buy me a secondhand piano, a black Wurlitzer spinet with a scarred bench. It was the showpiece of our living room.

For the talent show, I was to play a piece called "Pleading Child" from Schumann's[12] *Scenes from Childhood.* It was a simple, moody piece that sounded more difficult than it was. I was supposed to memorize the whole thing, playing the repeat parts twice to make the piece sound longer. But I dawdled over it, playing a few bars and then cheating, looking up to see what notes followed. I never really listened to what I was playing. I daydreamed about being somewhere else, about being someone else.

The part I liked to practice best was the fancy curtsy: right foot out, touch the rose on the carpet with a pointed foot, sweep to the side, left leg bends, look up and smile.

My parents invited all the couples from the Joy Luck Club[13] to witness my debut.[14] Auntie Lindo and Uncle Tin were there. Waverly and her two older brothers had also come. The first two rows were filled with children both younger and older than I was. The littlest ones got to go first. They recited simple nursery rhymes, squawked out tunes on miniature violins, twirled Hula-Hoops,[15] pranced in pink ballet tutus,[16] and when they bowed or curtsied, the audience would sigh in unison, "Awww," and then clap enthusiastically.

When my turn came, I was very confident. I remember my childish excitement. It was as if I knew, without a doubt, that the prodigy side of me really did exist. I had no fear whatsoever, no nervousness. I remember thinking to myself, This is it! This is it! I looked out over the audience, at my mother's blank face, my father's yawn, Auntie Lindo's stiff-lipped smile, Waverly's sulky expression. I had on a white dress layered with sheets of lace, and a pink bow in my Peter Pan haircut. As I sat down I envisioned people jumping to their feet and Ed Sullivan rushing up to introduce me to everyone on TV.

And I started to play. It was so beautiful. I was so caught up in how lovely I looked that at first I didn't worry how I would sound. So it was a surprise to me when I hit the first wrong note and I realized something didn't sound quite right. And then I hit another, and another followed that. A chill started at the top of my head and began to trickle down. Yet I couldn't stop playing, as though my hands were bewitched. I kept thinking my fingers would adjust themselves back, like a train switching to the right track. I played this strange jumble through two repeats, the sour notes staying with me all the way to the end.

When I stood up, I discovered my legs were shaking. Maybe I had just been nervous and the audience, like Old Chong, had seen me go through the right motions and had not heard anything wrong at all. I swept my right foot out, went down on my knee, looked up and smiled.

---

12. **Schumann** (sho͞o′män): Robert Schumann (1810–1856), German composer.
13. **Joy Luck Club:** social club to which Jing-mei's mother and three other Chinese mothers belong.
14. **debut** (dā·byo͞o′) *n.:* first appearance in public of a performer.

---

15. **Hula-Hoops** (ho͞o′lə ho͞ops′): trademark for plastic hoops usually twirled around the hips.
16. **tutus** (to͞o′to͞oz′) *n.:* short skirts worn by ballerinas.

Vocabulary
dawdled (dôd′′ld) *v.:* wasted time; lingered.

The room was quiet, except for Old Chong, who was beaming and shouting, "Bravo! Bravo! Well done!" But then I saw my mother's face, her stricken face. The audience clapped weakly, and as I walked back to my chair, with my whole face quivering as I tried not to cry, I heard a little boy whisper loudly to his mother, "That was awful," and the mother whispered back, "Well, she certainly tried."

When I stood up, I discovered my legs were shaking.

And now I realized how many people were in the audience, the whole world it seemed. I was aware of eyes burning into my back. I felt the shame of my mother and father as they sat stiffly throughout the rest of the show.

We could have escaped during intermission. Pride and some strange sense of honor must have anchored my parents to their chairs. And so we watched it all: the eighteen-year-old boy with a fake mustache who did a magic show and juggled flaming hoops while riding a unicycle. The breasted girl with white makeup who sang from *Madama Butterfly*[17] and got honorable mention. And the eleven-year-old boy who won first prize playing a tricky violin song that sounded like a busy bee.

After the show, the Hsus, the Jongs, and the St. Clairs from the Joy Luck Club came up to my mother and father.

"Lots of talented kids," Auntie Lindo said vaguely, smiling broadly.

"That was somethin' else," said my father, and I wondered if he was referring to me in a humorous way, or whether he even remembered what I had done.

Waverly looked at me and shrugged her shoulders. "You aren't a genius like me," she said matter-of-factly. And if I hadn't felt so bad, I would have pulled her braids and punched her stomach.

But my mother's expression was what devastated me: a quiet, blank look that said she had lost everything. I felt the same way, and it seemed as if everybody were now coming up, like gawkers at the scene of an accident, to see what parts were actually missing. When we got on the bus to go home, my father was humming the busy-bee tune and my mother was silent. I kept thinking she wanted to wait until we got home before shouting at me. But when my father unlocked the door to our apartment, my mother walked in and then went to the back, into the bedroom. No accusations. No blame. And in a way, I felt disappointed. I had been waiting for her to start shouting, so I could shout back and cry and blame her for all my misery.

---

17. *Madama Butterfly:* opera by the Italian composer Giacomo Puccini (1858–1924).

Vocabulary
stricken (strik′ən) *adj.*: heartbroken; affected by or suffering from something painful or distressing.

I assumed my talent-show fiasco meant I never had to play the piano again. But two days later, after school, my mother came out of the kitchen and saw me watching TV.

"Four clock," she reminded me as if it were any other day. I was stunned, as though she were asking me to go through the talent-show torture again. I wedged myself more tightly in front of the TV.

"Turn off TV," she called from the kitchen five minutes later.

I didn't budge. And then I decided. I didn't have to do what my mother said anymore. I wasn't her slave. This wasn't China. I had listened to her before and look what happened. She was the stupid one.

She came out from the kitchen and stood in the arched entryway of the living room. "Four clock," she said once again, louder.

"I'm not going to play anymore," I said nonchalantly. "Why should I? I'm not a genius."

She walked over and stood in front of the TV. I saw her chest was heaving up and down in an angry way.

"No!" I said, and I now felt stronger, as if my true self had finally emerged. So this was what had been inside me all along.

"No! I won't!" I screamed.

She yanked me by the arm, pulled me off the floor, snapped off the TV. She was frighteningly strong, half pulling, half carrying me toward the piano as I kicked the throw rugs under my feet. She lifted me up and onto the hard bench. I was sobbing by now, looking at her bitterly. Her chest was heaving even more and her mouth was open, smiling crazily, as if she were pleased I was crying.

"You want me to be someone that I'm not!" I sobbed. "I'll never be the kind of daughter you want me to be!"

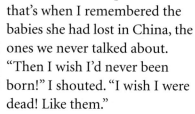

"Only two kinds of daughters," she shouted in Chinese. "Those who are obedient and those who follow their own mind! Only one kind of daughter can live in this house. Obedient daughter!"

"Then I wish I wasn't your daughter. I wish you weren't my mother," I shouted. As I said these things, I got scared. It felt like worms and toads and slimy things crawling out of my chest, but it also felt good, as if this awful side of me had surfaced, at last.

"Too late change this," said my mother shrilly.

And I could sense her anger rising to its breaking point. I wanted to see it spill over. And that's when I remembered the babies she had lost in China, the ones we never talked about. "Then I wish I'd never been born!" I shouted. "I wish I were dead! Like them."

It was as if I had said the magic words. Alakazam!—and her face went blank, her mouth closed, her arms went slack, and she backed out of the room, stunned, as if she were blowing away like a small brown leaf, thin, brittle, lifeless.

It was not the only disappointment my mother felt in me. In the years that followed, I failed her so many times, each time asserting my own will, my right to fall short of expectations. I didn't get straight A's. I didn't become class president. I didn't get into Stanford.[18] I dropped out of college.

For unlike my mother, I did not believe I could be anything I wanted to be. I could only be me.

---

18. **Stanford:** high-ranking university in Stanford, California.

Vocabulary

fiasco (fē·as′kō) *n.:* total failure.

nonchalantly (nän′shə·länt′lē) *adv.:* without interest or concern; indifferently.

And for all those years, we never talked about the disaster at the recital or my terrible accusations afterward at the piano bench. All that remained unchecked, like a betrayal that was now unspeakable. So I never found a way to ask her why she had hoped for something so large that failure was inevitable.

And even worse, I never asked her what frightened me the most: Why had she given up hope?

For after our struggle at the piano, she never mentioned my playing again. The lessons stopped. The lid to the piano was closed, shutting out the dust, my misery, and her dreams.

So she surprised me. A few years ago, she offered to give me the piano, for my thirtieth birthday. I had not played in all those years. I saw the offer as a sign of forgiveness, a tremendous burden removed.

"Are you sure?" I asked shyly. "I mean, won't you and Dad miss it?"

"No, this your piano," she said firmly. "Always your piano. You only one can play."

"Well, I probably can't play anymore," I said. "It's been years."

"You pick up fast," said my mother, as if she knew this was certain. "You have natural talent. You could been genius if you want to."

"No, I couldn't."

"You just not trying," said my mother. And she was neither angry nor sad. She said it as if to announce a fact that could never be disproved. "Take it," she said.

But I didn't at first. It was enough that she had offered it to me. And after that, every time I saw it in my parents' living room, standing in front of the bay windows, it made me feel proud, as if it were a shiny trophy I had won back.

Last week I sent a tuner over to my parents' apartment and had the piano reconditioned, for purely sentimental reasons. My mother had died a few months before, and I had been getting things in order for my father, a little bit at a time. I put the jewelry in special silk pouches. The sweaters she had knitted in yellow, pink, bright orange—all the colors I hated—I put those in mothproof boxes. I found some old Chinese silk dresses, the kind with little slits up the sides. I rubbed the old silk against my skin, then wrapped them in tissue and decided to take them home with me.

After I had the piano tuned, I opened the lid and touched the keys. It sounded even richer than I remembered. Really, it was a very good piano. Inside the bench were the same exercise notes with handwritten scales, the same second-hand music books with their covers held together with yellow tape.

I opened up the Schumann book to the dark little piece I had played at the recital. It was on the left-hand side of the page, "Pleading Child." It looked more difficult than I remembered. I played a few bars, surprised at how easily the notes came back to me.

And for the first time, or so it seemed, I noticed the piece on the right-hand side. It was called "Perfectly Contented." I tried to play this one as well. It had a lighter melody but the same flowing rhythm and turned out to be quite easy. "Pleading Child" was shorter but slower; "Perfectly Contented" was longer but faster. And after I played them both a few times, I realized they were two halves of the same song. ∎

Vocabulary
betrayal (bē·trā′əl) *n.*: failure to fulfill another's hopes. *Betrayal* also means "act of disloyalty; deception."

Meet the Writer

Amy Tan

Many Englishes

Amy Tan (1952–   ) says that she grew up with several Englishes. The Englishes were primarily American English and Chinese English. Tan was born in Oakland, California, two and a half years after her parents fled China's Communist revolution and settled in the United States. Although Tan's parents had wanted her to become a surgeon, with piano as a hobby, she got a master's degree in linguistics instead. Her first short story, written at a writers' workshop in 1985, was eventually published in *Seventeen*.

At the request of a literary agent, Tan next drafted a proposal for a novel based on the lives of four Chinese mothers and their American daughters. Then Tan left on a trip to China with her own mother, who had just recovered from a serious illness.

When she returned, Tan was amazed to find that her agent had obtained a sizable advance for a book she hadn't even written yet. She immediately devoted herself full time to writing *The Joy Luck Club*—a collection of related stories told from the points of view of four mothers and four daughters.

"When I wrote these stories, it was as much a discovery to me as to any reader reading them for the first time," Tan has said. "Things would surprise me. I would sit there laughing and I would say, 'Oh you're kidding!' It was like people telling me the stories, and I would write them down as fast as I could." Published in 1989 to rave reviews, *The Joy Luck Club* became an instant bestseller.

Afraid of failing after the huge success of *The Joy Luck Club,* Tan agonized over her second novel, *The Kitchen God's Wife* (1991). In writing that book, she says, she "had to fight for every single character, every image, every word." She needn't have worried. The novel, the story of a woman's harrowing life in pre-Communist China, was another blockbuster. Tan followed her first two successes with two more: *The Hundred Secret Senses* (1995) and *The Bonesetter's Daughter* (2001).

Here is what Tan says about being a writer who knows two cultures:

> **❝** I am a writer. I am fascinated by language in daily life. I spend a great deal of my time thinking about the power of language— the way it can evoke an emotion, a visual image, a complex idea, or a simple truth. Language is the tool of my trade. And I use them all—all the Englishes I grew up with. **❞**

For Independent Reading

If you enjoyed "Two Kinds," you might want to read *The Joy Luck Club* (mentioned above), from which "Two Kinds" is taken.

Response and Analysis

Reading Check

1. What does Jing-mei's mother want for her daughter?

2. How does Jing-mei feel about her mother's plans for her?

3. What happens when Jing-mei plays the piano in front of an audience?

4. What does Jing-mei say to hurt her mother in their last struggle over the piano lessons?

Thinking Critically

5. Identify the story's central **conflict,** and tell what causes it. What does the **main character** desire, and what blocks her from achieving it?

6. What **inferences** can you make about the mother's **motivation** for pushing Jing-mei to be a prodigy? Consider
   • the mother's life in China
   • her life in America

7. Why might Jing-mei's mother want her to keep playing the piano even after her disastrous performance? What kind of daughter does she really want Jing-mei to be?

8. How do you think other children might respond to the pressure to become a prodigy? What **inferences** can you make about Jing-mei's **character traits** from her response to her mother's pressure?

9. What do you think the **title** of the story means? How does Jing-mei's discovery concerning the two Schumann songs relate to the story's title?

10. Near the end of the story, Jing-mei says, "In the years that followed, I failed her so many times. . . ." What does she mean by that? Do you think author Amy Tan agrees with her? Why?

Extending and Evaluating

11. Do you think the demands and high expectations of others can make us want to fail (out of spite or hopelessness, perhaps), or do you think such expectations can motivate us to greater success? Explain your opinion, drawing examples from your own experiences and those of people you know. (Your Quickwrite notes may help you answer this question.)

WRITING

Mother Versus Daughter

Do you think Jing-mei's mother is right to push Jing-mei so hard, or do you agree with Jing-mei that her mother's pride is foolish? Do you think that Jing-mei is cruel to her mother or that her mother is cruel to her? Write a paragraph or two analyzing the relationship between the mother and daughter. Support your statements with details from the story.

My Unforgettable Character

Amy Tan's story is interesting in part because it lets us meet some unusual characters. Write a **character sketch** of your own about a person you know— preferably someone you can observe. You might find a subject by thinking about the characters in "Two Kinds." Does anyone in the story remind you of someone in your own life? Use descriptive details to tell what your character looks like, how he or she acts, what characteristic things he or she says, what he or she likes to do. How do you know this person? Open your sketch with a sentence that hooks your readers' interest.

▶ **Use "Describing a Person," pages 540–547, for help with this assignment.**

SKILLS FOCUS

Literary Skills
Analyze conflict and motivation.

Reading Skills
Make inferences about motivation.

Writing Skills
Write an analysis of the relationship between two characters. Write a character sketch.

Vocabulary Development

Clarifying Word Meanings: Comparison and Contrast

Comparison means finding similarities, and **contrast** means finding differences. How can you use these skills to help build your vocabulary?

Clues to a word's meaning can often be found in a sentence by identifying **synonyms** (words with *similar* meanings) or **antonyms** (words with *opposite* meanings). Look also for **signal words.** Words such as *similarly, like, as, also, too,* and *resembling* signal comparison. Words and phrases such as *although, but, yet, still, unlike, not, in contrast, instead,* and *however* signal contrast.

COMPARISON Jing-mei's mother had a <u>stricken</u> look, **like** a woman who was **heartbroken.**

CONTRAST Jing-mei's mother expected **loyalty** and **trustworthiness, not** <u>betrayal</u>, from her daughter.

PRACTICE

Make a word map like the one below for each Word Bank word. First, list at least one synonym and, when possible, an antonym (many words do not have antonyms). Consult a dictionary and a thesaurus if necessary. Then, write a sentence clarifying each word's meaning. In your sentences, use synonyms or antonyms to compare and contrast the words' meanings.

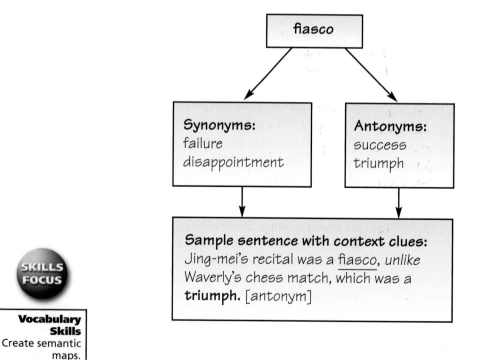

SKILLS FOCUS

Vocabulary Skills
Create semantic maps.

Grammar Link

Main or Subordinate Clause: Can It Stand Alone?

A **clause** is a group of words that has a subject and a verb. A **main clause** (also called an **independent clause**) can stand alone as a sentence because it has a subject and a verb, *and* it expresses a complete thought.

MAIN CLAUSE	Jing-mei's mother argued with her daughter. [sentence]

A **subordinate clause,** on the other hand, has a subject and verb, but it does *not* express a complete thought, and so it cannot stand on its own as a sentence. A subordinate clause must be attached to a main clause to communicate a whole idea.

A subordinate clause that stands by itself is a sentence fragment. A **sentence fragment** does not express a complete thought.

SUBORDINATE CLAUSE	Because Jing-mei didn't want to be a prodigy. [sentence fragment]

Whenever you write, make sure that every subordinate clause is firmly attached to a main clause. The subordinate clause may come at the beginning of the sentence, at the end, or in the middle.

COMPLETE SENTENCE	Jing-mei's mother argued with her daughter because Jing-mei didn't want to be a prodigy.

PRACTICE

Edit and rewrite the following paragraph, correcting all errors in the use of subordinate clauses. (Make any capitalization and punctuation changes that are necessary as well.)

The plot of this story would not have been believable. If Old Chong, the piano teacher, weren't completely deaf. Anyone can hear the terribly wrong notes. Who listens to Jing-mei's playing. When she starts playing before a hearing audience. Jing-mei realizes for the first time what she has done. She feels terrible. Because she has humiliated herself and her parents.

▶ **For more help, see Kinds of Clauses, 7b–c, in the Language Handbook.**

SKILLS FOCUS

Grammar Skills
Use subordinate clauses correctly.

By Any Other Name

Make the Connection

Quickwrite ✏️

This essay's title comes from Shakespeare's *Romeo and Juliet*. Juliet wishes that Romeo had a different surname because his family and hers are enemies. "What's in a name?" she asks. "That which we call a rose / By any other name would smell as sweet."

How important is a person's name? How would you react if someone took your name away and then referred to you only by a number? Quickwrite your response.

Literary Focus

Character and Autobiography

You've seen how fiction writers use methods of **indirect characterization** to create characters that seem real. They *show* (rather than *tell*) what their characters look like and what they say, do, and think. So how does a nonfiction writer (in this case a writer of **autobiography**) reveal what her real-life characters are like? Notice how Santha Rama Rau brings her characters and their conflicts to life. Are her techniques the same as a fiction writer's, or are they different?

Reading Skills

Comparison and Contrast

When the sisters in this account enroll in a school run by teachers from England in their native India, they encounter cultural differences ranging from the different foods the students eat to more important conflicts of values and attitudes. As you read, **compare and contrast** these cultures and the different reactions of the sisters.

INTERNET

Vocabulary Practice

Keyword: LE5 10-2

Literary Skills
Understand character and autobiography.

Reading Skills
Compare and contrast.

Background

At the time of this account (around 1928), India was a colony of Great Britain, and educated Indians were expected to learn English in addition to their native languages. (Many languages are spoken in India.) The headmistress of Rama Rau's school is British, as are most of the students, children of British civil servants sent to India as colonial rulers.

Vocabulary Development

precarious (pri·ker′ē·əs) *adj.*: in danger of falling down; unstable.

intimidated (in·tim′ə·dāt′id) *v.*: made afraid.

provincial (prə·vin′shəl) *adj.*: belonging to a province, especially a rural one; also, unsophisticated.

insular (in′sə·lər) *adj.*: isolated from one's surroundings; narrow-minded.

valid (val′id) *adj.*: meeting the requirements of established standards.

palpitating (pal′pə·tāt′iŋ) *v.* used as *adj.*: throbbing; quivering.

wizened (wiz′ənd) *adj.*: wrinkled and dried up.

sedately (si·dāt′lē) *adv.*: in a calm and dignified manner.

tepid (tep′id) *adj.*: neither hot nor cold; lukewarm.

peevishness (pē′vish·nis) *n.*: irritability.

> "Suppose we give you pretty English names."

Santha Rama Rau (right), her older sister, Premila, and their dog in Simla, India, 1927.

By Any Other Name

Santha Rama Rau

At the Anglo-Indian[1] day school in Zorinabad to which my sister and I were sent when she was eight and I was five and a half, they changed our names. On the first day of school, a hot, windless morning of a north Indian September, we stood in the headmistress's study, and she said, "Now you're the *new* girls. What are your names?"

My sister answered for us. "I am Premila, and she"—nodding in my direction—"is Santha."

The headmistress had been in India, I suppose, fifteen years or so, but she still smiled her helpless inability to cope with Indian names. Her rimless half-glasses glittered, and the precarious bun on the top of her head trembled as she shook her head. "Oh, my dears, those are much too hard for me. Suppose we give you pretty English names. Wouldn't that be more jolly? Let's see, now—Pamela for you, I think." She shrugged in a baffled way at my sister. "That's as close as I can get. And for *you,*" she said to me, "how about Cynthia? Isn't that nice?"

My sister was always less easily intimidated than I was, and while she kept a stubborn silence, I said "Thank you," in a very tiny voice.

We had been sent to that school because my father, among his responsibilities as an officer of the civil service, had a tour of duty to perform in the villages around that steamy little provincial town, where he had his headquarters at that time. He used to make his shorter inspection tours on horseback, and a week before, in the stale heat of a typically postmonsoon[2] day, we had waved goodbye to him and a little procession—an assistant, a secretary, two bearers, and the man to look after the bedding rolls and luggage. They rode away through our large garden, still bright green from the rains, and we turned back into the twilight of the house and the sound of fans whispering in every room.

Up to then, my mother had refused to send Premila to school in the British-run establishments of that time, because, she used to say, "You can bury a dog's tail for seven years and it still comes out curly, and you can take a Britisher away from his home for a lifetime and he still remains insular." The examinations and degrees from entirely Indian schools were not, in those days, considered valid. In my case, the question had never come up and probably never would have come up if Mother's extraordinary good health had not broken down. For the first time in my life, she was not able to continue the lessons she had been giving us every morning. So our Hindi[3] books were put away, the stories of the Lord Krishna[4] as a little boy were left in midair, and we were sent to the Anglo-Indian school.

That first day at school is still, when I think of it, a remarkable one. At that age, if one's name is changed, one develops a curious form of dual personality. I remember having a certain detached and disbelieving concern in the actions of "Cynthia," but certainly no responsibility. Accordingly, I followed the thin, erect back of the headmistress down the veranda to my classroom, feeling, at most, a passing interest in what was going to happen to me in this strange, new atmosphere of School.

---

1. **Anglo-Indian:** English and Indian; also refers to the British colonists living in India.
2. **postmonsoon** *adj.:* after the monsoon, or seasonal heavy rains.
3. **Hindi:** official language of India.
4. **Lord Krishna:** in the Hindu religion, human form taken by the god Vishnu. Many Hindu stories recount episodes in the life of Krishna.

Vocabulary

precarious (pri·ker′ē·əs) *adj.:* in danger of falling down; unstable.

intimidated (in·tim′ə·dāt′id) *v.:* made afraid.

provincial (prə·vin′shəl) *adj.:* belonging to a province, especially a rural one; also, unsophisticated.

insular (in′sə·lər) *adj.:* isolated from one's surroundings; narrow-minded.

valid (val′id) *adj.:* meeting the requirements of established standards.

The building was Indian in design, with wide verandas opening onto a central courtyard, but Indian verandas are usually whitewashed, with stone floors. These, in the tradition of British schools, were painted dark brown and had matting on the floors. It gave a feeling of extra intensity to the heat.

I suppose there were about a dozen Indian children in the school—which contained perhaps forty children in all—and four of them were in my class. They were all sitting at the back of the room, and I went to join them. I sat next to a small, solemn girl, who didn't smile at me. She had long, glossy black braids and wore a cotton dress, but she still kept on her Indian jewelry—a gold chain around her neck, thin gold bracelets, and tiny ruby studs in her ears. Like most Indian children, she had a rim of black kohl[5] around her eyes. The cotton dress should have looked strange, but all I could think of was that I should ask my mother if I couldn't wear a dress to school, too, instead of my Indian clothes.

I can't remember too much about the proceedings in class that day, except for the beginning. The teacher pointed to me and asked me to stand up. "Now, dear, tell the class your name."

I said nothing.

"Come along," she said, frowning slightly. "What's your name, dear?"

"I don't know," I said, finally.

The English children in the front of the class—there were about eight or ten of them—giggled and twisted around in their chairs to look at me. I sat down quickly and opened my eyes very wide, hoping in that way to dry them off. The little girl with the braids put out her hand and very lightly touched my arm. She still didn't smile.

Most of that morning I was rather bored. I looked briefly at the children's drawings pinned to the wall, and then concentrated on a lizard

clinging to the ledge of the high, barred window behind the teacher's head. Occasionally it would shoot out its long yellow tongue for a fly, and then it would rest, with its eyes closed and its belly palpitating, as though it were swallowing several times quickly. The lessons were mostly concerned with reading and writing and simple numbers—things that my mother had already taught me—and I paid very little attention. The teacher wrote on the easel-blackboard words like "bat" and "cat," which seemed babyish to me; only "apple" was new and incomprehensible.

When it was time for the lunch recess, I followed the girl with braids out onto the veranda. There the children from the other classes were assembled. I saw Premila at once and ran over to her, as she had charge of our lunchbox. The children were all opening packages and sitting down to eat sandwiches. Premila and I were the only ones who had Indian food—thin wheat chapatis,[6] some vegetable curry, and a bottle of buttermilk. Premila thrust half of it into my hand and whispered fiercely that I should go and sit with my class, because that was what the others seemed to be doing.

The enormous black eyes of the little Indian girl from my class looked at my food longingly, so I offered her some. But she only shook her head and plowed her way solemnly through her sandwiches.

I was very sleepy after lunch, because at home we always took a siesta. It was usually a pleasant time of day, with the bedroom darkened against the harsh afternoon sun, the drifting off into sleep with the sound of Mother's voice reading a story in one's mind, and, finally, the shrill, fussy voice of the ayah[7] waking one for tea.

---

5. **kohl** (kōl) *n.:* dark powder used as eye makeup.

6. **chapatis** (chə·pät′ēz) *n.:* thin, flat bread.
7. **ayah** (ä′yə) *n.:* Anglo-Indian for "nanny" or "maid."

Vocabulary
palpitating (pal′pə·tāt′iŋ) *v.* used as *adj.:* throbbing; quivering.

At school, we rested for a short time on low, folding cots on the veranda, and then we were expected to play games. During the hot part of the afternoon we played indoors, and after the shadows had begun to lengthen and the slight breeze of the evening had come up, we moved outside to the wide courtyard.

I had never really grasped the system of competitive games. At home, whenever we played tag or guessing games, I was always allowed to "win"—"because," Mother used to tell Premila, "she is the youngest, and we have to allow for that." I had often heard her say it, and it seemed quite reasonable to me, but the result was that I had no clear idea of what "winning" meant.

When we played twos-and-threes[8] that afternoon at school, in accordance with my training I let one of the small English boys catch me but was naturally rather puzzled when the other children did not return the courtesy. I ran about for what seemed like hours without ever catching anyone, until it was time for school to close. Much later I learned that my attitude was called "not being a good sport," and I stopped allowing myself to be caught, but it was not for years that I really learned the spirit of the thing.

When I saw our car come up to the school gate, I broke away from my classmates and rushed toward it yelling, "Ayah! Ayah!" It seemed like an eternity since I had seen her that morning—a wizened, affectionate figure in her white cotton sari,[9] giving me dozens of urgent and useless instructions on how to be a good girl at school. Premila followed more sedately, and she told me on the way home never to do that again in front of the other children.

When we got home, we went straight to Mother's high, white room to have tea with her, and I immediately climbed onto the bed and bounced gently up and down on the springs. Mother asked how we had liked our first day in school. I was so pleased to be home and to have left that peculiar Cynthia behind that I had nothing whatever to say about school, except to ask what "apple" meant. But Premila told Mother about the classes, and added that in her class they had weekly tests to see if they had learned their lessons well.

I asked, "What's a test?"

Premila said, "You're too small to have them. You won't have them in your class for donkey's years."[10] She had learned the expression that day and was using it for the first time. We all laughed enormously at her wit. She also told Mother, in an aside, that we should take sandwiches to school the next day. Not, she said, that *she* minded. But they would be simpler for me to handle.

That whole lovely evening I didn't think about school at all. I sprinted barefoot across the lawns with my favorite playmate, the cook's son, to the stream at the end of the garden. We quarreled in our usual way, waded in the tepid water under the lime trees, and waited for the night to bring out the smell of the jasmine.[11] I listened with fascination to his stories of ghosts and demons, until I was too frightened to cross the garden alone in the semidarkness. The ayah found me, shouted at the cook's son, scolded me, hurried me in to supper—it was an entirely usual, wonderful evening.

---

10. **donkey's years:** expression meaning "a very long time."
11. **jasmine** (jaz'min) *n.:* tropical plant with fragrant flowers.

Vocabulary

wizened (wiz'ənd) *adj.:* wrinkled and dried up.

sedately (si·dāt'lē) *adv.:* in a calm and dignified manner.

tepid (tep'id) *adj.:* neither hot nor cold; lukewarm.

---

8. **twos-and-threes:** game similar to tag.
9. **sari** (sä'rē) *n.:* long piece of cloth wrapped around the body. One end forms a skirt; the other end goes across the chest and over one shoulder.

It was a week later, the day of Premila's first test, that our lives changed rather abruptly. I was sitting at the back of my class, in my usual inattentive way, only half listening to the teacher. I had started a rather guarded friendship with the girl with the braids, whose name turned out to be Nalini (Nancy in school). The three other Indian children were already fast friends. Even at that age, it was apparent to all of us that friendship with the English or Anglo-Indian children was out of the question. Occasionally, during the class, my new friend and I would draw pictures and show them to each other secretly.

The door opened sharply and Premila marched in. At first, the teacher smiled at her in a kindly and encouraging way and said, "Now, you're little Cynthia's sister?"

Premila didn't even look at her. She stood with her feet planted firmly apart and her shoulders rigid and addressed herself directly to me. "Get up," she said. "We're going home."

I didn't know what had happened, but I was aware that it was a crisis of some sort. I rose obediently and started to walk toward my sister.

"Bring your pencils and your notebook," she said.

I went back for them, and together we left the room. The teacher started to say something just as Premila closed the door, but we didn't wait to hear what it was.

In complete silence we left the school grounds and started to walk home. Then I asked Premila what the matter was. All she would say was, "We're going home for good."

It was a very tiring walk for a child of five and a half, and I dragged along behind Premila with my pencils growing sticky in my hand. I can still remember looking at the dusty hedges and the tangles of thorns in the ditches by the side of the road, smelling the faint fragrance from the eucalyptus trees, and wondering whether we would ever reach home. Occasionally a horse-drawn

Interior of a historic mansion in Goa, India.

tonga[12] passed us, and the women, in their pink or green silks, stared at Premila and me trudging along on the side of the road. A few coolies[13] and a line of women carrying baskets of vegetables on their heads smiled at us. But it was nearing the hottest time of day, and the road was almost deserted. I walked more and more slowly, and shouted to Premila, from time to time, "Wait for me!" with increasing peevishness.

---

12. **tonga** *n.:* two-wheeled carriage.
13. **coolies** *n.:* unskilled laborers.

Vocabulary
peevishness (pē′vish·nis) *n.:* irritability.

She spoke to me only once, and that was to tell me to carry my notebook on my head, because of the sun.

When we got to our house, the ayah was just taking a tray of lunch into Mother's room. She immediately started a long, worried questioning about what are you children doing back here at this hour of the day.

Mother looked very startled and very concerned and asked Premila what had happened.

Premila said, "We had our test today, and She made me and the other Indians sit at the back of the room, with a desk between each one."

Mother said, "Why was that, darling?"

"She said it was because Indians cheat," Premila added. "So I don't think we should go back to that school."

Mother looked very distant and was silent a long time. At last she said, "Of course not, darling." She sounded displeased.

We all shared the curry she was having for lunch, and afterward I was sent off to the beautifully familiar bedroom for my siesta. I could hear Mother and Premila talking through the open door.

Mother said, "Do you suppose she understood all that?"

Premila said, "I shouldn't think so. She's a baby."

Mother said, "Well, I hope it won't bother her."

Of course, they were both wrong. I understood it perfectly, and I remember it all very clearly. But I put it happily away, because it had all happened to a girl called Cynthia, and I never was really particularly interested in her. ■

Meet the Writer

Santha Rama Rau

A Stranger in Her Own Land

Santha Rama Rau (1923–   ) was born into one of India's most influential families but has spent most of her life in other lands. Her father was a knighted diplomat, her mother a social reformer. Santha Rama Rau made her first trip to England at the age of six and returned for a much longer stay when she was eleven. In 1939, as war was breaking out in Europe, Lady Rama Rau took her two daughters back to India for safety. Feeling somewhat like an outsider, Santha made a conscious effort to reorient herself to her homeland and her extended family, and she recorded her impressions in her first book, *Home to India* (1944). In 1947, she witnessed the turmoil of India's independence from Britain. Five years later she married an American and settled in New York City.

Rama Rau eventually published many insightful travel books, as well as two novels, *Remember the House* (1956) and *The Adventuress* (1970). She also adapted E. M. Forster's novel *A Passage to India* into a play. Her autobiography *Gifts of Passage,* from which this selection is excerpted, was published in 1961.

Response and Analysis

Reading Check

1. Why are Santha and Premila sent to the English school?

2. How does the headmistress react to their names? What does she do?

3. Name two ways in which the Indian girls who have been at the school awhile imitate the English girls.

4. Why does Premila take Santha out of school in the middle of the day?

Thinking Critically

5. What does the mother mean when she makes the remark on page 114 about burying a dog's tail? Do her daughters' experiences in school prove she is right or wrong? Explain.

6. **Compare and contrast** aspects of Indian life and values with the values promoted in the English school. What other examples of cultural differences do you find in this story?

7. The selection has two **main characters** (Santha and Premila) and two **subordinate characters** (the mother and the headmistress). How would you describe each character's traits? Find details of **characterization** to support your descriptions.

8. Based on the last paragraph, explain how Santha resolves her **conflict** with the headmistress.

9. How do you think Santha Rama Rau would answer Juliet's question "What's in a name?" How important do you think a person's name is to his or her sense of identity? (Look back at your Quickwrite notes from page 112—have your ideas changed? How?) 🖉

10. This story takes place more than seventy years ago and half a world away. Do you think events like these stemming from prejudice take place today in other settings? Explain. Then, express what you think is the story's **theme,** or insight about life.

Extending and Evaluating

11. Santha Rama Rau doesn't directly tell us her thoughts and feelings as she looks back on her experiences as a five-year-old. Do you think her story would have been more powerful, or less, if she'd stated her thoughts and feelings directly? Explain.

WRITING

Between Two Worlds

Rama Rau had the experience of living in two cultures. Can you think of someone— a relative, friend, or neighbor—who has come to this country and has had to adapt to American ways? Write a short biographical narrative describing the person and some experiences he or she had. If you don't know anyone personally, research and write about an author such as Julia Alvarez or Judith Ortiz Cofer.

▶ **Use "Writing a Biographical Narrative," pages 122–129, for help with this assignment.**

Name Yourself

Think about a different name you'd choose for yourself. It might be a name you've sometimes wished you had; it might be a perfectly ordinary name that just happens to be different from yours. It might be a name you'd take if you lived in another culture. Visualize yourself as the bearer of that name. Then, write a brief **character sketch** of yourself with your new name.

SKILLS FOCUS

Literary Skills
Analyze character.

Reading Skills
Compare and contrast.

Writing Skills
Write a biographical narrative. Write a character sketch.

Vocabulary Development

Putting Words in Context: Cluster Diagrams

PRACTICE

Organize what you know about each word in the Word Bank (you can skip *precarious*) by making a cluster diagram like the one below. Work with a partner to brainstorm several questions that suggest **contexts** in which the word is used appropriately. Then, list words or phrases that answer your questions.

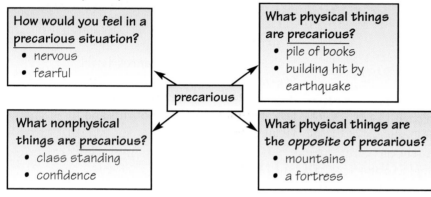

How would you feel in a precarious situation?
- nervous
- fearful

What physical things are precarious?
- pile of books
- building hit by earthquake

precarious

What nonphysical things are precarious?
- class standing
- confidence

What physical things are the *opposite* of precarious?
- mountains
- a fortress

Grammar Link

Who's Who? Making Pronouns Clear

SKILLS FOCUS

Vocabulary Skills
Use words in context.

Grammar Skills
Use clear pronoun references.

Unclear pronoun reference, a common mistake, causes misunderstandings. A **pronoun** must clearly refer to its **antecedent,** the noun or pronoun that the pronoun replaces. Avoid unclear, or **ambiguous,** pronoun references, which occur when a pronoun can have more than one antecedent. One way to pin down your meaning is to replace the unclear pronoun with the noun to which it refers.

UNCLEAR Although Santha is five and her sister, Premila, is eight, she understands what happened. [Who understands— Santha or Premila?]

CLEAR Although Santha is five and her sister, Premila, is eight, Santha understands what happened.

PRACTICE

Reword the following sentences to correct any unclear pronoun references.

1. The British girls and the Indian girls eat sandwiches for lunch, but they do not like them.

2. Premila and Santha like the school at first, but soon she is angered by something that happens to her.

3. Premila and Santha enter the mother's room, and she talks to her about whether the incident had upset her.

▶ **For more help, see Clear Pronoun Reference, 4i, in the Language Handbook.**

FICTION

Money Isn't Everything

It's the mid–nineteenth century, and Catherine Sloper lives with her father in New York City's fashionable Washington Square. Catherine, a plain, awkward, and soft-spoken young woman, is generally thought to be "unmarriageable." When a poor but handsome suitor begins to court her, her father tries to end the relationship, believing that the young man has eyes only for the family fortune. Should Catherine listen to her father or to her heart? *Washington Square,* a novel by Henry James, reveals a woman's inner strength in a way that you might not expect.

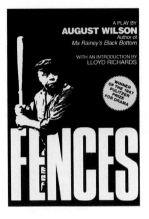

DRAMA

Father and Son

The father and son in August Wilson's 1987 Pulitzer Prize–winning play **Fences** have conflicting visions for the boy's future. Having once been excluded from baseball's Major Leagues because of his race, fifty-three-year-old Troy Maxson finds it difficult to encourage his son's ball-playing ambitions. Is he an overbearing dad, or is he just looking out for his son's best interests?

NONFICTION

Growing Up Despite It All

Gary Soto's **A Summer Life** reveals what it was like to grow up in a Mexican American family in California's San Joaquin Valley. In a series of funny and often touching essays, Soto focuses on topics like "The Shirt," "The Haircut," "The Drive-In Movies," "The Computer Date," and other vivid scenes and memories from a mischievous boy's life.

NONFICTION

The Smart One

Jade Snow Wong was one of many children in her parents' California home, but she was always regarded as the smart member of her family. She excelled in school and received tutoring from her father, learning the honorable, traditional ways of Chinese culture. However, Jade Snow's education afforded her the opportunity to have a life that the traditional Chinese girl didn't have. You can read about Jade Snow's struggle to unite her roots with her newfound American ways in her acclaimed autobiography, **Fifth Chinese Daughter.**

Writing a Biographical Narrative

Writing Assignment
Write a biographical narrative about a person you know well, creating a controlling impression that communicates the significance of your subject.

Earlier in this collection you read a fictional narrative—Alice Walker's short story "Everyday Use." In that story, the narrator sketches vivid portraits of her daughters by noting Maggie's thin, awkward arms and Dee's haughty walk. Now it's your turn to describe a person by writing a **biographical narrative,** a nonfiction account of someone who is important to you. In your narrative, you'll share anecdotes and concrete details that show how you feel about that person and your relationship.

Prewriting

Choose a Subject

A Face in the Crowd To pick a subject for your biographical narrative, make a list of the most interesting people you know well. Picture the face of each person on the list and jot down what makes that person both interesting and **significant** to you. Then, list anecdotes—short, true stories—about each person on your list. Pick anecdotes that show why each person is meaningful to you. Look at how one writer took notes in a three-column chart.

Who	Significance	Anecdotes
Kelly	Her way of looking at life makes her interesting. She always helps me see a different side of things. We've been good friends since we both joined the Photography Club.	1. First notice of Kelly in middle school during a class discussion 2. My visit to Kelly's home 3. Kelly in the photography darkroom 4. Kelly's visit to my home
Aunt Thelma	Her wide-ranging knowledge makes her interesting. I've known her all my life.	1. Aunt Thelma teaching me to ride a bike 2. Aunt Thelma trying to teach me to sew 3. My trip to the museum with Aunt Thelma

SKILLS FOCUS

Writing Skills
Write a biographical narrative. Choose a subject.

Now, choose the subject from your list that prompts the strongest and most specific memories and feelings in you; when you write your biographical narrative, you'll need an abundance of details about your subject.

Create a Controlling Impression

Show, Don't Tell Because a biographical narrative is different from an essay, don't blurt out the importance of your subject in a traditional thesis statement. Instead, *hint* at your subject's significance in the beginning anecdote and let the rest of the anecdotes in your narrative—and the narrative as a whole—confirm the hint by creating a **controlling impression** of your subject, from which your readers can infer the subject's significance.

How do you create a controlling impression? The answer is in the **anecdotes** you narrate and the **details** you choose to include in each of them. For example, the student chose to write about her friend Kelly, whose significance is that she helps the writer see the world around her in different ways. The anecdotes and details in her narrative contribute convincingly to a single controlling impression of Kelly: She is generous in sharing her thoughtful and unique way of looking at the world around her.

Gather Details

Down to the Last Detail Create the controlling impression you desire by using **concrete sensory details**—details of sight, sound, smell, touch, and taste—to describe the actions, movements, and gestures of your subject. In addition, describe your thoughts and feelings about your subject and your relationship with that person. To share your thoughts and feelings, use **interior monologue**—the words you say to yourself in your head.

Also, use sensory details to describe the **specific places,** or **settings,** where each anecdote occurred. The sensory details you use will create **images** of place and time in your readers' minds and create a sense of the mood or atmosphere of the setting. For example, the writer of the sample narrative on page 125 included a description of birds in one setting—"their dark bodies distinctly silhouetted against the orange sun setting behind them"—to create an image that communicates an atmosphere of peacefulness and warmth.

Talk the Talk Using **dialogue** is another way to develop a controlling impression of your subject. Re-create your subject's own words and manner of speaking as exactly as you can. That means you can use slang and contractions. Using realistic dialogue in your paper will allow your readers to imagine a complete picture of your subject.

SKILLS FOCUS

Writing Skills
Create a controlling impression. Gather details.

Look below at the notes the student took for the opening anecdote of her narrative. Notice how she divided her notes into categories.

Anecdote 1

- **Where and when:** three years ago in our overcrowded English classroom at Pinewood Middle School
- **How Kelly looked:** dark red hair; wild curls escaping ponytail; infectious smile
- **What happened:** Kelly explained to the class why a character everybody disliked was really a likable character.
- **How Kelly acted:** Kelly spoke earnestly; she leaned forward and chopped the air with her hand for emphasis as she talked.
- **What Kelly said:** "I *do* like him."
- **What I thought:** I thought she looked friendly. Her explanation of the class's misunderstanding of the character gave me a glimpse into her unique way of seeing things.

Plan Organization and Pacing

Plot Your Course After collecting details, think of the most logical **organizational strategies** you can use to present those details. Most narratives are related in **chronological order,** beginning with the anecdote that occurred first and going on to the second, third, and so on. You will probably want to relate the **sequence of events** that make up an anecdote in chronological order, too. Within that framework, you may also want to organize some details **spatially,** or according to their location. For example, you might describe the setting of your aunt's wedding from left to right, top to bottom, or near to far. Alternatively, you could describe a friend's appearance from the top of her cinnamon-colored mop of a hairdo down to the tips of her aqua-blue painted toenails.

Pace Yourself Vary the **pace** of your narrative to show the passage of time or a change in the mood of your narrative. Pace can be conveyed by your choice of words and sentences. Short words and simple sentences are easier and quicker to read, so they speed up the events and make the mood seem hurried. Longer words and complex sentences tend to cause readers to slow down, drawing out the events and creating a serious mood.

SKILLS FOCUS

PRACTICE & APPLY 1 Use the prewriting steps in this section to choose a subject and decide upon the controlling impression you want to create. Then, gather the details you will need and plan the organization and pace of your narrative.

Writing Skills
Plan the organization and pacing.

Writing

Writing a Biographical Narrative

A Writer's Model

The View from a Different Angle

The first time I really noticed Kelly was during the first week of school at Pinewood Middle School three years ago. I spied her three rows over in English class and thought she looked friendly and confident. Her cinnamon-colored hair was pulled up in a haphazard ponytail from which a dozen mischievous curls had escaped. Her eyes crinkled merrily when she smiled.

Our class was discussing a character in the story we'd just read, someone who nearly everyone agreed was completely unlikable. Just then, Kelly raised her hand and said earnestly, "But I *do* like him." She leaned forward, emphatically chopping the air with her hands as she explained the ways she thought we had misunderstood the character. Slowly, our classmates began to nod in agreement. That was my first glimmer into Kelly's unique way of seeing things.

Later in the semester, we both joined the Photography Club and were matched as partners so we could share equipment. I hadn't realized that Kelly had a lot of her own photography equipment until she invited me over to try it out. When I arrived at her magnificent home—really a mansion—the first thing I noticed was a long hallway filled with pictures both old and new. I asked Kelly if the pictures in the hall had anything to do with why she wanted to be in the Photography Club. She looked puzzled for a minute, then smiled and

(continued)

BEGINNING
Background information

Details of appearance

Opening anecdote

Details of speech, gestures

Hint at subject's significance

MIDDLE
Second anecdote

Details of setting and action

(continued)

Sensory details

said, "Not really, but what I *do* like about some of these pictures are the frames." I hadn't noticed them at all before, but it was true—some of the pictures had very intricate, hand-carved wooden frames around them. Kelly told me about the wood used in the frames, olive wood from hillside groves by the sea near her family's village in Italy. She described it so vividly that I could smell the salt in the air! As I came to know Kelly better, I realized that noticing the frame, as opposed to the picture, was just one way Kelly saw things differently.

Hint at controlling impression

Third anecdote

In the same way, Kelly deliberated on the details of her work in the Photography Club. While I focused on the technical aspects of the camera, Kelly concentrated very intensely on the "art" of photography, especially in the darkroom. One time she spent hours bent over her work in the darkroom, developing a photograph of the moon rising at sunset. It came out beautifully, with both the moon and the sun appearing with almost exactly the same brightness against the sky. I knew I would never have her vision—or patience.

Sensory details
Writer's thoughts

Fourth anecdote

Details of setting

Although I didn't want to, I soon invited Kelly to my house. I was a little embarrassed because, well, my apartment seems sort of meager compared to a big house like Kelly's. I knew she had arrived when I heard her singing my name from my open bedroom window. When I looked down, she waved, and I ran down to let her in through the gate. When she came into my room, she made me flush with warmth as she praised the job I had done painting my room.

Writer's feeling

END

Interior monologue
Slow pace
Image

Summary of significance

We sat on my bed, looking out my small, three-by-four window. "I wish we had a yard," I said as I looked down to the ground outside. "Like your family," I thought, more than a little jealous of Kelly's lush yard. Kelly replied by pointing out the sixth-story window to the expansive sky as a flock of Canada geese flew by. The birds moved in unison, their dark bodies distinctly silhouetted against the orange sun setting behind them. "You have the whole sky," she said. Kelly was always opening my eyes, teaching me to see the precious things I hadn't noticed and to understand the value of what I have instead of what I do not.

PRACTICE & APPLY 2 Using the framework on page 125 and the Writer's Model above, write the first draft of your biographical narrative. Return to the Prewriting section to freshen your understanding of basic concepts, as necessary.

Revising

Evaluate and Revise Your Narrative

Methodical Mending Even the best editors can't revise a piece of writing after just one reading. To edit your draft thoroughly, read it at least twice. In the first reading, focus on content and organization. In the second reading, consider style.

▶ **First Reading: Content and Organization** Using the questions in the following chart, carefully evaluate the content and organization of your narrative. As you work through the list, keep your **purpose** and intended **audience** in mind. Because the purpose of this biography is, in large part, to express your feelings and observations about your subject, your language may be **less formal** than in other papers you write in school. First-person pronouns and informal language, especially in dialogue, are acceptable here.

PEER REVIEW

Ask a classmate to read your narrative and suggest ways you might improve its content, organization, or style. For example, a classmate might suggest ways to better communicate the controlling impression of your narrative.

Rubric: Writing a Biographical Narrative

Evaluation Questions	▶ Tips	▶ Revision Techniques
① Does the narrative provide an interesting introduction to the subject and hint at the subject's significance to the writer?	▶ **Underline** the vivid introduction of the subject. **Double underline** any hint of the subject's significance.	▶ **Replace** the opening sentences with a striking or intriguing view of the subject. **Add** a hint about the subject's significance to you.
② Do all anecdotes contribute to the controlling impression of the subject?	▶ **Star** each sentence that begins a separate anecdote. In the margin **write a phrase** that tells the impression of the subject each anecdote gives.	▶ **Cut** anecdotes that do not support the controlling impression. **Add** relevant anecdotes.
③ Are concrete sensory details used to describe all people and places? Are the writer's and others' thoughts and feelings described?	▶ **Highlight** all concrete sensory details. **Check** the thoughts and feelings of the writer and others.	▶ **Add** concrete sensory details or **elaborate** on existing details. **Add** thoughts and feelings of the writer and others.
④ Are anecdotes and descriptions organized logically?	▶ **Number** the anecdotes narrated. **Bracket** each description of a person or setting.	▶ **Reorder** incidents in chronological order or descriptions in spatial order.
⑤ Does the conclusion reinforce the controlling impression and sum up the subject's significance to the writer?	▶ **Box** sentences enhancing the controlling impression. **Circle** sentences that sum up the subject's significance.	▶ **Add** a final comment, quotation, or image to enhance the controlling impression. **Add** a clear statement of the subject's significance, if necessary.

Second Reading: Style During your second reading, focus your attention on the style of your narrative. Look carefully at the words you have chosen, particularly **adverbs**—words that modify verbs, adjectives, and other adverbs. Some adverbs are used so often that they have lost their punch. Use the following style guidelines to help you eliminate overused adverbs.

Style Guidelines

Evaluation Question	▶ **Tip**	▶ **Revision Technique**
● Does the narrative contain worn-out adverbs?	▶ **Highlight** worn-out adverbs, such as *very, really, awfully, rather, extremely,* and *somewhat*.	▶ **Replace** the overused adverbs with more precise ones, or **delete** the adverbs.

ANALYZING THE REVISION PROCESS
Study these revisions, and answer the questions that follow.

Our class was discussing a character in the story we'd just

read, someone who nearly everyone agreed was ~~very~~ *completely* unlikable.

replace

Just then, Kelly raised her hand and said ~~really~~ earnestly, "But I

delete

do like him." She explained the ways she thought we had mis- *leaned forward, emphatically chopping the air* *with her hands as she*

add

understood the character. Slowly, our classmates began to nod

in agreement. That was my first glimmer into Kelly's unique

way of seeing things.

Responding to the Revision Process
1. Why did the writer replace *very* with *completely* in the first sentence and delete *really* from the second sentence?
2. Why did the writer make the addition to the third sentence?

PRACTICE & APPLY ⑧ Using the guidelines in this section, evaluate and revise the content, organization, and style of your narrative. You may want to work with a classmate throughout the revision process.

SKILLS FOCUS

Writing Skills
Revise for content and style.

Publishing

Proofread and Publish Your Narrative

Put Your Best Foot Forward You want your final draft to make a good impression, of course. To ensure that it does, carefully proofread it for errors in grammar, usage, and mechanics, and correct any mistakes you may find. When in doubt, consult a peer or your teacher.

May I Introduce You? You've worked exceptionally hard to capture the essence of your subject—what makes him or her a unique individual of great significance to you. Now, introduce your subject to the wider world with one of these suggestions.

- Give or send a copy of your narrative to your subject and ask for a response. In particular, you might ask if your portrait matches the way your subject sees himself or herself.

- Stage a group reading with other classmates. You might even hold your reading at a time when the people you have written about—or others who know them well—can attend.

- Submit your narrative to a student magazine. Many periodicals regularly publish biographical narratives. Ask your teacher or school librarian for the names of periodicals that publish biographical narratives.

- Exchange narratives with a peer from your English class. Then, discuss which literary characters have something in common with the subjects of your biographies. Be sure to offer specific evidence for your ideas.

Reflect on Your Narrative

A Backward Glance Before writing, you thought deeply about your subject and what makes him or her special to you. Now, reflect on the process of writing about that person. Use these questions to help you sort out your thoughts.

- What is your favorite line or passage in your narrative? Why?

- Did your view of your subject change as you worked on your narrative? Why do you think so?

- If someone wrote a biographical narrative about *you*, what controlling impression might it offer? Why do you think so?

 PRACTICE & APPLY 4 If possible, collaborate with a classmate to proofread your narrative for errors in grammar, usage, and mechanics. Then, publish and reflect on your biographical narrative using the suggestions and questions above.

TIP As you proofread, keep a sharp eye out for errors in the **conventions** of standard American English usage. In particular, watch for errors in punctuating dialogue, a common problem in biographical writing. For more on **using quotation marks,** see Quotation Marks, 13c–l, in the Language Handbook.

SKILLS FOCUS

Writing Skills
Proofread, especially for correct use of quotation marks.

Test Practice

Character

DIRECTIONS: Read the following short story. Then, read and respond to the questions that follow.

Powder

Tobias Wolff

Just before Christmas my father took me skiing at Mount Baker. He'd had to fight for the privilege of my company, because my mother was still angry with him for sneaking me into a nightclub during our last visit, to see Thelonious Monk.[1]

He wouldn't give up. He promised, hand on heart, to take good care of me and have me home for dinner on Christmas Eve, and she relented. But as we were checking out of the lodge that morning it began to snow, and in this snow he observed some quality that made it necessary for us to get in one last run. We got in several last runs. He was indifferent to my fretting.[2] Snow whirled around us in bitter, blinding squalls, hissing like sand, and still we skied. As the lift bore us to the peak yet again, my father looked at his watch and said, "Criminey. This'll have to be a fast one."

By now I couldn't see the trail. There was no point in trying. I stuck to him like white on rice and did what he did and somehow made it to the bottom without sailing off a cliff. We returned our skis and my father put chains on the Austin-Healy while I swayed from foot

to foot, clapping my mittens and wishing I were home. I could see everything. The green tablecloth, the plates with the holly pattern, the red candles waiting to be lit.

We passed a diner on our way out. "You want some soup?" my father asked. I shook my head. "Buck up," he said. "I'll get you there. Right, doctor?"

I was supposed to say, "Right, doctor," but I didn't say anything.

A state trooper waved us down outside the resort. A pair of sawhorses were blocking the road. The trooper came up to our car and bent down to my father's window. His face was bleached by the cold. Snowflakes clung to his eyebrows and to the fur trim of his jacket and cap.

"Don't tell me," my father said.

The trooper told him. The road was closed. It might get cleared, it might not. Storm took everyone by surprise. So much, so fast. Hard to get people moving. Christmas Eve. What can you do?

My father said, "Look. We're talking about four, five inches. I've taken this car through worse than that."

The trooper straightened up, boots creaking. His face was out of sight but I could hear him. "The road is closed."

My father sat with both hands on the wheel, rubbing the wood with his thumbs. He looked at the barricade for a long time. He seemed to be trying to master the idea

---

1. **Thelonious Monk** (1917–1982): American jazz musician, famed as a pianist and composer; one of the creators of the bop style of jazz.
2. **fretting** *v.* used as *n.*: worrying.

SKILLS FOCUS

Pages 130–133 cover
Literary Skills
Analyze character traits and interactions.

of it. Then he thanked the trooper, and with a weird, old-maidy show of caution turned the car around. "Your mother will never forgive me for this," he said.

"We should have left before," I said. "Doctor."

He didn't speak to me again until we were both in a booth at the diner, waiting for our burgers. "She won't forgive me," he said. "Do you understand? Never."

"I guess," I said, but no guesswork was required; she wouldn't forgive him.

"I can't let that happen." He bent toward me. "I'll tell you what I want. I want us to be together again. Is that what you want?"

I wasn't sure, but I said, "Yes, sir."

He bumped my chin with his knuckles. "That's all I needed to hear."

When we finished eating he went to the pay phone in the back of the diner, then joined me in the booth again. I figured he'd called my mother, but he didn't give a report. He sipped at his coffee and stared out the window at the empty road. "Come on!" When the trooper's car went past, lights flashing, he got up and dropped some money on the check. "Okay. *Vámonos.*"[3]

The wind had died. The snow was falling straight down, less of it now; lighter. We drove away from the resort, right up to the barricade. "Move it," my father told me. When I looked at him he said, "What are you waiting for?" I got out and dragged one of the sawhorses aside, then pushed it back after he drove through. When I got inside the car, he said, "Now you're an accomplice.[4] We go down

together." He put the car in gear and looked at me. "Joke, doctor."

"Funny, doctor."

Down the first long stretch I watched the road behind us, to see if the trooper was on our tail. The barricade vanished. Then there was nothing but snow: snow on the road, snow kicking up from the chains, snow on the trees, snow in the sky; and our trail in the snow. I faced around and had a shock. The lie of the road behind us had been marked by our own tracks, but there were no tracks ahead of us. My father was breaking virgin snow between a line of tall trees. He was humming "Stars Fell on Alabama." I felt snow brush along the floorboards under my feet. To keep my hands from shaking I clamped them between my knees.

My father grunted in a thoughtful way and said, "Don't ever try this yourself."

"I won't."

"That's what you say now, but someday you'll get your license and then you'll think you can do anything. Only you won't be able to do this. You need, I don't know—a certain instinct."

"Maybe I have it."

"You don't. You have your strong points, but not . . . you know. I only mention it because I don't want you to get the idea this is something just anybody can do. I'm a great driver. That's not a virtue, okay? It's just a fact, and one you should be aware of. Of course you have to give the old heap some credit, too—there aren't many cars I'd try this with. Listen!"

I listened. I heard the slap of the chains, the stiff, jerky rasp of the wipers, the purr of the engine. It really did purr. The car was almost new. My father couldn't afford it, and

---

3. *Vámonos* (vä′mō·nōs): Spanish for "Let's go."
4. **accomplice** (ə·käm′plis) *n.:* partner in crime.

kept promising to sell it, but here it was.

I said, "Where do you think that police-man went to?"

"Are you warm enough?" He reached over and cranked up the blower. Then he turned off the wipers. We didn't need them. The clouds had brightened. A few sparse, feathery flakes drifted into our slipstream and were swept away. We left the trees and entered a broad field of snow that ran level for a while and then tilted sharply downward. Orange stakes had been planted at intervals in two parallel lines and my father ran a course between them, though they were far enough apart to leave considerable doubt in my mind as to where exactly the road lay. He was humming again, doing little scat riffs[5] around the melody.

"Okay then. What are my strong points?"

"Don't get me started," he said. "It'd take all day."

"Oh, right. Name one."

"Easy. You always think ahead."

True. I always thought ahead. I was a boy who kept his clothes on numbered hangers to ensure proper rotation. I both-ered my teachers for homework assign-ments far ahead of their due dates so I could make up schedules. I thought ahead, and that was why I knew that there would

be other troopers waiting for us at the end of our ride, if we got there. What I did not know was that my father would wheedle and plead his way past them—he didn't sing "O Tannenbaum"[6] but just about—and get me home for dinner, buying a little more time before my mother decided to make the split final. I knew we'd get caught; I was resigned to it. And maybe for this reason I stopped moping and began to enjoy myself.

Why not? This was one for the books. Like being in a speedboat, only better. You can't go downhill in a boat. And it was all ours. And it kept coming, the laden trees, the unbroken surface of snow, the sudden white vistas. Here and there I saw hints of the road, ditches, fences, stakes, but not so many that I could have found my way. But then I didn't have to. My father in his forty-eighth year, rumpled, kind, bankrupt of honor, flushed with certainty. He was a great driver. All persuasion, no coercion.[7] Such subtlety at the wheel, such tactful pedalwork. I actually trusted him. And the best was yet to come—switchbacks and hairpins impossible to describe. Except maybe to say this: If you haven't driven fresh powder,[8] you haven't driven.

---

5. **scat riffs:** short, improvised musical phrases in the style of scat, a kind of jazz singing.

6. **"O Tannenbaum":** title of a German Christ-mas carol, known in English as "O Christmas Tree."
7. **coercion** (kō · ur′shən) *n.:* use of force.
8. **powder** *n.:* light, dry snow, considered to be best for skiing.

Collection 2: Skills Review

1. Two adjectives that can be used to describe the father's **character traits** are —
   - **A** daring, humorous
   - **B** dull, hesitant
   - **C** mean, responsible
   - **D** fearful, serious

2. The father's drive down the mountain is **motivated** by his desire to —
   - **F** seek thrills no matter how great the danger
   - **G** prove his skill as a driver
   - **H** prove his concern for his son's safety
   - **J** keep his promise to his wife

3. The boy's mother, whom we never meet, influences the events of the **plot** since we infer that she might —
   - **A** punish the son for being late
   - **B** send out a search party
   - **C** celebrate Christmas without him
   - **D** prevent the father from seeing his son again

4. The relationship between which of the following characters in the story does *not* involve **conflict**?
   - **F** The father and the state trooper
   - **G** The father and the mother
   - **H** The son and his mother
   - **J** The father and his son

5. From what the **narrator** says about himself, which of the following statements can we infer?
   - **A** He misses his mother.
   - **B** He is very self-confident.
   - **C** He is a bully.
   - **D** He is a worrier.

6. From what the **narrator** says about his habits, we learn that he is —
   - **F** sloppy and reckless
   - **G** cautious and organized
   - **H** carefree and fun loving
   - **J** angry and depressed

7. When the son calls his father "rumpled, kind, bankrupt of honor, flushed with certainty," we can infer that the son —
   - **A** fears his father
   - **B** loves his father
   - **C** despises his father
   - **D** doesn't know his father well

8. The **dialogue** in the story between the father and son reveals the father's —
   - **F** love for his son
   - **G** need to be serious
   - **H** lack of self-confidence
   - **J** lack of humor

Constructed Response

9. How does the narrator feel at the end of the story? Support your answer with details from the text.

Collection 2: Skills Review

Vocabulary Skills

Context Clues

DIRECTIONS: Using context clues to help you, choose the answer that gives the best definition of the underlined word.

1. Always nervous and shy, Maggie was cowering behind Mama's back when Dee took their pictures. *Cowering* means —

   A huddling in fear
   B laughing with amusement
   C making strange faces
   D protesting loudly

2. Dee's boyfriend had built his philosophy of life on certain doctrines. *Doctrines* means —

   F famous sayings
   G principles
   H relationships
   J medical procedures

3. In her desire to find family heirlooms, Dee was caught rifling through Mama's belongings. *Rifling* means —

   A slashing
   B shooting
   C searching roughly
   D stealing

4. Jing-mei's mother wanted her to be a prodigy like Waverly Jong, who was an extraordinarily talented chess champion. *Prodigy* means —

   F daughter
   G young genius
   H musician
   J scholar

5. Jing-mei performed listlessly, her head resting on one arm. She seemed tired and bored. *Listlessly* means —

   A without fear
   B without embarrassment
   C without talent
   D without energy

6. Jing-mei played only discordant music, and Old Chong, her deaf teacher, had no idea how earsplitting her playing sounded. *Discordant* means —

   F unharmonious
   G melodious
   H popular
   J rhythmic

7. Unlike the success Jing-mei had imagined, her performance was a fiasco that shamed her parents. *Fiasco* means —

   A misunderstanding
   B failure
   C triumph
   D surprise

8. Santha shyly entered the classroom of strange, unfriendly-looking students and was immediately intimidated by them. *Intimidated* means —

   F made to feel afraid
   G surprised
   H delighted
   J questioned

SKILLS FOCUS

Vocabulary Skills
Use context clues.

Test Practice

DIRECTIONS: Read the following paragraph from a draft of a student's biographical narrative. Then, answer the questions below it.

(1) Before my next-door neighbor became my friend, I saw her only once a day when she shuffled out of her house to get her mail. (2) Her appearance frightened me for a while. (3) One day I was locked out of my house after school and needed to borrow her telephone. (4) "She's going to slam this door right in my face," I thought as I knocked, but to my surprise she greeted me warmly and let me call my mom. (5) While I waited for my mother, my neighbor showed me her collection of glass animal figures and told me to keep the one I liked best. (6) I chose a tiny glass chameleon that changed colors as the light struck it from different angles—a reminder that appearances can be deceiving.

1. Which of the following techniques of narrative writing did the writer use in the first part of sentence 4?

   A imagery

   B sensory details

   C dialogue

   D interior monologue

2. To portray the setting of the passage better, the writer could

   F relate how scary it was to knock on the neighbor's door

   G describe her neighbor's home

   H tell what her neighbor was wearing

   J describe the writer's own room

3. Which character description would support the ideas in sentence 2?

   A My neighbor is retired and lives alone, but her son often visits.

   B She bought a bright red leash for her white poodle.

   C She talks to everyone and leaves little presents for the mail carrier.

   D Her wild gray hair frames her dark eyes that dart suspiciously.

4. Which clause could replace the last clause of sentence 6 and eliminate a cliché?

   F that beauty is in the eye of the beholder

   G that you shouldn't judge a book by its cover

   H that things appear different from different perspectives

   J that the apple doesn't fall far from the tree

5. Which sentence could the writer add to summarize the significance of the subject?

   A I learned that my neighbor's appearance contrasts with her personality.

   B I learned that I live next door to a scary woman who is evil.

   C I learned that people's appearances often reflect their natures.

   D I learned that my neighborhood is full of interesting people.

SKILLS FOCUS

Writing Skills
Write a biographical narrative.

Collection 3

Narrator and Voice

INFORMATIONAL READING FOCUS

GENERATING RESEARCH QUESTIONS

What I am trying to achieve is a voice
sitting by a fireplace telling you a story
on a winter's evening.

—Truman Capote

Let Me Help (1953) by Anna Mary Robertson
("Grandma") Moses.
Oil on panel (18″ × 22″).

Copyright © 1953 (renewed 1981), Grandma Moses Properties
Co., New York. Photo courtesy of Owen Gallery, New York, NY.

go.hrw.com

INTERNET

Collection
Resources

Keyword: LE5 10-3

Elements of Literature

Point of View *by* John Leggett
THE STORY'S VOICE

Omniscient Point of View: Know-It-All

Point of view—the vantage point from which a writer tells a story—has a powerful effect. The traditional vantage point is the **omniscient** (äm·nish′ənt) **point of view.** The **omniscient** ("all-knowing") **narrator,** a godlike observer who knows everything that is going on in the story, can see into every character's heart and mind—and tell us what each character is thinking. This storyteller is altogether outside the story's action.

A newly married pair had boarded this coach at San Antonio. The man's face was reddened from many days in the wind and sun. . . . From time to time he looked down respectfully at his attire. He sat with a hand on each knee, like a man waiting in a barber's shop. The glances he devoted to other passengers were furtive and shy.

    The bride was not pretty, nor was she very young. She wore a dress of blue cashmere with small reservations of velvet here and there, and with steel buttons abounding. She continually twisted her head to regard her puff sleeves, very stiff, straight, and high. They embarrassed her.
—Stephen Crane, from "The Bride Comes to Yellow Sky"

First-Person Point of View: "I" Speaks

At the opposite extreme from the omniscient point of view is the **first-person point of view.** In stories told in the **first person,** an "I" tells the story. This "I" also participates in the action, usually as the main character. (Literary critics often use the term **persona** to refer to this fictional first-person narrator.) The first-person point of view presents only what the "I" character sees, hears, knows, thinks, and feels. Suppose, for instance, Stephen Crane had the bride telling her own story.

We boarded the Pullman car at San Antonio and sat stiffly in the plush seat. I was so nervous, and I noticed that my new husband seemed ill at ease. Did he regret our marriage already? I felt myself falling in love with his shyness.

A first-person narrator may or may not be **credible** or **reliable**—that is, he or she may not be objective, honest, or even perceptive about what's happening. In fact, the whole point of a story told from the first-person point of view may lie in the contrast between what the narrator tells us and what the writer allows us to understand in spite of the narrator.

Third-Person-Limited Point of View: Zooming In

Between the two extremes of the omniscient and first-person points of view lies the **third-person-limited point of view.** Here the story is told by an outside observer, who frequently refers to characters with third-person pronouns *(he, she, they)*. Unlike the omniscient narrator this narrator views the action from the vantage point of one character, and plot events are limited to what this character experiences or observes. Suppose Crane used a third-person-limited narrator

INTERNET
More About Point of View
Keyword: LE5 10-3

SKILLS FOCUS

Literary Skills
Understand narrators, or points of view (omniscient, first-person, and third-person limited), tone, and voice.

to tell his story and zoomed in on the husband:

He was a working man—a sheriff—and dressed in a new suit for the first time in his life. His face was like a map, full of lines from exposure to the sun. He was terrified of what he'd done—married a woman he hardly knew—but pleased with himself and his quiet bride.

Determining a Story's Point of View

When you read fiction, ask the following five questions about point of view:

1. Who is telling the story?
2. How much does this narrator know and understand?
3. How much does this narrator want me to know?
4. Can I trust this narrator?
5. In what ways would the story be different if someone else were telling it?

Voice: Hearing the Writer

Voice refers to the writer's distinctive use of language in a story, the choice of words (**diction**), and the attitude expressed (see **tone,** below). In fact, all the stylistic decisions a writer makes in a story contribute to the writer's voice. Although a writer's voice may evolve or vary, it tends to be consistent and recognizable from work to work.

In fiction a narrator can also be said to have a voice, as expressed by his or her way of speaking, use of language, and tone. The voice the author gives a narrator can strongly influence the story's tone and believability and even its plot. Imagine, for example, if "Everyday Use" were narrated

by a meek, listless character with no gift for observation, description, or speech.

Tone: It's an Attitude

Tone is the attitude a speaker or writer takes toward a subject, a character, or the reader. Like the tone of a spoken voice, the tone of a story may be sympathetic, critical, ironic, humorous, tragic, hopeful, bitter, and so on.

Point of view has a tremendous effect on a story's tone. A story told from the perspective of a madman who hates everyone but his saintly mother will be different in tone from the same story told by the saintly mother herself. It will be still more different from the story told by an outside narrator who can penetrate the mysteries of both mother and son.

Reproduced from the Saturday Evening Post.

Practice

Take a story you've read recently, and do the following exercises:

- Imagine the story as told from a different point of view, and write the opening paragraphs.
- Explain how changing the point of view affects the story.

By the Waters of Babylon

Make the Connection

Quickwrite 🖉

In Stephen Vincent Benét's fantasy you'll accompany John, the narrator, as he catches glimpses of a past civilization. Using what you know of world history, jot down some of the reasons why civilizations might disappear. What role do people play in their destruction?

Literary Focus

First-Person Point of View: "I" Tells the Story

When a story is told from the **first-person point of view,** two important things happen. First, we share immediately in the narrator's experience and feelings. Second, we know *only* what the narrator knows. All that we learn about the story's events and the other characters comes from the narrator's observations.

Writers often choose the first-person point of view to create a sense of intimacy, as if the narrator were a friend talking directly to us. In other words, writers create a **persona**—a "mask" or voice for their fictional narrator.

Sometimes a writer will purposely use an unreliable narrator, one that the reader suspects can't be trusted, to report events. In this story, Benét uses the point of view to limit our knowledge—we know only what the narrator tells us as he makes his journey to the Place of the Gods.

Setting: Where and When

The **setting** of a story is the time and place in which the action occurs. Writers use setting in various ways: to create a **mood,** or atmosphere (such as gloomy, peaceful, or ominous); to help reveal character; and sometimes to provide the story's main conflict. In "The Cold Equations" (page 164), for example, the characters are in conflict with their setting—the cold, harsh, and dangerous frontier of space. As you read, think about the role the setting plays in this story.

Reading Skills 📖

Drawing Conclusions: Detective Work

When you read mystery stories and other stories that present a puzzle, as "By the Waters of Babylon" does, you must act like a detective. You must look for clues and draw **conclusions** about what certain details in the story mean. As you read this story, be especially alert to clues to the **setting.** Read carefully the descriptions of objects and places. Think about what the narrator and the writer may *not* be telling you. Then, throw your own experience and knowledge into the mix as you try to solve the story's puzzles. Remember: Like a detective, you'll have to keep monitoring and revising your conclusions as new clues surface.

Background

The title of this story is an **allusion,** or reference, to Psalm 137 in the Bible. The psalm tells of the Israelites' sorrow over the destruction of their Temple in Zion (a reference to Jerusalem) and their enslavement in Babylon. The psalm begins, "By the waters of Babylon, there we sat down and wept, when we remembered Zion."

SKILLS FOCUS

Literary Skills
Understand first-person point of view.
Understand setting.

Reading Skills
Draw conclusions.

By the Waters of Babylon

Stephen Vincent Benét

*At night, I would lie awake and listen to the wind—
it seemed to me that it was the voice of the gods.*

The north and the west and the south are good hunting ground, but it is forbidden to go east. It is forbidden to go to any of the Dead Places except to search for metal, and then he who touches the metal must be a priest or the son of a priest. Afterward, both the man and the metal must be purified. These are the rules and the laws; they are well made. It is forbidden to cross the great river and look upon the place that was the Place of the Gods— this is most strictly forbidden. We do not even say its name though we know its name. It is there that spirits live, and demons—it is there that there are the ashes of the Great Burning. These things are forbidden—they have been forbidden since the beginning of time.

My father is a priest; I am the son of a priest. I have been in the Dead Places near us, with my father—at first, I was afraid. When my father went into the house to search for the metal, I stood by the door and my heart felt small and weak. It was a dead man's house, a spirit house. It did not have the smell of man, though there were old bones in a corner. But it is not fitting that a priest's son should show fear. I looked at the bones in the shadow and kept my voice still.

Then my father came out with the metal—a good, strong piece. He looked at me with both eyes but I had not run away. He gave me the metal to hold—I took it and did not die. So he knew that

I was truly his son and would be a priest in my time. That was when I was very young—nevertheless, my brothers would not have done it, though they are good hunters. After that, they gave me the good piece of meat and the warm corner by the fire. My father watched over me—he was glad that I should be a priest. But when I boasted or wept without a reason, he punished me more strictly than my brothers. That was right.

After a time, I myself was allowed to go into the dead houses and search for metal. So I learned the ways of those houses—and if I saw bones, I was no longer afraid. The bones are light and old—sometimes they will fall into dust if you touch them. But that is a great sin.

I was taught the chants and the spells—I was taught how to stop blood from a wound and many secrets. A priest must know many secrets—that was what my father said. If the hunters think we do all things by chants and spells, they may believe so—it does not hurt them. I was taught how to read in the old books and how to make the old writings—that was hard and took a long time. My knowledge made me happy—it was like a fire in my heart. Most of all, I liked to hear of the Old Days and the stories of the gods. I asked myself many questions that I could not answer, but it was good to ask them. At night, I would lie awake and listen to the wind—it seemed to me that it was the voice of the gods as they flew through the air.

We are not ignorant like the Forest People—our women spin wool on the wheel, our priests wear a white robe. We do not eat grubs from the tree, we have not forgotten the old writings, although they are hard to understand. Nevertheless, my knowledge and my lack of knowledge burned in me—I wished to know more. When I was a man at last, I came to my father and said, "It is time for me to go on my journey. Give me your leave."

He looked at me for a long time, stroking his beard, then he said at last, "Yes. It is time." That night, in the house of the priesthood, I asked for and received purification. My body hurt but my spirit was a cool stone. It was my father himself who questioned me about my dreams.

He bade me look into the smoke of the fire and see—I saw and told what I saw. It was what I have always seen—a river, and, beyond it, a great Dead Place and in it the gods walking. I have always thought about that. His eyes were stern when I told him—he was no longer my father but a priest. He said, "This is a strong dream."

"It is mine," I said, while the smoke waved and my head felt light. They were singing the Star song in the outer chamber and it was like the buzzing of bees in my head.

He asked me how the gods were dressed and I told him how they were dressed. We know how they were dressed from the book, but I saw them as if they were before me. When I had finished, he threw the sticks three times and studied them as they fell.

"This is a very strong dream," he said. "It may eat you up."

"I am not afraid," I said and looked at him with both eyes. My voice sounded thin in my ears but that was because of the smoke.

He touched me on the breast and the forehead. He gave me the bow and the three arrows.

"Take them," he said. "It is forbidden to travel east. It is forbidden to cross the river. It is forbidden to go to the Place of the Gods. All these things are forbidden."

"All these things are forbidden," I said, but it was my voice that spoke and not my spirit. He looked at me again.

"My son," he said. "Once I had young dreams. If your dreams do not eat you up, you may be a great priest. If they eat you, you are still my son. Now go on your journey."

I went fasting, as is the law. My body hurt but not my heart. When the dawn came, I was out of sight of the village. I prayed and purified myself, waiting for a sign. The sign was an eagle. It flew east.

Lake George with Crows (1921) by Georgia O'Keeffe. Oil on canvas (28″ × 25″).

Sometimes signs are sent by bad spirits. I waited again on the flat rock, fasting, taking no food. I was very still—I could feel the sky above me and the earth beneath. I waited till the sun was beginning to sink. Then three deer passed in the valley, going east—they did not wind[1] me or see me. There was a white fawn with them—a very great sign.

I followed them, at a distance, waiting for what would happen. My heart was troubled about going east, yet I knew that I must go. My head hummed with my fasting—I did not even see the panther spring upon the white fawn. But, before I knew it, the bow was in my hand. I shouted and the panther lifted his head from the fawn. It is not easy to kill a panther with one arrow but the arrow went through his eye and into his brain. He died as he tried to spring—he rolled over, tearing at the ground. Then I knew I was meant to go east—I knew that was my journey. When the night came, I made my fire and roasted meat.

It is eight suns' journey to the east and a man passes by many Dead Places. The Forest People are afraid of them but I am not. Once I made my fire on the edge of a Dead Place at night and, next morning, in the dead house, I found a good knife, little rusted. That was small to what came afterward but it made my heart feel big. Always when I looked for game, it was in front of my arrow, and twice I passed hunting parties of the Forest People without their knowing. So I knew my magic was strong and my journey clean, in spite of the law.

Toward the setting of the eighth sun, I came to the banks of the great river. It was half a day's journey after I had left the god-road—we do not use the god-roads now, for they are falling apart into great blocks of stone, and the forest is safer going. A long way off, I had seen the water through trees but the trees were thick. At last,

> Everywhere there are the ruins of the high towers of the gods.

I came out upon an open place at the top of a cliff. There was the great river below, like a giant in the sun. It is very long, very wide. It could eat all the streams we know and still be thirsty. Its name is Ou-dis-sun, the Sacred, the Long. No man of my tribe had seen it, not even my father, the priest. It was magic and I prayed.

Then I raised my eyes and looked south. It was there, the Place of the Gods.

How can I tell what it was like—you do not know. It was there, in the red light, and they were too big to be houses. It was there with the red light upon it, mighty and ruined. I knew that in another moment the gods would see me. I covered my eyes with my hands and crept back into the forest.

Surely, that was enough to do, and live. Surely it was enough to spend the night upon the cliff. The Forest People themselves do not come near. Yet, all through the night, I knew that I should have to cross the river and walk in the places of the gods, although the gods ate me up. My magic did not help me at all and yet there was a fire in my bowels, a fire in my mind. When the sun rose, I thought, "My journey has been clean. Now I will go home from my journey." But, even as I thought so, I knew I could not. If I went to the Place of the Gods, I would surely die, but, if I did not go, I could never be at peace with my spirit again. It is better to lose one's life than one's spirit, if one is a priest and the son of a priest.

Nevertheless, as I made the raft, the tears ran out of my eyes. The Forest People could have killed me without fight, if they had come upon me then, but they did not come. When the raft was made, I said the sayings for the dead and painted myself for death. My heart was cold as a frog and my knees like water, but the burning in my mind would not let me have peace. As I pushed the raft from the shore, I began my death song—I had the right. It was a fine song.

---

1. **wind** (wind) *v.*: detect the scent of.

"I am John, son of John," I sang. *"My people*
are the Hill People. They are the men.
I go into the Dead Places but I am not slain.
I take the metal from the Dead Places but
I am not blasted.
I travel upon the god-roads and am not
afraid. E-yah! I have killed the panther,
I have killed the fawn!
E-yah! I have come to the great river. No
man has come there before.
It is forbidden to go east, but I have gone,
forbidden to go on the great river, but
I am there.
Open your hearts, you spirits, and hear my
song. Now I go to the Place of the Gods,
I shall not return.
My body is painted for death and my limbs
weak, but my heart is big as I go to the
Place of the Gods!"

All the same, when I came to the Place of the Gods, I was afraid, afraid. The current of the great river is very strong—it gripped my raft with its hands. That was magic, for the river itself is wide and calm. I could feel evil spirits about me, in the bright morning; I could feel their breath on my neck as I was swept down the stream. Never have I been so much alone—I tried to think of my knowledge, but it was a squirrel's heap of winter nuts. There was no strength in my knowledge anymore and I felt small and naked as a new-hatched bird—alone upon the great river, the servant of the gods.

Yet, after a while, my eyes were opened and I saw. I saw both banks of the river—I saw that once there had been god-roads across it, though now they were broken and fallen like broken vines. Very great they were, and wonderful and broken—broken in the time of the Great Burning when the fire fell out of the sky. And always the current took me nearer to the Place of the Gods, and the huge ruins rose before my eyes.

I do not know the customs of rivers—we are the People of the Hills. I tried to guide my raft with the pole but it spun around. I thought the river meant to take me past the Place of the Gods and out into the Bitter Water of the legends. I grew angry then—my heart felt strong. I said aloud, "I am a priest and the son of a priest!" The gods heard me—they showed me how to paddle with the pole on one side of the raft. The current changed itself—I drew near to the Place of the Gods.

When I was very near, my raft struck and turned over. I can swim in our lakes—I swam to the shore. There was a great spike of rusted metal sticking out into the river—I hauled myself up upon it and sat there, panting. I had saved my bow and two arrows and the knife I found in the Dead Place but that was all. My raft went whirling downstream toward the Bitter Water. I looked after it, and thought if it had trod me under, at least I would be safely dead. Nevertheless, when I had dried my bowstring and restrung it, I walked forward to the Place of the Gods.

It felt like ground underfoot; it did not burn me. It is not true what some of the tales say, that the ground there burns forever, for I have been there. Here and there were the marks and stains of the Great Burning, on the ruins, that is true. But they were old marks and old stains. It is not true either, what some of our priests say, that it is an island covered with fogs and enchantments. It is not. It is a great Dead Place—greater than any Dead Place we know. Everywhere in it there are god-roads, though most are cracked and broken. Everywhere there are the ruins of the high towers of the gods.

How shall I tell what I saw? I went carefully, my strung bow in my hand, my skin ready for danger. There should have been the wailings of spirits and the shrieks of demons, but there were not. It was very silent and sunny where I had landed—the wind and the rain and the birds that drop seeds had done their work—the grass grew in the cracks of the broken stone. It is a fair island—no wonder the gods built there. If I had come there, a god, I also would have built.

How shall I tell what I saw? The towers are not all broken—here and there one still stands, like a great tree in a forest, and the birds nest high. But the towers themselves look blind, for the gods are gone. I saw a fish-hawk, catching fish in the river. I saw a little dance of white butterflies over a great heap of broken stones and columns. I went there and looked about me—there was a carved stone with cut-letters, broken in half. I can read letters but I could not understand these. They said UBTREAS. There was also the shattered image of a man or a god. It had been made of white stone and he wore his hair tied back like a woman's. His name was ASHING, as I read on the cracked half of a stone. I thought it wise to pray to ASHING, though I do not know that god.

How shall I tell what I saw? There was no smell of man left, on stone or metal. Nor were there many trees in that wilderness of stone. There are many pigeons, nesting and dropping in the towers—the gods must have loved them, or, perhaps, they used them for sacrifices. There are wild cats that roam the god-roads, green-eyed, unafraid of man. At night they wail like demons but they are not demons. The wild dogs are more dangerous, for they hunt in a pack, but them I did not meet till later. Everywhere there are the carved stones, carved with magical numbers or words.

I went north—I did not try to hide myself. When a god or a demon saw me, then I would die, but meanwhile I was no longer afraid. My hunger for knowledge burned in me—there was so much that I could not understand. After a while, I knew that my belly was hungry. I could have hunted for my meat, but I did not hunt. It is known that the gods did not hunt as we do—they got their food from enchanted boxes and jars. Sometimes these are still found in the Dead Places—once, when I was a child and foolish,

I opened such a jar and tasted it and found the food sweet. But my father found out and punished me for it strictly, for, often, that food is death. Now, though, I had long gone past what was forbidden, and I entered the likeliest towers, looking for the food of the gods.

I found it at last in the ruins of a great temple in the midcity. A mighty temple it must have been, for the roof was painted like the sky at night with its stars—that much I could see, though the colors were faint and dim. It went down into great caves and tunnels—perhaps they kept their slaves there. But when I started to climb down, I heard the squeaking of rats, so I did not go—rats are unclean, and there must have been many tribes of them, from the squeaking. But near there, I found food, in the heart of a ruin, behind a door that still opened. I ate only the fruits from the jars—they had a very sweet taste. There was drink, too, in bottles of glass—the drink of the gods was strong and made my head swim. After I had eaten and drunk, I slept on the top of a stone, my bow at my side.

When I woke, the sun was low. Looking down from where I lay, I saw a dog sitting on his haunches. His tongue was hanging out of his mouth; he looked as if he were laughing. He was a big dog, with a gray-brown coat, as big as a wolf. I sprang up and shouted at him but he did not move—he just sat there as if he were laughing. I did not like that. When I reached for a stone to throw, he moved swiftly out of the way of the stone. He was not afraid of me; he looked at me as if I were meat. No doubt I could have killed him with an arrow, but I did not know if there were others. Moreover, night was falling.

I looked about me—not far away there was a great, broken god-road, leading north. The towers were high enough, but not so high, and while many of the dead houses were wrecked, there were some that stood. I went toward this god-road, keeping to the heights of the ruins, while the dog followed. When I had reached the god-road, I saw that there were others behind him. If I had slept later, they would have come upon me asleep and torn out my throat. As it was, they were sure enough of me; they did not hurry. When I went into the dead house, they kept watch at the entrance—doubtless they thought they would have a fine hunt. But a dog cannot open a door and I knew, from the books, that the gods did not like to live on the ground but on high.

I had just found a door I could open when the dogs decided to rush. Ha! They were surprised when I shut the door in their faces—it was a good door, of strong metal. I could hear their foolish baying beyond it but I did not stop to answer them. I was in darkness—I found stairs and climbed. There were many stairs, turning around till my head was dizzy. At the top was another door—I found the knob and opened it. I was in a long small chamber—on one side of it was a bronze door that could not be opened, for it had no handle. Perhaps there was a magic word to open it but I did not have the word. I turned to the door in the opposite side of the wall. The lock of it was broken and I opened it and went in.

Within, there was a place of great riches. The god who lived there must have been a powerful god. The first room was a small anteroom—I waited there for some time, telling the spirits of the place that I came in peace and not as a robber. When it seemed to me that they had had time to hear me, I went on. Ah, what riches! Few, even, of the windows had been broken—it was all as it had been. The great windows that looked over the city had not been broken at all though they were dusty and streaked with many years. There were coverings on the floors, the colors not greatly faded, and the chairs were soft and deep. There were pictures upon the walls, very strange, very wonderful—I remember one of a bunch of flowers in a jar—if you came close to it, you could see nothing but bits of color, but if you stood away from it, the flowers might have been picked yesterday. It made my heart feel strange to look at this picture—and to look at the figure of a bird, in some hard clay, on a table and see it so like our birds. Everywhere there were books and writings, many in tongues that I could not read. The god who lived there must have been a wise god and full of knowledge. I felt I had right there, as I sought knowledge also.

Nevertheless, it was strange. There was a washing-place but no water—perhaps the gods washed in air. There was a cooking-place but no wood, and though there was a machine to cook food, there was no place to put fire in it. Nor were there candles or lamps—there were things that looked like lamps but they had neither oil nor wick. All these things were magic, but I touched them and lived—the magic had gone out of them. Let me tell one thing to show. In the washing-place, a thing said "Hot" but it was not hot to the touch—another thing said "Cold" but it was not cold. This must have been a strong magic but the magic was gone. I do not understand—they had ways—I wish that I knew.

It was close and dry and dusty in their house of the gods. I have said the magic was gone but that is not true—it had gone from the magic things but it had not gone from the place. I felt the spirits about me, weighing upon me. Nor had I ever slept in a Dead Place before—and yet, tonight, I must sleep there. When I thought of it, my tongue felt dry in my throat, in spite of my wish for knowledge. Almost I would have gone down again and faced the dogs, but I did not.

I had not gone through all the rooms when the darkness fell. When it fell, I went back to the big room looking over the city and made fire. There was a place to make fire and a box with wood in it, though I do not think they cooked there. I wrapped myself in a floor-covering and slept in front of the fire—I was very tired.

> Within, there was a place of great riches.

Now I tell what is very strong magic. I woke in the midst of the night. When I woke, the fire had gone out and I was cold. It seemed to me that all around me there were whisperings and voices. I closed my eyes to shut them out. Some will say that I slept again, but I do not think that I slept. I could feel the spirits drawing my spirit out of my body as a fish is drawn on a line.

Why should I lie about it? I am a priest and the son of a priest. If there are spirits, as they say, in the small Dead Places near us, what spirits must there not be in that great Place of the Gods? And would not they wish to speak? After such long years? I know that I felt myself drawn as a fish is drawn on a line. I had stepped out of my body—I could see my body asleep in front of the cold fire, but it was not I. I was drawn to look out upon the city of the gods.

It should have been dark, for it was night, but it was not dark. Everywhere there were lights— lines of light—circles and blurs of light—ten thousand torches would not have been the same. The sky itself was alight—you could barely see the stars for the glow in the sky. I thought to myself, "This is strong magic," and trembled. There was a roaring in my ears like the rushing of rivers. Then my eyes grew used to the light and my ears to the sound. I knew that I was seeing the city as it had been when the gods were alive.

That was a sight indeed—yes, that was a sight: I could not have seen it in the body—my body would have died. Everywhere went the gods, on foot and in chariots—there were gods beyond number and counting and their chariots blocked the streets. They had turned night to day for their pleasure—they did not sleep with the sun. The noise of their coming and going was the noise of many waters. It was magic what they could do—it was magic what they did.

I looked out of another window—the great vines of their bridges were mended and the god-roads went east and west. Restless, restless were the gods, and always in motion! They burrowed tunnels under rivers—they flew in the air. With unbelievable tools they did giant works— no part of the earth was safe from them, for, if they wished for a thing, they summoned it from the other side of the world. And always, as they labored and rested, as they feasted and made love, there was a drum in their ears—the pulse of the giant city, beating and beating like a man's heart.

Were they happy? What is happiness to the gods? They were great, they were mighty, they were wonderful and terrible. As I looked upon them and their magic, I felt like a child—but a little more, it seemed to me, and they would pull down the moon from the sky. I saw them with wisdom beyond wisdom and knowledge beyond knowledge. And yet not all they did was well done—even I could see that—and yet their wisdom could not but grow until all was peace.

Then I saw their fate come upon them and that was terrible past speech. It came upon them as they walked the streets of their city. I have been in the fights with the Forest People—I have seen men die. But this was not like that. When gods war with gods, they use weapons we do not know. It was fire falling out of the sky and a mist that poisoned. It was the time of the Great Burning and the Destruction. They ran about like ants in the streets of their city—poor gods, poor gods! Then the towers began to fall. A few escaped—yes, a few. The legends tell it. But, even after the city had become a Dead Place, for many years the poison was still in the ground. I saw it happen, I saw the last of them die. It was darkness over the broken city and I wept.

All this, I saw. I saw it as I have told it, though not in the body. When I woke in the morning, I was hungry, but I did not think first of my hunger, for my heart was perplexed and

Now I tell what is very strong magic.

Radiator Building—Night, New York (1927) by Georgia O'Keeffe. Oil on canvas (48″ × 30″).

confused. I knew the reason for the Dead Places but I did not see why it had happened. It seemed to me it should not have happened, with all the magic they had. I went through the house looking for an answer. There was so much in the house I could not understand—and yet I am a priest and the son of a priest. It was like being on one side of the great river, at night, with no light to show the way.

Then I saw the dead god. He was sitting in his chair, by the window, in a room I had not entered before and, for the first moment, I thought that he was alive. Then I saw the skin on the back of his hand—it was like dry leather. The room was shut, hot and dry—no doubt that had kept him as he was. At first I was afraid to approach him—then the fear left me. He was sitting looking out over the city— he was dressed in the clothes of the gods. His age was neither young nor old—I could not tell his age. But there was wisdom in his face and great sadness. You could see that he would have not run away. He had sat at his window, watching his city die—then he himself had died. But it is better to lose one's life than one's spirit—and you could see from the face that his spirit had not been lost. I knew that, if I touched him, he would fall into dust—and yet, there was something unconquered in the face.

That is all of my story, for then I knew he was a man—I knew then that they had been men, neither gods nor demons. It is a great knowledge, hard to tell and believe. They were men— they went a dark road, but they were men. I had no fear after that—I had no fear going home, though twice I fought off the dogs and I was hunted for two days by the Forest People. When I saw my father again, I prayed and was purified. He touched my lips and my breast, he said, "You went away a boy. You come back a man and a priest." I said, "Father, they were men! I have been in the Place of the Gods and seen it! Now slay me, if it is the law—but still I know they were men."

He looked at me out of both eyes. He said, "The law is not always the same shape—you have done what you have done. I could not have done it my time, but you come after me. Tell!"

I told and he listened. After that, I wished to tell all the people but he showed me otherwise. He said, "Truth is a hard deer to hunt. If you eat too much truth at once, you may die of the truth. It was not idly that our fathers forbade the Dead Places." He was right—it is better the truth should come little by little. I have learned that, being a priest. Perhaps, in the old days, they ate knowledge too fast.

Perhaps, in the old days, they ate knowledge too fast.

Nevertheless, we make a beginning. It is not for the metal alone we go to the Dead Places now—there are the books and the writings. They are hard to learn. And the magic tools are broken—but we can look at them and wonder. At least, we make a beginning. And, when I am chief priest we shall go beyond the great river. We shall go to the Place of the Gods—the place newyork—not one man but a company. We shall look for the images of the gods and find the god ASHING and the others—the gods Lincoln and Biltmore[2] and Moses.[3] But they were men who built the city, not gods or demons. They were men. I remember the dead man's face. They were men who were here before us. We must build again. ∎

---

2. **Biltmore:** New York City hotel.
3. **Moses:** Robert Moses (1888–1981): New York City public official who oversaw many large construction projects, such as bridges and public buildings.

Meet the Writer

Stephen Vincent Benét

Mr. American History

According to one biographer, Stephen Vincent Benét (1898–1943) "wrote short stories for money and poetry for love." Yet despite his preference for poetry, some of Benét's stories have remained his best-known works. The story you have just read, "By the Waters of Babylon," first appeared as "The Place of the Gods" in *The Saturday Evening Post* magazine in July 1937. Benét later changed its title.

Benét was the grandson of an important general and the son of a well-known colonel who instilled a love of literature and American history in his children. (Benét's brother and sister also became writers.) With this background it's not surprising that Benét turned to American history, folklore, and legend as topics for his stories and poems. *John Brown's Body* (1928), a book-length narrative poem about the fiery abolitionist who led an attack on Harper's Ferry in 1859 and was hanged for treason, won Benét the Pulitzer Prize for poetry.

Benét always emphasized the importance of clear style. He advised one young writer,

66 Don't use four adjectives when one will do. Don't use five long words to say, 'We were happy.' 'It rained.' 'It was dark.' Write of the simple things simply. 99

For Independent Reading

"The Devil and Daniel Webster," probably Benét's most widely anthologized story, pits the real-life American statesman and orator Daniel Webster against the devil in a fierce struggle to save the soul of a New Hampshire farmer. The story won the O. Henry Award in 1937 and was made into an opera, a play, and a movie.

Response and Analysis

Reading Check

1. Imagine that you are John, the narrator, telling the Hill People about your journey. Briefly **summarize** the **main events** of your journey, either orally or in writing.

Thinking Critically

2. To understand what is really happening in this story, you have to **draw conclusions** based on the writer's clues and your own experience and knowledge. What do you think John is really seeing (and how are you able to tell) when he describes these elements of the story's **setting**?
   - the god-roads
   - the high towers of the gods
   - the statue of ASHING
   - the Great Burning
   - the caves and tunnels

3. How does Benét use **setting** to create a **mood** of suspense and hold our interest? What does this particular setting (the time, place, and culture) reveal about John's character?

4. How does Benét's use of the **first-person point of view** affect what the reader knows about John and about what happens in the story? How does it affect the **tone** of the story?

5. Find a place in the story where John achieves a breakthrough, and explain what he discovers. How does the **first-person point of view** help you appreciate his breakthrough?

6. How would you describe the **persona** Benét has created for the narrator, John? Why is it important that someone like John tell this story?

7. At what point in the story did you first begin to guess what the Place of the Gods was?

8. Near the end of the story, John says, "Perhaps, in the old days, they ate knowledge too fast." What do you think he means? Are we "eating knowledge" too fast today? Explain.

9. The Background on page 140 explains the biblical **allusion,** or reference, in the story's **title.** Now that you have read the story, explain how the words of the psalm connect to it.

Extending and Evaluating

10. Benét wrote this story in 1937, before the first atom bomb was built. World War II and the cold war are over now. Do Benét's warnings about the complete destruction of a civilization still have relevance? Why? (Your Quick-write notes may help you answer.)

11. Do you think Benét made the secret of the Place of the Gods too easy to guess or too hard, or were the clues just difficult enough? Explain.

WRITING

Babylon II?

What happened to the city that John calls the Place of the Gods? Write a **prequel,** a story of the events that led up to "By the Waters of Babylon." You might write your story from the **first-person point of view** of the man John finds "sitting looking out over the city," or you might write the story in the form of the man's last journal entries.

▶ **Use "Writing a Short Story," pages 602–609, for help with this assignment.**

INTERNET

Projects and
Activities

Keyword: LE5 10-3

**SKILLS
FOCUS**

Literary Skills
Analyze first-person point of view. Analyze setting.

Reading Skills
Draw conclusions.

Writing Skills
Write a short story from the first-person point of view.

Vocabulary Development

Suffixes: Meaningful Endings

It's suffixes that change *say* into *say**ings*** and *true* into *tru**ly***. A **suffix** is a word part (a group of letters) that is added to a word or word root to change the word's meaning and, often, its part of speech. Suffixes are tacked on to the end of a word. The most common suffixes are those that we use to create noun plurals and verb forms (*–es, –s, –ed, –ing, –en*) as well as adjectives and adverbs (*–er, –est, –ly*).

When you find an unfamiliar word, look for suffixes that provide clues to how the **root** (the base element of the word) changes. The chart below gives meanings and examples for some common suffixes and combining forms (a combining form is a kind of suffix). Remember that some suffixes have more than one meaning.

Latin Suffixes	Meaning	Example
–fy (forming *v.*)	to make; to become	liquefy
–ious (forming *adj.*)	characterized by	rebellious
–ity (forming *n.*)	state or condition of being	prosperity
–ous (forming *adj.*)	characterized by	dangerous

Greek Suffixes / Combining Forms	Meaning	Example
–cracy (forming *n.*)	form of government; rule by	democracy
–gram (forming *n.*)	something written or recorded	telegram
–logy (forming *n.*)	science or study of	zoology
–phobia (forming *n.*)	fear of	claustrophobia

Anglo-Saxon Suffixes	Meaning	Example
–wise (forming *adv.*)	in a direction or manner	clockwise
–dom (forming *n.*)	domain or dominion; fact or state of being	kingdom wisdom
–hood (forming *n.*)	state or condition; the whole group of	childhood priesthood
–some (forming *adj.*)	like; tending to be	lonesome

PRACTICE 1

Choose five suffixes from the chart. Then, work with a partner to list all the additional examples you can think of that use each suffix. Exchange your completed lists with those of another team.

PRACTICE 2

The words below are from the story. Each contains a suffix that is not on the chart above. Make a similar chart for these words. If you need help determining the meaning of a suffix, check a dictionary.

enchant<u>ments</u>   wilder<u>ness</u>   doubt<u>less</u>   wonder<u>ful</u>

SKILLS FOCUS

Vocabulary Skills
Understand and use suffixes.

The Storyteller

Make the Connection

Quickwrite ✏️

What do you expect from a children's story—a happy ending, a strong moral, surprising reversals? Think back to your favorite stories and books from when you were very young, and try to figure out why they captured your interest. Jot down your ideas.

Literary Focus

Omniscient Point of View: Knowing It All

An **omniscient** ("all-knowing") narrator plays no part in the action of a story. Instead, the narrator is an all-knowing observer who has the power to reveal the thoughts, feelings, and motives of every character and sometimes comments directly on the characters. Unlike stories written from the first-person point of view, stories with an omniscient point of view generally give us a more reliable perspective. We are in the hands of an all-knowing narrator, whom we are usually inclined to trust.

Satire: Isn't It Ridiculous?

Satire is any writing that ridicules the shortcomings of people or institutions in an attempt to bring about a change. Greed, injustice, cruelty, stupidity, and deceit are all targets of the satirist. Satire often uses both exaggeration and humor to invite laughter at someone's expense. As you read this story, try to figure out whom or what Saki is ridiculing.

Reading Skills

Does the Writer Have a Purpose?

Saki and other writers of humorous stories seem to create works that are pure entertainments. However, many of these writers, including Saki, often have a more serious purpose than simply to entertain their readers. To discover the purpose in a tale like "The Storyteller," you have to read closely. Look for key passages or loaded words that reveal the author's attitude toward the characters. Notice which characters Saki seems to poke fun at and which ones he seems sympathetic toward.

Vocabulary Development

sultry (sul′trē) *adj.*: hot and humid; sweltering.

persistent (pər·sist′ənt) *adj.*: continuing.

diversion (də·vur′zhən) *n.*: something that distracts the attention.

resolute (rez′ə·lōōt′) *adj.*: determined.

petulant (pech′ə·lənt) *adj.*: impatient; irritable; peevish.

deplorably (dē·plôr′ə·blē) *adv.*: very badly.

conviction (kən·vik′shən) *n.*: strong belief; certainty.

retort (ri·tôrt′) *n.*: sharp reply.

assail (ə·sāl′) *v.*: attack.

INTERNET

Vocabulary Practice
•
More About Saki

Keyword: LE5 10-3

Literary Skills
Understand omniscient point of view. Understand satire.

Reading Skills
Understand the writer's purpose.

The Story

The Storyteller
Saki

It was a hot afternoon, and the railway carriage was correspondingly <u>sultry</u>, and the next stop was at Templecombe, nearly an hour ahead. The occupants of the carriage were a small girl, and a smaller girl, and a small boy. An aunt belonging to the children occupied one corner seat, and the further corner seat on the opposite side was occupied by a bachelor who was a stranger to their party, but the small girls and the small boy emphatically occupied the compartment. Both the aunt and the children were conversational in a limited, <u>persistent</u> way, reminding one of the attentions of a housefly that refused to be discouraged. Most of the aunt's remarks seemed to begin with "Don't," and nearly all the children's remarks began with "Why?" The bachelor said nothing out loud.

"Don't, Cyril, don't," exclaimed the aunt, as the small boy began smacking the cushions of the seat, producing a cloud of dust at each blow.

"Come and look out of the window," she added.

The child moved reluctantly to the window. "Why are those sheep being driven out of that field?" he asked.

"I expect they are being driven to another field where there is more grass," said the aunt weakly.

"But there is lots of grass in that field," protested the boy; "there's nothing else but grass there. Aunt, there's lots of grass in that field."

"Perhaps the grass in the other field is better," suggested the aunt fatuously.[1]

"Why is it better?" came the swift, inevitable question.

---

1. **fatuously** (fach′o͞o·əs·lē) *adv.:* foolishly.

Vocabulary
sultry (sul′trē) *adj.:* hot and humid; sweltering.
persistent (pər·sist′ənt) *adj.:* continuing.

teller

"Oh, look at those cows!" exclaimed the aunt. Nearly every field along the line had contained cows or bullocks, but she spoke as though she were drawing attention to a rarity.

"Why is the grass in the other field better?" persisted Cyril.

The frown on the bachelor's face was deepening to a scowl. He was a hard, unsympathetic man, the aunt decided in her mind. She was utterly unable to come to any satisfactory decision about the grass in the other field.

The smaller girl created a diversion by beginning to recite "On the Road to Mandalay."[2] She only knew the first line, but she put her limited knowledge to the fullest possible use. She repeated the line over and over again in a dreamy but resolute and very audible voice; it seemed to the bachelor as though someone had had a bet with her that she could not repeat the line aloud two thousand times without stopping. Whoever it was who had made the wager was likely to lose his bet.

"Come over here and listen to a story," said the aunt, when the bachelor had looked twice at her and once at the communication cord.[3]

The children moved listlessly toward the aunt's end of the carriage. Evidently her reputation as a storyteller did not rank high in their estimation.

In a low, confidential voice, interrupted at frequent intervals by loud, petulant questions from her listeners, she began an unenterprising and deplorably uninteresting story about a little girl who was good, and made friends with everyone on account of her goodness, and was finally saved from a mad bull by a number of rescuers who admired her moral character.

"Wouldn't they have saved her if she hadn't been good?" demanded the bigger of the small girls. It was exactly the question that the bachelor had wanted to ask.

"Well, yes," admitted the aunt lamely, "but I don't think they would have run quite so fast to her help if they had not liked her so much."

"It's the stupidest story I've ever heard," said the bigger of the small girls, with immense conviction.

"I didn't listen after the first bit, it was so stupid," said Cyril.

The smaller girl made no actual comment on the story, but she had long ago recommenced a murmured repetition of her favorite line.

"You don't seem to be a success as a storyteller," said the bachelor suddenly from his corner.

The aunt bristled in instant defense at this unexpected attack.

"It's a very difficult thing to tell stories that children can both understand and appreciate," she said stiffly.

"I don't agree with you," said the bachelor.

"She was horribly good."

Vocabulary

diversion (də·vʉr′zhən) *n.*: something that distracts the attention.

resolute (rez′ə·lo̅o̅t′) *adj.*: determined.

petulant (pech′ə·lənt) *adj.*: impatient; irritable; peevish.

deplorably (dē·plôr′ə·blē) *adv.*: very badly.

conviction (kən·vik′shən) *n.*: strong belief; certainty.

---

2. **"On the Road to Mandalay"**: long poem in dialect by the English writer Rudyard Kipling (1865–1936). The first line is "By the old Moulmein Pagoda, lookin' eastward to the sea."

3. **communication cord:** on a train, signal used in emergencies to call the conductor.

"she was so good," co
bachelor, "that she wo
for goodness, which s
pinned onto her dres
medal for obedience
punctuality, and

"Perhaps *you* would like to tell them a story," was the aunt's retort.

"Tell us a story," demanded the bigger of the small girls.

"Once upon a time," began the bachelor, "there was a little girl called Bertha, who was extraordinarily good."

The children's momentarily aroused interest began at once to flicker; all stories seemed dreadfully alike, no matter who told them.

"She did all that she was told, she was always truthful, she kept her clothes clean, ate milk puddings as if they were jam tarts, learned her lessons perfectly, and was polite in her manners."

"Was she pretty?" asked the bigger of the small girls.

"Not as pretty as any of you," said the bachelor, "but she was horribly good."

There was a wave of reaction in favor of the story; the word horrible in connection with goodness was a novelty that commended itself. It seemed to introduce a ring of truth that was absent from the aunt's tales of infant life.

"She was so good," continued the bachelor, "that she won several medals for goodness, which she always wore, pinned onto her dress. There was a medal for obedience, another medal for punctuality, and a third for good behavior. They were large metal medals and they clicked against one another as she walked. No other child in the town where she lived had as many as three medals, so everybody knew that she must be an extra good child."

"Horribly good," quoted Cyril.

"Everybody talked about her goodness, and the Prince of the country got to hear about it, and he said that as she was so very good she might be allowed once a week to walk in his park, which was just outside the town. It was a beautiful park, and no children were ever allowed in it, so it was a great honor for Bertha to be allowed to go there."

"Were there any sheep in the park?" demanded Cyril.

"No," said the bachelor, "there were no sheep."

"Why weren't there any sheep?" came the inevitable question arising out of that answer.

The aunt permitted herself a smile, which might almost have been described as a grin.

"There were no sheep in the park," said the bachelor, "because the Prince's mother had once had a dream that her son would either be killed by a sheep or else by a clock falling on him. For that reason the Prince never kept a sheep in his park or a clock in his palace."

Vocabulary
retort (ri·tôrt′) *n.:* sharp reply.

The aunt suppressed a gasp of admiration.

"Was the Prince killed by a sheep or by a clock?" asked Cyril.

"He is still alive, so we can't tell whether the dream will come true," said the bachelor unconcernedly; "anyway, there were no sheep in the park, but there were lots of little pigs running all over the place."

"What color were they?"

"Black with white faces, white with black spots, black all over, gray with white patches, and some were white all over."

The storyteller paused to let a full idea of the park's treasures sink into the children's imaginations; then he resumed:

"Bertha was rather sorry to find that there were no flowers in the park. She had promised her aunts, with tears in her eyes, that she would not pick any of the kind Prince's flowers, and she had meant to keep her promise, so of course it made her feel silly to find that there were no flowers to pick."

"Why weren't there any flowers?"

"Because the pigs had eaten them all," said the bachelor promptly. "The gardeners had told the Prince that you couldn't have pigs and flowers, so he decided to have pigs and no flowers."

There was a murmur of approval at the excellence of the Prince's decision; so many people would have decided the other way.

"There were lots of other delightful things in the park. There were ponds with gold and blue and green fish in them, and trees with beautiful parrots that said clever things at a moment's notice, and hummingbirds that hummed all the popular tunes of the day. Bertha walked up and down and enjoyed herself immensely, and thought to herself: 'If I were not so extraordinarily good I should not have been allowed to come into this beautiful park and enjoy all that there is to be seen in it,' and her three medals clinked against one another as she walked and helped to remind her how very good she really was. Just then an enormous wolf came prowling into the park to see if it could catch a fat little pig for its supper."

"What color was it?" asked the children, amid an immediate quickening of interest.

"Mud-color all over, with a black tongue and pale gray eyes that gleamed with unspeakable

medal for obedience clinked
medals for good conduct
...lity. The wolf was just
...when he heard the sound
...clinking and stopped to
...nked again in a bush
...l. He dashed into the bush,
...eyes gleaming with
...iumph, and dragged
...l devoured her to the last
...t was left of her were her
...thing, and the three
...ness."

ferocity. The first thing that it saw in the park was Bertha; her pinafore[4] was so spotlessly white and clean that it could be seen from a great distance. Bertha saw the wolf and saw that it was stealing toward her, and she began to wish that she had never been allowed to come into the park. She ran as hard as she could, and the wolf came after her with huge leaps and bounds. She managed to reach a shrubbery of myrtle bushes and she hid herself in one of the thickest of the bushes. The wolf came sniffing among the branches, its black tongue lolling out of its mouth and its pale gray eyes glaring with rage. Bertha was terribly frightened and thought to herself: 'If I had not been so extraordinarily good I should have been safe in the town at this moment.' However, the scent of the myrtle was so strong that the wolf could not sniff out where Bertha was hiding, and the bushes were so thick

---

4. **pinafore** (pin′ə·fôr′) *n.*: apronlike garment that young girls used to wear over their dresses.

that he might have hunted about in them for a long time without catching sight of her, so he thought he might as well go off and catch a little pig instead. Bertha was trembling very much at having the wolf prowling and sniffing so near her, and as she trembled the medal for obedience clinked against the medals for good conduct and punctuality. The wolf was just moving away when he heard the sound of the medals clinking and stopped to listen; they clinked again in a bush quite near him. He dashed into the bush, his pale gray eyes gleaming with ferocity and triumph, and dragged Bertha out and devoured her to the last morsel. All that was left of her were her shoes, bits of clothing, and the three medals for goodness."

"Were any of the little pigs killed?"

"No, they all escaped."

"The story began badly," said the smaller of the small girls, "but it had a beautiful ending."

"It is the most beautiful story that I ever heard," said the bigger of the small girls, with immense decision.

"It is the *only* beautiful story I have ever heard," said Cyril.

A dissentient[5] opinion came from the aunt.

"A most improper story to tell young children! You have undermined the effect of years of careful teaching."

"At any rate," said the bachelor, collecting his belongings preparatory to leaving the carriage, "I kept them quiet for ten minutes, which was more than you were able to do."

"Unhappy woman!" he observed to himself as he walked down the platform of Templecombe station; "for the next six months or so those children will assail her in public with demands for an improper story!" ∎

---

5. **dissentient** (di·sen′shənt) *adj.*: dissenting; disagreeing.

Vocabulary
assail (ə·sāl′) *v.*: attack.

Meet the Writer

Saki (Hector Hugh Munro)

An Unusual Sense of Humor

Saki is the pen name of Hector Hugh Munro (1870–1916), who was born in Burma, the son of a British military officer. His mother died before he was two, and he and his older brother and sister were raised in Devonshire, England, by their grandmother and two strict aunts. (We find bad-tempered aunts in several Saki stories, including "The Storyteller.")

From an early age, Munro displayed an unusual temperament and sense of humor. In her biography of Munro, his sister Ethel recalls their childhood and describes Munro's mischievous delight in getting a well-behaved playmate in trouble:

> He saw to it that Claud did all the things we must never do, the easier to accomplish since his mother would be indoors tongue-wagging with Granny and the aunts. Poor Claud really was a good child, with no inclination to be anything else, but under Hector's ruthless tuition . . . he put in a breathless day of bad deeds.
>
> And when Aunt Tom (Charlotte she was never called), after the visitor's departure, remarked, 'Claud is not the good child I imagined him to be,' Hector felt it was the end of a perfect day.

Munro was a sickly child and had little formal schooling until he was sent to a boarding school at fourteen. "You can't expect a boy to be vicious till he's been to a good school," Munro wrote somewhat acidly in one of his stories.

At twenty-three, Munro returned to Burma to join his father and older brother. He took a police job arranged by his father but fell ill at once and returned to England a little more than a year later.

Early in his writing career he worked as a political satirist and a foreign correspondent for various newspapers. Eventually he found a wide audience for his humorous, satiric, and often cynical short stories.

Munro took his pen name from the Persian poem the *Rubáiyát of Omar Khayyám*, which was popular in England at the time. Saki is the name of the cupbearer, the servant who fills the wine cups.

Though Munro was forty-three when World War I began, he enlisted in the British army, eager for "the excitement of real warfare." He was killed on the front lines in France by a German sniper.

For Independent Reading

You can enjoy more of Saki's delicious twists in these short stories: "The Open Window" (about a girl whose story terrifies a visitor), "The Schartz-Metterklume Method" (in which a mischievous aristocrat plays a devious trick on an unsuspecting family), and "Sredni Vashtar" (about a boy's revenge on his overbearing guardian).

Response and Analysis

Reading Check

1. This is a **frame story,** in which one or more stories are told within another. Describe the **basic situation** that provides the frame for both the aunt's and the bachelor's stories.

2. In the aunt's story, why is the little girl saved? How do the children respond to the aunt's story?

3. What is the first "ring of truth" that the children notice in the bachelor's story?

4. In the bachelor's story, why does Bertha come to an unhappy end?

Thinking Critically

5. How would the story be different if either the aunt or the bachelor, rather than the **omniscient narrator,** were telling it from the **first-person point of view**? What would be lost?

6. What a vastly superior storyteller the bachelor is! He supplies both logic and information as he builds his extraordinary setting for Bertha's downfall. What surprises does he fill the park with? Why do you think he is able to make these surprises seem believable to the children?

7. When the bachelor calls Bertha "horribly good," the children are shocked and delighted. Find other **key passages** and **loaded words** that reveal the writer's **tone,** or attitude, toward the aunt, the bachelor, and their stories. What do you think Saki's **purpose** was in writing this story?

8. What would you say is the **theme,** or message, of the bachelor's story? How about the aunt's? Consult your Quick-write notes to see how each story measures up to your own ideas of what's important in children's literature.

9. In what ways can "The Storyteller" be considered a **satire**? What is Saki ridiculing? How does he use humor and exaggeration to make his point? Support your answers with examples from the story.

Literary Criticism

10. Respond to the following comment by Saki's biographer A. J. Langguth. Cite examples from the story to support your opinion.

> By now Hector was carving his stories with a keen blade, suffering no extraneous word or commonplace phrase. He had reached that degree of proficiency where the humor came less from his jokes than from the precision of each sentence.

WRITING

Imagine a Park

Suppose you were telling a story about someone who could equip a park with unusual or unexpected attractions. Write a paragraph **describing** an imaginary park setting—one that is very different from the parks that we are used to.

Literary Skills
Analyze omniscient point of view. Analyze satire.

Reading Skills
Analyze the writer's purpose.

Writing Skills
Write a description of a setting.

Vocabulary Development

Using Context Clues

PRACTICE

Explain the meaning of each underlined word, and point out the **context clues** in the sentence that helped you guess the meaning. Then, go back to Saki's story, and see if you can find context clues for the same underlined words. Write down any clues that you find.

Word Bank

sultry
persistent
diversion
resolute
petulant
deplorably
conviction
retort
assail

1. The bright August afternoon was typically sultry.
2. It was a persistent problem, one that would never go away.
3. The whole event became a welcome diversion for the bored onlookers.
4. He was resolute about never leaving his beloved boyhood home.
5. The girl's sharp, nagging questions were both petulant and rude.
6. Everyone was angry that she behaved deplorably.
7. She was a woman of great willpower and conviction.
8. The bad-tempered clerk gave the customer a quick retort.
9. The lawyer feared reporters would assail her as she left the courtroom.

Grammar Link

Inverted Order: Verbs Before Subjects

English sentences have a usual order: subjects first, then verbs. Some sentences, though, use **inverted order**—that is, the subject follows the verb. Inverted order is often used in questions and in sentences or clauses that begin with the word *here* or *there*. (Sometimes a sentence in inverted order will begin with a phrase or an adjective or adverb.) In these examples from "The Storyteller," the subject is underlined, and the verb is in boldface type:

"**Was** she pretty?"

"There **were** lots of other delightful things in the park."

PRACTICE

For each sentence, first find the subject. Then, choose the verb that agrees with the subject.

1. "(Were/was) there any sheep in the park?"
2. "Why (wasn't/weren't) there any flowers?"
3. "What color (was/were) they?"
4. "There (were/was) ponds with gold and blue and green fish in them. . . ."

▶ **For more help, see Agreement of Subject and Verb, 2a–n, in the Language Handbook.**

SKILLS FOCUS

Vocabulary Skills
Use context clues.

Grammar Skills
Use subjects and verbs in inverted order correctly.

 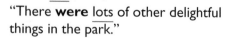

The Cold Equations

Make the Connection

Quickwrite ✏️

Nobody gets through life without having to make hard decisions. What kinds of choices might have difficult consequences no matter what we decide to do? Freewrite about such a choice. How would you make a decision when faced with such a hard choice?

Literary Focus

Third-Person-Limited Point of View

Like the omniscient narrator, the narrator of a story written from the **third-person-limited point of view** stands outside the action and refers to all the characters by name or as *he* or *she*. Unlike the omniscient narrator, however, this narrator zooms in on the thoughts, actions, and feelings of only *one* character. We almost never know what the others are thinking.

This point of view is popular with modern writers because it combines the possibilities of the omniscient point of view with the intense, personal focus of first-person narration. In "The Cold Equations" the third-person-limited narrator provides a calm voice in an increasingly tense, emotional situation.

Reading Skills 📖

Monitoring Your Reading: Questioning

Good readers ask questions as they read—whether they're reading a detective story or a serious novel. As you read "The Cold Equations," answer the questions at the open-book signs. They will serve as a guide for you to ask additional questions of your own as you read. You may keep wondering what is going to happen next in this suspenseful tale. You may have questions about the characters and the unusual setting and circumstances or about the choice of narrator. You may even have questions about Godwin's use of science.

Vocabulary Development

inured (in·yo͞ord′) *v.* used as *adj.*: accustomed to something difficult or painful.

increments (in′krə·mənts) *n.*: small increases.

recoiled (ri·koild′) *v.*: drew back in fear, surprise, or disgust.

paramount (par′ə·mount′) *adj.*: supreme; dominant.

annihilate (ə·nī′ə·lāt′) *v.*: destroy; demolish.

irrevocable (i·rev′ə·kə·bəl) *adj.*: irreversible; incapable of being canceled or undone.

immutable (i·myo͞ot′ə·bəl) *adj.*: unchangeable; never changing or varying.

ponderous (pän′dər·əs) *adj.*: heavy and slow moving.

apprehension (ap′rē·hen′shən) *n.*: dread; fear of a future event.

ineffably (in·ef′ə·blē) *adv.*: indescribably; inexpressibly.

go.hrw.com

INTERNET

Vocabulary Practice

Keyword: LE5 10-3

SKILLS FOCUS

Literary Skills Understand third-person-limited point of view.

Reading Skills Monitor your reading.

THE COLD EQUATIONS

Tom Godwin

It was the law, and there could be no appeal.

He was not alone.

There was nothing to indicate the fact but the white hand of the tiny gauge on the board before him. The control room was empty but for himself; there was no sound other than the murmur of the drives—but the white hand had moved. It had been on zero when the little ship was launched from the *Stardust;* now, an hour later, it had crept up. There was something in the supply closet across the room, it was saying, some kind of a body that radiated heat.

It could be but one kind of a body—a living, human body.

He leaned back in the pilot's chair and drew a deep, slow breath, considering what he would have to do. He was an EDS pilot, inured to the sight of death, long since accustomed to it and to viewing the dying of another man with an objective lack of emotion, and he had no choice in what he must do. There could be no alternative—but it required a few moments of conditioning for even an EDS pilot to prepare himself to walk across the room and coldly, deliberately, take the life of a man he had yet to meet.

He would, of course, do it. It was the law, stated very bluntly and definitely in grim Paragraph L, Section 8, of Interstellar Regulations: *"Any stowaway discovered in an EDS shall be jettisoned immediately following discovery."*

It was the law, and there could be no appeal.

> **QUESTIONING**
> 1. The story opens with suspense and conflict. What do you **predict** will happen next?

It was a law not of men's choosing but made imperative by the circumstances of the space frontier. Galactic expansion had followed the development of the hyperspace drive, and as men scattered wide across the frontier, there had come the problem of contact with the isolated first colonies and exploration parties. The huge hyperspace cruisers were the product of the combined genius and effort of Earth and were long and expensive in the building. They were not available in such numbers that small colonies could possess them. The cruisers carried the colonists to their new worlds and made periodic visits, running on tight schedules, but they could not stop and turn aside to visit colonies scheduled to be visited at another time; such a delay would destroy their schedule and produce a confusion and uncertainty that would wreck the complex interdependence between old Earth and the new worlds of the frontier.

Some method of delivering supplies or assistance when an emergency occurred on a world not scheduled for a visit had been needed, and the Emergency Dispatch Ships had been the answer. Small and collapsible, they occupied little room in the hold of the cruiser; made of light metal and plastics, they were driven by a small rocket drive that consumed relatively little fuel. Each cruiser carried four EDSs, and when a call for aid was received, the nearest cruiser would drop into normal space long enough to launch an EDS with the needed supplies or personnel, then vanish again as it continued on its course.

The cruisers, powered by nuclear converters, did not use the liquid rocket fuel, but nuclear converters were far too large and complex to permit their installation in the EDSs. The cruisers were forced by necessity to carry a limited amount of bulky rocket fuel, and the fuel was rationed[1] with care, the cruiser's computers determining the exact amount of fuel each EDS would require for its mission. The computers considered the course coordinates, the mass of the EDS, the mass of pilot and cargo; they were very precise and accurate and omitted nothing from their calculations. They could not, however, foresee and allow for the added mass of a stowaway.

> **QUESTIONING**
> 2. What questions do you have about the story's **basic situation** and the details of its **setting**?

The *Stardust* had received the request from one of the exploration parties stationed on Woden, the six men of the party already being stricken with the fever carried by the green kala midges and their own supply of serum destroyed by the tornado that had torn through their camp.

---

1. **rationed** (rash′ənd) *n.*: distributed.

Vocabulary
inured (in·yŏŏrd′) *v.* used as *adj.*: accustomed to something difficult or painful.

The *Stardust* had gone through the usual procedure, dropping into normal space to launch the EDS with the fever serum, then vanishing again in hyperspace. Now, an hour later, the gauge was saying there was something more than the small carton of serum in the supply closet.

He let his eyes rest on the narrow white door of the closet. There, just inside, another man lived and breathed and was beginning to feel assured that discovery of his presence would now be too late for the pilot to alter the situation. It *was* too late; for the man behind the door it was far later than he thought and in a way he would find it terrible to believe.

There could be no alternative. Additional fuel would be used during the hours of deceleration[2] to compensate for the added mass of the stowaway, infinitesimal increments of fuel that would not be missed until the ship had almost reached its destination. Then, at some distance above the ground that might be as near as a thousand feet or as far as tens of thousands of feet, depending upon the mass of ship and cargo and the preceding period of deceleration, the unmissed increments of fuel would make their absence known;

the EDS would expend its last drops of fuel with a sputter and go into whistling free fall. Ship and pilot and stowaway would merge together upon impact as a wreckage of metal and plastic, flesh and blood, driven deep into the soil. The stowaway had signed his own death warrant[3] when he concealed himself on the ship; he could not be permitted to take seven others with him.

He looked again at the telltale[4] white hand, then rose to his feet. What he must do would be unpleasant for both of them; the sooner it was over, the better. He stepped across the control room to stand by the white door.

"Come out!" His command was harsh and abrupt above the murmur of the drive.

It seemed he could hear the whisper of a furtive movement inside the closet, then nothing. He visualized the stowaway cowering closer into one corner, suddenly worried by the possible consequences of his act, his self-assurance evaporating.

"I said *out*!"

He heard the stowaway move to obey, and he waited with his eyes alert on the door and his hand near the blaster at his side.

The door opened and the stowaway stepped through it, smiling. "All right—I give up. Now what?"

It was a girl.

He stared without speaking, his hand dropping away from the blaster, and acceptance of what he saw coming like a heavy and unexpected physical blow. The stowaway was not a man—she was a girl in her teens, standing before him in little white gypsy sandals, with the top of her brown, curly head hardly higher than his shoulder, with a faint, sweet scent of perfume coming from her, and her smiling face tilted up so her

---

2. **deceleration** (dē·sel'ər·ā'shən) *n.:* act of slowing down.

3. **death warrant:** anything that makes someone's death inevitable.

4. **telltale** *adj.:* revealing what is meant to be hidden.

Vocabulary
increments (in'krə·mənts) *n.:* small increases.

eyes could look un- knowing and unafraid into his as she waited for his answer.

QUESTIONING
3. What questions would you ask the stowaway?

Now what? Had it been asked in the deep, defiant voice of a man, he would have answered it with action, quick and efficient. He would have taken the stowaway's identification disk and ordered him into the air lock. Had the stowaway refused to obey, he would have used the blaster. It would not have taken long; within a minute the body would have been ejected into space— had the stowaway been a man.

He returned to the pilot's chair and motioned her to seat herself on the boxlike bulk of the drive-control units that were set against the wall beside him. She obeyed, his silence making the smile fade into the meek and guilty expression of a pup that has been caught in mischief and knows it must be punished.

"You still haven't told me," she said. "I'm guilty, so what happens to me now? Do I pay a fine, or what?"

"What are you doing here?" he asked. "Why did you stow away on this EDS?"

"I wanted to see my brother. He's with the government survey crew on Woden and I haven't seen him for ten years, not since he left Earth to go into government survey work."

"What was your destination on the *Stardust*?"

"Mimir. I have a position waiting for me there. My brother has been sending money home all the time to us—my father and mother and me—and he paid for a special course in linguistics I was taking. I graduated sooner than expected and I was offered this job in Mimir. I knew it would be almost a year before Gerry's job was done on Woden so he could come on to Mimir, and that's why I hid in the closet there. There was plenty of room for me and I was willing to pay the fine. There were only the two of us kids—Gerry and I—and I haven't seen him for so long, and I didn't want to wait another year when I could see him now, even though I knew I would be breaking some kind of a regulation when I did it."

I knew I would be breaking some kind of a regulation. In a way, she could not be blamed for her ignorance of the law; she was of Earth and had not realized that the laws of the space frontier must, of necessity, be as hard and relentless as the environment that gave them birth. Yet, to protect such as her from the results of their own ignorance of the frontier, there had been a sign over the door that led to the section of the *Stardust* that housed the EDSs, a sign that was plain for all to see and heed: UNAUTHORIZED PERSONNEL KEEP OUT!

"Does your brother know that you took passage on the *Stardust* for Mimir?"

"Oh, yes. I sent him a spacegram telling him about my graduation and about going to Mimir on the *Stardust* a month before I left Earth. I already knew Mimir was where he would be stationed in a little over a year. He gets a promotion then, and he'll be based on Mimir and not have to stay out a year at a time on field trips, like he does now."

There were two different survey groups on Woden, and he asked, "What is his name?"

"Cross—Gerry Cross. He's in Group Two— that was the way his address read. Do you know him?"

Group One had requested the serum: Group Two was eight thousand miles away, across the Western Sea.

"No, I've never met him," he said, then turned to the control board and cut the deceleration to a fraction of a gravity, knowing as he did so that it could not avert the ultimate end, yet doing the only thing he could do to prolong that ultimate end. The sensation was like that of the ship suddenly dropping, and the girl's involuntary movement of surprise half lifted her from her seat.

"We're going faster now, aren't we?" she asked. "Why are we doing that?"

He told her the truth. "To save fuel for a little while."

"You mean we don't have very much?"

He delayed the answer he must give her so soon to ask, "How did you manage to stow away?"

"I just sort of walked in when no one was looking my way," she said. "I was practicing my Gelanese on the native girl who does the cleaning in the Ship's Supply office when someone came in with an order for supplies for the survey crew on Woden. I slipped into the closet there after the ship was ready to go just before you came in. It was an impulse of the moment to stow away, so I could get to see Gerry—and from the way you keep looking at me so grim, I'm not sure it was a very wise impulse. But I'll be a model criminal—or do I mean prisoner?" She smiled at him again. "I intended to pay for my keep on top of paying the fine. I can cook and I can patch clothes for everyone and I know how to do all kinds of useful things, even a little bit about nursing."

There was one more question to ask:

"Did you know what the supplies were that the survey crew ordered?"

"Why, no. Equipment they needed in their work, I supposed."

Why couldn't she have been a man with some ulterior motive? A fugitive from justice hoping to lose himself on a raw new world; an opportunist seeking transportation to the new colonies where he might find golden fleece[5] for the taking; a crackpot with a mission. Perhaps once in his lifetime an EDS pilot would find such a stowaway on his ship—warped men, mean and selfish men, brutal and dangerous men—but never before a smiling, blue-eyed girl who was willing to pay her fine and work for her keep that she might see her brother.

---

5. golden fleece: The reference is to the Greek myth of Jason and the Argonauts, who sailed to a faraway land to capture a golden sheepskin.

He turned to the board and turned the switch that would signal the *Stardust*. The call would be futile, but he could not, until he had exhausted that one vain hope, seize her and thrust her into the air lock as he would an animal— or a man. The delay, in the meantime, would not be dangerous with the EDS decelerating at fractional gravity.

📖 **QUESTIONING**

4. The **third-person-limited point of view** lets us witness the pilot's inner conflict. What do you learn about him in these last two paragraphs?

A voice spoke from the communicator. "*Stardust*. Identify yourself and proceed."

"Barton, EDS 34GII. Emergency. Give me Commander Delhart."

There was a faint confusion of noises as the request went through the proper channels. The girl was watching him, no longer smiling.

"Are you going to order them to come back after me?" she asked.

The communicator clicked and there was the sound of a distant voice saying, "Commander, the EDS requests . . ."

"Are they coming back after me?" she asked again. "Won't I get to see my brother after all?"

"Barton?" The blunt, gruff voice of Commander Delhart came from the communicator. "What's this about an emergency?"

"A stowaway," he answered.

"A stowaway?" There was a slight surprise to the question. "That's rather unusual—but why the 'emergency' call? You discovered him in time, so there should be no appreciable danger, and I presume you've informed Ship's Records so his nearest relatives can be notified."

"That's why I had to call you, first. The stowaway is still aboard and the circumstances are so different—"

"Different?" the commander interrupted, impatience in his voice. "How can they be different? You know you have a limited supply of fuel; you also know the law as well as I do: 'Any

stowaway discovered in an EDS shall be jettisoned immediately following discovery.'"

There was the sound of a sharply indrawn breath from the girl. "*What does he mean?*"

"The stowaway is a girl."

"*What?*"

"She wanted to see her brother. She's only a kid and she didn't know what she was really doing."

"I see." All the curtness was gone from the commander's voice. "So you called me in the hope I could do something?" Without waiting for an answer he went on, "I'm sorry—I can do nothing. This cruiser must maintain its schedule; the life of not one person but the lives of many depend on it. I know how you feel but I'm powerless to help you. You'll have to go through with it. I'll have you connected with Ship's Records."

The communicator faded to a faint rustle of sound, and he turned back to the girl. She was leaning forward on the bench, almost rigid, her eyes fixed wide and frightened.

"What did he mean, to go through with it? To jettison[6] me . . . to go through with it—what did he mean? Not the way it sounded . . . he couldn't have. What did he mean—what did he really mean?"

Her time was too short for the comfort of a lie to be more than a cruelly fleeting delusion.

"He meant it the way it sounded."

"*No!*" She recoiled from him as though he had struck her, one hand half raised as though to fend him off and stark unwillingness to believe in her eyes.

"It will have to be."

"No! You're joking—you're insane! You can't mean it!"

---

6. **jettison** (jet′ə·sən) *v.*: throw overboard, usually used in reference to goods.

Vocabulary
recoiled (ri·koild′) *v.*: drew back in fear, surprise, or disgust.

"I'm sorry." He spoke slowly to her, gently. "I should have told you before—I should have, but I had to do what I could first; I had to call the *Stardust*. You heard what the commander said."

"But you can't—if you make me leave the ship, I'll *die*."

"I know."

She searched his face, and the unwillingness to believe left her eyes, giving way slowly to a look of dazed horror.

"You know?" She spoke the words far apart, numbly and wonderingly.

"I know. It has to be like that."

"You mean it—you really mean it." She sagged back against the wall, small and limp like a little rag doll, and all the protesting and disbelief gone. "You're going to do it—you're going to make me die?"

"I'm sorry," he said again. "You'll never know how sorry I am. It has to be that way and no human in the universe can change it."

"You're going to make me die and I didn't do anything to die for—I didn't *do* anything—"

He sighed, deep and weary. "I know you didn't, child. I know you didn't."

"EDS." The communicator rapped brisk and metallic. "This is Ship's Records. Give us all information on subject's identification disk."

He got out of his chair to stand over her. She clutched the edge of the seat, her upturned face white under the brown hair and the lipstick standing out like a blood-red cupid's bow.

"*Now?*"

"I want your identification disk," he said.

She released the edge of the seat and fumbled at the chain that suspended the plastic disk from her neck with fingers that were trembling and awkward. He reached down and unfastened the clasp for her, then returned with the disk to his chair.

QUESTIONING

5. How do you **predict** the story will end? What do you think will happen to the stowaway?

"Here's your data, Records: Identification Number T837—"

"One moment," Records interrupted. "This is to be filed on the gray card, of course?"

"Yes."

"And the time of execution?"

"I'll tell you later."

"Later? This is highly irregular; the time of the subject's death is required before—"

He kept the thickness out of his voice with an effort. "Then we'll do it in a highly irregular manner—you'll hear the disk read first. The subject is a girl and she's listening to everything that's said. Are you capable of understanding that?"

There was a brief, almost shocked silence; then Records said meekly, "Sorry. Go ahead."

He began to read the disk, reading it slowly to delay the inevitable for as long as possible, trying to help her by giving her what little time he could to recover from her first horror and let it resolve into the calm of acceptance and resignation.

"Number T8374 dash Y54. Name, Marilyn Lee Cross. Sex, female. Born July 7, 2160." *She was only eighteen.* "Height, five-three. Weight, a hundred and ten." *Such a slight weight, yet enough to add fatally to the mass of the shell-thin bubble that was an EDS.* "Hair, brown. Eyes, blue. Complexion, light. Blood type O." *Irrelevant data.* "Destination, Port City, Mimir." *Invalid data.*

He finished and said, "I'll call you later," then turned once again to the girl. She was huddled back against the wall, watching him with a look of numb and wondering fascination.

"They're waiting for you to kill me, aren't they? They want me dead, don't they? You and everybody on the cruiser want me dead, don't you?" Then the numbness broke and her voice was that of a frightened and bewildered child. "Everybody wants me dead and I didn't *do* anything. I didn't hurt anyone—I only wanted to see my brother."

"It's not the way you think—it isn't that way at all," he said. "Nobody wants it this way; nobody would ever let it be this way if it was humanly possible to change it."

"Then why is it? I don't understand. Why is it?"

"This ship is carrying kala fever serum to Group One on Woden. Their own supply was destroyed by a tornado. Group Two—the crew your brother is in—is eight thousand miles away across the Western Sea, and their helicopters can't cross it to help Group One. The fever is invariably fatal unless the serum can be had in time, and the six men in Group One will die unless this ship reaches them on schedule. These little ships are always given barely enough fuel to reach their destination, and if you stay aboard, your added weight will cause it to use up all its fuel before it reaches the ground. It will crash then, and you and I will die and so will the six men waiting for the fever serum."

It was a full minute before she spoke, and as she considered his words, the expression of numbness left her eyes.

"Is that it?" she asked at last. "Just that the ship doesn't have enough fuel?"

"Yes."

"I can go alone or I can take seven others with me—is that the way it is?"

"That's the way it is."

"And nobody wants me to have to die?"

"Nobody."

"Then maybe— Are you sure nothing can be done about it? Wouldn't people help me if they could?"

"Everyone would like to help you, but there is nothing anyone can do. I did the only thing I could do when I called the *Stardust*."

"And it won't come back—but there might be other cruisers, mightn't there? Isn't there any hope at all that there might be someone, somewhere, who could do something to help me?"

She was leaning forward a little in her eagerness as she waited for his answer.

"No."

The word was like the drop of a cold stone and she again leaned back against the wall, the hope and eagerness leaving her face. "You're sure—you *know* you're sure?"

"I'm sure. There are no other cruisers within forty light-years; there is nothing and no one to change things."

She dropped her gaze to her lap and began twisting a pleat of her skirt between her fingers, saying no more as her mind began to adapt itself to the grim knowledge.

It was better so; with the going of all hope would go the fear; with the going of all hope would come resignation. She needed time and she could have so little of it. How much?

The EDSs were not equipped with hull-cooling units; their speed had to be reduced to a moderate level before they entered the atmosphere. They were decelerating at .10 gravity, approaching their destination at a far higher speed than the computers had calculated on. The *Stardust* had been quite near Woden when she launched the EDS; their present velocity was putting them nearer by the second. There would be a critical point, soon to be reached, when he would have to resume deceleration. When he did so, the girl's weight would be multiplied by the gravities of deceleration, would become, suddenly, a factor of paramount importance, the factor the computers had been ignorant of when they determined the amount of fuel the EDS should have. She would have to go when deceleration began; it could be no other way. When would that be—how long could he let her stay?

"How long can I stay?"

He winced involuntarily from the words that were so like an echo of his own thoughts. How long? He didn't know; he would have to ask the

Vocabulary
paramount (par′ə·mount′) *adj.*: supreme; dominant.

ship's computers. Each EDS was given a meager surplus of fuel to compensate for unfavorable conditions within the atmosphere, and relatively little fuel was being consumed for the time being. The memory banks of the computers would still contain all data pertaining to the course set for the EDS; such data would not be erased until the EDS reached its destination. He had only to give the computers the new data—the girl's weight and the exact time at which he had reduced the deceleration to .10.

"Barton." Commander Delhart's voice came abruptly from the communicator as he opened his mouth to call the *Stardust*. "A check with Records shows me you haven't completed your report. Did you reduce the deceleration?"

So the commander knew what he was trying to do.

"I'm decelerating at point ten," he answered. "I cut the deceleration at seventeen fifty and the weight is a hundred and ten. I would like to stay at point ten as long as the computers say I can. Will you give them the question?"

It was contrary to regulations for an EDS pilot to make any changes in the course or degree of deceleration the computers had set for him, but the commander made no mention of the violation. Neither did he ask the reason for it. It was not necessary for him to ask; he had not become commander of an interstellar cruiser without both intelligence and an understanding of human nature. He said only, "I'll have that given to the computers."

The communicator fell silent and he and the girl waited, neither of them speaking. They would not have to wait long; the computers would give the answer within moments of the asking. The new factors would be fed into the steel maw[7] of the first bank, and the electrical impulses would go through the complex circuits. Here and there a relay might click, a tiny cog turn over, but it would be essentially the electrical impulses that found the answer; formless, mindless, invisible, determining with utter precision how long the pale girl beside him might live. Then five little segments of metal in the second bank would trip in rapid succession against an inked ribbon and a second steel maw would spit out the slip of paper that bore the answer.

QUESTIONING

6. Do the technological and scientific details seem believable to you? What questions would you ask the author?

The chronometer[8] on the instrument board read 18:10 when the commander spoke again.

"You will resume deceleration at nineteen ten."

She looked toward the chronometer, then quickly away from it. "Is that when . . . when I go?" she asked. He nodded and she dropped her eyes to her lap again.

"I'll have the course correction given to you," the commander said. "Ordinarily I would never permit anything like this, but I understand your position. There is nothing I can do, other than what I've just done, and you will not deviate[9] from these new instructions. You will complete your report at nineteen ten. Now—here are the course corrections."

The voice of some unknown technician read them to him, and he wrote them down on the pad clipped to the edge of the control board. There would, he saw, be periods of deceleration when he neared the atmosphere when the deceleration would be five gravities—and at five gravities, one hundred ten pounds would become five hundred fifty pounds.

The technician finished and he terminated the contact with a brief acknowledgment. Then, hesitating a moment, he reached out and shut off the communicator. It was 18:13 and he would have

---

7. **maw** *n.*: huge, all-consuming mouth.

8. **chronometer** (krə·näm′ət·ər) *n.*: instrument for measuring time scientifically.

9. **deviate** (dē′vē·āt′) *v.*: turn aside or away from a given course of action or practice.

nothing to report until 19:10. In the meantime, it somehow seemed indecent to permit others to hear what she might say in her last hour.

He began to check the instrument readings, going over them with unnecessary slowness. She would have to accept the circumstances, and there was nothing he could do to help her into acceptance; words of sympathy would only delay it.

It was 18:20 when she stirred from her motionlessness and spoke.

"So that's the way it has to be with me?"

He swung around to face her. "You understand now, don't you? No one would ever let it be like this if it could be changed."

"I understand," she said. Some of the color had returned to her face and the lipstick no longer stood out so vividly red. "There isn't enough fuel for me to stay. When I hid on this ship, I got into something I didn't know anything about and now I have to pay for it."

She had violated a man-made law that said KEEP OUT, but the penalty was not for men's making or desire and it was a penalty men could not revoke. A physical law had decreed: *h amount of fuel will power an EDS with a mass of m safely to its destination;* and a second physical law had decreed: *h amount of fuel will not power an EDS with a mass of m plus x safely to its destination.*

EDSs obeyed only physical laws, and no amount of human sympathy for her could alter the second law.

"But I'm afraid. I don't want to die—not now. I want to live, and nobody is doing anything to help me; everybody is letting me go ahead and acting just like nothing was going to happen to me. I'm going to die and nobody *cares.*"

"We all do," he said. "I do and the commander does and the clerk in Ship's Records; we all care

> ### 📖 QUESTIONING
> 7. Since this story is told from Barton's **point of view,** how do we learn about Marilyn? What do we learn about her in this paragraph?

and each of us did what little he could to help you. It wasn't enough—it was almost nothing—but it was all we could do."

"Not enough fuel—I can understand that," she said, as though she had not heard his own words. "But to have to die for it. *Me* alone . . ."

How hard it must be for her to accept the fact. She had never known danger of death, had never known the environments where the lives of men could be as fragile and fleeting as sea foam tossed against a rocky shore. She belonged on gentle Earth, in that secure and peaceful society where she could be young and gay and laughing with the others of her kind, where life was precious and well guarded and there was always the assurance that tomorrow would come. She belonged in that world of soft winds and a warm sun, music and moonlight and gracious manners, and not on the hard, bleak frontier.

"How did it happen to me so terribly quickly? An hour ago I was on the *Stardust,* going to Mimir. Now the *Stardust* is going on without me and I'm going to die and I'll never see Gerry and Mama and Daddy again—I'll never see anything again."

He hesitated, wondering how he could explain it to her so she would really understand and not feel she had somehow been the victim of a reasonlessly cruel injustice. She did not know what the frontier was like; she thought in terms of safe, secure Earth. Pretty girls were not jettisoned on Earth; there was a law against it. On Earth her plight would have filled the newscasts and a fast black patrol ship would have been racing to her rescue. Everyone, everywhere, would have known of Marilyn Lee Cross, and no effort would have been spared to save her life. But this was not Earth and there were no patrol ships; only the *Stardust,* leaving them behind at many times the speed of light. There was no one to help her; there would be no Marilyn Lee Cross smiling from the newscasts tomorrow.

Marilyn Lee Cross would be but a poignant memory for an EDS pilot and a name on a gray card in Ship's Records.

"It's different here; it's not like back on Earth," he said. "It isn't that no one cares; it's that no one can do anything to help. The frontier is big, and here along its rim the colonies and exploration parties are scattered so thin and far between. On Woden, for example, there are only sixteen men—sixteen men on an entire world. The exploration parties, the survey crews, the little first colonies—they're all fighting alien environments, trying to make a way for those who will follow after. The environments fight back, and those who go first usually make mistakes only once. There is no margin of safety along the rim of the frontier; there can't be until the way is made for the others who will come later, until the new worlds are tamed and settled. Until then men will have to pay the penalty for making mistakes, with no one to help them, because there is no one *to* help them."

"I was going to Mimir," she said. "I didn't know about the frontier; I was only going to Mimir and *it's* safe."

"Mimir is safe, but you left the cruiser that was taking you there."

She was silent for a little while. "It was all so wonderful at first; there was plenty of room for me on this ship and I would be seeing Gerry so soon. I didn't know about the fuel, didn't know what would happen to me. . . ."

Her words trailed away, and he turned his attention to the viewscreen, not wanting to stare at her as she fought her way through the black horror of fear toward the calm gray of acceptance.

Woden was a ball, enshrouded in the blue haze of its atmosphere, swimming in space against the background of star-sprinkled dead blackness. The great mass of Manning's Continent sprawled like a gigantic hourglass in the Eastern Sea, with the western half of the Eastern Continent still visible. There was a thin line of shadow along the right-hand edge of the globe, and the Eastern Continent was disappearing into it as the planet turned on its axis. An hour before, the entire continent had been in view; now a thousand miles of it had gone into the thin edge of shadow and around to the night that lay on the other side of the world. The dark blue spot that was Lotus Lake was approaching the shadow. It was somewhere near the southern edge of the lake that Group Two had their camp. It would be night there soon, and quick behind the coming of night the rotation of Woden on its axis would put Group Two beyond the reach of the ship's radio.

He would have to tell her before it was too late for her to talk to her brother. In a way, it would be better for both of them should they not do so, but it was not for him to decide. To each of them the last words would be something to hold and cherish, something that would cut like the blade of a knife yet would be infinitely precious to remember, she for her own brief moments to live and he for the rest of his life.

He held down the button that would flash the grid lines on the viewscreen and used the known diameter of the planet to estimate the distance the southern tip of Lotus Lake had yet to go until it passed beyond radio range. It was approximately five hundred miles. Five hundred miles; thirty minutes—and the chronometer read 18:30. Allowing for error in estimating, it would not be later than 19:05 that the turning of Woden would cut off her brother's voice.

The first border of the Western continent was already in sight along the left side of the world. Four thousand miles across it lay the shore of the Western Sea and the camp of Group One. It had been in the Western Sea that the tornado had originated, to strike with such fury at the camp and destroy half their prefabricated buildings, including the one that housed the medical supplies. Two days before, the tornado had not existed; it had been no more than great gentle masses of air over the calm Western Sea. Group One had gone about their routine survey work, unaware of the meeting of air masses out at sea, unaware of the force the union was spawning. It had struck their camp without warning—a thundering, roaring destruction that sought to annihilate all that lay before it. It had passed on, leaving the wreckage in its wake. It had destroyed the labor of months and had doomed six men to die and then, as though its task was accomplished, it once more began to resolve into gentle masses of air. But, for all its deadliness, it had destroyed with neither malice nor intent. It had been a blind and mindless force, obeying the laws of nature, and it would have followed the same course with the same fury had men never existed.

Existence required order, and there was order; the laws of nature, irrevocable and immutable. Men could learn to use them, but men could not change them. The circumference of a circle was always pi times the diameter, and no science of man would ever make it otherwise. The combination of chemical A with chemical B under condition C invariably produced reaction D. The law of gravitation was a rigid equation, and it made no distinction between the fall of a leaf and the ponderous circling of a binary star system. The nuclear conversion process powered the cruisers that carried men to the stars; the same process in the form of a nova would destroy a world with equal efficiency. The laws *were,* and the universe moved in obedience to them. Along the frontier were arrayed all the forces of nature, and sometimes they destroyed those who were fighting their way outward from Earth. The men of the frontier had long ago learned the bitter futility of cursing the forces that would destroy them, for the forces were blind and deaf; the futility of looking to the heavens for mercy, for the stars of the galaxy swung in their long, long sweep of two hundred million years, as inexorably[10] controlled as they

by the laws that knew neither hatred nor compassion. The men of the frontier knew—but how was a girl from Earth to fully understand? *h amount of fuel will not power an EDS with a mass of m plus x safely to its destination.* To him and her brother and parents she was a sweet-faced girl in her teens; to the laws of nature she was x, the unwanted factor in a cold equation.

QUESTIONING
8. What do you think of this view of humans and the "laws of nature"?

She stirred again on the seat. "Could I write a letter? I want to write to Mama and Daddy. And I'd like to talk to Gerry. Could you let me talk to him over your radio there?"

"I'll try to get him," he said.

He switched on the normal-space transmitter and pressed the signal button. Someone answered the buzzer almost immediately.

"Hello. How's it going with you fellows now—is the EDS on its way?"

"This isn't Group One; this is the EDS," he said. "Is Gerry Cross there?"

"Gerry? He and two others went out in the helicopter this morning and aren't back yet. It's almost sundown, though, and he ought to be back right away—in less than an hour at the most."

"Can you connect me through to the radio in his copter?"

"Huh-uh. It's been out of commission for two months—some printed circuits went haywire[11] and we can't get any more until the next cruiser

---

10. **inexorably** (in·eks′ə·rə·blē) *adv.:* in an unchanged manner.

11. **haywire** *adj.:* out of order.

Vocabulary
annihilate (ə·nī′ə·lāt′) *v.:* destroy; demolish.

irrevocable (i·rev′ə·kə·bəl) *adj.:* irreversible; incapable of being canceled or undone.

immutable (i·myoot′ə·bəl) *adj.:* unchangeable; never changing or varying.

ponderous (pän′dər·əs) *adj.:* heavy and slow moving.

stops by. Is it something important—bad news for him, or something?"

"Yes—it's very important. When he comes in, get him to the transmitter as soon as you possibly can."

"I'll do that; I'll have one of the boys waiting at the field with a truck. Is there anything else I can do?"

"No, I guess that's all. Get him there as soon as you can and signal me."

He turned the volume to an inaudible minimum, an act that would not affect the functioning of the signal buzzer, and unclipped the pad of paper from the control board. He tore off the sheet containing his flight instructions and handed the pad to her, together with pencil.

"I'd better write to Gerry too," she said as she took them. "He might not get back to camp in time."

She began to write, her fingers still clumsy and uncertain in the way they handled the pencil, and the top of it trembling a little as she poised it between words. He turned back to the viewscreen, to stare at it without seeing it.

She was a lonely little child trying to say her last goodbye, and she would lay out her heart to them. She would tell them how much she loved them and she would tell them to not feel bad about it, that it was only something that must happen eventually to everyone and she was not afraid. The last would be a lie and it would be there to read between the sprawling, uneven lines: a valiant little lie that would make the hurt all the greater for them.

Her brother was of the frontier and he would understand. He would not hate the EDS pilot for doing nothing to prevent her going; he would know there had been nothing the pilot could do. He would understand, though the understanding would not soften the shock and pain when he learned his sister was gone. But the others, her father and mother—they would not understand. They were of Earth and they would think in the manner of those who had never lived where the safety margin of life was a thin, thin line—and sometimes nothing at all. What would they think of the faceless, unknown pilot who had sent her to her death?

They would hate him with cold and terrible intensity, but it really didn't matter. He would never see them, never know them. He would have only the memories to remind him; only the nights of fear, when a blue-eyed girl in gypsy sandals would come in his dreams to die again. . . .

He scowled at the viewscreen and tried to force his thoughts into less emotional channels. There was nothing he could do to help her. She had unknowingly subjected herself to the penalty of a law that recognized neither innocence nor youth nor beauty, that was incapable of sympathy or leniency. Regret was illogical—and yet, could knowing it to be illogical ever keep it away?

She stopped occasionally, as though trying to find the right words to tell them what she wanted them to know; then the pencil would resume its whispering to the paper. It was 18:37 when she folded the letter in a square and wrote a name on it. She began writing another, twice looking up at the chronometer, as though she feared the black hand might reach its rendezvous[12] before she had finished. It was 18:45 when she folded it as she had done the first letter and wrote a name and address on it.

She held the letters out to him. "Will you take care of these and see that they're enveloped and mailed?"

"Of course." He took them from her hand and placed them in a pocket of his gray uniform shirt.

"These can't be sent off until the next cruiser stops by, and the *Stardust* will have long since told them about me, won't it?" she asked. He nodded and she went on: "That makes the letters

---

12. **rendezvous** (rän′dā·vōō′) *n.:* appointed meeting; here, the movement of a clock's hand to the next digit.

not important in one way, but in another way they're very important—to me, and to them."

"I know. I understand, and I'll take care of them."

She glanced at the chronometer, then back to him. "It seems to move faster all the time, doesn't it?"

He said nothing, unable to think of anything to say, and she asked, "Do you think Gerry will come back to camp in time?"

"I think so. They said he should be in right away."

She began to roll the pencil back and forth between her palms. "I hope he does. I feel sick and scared and I want to hear his voice again and maybe I won't feel so alone. I'm a coward and I can't help it."

"No," he said, "you're not a coward. You're afraid, but you're not a coward."

"Is there a difference?"

He nodded. "A lot of difference."

"I feel so alone. I never did feel like this before; like I was all by myself and there was nobody to care what happened to me. Always, before, there were Mama and Daddy there and my friends around me. I had lots of friends, and they had a going-away party for me the night before I left."

Friends and music and laughter for her to remember—and on the viewscreen Lotus Lake was going into the shadow.

"Is it the same with Gerry?" she asked. "I mean, if he should make a mistake, would he have to die for it, all alone and with no one to help him?"

"It's the same with all, along the frontier; it will always be like that so long as there is a frontier."

"Gerry didn't tell us. He said the pay was good, and he sent money home all the time because Daddy's little shop just brought in a bare living, but he didn't tell us it was like this."

"He didn't tell you his work was dangerous?"

"Well—yes. He mentioned that, but we didn't understand. I always thought danger along the frontier was something that was a lot of fun; an exciting adventure, like in the three-D shows." A wan smile touched her face for a moment. "Only it's not, is it? It's not the same at all, because when it's real you can't go home after the show is over."

"No," he said. "No, you can't."

Her glance flicked from the chronometer to the door of the air lock, then down to the pad and pencil she still held. She shifted her position slightly to lay them on the bench beside her, moving one foot out a little. For the first time he saw that she was not wearing Vegan gypsy sandals, but only cheap imitations; the expensive Vegan leather was some kind of grained plastic, the silver buckle was gilded iron, the jewels were colored glass. *Daddy's little shop just brought in a bare living. . . .* She must have left college in her second year, to take the course in linguistics that would enable her to make her own way and help her brother provide for her parents, earning what she could by part-time work after classes were over. Her personal possessions on the *Stardust* would be taken back to her parents—they would neither be of much value nor occupy much storage space on the return voyage.

"Isn't it—" She stopped, and he looked at her questioningly. "Isn't it cold in here?" she asked, almost apologetically. "Doesn't it seem cold to you?"

"Why, yes," he said. He saw by the main temperature gauge that the room was at precisely normal temperature. "Yes, it's colder than it should be."

"I wish Gerry would get back before it's too late. Do you really think he will, and you didn't just say so to make me feel better?"

"I think he will—they said he would be in pretty soon." On the viewscreen Lotus Lake had gone into the shadow but for the thin blue line of its western edge, and it was apparent he had overestimated the time she would have in which to talk to her brother. Reluctantly, he said to her, "His camp will be out of radio range in a few minutes; he's on that part of Woden that's in the shadow"—he indicated the viewscreen—"and the turning of Woden will put him beyond contact. There may not be much time left when he comes in—not much time to talk to him before he fades out. I wish I could do something about it—I would call him right now if I could."

"Not even as much time as I will have to stay?"

"I'm afraid not."

"Then—" She straightened and looked toward the air lock with pale resolution. "Then I'll go when Gerry passes beyond range. I won't wait any longer after that—I won't have anything to wait for."

Again there was nothing he could say.

"Maybe I shouldn't wait at all. Maybe I'm selfish—maybe it would be better for Gerry if you just told him about it afterward."

There was an unconscious pleading for denial in the way she spoke and he said, "He wouldn't want you to do that, to not wait for him."

"It's already coming dark where he is, isn't it? There will be all the long night before him, and Mama and Daddy don't know yet that I won't ever be coming back like I promised them I would. I've caused everyone I love to be hurt, haven't I? I didn't want to—I didn't intend to."

"It wasn't your fault," he said. "It wasn't your fault at all. They'll know that. They'll understand."

"At first I was so afraid to die that I was a coward and thought only of myself. Now I see how selfish I was. The terrible thing about dying like this is not that I'll be gone but that I'll never see them again; never be able to tell them that I didn't take them for granted; never be able to tell them I knew of the sacrifices they made to make my life happier, that I knew all the things they did for me and that I loved them so much more than I ever told them. I've never told them any of those things. You don't tell them such things when you're young and your life is all before you—you're so afraid of sounding sentimental and silly. But it's so different when you have to die—you wish you had told them while you could, and you wish you could tell them you're sorry for all the little mean things you ever did or said to them. You wish you could tell them that you didn't really mean to ever hurt their feelings and for them to only remember that you always loved them far more than you ever let them know."

"You don't have to tell them that," he said. "They will know—they've always known it."

"Are you sure?" she asked. "How can you be sure? My people are strangers to you."

"Wherever you go, human nature and human hearts are the same."

tears and told me not to cry, that Flossy was gone for just a little while, for just long enough to get herself a new fur coat, and she would be on the foot of my bed the very next morning. I believed him and quit crying and went to sleep dreaming about my kitten coming back. When I woke up the next morning, there was Flossy on the foot of my bed in a brand-new white fur coat, just like he had said she would be. It wasn't until a long time later that Mama told me Gerry had got the pet-shop owner out of bed at four in the morning and, when the man got mad about it, Gerry told him he was either going to go

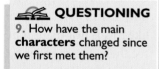

"And they will know what I want them to know—that I love them?"

"They've always known it, in a way far better than you could ever put in words for them."

QUESTIONING
9. How have the main **characters** changed since we first met them?

"I keep remembering the things they did for me, and it's the little things they did that seem to be the most important to me, now. Like Gerry—he sent me a bracelet of fire rubies on my sixteenth birthday. It was beautiful—it must have cost him a month's pay. Yet I remember him more for what he did the night my kitten got run over in the street. I was only six years old and he held me in his arms and wiped away my

down and sell him the white kitten right then or he'd break his neck."

"It's always the little things you remember people by, all the little things they did because they wanted to do them for you. You've done the same for Gerry and your father and mother; all kinds of things that you've forgotten about, but that they will never forget."

"I hope I have. I would like for them to remember me like that."

"They will."

"I wish—" She swallowed. "The way I'll die—I wish they wouldn't ever think of that. I've read how people look who die in space—their insides all ruptured and exploded and their lungs out between their teeth and then, a few seconds later, they're all dry and shapeless and horribly ugly. I don't want them to ever think of me as something dead and horrible like that."

"You're their own, their child and their sister. They could never think of you other than the way you would want them to, the way you looked the last time they saw you."

"I'm still afraid," she said. "I can't help it, but I don't want Gerry to know it. If he gets back in time, I'm going to act like I'm not afraid at all and—"

The signal buzzer interrupted her, quick and imperative.

"I wanted to see you," she said again. "I wanted to see you, so I hid on this ship—"

"You *hid* on it?"

"I'm a stowaway. . . . I didn't know what it would mean—"

"*Marilyn!*" It was the cry of a man who calls, hopeless and desperate, to someone already and forever gone from him. "What have you done?"

"I . . . it's not—" Then her own composure broke and the cold little hand gripped his shoulder convulsively. "Don't, Gerry—I only wanted to see you; I didn't intend to hurt you. Please, Gerry, don't feel like that—"

"Gerry!" She came to her feet. "It's Gerry now!"

He spun the volume control knob and asked, "Gerry Cross?"

"Yes," her brother answered, an undertone of tenseness to his reply. "The bad news—what is it?"

She answered for him, standing close behind him and leaning down a little toward the communicator, her hand resting small and cold on his shoulder.

"Hello, Gerry." There was only a faint quaver to betray the careful casualness of her voice. "I wanted to see you—"

"Marilyn!" There was sudden and terrible apprehension in the way he spoke her name. "What are you doing on that EDS?"

Something warm and wet splashed on his wrist, and he slid out of the chair to help her into it and swing the microphone down to her level.

"Don't feel like that. Don't let me go knowing you feel like that—"

The sob she had tried to hold back choked in her throat, and her brother spoke to her. "Don't cry, Marilyn." His voice was suddenly deep and infinitely gentle, with all the pain held out of it. "Don't cry, Sis—you mustn't do that. It's all right, honey—everything is all right."

Vocabulary
apprehension (ap′rē·hen′shən) *n.*: dread; fear of a future event.

"I—" Her lower lip quivered and she bit into it. "I didn't want you to feel that way—I just wanted us to say goodbye, because I have to go in a minute."

"Sure—sure. That's the way it'll be, Sis. I didn't mean to sound the way I did." Then his voice changed to a tone of quick and urgent demand. "EDS—have you called the *Stardust*? Did you check with the computers?"

"I called the *Stardust* almost an hour ago. It can't turn back; there are no other cruisers within forty light-years, and there isn't enough fuel."

"Are you sure that the computers had the correct data—sure of everything?"

"Yes—do you think I could ever let it happen if I wasn't sure? I did everything I could do. If there was anything at all I could do now, I would do it."

"He tried to help me, Gerry." Her lower lip was no longer trembling and the short sleeves of her blouse were wet where she had dried her tears. "No one can help me and I'm not going to cry anymore and everything will be all right with you and Daddy and Mama, won't it?"

"Sure—sure it will. We'll make out fine."

Her brother's words were beginning to come in more faintly, and he turned the volume control to maximum. "He's going out of range," he said to her. "He'll be gone within another minute."

"You're fading out, Gerry," she said. "You're going out of range. I wanted to tell you—but I can't now. We must say goodbye so soon—but maybe I'll see you again. Maybe I'll come to you in your dreams with my hair in braids and crying because the kitten in my arms is dead; maybe I'll be the touch of a breeze that whispers to you as it goes by; maybe I'll be one of those gold-winged larks you told me about, singing my silly head off to you; maybe, at times, I'll be nothing you can see, but you will know I'm there beside you. Think of me like that, Gerry; always like that and not—the other way."

Dimmed to a whisper by the turning of Woden, the answer came back:

"Always like that, Marilyn—always like that and never any other way."

"Our time is up, Gerry—I have to go now. Good—" Her voice broke in midword and her mouth tried to twist into crying. She pressed her hand hard against it and when she spoke again the words came clear and true:

"Goodbye, Gerry."

Faint and ineffably poignant and tender, the last words came from the cold metal of the communicator:

"Goodbye, little sister . . ."

She sat motionless in the hush that followed, as though listening to the shadow-echoes of the words as they died away; then she turned away from the communicator, toward the air lock, and he pulled down the black lever beside him. The inner door of the air lock slid swiftly open to reveal the bare little cell that was waiting for her, and she walked to it.

She walked with her head up and the brown curls brushing her shoulders, with the white sandals stepping as sure and steady as the fractional gravity would permit and the gilded buckles twinkling with little lights of blue and red and crystal. He let her walk alone and made no move to help her, knowing she would not want it that way. She stepped into the air lock and turned to face him, only the pulse in her throat to betray the wild beating of her heart.

"I'm ready," she said.

He pushed the lever up and the door slid its quick barrier between them, enclosing her in black and utter darkness for her last moments of life. It clicked as it locked in place and he jerked down the red lever. There was a slight waver of the ship as the air gushed from the

Vocabulary
ineffably (in·ef′ə·blē) *adv.*: indescribably; inexpressibly.

lock, a vibration to the wall as though something had bumped the outer door in passing; then there was nothing and the ship was dropping true and steady again. He shoved the red lever back to close the door on the empty air lock and turned away, to walk to the pilot's chair with the slow steps of a man old and weary.

Back in the pilot's chair he pressed the signal button of the normal-space transmitter. There was no response; he had expected none. Her brother would have to wait through the night until the turning of Woden permitted contact through Group One.

It was not yet time to resume deceleration, and he waited while the ship dropped endlessly downward with him and the drives purred softly. He saw that the white hand of the supply-closet temperature gauge was on zero. A cold equation had been balanced and he was alone on the ship. Something shapeless and ugly was hurrying ahead of him, going to Woden, where her brother was waiting through the night, but the empty ship still lived for a little while with the presence of the girl who had not known about the forces that killed with neither hatred nor malice. It seemed, almost, that she still sat, small and bewildered and frightened, on the metal box beside him, her words echoing hauntingly clear in the void she had left behind her:

I didn't do anything to die for. . . .
I didn't do anything. . . . ▪

QUESTIONING

10. What is your response to the story's ending?

Meet the Writer

Tom Godwin

A Sci-fi Pioneer

Tom Godwin (1915–1980) had a difficult start in life. He had to leave school after third grade because of family problems, and he suffered from a curvature of the spine. He later tried to earn a living in two very different fields—as a prospector and as a writer of science fiction.

Godwin lived for many years in various small towns in the Mojave Desert in southeastern California—a harsh environment that many people might consider as alien as outer space. Perhaps his surroundings influenced his first sci-fi stories, which appeared in 1953 in a pioneering sci-fi magazine called *Astounding Science Fiction.*

When "The Cold Equations," his most popular and controversial short story, appeared in the August 1954 issue of *Astounding,* many readers were shocked and angry. They wanted Godwin's "problem story" to have a happy ending, a last-minute way of saving the young stowaway.

Godwin published more than a dozen short stories and several novels, including *The Survivors* (1958) and *The Space Barbarians* (1964), but none of his works caused the stir of "The Cold Equations." His later writing continued to explore similar themes about the harsh indifference of nature to human survival.

All Watched Over by Machines of Loving Grace

Richard Brautigan

I like to think (and
the sooner the better!)
of a cybernetic° meadow
where mammals and computers
5   live together in mutually
programming harmony
like pure water
touching clear sky.

I like to think
10   (right now, please!)
of a cybernetic forest
filled with pines and electronics
where deer stroll peacefully
past computers
15   as if they were flowers
with spinning blossoms.

I like to think
   (it has to be!)
of a cybernetic ecology
20   where we are free of our labors
and joined back to nature,
returned to our mammal
brothers and sisters,
and all watched over
25   by machines of loving grace.

---

3. cybernetic (sī′bər·net′ik) *adj.:* having
   to do with computers.

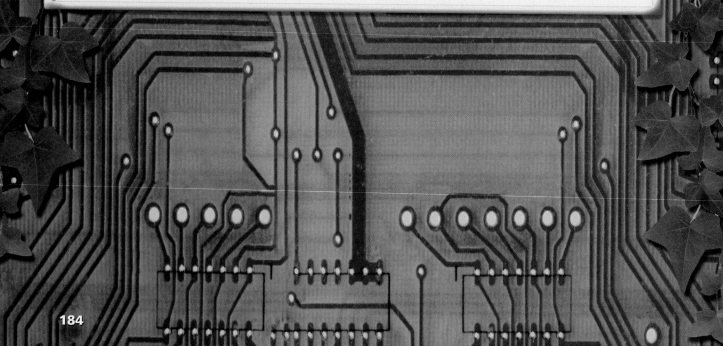

Response and Analysis

Reading Check

1. **Summarize** the main events of this story in a paragraph. Open with a note describing the **setting,** and then tell who the **characters** are and what their **problem** is. Be sure to explain how the problem is resolved.

Thinking Critically

2. What is the source of the story's **suspense**—that is, what questions kept you turning the pages? Did you have questions that the story didn't answer? Explain.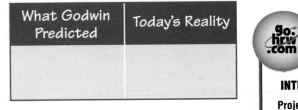

3. This story contrasts life on earth with life on the space frontier. In what important ways are those **settings** different? Do you find Godwin's space frontier believable? Why or why not?

4. Find the passage toward the middle of the story that explains its **title.** What are the "cold equations"? What other **images** of coldness can you find in the story?

5. Why do you suppose Godwin chose the **third-person-limited point of view** instead of making Barton the **first-person narrator**? How does the third-person-limited point of view affect the story's **tone, plot,** and **believability**? For help answering, try rewriting a brief passage in Barton's first-person voice.

6. How believable are Marilyn's choice to stow away and her later responses to her fate? If you were in her situation, how do you think you would react? Be sure to check your Quickwrite notes.

7. Do you think that Godwin and Brautigan (see the *Connection* on page 184) have similar or different attitudes toward technology? Explain your answer.

Extending and Evaluating

8. On page 167, we learn that Barton would have immediately carried out the regulation to eject the stowaway if it had been a man. What do you think of this attitude?

9. "The Cold Equations" was published in 1954, at a time when technology was far less advanced than it is now. Today we are living in what, to Godwin, was the future (though not as far in the future as the story is set). Do you think the technological "future" is turning out to be as cold and harsh as Godwin predicted? Explain your answer with specific examples from your own experience.

What Godwin Predicted	Today's Reality

WRITING

The Best Solution?

Do you agree that Barton has no choice but to let Marilyn die? Consider the problem presented in the story, and write a **problem-solution essay** in which you develop and support your ideas about what could have been done differently in "The Cold Equations."

▶ **Use "Analyzing Problems and Solutions," pages 212–219, for help with this assignment.**

go.
hrw
.com

INTERNET
Projects and
Activities
Keyword: LE5 10-3

SKILLS
FOCUS

Literary Skills
Analyze third-person-limited point of view.

Writing Skills
Write an essay analyzing problems and solutions.

Vocabulary Development

Using a Thesaurus to Find Synonyms

A **synonym** is a word that has the same or nearly the same meaning as another word. To find synonyms, writers use a **thesaurus** (a dictionary of synonyms). Most thesauri list synonyms based on a word's different shades of meaning, or **connotations.** You might want to look at all the synonyms and follow the cross-references given until you find the exact meaning you want to convey. See the example.

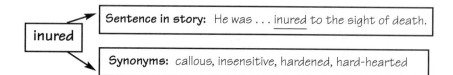

inured

Sentence in story: He was . . . inured to the sight of death.

Synonyms: callous, insensitive, hardened, hard-hearted

PRACTICE

Using a thesaurus, make **synonym charts** like the one above for the other Word Bank words. Before you list a synonym, check to be sure that it fits the meaning of the Word Bank word as it is used in the story.

Grammar Link

They Always Agree—Subject and Verb

One of the most common errors that people make in their writing and speaking has to do with subject-verb agreement. The rule is simple: **Singular subjects take singular verbs; plural subjects take plural verbs.** The trick is to find the subject and determine its **number.**

1. The number of the subject is not changed by a phrase following the subject.

    The <u>dials</u> in the EDS control room <u>were</u> flashing.

2. Singular subjects joined by *or* or *nor* take a singular verb.

    Neither <u>Barton</u> nor his <u>supervisor</u> <u>wants</u> to carry out the rules.

3. When a singular subject and a plural subject are joined by *or* or *nor,* the verb agrees with the subject nearer the verb.

    Neither <u>Barton</u> nor his <u>supervisors</u> <u>want</u> to eject the girl.

PRACTICE

Identify each subject below, and determine its number. Then, choose the correct verb.

1. Marilyn or her brother (is/are) going to die.

2. Neither Barton nor his supervisors (was/were) willing to make an exception to the rule.

3. The men on the EDS team (is/are) obliged to eject Marilyn.

Tip: When you proofread your writing, always check the subject of each sentence, and be sure the verb agrees with it in number.

▶ **For more help, see Agreement of Subject and Verb, 2a–n, in the Language Handbook.**

SKILLS FOCUS

Vocabulary Skills
Understand synonyms.

Grammar Skills
Use correct subject-verb agreement.

Taste—The Final Frontier

Generating Research Questions

When you set out to do a research project, your first, crucial step is to generate good research questions that will yield specific, relevant information. To help jump-start your questions, you may want to read a general encyclopedia article about your subject.

Helpful Hints

Here are some guidelines for generating productive research questions from materials you read:

- **Stay focused.** Don't write a long list of questions that cover everything you could possibly ask about a broad, general subject. Instead, zoom in on one aspect of your subject, and stick to questions about your narrowed topic. Try to identify the **main idea** of your topic to focus your questions better.

- **Check the subheads.** In an informational article, subheads indicate smaller divisions of the article's subject. They may give you ideas for a limited topic to research.

- **Do what reporters do.** Research questions that can be answered with yes or no will get you nowhere. When reporters investigate a story, their questions begin with *who, what, where, when, why,* and *how?* (For example, Who are the people involved? What happened?) Asking these **5W-How? questions** will lead you to specific information.

- **Be realistic.** Ask questions that you think you can find answers to with the resources available to you.

To sum up: Your first research task is to generate productive questions. Keep your questions on target (focused on your limited topic), and make them specific.

Vocabulary Development

breached (brēcht) *v.:* broken through.

palatable (pal'it·ə·bəl) *adj.:* tasty; fit to be eaten or drunk.

rancid (ran'sid) *adj.:* stale or spoiled.

mutiny (myo͞ot''n·ē) *n.:* rebellion or revolt against authority.

impoverished (im·päv'ər·isht) *v.* used as *adj.:* poor; without funds.

habitat (hab'i·tat') *n.:* person's environment or living space.

judicious (jo͞o·dish'əs) *adj.:* wise and careful.

metabolism (mə·tab'ə·liz'əm) *n.:* process by which living organisms turn food into energy and living tissue.

arresting (ə·rest'iŋ) *adj.:* interesting; striking.

Connecting to the Literature

Someday the space travel and colonization of other planets that is described in "The Cold Equations" may become a reality. Will space travelers be able to eat tasty and fresh foods, which until now have been missing from space missions? The following article discusses the plans and recipes that scientists are currently cooking up.

INTERNET
Interactive
Reading Model
Keyword: LE5 10-3

SKILLS FOCUS

Reading Skills
Generate relevant research questions.

Taste—The Final Frontier

from *The Guardian*, April 21, 2000

Esther Addley

Yuri Gagarin's first trip into space on April 12, 1961, was a brief one, which is perhaps just as well. If he'd stayed up any longer than his brief 108-minute orbit, he might have started getting peckish.[1] And since no one had any idea whether humans could swallow in zero gravity, he hadn't been allowed to take any food. The Soviets were ignoring the recommendations of the British interplanetary society in 1939, which advised that astronauts should be fattened up in advance, then given a daily pound of butter while on board to fulfill their calorific needs.

Space nutrition has completed several missions of its own in the four decades since the final frontier was breached, and the popular image of high-protein slop that tastes like liquidized cardboard is now largely outdated. But while the presentation may have improved, astronauts broadly agree that food in space has remained pretty awful since John Glenn returned from his mission in 1962 demanding a real sandwich instead of mush in a tube.

The way we feed ourselves in space has actually changed very little. Foods are freeze-dried and vacuum-packed to weigh next to nothing; when you feel like lunch you select a sachet,[2] add water, stir, and suck it out of the carton. Delicious.

The main challenge in cooking for long-haul astronauts, as anyone who has taken a transatlantic flight will know, is making the food palatable. NASA is careful to supply every vitamin, mineral, and calorie an astronaut requires, calculated to the minutest scale. But that doesn't mean it tastes nice. French astronaut Jean-Loup Chrétien described the Russian prepacked pot noodles on Mir as tasting like "rancid almonds"; his countryman Richard Filippi was so appalled at the menus that he devised a culinary art he called "gastronautics" to cater to the space station's final missions. "It was clearly unacceptable that a Frenchman should eat poorly in space," said Filippi. "Something had to be done." Astronauts, he figured, are like armies; they march—or spacewalk—on their stomachs.

Rehydratable food.

It's not just that astronauts are fussy eaters. Russian cosmonauts were rumoured at one point to be close to mutiny, so bad

---

1. **peckish** *adj.*: chiefly British for "slightly hungry."
2. **sachet** (sa·shā′) *n.*: small bag.

Vocabulary
breached (brēcht) *v.*: broken through.
palatable (pal′it·ə·bəl) *adj.*: tasty; fit to be eaten or drunk.
rancid (ran′sid) *adj.*: stale or spoiled.
mutiny (myo͞ot′′n·ē) *n.*: rebellion or revolt against authority.

was the food provided by their impoverished space agency. "It is extremely important that you have a varied diet in space," says Jean Hunter, associate professor of agricultural and biological engineering at Cornell University. "Food assumes an especially large role in psychological support of the crew. The astronauts are living in a habitat that doesn't change from day to day, so the most reliable source of variety in those conditions comes from the food."

The main gripe, unsurprisingly, is that nothing is fresh. Despite the introduction of refrigeration facilities, a locker of fresh apples and oranges will last only 48 hours. Then it's back to cartons, cans, and hot water, at least until a considerate shuttle drops by.

The solution? Grow the crops yourself. As well as providing variety, space crops would allow a future colony to be more self-sufficient. And it's not such a distant prospect. NASA has been investigating for some years the possibility of growing crops in space—artificially lit, watered, and temperature-controlled, of course. The atmosphere of Mars, 95% carbon dioxide, could be relatively easily managed for grain or vegetable production, the byproduct oxygen being used to produce water combined with imported hydrogen. And if the claims of ice having been discovered on the moon prove true, agriculture galactic[3]-style could really be in business.

Enter Hunter and her colleagues at Cornell. Raw grain or potato, after all, is unlikely to prove any more popular than in freeze-dried form. What astronauts will need is recipes, culinary tips, a cookbook. And this month 16 volunteers completed the first extended trial of moon food, for 30 days eating nothing but food that could, in theory, be grown and harvested on the moon or Mars.

"We developed more than 200 recipes using plants that could be grown in a lunar colony, in hydroponic cultures (that is, using nutrient-enriched fluid instead of soil) with artificial lighting, and looked at the ways they would have to be processed to turn them into food that people would want to eat," says Hunter.

Considering the restrictions on which plants can be cultivated—they need to be short, high yielding, and require little maintenance—the potential variety of diet is impressive. Rice, wheat, potato, sweet potato, tomato, and other vegetables are all seen as prime candidates. Soy

(From left to right) Mission Specialist Robert A. R. Parker, Payload Specialist Ronald A. Parise, and Commander Vance D. Brand enjoy a meal aboard the space shuttle *Columbia*.

3. **galactic** *adj.:* having to do with the Milky Way or another galaxy.

Vocabulary
impoverished (im·päv′ər·isht) *v.* used as *adj.:* poor; without funds.
habitat (hab′i·tat′) *n.:* person's environment or living space.

beans would give oil and milk; meat substitute could be made from wheat. With judicious use of flavoring, believe the researchers, the food produced could be extremely tasty. Sweet potato pancakes, lentil loaf sandwiches, or chocolate soy candy, anyone?

Rupert Spies, senior lecturer at the university's school of hotel administration and developer of most of the recipes, admits to being frustrated that all Mars menus must be low in salt, but says he got round it by adding "a lot of herbs." "The lack of salt is very important because it affects the metabolism in space. Salt and bone loss is a very specific issue if you are in microgravity."

At this stage, of course, all the recipes are necessarily vegan[4]—tethering a cow to a star-spangled banner on the surface of the moon is not yet a viable option. But not all animal protein will eventually need to be imported. "It is a very, very long way off until we will be farming animals in space," says Hunter. "But it does seem likely that the first meat animals will probably be fish, such as carp, because they can be grown in a closed system with very low water use."

Captain Loren J. Shriver, mission commander, pursues several floating chocolate candies on the flight deck of the space shuttle *Atlantis*.

The prospect of allotments[5] or fish farms dotted across the surface of Mars is an arresting one. But it is unlikely that astronauts will be training tomatoes up their mass spectrometers[6] for a while yet. And it will take considerably longer before they can cut ties with mother earth altogether.

"It's not worth attempting to be fully self-sufficient as a colony," says Hunter. "There are so many other things you'd have to bring from earth, you might as well bring some food as well." Exhausted astronauts might well agree. The average man requires 2.5 pounds of food a day. Tell an astronaut that he has to head off to the inflatable pod, harvest some grain, shell, grind, and cook it, and he might settle for powdered steak sandwich after all.

---

5. **allotments** *n.:* in Britain, small plots or parcels of public land set aside for growing vegetables or flowers.
6. **mass spectrometers** (spek·träm′ət·ərz): instruments used by scientists to identify chemical substances.

Vocabulary

judicious (jōō·dish′əs) *adj.:* wise and careful.

metabolism (mə·tab′ə·liz′əm) *n.:* process by which living organisms turn food into energy and living tissue.

arresting (ə·rest′iŋ) *adj.:* interesting; striking.

---

4. **vegan** (vē′gən) *n.* used as *adj.:* strictly vegetarian; not containing any animal products.

Analyzing Informational Text

Reading Check

1. What is the astronauts' main complaint about food in space?

2. Why do astronauts use freeze-dried food instead of fresh vegetables and fruits?

3. How might colonists on Mars grow fresh vegetables and raise carp?

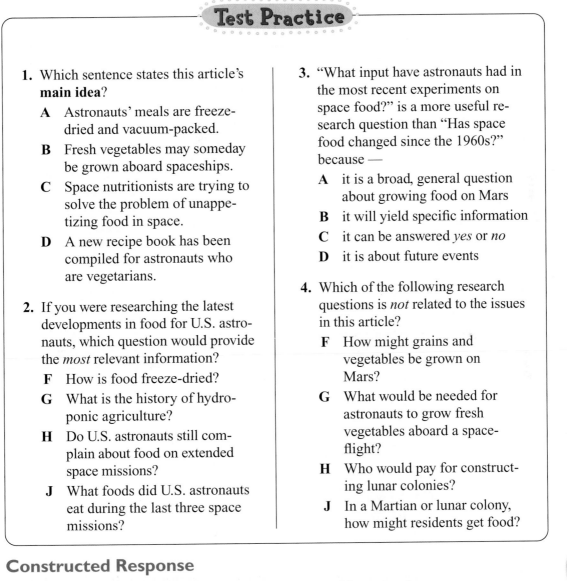

Test Practice

1. Which sentence states this article's **main idea**?
   - **A** Astronauts' meals are freeze-dried and vacuum-packed.
   - **B** Fresh vegetables may someday be grown aboard spaceships.
   - **C** Space nutritionists are trying to solve the problem of unappetizing food in space.
   - **D** A new recipe book has been compiled for astronauts who are vegetarians.

2. If you were researching the latest developments in food for U.S. astronauts, which question would provide the *most* relevant information?
   - **F** How is food freeze-dried?
   - **G** What is the history of hydroponic agriculture?
   - **H** Do U.S. astronauts still complain about food on extended space missions?
   - **J** What foods did U.S. astronauts eat during the last three space missions?

3. "What input have astronauts had in the most recent experiments on space food?" is a more useful research question than "Has space food changed since the 1960s?" because —
   - **A** it is a broad, general question about growing food on Mars
   - **B** it will yield specific information
   - **C** it can be answered *yes* or *no*
   - **D** it is about future events

4. Which of the following research questions is *not* related to the issues in this article?
   - **F** How might grains and vegetables be grown on Mars?
   - **G** What would be needed for astronauts to grow fresh vegetables aboard a spaceflight?
   - **H** Who would pay for constructing lunar colonies?
   - **J** In a Martian or lunar colony, how might residents get food?

Constructed Response

Write five **research questions** about humans in space. Your questions may further explore space nutrition or a related topic that this article has made you curious about. Then, get together with three or four classmates to evaluate one another's questions. Decide which questions seem likeliest to yield good research results.

SKILLS FOCUS

Reading Skills
Generate relevant research questions.

Vocabulary Development

Word Mapping: How to Own a New Word

Sometimes you can figure out a word from its context, but sometimes you can't. On page 188, the writer gives **context clues**—spread over three sentences—to help you understand what the word *palatable* means:

> "The main challenge in cooking for long-haul astronauts, as anyone who has taken a transatlantic flight will know, is making the food palatable. NASA is careful to supply every vitamin, mineral, and calorie an astronaut requires, calculated to the minutest scale. But that doesn't mean it tastes nice."

Making a **semantic map,** or **meaning map,** can help you pin down the meaning of a new word. Here is a sample map for the word *palatable*. Note how the questions, answers, and examples show the word in action and help to clarify its meaning.

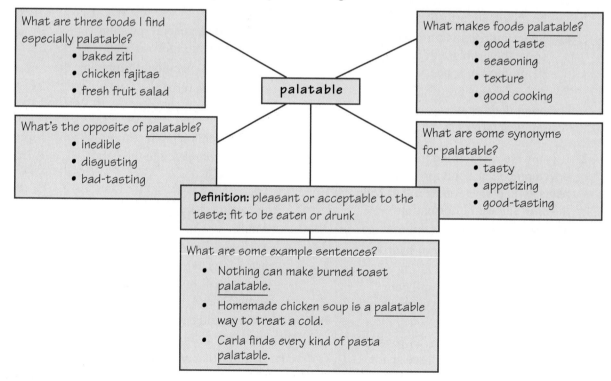

What are three foods I find especially <u>palatable</u>?
- baked ziti
- chicken fajitas
- fresh fruit salad

What makes foods <u>palatable</u>?
- good taste
- seasoning
- texture
- good cooking

palatable

What's the opposite of <u>palatable</u>?
- inedible
- disgusting
- bad-tasting

What are some synonyms for <u>palatable</u>?
- tasty
- appetizing
- good-tasting

Definition: pleasant or acceptable to the taste; fit to be eaten or drunk

What are some example sentences?
- Nothing can make burned toast <u>palatable</u>.
- Homemade chicken soup is a <u>palatable</u> way to treat a cold.
- Carla finds every kind of pasta <u>palatable</u>.

Vocabulary Skills
Make semantic maps.

PRACTICE

With a partner, divide the remaining Word Bank words so that you each have four. Then, make a **semantic map** for each of your words. You may need to create some of your own questions and answers. When you finish, share your maps with those of your partner.

Typhoid Fever

Make the Connection

Quickwrite

What do you remember from your childhood that is important, unusual, or funny? Make some notes about an early memory; think as a child. Ideas might come to you if you begin like this, in the present tense and the first person: "I am seven years old . . ." or "I'm in a playground . . ."

Literary Focus

Voice: The Sound of the Author

In literature the term **voice** refers to our sense of the writer who has created the work. (In fiction it can also refer to our sense of the narrator.) Writers express their voices by their distinctive use of language, including their **diction** (the kinds of words they choose), the complexity or simplicity of their sentence structure, and the **tone,** or attitude, that they take toward their subject and characters. In his memoirs, Frank McCourt uses a unique voice to tell his tragic story of growing up poor in Ireland. Read a passage aloud, and you'll hear McCourt's strong, true voice spring to life.

Reading Skills

Evaluating Credibility: Testing/Trusting Memory

"People are always asking, how does he remember so much," McCourt told an interviewer, "and how much is an Irish storyteller's embroidery?"

Credibility means "believability." How can you judge the credibility of an autobiography? Can adults remember exact conversations, events, and thoughts that took place when they were ten years old? Is accuracy important, or is the significance of an event of greater interest? Keep all these questions in mind as you read "Typhoid Fever." Does it ring true to you? Could the story's facts be checked?

Background

Angela's Ashes is Frank McCourt's gritty, moving memoir of growing up in Limerick, Ireland, in the 1930s and 1940s. McCourt's family lived in a filthy, overcrowded slum, and bacterial diseases such as typhoid fever and diphtheria were common.

Typhoid fever, caused by contaminated food or water, wastes the whole body. Diphtheria, spread by contact with an infected person, starts with a sore throat and can end in suffocation. Because both infections spread easily, people with these illnesses are quarantined. In Ireland they were isolated in "fever hospitals." Most of these hospitals were run by the Catholic Church and staffed by nuns. McCourt caught typhoid fever at age ten and was sent to a fever hospital.

INTERNET

Vocabulary Practice

Keyword: LE5 10-3

Vocabulary Development

induced (in·dōōst′) *v.* used as *adj.*: persuaded; led on.

potent (pōt′′nt) *adj.*: powerful; convincing.

torrent (tôr′ənt) *n.*: violent, forceful rush.

clamoring (klam′ər·iŋ) *v.* used as *adj.*: crying out; asking.

SKILLS FOCUS

Literary Skills
Understand the writer's voice, diction, and tone.

Reading Skills
Evaluate credibility.

TYPHOID FEVER

from Angela's Ashes

Frank McCourt

Yoo hoo, are you there, typhoid boy?

The room next to me is empty till one morning a girl's voice says, Yoo hoo, who's there?

I'm not sure if she's talking to me or someone in the room beyond.

Yoo hoo, boy with the typhoid, are you awake?

I am.

Are you better?

I am.

Well, why are you here?

I don't know. I'm still in the bed. They stick needles in me and give me medicine.

What do you look like?

I wonder, What kind of a question is that? I don't know what to tell her.

Yoo hoo, are you there, typhoid boy?

I am.

What's your name?

Frank.

That's a good name. My name is Patricia Madigan. How old are you?

Ten.

Oh. She sounds disappointed.

But I'll be eleven in August, next month.

Well, that's better than ten. I'll be fourteen in September. Do you want to know why I'm in the Fever Hospital?

I do.

I have diphtheria and something else.

What's something else?

They don't know. They think I have a disease from foreign parts because my father used to be in Africa. I nearly died. Are you going to tell me what you look like?

I have black hair.

You and millions.

I have brown eyes with bits of green that's called hazel.

You and thousands.

I have stitches on the back of my right hand and my two feet where they put in the soldier's blood.

Oh, did they?

They did.

You won't be able to stop marching and saluting.

There's a swish of habit and click of beads and then Sister Rita's voice. Now, now, what's this? There's to be no talking between two rooms especially when it's a boy and a girl. Do you hear me, Patricia?

I do, Sister.

Do you hear me, Francis?

I do, Sister.

You could be giving thanks for your two remarkable recoveries. You could be saying the rosary.[1] You could be reading *The Little Messenger of the Sacred Heart*[2] that's beside your beds. Don't let me come back and find you talking.

She comes into my room and wags her finger at me. Especially you, Francis, after thousands of boys prayed for you at the Confraternity.[3] Give thanks, Francis, give thanks.

She leaves and there's silence for awhile. Then Patricia whispers, Give thanks, Francis, give thanks, and say your rosary, Francis, and I laugh so hard a nurse runs in to see if I'm all right. She's a very stern nurse from the County Kerry and she frightens me. What's this, Francis? Laughing? What is there to laugh about? Are you and that Madigan girl talking? I'll report you to Sister Rita. There's to be no laughing for you could be doing serious damage to your internal apparatus.

She plods out and Patricia whispers again in a heavy Kerry accent, No laughing, Francis, you could be doin' serious damage to your internal apparatus. Say your rosary, Francis, and pray for your internal apparatus.

Mam visits me on Thursdays. I'd like to see my father, too, but I'm out of danger, crisis time is over, and I'm allowed only one visitor. Besides, she says, he's back at work at Rank's Flour Mills and please God this job will last a while with the war on and the English desperate for flour. She brings me a chocolate bar and that proves Dad is working. She could never afford it on the dole.[4] He sends me notes. He tells me my brothers are all praying for me, that I should be a good boy, obey the doctors, the nuns, the nurses, and don't forget to say my prayers. He's sure St. Jude pulled me through the crisis because he's the patron saint of desperate cases and I was indeed a desperate case.

Patricia says she has two books by her bed. One is a poetry book and that's the one she loves. The other is a short history of England and do I want it? She gives it to Seamus, the man who mops the floors every day, and he brings it to me. He says, I'm not supposed to be bringing anything from a dipteria room to a typhoid room with all the germs flying around and hiding between the pages and if you ever catch dipteria on top of the typhoid they'll know and I'll lose my good job and be out on the street singing patriotic songs with a tin cup in my hand, which I could easily do because there isn't a song ever written about Ireland's sufferings I don't know and a few songs about the joy of whiskey too.

---

1. **rosary** *n.:* group of prayers that Roman Catholics recite while holding a string of beads.
2. ***The Little Messenger of the Sacred Heart:*** religious publication for children.
3. **Confraternity:** here, a religious organization made up of nonclergy, or laypersons.

---

4. **dole** *n.:* government payment to the unemployed; also, money or food given to those in need.

Oh, yes, he knows Roddy McCorley. He'll sing it for me right enough but he's barely into the first verse when the Kerry nurse rushes in. What's this, Seamus? Singing? Of all the people in this hospital you should know the rules against singing. I have a good mind to report you to Sister Rita.

Ah, don't do that, nurse.

Very well, Seamus. I'll let it go this one time. You know the singing could lead to a relapse in these patients.

When she leaves he whispers he'll teach me a few songs because singing is good for passing the time when you're by yourself in a typhoid room. He says Patricia is a lovely girl the way she often gives him sweets from the parcel her mother sends every fortnight.[5] He stops mopping the floor and calls to Patricia in the next room, I was telling Frankie you're a lovely girl, Patricia, and she says, You're a lovely man, Seamus. He smiles because he's an old man of forty and he never had children but the ones he can talk to here in the Fever Hospital. He says, Here's the book, Frankie. Isn't it a great pity you have to be reading all about England after all they did to us, that there isn't a history of Ireland to be had in this hospital.

The book tells me all about King Alfred and William the Conqueror and all the kings and queens down to Edward, who had to wait forever for his mother, Victoria, to die before he could be king. The book has the first bit of Shakespeare I ever read.

> *I do believe, <u>induced</u> by <u>potent</u>*
> *circumstances,*
> *That thou art mine enemy.*

The history writer says this is what Catherine, who is a wife of Henry the Eighth, says to Cardinal Wolsey, who is trying to have her head cut off. I don't know what it means and I don't care because it's Shakespeare and it's like having jewels in my mouth when I say the words. If I had a whole book of Shakespeare they could keep me in the hospital for a year.

Patricia says she doesn't know what induced means or potent circumstances and she doesn't care about Shakespeare, she has her poetry book and she reads to me from beyond the wall a poem about an owl and a pussycat that went to sea in a green boat with honey and money and it makes no sense and when I say that Patricia gets huffy and says that's the last poem she'll ever read to me. She says I'm always reciting the lines from Shakespeare and they make no sense either. Seamus stops mopping again and tells us we shouldn't be fighting over poetry because we'll have enough to fight about when we grow up and get married. Patricia says she's sorry and I'm sorry too so she reads me part of another poem[6] which I have to remember so I can say it back to her early in the morning or late at night when there are no nuns or nurses about,

---

6. **part...poem:** The reference is to "The Highwayman" by the British poet Alfred Noyes (1880–1958). The poem is based on a true story about a highwayman who fell in love with an innkeeper's daughter in eighteenth-century England. Highwaymen, who robbed wealthy stagecoach passengers, were at that time popular romantic figures.

Vocabulary

induced (in·do͞ost′) v. used as adj.: persuaded; led on.

potent (pōt′'nt) adj.: powerful; convincing.

---

5. **fortnight** n.: chiefly British for "two weeks."

The wind was a <u>torrent</u> of darkness among the
  gusty trees,
The moon was a ghostly galleon tossed upon
  cloudy seas,
The road was a ribbon of moonlight over the
  purple moor,
And the highwayman came riding—
      Riding—riding—
The highwayman came riding, up to the old inn
  door.

He'd a French cocked-hat on his forehead, a
  bunch of lace at his chin,
A coat of the claret velvet, and breeches of
  brown doeskin,
They fitted with never a wrinkle. His boots were
  up to the thigh.
And he rode with a jeweled twinkle,
      His pistol butts a-twinkle,
His rapier hilt a-twinkle, under the jeweled sky.

Every day I can't wait for the doctors and nurses to leave me alone so I can learn a new verse from Patricia and find out what's happening to the highwayman and the landlord's red-lipped daughter. I love the poem because it's exciting and almost as good as my two lines of Shakespeare. The redcoats are after the highwayman because they know he told her, I'll come to thee by moonlight, though hell should bar the way.

I'd love to do that myself, come by moonlight for Patricia in the next room not giving a hoot though hell should bar the way. She's ready to read the last few verses when in comes the nurse from Kerry shouting at her, shouting at me, I told ye there was to be no talking between rooms. Dipthteria is never allowed to talk to typhoid and visa versa. I warned ye. And she calls out, Seamus, take this one. Take the by. Sister Rita said one more word out of him and upstairs with him. We gave ye a warning to stop the blathering but ye wouldn't. Take the by, Seamus, take him.

Ah, now, nurse, sure isn't he harmless. 'Tis only a bit o' poetry.

Take that by, Seamus, take him at once.

He bends over me and whispers, Ah, I'm sorry, Frankie. Here's your English history book. He slips the book under my shirt and lifts me from the bed. He whispers that I'm a feather. I try to see Patricia when we pass through her room but all I can make out is a blur of dark head on a pillow.

Sister Rita stops us in the hall to tell me I'm a great disappointment to her, that she expected me to be a good boy after what God had done for me, after all the prayers said by hundreds of boys at the Confraternity, after all the care from the nuns and nurses of the Fever Hospital, after the way they let my mother and father in to see me, a thing rarely allowed, and this is how I repaid them lying in the bed reciting silly poetry back and forth with Patricia Madigan knowing very well there was a ban on all talk between typhoid and diphtheria. She says I'll have plenty of time to reflect on my sins in the big ward upstairs and I should beg God's forgiveness for my disobedience reciting a pagan[7] English poem about a thief on a horse and a maiden with red lips who commits a terrible sin when I could have been praying or reading the life of a saint. She made it her business to read that poem so she did and I'd be well advised to tell the priest in confession.

The Kerry nurse follows us upstairs gasping and holding on to the banister. She tells me I better not get the notion she'll be running up to this part of the world every time I have a little pain or a twinge.

There are twenty beds in the ward, all white, all empty. The nurse tells Seamus put me at the far end of the ward against the wall to make sure I don't talk to anyone who might be passing the door, which is very unlikely since there isn't

---

7. **pagan** (pā'gən) *adj.*: here, non-Christian.

Vocabulary
torrent (tôr'ənt) *n.*: violent, forceful rush.

another soul on this whole floor. She tells Seamus this was the fever ward during the Great Famine[8] long ago and only God knows how many died here brought in too late for anything but a wash before they were buried and there are stories of cries and moans in the far reaches of the night. She says 'twould break your heart to think of what the English did to us, that if they didn't put the blight[9] on the potato they didn't do much to take it off. No pity. No feeling at all for the people that died in this very ward, children suffering and dying here while the English feasted on roast beef and guzzled the best of wine in their big houses, little children with their mouths all green from trying to eat the grass in the fields beyond, God bless us and save us and guard us from future famines.

Seamus says 'twas a terrible thing indeed and he wouldn't want to be walking these halls in the dark with all the little green mouths gaping at him. The nurse takes my temperature, 'Tis up a bit, have a good sleep for yourself now that you're away from the chatter with Patricia Madigan below who will never know a gray hair.

She shakes her head at Seamus and he gives her a sad shake back.

Nurses and nuns never think you know what they're talking about. If you're ten going on eleven you're supposed to be simple like my uncle Pat Sheehan who was dropped on his head. You can't ask questions. You can't show you understand what the nurse said about Patricia Madigan, that she's going to die, and you can't show you want to cry over this girl who taught you a lovely poem which the nun says is bad.

The nurse tells Seamus she has to go and he's to sweep the lint from under my bed and mop up a bit around the ward. Seamus tells me she's a right oul' witch for running to Sister Rita and complaining about the poem going between the two rooms, that you can't catch a disease from a poem unless it's love ha ha and that's not bloody likely when you're what? ten going on eleven? He never heard the likes of it, a little fella shifted upstairs for saying a poem and he has a good mind to go to the *Limerick Leader* and tell them print the whole thing except he has this job and he'd lose it if ever Sister Rita found out. Anyway, Frankie, you'll be outa here one of these fine days and you can read all the poetry you want though I don't know about Patricia below, I don't know about Patricia, God help us.

He knows about Patricia in two days because she got out of the bed to go to the lavatory when she was supposed to use a bedpan and collapsed and died in the lavatory. Seamus is mopping the floor and there are tears on his cheeks and he's saying, 'Tis a dirty rotten thing to die in a lavatory when you're lovely in yourself. She told me she was sorry she had you reciting that poem and getting you shifted from the room, Frankie. She said 'twas all her fault.

It wasn't, Seamus.

I know and didn't I tell her that.

Patricia is gone and I'll never know what happened to the highwayman and Bess, the landlord's daughter. I ask Seamus but he doesn't know any poetry at all especially English poetry. He knew an Irish poem once but it was about fairies and had no sign of a highwayman in it. Still he'll ask the men in his local pub where there's always someone reciting something and he'll bring it back to me. Won't I be busy meanwhile reading my short history of England and finding out all about their perfidy.[10] That's what Seamus says, perfidy, and I don't know what it means and he doesn't know what it means but if it's something the English do it must be terrible.

---

8. **Great Famine:** refers to the great famine in Ireland from 1845 to 1849, when failed potato crops resulted in the starvation and death of about one million people.
9. **blight** (blīt) *n.*: kind of plant disease.

---

10. **perfidy** (pʉr′fə·dē) *n.*: treachery; betrayal.

He comes three times a week to mop the floor and the nurse is there every morning to take my temperature and pulse. The doctor listens to my chest with the thing hanging from his neck. They all say, And how's our little soldier today? A girl with a blue dress brings meals three times a day and never talks to me. Seamus says she's not right in the head so don't say a word to her.

The July days are long and I fear the dark. There are only two ceiling lights in the ward and they're switched off when the tea tray is taken away and the nurse gives me pills. The nurse tells me go to sleep but I can't because I see people in the nineteen beds in the ward all dying and green around their mouths where they tried to eat grass and moaning for soup Protestant soup any soup and I cover my face with the pillow hoping they won't come and stand around the bed clawing at me and howling for bits of the chocolate bar my mother brought last week.

No, she didn't bring it. She had to send it in because I can't have any more visitors. Sister Rita tells me a visit to the Fever Hospital is a privilege and after my bad behavior with Patricia Madigan and that poem I can't have the privilege anymore. She says I'll be going home in a few weeks and my job is to concentrate on getting better and learn to walk again after being in bed for six weeks and I can get out of bed tomorrow after breakfast. I don't know why she says I have to learn how to walk when I've been walking since I was a baby but when the nurse stands me by the side of the bed I fall to the floor and the nurse laughs, See, you're a baby again.

I practice walking from bed to bed back and forth back and forth. I don't want to be a baby. I don't want to be in this empty ward with no Patricia and no highwayman and no red-lipped landlord's daughter. I don't want the ghosts of children with green mouths pointing bony fingers at me and <u>clamoring</u> for bits of my chocolate bar.

Seamus says a man in his pub knew all the verses of the highwayman poem and it has a very sad end. Would I like him to say it because he never learned how to read and he had to carry the poem in his head? He stands in the middle of the ward leaning on his mop and recites,

> Tlot-tlot, *in the frosty silence!* Tlot-tlot, *in the echoing night!*
> Nearer he came and nearer! Her face was like a light!
> Her eyes grew wide for a moment; she drew one last deep breath,
> Then her fingers moved in the moonlight,
> Her musket shattered the moonlight,
> Shattered her breast in the moonlight and warned him—with her death.

He hears the shot and escapes but when he learns at dawn how Bess died he goes into a rage and returns for revenge only to be shot down by the redcoats.

> Blood-red were his spurs in the golden noon; wine-red was his velvet coat,
> When they shot him down on the highway,
> Down like a dog on the highway,
> And he lay in his blood on the highway, with a bunch of lace at his throat.

Seamus wipes his sleeve across his face and sniffles. He says, There was no call at all to shift you up here away from Patricia when you didn't even know what happened to the highwayman and Bess. 'Tis a very sad story and when I said it to my wife she wouldn't stop crying the whole night till we went to bed. She said there was no call for them redcoats to shoot that highwayman, they are responsible for half the troubles of the world and they never had any pity on the Irish, either. Now if you want to know any more poems, Frankie, tell me and I'll get them from the pub and bring 'em back in my head. ∎

Vocabulary
clamoring (klam'ər·iŋ) *v.* used as *adj.*: crying out; asking.

Meet the Writer

Frank McCourt

"We Were Street Kids"

Frank McCourt (1930–   ), who regards himself as more a New Yorker than an Irishman, was born in Brooklyn, New York, the first child of Irish immigrants. When Frank was four, the McCourts made a bad decision—to move back to Ireland, where they lived in worse conditions than those they had fled in Brooklyn. Eventually Frank's father abandoned his wife, Angela, and their three surviving children.

Frank McCourt returned to New York City at age nineteen. Nine years later he began teaching writing to high school students. Encouraged by his students to write about his own experiences (see the **Connection** on page 201), he finally published his first book, *Angela's Ashes,* when he was sixty-six. The book dominated bestseller lists, won the 1997 Pulitzer Prize and the 1996 National Book Critics Circle Award for autobiography, and was made into a movie.

A sequel to his first novel, titled *'Tis* (1999), recounts McCourt's life as a young man in New York City, where he held a variety of jobs, from housekeeping at a hotel to acting to unloading meat trucks.

When he was asked how he found such humor in his poverty-stricken childhood, McCourt replied:

66 When you have nothing—no TV, no radio, no music—you have only the language. So you use it. We were street kids—we saw the absurdity and laughed at it. And we were fools; we were always dreaming. Bacon and eggs—we dreamed of that. 99

For Independent Reading

Don't miss the rest of *Angela's Ashes,* McCourt's moving, searing memoir of his growing-up years, or its sequel, *'Tis.*

The Education of Frank McCourt
Barbara Sande Dimmitt

"Yo, Teach!" a voice boomed. Frank McCourt scanned the adolescents in his classroom. It was the fall of 1970 and his first week of teaching at Seward Park High School, which sat in the midst of dilapidated tenement buildings on Manhattan's Lower East Side. McCourt located the speaker and nodded. "You talk funny," the student said. "Where ya from?"

"Ireland," McCourt replied. With more than ten years of teaching experience under his belt, this kind of interrogation no longer surprised him. But one question in particular still made him squirm: "Where'd you go to high school?" someone else asked.

If I tell them the truth, they'll feel superior to me, McCourt thought. *They'll throw it in my face.* Most of all, he feared an accusation he'd heard before—from himself: *You come from nothing, so you are nothing.*

But McCourt's heart whispered another possibility: Maybe these kids are yearning for a way of figuring out this new teacher. *Am I willing to risk being humiliated in the classroom to find out?*

"Come on, tell us! Where'd you go to high school?"

"I never did," McCourt replied.

"Did you get thrown out?"

I was right, the teacher thought. *They're curious.* McCourt explained he'd left school after the eighth grade to take a job.

"How'd you get to be a teacher, then?" they asked.

"When I came to America," he began, "I dreamed bigger dreams. I loved reading and writing, and teaching was the most exalted profession I could imagine. I was unloading sides of beef down on the docks when I decided enough was enough. By then I'd done a lot of reading on my own, so I persuaded New York University to enroll me."

McCourt wasn't surprised that this story fascinated his students. Theirs wasn't the kind of poverty McCourt had known; they had electricity and food. But he recognized the telltale signs of need in some of his students' threadbare clothes, and sensed the bitter shame and hopelessness he knew all too well. If recounting his own experiences would jolt these kids out of their defeatism so he could teach them something, that's what he would do.

A born storyteller, McCourt drew from a repertoire of accounts about his youth. His students would listen, spellbound by the gritty details, drawn by something more powerful than curiosity. He'd look from face to face, recognizing a bit of himself in each sober gaze.

Since humor had been the McCourts' weapon against life's miseries in Limerick, he used it to describe those days. "Dinner usually was bread and tea," he told the students. "Mam used to say, 'We've got our balanced diet: a solid and a liquid. What more could we want?'"

The students roared with laughter. . . .

One day McCourt lugged a tape recorder to class. "We're going to work on writing. Each of you will tell a story into this," he announced. McCourt then transcribed the stories. One boy described the time he was climbing down a fire escape past an open window when an awful smell hit him. "There was a body in the bed," McCourt typed. "The corpse was all juicy and swollen."

McCourt handed back the essay the next day. "See? You're a writer!"

"I was just talking," the boy protested. "I didn't write this."

"Yes, you did. These words came out of your head. They helped me understand something that was important to you. That's what writing's about. Now, learn to do it on paper." The boy's shoulders squared with pride.

The incident reminded McCourt of something that had happened at college. A creative-writing professor had asked him to describe an object from his childhood. McCourt chose the decrepit bed he and his brothers had shared. He wrote of their being scratched by the stiff stuffing protruding from the mattress and of ending up jumbled together in the sagging center with fleas leaping all over their bodies. The professor gave McCourt an A, and asked him to read the essay to the class.

"No!" McCourt said, recoiling at the thought. But for the first time, he began to see his sordid childhood, with all the miseries, betrayals, and longings that tormented him still, as a worthy topic. *Maybe that's what I was born to put on the page,* he thought.

While teaching, McCourt wrote occasional articles for newspapers and magazines. But his major effort, a memoir of 150 pages that he churned out in 1966, remained unfinished. Now he leafed through his students' transcribed essays. They lacked polish, but somehow they worked in a way his writing didn't. *I'm trying to teach these kids to write,* he thought, *yet I haven't found the secret myself.*

The bell rang in the faculty lounge at Stuyvesant High School in Manhattan. When McCourt began teaching at the prestigious public high school in 1972, he joked that he'd finally made it to paradise. . . .

The bits and pieces that bubbled into his consciousness enlivened the stories he told in class. "Everyone has a story to tell," he said. "Write about what you know with conviction, from the heart. Dig deep," he urged. "Find your own voice and dance your own dance!"

On Fridays the students read their compositions aloud. To draw them out, McCourt would read excerpts from his duffel bag full of notebooks. "You had such an interesting childhood, Mr. McCourt," they said. "Why don't you write a book?" They threw his own words back at him: "It sounds like there's more to that story; dig deeper. . . ."

McCourt was past fifty and painfully aware of the passage of time. But despite his growing frustration at his unfinished book, he never tired of his students' work.

Over the years some talented writers passed through McCourt's popular classes. Laurie Gwen Shapiro, whose first novel will be published in the spring, was one of them. He decided she was coasting along on her technical skills. "You're capable of much more," McCourt told her. "Try writing something that's meaningful to you for a change."

Near the end of the semester, McCourt laid an essay—graded 100—on Laurie's desk. "If Laurie is willing to read her essay," he announced to the class, "I think we'll all benefit."

Laurie began to read a portrait of love clouded by anger and shame. She told of her father, partially paralyzed, and of resenting his inability to play with her or help her ride a bicycle. The paper shook in her trembling hands, and McCourt understood all too well what it cost her to continue. She also admitted she was embarrassed by her father's limp. The words, McCourt knew, were torn straight from her soul.

When Laurie finished, with tears streaming down her face, the students broke into applause. McCourt looked around the room, his own vision blurred.

These young people have been giving you lessons in courage, he thought. *When will you dare as mightily as they?*

It was October 1994. Frank McCourt, now retired, sat down and read his book's new opening, which he had written a few days before and still found satisfying. But many blank pages lay before him. *What if I never get it right?* he wondered grimly.

He stared at the logs glowing in the fireplace and could almost hear students' voices from years past, some angry, some defeated, others confused and seeking guidance. "It's no good, Mr. McCourt. I don't have what it takes."

Then Frank McCourt, author, heard the steadying tones of Frank McCourt, teacher: *Of course you do. Dig deeper. Find your own voice and dance your own dance.*

He scribbled a few lines. "I'm in a playground on Classon Avenue in Brooklyn with my brother Malachy. He's two, I'm three. We're on the seesaw." In the innocent voice of an unprotected child who could neither comprehend nor control the world around him, Frank McCourt told his tale of poverty and abandonment.

—from *Reader's Digest,* November 1997

Response and Analysis

Reading Check

1. Why are Frankie and Patricia in the hospital?

2. Why is Frankie moved to another floor?

3. What happens to Frankie in the end?

4. What happens to Patricia?

5. How does Frankie learn the remaining verses of "The Highwayman"?

Thinking Critically

6. How do the lines from "The Highwayman" contrast with the stark reality of the Fever Hospital? Why do you think the poem appeals to the two children?

7. What do you think Frankie discovers about himself in the hospital? Be sure to consider the role that language—and, especially, poetry—plays in this story.

8. Frank McCourt repeatedly told his students, "Find your own voice" (see the **Connection** on page 201). When McCourt found his voice, his memoirs took off. How would you describe that **voice**? How does he create it?

9. What adjectives would you use to describe the **tone** of this memoir? How does tone help create McCourt's **voice**?

10. The Kerry nurse asks sharply, "What is there to laugh about?" Find two examples of **comic relief** in McCourt's memoir. How do you feel about the use of comedy in such a sad story?

11. Explain why you would—or would not—want Frank McCourt as a writing teacher. Base your answer on what you learn about him in "Typhoid Fever" and in the **Connection** on page 201.

Extending and Evaluating

12. How credible do you think "Typhoid Fever" is, and how much of it seems like "embroidery"? Support your opinion with examples from the text.

WRITING

Putting Us There

Frank McCourt puts us right inside a young boy's head, right in his Fever Hospital bed, right in the midst of a pack of colorful characters. Review the notes you made for the Quickwrite about a childhood memory. In a short **autobiographical narrative,** make that memory come alive by answering these questions:

- Who was there?

- What did people say?

- How did you feel?

- Did anything comical happen?

Help the reader enter your scene.

▶ **Use "Writing an Autobiographical Narrative," pages 56–63, for help with this assignment.**

LISTENING AND SPEAKING

Live from Limerick!

"Typhoid Fever" is full of interesting characters, each with a unique way of speaking: Frankie, Patricia, Sister Rita, the Kerry nurse, Seamus, even Seamus's wife. It also contains singing and poetry recitations. With a group, plan, practice, and present to the class an **oral reading** of part of "Typhoid Fever." Try to include some of the parts that include lines from "The Highwayman."

Vocabulary Development

Antonyms: Just the Opposite

PRACTICE

An **antonym** is a word that has the opposite or nearly opposite meaning of another word. Choose the best antonym for each word in capital letters. This exercise format will give you practice for taking standardized tests. Remember: You're looking for the best antonym—*not* **synonym** (word with the same meaning).

Word Bank

induced
potent
torrent
clamoring

1. INDUCED
   a. persuaded
   b. attempted
   c. increased
   d. discouraged

2. POTENT
   a. impossible
   b. weak
   c. strong
   d. safe

3. TORRENT
   a. trickle
   b. flood
   c. law
   d. tornado

4. CLAMORING
   a. creating
   b. whispering
   c. opening
   d. studying

Grammar Link

Usage and Style: Creating Voice

To help create the distinctive **voice** of his memoir, McCourt decided not to use standard punctuation and quotation marks. He wanted us to sense that we are overhearing someone's thoughts. He also wanted to represent realistic **dialect,** the characteristic way people talk in different regions. To appreciate the effect, read these passages aloud.

1. "Patricia says she doesn't know what induced means or potent circumstances and she doesn't care about Shakespeare, she has her poetry book and she reads to me from beyond the wall a poem about an owl and a pussycat that went to sea in a green boat with honey and money and it makes no sense and when I say that Patricia gets huffy and says that's the last poem she'll ever read to me."

2. "We gave ye a warning to stop the blathering but ye wouldn't. Take the by, Seamus, take him.
   Ah, now, nurse, sure isn't he harmless. 'Tis only a bit o' poetry."

PRACTICE

Suppose you are a very diligent editor in the publishing house that has accepted McCourt's manuscript. Your job is to "clean up" his writing, to make it conform to accepted usage. Correct the passages on the left. Correct spelling, and punctuate sentences for clarity. Compare your edited manuscripts in class. What has happened to McCourt's voice?

▶ **For more help, see Run-on Sentences, 9b, and Quotation Marks, 13c–l, in the Language Handbook.**

SKILLS FOCUS

Vocabulary Skills
Use antonyms.

Grammar Skills
Understand usage and style.

An Ancient Enemy Gets Tougher

Researching Information

Once you have thought of several good research questions, it's time to search for answers. Consult as many reliable sources as you can in a library and on the Internet.

In a Library

Here are some useful library resources:

- **Reference materials** include encyclopedias, atlases, almanacs, and biographical sources, such as
  Encyclopaedia Britannica
  The Times Atlas of the World
  The World Almanac and Book of Facts
  Contemporary Authors
- **Other nonfiction books,** such as biographies, autobiographies, and works by experts on history and science, may be found in a library catalog.
- Use the subject index in the *Readers' Guide to Periodical Literature*—a print index—or an online index to find **periodicals,** such as newspaper and magazine articles.
- **Computer databases** may provide access to sources you can't reach on a home computer.

The Internet

Here are some Internet research tips:

- **Use Web sites.** You can go directly to a Web site if you know its URL (uniform resource locator), or address.
- **Use search engines.** If you don't know the address of the Web site you want, use one or more search engines. Enter a **search term,** and the engine will respond with sites having that term.

If you get too many or unrelated results, use a more limited search term.

- **Evaluate sources.** Are you reading someone's opinion on a bulletin board, a home page by a high school student, or data from a government agency's site? Learn to evaluate each Web source. Is its creator reliable, expert, and objective? Is the site updated frequently?

Using a Web Site

Here are some common Web-site features:

- The **table of contents,** usually located near the top or at the side of a page, lists the site's other pages.
- Highlighted or underlined **links** connect you to other sources of information on your topic. Click on **internal links** to reach other pages in the same Web site. Click on **external links** to go to different Web sites.
- **Multimedia and interactive features** link you to sound and video components and allow you to interact with other users of the Web site.

SKILLS FOCUS

Reading Skills
Understand how to use research resources, including print resources and the Internet.

Connecting to the Literature

In "Typhoid Fever" the narrator recounts his ordeal with typhoid fever. This Web page discusses another terrible disease that has long been a part of human history. It begins with a reference to the biblical tale of David and Goliath. David was a small shepherd boy who defeated the giant Goliath.

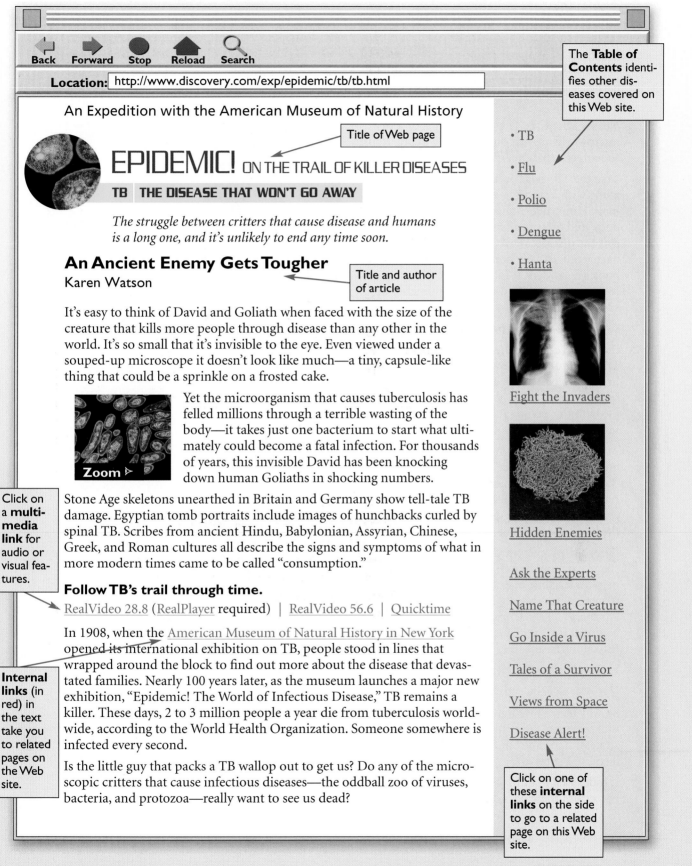

Back **Forward** **Stop** **Reload** **Search**

Location: http://www.discovery.com/exp/epidemic/tb/tb.html

An Expedition with the American Museum of Natural History

The **Table of Contents** identifies other diseases covered on this Web site.

Title of Web page

EPIDEMIC! ON THE TRAIL OF KILLER DISEASES

TB THE DISEASE THAT WON'T GO AWAY

The struggle between critters that cause disease and humans is a long one, and it's unlikely to end any time soon.

An Ancient Enemy Gets Tougher
Karen Watson

Title and author of article

It's easy to think of David and Goliath when faced with the size of the creature that kills more people through disease than any other in the world. It's so small that it's invisible to the eye. Even viewed under a souped-up microscope it doesn't look like much—a tiny, capsule-like thing that could be a sprinkle on a frosted cake.

Zoom ▷

Yet the microorganism that causes tuberculosis has felled millions through a terrible wasting of the body—it takes just one bacterium to start what ultimately could become a fatal infection. For thousands of years, this invisible David has been knocking down human Goliaths in shocking numbers.

Click on a **multimedia link** for audio or visual features.

Stone Age skeletons unearthed in Britain and Germany show tell-tale TB damage. Egyptian tomb portraits include images of hunchbacks curled by spinal TB. Scribes from ancient Hindu, Babylonian, Assyrian, Chinese, Greek, and Roman cultures all describe the signs and symptoms of what in more modern times came to be called "consumption."

Follow TB's trail through time.

RealVideo 28.8 (RealPlayer required) | RealVideo 56.6 | Quicktime

In 1908, when the American Museum of Natural History in New York opened its international exhibition on TB, people stood in lines that wrapped around the block to find out more about the disease that devastated families. Nearly 100 years later, as the museum launches a major new exhibition, "Epidemic! The World of Infectious Disease," TB remains a killer. These days, 2 to 3 million people a year die from tuberculosis worldwide, according to the World Health Organization. Someone somewhere is infected every second.

Internal links (in red) in the text take you to related pages on the Web site.

Is the little guy that packs a TB wallop out to get us? Do any of the microscopic critters that cause infectious diseases—the oddball zoo of viruses, bacteria, and protozoa—really want to see us dead?

- TB
- Flu
- Polio
- Dengue
- Hanta

Fight the Invaders

Hidden Enemies

Ask the Experts

Name That Creature

Go Inside a Virus

Tales of a Survivor

Views from Space

Disease Alert!

Click on one of these **internal links** on the side to go to a related page on this Web site.

Back   Forward   Stop   Reload   Search

Location: http://www.discovery.com/exp/epidemic/tb/tb.html

No, say scientists. These inhabitants of a vast microworld are just out to make a living. It just so happens that the living is on us.

Take the TB "bug." It likes us for some reason, along with a startling collection of other animals. Lions, tigers, sheep, cows, guinea pigs, dogs, and cats are a few. Name it, and it likely gets the disease. Why? For some reason, the TB bacterium actually prefers life inside one of the body's defenders. It makes a living from an immune system cell that normally munches up such invaders.

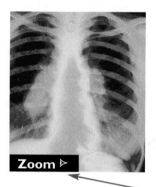

Click on **zoom** for enlargement of photo and more information.

Ask the experts about TB and our struggles with it.

Breathe in an airborne TB bacterium and it typically lands in the lungs. There, immune system cells quickly surround it and wall it off, forming a firm white ball the size of a pinhead. Inside this ball, the bug persists, perhaps for years. Exactly what happens there remains unclear, and most people with the TB bug inside them never experience the disease or become infectious themselves. Their body successfully keeps the invader in check.

But if there's a glitch in the body's defense system, and it doesn't work quite right, these once tiny balls can grow, some to the size of a baseball, as the bacteria inside them reproduce. These balls can erupt, spreading bacteria to other parts of the body through the blood. More balls, or "tubercles," grow, eventually clogging up the way the body does its daily business.

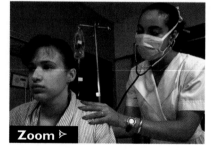

Every time someone sick with TB sneezes or coughs or exhales, they help the bacterium out. "Spreading is survival for the bug," says Dr. Ann Ginsberg, a TB scientist with the National Institute of Allergy and Infectious Diseases.

Hear about how tough TB is to tackle.

(RealPlayer required)

So why haven't we figured out a way to knock TB off the planet? The bug that scientists now call *Mycobacterium tuberculosis,* which long ago made a successful jump from living in dirt to living off animals, has turned out to be quite a survivor.

It hides well in humans—nearly 2 billion people are thought to carry the bacterium these days, though they show no signs. When symptoms do pop up, they are easily confused with those of other illnesses. The bug lives off lots of other animals besides humans, and it has so far proved to be a tricky adversary when it comes to the creation of an effective vaccine, says Dr. Rick O'Brien, chief of research and development of TB elimination at the Centers for Disease Control and Prevention.

In cities worldwide, though mostly in Africa and East Asia where the disease is most prevalent, TB now has a new ally of sorts in the virus that

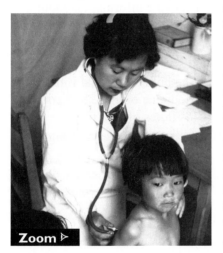

Zoom ▷

causes AIDS. It weakens the immune system, giving TB a kickstart.

This has doctors and researchers worried, since it creates a double-disease whammy in places where people were just getting a handle on TB. Moreover, those who have the disease must take a special combination of antibiotics for at least six months. If they don't complete their treatment, they risk nurturing new strains of drug-resistant TB.

The deceptively tiny David carries a big bag of survival tricks.

For more about TB:

Centers for Disease Control and Prevention

World Health Organization

National Tuberculosis Center, NJ

National Tuberculosis Center, NY

National Tuberculosis Center, CA

National Institute of Allergy and Infectious Diseases

Click on these **external links** to leave the Web site and go to other Web sites with related information. Phrases such as "For more about ..." and "Other sources" often identify these links.

Got a question about TB? Ask the experts.

Find out what happens when a microbe invades your body:
Fight the Invaders.

Turn to Disease Alert! for the latest on outbreaks.

EPIDEMIC!

| TB | Flu | Polio | Dengue | Hanta | At the Museum |

Disease Alert   Tune In

EXPEDITIONS

Analyzing Informational Text

Reading Check

1. What evidence do scientists have that tuberculosis is an ancient disease?
2. How widespread is tuberculosis today?
3. What happens when a tuberculosis bacterium enters a human body?

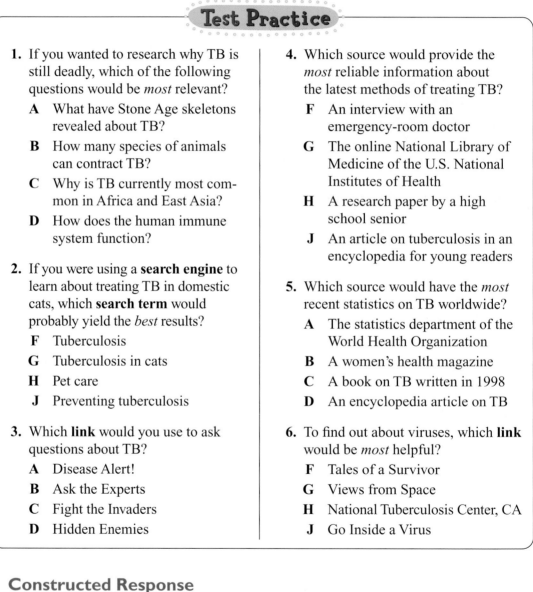

Test Practice

1. If you wanted to research why TB is still deadly, which of the following questions would be *most* relevant?
   A   What have Stone Age skeletons revealed about TB?
   B   How many species of animals can contract TB?
   C   Why is TB currently most common in Africa and East Asia?
   D   How does the human immune system function?

2. If you were using a **search engine** to learn about treating TB in domestic cats, which **search term** would probably yield the *best* results?
   F   Tuberculosis
   G   Tuberculosis in cats
   H   Pet care
   J   Preventing tuberculosis

3. Which **link** would you use to ask questions about TB?
   A   Disease Alert!
   B   Ask the Experts
   C   Fight the Invaders
   D   Hidden Enemies

4. Which source would provide the *most* reliable information about the latest methods of treating TB?
   F   An interview with an emergency-room doctor
   G   The online National Library of Medicine of the U.S. National Institutes of Health
   H   A research paper by a high school senior
   J   An article on tuberculosis in an encyclopedia for young readers

5. Which source would have the *most* recent statistics on TB worldwide?
   A   The statistics department of the World Health Organization
   B   A women's health magazine
   C   A book on TB written in 1998
   D   An encyclopedia article on TB

6. To find out about viruses, which **link** would be *most* helpful?
   F   Tales of a Survivor
   G   Views from Space
   H   National Tuberculosis Center, CA
   J   Go Inside a Virus

Constructed Response

Imagine that you are writing an article on TB or another disease. Write **questions** that focus on one aspect of your topic, and look for answers on the Internet or in a library. Keep a list of the sources you explore, and rate their usefulness.

FICTION

Stories with a Twist

Surprise endings and outrageous characters abound in the stories of Saki (H. H. Munro). Two of Saki's best-known protagonists, Reginald and Clovis, are rebellious youths who make fun of polite society with mischievous thoughts and deeds. Their bird's-eye view of everything from far-away lands to their neighbors' parlors can be glimpsed in the stories in **The Complete Saki.**

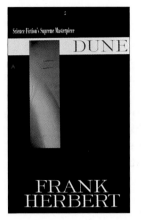

FICTION

Sand, Sand, Everywhere

Frank Herbert's classic science fiction novel **Dune** takes place on the strange desert planet Arrakis. There, under the shifting sands, live enormous worms that produce a precious life-sustaining spice valued through-out the universe. The young hero, Paul Atreides, must defend his noble family in a struggle to the death with rivals for control of the spice.

NONFICTION

A Special Friendship

"We understand each other. I let him go wherever he wishes and always he takes me where it is I wish to go." Such is the narrator's description of his faithful donkey, who brings a kind of enchantment to his small Spanish village. Juan Ramón Jiménez, winner of the 1956 Nobel Prize in literature, creates a tribute to friendship and the imagination through the deceptively simple autobiographical prose poems in **Platero and I.**

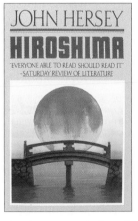

NONFICTION

Countdown to Terror

Hiroshima, by the Pulitzer Prize–winner John Hersey, gives us a moment-to-moment look at what hap-pened on August 6, 1945, the day the United States dropped the first atomic bomb on Hiroshima, Japan. In 1946, Hersey visited Hiroshima and inter-viewed survivors. The product of that visit is this detailed, compelling narrative that takes us into the minds of six people who relied on wits and luck to survive that terrible day.

Analyzing Problems and Solutions

Have you ever tried to convince someone that you have a good solution to a common problem? Perhaps you didn't face the kind of dilemma that the pilot does in Tom Godwin's "The Cold Equations." However, like the pilot, you may have found that arguing convincingly first means analyzing the problem before you can explain it to others. To **analyze** a problem, break it into its parts in order to understand it better. Then, present what you believe to be the best solution and try to persuade others to accept your solution.

Prewriting

Find a Problem to Analyze

Problems, Problems, Problems Solving problems is not an activity reserved for geometry or physics classes. To choose an interesting problem—one that matters both to you and to your readers—read a weekly newsmagazine or watch the national and local news on TV. Browse the Web for information about government and community groups devoted to solving problems, or check the editorials in your local newspaper. Then, make a list of possible topics. Keep in mind that your topic should be one for which you could write a 1,500-word essay.

Consider Purpose and Audience

Best of All Your **purpose** for writing is **expository**—that is, to analyze the problem and the possible solutions. You also want to **persuade** your **audience,** or readers, that the solution you think is best is the one they should adopt. Before you begin your analysis, however, ask yourself, "What does the audience already know about the problem?" and "What **expectations** might my audience have about possible ways to solve this problem?"

Thinking beforehand about how much your audience knows or how your audience might solve the problem may help you sort through the possible solutions. Also, brainstorm any possible objections—or **counterclaims**—that your audience might raise to the solutions you consider. Addressing any **concerns** your audience may have—any **biases** and **misunderstandings**—will later help you convince your audience that your proposed solution is best.

Investigate the Problem and Solutions

First Things First   Before you can persuade others that one solution is the best, you first need to explain the problem. One of the best ways to explain a problem is to provide answers to the *5W-How?* questions, as one student did in the following chart.

DO THIS

Problem: Teenagers' poor driving practices

Who is affected by the problem?	Parents, teenagers, police, insurance companies, doctors, and the general public are affected.
What has already been done about the problem?	Lawmakers may license teenagers in stages, only after a training period of several weeks.
Why is the problem occurring?	Teenagers lack driving experience and are faced with many new distractions on the road.
When did this problem become evident?	The problem has probably been around as long as teenagers have been driving.
Where is this a problem?	It's a national—maybe even worldwide—problem.
How does this problem affect me and my audience?	Bad driving puts everyone at risk.

   To find answers to the *5W-How?* questions, do research in the library or on the Internet, or interview someone who is knowledgeable about the problem. If the problem is local, observe it directly. Remember to take careful notes from your sources so that you can convey the information and ideas accurately and coherently.

What Works   While you are researching the problem, you should be researching solutions as well. Ask yourself, "What solutions have been suggested or attempted? What were the outcomes of the solutions?" The information you gather through your research should help you decide which solution you think may be the best for the problem.

What Works for You   After you've analyzed the problem and gathered information about the possible solutions, look back over your notes. Do you agree with any of the proposed solutions, or do you have another solution to offer for the problem? Look at the following proposed solutions to the problem of teenagers' poor driving records and one student's own solution.

TIP   As you do research to answer the *5W-How?* questions, record facts and quotations that you can use as **evidence** in your analysis of the problem. Be sure to record the page numbers and source titles of direct quotations.

Solution 1: Institute a graduated licensing program. (Disagree)
Solution 2: Raise driving age to eighteen. (Disagree)
My solution: Develop high school driving safety clubs.

SKILLS FOCUS

Writing Skills
Research the problem and solutions.

Reference Note

For more on **rhetorical devices,** see page 295.

TIP Use evidence to build a persuasive case with **logical reasoning.**

Build an Argument

Supporting Devices Give strong **reasons** to support your choice of solutions. Your reasons may include **rhetorical devices**—logical, emotional, and ethical appeals. **Logical appeals** provide solid reasoning. **Emotional appeals** use language to inspire strong feelings. **Ethical appeals** address the readers' sense of right and wrong and establish the credibility of the writer.

Legs to Stand On To back up your reasons and convince readers to accept your solution, use your collected **evidence** or gather additional evidence. Provide information that is precise and relevant to the point you are making. Here are different kinds of evidence you can use.

KINDS OF EVIDENCE

Facts are pieces of information that can be proven correct by testing or by consulting reliable sources. **Statistics** are facts expressed with numerical information.

Examples are specific instances of an idea or situation.

Expert opinions are statements by people who are considered experts in their fields. The opinion may include quotations or paraphrases of their ideas.

Anecdotes are brief personal stories that illustrate a point.

Commonly accepted beliefs are those beliefs shared by the writer and audience.

Case studies are examples from scientific studies.

Analogies are comparisons showing the similarities between two unrelated ideas or facts.

Write Your Thesis Statement

Make a Statement Generate a **thesis statement** that makes readers aware of the problem you are discussing and the solution you think is best. For example, one student's thesis statement was "Teens can take action to correct their poor driving practices by forming driving safety clubs."

Organize Your Analysis

Put Things in Order To present your analysis of the problem and the solution you recommend in a logical progression, use **chronological order:** Tell how the problem has developed over time, what solutions have been proposed, and what the best solution is for the future. Use **order of importance** if you want your most important idea to fall at the end.

SKILLS FOCUS

Writing Skills
Build an argument. Make a thesis statement. Organize information.

PRACTICE & APPLY 1 Follow the instructions on the previous pages to analyze a problem, decide on the solution you think is best, and support your ideas with evidence.

Writing

Analyzing Problems and Solutions

A Writer's Framework

Introduction

- Catch your audience's attention with an interesting anecdote or example.
- Provide background information if necessary.
- Include a thesis statement that identifies the problem and mentions the solution you think is best.

Body

- Analyze the problem.
- Explain the proposed solutions, and present the solution you think is best.
- Use reasons, evidence, and rhetorical devices to support your analysis.
- Address readers' counterclaims.

Conclusion

- Remind readers why your solution is best.
- Issue a call to action for readers to participate in your solution to the problem.
- Restate your thesis in a new and different way.

A Writer's Model

Licensed AND Safe!

Teenagers, has something like this happened to you? You are driving through the neighborhood in your car, talking to your friends, and changing the radio station. As you round a corner, a car that you didn't see crashes into you with a terrifying *crunch!* Everyone is okay, but the car is a wreck. While this unfortunate scenario is all too common for teenage drivers, it is a problem that can be solved. Teens can take action to correct their poor driving practices by forming driving safety clubs that increase teens' awareness of driving safety.

The problem of poor driving practices is not a new one for teens, nor is it limited to one area of the country. Although national studies show that teenage males may be more prone to accidents involving speed, a large percentage of fatal accidents for teen passengers occur with both male and female teenage drivers. Such a problem puts everyone at risk, affecting parents, teenagers, police, insurance companies, and the general public.

Why is this problem occurring? Of all the factors contributing to teens' poor safety record, a lack of driving experience is probably the leading cause of accidents involving teenagers. Frank Rodriguez, driving instructor for All Right Driving School, says, "A newly licensed driver needs about six more months of regular, non-stress

INTRODUCTION
Attention-grabbing anecdote

Thesis statement

BODY
Analysis of problem
Evidence: Fact

Further analysis

Evidence: Expert opinion

(continued)

(continued)

Evidence: Statistics

driving to develop confidence and skills." Once licensed, however, teens are often too unfamiliar with the roads and too distracted by conversation, food, music, and cell phones to drive safely. Studies show that half of all teenage drivers have an accident within a year of getting a license, and more than six thousand teenagers die in auto accidents every year.

Solutions already proposed

Counterclaims addressed

The solutions offered for this problem vary widely. Many lawmakers are pushing for a graduated licensing program to grant driving privileges over several months. Other lawmakers simply want to raise the driving age to eighteen, an age at which they believe teenagers will be more responsible. However, these solutions don't satisfy the multitude of mature, safe teenage drivers who desire freedom and depend on their cars for transportation to work or school. For those teens, raising the driving age or complicating the licensing requirements is more of a punishment than a solution to a problem.

Best solution
Reason, with logical appeal
Evidence: Anecdote

Teens can best address the problem of their poor driving practices by forming safe-driving clubs. Such clubs would increase teen drivers' awareness of safe driving practices. When I joined the Safe Driving for Teens Club, I helped print and distribute local street maps and brochures with tips for good driving habits. My club also developed an informative Web page with statistics about teenage driving, suggestions for parental supervision of teen driving, and advice for teens about driving in hazardous conditions. Our Web page received two community-service awards. Establishing safe-driving clubs for teens is also the right thing to do. Clubs like Safe Driving for Teens encourage teens to be safe drivers. More clubs like these should be started in school districts around the nation.

Reason, with ethical appeal

Evidence: Example

CONCLUSION
Importance
Emotional appeal
Call to action
Restatement of thesis

The problem of poor teenage driving practices is a serious one, but it can be reckoned with by the student community. If you don't want to see yourself or a friend hurt in an accident or wait until you're eighteen to drive, join an organization dedicated to increasing and improving teen responsibility on the road. By coming together to share and spread information on responsible driving, we can all work to make our communities safer places to live and drive.

INTERNET
More Writer's Models
Keyword: LE5 10-3

PRACTICE & APPLY 2 Use the framework on page 215 and the Writer's Model above as guides to write a first draft of your problem-solution analysis. Remember to investigate your problem and the possible solutions before you build an argument and support it with reasons and evidence.

Revising

Evaluate and Revise Your Draft

Take a Second Look How do good writers produce such polished work? They revise their drafts—often more than once—to make the final product the best it can be. Use the following guidelines to evaluate and revise the content and organization of your problem-solution analysis. Use the guidelines on page 218 to improve the style of your analysis.

PEER REVIEW

Before you revise, ask a peer to read your paper and to evaluate your use of precise and relevant evidence.

▶ **First Reading: Content and Organization** Use the chart below to evaluate the content and organization of your analysis. As you answer the evaluation questions, put yourself in your audience's place. Make sure that you have adequately explained the problem and given a sensible solution.

Rubric: Analyzing Problems and Solutions		
▶ **Evaluation Questions**	▶ **Tips**	▶ **Revision Techniques**
❶ Does the introduction grab the reader's attention?	**Circle** any attention-grabbing sentence or sentences.	**Add** an attention-grabbing opener—such as an anecdote or example.
❷ Does the thesis statement identify the problem and suggest the solution you think best?	**Underline** the thesis statement. **Double underline** the solution you suggest as the best one.	**Reword** your thesis statement to present the problem clearly and to suggest the solution you think best.
❸ Does the essay provide a clear and complete analysis of the problem?	**Highlight** the sentences that show the analysis of the problem.	**Elaborate** upon the problem with a complete analysis. **Add** details to make the problem clear.
❹ Does the essay address any counterclaims that readers may have?	**Bracket** the sentence that addresses a counterclaim that readers may have.	**Add** a sentence or sentences to address readers' counterclaims.
❺ Does the essay present the best solution and provide reasons and evidence to support it?	**Put a star** beside the best solution. **Draw arrow brackets** around the reasons and supporting evidence.	**Add** reasons to support the best solution. **Elaborate** with facts or statistics, an expert opinion, or an example.
❻ Does the conclusion restate the thesis of the essay? Does it contain a call to action?	**Label in the margin** the sentence that restates the thesis of the essay. **Put a check** beside the call to action.	**Reword** a concluding sentence to restate the thesis. **Add** a call to action.

Second Reading: **Style** When you are sure that you have presented a clear, thorough analysis of the problem and solutions, read your analysis again to concentrate on its style. Your analysis should excite readers and prepare them for action. Nothing will make readers tune out faster than **clichés**—tired, overused expressions, such as "the real thing" or "make a difference." Use the following guidelines to eliminate clichés from your essay.

Style Guidelines

Evaluation Question	▶ Tip	▶ Revision Technique
● Does the essay include clichés?	▶ **Draw a wavy line** under any phrases that sound familiar. Revise any underlined phrases.	▶ **Replace** clichés with straightforward or original language.

ANALYZING THE REVISION PROCESS

Study these revisions, and answer the questions that follow.

replace   Teens can ~~take matters into their own hands~~ *best address the problem of their poor driving practices* by forming safe-

add   driving clubs. Such clubs would increase teen drivers' awareness *of safe driving practices.*

elaborate   *When* I joined the Safe Driving for Teens Club, *I helped print and distribute local street maps and brochures with tips for good driving habits.*

Responding to the Revision Process

1. How did replacing the cliché improve the first sentence?

2. Why do you think the writer added information after the second sentence?

3. How did the additions to the last sentence strengthen the evidence the writer used?

SKILLS FOCUS

Writing Skills
Revise for content and style.

PRACTICE & APPLY 3 Use the guidelines in this section to revise the content, organization, and style of your analysis of a problem and its solution. Make sure that you have included reasons, evidence, and rhetorical devices. Remember also to read through your paper and eliminate any clichés you may find.

Publishing

Proofread and Publish Your Analysis

A Real Fixer-Upper If you want to be taken seriously, your analysis must be as error-free as possible. Set your analysis aside for a day or two so that you can look at it again with fresh eyes. Then, proofread it thoroughly and eliminate mistakes in grammar, usage, and mechanics.

Put the Gears in Motion Your analysis cannot help solve the problem unless you share it with others. Try one or more of the following ideas to find an audience for your analysis.

- Create a "problem bank." Gather copies of your class's problem-solution analyses, put them into a binder, and ask your school librarian to place the binder in the library for use as a problem bank. Other students at your school who are interested in problem solving and analyzing problems can use the problem bank as a resource.

- Schedule a debate. If your school has a debate team, share your essay with the debate coach, and ask him or her to consider using your problem as the topic for a schoolwide debate. This may help generate solutions that you may not have considered.

- Form a task force if your problem is school related. Does your problem directly affect students at your school? Is it something the students may be able to solve? If so, submit your analysis of a problem to your school newspaper and, with the school administration's permission, invite students, teachers, and parents to form a task force to put the solution you analyze into action.

Reflect on Your Analysis

Look Back After you have completed your analysis, take a moment to answer the following questions and find out what you have learned from this writing experience.

- What new ideas or information did you discover about the problem you researched?

- What kind of evidence did you find most helpful in writing your problem-solution essay? Explain your response.

PRACTICE & APPLY 4 Use the instruction on this page to proofread your analysis, share it with a wider audience, and reflect on what you have learned. Keep track of any responses you get from your audience about your essay.

TIP As you read your analysis, make sure that your sentences follow the **conventions** of American English. For example, avoid sentence fragments—groups of words that are not sentences. Take note of each sentence, and ask yourself, "Does the sentence have a subject? Does it have a verb? Does it express a complete thought?" For more information on **sentence fragments,** see Sentence Fragments, 9a, in the Language Handbook.

SKILLS FOCUS

Writing Skills
Proofread, especially for sentence fragments.

Giving a Persuasive Speech

Speaking Assignment
Adapt a written analysis into a formal persuasive speech that addresses a problem and presents a solution.

Do you remember the last public speech you heard? Chances are it was a persuasive speech that presented the speaker's solution to a common problem. Public officials—from city mayors right up to the President—and professionals in business usually take great care in crafting speeches that will convince their audiences to agree on an action or unite behind a common belief or cause. You can convince an audience, too, by adapting the problem-solution analysis you have just completed into a persuasive speech.

Adapt Your Written Analysis

Make a Statement Your **purpose** in giving a persuasive speech is to point out a particular problem and to convince an **audience** that you have the best solution for it. To help you begin adapting your problem-solution analysis, follow these suggestions.

- Rewrite your thesis, if necessary, to make clear for your listeners your opinion about the problem and the solution you propose as the best. (The thesis of a persuasive speech is an **assertion**—a statement that identifies the issue and expresses your opinion about it.)

- Read your analysis aloud and time yourself. Add or subtract information to clarify your assertion and to remain within the time limit. Simplify the explanations of the problem and solutions, if necessary.

- If you find that you need more information, gather more details through research or interviews. By interviewing others, you may gain additional **reasons** and **evidence** to support your proposed solutions, or you may learn of other **concerns** and **counterarguments** your listeners will have. The following chart provides guidelines for conducting interviews.

INTERNET
Speeches
Keyword: LE5 10-3

TIP Reasons may include rhetorical devices—logical, ethical, or emotional appeals. For more on **evidence** and **rhetorical devices,** see pages 214 and 295.

GUIDELINES FOR CONDUCTING INTERVIEWS

Before the interview

- Select a reliable source for your interview and set up a time that is convenient for the other person to meet you.

- Make a list of questions to ask. Make sure the questions are arranged in a logical order and require more than yes or no answers.

Listening and Speaking Skills
Present a persuasive speech.

(continued)

(continued)

During the interview

- Arrive on time. Ask the other person's permission to use a tape recorder or a video recorder. Also, be ready to take handwritten notes of responses.

- Listen carefully. Be respectful and sensitive if you ask follow-up questions. Respond politely and effectively if the interviewee asks you a question to show that you have knowledge of the subject.

After the interview

- Review your notes and write a summary of the material you have gathered.

- Send a note expressing your appreciation for the interview.

- Evaluate the effectiveness of your interview: What would you change?

Save the Best for Last As in your written analysis, the order of your speech should be coherent and logical. Begin with your thesis statement so that your audience is aware of your opinion. Then, provide background information and present the best solution with the reasons and evidence that show why this solution is the best. Arrange the reasons in **order of importance,** presenting the strongest reason last. End your speech with a call to action.

Rehearse and Deliver Your Speech

Speak Up, Speak Out For a formal presentation, memorize and then deliver your speech. Use only brief notes to help you. To help you gain confidence and to learn effective delivery techniques, rehearse your speech in front of a mirror or a few friends to help you maintain eye contact as you speak. Practice speaking loudly, slowly, and expressively enough to make your arguments clear even to listeners at the back of the room. Use standard American English for your formal presentation.

Ask for a Response After you deliver your speech, ask for feedback on your content and delivery techniques. Have your classmates answer questions such as, "What concerns or counterarguments did you have that the speaker did not address?" or "What was especially effective in the speaker's delivery and why?" Evaluate the responses to your questions so that you can make adjustments the next time you deliver a speech.

PRACTICE & APPLY 5 Plan and practice giving a formal persuasive speech by adapting your problem-solution analysis. Deliver the speech in front of an audience and ask for feedback to help your future presentations.

SKILLS FOCUS

Listening and Speaking Skills
Rehearse and deliver your presentation.

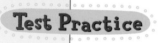
Test Practice

Generating Research Questions

DIRECTIONS: Read the following article. Then, read and respond to the questions that follow.

Local Hands on a New Space Project

Seema Mehta

Crystal capsules prepared by UC Irvine[1] scientist Alexander McPherson and schoolchildren across the United States are scheduled to be launched into space this morning on the shuttle *Atlantis,* destined for the International Space Station, a gigantic laboratory taking shape about 200 miles above earth.

Students helping with experiments for the International Space Station prepared solutions to grow crystals like the ones pictured here.

The station is a 16-nation effort led by the U.S. that should be completed in 2005. The finished lab, which will house scientists, should be as big as a football field and would weigh 1 million pounds on the ground.

The growing of protein crystals is the first experiment aboard the massive lab. Protein crystals, used for new HIV inhibitors, cancer drugs, nonpolluting laundry detergent, and more, grow better in the low-gravity environment of space.

SKILLS FOCUS

Pages 222–225 cover
Reading Skills
Generate relevant research questions.

---

1. **UC Irvine:** University of California campus at Irvine.

High school students working with solutions at NASA's Marshall Space Flight Center in Huntsville, Alabama. Their samples will be carried by the space shuttle *Atlantis* for experiments on the International Space Station.

About 150 of the 500 crystal samples being sent up were made by students in California, Alabama, Florida, and Tennessee. A total of 87 California students and teachers participated, most in Los Angeles and Orange counties.

"Our intention is not just to use the space station as a lab, but as a scientific classroom for the United States," McPherson said.

McPherson said student participation is a key element, because today's students are tomorrow's scientists. He traces his own interest in science to his youth.

A Mission to Excite Kids About Science

"Since I grew up in Orlando, I saw all the early missions. I've been following the space program since Alan Shepard went up in the early 1960s," he said.

But today, "the students are simply not going into science and mathematics—they think it's too hard or intimidating or not interesting," he said. "We're trying to turn that around. Science is the most interesting thing in the world."

Researchers and the students, working under McPherson's direction, sealed chemicals into small tubes that were then frozen to minus 320 degrees Fahrenheit. Scientists placed the samples into thermoslike containers that are kept cool with liquid nitrogen. Once in orbit, the nitrogen naturally boils off, thawing the samples and allowing the protein crystals to begin growing, according to the National Aeronautics and Space Administration.

The crystals will remain in orbit until October, when they will be retrieved by another manned space shuttle.

Once the crystals are brought back to earth, scientists will use X-rays to deduce the detailed atomic structure of the molecules.

Such studies have significant implications for humans because information gathered from the crystals can ultimately be used for manufacturing pharmaceuticals[2] and to learn more about human ailments such as genetic defects.[3]

"Those protein molecules are extremely important because they are the major biochemical element of all living tissue," said McPherson, who has been involved with NASA protein crystal projects since 1984. He received the agency's Exceptional Scientific Achievement Medal in 1999. "We can use our knowledge of those to design new drugs."

The information also has applications in the manufacturing of insecticides,[4] herbicides,[5] and industrial products, such as laundry detergents that use enzymes.[6]

—from the *Los Angeles Times,* September 8, 2000

---

2. **pharmaceuticals** (fär′mə·sōōt′i·kəls) *n.:* medicines.
3. **genetic defects:** disorders carried in the body's genes that can be passed from parent to child.
4. **insecticides** (in·sek′tə·sīdz′) *n.:* substances used to kill insects.
5. **herbicides** (hur′bə·sīdz′) *n.:* substances used to destroy plants, especially weeds.
6. **enzymes** (en′zīmz′) *n.:* here, synthetic proteins used to create kinds of chemical reactions.

Collection 3: Skills Review

1. Which research question is *most* relevant to the information in the article?

   A What have scientists deduced about the atomic structure of the molecules of a protein crystal?

   B What techniques do teachers use to make science and math more appealing to high school students?

   C What is the history of the U.S. space program?

   D Who is Alan Shepard?

2. Which research question would probably yield the *most* relevant information about future experiments planned for the ISS?

   F What is the likelihood of future experimentation in space?

   G How profitable is experimentation on the ISS?

   H What do scientists hope to learn from space experiments?

   J What are the research plans for the ISS for the next two years?

3. Which of the following research questions about protein crystals is the *most* narrow and focused?

   A Why are protein crystals important?

   B What are the results of some recent experiments in space?

   C How will the information gained from protein-crystal research be used practically?

   D What are the different types of crystals, and how does each grow?

4. If you were using an Internet search engine to try to find out more about the research experiment described in this article, which search term would probably be *most* helpful?

   F UC Irvine

   G Space science

   H International Space Station

   J Exceptional Scientific Achievement Medal

5. To find out the design of the ISS (what it looks like), which resource would be the *most* helpful?

   A A recent magazine article about experiments aboard the ISS

   B The ISS NASA-sponsored Web site

   C An encyclopedia article about Alexander McPherson

   D A book about the history of the U.S. space program published in 1997

Constructed Response

6. List three kinds of Web sites that would probably provide reliable information on the ISS. Explain why you think they would be useful.

Collection 3: Skills Review
Vocabulary Skills

Synonyms

DIRECTIONS: Choose the best synonym for the underlined word in each sentence.

1. In "The Storyteller" the little girl criticizes the aunt's story with great conviction.
   - A certainty
   - B annoyance
   - C disapproval
   - D skill

2. The children's questions are loud and petulant.
   - F intelligent
   - G ill-tempered
   - H repetitive
   - J comical

3. The smaller girl keeps repeating the line of poetry over and over in a stubborn and resolute way.
   - A creative
   - B dreamy
   - C ridiculous
   - D determined

4. In "The Cold Equations" the stowaway's weight is of paramount importance.
   - F little
   - G relative
   - H usual
   - J supreme

5. The laws of nature are irrevocable.
   - A complicated
   - B universal
   - C irreversible
   - D changeable

6. A tornado threatened to annihilate the Group One camp on Woden.
   - F strike
   - G destroy
   - H close
   - J rearrange

7. An example of an immutable natural law is the force of gravity, which pulls toward the earth's center.
   - A unchanging
   - B powerful
   - C unfamiliar
   - D unproven

8. The first lines from Shakespeare that young Frank reads are, "I do believe, induced by potent circumstances, / That thou art mine enemy."
   - F overcome
   - G persuaded
   - H defeated
   - J upset

9. Frankie finds Shakespeare's poetry very potent.
   - A powerful
   - B harsh
   - C difficult
   - D pleasing

SKILLS FOCUS

Vocabulary Skills
Use synonyms.

Collection 3: Skills Review
Writing Skills

Test Practice

DIRECTIONS: Read the following paragraph from a draft of a student's problem-solution analysis. Then, read the questions below it. Choose the best answer to each question.

(1) Asthma is a chronic lung disease that causes episodes of coughing, wheezing, and shortness of breath. (2) It can be triggered by allergens such as pollen and mold, and for that reason many doctors have recommended staying inside to prevent lung irritation. (3) By performing specific exercises to strengthen your lungs, you can manage asthma attacks and be able to live a more active life as well. (4) Asthma can be a pain in the neck, but it doesn't have to control your life.

1. To support the ideas in sentence 3, the writer could
   A provide an expert opinion on why air-cleaning devices are important
   B describe the other environmental factors that lead to asthma attacks
   C relate in detail the breathing activity that should be performed
   D include facts that prove the effectiveness of breathing exercises

2. Which sentence would add an emotional appeal to the passage?
   F Don't let asthma ruin your social life—exercise and fight back!
   G Some of the U.S. athletes in the 1996 Olympics had asthma.
   H Stay inside to avoid the perilous allergens that assault your lungs.
   J Because of asthma, I can't play basketball anymore.

3. To address a reader's concern that exercising with asthma could be dangerous, the writer could
   A provide an expert opinion on how exercising with asthma is helpful
   B tell readers to do more research

   C tell non-asthmatic readers that they shouldn't be concerned
   D provide a list of professional athletes from all sports

4. Which of the sentences below would best replace sentence 4 in order to eliminate the use of clichés?
   F Asthma can be a serious disease, but it's not as bad as other diseases.
   G Asthma can be a serious disease, but it doesn't have to conquer you.
   H Asthma can be a serious disease, and you can't do much about it.
   J Asthma can be a serious disease, but exercising can put you on cloud nine.

5. What might the student do to adapt the analysis into a persuasive speech?
   A cut the introduction to save time
   B read directly from note cards
   C provide additional information that relates to the audience
   D make arguments more complex so as to impress the audience

SKILLS FOCUS

Writing Skills
Write a problem-solution analysis.

Comparing Themes

INFORMATIONAL READING FOCUS

EVALUATING ARGUMENTS: PRO AND CON

There are only two or three human stories, and they go on repeating themselves as fiercely as if they had never happened before.

—Willa Cather

INTERNET

Collection Resources

Keyword: LE5 10-4

The Couple at the Eiffel Tower by Marc Chagall (1887–1985).
Oil on canvas.
Giraudon/Art Resource, New York.

229

Elements of Literature

Theme *by* John Leggett
WHAT DOES IT MEAN?

An Insight About Life

I once read a student's story that was full of action—two mountain climbers were about to plunge down a ravine, a skier was schussing into peril, and a killer was waiting in the valley below. Despite all this action and intrigue, however, the story was uninteresting because the action didn't seem to have any meaning.

A story's characters and events take on significance only when we recognize what they mean to us. In other words, all the elements of a good story must add up to a **theme**—an idea or insight about life and human nature that gives the story meaning. Themes are important to all forms of literature, and similar themes can often be found in different **genres**—in stories, novels, plays, poems, even in nonfiction.

What Do We Mean by Theme?

The theme of a work of literature is really its root. Theme is unseen and usually unstated, yet it is vital. It gives meaning to the characters and events, and at the same time it reveals the writer's personal attitude toward the world, toward how people should behave and how they actually do behave.

Theme is neither a summary of the plot (what happens) nor the work's subject (which might be boxing or prospecting for gold). Rather, theme is what the writer *means* by everything he or she has set down. A theme may give us insight into some aspect of life that we have never really thought about before, or it may

make us understand something we always knew but never realized we knew.

Another student's story I once read was a good story, about a girl who finds her car broken into and her stereo stolen. The girl is crazy with rage, and all she can think to do is to call up an ex-boyfriend because she believes he'll know what to do. He does. He calms her, gets the car fixed, and talks her out of her anger.

As I read the story, I realized that the girl is still in love with her ex-boyfriend, though he is no longer in love with her, and the story is really about *that* misfortune. In the end the girl accepts both facts. I realized, with all the force of sudden revelation, that the heroine has been undergoing a major growing-up experience: She has learned to accept loss.

Now *that's* a theme. Telling that by means of a story is much more memorable and emotionally compelling than simply stating the story's theme: "One of the lessons that everyone must learn in growing up is how to deal with loss."

Discovering a Theme

It's often difficult for a reader to state the theme of a literary work. (Remember that the writer has had to write the whole work to get that theme across to us.) Yet the attempt to put a theme into words can often help us understand the work more fully. Here are some guidelines for discovering and stating a theme:

 One of the best ways to discover the theme of a literary work is to

ask how the protagonist *changes* during the course of the story. Often what this character learns about life is the truth the writer wants to reveal to the reader.

2 Because conflict is so central to most literature, a good clue to theme is how the conflict is resolved.

3 Another way to discover the theme is to think about the title of a work, which often—but not always—has a special significance and hints at the theme.

4 We must use at least one complete sentence to state a theme. In other words, a theme must be a statement about the subject of the work rather than a phrase such as "the rewards of old age." (Sometimes you can reword this kind of phrase to form a sentence: "Old age can be a time of great satisfaction.")

5 Remember that a theme is not the same as a moral, which is a rule of conduct. In getting at theme, we should ask ourselves, "What does this work reveal?" rather than "What does this work teach?" Thus, it is a mistake to reduce a theme (at least a serious writer's theme) to a familiar saying or cliché, such as "Crime doesn't pay." A theme is usually a much more complex and original revelation about life.

6 A theme must be expressed as a **generalization** about life or human nature; it should not refer to specific characters or events in the work. Themes are often **universal**—that is, they apply to people everywhere—because people all over the world have common desires, needs, and experiences. We all know about love and loss, dreams and dashed hopes.

7 There is no single correct way to state the theme of a literary work. If there are thirty-five students in your English class, for instance, there will probably be thirty-five distinct ways of putting a story's central insight into words. Your classmates may also have several different ideas about what the story's major theme is. In fact, if a story or work of literature is rich and complex, it may have more than one theme.

Practice

Choose a story you have recently read that meant something to you. Using a chart like the one below, go step by step to discover, and then state, the story's theme. Compare your statement of the theme with the statements of classmates who have chosen the same story.

Steps to a Theme
How the main character changes:
How the conflict is resolved:
What the title suggests:
What, in general, the story reveals about life or people:
The story's theme:

Elements of Literature

Comparing Universal Themes

"Catch the Moon" . . . . by Judith Ortiz Cofer . . . short story . . . page 234
"The Bass, the River, and Sheila Mant" . . . by W. D. Wetherell . . . . . short story . . . page 244

A Universe of People and Themes

People all over the world and throughout time have shared common emotions, concerns, and experiences—it's what makes us human. We all want to be loved; we have hopes and dreams; we cope with loss, death, and disappointment. Our universal concerns are reflected in literature as **universal themes.** These broad themes come up again and again in literature, yet each writer gives a personal insight, or "twist," to these themes.

Love—You Can't Live with It, and You Can't Live Without It

Love is such a universal experience that sayings about it pepper our everyday conversation. Writers have explored the theme of love for thousands of years. The next two stories are about falling in love. You'll need to read on to find out how each story treats that universal experience.

Although we talk of love as a universal theme, remember that the theme of a work of literature is never expressed with a single word but rather in a complete sentence that makes a statement about life. For example, the theme of a story would never be stated simply as "love." Instead, the statement of the theme would express a view of love, such as "Love, despite its joys, also brings sorrow."

Reading Skills

Comparing and Contrasting Themes

For help comparing the themes in these two stories, review the guidelines for discovering and stating theme on pages 230–231. After you have read and discussed each story, fill in comments about the story's plot, characters, and theme in a chart like the one below. Then, turn to page 254.

	"Catch the Moon"	"The Bass, The River, and Sheila Mant"
Main character		
Changes main character undergoes		
Conflict between characters		
How conflict is resolved		
How character's change relates to theme		
How conflict relates to theme		
Statement of theme		

SKILLS FOCUS

Pages 232–254 cover
Literary Skills
Understand and compare universal themes.

Reading Skills
Compare and contrast themes.

Before You Read

Catch the Moon

Make the Connection

Quickwrite ✏️

Does falling in love change a person? What might motivate someone in love to behave as he or she would never have behaved before? Quickwrite about your ideas. You might think about your own experiences and observations as well as about love stories you have read or seen in the movies.

Literary Focus

Theme and Character

A story's **theme** is the message it communicates about life or people. When you're trying to determine the theme, keep your eyes on the **main character.** How the main character changes and what he or she learns are important clues to the theme. The change in the main character may be an outside change that everyone can see or an inner change— perhaps a sudden realization—that only the main character and the reader can recognize.

Reading Skills 📖

Making a Generalization

When you state the **theme** of a story or another work of literature, you state it as a **generalization**—a broad statement that takes into account all the details in the text, not just one. Generalizations help people make sense of the world. Just think how complicated life would be if we couldn't make generalizations about natural laws (wet climates produce lush foliage) or about people (everyone wants to be loved). As you read this story, think about what generalizations the characters and events suggest to you.

Vocabulary Development

harassing (har′əs·iŋ) v. used as n.: bothering; troubling.

dismantled (dis·mant′'ld) v.: took apart.

vintage (vin′tij) adj.: dating from a time long past.

ebony (eb′ə·nē) adj.: dark or black.

sarcastic (sär·kas′tik) adj.: mocking; taunting; in a manner that makes fun of something or someone.

relics (rel′iks) n.: objects or things from the past that may have special meanings or associations, sometimes religious ones.

---

go.hrw.com

INTERNET

Vocabulary Practice
•
More About Judith Ortiz Cofer

Keyword: LE5 10-4

SKILLS FOCUS

Literary Skills
Understand theme and character.

Reading Skills
Make a generalization.

CATCH THE MOON

Judith Ortiz Cofer

Luis watched the most beautiful girl he had ever seen.

Luis Cintrón sits on top of a six-foot pile of hubcaps and watches his father walk away into the steel jungle of his car junkyard. Released into his old man's custody[1] after six months in juvenile hall—for breaking and entering—and he didn't even take anything. He did it on a dare. But the old lady with the million cats was a light sleeper, and good with her aluminum cane. He has a scar on his head to prove it.

Now Luis is wondering whether he should have stayed in and done his full time. Jorge Cintrón of Jorge Cintrón & Son, Auto Parts and Salvage, has decided that Luis should wash and polish every hubcap in the yard. The hill he is sitting on is only the latest couple of hundred wheel covers that have come in. Luis grunts and stands up on top of his silver mountain. He yells at no one, "Someday, son, all this will be yours," and sweeps his arms like the Pope blessing a crowd over the piles of car sandwiches and mounds of metal parts that cover this acre of land outside the city. He is the "Son" of Jorge Cintrón & Son, and so far his father has had more than one reason to wish it was plain Jorge Cintrón on the sign.

---

1. **custody** *n.:* term describing the legal responsibility of one person for another.

Luis has been getting in trouble since he started high school two years ago, mainly because of the "social group" he organized—a bunch of guys who were into harassing the local authorities. Their thing was taking something to the limit on a dare or, better still, doing something dangerous, like breaking into a house, not to steal, just to prove that they could do it. That was Luis's specialty, coming up with very complicated plans, like military strategies, and assigning the "jobs" to guys who wanted to join the Tiburones.

Tiburón means "shark," and Luis had gotten the name from watching an old movie about a Puerto Rican gang called the Sharks with his father. Luis thought it was one of the dumbest films he had ever seen. Everybody sang their lines, and the guys all pointed their toes and leapt in the air when they were supposed to be slaughtering each other. But he liked their name, the Sharks, so he made it Spanish and had it air-painted on his black T-shirt with a killer shark under it, jaws opened wide and dripping with blood. It didn't take long for other guys in the barrio[2] to ask about it.

Man, had they had a good time. The girls were interested too. Luis outsmarted everybody by calling his organization a social club and registering it at Central High. That meant they were legal, even let out of last-period class on Fridays for their "club" meetings. It was just this year, after a couple of botched jobs, that the teachers had started getting suspicious. The first one to go wrong was when he sent Kenny Matoa to *borrow* some "souvenirs" out of Anita Robles's locker. He got caught. It seems that Matoa had been reading Anita's diary and didn't hear her coming down the hall. Anita was supposed to be in the gym at that time but had copped out with the usual female excuse of cramps. You could hear her screams all the way to Market Street.

She told the principal all she knew about the Tiburones, and Luis had to talk fast to convince old Mr. Williams that the club did put on cultural activities such as the Save the Animals talent show. What Mr. Williams didn't know was that the animal that was being "saved" with the ticket sales was Luis's pet boa, which needed quite a few live mice to stay healthy and happy. They kept E. S. (which stood for "Endangered Species") in Luis's room, but she belonged to the club and it was the members' responsibility to raise the money to feed their mascot.[3] So last year they had sponsored their first annual Save the Animals talent show, and it had been a great success. The Tiburones had come dressed as Latino Elvises and did a grand finale to "All Shook Up" that made the audience go wild. Mr. Williams had smiled while Luis talked, maybe remembering how the math teacher, Mrs. Laguna, had dragged him out in the aisle to rock-and-roll with her. Luis had gotten out of that one, but barely.

His father was a problem too. He objected to the T-shirt logo, calling it disgusting and vulgar. Mr. Cintrón prided himself on his own neat, elegant style of dressing after work, and on his manners and large vocabulary, which he picked up by taking correspondence courses[4] in just about everything. Luis thought it was just his way of staying busy since Luis's mother had died, almost three years ago, of cancer. He had never gotten over it.

All this was going through Luis's head as he slid down the hill of hubcaps. The tub full of soapy water, the can of polish, and the bag of rags had been neatly placed in front of a makeshift table made from two car seats and

---

3. **mascot** *n.:* person, animal, or thing kept by a group or team as its symbol or for good luck.
4. **correspondence courses** *n.:* courses of study conducted through the mail.

Vocabulary
harassing (har′əs·iŋ) *v.* used as *n:* bothering; troubling.

---

2. **barrio** (bär′ē · ō) *n.:* in the United States, a Spanish-speaking neighborhood.

a piece of plywood. Luis heard a car drive up and someone honk their horn. His father emerged from inside a new red Mustang that had been totaled. He usually <u>dismantled</u> every small feature by hand before sending the vehicle into the *cementerio,*[5] as he called the lot. Luis watched as the most beautiful girl he had ever seen climbed out of a <u>vintage</u> white Volkswagen Bug. She stood in the sunlight in her white sundress waiting for his father, while Luis stared. She was like a smooth wood carving. Her skin was mahogany, almost black, and her arms and legs were long and thin, but curved in places so that she did not look bony and hard—more like a ballerina. And her <u>ebony</u> hair was braided close to her head. Luis let his breath out, feeling a little dizzy. He had forgotten to breathe. Both the girl and his father heard him. Mr. Cintrón waved him over.

"Luis, the señorita here has lost a wheel cover. Her car is twenty-five years old, so it will not be an easy match. Come look on this side."

Luis tossed a wrench he'd been holding into a toolbox like he was annoyed, just to make a point about slave labor. Then he followed his father, who knelt on the gravel and began to point out every detail of the hubcap. Luis was

hardly listening. He watched the girl take a piece of paper from her handbag.

"Señor Cintrón, I have drawn the hubcap for you, since I will have to leave soon. My home address and telephone number are here, and also my parents' office number." She handed the paper to Mr. Cintrón, who nodded.

"Sí, señorita, very good. This will help my son look for it. Perhaps there is one in that stack there." He pointed to the pile of caps that Luis was supposed to wash and polish. "Yes, I'm almost certain that there is a match there. Of course, I do not know if it's near the top or the bottom. You will give us a few days, yes?"

Luis just stared at his father like he was crazy. But he didn't say anything because the girl was smiling at him with a funny expression on her face. Maybe she thought he had X-ray eyes like Superman, or maybe she was mocking him.

"Please call me Naomi, Señor Cintrón. You know my mother. She is the director of the funeral home. . . ." Mr. Cintrón seemed surprised at first; he prided himself on having a great memory. Then his friendly expression changed to one of sadness as he recalled the day of his wife's burial. Naomi did not finish her sentence. She reached over and placed her hand on Mr. Cintrón's arm for a moment. Then she said "Adiós" softly, and got in her shiny white car. She waved to them as she left, and her gold bracelets flashing in the sun nearly blinded Luis.

Mr. Cintrón shook his head. "How about that," he said as if to himself. "They are the Dominican owners of Ramirez Funeral Home." And, with a sigh, "She seems like such a nice young woman. Reminds me of your mother when she was her age."

---

5. **cementerio** (se·men·te′rē·ō) *n.:* Spanish for "cemetery."

Vocabulary

dismantled (dis·mant′'ld) *v.:* took apart.

vintage (vin′tij) *adj.:* dating from a time long past.

ebony (eb′ə·nē) *adj.:* dark or black.

Hearing the funeral parlor's name, Luis remembered too. The day his mother died, he had been in her room at the hospital while his father had gone for coffee. The alarm had gone off on her monitor and nurses had come running in, pushing him outside. After that, all he recalled was the anger that had made him punch a hole in his bedroom wall. And afterward he had refused to talk to anyone at the funeral. Strange, he did see a black girl there who didn't try like the others to talk to him, but actually ignored him as she escorted family members to the viewing room and brought flowers in. Could it be that the skinny girl in a frilly white dress had been Naomi? She didn't act like she had recognized him today, though. Or maybe she thought that he was a jerk.

Luis grabbed the drawing from his father. The old man looked like he wanted to walk down memory lane. But Luis was in no mood to listen to the old stories about his falling in love on a tropical island. The world they'd lived in before he was born wasn't his world. No beaches and palm trees here. Only junk as far as he could see. He climbed back up his hill and studied Naomi's sketch. It had obviously been done very carefully. It was signed "Naomi Ramirez" in the lower right-hand corner. He memorized the telephone number.

Luis washed hubcaps all day until his hands were red and raw, but he did not come across the small silver bowl that would fit the VW. After work he took a few practice Frisbee shots across the yard before showing his father what he had accomplished: rows and rows of shiny rings drying in the sun. His father nodded and showed him the bump on his temple where one of Luis's flying saucers had gotten him. "Practice makes perfect, you know. Next time you'll probably decapitate[6] me." Luis heard him struggle with the word *decapitate*, which Mr. Cintrón pronounced in syllables. Showing off his big vocabulary

again, Luis thought. He looked closely at the bump, though. He felt bad about it.

"They look good, hijo,[7]" Mr. Cintrón made a sweeping gesture with his arms over the yard. "You know, all this will have to be classified. My dream is to have all the parts divided by year, make of car, and condition. Maybe now that you are here to help me, this will happen."

"Pop . . ." Luis put his hand on his father's shoulder. They were the same height and build, about five foot six and muscular. "The judge said six months of free labor for you, not life, okay?" Mr. Cintrón nodded, looking distracted. It was then that Luis suddenly noticed how gray his hair had turned—it used to be shiny black like his own—and that there were deep lines in his face. His father had turned into an old man and he hadn't even noticed.

"Son, you must follow the judge's instructions. Like she said, next time you get in trouble, she's going to treat you like an adult, and I think you know what that means. Hard time, no breaks."

"Yeah, yeah. That's what I'm doing, right? Working my hands to the bone instead of enjoying my summer. But listen, she didn't put me under house arrest, right? I'm going out tonight."

"Home by ten. She did say something about a curfew, Luis." Mr. Cintrón had stopped smiling and was looking upset. It had always been hard for them to talk more than a minute or two before his father got offended at something Luis said, or at his sarcastic tone. He was always doing something wrong.

Luis threw the rag down on the table and went to sit in his father's ancient Buick, which was in mint condition. They drove home in silence.

After sitting down at the kitchen table with his father to eat a pizza they had picked up on

---

6. **decapitate** (dē·kap′ə·tāt′) *v.*: cut off the head of.

7. **hijo** (ē′hō) *n.*: Spanish for "son."

Vocabulary

sarcastic (sär·kas′tik) *adj.*: mocking; taunting; in a manner that makes fun of something or someone.

the way home, Luis asked to borrow the car. He didn't get an answer then, just a look that meant "Don't bother me right now."

Before bringing up the subject again, Luis put some ice cubes in a Baggie and handed it to Mr. Cintrón, who had made the little bump on his head worse by rubbing it. It had GUILTY written on it, Luis thought.

"Gracias, hijo." His father placed the bag on the bump and made a face as the ice touched his skin.

They ate in silence for a few minutes more; then Luis decided to ask about the car again.

"I really need some fresh air, Pop. Can I borrow the car for a couple of hours?"

"You don't get enough fresh air at the yard? We're lucky that we don't have to sit in a smelly old factory all day. You know that?"

"Yeah, Pop. We're real lucky." Luis always felt irritated that his father was so grateful to own a junkyard, but he held his anger back and just waited to see if he'd get the keys without having to get in an argument.

"Where are you going?"

"For a ride. Not going anywhere. Just out for a while. Is that okay?"

His father didn't answer, just handed him a set of keys, as shiny as the day they were manufactured. His father polished everything that could be polished: doorknobs, coins, keys, spoons, knives, and forks, like he was King Midas counting his silver and gold. Luis thought his father must be really lonely to polish utensils only he used anymore. They had been picked out by his wife, though, so they were like relics. Nothing she had ever owned could be thrown away. Only now the dishes, forks, and spoons were not used to eat the yellow rice and red beans, the fried chicken, or the mouth-watering sweet plantains that his mother had cooked for them. They were just kept in the cabinets that

his father had turned into a museum for her. Mr. Cintrón could cook as well as his wife, but he didn't have the heart to do it anymore. Luis thought that maybe if they ate together once in a while things might get better between them, but he always had something to do around dinnertime and ended up at a hamburger joint.

Tonight was the first time in months they had sat down at the table together.

Luis took the keys. "Thanks," he said, walking out to take his shower. His father kept looking at him with those sad, patient eyes. "Okay. I'll be back by ten, and keep the ice on that egg," Luis said without looking back.

He had just meant to ride around his old barrio, see if any of the Tiburones were hanging out at El Building, where most of them lived. It wasn't far from the single-family home his father had bought when the business starting paying off: a house that his mother lived in for three months before she took up residence at St. Joseph's Hospital. She never came home again. These days Luis wished he still lived in that tiny apartment where there was always something to do, somebody to talk to.

Instead Luis found himself parked in front of the last place his mother had gone to: Ramirez Funeral Home. In the front yard was a huge oak tree that Luis remembered having climbed during the funeral to get away from people. The tree looked different now, not like a skeleton, as it had then, but green with leaves. The branches reached to the second floor of the house, where the family lived.

For a while Luis sat in the car allowing the memories to flood back into his brain. He

It had GUILTY written on it.

Vocabulary

relics (rel'iks) *n.*: objects or things from the past that may have special meanings or associations, sometimes religious ones.

remembered his mother before the illness changed her. She had not been beautiful, as his father told everyone; she had been a sweet lady, not pretty but not ugly. To him, she had been the person who always told him that she was proud of him and loved him. She did that every night when she came to his bedroom door to say good-night. As a joke he would sometimes ask her, "Proud of what? I haven't done anything." And she'd always say, "I'm just proud that you are my son." She wasn't perfect or anything. She had bad days when nothing he did could make her smile, especially after she got sick. But he never heard her say anything negative about anyone. She always blamed *el destino*, fate, for what went wrong. He missed her. He missed her so much. Suddenly a flood of tears that had been building up for almost three years started pouring from his eyes. Luis sat in his father's car, with his head on the steering wheel, and cried, "Mami, I miss you."

When he finally looked up, he saw that he was being watched. Sitting at a large window with a pad and a pencil on her lap was Naomi. At first Luis felt angry and embarrassed, but she wasn't laughing at him. Then she told him with her dark eyes that it was okay to come closer. He walked to the window, and she held up the sketch pad on which she had drawn him, not crying like a baby, but sitting on top of a moun-tain of silver disks, holding one up over his head. He had to smile.

The plate-glass window was locked. It had a security bolt on it. An alarm system, he figured, so nobody would steal the princess. He asked her if he could come in. It was sound-proof too. He mouthed the words slowly for her to read his lips. She wrote on the pad, "I can't let you in. My mother is not home tonight." So they looked at each other and talked

through the window for a little while. Then Luis got an idea. He signed to her that he'd be back, and drove to the junkyard.

Luis climbed up on his mountain of hubcaps. For hours he sorted the wheel covers by make, size, and condition, stopping only to call his father and tell him where he was and what he was doing. The old man did not ask him for expla-nations, and Luis was grateful for that. By lamp-post light, Luis worked and worked, beginning to understand a little why his father kept busy all the time. Doing something that had a beginning, a middle, and an end did something to your head. It was like the satisfaction Luis got out of planning "adventures" for his Tiburones, but there was another element involved here that had nothing to do with showing off for others. This was a treasure hunt. And he knew what he was looking for.

Finally, when it seemed that it was a hopeless search, when it was almost midnight and Luis's hands were cut and bruised from his work, he found it. It was the perfect match for Naomi's drawing, the moon-shaped wheel cover for her car, Cinderella's shoe. Luis jumped off the small mound of disks left under him and shouted, "Yes!" He looked around and saw neat stacks of hubcaps that he would wash the next day. He would build a display wall for his father. People would be able to come into the yard and point to whatever they wanted.

Luis washed the VW hubcap and polished it until he could see himself in it. He used it as a mirror as he washed his face and combed his hair. Then he drove to the Ramirez Funeral Home. It was almost pitch-black, since it was a moonless night. As quietly as possible, Luis put some gravel in his pocket and climbed the oak tree to the second floor. He knew he was in front of Naomi's window—he could see her shadow through the curtains. She was at a table, apparently writing or drawing, maybe waiting for him. Luis hung the silver disk carefully on a branch near the window, then threw the gravel at the glass. Naomi ran to the window and drew the curtains aside while Luis held on to the thick branch and waited to give her the first good thing he had given anyone in a long time. ■

Meet the Writer

Judith Ortiz Cofer

Bridging Cultures

Judith Ortiz Cofer (1952–   ) has always traveled between two cultures. She was born in Puerto Rico and began her visits to the United States mainland when she was four. Whenever her father, a career navy man, was overseas, his family would return to Puerto Rico. Then, when he sailed back to the States, his family would rejoin him in Paterson, New Jersey.

Cofer grew up listening to her grandmother's fascinating *cuentos* (Spanish for "stories") and soon knew that she wanted to write.

66 When I was growing up, I absorbed literature, both the spoken *cuentos* and books, as a creature who breathed ink. Each writer provided poems, novels, taught me that language could be tamed. I realized that I could make it perform. I had to believe the work was important to my being: to use my art as a bridge between my cultures. Unlike my parents, I was not always straddling. I began crossing the bridge, traveling back and forth without fear and confusion. 99

Cofer writes from 5:00 to 7:00 A.M. before her day begins as wife, mother, and professor of English and creative writing at the University of Georgia in Athens. First known as a poet, she has said, "I'm still hoping to write that one poem that will outlast me." Among her works are a novel, *The Line of the Sun* (1989); a book of personal essays, *Silent Dancing* (1990); and two collections of prose and poetry, *The Latin Deli* (1993) and *The Year of Our Revolution* (1998).

For Independent Reading

If you enjoyed this story, try reading Cofer's *An Island Like You: Stories of the Barrio* (1995). The anthology includes "Catch the Moon" and other stories about the experiences of Puerto Rican teenagers growing up in the United States today.

Response and Analysis

Reading Check

1. Why is Luis working for his father?

2. Who are the Tiburones, and what does their name mean?

3. What "treasure hunt" does Luis go on late one night?

4. Find the passage that explains the story's title.

Thinking Critically

5. Describe Luis's attitude at the beginning of the story toward his job in his father's junkyard. How has his attitude changed by the end of the story? Why?

6. What role does Naomi play in the story? What **character traits,** aside from her beauty, make her attractive to Luis?

7. Even though she has been dead for almost three years, the mother plays an important role in this story. How does she continue to influence Luis and his father? Why do you think Luis is able to cry "a flood of tears" when he does?

8. How does Luis's relationship with his father change in the story? Do you think it will continue to change? Support your answers with evidence from the story.

9. In light of the changes Luis undergoes and the reasons for those changes, what would you say is the story's **theme,** or broad **generalization** about life? Remember to state the theme as a complete sentence.

Extending and Evaluating

10. How believable is the change that Luis undergoes? Look back at your Quick-write notes to see whether his behavior fits your ideas about the things people do for love.

Literary Criticism

11. In an essay about cultural awareness titled "I Am Latina Wherever I Am," Judith Ortiz Cofer says:

> I believe my role as an artist is to build bridges. To unite us with the world and fellow beings.

Do you think "Catch the Moon" accomplishes Cofer's goal of building bridges between cultures? Does the story express **universal** concerns and **themes**? Explain your answers.

WRITING

Memory and Imagination

Cofer gives us her writing formula:

> I follow *cuentos,* memories, characters that take me back to moments of being in my life. I re-create the scenes of my youth and transform them with my imagination.

Test Cofer's technique. Reach into your memories, and pull out one actual scene—a real event and a character or two—and don't forget to add your imagination. Make up details, vary what really happened, and write a short piece of what Cofer calls "creative nonfiction," a hybrid of reality and imagination.

SKILLS FOCUS

Literary Skills
Analyze theme and character.

Reading Skills
Make a generalization.

Writing Skills
Write a brief story that combines a memory and imagination.

Vocabulary Development

Word Meanings—Yes or No?

Be sure to justify your yes-or-no answers to these questions.

1. Would you expect a kind person to be <u>harassing</u> a child?
2. If you <u>dismantled</u> a clock, would it still tell time?
3. Could a dress be described as <u>vintage</u>?
4. Would a blonde's hair be described as <u>ebony</u>?
5. Would a <u>sarcastic</u> person hurt people's feelings?
6. Could you find <u>relics</u> in a museum?

> **Word Bank**
>
> harassing
> dismantled
> vintage
> ebony
> sarcastic
> relics

Figurative Language—Don't Take It Literally

Figurative language is language that is not meant to be taken literally. Here are three common types of figurative language:

- An **idiom** is an expression that is peculiar to a language and cannot be understood from the literal definitions of its words.

   "The old man looked like he wanted to <u>walk down memory lane</u>." [When you take a walk down memory lane, you're not literally walking anywhere—you're just recalling fond memories.]

- A **simile** uses the word *like, as, than,* or *resembles* to compare two unlike things.

   "The tree looked different now, not <u>like a skeleton</u>, as it had then, but green with leaves." [How can a tree look like a skeleton? When it is down to its "bare bones"—its trunk and branches.]

- A **metaphor** compares two unlike things by saying that something is something else. It also omits the word *like, as, than,* or *resembles*.

   "Luis Cintrón sits on top of a six-foot pile of hubcaps and watches his father walk away into the <u>steel jungle</u> of his car junkyard." [The jumbled auto parts are compared to a densely overgrown jungle.]

SKILLS FOCUS

Vocabulary Skills
Demonstrate word knowledge. Identify types of figurative language.

Tell whether each underlined expression is an **idiom,** a **simile,** or a **metaphor.** Then, write a sentence that expresses the same idea in literal, not figurative, language. Which sentence do you prefer? Why?

1. "He yells at no one, 'Someday, son, all this will be yours,' and sweeps his arms <u>like the Pope blessing a crowd</u> over the piles of car sandwiches and mounds of metal parts. ..."
2. "'That's what I'm doing, right? <u>Working my hands to the bone</u>. ...'"
3. "'I'll be back by ten, and <u>keep the ice on that egg</u>.'..."

Before You Read

The Bass, the River, and Sheila Mant

Make the Connection

Quickwrite 🖉

Think back to some time when you had to give up one thing for something else. Write down what happened. Looking back, do you feel that you made the right choice? Do you have any regrets? Explain.

Literary Focus

Theme and Conflict: Struggle Toward Meaning

Often the **theme** of a story—its message about life—is directly tied to the main character's **conflict,** or struggle, and to how that conflict is resolved. Remember that a conflict may be **external** (a show-down with another character or a struggle with nature) or **internal** (a struggle between competing desires or between two aspects of a character's personality). Internal conflicts force us to choose, and that choice can be agonizing.

In this story the main character is caught up in both external and internal conflicts. Watch to see how he deals with them and what the story's ending suggests about its theme.

Reading Skills 📖

Making Inferences About Character Motivation

Why do characters act the way they do? In order for a story to be convincing, we need to be able to infer the characters' **motivations**—the causes of their behavior. Literary characters, like real-life people, are motivated by their wants and needs. As you read this story, see if you can infer the narrator's motivations for the choices he makes. Do his motivations seem believable?

Vocabulary Development

denizens (den′ə·zenz) *n.*: inhabitants or occupants.

pensive (pen′siv) *adj.*: dreamily thoughtful.

dubious (dōō′bē·əs) *adj.*: doubtful; not sure.

antipathy (an·tip′ə·thē) *n.*: feeling of hatred; powerful and deep dislike.

filial (fil′ē·əl) *adj.*: pertaining to or due from a son or a daughter.

surreptitiously (sur′əp·tish′əs·lē) *adv.*: stealthily; sneakily.

conspicuous (kən·spik′yōō·əs) *adj.*: obvious or easy to see.

concussion (kən·kush′ən) *n.*: powerful shock or impact.

luminous (lōō′mə·nəs) *adj.*: glowing; giving off light.

quizzical (kwiz′i·kəl) *adj.*: puzzled; questioning.

INTERNET

Vocabulary Practice

Keyword: LE5 10-4

SKILLS FOCUS

Literary Skills
Understand theme and conflict.

Reading Skills
Make inferences about character motivation.

THE BASS, THE RIVER, AND SHEILA MANT

W. D. Wetherell

I never made the
same mistake again.

There was a summer in my life when the only creature that seemed lovelier to me than a largemouth bass was Sheila Mant. I was fourteen. The Mants had rented the cottage next to ours on the river; with their parties, their frantic games of softball, their constant comings and goings, they appeared to me <u>denizens</u> of a brilliant existence. "Too noisy by half," my mother quickly decided, but I would have given anything to be invited to one of their parties, and when my parents went to bed I would sneak through the woods to their hedge and stare enchanted at the candlelit swirl of white dresses and bright, paisley skirts.

Sheila was the middle daughter—at seventeen, all but out of reach. She would spend her days sunbathing on a float my Uncle Sierbert had moored in their cove, and before July was over I had learned all her moods. If she lay flat on the diving board with her hand trailing idly in the water, she was <u>pensive</u>, not to be disturbed. On her side, her head propped up by her arm, she was observant, considering those around her with a look that seemed queenly and severe. Sitting up, arms tucked around her long, suntanned legs, she was approachable, but barely, and it was only in those glorious moments when she stretched herself prior to entering the water that her various suitors found the courage to come near.

These were many. The Dartmouth heavyweight crew would scull[1] by her house on their way upriver, and I think all eight of them must have been in love with her at various times during the summer; the coxswain[2] would curse them through his megaphone, but without effect—there was always a pause in their pace when they passed Sheila's float. I suppose to these jaded twenty-year-olds she seemed the incarnation of innocence and youth, while to me she appeared unutterably suave, the epitome[3] of sophistication. I was on the swim team at school, and to win her attention would do endless laps between my house and the Vermont shore, hoping she would notice the beauty of my flutter kick, the power of my crawl. Finishing, I would boost myself up onto our dock and glance casually over toward her, but she was never watching, and the miraculous day she was, I immediately climbed the diving board and did my best tuck and a half for her and continued diving until she had left and the sun went down and my longing was like a madness and I couldn't stop.

It was late August by the time I got up the nerve to ask her out. The tortured will-I's, won't-I's, the agonized indecision over what to say, the false starts toward her house and embarrassed retreats—the details of these have been seared from my memory, and the only part I remember clearly is emerging from the woods toward dusk

---

1. **scull** (skul) *v.*: row, as a rowboat.
2. **coxswain** (käk′sən) *n.*: person steering a racing shell and calling out the rhythm of the strokes for the crew.
3. **epitome** (ē·pit′ə·mē′) *n.*: embodiment; one that is representative of a type or class.

Vocabulary
denizens (den′ə·zənz) *n.*: inhabitants or occupants.
pensive (pen′siv) *adj.*: dreamily thoughtful.

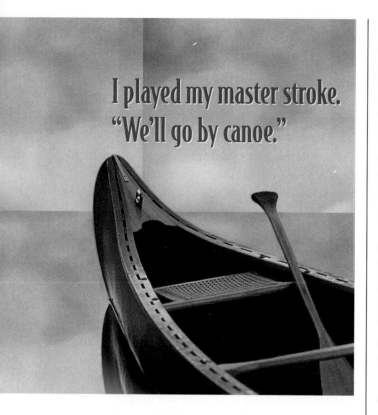

I played my master stroke. "We'll go by canoe."

while they were playing softball on their lawn, as bashful and frightened as a unicorn.

Sheila was stationed halfway between first and second, well outside the infield. She didn't seem surprised to see me—as a matter of fact, she didn't seem to see me at all.

"If you're playing second base, you should move closer," I said.

She turned—I took the full brunt of her long red hair and well-spaced freckles.

"I'm playing outfield," she said, "I don't like the responsibility of having a base."

"Yeah, I can understand that," I said, though I couldn't. "There's a band in Dixford tomorrow night at nine. Want to go?"

One of her brothers sent the ball sailing over the left-fielder's head; she stood and watched it disappear toward the river.

"You have a car?" she said, without looking up.

I played my master stroke. "We'll go by canoe."

I spent all of the following day polishing it. I turned it upside down on our lawn and rubbed every inch with Brillo, hosing off the dirt, wiping it with chamois[4] until it gleamed as bright as aluminum ever gleamed. About five, I slid it into the water, arranging cushions near the bow so Sheila could lean on them if she was in one of her pensive moods, propping up my father's transistor radio by the middle thwart[5] so we could have music when we came back. Automatically, without thinking about it, I mounted my Mitchell reel on my Pfleuger spinning rod and stuck it in the stern.

I say automatically, because I never went anywhere that summer without a fishing rod. When I wasn't swimming laps to impress Sheila, I was back in our driveway practicing casts, and when I wasn't practicing casts, I was tying the line to Tosca, our springer spaniel, to test the reel's drag, and when I wasn't doing any of those things, I was fishing the river for bass.

Too nervous to sit at home, I got in the canoe early and started paddling in a huge circle that would get me to Sheila's dock around eight. As automatically as I brought along my rod, I tied on a big Rapala plug, let it down into the water, let out some line, and immediately forgot all about it.

It was already dark by the time I glided up to the Mants' dock. Even by day the river was quiet, most of the summer people preferring Sunapee or one of the other nearby lakes, and at night it was a solitude difficult to believe, a corridor of hidden life that ran between banks like a tunnel. Even the stars were part of it. They weren't as sharp anywhere else; they seemed to have chosen the river as a guide on their slow wheel toward morning, and in the course of the summer's fishing, I had learned all their names.

I was there ten minutes before Sheila appeared. I heard the slam of their screen door first, then saw her in the spotlight as she came slowly down the path. As beautiful as she was on the float, she

4. **chamois** (sham'ē) *n.:* soft leather used for polishing.
5. **middle thwart:** brace across the middle of a canoe.

was even lovelier now—her white dress went perfectly with her hair, and complimented her figure even more than her swimsuit.

It was her face that bothered me. It had on its delightful fullness a very <u>dubious</u> expression.

"Look," she said. "I can get Dad's car."

"It's faster this way," I lied. "Parking's tense up there. Hey, it's safe. I won't tip it or anything."

She let herself down reluctantly into the bow. I was glad she wasn't facing me. When her eyes were on me, I felt like diving in the river again from agony and joy.

I pried the canoe away from the dock and started paddling upstream. There was an extra paddle in the bow, but Sheila made no move to pick it up. She took her shoes off and dangled her feet over the side.

Ten minutes went by.

"What kind of band?" she said.

"It's sort of like folk music. You'll like it."

"Eric Caswell's going to be there. He strokes number four."[6]

"No kidding?" I said. I had no idea whom she meant.

"What's that sound?" she said, pointing toward shore.

"Bass. That splashing sound?"

"Over there."

"Yeah, bass. They come into the shallows at night to chase frogs and moths and things. Big largemouths. *Micropterus salmoides,*"[7] I added, showing off.

"I think fishing's dumb," she said, making a face. "I mean, it's boring and all. Definitely dumb."

Now I have spent a great deal of time in the years since wondering why Sheila Mant should come down so hard on fishing. Was her father a fisherman? Her <u>antipathy</u> toward fishing nothing

more than normal <u>filial</u> rebellion? Had she tried it once? A messy encounter with worms? It doesn't matter. What does is that at that fragile moment in time I would have given anything not to appear dumb in Sheila's severe and unforgiving eyes.

She hadn't seen my equipment yet. What I *should* have done, of course, was push the canoe in closer to shore and carefully slide the rod into some branches where I could pick it up again in the morning. Failing that, I could have <u>surreptitiously</u> dumped the whole outfit overboard, written off the forty or so dollars as love's tribute. What I actually *did* do was gently lean forward, and slowly, ever so slowly, push the rod back through my legs toward the stern where it would be less <u>conspicuous</u>.

It must have been just exactly what the bass was waiting for. Fish will trail a lure sometimes, trying to make up their mind whether or not to attack, and the slight pause in the plug's speed caused by my adjustment was tantalizing enough to overcome the bass's inhibitions. My rod, safely out of sight at last, bent double. The line, tightly coiled, peeled off the spool with the shrill, tearing zip of a high-speed drill.

Four things occurred to me at once. One, that it was a bass. Two, that it was a big bass. Three, that it was the biggest bass I had ever hooked. Four, that Sheila Mant must not know.

"What was that?" she said, turning half around.

"Uh, what was what?"

---

6. **strokes number four:** rows in the fourth position on a sculling crew.
7. *Micropterus salmoides:* scientific name for a large-mouth bass.

Vocabulary

dubious (do͞o′bē·əs) *adj.:* doubtful; not sure.

antipathy (an·tip′ə·thē) *n.:* feeling of hatred; powerful and deep dislike.

filial (fil′ē·əl) *adj.:* pertaining to or due from a son or a daughter.

surreptitiously (sʉr′əp·tish′əs·lē) *adv.:* stealthily; sneakily.

conspicuous (kən·spik′yo͞o·əs) *adj.:* obvious or easy to see.

"That buzzing noise."

"Bats."

She shuddered, quickly drew her feet back into the canoe. Every instinct I had told me to pick up the rod and strike back at the bass, but there was no need to—it was already solidly hooked. Downstream, an awesome distance downstream, it jumped clear of the water, landing with a <u>concussion</u> heavy enough to ripple the entire river. For a moment, I thought it was gone, but then the rod was bending again, the tip dancing into the water. Slowly, not making any motion that might alert Sheila, I reached down to tighten the drag.

While all this was going on, Sheila had begun talking, and it was a few minutes before I was able to catch up with her train of thought.

"I went to a party there. These fraternity men. Katherine says I could get in there if I wanted. I'm thinking more of UVM or Bennington.[8] Somewhere I can ski."

The bass was slanting toward the rocks on the New Hampshire side by the ruins of Donaldson's boathouse. It had to be an old bass—a young one probably wouldn't have known the rocks were there. I brought the canoe back into the middle of the river, hoping to head it off.

"That's neat," I mumbled. "Skiing. Yeah, I can see that."

"Eric said I have the figure to model, but I thought I should get an education first. I mean, it might be a while before I get started and all. I was thinking of getting my hair styled, more swept back? I mean, Ann-Margret?[9] Like hers, only shorter."

She hesitated. "Are we going backward?"

We were. I had managed to keep the bass in the middle of the river away from the rocks, but it had plenty of room there, and for the first

time a chance to exert its full strength. I quickly computed the weight necessary to draw a fully loaded canoe backward—the thought of it made me feel faint.

"It's just the current," I said hoarsely. "No sweat or anything."

I dug in deeper with my paddle. Reassured, Sheila began talking about something else, but all my attention was taken up now with the fish. I could feel its desperation as the water grew shallower. I could sense the extra strain on the line, the frantic way it cut back and forth in the water. I could visualize what it looked like—the gape of its mouth, the flared gills and thick, vertical tail. The bass couldn't have encountered many forces in its long life that it wasn't capable of handling, and the unrelenting tug at its mouth must have been a source of great puzzlement and mounting panic.

Me, I had problems of my own. To get to Dixford, I had to paddle up a sluggish stream that came into the river beneath a covered bridge. There was a shallow sandbar at the mouth of this stream—weeds on one side, rocks on the other. Without doubt, this is where I would lose the fish.

"I have to be careful with my complexion. I tan, but in segments. I can't figure out if it's even worth it. I wouldn't even do it probably. I saw Jackie Kennedy[10] in Boston, and she wasn't tan at all."

Taking a deep breath, I paddled as hard as I could for the middle, deepest part of the bar. I could have threaded the eye of a needle with the canoe, but the pull on the stern threw me off, and I overcompensated—the canoe veered

10. **Jackie Kennedy** (1929–1994): First Lady during the administration of President John F. Kennedy; greatly admired by the public for her dignity and sense of style.

8. **UVM or Bennington:** University of Vermont or Bennington College, Bennington, Vermont.
9. **Ann-Margret** (1941–   ): movie star who was very popular at the time of this story.

Vocabulary

concussion (kən·kush′ən) *n*.: powerful shock or impact.

left and scraped bottom. I pushed the paddle down and shoved. A moment of hesitation . . . a moment more. . . . The canoe shot clear into the deeper water of the stream. I immediately looked down at the rod. It was bent in the same tight arc—miraculously, the bass was still on.

The moon was out now. It was low and full enough that its beam shone directly on Sheila there ahead of me in the canoe, washing her in a creamy, <u>luminous</u> glow. I could see the lithe,[11] easy shape of her figure. I could see the way her hair curled down off her shoulders, the proud, alert tilt of her head, and all these things were as a tug on my heart. Not just Sheila, but the aura she carried about her of parties and casual touchings and grace. Behind me, I could feel the strain of the bass, steadier now, growing weaker, and this was another tug on my heart, not just the bass but the beat of the river and the slant of the stars and the smell of the night, until finally it seemed I would be torn apart between longings, split in half. Twenty yards ahead of us was the road, and once I pulled the canoe up on shore, the bass would be gone, irretrievably gone. If instead I stood up, grabbed the rod, and started pumping, I would have it—as tired as the bass was, there was no chance it could get away. I reached down for the rod, hesitated, looked up to where Sheila was stretching herself lazily toward the sky, her small breasts rising beneath the soft fabric of her dress, and the tug was too much for me, and quicker than it takes to write down, I pulled a penknife from my pocket and cut the line in half.

With a sick, nauseous feeling in my stomach, I saw the rod unbend.

With a sick, nauseous feeling in my stomach, I saw the rod unbend.

"My legs are sore," Sheila whined. "Are we there yet?"

Through a superhuman effort of self-control, I was able to beach the canoe and help Sheila off. The rest of the night is much foggier. We walked to the fair—there was the smell of popcorn, the sound of guitars. I may have danced once or twice with her, but all I really remember is her coming over to me once the music was done to explain that she would be going home in Eric Caswell's Corvette.

"Okay," I mumbled.

For the first time that night she looked at me, really looked at me.

"You're a funny kid, you know that?"

Funny. Different. Dreamy. Odd. How many times was I to hear that in the years to come, all spoken with the same <u>quizzical</u>, half-accusatory tone Sheila used then. Poor Sheila! Before the month was over, the spell she cast over me was

---

11. **lithe** (līth) *adj.:* flexible; limber.

Vocabulary
luminous (lōō′mə·nəs) *adj.:* glowing; giving off light.
quizzical (kwiz′i·kəl) *adj.:* puzzled; questioning.

gone, but the memory of that lost bass haunted me all summer and haunts me still. There would be other Sheila Mants in my life, other fish, and though I came close once or twice, it was these secret, hidden tuggings in the night that claimed me, and I never made the same mistake again. ■

Meet the Writer

W. D. Wetherell

An Eye for Detail

W. D. Wetherell (1948–   ) lives in New Hampshire. He was born in Mineola, New York, and earned a bachelor's degree at Hofstra University, on Long Island. Like many writers he has worked at various jobs—he has been a magazine editor, a movie extra, a teacher, a journalist, and a tour guide. Wetherell's works have won numerous awards, including the O. Henry Award, the Drue Heinz Literature Prize, and a fellowship in fiction from the National Endowment for the Arts. "The Bass, the River, and Sheila Mant" won the 1983 PEN Syndicated Fiction Prize. Having read this story, you won't be surprised to learn that Wetherell has also written essays about nature and fishing.

In one essay he relates a "fish story" with an ending quite different from the one you just read. In the Pacific Northwest his wife asked him to take a photograph of her and the fish she had caught.

❝And I did, and as I focused the lens, the fog lifted, and behind her I saw the snowbanks and glacier and cliffs that framed the pond, revealing themselves only now when the moment was perfect. I held the camera steady until the beauty of the water and the woman and the trout came together, then—the moment captured—I crossed over the logs and took my wife by the hand. **❞**

It's Raining in Love
Richard Brautigan

I don't know what it is,
but I distrust myself
when I start to like a girl
    a lot.

5   It makes me nervous.
I don't say the right things
or perhaps I start
    to examine,
        evaluate,
10   compute
    what I am saying.

If I say, "Do you think it's going to rain?"
and she says, "I don't know,"
I start thinking: Does she really like me?

15   In other words
I get a little creepy.

A friend of mine once said,
"It's twenty times better to be friends
    with someone
20   than it is to be in love with them."

I think he's right and besides,
it's raining somewhere, programming flowers
and keeping snails happy.
    That's all taken care of.

25   BUT
if a girl likes me a lot
and starts getting real nervous
and suddenly begins asking me funny questions
and looks sad if I give the wrong answers
30   and she says things like,
"Do you think it's going to rain?"
and I say, "It beats me,"
and she says, "Oh,"
and looks a little sad
35   at the clear blue California sky,
I think: Thank God, it's you, baby, this time
    instead of me.

The Heart in Bliss (1992) by Jim Dine.
Oil, enamel, pencil, and wood fragment
on canvas (82½″ × 86⅞″).

© Christie's Images.

Response and Analysis

Reading Check

1. At the beginning of the story, what does the narrator try to find the courage to do?

2. How does the narrator know the bass on his line is very large?

3. Why doesn't the narrator tell Sheila that he has caught the bass?

4. How does Sheila behave toward the narrator when they get to the dance?

Thinking Critically

5. How does the story's **title** suggest the narrator's **external** and **internal conflicts**?

6. What is the story's **climax**—the moment of greatest excitement, when the conflict is resolved?

7. What two conflicting desires, or **motivations,** does the narrator have? Is his choice between them believable? Explain your answers.

8. What do you think the "secret, hidden tuggings in the night" are that the narrator mentions in the last sentence? What mistake has he never repeated?

9. Express the story's **theme** in one or more sentences. Remember that the theme makes a general statement about life and people. Find evidence in the story to support the theme.

Extending and Evaluating

10. Does the narrator's experience remind you of any personal experience with making a difficult choice? Looking back, are you now happy with your choice? Explain. (Be sure to check your Quickwrite notes.)

11. Some readers object to the **characterization** of Sheila Mant as a beautiful airhead, a stereotype. How would you respond to this criticism?

12. Would you recommend this story to other students? Rate the story on a scale from zero (worst) to ten (best). Give at least three reasons for your rating. Consider the plot, the characters, and the theme.

WRITING

Poem Versus Story— Alike and Yet . . .

Although "It's Raining in Love" (see the **Connection** on page 251) is a poem and "The Bass, the River, and Sheila Mant" is a story, the two works are similar in many ways. Write a paragraph or two in which you **compare** the conflicts of the narrators and the way the conflicts relate to the themes of the two works. In what ways are the themes similar? In what ways are they different?

> **Comparing Themes**
> For a writing assignment comparing the themes in "Catch the Moon" and "The Bass, the River, and Sheila Mant," see page 254.

Vocabulary Development

Synonyms and Antonyms

Synonyms are words with similar meanings. **Antonyms** are words with opposite meanings: *warm/cool, happy/sad*. Make a synonym or antonym map for each Word Bank word. *Filial* has been done for you. Not all words have antonyms, so make antonym maps for these words: *dubious, antipathy, surreptitiously, conspicuous,* and *luminous*. For the rest of the words, make synonym maps.

Word Bank

denizens
pensive
dubious
antipathy
filial
surreptitiously
conspicuous
concussion
luminous
quizzical

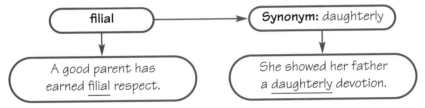

filial → Synonym: daughterly

A good parent has earned <u>filial</u> respect.

She showed her father a <u>daughterly</u> devotion.

Grammar Link

Stop That Run-on Sentence

A **run-on sentence** is made up of two or more sentences that are separated by a comma or are not set off with any punctuation. Here are three strategies for correcting run-ons:

1. Separate the run-on into two sentences.

   RUN-ON The narrator cuts the bass loose, he regrets it later.

   CORRECT The narrator cuts the bass loose. He regrets it later.

2. Change the run-on sentence to a compound sentence by using either a comma and a coordinating conjunction (such as *and, but, or,* or *so*) or a semicolon.

   CORRECT The narrator cuts the bass loose, but he regrets it later.

   CORRECT The narrator cuts the bass loose; he regrets it later.

3. Turn one sentence into a subordinate clause.

   CORRECT Although the narrator cuts the bass loose, he regrets it later.

Act as an editor, and rewrite the following paragraph. Use all three strategies for correcting run-on sentences.

Sheila wanted to drive to the dance the narrator said they'd go in his canoe she didn't seem very happy about it, on the way to the dance all she did was talk about herself. They got to the dance, the narrator cut the bass loose, he didn't see Sheila much that night he didn't take her home probably that was their last date.

▶ **For more help, see Run-on Sentences, 9b, in the Language Handbook.**

SKILLS FOCUS

Vocabulary Skills
Understand synonyms and antonyms.

Grammar Skills
Correct run-on sentences.

Writing a Comparison-Contrast Essay

Comparing Universal Themes

"Catch the Moon" . . . . page 234

"The Bass, the River, and Sheila Mant" . . . . page 244

Now that you have read "Catch the Moon" and "The Bass, the River, and Sheila Mant," you can compare the themes of the two stories in a comparison-contrast essay. When you write a **comparison-contrast essay,** you use the skills of **comparing** (finding similarities) and **contrasting** (finding differences).

Gather Your Information, and Organize It

Go back to your chart on page 232, in which you compared different elements of the two stories. It should give you plenty of information to use in writing your essay.

There are two main methods for organizing a comparison-contrast essay. One is the **block method,** which you will practice in this exercise. The other is the **point-by-point method,** which you will practice on page 283.

The Block Method

With this organization you discuss each of the *stories,* one at a time. First you write about the elements of one story. Then you discuss the same elements in the same order for the second story. The chart on the right gives an example of how to organize your comparison-contrast essay using the block method.

Use Three Basic Parts

Like most essays, comparison-contrast essays have three parts:

1. The **introduction,** usually a single paragraph, provides the title, author, and necessary background. It also includes your **thesis statement,** in which you explain briefly how the themes are alike or different.

2. The **body** of your essay is the part where you explain the information you've gathered in your chart. Make sure you discuss at least two different elements for each story. You might want to devote a separate paragraph to each story.

3. In the **conclusion,** sum up your major points, and add a new thought or a personal response.

Elaborate: Get Down to Specifics

You should elaborate on every general statement you make, using details, examples, and quotations from the stories.

▶ **For more help writing comparison-contrast essays, see pages 382–389.**

Block Method	
Story 1: "Catch the Moon"	
Element 1:	Main character
Element 2:	Main conflict and resolution
Element 3:	How character changes
Element 4:	Theme
Story 2: "The Bass, the River, and Sheila Mant"	
Element 1:	Main character
Element 2:	Main conflict and resolution
Element 3:	How character changes
Element 4:	Theme

SKILLS FOCUS

Literary Skills
Understand and compare universal themes.

Writing Skills
Write a comparison-contrast essay.

Elements of Literature

Comparing a Theme Across Genres

"And of Clay Are We Created" . . . . *by* Isabel Allende . . . . . short story . . page 257
"The Man in the Water" . . . . *by* Roger Rosenblatt . . . essay . . . . page 273

How Does Genre Affect Theme?

You'd probably agree that reading a short story about heroism affects you differently from reading a newspaper article or a poem about it. Why? For help understanding how genre shapes your reactions, consider the following:

- **How does the choice of genre relate to the author's purpose for writing?** For example, nonfiction authors usually want to examine an issue or make a point. Fiction authors want to share their particular insights into life. Poets often want to convey a theme in an intensified way.

- **What is the theme, or main idea, and is it stated or implied?** Generally in nonfiction the author states a main idea rather directly. In a story or poem, however, the author usually implies the theme, which can often make it more difficult for the reader to figure out.

- **How does the author use the characteristics of the genre to support the theme, or main idea?** For example, nonfiction authors usually supply facts and examples as support. Fiction authors use characters, conflict, point of view, and other literary elements to develop their themes. Poets often rely on imagery, figurative language, and mood.

Exploring a Theme

The short story and the essay you are about to read treat a similar theme and topic. Each centers on a person who heroically and unselfishly goes out of his way to help others. These selections are from different genres, and you'll be examining how the choice of genre shapes the theme and topic.

Reading Skills

Comparing and Contrasting a Theme Across Genres

For help comparing the themes in these two works, review the essay on theme on pages 230–231. After you have read and discussed each selection, fill in comments in a chart like the one below. Then, turn to page 283.

	"And of Clay Are We Created"	"The Man in the Water"
Genre		
Author's purpose		
How genre relates to purpose		
Theme or main idea (stated or implied)		
How elements of genre support theme or main idea		

SKILLS FOCUS

Pages 255–283 cover
Literary Skills Understand how genre affects theme.

Reading Skills Compare and contrast a theme across genres.

And of Clay Are We Created

Make the Connection

Quickwrite ✏️

Do you agree or disagree with the following statements? Explain why, and give an example. Save your notes.

- People are helpless when a natural disaster hits.
- Most people would risk their lives to try to save a stranger.

Literary Focus

Fact Versus Fiction

You are about to read two versions of the same event in different **genres** (a short story and a newspaper article). Allende's story, a work of **fiction,** sounds so real that you might think it a **nonfiction** report of what actually happened. As you read the two accounts, think about how they differ and how they are alike.

Theme and Purpose

Fiction writers with an important message to convey have powerful tools at their disposal—especially **theme.** Determining the theme of a work of literature often gives us a good idea of the author's purpose for writing—and vice versa.

INTERNET

Vocabulary
Practice
•
More About
Isabel Allende
Keyword: LE5 10-4

SKILLS FOCUS

Literary Skills
Understand fiction and non-fiction genres. Understand theme and purpose.

Reading Skills
Determine an author's purpose.

Reading Skills 📖

Determining an Author's Purpose

The three most common broad purposes of writing are **to inform, to persuade,** and **to entertain.** Allende took a real event and fictionalized it. What was her purpose? To figure it out, ask yourself why this subject was important to her and what she wants us to think about it. The questions at the open-book signs will help you.

Background

On November 13, 1985, the long-dormant Nevado del Ruiz volcano erupted in Colombia, South America. Molten rock and hot gases melted the volcano's thick ice cap and sent deadly mudslides down its slopes. More than 23,000 people died in the disaster—most of them in a village called Armero (är·me′rō).

Vocabulary Development

subterranean (sub′tə·rā′nē·ən) *adj.:* underground.

magnitude (mag′nə·tōōd′) *n.:* greatness or size.

presentiments (prē·zent′ə·mənts) *n.:* forebodings; feelings that something bad is about to happen.

tenacity (tə·nas′ə·tē) *n.:* stubborn persistence and determination.

equanimity (ek′wə·nim′ə·tē) *n.:* calmness; composure.

fortitude (fôrt′ə·tōōd′) *n.:* firm courage; strength to endure pain or danger.

ingenuity (in′jə·nōō′ə·tē) *n.:* cleverness; originality; skill.

resignation (rez′ig·nā′shən) *n.:* passive acceptance; submission.

pandemonium (pan′də·mō′nē·əm) *n.:* wildly noisy, chaotic scene.

commiserate (kə·miz′ər·āt′) *v.:* show or express sympathy.

The mud was like quicksand around her.

And of Clay Are We Created

Isabel Allende

translated by
Margaret Sayers Peden

They discovered the girl's head protruding from the mudpit, eyes wide open, calling soundlessly. She had a First Communion name, Azucena.[1] Lily. In that vast cemetery where the odor of death was already attracting vultures from far away, and where the weeping of orphans and wails of the injured filled the air, the little girl obstinately clinging to life became the symbol of the tragedy. The television cameras transmitted so often the unbearable image of the head budding like a black squash from the clay that there was no one who did not recognize her and know her name. And every time we saw her on the screen, right behind her was Rolf Carlé,[2] who had gone there on assignment, never suspecting that he would find a fragment of his past, lost thirty years before.

First a subterranean sob rocked the cotton fields, curling them like waves of foam. Geologists had set up their seismographs[3] weeks before and knew that the mountain had awakened again. For some time they had predicted that the heat of the eruption could detach the eternal ice from the slopes of the volcano, but no one heeded their warnings; they sounded like the tales of frightened old women. The towns in the valley went about their daily life, deaf to the moaning of the earth, until that fateful Wednesday night in November when a prolonged roar announced the end of the world, and walls of snow broke loose, rolling in an avalanche of clay, stones, and water that descended on the villages and buried them beneath unfathomable meters of telluric[4] vomit. As soon as the survivors emerged from the paralysis of that first awful terror, they could see that houses, plazas, churches, white cotton plantations, dark coffee forests, cattle pastures—all had disappeared.

Much later, after soldiers and volunteers had arrived to rescue the living and try to assess the magnitude of the cataclysm,[5] it was calculated that beneath the mud lay more than twenty thousand human beings and an indefinite number of animals putrefying in a viscous soup.[6] Forests and rivers had also been swept away, and there was nothing to be seen but an immense desert of mire.[7]

> **AUTHOR'S PURPOSE**
> 1. What is the **author's purpose** in this paragraph?

When the station called before dawn, Rolf Carlé and I were together. I crawled out of bed, dazed with sleep, and went to prepare coffee while he hurriedly dressed. He stuffed his gear in the green canvas backpack he always carried, and we said goodbye, as we had so many times before. I had no presentiments. I sat in the kitchen, sipping my coffee and planning the long hours without him, sure that he would be back the next day.

He was one of the first to reach the scene, because while other reporters were fighting their way to the edges of that morass[8] in jeeps, bicycles, or on foot, each getting there however he could, Rolf Carlé had the advantage of the television helicopter, which flew him over the avalanche. We watched on our screens the footage captured by his assistant's camera, in which he was up to his knees in muck, a microphone in his hand, in the midst of a

---

1. **Azucena** (ä·sōō·sä′nä): Spanish for "lily."
2. **Rolf Carlé** (rôlf kär·lā′).
3. **seismographs** (sīz′mə·grafs′) *n.*: instruments that measure and record earthquakes and other tremors.
4. **telluric** (te·loor′ik) *adj.*: of or from the earth.

---

5. **cataclysm** (kat′ə·kliz′əm) *n.*: disaster; great upheaval causing sudden, violent changes.
6. **putrefying in a viscous soup**: rotting in a thick mixture.
7. **mire** *n.*: deep mud.
8. **morass** (mə·ras′) *n.*: bog or swamp.

Vocabulary

subterranean (sub′tə·rā′nē·ən) *adj.*: underground.

magnitude (mag′nə·tōōd′) *n.*: greatness or size.

presentiments (prē·zent′ə·mənts) *n.*: forebodings; feelings that something bad is about to happen.

The Nevado del Ruiz volcano after eruption, Colombia (1985).

Photograph by J. Marso.

bedlam[9] of lost children, wounded survivors, corpses, and devastation. The story came to us in his calm voice. For years he had been a familiar figure in newscasts, reporting live at the scene of battles and catastrophes with awesome tenacity. Nothing could stop him, and I was always amazed at his equanimity in the face of danger and suffering; it seemed as if nothing could shake his fortitude or deter his curiosity. Fear seemed never to touch him, although he had confessed to me that he was not a courageous man, far from it. I believe that the lens of the camera had a strange effect on him; it was as if it transported him to a different time from which he could watch events without actually participating in them. When I knew him better, I came to realize that this fictive distance seemed to protect him from his own emotions.

Rolf Carlé was in on the story of Azucena from the beginning. He filmed the volunteers who discovered her, and the first persons who tried to reach her; his camera zoomed in on the girl, her dark face, her large desolate eyes, the plastered-down tangle of her hair. The mud was like quicksand around her, and anyone attempting to reach her was in danger of sinking. They threw a rope to her that she made no effort to grasp until they shouted to her to catch it; then she pulled a hand from the mire and tried to

---

9. **bedlam** (bed′ləm) *n.:* place or situation filled with noise and confusion (from the name of an old insane asylum in London).

Vocabulary

tenacity (tə·nas′ə·tē) *n.:* stubborn persistence and determination.

equanimity (ek′wə·nim′ə·tē) *n.:* calmness; composure.

fortitude (fôrt′ə·tōōd′) *n.:* firm courage; strength to endure pain or danger.

move, but immediately sank a little deeper. Rolf threw down his knapsack and the rest of his equipment and waded into the quagmire, commenting for his assistant's microphone that it was cold and that one could begin to smell the stench of corpses.

"What's your name?" he asked the girl, and she told him her flower name. "Don't move, Azucena," Rolf Carlé directed, and kept talking to her, without a thought for what he was saying, just to distract her, while slowly he worked his way forward in mud up to his waist. The air around him seemed as murky as the mud.

It was impossible to reach her from the approach he was attempting, so he retreated and circled around where there seemed to be firmer footing. When finally he was close enough, he took the rope and tied it beneath her arms, so they could pull her out. He smiled at her with that smile that crinkles his eyes and makes him look like a little boy; he told her that everything was fine, that he was here with her now, that soon they would have her out. He signaled the others to pull, but as soon as the cord tensed, the girl screamed. They tried again, and her shoulders and arms appeared, but they could move her no farther; she was trapped. Someone suggested that her legs might be caught in the collapsed walls of her house, but she said it was not just rubble, that she was also held by the bodies of her brothers and sisters clinging to her legs.

"Don't worry, we'll get you out of here," Rolf promised. Despite the quality of the transmission, I could hear his voice break, and I loved him more than ever. Azucena looked at him, but said nothing.

NARRATOR

2. Who is telling this story? What device enables the **narrator** to witness the action at Armero?

During those first hours Rolf Carlé exhausted all the resources of his ingenuity to rescue her. He struggled with poles and ropes, but every tug was an intolerable torture for the imprisoned girl. It occurred to him to use one of the poles as a lever but got no result and had to abandon the idea. He talked a couple of soldiers into working with him for a while, but they had to leave because so many other victims were calling for help. The girl could not move, she barely could breathe, but she did not seem desperate, as if an ancestral resignation allowed her to accept her fate. The reporter, on the other hand, was determined to snatch her from death. Someone brought him a tire, which he placed beneath her arms like a life buoy, and then laid a plank near the hole to hold his weight and allow him to stay closer to her. As it was impossible to remove the rubble blindly, he tried once or twice to dive toward her feet, but emerged frustrated, covered with mud, and spitting gravel. He concluded that he would have to have a pump to drain the water, and radioed a request for one, but received in return a message that there was no available transport and it could not be sent until the next morning.

"We can't wait that long!" Rolf Carlé shouted, but in the pandemonium no one stopped to commiserate. Many more hours would go by before he accepted that time had stagnated and reality had been irreparably distorted.

A military doctor came to examine the girl, and observed that her heart was functioning well and that if she did not get too cold she could survive the night.

"Hang on, Azucena, we'll have the pump tomorrow," Rolf Carlé tried to console her.

Vocabulary

ingenuity (in′jə·nōō′ə·tē) *n.:* cleverness; originality; skill.

resignation (rez′ig·nā′shən) *n.:* passive acceptance; submission.

pandemonium (pan′də·mō′nē·əm) *n.:* wildly noisy, chaotic scene.

commiserate (kə·miz′ər·āt′) *v.:* show or express sympathy.

"Don't leave me alone," she begged.

"No, of course I won't leave you."

Someone brought him coffee, and he helped the girl drink it, sip by sip. The warm liquid revived her and she began telling him about her small life, about her family and her school, about how things were in that little bit of world before the volcano had erupted. She was thirteen, and she had never been outside her village. Rolf Carlé, buoyed by a premature optimism, was convinced that everything would end well: the pump would arrive, they would drain the water, move the rubble, and Azucena would be transported by helicopter to a hospital where she would recover rapidly and where he could visit her and bring her gifts. He thought, She's already too old for dolls, and I don't know what would please her; maybe a dress. I don't know much about women, he concluded, amused, reflecting that although he had known many women in his lifetime, none had taught him these details. To pass the hours he began to tell Azucena about his travels and adventures as a newshound, and when he exhausted his memory, he called upon imagination, inventing things he thought might entertain her. From time to time she dozed, but he kept talking in the darkness, to assure her that he was still there and to overcome the menace of uncertainty.

That was a long night.

Many miles away, I watched Rolf Carlé and the girl on a television screen. I could not bear the wait at home, so I went to National Television, where I often spent entire nights with Rolf editing programs. There, I was near his world, and I could at least get a feeling of what he lived through during those three decisive days. I called

"Don't leave me alone," she begged.

all the important people in the city, senators, commanders of the armed forces, the North American ambassador, and the president of National Petroleum, begging them for a pump to remove the silt, but obtained only vague promises. I began to ask for urgent help on radio and television, to see if there wasn't *someone* who could help us. Between calls I would run to the newsroom to monitor the satellite transmissions that periodically brought new details of the catastrophe. While reporters selected scenes with most impact for the news report, I searched for footage that featured Azucena's mudpit. The screen reduced the disaster to a single plane and accentuated the tremendous distance that separated me from Rolf Carlé; nonetheless, I was there with him. The child's every suffering hurt me as it did him; I felt his frustration, his impotence. Faced with the impossibility of communicating with him, the fantastic idea came to me that if I tried, I could reach him by force of mind and in that way give him encouragement. I concentrated until I was dizzy—a frenzied and futile activity. At times I would be overcome with compassion and burst out crying; at other times, I was so drained I felt as if I were staring through a telescope at the light of a star dead for a million years.

I watched that hell on the first morning broadcast, cadavers of people and animals awash in the current of new rivers formed overnight from the melted snow. Above the mud rose the tops of trees and the bell towers of a church where several people had taken refuge and were patiently awaiting rescue teams. Hundreds of soldiers and volunteers from the Civil Defense were clawing through rubble searching for survivors, while long rows of ragged specters[10] awaited their turn for a cup of hot broth. Radio networks announced that their phones were jammed with calls from families offering shelter to orphaned children. Drinking water was in scarce supply, along with gasoline and food. Doctors, resigned to amputating arms and legs without anesthesia, pled that at least they be sent serum and painkillers and antibiotics; most of the roads, however, were impassable, and worse were the bureaucratic obstacles that stood in the way. To top it all, the clay contaminated by decomposing bodies threatened the living with an outbreak of epidemics.

AUTHOR'S PURPOSE

3. What do you think the author wants us to feel about the tragedy at Armero?

Azucena was shivering inside the tire that held her above the surface. Immobility and tension had greatly weakened her, but she was conscious and could still be heard when a microphone was held out to her. Her tone was humble, as if apologizing for all the fuss. Rolf Carlé had a growth of beard, and dark circles beneath his eyes; he looked near exhaustion. Even from that enormous distance I could sense the quality of his weariness, so different from the fatigue of other adventures. He had completely forgotten the camera; he could not look at the girl through a lens any longer. The pictures we were receiving were not his assistant's but those of other reporters who had appropriated Azucena, bestowing on her the pathetic responsibility of embodying the horror of what had happened in that place. With the first light Rolf tried again to dislodge the obstacles that held the girl in her tomb, but he had only his hands to work with; he did not dare use a tool for fear of injuring her. He fed Azucena a cup of the corn-meal mush and bananas the Army was distributing, but she immediately vomited it up. A doctor

stated that she had a fever, but added that there was little he could do: Antibiotics were being reserved for cases of gangrene.[11] A priest also passed by and blessed her, hanging a medal of the Virgin around her neck. By evening a gentle, persistent drizzle began to fall.

"The sky is weeping," Azucena murmured, and she, too, began to cry.

"Don't be afraid," Rolf begged. "You have to keep your strength up and be calm. Everything will be fine. I'm with you, and I'll get you out somehow."

Reporters returned to photograph Azucena and ask her the same questions, which she no longer tried to answer. In the meanwhile, more television and movie teams arrived with spools of cable, tapes, film, videos, precision lenses, recorders, sound consoles, lights, reflecting screens, auxiliary motors, cartons of supplies, electricians, sound technicians, and cameramen: Azucena's face was beamed to millions of screens around the world. And all the while Rolf Carlé kept pleading for a pump. The improved technical facilities bore results, and National Television began receiving sharper pictures and clearer sound; the distance seemed suddenly compressed, and I had the horrible sensation that Azucena and Rolf were by my side, separated from me by impenetrable glass. I was able to follow events hour by hour; I knew everything my love did to wrest the girl from her prison and help her endure her suffering; I overheard fragments of what they said to one another and could guess the rest; I was present when she taught Rolf to pray, and when he distracted her with the stories I had told him in a thousand and one nights beneath the white mosquito netting of our bed.

When darkness came on the second day, Rolf tried to sing Azucena to sleep with old Austrian

---

10. **specters** *n.*: ghostlike figures.

11. **gangrene** (gaŋ'grēn') *n.*: death or decay of flesh, usually caused by disease.

folk songs he had learned from his mother, but she was far beyond sleep. They spent most of the night talking, each in a stupor of exhaustion and hunger, and shaking with cold. That night, imperceptibly, the unyielding floodgates that had contained Rolf Carlé's past for so many years began to open, and the torrent of all that had lain hidden in the deepest and most secret layers of memory poured out, leveling before it the obstacles that had blocked his consciousness for so long. He could not tell it all to Azucena; she perhaps did not know there was a world beyond the sea or time previous to her own; she was not capable of imagining Europe in the years of the war. So he could not tell her of defeat, nor of the afternoon the Russians had led them to the concentration camp to bury prisoners dead from starvation. Why should he describe to her how the naked bodies piled like a mountain of firewood resembled fragile china? How could he tell this dying child about ovens and gallows? Nor did he mention the night that he had seen his mother naked, shod in stiletto-heeled red boots, sobbing with humiliation. There was much he did not tell, but in those hours he relived for the first time all the things his mind had tried to erase. Azucena had surrendered her fear to him and so, without wishing it, had obliged Rolf to confront his own. There, beside that hellhole of mud, it was impossible for Rolf to flee from himself any longer, and the visceral[12] terror he had lived as a boy suddenly invaded him. He reverted to the years when he was the age of Azucena, and younger, and, like her, found himself trapped in a pit without escape, buried in life, his head barely above ground; he saw before his eyes the boots and

"I'm with you, and I'll get you out somehow."

legs of his father, who had removed his belt and was whipping it in the air with the never-forgotten hiss of a viper coiled to strike. Sorrow flooded through him, intact and precise, as if it had lain always in his mind, waiting. He was once again in the armoire[13] where his father locked him to punish him for imagined misbehavior, there where for eternal hours he had crouched with his eyes closed, not to see the darkness, with his hands over his ears, to shut out the beating of his heart, trembling, huddled like a cornered animal. Wandering in the mist of his memories he found his sister Katharina, a sweet, retarded child who spent her life hiding, with the hope that her father would forget the disgrace of her having been born. With Katharina, Rolf crawled beneath the dining room table, and with her hid there under the long white tablecloth, two children forever embraced, alert to footsteps and voices. Katharina's scent melded with his own sweat, with aromas of cooking, garlic, soup, freshly baked bread, and the unexpected odor of putrescent[14] clay. His sister's hand in his, her frightened breathing, her silk hair against his cheek, the candid gaze of her eyes. Katharina . . . Katharina materialized before him, floating on the air like a flag, clothed in the white tablecloth, now a winding sheet, and at last he could weep for her death and for the guilt of having abandoned her. He understood then that all his exploits as a reporter, the feats that had won him such recognition and fame, were merely an attempt to keep his most ancient fears at bay, a stratagem[15] for taking

---

12. **visceral** (vis′ər·əl) *adj.:* intuitive or emotional rather than intellectual.

13. **armoire** (är·mwär′) *n.:* large cupboard for holding clothes.

14. **putrescent** (pyoo·tres′ənt) *adj.:* rotting.

15. **stratagem** (strat′ə·jəm) *n.:* plan or scheme for achieving some goal.

refuge behind a lens to test whether reality was more tolerable from that perspective. He took excessive risks as an exercise of courage, training by day to conquer the monsters that tormented him by night. But he had come face to face with the moment of truth; he could not continue to escape his past. He *was* Azucena; he was buried in the clayey mud; his terror was not the distant emotion of an almost forgotten childhood, it was a claw sunk in his throat. In the flush of his tears he saw his mother, dressed in black and clutching her imitation-crocodile pocketbook to her bosom, just as he had last seen her on the dock when she had come to put him on the boat to South America. She had not come to dry his tears, but to tell him to pick up a shovel: the war was over and now they must bury the dead.

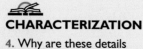

"Don't cry. I don't hurt anymore. I'm fine."

CHARACTERIZATION

4. Why are these details about Rolf's childhood important?

"Don't cry. I don't hurt anymore. I'm fine," Azucena said when dawn came.

"I'm not crying for you," Rolf Carlé smiled. "I'm crying for myself. I hurt all over."

The third day in the valley of the cataclysm began with a pale light filtering through storm clouds. The President of the Republic visited the area in his tailored safari jacket to confirm that this was the worst catastrophe of the century; the country was in mourning; sister nations had offered aid; he had ordered a state of siege; the Armed Forces would be merciless, anyone caught stealing or committing other offenses would be shot on sight. He added that it was impossible to remove all the corpses or count the thousands who had disappeared; the entire valley would be declared holy ground, and bishops would come to celebrate a solemn mass for the souls of the victims. He went to the Army field tents to offer relief in the form of vague promises to crowds of the rescued, then to the improvised hospital to offer a word of encouragement to doctors and nurses worn down from so many hours of tribulations.[16] Then he asked to be taken to see Azucena, the little girl the whole world had seen. He waved to her with a limp statesman's hand, and microphones recorded his emotional voice and paternal[17] tone as he told her that her courage had served as an example to the nation. Rolf Carlé interrupted to ask for a pump, and the President assured him that he personally would attend to the matter. I caught a glimpse of Rolf for a few seconds kneeling beside the mudpit. On the evening news broadcast, he was still in the same position; and I, glued to the screen like a fortuneteller to her crystal ball, could tell that something fundamental had changed in him. I knew somehow that during the night his defenses had crumbled and he had given in to grief; finally he was vulnerable. The girl had touched a part of him that he himself had no access to, a part he had never shared with me. Rolf had wanted to console her, but it was Azucena who had given him consolation.

I recognized the precise moment at which Rolf gave up the fight and surrendered to the torture of watching the girl die. I was with them, three days and two nights, spying on them from the other side of life. I was there when she told

---

16. **tribulations** (trib′yə‧lā′shənz) *n.:* miseries or sufferings.
17. **paternal** *adj.:* fatherly.

him that in all her thirteen years no boy had ever loved her and that it was a pity to leave this world without knowing love. Rolf assured her that he loved her more than he could ever love anyone, more than he loved his mother, more than his sister, more than all the women who had slept in his arms, more than he loved me, his life companion, who would have given anything to be trapped in that well in her place, who would have exchanged her life for Azucena's, and I watched as he leaned down to kiss her poor forehead, consumed by a sweet, sad emotion he could not name. I felt how in that instant both were saved from despair, how they were freed from the clay, how they rose above the vultures and helicopters, how together they flew above the vast swamp of corruption and laments. How, finally, they were able to accept death. Rolf Carlé prayed in silence that she would die quickly, because such pain cannot be borne.

By then I had obtained a pump and was in touch with a general who had agreed to ship it the next morning on a military cargo plane. But on the night of that third day, beneath the unblinking focus of quartz lamps and the lens of a hundred cameras, Azucena gave up, her eyes locked with those of the friend who had sustained her to the end. Rolf Carlé removed the life buoy, closed her eyelids, held her to his chest for a few moments, and then let her go. She sank slowly, a flower in the mud.

AUTHOR'S PURPOSE AND THEME

5. What does the tragic ending suggest about the **author's purpose** and the story's **theme**?

You are back with me, but you are not the same man. I often accompany you to the station and we watch the videos of Azucena again; you study them intently, looking for something you could have done to save her, something you did not think of in time. Or maybe you study them to see yourself as if in a mirror, naked. Your cameras lie forgotten in a closet; you do not write or sing; you sit long hours before the window, staring at the mountains. Beside you, I wait for you to complete the voyage into yourself, for the old wounds to heal. I know that when you return from your nightmares, we shall again walk hand in hand, as before. ■

Meet the Writer

Isabel Allende

"I Am a Story Hunter"

Isabel Allende (ēs'ä·bel ä·yen'de) (1942–   ) describes herself as a "good listener and a story hunter" who reads newspapers to search for story ideas. Allende vividly recalls the Armero disaster:

66 Thousands perished, but the world remembers the catastrophe specifically because of Omaira Sanchez, a thirteen-year-old girl who was trapped in the mud from the slide. . . . Her eyes staring from the television screen have haunted me ever since. I still have her photograph on my desk; again and again I studied it, trying to comprehend the meaning of her martyrdom. **99**

Three years after Armero, Allende wrote the story you have just read. Thoughts of Omaira would still not leave her, though, and four years later, as her own daughter lay dying, Allende says she "finally could decipher the message in those intense black eyes: patience, courage, resignation, dignity in the face of death."

Allende was born in Lima, Peru, where her father served as a diplomat for the Chilean government. When her parents divorced, three-year-old Isabel returned with her mother to her grandparents' home in Santiago. She eventually became a journalist, conducting TV interviews, writing for a feminist magazine, and making documentary films.

Her uncle, Salvador Allende, president of Chile, was killed during a military takeover of the government in 1973. Isabel and her husband and children soon fled to Caracas, Venezuela. For the thirteen years they lived there in exile, Allende wrote columns for a Venezuelan newspaper. In 1987, she moved to the United States, where she taught literature at several colleges. She now lives in California.

In 1981, Allende began writing a long goodbye letter to her ailing grandfather, who was nearly one hundred years old and preparing to die. That letter grew into her first novel, *The House of the Spirits* (1982), which became an international bestseller. Her next three novels established her reputation as a major writer: *Of Love and Shadows* (1984), *Eva Luna* (1988), and *The Stories of Eva Luna* (1990), from which "And of Clay Are We Created" is taken.

This newspaper article is an account of the real event in Armero, Colombia, that inspired Allende's story. Her character Azucena is based on Omaira Sanchez.

Ill-Equipped Rescuers Dig Out Volcano Victims; Aid Slow to Reach Colombian Town

Bradley Graham

Frank Fournier/Contact Press Images.

Thirteen-year-old Omaira Sanchez was trapped in a mudflow from the Nevado del Ruiz eruption. Rescue workers could not manage to release her from the hardening mud and debris, and she died within forty-eight hours.

ARMERO, Colombia, Nov. 15, 1985—From beneath the rubble of what was Armero, now a mass of broken concrete slabs and twisted corrugated metal, of scattered belongings and crushed bodies buried under brown watery slush, came the cries today of survivors alive two days after a volcanic eruption caused a flood of mud that swallowed this town.

But few were here to save them.

Officials in Bogota, who had declared a national emergency after the eruption Wednesday of Nevado del Ruiz volcano, reported that aid had begun to arrive from the United States, Europe, and international agencies. But only a tiny amount of material and a small number of volunteers have arrived so far to this main scene of disaster.

Relief workers, laboring in hot, humid

weather amid the rising stench of spoiled food and decomposing bodies, said there was a desperate shortage of supplies and personnel. As they worked, more tremors and rumbles were felt from the volcano.

Government and relief officials estimated that as many as 20,000 people may have died in the disaster, and thousands more have been injured. But those on the scene stressed that a complete casualty count would not be possible for a long time.

Walter Cotte of the Red Cross said many of the dead were buried in mass graves without being photographed or fingerprinted. One relief official said it would probably be necessary to declare Armero "holy ground," leaving many of the dead buried where they died. Hastily constructed tent hospitals were set up in the nearby towns of Mariquita, Lerida, and Guayabal, civil defense officials said, but there were few helicopters to carry the victims there, and no roads were passable in the narrow Andean valleys near Armero. "We don't have the help we need," said Raul Alferez, who is in charge of the Red Cross medical unit here. "We need people, we need equipment, but we have next to nothing."

The magnitude of what has to be done is overwhelming. What was once a picturesque country city of 25,000 people is now a mangled mass of junk and corpses.

In the low hills above the city, several hundred people have camped in makeshift huts with tin roofs. They are the lucky ones, those who managed somehow to escape the waves of hot mud and debris[1] that swept through Armero.

But they were not being evacuated. Relief officials said priority for seats in the nine or ten helicopters ferrying people to and from the disaster site was given to the injured.

On the northwest side of Armero, several bulldozers were pushing back the mud, trying to open a road into the town. But it could be days before emergency land vehicles can reach here.

The Red Cross has set up a tent and evacuation area in a clearing several hundred yards from where the mud stopped. Only five medics and fifteen volunteers made up the Red Cross team today, according to Alferez. Also helping in the rescue effort here were about ten blue-suited Air Force members and about the same number of orange-suited Civil Defense workers. Yesterday, emergency teams pulled survivors off the roofs and trees where they had climbed to escape the avalanche. Today, the rescuers searched for those buried alive in the mud.

Alferez estimated that 1,000 people could be trapped alive in the city's ruins. An Argentine medic participating in the relief effort, 23-year-old Alejandro Jimenez, guessed that there could be 2,000.

As of early this afternoon, Alferez, who was not keeping exact records, said about 65 injured survivors had been found and flown out today.

But there is no organization, no plan, to search for the living. It is a hit-or-miss operation. Survivors have been located most often when their screams or cries were heard by passersby.

Once survivors are found, the process of freeing them is a lengthy, arduous effort.

One team of workers spent much of this morning trying to pry a 34-year-old man from his collapsed house while, a few yards away, another team chest-deep in water sought desperately to lift to safety a 13-year-old girl whose feet were pinned by fallen concrete.

---

1. **debris** (də·brē′) *n.:* rubble; broken glass, stone, and other materials resulting from destruction.

The man, Efrain Gomez Primo, a peanut farmer and candy vendor, was stuck under his collapsed house. He talked about his ordeal as rescue workers hacked away with machetes[2] at the boards that imprisoned him.

He said the walls of his house fell in Wednesday night as he was trying to flee the raging current. After the volcanic storm had subsided, he said, he started screaming for help. His brother found him at 6:30 yesterday morning and told him not to worry, that the Red Cross, Civil Defense, and Army were on their way. The brother never returned.

A Civil Defense worker who arrived soon afterward lacked the necessary tools and left. It was not until late this morning that a rescue squad arrived.

By then, a middle-aged woman, who had been caught in the wreckage with him and was in great pain through last night, had died. Her corpse lay facing up on a sheet of tin.

"I'm half dead," he said, as the effort to free him began. No one had given him anything to eat or drink for more than 36 hours. Gasping for air, he exclaimed, "I can barely breathe."

When he was finally pried loose and carried to the evacuation zone, medics had no splint for Gomez's broken right leg. They tied a strip of cardboard around it.

Just a few yards from Gomez was the girl, Omaira Sanchez. She had been found just after dawn yesterday by an Air Force officer working in the rescue campaign. The first problem was how to pry loose the stiff arms of the girl's dead aunt, who had grasped the child the night of the tragedy.

Sanchez said the waters of the ravaging Lagunilla River had prevented her aunt from opening the door of their house. All during that stormy night, before she died, the aunt kept apologizing for not having managed to rush the family to freedom, the niece recalled.

The girl's eyes were bright red and swollen. When rescue workers called for an anesthetic,[3] there was none.

She asked for cookies, but there were none of those either. Somehow the girl managed to stay calm and lucid,[4] closing her eyes in pain at times, breaking into tears at other moments.

She would wrap her hands around the neck of a rescue worker standing in the water in front of her and try, with all her might, to tear herself free of whatever was keeping her feet pinned down. But she could not budge.

Workers dug around her, lifting out huge blocks of broken concrete. Rescuers feared that rising water would drown the girl if they couldn't get her out soon. Her head was just above the water line.

Watching the desperate attempts to save the girl, Alferez, the Red Cross chief, shook his head in despair.

"This makes one feel useless," he said. "What can we do?"

—from *The Washington Post*, November 16, 1985

---

2. **machetes** (mə·shet′ēz) *n.:* large blades used to cut underbrush and crops like sugar cane.

3. **anesthetic** (an′es·thet′ik) *n.:* drug used to eliminate pain.
4. **lucid** (loo′sid) *adj.:* clearheaded.

Response and Analysis

Reading Check

1. Describe the event that occurs before the story begins.

2. Describe Azucena's situation when the story opens.

3. Summarize Rolf Carlé's efforts to save Azucena.

4. How does the narrator try to help Azucena?

5. At the end of the story, what happens to Azucena?

Thinking Critically

6. What is the relationship between Rolf and Azucena? What do they give to each other?

7. Why do you think Allende chose to write a story about the events described in the newspaper article, rather than a nonfiction account? What do you think her **purpose** is in this story?

8. What do you think the **title** of the story means?

9. Consider Rolf's efforts to help Azucena and what happens to Rolf and Azucena at the end. Then, in a sentence or two, express what you think is the story's **theme,** its insight or message about life.

10. **Compare and contrast** Allende's story with the newspaper account of the same events (see the **Connection** on page 267). Think about how the choice of **genre** affects how the story is told. Consider especially these elements:

    • writer's purpose

    • point of view

    • tone

    • descriptive details

    • figurative language

    • theme or main idea

    Which account do you find more moving? Which do you find more informative? Explain why.

Extending and Evaluating

11. Look back at your Quickwrite notes. Do you think most people would behave as Rolf Carlé does? Explain why or why not.

12. Allende has written:

> Writing a short story is like shooting an arrow; it requires the instinct, practice, and precision of a good archer . . . and good luck—to hit the bull's eye.

    In your opinion, has she hit the bull's-eye with this story? Support your evaluation by referring to details in the story.

WRITING

Tell It Again

Retell the events of the Armero disaster in still **another genre.** You might write a poem or song, an interview with a survivor, or journal entries that Rolf Carlé might have written after the disaster.

You Are a Story Hunter

Take a newspaper article from today's paper, and use it as the basis for a **short story.** Elaborate on the facts in the article with believable characters, dialogue, sensory details, and figurative language. Feel free to change or add characters and plot events. Before you start writing, decide on your purpose, and choose the point of view that you think will be most useful for that purpose.

SKILLS FOCUS

Literary Skills
Analyze fiction and nonfiction genres. Analyze theme and purpose.

Reading Skills
Determine an author's purpose.

Writing Skills
Retell the events in the selection in another genre. Write a short story based on a newspaper article.

Vocabulary Development

Mapping a Word's Origin

Every word has a history, which you can discover by checking its **etymology,** or **origin,** in a dictionary. (Since etymologies trace a word's history backward in time, the oldest form of the word is normally listed last.) Here is a word map for *subterranean:*

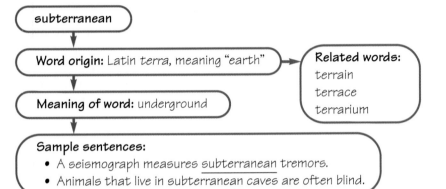

subterranean

Word origin: Latin *terra,* meaning "earth"

Related words:
terrain
terrace
terrarium

Meaning of word: underground

Sample sentences:
- A seismograph measures <u>subterranean</u> tremors.
- Animals that live in <u>subterranean</u> caves are often blind.

Word Bank

subterranean
magnitude
presentiments
tenacity
equanimity
fortitude
ingenuity
resignation
pandemonium
commiserate

PRACTICE 1

For each word in the Word Bank, work with a partner to make a word map like the one for *subterranean.* (Hint: For some words the dictionary may send you to another word to find the origin.)

Word Roots

When you trace word origins, you find that many words come from common roots. **A root** is the part of a word that carries its core meaning. The chart below lists some common Greek and Latin roots.

Greek Roots	Meaning	Example
–log–	study or science of	anthropology
–poly–	many; much	polygon
–therm–	heat	thermometer
Latin Roots	**Meaning**	**Example**
–cred–	belief; trust	credibility
–fid–	belief; faith	confidential
–luc–, –lum–	light	lucid, luminous
–vid–, –vis–	see; seeing	video, revise

PRACTICE 2

List as many example words as you can for each Greek or Latin root in the chart. Get together in a small group to compare lists.

SKILLS FOCUS

Vocabulary Skills
Make semantic maps. Understand word roots.

Before You Read

The Man in the Water

Make the Connection

Quickwrite ✏️

In your notebook, define *hero* and *heroism* in a sentence or two. Then, list some people, past or present, famous or ordinary, whom you regard as heroes. Briefly tell why you think each person is a hero. Save your notes.

Literary Focus

Essays: Thinking on Paper

The subject matter of today's **personal** (or **informal**) **essays** is as wide as human experience—from the mysteries of the cosmos to the clothes dryer's habit of eating socks. The tone can range from serious and thoughtful, as in the essay you're about to read, to comic, as in essays by James Thurber, Dave Barry, and Erma Bombeck.

Essays are thought journeys. Essay writers take a subject—any subject—and examine it from different perspectives, like looking at an object through a telescope, then a microscope, and then a kaleidoscope. Essayists, writing about their own thoughts and feelings, touch us because they are writing about us all.

INTERNET

Vocabulary Practice

Keyword: LE5 10-4

The Main Idea

When Roger Rosenblatt sat down to write about the man in the water, he probably had his **main idea** in mind— the insight or message he wished to communicate about the tragedy. He was not writing a news article in which he'd have to report the facts of the event. Instead, he wanted to talk about something important that he saw in the incident. He had an idea to share.

Literary Skills
Understand personal essays. Understand the main idea.

Reading Skills
Summarize the main idea.

Reading Skills 📖

Summarizing the Main Idea

When you **summarize** an essay, you state its most important idea in your own words. You should also cite some of the essay's key **supporting details.** To find the **main idea** of Rosenblatt's—or any— essay, look for key statements that express the writer's opinion.

Background

The disaster described in this essay occurred on January 13, 1982. Washington, D.C., was blanketed in wet snow flurries when Air Florida Flight 90 took off from Washington National Airport. Just after takeoff the plane hit the Fourteenth Street Bridge, crushed five cars and tipped over a truck, and then crashed into the Potomac River. Seventy-eight people died, including four motorists. Of the seventy-nine people aboard the plane, only five survived—four passengers and one flight attendant. The probable cause of the accident was ice on the plane's wings.

Vocabulary Development

flailing (flāl′iŋ) *v.* used as *adj.*: waving wildly.

extravagant (ek·strav′ə·gənt) *adj.*: excessive; showy.

abiding (ə·bīd′iŋ) *adj.*: continuing; lasting.

pitted (pit′id) *v.*: placed in competition.

implacable (im·plak′ə·bəl) *adj.*: relentless; not affected by attempts at change.

Like every other person on that flight,
he was desperate to live.

The MAN in the WATER

Roger Rosenblatt

As disasters go, this one was terrible but not unique, certainly not among the worst on the roster of U.S. air crashes. There was the unusual element of the bridge, of course, and the fact that the plane clipped it at a moment of high traffic, one routine thus intersecting[1] another and disrupting both. Then, too, there was the location of the event. Washington, the city of form and regulations, turned chaotic, deregulated,[2] by a blast of real winter and a single slap of metal on metal. The jets from Washington National Airport that normally swoop around the presidential monuments like famished gulls were, for the moment, emblemized[3] by the one that fell; so there was that detail. And there was the aesthetic clash[4] as well—blue-and-green Air Florida, the name a flying garden, sunk down among gray chunks in a black river. All that was worth noticing, to be sure. Still, there was nothing very special in any of it, except death, which, while always special, does not necessarily bring millions to tears or to attention. Why, then, the shock here?

Perhaps because the nation saw in this disaster something more than a mechanical failure. Perhaps because people saw in it no failure at all, but rather something successful about their makeup. Here, after all, were two forms of nature in collision: the elements and human character. Last Wednesday, the elements, indifferent as ever, brought down Flight 90. And on that same afternoon, human nature—groping and <u>flailing</u> in mysteries of its own—rose to the occasion.

Of the four acknowledged heroes of the event, three are able to account for their behavior. Donald Usher and Eugene Windsor, a park-police helicopter team, risked their lives every time they dipped the skids[5] into the water to pick up survivors. On television, side by side in bright blue jumpsuits, they described their courage as all in the line of duty. Lenny Skutnik, a 28-year-old employee of the Congressional Budget Office, said: "It's something I never thought I would do"—referring to his jumping into the water to drag an injured woman to shore. Skutnik added that

---

1. **intersecting** *v.* used as *adj.*: cutting across.
2. **deregulated** *v.* used as *adj.*: removed from government control; here, an ironic reference to the disorder caused by a winter storm.
3. **emblemized** (em′blə·mīzd′) *v.*: represented; symbolized.
4. **aesthetic** (es·thet′ik) **clash:** unpleasant visual contrast.
5. **skids** *n.*: long, narrow pieces used in place of wheels for aircraft landing gear.

Vocabulary
flailing (flāl′iŋ) *v.* used as *adj.*: waving wildly.

"somebody had to go in the water," delivering every hero's line that is no less admirable for its repetitions. In fact, nobody had to go into the water. That somebody actually did so is part of the reason this particular tragedy sticks in the mind.

But the person most responsible for the emotional impact of the disaster is the one known at first simply as "the man in the water." (Balding, probably in his 50s, an <u>extravagant</u> moustache.) He was seen clinging with five other survivors to the tail section of the airplane. This man was described by Usher and Windsor as appearing alert and in control. Every time they lowered a lifeline and flotation ring to him, he passed it on to another of the passengers. "In a mass casualty, you'll find people like him," said Windsor. "But I've never seen one with that commitment." When the helicopter came back for him, the man had gone under. His selflessness was one reason the story held national attention; his anonymity[6] another. The fact that he went unidentified invested him with a universal character. For a while he was Everyman, and thus proof (as if one needed it) that no man is ordinary.

---

6. anonymity (an'ə·nim'ə·tē) *n.:* unknown identity.

Vocabulary
extravagant (ek·strav'ə·gənt) *adj.:* excessive; showy.

A Closer Look

Black Box: Air Florida Flight 90

The following conversation took place just before the crash of Air Florida Flight 90. It was recorded on the plane's black box, later retrieved from the wreckage.

Copilot. It's been a while since we've been de-iced.
Pilot. Think I'll go home and . . .
Copilot. Boy . . . this is a losing battle here on trying to de-ice those things . . . a false sense of security, that's all that does.
Pilot. That, ah, satisfies the Feds. Right there is where the icing truck, they oughta have two . . .
Copilot. Yeah, and you taxi through kinda like a carwash or something.
Pilot. Hit that thing with about eight billion gallons of glycol . . .
Copilot. Slushy runway. Do you want me to do anything special for this or just go for it?
Pilot. Unless you got anything special you'd like to do.
Copilot. . . . just take off the nose wheel early like a soft-field takeoff . . . I'll pull it [the throttle] back to about one point five . . . supposed to be about one six depending on how scared we are . . . *(laughter)*

[The plane is cleared for takeoff at 3:59 P.M., 45 minutes after its last de-icing.]

Copilot. God, look at that thing.
Copilot. That doesn't seem right, does it?
Copilot. Ah, that's not right.
Pilot. Yes, it is, there's eighty.
Copilot. Naw, I don't think that's right.
Copilot. Ah, maybe it is.
Pilot. Hundred and twenty.
Copilot. I don't know. . . .
Pilot. Come on, forward. . . .
Pilot. Just barely climb.
Speaker Undetermined. Stalling, we're [falling].
Copilot. Larry, we're going down, Larry.
Pilot. I know it.

[Sound of impact]

Still, he could never have imagined such a capacity in himself. Only minutes before his character was tested, he was sitting in the ordinary plane among the ordinary passengers, dutifully listening to the stewardess telling him to fasten his seat belt and saying something about the "No Smoking" sign. So our man relaxed with the others, some of whom would owe their lives to him. Perhaps he started to read, or to doze, or to regret some harsh remark made in the office that morning. Then suddenly he knew that the trip would not be ordinary. Like every other person on that flight, he was desperate to live, which makes his final act so stunning.

For at some moment in the water he must have realized that he would not live if he continued to hand over the rope and ring to others. He *had* to know it, no matter how gradual the effect of the cold. In his judgment he had no choice. When the helicopter took off with what was to be the last survivor, he watched everything in the world move away from him, and he deliberately let it happen.

Yet there was something else about our man that kept our thoughts on him, and which keeps our thoughts on him still. He was *there,* in the essential, classic circumstance. Man in nature. ~~Man~~ in the water. For its part, nature cared ~~nothing~~ out the five passengers. Our man, on the other hand, cared totally. So the timeless battle commenced in the Potomac. For as long as that man could last, they went at each other, nature and man; the one making no distinctions of good and evil, acting on no principles, offering no lifelines; the other acting wholly on distinctions, principles, and, one supposes, on faith.

Since it was he who lost the fight, we ought to come again to the conclusion that people are powerless in the world. In reality, we believe the reverse, and it takes the act of the man in the water to remind us of our true feelings in this matter. It is not to say that everyone would have acted as he did, or as Usher, Windsor, and Skutnik. Yet whatever moved these men to challenge death on behalf of their fellows is not peculiar to them. Everyone feels the possibility in himself. That is the abiding wonder of the story. That is why we would not let go of it. If the man in the water gave a lifeline to the people gasping for survival, he was likewise giving a lifeline to those who observed him.

The odd thing is that we do not even really believe that the man in the water lost his fight. "Everything in Nature contains all the powers of

---

Vocabulary
abiding (ə·bīd′iŋ) *adj.:* continuing; lasting.

Nature," said Emerson. Exactly. So the man in the water had his own natural powers. He could not make ice storms, or freeze the water until it froze the blood. But he could hand life over to a stranger, and that is a power of nature too. The man in the water <u>pitted</u> himself against an <u>implacable</u>, impersonal enemy; he fought it with charity; and he held it to a standoff. He was the best we can do. ■

Meet the Writer

Roger Rosenblatt

Searching for the Good and the Mysterious

Roger Rosenblatt (1940–   ) says that an expression of mystery characterizes his best essays and stories.

❝ Often I will wait to write till the last possible minute before deadline, hoping not to solve a particular mystery, but to feel it more deeply. 'The Man in the Water' . . . was written in forty-five minutes, but I brooded about it for many days. . . .

Three full days that air crash led the evening news. I came to believe that the man in the water was the reason, yet no one had said so because he had done something people could not understand.

In too many ways the piece shows that it was written in forty-five minutes, but it resonated with readers at the time because it dwelt on the mystery of an act that people did not understand, or want to understand. Certain stories people do not want to understand. The mystery makes them feel closer to one another than would any solution. ❞

Rosenblatt has had a career's worth of practice as a columnist and editorial writer for publications including *The New Republic, The Washington Post,* and *Time.* He appears regularly on PBS's *The NewsHour with Jim Lehrer* as a commentator on current issues.

Rosenblatt, who has a doctorate degree in English and American literature from Harvard University, began his career teaching literature and writing at Harvard before turning to journalism. In 1996, he returned to teaching as professor of English at Southampton College on Long Island.

He has written and coauthored more than a dozen books, among them *Children of War* (1983), *Witness: The World Since Hiroshima* (1985), *The Man in the Water: Essays and Stories* (1994), and *Rules for Aging* (2000). Many of Rosenblatt's books and essays show his search for the redeeming aspects of human existence and its mysteries.

*A **parable** is a brief story that teaches a lesson about life. In this well-known parable from the Bible, the lesson is about helping others.*

The Parable of the Good Samaritan

The Good Samaritan (1890) by Vincent van Gogh, after Delacroix. Oil on canvas.

Rijksmuseum Kröller-Müller, Otterlo, the Netherlands.

A certain man went down from Jerusalem to Jericho and fell among thieves, which stripped him of his raiment[1] and wounded him and departed, leaving him half dead.

And by chance there came down a certain priest that way, and when he saw him, he passed by on the other side.

And likewise a Levite,[2] when he was at the place, came and looked on him and passed by on the other side.

But a certain Samaritan,[3] as he journeyed, came where he was, and when he saw him, he had compassion[4] on him and went to him and bound up his wounds, pouring in oil and wine, and set him on his own beast and brought him to an inn and took care of him.

And on the morrow when he departed, he took out two pence and gave them to the host and said unto him, "Take care of him, and whatsoever thou spendest more, when I come again, I will repay thee."

Which now of these three, thinkest thou, was neighbor unto him that fell among the thieves?

—Luke 10:30–36, from the King James Bible

1. **raiment** (rā′mənt) *n.:* archaic word for "clothing."
2. **Levite** (lē′vīt′): member of the ancient Israelite tribe of Levi.
3. **Samaritan** (sə·mer′ə·tən): person from Samaria, a region neighboring ancient Israel.
4. **compassion** *n.:* pity for the sufferings of others.

A State Championship Versus Runner's Conscience

John Christian Hoyle

A light drizzle and fog fill the vast margin between gray clouds and muddy ground. The temperature is 42 degrees. The weather envelops and entices me and my six cross-country teammates as we exit the school van.

Our previous performance under similar atmospheric conditions was impressive. It got us here—the final meet of the season, the high school state championship. Physically and mentally, we are overprepared. We're cocky.

Jogging toward the starting line, I feel the eyes of our competition burn into my back. I reciprocate[1] glares while laughing at a joke a teammate shares. I savor knowing that these 180-odd runners know we are the team to beat. I feel powerful.

As we stretch ligaments, I catch a glimpse of our coach smiling—a configuration his mouth and cheeks are not used to. He knows

1. **reciprocate** (ri·sip′rə·kāt′) *v.*: return; exchange.

the probability of our placing first is better than excellent.

"This is the best opportunity your school has ever had to win a state title," he says in a gruff voice. "Don't let the school down. Don't let me down. Don't let your teammates down. And, most importantly, don't let yourselves down."

Coach is still speaking. But I've stopped listening. I dream of the big, shiny trophy.

We take our places: The gun fires. As I accelerate, I inhale deep breaths. Most of the racers are behind me. I'm hitting stride. A strong finish is mine.

Rounding a corner of a remote leg of the winding course, my eyes zero in on a runner in red shorts. He's sitting down, crying in pain, clutching his foot. I sidestep him and glance at my watch. I'm making good time. I take comfort in knowing there's one fewer runner ahead of me.

But suddenly I freeze. Cold. I'm breathing heavily. My mind tells my legs to keep moving. But I don't. I swivel around, spotting the downed runner. He's now lying on his back—in the mud. I'm about 20 feet from him. I think for a moment. Do I help? Will someone else in the pack stop to help? Can I come back or send someone when I cross the finish line? I'm losing precious minutes. The agony on his face disturbs me. He's in trouble. Our eyes connect, and at this moment the race has ended for me. Arguments against helping become moot.[2] I can think of nothing other than helping this fellow.

I help him to his feet. We look for someone else to help, but no one does. About 25 runners have whizzed by. Finally, two or three minutes later, a man comes to take over for me.

"Finish the race," he encourages. "Finish the race!" I do. When I cross the finish line, my coach and teammates are waiting to find out what happened.

"Where were you?" Coach asks in a tone that would have dwarfed Lombardi.[3]

I explain.

"You what?" he says, tossing his arms in the air in disbelief. "You stopped to help someone."

"Yes," I mumble sheepishly. "It seemed right. I'm sorry."

He laughs at me. His face is fiery red. The six-hour ride back takes days in my mind. It's lonely and silent. Drumbeats from headphones are the only sounds that break the stale air.

My team placed fourth. Almost three weeks will go by until Coach speaks to me. Sports make my world revolve. It seems everyone thinks I failed, that I should have breezed by the guy.

I think about it a lot, even now, several years later. Did I do the right thing? Was it worth it?

Yes, because when his eyes connected with mine, my conscience demanded I stop and help. Though I had to think about it for a moment, I couldn't keep running. I would have felt awful if I had—and that would have smoldered in my mind a lot longer than the disapproval of Coach and my team. Basking in personal glory on the altar of ego, I figure, is never worth it.

—from *The Christian Science Monitor,* February 5, 1999

---

2. **moot** *adj.:* no longer worthy of consideration; pointless.

3. **Lombardi:** Vince Lombardi coached the Green Bay Packers football team from 1959 to 1967 and led them to five championships.

Response and Analysis

Reading Check

1. Briefly describe the disaster.

2. According to Rosenblatt, the disaster was a clash between "the elements, indifferent as ever," and what else?

3. Besides the man in the water, who are the three other heroes, and what does each one do?

4. Describe what the man in the water looks like and what he does. What ultimately happens to him?

Thinking Critically

5. According to Rosenblatt, the man in the water symbolizes the **conflict** between human beings and nature. How does Rosenblatt characterize nature? How does nature differ from the man in the water?

6. Rosenblatt says that the man in the water is proof that "no man is ordinary." What do you think he means by this?

7. **Summarize** Rosenblatt's most important points, and state his **main idea**. Which passages support this idea most effectively?

8. Briefly state what you think is the **theme** of Rosenblatt's essay. In this case, is the theme the same as the main idea? Explain why or why not.

9. How is John Hoyle, the author of "A State Championship Versus Runner's Conscience" (see the **Connection** on page 279), like the Samaritan in the Bible parable (see the **Connection** on page 278)? How are they both like the heroes in Rosenblatt's essay? Are all these people good Samaritans? Explain your responses.

Extending and Evaluating

10. How would you react in a situation in which you might save a stranger's life but would risk losing your own? Talk about your responses to what the four heroes in Rosenblatt's essay did.

11. The final two paragraphs of the essay make specific points about human nature. Explain in your own words what Rosenblatt is saying, and then give your opinion of his ideas.

WRITING

Right or Wrong?

Think about the writer of "A State Championship Versus Runner's Conscience" (see the **Connection** on page 279). Did he do the right thing? Write a **persuasive essay** in which you argue either that he should have helped the other runner *or* that he should have been more loyal to himself, his team, and his school. Be sure to include a thesis statement and supporting details.

▶ **Use "Writing a Persuasive Essay," pages 294–301, for help with this assignment.**

My Hero

Create a brief **biographical sketch** of one of the heroes you listed in your Quickwrite notes. Show your hero in his or her surroundings, and tell a little about the person's life and why he or she is a hero to you.

INTERNET

Projects and Activities

Keyword: LE5 10-4

SKILLS FOCUS

Literary Skills
Analyze a personal essay. Analyze the main idea.

Reading Skills
Summarize the main idea.

Writing Skills
Write a persuasive essay. Write a biographical sketch.

Comparing Themes

For a writing assignment comparing the themes in "And of Clay Are We Created" and "The Man in the Water," see page 283.

Vocabulary Development

In Other Words: Synonyms and Connotations

PRACTICE

From a number of **synonyms,** Rosenblatt chose the words that had the **connotations**—the emotional overtones—he wanted. Answer the questions below about his word choices.

1. Rosenblatt says that in the aftermath of the crash, human nature found itself "groping and flailing in mysteries of its own." Why wouldn't *waving* have the same effect as *flailing*?

2. The author mentions the man's "extravagant moustache." Why is *extravagant* a more effective word to use than *large*?

3. What does *abiding* add to the author's conclusion about the "wonder of the story" that *lingering* wouldn't convey?

4. The man in the water "pitted" himself against nature. Why wouldn't substituting *set* for *pitted* work as well?

5. Why would the author call nature *implacable* rather than *firm*?

> **Word Bank**
> flailing
> extravagant
> abiding
> pitted
> implacable

Grammar Link

Say It Straight: Eliminating Wordiness

Knowing when and how to use clauses and phrases is important because they can add information and variety to your sentences. Don't overdo them, though, and create a wordy disaster. Compare these two sentences, for example:

1. Every time, hoping to rescue him, they lowered a lifeline and flotation ring and hoped that he would allow himself to be rescued out of the water; but he conveyed the rescue device to yet another one of the passengers who had been in the plane with him, waiting in the water to be rescued after the crash.

2. ROSENBLATT
"Every time they lowered a lifeline and flotation ring to him, he passed it on to another of the passengers."

Rosenblatt's sentence is not only much better than the first sentence; it was also harder to write. That's because it's easier to be wordy than concise. In your writing, don't add too many phrases and clauses to a sentence.

▶ **For more help, see Revising Wordy Sentences, 10h, in the Language Handbook.**

PRACTICE 1

Pick another short passage from "The Man in the Water," and inflate it as in the first example. (By rewriting good, spare prose, you'll appreciate what makes it good.) Then, ask a partner to streamline the passage. Compare the shortened version with Rosenblatt's. Did your partner come close to finding the original amid the wordiness?

PRACTICE 2

Take a piece of prose you're working on or a piece from your writer's portfolio. See whether you can improve it by doing some pruning.

SKILLS FOCUS

Vocabulary Skills
Understand synonyms and connotations.

Grammar Skills
Eliminate wordiness.

Writing a Comparison-Contrast Essay

Comparing a Theme Across Genres

"And of Clay Are We Created" .... page 257
"The Man in the Water" .... page 273

Now that you have read Allende's story and Rosenblatt's essay, you can compare their themes in a comparison-contrast essay. When you write a **comparison-contrast essay,** you use the skills of **comparing** (finding similarities) and **contrasting** (finding differences).

Gather Your Information, and Organize It

For help writing your essay, go back to the chart you completed on page 255.

There are two main methods for organizing a comparison-contrast essay. The one you will practice here is the **point-by-point method.** (The **block method** was covered on page 254.)

The Point-by-Point Method

With this organization you discuss the *elements,* one at a time. You might discuss the author's purpose in work 1 and then the author's purpose in work 2, and so on for other elements. The chart on the right shows an example.

Use Three Basic Parts, and Elaborate

As with most essays, use three basic parts:

• **introduction**—includes background and **thesis statement**
• **body**—includes a separate paragraph for each element
• **conclusion**—sums up and adds a personal comment

Be sure to **elaborate** on every general statement you make; use details, examples, and quotations from the selections.

Revise Your Essay

Revise your paper after peer evaluation or self-evaluation. Ask yourself:

• Does the thesis statement clearly state the main point of the essay?

• Does the essay elaborate on the elements of both selections?

• Does the essay follow point-by-point organization? Is each point about an element in work 1 followed by a point about that element in work 2?

• Is the conclusion clear and effective?

▶ **For more help writing a comparison-contrast essay, see pages 382–389.**

Point-by-Point Method
Element 1: How Genre Relates to Author's Purpose
Work 1: "And of Clay Are We Created"   Work 2: "The Man in the Water"
Element 2: Theme/Main Idea and Whether Stated or Implied
Work 1: "And of Clay Are We Created"   Work 2: "The Man in the Water"
Element 3: Genre Elements That Support Theme/Main Idea
Work 1: "And of Clay Are We Created"   Work 2: "The Man in the Water"

SKILLS FOCUS

Literary Skills
Understand how genre affects theme.

Writing Skills
Write a comparison-contrast essay.

If Decency Doesn't, Law Should Make Us Samaritans ◆
Good Samaritans U.S.A. Are Afraid to Act

Evaluating Arguments: Pro and Con

Are You Convinced?

It's hard to get through a day without someone trying to persuade you, usually through an **argument,** a series of statements designed to convince you of something. For starters, consider politicians' speeches and all the editorials in newspapers. Often you are faced with opposing arguments (pro and con) on an issue, as in the two opinion essays you are about to read. How can you evaluate all these arguments? Whose position is believable and backed up by evidence, and whose isn't?

The following questions and the chart on the next page will help you evaluate the **credibility,** or believability, of an author's argument:

1. **What's the claim, or opinion?**
   If you're reading a persuasive piece, first read through it to get the big picture—the whole idea of what the writer is saying. Then, determine the author's **claim,** which is also called an **opinion.** This opinion is often stated in the form of a **generalization** (a broad statement that covers many situations). For example, this is a generalization that states an opinion: "Every eligible citizen should be required to vote."

2. **What's the support?** Here are some common ways in which authors support their views:

   Logical appeals. Logical appeals include convincing reasons and evidence.

Reasons are statements that explain *why* the author holds an opinion. (For example, this statement includes a reason for the author's opinion: "Citizens should be required to vote because only then will elected officials represent all the people.")

Evidence is the specific information that is used to back up a reason. Remember that evidence must be **relevant** to the reason—that is, it must be directly and logically related to it. Remember, too, that every generalization, in order to be believable, should be backed up by evidence.

The types of evidence most frequently used include

- facts
- statistics (number facts)
- examples
- quotations or opinions by experts

Emotional appeals. Arguments can also be supported by emotional appeals. These appeals stir feelings such as happiness or anger in readers. Authors often use emotional appeals because they know that our emotions may override our reason. You should be wary of a writer who mainly uses emotional appeals in an argument. Emotional appeals are usually accomplished through

- loaded words (words with strong emotional connotations, or associations)
- anecdotes (brief stories or personal accounts of an event or happening)

SKILLS FOCUS

Reading Skills
Evaluate author arguments.

Evaluating an Author's Argument	
Claim, or Opinion	
Logical Appeals	
Reason 1	
Evidence	
Reason 2	
Evidence	
Emotional Appeals	
Loaded words, etc.	

3. Is the evidence comprehensive?

Evidence can make or break an argument, so an author must provide sufficient evidence to back up generalizations and to make an argument convincing. Ask yourself whether the author has done his or her job. If the argument is filled with emotional appeals but no relevant evidence is presented, you need to ask yourself why. Could it be there is no real evidence to support the author's claim?

4. What's the author's intent?

Consider the author's intent. Does he or she hold a biased or prejudiced interest in the topic and have an ax to grind, or is the author trying to present a reasoned, objective-sounding argument? Note how the author's intent affects the **tone**. For example, an angry or insulting tone should send up red flags, telling the reader that the author's argument is based more on opinion or strong feeling than on evidence.

▶ **For more about persuasive writing, see "Writing a Persuasive Essay," pages 294–301, at the end of this collection.**

Vocabulary Development

allegations (al′·ə·gā′shənz) *n.:* in law, assertions, or positive statements, made without proof.

depraved (dē·prāvd′) *adj.:* immoral.

liability (lī′·ə·bil′·ə·tē) *n.:* legal obligation or responsibility to make good a damage or loss.

rationalizations (rash′·ən··ə·lə·zā′shənz) *n.:* seemingly reasonable excuses or explanations for one's behavior—but not the real reasons.

solidarity (säl′·ə·dar′·ə·tē) *n.:* complete unity in a group or organization.

callous (kal′·əs) *adj.:* unfeeling.

feigning (fān′·iŋ) *v.:* pretending.

immunity (i·myo͞on′·ə·tē) *n.:* freedom from a legal obligation.

construed (kən·stro͞od′) *v.:* interpreted.

indemnifies (in·dem′ni·fīz′) *v.:* in a legal sense, protects.

Connecting to the Literature

Rolf Carlé in "And of Clay Are We Created" and the selfless hero in "The Man in the Water" are examples of people helping others in situations of extreme danger. The following two articles discuss whether such help should be required by law.

If Decency Doesn't, Law Should Make Us Samaritans

from the *Houston Chronicle*, September 18, 1997

Gloria Allred *and* Lisa Bloom

Witnesses' allegations that paparazzi[1] stood by and snapped photos while Princess Diana[2] and her companions were bleeding, injured, and dying, rather than aiding the accident victims, have shocked the world and offended our deepest sense of decency.

If the photographers did so, they may be charged with violating France's "Good Samaritan"[3] law requiring people to assist others in distress. Yet in the United States there is no civil or criminal law[4] requiring a bystander to come to the aid of another. If the accident had occurred in the United States, the paparazzi could not have been charged with violating any law as a result of photographing rather than assisting. If any good is to come of the Princess Diana tragedy and the depraved image of people trying to make a buck off of the dying, it should be a call to change U.S. law to require each of us to render at least minimal assistance, where possible, to those at risk of suffering grievous injury or death. ❶

For example, it is not too much to ask that we call the police or an ambulance when we come upon a major car accident with severely injured people. In that situation a few minutes' delay can be the difference between life and death.

The American "no duty to come to the aid of another" rule has been criticized by legal scholars, yet the issue has generally been ignored by the public. It should insult our values to think that a healthy adult could come upon a baby drowning face down in an inch of water and walk right by when a mere nudge would save the baby's life. Law students are taught that if someone is choking on a chicken bone in a restaurant, not only are other patrons not required to give the Heimlich maneuver,[5] call an ambulance, or

> ❶ **EMOTIONAL APPEALS**
> What **loaded words** can you find in the first two paragraphs?

---

1. **paparazzi** (pä′pä·rät′tsē) *n.:* photographers (especially intrusive photographers who take candid pictures of celebrities).
2. **Princess Diana:** Diana, Princess of Wales (1961–1997), who was killed in a highly publicized car crash in Paris on August 31, 1997. Photographers were later criticized for taking photos of the accident without trying to help the victims.
3. **Good Samaritan:** someone who unselfishly helps others in need. The term comes from a Bible parable (see page 278).
4. **civil or criminal law:** Civil law is the body of law relating to individuals' private rights; criminal law deals with crimes and their punishments.
5. **Heimlich maneuver:** emergency technique used to remove something blocking a person's windpipe by delivering a sudden, sharp, upward blow to the abdomen below the ribs.

Vocabulary

allegations (al′ə·gā′shənz) *n.:* in law, assertions, or positive statements, made without proof.

depraved (dē·prāvd′) *adj.:* immoral.

A paramedic assists an accident victim at the scene of a car crash.

do CPR,[6] but in fact the other patrons could, without violating any law, even dance around the gasping victim, singing, "Chicken bone! Chicken bone! Choking on a chicken bone!" ②

Under American law, liability generally exists for action, not inaction. We are each responsible for the harm we cause to others due to the lack of reasonable care. If my careless actions, however innocent, injure you, you have the right to sue me for your damages. Yet even if I maliciously, hatefully, and with evil intent stand by and watch you die without giving simple assistance, there is no legal remedy. This is indecent and should be changed. It is time to join with countries like France and insist that there be legal consequences for turning one's back on someone in desperate need. ③

Why do so many people ignore the needs of accident and crime victims? Rationalizations range from fear that getting involved will be unduly time consuming or cause personal injury to the Good Samaritan to doubts as to what to do in a crisis. While the untrained should not attempt medical assistance, it takes so little time and effort to phone paramedics.[7]

The real reason people don't reach out is because they feel disconnected from strangers in need. Yet the child at risk, the injured motorist, the choking restaurant patron could be any one of us or our loved ones. If each of us recognized a moral responsibility to come to the aid of others, we would all gain the benefits of a stronger and safer community. ④

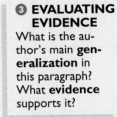

② **EVALUATING TONE**
What **tone** does this paragraph have? What phrases and sentences create the tone?

③ **EVALUATING EVIDENCE**
What is the author's main **generalization** in this paragraph? What **evidence** supports it?

④ **EVALUATING EVIDENCE**
What **types of evidence** have the authors used to support their argument in this article? Cite examples of each type.

---

6. **CPR:** short for "cardiopulmonary resuscitation," an emergency first-aid technique using cardiac massage and mouth-to-mouth breathing to keep someone alive.

7. **paramedics** (par′ə·med′iks) *n.:* people who are trained to provide emergency medical services.

Vocabulary

liability (lī′ə·bil′ə·tē) *n.:* legal obligation or responsibility to make good a damage or loss.

rationalizations (rash′ən·ə·lə·zā′shənz) *n.:* seemingly reasonable excuses or explanations for one's behavior—but not the real reasons.

Good Samaritans U.S.A. Are Afraid to Act

from *The Virginian-Pilot*, September 15, 1997

Ann Sjoerdsma

On the streets of Paris and other European cities, as we've learned since Princess Diana's fatal crash on August 31, passersby—even pursuing paparazzi—are required by law to assist victims of accidents. To be "Good Samaritans."

On the streets of most-towns, U.S.A., passersby who happen upon an accident—even physicians—can look the other way, ignore the victims. We have no legal obligation to assist.

Thanks to our English common-law origins,[1] Americans have a legal system strong on individualism, whereas Europeans, whose "civil law" is Roman, prize social solidarity. ❶

> ❶ **PARAPHRASING GENERALIZATIONS**
> In your own words, explain the **generalization** the author makes here.

Increasingly, however, in reaction to cases of callous indifference, states such as Minnesota and Wisconsin are mandating citizen help in emergencies. They are imposing on us a duty to assist, provided we don't put ourselves at risk.

As much as I'd like to encourage compassion and community, I think it's too late to legislate such morality. It's too late because it's too dangerous. This isn't France.

The Good Samaritan of Biblical parable didn't have to fear that the man he found beaten and robbed in the road was feigning injury and might ambush him. He also didn't have to worry about being sued. Today's Good Samaritan U.S.A. does.

Instead of compelling reluctant or even incompetent people to intervene, we should concentrate on protecting Good Samaritans who act now, without force of law. ❷

> ❷ **EVALUATING EVIDENCE**
> What two **reasons** has the writer previously given to support the opinion in this paragraph?

All states have "Good-Sam" statutes, but "they're all over the place," says Ken King of the Dallas-based American College of Emergency Physicians.

In general, if a Good Samaritan does what a "reasonable person"—in France, he's called a *bon père de famille*[2]—would do under the circumstances, he won't be held liable in negligence[3] for any harm he may cause the accident victim.

But he still might get sued.

Let me back up a bit. . . .

At common law there was no duty to

---

1. **English common-law origins:** reference to the English system of laws based on custom, usage, and legal decisions that forms the basis of the American legal system.

2. ***bon père de famille*** (bôn per də fä·mē′y′): French expression for "good family man."
3. **liable in negligence:** legally responsible to pay for loss or damage caused by *not* doing something.

Vocabulary

solidarity (säl′ə · dar′ə · tē) *n.:* complete unity in a group or organization.

callous (kal′əs) *adj.:* unfeeling.

feigning (fān′iŋ) *v.:* pretending.

render aid to a person in an emergency. A man could sit on a dock, smoke a cigar, and watch a person drown without risking any civil or criminal liability.

But there were exceptions.

A key one was a "special relationship" between the victim and the would-be rescuer. Certain people have a duty of care toward others because of their relationship, usually one of dependency: the physician toward his patient, the shopkeeper toward his customer, the employer-employee, parent-child.

If that man on the dock were a lifeguard, he'd have to dive in. Duty would call.

But suppose the man on the dock—or a passerby on the road—attempts to rescue the victim, does a poor job of it, and actually worsens the situation? Can he just quit? Others may have held up their rescues in reliance on his efforts.

No, a non-duty can become an affirmative duty after a person chooses to intervene. At common law, interfering had its price. Which is why we have "Good Samaritan" statutes[4] —to make it clear that good-faith efforts voluntarily undertaken by would-be rescuers, especially physicians, who lobbied for these laws, are protected and encouraged.

California passed the first Good Samaritan law in 1959.

Ironically, however, these statutes, which typically do not grant absolute immunity, have confused the issue. Why? Because they have to be construed, and when lawyers are around, interpretations of seemingly clear terms multiply.

North California law shields from civil liability "any person who renders first aid or emergency assistance" at a motor-vehicle accident unless the person's actions amount to "wanton[5] conduct or intentional wrongdoing."

---

4. **statutes** (stach′o͞ots) *n.*: laws.
5. **wanton** (wänt′'n) *adj.*: deliberately harmful; immoral.

Though it may seem unlikely that Good Samaritans would act wantonly, the term is subject to a lawyer's spin. And what exactly are the limits of "first aid" and "emergency assistance"?

Virginia, which has exemplary[6] Good-Sam laws covering a variety of personnel and crises, indemnifies "any person who, in good faith, renders emergency care or assistance, without compensation"[7] to injured people at an accident, fire, or other "life-threatening emergency."

Does this law safeguard doctors?

Though physicians without "a duty to treat" (based on an existing doctor-patient relationship) rarely get sued for their emergency treatment, lawyers can be creative about arguing that such a duty has arisen.

I wish we could do as the French do. But our nation is much too litigious[8] and dangerous. The "duty to assist" criminal laws that Minnesota and Wisconsin have enacted are largely symbolic, and likely to be selectively enforced.

For Americans, moral conscience, not legal duty, remains the best guide to emergency aid. But if ever there were an argument for a cellular phone, the plight of the Good Samaritan is it. ❸

> ❸ **EVALUATING EVIDENCE**
> Cite **evidence** the writer has given in her article to support the **generalizations** made in these last two paragraphs.

---

6. **exemplary** (eg · zem′plə · rē) *adj.*: serving as a good example; worth imitating.
7. **compensation** *n.*: payment.
8. **litigious** (li · tij′əs) *adj.*: quick to sue.

Vocabulary

immunity (i · myo͞on′ə · tē) *n.*: freedom from a legal obligation.

construed (kən · stro͞od′) *v.*: interpreted.

indemnifies (in · dem′ni · fīz′) *v.*: in a legal sense, protects.

Analyzing Informational Text

Reading Check

1. What event prompted the writing of both opinion pieces?
2. Explain France's good-Samaritan law.
3. Under common law, what is a person's duty when it comes to helping a stranger in an emergency?
4. Which states are mentioned in the articles as having good-Samaritan laws or statutes?

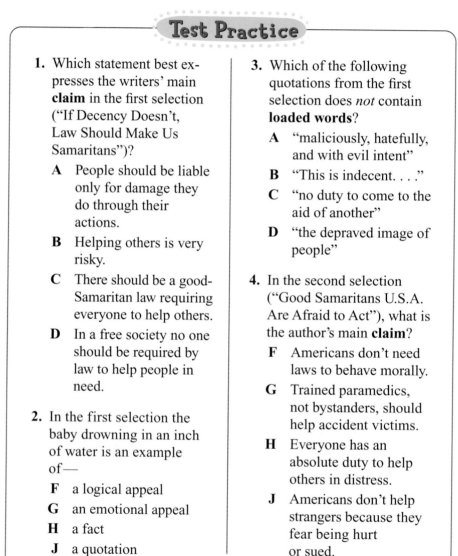

Test Practice

1. Which statement best expresses the writers' main **claim** in the first selection ("If Decency Doesn't, Law Should Make Us Samaritans")?

   A People should be liable only for damage they do through their actions.

   B Helping others is very risky.

   C There should be a good-Samaritan law requiring everyone to help others.

   D In a free society no one should be required by law to help people in need.

2. In the first selection the baby drowning in an inch of water is an example of—

   F a logical appeal
   G an emotional appeal
   H a fact
   J a quotation

3. Which of the following quotations from the first selection does *not* contain **loaded words**?

   A "maliciously, hatefully, and with evil intent"
   B "This is indecent. . . ."
   C "no duty to come to the aid of another"
   D "the depraved image of people"

4. In the second selection ("Good Samaritans U.S.A. Are Afraid to Act"), what is the author's main **claim**?

   F Americans don't need laws to behave morally.
   G Trained paramedics, not bystanders, should help accident victims.
   H Everyone has an absolute duty to help others in distress.
   J Americans don't help strangers because they fear being hurt or sued.

SKILLS FOCUS

Reading Skills
Evaluate author arguments.

5. In the second selection the author expresses disappointment because the state laws that have been passed protecting good Samaritans—

A are not consistent for every state

B are unnecessary

C have not been passed in enough states to evaluate their effectiveness

D confuse the issue because they are subject to varying legal interpretations

6. In the second selection the references to North Carolina and Virginia good-Samaritan laws are examples of—

F facts

G loaded words

H anecdotes

J statistics

7. To support her **argument,** the author of the second selection relies most heavily on—

A quotations from experts

B emotional appeals

C examples and facts

D statistics

8. Both articles seem to blame the difficulties in helping accident victims in the United States on the—

F U.S. legal system

G lack of adequate paramedic services

H decline of values and religion in the United States

J high number of car accidents on U.S. highways

Constructed Response

In a short essay, evaluate the **credibility** of the **arguments** in the two opinion pieces you have just read. First, summarize the writers' main **claim** in each piece. Then, evaluate the **evidence** and other support the writers used in their arguments. Finally, tell which article you found more convincing, and explain why.

Vocabulary Development

Jargon: Legalese—Words That Lawyers Use

If someone trips over your outstretched foot, falls, and breaks a leg, are you *liable*—or are you *indemnified*? If that person sues you, are you the *plaintiff* or the *defendant*? Law—like every profession, hobby, and sport—has its own **jargon,** or specialized vocabulary. You already know a lot of legalese (the jargon that lawyers use) from watching TV shows and movies about crime, detectives, and courtroom trials.

PRACTICE 1

Choose one of these Word Bank words to fill in each blank below: *allegations, liability, immunity, indemnifies*. Use **context clues** to figure out which word goes where.

1. The judge charged the defendant with _____ for the damages.

2. Are you sure this insurance policy _____ the homeowner against losses caused by flooding?

3. She offered no documents or other proof to support her _____ of wrongdoing at her place of employment.

4. The defendant asked for _____ in exchange for testifying against members of his gang.

Use a Word, and "Own" It

PRACTICE 2

When you can use a word correctly, you should feel that you "own" it. Follow the instructions below for each item, writing at least one sentence that uses the underlined word.

1. Use the word <u>depraved</u> in a sentence from a movie review of a violent horror film.

2. Use the word <u>rationalizations</u> in a note to your teacher explaining why your research paper is a week late.

3. Write a sentence from a TV newscast reporting a landslide election victory in your community; use the word <u>solidarity</u>.

4. In a letter to a friend, use the word <u>callous</u> in a sentence explaining why your feelings are hurt.

5. Describe a person who is <u>feigning</u> interest in a boring speech.

6. Write a sentence a politician might use who felt her remarks had been misinterpreted; use <u>construed</u>.

SKILLS FOCUS

Vocabulary Skills
Understand jargon. Demonstrate word knowledge.

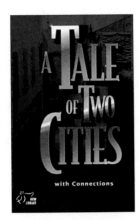

FICTION

"It Is a Far, Far Better Thing . . ."

Sydney Carton is a lazy ne'er-do-well who is disappointed by the course his life has taken. Charles Darnay is a French nobleman whose good deeds can't save him from a certain death. These two men's lives are at the heart of Charles Dickens's *A Tale of Two Cities*—a novel about the passion, power, and discord of the French Revolution and an unlikely hero who sacrifices everything for a friend.

This title is available in the HRW Library.

FICTION

Forbidden Love

When Shinji first glimpsed Hatsue resting on the sand at twilight, he thought she was the most beautiful girl he had ever seen. What begins as an awkward friendship soon blossoms into a relationship of great tenderness and trust. Soon the young couple's families are doing everything to tear them apart—and Shinji must prove his worth at great risk to himself. Set in a small Japanese fishing village, Yukio Mishima's *The Sound of Waves* is one of the great love stories of the twentieth century.

FICTION

A Navajo Romance

Oliver La Farge's *Laughing Boy* takes us back to the American Southwest in 1915. Laughing Boy is an idealistic young man who follows the traditional ways of his Navajo culture. The woman he loves, Slim Girl, has been stripped of her heritage and forced to attend white-run schools. These two young people enter into a marriage marked by miscommunication and strife. Will their love be enough to hold them together, or will a fateful turn of events be their undoing?

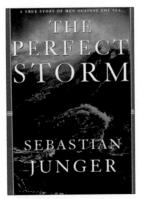

NONFICTION

Stormy Weather

What began as a routine swordfishing expedition became a nightmare for six young fishermen from Gloucester, Massachusetts. A freakish combination of three weather systems resulted in *The Perfect Storm*—a monstrous tempest with one-hundred-foot waves that overpowered the *Andrea Gail*'s crew on one fateful night in October. This riveting true story by Sebastian Junger boasts many heroes: the fishermen, the search-and-rescue crews, and the courageous families of the men who vanished at sea.

Writing a Persuasive Essay

Writing Assignment
Write a persuasive essay on an issue about which you have a strong opinion.

In Roger Rosenblatt's essay "The Man in the Water," you read about several heroes who made a difference for crash victims in the frozen waters of the Potomac River. Have you ever wanted to make a difference? Perhaps you want to change laws governing an endangered species' habitat or motivate people to do volunteer work in your community. Writing a persuasive essay on an issue is one way to turn your ideas into a reality and to make a difference in others' lives.

Prewriting

Choose an Issue

Powerful Beliefs By definition, an **issue** is something about which people have opposing opinions. As you choose an issue to write about, keep in mind that you will probably not convince anyone to agree with you if you do not feel strongly about the issue you choose. To find an issue that matters to you, watch television news shows for current issues, or brainstorm with classmates about issues that affect your school or community.

State Your Position

No Fence-Sitting Allowed You've chosen an issue. Now make your position, or opinion, on the issue absolutely clear by writing a focused **opinion statement** that names the issue and states your position on it. The following notes show the opinion statement one student wrote.

> [position]   [issue]
> State government should not create a law to limit the noise levels coming from car stereos.

Consider Your Purpose and Audience

Rabble-Rousing Once you've written an opinion statement, your **purpose** for writing should be clear—to convince others to share your opinion or to take the action you recommend. Next, consider who your **audience** will be. Obviously, you don't need to worry about people who agree with you. Instead, you need to concern yourself with those who either disagree with you or have no opinion at all. Consider this audience by answering the questions on the next page.

SKILLS FOCUS

Writing Skills
Write a persuasive essay. Choose an issue, and state your position. Consider purpose and audience.

- **What are my audience's concerns?** Think about **biases,** or prejudices, your audience might have. Be prepared to address any objections, or **counterarguments,** readers may propose.

TIP Readers' counter-arguments can also be called **counterclaims.**

- **What are my audience's expectations?** Your audience will expect a tightly reasoned **argument** that includes solid reasons supported by evidence. Read on to learn how to meet this expectation.

Support Your Opinion

Voice of Reason Strong **reasons** are the foundation of a persuasive argument. The reasons you give to back up your opinion statement will communicate your perspective on the issue and show why you think your opinion is correct. Your reasons should include the **rhetorical devices** of logical appeals, emotional appeals, and ethical appeals.

- **Logical appeals** speak to your readers' minds. They rely on your audience's ability to be reasonable and to use their common sense.

TIP Your teacher may want you to include more logical appeals than emotional or ethical appeals in your essay.

- **Emotional appeals** speak to readers' emotions, such as sympathy, fear, and hope.

- **Ethical appeals** appeal to your readers' ethics, or moral values. They rely upon commonly accepted beliefs or values. For example, honesty and fairness are values that most people accept as worthwhile. A writer uses an ethical appeal to establish that he or she is **credible,** or trustworthy.

Trust the Evidence It's not enough to state your opinion and tell why people should agree with you. You also need to provide **evidence** that supports your reasons. You can gather evidence through research or by interviewing local experts on your topic. The chart below shows the kinds of evidence you can look for while researching.

TYPES OF EVIDENCE	
Facts	information that can be proven true. Some facts are in the form of **statistics,** or numerical information.
Examples	specific instances of an idea or situation
Expert opinions	statements (either **quotations** or **paraphrases**) by people who are considered experts on the issue
Analogies	comparisons that show the similarities between two otherwise unrelated facts or ideas
Case studies	examples from scientific studies
Anecdotes	brief, personal stories that illustrate a point

SKILLS FOCUS

Writing Skills
Support your opinion.

Make sure that all of your evidence has the three *R*'s. It should be

Relevant—tied closely to your issue

Reliable—from trustworthy sources

Representative—not all from one or two sources

In the chart below, a student lists several reasons—containing logical, emotional, and ethical appeals—to explain why a law should not be passed to limit the noise levels of car stereos. She also gives at least two pieces of evidence for each of her reasons.

Opinion: The state government should not create a law to limit the noise levels coming from car stereos.

Reasons	Evidence
There are laws about disturbing the peace that cover this situation. (contains logical appeal)	**Fact:** Noise pollution laws exist. **Expert opinion:** Sheriff Tharpe says that he just enforces existing laws.
A law like this will add to the burden of overworked police. (contains emotional appeal)	**Fact:** information from newspaper article about police-staffing shortages **Anecdote:** John's father, Deputy Marquez, working double shifts **Expert opinion:** Deputy Marquez: officers spend too much time enforcing misdemeanor laws.
Singling out noise from car stereos is a form of discrimination. (contains ethical appeal)	**Fact:** Other public noises are loud but do not have laws against them. **Examples:** the noise at football games and other places

DO THIS ➤ Create a chart like the one above in which you list the reasons and evidence that you will give to support your opinion statement.

Organize Your Essay

The Importance of Order The way you organize your essay is important to its effectiveness. Most writers of persuasive essays arrange their reasons in **order of importance.** Some writers feel that it is important to grab the audience's attention immediately by beginning with the strongest reason. Others feel that it is more effective to put the strongest reason last to leave the audience with a powerful last impression. Decide which order you prefer, and number the reasons in your support chart in the order in which you want to present them.

SKILLS FOCUS

Writing Skills
Organize your essay in order of importance.

PRACTICE & APPLY 1 Follow the instructions in this section to choose an issue, write an opinion statement, gather support, and organize your ideas.

Writing

Writing a Persuasive Essay

A Writer's Framework		
Introduction	**Body**	**Conclusion**
• Grab your readers' attention by asking a question, relating an anecdote, or presenting a startling statistic. • Give background information so readers understand the issue. • Give an opinion statement that clearly states your position on the issue.	• Give at least three reasons that support your opinion statement. • Make sure your reasons reflect logical, emotional, and ethical appeals. • Organize the reasons in an effective way to reach your audience. • Provide at least two pieces of evidence for each reason.	• Restate, but do not repeat, your opinion. • Summarize the reasons for your opinion if you like. • Include a call to action that tells readers what they can do to help change a situation.

A Writer's Model

Music to Whose Ears?

Warm spring weather had finally arrived. I got in the passenger seat of my brother's car. He got in the driver's seat. We rolled down the windows, and he popped a CD in the stereo, turned up the volume, and headed out for the lake. This is a recipe for a great feeling and harmless fun, right? Some state senators do not think so. They have proposed a law that bans car speakers above a certain size and sets legal volume levels. This law is misguided and unfair. State government should not create a law to limit the noise levels coming from car stereos.

Some people may think that a law should be passed because they believe loud car stereos are a public nuisance—or even dangerous. However, existing state laws already cover the problem of loud noises. According to Richard Tharpe, Hamilton County sheriff, "Right now we can arrest people for disturbing the peace, and state law even sets noise pollution levels. So a new law just doesn't seem necessary." In addition, if a stereo causes a traffic accident—which Tharpe notes is uncommon and hard to prove—the driver can be charged. However, in the past five years, only one such accident has been reported. To institute the proposed law, then, is simply unnecessary.

INTRODUCTION
Attention-grabbing opener

Background information

Opinion statement

BODY/Addresses counterargument

First reason: Logical appeal

Expert opinion

Fact and statistic

(continued)

(continued)

Second reason:
Emotional appeal

Fact
Anecdote

Expert opinion

Third reason:
Ethical appeal

Fact and examples

CONCLUSION
Restatement of
opinion

Summary of reasons

Call to action

Another reason the legislature should vote down this proposal is that it will add to the burden of already overworked police. A number of towns and cities in the state have admitted to staffing shortages. In fact, Deputy Dennis Marquez, the father of a close friend, has had to work double shifts the last six months in order to ensure that all patrols are covered. According to Deputy Marquez, this shortage results from officers spending too much of their time enforcing misdemeanor laws similar to the proposed ban on loud car stereos. Just because serious crime is no longer on the rise, the police should not have to add another misdemeanor to their workload. Do they really have time to point decibel monitors at passing cars?

The most compelling reason to put a halt to this proposal is that setting legal limits on the volume of car stereos is a form of discrimination. After all, many other public noises are just as loud. Parades and rallies often use high-volume sound trucks. Radio stations broadcast live from stores and parking lots. Loudspeakers, bands, and cheering crowds at football games can be heard for blocks. For example, the cheering during last week's victorious game against the Tigers could be heard as far away as 135th Street. Also, what about the noise from tools? I have been awakened from a peaceful sleep on many Saturday mornings by neighbors' lawnmowers, yet I see no proposals for laws to regulate noise made under these circumstances. Why should car stereos be singled out?

We all want our streets to be calm and safe, but the senators' approach is misguided. An existing law already addresses the problem, and creating a new one would cause more work for police officers. In addition, the new law would not take into account other noises. A law restricting the volume of car stereos is unnecessary and unfair, and each of us should write or call our legislators to say so.

INTERNET
More Writer's Models
Keyword: LE5 10-4

PRACTICE & APPLY 2 Now it's your turn to draft a persuasive essay. As you write, clearly state your opinion and use the strongest reasons and evidence to provide support. Make sure you organize the support in a way that will persuade your readers. Refer to the framework on page 297 and the Writer's Model above as guides.

Revising

Evaluate and Revise Your Paper

The Once-over, Twice Revising is possibly the most important part of the writing process. Read your paper at least twice. In the first reading, focus on the content and organization, using the guidelines below. In the second reading, focus on your essay's style, using the guidelines on page 300.

> **First Reading: Content and Organization** Use the chart below as a **think sheet.** The questions, tips, and revision techniques can help you look for ways to improve the content and organization of your persuasive essay. As you revise, consider your audience, purpose, and tone. Make changes that will appeal to your audience, match your purpose, and enhance a formal tone.

PEER REVIEW

Exchange your essay with a classmate. He or she may be able to spot reasons that need more evidence to support them.

Rubric: Writing a Persuasive Essay

Evaluation Questions	▶ Tips	▶ Revision Techniques
❶ Does the introduction grab the reader's attention and give background information on the issue? Does it present a clear opinion statement?	▶ **Put a check mark** by sentences that get the reader interested. **Put a star** by sentences that give background information on the issue. **Underline** the opinion statement.	▶ **Add** an interesting statement and background information. **Add** an opinion statement that clearly states your position on the issue.
❷ Does the essay include at least three reasons? Do the reasons contain logical, emotional, or ethical appeals?	▶ **Highlight** each reason. **Draw a box** around the part that indicates a logical, emotional, or ethical appeal.	▶ **Add** reasons that appeal to readers' logic, emotions, or ethics.
❸ Is each reason supported by at least two pieces of relevant evidence?	▶ **Circle** each piece of evidence (facts, examples, and so on). **Draw an arrow** from each item to the reason it supports.	▶ **Add** evidence to support your reasons. **Rearrange** evidence so it is in the paragraph with the reason it supports.
❹ Are the reasons organized effectively?	▶ **Number** reasons in the order of their importance. If the order seems illogical or ineffective, revise.	▶ **Rearrange** the reasons by putting the most important reason first or last.
❺ Does the conclusion restate the opinion on the issue? Does it include a call to action?	▶ **Underline** the sentence that restates the writer's opinion. **Put a check mark** next to sentences that make a call to action.	▶ **Add** a restatement of your opinion on the issue. **Add** a call to action.

Second Reading: Style To be persuasive, you must present your ideas forcefully. To maintain a powerful tone, avoid using too many passive sentences, in which the subject does not perform the action in the sentence. Instead, use the **active voice** to spur readers to action. The guidelines below can help you turn passive sentences into active ones.

Style Guidelines

Evaluation Question	▶ **Tip**	▶ **Revision Technique**
● **Does the essay include active-voice sentences?**	▶ **Put a minus sign** above each subject that does not perform the action in its sentence.	▶ **Rewrite** sentences so that the subject of the sentence performs the action of the verb.

ANALYZING THE REVISION PROCESS
Study these revisions, and answer the questions that follow.

> Some people may think that a law should be passed because
>
> they believe loud car stereos are a public nuisance—or even
>
> *However, existing state laws already cover the*
> dangerous. ∧According to Richard Tharpe, Hamilton County
> *problem of loud noises.*
>
> sheriff, "Right now we can arrest people for disturbing the
>
> peace, and state law even sets noise pollution levels. So a new
>
> *a stereo causes*
> law just doesn't seem necessary." In addition, if∧ ~~an accident is~~
>
> *a traffic accident*
> ~~caused by a stereo~~—which Tharpe notes is uncommon and
>
> hard to prove—the driver can be charged.

add (beside "dangerous" paragraph)

rewrite (beside "law just doesn't seem" paragraph)

Responding to the Revision Process
1. Why did the writer add the sentence before the quotation?
2. Why did the writer revise the last sentence?

SKILLS FOCUS

Writing Skills
Revise for content and style.

PRACTICE & APPLY 3 Use the guidelines on these pages to evaluate and revise the content, organization, and style of your essay. If a peer reviewed your essay, consider his or her comments, too.

Publishing

Proofread and Publish Your Essay

One More Time Don't ruin the impact of your well-crafted words by letting little mistakes show up in your final draft. Review your paper to make sure it is free of mistakes in grammar, spelling, and punctuation. If you find it hard to inspect your own paper for these mistakes, trade papers with a partner and examine each other's work closely.

A Wider Audience You cannot persuade anyone if you are the only one who reads your essay. Take the next step in making your opinion heard by publishing your essay. Here are some ideas to help you gain a wider reading audience for your persuasive essay.

- Submit your paper to the opinion page of your school or local newspaper.

- Submit your essay to a local Internet bulletin board where public exchanges are welcome.

- Turn your persuasive essay into a pamphlet that contains photos or graphics by using publishing software or graphic programs. With your teacher's permission, distribute pamphlets to your classmates.

- With a partner who opposes your position, debate the issue you chose for your essay. For more on **participating in a debate,** see page 302.

Reflect on Your Essay

Take a Deep Breath Now that the hard work is over, think about your essay and the process you used to create it. Answering the following questions can help you think about the process of writing a persuasive essay and identify ways you and others use persuasion outside this class.

- Which of the reasons in your paper do you think is the weakest or least convincing? How could you revise the reason or the evidence that supports it to make it more convincing?

- How did you go about finding reasons to support your opinion or evidence to support your reasons? For what other types of writing might you use the same process for gathering support?

- How do you see logical, emotional, and ethical appeals used in other areas of life such as at home, on television, and in politics?

PRACTICE & APPLY 4 First, proofread your essay. Then, choose one of the options above to publish your essay for an audience. Finally, answer the reflection questions.

TIP Check that you have used English-language **conventions** properly. For example, if you include a quotation from an expert as a piece of evidence, don't forget to use quotation marks properly. For more on **quotation marks,** see Quotation Marks, 13c–l, in the Language Handbook.

COMPUTER TIP

For more on **incorporating graphics,** see Designing Your Writing in the Writer's Handbook.

Writing Skills
Proofread, especially for correct use of quotation marks.

Participating in a Debate

Speaking Assignment

With other students, stage a debate in which you present both sides of an issue.

"That's debatable" is an expression people often use to cast doubt on something that has just been said. If a statement is debatable, good arguments can be made both for and against it. While a persuasive essay or speech presents only one side of an issue, a **debate** involves two teams on opposite sides of an issue who publicly compete for the hearts and minds of an audience.

Prepare for a Debate

A Winning Proposition If you are asked to participate in a debate, you must first know what proposition you will be debating. A **proposition** focuses on one narrow, controversial issue. The proposition suggests a change in the **status quo**—the current state of things—and is worded as a **resolution.** An example of a proposition is "Resolved: That Chavez High School should build a parking lot west of the main soccer fields." Most often the person in charge of the debate assigns the proposition that the teams will debate.

Participants in a debate are usually also assigned a side of the proposition—pro (for) or con (against). If you are participating in a debate, your challenge is to present a good argument, based on solid reasoning, for your side of the issue—regardless of your personal feelings on the issue.

Who's Who? A traditional debate requires two teams of two people each, plus a chairperson in charge of running the debate.

Affirmative Team The **affirmative team** argues that the proposition should be accepted. Because the affirmative team argues for a change in the status quo, it has the **burden of proof**—an obligation to prove that change must be made.

Negative Team The **negative team** argues that the proposition should be rejected and that the status quo should remain unchanged.

Chairperson A **chairperson** rules over a debate, keeping the debate organized, courteous, and fair. A debater may appeal to the chairperson if he or she believes that the other team has broken any rules.

Research the Proposition To debate effectively, you must prepare by thoroughly researching the proposition. First, identify the differences between your position and the other team's position. These differences often revolve around the following questions.

- Is there a significant problem?

- What is causing the problem?

SKILLS FOCUS

Listening and Speaking Skills
Participate in a debate.
Research the proposition.

- Would this proposition solve the problem?
- What would the proposition cost (in time, money, or other resources)?

Next, develop specific **reasons,** which may include rhetorical devices, that will show people why they should support your side of the proposition. In turn, you must also find **proof**—evidence to support each reason. Three types of evidence commonly used in debates are defined below.

Facts and Statistics **Facts** are statements that can be proven true. **Statistics** are information based on numbers. For example, the following statistic might support an argument proposing a new school parking lot: "Our parking lot has 150 spaces, yet 297 teachers, staff, and students drive to school."

Specific Instances **Specific instances** are examples that illustrate a point, such as, "Parents who come to school during school hours have said that they had to park their cars blocks away on residential streets."

Testimony **Testimony** includes comments or opinions from people who have studied or experienced the problem. Here is an example of supporting testimony: "According to Principal Cho, 'School parking is a serious problem. Students with after-school jobs need to drive rather than take the bus. We don't have enough space for all of them.'"

Be sure that all evidence—facts, statistics, specific instances, and testimony—that supports your reasons meets the tests in the chart below.

TIP Additional types of evidence you can use are case studies, anecdotes, and analogies. For more on **types of evidence,** see page 295.

TESTS FOR EVIDENCE

Evidence should have . . .	That means . . .
credibility	evidence should come from a source recognized as an authority on the subject. The source should be objective rather than biased toward one side of the issue.
validity	evidence should clearly support the position it is being used to support. Valid evidence should not be interpreted to support the opposite side of the issue.
relevance	evidence should have a close, logical relationship to the reason it supports. Relevant information is also recent enough to directly relate to the issue being addressed.

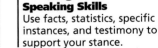

SKILLS FOCUS

Listening and Speaking Skills
Use facts, statistics, specific instances, and testimony to support your stance.

Organize Your Debate Information

To Each Its Own Organize the reasons and evidence you find into three categories.

- **Constructive arguments**—support for your side

- **Refutations**—attacks on the other side's position

- **Rebuttals**—material that answers challenges to your position

Constructive Speeches A traditional debate is divided into two parts: **constructive speeches** and **rebuttal speeches** (which include both rebuttals and refutations).

First, teams make **constructive speeches,** which build their arguments for or against the proposition.

- If you are presenting a constructive speech for the **affirmative** (pro) side of an issue, you should provide two to four reasons for your position, each reason backed with strong evidence.

- To present a constructive speech for the **negative** (con) side of an issue, plan to defend the status quo. In other words, your speech should make clear either that no problem exists or that any existing problem can be corrected through existing solutions. Again, you will use reasons and evidence to build your position.

Rebuttal Speeches After the constructive speeches, both teams make **rebuttal speeches.** In spite of their name, rebuttal speeches should include both rebuttals and refutations. In a **rebuttal** you rebuild your own arguments that the other team has damaged, while in a **refutation** you attempt to disprove your opponents' constructive arguments. Effective refutations focus on these elements:

- **Quantity**—Does the other team provide enough evidence?

- **Quality**—Is the other team's evidence credible, valid, and relevant?

- **Reasoning**—Has the other team drawn logical conclusions based on the evidence?

Making an effective rebuttal speech depends on your ability to listen to the opposing team's arguments and respond with convincing arguments and evidence of your own.

Conduct the Debate

Present Yourself As a debater, you must follow proper **debate etiquette.** No matter what your opponent may say, you should remain respectful and courteous, avoiding sarcasm and personal attacks. Be polite. It is traditional to refer to other debate participants with terms such as "the first affirmative speaker" or "my worthy opponent."

TIP Because time for rebuttal speeches is short, focus only on the most important points the opposing team made, not on everything they said.

Listening and Speaking Skills
Organize your debate into constructive arguments, refutations, and rebuttals.

Present Your Ideas Your reasons and evidence will have the greatest impact if you are well prepared. As you speak, maintain eye contact with your audience and speak slowly, clearly, and loudly enough that everyone can understand you. Use your voice and facial expressions to emphasize important points.

Speaking in Turn A traditional debate follows this schedule. Each team member delivers one constructive and one rebuttal speech.

TRADITIONAL DEBATE SCHEDULE

First Part: Constructive Speeches		Second Part: Rebuttal Speeches
(10 minutes each)		(5 minutes each)
1st Affirmative Team Speaker	I	1st Negative Team Speaker
1st Negative Team Speaker	n	1st Affirmative Team Speaker
2nd Affirmative Team Speaker	t e r m i s s i o n	2nd Negative Team Speaker
2nd Negative Team Speaker		2nd Affirmative Team Speaker

And the Winner Is . . . Judges usually determine the winner of a debate. Occasionally, an audience may vote to determine the winning team. To make your own judgment about which team won a debate, answer the questions in the following chart. You can use the chart to evaluate both the affirmative and negative teams.

QUESTIONS FOR JUDGING A DEBATE

Content

1. What arguments did the team provide to prove or disprove that a significant problem exists? Were these arguments effective? Explain why or why not.

2. Did the team convince you that the proposition is or is not the best solution to solving the problem (if any exists)? Explain.

3. What reasons and evidence did the team provide to support the case? How credible, valid, and relevant was the evidence?

4. How did the team refute and rebut arguments made by the opposing team? Were the rebuttal speeches effective? Explain why or why not.

Delivery

1. How confident and well prepared were the speakers? How could they improve their delivery?

2. How well did each speaker maintain eye contact? How effective were the rate and volume at which each spoke?

3. Describe any incidents in which the speakers did not observe proper debate etiquette.

PRACTICE & APPLY 5 Follow the steps in this workshop to plan, participate in, and judge a debate.

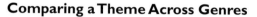

Comparing a Theme Across Genres

Test Practice

DIRECTIONS: Read the following short story and poem. Then, read and respond to the questions that follow.

What Happened During the Ice Storm
Jim Heynen

One winter there was a freezing rain. "How beautiful!" people said when things outside started to shine with ice. But the freezing rain kept coming. Tree branches glistened like glass. Then broke like glass. Ice thickened on the windows until everything outside blurred. Farmers moved their livestock into the barns, and most animals were safe. But not the pheasants. Their eyes froze shut.

Some farmers went ice-skating down the gravel roads with clubs to harvest pheasants that sat helplessly in the roadside ditches. The boys went out into the freezing rain to find pheasants too. They saw dark spots along a fence. Pheasants, all right. Five or six of them. The boys slid their feet along slowly, trying not to break the ice that covered the snow. They slid up close to the pheasants. The pheasants pulled their heads down between their wings. They couldn't tell how easy it was to see them huddled there.

The boys stood still in the icy rain. Their breath came out in slow puffs of steam. The pheasants' breath came out in quick little white puffs. Some of them lifted their heads and turned them from side to side, but they were blindfolded with ice and didn't flush. The boys had not brought clubs, or sacks, or anything but themselves. They stood over the pheasants, turning their own heads, looking at each other, each expecting the other to do something. To pounce on a pheasant, or to yell "Bang!"

SKILLS FOCUS

Pages 306–309 cover
Literary Skills
Compare a theme across genres.

306 Collection 4 Comparing Themes • Evaluating Arguments: Pro and Con

Things around them were shining and dripping with icy rain. The barbed-wire fence. The fence posts. The broken stems of grass. Even the grass seeds. The grass seeds looked like little yolks inside gelatin whites. And the pheasants looked like unborn birds glazed in egg white. Ice was hardening on the boys' caps and coats. Soon they would be covered with ice too.

Then one of the boys said, "Shh." He was taking off his coat, the thin layer of ice splintering in flakes as he pulled his arms from the sleeves. But the inside of the coat was dry and warm. He covered two of the crouching pheasants with his coat, rounding the back of it over them like a shell. The other boys did the same. They covered all the helpless pheasants. The small gray hens and the larger brown cocks. Now the boys felt the rain soaking through their shirts and freezing. They ran across the slippery fields, unsure of their footing, the ice clinging to their skin as they made their way toward the blurry lights of the house.

Gracious Goodness

Marge Piercy

On the beach where we had been idly
telling the shell coins
cat's paw, crossbarred Venus, china cockle,
we both saw at once
5   the sea bird fall to the sand
and flap grotesquely.
He had taken a great barbed hook
out through the cheek and fixed
in the big wing.
10 He was pinned to himself to die,
a royal tern with a black crest blown back
as if he flew in his own private wind.
He felt good in my hands, not fragile
but muscular and glossy and strong,
15 the beak that could have split my hand
opening only to cry
as we yanked on the barbs.
We borrowed a clippers, cut and drew
        out the hook.
Then the royal tern took off, wavering,
20 lurched twice,
then acrobat returned to his element,
        dipped,
zoomed, and sailed out to dive for a fish.
Virtue: what a sunrise in the belly.
Why is there nothing
25 I have ever done with anybody
that seems to me so obviously right?

1. In "What Happened During the Ice Storm," which element is important in establishing the **theme**?
   A Setting
   B Dialogue
   C Point of view
   D Tone

2. Which of the following influences provides the main source of **conflict** in the short story?
   F The boys' sympathy for the birds
   G The farmers' actions
   H The pretty landscape
   J The boys' fear of the birds

3. In "Gracious Goodness" the **narrator** seems to experience —
   A conflict
   B boredom
   C satisfaction
   D regret

4. One way the story *differs* from the poem is in the story's —
   F unexpected ending
   G humorous tone
   H first-person narration
   J outdoor setting

5. Which word *best* describes the **tone** of the poem?
   A angry
   B ironic
   C sad
   D reflective

6. Which statement *best* describes the common **theme** of both selections?
   F Helping others can be a rewarding experience.
   G Nature is both inspiring and terrifying.
   H No matter what we do, death comes to all living things.
   J Life is full of unexpected turns.

7. Despite their different **genres,** these two selections share a basically similar —
   A setting and plot
   B plot and cast of characters
   C point of view and theme
   D theme and subject matter

8. How does the **genre** of each selection affect the way the **theme** is developed?
   F Since the poem is shorter, its theme is not as rich.
   G Since the poem is shorter, it expresses its theme and subject matter more compactly.
   H The story can reveal characters' thoughts, but the poem cannot.
   J Since the poem has no plot, its theme must be inferred from imagery.

Constructed Response

9. Describe the character traits of the boys in the story and the narrator in the poem. Use details from the texts to support your answer.

Collection 4: Skills Review

Vocabulary Skills

Test Practice

Multiple-Meaning Words

DIRECTIONS: Choose the answer in which the underlined word is used in the same way as it is used in each numbered passage from "And of Clay Are We Created."

1. "I watched that hell on the first morning broadcast, cadavers of people and animals awash in the <u>current</u> of new rivers formed overnight . . . ."
   A They paddled against the <u>current</u>.
   B Turn off the electric <u>current</u> before you install the new light.
   C She is critical of <u>current</u> government policies.
   D What was the general <u>current</u> of the discussion?

2. "Despite the quality of the transmission, I could hear his voice <u>break</u>, and I loved him more than ever."
   F He took a <u>break</u> from studying.
   G A <u>break</u> in a pipe caused the leak.
   H "Give me a <u>break</u>," she told the wildly barking dog.
   J There was a sudden <u>break</u> in the singer's high note.

3. "The screen reduced the disaster to a single <u>plane</u> and accentuated the tremendous distance that separated me from Rolf Carlé; nonetheless, I was there with him."
   A We heard a <u>plane</u> circling above.
   B A picture painted on a flat <u>plane</u> can look three-dimensional.
   C Her comments brought the discussion to a higher <u>plane</u>.
   D Use a <u>plane</u> to smooth rough boards.

4. "I could not <u>bear</u> the wait at home, so I went to National Television, . . ."
   F Remember to <u>bear</u> to the right.
   G He tried to <u>bear</u> in mind the cost.
   H The project will soon <u>bear</u> results.
   J She could hardly <u>bear</u> the pain.

5. "For years he had been a familiar <u>figure</u> in newscasts, reporting live at the scene of battles and catastrophes with awesome tenacity."
   A Models must have a slender <u>figure</u>.
   B She was a famous <u>figure</u> in history.
   C The skater completed a <u>figure</u> eight.
   D The <u>figure</u> for the sale was high.

6. "Her <u>tone</u> was humble, as if apologizing for all the fuss."
   F He set a moral <u>tone</u> for the others.
   G The painting had a rich <u>tone</u> of red.
   H Exercise can improve muscle <u>tone</u>.
   J He always has a friendly <u>tone</u>.

7. "He took excessive risks as an <u>exercise</u> of courage, training by day to conquer the monsters that tormented him by night."
   A Rowing is a form of <u>exercise</u>.
   B That grammar <u>exercise</u> is too easy.
   C Losing an election is an <u>exercise</u> in humility.
   D Lorna is practicing a finger <u>exercise</u> on the piano.

SKILLS FOCUS

Vocabulary Skills
Understand multiple-meaning words.

Collection 4: Skills Review

Writing Skills

DIRECTIONS: Read the following paragraph from a draft of a student's persuasive essay. Then, read the questions below it. Choose the best answer to each question.

(1) Every day, children are bombarded with violent behavior on TV, and parents need to take action to protect their children. (2) With each passing year, the amount of violence on TV increases dramatically. (3) Watching too much TV has negative effects on children's health. (4) However, parental monitoring of TV programs is not enough. (5) Not only should parents remove televisions from the reach of vulnerable children, but they should also explain to those children that they are only allowed to watch TV with an adult.

1. Which sentence could be added as evidence to support the claim that there is too much violence on TV?

   A A recent study shows that 85 percent of cable TV contains violence.

   B Most of the violent programming comes on late at night.

   C Think about the violence in the television shows you watch.

   D Many parents do not watch television with their children.

2. How might the writer address the bias of some readers who think parental monitoring is a reasonable solution?

   F by telling them that their opinion will be discussed in detail at a later time

   G by ignoring their opinion

   H by providing evidence—only 38 percent of parents monitor their children

   J by restating his position

3. Which sentence would add an emotional appeal?

   A Children should read books.

   B Many TV shows contain violence.

   C Removing televisions from the reach of children is important.

   D Children often mimic what they see on TV—with harmful results.

4. Which of the following sentences should be deleted to improve the organization of the evidence?

   F 1   **H** 3

   G 2   **J** 5

5. If you were listening to the paragraph in a debate, which of the following would best state the speaker's position?

   A The amount of violence on TV rises each year.

   B Violent episodes are shown on many channels.

   C Parents should not allow children to watch TV unsupervised.

   D Children should not watch prime-time shows.

SKILLS FOCUS

Writing Skills
Write a persuasive essay.

Irony and Ambiguity

INFORMATIONAL READING FOCUS

GENERATING RESEARCH QUESTIONS AND EVALUATING SOURCES

irony is bitter truth

wrapped up in a little joke

—H. D.

The Human Condition (1934) by
René Magritte. Oil on canvas.

Peter Willi/SuperStock.

Elements of Literature

Irony and Ambiguity *by* John Leggett
SURPRISES AND UNCERTAINTIES

Good stories entertain us and offer some insight into human experience, those joys and sorrows that are common to us all. For the magic of storytelling to work, the story must first persuade us that it is life-like, which often means full of surprises and uncertainties. After all, we know that our own expectations are rarely fulfilled as we imagined they would be and that the future remains unknown. In fiction the representation of such surprises and un-certainties is often achieved through the use of **irony** and **ambiguity.**

Verbal Irony: Meaning Something Else

There are three kinds of irony, each of which involves some kind of contrast be-tween expectation and reality. **Verbal irony**—the simplest kind—is being used when someone *says* one thing but *means* the opposite. The man who remarks "You sure can pick 'em" to his friend whose team finished last or the woman who says "Fine day for a picnic" in the middle of a torrential rainfall is using verbal irony. When we recognize verbal irony, we often laugh in appreciation.

Situational Irony: Reversing Expectations

Situational irony is much more impor-tant to the storyteller than other kinds of irony. It describes an occurrence that is not just surprising; it is the *opposite* of what we expected. In an ironic situation what actually happens is so contrary to

our expectations that it seems to mock human intentions and the confidence with which we plan our futures. The ironic pos-sibility that some haughty rich man will come begging from us tomorrow or that a woman who is dreading tonight's party will meet her future husband there keeps life interesting.

Situational irony cuts deeply into our feelings. When irony is put to work in fiction, it is often what touches us most. Irony can move us toward tears or laugh-ter because we sense we are close to the truth of life.

Dramatic Irony: Withholding Knowledge

Dramatic irony is the kind of irony that occurs when *we* know what is in store for a character but the character does not know. This is called dramatic irony be-cause it's so often used in plays and films. In an action movie, for example, we know (but the hero doesn't know) that one of the cables of the elevator she's about to enter has been cut.

Dramatic irony is used in novels and short stories too. What about Little Red Riding Hood knocking innocently on Grandma's front door? We know about the wolf under Grandma's bedclothes, wearing her bonnet, but Little Red is unaware of the toothy surprise that awaits her.

Dramatic irony adds to our enjoyment of a story because it mimics life, which is forever pulling surprises on us. Irony of all kinds is somehow enormously satisfying, perhaps because we know instinctively that our carefully laid plans, ambitions, and strivings often come to little, whereas good luck (or bad) often finds unlikely targets.

Ambiguity: Multiple Meanings

While irony presents an outcome that is the opposite of what we expect, **ambiguity** offers us a choice of more than one meaning or interpretation. Ambiguity keeps us guessing, wondering, and reflecting. In an ambiguous story the choices are up in the air, but they are also ours for the taking. Think of the bright young singer who, after a terrible struggle, conquers the entertainment world and wins admiration and fame. By the end of the story, she is surrounded by fair-weather friends who insist she leave her past behind, including a boyfriend deeply troubled by her success. The confused hero then goes away alone on a long trip—and we are left to puzzle over her future. The point of ambiguity is to make us figure out our own interpretation of a story, our own reactions, based on the clues we uncover.

Ambiguity is not only rooted in a particular event or an ending, though. An ambiguous **theme** or **mood** can filter its way through an entire story. Is the tale of a nineteenth-century boy who becomes gravely ill from working in the coal mines—yet somehow retains his cheerful outlook—a moral lesson in keeping a positive attitude through hardship? Is it a comment on the society whose labor practices made him ill in the first place? Is the mood upbeat, tragic, or both? The opinions may vary from reader to reader as each finds a different answer within the delicate workings of the story.

Ambiguous stories generally linger in our minds the longest, because ambiguity challenges our imaginations. It gets us thinking and feeling, and it encourages us to talk about our reactions—to share our thoughts and ideas with others. What better purpose can a story have than that?

Imagine that you have been asked to contribute to a book that examines the many sides of irony, titled *The Irony of It All!* Review the discussion of irony in this essay, and use the chart below for a guide. Then, for each of the three types of **irony—verbal, situational,** and **dramatic—** come up with an example. Describe each example in a brief paragraph that you will contribute to the book. Be imaginative, but make sure your ironies ring true to life.

Verbal irony	Say one thing but mean the opposite	Example:
Situational irony	What happens is the opposite of what is expected	Example:
Dramatic irony	We know something a character does not know	Example:

Before You Read

Lamb to the Slaughter

Make the Connection
Quickwrite 🖉

Have you ever heard someone described as going "like a lamb to the slaughter"? The saying comes from the Bible, which describes many instances of lambs used as sacrifices. Roald Dahl chose that biblical **allusion,** or reference, as the title of his story. Knowing that, what do you think this story might be about? Jot down your ideas.

Literary Focus

Two Kinds of Irony

The story you are about to read starts out with a pleasant domestic scene that suddenly turns sinister. It's not scary the way a horror film is, but there are plenty of strange twists and surprises.

As you read the story, see if you can find both situational irony and dramatic irony. **Situational irony** occurs when something that happens is the opposite of what we would normally expect to happen or would find appropriate. In **dramatic irony** the reader knows something important that some or all of the characters do not know.

INTERNET

More About Roald Dahl
Keyword: LE5 10-5

Literary Skills
Understand situational irony and dramatic irony.

Reading Skills
Make predictions.

Reading Skills 📖

Making Predictions

When you read a story or a novel, your brain automatically darts ahead, wondering, "What's next? Then what happens? And then what? How will it end?" Part of the fun of reading comes from your providing answers—guesses—to these "what's next" questions. You **make predictions** based on what you know about the story's characters and events and what you know about real-life people.

Stories with **ironic** twists, turns, and surprises are deliciously satisfying for making predictions. As you read this story, jot down your predictions—whenever you think you know what's coming next.

Vocabulary Development

anxiety (aŋ·zī'ə·tē) *n.*: state of being worried or uneasy.

placid (plas'id) *adj.*: calm; tranquil.

luxuriate (lug·zhoor'ē·āt') *v.* (used with *in*): take great pleasure.

administered (ad·min'is·tərd) *v.* used as *adj.*: given; applied.

premises (prem'is·iz) *n.*: house or building and its surrounding property.

consoling (kən·sōl'iŋ) *v.* used as *adj.*: comforting.

hospitality (häs'pi·tal'ə·tē) *n.*: friendly, caring treatment of guests.

Lamb to the Slaughter

Roald Dahl

"It's the old story. Get the weapon,
and you've got the man."

The room was warm and clean, the curtains drawn, the two table lamps alight—hers and the one by the empty chair opposite. On the sideboard behind her, two tall glasses, soda water, whisky. Fresh ice cubes in the Thermos bucket.

Mary Maloney was waiting for her husband to come home from work.

Now and again she would glance up at the clock, but without <u>anxiety</u>, merely to please herself with the thought that each minute gone by made it nearer the time when he could come. There was a slow smiling air about her, and about everything she did. The drop of the head as she bent over her sewing was curiously tranquil. Her skin—for this was her sixth month with child—had acquired a wonderful translucent[1] quality, the mouth was soft, and the eyes, with their new <u>placid</u> look, seemed larger, darker than before.

---

1. **translucent** (trans·lōo'sənt) *adj.:* glowing; clear.

Vocabulary
anxiety (aŋ·zī'ə·tē) *n.:* state of being worried or uneasy.
placid (plas'id) *adj.:* calm; tranquil.

When the clock said ten minutes to five, she began to listen, and a few moments later, punctually as always, she heard the tires on the gravel outside, and the car door slamming, the footsteps passing the window, the key turning in the lock. She laid aside her sewing, stood up, and went forward to kiss him as he came in.

"Hullo, darling," she said.

"Hullo," he answered.

She took his coat and hung it in the closet. Then she walked over and made the drinks, a strongish one for him, a weak one for herself; and soon she was back again in her chair with the sewing, and he in the other, opposite, holding the tall glass with both his hands, rocking it so the ice cubes tinkled against the side.

For her, this was always a blissful time of day. She knew he didn't want to speak much until the first drink was finished, and she, on her side, was content to sit quietly, enjoying his company after the long hours alone in the house. She loved to luxuriate in the presence of this man, and to feel—almost as a sunbather feels the sun—that warm male glow that came out of him to her when they were alone together. She loved him for the way he sat loosely in a chair, for the way he came in a door, or moved slowly across the room with long strides. She loved the intent, far look in his eyes when they rested on her, the funny shape of the mouth, and especially the way he remained silent about his tiredness, sitting still with himself until the whisky had taken some of it away.

"Tired, darling?"

"Yes," he said. "I'm tired." And as he spoke, he did an unusual thing. He lifted his glass and drained it in one swallow although there was still half of it, at least half of it left. She wasn't really watching him, but she knew what he had done because she heard the ice cubes falling back against the bottom of the empty glass when he lowered his arm. He paused a moment, leaning forward in the chair, then he got up and went slowly over to fetch himself another.

"I'll get it!" she cried, jumping up.

"Sit down," he said.

When he came back, she noticed that the new drink was dark amber with the quantity of whisky in it.

"Darling, shall I get your slippers?"

"No."

She watched him as he began to sip the dark yellow drink, and she could see little oily swirls in the liquid because it was so strong.

"I think it's a shame," she said, "that when a policeman gets to be as senior as you, they keep him walking about on his feet all day long."

He didn't answer, so she bent her head again and went on with her sewing; but each time he lifted the drink to his lips, she heard the ice cubes clinking against the side of the glass.

"Darling," she said. "Would you like me to get you some cheese? I haven't made any supper because it's Thursday."

"No," he said.

"If you're too tired to eat out," she went on, "it's still not too late. There's plenty of meat and stuff in the freezer, and you can have it right here and not even move out of the chair."

Her eyes waited on him for an answer, a smile, a little nod, but he made no sign.

"Anyway," she went on, "I'll get you some cheese and crackers first."

"I don't want it," he said.

She moved uneasily in her chair, the large eyes still watching his face. "But you *must* have supper. I can easily do it here. I'd like to do it. We can have lamb chops. Or pork. Anything you want. Everything's in the freezer."

"Forget it," he said.

"But, darling, you *must* eat! I'll fix it anyway, and then you can have it or not, as you like."

She stood up and placed her sewing on the table by the lamp.

Vocabulary

luxuriate (lug·zhoor′ē·āt′) v. (used with *in*): take great pleasure.

"Sit down," he said. "Just for a minute, sit down."

It wasn't till then that she began to get frightened.

"Go on," he said. "Sit down."

She lowered herself back slowly into the chair, watching him all the time with those large, bewildered eyes. He had finished the second drink and was staring down into the glass, frowning.

"Listen," he said. "I've got something to tell you."

"What is it, darling? What's the matter?"

He had now become absolutely motionless, and he kept his head down so that the light from the lamp beside him fell across the upper part of his face, leaving the chin and mouth in shadow. She noticed there was a little muscle moving near the corner of his left eye.

"This is going to be a bit of a shock to you, I'm afraid," he said. "But I've thought about it a good deal and I've decided the only thing to do is tell you right away. I hope you won't blame me too much."

"This is going to be a bit of a shock to you, I'm afraid," he said.

And he told her. It didn't take long, four or five minutes at most, and she sat very still through it all, watching him with a kind of dazed horror as he went further and further away from her with each word.

"So there it is," he added. "And I know it's kind of a bad time to be telling you, but there simply wasn't any other way. Of course I'll give you money and see you're looked after. But there needn't really be any fuss. I hope not anyway. It wouldn't be very good for my job."

Her first instinct was not to believe any of it, to reject it all. It occurred to her that perhaps he hadn't even spoken, that she herself had imagined the whole thing. Maybe, if she went about her business and acted as though she hadn't been listening, then later, when she sort of woke up again, she might find none of it had ever happened.

"I'll get the supper," she managed to whisper, and this time he didn't stop her.

When she walked across the room she couldn't feel her feet touching the floor. She couldn't feel anything at all—except a slight nausea and a desire to vomit. Everything was automatic now—down the steps to the cellar, the light switch, the deep freeze, the hand inside the cabinet taking hold of the first object it met. She lifted it out, and looked at it. It was wrapped in paper, so she took off the paper and looked at it again.

A leg of lamb.

All right then, they would have lamb for supper. She carried it upstairs, holding the thin bone-end of it with both her hands, and as she went through the living room, she saw him standing over by the window with his back to her, and she stopped.

"For God's sake," he said, hearing her, but not turning round.

"Don't make supper for me. I'm going out."

At that point, Mary Maloney simply walked up behind him and without any pause she swung the big frozen leg of lamb high in the air and brought it down as hard as she could on the back of his head.

She might just as well have hit him with a steel club.

She stepped back a pace, waiting, and the funny thing was that he remained standing there for at least four or five seconds, gently swaying. Then he crashed to the carpet.

The violence of the crash, the noise, the small table overturning, helped bring her out of the shock. She came out slowly, feeling cold and surprised, and she stood for a while blinking at the body, still holding the ridiculous piece of meat tight with both hands.

All right, she told herself. So I've killed him.

It was extraordinary, now, how clear her mind became all of a sudden. She began thinking very fast. As the wife of a detective, she knew quite well what the penalty would be. That was fine. It made no difference to her. In fact, it would be a relief. On the other hand, what about the child? What were the laws about murderers with unborn children? Did they kill them both—mother and child? Or did they wait until the tenth month? What did they do?

Mary Maloney didn't know. And she certainly wasn't prepared to take the chance.

She carried the meat into the kitchen, placed it in a pan, turned the oven on high, and shoved it inside. Then she washed her hands and ran

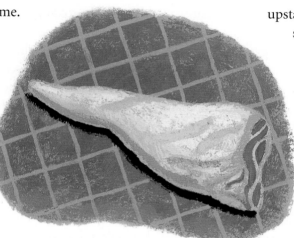

"I got a nice leg of lamb, from the freezer."

upstairs to the bedroom. She sat down before the mirror, tidied her face, touched up her lips and face. She tried a smile. It came out rather peculiar. She tried again.

"Hullo Sam," she said brightly, aloud.

The voice sounded peculiar too.

"I want some potatoes please, Sam. Yes, and I think a can of peas."

That was better. Both the smile and the voice were coming out better now. She rehearsed it several times more. Then she ran downstairs, took her coat, went out the back door, down the garden, into the street.

It wasn't six o'clock yet and the lights were still on in the grocery shop.

"Hullo Sam," she said brightly, smiling at the man behind the counter.

"Why, good evening, Mrs. Maloney. How're *you*?"

"I want some potatoes please, Sam. Yes, and I think a can of peas."

The man turned and reached up behind him on the shelf for the peas.

"Patrick's decided he's tired and doesn't want to eat out tonight," she told him. "We usually go out Thursdays, you know, and now he's caught me without any vegetables in the house."

"Then how about meat, Mrs. Maloney?"

"No, I've got meat, thanks. I got a nice leg of lamb, from the freezer."

"Oh."

"I don't much like cooking it frozen, Sam, but I'm taking a chance on it this time. You think it'll be all right?"

"Personally," the grocer said, "I don't believe it makes any difference. You want these Idaho potatoes?"

"Oh yes, that'll be fine. Two of those."

"Anything else?" The grocer cocked his head on one side, looking at her pleasantly. "How about afterwards? What you going to give him for afterwards?"

"Well—what would you suggest, Sam?"

The man glanced around his shop. "How about a nice big slice of cheesecake? I know he likes that."

"Perfect," she said. "He loves it."

And when it was all wrapped and she had paid, she put on her brightest smile and said, "Thank you, Sam. Good night."

"Good night, Mrs. Maloney. And thank *you*."

And now, she told herself as she hurried back, all she was doing now, she was returning home to her husband and he was waiting for his supper; and she must cook it good, and make it as tasty as possible because the poor man was tired; and if, when she entered the house, she happened to find anything unusual, or tragic, or terrible, then naturally it would be a shock and she'd become frantic with grief and horror. Mind you, she wasn't *expecting* to find anything. She was just going home with the vegetables. Mrs. Patrick Maloney going home with the vegetables on Thursday evening to cook supper for her husband.

That's the way, she told herself. Do everything right and natural. Keep things absolutely natural and there'll be no need for any acting at all.

Therefore, when she entered the kitchen by the back door, she was humming a little tune to herself and smiling.

"Patrick!" she called. "How are you, darling?"

She put the parcel down on the table and went through into the living room; and when she saw him lying there on the floor with his legs doubled up and one arm twisted back underneath his body, it really was rather a shock. All the old love and longing for him welled up inside her, and she ran over to him, knelt down beside him, and began to cry her heart out. It was easy. No acting was necessary.

A few minutes later she got up and went to the phone. She knew the number of the police station, and when the man at the other end answered, she cried to him, "Quick! Come quick! Patrick's dead!"

"Who's speaking?"

"Mrs. Maloney. Mrs. Patrick Maloney."

"You mean Patrick Maloney's dead?"

"I think so," she sobbed. "He's lying on the floor and I think he's dead."

"Be right over," the man said.

The car came very quickly, and when she opened the front door, two policemen walked in. She knew them both—she knew nearly all the men at that precinct—and she fell right into Jack Noonan's arms, weeping hysterically. He put her gently into a chair, then went over to join the other one, who was called O'Malley, kneeling by the body.

"Is he dead?" she cried.

"I'm afraid he is. What happened?"

Briefly, she told her story about going out to the grocer and coming back to find him on the

"Quick! Come quick! Patrick's dead!"

floor. While she was talking, crying and talking, Noonan discovered a small patch of congealed[2] blood on the dead man's head. He showed it to O'Malley who got up at once and hurried to the phone.

Soon, other men began to come into the house. First a doctor, then two detectives, one of whom she knew by name. Later, a police photographer arrived and took pictures, and a man who knew about fingerprints. There was a great deal of whispering and muttering beside the corpse, and the detectives kept asking her a lot of questions. But they always treated her kindly. She told her story again, this time right from the beginning, when Patrick had come in, and she was sewing, and he was tired, so tired he hadn't wanted to go out for supper. She told how she'd put the meat in the oven—"it's there now, cooking"—and how she'd slipped out to the grocer for vegetables, and come back to find him lying on the floor.

"Which grocer?" one of the detectives asked.

She told him, and he turned and whispered something to the other detective who immediately went outside into the street.

In fifteen minutes he was back with a page of notes, and there was more whispering, and through her sobbing she heard a few of the whispered phrases—". . . acted quite normal . . . very cheerful . . . wanted to give him a good supper . . . peas . . . cheesecake . . . impossible that she . . ."

After a while, the photographer and the doctor departed and two other men came in and took the corpse away on a stretcher. Then the fingerprint man went away. The two detectives remained, and so did the two policemen. They were exceptionally nice to her, and Jack Noonan asked if she wouldn't rather go somewhere else, to her sister's house perhaps, or to his own wife who would take care of her and put her up for the night.

No, she said. She didn't feel she could move even a yard at the moment. Would they mind awfully if she stayed just where she was until she felt better? She didn't feel too good at the moment, she really didn't.

Then hadn't she better lie down on the bed? Jack Noonan asked.

No, she said. She'd like to stay right where she was, in this chair. A little later perhaps, when she felt better, she would move.

So they left her there while they went about their business, searching the house. Occasionally one of the detectives asked her another question. Sometimes Jack Noonan spoke to her gently as he passed by. Her husband, he told her, had been killed by a blow on the back of the head administered with a heavy blunt instrument, almost certainly a large piece of metal. They were looking for the weapon. The murderer may have taken it with him, but on the other hand he may've thrown it away or hidden it somewhere on the premises.

"It's the old story," he said. "Get the weapon, and you've got the man."

Later, one of the detectives came up and sat beside her. Did she know, he asked, of anything in the house that could've been used as the weapon? Would she mind having a look around to see if anything was missing—a very big spanner,[3] for example, or a heavy metal vase.

They didn't have any heavy metal vases, she said.

"Or a big spanner?"

She didn't think they had a big spanner. But there might be some things like that in the garage.

---

3. **spanner** *n.:* British English for "wrench."

Vocabulary

administered (ad·min′is·tərd) *v.* used as *adj.:* given; applied.

premises (prem′is·iz) *n.:* house or building and its surrounding property.

---

2. **congealed** (kən·jēld′) *v.* used as *adj.:* thickened; made solid.

They were looking for the weapon.

The search went on. She knew that there were other policemen in the garden all around the house. She could hear their footsteps on the gravel outside, and sometimes she saw the flash of a torch through a chink in the curtains. It began to get late, nearly nine she noticed by the clock on the mantel. The four men searching the rooms seemed to be growing weary, a trifle exasperated.

"Jack," she said, the next time Sergeant Noonan went by. "Would you mind giving me a drink?"

"Sure I'll give you a drink. You mean this whisky?"

"Yes, please. But just a small one. It might make me feel better."

He handed her the glass.

"Why don't you have one yourself," she said. "You must be awfully tired. Please do. You've been very good to me."

"Well," he answered. "It's not strictly allowed, but I might take just a drop to keep me going."

One by one the others came in and were persuaded to take a little nip of whisky. They stood around rather awkwardly with the drinks in their hands, uncomfortable in her presence, trying to say consoling things to her. Sergeant Noonan wandered into the kitchen, came out quickly and said, "Look, Mrs. Maloney. You know that oven of yours is still on, and the meat still inside."

"Oh *dear* me!" she cried. "So it is!"

"I better turn it off for you, hadn't I?"

"Will you do that, Jack. Thank you so much."

When the sergeant returned the second time, she looked at him with her large, dark, tearful eyes. "Jack Noonan," she said.

"Yes?"

"Would you do me a small favor—you and these others?"

"We can try, Mrs. Maloney."

Vocabulary
consoling (kən·sōl′iŋ) v. used as *adj.*: comforting.

"She *wants* us to finish it.
She said so. Be doing her a favor."

"Well," she said. "Here you all are, and good friends of dear Patrick's too, and helping to catch the man who killed him. You must be terrible hungry by now because it's long past your supper time, and I know Patrick would never forgive me, God bless his soul, if I allowed you to remain in his house without offering you decent hospitality. Why don't you eat up that lamb that's in the oven? It'll be cooked just right by now."

"Wouldn't dream of it," Sergeant Noonan said.

"Please," she begged. "Please eat it. Personally I couldn't touch a thing, certainly not what's been in the house when he was here. But it's all right for you. It'd be a favor to me if you'd eat it up. Then you can go on with your work again afterwards."

There was a good deal of hesitating among the four policemen, but they were clearly hungry, and in the end they were persuaded to go into the kitchen and help themselves. The woman stayed where she was, listening to them through the open door, and she could hear them speaking among themselves, their voices thick and sloppy because their mouths were full of meat.

"Have some more, Charlie?"

"No. Better not finish it."

"She *wants* us to finish it. She said so. Be doing her a favor."

"Okay then. Give me some more."

"That's the hell of a big club the guy must've used to hit poor Patrick," one of them was saying. "The doc says his skull was smashed all to pieces just like from a sledgehammer."

"That's why it ought to be easy to find."

"Exactly what I say."

"Whoever done it, they're not going to be carrying a thing like that around with them longer than they need."

One of them belched.

"Personally, I think it's right here on the premises."

"Probably right under our very noses. What you think, Jack?"

And in the other room, Mary Maloney began to giggle. ∎

Vocabulary
hospitality (häs′pi·tal′ə·tē) *n.:* friendly, caring treatment of guests.

Meet the Writer

Roald Dahl

Master of the Delightfully Sinister

When Roald (roo′äl) Dahl (1916–1990) was fifteen, a teacher in a British boarding school wrote on his report card: "A persistent muddler. Vocabulary negligible, sentences malconstructed. He reminds me of a camel." So much for accurately assessing Dahl's talents, for he became one of Britain's most popular writers of children's fiction and adult short stories, famous for his delightfully sinister fantasies.

The son of Norwegian parents, Roald Dahl was born in the south of Wales. Though his father died when Dahl was four, the family remained in England so the children could go to English schools, which his father had thought the best in the world. Dahl hated the boarding schools, which he began attending when he was nine. He recalled "just rules, rules and still more rules that had to be obeyed."

In 1934, when he graduated from prep school, Dahl turned down his mother's offer to send him to college. Instead, he took a job with an oil company and was sent to Tanzania, in East Africa. When World War II broke out, Dahl joined the British Royal Air Force in Nairobi as a fighter pilot, and he was badly injured when his plane crash-landed in the Libyan desert. In 1942, he was assigned as assistant air attaché to the British embassy in Washington, D.C. There he began writing, at first about his wartime experiences. "As I went on," he later said in an interview, "the stories become less and less realistic and more fantastic."

Dahl became especially interested in children's stories. In his first effort, *The Gremlins* (1943), he claimed to have coined the word for the imaginary gnomes that sabotage fighter planes and bombers, causing them to crash. Dahl's most successful children's books, inspired by the long bedtime stories he used to tell his five children, are *James and the Giant Peach* (1961) and *Charlie and the Chocolate Factory* (1964).

Dahl crafted his tales carefully, often spending six months on a single story. He once wrote this comment about being a writer:

> **66** A person is a fool to become a writer. His only compensation is absolute freedom. He has no master except his own soul, and that, I am sure, is why he does it. **99**

For Independent Reading

Want to learn more about the early life of the author? In *Boy: Tales of Childhood* (1984), Dahl relates his memorable boyhood experiences.

Response and Analysis

Reading Check

1. At the beginning of the story, what do we learn about Mary's feelings for her husband, Patrick?

2. What happens to upset Mary?

3. Why does Mary go out to the grocer's?

4. What do the police think happened to Patrick?

Thinking Critically

5. Dahl does not tell us the exact details of what Patrick tells Mary. What can we **infer** that Patrick tells her?

6. Cite two examples of **situational irony** in the story. What clues, or **foreshadowing,** if any, does Dahl give to prepare us for the unexpected?

7. How does Dahl also make use of **dramatic irony**? Which did you find more powerful—the dramatic irony or the situational irony? Explain why.

8. Find the passage in which Mary asks the police officers to do her a "small favor" and eat the lamb. What kind of **irony** is at work here?

9. Look back at the notes you made as you read the story to see when, if at all, you **predicted** the following developments:

   • that Mary would murder her husband

   • what Mary would use for a weapon

   • how Mary would dispose of the weapon

10. Now that you have read the story, what do you think the **title** means? Is it appropriate? Is it **ironic**? Check your Quickwrite notes, and then explain your answers.

Extending and Evaluating

11. Do you think Dahl intends his characters and plot to be **credible**? Explain your answer.

Literary Criticism

12. Children, Dahl said,

> invariably pick out the most grue-some events as the favorite parts of [my] books. . . . They don't relate it to life. They enjoy the fantasy. And my nastiness is never gratuitous. It's retribution. Beastly people must be punished.

In your opinion, what does Dahl want us to think about Mary and the murder of her husband? How does he manage to make us react as we do?

WRITING

Analyzing Character

What do you make of Mary's giggling at the end of the story? This ending is somewhat **ambiguous** and hard to interpret. On the one hand, you might think it shows a newly revealed, more sinister side to her nature. On the other hand, you might think it merely reflects her need for a small release from the great stress and strain of her recent experience. Perhaps you have yet another interpretation. Write a brief **character analysis** of Mary as she is depicted throughout the story. Be sure to explain what you think Mary's giggling at the end reveals about her.

Vocabulary Development

Using Context Clues

PRACTICE 1

Fill in the blanks below by using the **context clues** in each sentence and then choosing the Word Bank word that best fits each context.

    Later in life, Roald Dahl complained that life at school was hardly calm and _____. Instead of discovering a pleasant atmosphere of _____, he lived in constant _____ over all the rules that had to be followed. He especially disliked the awful punishments that were _____ if any rules were broken. He couldn't even _____ in a chat in the dormitory— it was forbidden. When asked by his mother if he wanted to continue his education at university, he revealed his wish to leave the school's _____ and get a job far away— in China or Africa. He found his dream of future travel _____ during that difficult time.

PRACTICE 2

Now, identify the context clues in each sentence that helped you guess the correct missing word.

Word Bank

anxiety
placid
luxuriate
administered
premises
consoling
hospitality

Grammar Link

Active or Passive Voice

Verbs that express action can be used in either the **active voice** or the **passive voice.**

ACTIVE Mary <u>cooked</u> the leg of lamb.
          [The action is done *by* the subject, *Mary.*]

PASSIVE The leg of lamb <u>was cooked</u>.
          [The action is done *to* the subject, *the leg of lamb.* The doer of the action is not even mentioned.]

For most kinds of writing, you are better off using the active voice, which is stronger and more direct. Use the passive voice only when you don't know the performer of the action or when you wish to conceal or give less emphasis to the performer.

PASSIVE According to the detective, Mr. Maloney <u>was hit</u> in the back of the head with a heavy object.
          [The detective does not know who hit Mr. Maloney.]

PRACTICE

Rewrite the following paragraph so that all the verbs are in the active voice. (You may have to add new subjects for some sentences.)

    Mary Maloney was told some shocking news by her husband. He was then killed by Mary with a frozen leg of lamb. The house was thoroughly searched, but nothing suspicious was found. Mary and the grocer were carefully questioned by detectives. The dreadful leg of lamb was cooked, and the murder weapon was eaten by the hungry detectives. The identity of the murderer was not guessed by the police. In fact, Mary was never suspected as the murderer.

▶ **For more help, see Active and Passive Voice, 3g–h, in the Language Handbook.**

SKILLS FOCUS

Vocabulary Skills
Use context clues.

Grammar Skills
Understand active voice and passive voice.

R.M.S. Titanic

Make the Connection

Quickwrite ✏️

Choose any kind of disaster—a sinking ship, an earthquake, a raging tornado, a flood, an avalanche. Put yourself there. Write briefly about how you think you'd feel and what you'd do. Save your notes.

Literary Focus

Irony: It's Unexpected

The following account of the *Titanic*'s maiden voyage illustrates both **situational irony** (which occurs when what happens is the opposite of what we expect to happen or should happen) and **dramatic irony** (which occurs in literature when the reader knows something important that the characters do not know).

The passengers on the *Titanic,* including the great ship's builders and its financial backers, believed that they were on an unsinkable vessel. Their confidence, or arrogance, is one of the great ironies of twentieth-century history. Even the naming of the ship is ironic. The Titans were ancient Greek gods possessing enormous size and incredible strength. For eons they reigned supreme in the universe, according to Greek mythology. Perhaps those who named the ship had forgotten that even the Titans did not rule forever.

Objective and Subjective Writing

This account of the sinking of the *Titanic* may remind you of other disasters. When reporting on a catastrophe, different writers may begin with the same facts yet present the event in vastly differing ways.

In **objective writing** only the **facts** are included; the writer's views aren't revealed. Those facts, however, can be presented in an engaging and compelling manner. In **subjective writing** the writer adds his or her **opinions,** judgments, or feelings. As you read, determine Hanson Baldwin's approach. What stance does he strike immediately in his first paragraph?

Reading Skills

Understanding Text Structures

The sinking of the *Titanic* involved a complex series of actions occurring within a few hours. In writing his account of the disaster, Baldwin uses the **headings I–V** as **text structures** to organize and divide that complicated rush of events. Each numbered part covers a different stage in the tragedy. Another chronological text

The *Titanic,* underwater 375 miles southeast of Newfoundland, in the summer of 1991.

INTERNET

Vocabulary Practice

Keyword: LE5 10-5

SKILLS FOCUS

Literary Skills
Understand situational irony and dramatic irony.
Understand objective writing and subjective writing.

Reading Skills
Understand text structures.

The *Titanic*'s captain, E. J. Smith.

structure is the notation of time—as the minutes tick by in Part II. These reminders build suspense and help you keep stark track of the unfolding disaster.

Background

The following article on the *Titanic* disaster was written by Hanson Baldwin in 1934. Baldwin's account was based on exhaustive factual research at the time, including a review of ship logs and other records as well as numerous interviews.

Since the publication of this landmark article, public fascination with the *Titanic* disaster has continued to grow, and more information has been revealed. For example, a pioneering underwater exploration of the wreck in 1986 was unable to find a three-hundred-foot gash in the ship, which Baldwin described. Instead, divers in a mini-submarine saw buckled seams and separated plates in the ship's hull, which are probably what caused the ship to flood and sink.

Vocabulary Development

superlative (sə·pʉr′lə·tiv) *adj.:* supreme; better than all others.

ascertain (as′ər·tān′) *v.:* find out with certainty; determine.

corroborated (kə·räb′ə·rāt′id) *v.:* supported; upheld the truth of.

quelled (kweld) *v.:* quieted; subdued.

poised (poizd) *adj.:* balanced; in position.

perfunctory (pər·fuŋk′tə·rē) *adj.:* not exerting much effort; unconcerned.

garbled (gär′bəld) *v.* used as *adj.:* confused; mixed up.

recriminations (ri·krim′ə·nā′shənz) *n.:* accusations against an accuser; countercharges.

pertinent (pʉrt′ʼn·ənt) *adj.:* having some connection with the subject.

vainly (vān′lē) *adv.:* without success; fruitlessly.

R.M.S. TITANIC

Hanson W. Baldwin

OUT OF THE DARK SHE CAME,
A VAST, DIM, WHITE,
MONSTROUS SHAPE . . .

I

The White Star liner *Titanic,* largest ship the world had ever known, sailed from Southampton on her maiden voyage to New York on April 10, 1912. The paint on her strakes[1] was fair and bright; she was fresh from Harland and Wolff's Belfast yards, strong in the strength of her forty-six thousand tons of steel, bent, hammered, shaped, and riveted through the three years of her slow birth.

---

1. **strakes** *n.:* single lines of metal plating extending the whole length of a ship.

There was little fuss and fanfare at her sailing; her sister ship, the *Olympic*—slightly smaller than the *Titanic*—had been in service for some months and to her had gone the thunder of the cheers.

But the *Titanic* needed no whistling steamers or shouting crowds to call attention to her superlative qualities. Her bulk dwarfed the ships near her as longshoremen singled up her mooring lines and cast off the turns of heavy rope from the dock bollards.[2] She was not only the largest ship afloat, but was believed to be the safest. Carlisle, her builder, had given her double bottoms and had divided her hull into sixteen watertight compartments, which made her, men thought, unsinkable. She had been built to be and had been described as a gigantic lifeboat. Her designers' dreams of a triple-screw[3] giant, a luxurious, floating hotel, which could speed to New York at twenty-three knots, had been carefully translated from blueprints and mold loft lines at the Belfast yards into a living reality.

The *Titanic*'s sailing from Southampton, though quiet, was not wholly uneventful. As the liner moved slowly toward the end of her dock that April day, the surge of her passing sucked away from the quay[4] the steamer *New York,* moored just to seaward of the *Titanic*'s berth. There were sharp cracks as the manila mooring lines of the *New York* parted under the strain. The frayed ropes writhed and whistled through the air and snapped down among the waving crowd on the pier; the *New York* swung toward the *Titanic*'s bow, was checked and dragged back to the dock barely in time to avert a collision. Seamen muttered, thought it an ominous start.

Past Spithead and the Isle of Wight the *Titanic* steamed. She called at Cherbourg at dusk and then laid her course for Queenstown. At 1:30 P.M.

on Thursday, April 11, she stood out of Queenstown harbor, screaming gulls soaring in her wake, with 2,201 persons—men, women, and children—aboard.

Occupying the Empire bedrooms and Georgian suites of the first-class accommodations were many well-known men and women— Colonel John Jacob Astor and his young bride; Major Archibald Butt, military aide to President Taft, and his friend Frank D. Millet, the painter; John B. Thayer, vice president of the Pennsylvania Railroad, and Charles M. Hays, president of the Grand Trunk Railway of Canada; W. T. Stead, the English journalist; Jacques Futrelle, French novelist; H. B. Harris, theatrical manager, and Mrs. Harris; Mr. and Mrs. Isidor Straus; and J. Bruce Ismay, chairman and managing director of the White Star Line.

Down in the plain wooden cabins of the steerage class were 706 immigrants to the land of promise, and trimly stowed in the great holds was a cargo valued at $420,000: oak beams, sponges, wine, calabashes,[5] and an odd miscellany of the common and the rare.

The *Titanic* took her departure on Fastnet Light[6] and, heading into the night, laid her course for New York. She was due at quarantine[7] the following Wednesday morning.

Sunday dawned fair and clear. The *Titanic* steamed smoothly toward the west, faint

---

2. **bollards** (bäl′ərdz) *n.:* strong posts on a pier or wharf for holding a ship's mooring ropes.
3. **triple-screw:** three-propellered.
4. **quay** (kē) *n.:* dock.

5. **calabashes** (kal′ə·bash′əz) *n.:* large smoking pipes made from the necks of gourds.
6. **Fastnet Light:** lighthouse at the southwestern tip of Ireland. After the Fastnet Light there is only open sea until the coast of North America.
7. **quarantine** (kwôr′ən·tēn) *n.:* place where a ship is held in port after arrival to determine whether its passengers and cargo are free of communicable diseases. *Quarantine* can also be used for the length of time a ship is held.

Vocabulary
superlative (sə·pʉr′lə·tiv) *adj.:* supreme; better than all others.

Message from the *Caronia*, warning of icebergs and tracts of floating ice.

Second Operator Harold Bride.

streamers of brownish smoke trailing from her funnels. The purser held services in the saloon in the morning; on the steerage deck aft[8] the immigrants were playing games and a Scotsman was puffing "The Campbells Are Coming" on his bagpipes in the midst of the uproar.

At 9:00 A.M. a message from the steamer *Caronia* sputtered into the wireless shack:

Captain, *Titanic*—Westbound steamers report bergs growlers and field ice 42 degrees N. from 49 degrees to 51 degrees W. 12th April.

Compliments—Barr.

It was cold in the afternoon; the sun was brilliant, but the *Titanic,* her screws turning over at seventy-five revolutions per minute, was approaching the Banks.[9]

In the Marconi cabin[10] Second Operator Harold Bride, earphones clamped on his head, was figuring accounts; he did not stop to answer when he heard *MWL,* Continental Morse for

the nearby Leyland liner, *Californian,* calling the *Titanic.* The *Californian* had some message about three icebergs; he didn't bother then to take it down. About 1:42 P.M. the rasping spark of those days spoke again across the water. It was the *Baltic,* calling the *Titanic,* warning her of ice on the steamer track. Bride took the message down and sent it up to the bridge.[11] The officer-of-the-deck glanced at it; sent it to the bearded master of the *Titanic,* Captain E. C. Smith,[12] a veteran of the White Star service. It was lunchtime then; the captain, walking along the promenade deck, saw Mr. Ismay, stopped, and handed him the message without comment. Ismay read it, stuffed it in his pocket, told two ladies about the icebergs, and resumed his walk. Later, about 7:15 P.M., the captain requested the return of the message in order to post it in the chart room for the information of officers.

Dinner that night in the Jacobean dining room was gay. It was bitter on deck, but the night was calm and fine; the sky was moonless but studded with stars twinkling coldly in the clear air.

After dinner some of the second-class passengers gathered in the saloon, where the Reverend Mr. Carter conducted a "hymn singsong." It was almost ten o'clock and the stewards were waiting with biscuits and coffee as the group sang:

O, hear us when we cry to Thee
For those in peril on the sea.

On the bridge Second Officer Lightoller—short, stocky, efficient—was relieved at ten o'clock by First Officer Murdoch. Lightoller had talked with other officers about the proximity of ice; at least five wireless ice warnings had

---

8. **aft** *adv.:* in the rear of a ship.
9. **Banks:** Grand Banks, shallow waters near the southeast coast of Newfoundland.
10. **Marconi cabin:** room where messages were received and sent by radio.

---

11. **bridge** *n.:* raised structure on a ship. The ship is controlled from the bridge.
12. Smith's initials were actually E. J., not E. C.

reached the ship; lookouts had been cautioned to be alert; captains and officers expected to reach the field at any time after 9:30 P.M. At twenty-two knots, its speed unslackened, the *Titanic* plowed on through the night.

Lightoller left the darkened bridge to his relief and turned in. Captain Smith went to his cabin. The steerage was long since quiet; in the first and second cabins lights were going out; voices were growing still; people were asleep. Murdoch paced back and forth on the bridge, peering out over the dark water, glancing now and then at the compass in front of Quartermaster Hichens at the wheel.

In the crow's-nest, lookout Frederick Fleet and his partner, Leigh, gazed down at the water, still and unruffled in the dim, starlit darkness. Behind and below them the ship, a white shadow with here and there a last winking light; ahead of them a dark and silent and cold ocean.

There was a sudden clang. "Dong-dong. Dong-dong. Dong-dong. Dong!" The metal clapper of the great ship's bell struck out 11:30. Mindful of the warnings, Fleet strained his eyes, searching the darkness for the dreaded ice. But there were only the stars and the sea.

In the wireless room, where Phillips, first operator, had relieved Bride, the buzz of the *Californian*'s set again crackled into the earphones:

Californian: "Say, old man, we are stuck here, surrounded by ice."

Titanic: "Shut up, shut up; keep out. I am talking to Cape Race; you are jamming my signals."

Then, a few minutes later—about 11:40 . . .

Lookout Frederick Fleet.

First Operator Jack Phillips.

II

Out of the dark she came, a vast, dim, white, monstrous shape, directly in the *Titanic*'s path. For a moment Fleet doubted his eyes. But she was a deadly reality, this ghastly *thing*. Frantically, Fleet struck three bells—*something dead ahead*. He snatched the telephone and called the bridge:

"Iceberg! Right ahead!"

The first officer heard but did not stop to acknowledge the message.

"Hard-a-starboard!"

Hichens strained at the wheel; the bow swung slowly to port. The monster was almost upon them now.

Murdoch leaped to the engine-room telegraph. Bells clanged. Far below in the engine room those bells struck the first warning. Danger! The indicators on the dial faces swung round to "Stop!" Then "Full speed astern!" Frantically the engineers turned great valve wheels; answered the bridge bells . . .

There was a slight shock, a brief scraping, a small list to port. Shell ice—slabs and chunks of it—fell on the foredeck. Slowly the *Titanic* stopped.

Captain Smith hurried out of his cabin.

"What has the ship struck?"

Murdoch answered, "An iceberg, sir. I hard-a-starboarded and reversed the engines, and I was going to hard-a-port around it, but she was too close. I could not do any more. I have closed the watertight doors."

Fourth Officer Boxhall, other officers, the carpenter, came to the bridge. The captain sent Boxhall and the carpenter below to <u>ascertain</u> the damage.

A few lights switched on in the first and second cabins; sleepy passengers peered through porthole glass; some casually asked the stewards:

"Why have we stopped?"

"I don't know, sir, but I don't suppose it is anything much."

In the smoking room a quorum[13] of gamblers and their prey were still sitting round a poker table; the usual crowd of kibitzers[14] looked on. They had felt the slight jar of the collision and had seen an eighty-foot ice mountain glide by the smoking-room windows, but the night was calm and clear, the *Titanic* was "unsinkable"; they hadn't bothered to go on deck.

But far below, in the warren of passages on the starboard side forward, in the forward holds and boiler rooms, men could see that the *Titanic*'s hurt was mortal. In No. 6 boiler room, where the red glow from the furnaces lighted up the naked, sweaty chests of coal-blackened firemen, water was pouring through a great gash about two feet above the floor plates. This was no slow leak; the ship was open to the sea; in ten minutes there were eight feet of water in No. 6. Long before then the stokers had raked the flaming fires out of the furnaces and had scrambled through the watertight doors in No. 5 or had climbed up the long steel ladders to safety. When Boxhall looked at the mailroom in No. 3 hold, twenty-four feet above the keel, the mailbags were already floating about in the slushing water. In No. 5 boiler room a stream of water spurted into an empty bunker. All six compartments forward of No. 4 were open to the sea; in ten seconds the iceberg's jagged claw had ripped a three-hundred-foot slash in the bottom of the great *Titanic*.[15]

Reports came to the bridge; Ismay in dressing gown ran out on deck in the cold, still, starlit night, climbed up the bridge ladder.

"What has happened?"

Captain Smith: "We have struck ice."

"Do you think she is seriously damaged?"

Captain Smith: "I'm afraid she is."

Ismay went below and passed Chief Engineer William Bell, fresh from an inspection of the damaged compartments. Bell <u>corroborated</u>

---

15. An underwater expedition to the *Titanic* wreck in 1986 led by the explorer Dr. Robert Ballard revealed loosened or buckled seams in the ship's hull but no three-hundred-foot gash. Ballard concluded that the collision of the ship with the iceberg caused the buckling of the seams and a separation of the hull's plates, which in turn allowed water to enter the ship and sink it. This theory explains why survivors said they barely felt the fatal collision when it occurred.

Vocabulary

ascertain (as'ər·tān') *v.*: find out with certainty; determine.

corroborated (kə·räb'ə·rāt'id) *v.*: supported; upheld the truth of.

---

13. **quorum** (kwôr'əm) *n.*: number of people required for a particular activity—in this case, for a game.

14. **kibitzers** (kib'it·sərz) *n.*: talkative onlookers who often give unwanted advice.

the captain's statement; hurried back down the glistening steel ladders to his duty. Man after man followed him—Thomas Andrews, one of the ship's designers, Archie Frost, the builder's chief engineer, and his twenty assistants—men who had no posts of duty in the engine room but whose traditions called them there.

On deck, in corridor and stateroom, life flowed again. Men, women, and children awoke and questioned; orders were given to uncover the lifeboats; water rose into the firemen's quarters; half-dressed stokers streamed up on deck. But the passengers—most of them—did not know that the *Titanic* was sinking. The shock of the collision had been so slight that some were not awakened by it; the *Titanic* was so huge that she must be unsinkable; the night was too calm, too beautiful, to think of death at sea.

Captain Smith half ran to the door of the radio shack. Bride, partly dressed, eyes dulled with sleep, was standing behind Phillips, waiting.

"Send the call for assistance."

The blue spark danced: "CQD—CQD— CQD—CQ—"[16]

Miles away Marconi men heard. Cape Race heard it, and the steamships *La Provence* and *Mt. Temple.*

The sea was surging into the *Titanic*'s hold. At 12:20 the water burst into the seamen's quarters through a collapsed fore-and-aft wooden bulkhead. Pumps strained in the engine rooms— men and machinery making a futile fight against the sea. Steadily the water rose.

The boats were swung out—slowly, for the deckhands were late in reaching their stations; there had been no boat drill, and many of the crew did not know to what boats they were assigned. Orders were shouted; the safety valves had lifted, and steam was blowing off in a great rushing roar. In the chart house Fourth Officer

Boxhall bent above a chart, working rapidly with pencil and dividers.

12:25 A.M. Boxhall's position is sent out to a fleet of vessels: "Come at once; we have struck a berg."

To the Cunarder *Carpathia* (Arthur Henry Rostron, Master, New York to Liverpool, fifty-eight miles away): "It's a CQD, old man. Position 41–46N.; 50–14 W."

The blue spark dancing: "Sinking; cannot hear for noise of steam."

12:30 A.M. The word is passed: "Women and children in the boats." Stewards finish waking their passengers below; life preservers are tied on; some men smile at the precaution. "The *Titanic* is unsinkable." The *Mt. Temple* starts for the *Titanic;* the *Carpathia,* with a double watch in her stokeholds, radios, "Coming hard." The CQD changes the course of many ships—but not of one; the operator of the *Californian,* nearby, has just put down his earphones and turned in.

The CQD flashes over land and sea from Cape Race to New York; newspaper city rooms leap to life and presses whir.

On the *Titanic,* water creeps over the bulkhead between Nos. 5 and 6 firerooms. She is going down by the head; the engineers—fighting a losing battle—are forced back foot by foot by the rising water. Down the promenade deck, Happy Jock Hume, the bandsman, runs with his instrument.

12:45 A.M. Murdoch, in charge on the starboard side, eyes tragic, but calm and cool, orders boat No. 7 lowered. The women hang back; they want no boat ride on an ice-strewn sea; the *Titanic* is unsinkable. The men encourage them, explain that this is just a precautionary measure: "We'll see you again at breakfast." There is little confusion; passengers stream slowly to the boat deck. In the steerage the immigrants chatter excitedly.

A sudden sharp hiss—a streaked flare against the night; Boxhall sends a rocket toward the sky. It explodes, and a parachute of white stars lights

---

16. **CQD:** call by radio operators, inviting others to communicate with them.

Molly Brown (nicknamed "unsinkable" by the Associated Press) helped row a lifeboat and nurse survivors.

Colonel John Jacob Astor, wealthy hotel owner, went down with the *Titanic*.

up the icy sea. "God! Rockets!" The band plays ragtime.

No. 8 is lowered, and No. 5. Ismay, still in dressing gown, calls for women and children, handles lines, stumbles in the way of an officer, is told to "get the hell out of here." Third Officer Pitman takes charge of No. 5; as he swings into the boat, Murdoch grasps his hand. "Goodbye and good luck, old man."

No. 6 goes over the side. There are only twenty-eight people in a lifeboat with a capacity of sixty-five.

A light stabs from the bridge; Boxhall is calling in Morse flashes, again and again, to a strange ship stopped in the ice jam five to ten miles away. Another rocket drops its shower of sparks above the ice-strewn sea and the dying ship.

1:00 A.M. Slowly the water creeps higher; the fore ports of the *Titanic* are dipping into the sea. Rope squeaks through blocks; lifeboats drop jerkily seaward. Through the shouting on the decks comes the sound of the band playing ragtime.

The "Millionaires' Special" leaves the ship—boat No. 1, with a capacity of forty people, carries only Sir Cosmo and Lady Duff Gordon and ten others. Aft, the frightened immigrants mill and jostle and rush for a boat. An officer's fist flies out; three shots are fired in the air, and the panic is <u>quelled</u>. . . . Four Chinese sneak unseen into a boat and hide in the bottom.

1:20 A.M. Water is coming into No. 4 boiler room. Stokers slice and shovel as water laps about their ankles—steam for the dynamos, steam for the dancing spark! As the water rises, great ash hoes rake the flaming coals from the furnaces. Safety valves pop; the stokers retreat aft, and the watertight doors clang shut behind them.

The rockets fling their splendor toward the stars. The boats are more heavily loaded now, for the passengers know the *Titanic* is sinking. Women cling and sob. The great screws aft are rising clear of the sea. Half-filled boats are ordered to come alongside the cargo ports and take on more passengers, but the ports are never opened—and the boats are never filled. Others pull for the steamer's light miles away but never reach it; the lights disappear; the unknown ship steams off.

The water rises and the band plays ragtime.

1:30 A.M. Lightoller is getting the port boats off; Murdoch, the starboard. As one boat is lowered into the sea, a boat officer fires his gun along

Vocabulary
quelled (kweld) *v.*: quieted; subdued.

the ship's side to stop a rush from the lower decks. A woman tries to take her Great Dane into a boat with her; she is refused and steps out of the boat to die with her dog. Millet's "little smile which played on his lips all through the voyage" plays no more; his lips are grim, but he waves goodbye and brings wraps for the women.

Benjamin Guggenheim, in evening clothes, smiles and says, "We've dressed up in our best and are prepared to go down like gentlemen."

1:40 A.M. Boat 14 is clear, and then 13, 16, 15, and C. The lights still shine, but the *Baltic* hears the blue spark say, "Engine room getting flooded."

The *Olympia* signals, "Am lighting up all possible boilers as fast as can."

Major Butt helps women into the last boats and waves goodbye to them. Mrs. Straus puts her foot on the gunwale of a lifeboat; then she draws back and goes to her husband: "We have been together many years; where you go, I will go." Colonel John Jacob Astor puts his young wife in a lifeboat, steps back, taps cigarette on fingernail: "Goodbye, dearie; I'll join you later."

1:45 A.M. The foredeck is under water; the fo'c'sle[17] head almost awash; the great stern is lifted high toward the bright stars; and still the band plays. Mr. and Mrs. Harris approach a lifeboat arm in arm.

Officer: "Ladies first, please."

Harris bows, smiles, steps back: "Of course, certainly; ladies first."

Boxhall fires the last rocket, then leaves in charge of boat No. 2.

2:00 A.M. She is dying now; her bow goes deeper, her stern higher. But there must be steam. Below in the stokeholds the sweaty firemen keep steam up for the flaring lights and the dancing spark. The glowing coals slide and tumble over the slanted grate bars; the sea pounds behind that yielding bulkhead. But the spark dances on.

The *Asian* hears Phillips try the new signal—SOS.

Boat No. 4 has left now; boat D leaves ten minutes later. Jacques Futrelle clasps his wife: "For God's sake, go! It's your last chance; go!" Madame Futrelle is half forced into the boat. It clears the side.

---

17. fo'c'sle (fōk′səl) *n.:* forecastle, front upper deck of a ship.

There are about 660 people in the boats and 1,500 still on the sinking *Titanic.*

On top of the officers' quarters, men work frantically to get the two collapsibles stowed there over the side. Water is over the forward part of A deck now; it surges up the companion-ways toward the boat deck. In the radio shack, Bride has slipped a coat and life jacket about Phillips as the first operator sits hunched over his key, sending—still sending—"41–46 N.; 50–14 W. CQD—CQD—SOS—SOS—"

The captain's tired white face appears at the radio-room door. "Men, you have done your full duty. You can do no more. Now, it's every man for himself." The captain disappears—back to his sinking bridge, where Painter, his personal stew-ard, stands quietly waiting for orders. The spark dances on. Bride turns his back and goes into the inner cabin. As he does so, a stoker, grimed with coal, mad with fear, steals into the shack and reaches for the life jacket on Phillips's back. Bride wheels about and brains him with a wrench.

2:10 A.M. Below decks the steam is still hold-ing, though the pressure is falling—rapidly. In the gymnasium on the boat deck, the athletic in-structor watches quietly as two gentlemen ride the bicycles and another swings casually at the punching bag. Mail clerks stagger up the boat-deck stairways, dragging soaked mail sacks. The spark still dances. The band still plays—but not ragtime:

Nearer my God to Thee.
Nearer to Thee . . .

A few men take up the refrain; others kneel on the slanting decks to pray. Many run and scramble aft, where hundreds are clinging above the silent screws on the great uptilted stern. The spark still dances and the lights still flare; the en-gineers are on the job. The hymn comes to its close. Bandmaster Hartley, Yorkshireman violin-ist, taps his bow against a bulkhead, calls for "Autumn" as the water curls about his feet, and

the eight musicians brace themselves against the ship's slant. People are leaping from the decks into the nearby water—the icy water. A woman cries, "Oh, save me, save me!" A man answers, "Good lady, save yourself. Only God can save you now." The band plays "Autumn":

God of Mercy and Compassion!
Look with pity on my pain . . .

The water creeps over the bridge where the *Titanic's* master stands; heavily he steps out to meet it.

2:17 A.M. "CQ—" The *Virginian* hears a ragged, blurred CQ, then an abrupt stop. The blue spark dances no more. The lights flicker out; the engineers have lost their battle.

2:18 A.M. Men run about blackened decks; leap into the night; are swept into the sea by the curling wave that licks up the *Titanic's* length. Lightoller does not leave the ship; the ship leaves him; there are hundreds like him, but only a few who live to tell of it. The funnels still swim above the water, but the ship is climbing to the perpendicular; the bridge is under and most of the foremast; the great stern rises like a squat leviathan.[18] Men swim away from the sinking ship; others drop from the stern.

The band plays in the darkness, the water lap-ping upward:

Hold me up in mighty waters,
Keep my eyes on things above,
Righteousness, divine atonement,
Peace and everlas . . .

The forward funnel snaps and crashes into the sea; its steel tons hammer out of existence swimmers struggling in the freezing water. Streams of sparks, of smoke and steam, burst from the after funnels. The ship upends to 50—to 60 degrees.

---

18. **leviathan** (lə·vī′ə·thən) *n.:* biblical sea monster, perhaps a whale.

Down in the black abyss of the stokeholds, of the engine rooms, where the dynamos have whirred at long last to a stop, the stokers and the engineers are reeling against the hot metal, the rising water clutching at their knees. The boilers, the engine cylinders, rip from their bed plates; crash through bulkheads; rumble—steel against steel.

The *Titanic* stands on end, <u>poised</u> briefly for the plunge. Slowly she slides to her grave—slowly at first, and then more quickly—quickly—quickly.

2:20 A.M.   The greatest ship in the world has sunk. From the calm, dark waters, where the floating lifeboats move, there goes up, in the white wake of her passing, "one long continuous moan."

III

The boats that the *Titanic* had launched pulled safely away from the slight suction of the sinking ship, pulled away from the screams that came from the lips of the freezing men and women in the water. The boats were poorly manned and badly equipped, and they had been unevenly loaded. Some carried so few seamen that women bent to the oars. Mrs. Astor tugged at an oar handle; the Countess of Rothes took a tiller. Shivering stokers in sweaty, coal-blackened singlets and light trousers steered in some boats; stewards in white coats rowed in others. Ismay was in the last boat that left the ship from the starboard side; with Mr. Carter of Philadelphia and two seamen he tugged at the oars. In one of the lifeboats an Italian with a broken wrist—disguised in a woman's shawl and hat—huddled on the floorboards, ashamed now that fear had left him. In another rode the only baggage saved from the *Titanic*—the carryall of Samuel L. Goldenberg, one of the rescued passengers.

There were only a few boats that were heavily loaded; most of those that were half empty made but <u>perfunctory</u> efforts to pick up the moaning swimmers, their officers and crew fearing they would endanger the living if they pulled back into the midst of the dying. Some boats beat off the freezing victims; fear-crazed men and women struck with oars at the heads of swimmers. One woman drove her fist into the face of a half-dead man as he tried feebly to climb over the gunwale. Two other women helped him in and staunched the flow of blood from the ring cuts on his face.

One of the collapsible boats, which had floated off the top of the officers' quarters when the *Titanic* sank, was an icy haven for thirty or forty men. The boat had capsized as the ship sank; men swam to it, clung to it, climbed upon its slippery bottom, stood knee-deep in water in the freezing air. Chunks of ice swirled about their legs; their soaked clothing clutched their bodies in icy folds. Colonel Archibald Gracie was cast up there, Gracie who had leaped from the stern as the *Titanic* sank; young Thayer who had seen his father die; Lightoller who had twice been sucked down with the ship and twice blown to the surface by a belch of air; Bride, the second operator, and Phillips, the first. There were many stokers, half naked; it was a shivering company. They stood there in the icy sea, under the far stars, and sang and prayed—the Lord's Prayer. After a while a lifeboat came and picked them off, but Phillips was dead then or died soon afterward in the boat.

Only a few of the boats had lights; only one—No. 2—had a light that was of any use to the *Carpathia*, twisting through the ice field to the rescue. Other ships were "coming hard" too; one, the *Californian*, was still dead to opportunity.

Vocabulary

poised (poizd) *adj.:* balanced; in position.

perfunctory (pər·fuŋk′tə·rē) *adj.:* not exerting much effort; unconcerned.

The blue sparks still danced, but not the *Titanic*'s. *La Provence* to *Celtic:* "Nobody has heard the *Titanic* for about two hours."

It was 2:40 when the *Carpathia* first sighted the green light from No. 2 boat; it was 4:10 when she picked up the first boat and learned that the *Titanic* had foundered.[19] The last of the moaning cries had just died away then.

Captain Rostron took the survivors aboard, boatload by boatload. He was ready for them, but only a small minority of them required much medical attention. Bride's feet were twisted and frozen; others were suffering from exposure; one died, and seven were dead when taken from the boats, and were buried at sea.

It was then that the fleet of racing ships learned they were too late; the *Parisian* heard the weak signals of *MPA*, the *Carpathia*, report the death of the *Titanic*. It was then—or soon afterward, when her radio operator put on his earphones—that the *Californian*, the ship that had been within sight as the *Titanic* was sinking, first learned of the disaster.

And it was then, in all its white-green majesty, that the *Titanic*'s survivors saw the iceberg, tinted with the sunrise, floating idly, pack ice jammed about its base, other bergs heaving slowly nearby on the blue breast of the sea.

IV

But it was not until later that the world knew, for wireless then was not what wireless is today, and garbled messages had nourished a hope that all of the *Titanic*'s company were safe. Not until Monday evening, when P.A.S. Franklin, vice president of the International Mercantile Marine Company, received relayed messages in New York that left little hope, did the full extent of the disaster begin to be known. Partial and garbled lists of the survivors; rumors of heroism and cowardice; stories spun out of newspaper imagination, based on a few bare facts and many false reports, misled the world, terrified and frightened it. It was not until Thursday night, when the *Carpathia* steamed into the North River, that the full truth was pieced together.

Flashlights flared on the black river when the *Carpathia* stood up to her dock. Tugs nosed about her, shunted her toward Pier 54. Thirty thousand people jammed the streets; ambulances and stretchers stood on the pier; coroners and physicians waited.

In midstream the Cunarder dropped over the *Titanic*'s lifeboats; then she headed toward the dock. Beneath the customs letters on the pier stood relatives of the 711 survivors, relatives of the missing—hoping against hope. The *Carpathia* cast her lines ashore; stevedores[20] looped them over bollards. The dense throngs stood quiet as the first survivor stepped down the gangway. The woman half staggered—led by customs guards—beneath her letter. A "low wailing" moan came from the crowd; fell, grew in volume, and dropped again.

Thus ended the maiden voyage of the *Titanic*. The lifeboats brought to New York by the *Carpathia*, a few deck chairs and gratings awash in the ice field off the Grand Bank eight hundred miles from shore, were all that was left of the world's greatest ship.

V

The aftermath of weeping and regret, of recriminations and investigations, dragged

---

20. stevedores (stē′və·dôrz′) *n.:* persons who load and unload ships.

Vocabulary

garbled (gär′bəld) *v.* used as *adj.:* confused; mixed up.

recriminations (ri·krim′ə·nā′shənz) *n.:* accusations against an accuser; countercharges.

---

19. foundered *v.:* filled with water, so that it sank; generally, collapsed; failed.

on for weeks. Charges and countercharges were hurled about; the White Star Line was bitterly criticized; Ismay was denounced on the floor of the Senate as a coward but was defended by those who had been with him on the sinking *Titanic* and by the Board of Trade investigation in England.

It was not until weeks later, when the hastily convened Senate investigation in the United States and the Board of Trade report in England had been completed, that the whole story was told. The Senate investigating committee, under the chairmanship of Senator Smith, who was attacked in both the American and the British press as a "backwoods politician," brought out numerous pertinent facts, though its proceedings verged at times on the farcical.[21] Senator Smith was ridiculed for his lack of knowledge of the sea when he asked witnesses, "Of what is an iceberg composed?" and "Did any of the passengers take refuge in the watertight compartments?" The senator seemed particularly interested in the marital status of Fleet, the lookout, who was saved. Fleet, puzzled, growled aside, "Wot questions they're arskin' me!"

The report of Lord Mersey, wreck commissioner in the British Board of Trade's investigation, was tersely damning.

The *Titanic* had carried boats enough for 1,178 persons, only one third of her capacity. Her sixteen boats and four collapsibles had saved but 711 persons; 400 people had needlessly lost their lives. The boats had been but partly loaded; officers in charge of launching them had been afraid the falls[22] would break or the boats buckle under their rated loads; boat crews had been slow in reaching their stations; launching arrangements were confused because no boat drill had been held; passengers were loaded into the boats haphazardly because no boat assignments had been made.

But that was not all. Lord Mersey found that sufficient warnings of ice on the steamer track had reached the *Titanic*, that her speed of twenty-two knots was "excessive under the circumstances," that "in view of the high speed at which the vessel was running it is not considered that the lookout was sufficient," and that her master made "a very grievous mistake"—but should not be blamed for negligence. Captain Rostron of the *Carpathia* was highly praised. "He did the very best that could be done." The *Californian* was damned. The testimony of her master, officers, and crew showed that she was not, at the most, more than nineteen miles away from the sinking *Titanic* and probably no more than five to ten miles distant. She had seen the *Titanic*'s lights; she had seen the rockets; she had not received the CQD calls because her radio operator was asleep. She had attempted to get in communication with the ship she had sighted by flashing a light, but vainly.

"The night was clear," reported Lord Mersey, "and the sea was smooth. When she first saw the rockets, the *Californian* could have pushed through the ice to the open water without any serious risk and so have come to the assistance of the *Titanic*. Had she done so she might have saved many if not all of the lives that were lost.

"She made no attempt." ■

---

21. **farcical** (fär′si·kəl) *adj.:* absurd; ridiculous; like a farce (an exaggerated comedy).
22. **falls** *n.:* chains used for hoisting.

Vocabulary
pertinent (pʉrt′'n·ənt) *adj.:* having some connection with the subject.
vainly (vān′lē) *adv.:* without success; fruitlessly.

Meet the Writer

Hanson W. Baldwin

Journalist and Seaman

Hanson W. Baldwin (1903–1991) was one of America's great journalists. He graduated with an ensign's commission from the U.S. Naval Academy at Annapolis. After only three years of service aboard battleships, Baldwin resigned from the Navy and launched a career as a military correspondent and editor. His longest hitch was with *The New York Times.*

During World War II Baldwin covered battles in North Africa and the D-day invasion of Normandy. His series of articles on the war in the South Pacific won him a Pulitzer Prize in 1943. After the war, he reported on the second atomic bomb test at Bikini Island, on guided-missile and rocket-firing installations, and on the organization of U.S. military forces in the nuclear age.

Relatively early in his writing career (1934), Baldwin wrote an article for *Harper's Magazine* about the sinking of the *Titanic,* which had occurred twenty-two years earlier. His research was thorough: He pieced together information from ship logs, from interviews with survivors, and from written reports detailing the ship's design and launching. The subject of the *Titanic* was by no means new for Baldwin's readers. The sinking of the "unsinkable" ship had been fictionalized, sensationalized, and sentimentalized many times before 1934. Nevertheless, Baldwin's article became a textbook example of excellent reporting. His fast-paced account, with its mixture of factual details and irony, makes the disaster and all the human foibles associated with it seem tragically real again.

The lifeboats of the "unsinkable" Titanic carried fewer than one third of the approximately 2,200 people aboard. A U.S. Senate investigating committee in 1912 found that a total of 1,517 lives were lost—a high proportion of them poor passengers who were far below deck, in steerage. Here are two eyewitness accounts of survivors:

A Fireman's Story

Harry Senior

Mrs. J. Bruce Ismay.

J. Bruce Ismay, director of the White Star Line.

I was in my bunk when I felt a bump. One man said, "Hello. She has been struck." I went on deck and saw a great pile of ice on the well deck before the forecastle, but we all thought the ship would last some time, and we went back to our bunks. Then one of the firemen came running down and yelled, "All muster for the lifeboats." I ran on deck, and the captain said, "All firemen keep down on the well deck. If a man comes up, I'll shoot him."

Then I saw the first lifeboat lowered. Thirteen people were on board, eleven men and two women. Three were millionaires, and one was Ismay [J. Bruce Ismay, managing director of the White Star Line; a survivor].

Then I ran up onto the hurricane deck and helped to throw one of the collapsible boats onto the lower deck. I saw an Italian woman holding two babies. I took one of them and made the woman jump overboard with the baby, while I did the same with the other. When I came to the surface, the baby in my arms was dead. I saw the woman strike out in good style, but a boiler burst on the *Titanic* and started a big wave. When the woman saw that wave, she gave up. Then, as the child was dead, I let it sink too.

I swam around for about half an hour, and was swimming on my back when the *Titanic* went down. I tried to get aboard a boat, but some chap hit me over the head with an oar. There were too many in her. I got around to the other side of the boat and climbed in.

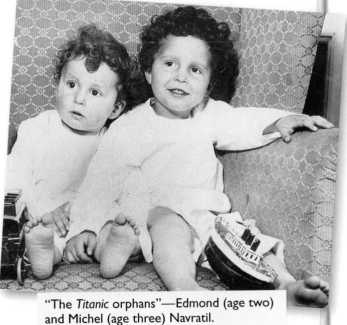

"The *Titanic* orphans"—Edmond (age two) and Michel (age three) Navratil.

From a Lifeboat

Mrs. D. H. Bishop

We did not begin to understand the situation till we were perhaps a mile or more away from the *Titanic.* Then we could see the rows of lights along the decks begin to slant gradually upward from the bow. Very slowly, the lines of light began to point downward at a greater and greater angle. The sinking was so slow that you could not perceive the lights of the deck changing their position. The slant seemed to be greater about every quarter of an hour. That was the only difference.

In a couple of hours, though, she began to go down more rapidly. Then the fearful sight began. The people in the ship were just beginning to realize how great their danger was. When the forward part of the ship dropped suddenly at a faster rate, so that the upward slope became marked, there was a sudden rush of passengers on all the decks toward the stern. It was like a wave. We could see the great black mass of people in the steerage sweeping to the rear part of the boat and breaking through into the upper decks. At the distance of about a mile, we could distinguish everything through the night, which was perfectly clear. We could make out the increasing excitement on board the boat as the people,

Ruth Becker and her brother Richard survived in separate lifeboats.

Marion Wright from Somerset, England, married her fiancé when she arrived in New York City.

rushing to and fro, caused the deck lights to disappear and reappear as they passed in front of them.

This panic went on, it seemed, for an hour. Then suddenly the ship seemed to shoot up out of the water and stand there perpendicularly. It seemed to us that it stood upright in the water for four full minutes.

Then it began to slide gently downward. Its speed increased as it went down headfirst, so that the stern shot down with a rush.

The lights continued to burn till it sank. We could see the people packed densely in the stern till it was gone. . . .

As the ship sank, we could hear the screaming a mile away. Gradually it became fainter and fainter and died away. Some of the lifeboats that had room for more might have gone to their rescue, but it would have meant that those who were in the water would have swarmed aboard and sunk them.

Response and Analysis

Reading Check

1. According to the Baldwin article, what caused the *Titanic* to sink?

2. Why didn't the closest ship rush to the rescue?

3. Why weren't the lifeboats full?

4. Cite two heroic acts and two cowardly acts that took place aboard the *Titanic*.

Thinking Critically

5. Baldwin uses numbered **headings** as **text structures** to organize his article. Briefly summarize what is covered in each numbered part. Why are these divisions logical?

6. Find as many examples as you can of **irony**—both **situational** and **dramatic**—in this story of the *Titanic*. Which instance of irony do you think is the most incredible?

7. Baldwin combines a **chronological** account (a **narrative,** or story) with **factual** information (**exposition**). What do you think is his **purpose** in combining these two types of writing?

8. What techniques does Baldwin use to create drama and **suspense** in this story, whose outcome we already know? Notice, for example, the switch to present-tense verbs in Part II. What other devices help make the article as compelling as a fast-paced adventure novel?

9. Baldwin returns many times to the music played by the ship's band. What **moods** are suggested by the music? What other examples of **repetition** can you find?

10. What truths about human nature can you **infer** from this story and from the survivors' accounts (see the **Connection** on page 345)?

Extending and Evaluating

11. After reading about the events on board the *Titanic,* as well as the **Connection** on page 345, how do you think (or hope) you would have acted if you'd been a passenger? a crew member? Look back at your Quickwrite to see whether you've changed your mind about how you'd behave in a catastrophe.

12. Baldwin spent hundreds of hours reading reports, ships' records, eyewitness accounts, and court proceedings. How **objective** or **subjective** do you think Baldwin's report is? Explain your evaluation.

WRITING

Summary of a Disaster

Write a one-page **summary** of "R.M.S. Titanic," including the most significant facts and Baldwin's most important conclusions. Before you begin writing, **outline** the article, showing what Baldwin covers in each of the five numbered sections. Include with your summary a graphic organizer in the form of a **time line** to show the major events in the disaster.

Titanic Update

We now know that Baldwin's article contains errors (such as Captain Smith's initials and the description of a three-hundred-foot gash that later exploration has not been able to find). Using the Internet and recent books and articles on the subject, determine what other information has been revealed about the *Titanic* since the Baldwin article was written. Record your findings in a **brief report**.

SKILLS FOCUS

Literary Skills
Analyze situational irony and dramatic irony. Analyze objective writing and subjective writing.

Reading Skills
Analyze text structures.

Writing Skills
Write a summary containing a time line. Write a brief research report.

Vocabulary Development

Word Maps: Showing Words in Action

PRACTICE 1

You can pin down a new word's meaning by asking—and answering—questions about it. Work alone or with a partner to make a **word map** like the one below for *superlative* for the other words in the Word Bank. The questions you ask will vary.

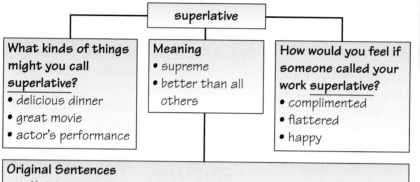

superlative

What kinds of things might you call superlative?
• delicious dinner
• great movie
• actor's performance

Meaning
• supreme
• better than all others

How would you feel if someone called your work superlative?
• complimented
• flattered
• happy

Original Sentences
• Jeff did a superlative job of painting the kitchen.
• The conductor complimented Sheila for her superlative trumpet solo.

Words from Mythology: So That's Where That Word Comes From

Many words in English derive from the myths of ancient Greece. For example, *Titanic,* as you read earlier, comes from the Greek myth of the Titans. *Ocean* is another word that comes from the myth of the Titans. Ocean, or Oceanus, was lord of the great river (also called Ocean) that was believed to circle the earth.

SKILLS FOCUS

Vocabulary Skills
Make semantic maps. Understand words derived from Greek mythology.

PRACTICE 2

Match the words below to the numbered items that follow. Then, use a dictionary to define the modern meaning of the words. (For more about words from mythology, see pages 672 and 684–685.)

echo   panic
narcissism   tantalize

1. Pan, the Greek god of shepherds, was depicted as half-man and half-goat. His great shout struck fear in humans.

2. Echo was a nymph, a kind of goddess. She angered the goddess Hera, who took away her power to speak, except to repeat what others said. Echo was in love with a youth who rejected her, and she pined away for him until all that was left was her voice.

3. Narcissus, a beautiful youth loved by all the nymphs who saw him, rejected them, and they prayed for revenge. In answer to their prayers, the goddess Nemesis made him fall in love with his own reflection.

4. Tantalus, a king who stole the food of the gods, was punished with eternal hunger and thirst while food and drink were kept just out of his reach.

Before You Read

from Into Thin Air

Make the Connection

Quickwrite ✏

Can you imagine yourself standing on the 29,035-foot top of the world? The cold has numbed your body, the altitude has dulled your brain, and you are exhausted beyond belief. Now you have to get down—the most dangerous part of the climb.

Jon Krakauer, the author of this magazine article, lived through that experience. Why do you think some people, like Krakauer, are so drawn to climbing mountains? Would you like to do it? Briefly jot down why you would or wouldn't.

Literary Focus

Ironies and Contradictions That Spell Real-Life Disaster

In this true story of climbers struggling on Mount Everest, Murphy's law seems to have taken hold: "If there's a possibility that something can go wrong, it will." As you read, look for examples of **situational irony**—when the opposite of what's expected or appropriate occurs.

Look also for the real-life **contradictions** and **incongruities** that lead to disaster—instances in which people don't do what they say they will do or when things don't come together as they should. For example, expedition leader Rob Hall contradicts his own rule of an absolute cutoff time for reaching the summit. These and other fateful twists combine to spell tragedy for the climbers.

Reading Skills

Understanding Cause and Effect

A **cause** is the reason why something happens; an **effect** is the result of some event. A single effect may have several causes, and a single cause may lead to many effects.

Everything that happens in this tragic story is connected by a complex pattern of causes and effects, many of which are filled with **irony.** As you read, look for the causes that led to the disasters on Mount Everest. Look for the effects of certain decisions made by the climbers. The questions at the open-book signs will help you.

Vocabulary Development

deteriorate (dē·tir′ē·ə·rāt′) *v.:* worsen.

innocuous (i·näk′yoo·əs) *adj.:* harmless.

notorious (nō·tôr′ē·əs) *adj.:* famous, usually in an unfavorable sense.

benign (bi·nīn′) *adj.:* here, favorable or harmless.

apex (ā′peks′) *n.:* highest point; top.

crucial (kroo′shəl) *adj.:* extremely important; decisive.

speculate (spek′yə·lāt′) *v.:* think; guess.

traverse (trə·vurs′) *v.:* cross.

jeopardize (jep′ər·dīz′) *v.:* endanger.

tenuous (ten′yoo·əs) *adj.:* weak; slight.

INTERNET

Vocabulary Practice

Keyword: LE5 10-5

SKILLS FOCUS

Literary Skills
Understand situational irony, contradictions, and incongruities.

Reading Skills
Understand cause and effect.

(*continued*)

Background

Hot Story, Cold Mountain

The man who said he wanted to climb Mount Everest "because it's there," George Leigh Mallory, disappeared in a mist near the summit in 1924. The first recorded conquest of the 29,035-foot peak was achieved by Edmund Hillary of New Zealand and Tenzing Norgay of Nepal in 1953. Since then more than 1,300 climbers have reached the summit, but about 170 have lost their lives to the mountain.

The journalist who wrote this magazine article barely escaped with his life. In 1996, *Outside* magazine financed Jon Krakauer's climb, which he undertook as a client of a commercial expedition. The day he reached the summit of Everest, eight other climbers (including Krakauer's tour leader) died on the mountain. (This is the riskiest form of **participatory journalism,** in which a reporter takes part in the events he or she is reporting.)

Since the May 1996 tragedy, more and more people have caught Everest fever, some paying as much as seventy thousand dollars for a guided climb. Although many of these climbers are experts, some are inexperienced—a problem that creates grave dangers.

Making a Climb

Everest expeditions ascend the mountain in stages. From Base Camp, at 17,600 feet, they make short trips up and down to acclimatize, or get used to higher elevations. This process may last several weeks before the final climb to the top, which is also done in stages. Krakauer's group made camp at 19,500 feet, 21,300 feet, 24,000 feet, and 26,000 feet. The area above 25,000 feet is known as the Death Zone. Here the air is so poor in oxygen that it's almost impossible for climbers to make rational decisions.

Some of the Climbers Involved in the Tragedy

New Zealand–Based Team
① Rob Hall, *leader; head guide*
② Mike Groom, *guide*
③ Andy "Harold" Harris, *guide*
④ Doug Hansen, *client*
⑤ Jon Krakauer, *client; journalist*
⑥ Yasuko Namba, *client*
⑦ Beck Weathers, *client*
  Lhakpa Chhiri Sherpa,
    climbing Sherpa

American-Based Team
Scott Fischer, *leader; head guide*
Anatoli Boukreev, *guide*

Taiwan Team
"Makalu" Gau Ming-Ho, *leader*

IMAX Film Crew
David Breashears, *leader;*
  film director
Ed Viesturs, *climber;*
  film talent

Everest Summit 29,035 feet

The Hillary Step

The South Summit 28,710 feet

The Balcony 27,600 feet

TIBET (Self-governing region of China)

HIMALAYA

Annapurna 26,504 ft.

Everest 29,035 ft.

NEPAL

North

Katmandu

INDIA

Scale in miles

0   100   200   300   400   500

Camp Four 26,000 feet

To Camp Three

South Col

Members of Jon Krakauer's expedition team, led by Rob Hall. The numbers identify the team members named in the list of expedition members on page 350.

Into

Everest deals with trespassers harshly: The dead vanish beneath the snows, while the living struggle to explain what happened, and why. A survivor of the mountain's worst disaster examines the business of Mount Everest and the steep price of ambition.

Thin Air

Jon Krakauer

Straddling the top of the world, one foot in Tibet and the other in Nepal, I cleared the ice from my oxygen mask, hunched a shoulder against the wind, and stared absently at the vast sweep of earth below. I understood on some dim, detached level that it was a spectacular sight. I'd been fantasizing about this moment, and the release of emotion that would accompany it, for many months. But now that I was finally here, standing on the summit of Mount Everest, I just couldn't summon the energy to care.

It was the afternoon of May 10. I hadn't slept in 57 hours. The only food I'd been able to force down over the preceding three days was a bowl of Ramen soup and a handful of peanut M&M's. Weeks of violent coughing had left me with two separated ribs, making it excruciatingly painful to breathe. Twenty-nine thousand twenty-eight feet[1] up in the troposphere,[2] there was so little oxygen reaching my brain that my mental capacity was that of a slow child. Under the circumstances, I was incapable of feeling much of anything except cold and tired.

I'd arrived on the summit a few minutes after Anatoli Boukreev,[3] a Russian guide with an American expedition, and just ahead of Andy Harris, a guide with the New Zealand–based commercial team that I was a part of and someone with whom I'd grown to be friends during the last six weeks. I snapped four quick photos of Harris and Boukreev striking summit poses, and then turned and started down. My watch read 1:17 P.M. All told, I'd spent less than five minutes on the roof of the world.

---

1. In 1999, after this article was written, scientists using sophisticated equipment determined the elevation of Everest to be 29,035 feet, not 29,028 feet as previously believed.
2. **troposphere** (trō′pə·sfir′) *n.*: portion of the atmosphere directly below the stratosphere (it extends from 6 to 8 miles above the earth's surface).
3. **Anatoli Boukreev:** Boukreev (pictured at left on Mount Everest) was killed in an avalanche about a year and a half later, on December 25, 1997, while climbing Annapurna in the Himalayas.

After a few steps, I paused to take another photo, this one looking down the Southeast Ridge, the route we had ascended. Training my lens on a pair of climbers approaching the summit, I saw something that until that moment had escaped my attention. To the south, where the sky had been perfectly clear just an hour earlier, a blanket of clouds now hid Pumori, Ama Dablam, and the other lesser peaks surrounding Everest.

Days later—after six bodies had been found, after a search for two others had been abandoned, after surgeons had amputated[4] the gangrenous[5] right hand of my teammate Beck Weathers—people would ask why, if the weather had begun to deteriorate, had climbers on the upper mountain not heeded the signs? Why did veteran Himalayan guides keep moving upward, leading a gaggle of amateurs, each of whom had paid as much as $65,000 to be ushered safely up Everest, into an apparent death trap?

Nobody can speak for the leaders of the two guided groups involved, for both men are now dead. But I can attest that nothing I saw early on the afternoon of May 10 suggested that a murderous storm was about to bear down on us. To my oxygen-depleted mind, the clouds drifting up the grand valley of ice known as the Western Cwm looked innocuous, wispy, insubstantial. Gleaming in the brilliant midday sun, they appeared no different from the harmless puffs of convection condensation that rose from the valley almost daily. As I began my descent, I was indeed anxious, but my concern had little to do with the weather. A check of the gauge on my oxygen tank had revealed that it was almost empty. I needed to get down, fast.

> **Nobody can speak for the leaders . . . for both men are now dead.**

The uppermost shank of the Southeast Ridge is a slender, heavily corniced fin[6] of rock and wind-scoured snow that snakes for a quarter-mile toward a secondary pinnacle known as the South Summit. Negotiating the serrated[7] ridge presents few great technical hurdles, but the route is dreadfully exposed. After 15 minutes of cautious shuffling over a 7,000-foot abyss,[8] I arrived at the notorious Hillary Step, a pronounced notch in the ridge named after Sir Edmund Hillary, the first Westerner to climb the mountain, and a spot that does require a fair amount of technical maneuvering. As I clipped into a fixed rope and prepared to rappel[9] over the lip, I was greeted by an alarming sight.

Thirty feet below, some 20 people were queued up[10] at the base of the Step, and three climbers were hauling themselves up the rope that I was attempting to descend. I had no choice but to unclip from the line and step aside.

The traffic jam comprised climbers from three separate expeditions: the team I belonged to, a group of paying clients under the leadership of the celebrated New Zealand guide Rob Hall; another guided party headed by American Scott Fischer; and a nonguided team from Taiwan. Moving at the snail's pace that is the norm above 8,000 meters, the throng labored up the

---

6. **corniced** (kôr′nist) **fin:** curving and narrow ridge.
7. **serrated** v. used as adj.: notched like a saw.
8. **abyss** (ə·bis′) n.: deep crack or opening in the earth's surface.
9. **rappel** (ra·pel′) v.: descend a mountain by means of a double rope arranged around the climber's body so that he or she can control the slide downward.
10. **queued** (kyo͞od) **up:** lined up.

Vocabulary

deteriorate (dē·tir′ē·ə·rāt′) v.: worsen.

innocuous (i·näk′yo͞o·əs) adj.: harmless.

notorious (nō·tôr′ē·əs) adj.: famous, usually in an unfavorable sense.

---

4. **amputated** v.: cut off (a limb or body part) through surgery.
5. **gangrenous** (gaŋ′grə·nəs) adj.: affected by the decay of tissue resulting from a lack of blood supply.

Hillary Step one by one, while I nervously bided my time.

Harris, who left the summit shortly after I did, soon pulled up behind me. Wanting to conserve whatever oxygen remained in my tank, I asked him to reach inside my backpack and turn off the valve on my regulator, which he did. For the next ten minutes I felt surprisingly good. My head cleared. I actually seemed less tired than with the gas turned on. Then, abruptly, I felt like I was suffocating. My vision dimmed and my head began to spin. I was on the brink of losing consciousness.

Instead of turning my oxygen off, Harris, in his hypoxically[11] impaired state, had mistakenly cranked the valve open to full flow, draining the tank. I'd just squandered the last of my gas going nowhere. There was another tank waiting for me at the South Summit, 250 feet below, but to get there I would have to descend the most exposed terrain on the entire route without benefit of supplemental oxygen.

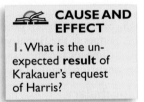

CAUSE AND EFFECT

1. What is the unexpected **result** of Krakauer's request of Harris?

But first I had to wait for the crowd to thin. I removed my now useless mask, planted my ice ax into the mountain's frozen hide, and hunkered on the ridge crest. As I exchanged banal[12] congratulations with the climbers filing past, inwardly I was frantic: "Hurry it up, hurry it up!" I silently pleaded. "While you guys are messing around here, I'm losing brain cells by the millions!"

Most of the passing crowd belonged to Fischer's group, but near the back of the parade two of my teammates eventually appeared: Hall and Yasuko Namba. Girlish and reserved, the 47-year-old Namba was 40 minutes away from becoming the oldest woman to climb Everest and the second Japanese woman to reach the highest point on each continent, the so-called Seven Summits.

Later still, Doug Hansen—another member of our expedition, a postal worker from Seattle who had become my closest friend on the mountain—arrived atop the Step. "It's in the bag!" I yelled over the wind, trying to sound more upbeat than I felt. Plainly exhausted, Doug mumbled something from behind his oxygen mask that I didn't catch, shook my hand weakly, and continued plodding upward.

The last climber up the rope was Fischer, whom I knew casually from Seattle, where we both lived. His strength and drive were legendary—in 1994 he'd climbed Everest without using bottled oxygen—so I was surprised at how slowly he was moving and how hammered he looked when he pulled his mask aside to say hello. "Bruuuuuuce!" he wheezed with forced cheer, employing his trademark, fratboyish greeting. When I asked how he was doing, Fischer insisted he was feeling fine: "Just dragging a little today for some reason. No big deal." With the Hillary Step finally clear, I clipped into the strand of orange rope, swung quickly around Fischer as he slumped over his ice ax, and rappelled over the edge.

It was after 2:30 when I made it down to the South Summit. By now tendrils of mist were wrapping across the top of 27,890-foot Lhotse and lapping at Everest's summit pyramid. No longer did the weather look so <u>benign</u>. I grabbed a fresh oxygen cylinder, jammed it onto my regulator, and hurried down into the gathering cloud.

Four hundred vertical feet above, where the summit was still washed in bright sunlight under an immaculate cobalt sky, my

---

11. **hypoxically** *adv.:* characterized by hypoxia, a condition resulting from a decrease in the oxygen reaching body tissues. Hypoxia is a common condition at very high altitudes.
12. **banal** *adj.:* everyday; commonplace.

Vocabulary
benign (bi·nīn′) *adj.:* here, favorable or harmless.

compadres[13] were dallying,[14] memorializing their arrival at the apex of the planet with photos and high-fives—and using up precious ticks of the clock. None of them imagined that a horrible ordeal was drawing nigh. None of them suspected that by the end of that long day, every minute would matter. . . .

At 3 P.M., within minutes of leaving the South Summit, I descended into clouds ahead of the others. Snow started to fall. In the flat, diminishing light, it became hard to tell where the mountain ended and where the sky began. It would have been very easy to blunder off the edge of the ridge and never be heard from again. The lower I went, the worse the weather became.

When I reached the Balcony again, about 4 P.M., I encountered Beck Weathers standing alone, shivering violently. Years earlier, Weathers had undergone radial keratotomy to correct his vision. A side effect, which he discovered on Everest and consequently hid from Hall, was that in the low barometric pressure at high altitude, his eyesight failed. Nearly blind when he'd left Camp Four in the middle of the night but hopeful that his vision would improve at daybreak, he stuck close to the person in front of him and kept climbing.

Upon reaching the Southeast Ridge shortly after sunrise, Weathers had confessed to Hall that he was having trouble seeing, at which point Hall declared, "Sorry, pal, you're going down. I'll send one of the Sherpas[15] with you." Weathers countered that his vision was likely to improve as soon as the sun crept higher in the sky; Hall said he'd give Weathers 30 minutes to find out—after that, he'd have to wait there at 27,500 feet for Hall and the rest of the group to come back down. Hall didn't want Weathers descending alone. "I'm dead serious about this," Hall

---

13. **compadres** (kəm·pä′drāz′) *n.:* close friends; in this case, fellow members of the climbing team.
14. **dallying** *v.:* wasting time.

---

15. **Sherpas:** Tibetan people living on the southern slopes of the Himalayas. As experienced mountain climbers, the Sherpas are hired by expeditions to haul loads and set up camps and ropes.

Vocabulary
apex (ā′peks′) *n.:* highest point; top.

Doug Hansen approaching the summit.

admonished his client. "Promise me that you'll sit right here until I return."

"I crossed my heart and hoped to die," Weathers recalls now, "and promised I wouldn't go anywhere." Shortly after noon, Hutchison, Taske, and Kasischke[16] passed by with their Sherpa escorts, but Weathers elected not to accompany them. "The weather was still good," he explains, "and I saw no reason to break my promise to Rob."

By the time I encountered Weathers, however, conditions were turning ugly. "Come down with me," I implored, "I'll get you down, no problem." He was nearly convinced, until I made the mistake of mentioning that Groom was on his way down, too. In a day of many mistakes, this would turn out to be a crucial one. "Thanks anyway," Weathers said. "I'll just wait for Mike. He's got a rope; he'll be able to short-rope[17] me." Secretly relieved, I hurried toward the South Col, 1,500 feet below.

CAUSE AND EFFECT

2. What is the **effect** of Weathers's promise to Hall?

These lower slopes proved to be the most difficult part of the descent. Six inches of powder snow blanketed outcroppings of loose shale. Climbing down them demanded unceasing concentration, an all but impossible feat in my current state. By 5:30, however, I was finally within 200 vertical feet of Camp Four, and only one obstacle stood between me and safety: a steep bulge of rock-hard ice that I'd have to descend without a rope. But the weather had deteriorated into a full-scale blizzard. Snow pellets born on 70-mph winds stung my face; any exposed skin was instantly frozen. The tents, no more than 200 horizontal yards away, were only intermittently visible through the whiteout. There was zero margin for error. Worried about making a critical blunder, I sat down to marshal my energy.

Suddenly, Harris[18] appeared out of the gloom and sat beside me. At this point there was no mistaking that he was in appalling shape. His cheeks were coated with an armor of frost, one eye was frozen shut, and his speech was slurred. He was frantic to reach the tents. After briefly discussing the best way to negotiate the ice, Harris started scooting down on his butt, facing forward. "Andy," I yelled after him, "it's crazy to try it like that!" He yelled something back, but the words were carried off by the screaming wind. A second later he lost his purchase[19] and was rocketing down on his back.

Two hundred feet below, I could make out Harris's motionless form. I was sure he'd broken at least a leg, maybe his neck. But then he stood up, waved that he was OK, and started stumbling toward camp, which was for the moment in plain sight, 150 yards beyond.

I could see three or four people shining lights outside the tents. I watched Harris walk across the flats to the edge of camp, a distance he covered in less than ten minutes. When the clouds closed in a moment later, cutting off my view, he was within 30 yards of the tents. I didn't see him again after that, but I was certain that he'd reached the security of camp, where Sherpas would be waiting with hot tea. Sitting out in the storm, with the ice bulge still standing between me and the tents, I felt a pang of envy. I was angry that my guide hadn't waited for me.

Twenty minutes later I was in camp. I fell into my tent with my crampons still on, zipped the door tight, and sprawled across the frost-covered floor. I was drained, more exhausted than I'd ever

---

16. Stuart Hutchison, Dr. John Taske, and Lou Kasischke were three clients on Rob Hall's team.
17. **short-rope** *n.* used as *v.*: assist a weak or injured climber by hauling him or her.

---

18. After writing this article, Krakauer discovered through conversations with Martin Adams (a client on Scott Fischer's team) that the person he thought was Harris was, in fact, Martin Adams.
19. **purchase** *n.*: firm hold.

Vocabulary
crucial (kroo′shəl) *adj.*: extremely important; decisive.

been in my life. But I was safe. Andy was safe. The others would be coming into camp soon. We'd done it. We'd climbed Mount Everest.

It would be many hours before I learned that everyone had in fact not made it back to camp— that one teammate was already dead and that 23 other men and women were caught in a desperate struggle for their lives. . . .

Meanwhile, Hall and Hansen were still on the frightfully exposed summit ridge, engaged in a grim struggle of their own. The 46-year-old Hansen, whom Hall had turned back just below this spot exactly a year ago, had been determined to bag the summit this time around. "I want to get this thing done and out of my life," he'd told me a couple of days earlier. "I don't want to have to come back here."

Indeed Hansen had reached the top this time, though not until after 3 P.M., well after Hall's predetermined turnaround time. Given Hall's conservative, systematic nature, many people wonder why he didn't turn Hansen around when it became obvious that he was running late. It's not far-fetched to speculate that because Hall had talked Hansen into coming back to Everest this year, it would have been especially hard for him to deny Hansen the summit a second time—especially when all of Fischer's clients were still marching blithely toward the top.

"It's very difficult to turn someone around high on the mountain," cautions Guy Cotter, a New Zealand guide who summited Everest with Hall in 1992 and was guiding the peak for him in 1995 when Hansen made his first attempt. "If a client sees that the summit is close and they're dead set on getting there, they're going to laugh in your face and keep going up."

In any case, for whatever reason, Hall did not turn Hansen around. Instead, after reaching the summit at 2:10 P.M., Hall waited for more than an hour for Hansen to arrive and then headed

down with him. Soon after they began their descent, just below the top, Hansen apparently ran out of oxygen and collapsed. "Pretty much the same thing happened to Doug in '95," says Ed Viesturs, an American who guided the peak for Hall that year. "He was fine during the ascent, but as soon as he started down he lost it mentally and physically. He turned into a real zombie, like he'd used everything up."

CAUSE AND EFFECT

3. What **contradiction** is evident in Hall's behavior? What is the **result**?

At 4:31 P.M., Hall radioed Base Camp to say that he and Hansen were above the Hillary Step and urgently needed oxygen. Two full bottles were waiting for them at the South Summit; if Hall had known this he could have retrieved the gas fairly quickly and then climbed back up to give Hansen a fresh tank. But Harris, in the throes of his oxygen-starved dementia,[20] overheard the 4:31 radio call while descending the Southeast Ridge and broke in to tell Hall that all the bottles at the South Summit were empty. So Hall stayed with Hansen and tried to bring the helpless client down without oxygen, but could get him no farther than the top of the Hillary Step.

Cotter, a very close friend of both Hall and Harris, happened to be a few miles from Everest Base Camp at the time, guiding an expedition on Pumori. Overhearing the radio conversations between Hall and Base Camp, he called Hall at 5:36 and again at 5:57, urging his mate to leave Hansen and come down alone. . . . Hall, however, wouldn't consider going down without Hansen.

---

20. **dementia** (di·men′shə) *n.:* mental impairment; madness.

Vocabulary
speculate (spek′yə·lāt′) *v.:* think; guess.

There was no further word from Hall until the middle of the night. At 2:46 A.M. on May 11, Cotter woke up to hear a long, broken transmission, probably unintended: Hall was wearing a remote microphone clipped to the shoulder strap of his backpack, which was occasionally keyed on by mistake. In this instance, says Cotter, "I suspect Rob didn't even know he was transmitting. I could hear someone yelling— it might have been Rob, but I couldn't be sure because the wind was so loud in the background. He was saying something like 'Keep moving! Keep going!' presumably to Doug, urging him on."

If that was indeed the case, it meant that in the wee hours of the morning Hall and Hansen were still struggling from the Hillary Step toward the South Summit, taking more than 12 hours to <u>traverse</u> a stretch of ridge typically covered by descending climbers in half an hour.

> **CAUSE AND EFFECT**
>
> **4.** Why does it take them so long to traverse the ridge?

Hall's next call to Base Camp was at 4:43 A.M. He'd finally reached the South Summit but was unable to descend farther, and in a series of transmissions over the next two hours he sounded confused and irrational. "Harold[21] was with me last night," Hall insisted, when in fact Harris had reached the South Col at sunset. "But he doesn't seem to be with me now. He was very weak."

Mackenzie[22] asked him how Hansen was doing. "Doug," Hall replied, "is gone." That was all he said, and it was the last mention he ever made of Hansen.

On May 23, when Breashears and Viesturs, of the IMAX team,[23] reached the summit, they found no sign of Hansen's body but they did find an ice ax planted about 50 feet below the Hillary Step, along a highly exposed section of ridge where the fixed ropes came to an end. It is quite possible that Hall managed to get Hansen down the ropes to this point, only to have him lose his footing and fall 7,000 feet down the sheer Southwest Face, leaving his ice ax jammed into the ridge crest where he slipped.

During the radio calls to Base Camp early on May 11, Hall revealed that something was wrong with his legs, that he was no longer able to walk and was shaking uncontrollably.

Guide Rob Hall.

---

21. **Harold:** Andy Harris's nickname.
22. **Mackenzie:** Dr. Caroline Mackenzie was Base Camp doctor for Rob Hall's team.
23. **IMAX team:** Another team of climbers, who were shooting a $5.5-million giant-screen movie about Mount Everest. The movie was released in 1998.

Vocabulary
traverse (trə·vʉrs') v.: cross.

This was very disturbing news to the people down below, but it was amazing that Hall was even alive after spending a night without shelter or oxygen at 28,700 feet in hurricane-force wind and minus-100-degree windchill.

At 5 A.M., Base Camp patched through a call on the satellite telephone to Jan Arnold, Hall's wife, seven months pregnant with their first child in Christchurch, New Zealand. Arnold, a respected physician, had summited Everest with Hall in 1993 and entertained no illusions about the gravity of her husband's predicament. "My heart really sank when I heard his voice," she recalls. "He was slurring his words markedly. He sounded like Major Tom[24] or something, like he was just floating away. I'd been up there; I knew what it could be like in bad weather. Rob and I had talked about the impossibility of being rescued from the summit ridge. As he himself had put it, 'You might as well be on the moon.'"

By that time, Hall had located two full oxygen bottles, and after struggling for four hours trying to de-ice his mask, around 8:30 A.M. he finally started breathing the life-sustaining gas. Several times he announced that he was preparing to descend, only to change his mind and remain at the South Summit. The day had started out sunny and clear, but the wind remained fierce, and by late morning the upper mountain was wrapped with thick clouds. Climbers at Camp Two reported that the wind over the summit sounded like a squadron of 747s, even from 8,000 feet below. . . .

Throughout that day, Hall's friends begged him to make an effort to descend from the South Summit under his own power. At 3:20 P.M., after one such transmission from Cotter, Hall began to sound annoyed. "Look," he said, "if I thought I could manage the knots on the fixed ropes with me frostbitten hands,

I would have gone down six hours ago, pal. Just send a couple of the boys up with a big thermos of something hot—then I'll be fine."

At 6:20 P.M., Hall was patched through a second time to Arnold in Christchurch. "Hi, my sweetheart," he said in a slow, painfully distorted voice. "I hope you're tucked up in a nice warm bed. How are you doing?"

"I can't tell you how much I'm thinking about you!" Arnold replied. "You sound so much better than I expected. . . . Are you warm, my darling?"

"In the context of the altitude, the setting, I'm reasonably comfortable," Hall answered, doing his best not to alarm her.

"How are your feet?"

"I haven't taken me boots off to check, but I think I may have a bit of frostbite."

"I'm looking forward to making you completely better when you come home," said Arnold. "I just know you're going to be rescued. Don't feel that you're alone. I'm sending all my positive energy your way!" Before signing off, Hall told his wife, "I love you. Sleep well, my sweetheart. Please don't worry too much."

These would be the last words anyone would hear him utter. Attempts to make radio contact with Hall later that night and the next day went unanswered. Twelve days later, when Breashears and Viesturs climbed over the South Summit on their way to the top, they found Hall lying on his right side in a shallow ice-hollow, his upper body buried beneath a drift of snow.

CAUSE AND EFFECT

5. Name several of the **causes** that led to Hall's death.

Early on the morning of May 11, when I returned to Camp Four, Hutchison, standing in for Groom, who was unconscious in his tent, organized a team of four Sherpas to locate the bodies of our teammates Weathers and Namba. The Sherpa search party, headed by Lhakpa Chhiri, departed ahead of Hutchison,

---

24. **Major Tom:** reference to the David Bowie song "Space Oddity," which is about an astronaut, Major Tom, who is lost and floating in space.

who was so exhausted and befuddled that he forgot to put his boots on and left camp in his light, smooth-soled liners. Only when Lhakpa Chhiri pointed out the blunder did Hutchison return for his boots. Following Boukreev's directions, the Sherpas had no trouble locating the two bodies at the edge of the Kang-shung Face.

The first body turned out to be Namba, but Hutchison couldn't tell who it was until he knelt in the howling wind and chipped a three-inch-thick carapace of ice from her face. To his shock, he discovered that she was still breathing. Both her gloves were gone, and her bare hands appeared to be frozen solid. Her eyes were dilated.[25] The skin on her face was the color of porcelain. "It was terrible," Hutchison recalls. "I was overwhelmed. She was very near death. I didn't know what to do."

He turned his attention to Weathers, who lay 20 feet away. His face was also caked with a thick armor of frost. Balls of ice the size of grapes were matted to his hair and eyelids. After cleaning the frozen detritus[26] from his face, Hutchison discovered that he, too, was still alive: "Beck was mumbling something, I think, but I couldn't tell what he was trying to say. His right glove was missing and he had terrible frostbite. He was as close to death as a person can be and still breathing."

Badly shaken, Hutchison went over to the Sherpas and asked Lhakpa Chhiri's advice. Lhakpa Chhiri, an Everest veteran respected by Sherpas and sahibs[27] alike for his mountain savvy, urged Hutchison to leave Weathers and Namba where they lay. Even if they survived long enough to be dragged back to Camp Four, they

> "He was as close to death as a person can be and still be breathing."

would certainly die before they could be carried down to Base Camp, and attempting a rescue would needlessly jeopardize the lives of the other climbers on the Col, most of whom were going to have enough trouble getting themselves down safely.

Hutchison decided that Chhiri was right. There was only one choice, however difficult: Let nature take its inevitable course with Weathers and Namba, and save the group's resources for those who could actually be helped. It was a classic act of triage.[28] When Hutchison returned to camp at 8:30 A.M. and told the rest of us of his decision, nobody doubted that it was the correct thing to do.

Later that day a rescue team headed by two of Everest's most experienced guides, Pete Athans and Todd Burleson, who were on the mountain with their own clients, arrived at Camp Four. Burleson was standing outside the tents about 4:30 P.M. when he noticed someone lurching slowly toward camp. The person's bare right hand, naked to the wind and horribly frostbitten, was outstretched in a weird, frozen salute. Whoever it was reminded Athans of a mummy in a low-budget horror film. The mummy turned out to be none other than Beck Weathers, somehow risen from the dead.

A couple of hours earlier, a light must have gone on in the reptilian core of Weathers' comatose[29] brain, and he regained consciousness. "Initially I thought I was in a dream," he recalls. "Then I saw how badly frozen my right hand was, and that helped bring me around to reality. Finally I woke up enough to recognize

---

25. **dilated** v. used as adj.: made wider; here, referring to the pupil of the eye.
26. **detritus** (dē·trīt′əs) n.: debris.
27. **sahibs** (sä′ibz′) n.: term used by Sherpas to refer to the paying members of the expeditions.

28. **triage** (trē·äzh′) n.: assigning of priorities of medical care based on chances for survival.
29. **comatose** adj.: deeply unconscious due to injury or disease.

Vocabulary
jeopardize (jep′ər·dīz′) v.: endanger.

that the cavalry[30] wasn't coming so I better do something about it myself."

Although Weathers was blind in his right eye and able to focus his left eye within a radius of only three or four feet, he started walking into the teeth of the wind, deducing correctly that camp lay in that direction. If he'd been wrong he would have stumbled immediately down the Kangshung Face, the edge of which was a few yards in the opposite direction. Ninety minutes later he encountered "some unnaturally smooth, bluish-looking rocks," which turned out to be the tents of Camp Four.

CAUSE AND EFFECT

6. How did Weathers save his own life? What is **ironic** about his situation?

The next morning, May 12, Athans, Burleson, and climbers from the IMAX team short-roped Weathers down to Camp Two. On the morning of May 13, in a hazardous helicopter rescue, Weathers and Gau[31] were evacuated from the top of the icefall by Lieutenant Colonel Madan Khatri Chhetri of the Nepalese army. A month later, a team of Dallas surgeons would amputate Weathers' dead right hand just below the wrist and use skin grafts to reconstruct his left hand.

After helping to load Weathers and Gau into the rescue chopper, I sat in the snow for a long while, staring at my boots, trying to get some grip, however tenuous, on what had happened

over the preceding 72 hours. Then, nervous as a cat, I headed down into the icefall for one last trip through the maze of decaying seracs.[32]

I'd always known, in the abstract, that climbing mountains was a dangerous pursuit. But until I climbed in the Himalayas this spring, I'd never actually seen death at close range. And there was so much of it: Including three members of an Indo-Tibetan team who died on the north side just below the summit in the same May 10 storm and an Austrian killed some days later, 11 men and women lost their lives on Everest in May 1996, a tie with 1982 for the worst single-season death toll in the peak's history. . . .[33]

Climbing mountains will never be a safe, predictable, rule-bound enterprise. It is an activity that idealizes risk-taking; its most celebrated figures have always been those who stuck their necks out the farthest and managed to get away with it. Climbers, as a species, are simply not distinguished by an excess of common sense. And that holds especially true for Everest climbers: When presented with a chance to reach the planet's highest summit, people are surprisingly quick to abandon prudence altogether. "Eventually," warns Tom Hornbein, 33 years after his ascent of the West Ridge, "what happened on Everest this season is certain to happen again." ∎

---

30. **cavalry** *n.:* soldiers on horseback or motorized transport; an allusion to the idea that troops were not coming to the rescue.
31. **Gau:** "Makalu" Gau Ming-Ho, leader of the Taiwanese National Expedition, another team climbing on Everest.

32. **seracs** *n.:* pointed masses of ice.
33. It actually was the worst death toll on record. After Krakauer wrote this article, a twelfth death was discovered.

Vocabulary
tenuous (ten′yo͞o·əs) *adj.:* weak; slight.

Meet the Writer

Jon Krakauer

Journalist Climber

Jon Krakauer (1954–   ) had mountain climbers as boyhood heroes instead of baseball players or movie stars. He made his first climb when he was only eight and after college became a "climbing bum." During the 1980s, he began writing articles on outdoor subjects.

In 1996, when *Outside* magazine asked Krakauer to write about Everest, he was an experienced climber but had never been above 17,200 feet. He later said,

"If you don't understand Everest and appreciate its mystique, you're never going to understand this tragedy and why it's quite likely to be repeated."

After the disaster, Krakauer conducted dozens of interviews with other survivors. His article, completed five weeks after his return from Nepal, was published in September 1996. Krakauer still felt such a need to get the experience off his chest that he soon expanded the article into a book, *Into Thin Air,* which was an immediate bestseller. Despite that success, Krakauer has suffered grief and guilt over the disaster on Mount Everest and has said,

"I'm never climbing it again, never. . . . I wish I hadn't gone this time."

For Independent Reading

If you enjoyed reading this excerpt from Krakauer's magazine article, you might want to read the book *Into Thin Air* (1997), Krakauer's full-length account of the ill-fated Everest expeditions. You might also enjoy *Into the Wild* (1996), Krakauer's terrifying true account of a young man's fateful wilderness adventure.

Response and Analysis

Reading Check

1. Make a list of the **main events** in this Everest story. Then, circle the events during which Krakauer or other climbers were in grave danger. Tell the outcome of each circled event.

Thinking Critically

2. Find and explain at least four examples of **situational irony, contradictions,** or **incongruities** in the article. (Hint: Consider what happens to Rob Hall and Beck Weathers for starters.)

3. **Situational irony** is a favorite device of short story writers. What impact does it have in this nonfiction narrative?

4. Choose one tragedy that happened on the mountain—for example, the death of Doug Hansen or the loss of Beck Weathers's right hand. Draw a **cause-and-effect diagram** similar to the one below to show the complex causes that led to the tragedy.

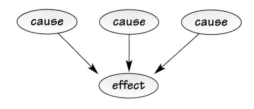

5. Are there any real-life heroes in this story? If so, who are they, and why do you think they are heroes?

6. What **conclusions** does Krakauer draw at the end of this selection? Do you think these conclusions apply to other "risk takers" as well? Explain.

7. What passages in this narrative impress you, puzzle you, shock you, or cause other strong reactions? Read those passages aloud in a group.

Discuss how the events described affected your previous opinion of mountain climbing. (Check your Quickwrite notes.) 🖉

8. In an interview Krakauer gave about his experience in 1996 on Everest, he said, "We should think of Everest not as a mountain, but as the geologic embodiment of **myth**." What do you think he means by that statement? In what way is Everest a "chunk of myth"?

Extending and Evaluating

9. Evaluate the article in terms of its **subjectivity** and **objectivity.** Find some of the subjective details (thoughts, feelings, personal information) that Krakauer includes. Would you prefer reading a totally objective (factual) account? Explain.

WRITING

Comparing Media Coverage

Today most important news events are covered in a variety of media genres—for example, newspapers, newsmagazines, TV news reports, TV newsmagazines, even TV talk shows. In 1996, the tragic Everest expedition was a hot news story for some time. Several of the survivors, such as Beck Weathers, became instant celebrities and appeared on TV talk shows.

Pick an event from today's news that interests you—any event that is widely covered in both newspapers and on television. Follow coverage of the event in different genres, and write a **brief report** comparing the coverage in those genres.

▶ **Use "Comparing Media Genres," pages 382–389, for help with this assignment.**

go.
hrw
.com

INTERNET

Projects and Activities

Keyword: LE5 10-5

SKILLS FOCUS

Literary Skills
Analyze situational irony, contradictions, and incongruities.

Reading Skills
Analyze cause and effect.

Writing Skills
Write a report comparing different media coverage.

Vocabulary Development

Analogies: Parallel Word Pairs

PRACTICE 1

In an **analogy** the words in one pair relate to each other in the same way as the words in a second pair. Fill in each blank below with the word from the Word Bank that best completes the analogy. (Two words on the list are synonyms and may be used interchangeably.) For more help with analogies, see pages 29–30.

1. BASE : BOTTOM :: _____ : top

2. SAFE : DANGEROUS :: _____ : harmful

3. MISLEAD : DECEIVE :: _____ : endanger

4. TRIVIAL : MINOR :: _____ : important

5. TRY : ATTEMPT :: _____ : guess

6. MINOR : MAJOR :: _____ : malignant

7. FAMOUS : STAR :: _____ : criminal

8. WEAKEN : STRENGTHEN :: _____ : improve

9. CLIMB : STAIRS :: _____ : bridge

10. STRONG : POWERFUL :: _____ : weak

Word Bank

deteriorate
innocuous
notorious
benign
apex
crucial
speculate
traverse
jeopardize
tenuous

Technical Vocabulary— Widgets, Whatsits, Thingamajigs

If you are a football fan, you know the meaning of *touchdown, off tackle,* and *scrimmage.* Before reading "Into Thin Air," did you know the meaning of *rappel* and *short-rope?*

"As I clipped into a fixed rope and prepared to <u>rappel</u> over the lip . . ." (page 354)

"'He's got a rope; he'll be able to <u>short-rope</u> me.'" (page 357)

Almost every kind of work or play has its own special **technical vocabulary,** or **jargon.** When writers cover a technical subject for a general audience, they usually include **context clues** to help the reader guess the meaning, and sometimes they

also provide footnotes. (Check the context clues and footnotes for *rappel* and *short-rope.* Can you explain these words to a friend?)

PRACTICE 2

1. Review the footnotes for these words from "Into Thin Air": *troposphere, dementia, triage, comatose.* List any context clues in the text that can help you determine the meanings of the words.

2. Write a list of technical terms for any field that you know well (perhaps a sport or a favorite hobby). Choose two of the most obscure terms, and write sentences using context clues that would enable a reader to understand the terms. See whether a classmate can guess the words' meanings.

SKILLS FOCUS

Vocabulary Skills
Complete word analogies. Understand technical vocabulary.

Explorers Say There's Still Lots to Look For

Generating Research Questions and Evaluating Sources

To research a topic, you need to generate specific, focused research questions. Then, you look for answers. Before you decide to use a source, evaluate it.

1. **Check relevance.** Always skim a source to make sure it has relevant information.

2. **Check the source's credentials.** Is the source a well-known newspaper, magazine, encyclopedia, or other reputable source? Does the writer seem qualified to speak on the subject? Has the writer written other books or articles on the topic?

3. **Check for bias.** Are you reading someone's subjective **opinion** or objective **facts**? If an opinion, ask whether the writer has any **bias,** or prejudice, toward the topic. This issue is especially important if you are researching a controversial topic.

4. **Check for accuracy.** Verify factual information in at least two reputable sources, such as encyclopedias or other reference sources.

5. **Check the source's timeliness.** Check publication dates. The most recent sources will have the most up-to-date information, but older information may provide historical details.

Be Wary of the Internet

Because the Internet is not monitored for accuracy as most publications are, you must carefully evaluate any information you find on it. The most accurate, reliable, and unbiased information can be found on sites that are affiliated with and created by reputable organizations, such as universities, government agencies, museums, and national news organizations. (The addresses for these sites usually include *edu, gov,* or *org.*) An individual's home page is not considered reliable. Always ask yourself:

- What qualifications does the Web site author have to speak on the topic?
- What is the purpose of the site?
- Does the site appear to be objective?
- When was the site created or updated?

Vocabulary Development

illusion (i·lōō′zhən) *n.:* misleading or inaccurate idea.

marooned (mə·rōōnd′) *v.* used as *adj.:* left stranded, helpless, or isolated.

nudged (nujd) *v.:* lightly pushed; bumped.

whimsy (hwim′zē) *n.:* quaint or odd humor.

navigator (nav′ə·gāt′ər) *n.:* person who plots the course of a vehicle, usually a ship or plane.

Connecting to the Literature

Would you call the climbers on Mount Everest who are described in "Into Thin Air" adventurers or explorers? The following article discusses the difference between adventure and exploration and introduces you to some of the daring women and men who probe earth's unexplored regions.

go.
hrw
.com

INTERNET
Interactive
Reading Model
Keyword: LE5 10-5

SKILLS FOCUS

Reading Skills
Generate research questions,
and evaluate
sources.

Explorers Say There's Still Lots to Look For

from *The Seattle Times*, May 21, 2000

Helen O'Neill

NEW YORK—The crickets were roasted to perfection. Baby scorpions adorned points of savory toast. And the saddle of beaver simmered gently in a decorative silver tureen.

Oceanographer[1] Sylvia Earle glided across the room in a shimmering red gown and golden shawl. She'd rather have been in her wet suit. She'd rather have been diving to the darkest corners of the abyss. Instead, "Her Deepness," as Earle is known, was busy in her role as honorary president of the Explorers Club, charming the cocktail crowd with her latest exploit: dancing a solitary dance with a giant octopus at the bottom of the Pacific.

Across the room, tuxedoed archaeologist[2] Johan Reinhard clutched his wineglass and chatted about his latest find—a 500-year-old Inca mummy unearthed atop a remote Andean peak. Next to him, Bertrand Piccard, first man to circumnavigate[3] earth in a balloon, engaged in intense debate about the future of solar-powered planes.

All around were people who have bushwhacked[4] through jungles, trekked across deserts, floated in space. Dripping medals and jewels and tales from afar, they gathered in the ballroom of the Waldorf-Astoria hotel for the annual Explorers Club banquet. Once a year they come here, to mingle with sponsors and troll[5] for support, to nibble on loin of kangaroo and explain to the world that there are still places to be discovered.

A Great Era of Exploration

"There is a popular illusion that all corners of the earth have been explored," Earle says. "The greatest mountain ranges on the planet are underwater, where there is a whole continent waiting to be explored."

In the past two years alone, Ian Baker reported discovering the fabled Shangri-La waterfall on Tibet's mighty Tsangpo River; Reinhard recovered three frozen Inca mummies from an Andean volcano; the body of English climber George Mallory,[6] who disappeared in 1924, was discovered on Mount Everest; and Robert Ballard located the world's oldest shipwrecks—two Phoenician cargo vessels in the Mediterranean. The same trip led him to uncover evidence of a giant flood about 7,000 years ago—perhaps the biblical flood of Noah.

---

1. **oceanographer** (ō′shə·näg′rə·fər) *n.:* scientist who studies the environment in the oceans.
2. **archaeologist** (är′kē·äl′ə·jist) *n.:* scientist who studies the life and cultures of the past, often through excavation of ancient sites and artifacts.
3. **circumnavigate** (sʉr′kəm·nav′ə·gāt′) *v.:* fly or sail completely around a geographic place.
4. **bushwhacked** *v.:* beat or cut one's way through bushes.

5. **troll** *v.:* literally, to fish with bait behind a slow-moving boat; in this instance it refers to "fishing" for funding.
6. **George Mallory:** In 1924, the British climbers George Mallory and Andrew Irvine disappeared in an attempt to reach Mount Everest's summit. In 1999, climbers discovered Mallory's frozen corpse near the summit.

Vocabulary
illusion (i·lōō′zhən) *n.:* misleading or inaccurate idea.

Explorers still scale peaks that never have been climbed, crawl through caves to the insides of earth, hurtle into space to walk among the stars. They find ancient tribes and ancient cities. They dig up dinosaurs. They journey to places where no one has reported being before: the jungles of central Congo, the Amazon and Peru, the deserts of Tibet and China, vast underwater caves in Mexico and Belize. They are only beginning to probe the oceans; 5 percent has been explored, though water covers 71 percent of the planet.

All of which makes Earle say, "I think the great era of exploration has just begun."

What Sets Them Apart

"Men wanted for hazardous journey. Small wages, bitter cold, long months of complete darkness, constant danger, safe return doubtful. Honor and recognition in case of success."—Ernest Shackleton's 1914 advertisement for crew members for *Endurance*.

The ship was aptly named. Although Shackleton failed in his quest to cross the Antarctic,[7] his journey became one of the great epics of survival. Marooned for months on an ice floe, his ship crushed by pack ice, Shackleton managed to sail a lifeboat 800 miles, scale an unmapped mountain range, reach a Norwegian whaling station, and return to rescue all of his men.

Seventy-five years later, Robert Ballard wants to dig through the ice and find his hero's ship.

The ship from the Shackleton expedition, the *Endurance,* keeling over in the ice. Photo taken by expedition member Frank Hurley in 1915.

Ballard is one of the most famous living explorers, and not just because he discovered the world's most famous shipwreck. Long before the lights of his little roaming robot lit up *Titanic*'s ghostly bow in 1985, the former naval officer and oceanographer dedicated his life to exploration. *Bismarck.* U.S.S. *Yorktown. Lusitania.*[8] Ballard has explored them all.

"When I die," Ballard says, "I want one word on my tombstone: Explorer."

---

8. **Bismarck. U.S.S. Yorktown. Lusitania:** The *Bismarck* was an important German battleship that was sunk by the British navy during World War II. The U.S.S. *Yorktown* was an American aircraft carrier that was sunk by the Japanese navy during World War II. The *Lusitania* was a British ocean liner that was sunk by a German submarine during World War I.

Vocabulary

marooned (mə·rōōnd') *v.* used as *adj.:* left stranded, helpless, or isolated.

---

7. **Antarctic:** ice-covered continent at the South Pole.

He is standing in his Institute of Exploration in Mystic, Connecticut, in a replica of the control room from which he discovered *Titanic*. The institute, which opened last year, is packed with videos and displays from Ballard's finds. On one wall, a large chart details his plans: searching for ancient wrecks in the Black Sea, the lost ships of the Franklin expedition[9] in the Canadian Arctic, Shackleton's *Endurance*.

"A lot of people do adventure," Ballard says. "They retrace Hannibal's route[10] in a Winnebago. They take a helicopter to the North Pole and have cocktails. That is not exploration."

True exploration, he says, is about having a vision and following it, about going where no one has dared go before, about bringing back scientific information and publishing it in journals.

"It's about having the heart to push on when you want to turn back," he says. "That is what sets explorers apart."

Seeking Knowledge

"Explorers are foragers,"[11] says Anna Roosevelt, curator of archaeology at the Field Museum of Natural History in Chicago and professor of anthropology at the University of Illinois. "They will seek until they find."

The great-granddaughter of Theodore Roosevelt spends much of her time foraging in the Amazon River basin, challenging conventional wisdom about early settlements there. She also challenges any notion that she is following in the footsteps of her famous ancestor, whose faded expedition photographs decorate the walls of the Explorers Club. Teddy Roosevelt, she says, was a great adventurer and a great president, but he wasn't an explorer in the true sense.

"People and animals died on his expeditions," she said of his legendary African safaris and canoe trips down the Amazon's River of Doubt. "They don't die on mine."

Roosevelt was one of the first women inducted into the Explorers Club after it opened its doors to women in 1981. Another was astronaut Kathryn Sullivan, first American woman to walk in space.

Sullivan didn't particularly feel like an explorer when she nudged her spaceship out of

Astronaut Kathryn Sullivan checks the antenna of the spaceship *Challenger*.

---

9. **Franklin expedition:** In 1845, the British explorer John Franklin led an expedition of two ships to the Arctic in search of a "northwest passage" linking the Atlantic and Pacific Oceans. The explorers and crew had to abandon ship and died one and a half years later in the Arctic wilderness. The ships were never found.

10. **Hannibal's route:** Hannibal (247–183 B.C.), a general in the ancient North African kingdom of Carthage, crossed the Alps to invade the Italian peninsula in 218 B.C.

11. **foragers** (fôr′ij·ərz) *n.*: those who search for what is needed or wanted.

Vocabulary
nudged (nujd) *v.*: lightly pushed; bumped.

Amelia Earhart in the cockpit of a small airplane.

Much Still to Discover

"A few toes aren't much to give to achieve the pole," Peary exclaimed in 1898.

So what is left for modern-day explorers to achieve, or sacrifice? Plenty, says Bradford Washburn, a ninety-year-old cartographer[12] and mountaineer from Boston. Washburn was friends with Richard Byrd.[13] He interviewed for the position of navigator on Amelia Earhart's round-the-world flight, dropping out because he thought the radios were inadequate. In the 1930s he knocked out the door of a Lockheed Vega airplane and tied himself to the opposite bulkhead in order to map glaciers on Alaska's St. Elias Range. Last year, he directed an expedition that led to the discovery of a new altitude of Everest—29,035 feet, 7 feet higher than previously recorded.

"It was exciting," Washburn says, "but nothing as exciting as when Ed Hillary got to the top."

Still, Washburn marvels at the technology that hurtles modern explorers toward new frontiers, and at the spirit propelling them.

the way so she could get a better view of earth. She was more amused by the whimsy of it all: Having trained for this moment so long, it actually felt normal. It wasn't until she got back to earth that she pondered its meaning.

"I think sometimes we learn more about ourselves and our place in society and in the universe than the places we thought we were going to explore."

Clinging to a cliff in Cameroon, thirty-two-year-old South African climber Edmund February agreed. Sure it's an adventure, he said, in a phone interview from the mountain in December. But it's exploration, too.

"When we make these climbs, we are exploring a new dimension, a new theater," said February, who was pioneering a first ascent on the volcanic spires of the Mandara Mountains. "It's not with the same parameters as Scott or Amundsen. But it's more than just a thirst for adventure. It's a thirst for knowledge, too."

---

12. **cartographer** (kär·tăg′rə·fər) *n.:* person who makes maps or charts.
13. **Richard Byrd** (1888–1957): U.S. naval officer who pioneered the exploration of Arctic and Antarctic regions by air.

Vocabulary

whimsy (hwĭm′zē) *n.:* quaint or odd humor.

navigator (năv′ə·gāt′ər) *n.:* person who plots the course of a vehicle, usually a ship or plane.

Ballard discovering the *Titanic*, Reinhard staring into the mummified face of an Inca child, Earle dancing with a giant octopus. All of them, Washburn says, are driven by the same spirit that drove Columbus and Peary and Byrd: to discover new worlds and document them.

At the Boston Museum of Science, where he is honorary director and where he still works several days a week, Washburn breaks into a poem.

"Something hidden. Go and find it. . . . Something lost behind the Ranges. Lost and waiting for you. Go!"

The poem is by Kipling.[14] It's one of Washburn's favorites. It's called "The Explorer."

---

14. **Rudyard Kipling** (1865–1936): British writer, poet, and Nobel Prize winner.

The following men and women, all mentioned in the article, make up a short list of some of the world's most famous explorers of the twentieth century.

Notable Explorers of the Twentieth Century

Roald Amundsen (1872–1928)	Norwegian explorer; first person to reach the South Pole and to sail through the Northwest Passage in the Arctic.
Robert Ballard (1942–)	American deep-sea explorer who discovered the wreck of the *Titanic* in 1985 and has pioneered use of underwater robots.
Amelia Earhart (1897–1937)	First woman to fly solo across the Atlantic. She disappeared over the Pacific Ocean during a round-the-world flight.
Sylvia Earle (1935–)	Pioneer researcher on marine ecosystems; has led over fifty deep-sea expeditions.
Edmund Hillary (1919–)	New Zealand mountain climber. He and Tenzing Norgay were the first to reach the top of Mount Everest, in 1953.
Robert Peary (1856–1920)	American explorer and naval officer credited with being first to reach the North Pole, in 1909.
Johan Reinhard (1943–)	High-altitude archaeologist specializing in ancient ceremonial sites in South America.
Anna Roosevelt (1946–)	Anthropologist and archaeologist who has documented civilization of the Amazon region dating back eleven thousand years.
Robert Scott (1868–1912)	British naval officer and explorer who died during an expedition that tried to reach the South Pole in 1912.
Ernest Shackleton (1874–1922)	British explorer and naval reserve officer whose third expedition to the Antarctic resulted in a heroic two-year struggle for survival.

Analyzing Informational Text

Reading Check

1. According to Earle, where is there a "continent waiting to be explored"?
2. What happened on Ernest Shackleton's expedition?
3. According to Ballard, what defines true exploration?

Test Practice

1. If you were looking for the facts about the *Endurance* crew's months on the ice floe, which source would probably be *most* useful?

    A "Sir Ernest Shackleton and the Antarctic," lecture at Explorers Club (May 7, 2001) by Dr. William Rom

    B An entry on Antarctica in *The Columbia Encyclopedia*

    C *The Endurance: Shackleton's Legendary Antarctic Expedition* by Caroline Alexander with photos of the expedition by Frank Hurley

    D Ernest Shackleton's testimony (June 18, 1912) on the sinking of the *Titanic*

2. Who would probably have the *most* biased view of the importance of further deep-sea exploration?

    F Sylvia Earle

    G Anna Roosevelt

    H Ian Baker

    J Johan Reinhard

3. If you wanted to do further research on Ballard's career and his explorations, which source would be *most* useful?

    A An article on robotics and exploration in *Time* magazine

    B An encyclopedia article on deep-sea exploration

    C A history of great shipwrecks of the Atlantic Ocean

    D A feature article in a national newsmagazine on Ballard and his career

4. Which of the following sources would be *most* reliable if you were researching the history of the Explorers Club?

    F The Web site of Explorers Club Lodge and Safaris, a lodge for backpackers in South Africa

    G The Web site of the Explorers Club; its section on the club's history

    H An interview with a friend whose grandfather was a member of the Explorers Club

    J An entry on "Explorers Club" in a guidebook to New York City

SKILLS FOCUS

Reading Skills
Generate research questions, and evaluate sources.

Constructed Response

Think of several good **research questions** suggested by the article. Choose one question, and start your research. Evaluate all the sources you discover. Then, summarize your research experience in a few paragraphs.

Vocabulary Development

Words in Context: Clues All Around

The words in the Word Bank are defined for you, but what if they weren't? Look back at the text, and see whether there are any **clues** in the surrounding words and sentences (the **context**) that tell you what each word means. Then, sharpen your understanding of these words with the practice below.

Word Bank

illusion
marooned
nudged
whimsy
navigator

PRACTICE 1

Write your answer to each of the following questions.

1. Why is an illusion different from the truth?
2. If you had to be marooned somewhere for a month, where would you choose to be, and what would you take with you?
3. If you nudged an object, what would happen to it? Have you nudged anything recently? Explain.
4. Is whimsy a quality that makes you laugh or not? Why?
5. A deep-sea research team has a job for a navigator. What responsibility does that position involve?

Word Clues: Greek and Latin Roots and Relations

What do a seismograph, an autobiography, and a telegraph have in common? Sound like a riddle? In fact, all three words share the Greek root —graph—, so they're related. Learning to recognize familiar Greek and Latin roots will help you fathom the meanings of many English words. Many of the roots in the chart below can be found in words in the selection.

Greek Root	Meaning	Example
—anthropo—	human being	anthropology
—auto—	self	autobiography
—bio—	life	biology
—graph—	to write	graphic
—photo—	light	photocopy
—psycho—	mind	psychoanalysis
Latin Root	**Meaning**	**Example**
—scrib—	write	script
—labor—	work	laboratory

PRACTICE 2

Think of at least one other word for each of the Greek and Latin roots listed above, and then write the word's meaning. Explain how knowing the meaning of the root helps you understand the word. Use a dictionary for help.

SKILLS FOCUS

Vocabulary Skills
Use context clues. Understand Greek and Latin roots.

Before You Read

Notes from a Bottle

Make the Connection

Quickwrite ✏️

Attacking aliens, a giant asteroid, global warming, nuclear war—writers and scientists have made dire predictions about dangers that threaten to wipe out human life on earth. Choose one serious, life-threatening problem. Tell how you think you would react and what you would do in the three days before the dire prediction comes true.

Literary Focus

Ambiguities and Subtleties: Open to Interpretation

Often the stories we find most memorable are the ones that leave us thinking and guessing. Knowing this, writers sometimes challenge and baffle readers, presenting a kind of puzzle with important information omitted. They purposely make events or characters or even the theme of a work **ambiguous** or **subtle**—that is, unclear or open to different interpretations.

When we read such stories, we struggle to figure out what's happening, what has happened, what will happen—and why. It's up to each reader to piece things together and ponder the facts. The unusual story you're about to read focuses on a single apartment building in New York City; that much is clear. The rest—well, have fun figuring it out.

Reading Skills

Making Inferences

An **inference** is an educated guess—you make such guesses all the time. Suppose your friend, who's never late, doesn't appear at the usual time to pick you up for school. You infer that something's happened (like a traffic jam or an accident) to delay her or that maybe she's sick.

Similarly, when you read a story, you fill in missing information, reading between the lines to make guesses about what's left unsaid or unclear. In an ambiguous story like the one you are about to read, the writer has purposely left out important information. You must therefore work even harder to make inferences and decide what is happening and why.

Vocabulary Development

portable (pôr′tə·bəl) *adj.:* able to be carried.

presumably (prē·zoom′ə·blē) *adv.:* probably.

speculation (spek′yə·lā′shən) *n.:* thought; guesswork.

submerged (səb·murjd′) *v.:* covered with water.

recede (ri·sēd′) *v.:* move back or away.

go.
hrw
.com

INTERNET

Vocabulary
Practice

Keyword: LE5 10-5

SKILLS FOCUS

Literary Skills
Understand ambiguities and subtleties.

Reading Skills
Make inferences.

Notes from a Bottle

James Stevenson

(A bottle containing the following notes was discovered on a mountainside on Ascension Island, in the South Atlantic.)

March 23rd. 7 A.M.: Looked out the window of my apartment, saw that the water was up to the second story all along Eighty-sixth Street. Yesterday, the movie marquees[1] toward Lexington were still visible at twilight, but this morning they are gone. There were, of course, no lights last night—there has been no electricity in the city for three days. (No telephones, no water, no heat, no television. Heat and telephone service had been gone for several days before that, owing to the fuel strike and the phone strike. Some portable radios still work, but they receive only the grainy sound of static.) A light snow is falling.

4 P.M.: It is almost dark again, and the water is approaching the fourth floor. No planes or helicopters were seen today; the airports were probably the first to flood, and any planes that managed to get aloft would have run out of fuel by now. It looks like another night of parties and celebrations. Across the street, candles and flashlight beams move about in the windows, and in our building loud, cheerful voices can be heard echoing in the fire stairs. There is a lot of shrieking and laughter. The children, as usual, are riding bicycles up and down the halls, as adults—bundled up in all manner of

---

1. **movie marquees:** structures projecting over the entrances to movie theaters that are usually lit up and display the name of the movie being shown.

Vocabulary
portable (pôr′tə·bəl) *adj.:* able to be carried.

clothing, and carrying drinks and candles—roam the building, going from one party to another. The Williamses, who were supposed to go on a cruise, have been dancing around in their vacation clothes—Audrey in a fur coat and bathing suit, Harold in a mask and flippers. A lot of things have been thrown out of windows; Ed Shea on 7 was tossing an orange back and forth to somebody in the building across the street; one group was skimming L.P. records,[2] throwing them like Frisbees. There has been a good deal of horseplay. Carson on 8 would lean out his window and drop a paper bag full of flour on any head that was sticking out below. The biggest party last night was in the Mac-Neills' on 4—Alice played the piano, and everyone sang and danced until around three. (Today, a group of volunteers is moving the piano up to the Webers' on 6, just in case, and the Webers intend to have everybody in.) Phil Lewis amused everybody last night, saying that an ark[3] was on its way and that it was going to take two people from the Upper East Side. Martin, the doorman, has been drunk for a couple of days; he opened the Wenkers' apartment on 10—they're in Spain—and he has been holding court up there, dispensing the Wenkers' liquor with a free hand. There is still no explanation for the flood, beyond rumors

> ### There is still no explanation for the flood . . .

shouted from one building to another. A lot of activity on Eighty-sixth Street during the day. For a while, everyone was throwing piles of flaming newspapers out their windows and watching them float away, burning, and there was considerable boat traffic—outboards, rowboats, a Circle Line boat with a crowd aboard, a small tug,[4] a speedboat full of howling drunks towing a water skier in a black wet suit. An hour ago, the mayor went by, smiling grimly, in a large Chris-Craft cruiser with the city flag on the stern, the deck jammed with officials. Presumably, the water has reached Gracie Mansion[5] by now, although the mansion is on high ground.

March 24th. 3 P.M.: The water is now just below my windows on the ninth floor. There is nothing to do but watch. The water is filthy—there had been the six-week garbage strike, and all the city's garbage is awash—and the sea gulls are everywhere, feasting. A number of people came up to stay in my apartment during the night, but they have left now and gone to a higher floor. They all arrived with apologies and genial remarks, but when they left they did so without

---

2. **L.P. records:** long-playing phonograph records, playing at 33⅓ revolutions per minute.
3. **ark** *n.:* large boat; reference to the Bible story of Noah's ark, which saved two of every creature from the great flood.

---

4. **tug** *n.:* small, powerful boat used to tow and push larger ships and barges.
5. **Gracie Mansion:** official residence of New York City's mayor.

Vocabulary
presumably (prē·zōōm′ə·blē) *adv.:* probably.

fanfare[6]—simply disappeared, one or two at a time, when I wasn't looking. I'd hear the door click shut, and I'd know they'd gone upstairs. There has been constant speculation on the cause of the flood—an atomic test in the Arctic is a popular explanation—but no one has any information at all, and no one really expects any. Those of us who have lived here for any length of time have become hardened: One simply waits. Langford, the lawyer, who recently moved to New York and lives on 8, was furious at first. "Why haven't we been informed?" he kept demanding. "I have contacts in Washington. . . ." But when I saw him a few minutes ago—he was standing in the hall, eating a once-frozen TV dinner—he was brooding, and when others spoke to him he didn't reply.

5 P.M.: The strangest thing is the silence of the city. No car noises, honking, sirens. Bodies float by, tangled in wreckage—furniture, lumber, trash. Suddenly a boat's horn, but then it is silent again—extraordinary silence. The loudest sound, except when the gulls come near, is the slap of water just below the windowsill, or the scrape of something bumping the window air conditioner.

March 25th: We are on the roof now. I have no idea what time it is, but it is daylight. The lower buildings have been submerged, the tall office buildings stand like tombstones above the heaving waves. There are whitecaps[7] toward Central Park. An ocean liner stood by the Pan Am Building for a while, then moved out to sea. Our rooftop is packed with people; many huddle against the chimneys, trying to keep away from the bitter wind. Alice MacNeill—her piano was abandoned on 8—tried to get everyone to sing "Nearer My God to Thee,"[8] but there was little response. No one wants to accept the situation as final, and yet everyone is keeping to himself. Langford, I notice, has moved toward the tallest TV antenna and has stationed himself near its base. He dreams, I suppose, that when the water covers the roof and the skylights and the chimneys, he will shinny up the pole and cling to the top. In his mind, probably, the water will rise until it reaches his ankles, and then stop. That is his hope. Then the water will recede, go down, down, down—and he will be saved. The water is swirling around the skylights now. The wind shifts. The waves are coming straight in from the Atlantic. ■

> ## The strangest thing is the silence of the city.

---

7. **whitecaps** *n.:* waves with white, foamy crests.
8. **"Nearer My God to Thee":** hymn reportedly played by the *Titanic*'s musicians as the ship was sinking.

Vocabulary

speculation (spek'yə·lā'shən) *n.:* thought; guesswork.

submerged (səb·murjd') *v.:* covered with water.

recede (ri·sēd') *v.:* move back or away.

---

6. **fanfare** *n.:* showy display.

Meet the Writer

James Stevenson

Writer, Illustrator, and Cartoonist

James Stevenson (1929–   ) works at two desks—one for writing and one for drawing. He's had an almost-fifty-year career as a cartoonist, reporter, and satirist on political and contemporary subjects. He is best known, however, as a writer and illustrator of whimsical, gently humorous books for young children.

Stevenson credits his elementary school in a suburb of New York City as a major influence on his creative life. His school, he recalls, encouraged its students to get involved in the social and political issues of the day and to express themselves artistically. It had a "policy of telling you that everybody could do everything. Everybody could sing, dance, act, play musical instruments, write stories, make pictures, and change the world."

By the time he was in college (and later, when he served as a U.S. Marine during the Korean War), Stevenson was selling cartoon ideas to *The New Yorker* magazine. He later worked as a reporter for *Life* magazine before joining *The New Yorker* as an editor, cartoonist, and staff writer.

Stevenson began his career by humorously depicting life in the suburbs, but by the 1960s, he was also satirizing political and national topics, such as the nuclear arms race and government bureaucracy. His major achievement, however, has been as a writer and illustrator of almost one hundred children's books, many of them winners of prestigious awards. Critics praised his ability to explore the difficulties of childhood with an insightful, lighthearted touch.

Stevenson credits movies and comic books, not the books he read as a child, with influencing his career:

> 66 I think that my experience and creative mind have been formed much more by movies and comic books. I like the idea of a storyboard, and I like the idea of a movie and all the different angles from which things can be viewed. 99

Response and Analysis

Reading Check

1. **Summarize** what happens in the story by filling out a chart like the one below. Write a question mark next to items the story doesn't answer.

Where and when the story takes place	
What has happened before the story starts	
What happens during the story	
What happens as the story ends	

Thinking Critically

2. The story begins *in medias res* (in the middle of the action), with important information omitted. What **inferences** can you make about each of the following **ambiguities** in the story? What details help you make these inferences?

   - the cause of the flood
   - how widespread the flood is
   - the outcome for the narrator and his or her neighbors

3. What do the **title** and **subtitle** add to your knowledge of the story?

4. Trace the subtle changes in **mood,** or feeling, as the story progresses. Find sensory details and other details that help create the moods.

5. What do the **minor characters** (about whom we know almost nothing) add to the story?

6. What do the writer's choice of **point of view** and the story's **form** (journal entries) enable the writer to do?

7. An **allusion** is a reference to a real or literary character or event that's not explained—just mentioned. Find allusions to the biblical story of Noah and to the sinking of the *Titanic* (check the footnotes). What do these allusions add to the story?

8. What do you think is the author's **purpose** in this story? Explain. (Hint: The Meet the Writer feature on page 378 may give you some help.)

Extending and Evaluating

9. Evaluate the story's **credibility.** Which details seem credible and which incredible? Do you find the behavior of the characters credible? How does their behavior compare with what your own might be? (Check your Quickwrite notes.)

WRITING

The Prequel or the Sequel

Write a brief **prequel** or **sequel**—a story that explains either what happens to cause the flood before Stevenson's story begins or what happens after the bottle is found. This is your chance to offer your interpretation of the story's **ambiguities** or **subtleties.** Make sure your details and interpretations are consistent with the details in Stevenson's story. For a challenge, make your story ambiguous as well.

▶ **Use "Writing a Short Story," pages 602–609, for help with this assignment.**

SKILLS FOCUS

Literary Skills
Analyze ambiguities and subtleties.

Reading Skills
Make inferences.

Writing Skills
Write a prequel or sequel.

Vocabulary Development

Word Roots and Their Families

Some words have lots of relatives—other words that come from the same **root** (the part of the word that carries its core meaning). Knowing common roots can help you figure out the meanings of unfamiliar words.

PRACTICE 1

Using the chart, find the root of each Word Bank word. Then, explain how the root relates to the word's meaning.

Latin Root	Meaning	Example Word
–ced–	yield	precede
–merg–	plunge	merge
–port–	carry	export
–spec–	see	spectacle
–sum–	take	consume

PRACTICE 2

For each word below, indicate its Latin root from the chart at the left. Then, give the word's meaning. Use a dictionary for help. When you are done, group the words into "families"—words with the same root.

1. consumable
2. emerge
3. import
4. transport
5. intercede
6. resume
7. emergence
8. proceed
9. inspect
10. prospect

Grammar Link

Using Modifiers Correctly

Most **modifiers** (adjectives and adverbs) use the suffixes –er and –est or the words more and most or less and least to form their **degrees of comparison.**

1. Use the **comparative form** (taller, more unusual, less patient) to compare two things. Use the **superlative form** (tallest, most unusual, least patient) to compare more than two things.

   The building across the street is higher than ours. [comparative]

   That is the highest building on the block. [superlative]

2. Avoid **double comparisons.** Do not use both –er and more/less or both –est and most/least to modify the same word.

   INCORRECT   The water rises more faster every hour.

   CORRECT   The water rises faster every hour.

PRACTICE

For each underlined comparative or superlative modifier in the paragraph below, indicate whether it is correct, and if not, supply the correct form.

Every day the waters rise (1) more higher than the day before, and the city looks (2) stranger and stranger. Some people seem much (3) most resigned to their fate than others. They act (4) more calmly than their hysterical neighbors. The (5) more maddening thing of all is that no one knows the cause of the flooding. Do you suppose areas at (6) more higher elevations are (7) more better or (8) more worse off?

▶ **For more help, see Comparison of Modifiers, 5c–g, in the Language Handbook.**

SKILLS FOCUS

Vocabulary Skills
Understand word roots.

Grammar Skills
Use comparative modifiers correctly.

FICTION
Expect the Unexpected

Roald Dahl's wicked imagination is showcased to perfection in *Tales of the Unexpected.* Here you'll encounter unusual characters and entertainingly horrible situations, from a long-suffering wife's revenge on an annoying husband to a "royal jelly" that has a startling effect on the baby who consumes it. These stories, collected from among Dahl's best, have only two things in common: All feature Dahl's dark sense of humor—and all will surprise you.

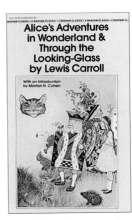

FICTION
The Other Side of the Mirror

Lewis Carroll's *Alice's Adventures in Wonderland* and *Through the Looking-Glass* follow its young heroine through the twists and turns of a strange new world where logic is turned completely on its head. After falling down a rabbit hole, Alice finds herself amid a host of odd characters who speak in baffling riddles. These tales are presented with further explanations in *The Annotated Alice,* which describes how the Alice stories were partly intended as witty social allegories.

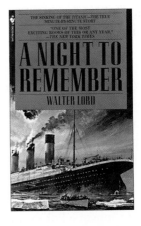

NONFICTION
They Called It Unsinkable

Walter Lord's *A Night to Remember,* first published in 1955, is still regarded as one of the finest books about the *Titanic* disaster of 1912. Lord interviewed hundreds of the *Titanic*'s passengers to create a gripping, authentic narrative of what happened before and after the ship's fatal collision. Filled with deeply personal accounts of those who survived as well as tributes to those who didn't, *A Night to Remember* provides a fascinating look at an unforgettable event in history.

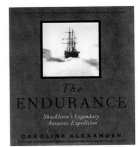

NONFICTION
Fearless Leader

In 1914, Sir Ernest Shackleton, a seasoned polar explorer, wanted to be the first man to cross the Antarctic continent. He assembled a team of experienced men to accompany him on what promised to be a career-making voyage. Little did Shackleton know that his ship, the *Endurance,* would be destroyed. Caroline Alexander's *The Endurance: Shackleton's Legendary Antarctic Expedition* uses journals, documents, and original photographs to reconstruct a historic voyage gone terribly wrong.

Comparing Media Genres

Writing Assignment
Write an essay in which you compare and contrast the coverage of a single news event by two different news media.

As you know from reading the selections in the previous section, the truth is often ambiguous. Two characters may view the same event in wildly different—even opposite—ways. A similar ambiguity can be found in two different media accounts, or retellings, of the same event. For example, a news story in a newspaper may focus on one person's point of view of an event, whereas an Internet news story about the same event may provide several perspectives. In this workshop you will examine how news accounts vary and how different media shape those accounts.

Prewriting

INTERNET
Media
Tutorials
Keyword: LE5 10-5

SKILLS FOCUS

Writing Skills
Write an essay comparing and contrasting media genres. Choose a news event. Compare and contrast media coverage.

Choose a News Event

A Nose for News To find a news event for your comparison-contrast essay, scan the front section of a newspaper or watch a national news program. Once you've focused on one event that interests you, search for coverage in other news media, including news Web sites, magazines, and radio programs. If you have trouble finding an event covered in two different media, you may need to consider one that has greater appeal to a national or an international audience.

Compare Coverage

Two Roads, Same Destination News organizations share the same purpose—to provide accurate information about events that interest people. However, the ways news organizations report the information can be very different. Each story is molded into a unique account by the people involved in creating the story and by the technology used to present the story. Every word and picture you see in a news story has been chosen by a journalist, editor, or producer to fit the strengths of the medium in which the story appears. For example, television is uniquely suited to capture the roar of a crowd as a marathoner crosses the finish line, while a newspaper is better able to present a list of the runners and a map of the route.

As you compare the coverage of an event by two media, consider the **points of comparison** in the left-hand column of the chart on the next page. Answer the questions beside each point for both media. The answers will lead you to the specific ways the coverage of the two media is alike and different.

COMPARING MEDIA: POINTS OF COMPARISON

Attention-getting techniques	• What words, sounds, and images are used to grab the audience's attention? • Does the story build suspense by slowly revealing the outcome of the event? Explain.
Structure	• What sequence does the information follow? • Does the story close with a neutral, positive, or negative view of the event?
Complexity	• How much information is given? • How many points of view are represented? • Is the event put in a broad enough context to explain most of its causes and consequences?
Objectivity	• Do the words in the story show an overtly positive or negative view of the subject? • Does the story seem to side with one person or group over another?
Emotional impact	• What feelings does the story arouse, if any? • What techniques are used to arouse these feelings?

A student used the questions in the chart above to compare the coverage of major Midwestern floods by a TV newsmagazine and a print newsmagazine. He organized his findings in the analysis log you see below, dividing information about the TV newsmagazine and the print newsmagazine into two columns. Then, he went back and underlined the similarities between the two stories. When he writes his essay, he will use the information in this log as evidence to support his thesis.

Analysis Log: TV Newsmagazine and Print Newsmagazine

Attention-getting techniques	TV: Used the words "horror," "heartbreak," and "terrible." Shots of the destruction and people crying.	Print: Used the words "horror," "tragedy," and "heartbreak in the heartland." Photos of rising floodwaters and upset people.
Structure	TV: Gave day-by-day accounts of the hardships two families must face. Ended with the families saying they would rebuild their homes and lives.	Print: Gave estimates of how many people lost property. Ended with a meteorologist's prediction of when flooding may occur again.
Complexity	TV: Focused on the points of view of two families. Included interviews with rescue workers.	Print: Gave many points of view—residents, rescue workers, government officials, meteorologists.

Develop a Thesis

The Verdict Is . . . Just as judges pass judgment on legal cases, you will pass judgment on the coverage by the two news media. Did one story give more information? Was one story more dramatic? The conclusions or judgments you make will be the **thesis** of your essay. Write your thesis in a **clear and coherent** thesis statement, a sentence or two that tells your audience the conclusions you drew about each medium's coverage. An example of a thesis statement follows.

> While the television show could offer its audience a more vivid sense of the frightened families and enormous damage, the magazine ended up presenting a much more in-depth and informative account.

Organize Your Essay

What Goes Where? Everything has a place—even the details of a comparison-contrast essay. To write a **focused** comparison-contrast essay, use one of the organizational patterns below.

- **Block style**—If you organize your essay in block style you will either discuss all the similarities and then all the differences of the two media, or you will tell everything about one medium first before discussing the second medium. Block style works best for essays that contain few comparisons.

- **Point-by-point style**—If you organize your essay in point-by-point style, you will go back and forth between the two media. You will first explain how the media are alike and different for *one* point of comparison, then how they are alike and different for the *next* point of comparison, and so on. This style is best suited for essays that contain more comparisons.

- **Modified block style**—If you arrange your essay in modified block style, you will use a combination of block style and point-by-point style. The overall organization of the essay will be block: a discussion of similarities and then a discussion of differences. Within each section, though, the specific similarities and differences will be organized in point-by-point style. For example, the first section of the paper about the Midwestern floods would discuss the points of comparison that have similarities. The second section would discuss the points of comparison that have differences.

SKILLS FOCUS

Writing Skills
Write a thesis statement.
Organize your essay.

PRACTICE & APPLY 1 Use the instructions in this section to compare the coverage of a news event by two different media, write a thesis statement, and organize your ideas.

Writing

Comparing Media Genres

A Writer's Framework

Introduction

- Start with an interesting opener.
- Provide background information about the news event.
- Introduce the two media you will compare and contrast.
- Present a clear thesis statement.

Body

- Organize your essay in block style, point-by-point style, or modified block style.
- Discuss the points of comparison.
- Include specific references to each news story as evidence for each point.

Conclusion

- Summarize your main points by restating your thesis.
- Offer ideas about how the two stories were shaped by the media that delivered them.
- Close with a final impression or insight.

A Writer's Model

More Than News

The weather is not what you usually think of as a fascinating news story. Sometimes, however, it grabs the attention of the entire country. Last month, several Midwestern states suffered the worst flooding in decades. One widely read newsmagazine published a long cover story on the flood, and a national weekly television newsmagazine devoted an entire broadcast to it. While the television show offered its audience a more vivid sense of the frightened families and enormous damage, the magazine ended up presenting a much more in-depth and informative account.

There were a number of similarities between the two stories. Both stories focused mostly on the human-interest angle, using similar shots of water rising over rooftops along with the worried or weeping faces of the newly homeless. In addition, both offered several interviews with residents who lost homes and with exhausted rescue workers. Perhaps because the event involved the kind of loss that everyone fears, both the television show and magazine also used a variety of attention-getting techniques to prompt an emotional response. Aside from the shocking visuals, both also used loaded words like "horror" and "tragedy" to describe the landscape.

(continued)

INTRODUCTION

Interesting opener

Background information

Reference to two media

Thesis statement

BODY/Similarities:

1. **Emotional impact**

2. **Complexity**

3. **Attention-getting techniques**

(continued)

Differences:
I. Complexity

Despite their similarities, the two stories also had important differences. Among the most noticeable were the differing points of view each presented. The television show primarily focused on two families whose houses were in the path of the flood. This restricted point of view made the story quite personal. In contrast, the magazine article offered many points of view, including those of residents affected by the floods, rescue workers, government officials, and meteorologists. This number of different voices made the story less intimate, but provided readers with greater depth and clarity. By reading the magazine story, a reader understood more about how many people were in danger and how the flooding would affect the entire area.

2. Structure

Another major difference between the two stories was the way they structured their information. The TV report was structured like a mystery, suspensefully tracking the water as it rose day by day and concealing the fates of the two families' homes until the end of the program. In addition, despite the eventual ruin of both families' homes, the TV report offered a positive, storybook ending, with family members all pledging to rebuild their houses and lives. In contrast, the first paragraphs of the magazine story presented detailed estimates of how many people were affected by the flood. The magazine chose to close the article with a meteorologist's prediction about how soon the next round of flooding might occur in the region.

CONCLUSION
Restatement of thesis

Ideas about how stories were shaped

Final insight

It is true that the magazine and television stories both communicated the emotional impact of the story. However, the television story focused narrowly on the suffering of just a few people, while the print story provided a broader context and more factual information. Television has many strengths that make it appealing to viewers, especially the ways it can produce emotional responses with intimate interviews and dramatic visuals. However, television newsmagazine stories often stop there, failing to provide the context and depth that print newsmagazines can offer. The next time you think a television news story has given you the complete picture, you might check out a magazine article, too.

INTERNET

More Writer's Models

Keyword: LE5 10-5

PRACTICE & APPLY 2 Use the framework on page 385 and the Writer's Model above to guide you as you write a first draft of your comparison-contrast essay.

Revising

Evaluate and Revise Your Draft

Twice Is Nice Your job isn't done until you've given your essay at least two readings. Have you provided enough detail to show the strengths and weaknesses of the news stories you compared? Is your essay logically organized and smoothly written? As you revise, be sure to keep in mind your **audience** and the degree of **formality** your readers might expect in a comparison-contrast essay. Also, think about how the essay achieves your **purpose**—to provide information.

▶ **First Reading: Content and Organization** Use the guidelines in the chart below as a **think sheet.** The questions, tips, and revision techniques can help you revise the content and organization of your essay.

Rubric: Comparing Media Genres		
Evaluation Questions ▶	**Tips** ▶	**Revision Techniques**
① Does the introduction engage the reader and include any necessary background information?	▶ **Bracket** the sentences that capture the reader's attention. **Underline** the sentences that explain the event covered in the stories.	▶ **Replace** the opening with one or two sentences that will grab the reader's attention. If necessary, **add** a few sentences that explain the event.
② Does the introduction offer a clear thesis statement that presents the conclusions the writer drew about the media coverage?	▶ **Draw a wavy line** under the thesis statement.	▶ **Add** a statement that expresses the conclusions about the media coverage, or **revise** the existing statement to make it clearer.
③ Is the pattern of organization easy to follow?	▶ **Label** the points of comparison, for example, structure, complexity, and so on. If the order is not logical, revise.	▶ **Reorder** the points in a clear block style, point-by-point style, or modified block style.
④ Is each point of comparison supported by specific details and references to the news stories?	▶ **Put a check** beside each detail or reference to a news story.	▶ **Elaborate** on the points by offering examples, quotations, and other specific evidence from the two news stories.
⑤ Does the conclusion restate the thesis and reflect on how each story was shaped by the media? Does it offer a final impression?	▶ **Draw a box** around the sentence that summarizes the thesis. **Highlight** the sentences that comment on how each story was shaped. **Star** any final impression or insight.	▶ If necessary, **add** a brief restatement of the thesis. **Add** sentences that explain how media shaped the stories. **Add** a final impression of the media being compared.

Second Reading: Style Now, focus on the style of your essay. Unvaried sentence length is a common problem in comparison-contrast essays. In comparing subject A to subject B, a writer's sentences often start to sound the same—either short and choppy or tongue-trippingly long. Consequently, the reader may become bored or confused. Use the chart below to help you **vary the sentence length** in your comparison-contrast essay.

Style Guidelines

Evaluation Question ▶	**Tip**	▶ **Revision Technique**
● Is there a series of sentences that are all the same length?	▶ **Put a jagged line** beneath three or more short sentences or long sentences in succession.	▶ **Combine** a short sentence with another one, or **break** a longer sentence into two or more shorter ones.

ANALYZING THE REVISION PROCESS
Study these revisions, and answer the questions that follow.

Another major difference between the two stories was

the way they structured their information. The TV report was

, *suspensefully tracking*

combine   structured like a mystery. ~~It suspensefully tracked~~ the water as

and concealing

it rose day by day. ~~It concealed~~ the fates of the two families'

homes until the end of the program. In addition, despite the

eventual ruin of both families' homes, the TV report

add   offered a positive, storybook ending , *with family members*
all pledging to rebuild their houses and lives.

Responding to the Revision Process

1. Why did the writer combine the second, third, and fourth sentences?

2. How does the addition to the last sentence improve the passage?

SKILLS FOCUS

Writing Skills
Revise for content and style.

PRACTICE & APPLY 3 Use the content, organization, and style guidelines on this page and the previous page to revise your draft. If a peer reviewed your essay, consider his or her comments as you revise.

Publishing

Proofread and Publish Your Essay

A Critical Eye Imagine finding a misspelled word or an ungrammatical sentence in a news article. Would it lead you to question the accuracy of the content, too? It probably would. The same is true of *your* readers. Show them that you have done a reliable job by carefully proofreading for grammar, usage, and mechanics errors. If you choose, ask a partner to help. Once you have found and corrected any mistakes, make a clean final copy of your essay.

Extra, Extra! Read All About It! You've thought deeply about how media messages shape events for readers, listeners, and viewers. Now, help others reflect on media by getting your essay to an audience of your own.

- Send your essay to the two news media you compared. (Look for an address within the publication or on the Web.) Ask for a response from the journalist or producer who created each story.

- Exchange essays with a group of classmates and then stage a discussion session. Perhaps this will lead you to form a group that monitors how different media present information.

- Working with a small group of classmates, turn your essay into a short multimedia presentation to teach younger children about the characteristics of different media.

Reflect on Your Essay

Analyze the Analysis What have you learned about news media—and about your own writing process—while drafting and polishing your essay? Use these questions to reflect on your experience:

- How was writing this essay similar to other essays you write in school? How was it different?

- How has writing this essay affected the way you understand and respond to news stories?

- Choose one of the stories you analyzed, and put yourself in the journalist's or producer's shoes. What would you have done differently in presenting the story? Explain your answer.

PRACTICE & APPLY 4 Proofread and publish your essay in one of the ways suggested on this page or in another interesting way. Then, reflect on news media and your writing process by answering the questions above.

> **TIP** Proofreading will help you ensure that you follow the **conventions** of standard American English. In particular, watch for errors in parallel structure, which often occur when you are making comparisons and contrasts. For more on using **parallel structure,** see Using Parallel Structure, 10f, in the Language Handbook.

SKILLS FOCUS

Writing Skills
Proofread, especially for correct use of parallel structure.

Generating Research Questions and Evaluating Sources

DIRECTIONS: Read the following article. Then, read and respond to the questions that follow.

The Last Frontier

Michael D. Lemonick

The irony of twentieth-century scientists venturing out to explore waters that have been navigated for thousands of years is not lost on oceanographers. More than one hundred expeditions have reached Everest, the 29,028-foot pinnacle of the Himalayas;[1] manned voyages to space have become commonplace; and robot probes have ventured to the outer reaches of the solar system. But only now are the deepest parts of the ocean coming within reach. "I think there's a perception that we have already explored the sea," says marine biologist Sylvia Earle, a former chief scientist at the National Oceanographic and Atmospheric Administration and a cofounder of Deep Ocean Engineering, the San Leandro, California, company where construction of *Deep Flight I*[2] began: "The reality is we know more about Mars than we know about the oceans."

That goes not only for the sea's uttermost depths but also for the still-mysterious middle waters three or four miles down, and even for the "shallows" a few hundred feet deep. For while the push to reach the very bottom of the sea has fired the imagination of some of the world's most daring explorers, it is just the most visible part of a broad international effort to probe the oceans' depths. It's a high-sea adventure fraught[3] with danger, and—because of the expense—with controversy as well.

But the rewards could be enormous: oil and mineral wealth to rival Alaska's North Slope and California's Gold Rush;[4] scientific discoveries that could change our view of how the planet—and the life-forms on it—evolved; natural substances that could yield new medicines and whole new classes of industrial chemicals. Beyond those practical benefits there is the intangible but real satisfaction that comes from exploring earth's last great frontier.

There's a lot to explore. Oceans cover nearly three quarters of the planet's surface—336 million cubic miles of water that reaches an average depth of 2.3 miles.

---

1. Since this article was written, the elevation of Mount Everest has been recalculated as 29,035 feet.
2. *Deep Flight I:* small, experimental submarine designed for deep-sea exploration.
3. **fraught** (frôt) *adj.:* filled.
4. **Alaska's North Slope and California's Gold Rush:** reference to the oil fields in Alaska's northern coast and the great California gold rush of 1849.

SKILLS FOCUS

Pages 390–393 cover **Reading Skills** Generate research questions, and evaluate sources.

390 Collection 5 Irony and Ambiguity • Generating Research Questions and Evaluating Sources

The sea's intricate food webs support more life by weight and a greater diversity of animals than any other ecosystem,[5] from sulfur-eating bacteria clustered around deep-sea vents to fish that light up like Times Square billboards to lure their prey. Somewhere below, there even lurks the last certified sea monster left from prescientific times: the 64-foot-long giant squid.

The sea's economic potential is equally enormous. Majestically swirling ocean currents influence much of the world's weather patterns; figuring out how they operate could save trillions of dollars in weather-related disasters. The oceans also have vast reserves of commercially valuable minerals, including nickel, iron, manganese, copper, and cobalt. Pharmaceutical[6] and biotechnology[7] companies are already analyzing deep-sea bacteria, fish, and marine plants, looking for substances that they might someday turn into miracle drugs. Says Bruce Robison, of the Monterey Bay Aquarium Research Institute (MBARI) in California: "I can guarantee you that the discoveries beneficial to mankind will far outweigh those of the space program over the next couple of decades. If we can get to the abyss regularly, there will be immediate payoffs."

Getting there, though, will force explorers to cope with an environment just as perilous as outer space. Unaided, humans can't dive much more than 10 feet down—less than one three-thousandth of the way to the very bottom—before increasing pressure starts to build up painfully on the inner ear, sinuses, and lungs. Frigid subsurface water rapidly sucks away body heat. And even the most leathery of lungs can't hold a breath for more than two or three minutes.

For these reasons the modern age of deep-sea exploration had to wait for two key technological developments: engineer Otis Barton's 1930 invention of the bathysphere—essentially a deep-diving tethered steel ball—and the invention of scuba (short for "self-contained underwater breathing apparatus") by Jacques-Yves Cousteau and Emile Gagnan in 1943. Swimmers had been trying to figure out how to get oxygen underwater for thousands of years. Sponge divers in ancient Greece breathed from air-filled kettles; bulky-helmeted diving suits linked by hose to the surface first appeared in the 1800s. But it wasn't until scuba came along that humans, breathing compressed air, were able to move about freely underwater at depths of more than 100 feet.

Even the most experienced scuba divers rarely venture below 150 feet, however, owing to increasingly crushing pressure and the laborious decompression process required to purge the blood of nitrogen (which can form bubbles as a diver returns to the surface and cause the excruciating and sometimes-fatal condition known as

---

5. **ecosystem** (ē′kō·sis′təm) *n.:* community of animals and plants related to each other and to their environment.
6. **pharmaceutical** (fär′mə·sōōt′i·kəl) *adj.:* relating to drugs and medicines.
7. **biotechnology** (bī′ō·tek·näl′ə·jē) *n.* used as *adj.:* use of technology to study living organisms and solve problems involving them.

the bends). And pressurized diving suits make it possible for humans to descend only to 1,440 feet—far short of the deepest reaches of the oceans. . . .

Do scientists expect even more surprises as they venture farther below the surface? The question is a crucial one, as both scientists and policy makers debate the finances of deep-sea exploration. Most everyone acknowledges that there is some value in studying the oceans. It's expensive, though, and because of generally tight budgets, even the few existing manned submersibles[8] (which in any case are rated only for depths above 20,000 feet) often have to sit idle. Building more strikes some as a waste of money.

That includes some scientists. Although he has never been to the very deepest trenches, ocean explorer Robert Ballard of Woods Hole,[9] who is best known for discovering the wreck of the *Titanic* in 1985, is convinced that the action lies in the relative

---

8. **submersibles** (səb·mʉr′sə·bəlz) *n.:* vessels that operate underwater, such as submarines.
9. **Woods Hole:** Woods Hole Oceanographic Institution, a research center located in Woods Hole, Massachusetts.

shallows. "I believe that the deep sea has very little to offer," he says. "I've been there. I've spent a career there. I don't see the future there." The French have decided not even to bother trying to break the 20,000-foot barrier—the range of their deepest-diving submersible, the three-person *Nautile.* Says Jean Jarry, director of the Toulon-sur-Mer research center of IFREMER, France's national oceanographic institute: "We think that's a good depth because it covers 97 percent of the ocean. To go beyond that is not very interesting and is very expensive."

But that attitude is far from universal. Biologist Greg Stone, of the New England Aquarium in Boston, compares reaching the deepest abyss with Christopher Columbus's search for the New World. "Why should we care about the deepest 3 percent of the oceans, and why do we need to reach it?" he asks rhetorically. "For one, we won't know what it holds until we've been there. There will certainly be new creatures. We'll be able to learn where gases from the atmosphere go in the ocean. We'll be able to get closest to where the geological action is. We know very little about the details of these processes. And once we're there, I'm sure studies will open up whole sets of new questions." . . .

—from *Time,* August 14, 1995

1. Which statement *best* expresses the **main idea** of "The Last Frontier"?

   A Scuba divers are equipped to explore depths below 20,000 feet.

   B Exploring the oceans could have many practical and scientific benefits.

   C No scientist wants to explore the ocean below 20,000 feet.

   D More than half of the earth's surface is covered by oceans.

2. Which research question will yield the *most* useful information for a report on deep-sea exploration?

   F What is marine biology?

   G What did Emile Gagnan invent?

   H What percentage of the earth's oceans are below 20,000 feet?

   J What deep-sea discoveries have been made using manned submersibles?

3. Which of the following research questions is *not* directly related to topics discussed in this article?

   A What minerals have been discovered beneath the sea?

   B What groups are currently exploring the ocean below 20,000 feet?

   C What are the scientific benefits of exploring the frozen waters of the South Pole?

   D How is deep-sea exploration funded?

4. If you were researching the invention of the bathysphere, which source would be *most* useful?

   F A TV documentary about the life and work of Jacques-Yves Cousteau

   G An article on Otis Barton in *Encyclopaedia Britannica,* published in 2002

   H A Web page on deep-sea marine life maintained by the American Museum of Natural History

   J A national magazine article on underwater volcanos

5. If you were researching the funding for exploration of the deepest parts of the ocean, who would you expect to be *most* biased against the funding?

   A Jacques-Yves Cousteau

   B Robert Ballard

   C Greg Stone

   D Bruce Robison

Constructed Response

6. List three kinds of sources that would be useful for a research paper on recently discovered deep-sea animals. Explain why you chose those sources.

Collection 5: Skills Review
Vocabulary Skills

Context Clues

DIRECTIONS: Use context clues to help you choose the answer that gives the best definition for each underlined word.

1. The policemen felt sorry for Mary about her husband's death and tried to be consoling.

   Consoling means —

   A humorous
   B comforting
   C polite
   D religious

2. Built to be the very best ship of the era, the *Titanic* had several superlative qualities, including luxury and speed.

   Superlative means —

   F safety
   G supreme
   H rich
   J odd

3. Rather than causing upset, the shots the officers fired into the air quelled the panic among the passengers.

   Quelled means —

   A increased
   B repeated
   C renewed
   D quieted

4. In "Into Thin Air" the clouds drifting up the valley at first seemed completely innocuous, but later proved deadly.

   Innocuous means —

   F worrisome
   G dangerous
   H harmless
   J wispy

5. Because of the weather it took Hall and Hansen more than twelve hours to traverse a part of the ridge that climbers usually cross in half an hour.

   Traverse means —

   A retreat from
   B observe
   C cross over
   D go under

6. Following the Sherpas' advice, Hutchison decided not to jeopardize the other climbers' lives by making a risky effort to rescue Weathers and Namba, who were so close to death.

   Jeopardize means —

   F endanger
   G ensure
   H rescue
   J upset

7. In "Notes from a Bottle" the rising water has already submerged the lower buildings and will soon flood the city's tallest structures.

   Submerged means —

   A reacted to
   B covered with water
   C revealed
   D drawn attention to

SKILLS FOCUS

Vocabulary Skills
Use context clues.

Collection 5: Skills Review
Writing Skills

DIRECTIONS: Read the following paragraph from a draft of a student's comparison-contrast essay, and respond to the questions.

(1) Recently, two separate news sources carried articles about professional golfer Leon Dillard. (2) If you have access to the Web, you can read both articles online. (3) The newspaper article, "Young Egos Intruding on Sport," presents the opinion that Dillard is ruining the game by inspiring youths to take up the sport in hopes of making millions of dollars. (4) On the other hand, the magazine article, "Leon Dillard: On the Course and Off," presents a detailed account of Dillard's golfing career and the positive impact his sponsorship of urban golf leagues has had on the sport.

1. To present a clear, coherent thesis, which of these sentences could the writer add?
   - **A** While both stories discuss Dillard's impact on the game, the newspaper conveys a more negative perspective.
   - **B** Leon Dillard is an amazing golfer whose skills rival other greats.
   - **C** Leon Dillard has been interviewed by media sources worldwide.
   - **D** Newspaper articles are always more factual than magazine stories.

2. To support the ideas in sentence 3, which sentence could the writer add?
   - **F** It gives a graphic diagram of Dillard's powerful golf swing.
   - **G** It explains how Dillard began his golf career.
   - **H** It focuses on Dillard's hobbies outside of golf.
   - **J** It quotes youths who hope their golf lessons will lead to riches.

3. Which of the following would elaborate on the ideas in sentence 4?
   - **A** The newspaper article is biased, focusing on the writer's opinions.
   - **B** The magazine article is part of a series of stories on Leon Dillard.
   - **C** The article quotes a young golfer who admires Dillard's generosity.
   - **D** Statistics in the newspaper reveal Dillard's earnings.

4. Which sentence should be deleted to improve the passage's organization?
   - **F** 1
   - **G** 2
   - **H** 3
   - **J** 4

5. To discuss the similarities between the two media, the writer could
   - **A** explain that the newspaper is distributed only locally
   - **B** defend the credibility of the sources quoted in each article
   - **C** describe the photo of Dillard that accompanies the magazine article
   - **D** discuss how both articles credit Dillard for influencing young golfers

SKILLS FOCUS

Writing Skills
Write a comparison-contrast essay.

Collection 6

SYMBOLISM AND ALLEGORY

INFORMATIONAL READING FOCUS

SYNTHESIZING SOURCES

We are symbols, and inhabit symbols.

—Ralph Waldo Emerson

The Persistence of Memory (1931)
by Salvador Dali.
Oil on canvas (80.7 cm × 100.6 cm).

INTERNET
Collection
Resources
Keyword: LE5 10-6

Symbolism and Allegory *by* John Leggett

SIGNS OF SOMETHING MORE

Our everyday lives are full of symbols. The ring on your finger, though actually a piece of metal with a stone in it, may also be a symbol of something less concrete. For you it may symbolize love, calling to mind the special person who saved for months to buy it for you.

There are many symbols in our culture that we know and recognize at once. We automatically make the associations suggested by a cross, a six-pointed star, a crown, a skull and crossbones, and the Stars and Stripes. These commonly accepted symbols are **public symbols.**

Symbols in Literature: Making Associations

Writers of fiction, poetry, and drama create new, personal symbols in their work. Some literary symbols, like the great white whale in *Moby-Dick* and that stubborn spot of blood on Lady Macbeth's hand, become so widely known that eventually they too become a part of our public stockpile of symbols.

In literature a **symbol** is something (an object, a setting, an event, an animal, or even a person) that functions in a story the way you'd expect it to but also stands for something more than itself, usually something abstract. The white whale in *Moby-Dick* is a very real white whale in the novel, and Captain Ahab spends the whole book chasing it. Certain passages in that novel make clear to us that this whale is also associated with the mystery of evil in the world. That is how symbols work—by association. Most people associate the color green with new life and, therefore, with hope. In some cultures the color white is associated with innocence and purity; in others white is a color of death. We usually associate gardens with joy and wastelands with futility and despair. We associate winter with sterility and spring with fertility. We associate cooing doves with peace and pecking ravens with death, but these are associations, not equations.

A literary symbol isn't just a sign with one specific meaning. The picture of a cigarette in a circle with a diagonal line drawn through it is a sign meaning, precisely and specifically, "No Smoking." The white whale, on the other hand, doesn't mean, precisely and specifically, "the mystery of evil." Instead, the associations suggested by the writer, made by the characters in the story, and ultimately made by the reader evoke images of evil (and perhaps other elements), suggest aspects of the darker side of life, and hint at possible ways of seeing and thinking about the events portrayed.

Symbols invite the reader to participate in making sense of the text by building on the associations and connections that the symbols suggest.

Is It a Symbol?

However, you must be careful not to start looking for symbols in everything you read: They won't be there. Here are some hints to pay attention to when you sense that a story is operating on a symbolic level:

SKILLS FOCUS

Literary Skills
Understand symbolism and allegory.

1 Symbols are often visual.

2 When some event or object or setting is used as a symbol, it often reappears throughout the story.

3 A symbol in literature is a form of **figurative language.** Like a metaphor a symbol is something that is identified with something else that is very *different* from it but that shares some quality. When you are thinking about whether something is used symbolically, ask yourself this: "Does this item also stand for something essentially different from itself?"

4 A symbol usually has something to do with a story's **theme.**

Why Use Symbols?

Why do writers use symbols? Why don't they just come out and tell us directly what they want to say? One answer is that symbols have the power to move us. When they fit a human emotion just right, they stir us and last for years in our imaginations. You may well find that you remember a story's symbol long after you have forgotten other parts of the story's plot.

Allegory: When Symbols Get Specific

Allegories are stories in which characters and places stand for virtues and vices. Characters in an allegory might even have names that describe what they symbolize: Ignorance, Mr. Worldly Wiseman, Little-Faith, Mrs. Bubble.

Years ago allegories were very popular. An allegory written in the seventeenth century by John Bunyan, called *The Pilgrim's Progress,* was at one time second only to

the Bible in popularity in the English-speaking world. *The Pilgrim's Progress* is about a man named Christian and his progress through the world to the Celestial City. On the way he must conquer all kinds of dangers and temptations, such as the Giant Despair, the City of Destruction, and the Valley of Humiliation.

There are several types of allegory. In **fables,** animal characters that symbolize vices and virtues act out a story in order to teach a practical lesson about how to succeed in life. You might remember the sly fox, the slow-but-steady tortoise, the greedy crow.

Another kind of allegory is the parable. A **parable** is a brief story that is set in the ordinary everyday world and told to teach a lesson about ethics or morality. One of the most famous parables is that of the Good Samaritan (see page 278), who stops and helps a stranger who has been robbed and beaten. Today we still call caring strangers good Samaritans.

Practice

How many symbols can you find in public life? Try identifying what the following things stand for:

1. dove with an olive branch
2. blindfolded woman holding a pair of scales
3. yellow rose
4. yellow ribbon tied around a tree
5. dragon (dragons stand for different things in the East and the West)
6. pink ribbon in a lapel

Before You Read

Through the Tunnel

Make the Connection

Quickwrite ✏

Think of a time when you felt you needed to prove yourself by achieving something that was difficult and challenging. What did you have to go through to reach your goal? Did you get or do what you wanted? How did you feel at the end? Freewrite for a few minutes about your experience.

Literary Focus

Symbolic Meaning: More Than Meets the Eye

When we read, we often sense that a story means more than what happens on its surface. For instance, if a young woman in a story is in serious conflict with her parents over her earrings (she loves them; they hate them), we should suspect that those earrings represent something important to her. A **symbol** is a person, place, thing, or event that stands both for itself and for something beyond itself. To the young woman the earrings may symbolize her independence or maturity. A large part of the appeal of symbols is that they often carry associations, connections, and powerful emotions.

The **symbolic meaning** of a story emerges from an overall interpretation of the story's symbols. As you read "Through the Tunnel," look for elements that could be symbolically significant. What might they mean?

SKILLS FOCUS

Literary Skills
Understand symbolic meaning.

Reading Skills
Re-read and read for details.

Reading Skills 📖

Re-reading and Reading for Details

Many stories need only one reading because everything seems perfectly clear the first time through. Other stories puzzle, nag, and tease us. They seem to have layers that invite peeling away to get at the story's core meaning. Once you finish reading such a story, you may want—or need—to go round again, **re-reading** the text to mine its subtler, deeper meanings.

As you re-read, you may be searching for answers to questions you've asked yourself at the story's end. You may also notice details that your eye jumped over during your first reading. Writers plant significant details as signposts or clues, but we often don't recognize their importance until we've read the story all the way to its end.

Plan to read this story twice. Ask yourself questions when you finish the first time: "What puzzles me? What seems unclear?" Then, re-read the story, looking for important details and answers to your questions.

Vocabulary Development

contrition (kən·trish′ən) *n.*: regret or sense of guilt at having done wrong.

supplication (sup′lə·kā′shən) *n.*: humble appeal or request.

defiant (dē·fi′ənt) *adj.*: challenging authority.

inquisitive (in·kwiz′ə·tiv) *adj.*: questioning; curious.

minute (mī·nōōt′) *adj.*: small; tiny.

incredulous (in·krej′oo·ləs) *adj.*: disbelieving; skeptical.

Through the Tunnel

Doris Lessing

WATER SURGED INTO HIS MOUTH; HE CHOKED, SANK, CAME UP.

Going to the shore on the first morning of the vacation, the young English boy stopped at a turning of the path and looked down at a wild and rocky bay and then over to the crowded beach he knew so well from other years. His mother walked on in front of him, carrying a bright striped bag in one hand. Her other arm, swinging loose, was very white in the sun. The boy watched that white naked arm and turned his eyes, which had a frown behind them, toward the bay and back again to his mother. When she felt he was not with her, she swung around. "Oh, there you are, Jerry!" she said. She looked impatient, then smiled. "Why, darling, would you rather not come with me? Would you rather—" She frowned, conscientiously worrying over what amusements he might secretly be longing for, which she had been too busy or too careless to imagine. He was very familiar with that anxious, apologetic smile. Contrition sent him running after her. And yet, as he ran, he looked back over his shoulder at the wild bay; and all morning, as he played on the safe beach, he was thinking of it.

Next morning, when it was time for the routine of swimming and sunbathing, his mother said, "Are you tired of the usual beach, Jerry? Would you like to go somewhere else?"

"Oh, no!" he said quickly, smiling at her out of that unfailing impulse of contrition—a sort of chivalry.[1] Yet, walking down the path with her, he blurted out, "I'd like to go and have a look at those rocks down there."

She gave the idea her attention. It was a wild-looking place, and there was no one there, but she said, "Of course, Jerry. When you've had enough, come to the big beach. Or just go straight back to the villa, if you like." She walked away, that bare arm, now slightly reddened from yesterday's sun, swinging. And he almost ran after her again, feeling it unbearable that she should go by herself, but he did not.

She was thinking, Of course he's old enough to be safe without me. Have I been keeping him too close? He mustn't feel he ought to be with me. I must be careful.

He was an only child, eleven years old. She was a widow. She was determined to be neither possessive nor lacking in devotion. She went worrying off to her beach.

As for Jerry, once he saw that his mother had gained her beach, he began the steep descent to the bay. From where he was, high up among red-brown rocks, it was a scoop of moving bluish green fringed with white. As he went lower, he saw that it spread among small promontories and inlets of rough, sharp rock, and the crisping, lapping surface showed stains of purple and darker blue. Finally, as he ran sliding and scraping down the last few yards, he saw an edge of white surf and the shallow, luminous movement of water over white sand and, beyond that, a solid, heavy blue.

He ran straight into the water and began swimming. He was a good swimmer. He went out fast over the gleaming sand, over a middle region where rocks lay like discolored monsters under the surface, and then he was in the real sea—a warm sea where irregular cold currents from the deep water shocked his limbs.

When he was so far out that he could look back not only on the little bay but past the promontory that was between it and the big beach, he floated on the buoyant surface and looked for his mother. There she was, a speck of yellow under an umbrella that looked like a slice of orange peel. He swam back to shore, relieved at being sure she was there, but all at once very lonely.

On the edge of a small cape that marked the side of the bay away from the promontory was a loose scatter of rocks. Above them, some boys were stripping off their clothes. They came running, naked, down to the rocks. The English boy swam toward them but kept his distance at a stone's throw. They were of that coast; all of them were burned smooth dark brown and speaking a language he did not understand. To be with them, of them, was a craving that filled his whole body. He swam a little closer; they

---

1. **chivalry** (shiv′əl·rē) n.: here, an act of gentlemanly politeness.

Vocabulary

contrition (kən·trish′ən) n.: regret or sense of guilt at having done wrong.

turned and watched him with narrowed, alert dark eyes. Then one smiled and waved. It was enough. In a minute, he had swum in and was on the rocks beside them, smiling with a desperate, nervous supplication. They shouted cheerful greetings at him; and then, as he preserved his nervous, uncomprehending smile, they understood that he was a foreigner strayed from his own beach, and they proceeded to forget him. But he was happy. He was with them.

They began diving again and again from a high point into a well of blue sea between rough, pointed rocks. After they had dived and come up, they swam around, hauled themselves up, and waited their turn to dive again. They were big boys—men, to Jerry. He dived, and they watched him; and when he swam around to take his place, they made way for him. He felt he was accepted and he dived again, carefully, proud of himself.

Soon the biggest of the boys poised himself, shot down into the water, and did not come up. The others stood about, watching. Jerry, after waiting for the sleek brown head to appear, let out a yell of warning; they looked at him idly and turned their eyes back toward the water. After a long time, the boy came up on the other side of a big dark rock, letting the air out of his lungs in a sputtering gasp and a shout of triumph. Immediately the rest of them dived in. One moment, the morning seemed full of chattering boys; the next, the air and the surface of the water were empty. But through the heavy blue, dark shapes could be seen moving and groping.

Jerry dived, shot past the school of underwater swimmers, saw a black wall of rock looming at him, touched it, and bobbed up at once to the surface, where the wall was a low barrier he could see across. There was no one visible; under him, in the water, the dim shapes of the swimmers had disappeared. Then one and then another of the boys came up on the far side of the barrier of rock, and he understood that they had swum through some gap or hole in it. He plunged down again. He could see nothing through the stinging salt water but the blank rock. When he came up, the boys were all on the diving rock, preparing to attempt the feat again. And now, in a panic of failure, he yelled up, in English, "Look at me! Look!" and he began splashing and kicking in the water like a foolish dog.

They looked down gravely, frowning. He knew the frown. At moments of failure, when he clowned to claim his mother's attention, it was with just this grave, embarrassed inspection that she rewarded him. Through his hot shame, feeling the pleading grin on his face like a scar that he could never remove, he looked up at the group of big brown boys on the rock and shouted, *Bonjour! Merci! Au revoir! Monsieur, monsieur!*[2] while he hooked his fingers round his ears and waggled them.

Water surged into his mouth; he choked, sank, came up. The rock, lately weighted with boys, seemed to rear up out of the water as their

---

2. *Bonjour! Merci! Au revoir! Monsieur, monsieur!:* French for "Hello! Thank you! Goodbye! Mister, mister!"—probably the only French words Jerry knows.

Vocabulary
supplication (sup′lə·kā′shən) *n.:* humble appeal or request.

weight was removed. They were flying down past him now, into the water; the air was full of falling bodies. Then the rock was empty in the hot sunlight. He counted one, two, three . . .

At fifty, he was terrified. They must all be drowning beneath him, in the watery caves of the rock! At a hundred, he stared around him at the empty hillside, wondering if he should yell for help. He counted faster, faster, to hurry them up, to bring them to the surface quickly, to drown them quickly—anything rather than the terror of counting on and on into the blue emptiness of the morning. And then, at a hundred and sixty, the water beyond the rock was full of boys blowing like brown whales. They swam back to the shore without a look at him.

He climbed back to the diving rock and sat down, feeling the hot roughness of it under his thighs. The boys were gathering up their bits of clothing and running off along the shore to another promontory. They were leaving to get away from him. He cried openly, fists in his eyes. There was no one to see him, and he cried himself out.

It seemed to him that a long time had passed, and he swam out to where he could see his mother. Yes, she was still there, a yellow spot under an orange umbrella. He swam back to the big rock, climbed up, and dived into the blue pool among the fanged and angry boulders. Down he went, until he touched the wall of rock again. But the salt was so painful in his eyes that he could not see.

He came to the surface, swam to shore, and went back to the villa to wait for his mother. Soon she walked slowly up the path, swinging her striped bag, the flushed, naked arm dangling beside her. "I want some swimming goggles," he panted, defiant and beseeching.

She gave him a patient, inquisitive look as she said casually, "Well, of course, darling."

But now, now, now! He must have them this minute, and no other time. He nagged and pestered until she went with him to a shop. As soon as she had bought the goggles, he grabbed them from her hand as if she were going to claim them for herself, and was off, running down the steep path to the bay.

Jerry swam out to the big barrier rock, adjusted the goggles, and dived. The impact of the water broke the rubber-enclosed vacuum, and the goggles came loose. He understood that he must swim down to the base of the rock from the surface of the water. He fixed the goggles tight and firm, filled his lungs, and floated, face down, on the water. Now he could see. It was as if he had eyes of a different kind—fish eyes that showed everything clear and delicate and wavering in the bright water.

Under him, six or seven feet down, was a floor of perfectly clean, shining white sand, rippled firm and hard by the tides. Two grayish shapes steered there, like long, rounded pieces of wood or slate. They were fish. He saw them nose toward each other, poise motionless, make a dart forward, swerve off, and come around again. It was like a water dance. A few inches above them the water sparkled as if sequins were dropping through it. Fish again—myriads of minute fish, the length of his fingernail—were drifting through the water, and in a moment he could feel the innumerable tiny touches of them against his limbs. It was like swimming in flaked silver. The great rock the big boys had swum through rose sheer out of the white sand—black, tufted lightly with greenish weed. He could see no gap in it. He swam down to its base.

Again and again he rose, took a big chestful of air, and went down. Again and again he groped over the surface of the rock, feeling it, almost hugging it in the desperate need to find the entrance. And then, once, while he was clinging

Vocabulary

defiant (dē·fī′ənt) *adj.*: challenging authority.

inquisitive (in·kwiz′ə·tiv) *adj.*: questioning; curious.

minute (mī·noot′) *adj.*: small; tiny.

to the black wall, his knees came up and he shot his feet out forward and they met no obstacle. He had found the hole.

He gained the surface, clambered about the stones that littered the barrier rock until he found a big one, and with this in his arms, let himself down over the side of the rock. He dropped, with the weight, straight to the sandy floor. Clinging tight to the anchor of stone, he lay on his side and looked in under the dark shelf at the place where his feet had gone. He could see the hole. It was an irregular, dark gap; but he could not see deep into it. He let go of his anchor, clung with his hands to the edges of the hole, and tried to push himself in.

He got his head in, found his shoulders jammed, moved them in sidewise, and was inside as far as his wrist. He could see nothing ahead. Something soft and clammy touched his mouth; he saw a dark frond[3] moving against the grayish rock, and panic filled him. He thought of octopuses, of clinging weed. He pushed himself out backward and caught a glimpse, as he retreated, of a harmless tentacle of seaweed drifting in the mouth of the tunnel. But it was enough. He reached the sunlight, swam to shore, and lay on the diving rock. He looked down into the blue well of water. He knew he must find his way through that cave, or hole, or tunnel, and out the other side.

First, he thought, he must learn to control his breathing. He let himself down into the water with another big stone in his arms, so that he could lie effortlessly on the bottom of the sea. He counted. One, two, three. He counted steadily. He could hear the movement of blood in his chest. Fifty-one, fifty-two. . . . His chest was hurting. He let go of the rock and went up into the air. He saw that the sun was low. He rushed to the villa and found his mother at her supper. She said only, "Did you enjoy yourself?" and he said, "Yes."

All night the boy dreamed of the water-filled cave in the rock, and as soon as breakfast was over, he went to the bay.

That night, his nose bled badly. For hours he had been underwater, learning to hold his breath, and now he felt weak and dizzy. His mother said, "I shouldn't overdo things, darling, if I were you."

That day and the next, Jerry exercised his lungs as if everything, the whole of his life, all that he would become, depended upon it. Again his nose bled at night, and his mother insisted on his coming with her the next day. It was a torment to him to waste a day of his careful self-training, but he stayed with her on that other beach, which now seemed a place for small children, a place where his mother might lie safe in the sun. It was not his beach.

He did not ask for permission, on the following day, to go to his beach. He went, before his mother could consider the complicated rights and wrongs of the matter. A day's rest, he discovered, had improved his count by ten. The big boys had made the passage while he counted a hundred and sixty. He had been counting fast, in his fright. Probably now, if he tried, he could get through that long tunnel, but he was not going to try yet. A curious, most unchildlike persistence, a controlled impatience, made him wait. In the meantime, he lay underwater on the white sand, littered now by stones he had brought down from the upper air, and studied the entrance to the tunnel. He knew every jut and corner of it, as far as it was possible to see. It was as if he already felt its sharpness about his shoulders.

He sat by the clock in the villa, when his mother was not near, and checked his time. He was incredulous and then proud to find he could

---

3. **frond** (fränd) *n.:* large leaf or leaflike part of seaweed.

Vocabulary
incredulous (in·krej′ oo·ləs) *adj.:* disbelieving; skeptical.

hold his breath without strain for two minutes. The words "two minutes," authorized by the clock, brought close the adventure that was so necessary to him.

In another four days, his mother said casually one morning, they must go home. On the day before they left, he would do it. He would do it if it killed him, he said defiantly to himself. But two days before they were to leave—a day of triumph when he increased his count by fifteen—his nose bled so badly that he turned dizzy and had to lie limply over the big rock like a bit of seaweed, watching the thick red blood flow onto the rock and trickle slowly down to the sea. He was frightened. Supposing he turned dizzy in the tunnel? Supposing he died there, trapped? Supposing—his head went around, in the hot sun, and he almost gave up. He thought he would return to the house and lie down, and next summer, perhaps, when he had another year's growth in him—then he would go through the hole.

But even after he had made the decision, or thought he had, he found himself sitting up on the rock and looking down into the water; and he knew that now, this moment, when his nose had only just stopped bleeding, when his head was still sore and throbbing—this was the moment when he would try. If he did not do it now, he never would. He was trembling with fear that he would not go; and he was trembling with horror at the long, long tunnel under the rock, under the sea. Even in the open sunlight, the barrier rock seemed very wide and very heavy; tons of rock pressed down on where he would go. If he died there, he would lie until one day—perhaps not before next year—those big boys would swim into it and find it blocked.

He put on his goggles, fitted them tight, tested the vacuum. His hands were shaking. Then he chose the biggest stone he could carry and slipped over the edge of the rock until half of him was in the cool enclosing water and half in the hot sun. He looked up once at the empty sky, filled his lungs once, twice, and then sank fast to the bottom with the stone. He let it go and began to count. He took the edges of the hole in his hands and drew himself into it, wriggling his shoulders in sidewise as he remembered he must, kicking himself along with his feet.

Soon he was clear inside. He was in a small rock-bound hole filled with yellowish-gray water. The water was pushing him up against the roof. The roof was sharp and pained his back. He pulled himself along with his hands—fast, fast—and used his legs as levers. His head knocked against something; a sharp pain dizzied him. Fifty, fifty-one, fifty-two . . . He was without light, and the water seemed to press upon him with the weight of rock. Seventy-one, seventy-two . . . There was no strain on his lungs. He felt like an inflated balloon, his lungs were so light and easy, but his head was pulsing.

He was being continually pressed against the sharp roof, which felt slimy as well as sharp. Again he thought of octopuses, and wondered if the tunnel might be filled with weed that could tangle him. He gave himself a panicky, convulsive kick forward, ducked his head, and swam. His feet and hands moved freely, as if in open water. The hole must have widened out. He thought he must be swimming fast, and he was frightened of banging his head if the tunnel narrowed.

A hundred, a hundred and one . . . The water paled. Victory filled him. His lungs were beginning to hurt. A few more strokes and he would be out. He was counting wildly; he said a hundred and fifteen and then, a long time later, a hundred and fifteen again. The water was a clear jewel-green all around him. Then he saw, above his head, a crack running up through the rock. Sunlight was falling through it, showing the clean, dark rock of the tunnel, a single mussel[4] shell, and darkness ahead.

---

4. **mussel** *n.*: shellfish, similar to a clam or an oyster, that attaches itself to rocks.

He was at the end of what he could do. He looked up at the crack as if it were filled with air and not water, as if he could put his mouth to it to draw in air. A hundred and fifteen, he heard himself say inside his head—but he had said that long ago. He must go on into the blackness ahead, or he would drown. His head was swelling, his lungs cracking. A hundred and fifteen, a hundred and fifteen, pounded through his head, and he feebly clutched at rocks in the dark, pulling himself forward, leaving the brief space of sunlit water behind. He felt he was dying. He was no longer quite conscious. He struggled on in the darkness between lapses into unconsciousness. An immense, swelling pain filled his head, and then the darkness cracked with an explosion of green light. His hands, groping forward, met nothing; and his feet, kicking back, propelled him out into the open sea.

He drifted to the surface, his face turned up to the air. He was gasping like a fish. He felt he would sink now and drown; he could not swim the few feet back to the rock. Then he was clutching it and pulling himself up onto it. He lay face down, gasping. He could see nothing but a red-veined, clotted dark. His eyes must have burst, he thought; they were full of blood. He tore off his goggles and a gout[5] of blood went into the sea. His nose was bleeding, and the blood had filled the goggles.

He scooped up handfuls of water from the cool, salty sea, to splash on his face, and did not know whether it was blood or salt water he tasted. After a time, his heart quieted, his eyes cleared, and he sat up. He could see the local boys diving and playing half a mile away. He did not want them. He wanted nothing but to get back home and lie down.

In a short while, Jerry swam to shore and climbed slowly up the path to the villa. He flung himself on his bed and slept, waking at the sound of feet on the path outside. His mother was coming back. He rushed to the bathroom, thinking she must not see his face with blood-stains, or tearstains, on it. He came out of the bathroom and met her as she walked into the villa, smiling, her eyes lighting up.

---

5. **gout** (gout) *n.:* large glob.

A Closer Look

Initiation Rites

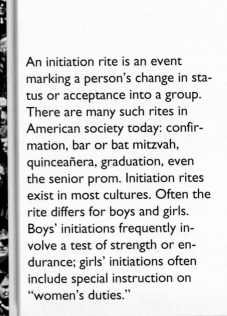

An initiation rite is an event marking a person's change in status or acceptance into a group. There are many such rites in American society today: confirmation, bar or bat mitzvah, quinceañera, graduation, even the senior prom. Initiation rites exist in most cultures. Often the rite differs for boys and girls. Boys' initiations frequently involve a test of strength or endurance; girls' initiations often include special instruction on "women's duties."

Two examples from different areas of the world demonstrate how an ordeal like Jerry's is similar to traditional ritual ordeals for boys, marking the transition to adulthood. The Hopi are American Indians who live in Arizona. In a traditional Hopi initiation, boys must sit almost motionless for four days with their knees touching their chins. When they emerge from this fetal position, they are reborn as men.

In a ritual practiced by the Mende of Sierra Leone in West Africa, boys are seized from their homes and carried into the bush. Their backs are marked with knives, and they spend several weeks away from the village. Small children are told that the Great Spirit has swallowed the boys and that when they emerge from his belly with the marks of his teeth on their backs, they will be men. When the boys return to the village, the people treat them as honored guests. They are now adults.

"Have a nice morning?" she asked, laying her hand on his warm brown shoulder a moment.

"Oh, yes, thank you," he said.

"You look a bit pale." And then, sharp and anxious, "How did you bang your head?"

"Oh, just banged it," he told her.

She looked at him closely. He was strained; his eyes were glazed-looking. She was worried. And then she said to herself, Oh, don't fuss! Nothing can happen. He can swim like a fish.

They sat down to lunch together.

"Mummy," he said, "I can stay underwater for two minutes—three minutes, at least." It came bursting out of him.

"Can you, darling?" she said. "Well, I shouldn't overdo it. I don't think you ought to swim anymore today."

She was ready for a battle of wills, but he gave in at once. It was no longer of the least importance to go to the bay. ∎

Meet the Writer

Doris Lessing

Out of Africa

Doris Lessing (1919–   ) was born in Persia (now Iran), where her father, who was British, was in charge of a bank. When she was five, her father, growing tired of the corruption around him and longing for a freer life, moved the family to a three-thousand-acre farm in Southern Rhodesia (now Zimbabwe). Life was extremely hard there. The farm's thirty to fifty African laborers lived in mud huts with no sanitation. Lessing's mother was homesick for England and often ill; her father was becoming increasingly unpredictable. The nearest neighbor was miles away. Lessing has described this childhood as "hellishly lonely." She has also acknowledged the advantage of such a childhood: Lacking company, she enriched her mind by reading classic European and American literature.

At the age of fourteen, Lessing quit school and went to work in Salisbury, the capital of Rhodesia, first as a nursemaid and then as a stenographer and telephone operator. Salisbury had a white population of about ten thousand and a larger black popu-lation that Lessing discovered "didn't count." During this period of her life, she became involved in radical politics and was twice married and twice divorced. In 1949, with her two-year-old son and the manuscript of her first novel, *The Grass Is Singing*, she fulfilled a lifelong wish by immigrating to England. The novel, about the complex relationship between a white farm wife and her African servant, was published in 1950, one of the earliest treatments in fiction of Africa's racial problems. From then on, Lessing supported herself by writing. Her powerful stories and novels are among the most admired writing of our day.

Lessing admits she writes to be "an instrument of change."

    ❝It is not merely a question of preventing evil, but of strengthening a vision of good which may defeat the evil.❞

Response and Analysis

Reading Check

1. Retell the **main events** of this story as Jerry might tell them to his best friend when he returns from vacation or to his own son later in life.

Thinking Critically

2. Why is it so important to Jerry to be with the boys on the wild beach? What significant details does the author provide to help us understand Jerry's feelings about the boys? (See pages 402–404.)

3. Identify the physical and mental "tortures" Jerry undergoes, first as he prepares for his ordeal and then as he swims through the tunnel. Which details suggest that Jerry's quest has great significance?

4. A ticking clock is usually good for creating **suspense.** What device does Lessing use to create a sort of "ticking clock" that increases our anxiety?

5. What breakthroughs has Jerry achieved by the story's end? Consider:
   - Jerry's conquest of the tunnel
   - his feelings about himself
   - his dependence on his mother

6. What do you think is the main message, or **theme,** of this story? Consider:
   - what the swim through the tunnel means to Jerry
   - why Jerry no longer feels he has to go to the bay

7. Read the information in A Closer Look on page 407. Do you think Jerry's experience can be viewed as an initiation rite? What similarities and differences can you find in his experience and the coming-of-age rites in other cultures?

8. Check the text to see what you learn about the thoughts and feelings of Jerry's mother. How would the story be different if she, rather than the **omniscient narrator,** were telling it?

Extending and Evaluating

9. Have you ever taken great risks to prove yourself? (Check your Quickwrite notes.) Do you find it convincing that Jerry takes such a risk and survives? Explain.

WRITING

Story Symbols

Symbols are appealing because they often carry powerful associations and emotional overtones. Write a brief **essay** analyzing the **symbolism** in "Through the Tunnel." First, consider the three **settings:** the wild beach, the safe beach, and the tunnel. Tell what you think each setting must symbolize for Jerry. Then, consider the larger **symbolic meaning** of Jerry's passage through the tunnel. What does his trip represent? Why is it a powerful symbol? Support your analysis, and elaborate with direct references to details in the story. (You can take notes in a chart like the one below.)

Symbol	Symbolic Meaning
Wild beach	
Safe beach	
Tunnel	
Trip through the tunnel	

▶ Use "Analyzing a Short Story," pages 440–447, for help with this assignment.

SKILLS FOCUS

Literary Skills
Analyze symbolic meaning.

Reading Skills
Re-read and read for details.

Writing Skills
Write an essay analyzing symbolism in a story.

Vocabulary Development

Analogies: Matching Relationships

In an **analogy** the words in a first pair relate to each other in the same way as the words in a second pair. Many kinds of relationships are possible. For example, a pair of words can be synonyms (*timid : meek*) or antonyms (*timid : bold*), or one word can describe a characteristic of the other (*knife : sharp*) or express a degree of intensity (*whisper : scream*). Analogies are frequently written like this:

HUGE : ELEPHANT :: _____ : gnat.

PRACTICE

Complete each analogy below with the word from the Word Bank that fits best. Begin by identifying the type of relationship in the first word pair. (For more help with analogies, see pages 29–30.)

1. HUGE : ELEPHANT :: _____ : gnat
2. SADNESS : MOURNING :: _____ : regretting
3. SECURE : SAFE :: _____ : curious
4. NEEDY : BEGGAR :: _____ : skeptic
5. WHISPER : SHOUT :: _____ : demand
6. BRILLIANT : SMART :: _____ : stubborn

Grammar Link

Powerful Participles

Participles are verb forms that can be used as adjectives to modify nouns and pronouns: *running* water, *cleared* land. Present participles always end in *–ing*, and most past participles end in *–ed* or *–d*. Because they combine the action of verbs and the descriptive power of adjectives, participles create vivid pictures in few words.

"He could see nothing through the stinging salt water but the blank rock."

"It was like swimming in flaked silver."

Participial phrases are participles with all their complements and modifiers.

"He was in a small rock-bound hole filled with yellowish-gray water."

PRACTICE

1. Write four sentences, using the following participles or any other participles you wish: *lapping, rippled, diving, glittering*. Make sure you use each participle as an adjective.

2. Now, write four more sentences, using the same participles in participial phrases. Compare your sentences with a partner's.

▶ **For more help, see Participles and Participial Phrases, 6c, in the Language Handbook.**

Coming of Age, Latino Style ◆ Vision Quest ◆ Crossing a Threshold to Adulthood

Synthesizing Sources

When you research a topic, you often need to get a balanced view by looking at different sources. Then you can **synthesize** what you've read—pull it all together so that you can better understand the subject. The following guidelines will help:

- **Determine the message.** Look for the writer's **main ideas** and for **supporting details** in each source.

- **Paraphrase the ideas.** To help you understand a source, try paraphrasing its ideas, which means restating them *in your own words*. When you put a difficult or complex text in your own words, you'll understand it better. A paraphrase should be about the same length as the original source, and it should cover all the significant information in the original in the same order.

- **Determine the author's purpose and audience.** Was the piece written, for example, to tell a story, to change your opinion, or to give information?

- **Evaluate each source.** Determine the kinds and amount of support the writer gives. Is there enough support to make the ideas **credible**? Evaluate the tone and reliability too. Is the source **objective** (based solely on facts) or **subjective** (expressing the writer's opinions and feelings)?

- **Compare and contrast.** Compare sources in terms of the type of information in each one. What do they have in common? How do they differ?

- **Connect to other sources.** Connect the ideas to related topics and to stories and other articles you've read.

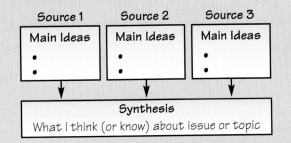

- **Synthesize.** Now, consider all your sources as a group. Do they work together to help you better understand a topic? Can you draw **conclusions** from the sources and form connections with other sources you have read?

Vocabulary Development

indigenous (in·dij′ə·nəs) *adj.:* native.

solitary (säl′ə·ter′ē) *adj.:* without others.

vigil (vij′əl) *n.:* watchful staying awake during the usual hours of sleep.

predominant (prē·däm′ə·nənt) *adj.:* most frequent or noticeable.

formidable (fôr′mə·də·bəl) *adj.:* remarkable; impressive.

inevitable (in·ev′i·tə·bəl) *adj.:* unavoidable; certain to happen.

INTERNET
Interactive
Reading Model
Keyword: LE5 10-6

Connecting to the Literature

In "Through the Tunnel," Jerry works hard to accomplish a difficult feat, and afterward he feels as if he's no longer a boy. The three articles that follow describe events that mark the passage to adulthood in various cultures.

Reading Skills
Synthesize information from several sources on a single topic.

Coming of Age, Latino Style

Special Rite Ushers Girls into Adulthood

from *Boston Globe*, January 5, 1997

Cindy Rodriguez

LOWELL—Iris Cancel's eyes filled with pride, not tears, as she watched her daughter Glenda glide down the church aisle, her tiny frame covered by a white satin and lace dress that flared at the hips and trailed behind her. Small white flowers speckled the bodice,[1] and her long, dark hair, wrapped in baby's breath,[2] was encircled by a shimmery crown.

"I think it's an exciting day for her and everyone involved," Iris Cancel said. "Her father's a nervous wreck. I keep telling him, 'She's not getting married.'"

Glenda, a sophomore at Greater Lowell Vocational Technical School, did not celebrate her wedding a week ago Saturday, although the ceremony did resemble one. She celebrated a special birthday. She turned fifteen on December 26 and toasted it two days later with a *quinceañera*,[3] a custom in Hispanic communities that marks a girl's entrance into adulthood.

Experts of Hispanic culture disagree on the origin of the quinceañera. The word literally means "fifteen-year-old girl" but is also used to describe the entire celebration. Some say coming-of-age traditions in general, though not the quinceañera in particular, can be traced back to indigenous cultures.

Then, it was a recognition that boys were ready to be warriors and girls were ready to bear children.

Some experts believe that for years the quinceañera was most often celebrated by upper-class Hispanics, who wrapped the social custom in religious symbolism and personal wealth. Elaborate celebrations similar to debutante balls[4] showed off a family's social status and daughter to possible suitors. A similar celebration for boys is uncommon among Hispanics.

Today the quinceañera is celebrated in the United States and abroad by Latinos of varied cultural backgrounds and economic classes. Glenda, one of six children, was born in Lowell to Puerto Rican parents. Iris, a mail handler at Holland Mark Martin in Burlington, and Marcos, a school-bus driver in Lowell, have lived in Massachusetts for twenty-nine years.

The celebration can be religious or secular,[5] inexpensive or costly. Some Hispanic families still host debutante-style balls that can cost up to $10,000, while others plan simple birthday parties.

---

1. **bodice** *n.:* upper part of a woman's dress.
2. **baby's breath** *n.:* a type of flower.
3. **quinceañera** (kēn'se · ä · nyer'ä).
4. **debutante balls** *n.:* formal dances held to introduce a group of young women into society.
5. **secular** (sek'yə · lər) *adj.:* worldly, as distinguished from religious.

Vocabulary
indigenous (in · dij'ə · nəs) *adj.:* native.

Still, the quinceañera in any form remains an important rite of passage for many Hispanic girls. For girls like Glenda, the purpose is not so much to find a future mate at the reception as to celebrate themselves.

"I feel like I deserve it," said Glenda, who gets good grades, has near-perfect school attendance, and attends church regularly. She plans to attend college to be a pediatrician[6] or a professional basketball player.

And, of course, it's fun to get dressed up for a celebration that in Glenda's case took a year to plan.

---

6. **pediatrician** (pē′dē·ə·trish′ən) *n.:* doctor who specializes in the care of children.

Vision Quest

from *Encyclopaedia Britannica*, 1995

vision quest, among the American Indian hunters of the eastern woodlands and the Great Plains, an essential part of a young boy's (or, more rarely, a girl's) initiation into adulthood. The youth was sent out from the camp on a solitary vigil involving fasting[1] and prayer in order to gain some sign of the presence and nature of his guardian spirit (*q.v.*).[2] The specific techniques varied from tribe to tribe, as did the age at which the quest was to be undertaken, its length and intensity, and the nature of the sign.

In some traditions the youth would watch for an animal who behaved in a significant way; in others he discovered an object (usually a stone), which resembled some animal. In the predominant form, he had a dream in which his guardian appeared (usually in animal form), instructed him, took him on a visionary journey, and taught him songs. Upon receiving these signs and visions he returned to his home, indicated his success, and sought out a religious specialist for help in interpreting his visions.

The techniques of the vision quest are not confined only to those at puberty. They underlie every visionary experience of the Indian, from those of the ordinary man who seeks to gain contact with and advice from his guardian to the visions of the great prophets and shamans (religious personages with healing and psychic transformation powers). Among the South American Indians, the vision quest, like the guardian spirit, is confined exclusively to the shaman.

---

1. **fasting** *v.* used as *n.:* not eating.
2. ***q.v.:*** abbreviation for Latin *quod vide,* "which see." This abbreviation indicates that the encyclopedia from which this entry was taken contains a separate entry for *guardian spirit.*

Vocabulary

solitary (säl′ə·ter′ē) *adj.:* without others.

vigil (vij′əl) *n.:* watchful staying awake during the usual hours of sleep.

predominant (prē·däm′ə·nənt) *adj.:* most frequent or noticeable.

Crossing a Threshold to Adulthood

from the *Times Union*, Albany, N.Y., September 24, 2000

Jessica Barnes

September is wedding season in Uzbekistan,[1] and every afternoon I hear the honking trumpet sound that announces the procession of men who accompany a groom to fetch his bride from her parents' home.

I go to a wedding almost every week now, and turn down invitations to several others. I'm surrounded by weddings. When I walk home from school, I'm passed by wedding processions; I go to sleep at night hearing the music from weddings in my neighborhood, occasionally interrupted by toasts spoken over a microphone.

The teachers at my school are more determined than ever to see me married in Uzbekistan; they can't bear the thought of sending me back to America next year as an old maid of twenty-five. I spend my lunch periods with them thinking up excuses for why I can't marry the Russian teacher's son or my director's cousin's neighbor.

When my local friends aren't attending weddings or plotting mine, they're watching the video from the latest wedding. Every wedding I've been to has been videotaped; the cameraman was such a formidable presence that when I think back on the wedding, I remember the married couple and the cameraman. We watch the videos over and over—or maybe we're not watching the same video more than once. Maybe I've seen a hundred different wedding videos. I can't tell because they're all the same. The same music, the same toasts, the same food. It's a ceremony with little room for variation.

Every video begins in the bride's home, just after the groom and his friends arrive. The bride is crying because she is about to leave the home where she grew up. Her girlfriends place a cloth over her head and lead her out of the house, where all the neighbors have gathered. The trumpets stop and the only sounds are the sobs of the bride and the murmured good wishes of her close family members.

The sadness of the moment always strikes me: How sad it is to grow up and leave others behind, and how inevitable. At the wedding, while everyone laughs and drinks and dances, the glum faces of the bride and groom preside over all. She is sad at leaving her family and he is thinking of responsibilities that lie ahead as husband and father. Starting a family is no laughing matter in Uzbekistan.

Afterward, the whole thing is there, in one small, black cartridge, to be watched over and over. The day a bride leaves her parents' home, she crosses from childhood into adulthood in one neat step. This rite of

---

1. **Uzbekistan** (o͞oz·bek′i·stan′): central Asian country that became independent upon the breakup of the Soviet Union in 1991.

Vocabulary

formidable (fôr′mə·də·bəl) *adj.*: remarkable; impressive.

inevitable (in·ev′i·tə·bəl) *adj.*: unavoidable; certain to happen.

People celebrating at an Uzbeki wedding.

passage signifies the change in her role as clearly as if she were given a list of her job expectations.

I don't think I'll ever experience a rite of passage like that one. In America, we grow up in fits and starts. I got a driver's license at sixteen, the first step toward independence, but I was still a child. After I voted for the first time, I was still a child. I moved away from home to go to college, then moved back, a child with a degree.

After finishing with the Peace Corps,[2] I'll go back to my parents' home, and then eventually to an apartment of my own, and

then, if I get married, to an apartment with my husband. At which of these points do I look in the mirror and say "childhood" is past and I am now an adult? I don't think it will happen in the few moments you can capture on videotape. I think, rather, one day I will realize that somewhere along the line it has happened. Or, worse, I'll never know.

In Uzbekistan, I've noticed the importance of these rites of passage for knowing yourself and what is expected of you. And there's comfort in the fact that everyone goes through them.

My Americanness wants to praise us for all growing up in different ways, at different paces. It's good to be different, but lonely and often confusing.

2. **Peace Corps:** U.S. agency that provides volunteers to assist people in underdeveloped countries.

Analyzing Informational Text

Reading Check

1. What special occasion does a quinceañera celebrate?

2. For certain American Indian tribes, what is the purpose of a vision quest?

3. What is the most typical rite of passage to adulthood in Uzbekistan?

Test Practice

1. What is the **purpose** of *each* of the three selections?
   - **A** To discuss one kind of initiation into adulthood
   - **B** To persuade readers of the importance of initiation rites
   - **C** To provide eyewitness accounts of coming-of-age rituals
   - **D** To compare initiation rites across cultures

2. From these three selections you can infer that in most societies the passage into adulthood is marked by some kind of —
   - **F** vision quest
   - **G** ceremony or ritual
   - **H** large party or dance
   - **J** painful ordeal

3. According to Jessica Barnes, American society —
   - **A** has a lower marriage rate than Uzbekistan
   - **B** places less emphasis on weddings than Uzbekistan
   - **C** demands that all its young people grow up at the same pace
   - **D** allows its young people to grow up at different paces

4. Which article is **subjective**? That is, in which does the writer express mostly personal thoughts?
   - **F** "Coming of Age, Latino Style"
   - **G** "Vision Quest"
   - **H** "Crossing a Threshold to Adulthood"
   - **J** None of the articles

5. Unlike Jerry's experience in "Through the Tunnel," the experiences described in these three articles —
   - **A** follow a cultural tradition
   - **B** are dangerous and life threatening
   - **C** take place indoors, surrounded by people
   - **D** take place when the individual is alone

SKILLS FOCUS

Reading Skills
Synthesize information from several sources on a single topic.

Constructed Response

To **synthesize** what you've learned, write a brief essay about a ceremony you are familiar with or one that you've seen or read about that marks a passage into another phase of life. Give details about the ceremony (its purpose, what the person does, where and when the ceremony takes place). Then, **compare and contrast** your ceremony with those described in the three articles. You may **paraphrase** the main ideas in the articles.

Vocabulary Development

Word Mapping: Pinning Down Meaning

Sometimes you can figure out the meaning of a word from its **context.**
Consider these two sentences from "Coming of Age, Latino Style":

"Some say coming-of-age traditions in general, though not the quinceañera
in particular, can be traced back to <u>indigenous</u> cultures. Then, it was a recognition that boys were ready to be <u>warriors</u> and girls were ready to
bear children."

Does this context help you understand *indigenous?* Probably not. You'll have
to use a dictionary to find the meaning that fits the context.

Creating a **word map,** or **semantic map,** will help you pin down the
precise meaning of any unfamiliar word. Make up questions about the word,
and then answer the questions. Here's how a student in Florida completed
a word map for *indigenous:*

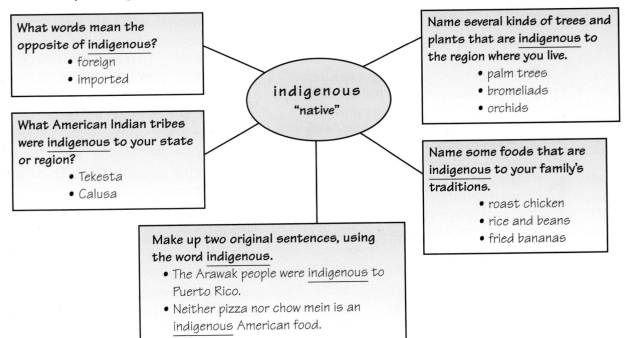

What words mean the opposite of indigenous?
- foreign
- imported

What American Indian tribes were indigenous to your state or region?
- Tekesta
- Calusa

Make up two original sentences, using the word indigenous.
- The Arawak people were indigenous to Puerto Rico.
- Neither pizza nor chow mein is an indigenous American food.

indigenous "native"

Name several kinds of trees and plants that are indigenous to the region where you live.
- palm trees
- bromeliads
- orchids

Name some foods that are indigenous to your family's traditions.
- roast chicken
- rice and beans
- fried bananas

PRACTICE

Work with a partner or small group to make a **word map** for each of the
other words in the Word Bank. The questions you ask will vary, but in each
map, try to include examples of times when you'd use the word and two
original sentences. Exchange your finished word maps with another group.

SKILLS FOCUS

Vocabulary Skills
Create semantic maps.

The Masque of the Red Death

Make the Connection

Quickwrite 🖉

Rich and powerful people often build huge houses. They build high walls around their estates so that they can block out the up-setting parts of life. What realities of life must people face, no matter who they are? Write down your thoughts.

Literary Focus

Allegory: A Story Behind a Story

An **allegory** is a narrative that is really a double story. One story takes place on the surface. Under the surface the story's characters and events represent abstract ideas or states of being, things like love or freedom, evil or goodness, hell or heaven.

To work, an allegory must operate on two levels. On the level of pure storytelling, an allegory must hold our attention. Its characters must seem believable and inter-esting enough for us to care about them. On the allegorical level the ideas in the story must be accessible to us. As you read, you should find that the allegorical level of the story gradually begins to strike you.

See if you find that Poe's story of arro-gance and death hooks you on both levels.

Reading Skills

Monitoring Your Reading: Asking Questions

As you read this story, you'll find questions at the open-book signs. The questions are designed to make you stop briefly and think about the text. They ask you to sum up what you have read. They ask you about the meanings of words. They remind you to visualize the action. These are issues that active readers think about all the time.

INTERNET

Vocabulary Practice

•

More About Edgar Allan Poe

Keyword: LE5 10-6

SKILLS FOCUS

Literary Skills Understand characteristics of allegory.

Reading Skills Monitor your reading by ask-ing questions.

Background

Poe's fictional Red Death is probably based on the Black Death, which swept fourteenth-century Europe and Asia, killing as many as two thirds of the population in some regions in less than twenty years. (See the **Con-nection** on page 429.) Poe calls the plague "the Red Death" because vic-tims oozed blood from painful sores.

In this story a fourteenth-century prince gives a costume party, or masque, to try to forget about the epidemic raging all around him.

Vocabulary Development

profuse (prō·fyoōs′) *adj.*: given or poured forth freely and abundantly; plentiful.

sagacious (sə·gā′shəs) *adj.*: wise; showing sound judgment.

contagion (kən·tā′jən) *n.*: spreading of disease.

imperial (im·pir′ē·əl) *adj.*: majestic; of great size or superior quality.

emanating (em′ə·nāt′iŋ) *v.*: coming forth; emerging, as from a source.

sedate (si·dāt′) *adj.* used as *n.*: calm; quiet.

pervaded (pər·vād′id) *v.*: spread throughout.

cessation (se·sā′shən) *n.*: ceasing or stopping.

propriety (prə·prī′ə·tē) *n.*: quality of being proper, fitting, or suitable.

tangible (tan′jə·bəl) *adj.*: that can be touched.

The Masque of the Red Death

Edgar Allan Poe

No pestilence had
ever been so fatal...

A. MONITOR YOUR READING
What is the Red Death?

3. dauntless (dônt′lis) *adj.*: fearless.
4. castellated (kas′tə·lāt′id) **abbeys:** monasteries built with towers.
5. august *adj.*: grand.
6. ingress or egress: entrance or exit.

7. improvisatori (im·prä· və·zə·tōr′ē) *n.*: poets who make up a verse on the spur of the moment.

B. MONITOR YOUR READING
How do the prince and his friends try to escape the Red Death?

(Page 419)

Masked Ball in the Card Room (c. 1757–1760) by Pietro Longhi. Oil on canvas (62.5 cm × 51 cm).

© Scala/Art Resource, New York.

The "Red Death" had long devastated the country. No pestilence had ever been so fatal, or so hideous. Blood was its Avatar[1] and its seal—the redness and the horror of blood. There were sharp pains, and sudden dizziness, and then profuse bleeding at the pores, with dissolution.[2] The scarlet stains upon the body and especially upon the face of the victim were the pest ban which shut him out from the aid and from the sympathy of his fellow men. And the whole seizure, progress, and termination of the disease were the incidents of half an hour.

But the Prince Prospero was happy and dauntless[3] and sagacious. When his dominions were half depopulated, he summoned to his presence a thousand hale and lighthearted friends from among the knights and dames of his court, and with these retired to the deep seclusion of one of his castellated abbeys.[4] This was an extensive and magnificent structure, the creation of the prince's own eccentric yet august[5] taste. A strong and lofty wall girdled it in. This wall had gates of iron. The courtiers, having entered, brought furnaces and massy hammers and welded the bolts. They resolved to leave means neither of ingress or egress[6] to the sudden impulses of despair or of frenzy from within. The abbey was amply provisioned. With such precautions the courtiers might bid defiance to contagion. The external world could take care of itself. In the meantime it was folly to grieve, or to think. The prince had provided all the appliances of pleasure. There were buffoons, there were improvisatori,[7] there were ballet dancers, there were musicians, there was Beauty, there was wine. All these and security were within. Without was the "Red Death."

It was toward the close of the fifth or sixth month of his seclusion, and while the pestilence raged most furiously abroad, that the Prince Prospero entertained his thousand friends at a masked ball of the most unusual magnificence.

It was a voluptuous scene, that masquerade. But first let me tell of the rooms in which it was held. There were seven—an imperial suite. In many palaces, however, such suites form a long and straight vista, while the folding doors slide back nearly to the walls on either hand, so that the view of the whole extent is scarcely impeded. Here the case was very different; as might have been expected from the duke's love of the *bizarre*. The apartments were so irregularly disposed that the vision embraced

Vocabulary

profuse (prō·fyōōs′) *adj.*: given or poured forth freely and abundantly; plentiful.

sagacious (sə·gā′shəs) *adj.*: wise; showing sound judgment.

contagion (kən·tā′jən) *n.*: spreading of disease.

imperial (im·pir′ē·əl) *adj.*: majestic; of great size or superior quality.

but little more than one at a time. There was a sharp turn at every twenty or thirty yards, and at each turn a novel effect. To the right and left, in the middle of each wall, a tall and narrow Gothic window looked out upon a closed corridor which pursued the windings of the suite. These windows were of stained glass whose color varied in accordance with the prevailing hue of the decorations of the chamber into which it opened. That at the eastern extremity was hung, for example, in blue—and vividly blue were its windows. The second chamber was purple in its ornaments and tapestries, and here the panes were purple. The third was green throughout, and so were the casements. The fourth was furnished and lighted with orange—the fifth with white—the sixth with violet. The seventh apartment was closely shrouded in black velvet tapestries that hung all over the ceiling and down the walls, falling in heavy folds upon a carpet of the same material and hue. But in this chamber only, the color of the windows failed to correspond with the decorations. The panes here were scarlet—a deep blood color. Now in no one of the seven apartments was there any lamp or candelabrum, amid the profusion of golden ornaments that lay scattered to and fro or depended from the roof. There was no light of any kind <u>emanating</u> from lamp or candle within the suite of chambers. But in the corridors that followed the suite, there stood, opposite to each window, a heavy tripod, bearing a brazier of fire that projected its rays through the tinted glass and so glaringly illumined the room. And thus were produced a multitude of gaudy and fantastic appearances. But in the western or black chamber the effect of the firelight that streamed upon the dark hangings through the blood-tinted panes was ghastly in the extreme, and produced so wild a look upon the countenances of those who entered that there were few of the company bold enough to set foot within its precincts at all.

It was in this apartment, also, that there stood against the western wall a gigantic clock of ebony. Its pendulum swung to and fro with a dull, heavy, monotonous clang; and when the minute hand made the circuit of the face, and the hour was to be stricken, there came from the brazen lungs of the clock a sound which was clear and loud and deep and exceedingly musical, but of so peculiar a note and emphasis that, at each lapse of an hour, the musicians of the orchestra were constrained to pause, momentarily, in their performance, to hearken to the sound; and thus the waltzers perforce ceased their evolutions;[8] and there was a brief disconcert[9] of the whole gay company; and, while the chimes of the clock yet rang, it was observed that the giddiest grew pale, and the more

C. MONITOR YOUR READING
Describe the seven rooms as you **visualize** them.

8. evolutions (ev′ə·lo̅o̅′shənz) *n*.: movements that are part of a pattern.
9. disconcert (dis′kən·sʉrt′) *n*.: upset.

Vocabulary
emanating (em′ə·nāt′iŋ) *v*.: coming forth; emerging, as from a source.

10. tremulousness
(trem′yo͞o·ləs·nis) *n.:* trembling; fearfulness.

![book icon]
D. MONITOR YOUR READING
What strange effect does the ebony clock have on the partygoers?

11. *decora* (də·kō′rə) *n.:* Latin for "accepted standards of good taste."

aged and <u>sedate</u> passed their hands over their brows as if in confused reverie or meditation. But when the echoes had fully ceased, a light laughter at once <u>pervaded</u> the assembly; the musicians looked at each other and smiled as if at their own nervousness and folly, and made whispering vows, each to the other, that the next chiming of the clock should produce in them no similar emotion; and then, after the lapse of sixty minutes (which embrace three thousand and six hundred seconds of the Time that flies), there came yet another chiming of the clock, and then were the same disconcert and tremulousness[10] and meditation as before. ![book icon]

But, in spite of these things, it was a gay and magnificent revel. The tastes of the duke were peculiar. He had a fine eye for colors and effects. He disregarded the *decora*[11] of mere fashion. His plans were bold and

Vocabulary
sedate (si·dāt′) *adj.* used as *n.:* calm; quiet.
pervaded (pər·vād′id) *v.:* spread throughout.

The Redoute by Francesco Guardi (1712–1793).

fiery, and his conceptions glowed with barbaric lustre. There are some who would have thought him mad. His followers felt that he was not. It was necessary to hear and see and touch him to be *sure* that he was not.

He had directed, in great part, the moveable embellishments of the seven chambers, upon occasion of this great *fête;*[12] and it was his own guiding taste which had given character to the masqueraders. Be sure they were grotesque. There were much glare and glitter and piquancy[13] and phantasm[14]—much of what has been since seen in *Hernani.*[15] There were arabesque[16] figures with unsuited limbs and appointments. There were delirious fancies such as the madman fashions. There was much of the beautiful, much of the wanton, much of the *bizarre,* something of the terrible, and not a little of that which might have excited disgust. To and fro in the seven chambers there stalked, in fact, a multitude of dreams. And these—the dreams—writhed in and about, taking hue[17] from the rooms, and causing the wild music of the orchestra to seem as the echo of their steps. And, anon,[18] there strikes the ebony clock which stands in the hall of the velvet. And then, for a moment, all is still, and all is silent

12. *fête* (fet′) *n.*: French for "celebration."

13. piquancy (pē′kən·sē) *n.*: quality of being pleasantly exciting.

14. phantasm (fan′taz′əm) *n.*: illusion.

15. *Hernani:* play by the French writer Victor Hugo.

16. arabesque (ar′ə·besk′) *adj.*: fantastic; elaborate.

17. hue (hyo͞o) *n.*: color or shade of color.

18. anon (ə·nän′) *adv.*: soon.

E. MONITOR YOUR READING
What details suggest that the party is, as Poe says, grotesque and bizarre? Why don't the revelers go into the seventh room?

20. disapprobation (dis′ap′ rə·bā′shən) *n.:* disapproval.

F. MONITOR YOUR READING
How does the masked figure affect the revelers?

21. license *n.:* here, excessive freedom.
22. Herod: evil biblical king who had baby boys slaughtered in his attempt to kill the infant Jesus. To "out-Herod Herod" is to be more evil than the worst tyrant.

save the voice of the clock. The dreams are stiff-frozen as they stand. But the echoes of the chime die away—they have endured but an instant— and a light, half-subdued laughter floats after them as they depart. And now again the music swells, and the dreams live, and writhe to and fro more merrily than ever, taking hue from the many-tinted windows through which stream the rays from the tripods. But to the chamber which lies most westwardly of the seven, there are now none of the maskers who venture; for the night is waning away; and there flows a ruddier light through the blood-colored panes; and the blackness of the sable drapery appalls;[19] and to him whose foot falls upon the sable carpet, there comes from the near clock of ebony a muffled peal more solemnly emphatic than any which reaches *their* ears who indulge in the more remote gaieties of the other apartments.

But these other apartments were densely crowded, and in them beat feverishly the heart of life. And the revel went whirlingly on, until at length there commenced the sounding of midnight upon the clock. And then the music ceased, as I have told; and the evolutions of the waltzers were quieted; and there was an uneasy cessation of all things as before. But now there were twelve strokes to be sounded by the bell of the clock; and thus it happened, perhaps, that more of thought crept, with more of time, into the meditations of the thoughtful among those who revelled. And thus, too, it happened, perhaps, that before the last echoes of the last chime had utterly sunk into silence, there were many individuals in the crowd who had found leisure to become aware of the presence of a masked figure which had arrested the attention of no single individual before. And the rumor of this new presence having spread itself whisperingly around, there arose at length from the whole company a buzz, or murmur, expressive of disapprobation[20] and sur-prise—then, finally, of terror, of horror, and of disgust.

In an assembly of phantasms such as I have painted, it may well be supposed that no ordinary appearance could have excited such sensa-tion. In truth the masquerade license[21] of the night was nearly un-limited; but the figure in question had out-Heroded Herod,[22] and gone beyond the bounds of even the prince's indefinite decorum. There are chords in the hearts of the most reckless which cannot be touched with-out emotion. Even with the utterly lost, to whom life and death are equally jests, there are matters of which no jest can be made. The whole company, indeed, seemed now deeply to feel that in the costume and bearing of the stranger neither wit nor propriety existed. The figure was

Vocabulary
cessation (se·sā′shən) *n.:* ceasing or stopping.
propriety (prə·prī′ə·tē) *n.:* quality of being proper, fitting, or suitable.

tall and gaunt, and shrouded from head to foot in the habiliments[23] of the grave. The mask which concealed the visage was made so nearly to resemble the countenance of a stiffened corpse that the closest scrutiny must have had difficulty in detecting the cheat. And yet all this might have been endured, if not approved, by the mad revelers around. But the mummer[24] had gone so far as to assume the type of the Red Death. His vesture[25] was dabbled in *blood*—and his broad brow, with all the features of the face, was besprinkled with the scarlet horror.

When the eyes of Prince Prospero fell upon this spectral[26] image (which with a slow and solemn movement, as if more fully to sustain its *role,* stalked to and fro among the waltzers), he was seen to be convulsed, in the first moment with a strong shudder either of terror or distaste; but, in the next, his brow reddened with rage.

"Who dares?" he demanded hoarsely of the courtiers who stood near him—"who dares insult us with this blasphemous[27] mockery? Seize him and unmask him—that we may know whom we have to hang at sunrise, from the battlements!"

It was in the eastern or blue chamber in which stood the Prince Prospero as he uttered these words. They rang throughout the seven rooms loudly and clearly—for the prince was a bold and robust man, and the music had become hushed at the waving of his hand.

23. habiliments (hə·bil′ə·mənts) *n.:* clothing.
24. mummer *n.:* person who wears a mask or disguise.
25. vesture (ves′chər) *n.:* clothing.

G. MONITOR YOUR READING
How is the masked guest costumed? Who do you **predict** this is?

26. spectral (spek′trəl) *adj.:* ghostly.
27. blasphemous (blas′fə·məs) *adj.:* here, highly disrespectful.

Masks and Death (1897) by James Ensor.

It was in the blue room where stood the prince, with a group of pale courtiers by his side. At first, as he spoke, there was a slight rushing movement of this group in the direction of the intruder, who at the moment was also near at hand, and now, with deliberate and stately step, made closer approach to the speaker. But from a certain nameless awe with which the mad assumptions of the mummer had inspired the whole party, there were found none who put forth hand to seize him; so that, unimpeded, he passed within a yard of the prince's person; and, while the vast assembly, as if with one impulse, shrank from the centers of the rooms to the walls, he made his way uninterruptedly, but with the same solemn and measured step which had distinguished him from the first, through the blue chamber to the purple—through the purple to the green—through the green to the orange—through this again to the white—and even thence to the violet, ere a decided movement had been made to arrest him. It was then, however, that the Prince Prospero, maddening with rage and the shame of his own momentary cowardice, rushed hurriedly through the six chambers, while none followed him on account of a deadly terror that had seized upon all. He bore aloft a drawn dagger, and had approached, in rapid impetuosity,[28] to within three or four feet of the retreating figure, when the latter, having attained the extremity of the velvet apartment, turned suddenly and confronted his pursuer. There was a sharp cry—and the dagger dropped gleaming upon the sable carpet, upon which, instantly afterwards, fell prostrate in death the Prince Prospero. Then, summoning the wild courage of despair, a throng of the revelers at once threw themselves into the black apartment, and, seizing the mummer, whose tall figure stood erect and motionless within the shadow of the ebony clock, gasped in unutterable horror at finding the grave cerements[29] and corpselike mask which they handled with so violent a rudeness, untenanted by any <u>tangible</u> form.

And now was acknowledged the presence of the Red Death. He had come like a thief in the night. And one by one dropped the revelers in the blood-bedewed halls of their revel, and died each in the despairing posture of his fall. And the life of the ebony clock went out with that of the last of the gay. And the flames of the tripods expired. And Darkness and Decay and the Red Death held illimitable dominion[30] over all. ■

Vocabulary
tangible (tan′jə·bəl) adj.: that can be touched.

(Opposite) "And Darkness and Decay and the Red Death held illimitable dominion over all." Illustration (1909) by John Byam Liston Shaw for "The Masque of the Red Death."

28. **impetuosity** (im·pech′ oo·äs′i·tē) n.: rashness; impulsiveness.

29. **grave cerements:** shrouds; cloths that cover a body for burial.

H. MONITOR YOUR READING
What happens when the guest is unmasked?

30. **dominion** n.: rule.

I. MONITOR YOUR READING
Who was the guest? What happens to the revelers?

Meet the Writer

Edgar Allan Poe

Nightmare Worlds

Edgar Allan Poe (1809–1849) was a moody, sensitive person whose stories and poems dwell on the supernatural and on crime, torture, premature burial, and death. His writing, which brought him little comfort or security, reflects the dark, nightmare side of the imagination.

Poe's stormy personal history began when his father deserted his mother, a popular young actress, who died in 1811 in a theatrical rooming house in Richmond, Virginia, just before Edgar was three years old.

The Allans, a wealthy, childless couple, took him in and gave him a good education, expecting him to go into business eventually. Edgar wanted to be a writer, though, not a businessman. This disagreement and John Allan's persistent refusal to adopt Edgar legally led to frequent fights. John Allan had severed all connections with him by the time he was twenty-one. Eventually Poe entered upon a hectic, full-time literary career, working for a number of periodicals in Baltimore and New York.

In 1836, Poe married a thirteen-year-old cousin, Virginia Clemm. Although a drinking problem often got him into destructive fights with other writers and critics, Poe managed somehow to keep his household together. In 1845, he sold his poem "The Raven" to a newspaper for about fifteen dollars. "The Raven" was soon on everyone's lips, as popular as a top-ten song is today.

Poe was to know no peace, however. Virginia had already fallen victim to that plague of nineteenth-century life, tuberculosis. In 1847, she died, and Poe's loneliness and drinking increased. On October 3, 1849, when he was only forty years old, Poe was found, disoriented and suffering from exposure, outside a tavern in rainy, windswept Baltimore. He died in a Baltimore hospital from unspecified causes several days later.

Poe, a meticulous writer who was devoted to his craft, invented two genres: the mystery story and the horror story. Both forms have flourished ever since.

For Independent Reading

Poe's horror tales include "Hop-Frog" and "The Cask of Amontillado," two stories about cold-blooded revenge; "The Tell-Tale Heart," about an irrational murder; and "The Pit and the Pendulum," set in a prison in Toledo, Spain.

The Black Death
from **When Plague Strikes**

James Cross Giblin

The bubonic plague—the Black Death—arrived in Sicily in October 1347, carried by the crew of a fleet from the east. All the sailors on the ships were dead or dying. In the words of a contemporary historian, they had "sickness clinging to their very bones."

The harbor masters at the port of Messina ordered the sick sailors to remain on board, hoping in this way to prevent the disease from spreading to the town. They had no way of knowing that the actual carriers of the disease had already left the ships. Under cover of night, when no one could see them, they had scurried down the ropes that tied the ships to the dock and vanished into Messina.

The carriers were black rats and the fleas that lived in their hair. Driven by an unending search for food, the rats' ancestors had migrated slowly westward along the caravan routes. They had traveled in bolts of cloth and bales of hay, and the fleas had come with them.

Although it was only an eighth of an inch long, the rat flea was a tough, adaptable creature. It depended for nourishment on the blood of its host, which it obtained through a daggerlike snout that could pierce the rat's skin. And in its stomach the flea often carried thousands of the deadly bacteria that caused the bubonic plague.

The bacteria did no apparent harm to the flea, and a black rat could tolerate a moderate amount of them, too, without showing ill effects. But sometimes the flea contained so many bacteria that they invaded the rat's lungs or nervous system when the flea injected its snout. Then the rat died a swift and horrible death, and the flea had to find a new host.

Aiding the tiny flea in its search were its powerful legs, which could jump more than 150 times the creature's length. In most instances the flea landed on another black rat. Not always, though. If most of the rats in the vicinity were already dead or dying from the plague, the flea might leap to a human being instead. As soon as it had settled on the human's skin, the flea would begin to feed, and the whole process of infection would be repeated. . . .

From Sicily, trading ships loaded with infected flea-bearing rats carried the Black Death to ports on the mainland of Italy. Peddlers and other travelers helped spread it to inland cities such as Milan and Florence.

Conditions in these medieval cities provided a splendid breeding ground for all types of vermin, including rats. There were no regular garbage collections, and refuse accumulated in piles in the streets. Rushes from wet or marshy places, not rugs, covered the floors in most homes. After a meal, it was customary to throw bits of leftover food onto the rushes for the dog or cat to eat. Rats and mice often got their share, too.

Because the cities had no running water, even the wealthy seldom washed their heavy clothing, or their own bodies. As a result, both rich and poor were prime targets for lice and fleas and the diseases they carried—the most deadly being the bubonic plague. . . .

The most complete account of the Black Death in Italy was given by the writer Giovanni Boccaccio, who lived in the city of Florence. In the preface to his classic book the *Decameron,* Boccaccio wrote: "Some say that the plague descended upon the human race through the influence of the heavenly bodies, others that it was a punishment signifying God's righteous anger at our wicked way of life." . . .

they were rich enough, abandoned their homes in the city and fled to villas in the countryside. They hoped in this way to escape the disease—but often it followed them.

Whatever steps they took, the same percentage of people in each group seemed to fall ill. So many died that the bodies piled up in the streets. A new occupation came into being: that of loading the bodies on carts and carrying them away for burial in mass graves.

The Plague (c. 1515–1516) by Marcantonio Raimondi.
© Historical Picture Archive/CORBIS.

"No more respect was accorded to dead people," Boccaccio wrote, "than would be shown toward dead goats."

The town of Siena, thirty miles south of Florence, suffered severe losses also. A man named Agnolo di Tura offered a vivid account of what happened there:

"The mortality in Siena began in May. It was a horrible thing, and I do not know where to begin to tell of the cruelty . . . . Members of a household brought their dead to a ditch

How did the people of Florence react to this mysterious and fatal disease? Some isolated themselves in their homes, according to Boccaccio. They ate lightly, saw no outsiders, and refused to receive reports of the dead or sick. Others adopted an attitude of "play today for we die tomorrow." They drank heavily, stayed out late, and roamed through the streets singing and dancing as if the Black Death were an enormous joke. Still others, if

as best they could, without a priest, without any divine services. Nor did the death bell sound. . . . And as soon as those ditches were filled, more were dug. I, Agnolo di Tura, buried my five children with my own hands. . . . And no bells tolled, and nobody wept no matter what his loss because almost everyone expected death. . . . And people said and believed, 'This is the end of the world.'"

Response and Analysis

Reading Check

1. How do Prince Prospero and his friends try to escape from the Red Death?

2. What kind of life do the prince and his guests lead in their world apart?

3. Describe the seven rooms of the prince's suite.

4. Why do the guests avoid the seventh room?

5. How do the guests respond to the chiming of the ebony clock?

6. How does the masked ball end?

Thinking Critically

7. In the long paragraph that describes the masquerade on pages 423–424, what details suggest madness?

8. What is the **climax** of this horror story—that moment of greatest suspense and emotion, when you know how the problem in the story is going to be resolved?

9. Most readers agree that this story can be interpreted as an **allegory.** What might each of the following characters, events, or colors, represent?

   - Prince Prospero (consider even the significance of his name)
   - the masked ball
   - the colors of the seven rooms
   - the seventh room itself
   - the ebony clock
   - the masked figure

10. In a sentence or two, summarize what you think is the story's **allegorical meaning**—the symbolic meaning behind the surface narrative. What does that additional level of meaning add to your appreciation of the story?

11. What unanswered questions do you have about this story?

12. Review the **Connection** on page 429. What parallels are there between the way Poe's characters react to the Red Death and the way people reacted to the Black Death in Europe?

Extending and Evaluating

13. According to Poe, every literary element in a story should be directed to achieve "a certain single effect." Decide what you think Poe's intended effect is in this story. Then, evaluate how well he achieves his goal. Support your evaluation with details from the story.

WRITING

The Great Escape

Write a **story** of your own about a group of people who retreat to an isolated place in order to escape some danger. Before you write, decide what emotional effect you want to create in your story: horror? humor? irony? You might even consider writing your story so that it parodies Poe's story, or imitates it in a comical way. Refer to your Quickwrite notes for ideas. Filling out a story map like the one below before you write might help you.

Setting:
Characters:
Problem:
Main events:
Climax:

Vocabulary Development

Context Clues: Filling In the Blanks

The **context,** the words and sentences that surround an unfamiliar word, may provide clues to its meaning. There are different kinds of context clues: **definition, restatement, synonym,** and **antonym.** The following sentences about "The Masque of the Red Death" contain context clues that will help you figure out the meaning of the underlined words. The context clues appear in *italic* type.

DEFINITION AND RESTATEMENT
The room's only light came from a brazier. *This metal pan filled with glowing coals* stood outside each window.

SYNONYM
The seventh room brought a ghastly look to the countenances, or *faces,* of all who entered it.

ANTONYM
Everyone at the ball viewed the masked stranger *not with approval* but with disapprobation.

Strategies for Using Context Clues

You've found a word you've never seen before, and you have no idea what it means.

- Think of that unfamiliar word as a blank that needs filling in.
- Determine the word's part of speech.
- Re-read the whole sentence, looking for context clues. Nothing in the sentence? Go back a couple of more sentences and forward one or two.
- Try a few synonyms (or definitions), and see if they make sense in the sentence.

SKILLS FOCUS

Vocabulary Skills
Use context clues.

Stopping by Woods on a Snowy Evening
After Apple-Picking

Make the Connection

Quickwrite 🖉

Jot down all of the **images, connotations,** and any other kinds of **associations** that occur to you for these words: *sleep, woods, dreaming, apples, apple-picking.* Take notes in a chart like this:

	Images	Connotations/ Associations
Sleep		
Woods		
Dreaming		
Apples		
Apple-picking		

Literary Focus

Symbolic Meaning: What Lies Beneath the Surface

Literally, snow is snow, a horse is a horse, and apples are apples. In the hands of a poet, however, ordinary things become **symbols**—that is, they stand for things other than themselves and suggest deeper layers of meaning. There's much more to these two poems by Robert Frost than a literal pause in a wintry journey and a rest after a hard day's apple-picking.

So how can you tell when a poem has **symbolic meaning?** Be alert to clues the poet plants—repetition, emphasis, word associations, and mysterious images. Even though symbolic meanings in a poem may be difficult to pin down and express precisely, symbols appeal powerfully to our emotions and our imaginations.

Reading Skills 📖

Monitoring Your Reading: Re-reading

Read each of these poems several times to understand them better.

As you re-read, take notes in a chart like the one below. Focus on one poem at a time, and follow these guidelines:

- On your second reading, jot down what you see in each poem—its visual images and what is happening.
- On your third reading of "Stopping by Woods on a Snowy Evening," jot down all the things you think are going through the traveler's mind as he gazes at the woods.
- On your third reading of "After Apple-Picking," jot down what you think "harvest" stands for on a deeper level.

Keep your notes.

	"Stopping by Woods on a Snowy Evening"	"After Apple-Picking"
Second Reading		
Third Reading		

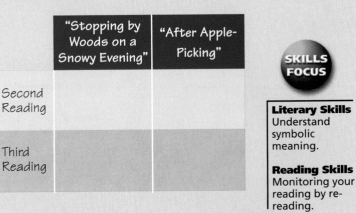

go.hrw.com

INTERNET

More About Robert Frost

Keyword: LE5 10-6

SKILLS FOCUS

Literary Skills Understand symbolic meaning.

Reading Skills Monitoring your reading by re-reading.

Stopping by Woods on a Snowy Evening

Robert Frost

Whose woods these are I think I know.
His house is in the village, though;
He will not see me stopping here
To watch his woods fill up with snow.

5   My little horse must think it queer
To stop without a farmhouse near
Between the woods and frozen lake
The darkest evening of the year.

He gives his harness bells a shake
10   To ask if there is some mistake.
The only other sound's the sweep
Of easy wind and downy flake.

The woods are lovely, dark, and deep,
But I have promises to keep,
15   And miles to go before I sleep,
And miles to go before I sleep.

After Apple-Picking

Robert Frost

My long two-pointed ladder's sticking
    through a tree
Toward heaven still,
And there's a barrel that I didn't fill
Beside it, and there may be two or three
5   Apples I didn't pick upon some bough.
But I am done with apple-picking now.
Essence of winter sleep is on the night,
The scent of apples: I am drowsing off.
I cannot rub the strangeness from my sight
10 I got from looking through a pane of glass
I skimmed this morning from the drinking
    trough
And held against the world of hoary° grass.
It melted, and I let it fall and break.
But I was well
15 Upon my way to sleep before it fell,
And I could tell
What form my dreaming was about to take.
Magnified apples appear and disappear,
Stem end and blossom end,
20 And every fleck of russet showing clear.
My instep arch not only keeps the ache,
It keeps the pressure of a ladder-round.
I feel the ladder sway as the boughs bend.
And I keep hearing from the cellar bin
25 The rumbling sound
Of load on load of apples coming in.
For I have had too much
Of apple-picking: I am overtired
Of the great harvest I myself desired.
There were ten thousand thousand fruit to
30   touch,
Cherish in hand, lift down, and not let fall.

Apples (1867) by Worthington Whittredge.

---

12. hoary: (hôr′ē) *adj.:* covered with hoarfrost, white
crystals of ice. *Hoary* also means "very old; ancient."

For all
That struck the earth,
No matter if not bruised or spiked with stubble,
35 Went surely to the cider-apple heap
As of no worth.
One can see what will trouble
This sleep of mine, whatever sleep it is.
Were he not gone,
40 The woodchuck could say whether it's like his
Long sleep, as I describe its coming on,
Or just some human sleep.

Apple Harvest by Levi Wells Prentice (1851–1935).

Meet the Writer

Robert Frost

Beneath the Surface

Robert Frost (1874–1963), whom most Americans consider the voice of rural New England, was born in San Francisco and lived as a child in the industrial city of Lawrence, Massachusetts. He attended Dartmouth College for a few months but left to write poetry and work in a cotton mill. Years later, after he had become a husband and father, Frost returned to college but left after two years, again to write seriously.

In 1912, Frost moved his young family to England. During the three years he spent there, he wrote and published two books of poems—*A Boy's Will* (1913) and *North of Boston* (1914)—which were immediate successes on both sides of the Atlantic.

Frost went home to New England in 1915, finally able to make his living as a poet. During his long career he won four Pulitzer Prizes and often gave public readings and lectures. One of his last public appearances was at the 1961 inauguration of President John F. Kennedy, where he recited his poem "The Gift Outright."

Like the independent New England farmers he frequently wrote about, Frost went his own way. He refused to join his contemporaries in their experimental search for new poetic forms, finding all the freedom he needed within the bounds of traditional verse. Despite their apparently homespun subjects and traditional form, Frost's poems are only seemingly simple. Beneath their surface is a complex and often dark view of human life and personality. Frost said:

> 66 Like a piece of ice on a hot stove, the poem must ride on its own melting. . . . Read it a hundred times; it will forever keep its freshness as a metal keeps its fragrance. It can never lose its sense of a meaning that once unfolded by surprise as it went. 99

For Independent Reading

In a collection of Frost's poetry, read these all-time favorites: "The Road Not Taken," "Birches," "Acquainted with the Night," "Design," "Desert Places," and "The Gift Outright." Browse a little, and you'll discover favorites of your own to share with your classmates.

Response and Analysis

Stopping by Woods on a Snowy Evening
After Apple-Picking

Reading Check

1. For each poem, summarize what is **literally** happening in the poem. (Check your re-reading notes.)

Thinking Critically

2. In "Stopping by Woods on a Snowy Evening," the speaker says he has miles to go before he can sleep. What is he probably thinking of? What other, **metaphorical** sleep might he be referring to?

3. The big question set up by the poem is what those lovely, dark, and deep woods **symbolize** to the traveler. What do you think? What has the speaker said no to in passing them by?

4. Whatever the woods stand for, what has the speaker said yes to in deciding to go on? In other words, how has he resolved his **conflict**?

5. On a **symbolic** level, what do you think is "the great harvest" that the speaker in "After Apple-Picking" once valued (see lines 28–36)?

6. What is suggested by the speaker's statement that he is "overtired" of the great harvest he once wanted?

7. In "After Apple-Picking," trace the speaker's state of drowsiness and dreaming. (Note, for example, how many times the word *sleep* occurs and when a dream passage begins.) What kind of sleep do you think the speaker is talking about? **Compare** it to the sleep in lines 15–16 of "Stopping by Woods on a Snowy Evening."

8. Look at your Quickwrite notes. How have your associations with the words *sleep, woods,* and *apple-picking* changed after reading these poems?

9. The **theme** of a poem is an insight into life that the poet wants to convey. Try to express what you think is the theme of each poem.

Comparing Poems
Alike yet Different

Write a brief **comparison-contrast essay** for these two poems. You might begin by taking notes in a chart like the one below. (See pages 254 and 283 for help with a comparison-contrast essay.)

	"Stopping by Woods on a Snowy Evening"	"After Apple-Picking"
Speaker		
Situation		
Setting/ season		
Repeated words		
Symbols		
Theme		

LISTENING AND SPEAKING
Oral Interpretation

Choose one of these poems to prepare for an **oral interpretation.** You'll have to make these decisions: Will you use a single voice or several? When will you slow down? speed up? pause for effect? Will you set the poem to music? Will you arrange it as a ballad? a hymn? a rock song? a rap song?

FICTION

A Rabbit Odyssey

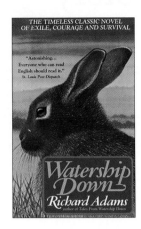

When land developers begin to dig up the English countryside, they have no idea that their labor means life or death for a band of talking rabbits. Led by brave Hazel, eleven of the rabbits set off on a dangerous journey—battling illness, injuries, and evil animals—in search of a new place to live. If you're in the mood for an action-packed fantasy—one that also serves as a rich allegorical tale of human beings and nature—then Richard Adams's *Watership Down* is the book for you.

FICTION

In a Faraway Land

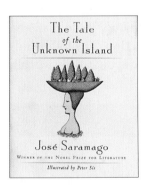

The Tale of the Unknown Island, by the Nobel Prize–winning author José Saramago, starts out as simply as a fairy tale: Wanting to discover an unknown island, a man goes to the king's door and asks for a boat. A palace cleaning woman overhears his request and follows the man, since she has never seen an unknown island herself. Their journey becomes a moving allegory of love and discovery, loss and gain—all revealed in a timeless story packed with substance, humor, and truth.

FICTION

Fateful Friendship

The Devon School, with its beautiful, tree-lined campus, seems a safe haven for boys during World War II. Gene, a lonely sixteen-year-old, is assigned the perfect roommate: athletic, fun-loving Finny, who drags Gene away from his schoolbooks and into the real world. Then friendship turns into rivalry, and rivalry turns into something far more sinister. *A Separate Peace* by John Knowles is the story of two boys whose struggle mirrors the terrible war being fought beyond campus walls.

This title is available in the HRW Library.

NONFICTION

Questions of Identity

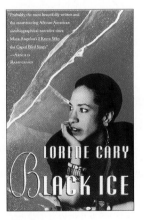

In her autobiography, *Black Ice,* Lorene Cary tells of the difficult choices she had to make when she moved from her African American neighborhood in Philadelphia to an elite, formerly all-white prep school in New Hampshire. Thrust into an intimidating and unfamiliar setting, Cary began to question how to become a part of school life without sacrificing her own very distinct identity and values. Cary's struggle to succeed without seeming to betray her heritage is recorded with gutsy honesty.

Analyzing a Short Story

Writing Assignment
Write a response to literature in which you analyze the literary elements of a short story.

What makes a short story like Tom Godwin's "The Cold Equations" (page 164) compelling and memorable? One way to find out is through analysis. When you do a **literary analysis,** you take a critical and objective look at how a writer uses the elements of literature to create a unique work of literary art. A close analysis of a piece of literature gives you insight into how the author crafted the work and adds to your understanding of it.

Prewriting

Choose a Story

The Choice Is Yours To choose an appropriate short story to analyze, consider stories you have already read and enjoyed as well as those recommended by others. Also consider stories by authors whose other works you have enjoyed. Your analysis will have to be 1,500 words long, so be sure to choose a story that is complex and rich in meaning.

Analyze the Story and Develop a Thesis

Take a Closer Look Read your story once to get an overall grasp of it. Then, discover what makes the story unique. To do that, analyze how the author uses the basic **elements of fiction**. The following chart defines these elements and provides questions you can answer about each one.

ANALYZING ELEMENTS OF FICTION

Element	Analysis Questions
Plot is the action or series of events depicted in the story.	• What is the **conflict,** or main problem, and who is involved in the story? • What is the story's **climax**—the most intense moment in the plot? • How is the conflict resolved? Is the **resolution** logical? • Do events happen in a predictable way, or does the writer build suspense by creating doubt about how the conflict will be resolved?
Setting is the time and place in which the story occurs.	• Where and when does the story take place? • Does the setting affect the plot, the characters, or the mood or atmosphere of the story? How?

(continued)

(continued)

Characters are the individuals in a story.	• What are the major characters like? • What motivates the characters to behave as they do? • Do any of the characters change? If so, how and why?
Theme is an important idea about life.	• What important idea about life or human nature does the story reveal? • Do other elements, such as plot or characters, play a role in the development of the theme? If so, how?
Stylistic devices are the techniques a writer uses to create certain effects in a work.	• Does the writer's **diction,** or choice of important words, affect the tone of the story? How? • Does the writer use **imagery**—language that appeals to the senses? What is the effect of such imagery on the story? • Does the writer make imaginative comparisons through the use of **figurative language**—metaphor, simile, and personification?

Pick Your Target   For your analysis, zero in on the element or elements that seem to dominate the story. Dominant elements will usually be the ones for which you have the most specific information. For example, based on his answers to the questions in the chart, one student analyzing "The Cold Equations" chose to focus on the story's plot.

Next, identify your main idea, or **thesis,** about the element or elements on which your analysis will focus. Draw a conclusion about the role of the focus element or elements in the story. Then, draft a thesis statement that includes the story's title and author and this conclusion. Here's one writer's working thesis statement, which he revised during drafting.

DO THIS

Focus element: plot

Conclusion: The story's powerful effect is a result of the suspense the writer builds into the plot.

Thesis statement: In "The Cold Equations," author Tom Godwin builds a plot tingling with suspense to create a memorable story.

Gather and Organize Support

Focusing In   Support for a literary analysis includes **key points** to support your thesis, **details** from the story to provide evidence for the key points, and **elaboration** to link the details to the key points.

Key Points   Key points are the aspects of the story that led you to the conclusion in your thesis statement. The student analyzing "The Cold Equations" decided that the suspense in the story came from the unknown identity of the stowaway, withheld information, and the question of whether Marilyn would contact her brother in time.

SKILLS FOCUS

Writing Skills
Write an analysis of a short story. Choose a story. Analyze the story, and develop a thesis statement.

Supporting Details To support your key points, use **references to the text**—details from the story in the form of direct quotations, paraphrases of passages, or summaries of ideas. You may also wish to consult professional works of literary analysis for support of your key points.

Elaboration Elaborate on supporting details to show that you have an understanding of the **significant ideas** in the short story. In other words, explain *how* your supporting details connect to key points.

Your elaboration might include a discussion of the **ambiguities, nuances,** and **complexities** of the work—three characteristics that give literature richness and depth.

- **Ambiguities** are situations that can be interpreted in more than one way.

- **Nuances** are slight variations in tone or meaning.

- **Complexities** exist when a story is rich in meaning but difficult to interpret.

Look at the partial chart below to see how the student writer started with a key point, found a detail to support that point, and then elaborated with an explanation. You can create a chart of your own to map out your key points, supporting details, and elaboration.

TIP When discussing events from a story, use the **literary present tense.** That is, refer to the events in the story as if they were happening right now. For example, write, "Marilyn hopes to visit her brother," not "Marilyn hoped to visit her brother."

Key Point	Supporting Detail	Elaboration
The author reveals the presence, but not the identity, of someone on the ship.	Quotation: "He was not alone. . . . There was something in the supply closet across the room . . . a living, human body."	The suspense comes from questions raised in the reader's mind: Why is the pilot supposed to be alone? Who is the stowaway in the closet? Is this person dangerous?

Get It in Order Your key points may suggest an **organizational pattern** for arranging your analysis. In an analysis of plot or character development, you might discuss key points in **chronological order**—the order in which they occurred in the story. For an analysis examining theme, you might use **order of importance,** explaining key points from most important to least important, or vice versa. Look at your key points. Which organizational pattern will you use?

SKILLS FOCUS

Writing Skills
Gather and organize supporting information.

PRACTICE & APPLY 1 Use the instructions on pages 440–442 to choose and analyze a short story. Find a focus element, develop a thesis statement, and back up the thesis statement with key points, supporting details, and elaboration.

Writing

Analyzing a Short Story

A Writer's Framework

Introduction

- Open with an interesting comment on the story, such as an observation related to your thesis.

- Include a thesis statement that names the story's title and author and states your conclusion about the element or elements your analysis focuses on.

Body

- Arrange your key points in chronological order or by order of importance.

- Back up key points with supporting details in the form of direct quotations, paraphrases, and summaries.

- Elaborate on supporting details by explaining how they support the key points.

Conclusion

- Summarize your key points.

- Restate your thesis, using different words.

- Leave readers with something to consider, such as a general comment about the story that relates to your thesis.

A Writer's Model

Suspense in "The Cold Equations"

Space is widely considered the last frontier, the last great challenge to human exploration. Because space exploration is dangerous, strict rules based on our understanding of the laws of nature must be made and followed. Can the dangers and demands of this final frontier also take human nature into account? In "The Cold Equations," author Tom Godwin uses plot developments to build suspense progressively as he explores this complex question.

Godwin begins creating suspense in the very first scene by revealing the presence, but not the identity, of someone aboard the Emergency Dispatch Ship other than Barton, the pilot: "He was not alone. . . . There was something in the supply closet across the room . . . a living, human body." These statements raise questions in the reader's mind. Is Barton supposed to be alone? Who is the stowaway, and is the person dangerous? Barton considers the necessary fate of all stowaways—death—making the reader more anxious. Then, when Barton realizes that the intruder is an innocent teenager, it hits him—and the reader—"like a heavy and unexpected physical blow." Now the question is: Will Barton really kill a defenseless teenager?

INTRODUCTION

Interesting comment

Complexity suggested

Thesis statement

BODY

Key point 1

Supporting detail

Elaboration

(continued)

(continued)

,2

g details

Godwin intensifies the suspense by withholding until nearly halfway through the story just how long Marilyn, the young stowaway, has to live. After Barton questions her about how and why she stowed away, he slows the rate of the ship's deceleration to conserve fuel. He does not believe that his action will change the outcome of events, but it is all he can do to postpone the unavoidable. Next, he calls Commander Delhart of the *Stardust*, the ship on which Marilyn had been traveling. He is sure this action is also "futile" since the spaceship will not be able to turn back for her. Still, he pursues this "one vain hope" to save Marilyn. Wanting to give her as much time as possible to accept her fate, he puts off calculating the deadline until Commander Delhart orders him to do so. All these delays create suspense by seeming to leave open the possibility that Marilyn may somehow be rescued. To add to this suspense, the author repeats both the cold rules of space travel and Marilyn's human, emotional pleas. Readers are forced to see the subtle difference in the tone created by the language of the rules and the tone created by Marilyn's language.

Elaboration

Nuance explained

Key point 3

Supporting details

With time running out for Marilyn, the author further increases the suspense by making her brother temporarily unreachable. When Barton contacts Gerry's base station on the planet Woden, Gerry is out in a helicopter that does not have a working radio. He is expected back at the camp soon—"in less than an hour at the most"—but Marilyn has less than an hour to live. Meanwhile, Woden is gradually turning, the camp slipping away from the range of the radio. The uncertainty about whether Gerry will return in time suggests that Marilyn may not even get to say goodbye to her beloved big brother.

Elaboration

CONCLUSION

Summary of key points

Restatement of thesis

General comment

At important points in the story, Godwin deliberately holds back crucial information—who the stowaway is, when she must die, and whether she will be able to contact her brother. The result is suspense, which keeps the reader uncertain and anxious right up to the story's tragic conclusion. If Godwin's vision of the grim world of future space travel is accurate, we must consider whether exploring the final frontier is worth the price.

PRACTICE & APPLY 2 As you turn your prewriting notes into the first draft of your literary analysis, be sure to consult the framework on page 443 and the Writer's Model above. Return to the Prewriting section as necessary.

Revising

Evaluate and Revise Your Draft

Check It Twice Carefully read your whole paper at least twice. First, examine the paper's content and organization, using the guidelines below. Then, use the guidelines on page 446 to help you focus on sentence style.

PEER REVIEW

Exchange your analysis with a peer. He or she may have ideas on how you can improve on your elaboration of supporting details.

▶ **First Reading: Content and Organization** Use the following chart as a **think sheet** to help you evaluate and revise the content and organization of your analysis. You can use the chart either alone or during a peer review.

Rubric: Analyzing a Short Story

Evaluation Questions	▶ Tips	▶ Revision Techniques
❶ Does the introduction grab the reader's attention with an interesting comment on the story?	▶ **Put a star** beside the interesting comment.	▶ **Add** an interesting comment about the story, such as an observation related to the thesis.
❷ Does the thesis statement identify the story's title and author, the literary element(s) discussed, and the conclusion about the element(s)?	▶ **Circle** the title, the author, and the literary element(s) discussed. **Bracket** the writer's conclusion about the element(s).	▶ If necessary, **add** any missing parts to the thesis statement: title and author, literary element(s), or conclusion about element(s).
❸ Are key points clearly identified and organized in the body of the analysis?	▶ **Draw a wavy line** under each key point. **Number** each body paragraph for chronological order or order of importance.	▶ **Add** a sentence clearly explaining the paragraph's key point. **Rearrange** paragraphs if they do not follow a clear order.
❹ Is each key point supported by details—direct quotations, summaries, and paraphrases—from the story?	▶ **Highlight** each quotation, summary, and paraphrase from the story that is used as support.	▶ **Add** supporting details to support your key points. **Delete** sentences that do not support a key point.
❺ Does elaboration connect key points and supporting details?	▶ **Draw an arrow** to each sentence that elaborates a detail.	▶ **Add** explanations that show how details relate to key points.
❻ Does the conclusion summarize the key points and restate the thesis? Does it include a comment about the story that relates to the thesis?	▶ **Circle** the summary of the key points and **highlight** the restatement of the thesis. **Put a check mark** by the final comment.	▶ **Add** a sentence that summarizes the key points or restates the thesis, if necessary. **Add** a final comment.

Second Reading: **Style** To keep readers interested, use a variety of sentence lengths. Avoid using several short, choppy sentences in a row. Instead, combine two or more such sentences by using **adjective clauses**—clauses that modify a noun or pronoun and are introduced by relative pronouns such as *who, whom, which,* and *that.* Notice how an adjective clause is used to combine the choppy sentences below.

Choppy <u>Barton</u> is the pilot of the EDS. <u>He</u> discovers a stowaway.

Combined Barton, <u>who</u> is the pilot of the EDS, discovers a stowaway.

Style Guidelines

Evaluation Question	▶ Tip	▶ Revision Technique
● Does the paper include a variety of sentence lengths (some short, some long)?	▶ **Underline** nouns and related pronouns that are repeated in short, back-to-back sentences.	▶ **Replace** a repeated noun or pronoun with *who, whom, which,* or *that,* and **add** the clause to the related sentence.

ANALYZING THE REVISION PROCESS

Study these revisions, and answer the questions that follow.

> With time running out for Marilyn, the author further increases the suspense by making her brother temporarily
>
> *delete* unreachable. ~~Marilyn explains that her sole reason for stowing away is to see her older brother.~~ When Barton contacts Gerry's base station on the planet Woden, Gerry is out in a
>
> *that*
> *replace/add* helicopter, ~~The helicopter~~ does not have a working radio.

Responding to the Revision Process

1. Why did the writer delete the second sentence?
2. Why did the writer combine the third and fourth sentences?

SKILLS FOCUS

Writing Skills
Revise for content and style.

PRACTICE & APPLY 3 Use the guidelines on pages 445 and 446 to evaluate and revise the content, organization, and style of your draft. Consider peer comments, too.

Publishing

Proofread and Publish Your Analysis

A Last Look Before publishing your analysis, work with a classmate to proofread it at least twice for errors in grammar, spelling, and punctuation. Two sets of eyes and two minds are much better than one when it comes to spotting and correcting major and minor errors in these areas. Major errors can ruin an analysis with strong content and even minor errors can distract readers from an otherwise excellent analysis.

Share Your Work Other people may be interested in what you have to say about the short story you analyzed. To get your analysis in front of an audience, consider the following publishing options.

- Surf the Web to find the sites of high school literary magazines in different parts of the country and submit your analysis for publication and feedback.

- Submit your analysis to your school's newspaper or to a student literary magazine.

- With other students who analyzed short stories, create and bind a collection of analyses to be placed in the school library.

- Deliver your analysis as an oral response to literature. For more on **presenting a literary response,** see page 448.

Reflect on Your Analysis

Looking Back Taking time to reflect on the process of writing a short story analysis will help you understand your strengths and weaknesses as a critical reader and writer. To think about what you have learned from this workshop, answer the following questions. If you add your analysis to your writing portfolio, include your written responses to these questions.

- How did you choose a story to analyze? Would you use this method to choose other stories or pieces of nonfiction to read for school or for enjoyment? Explain your response.

- How did your understanding of the story change as you wrote your analysis? Will this new understanding change how you approach reading other stories? Explain.

 **PRACTICE & APPLY 4** Proofread your short story analysis carefully for errors in language conventions. Then, publish your analysis, using one of the suggestions on this page. Finally, take stock of what you've learned by answering the reflection questions above.

TIP Proofreading will help you make sure that you follow the **conventions** of standard American English. Pay particular attention to your punctuation of the story's title and of direct quotations. For more on **punctuating quotations and titles,** see Quotation Marks, 13c–k, in the Language Handbook.

SKILLS FOCUS

Writing Skills
Proofread, especially for correct punctuation of quotations and titles.

Presenting a Literary Response

**SKILLS
FOCUS**

**Listening and Speaking
Skills**
Present an oral response to literature.

Quick guide!

A literary analysis doesn't have to be a written presentation only; it can also make an effective oral presentation. In this workshop you will adapt your written literary analysis for delivery as an **oral response to literature.** Your purpose will be to show your audience that you have a firm grasp of the significant ideas of the story you are analyzing. A listening audience has very different needs than a reading audience, even if both groups contain your classmates and teacher. You have much to consider as you plan your adaptation and delivery.

Adapt Your Written Analysis

Consider the Ingredients Your written analysis consisted of an introduction, a body, and a conclusion. So should your oral presentation. However, you might need to make changes beyond simplified sentence structure and vocabulary to make the points of your paper interesting to listeners and easy to understand. Here are some things to consider.

Introduction The **introduction** to an oral presentation needs to be more dramatic and personal than a written introduction. Here are some ways you can adapt the introduction of your written response to grab your listeners' attention.

DEVELOPING INTRODUCTIONS

Technique	Example
Begin with a quotation.	"It was the law, and there could be no appeal." The characters in Tom Godwin's "The Cold Equations" learn this lesson all too well. Despite the strong human concerns and emotions the author presents, the law is inescapable.
Begin with a personal observation or anecdote.	In my own experience, having a good reason for doing something I shouldn't has sometimes spared me the worst consequences. However, my experiences with human rules would not prepare me for the inescapable laws of space travel.
Begin with a reference to a familiar source.	According to Newton's laws of motion, the force of a planet's gravity is stronger on an object with more mass and increases the closer the object gets. It's one thing to read that in a science book, but it's completely different to think about how that law might affect human beings.

Your introduction should also identify the story's title and author and the conclusion about the story element or elements (plot, character, stylistic device, and so on) you plan to focus on. State this information in simple but strong language. That way your listeners will understand the basics of your presentation at the beginning, which will make the rest of your presentation easier to follow.

Body The **body** of your oral presentation is where you advance a **judgment** that shows you have a complete grasp of the important ideas in the short story. It will contain the same basic information your written analysis does. To adapt the written analysis, provide **extra elaboration** of the details that support your thesis. Extra elaboration makes an oral presentation easier to understand. If you need to provide **references to the text** (quotations, paraphrases, or summaries) to support a point, be sure you put the reference into context by explaining the circumstances or events that surround it.

Add plenty of **transitional words and phrases** to the body of your oral presentation to guide listeners through it. For chronological order, use words and phrases such as *after, then, next,* and *finally* to show the order of ideas. For order of importance, use words and phrases such as *mainly, to begin with,* and *more* (or *most*) *important.* Some transitional words such as *first, second, third,* and *last* can be used to show either order.

Conclusion The **conclusion** of your oral presentation should, like the introduction, be dramatic and personal. Summarize your key points and restate your thesis, all in simple but strong language. Then, close with a statement that shows your appreciation of the effects the author has created in the story.

Deliver Your Oral Response

Make a Note of It Make concise notes to guide you in delivering the ideas you have planned and organized. Your oral response will be **extemporaneous**—rehearsed extensively but not read or memorized. Your notes should contain clearly organized words and phrases to remind you of the ideas you will present. Write down word for word any quotations you will use from the story so that you will deliver them accurately.

Go Tell It Practice using your voice and body effectively. Speak loudly enough for everyone to hear and slowly enough for them to understand each word. Make eye contact with your audience, and vary your facial expressions to hold listener interest. Use both your voice and gestures to emphasize important ideas.

PRACTICE & APPLY **5** Adapt your written analysis as an oral presentation. Use your voice and gestures effectively as you deliver your oral response to literature.

TIP Don't forget to explain the **ambiguities, nuances,** and **complexities** that you discussed in your written analysis. Take extra care to explain how they are connected to your thesis statement. Also, be sure to point out **stylistic devices** that the author uses.

SKILLS FOCUS

Listening and Speaking Skills
Plan and deliver your oral response.

Test Practice **Symbolism and Allegory**

DIRECTIONS: Read the following short story. Then, read and respond to the questions that follow.

The Blue Stones

Isak Dinesen

There was once a skipper who named his ship after his wife. He had the figurehead of it beautifully carved, just like her, and the hair of it gilt. But his wife was jealous of the ship. "You think more of the figurehead than of me," she said to him. "No," he answered, "I think so highly of her because she is like you, yes, because she is you yourself. Is she not gallant, full-bosomed; does she not dance in the waves, like you at our wedding? In a way she is really even kinder to me than you are. She gallops along where I tell her to go, and she lets her long hair hang down freely, while you put up yours under a cap. But she turns her back to me, so that when I want a kiss I come home to Elsinore." Now once, when this skipper was trading at Trankebar, he chanced to help an old native king to flee traitors in his own country. As they parted, the king gave him two big blue, precious stones, and these he had set into the face of his figurehead, like a pair of eyes to it. When he came home he told his wife of his adventure, and said: "Now she has your blue eyes too." "You had better give me the stones for a pair of earrings," said she. "No," he said again, "I cannot do that, and you would not ask me

to if you understood." Still the wife could not stop fretting about the blue stones, and one day, when her husband was with the skippers' corporation, she had a glazier of the town take them out, and put two bits of blue glass into the figurehead instead, and the skipper did not find out, but sailed off to Portugal. But after some time the skipper's wife found that her eyesight was growing bad, and that she could not see to thread a needle. She went to a wise-woman, who gave her ointments and waters, but they did not help her and in the end the old woman shook her head, and told her that this was a rare and incurable disease, and that she was going blind. "Oh, God," the wife then cried, "that the ship was back in the harbor of Elsinore. Then I should have the glass taken out, and the jewels put back. For did he not say that they were my eyes?" But the ship did not come back. Instead the skipper's wife had a letter from the Consul of Portugal, who informed her that she had been wrecked, and gone to the bottom with all hands. And it was a very strange thing, the Consul wrote, that in broad daylight she had run straight into a tall rock, rising out of the sea.

SKILLS FOCUS

Pages 450–451 cover **Literary Skills** Analyze symbolism and allegory.

450 Collection 6 | Symbolism and Allegory • Synthesizing Sources

1. To the skipper the ship's figurehead represents —
   A   freedom
   B   his wife
   C   his success as a captain
   D   ideal feminine beauty

2. On a deeper level, what does the ship's figurehead **symbolize** in the story?
   F   The skipper's love for his wife
   G   The uncertainty of human relationships
   H   The wife's coldness toward her husband
   J   Innocence

3. The **conflict** between the skipper and his wife is caused by the wife's —
   A   sadness and fear
   B   compassion and understanding
   C   worry and loneliness
   D   jealousy and greed

4. In the story the big blue stones are a **symbol** of —
   F   beauty
   G   wealth and power
   H   the wife's eyes
   J   the sea

5. A clue that the stones are a **symbol** is their —
   A   appearance throughout the story
   B   unusual color and shape

C   strange history
D   great value

6. The story suggests that the wife goes blind and the ship sinks because —
   F   the wife steals the figurehead's eyes
   G   the skipper stops loving his wife
   H   the skipper is cursed by the foreign king
   J   the wife is an unlucky woman

7. Part of the appeal of reading "The Blue Stones" is that we realize that beneath the literal story lies —
   A   a comic intent
   B   an unhappy ending
   C   a moral lesson
   D   an allusion to the Bible

8. "The Blue Stones" can be interpreted as an **allegory** warning us about the dangers of —
   F   jealousy and greed
   G   loneliness
   H   unhappy marriages
   J   life at sea

Constructed Response

9. What does the skipper mean when he says, "No, I cannot do that, and you would not ask me to if you understood"? Use details from the story to explain your answer.

Collection 6: Skills Review
Vocabulary Skills

Synonyms

DIRECTIONS: Choose the best synonym for the underlined word in each sentence.

1. Jerry feels <u>contrition</u> at first when he thinks his mother feels abandoned.
   A   worry
   B   anger
   C   regret
   D   sympathy

2. When he asks for swimming goggles, his mother gives him an <u>inquisitive</u> look.
   F   startled
   G   concerned
   H   frightened
   J   curious

3. Jerry times how long he can hold his breath and is <u>incredulous</u> at the results.
   A   disappointed
   B   disbelieving
   C   happy
   D   encouraged

4. The masked ball took place in the elegant <u>imperial</u> suite in Prince Prospero's palace.
   F   majestic
   G   unfinished
   H   colorful
   J   imaginary

5. Prospero thinks of himself as <u>sagacious</u>.
   A   wise
   B   brave

C   cautious
D   cheerful

6. The masked figure had no <u>tangible</u> form.
   F   touchable
   G   recognizable
   H   colorful
   J   remarkable

7. The elderly and the <u>sedate</u> watched the young, lively revelers dance.
   A   quiet
   B   rich
   C   restless
   D   worried

8. The stranger's appearance and actions showed a complete lack of <u>propriety</u>.
   F   refinement
   G   humor
   H   correctness
   J   awkwardness

9. Coming-of-age rituals and traditions are thought to be common to many <u>indigenous</u> cultures.
   A   foreign
   B   native
   C   agricultural
   D   religious

SKILLS FOCUS

Vocabulary Skills
Identify synonyms.

Collection 6: Skills Review

Writing Skills

Test Practice

DIRECTIONS: Read the following paragraph from a draft of a student's analysis of a short story. Then, read the questions below it. Choose the best answer for each question.

(1) In "The Masque of the Red Death," Edgar Allan Poe creates a scene of nightmarish horror through his development of the story's setting. (2) Poe, a master of the Gothic story, is famous for his tales of horror and suspense. (3) He sets his story in a palace remarkable for its bizarre architecture, which gives the place an almost dreamlike quality. (4) The most frightening element of the setting, however, is the black room. (5) In it, "the effect of the firelight that streamed upon the dark hangings through the blood-tinted panes was ghastly in the extreme."

1. Which of the following statements containing direct quotations could be added to support the idea in sentence 3?

A "The 'Red Death' had long devastated the country," and people fled to the palace for protection.

B The main corridor has "a sharp turn at every twenty or thirty yards, and at each turn a novel effect."

C "Prince Prospero was happy and dauntless and sagacious" because he didn't believe that the plague could enter the palace.

D The uninvited guest's "broad brow, with all the features of the face, was besprinkled with the scarlet horror."

2. To elaborate sentence 4, which of the following would work best?

F relate the gruesome symptoms of the "Red Death"

G explain the other frightening elements of the story

H describe how the masked figure looked

J speculate on the symbolism of the black room

3. Which sentence might be added to elaborate the direct quotation in sentence 5?

A The prince provides entertainers to keep his guests happy.

B Prince Prospero becomes angry with the uninvited guest.

C The description of the room foreshadows the horror that follows.

D The party guests grow quiet every time the great clock chimes.

4. Which sentence should be deleted to improve the passage's organization?

F 1 **H** 4
G 2 **J** 5

5. How could a student presenting this passage in an oral response to literature conclude the presentation?

A sum up and show appreciation for the effects created by the setting

B give details on Poe's life, including his childhood and marriage

C restate, word for word, the main idea of the paragraph

D describe how Poe also uses symbolism and tone in all his writings

SKILLS FOCUS

Writing Skills
Write an analysis of a short story.

Collection 7

Poetry

Ink runs from the corners of my mouth.
There is no happiness like mine.
I have been eating poetry.

—Mark Strand

Poppies (late 17th century) by Yun Shouping.
Ink and color on silk.

INTERNET

Collection
Resources

Keyword: LE5 10-7

Elements of Literature

Imagery *by* John Malcolm Brinnin
SEEING WITH OUR MINDS

An **image** is a representation of anything we can see, hear, taste, touch, or smell. A painter or sculptor can create an image of an apple so true to life that we'd like to eat it or feel its weight and roundness in our hands. A poet, using only words, can make us see and feel, taste and smell an apple by describing it as "rosy," "shiny," "heavy," "mushy," "sweet." The language that appeals to our five senses and creates images in our minds is called **imagery.**

Imagery and Feelings

To see how imagery works, look at the two poems about the moon on this page and the next one. The first poem, by John Haines, introduces many variations on the image of the moon. Can you find the image that tells us that the poem was written sometime after 1969, when humans first disturbed the dust of the moon and left their debris on its surface? The second poem, by Emily Dickinson, was written more than a hundred years earlier than Haines's poem.

These two "moon" poems show us something else that imagery can do: The poets, through their evocative imagery, tell us how they *feel* about the moon. Haines's images of the "moon of the poet" are ironic and violent. As we see this moon in our minds, we share his sadness and even his anger over the human capacity for destruction.

Dickinson, on the other hand, uses romantic images that help us see another moon and share other feelings. Her moon is personified as a beautiful woman, even a queen, dressed in all the beauties of the night sky. Images of gold, beryl, dew, amber, silver, trinkets, and dimities help us share her feelings of wonder, admiration, and perhaps playfulness.

Moons

There are moons like continents,
diminishing to a white stone
softly smoking
in a fog-bound ocean.

5 Equinoctial° moons,
immense rainbarrels spilling
their yellow water.

Moons like eyes turned inward,
hard and bulging
10 on the blue cheek of eternity.

And moons half-broken,
eaten by eagle shadows . . .

But the moon of the poet
is soiled and scratched, its seas
15 are flowing with dust.

And other moons are rising,
swollen like boils—

in their bloodshot depths
the warfare of planets
20 silently drips and festers.

—John Haines

---

5. **equinoctial** (ē′kwi·näk′shəl) *adj.:* of the spring and fall equinoxes, when day and night are of equal length.

SKILLS FOCUS

Literary Skills
Understand imagery.

The Moon was but a Chin of Gold

The Moon was but a Chin of Gold
A Night or two ago—
And now she turns Her perfect Face
Upon the World below—

5   Her Forehead is of Amplest Blonde—
Her Cheek—a Beryl° hewn—
Her Eye unto the Summer Dew
The likest I have known—

Her Lips of Amber never part—
10 But what must be the smile
Upon Her Friend she could confer
Were such Her Silver Will—

And what a privilege to be
But the remotest Star—
15 For Certainty She takes Her Way
Beside Your Palace Door—

Her Bonnet is the Firmament°—
The Universe—Her Shoe—
The Stars—the Trinkets at Her Belt—
20 Her Dimities°—of Blue—

—Emily Dickinson

---

6. beryl *n.:* mineral that usually occurs in
crystals of blue, green, pink, or yellow.
17. firmament *n.:* sky.
20. dimities *n.:* dresses made of dimity,
a sheer, cool, cotton material.

Practice

Think of an object or scene (perhaps a snowy winter night or a half-time performance), and then choose a particular **mood** (maybe peacefulness, joy, excitement). Jot down **imagery**—sensory words—that relates to your object or scene and mood. Your notes can be raw material for a poem.

Object or scene:	
Mood:	
Sights:	
Smells:	
Sounds:	
Tastes:	
Touch:	

Thus, images are not made just for the eye. When we read poetry, we must arrive at that point where we can say to the poet not only "I see the picture you are creating" but also "I see what you are feeling. I see what you mean."

Before You Read

A Storm in the Mountains

Make the Connection

Quickwrite ✏️

Nature sometimes reminds us of how fragile we are (consider Jon Krakauer's harrowing experience on Mount Everest—see page 352). Can you think of a time when nature gave you a wake-up call? You might recall an earthquake, a bad storm, a tornado, a flood, or a forest fire. Use a chart like the one below to jot down the key details you remember about your experience with one of nature's dramatic events.

Where I was	
What happened	
What I saw and heard and touched	
What I thought/felt	

Literary Focus

Prose Poems: Prose Form, Poetic Language

The following **prose poem** is written in ordinary paragraph form, yet it uses the elements of poetry—especially very powerful **images** that make the speaker's world easy to see and feel. Like other poems, this prose poem, by a Russian novelist, allows us to enter the speaker's world and make our own meaning of it. After you've read Solzhenitsyn's work twice, read it aloud to yourself. Does it *sound* like a poem? Why?

Celestial Combat by Nikolai Roerich (1874–1947).

SKILLS FOCUS

Literary Skills
Understand characteristics of prose poems.

Russian State Museum, St. Petersburg, Russia.

A Storm in the Mountains

Aleksandr Solzhenitsyn
translated by Michael Glenny

It caught us one pitch-black night at the foot of the pass. We crawled out of our tents and ran for shelter as it came towards us over the ridge.

Everything was black—no peaks, no valleys, no horizon to be seen, only the searing flashes of lightning separating darkness from light, and the gigantic peaks of Belaya-Kaya and Djuguturlyuchat[1] looming up out of the night. The huge black pine trees around us seemed as high as the mountains themselves. For a split second we felt ourselves on terra firma;[2] then once more everything would be plunged into darkness and chaos.

The lightning moved on, brilliant light alternating with pitch blackness, flashing white, then pink, then violet, the mountains and pines always springing back in the same place, their hugeness filling us with awe; yet when they disappeared we could not believe that they had ever existed.

The voice of the thunder filled the gorge, drowning the ceaseless roar of the rivers. Like the arrows of Sabaoth,[3] the lightning flashes rained down on the peaks, then split up into serpentine streams as though bursting into spray against the rock face, or striking and then shattering like a living thing.

As for us, we forgot to be afraid of the lightning, the thunder, and the downpour, just as a droplet in the ocean has no fear of a hurricane. Insignificant yet grateful, we became part of this world—a primal world in creation before our eyes. ■

---

1. **Belaya-Kaya** (bye·lī′ə kī′ə) **and Djuguturlyuchat** (djo͞o·go͞o·to͞or·lyo͞o′chət): two mountains in Russia.
2. **terra firma** (ter′ə fur′mə): Latin expression meaning "solid ground."

---

3. **Sabaoth** (sab′ā·äth′): biblical term meaning "armies."

Meet the Writer

Aleksandr Solzhenitsyn

Russia's Nobel Laureate

Aleksandr Solzhenitsyn (sōl′zhə·nēt′sin) (1918–   ) spent many years in Soviet prisons. Solzhenitsyn catapulted to fame with the publication of his first novel, *One Day in the Life of Ivan Denisovich* (1962), which details the daily life of a political prisoner. Solzhenitsyn wrote from firsthand knowledge: In 1945, he was arrested for criticizing the Soviet leader Joseph Stalin and sentenced to eight years in prison and labor camps plus three years in exile. After his release he taught math-ematics and physics and continued writing. After the publication of *The Gulag Archipelago* (1974), he was exiled from Russia. In 1976, Solzhenitsyn and his wife settled quietly in Vermont, where he continued to write and publish novels about Soviet life under the Communist regime.

In his acceptance speech for the 1970 Nobel Prize in literature, Solzhenitsyn commented on the relationship between life and literature:

“The sole substitute for an experience which we have not ourselves lived through is art and literature. ”

In 1994, with the cold war over and Russia's Communist regime out of power, Solzhenitsyn and his wife returned at last to their homeland.

Response and Analysis

Reading Check

1. Fill out a chart like the one in the Quickwrite on page 458. Base it on the experience Solzhenitsyn describes.

Thinking Critically

2. What makes this description a **prose poem** rather than a news report—or some other kind of writing? Cite details from the poem.

3. Writers frequently use **allusions,** or references, to compare one thing to something else. What allusion to the Bible does Solzhenitsyn use to help us see the lightning as he saw it?

4. What **comparison** does Solzhenitsyn use to explain why he felt no fear?

5. What meaning or lesson does Solzhenitsyn draw from his experience? What other experience might also make a person feel "part of this world"?

WRITING

An Encounter with Nature

Write a **prose poem** in which you describe the experience you recalled in your Quickwrite notes. Use images to help your readers share your experience. What meaning did you find in your encounter?

Before You Read

Same Song

Make the Connection

Quickwrite ✏️

What are some of the things that high school students do to "look good"? How do they figure out what "looking good" should look like? How important is "looking good" anyway? Jot down your ideas.

Literary Focus

Imagery: Words You Can See, Hear, Smell, Taste, and Touch

Imagery is language that appeals to the five senses. An **image** helps us re-create a person, a scene, or an object in our imaginations. When you hear the words "red wheelbarrow," for example, you form a picture in your mind's eye.

In this poem the speaker makes an **allusion,** or reference, to a classic fairy tale. If you recognize the allusion, be aware of the image it instantly forms in your mind.

SKILLS FOCUS

Literary Skills
Understand imagery and allusion.

Same Song

Pat Mora

While my sixteen-year-old son sleeps,
my twelve-year-old daughter
stumbles into the bathroom at six a.m.
plugs in the curling iron
5   squeezes into faded jeans
curls her hair carefully
strokes Aztec Blue shadow on her eyelids
smooths Frosted Mauve blusher on her cheeks
outlines her mouth in Neon Pink
10 peers into the mirror, mirror on the wall
frowns at her face, her eyes, her skin,
not fair.

At night this daughter
stumbles off to bed at nine
15 eyes half-shut while my son
jogs a mile in the cold dark
then lifts weights in the garage
curls and bench presses
expanding biceps, triceps, pectorals,
20 one-handed push-ups, one hundred sit-ups
peers into that mirror, mirror and frowns too.

for Libby

Meet the Writer

Pat Mora

"Am I Lucky!"

If Pat Mora (1942–   ) has her way, every April 30 will be *Día de los niños/Día de los libros* (Children's Day/Book Day), a national celebration of language and literacy. Mora wants to bring to all children the power and pleasure of what she calls "bookjoy."

❝ I was born in El Paso, Texas, and grew up in a bilingual home where books were an important part of my life. I can speak and write in both English and Spanish— am I lucky! I've always enjoyed reading all kinds of books and now I get to write them too—to sit and play with words on my computer. **❞**

After receiving her master's degree from the University of Texas in El Paso, Mora taught in public schools and college. Her poetry has been collected in several volumes, including *Chants* (1984) and *Borders* (1986). Mora has also written *House of Houses* (1997), a memoir about her Mexican American ancestors, and she has written many children's books.

Response and Analysis

Reading Check

1. Identify the speaker in the poem, and briefly describe the subject.

2. What purpose does the stanza break serve?

Thinking Critically

3. What does the poem's **title** mean?

4. What **images** does Mora use to help you visualize the speaker's daughter?

5. What **images** help you see what the son is doing?

6. What old fairy tale is the poem **alluding,** or referring, to in lines 10 and 21? What **image** does this reference put in your mind? (Is it a pleasant or unpleasant image?)

7. How do the son and daughter feel about the way they look? What word gives you a clue?

8. How do you interpret line 12—"not fair"? What two meanings could the word *fair* have here?

9. What **theme,** or message, do you think the poem conveys? Is that message true only for young people? Explain your responses.

WRITING

Beautiful and Handsome— Who Decides?

Where, in your opinion, do women and men in our society get the standards for the way they think they should look? (Review your Quickwrite notes.) Write a brief **essay** giving your **opinion** on this question. Support your opinions with details, examples, or anecdotes from your own experience.

> ▶ Use "Writing a Persuasive Essay," pages 294–301, for help with this assignment.

Before You Read

Eating Together
Grape Sherbet

Make the Connection

If you were asked to name one food you associate with your family or with your childhood, what would it be? Jot down some notes.

Literary Focus

The Speaker in the Poem

The **speaker** in a poem is the voice that talks directly to us. It's a mistake to think that the writer and the speaker are always the same person. Sometimes we feel confident that the speaker is the poet. Often, however, the speaker is almost anyone (or anything) else—a fictional character, an animal, or even an object.

The choice of a speaker affects a poem's **tone,** the attitude expressed toward its subject or audience. The speaker's tone and his or her style of speaking create the speaker's **voice.**

go.hrw.com

INTERNET

More About
Li-Young Lee
•
More About
Rita Dove

Keyword: LE5 10-7

SKILLS FOCUS

Literary Skills
Identify a poem's speaker.

The Meal or *The Bananas* (1891) by Paul Gauguin.

© Réunion des Musées Nationaux/Art Resource, New York.

Eating Together
Li-Young Lee

In the steamer is the trout
seasoned with slivers of ginger,
two sprigs of green onion, and sesame oil.
We shall eat it with rice for lunch,
5   brothers, sister, my mother who will
taste the sweetest meat of the head,
holding it between her fingers
deftly, the way my father did
weeks ago. Then he lay down
10   to sleep like a snow-covered road
winding through pines older than him,
without any travelers, and lonely for no one.

Meet the Writer

Li-Young Lee

"A Guest in the Language"

For Li-Young Lee (1957–   ), like many Americans, English is a second language; Chinese is his first.

❝I'm highly aware that I'm a guest in the language. I'm wondering if that's not the truth for all of us, that somehow we're all guests in language, that once we start speaking any language somehow we bow to that language at the same time we bend that language to us. ❞

Li-Young Lee was born in Jakarta, Indonesia, of Chinese parents who were political refugees. His father spent nineteen months in an Indonesian jail as a political prisoner. The family later fled to Hong Kong, Macau, and Japan. Lee was six years old when his family arrived in the United States. He grew up in a small town in western Pennsylvania, where his father was the Presbyterian minister. He remembers his father teaching him how to read from the Bible.

❝On Sundays, if we weren't making rounds, we were at home observing silence. At least twice a week, our family kept a whole afternoon of quiet, neither speaking nor whispering, my father, my mother, my sister, three brothers, and I

keeping everything to ourselves in the one house of three floors of square rooms and identical doors. It was clarifying, the quiet, and our stillness felt like a deep liberty. It was one more detail of my life with my father which made me feel strange in a world which found my family strange, with our accented speech and permanent bewilderment at meatloaf. ❞

Ever since the publication of his first two books of poetry, *Rose* (1986) and *The City in Which I Love You* (1990), Lee has been widely acclaimed as a major new voice in American poetry. The poet Garrett Hongo (see page 475) calls Lee's poetic memoir, *The Winged Seed* (1995), "a memory palace of exile . . . and retribution."

Grape Sherbet
Rita Dove

The day? Memorial.
After the grill
Dad appears with his masterpiece—
swirled snow, gelled light.
5   We cheer. The recipe's
a secret and he fights
a smile, his cap turned up
so the bib resembles a duck.

That morning we galloped
10 through the grassed-over mounds
and named each stone
for a lost milk tooth. Each dollop
of sherbet, later,
is a miracle,
15 like salt on a melon that makes it sweeter.

Everyone agrees—it's wonderful!
It's just how we imagined lavender
would taste. The diabetic grandmother
stares from the porch,
20 a torch
of pure refusal.

We thought no one was lying
there under our feet,
we thought it
25 was a joke. I've been trying
to remember the taste,
but it doesn't exist.
Now I see why
you bothered,
30 father.

Spending Time by Jessie Coates (1950–   ).

Meet the Writer

Rita Dove

"I Know What You Meant . . . I Felt That Too"

Rita Dove (1952–   ), an avid reader, remembers that when she was growing up—in Akron, Ohio—there was a feeling in the household "that the only ticket you have to a happy life is to do the best you can in whatever you do. And the one place we were allowed to go practically any time was the library, but we had to read all the books that we got. . . ." In 1970, Rita Dove was a Presidential Scholar, one of the top one hundred high school seniors in the nation.

" I know that every time that I write a poem . . . I try to remember or try to imagine that reader—the reader that I was—curled up on the couch, the moment of opening a book and absolutely having my world fall away and entering into another one and feeling there was one other voice that was almost inside of me, we were so close. In writing a poem, if the reader on the other end can come up and say: 'I know what you meant, I mean, I felt that too'—then we are a little less alone in the world, and that to me is worth an awful lot. "

Rita Dove is the youngest person and the first African American to serve as poet laureate of the United States (1993–1995). She is now professor of English at the University of Virginia in Charlottesville.

Response and Analysis

Eating Together

Reading Check

1. Who is the **speaker** of this poem? Identify the other family members who are mentioned. What are they eating?

Thinking Critically

2. A **simile** is a figure of speech that compares two unlike things using a specific word of comparison, such as *like, as,* or *resembles.* What simile tells you what has happened to the father?

3. What is the **tone** of this poem—the feeling or attitude the **speaker** takes toward the events he describes? What details especially suggest that tone to you?

Grape Sherbet

Reading Check

1. Who is the **speaker** of "Grape Sherbet"? What details does the speaker remember about a family get-together on a Memorial Day in the past?

2. What are the speaker and the other children doing in lines 9–10?

Thinking Critically

3. A **metaphor** is a figure of speech that compares two unlike things. Unlike a simile, however, a metaphor makes the comparison without using a specific word of comparison. What metaphor describes the grandmother, in lines 18–21? What is she refusing?

4. What is the "joke" in line 25?

5. Why does the taste of the sherbet no longer exist (lines 25–27)?

Plate with Grapes and Peach (c. mid-1870s) by Paul Cezanne.

© The Barnes Foundation, Merion Station, Pennsylvania/CORBIS.

6. What does the **speaker** mean when she says, "Now I see why you bothered, father"? What **tone** do you hear in this poem—what feeling does the speaker reveal toward this family memory?

WRITING

Comparing Memories

In an essay, **compare and contrast** Li-Young Lee's poem with Rita Dove's. Before you write, gather your details in a chart like the following one:

	Li-Young Lee	Rita Dove
Speaker		
Speaker's memory		
Setting		
Food		
Tone		
Message		

SKILLS FOCUS

Literary Skills
Identify and analyze a poem's speaker.

Writing Skills
Write an essay comparing and contrasting two poems.

The Legend

Make the Connection

Quickwrite ✏️

What news story have you heard or seen lately that struck you as especially moving or inspiring or sad? Maybe it was a story buried on the newspaper's back page; maybe it was a front-page story or one that led the evening news on TV. Maybe the victim is someone you would like to memorialize. Whatever the story was, make a few notes about it. When you finish reading the poem and the **Connection** that follows, see whether you can use this incident as the basis of a poem of your own.

Literary Focus

Tone: An Attitude

When someone says, "I don't like your tone of voice," you know that person is complaining about your attitude. In the same way, **tone** in writing is the attitude the writer takes toward a subject, a character, or the reader. Tone may be sympathetic or critical, humorous or sarcastic, ironic or sentimental, bitter or sad—or any one of dozens of different feelings. In speech, tone is identified by voice. In writing, tone must be inferred from word choice, or **diction.**

Background

One night, Garrett Hongo saw a TV news story about an Asian man who had been killed in an act of street violence. Much later, Hongo claims, this poem "just appeared."

SKILLS FOCUS

Literary Skills
Understand tone.

Portrait of an Old Man (c. 1652–1654) by Rembrandt.
Oil on canvas (108 cm × 86 cm).

The Legend

Garrett Hongo

In Chicago, it is snowing softly
and a man has just done his wash for the week.
He steps into the twilight of early evening,
carrying a wrinkled shopping bag
5   full of neatly folded clothes,
and, for a moment, enjoys
the feel of warm laundry and crinkled paper,

flannellike against his gloveless hands.
There's a Rembrandt° glow on his face,
10 a triangle of orange in the hollow of his cheek
as a last flash of sunset
blazes the storefronts and lit windows of the street.

He is Asian, Thai or Vietnamese,
and very skinny, dressed as one of the poor
15 in rumpled suit pants and a plaid mackinaw,°
dingy and too large.
He negotiates the slick of ice
on the sidewalk by his car,
opens the Fairlane's back door,
20 leans to place the laundry in,
and turns, for an instant,
toward the flurry of footsteps
and cries of pedestrians
as a boy—that's all he was—
25 backs from the corner package store°
shooting a pistol, firing it,
once, at the dumbfounded man
who falls forward,
grabbing at his chest.

30 A few sounds escape from his mouth,
a babbling no one understands
as people surround him
bewildered at his speech.
The noises he makes are nothing to them.
35 The boy has gone, lost
in the light array of foot traffic
dappling the snow with fresh prints.
Tonight, I read about Descartes'
grand courage to doubt everything
40 except his own miraculous existence°
and I feel so distinct
from the wounded man lying on the concrete
I am ashamed.

Let the night sky cover him as he dies.
45 Let the weaver girl cross the bridge of heaven
and take up his cold hands.

IN MEMORY OF JAY KASHIWAMURA

9. Rembrandt: Dutch painter (1606–1669), famous for his dramatic use of color and of light and shadow. (See the painting by Rembrandt on page 472.)

15. mackinaw *n.*: short, double-breasted coat made of heavy woolen cloth, usually plaid.

25. package store: retail store where alcohol is sold.

38–40. Descartes' . . . existence: René Descartes (1596–1650), a French philosopher and mathematician, attempted to explain the universe by reason alone. In his search for truth, he discarded all traditional ideas and doubted everything. The one thing he could not doubt was the fact that he was doubting, which led him to conclude, "I think; therefore I am" (in Latin, *Cogito, ergo sum*).

Hongo Reflects on "The Legend"

When he was asked about "The Legend," here is what Hongo answered:

What I wanted, the city could not give me. I wanted *mercy*. I wanted the universe to bend down and kiss its own creation, like a parent does to a child just after it's born, as if a tenderness were the pure expression of the world for itself. I wanted to believe that what was not given could be given, that were a man or a woman to cry out for solace, that the world, for all of its steel plants and tire factories, for all of its liquor stores and razor wire, for all of its buses that belched carcinogenic poisons and people who passed you by on the freeway who cursed you with their eyes—for all of that, it would still lay its soft wings of blessing upon you if you cried out in need.

From time to time, I'd recollect a story I'd heard during childhood, probably in Hawaii, a legend about the creation of the universe. From an aunt baking *pan dulce*[1] or a cousin flinging stones with me into waves along Hau'ula Beach, into abandoned canefields or at the headboards of the Japanese graves on the promontory at the Kahuku plantation, I'd heard that, in order for the stars to turn and remain where they were, it took two creatures and their sacrifice. It took a Weaver Maid to make the stars—Being—and a Herd Boy to make sure they all stayed together or apart as they should. The Weaver Maid and the Herd Boy lived on opposite sides of the Milky Way, that band of stars that is our galaxy and which Asians see as a mighty river of stars. They call it The River of Heaven. The Herd Boy and Weaver Maid are stars on its opposite banks, the one in a cluster around Antares,[2] the other far away and down along the flow, in a spot near Aldebaran.[3] They labor, dutifully fabricating the web and warp of Being, herding the star bands in an eternal solitude, celibate, without love or companionship. Yet, for one night of the year, on an evening when the star sky is said to be clearest, the universe is supposed to succumb to an overwhelming pity for the two lovers, living out lives in exile from each other, lives in deprivation of passion, without emotional compass or root in material certainties. In the form of a flock of compassionate starlings or swallows in the

---

1. *pan dulce* (pän' dōōl'sā): sweet bread.

2. **Antares** (an · ter'ēz'): brightest star in the constellation Scorpius. Its name derives from the Greek for "rival of Ares" (Mars).
3. **Aldebaran** (al·deb'ə·rən): brightest star in the constellation Taurus.

Japanese or Chinese versions, in the folded and gigantic wing of Crow in the Tlingit and Haida versions of the North Coast Pacific Indians, the universe, *one turning*, responds by making a footbridge across the River of Heaven out of its own interlocking bodies, out of its own need to create mercy and requital in a night of love for the effortful sacrifices of two of its children.

It is a vision of the afterlife, in a sense, a promise that the world will provide for us a reward and a reason for our struggles. It is a parable[4] about mercy and fulfillment, the response of the universe to needs of the human heart. The poem is the story of the Weaver Girl and the Herd Boy, told in inner-city, contemporary terms. It is about my own needs for mercy, for a fulfillment to a broad, urban, and contemporary story that baffled me.

---

4. **parable** (par′ə·bəl) *n.:* brief story that teaches a moral or religious lesson.

Garrett Hongo

Looking for Mercy

Garrett Hongo (1951–   ) was born in Volcano, Hawaii, and grew up in Hawaii and Los Angeles. After graduating, with honors, from Pomona College, he toured Japan for a year and then returned to the United States to write and teach poetry. Hongo says he writes

“for my father in a very personal way. He was a great example to me of a man who refused to hate or, being different himself, to be afraid of difference. . . . I want my poems to be equal to his heart. ”

Response and Analysis

Reading Check

1. Describe the poem's **setting,** or time and place.

2. In this poem an ordinary street scene is suddenly transformed by a tragic event. What happens?

Thinking Critically

3. Why do you suppose the speaker in the poem says he feels ashamed? (Re-read lines 38–43.)

4. Read Hongo's explanation of how he came to write "The Legend" (see the **Connection** on page 474). How do lines 38–46 of the poem relate to the legend and to the death?

5. What **images** does Hongo use to help you feel as if you were an eye-witness to the setting, the characters, and the event (lines 1–37)?

6. How would you describe the poem's **tone?** In other words, what is the poet's attitude toward the event he's made into a poem? List some of the details and words the poet uses to create the tone.

WRITING

News Stories Are True Poems

"The true poem is the daily paper," wrote Walt Whitman in 1852. Write a **poem** that is based on a newspaper story or a television news report. (Check your Quickwrite notes.) Follow Hongo's pattern in "The Legend": Begin with a close observation of the scene, and focus on one or more unnamed characters. Then, tell what happens, using present-tense verbs. End your poem with a comment on your own feelings and thoughts about the event. Use your imagination to elaborate with **sensory images.** You might want to

gather notes in a chart like the one below before you write your poem.

News story that poem will be about:
Description of scene:
Character(s):
What happened:
Important sensory images:
My thoughts and feelings about the event:

A Letter to the Writer

In his reflection on the poem (see the **Connection** on page 474), Garrett Hongo expresses a hope that the world will lay its soft wings of mercy upon him if he cries out in need. Write a **letter** to the poet responding to his comment. Tell him of an incident in which the world did "have mercy" on someone in need.

Elements of Literature

Figurative Language *by* John Malcolm Brinnin

LANGUAGE OF THE IMAGINATION

Long before people began to communicate through writing, they uttered combinations of words having the sound of poetry. Yet after thousands of years no one has produced a single definition of poetry that takes into account all the ways in which poetry makes itself heard.

Yet we all know poetry when we hear it—whether it's a passage from the Bible, the chorus of a song, or a striking phrase heard on a city street. Poetry is different from the plain prose we speak and from the flat language of a business report.

Speaking Figuratively

One of the elements that make poetry is **figurative language**—language based on some sort of **comparison** that is not literally true. Such language is so natural to us that we use it every day. Let's say you read this in the newspaper:

The Budget Committee hammered at the Treasury secretary for three hours.

You don't ask in horror, "Will they be charged with murder?" You understand immediately from the context that the writer is speaking figuratively. A **figure of speech** is language in which one thing (here, the continual questioning) is compared to something that seems to be entirely different (repeated blows with a hammer). A figure of speech is never literally true, but a good one always suggests a powerful truth to our imaginations.

Stated Likenesses: Similes

A **simile** is a figure of speech that uses the word *like, as, than,* or *resembles* to compare things that seem to have little or nothing in common. In a literal comparison, we might say, "His face was as red as his father's." But when we use a simile, the comparison becomes more striking and imaginative: "His face was as red as a ripe tomato," or "His face was like a stoplight."

Similes are part of every poet's equipment. In a good simile the comparison is unexpected but entirely reasonable. The English poet William Wordsworth opens a poem with this now-famous simile:

I wandered lonely as a cloud. . . .

This simile helps us see at once that the wandering speaker has no more sense of purpose than a cloud driven by the wind.

"Remorse sits in my stomach like a piece of stale bread. How does that sound?"

(continued)

SKILLS FOCUS

Literary Skills
Understand figurative language, including simile, metaphor, and personification.

Making Identifications: Metaphors

A **metaphor** is another kind of comparison between unlike things, one in which some reasonable connection is instantly revealed. A metaphor is a more forceful version of a simile because the connective *like, as, resembles,* or *than* is not used. A **direct metaphor** says that something *is* something else: not "I wandered lonely as a cloud" but "I was a lonely cloud."

Metaphors, in fact, are basic to everyday conversation because they allow us to speak in a kind of imaginative shorthand. Suppose a man enters a diner and asks for two scrambled eggs on an English muffin. The waiter might call to the kitchen, "Two wrecks on a raft!" The waiter is using an **implied metaphor.**

Many of the metaphors we use in conversation are implied: "the long arm of the law," "this neck of the woods," "the foot of the mountain." All these metaphors suggest comparisons between parts of the body and things quite different from the body. Even single words can contain implied metaphors: "She *barked* her command" compares human speech to the sound a dog makes.

Metaphors in poetry can be startling. Here is how the American poet Robert Lowell uses metaphor to describe a construction site in Boston in a poem called "For the Union Dead":

> Behind their cage,
> yellow dinosaur steamshovels were
>   grunting
> as they cropped up tons of mush
>   and grass
> to gouge their underworld garage.

Metaphors are often **extended** over several lines of a poem and taken as far as they can logically go.

Humanizing the World: Personification

When we attribute human qualities to a nonhuman thing or to an abstract idea, we are using **personification.** We call computers "user-friendly," for example, or say that "misery loves company" or that "the future beckons." Personification is widely used by cartoonists, especially political cartoonists. You've probably seen justice personified as a blindfolded woman carrying scales and love personified as a chubby infant with a bow and arrow.

In poetry, figurative language is the most important means of imaginative expression. It is a tool that poets have used through the centuries to translate the experiences of their times into personal statements.

Practice

Turn up your imagination as you think about common objects, people, and places. Using each of the subjects listed below, write a **figure of speech**—a **simile,** a **metaphor,** or an instance of **personification.** Then, pick at least one subject of your own, and do the same. Here's an example: "The computer monitor stared back at her like an unfriendly, unblinking eye."

1. backpack
2. toaster
3. quarterback
4. drummer
5. schoolyard
6. beach

Simile

Make the Connection

Quickwrite ✏️

How do you feel after you've had a serious argument with someone you love? What images or figures of speech can you think of to describe your feelings? Jot down whatever words and phrases come to mind, and keep your notes.

Literary Focus

Simile: Extending the Comparison

A **simile** is a **figure of speech** that compares two unlike things by using a connecting word, such as *like, as, than,* or *resembles.* If you provide the missing words in the blanks below, you'll have four similes so overused that they're clichés: as quiet as a _____; like peas in a _____; as busy as a _____; as cold as _____. Poets hate clichés (you should too). They try to invent imaginative similes that no one's ever thought of before.

An **extended simile** continues the comparison for several lines or even through an entire poem.

SKILLS FOCUS

Literary Skills
Understand simile.

Simile

N. Scott Momaday

What did we say to each other
that now we are as the deer
who walk in single file
with heads high
with ears forward
with eyes watchful
with hooves always placed on firm ground
in whose limbs there is latent flight

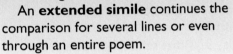

Meet the Writer

N. Scott Momaday

Rock-Tree Boy

When N. Scott Momaday (1934–   ) was six months old, his parents took him to a sacred place—Devils Tower in Wyoming, which the Kiowa people call Tsoai (Rock Tree). There an old storyteller gave Momaday the name Tsoai-talee, which means "Rock-Tree Boy." (Devils Tower looks like a steep-sided volcanic rock tower—it is 865 feet high.)

Momaday says that schooling was a problem at Jemez, in New Mexico, where he grew up, because there were no high schools nearby. He recalled his mother's influence:

66 My mother has been the inspiration of many people . . . certainly she was mine at Jemez, when inspiration was the nourishment I needed most. I was at that age in which a boy flounders. I had not much sense of where I must go or of what I must do and be in my life, and there were for me moments of great, growing urgency, in which I felt that I was imprisoned in the narrow quarters of my time and place. I wanted, needed, to conceive of what my destiny might be, and my mother allowed me to believe that it might be worthwhile. 99

Momaday received his bachelor's degree from the University of New Mexico and his doctorate in English from Stanford University. While teaching at several universities, he has created novels, memoirs, poems, and paintings that draw upon his American Indian heritage.

For Independent Reading

House Made of Dawn (1968), Momaday's first novel, won the Pulitzer Prize in fiction. His memoir *The Way to Rainy Mountain* (1969) combines Kiowa legend, history, personal memories, and poetry.

Response and Analysis

Thinking Critically

1. Whom is the **speaker** addressing? Before the poem begins, what has happened?

2. In the poem's **extended simile,** in what specific ways are the speaker and the person he or she is addressing like the deer?

3. What do you think is the special significance of the last line? (What is "latent flight"?)

WRITING

"We Are Like . . ."

When two people who loved each other walk away from each other, what do they remind you of? You might think of something from the animal, vegetable, or mineral worlds. Write a poem in which you extend your comparison for at least three lines. (Check your Quickwrite notes.) ✏

Comparing Similes

The poem below is by another American poet, Amy Lowell. Read the poem carefully, and then write a paragraph in which you **compare** this poem to Momaday's "Simile." First, summarize the text of each poem. Then, explain the terms of the comparison in the simile in each poem. Finally, tell which **simile** you think more powerfully describes the separation of lovers.

The Taxi

Amy Lowell

When I go away from you
The world beats dead
Like a slackened drum.
I call out for you against the jutted stars
5   And shout into the ridges of the wind.
Streets coming fast,
One after the other,
Wedge you away from me,
And the lamps of the city prick my eyes
10 So that I can no longer see your face.
Why should I leave you,
To wound myself upon the sharp edges
   of the night?

Literary Skills
Analyze simile.

Writing Skills
Write a poem containing an extended simile. Write a paragraph comparing two poems.

Before You Read

I Am Offering This Poem

Make the Connection

Quickwrite ✏

Suppose someone says to you, "I have nothing to give you—except love." How would you feel? Is love enough? Jot down your ideas, and save your notes.

Literary Focus

Lyric Poetry: Singing Your Feelings

Lyric poetry owes its name to the ancient Greeks, who used the word *lyrikos* to refer to brief poems they sang to the accompaniment of the lyre, a stringed instrument. Today most lyrics are short, and they are still musical. Unlike a narrative poem, which tells a story, a lyric poem uses language to suggest (rather than state directly) a single, strong emotion. Most of the poems in this chapter are lyric poems.

SKILLS FOCUS

Literary Skills
Understand characteristics of lyric poetry.

I Am Offering This Poem

Jimmy Santiago Baca

I am offering this poem to you,
since I have nothing else to give.
Keep it like a warm coat
when winter comes to cover you,
5 or like a pair of thick socks
the cold cannot bite through,

      I love you,

I have nothing else to give you,
so it is a pot full of yellow corn
10 to warm your belly in winter,
it is a scarf for your head, to wear
over your hair, to tie up around your face,

      I love you,

Keep it, treasure this as you would
15 if you were lost, needing direction,
in the wilderness life becomes when mature;
and in the corner of your drawer,
tucked away like a cabin or hogan
in dense trees, come knocking,
20 and I will answer, give you directions,
and let you warm yourself by this fire,
rest by this fire, and make you feel safe,

      I love you,

It's all I have to give,
25 and all anyone needs to live,
and to go on living inside,
when the world outside
no longer cares if you live or die;
remember,

30   I love you.

Meet the Writer

Jimmy Santiago Baca

To Prove That He Exists

Jimmy Santiago Baca (1952–   ) says he began to write so the world would know he existed. Born in New Mexico of Mexican American and Apache ancestry, he was abandoned by his parents when he was two. Baca's grandmother took care of him until he was sent to an orphanage at five. At eleven he ran away, living on the streets until he landed in prison at eighteen for possessing drugs. In prison, Baca felt sure he was going to die:

> 66 And I had to tell somebody that I was here. . . . It's unthinkable to come to a universe, to live as a human being, and then to die and not have anyone ever know you were there. 99

Baca taught himself to read and write in prison. He also began to keep a journal and eventually attended a poetry workshop. Then he "took a wild chance." He sent some poems to a magazine, and the magazine published them. Five books of poetry followed, along with essays, a screenplay, and a novel. Today Baca lives with his wife and sons in an old adobe house south of Albuquerque.

Before You Read

since feeling is first

Make the Connection

Feeling Your Way

At first sight this poem might look difficult. Its lines break at unusual places; there is no capitalization; the punctuation isn't standard; and words are used in odd ways. If you read the poem silently a couple of times, however, and then read it aloud, you'll quickly "own" it—you'll be able to say, "I see what you mean. I understand how you feel."

Literary Focus

Metaphors: Grammar and Love

Lovers cannot bear to think of their love ending or of death separating them. Here a poet sings of love and puts down death, in two metaphors that only a writer would think of.

Like a simile, a **metaphor** is a surprising comparison between two unlike things, but a metaphor is more direct than a simile—it states that something *is* something else.

Lovers (1929) by Marc Chagall. Oil on canvas.

Literary Skills
Understand metaphor.

since feeling is first

E. E. Cummings

since feeling is first
who pays any attention
to the syntax° of things
will never wholly kiss you;

5   wholly to be a fool
while Spring is in the world

my blood approves,
and kisses are a better fate
than wisdom
10   lady i swear by all flowers. Don't cry
—the best gesture of my brain is less than
your eyelids' flutter which says

we are for each other:then
laugh,leaning back in my arms
15   for life's not a paragraph

And death i think is no parenthesis

---

3. syntax (sin′taks′)*n.:* arrangement of words, phrases, and clauses in sentences; here, a systematic, orderly arrangement.

Meet the Writer

E. E. Cummings

"Nobody Else Can Be Alive for You"

E. E. (Edward Estlin) Cummings (1894–1962) was born in Cambridge, Massachusetts. This son of a Unitarian minister grew up "only a butterfly's glide" from Harvard and "attended four Cambridge schools: the first, private—where everybody was extraordinarily kind; and where (in addition to learning nothing) I burst into tears and nosebleeds—the other three, public; where I flourished like the wicked and learned what the wicked learn, and where almost nobody cared about somebody else."

After graduating from Harvard, Cummings joined a volunteer U.S. ambulance corps in France. (The United States had not yet entered World War I.) A French censor decided that one of Cummings's odd-looking letters home was suspicious. So Cummings was arrested as a spy and held for three months in a prison camp, an experience he wrote about in a novel he called *The Enormous Room* (1922).

In his poetry, Cummings liked to use lowercase letters, space his words oddly across the page, and punctuate in his own style, although those oddities are only typographical. His themes are familiar: the joy, wonder, and mystery of life and the miracle of individual identity. He once advised young poets to be themselves:

> 66 . . . remember one thing only: that it's you—nobody else—who determines your destiny and decides your fate. Nobody else can be alive for you; nor can you be alive for anybody else. 99

Response and Analysis

I Am Offering This Poem

Reading Check

1. Why is the speaker offering this poem? To whom is he offering it?

2. What **refrain** does Baca keep repeating?

Thinking Critically

3. Throughout his poem, what **figures of speech** does Baca use to suggest what his love will do for the person he is addressing?

4. The speaker says that love is "all anyone needs to live." Another American poet, Edna St. Vincent Millay, has a poem that opens, "Love is not all; It is not meat nor drink / Nor slumber nor a roof against the rain. . . ." How do you feel about these two assessments of the importance of love? (Before you answer, check your Quickwrite notes.) ✏

5. When we talk of "love poems," we usually think of romantic love. Could Baca's **lyric poem** be addressed to a child? to a good friend? to a parent? to anyone else? Discuss your responses.

since feeling is first

Reading Check

1. Divide this poem into sentences that express complete thoughts. Where does each sentence begin and end?

2. According to the speaker of this poem, what is better than wisdom?

3. In lines 10–12, how does the speaker again contrast thinking with feeling?

Thinking Critically

4. In his **lyric poem,** Cummings expresses his feelings about love and death in two powerful **metaphors.** What are they, and how would you explain the comparisons they are based on?

5. Notice the **opposites** Cummings uses. A person who pays attention to the "syntax of things" (lines 2–3) is contrasted with someone who is "wholly . . . a fool" (line 5). What opposites does he pose to wisdom (line 9), the brain (line 11), and life (line 15)? In each case, which of the opposites does the speaker choose?

WRITING

Twin Poems—Similar, Not Identical

In an essay, **compare and contrast** Baca's and Cummings's lyrics. For help finding the points of comparison between the poems, fill out a chart like the one below. At the end of your analysis, tell which of these love poems you would like to receive and why.

	Baca	Cummings
Speaker		
Person addressed		
Figures of speech		
Message		
Speaker's feelings		

Heart! We will forget him!

Make the Connection

Trying to Forget

In this poem, Emily Dickinson tells the old, sad story of unrequited love—of love that is not returned. The poem is about conflict between will and emotion, between the thinking mind and the feeling heart.

Which do you think is more powerful—the mind or the heart? Does one control the other, or are they completely separate systems?

Literary Focus

Personification

Personification is a kind of metaphor in which a nonhuman thing or quality is talked about as if it were human. In "Heart! We will forget him!" Emily Dickinson addresses her heart as if it were a person who can listen, act, and feel.

SKILLS FOCUS

Literary Skills
Understand personification.

Heart! We will forget him!

Emily Dickinson

Heart! We will forget him!
You and I— tonight!
You may forget the warmth he gave—
I will forget the light!

When you have done, pray tell me
That I may straight begin!
Haste! lest while you're lagging
I remember him!

Elvira Sitting at a Table (1919)
by Amedeo Modigliani.

© Francis G. Mayer/CORBIS.

Meet the Writer

Emily Dickinson

Shy Genius

Emily Dickinson (1830–1886) rarely left Amherst, Massachusetts, her birthplace. There she lived unknown as a poet except to her family and a few friends, and there she produced almost eighteen hundred exquisite short poems that are now regarded as one of the great expressions of American genius.

She was the bright daughter of a well-to-do religious family; her father was a lawyer. As a girl at boarding school, she seemed high-spirited and happy. But something happened when she was a young woman (a love that was not, could not be requited, biographers speculate), and at thirty-one, she simply withdrew from the world. She dressed all in white, refused to leave her home or meet strangers, and devoted her life to her family—and to writing poetry. Of her own poetry, she wrote,

66 This is my letter to the World / That never wrote to Me. . . . 99

She wrote her poems on little pieces of paper, tied them in neat packets, and occasionally gave them to relatives as valentine or birthday greetings or attached them to gifts of cookies or pies. In 1862, she sent four poems to the editor of *The Atlantic Monthly.* Only seven of her poems were published (anonymously) during her lifetime. When she died, at age fifty-six, she had no notion that one day she would be honored as one of America's greatest poets.

Emily Dickinson (1848). Oil over a photograph.

The Granger Collection, New York.

Three Japanese Tankas

Make the Connection

Quickwrite ✏️

A loves B more than B loves A; B used to love A but feared rejection and has decided to snub A. If you think you hear a lot of that kind of gossip in your cafeteria, take a look at love in Japan more than a thousand years ago. Jot down notes to fill out these metaphorical equations: Love is . . . Life is . . .

Literary Focus

Tanka Structure

The **tanka,** a Japanese poetic form, dates back to the seventh century and is written according to the strictest rules. In Japanese, tankas always have five unrhymed lines and a total of exactly thirty-one syllables. Lines 1 and 3 have five syllables each. Lines 2, 4, and 5 have seven each. (The English translations don't always follow this strict syllable count.) A tanka evokes a strong feeling with a single image.

SKILLS FOCUS

Literary Skills
Understand characteristics of the tanka.

A Closer Look

Poetry in the Golden Age of Japan

In the imperial court of Heian-era Japan (794–1185), poetry had both private and public functions. In private, poetry was the accepted language of love. A gentleman showed his interest in a lady of the court by sending her an admiring five-line poem (a tanka). If the poem she wrote in reply was encouraging, he paid her a visit. Their exchange of poems continued throughout their relationship, and each new message had to be original and intriguing.

Lovers also valued skillful calligraphy, exquisite paper, and a tasteful presentation. To match the mood of their poems, they covered tinted bamboo paper with scattered designs and tiny flecks of gold and silver foil. The final creation, carefully sealed with a twig or spray of flowers, was often lovely enough to decorate a folding screen.

Public poetry could be as romantic and beautiful as private poems, but it was presented and evaluated very differently. At popular poetry contests (*uta-awase*), competitors grouped themselves into two teams, Right and Left. A judge gave the teams a topic, such as "spring" or "names of things," and awarded a point to the side that created and recited the more pleasing composition. The team that had the most points after several rounds won. The government Office of Poetry preserved exceptional spoken poems in written anthologies.

Three Japanese Tankas
Ono Komachi

translated by Jane Hirshfield
with Mariko Aratani

1

*Sent anonymously to a man who had passed
in front of the screens of my room*

Should the world of love
end in darkness,
without our glimpsing
that cloud-gap
where the moon's light fills the sky?

2

*Sent to a man who seemed to have changed
his mind*

Since my heart placed me
on board your drifting ship,
not one day has passed
that I haven't been drenched
in cold waves.

3

*Sent in a letter attached to a rice stalk with
an empty seed husk*

How sad that I hope
to see you even now,
after my life has emptied itself
like this stalk of grain
into the autumn wind.

*Page from Ishiyamagire: Poems of Ki no Tsurayuki
(872?–c. 946). Calligraphy on paper.*

Courtesy of the Freer Gallery of Art/Smithsonian
Institution, Washington, D.C. (69.4).

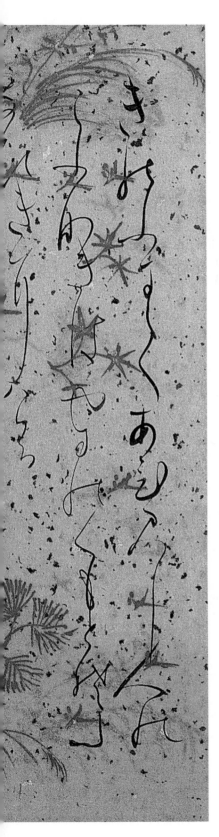

Meet the Writer

Ono Komachi

A Leading Lady and Poet

Ono Komachi (834–?) may have been the daughter of a ninth-century Japanese lord and may have served at the imperial court. Though little is known about her life, she is believed to have had at least one child and one grandchild. She was supposed to have been one of the most beautiful women of her time but is said to have died in poverty—aged and forgotten but still writing poetry.

Whatever the facts of her life, it is indisputable that Komachi was one of the great figures in an age when women dominated Japanese society and literature. In her hundred or so short poems that survive, she illuminates the subject of love through her understanding of Buddhist ideas about the fleeting nature of existence.

The Poetess Ono Komachi (c. 1820) by Hokkei. Surimono print (20 cm × 17 cm).

Spencer Museum of Art: The William Bridges Thayer Memorial (00.1561).

Response and Analysis

Heart! We will forget him! Three Japanese Tankas

Reading Check

1. Who is the **speaker** of Dickinson's poem, and whom is the speaker talking to?

2. What does the speaker in Dickinson's poem want to do?

3. Describe the situation of the speaker in each of the three tankas.

Thinking Critically

4. Dickinson **personifies** her heart by telling it to do things that only a person can do. What does she tell her heart? How would you paraphrase what she means by "warmth" and "light" (lines 3–4)?

5. Look back at the **images** and the **figures of speech** in the three **tankas.** What feelings do they suggest to you?

6. How does the **mood,** or feeling, in Dickinson's poem **compare** to the mood in Komachi's tankas?

7. All of these poems were written many years ago—the tankas are centuries old. Are they dated? Do they still apply to people's feelings and experiences today? Explain your responses to the lyrics.

WRITING

The Hidden Character

All of these poems contain hidden, unidentified characters—the men in Komachi's poems and the lost love in Dickinson's poem. If any one of these hidden characters could speak, what do you think he would say? Write a **letter** or **journal entry** in the character's voice (using the first-person pronoun *I*). Respond to what the speaker in the poem has written about you and about your love.

Try a Tanka

Review the information about the **tanka form** on page 489. Then, in tanka style, write a series of **poems** that trace a relationship. (You don't have to get exactly the right number of syllables in each line.) Try to use the **images** or **figures of speech** that you created for the Quickwrite on page 489. Finally, describe a symbolic object you might send with your tanka.

Bridge Across the Moon (1834) by Yashima Gakutei. Woodblock print.
Janette Ostier Gallery, Paris, France/Giraudon, Paris/SuperStock.

Before You Read

Shall I Compare Thee to a Summer's Day?

Make the Connection

Quickwrite ✏️

In Shakespeare's day every gentleman was expected to write sonnets in praise of his beloved. Writing a sonnet was a challenge, a kind of game. The speaker of this sonnet expresses passionate feelings within very strict rules—not an easy task.

Before you read this poem, write your response to this question: Why would someone want to compare the person he or she loves to a summer's day?

Literary Focus

The Sonnet: Strict Structure

The sonnet form favored (but not invented) by William Shakespeare is the **English sonnet** (also called, because he perfected the form, the **Shakespearean sonnet**). Its fourteen lines are divided into three **quatrains** (rhyming four-line stanzas) and a concluding **couplet** (pair of rhyming lines). Each quatrain makes a point or gives an example, and the couplet sums it all up.

For a biography of William Shakespeare, see page 741.

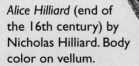

Alice Hilliard (end of the 16th century) by Nicholas Hilliard. Body color on vellum.

Victoria and Albert Museum, London/Art Resource, New York.

SKILLS FOCUS

Literary Skills
Understand characteristics of the English sonnet.

Shall I Compare Thee to a Summer's Day?

William Shakespeare

Shall I compare thee to a summer's day?
Thou art more lovely and more temperate.
Rough winds do shake the darling buds of May,
And summer's lease hath all too short a date.
5 Sometime too hot the eye of heaven shines,
And often is his gold complexion dimmed;
And every fair from fair sometime declines,
By chance, or nature's changing course, untrimmed;°
But thy eternal summer shall not fade,
10 Nor lose possession of that fair thou ow'st,°
Nor shall Death brag thou wand'rest in his shade,
When in eternal lines to time thou grow'st:
    So long as men can breathe or eyes can see,
    So long lives this, and this gives life to thee.

---

8. untrimmed *v.* used as *adj.*: without trimmings (decorations).

10. thou ow'st: you own.

494

Response and Analysis

Reading Check

1. The **speaker** opens the sonnet by wondering if he should compare his beloved to a summer's day. How does he answer his own question? What reasons does he give in line 2 for rejecting the comparison?

Thinking Critically

2. In lines 3–8, the speaker continues to think about his comparison. What **image** does he use to show that summer weather is unpredictable?

3. Explain the **metaphor** and **personification** in lines 5–8. Why is the "eye of heaven" neither constant nor trustworthy?

4. According to lines 7–8, what can happen to any kind of beauty?

5. In the third **quatrain** (lines 9–12), the speaker makes a daring statement to his beloved. What does he claim will never happen?

6. What does the speaker mean by "eternal lines to time" (line 12)? What is the connection between those eternal lines and the prediction he makes in lines 9–11?

7. Would you say that this sonnet is a love poem, or is it really about something else? Explain your interpretation.

8. If you were going to describe someone you love, what would you **compare** him or her to? (See what you thought of the speaker's suggested comparison in your Quickwrite.)

9. Has the poet's bold assertion in his **couplet** proved true? In what ways can other kinds of art immortalize someone? Give as many examples as you can think of.

WRITING

Are You Flattered—or Annoyed?

Imagine that you are the person addressed in Shakespeare's sonnet. Prepare a written or an oral **response** to this poem. What do you think of Shakespeare's rejection of the summer-day comparison? What do you think of the speaker's saying you'll never get old or die because of his poem? Decide what **tone** you'll take: flattered, irritated, sarcastic, confused, loving—something else? Meet with a classmate to present your responses.

William Shakespeare by David Levine.

Reprinted with permission from *The New York Review of Books.* Copyright ©1967 NYREV, Inc.

How Is It Made?

In an **essay,** take the sonnet apart to see how well Shakespeare has followed the blueprint for an English sonnet. Before you write, gather your notes in a chart like the following one:

Quatrain 1	Main point:
Quatrain 2	Main point:
Quatrain 3	Main point:
Couplet	Summation:

SKILLS FOCUS

Literary Skills
Analyze a sonnet.

Writing Skills
Write a response to a poem. Write an essay analyzing a sonnet.

Vocabulary Development

Archaic Words: Long Gone and Strange to Our Ears

Shakespeare's plays are sometimes presented in modern dress, set in the present or in the recent past. In a contemporary movie version of *Hamlet,* for example, young Hamlet works in a high-tech firm and intones his "To be or not to be" soliloquy (speech to himself) while browsing in a video store.

The English language has been through many changes and is changing still, adding new words and meanings, letting others drift out of use. For example, in Shakespeare's day the pronouns *thee* and *thou,* along with the other *th–* pronouns, *thy* and *thine,* were used to address people whom the speaker was familiar with or intimate with (wife, husband, close friend). *You,* on the other hand, and the other *y–* pronouns, *your* and *yours,* were used with people who were not intimate friends or who were the speaker's superior (parents, bosses, kings). Shakespeare also used the verb endings *–st* and *–th* (as in *didst* and *goeth*), which are no longer used today. In fact, even in Shakespeare's day these verb endings sounded a little old-fashioned. Today all these words are **archaic,** which means they are no longer used. (For more about archaic words in Shakespeare's plays, see pages 752–753.)

PRACTICE

What happens when you bring Shakespeare's language up to date?

Find all of the archaic words in this sonnet, and replace each one with its modern equivalent. Then, try reading the sonnet aloud—first with the archaic words and then with the modern ones. Does a "translation" work?

Grammar Link

Inverted Sentences—Variety and Challenge

Syntax refers to sentence structure, to the way words, phrases, and clauses are arranged to show their relationships. In his poem on page 485, E. E. Cummings lightly mocks people who worry about syntax, but without rules of syntax, language would be unintelligible.

English sentences usually begin with the **subject,** followed by the **verb** and, if there is one, a **complement.** Modifiers are placed near the words they modify. Some writers choose to wrench this syntax out of its usual order. Shakespeare, for example, in order to keep his rhymes and meter going, uses what we call **inverted sentences** (sentences in which the order is *not* subject-verb-complement and in which modifiers sometimes appear in unexpected places).

PRACTICE

1. What other word order could you use within lines 5 and 6 of the Shakespeare sonnet?

2. In line 7, where would the prepositional phrase "from fair" ordinarily be placed?

3. What other word order could you propose for line 12?

SKILLS FOCUS

Vocabulary Skills
Understand archaic words.

Grammar Skills
Recognize and use inverted sentences.

Before You Read

Ode to My Socks

Make the Connection

Quickwrite

If you could talk directly to a beloved article of clothing (a pair of jeans, say, or sneakers or a T-shirt), what might you say? Jot down some ideas, and save your notes.

Literary Focus

Ode: A Lofty Lyric

A traditional **ode** is a long lyric poem about a serious subject, written in a dignified style. In ancient Greece and Rome, odes were recited or sung in public, often to celebrate a triumph in the Olympic Games.

From 1954 to 1959, the Chilean poet Pablo Neruda published four volumes of odes to such unconventional everyday objects and experiences as soap, onions, love, summer, the color green, French fries, corn, bees—and a pair of socks.

Extended Metaphor and Simile: Continuing Comparisons

Who would think that a pair of socks could inspire an outpouring of **metaphors** and **similes** in which the poet sees his new socks as rabbits, fish, blackbirds, cannons—and even more. Many of these similes and metaphors are **extended** throughout the poem, which means that the poet continues to develop points of comparison between his socks and other things.

INTERNET

More About Pablo Neruda

Keyword: LE5 10-7

Literary Skills
Understand characteristics of the ode. Understand extended metaphor and simile.

Ode to My Socks

Pablo Neruda

translated by Robert Bly

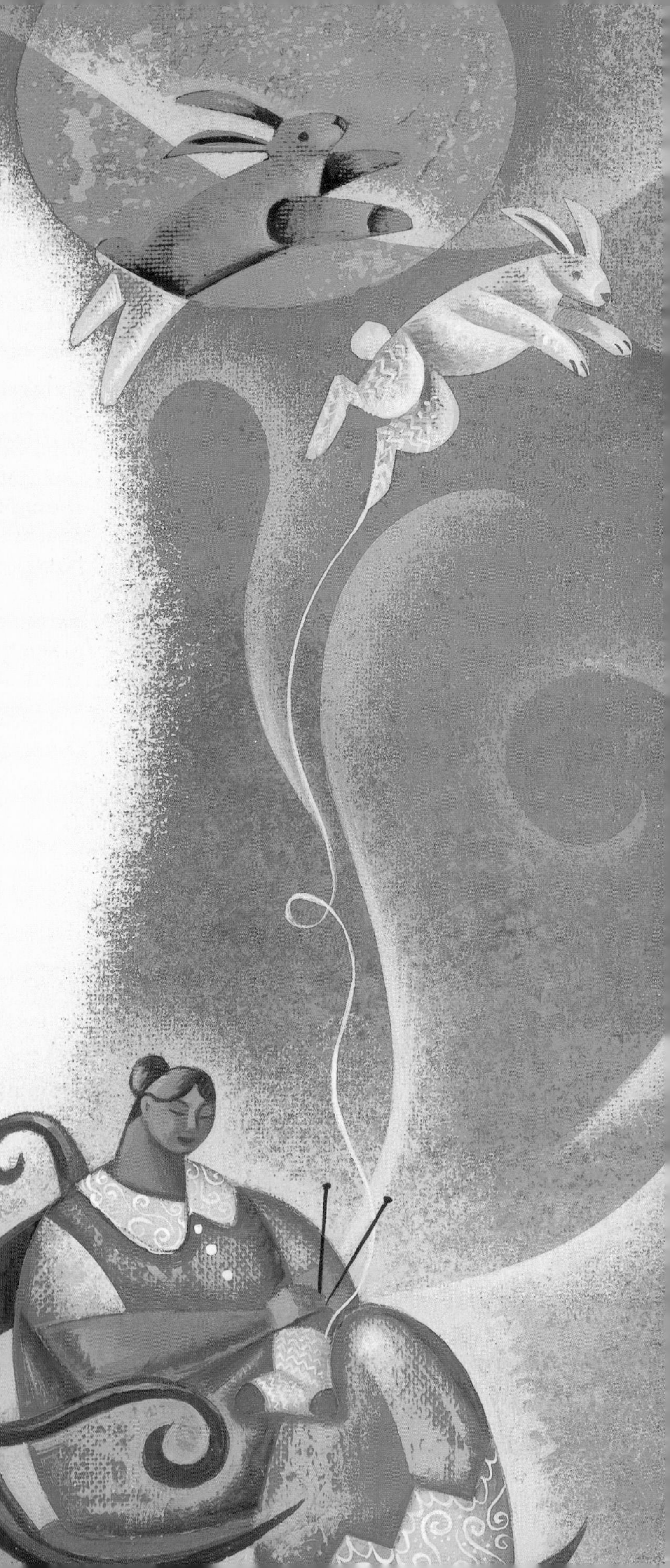

Maru Mori brought me
a pair
of socks
which she knitted herself
5 with her sheepherder's hands,
two socks as soft
as rabbits.
I slipped my feet
into them
10 as though into
two
cases
knitted
with threads of
15 twilight
and goatskin.
Violent socks,
my feet were
two fish made
20 of wool,
two long sharks
sea-blue, shot
through
by one golden thread,
25 two immense blackbirds,
two cannons:
my feet
were honored
in this way
30 by

these
heavenly
socks.
They were
35 so handsome
for the first time
my feet seemed to me
unacceptable
like two decrepit
40 firemen, firemen
unworthy
of that woven
fire,
of those glowing
45 socks.

Nevertheless
I resisted
the sharp temptation
to save them somewhere
50 as schoolboys
keep
fireflies,
as learned men
collect
55 sacred texts,
I resisted
the mad impulse
to put them
into a golden

60 cage
and each day give them
birdseed
and pieces of pink melon.
Like explorers
65 in the jungle who hand
over the very rare
green deer
to the spit°
and eat it
70 with remorse,
I stretched out
my feet
and pulled on
the magnificent
75 socks
and then my shoes.

The moral
of my ode is this:
beauty is twice
80 beauty
and what is good is doubly
good
when it is a matter of two socks
made of wool
85 in winter.

---

68. spit *n.:* thin rod or stick on which
meat is roasted.

Meet the Writer

Pablo Neruda

"To Roam, to Go Singing Through the World"

Pablo Neruda (1904–1973), the most important Latin American poet of the twentieth century, was baptized Neftalí Ricardo Reyes Basoalto. He changed his name when he began writing poetry, to avoid embarrassing his father, who frowned on his literary ambitions. Even as a child, Neruda observed nature closely—"birds, beetles, partridge eggs" and "the perfection of insects." In his *Memoirs* he writes,

> "Anyone who hasn't been in the Chilean forest doesn't know this planet. I have come out of that landscape, that mud, that silence, to roam, to go singing through the world."

Neruda wrote his first poems when he was very young, and by fifteen he'd had several poems published. He enrolled in the University of Chile in Santiago, Chile's capital, planning to become a French professor, but he took a detour to serve as Chile's consul to Rangoon, Burma, the first of several diplomatic postings in Asia. Throughout his diplomatic career in Spain, France, and Mexico, Neruda continued publishing prize-winning volumes of poetry. A lifelong political activist, he wrote and spoke eloquently in support of Chile's poor Indians and workers. He was elected to Chile's senate, but a speech highly critical of Chile's repressive government led to an order for his arrest. In 1949, Neruda fled Chile for three years

Pablo Neruda (1970) by Sofia Gandarias.

until the order for his arrest was dropped.

Neruda was awarded the Nobel Prize in literature in 1971 "for a poetry that with the action of an elemental force brings alive a continent's destiny and dreams." In his acceptance speech he wrote,

> "I have always maintained that the writer's task has nothing to do with mystery or magic, and that the poet's, at least, must be a personal effort for the benefit of all. The closest thing to poetry is a loaf of bread or a ceramic dish or a piece of wood lovingly carved, even if by clumsy hands."

The Word

Pablo Neruda

What a great language I have, it's a fine language we inherited from the fierce conquistadors[1] . . . They strode over the giant *cordilleras,*[2] over the rugged Americas, hunting for potatoes, sausages, beans, black tobacco, gold, corn, fried eggs, with a voracious appetite not found in the world since then . . . They swallowed up everything, religions, pyramids, tribes, idolatries[3] just like the ones they brought along in their huge sacks . . . Wherever they went, they razed the land . . . But words fell like pebbles out of the boots of the barbarians,[4] out of their beards, their helmets, their horseshoes, luminous words that were left glittering here . . . our language. We came up losers . . . We came up winners . . . They carried off the gold and left us the gold . . . They carried everything off and left us everything . . . They left us the words.

—from *Memoirs*

---

1. **conquistadors** (kän·kwis′tə·dôrz′) *n.:* sixteenth-century Spanish conquerors of much of Central and South America.
2. *cordilleras* (kôr·di·yer′äs) *n.:* mountain system of western South America.
3. **idolatries** (ī·däl′ə·trēz) *n.:* devotions to or worship of idols, or images of gods.
4. **barbarians** (bär·ber′ē·ənz) *n.:* here, foreigners; aliens.

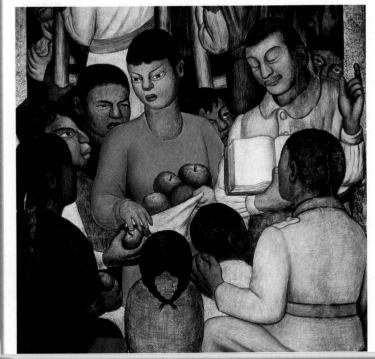

Fruit of the Earth (*Los Frutos*) (detail) (1926) by Diego Rivera. Mural in Mexico City.

© Schalkwijk/Art Resource, New York.

Response and Analysis

Reading Check

1. Where did the socks come from?

2. If the socks were lost or stolen, what factual description could you give someone searching for them?

3. What temptation and what mad impulse does the speaker resist?

4. What does the speaker end up doing with the pair of socks?

5. What does the speaker say is the "moral" of his ode?

Thinking Critically

6. Make a list of all of the poem's **similes** and **metaphors.** Which ones are **extended** over several or more lines? Which ones do you think are the most interesting or the most fun?

Similes	
Extended similes	
Metaphors	
Extended metaphors	

7. Based on how the **speaker** talks about his socks, describe how he feels about his gift.

8. John Keats's famous poem "Ode on a Grecian Urn" ends with these lines: "'Beauty is truth, truth beauty.' That is all / Ye know on earth, and all ye need to know." What do you think Neruda's stated moral in lines 77–85 means? How might it relate to Keats's lines?

9. How credible is it that anyone would be so passionate about a pair of socks? Do you think Neruda intends this ode to be taken seriously, or is he writing a **parody** of an ode? (A **parody** is a humorous imitation of a serious work of literature, art, or music.) Support your opinion with references to the poem and to the way it demonstrates the qualities of an ode (see page 497).

Extending and Evaluating

10. In the selection from his memoir (see the **Connection** on page 501), Neruda says that words are "everything." Do you think his love of language is evident in the similes and metaphors he uses in "Ode to My Socks"? Explain your opinion.

WRITING

Ode to a Common Thing

Write an **ode** to an object you see every day. Start by observing the object closely and making some notes about how it looks, what it resembles, and how it makes you feel. (Look back at your Quickwrite notes for ideas.) What **tone** will you give your ode?

Ode to My . . .
How it looks:
What it resembles:
How it makes me feel:

Elements of Literature

The Sounds of Poetry
RHYTHM, RHYME, AND OTHER SOUND EFFECTS
by John Malcolm Brinnin

Rhythm: Music in Speech

Poetry is a musical kind of speech. Like music, poetry is based on **rhythm**—that is, on the alternation of stressed and unstressed sounds that makes the voice rise and fall.

Poets have a choice of the kind of rhythm they can use. They can use **meter**—a strict rhythmic pattern of stressed and unstressed syllables in each line, or they can write in **free verse**—a loose kind of rhythm that sounds more like natural speech than like formal poetry.

Meter: Patterns of Sound

In **metrical poetry** (poetry that has a meter), stressed and unstressed syllables are arranged in a regular pattern. Here's a famous stanza from *The Rime of the Ancient Mariner* by Samuel Taylor Coleridge:

˘ ′ ˘ ′ ˘ ′ ˘ ′

He prayeth best, who loveth best

˘ ′ ˘ ′ ˘ ′

All things both great and small;

˘ ˘ ′ ˘ ′ ˘ ′

For the dear God who loveth us,

˘ ′ ˘ ′ ˘ ′

He made and loveth all.

The stress (′) indicates a stressed syllable. The breve (˘) indicates an unstressed syllable. Indicating the stresses this way is called **scanning** a poem.

In metrical poetry, variation is important. Without any variation at all, meter becomes mechanical and monotonous, like the steady ticktock of a clock. An occasional change in rhythm, as in the third line of the stanza from *The Rime of the Ancient Mariner,* also allows the poet to draw attention to key words in the poem.

Five Kinds of Feet

A line of metrical poetry is made up of metrical units called feet. A **foot** is a unit consisting of at least one stressed syllable and usually one or more unstressed syllables. Here are the five common types of feet used by poets in English and an example of a single word that matches each pattern:

˘ ′

iamb (insist)

′ ˘

trochee (double)

˘ ˘ ′

anapest (understand)

′ ˘ ˘

dactyl (excellent)

′ ′

spondee (football)

(*For more about these feet, see Meter in the Handbook of Literary Terms.*)

(*continued*)

SKILLS FOCUS

Literary Skills
Understand the sounds of poetry, including rhythm, meter, free verse, rhyme, alliteration, and onomatopoeia.

Free Verse: No Rules

Early in the twentieth century some American and English poets decided that they would rid poetry of its prettiness, sentimentality, and artificiality by concentrating on a new kind of poetry. Calling themselves **imagists,** they declared that imagery alone—without any elaborate metrics or stanza patterns—could carry the full emotional message of a poem. They called their poetry **free verse** because it is free from the old metric rules.

Robert Frost, who disliked free verse, said that writing without the metric rules was "like playing tennis with the net down." What he meant was that the net on the tennis court is like meter in poetry—the essential part of the game, which players must both respect and overcome. Nevertheless, more and more poets write in free-verse cadences that follow "curves of thought" or "shapes of speech."

Rhyme: Chiming Sounds

Rhyme is the repetition of the accented vowel sound and all subsequent sounds in a word (*time/dime, history/mystery, lobster/mobster*).

Chiming sounds that punctuate the rhythm of a poem also give the poem structure and make it easy to remember. In the cartoon on this page, Edgar Allan Poe searches for words to rhyme with the refrain "Nevermore" in his poem "The Raven."

In poetry the chiming sounds of rhymes may occur at the ends of lines—**end rhyme**—or within a line—**internal rhyme.** A perfect rhyme, like *cat/mat* or *verging/merging,* is called an **exact rhyme.** When sounds are similar but not exact, as in *fellow/follow* or *mystery/mastery,* the rhyme is called **approximate rhyme.** Approximate rhymes are also called half rhymes, slant rhymes, or imperfect rhymes. The following verse from "Father William," a comic poem by Lewis Carroll, contains exact rhymes:

"You are old, Father William," the young
    man said,
"And your hair has become very white;
And yet you incessantly stand on your
    head—
Do you think, at your age, it is right?"

Drawing by Chas. Addams. ©1983 The New Yorker Magazine, Inc.

In the next poem the rhymes are both approximate (*washes/rushes, bales/orioles*) and exact (*sea/mystery*):

This is the land the Sunset washes

This is the land the Sunset washes—
These are the banks of the Yellow Sea—
Where it rose—or whither it rushes—
There are the Western Mystery!

Night after night her purple traffic
Strews the landing with Opal Bales—
Merchantmen poise upon horizons—
Dip—and vanish like Orioles!

—Emily Dickinson

Alliteration: Repeated Beginning Sounds

Alliteration is the repetition of consonant sounds in words that appear close together; strictly speaking, alliteration occurs at the beginnings of words or on accented syllables. Alliteration used with restraint can result in lines as memorable as this one from Percy Bysshe Shelley's "Ode to the West Wind":

O wild West Wind, thou breath of
   Autumn's being

Or this one from Robert Frost's "Acquainted with the Night":

I have stood still and stopped the sound
   of feet

Onomatopoeia: Sounds into Words

Onomatopoeia (ăn′ō·mat′ō·pē′ə) is the use of words that sound like what they

mean (*snap, crackle, pop*). *Onomatopoeia,* Greek for "making of words," has come to refer to the making of words by imitating or suggesting sounds.

In its most basic form, onomatopoeia is a single word (*gurgle, bang, rattle, boom, hiss, buzz*) that echoes a natural or mechanical sound. For the poet, onomatopoeia is a way of conveying meaning through evocative words that also provide musical accompaniment—as background music in a movie can affect the mood of a scene.

In this famous example from Tennyson's *The Princess,* onomatopoeia is used with such exactness that the sounds of the poem voice a particular feeling that words alone could only approximate:

The moan of doves in immemorial elms
And murmuring of innumerable bees

Practice

As in ancient days, when poetry was not written but only spoken or sung, poetry today is addressed to the ear. You can't really say that you know a poem until you've heard it read aloud.

Choose one of the poems you've already read in this chapter (or any favorite poem), and **read it aloud** to yourself and then to a partner or a small group.

Then, write a paragraph or two discussing the poem's **rhythm, rhyme,** or other **sound effects.**

Sea Fever

Make the Connection

Feverish

What do you think this poem's title means? Does the title remind you of any other fever?

Literary Focus

Meter: Rhythms of the Sea

Meter is a pattern of stressed and unstressed syllables in poetry. Read this famous poem aloud to hear how the poet's use of meter suggests the motion of a ship on the high seas. Where do you hear and feel the rolling rhythm of the sea swells? Where do you hear and feel the slap of waves against the ship?

Rhyme

Rhyme is probably the one feature most people identify with poetry, especially rhyme at the ends of lines in a poem. (Of course, many poems, especially modern ones, do not rhyme.) **Rhyme** is the repetition of vowel sounds and all sounds following them in words that are close together (*sky/by, shaking/breaking*). Usually rhymes create a particular pattern in a poem, called a **rhyme scheme.** Poetry owes much of its music to the effect of rhyme. As you read, notice the rhymes in "Sea Fever." How do they contribute to the music of the poem?

SKILLS FOCUS

Literary Skills
Understand meter. Understand rhyme and rhyme scheme.

Background

Although supertankers and cruise ships are much taller than sailing ships, the term *tall ship* is still used for a sailing vessel with high masts. For millions of landlubbers, the image of a tall ship triggers dreams of romance, freedom, and adventure, just as it did for Masefield.

"The wheel's kick" in line 3 is a reference to what can happen when a sudden shift in the wind or tide causes a ship's steering wheel to "kick over"—to spin out of control until the person at the helm can grab it and put the ship back on course. "Trick" (line 12) is a sailing term for a round-trip voyage. Years ago a "long trick" might have involved a voyage from England to China and back, a trip that could last for more than a year.

Sea Fever

John Masefield

I must go down to the seas again, to the lonely sea and the sky,
And all I ask is a tall ship and a star to steer her by;
And the wheel's kick and the wind's song and the white sail's shaking,
And a gray mist on the sea's face and a gray dawn breaking.

5   I must go down to the seas again, for the call of the running tide
Is a wild call and a clear call that may not be denied;
And all I ask is a windy day with the white clouds flying,
And the flung spray and the blown spume,° and the sea gulls crying.

I must go down to the seas again, to the vagrant gypsy life,
10   To the gull's way and the whale's way where the wind's like a whetted knife;
And all I ask is a merry yarn from a laughing fellow-rover.
And a quiet sleep and a sweet dream when the long trick's over.

---

8. **spume** (spyo͞om) *n.:* foam or froth.

Meet the Writer

John Masefield

Sailor-Poet

John Masefield (1878–1967), born in England, was orphaned by the time he was thirteen years old. At once, as boys could do in those days, he joined the merchant navy and shipped around the world for several years. On a trip to New York, he jumped ship and lived for a time in the city as what we'd call today a homeless person. He began to write poetry after coming across a collection of Chaucer's *Canterbury Tales* in a New York bookstore.

Masefield is best remembered today for poems inspired by the years he spent as a seaman, first on windjammers in the last days of the sailing ships and then on tramp steamers and ocean liners. No one has better evoked for the landlubber the sense of freedom and adventure, the taste of salt and spray associated with sailing "before the mast," or the pride that marked the crews of even the rustiest and dingiest of freighters.

For more than thirty years, Masefield served as Britain's poet laureate. Of his passion for sailing ships, the poet said:

❝ They were the only youth I had, and the only beauty I knew in my youth, and now that I am old, not many greater beauties seem to be in the world. ❞

Response and Analysis

Reading Check

1. What does the speaker ask for?
2. What call does the speaker hear?
3. What kind of life does the speaker yearn for?

Thinking Critically

4. What do you think the "long trick" and the "quiet sleep" and "sweet dream" stand for in the last line?

5. You are probably familiar with a variety of expressions that use *fever* **metaphorically**—for example, "spring fever" and "gold-rush fever." What exactly is "sea fever," and why is it a good **title** for the poem? What other "fevers" might grip someone the way the sea has gripped this speaker?

6. What specific **images** in the poem help you see, hear, and even feel the kind of life the speaker longs for?

7. Read the poem aloud, and scan it line by line, marking the stressed syllables (′) and the unstressed syllables (˘). How many strong beats do you hear

in each line? Where do you hear variations in the **meter**?

8. After you have scanned the poem, read it aloud again. Where does the **meter** reinforce the sense of the poem—the kick of the wheel and the roll of the sea?

9. What pattern of **rhyme** is used in the poem? How does the **rhyme scheme** contribute to the overall sound and music of the poem?

10. Masefield uses **alliteration** throughout the poem to create his sea song. Where is alliteration especially strong?

WRITING

What's *Your* "Fever"?

Write a **poem** in imitation of Masefield's that opens "I must go . . ." Give your poem a title that uses the word *fever*. Describe the place you long to go back to. Try to find **images** that help your readers share what you can see, smell, taste, hear, and touch in this special place. You might enjoy imitating Masefield's **meter**.

SKILLS FOCUS

Literary Skills
Analyze meter.
Analyze rhyme and rhyme scheme.

Writing Skills
Write a poem.

508   Collection 7   Poetry

Bonny Barbara Allan

Make the Connection

Some Things Never Change

Think about the content of songs popular today. Are they happy or tragic? Are any songs about love? about betrayal? What are their refrains?

Literary Focus

The Ballad

"Bonny Barbara Allan" is a **ballad,** a story that is told in song. Most ballads use simple language and two of the oldest elements of poetry: a strong **meter** and a **refrain** (whole lines or stanzas repeated at regular intervals).

Folk ballads such as this one, which have been passed down orally from generation to generation, often tell tales of true love or domestic violence. Folk ballads also use certain formulas—phrases such as "white as milk," "red, red lips," and "true, true love." The images of trees and rose-bushes growing on lovers' graves is also a formula. All of these formulas were part of the ballad singer's repertoire; whenever the singer needed to describe a woman's skin, for example, a formula was available. The formulas also made the songs easy to memorize.

As you read this old ballad, think about whether its love story is timely or out of date. Could it happen today?

Background

The tragic story of Barbara Allan and her fickle lover originated in Scotland in the seventeenth century. Like many Scottish ballads, this one traveled to America in the eighteenth century with the Scots-Irish who settled in the mountains of Appalachia. There the song of Barbara Allan continued to be sung, often with changes that made it a local love story.

SKILLS FOCUS

Literary Skills
Understand characteristics of ballads.

A hunting party (14th century), School of Paris. Ivory.

Victoria and Albert Museum, London/Art Resource, New York.

Lovers in a garden (c. 1487–1495). Painting from a French illuminated manuscript.

Bonny Barbara Allan

Anonymous

Oh, in the merry month of May,
When all things were a-blooming,
Sweet William came from the Western states
And courted Barbara Allan.

5　But he took sick, and very sick
And he sent for Barbara Allan,
And all she said when she got there,
"Young man, you are a-dying."

"Oh yes, I'm sick, and I'm very sick,
10　And I think that death's upon me;
But one sweet kiss from Barbara's lips
Will save me from my dying."

"But don't you remember the other day
You were down in town a-drinking?
15　You drank your health to the ladies all around,
And slighted Barbara Allan."

"Oh yes, I remember the other day
I was down in town a-drinking;
I drank my health to the ladies all 'round.
20 But my love to Barbara Allan."

He turned his face to the wall;
She turned her back upon him;
The very last word she heard him say,
"Hardhearted Barbara Allan."

25 As she passed on through London Town,
She heard some bells a-ringing,
And every bell, it seemed to say,
"Hardhearted Barbara Allan."

She then passed on to the country road,
30 And heard some birds a-singing;
And every bird, it seemed to say,
"Hardhearted Barbara Allan."

She hadn't got more than a mile from town
When she saw his corpse a-coming;
35 "O bring him here, and ease him down,
And let me look upon him.

"Oh, take him away! Oh, take him away!
For I am sick and dying!
His death-cold features say to me,
40 'Hardhearted Barbara Allan.'

"O Father, O Father, go dig my grave,
And dig it long and narrow;
Sweet William died for me today;
I'll die for him tomorrow."

45 They buried them both in the old graveyard,
All side and side each other.
A red, red rose grew out of his grave,
And a green briar out of hers.

They grew and grew so very high
50 That they could grow no higher;
They lapped, they tied in a truelove knot—
The rose ran 'round the briar.

A Choral Reading: The Balladeers

As far as we know, ballads were sung by individuals. Even so, here are some ideas for a choral reading of a ballad—no instruments required!

- First, examine the ballad: How many people are speaking? Which lines could be recited by a chorus? (Refrains are often a good choice for several speakers.)
- Next, think of how the speakers are feeling. (Usually in a ballad, feelings run pretty strong.) How can you express those feelings, using volume, pitch, and tone of voice? Where do feelings change?
- Will you use gestures? props? How will you dress?
- Finally, mark up a copy of your choral reading to use as a script. Watch the punctuation, and let it guide you in deciding where to pause and when to speed up. Indicate words to emphasize.
- Practice. Evaluate and adjust your performance before you present it to an audience. Have you and your fellow balladeers caught the texture of this sad story of love and betrayal?

Response and Analysis

Reading Check

1. What problem does the ballad set up in stanzas 1 and 2?

2. In stanza 3, what favor does William ask of Barbara Allan? According to the next stanza, why does she refuse him?

3. How does William explain his "insult" to Barbara Allan?

4. What happens to Barbara Allan after William calls her "hardhearted"?

5. How are William and Barbara Allan united after death?

Thinking Critically

6. **Ballads** are **narrative poems,** but they never tell the whole story. What details are left out of this one? For example, what caused William's death? How about Barbara Allan's?

7. What evidence shows that Barbara Allan is indeed hardhearted? Does anything indicate that she is *not* hardhearted? Explain.

8. We'd expect the aggressive vines of a briar to grow around any nearby plant. Which plant entwines the other in this story? Which character and which emotion have triumphed?

9. Note all the different kinds of **repetition** you can find in this ballad. What is the **refrain**?

WRITING

In a News Flash

Ballads often took their subjects from stories of domestic tragedy that would today be featured on the evening news. Write your own version of this ballad as if it were tomorrow's **news story.** Remember that a good reporter answers the *5W-How?* questions—*who? what?*

when? where? why? and *how?* You might also want to invent interviews with relatives and friends of Barbara Allan and Sweet William. Write a news report for the morning paper, or record your story on videotape or audiotape for a TV or radio news broadcast. Even though reporters don't usually create their own headlines, you'll have to create your headline for this story.

Songs Yesterday and Today

In a brief **essay, compare and contrast** this popular old ballad with the kinds of songs popular today, such as country-and-western songs. Before you write, gather your details in a chart like the following one:

	Ballad	Today's Songs
Subjects		
Rhythms (musical effects)		
Refrains		
Level of violence		

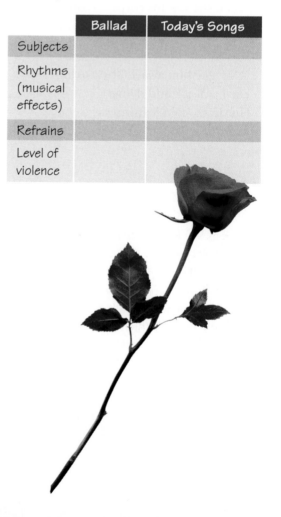

Before You Read

The Flying Cat

Make the Connection

Quickwrite ✏️

Do animals have feelings? Can they, for example, feel love or fear? Do they have thoughts and memories? Jot down your opinions, and save your notes.

Literary Focus

Free Verse: The Rhythms of Everyday Speech

Like many contemporary poets, Naomi Shihab Nye writes in **free verse.** Free verse uses no regular meter or rhyme scheme but instead attempts to imitate the natural rhythms of speech. Nye's poem has a distinct rhythm, created by the use of long and short sentences and many run-on lines (lines that do not end with any mark of punctuation). Read the poem aloud to hear its conversational rhythm.

SKILLS FOCUS

Literary Skills
Understand characteristics of free verse.

The Flying Cat
Naomi Shihab Nye

Never, in all your career of worrying, did you imagine
what worries could occur concerning the flying cat.
You are traveling to a distant city.
The cat must travel in a small box with holes.

5   Will the baggage compartment be pressurized?
       Will a soldier's footlocker fall on the cat during take-off?
       Will the cat freeze?

You ask these questions one by one, in different voices
over the phone. Sometimes you get an answer,
10   sometimes a click.
Now it's affecting everything you do.
At dinner you feel nauseous, like you're swallowing
at twenty thousand feet.
In dreams you wave fish-heads, but the cat has grown propellers,
15   the cat is spinning out of sight!

       Will he faint when the plane lands?
       Is the baggage compartment soundproofed?
       Will the cat go deaf?

"Ma'am, if the cabin weren't pressurized, your cat would explode."
20   And spoken in a droll impersonal tone, as if
the explosion of cats were another statistic!

Hugging the cat before departure, you realize again
the private language of pain. He purrs. He trusts you.
He knows little of planets or satellites,
25   black holes in space or the weightless rise of fear.

Meet the Writer

Naomi Shihab Nye

Stories in Everyday Objects

Naomi Shihab Nye (1952–   ) is a poet, a storyteller, an anthologist, an essayist, a teacher, and a songwriter. She also works in schools, encouraging students to find the poet in themselves. In her first two collections of poetry, *Different Ways to Pray* (1980) and *Hugging the Jukebox* (1982), Nye was writing on a topic she still feels passionately about: the experiences people from different cultures share. In *Yellow Glove* (1986), several poems deal with small, everyday objects—which are a recurring focus of her work.

“ Since I was a small child, I've felt that little inanimate things were very wise, that they had their own kind of wisdom, something to teach me if I would only pay the right kind of attention to them. ”

She thinks that poems about such objects say, "Pause. Take note. A story is being told through this thing."

For Independent Reading

Nye's young-adult novel *Habibi* (1997) draws on her experience as an American teenager of half-Palestinian descent as she describes a visit made by a Palestinian American teenager to her father's homeland in the 1970s.

Interview with Naomi Shihab Nye

Bill Moyers

The journalist Bill Moyers talked to Naomi Shihab Nye about writing, poetry, language, and life. Here is an excerpt from their conversation.

Moyers. Poetry is a form of conversation for you, isn't it?

Nye. Absolutely. Poetry is a conversation with the world; poetry is a conversation with the words on the page in which you allow those words to speak back to you; and poetry is a conversation with yourself. Many times I meet students and see a little look of wariness in their faces—"I'm not sure I *want* to do this or I'm not sure I *can* do this"—I like to say, "Wait a minute. How nervous are you about the conversation you're going to have at lunch today with your friends?" And they say, "Oh, we're not nervous at all about *that*. We do *that* every day." Then I tell them they can come to feel the same way about writing. Writing doesn't have to be an exotic or stressful experience. You can just sit down with a piece of paper and begin talking and see what speaks back.

Moyers. Talking out loud? When you're alone?

Nye. Well, sometimes, I often begin talking out loud, whether I'm alone or not. My son will say, "You were talking to yourself right now." And I say, "That's what I was doing; but I was so comfortable with you and I didn't notice it." I often just repeat a phrase I've heard or some words I want to write down so I won't forget them. In our culture especially I think we need to talk to ourselves more, and we also need to *listen* to ourselves more.

Moyers. Some people think there's so much talk in America—the talk shows, call-in shows, interviews, . . . press conferences, TV commercials—that it's all just a babble.

Nye. Maybe what I mean is a different kind of talk, because the kind I'm thinking about is a very slow and deliberate, delighted kind of talk. My favorite quote comes from Thailand: "Life is so short we must move very slowly." I think that poems help us to do that by allowing us to savor a single image, a single phrase. Think about haiku—those little seventeen-syllable poems—how many people have savored a single haiku poem over hundreds of years? Reading a poem slows you down, and when you slow down, you are likely to read it more than one time. You read it more slowly than you would speak to somebody in a store, and we *need* that slow experience with words, as well as those quick and jazzy ones.

—from *The Language of Life*

Response and Analysis

Reading Check

1. What anxiety is the speaker sharing with you?

2. What horrible things does the speaker ask you to imagine in regard to her cat?

3. What does she ask you to realize about the cat at the end of the poem?

Thinking Critically

4. Explain what you think the speaker means by "the private language of pain" (line 23). What significance do you see in the fact that she says she realizes that pain "again"?

5. Is this poem about more than the cat? How does the last stanza extend the meaning of the poem?

6. Although this poem is written without rhyme or meter—it is written in **free verse**—it is designed with care. What structural element do you notice immediately as you look at the poem on the page? What examples of **parallelism**—words, phrases, or sentences with a similar grammatical structure—can you find?

Extending and Evaluating

7. In Bill Moyers's interview with Nye (see the **Connection** on page 516), she says that reading poetry is important because we need the "slow experience with words" that poems give us. Do you agree with Nye? Are there words or phrases in "The Flying Cat" that had a special impact on you as you read the poem? Explain your answers.

WRITING

A Feline Point of View

Imagine you're the flying cat. Write a brief **free-verse** poem (or a few paragraphs of prose) describing the plane trip from your point of view. You might describe how you feel about your worried owner, what happens during the trip, what you think about during the trip, and how you feel when you arrive at your destination. (Check your Quickwrite notes before beginning.) ✏

LISTENING AND SPEAKING

Different Voices

Prepare Nye's poem for performance. First, determine whether you want to use more than one speaker. Then, decide how you'll read the questions. Will you do as the poet says she did and ask them in different voices? Rehearse your poem, and perform it for a small group or your class.

Ex–Basketball Player

Make the Connection

Sports and Life

Almost every school has a sports hero, someone who is a natural at the game. Like the glittering stars whose brilliance fades overnight, some of these bright heroes seem to dim after graduation.

How important are school athletics to you? Do you think they prepare young people for life? Why?

Literary Focus

Sound Effects

Even though Updike's poem sounds free and conversational, it's written within a tight **structure**. The basic beat is **iambic pentameter**—five iambs (⌣′) to a line. This meter is closest to the rhythm of everyday English speech, and its use gives the poem an informal, conversational sound. You'll find the same meter in a poem written centuries before Updike's: Shakespeare's sonnet on page 494. Updike uses other sound devices: **Internal rhymes** and **alliteration** lend his unrhymed poem verbal music. Read it aloud.

Ex–Basketball Player
John Updike

Pearl Avenue runs past the high-school lot,
Bends with the trolley tracks, and stops, cut off
Before it has a chance to go two blocks,
At Colonel McComsky Plaza. Berth's Garage
5   Is on the corner facing west, and there,
Most days, you'll find Flick Webb, who helps Berth out.

Flick stands tall among the idiot pumps—
Five on a side, the old bubble-head style,
Their rubber elbows hanging loose and low.
10   One's nostrils are two S's, and his eyes
An E and O. And one is squat, without
A head at all—more of a football type.

Once Flick played for the high-school team, the Wizards.
He was good: in fact, the best. In '46
15   He bucketed three hundred ninety points,
A county record still. The ball loved Flick.
I saw him rack up thirty-eight or forty
In one home game. His hands were like wild birds.

He never learned a trade, he just sells gas,
20   Checks oil, and changes flats. Once in a while,
As a gag, he dribbles an inner tube,
But most of us remember anyway.
His hands are fine and nervous on the lug wrench.
It makes no difference to the lug wrench, though.

25   Off work, he hangs around Mae's luncheonette.
Grease-gray and kind of coiled, he plays pinball,
Smokes thin cigars, and nurses lemon phosphates.
Flick seldom says a word to Mae, just nods
Beyond her face toward bright applauding tiers
30   Of Necco Wafers, Nibs, and Juju Beads.

Meet the Writer

John Updike

Observer of American Life

John Updike (1932–   ) was born in the small town of Shillington, Pennsylvania. A year after he graduated from Harvard University, he got a job on the staff of *The New Yorker* magazine, which has published much of his writing ever since.

Though he has won fame for his novels and short stories, Updike is also a poet of great wit and craft. He is particularly drawn to occasional poetry—pieces inspired by odd or funny incidents reported in the newspapers or observed in the American suburban landscape of housing developments, service stations, and supermarkets. Despite his humorous approach, Updike is a sharp social observer and a serious moralist.

Among the most successful of Updike's novels are the Rabbit tales (the last two of which won Pulitzer Prizes): *Rabbit, Run* (1960), *Rabbit Redux* (1971), *Rabbit Is Rich* (1981), and *Rabbit at Rest* (1990). These novels chronicle the life of Harry "Rabbit" Angstrom, an ex–basketball player. Rabbit lives an outwardly conventional life in a small Pennsylvania town, but his hidden yearnings and disappointing relationships reveal the uncertainties of contemporary American life.

In accepting the American Book Award in 1982, Updike spoke these words to young writers:

66 Have faith. May you surround yourselves with parents, editors, mates, and children as supportive as mine have been. But the essential support and encouragement of course comes from within, arising out of the mad notion that your society needs to know what only you can tell it. 99

miss rosie

Make the Connection

Portrait of a Woman

No one can say that Lucille Clifton's portrait of Miss Rosie is very pretty. Yet beauty—and what can happen to it—is the subject of the poem. Notice how figures of speech help you see contrasting pictures, past and present, of Miss Rosie.

Literary Focus

Idioms—Not Literally True

An **idiom** is an expression that is peculiar to a certain language and cannot be understood by a mere literal definition of its individual words. For example, the literal meaning of "to fall in love" would be absurd. Like many idioms, this one implies a comparison. The experience of love can be so overwhelming that it feels like losing your footing or falling into a trap, although not necessarily an unpleasant one.

Idioms are so common in English that you probably use them all the time.

Here are a few more common examples: "raining cats and dogs," "to have the upper hand," "to jump out of my skin." Can you think of others? Idioms present a particular difficulty for people learning a new language.

If an idiom is unfamiliar to you—as the idiom "i stand up" in "miss rosie" might be—the context might help you understand it.

Literary Skills
Understand idioms.

Mirage (1993)
by Catherine Howe.
Oil on canvas.

Collection Alan P. Power,
Venice, California.

miss rosie
Lucille Clifton

when i watch you
wrapped up like garbage
sitting, surrounded by the smell
of too old potato peels
5 or
when i watch you
in your old man's shoes
with the little toe cut out
sitting, waiting for your mind
10 like next week's grocery
i say
when i watch you
you wet brown bag of a woman
who used to be the best looking gal in georgia
15 used to be called the Georgia Rose
i stand up
through your destruction
i stand up

Meet the Writer

Lucille Clifton

Celebrating Survival

Lucille Clifton (1936–) writes both fiction and poetry and has published many books for children. One of Clifton's best-known works is *Generations* (1976), a poetic memoir composed of portraits of five generations of her family. It begins with her great-great-grandmother, who was brought from Africa to New Orleans and sold into slavery. Like all of Clifton's work, *Generations* is honest but rarely bitter. As one critic observed, her purpose is perpetuation and celebration, not judgment.

Clifton says that family stories are part of the ingredients that make us who we are. She remembers hearing her own family's stories when she was growing up.

" My father told those stories to me over and over. That made them seem important. He told the stories to whoever was present, but I was the only person who listened. I think there is a matter of preserving the past for the future's sake. I think if we see our lives as an ongoing story, it's important to include all the ingredients of it and not have it in little compartments. I like to think of it as not just that was then, this is now, but that they all connect. For some reason, I've always been a person who found more interesting the stories between the stories. I've always wondered the hows and the whys to things. Why is this like this? What has gone into making us who we are? Is it good or not so good? What is destroying us? What will keep us warm? **"**

Response and Analysis

Ex–Basketball Player

Reading Check

1. Find details in the poem that tell us how Flick spends his time now.

2. Find details that tell us about Flick's past.

Thinking Critically

3. What different kinds of **sound effects** can you identify? Look especially for **internal rhyme** and **alliteration.** Note them all, and give examples.

4. Look back at the opening description of Pearl Avenue. How can this street be seen as a **metaphor** for Flick's life?

5. In the second stanza, find words that **personify** the gas pumps—that make them seem as if they were alive. Do you think Flick is similar to the pumps? Why or why not?

6. In the last stanza, what is the candy **compared** to, and who sees it that way? What do you think this suggests about Flick's fantasies—or dreams?

7. Scan the first and second stanzas of the poem. Which lines vary the **iambic pentameter** to avoid a mechanical sound? Which lines are in regular iambic pentameter?

miss rosie

Reading Check

1. What details tell you how Miss Rosie looks now?

2. What details tell you how Miss Rosie used to look?

Thinking Critically

3. Which **figure of speech** in "miss rosie" do you think is the most powerful? What picture of Miss Rosie does it create for you?

4. The **idiom** "i stand up," used twice, gives the most important clue to how the writer wants us to feel about Miss Rosie. What does standing up in the face of Miss Rosie's destruction mean? Why might the speaker be moved to "stand up" for Miss Rosie?

5. In a way, Miss Rosie seems to represent something more than herself, something never named. What do you think she might **symbolize**?

WRITING

Portrait of a Person

In their poems, Updike and Clifton paint a memorable portrait of a person who has lost the glory of former times. Think of someone you know or someone famous (or create a character of your own). Write a **description** of that person in either the heyday of success or past his or her prime. Be sure to use vivid **sensory images** as you describe what the person looks like and what he or she does.

▶ **Use "Describing a Person," pages 540–547, for help with this assignment.**

SKILLS FOCUS

Literary Skills
Analyze sound effects. Analyze idioms.

Writing Skills
Write a description of a person. Take notes on a subject for a poem. Write a comparison-contrast essay.

The Poet in You

Here's what Lucille Clifton says about how she writes poetry:

> I have a feeling that sometimes rather than wrestle and look for words, you have to be still and let them come. I was not trained as a poet, and I've never taken poetry lessons or had workshops. Nobody taught me anything much, really. So I learned how to learn, and what I learned is that I could be still and allow the world and the impressions and the feelings—I'm very good with feelings—to come to me, and I could use our language to write them down.

Try it. Plant yourself in front of something that you love (or merely like)—or something that disturbs you. Jot down all of the feelings and words and phrases as they occur to you. When you're finished taking notes, see whether you've got the makings of a poem. Work on it until you're satisfied, adding whatever sound effects seem natural and easy.

Comparing Poems

In an **essay, compare and contrast** Updike's poem about Flick with Clifton's poem about Miss Rosie. Before you begin writing, take notes on the points of comparison between the two poems, using a chart like this one:

	"Ex-Basket-ball Player"	"miss rosie"
What character is like today		
What character was once like		
Speaker's attitude toward character		

Vocabulary Development

Idioms All Around You

PRACTICE 1

1. Look over both poems, and note all of the expressions that you'd classify as **idioms** (see page 521). Get together with classmates, and see whether you agree.

2. With a small group, survey students in your school, or survey your family or neighbors. Ask them to think of as many idioms as they can, in English or other languages. Read a few idioms to get them started—for example, "big shot," "go in one ear and out the other." You might prepare a dictionary of idioms to share with the class.

SKILLS FOCUS

Vocabulary Skills
Recognize and define idioms. Create semantic maps for jargon.

(continued)

Jargon: Job-Related Vocabulary

Jargon is the specialized vocabulary used by people in particular jobs or sharing particular interests. Doctors have jargon, as do athletes, actors, computer users, and sailors.

PRACTICE 2

Set up a word map similar to the one below for *dunk,* in order to study each of the basketball terms Updike uses in his poem. If you're hooked on sports jargon, do the same for other sports terms, or make charts for technical terms associated with your hobby or special interest.

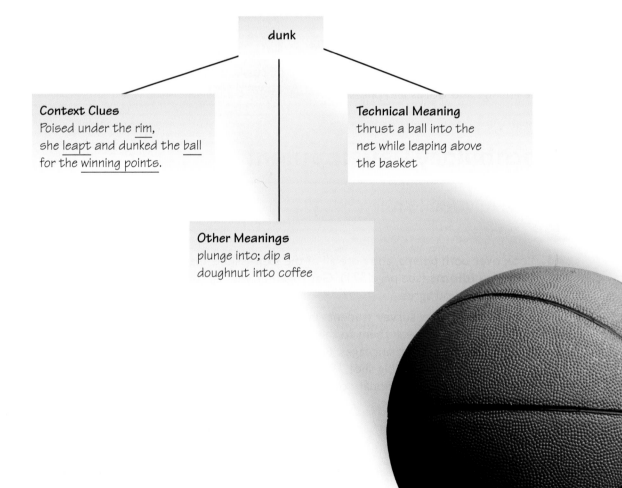

dunk

Context Clues
Poised under the rim,
she leapt and dunked the ball
for the winning points.

Technical Meaning
thrust a ball into the
net while leaping above
the basket

Other Meanings
plunge into; dip a
doughnut into coffee

Before You Read

Remember

Make the Connection

Quickwrite ✎

Many popular ballads list a series of memories in clear or interesting ways. On a piece of paper, list some of the events, objects, people, and places you can remember most vividly.

Literary Focus

Repetition and Refrain: Singing Sounds

Both poets and songwriters use **repetition** to create emotional effects. When certain words or phrases or sentences occur repeatedly in a kind of pattern, they're called a **refrain.** You can probably sing dozens of refrains (the part everyone remembers best) from your favorite songs. Refrains create musical effects because they repeat the exact sounds and sentence patterns again and again. Refrains also give emphasis to certain ideas. Sometimes a refrain can so draw out a story that it builds up tension and creates suspense.

Literary Skills
Understand repetition and refrain.

The Sun Dance (c. 1880s). Native American Plains Indian (probably Sioux) painting on animal hide.

Remember

Joy Harjo

Remember the sky that you were born under,
know each of the star's stories.
Remember the moon, know who she is.
Remember the sun's birth at dawn, that is the
5   strongest point of time. Remember sundown
and the giving away to night.
Remember your birth, how your mother struggled
to give you form and breath. You are evidence of
her life, and her mother's, and hers.
10   Remember your father. He is your life, also.
Remember the earth whose skin you are:
red earth, black earth, yellow earth, white earth
brown earth, we are earth.

Sun (1943) by Arthur G. Dove. Wax emulsion on canvas (24″ × 32″).

Remember the plants, trees, animal life who all have their
15 tribes, their families, their histories, too. Talk to them,
listen to them. They are alive poems.
Remember the wind. Remember her voice. She knows the
origin of this universe.
Remember that you are all people and that all people
20 are you.
Remember that you are this universe and that this
universe is you.
Remember that all is in motion, is growing, is you.
Remember that language comes from this.
25 Remember the dance that language is, that life is.
Remember.

Meet the Writer

Joy Harjo

"Enter the Poet's World"

Many of the poems of Joy Harjo (1951–   )
deal with her mixed Muscogee Creek and
Cherokee heritage and the themes of personal survival and mythic space. Harjo per-
forms her poetry and plays the saxophone
with a band, Poetic Justice.

When she writes, Harjo says, she often
feels the presence of her ancestors, and
sometimes an old Creek Indian within her
acts as her muse.

Here's what she tells her college students
about how to read a poem:

66 First of all, it's important to read the
poem out loud. Poetry is an oral art—it's
meant to be spoken and to be read out loud.
I have my students memorize at least two
poems a semester, which they usually don't
like doing, but they come to see why it's important. I've given thought to having everyone memorize a poem a week—for which
I'm sure I would not be very popular—but
there's such magic in doing that. Then it's
important to be willing to let go of your immediate reality and enter the poet's
world. 99

Response and Analysis

Reading Check

1. What single word, piled up throughout the poem, acts as a kind of **refrain**?

Thinking Critically

2. Whom do you suppose this **speaker** is talking to?

3. What elements of nature does the speaker **personify**—that is, in what way does she talk about them as if they were human?

4. What **metaphors** does the speaker use to describe our skin, which comes in all colors; the plants; animal life; and language itself?

5. What do you make of lines 19–22? Are these two statements logical? Do they sound true to you?

6. Someone has asked you what this poem is about. What will you say?

7. What lines from the poem do you think are especially important in delivering the speaker's message?

8. How does the **refrain** contribute to the poem's **tone** and message?

WRITING

Memories

Re-read your Quickwrite notes, and choose a number of the memories that are most meaningful to you. Then, imitate Harjo's poem by writing a series of sentences that begin "I remember . . ."

Orders

Harjo's poem is like a series of instructions to someone the poet addresses as "you." Write a series of **instructions** to a person *you* know: a child or a friend or an older person. Keep repeating one **verb** in your series of instructions (such as *love* or *read* or *hope*). You should include at least three things that you want the person to do.

Shell disc inscribed with a spider and sacred-cross-of-fire design (c. 1000 A.D.). Mississippi culture.
Field Museum of Natural History, Chicago.
©Werner Forman/Art Resource, New York.

SKILLS FOCUS

Literary Skills
Analyze repetition and refrain.

Writing Skills
Write sentences containing repetition. Write a series of instructions.

Before You Read

We Real Cool

Make the Connection

Quickwrite ✎

Read Gwendolyn Brooks's poem aloud several times, and imagine how the young people look, dress, and move. Jot down a description of what you visualize. Keep your notes to use on page 534.

Literary Focus

Alliteration: Repeated Consonant Sounds

Remember the old tongue twisters "*Peter Piper picked a peck of pickled peppers*" and "*She sells seashells by the seashore*"?

Both of those contain examples of **alliteration**—the repetition of the same or similar consonant sounds at the beginning (usually) of words that are close together. (A consonant is any letter that is not a vowel.)

By carefully choosing and arranging ordinary, everyday English words, poets make music with the sounds of words. The literary devices of rhyme, rhythm, repetition, onomatopoeia, and alliteration provide the special sound effects.

INTERNET

More About Gwendolyn Brooks

Keyword: LE5 10-7

SKILLS FOCUS

Literary Skills
Understand alliteration.

We Real Cool

The Pool Players.
Seven at The Golden Shovel.

We real cool. We
Left school. We

Lurk late. We
Strike straight. We

Sing sin. We
Thin gin. We

Jazz June. We
Die soon.

—Gwendolyn Brooks

Pool (1954) by Jacob Lawrence. Tempera on hardboard (9⅞″ × 13⅞″).

Meet the Writer

Gwendolyn Brooks

Chicago's Voice

Gwendolyn Brooks (1917–2000) was born in Topeka, Kansas, but for most of her life she was associated with Chicago, especially with its large African American population. Skilled in many different kinds of poetry, Brooks wrote with both formal elegance and an ear for the natural speech rhythms of the people of Chicago's South Side. In an interview, Brooks gave the following answers to questions about her work:

Q. Why do you write poetry?

Brooks. I like the concentration, the crush; I like working with language, as others like working with paints and clay or notes.

Q. Has much of your poetry a racial element?

Brooks. Yes. It is organic, not imposed. It is my privilege to state "Negroes" not as curios but as people.

Q. What is your poet's premise [basic principle]?

Brooks. "Vivify the contemporary fact," said Whitman. I like to vivify the *universal* fact, when it occurs to me. But the universal wears contemporary clothing very well.

For Independent Reading

You might enjoy Brooks's novel *Maud Martha* (1953), which follows a young African American girl as she grows up and finds her dream.

Response and Analysis

Reading Check

1. Who is the *we* in this poem?

2. What important facts do we learn about the speaker or speakers?

Thinking Critically

3. What purpose do the two lines immediately below the title serve? What **connotations,** or associations, do you have with the words *golden* and *shovel?*

4. What do you think is the poem's **theme,** or message?

5. Where does the poet use **alliteration?** When you read the poem aloud, how does the unusual repetition affect the sound of the poem?

6. Describe the poem's unusual use of **rhymes.**

7. The poem's **meter,** or pattern of stressed and unstressed syllables, is extremely unusual. It is clearly the work of a skilled poet. Scan the poem. What meter does Brooks use to pound out her story?

8. How would you describe the poem's **tone,** the poet's attitude toward the characters and subject? What words would you use to describe the speaker's tone?

Extending and Evaluating

9. Brooks wrote "We Real Cool" in 1960—more than forty years ago. Do you think the poem is outdated, or does it still apply to life today? Explain, referring to details in the poem and to your Quickwrite notes. ✏️

WRITING

A Poem with Sound Effects

Try to write your own **poem** in imitation of "We Real Cool." You could open with Brooks's title, or you could choose one of your own. You might build your poem on a series of statements that begin "I am . . ." or "We are . . ." Who will be the **speaker** (or speakers) of your poem? Work in as many examples of **alliteration** as you can.

LISTENING AND SPEAKING

An Oral Interpretation

Here's what Brooks said about reading her poem aloud:

> The *We's* in "We Real Cool" are tiny, wispy, weakly argumentative "Kilroy-is-here" announcements. The boys have no accented sense of themselves, yet they are aware of a semi-defined personal importance. Say the *We* softly.

With a group, prepare and present an **oral interpretation** of this poem. Decide whether you'll use a single voice or several voices or even a chorus. Will you use background music, and if so, what piece will you choose? Be sure to prepare scripts indicating where your speakers will pause and how they'll vary their volume. Ask the audience to evaluate the class performances.

SKILLS FOCUS

Literary Skills
Analyze alliteration.

Writing Skills
Write a poem containing alliteration.

Listening and Speaking Skills
Present an oral interpretation of a poem.

Jazz Fantasia

Make the Connection

Quickwrite 🖉

Choose a kind of music that you know and like. What sounds do you associate with that music? Jot down some ideas, and save your notes.

Literary Focus

Onomatopoeia: Sound Echoes Sense

No one is certain about the origins of language, but we do know that a few words in our languages are *echoic* in origin. That means that the words echo, or imitate, the sounds they name. Both nouns and verbs —such as *hush, buzz, whoosh, hiss,* and *hiccup*—can have echoic origins. The literary device that uses such words is called **onomatopoeia** (än′ō·mat′ō·pē′ə). Poets choose and place such words carefully to unify sound and meaning.

"Jazz Fantasia" is about jazz, so it's not surprising that the poet has used some words that echo the sounds of jazz. Read the poem once silently, and then read it aloud more than once. Listen to its sounds.

Bass by Gil Mayers (1947–   ). Mixed media.
Private collection.

Background

During the late nineteenth century small groups of African Americans in the South created a unique kind of music—jazz. Their music was improvised and unrehearsed, with a syncopated, irregular beat and many melodic variations. Jazz soloists wail and croon on the clarinet, saxophone, trumpet, and trombone. In the early days of jazz, though, musicians often played any object that could make a sound—for example, tin pans (see line 5 of the poem), coconuts, and sandpaper (line 6). Traps (line 9) are percussion instruments: drums, cymbals, blocks, and bells.

Jazz quickly spread from the South to Chicago, Kansas City, and New York. By the time Carl Sandburg wrote "Jazz Fantasia" (published in 1920), Americans and Europeans were enjoying what came to be known as the Jazz Age.

A **fantasia** is an unrehearsed, spontaneous musical composition with a structure determined by the composer's fancy.

SKILLS FOCUS

Literary Skills
Understand onomatopoeia.

Jazz Fantasia

Carl Sandburg

Drum on your drums, batter on your banjoes,
sob on the long cool winding saxophones.
Go to it, O jazzmen.

Sling your knuckles on the bottoms of the happy
5   tin pans, let your trombones ooze, and go husha-
husha-hush with the slippery sand-paper.

Moan like an autumn wind high in the lonesome treetops, moan soft like
you wanted somebody terrible, cry like a racing car slipping away from a
motorcycle cop, bang-bang! you jazzmen, bang altogether drums, traps,
10   banjoes, horns, tin cans—make two people fight on the top of a stairway
and scratch each other's eyes in a clinch tumbling down the stairs.

Can the rough stuff . . . now a Mississippi steamboat pushes up the night
river with a hoo-hoo-hoo-oo . . . and the green lanterns calling to the high
soft stars . . . a red moon rides on the humps of the low river hills . . .
15   go to it, O jazzmen.

Meet the Writer

Carl Sandburg

Poet of the Prairies

Carl Sandburg (1878–1967) wrote just about everything—poetry, history, biography, songs, newspaper articles, a novel, and children's books. He was a school dropout at thirteen, but he had a love of reading and writing from the time he was a little boy, and that love never left him. Like Walt Whitman, whose poetry influenced him greatly, the common man and America's history were the main focus of Sandburg's writings.

Sandburg was born and grew up in Galesburg, Illinois, a small town not far from the Mississippi River. He was one of seven children of poor Swedish immigrants. To supplement the family income, he left school at thirteen and began a series of odd jobs: driving a milk wagon, working in a barbershop, and serving as an apprentice tinsmith. At eighteen he traveled throughout the Midwest as a hobo. After a brief stint in the army during the Spanish-American War, Sandburg attended college in Galesburg. The big city—first Milwaukee, then Chicago—drew him, and he worked as a journalist from 1912 until the early 1930s.

Sandburg got his first break as a poet in 1914 when Harriet Monroe published six of his poems in *Poetry: A Magazine of Verse.* Monroe said of his early work: "One feels in all these poems a true and deep emotion of love as the central controlling motive—love of the prairie country, the prairie towns and city, and the people who struggle through toilsome lives there."

For many years, from the early 1920s to 1939, Sandburg also labored on a six-volume biography of his hero, Abraham Lincoln, a work that won Sandburg the Pulitzer Prize in history in 1940.

In his introduction to *Good Morning, America* (1928), a collection of poems, Sandburg lists thirty-eight definitions of poetry. Here are four of them:

> **❝** Poetry is the report of a nuance between two moments, when people say, 'Listen!' and 'Did you see it?' 'Did you hear it? What was it?'
>
> Poetry is a sliver of the moon lost in the belly of a golden frog.
>
> Poetry is a packsack of invisible keepsakes.
>
> Poetry is an echo asking a shadow dancer to be a partner. **❞**

Response and Analysis

Reading Check

1. Whom does the **speaker** of the poem address?

2. What message does the speaker give?

Thinking Critically

3. Point out the uses of **onomatopoeia** in the poem. What other **sound effects** can you identify?

4. Why is the poem's irregular **rhythm** appropriate? At what point in the poem does the rhythm change?

5. Which **images** convey the roughness and power of jazz? Which images create an altogether different **mood**?

6. Notice Sandburg's use of vivid **verbs** throughout the poem. Why do you think he chose these particular verbs? (Try substituting synonyms, and notice how the poem changes.)

7. Where does the poet use **similes, metaphors,** and **personification** to describe the jazzmen and their music?

WRITING

Playing Another Kind of Tune

Do what Carl Sandburg did: Write a **free-verse poem** that imitates a specific kind of music or sound. (Before you begin to write, look back at your Quickwrite notes for page 535. If you haven't settled on a subject yet, brainstorm ideas with a small group of classmates.) In your poem, include **sensory details, figurative language, onomatopoeia,** and all the **sound effects** you can think of.

LISTENING AND SPEAKING

Oral Interpretation

Here's a poem that *must* be read aloud. Practice your interpretation. Where will your voice rise and fall? What words will you emphasize? Which ones will you speak softly? Where will you take a breath? Practice reading the poem aloud until it sounds right to you, and then read it aloud to a small group or to a partner.

Literary Skills
Analyze onomatopoeia.

Writing Skills
Write a free-verse poem.

Listening and Speaking Skills
Present an oral interpretation of a poem.

Cherry Rouge (1976) by Bernard Rancillac. (1.6 m × 1.3 m).

Giraudon/Art Resource, New York.

POETRY

Now Hear This

You may think of poetry as a quiet pursuit, but *Poetry Out Loud,* edited by Robert Alden Rubin, reminds us that poems are meant to be heard as well as seen. You'll find more than one hundred poems suited for reading aloud in this collection—from Shakespeare's songs to Lewis Carroll's "Jabberwocky" to the American classic "Casey at the Bat." Limericks, lyrics, and rap are also featured in this collection of poems you'll want to read aloud.

POETRY

From East to West

One hundred and twenty-nine poets from sixty-eight countries are featured in *This Same Sky: A Collection of Poems from Around the World,* edited by Naomi Shahib Nye. These poems—many of which are translated here for the first time—address such universal yet individual subjects as dreamers and dreams, families, nature, loss, and the power of language and words. With titles like "A New Dress," "Bicycles," and "At the Ferry," *This Same Sky* shows us just how closely connected the entire world really is, despite great cultural differences.

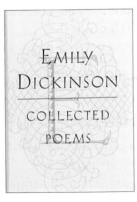

POETRY

Add a Dash of Dickinson

The reclusive nineteenth-century poet Emily Dickinson may have inspired more contemporary American poets than any other writer. To find out what all the fuss is about, take a look at *Emily Dickinson: Collected Poems,* with an insightful introduction by Martha Dickinson Bianchi. This collection includes poems that are alternately playful ("I'm nobody!"), exhilarating ("Wild nights!"), and reflective ("I felt a funeral in my brain").

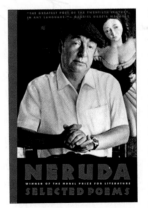

POETRY

Through Neruda's Eyes

Pablo Neruda is regarded as one of the greatest poets of the twentieth century. His poems tackle a range of universal themes, including love, peace, war, and the beauty and mystery of the natural world. For a sampling of his best works, read *Selected Poems,* a bilingual edition that allows you to read his poetry in English translation and Neruda's native Spanish. These soulful, impassioned, and humane works may change the way you view poetry . . . and life.

Describing a Person

Writing Assignment
Write a description of a specific person that you know well or that you can learn more about.

In this chapter you've read descriptive poetry that allowed you to experience the moments the poets wished to share with you. Did you find the people, places, and events described somewhat familiar or entirely new? Could you envision what the poets described? Good **description** uses words to create a picture. Now it's your turn to learn new strategies for creating vivid descriptions to share with others.

Prewriting

Choose a Subject

Snapshots Memorable photographs, such as those you have seen in calendars, in books and magazines, or on the Internet, compose a scene using light and shapes. When you describe a subject through writing, you use only words to compose a mental picture for your audience. Through words, you define your subject and highlight its importance to you. For this workshop you will describe a person. To find a suitable subject that will leave a lasting impression on your audience, consider the following.

- The person should be someone that you know well or someone that you can talk to and learn more about as you prepare to write.

- The person should be either someone that will immediately interest your essay's readers or someone that you can make interesting through your description.

Consider Purpose and Audience

Taking in the View Think about your **purpose,** or reason for writing. Knowing this can help you communicate a **clear and distinctive perspective,** or point of view—your unique thoughts and feelings about the subject. You will describe the subject and explain your relationship with him or her. Think of this purpose throughout the writing process to ensure that you maintain a consistent and focused perspective in your essay.

Next, think about who your **audience** will be. Who is likely to read your essay? What do they already know about your subject? What kind of details about the subject will they find interesting and appealing? Write with your audience in mind at all times.

SKILLS FOCUS

Writing Skills
Write a description of a person. Choose a subject. Consider purpose and audience.

Gather Your Details

Hunting and Gathering When you describe your subject, include details that will help your readers mentally create a complete portrait of the person—not just a visual re-creation of the person.

- Include details that give your readers a real sense of *knowing* the whole person, not just his or her physical **appearance.**

- Gather details by searching your memory, by observing your subject directly, or by talking with or interviewing the subject.

- Use **precise language** and **concrete details** rather than vague, general descriptions.

- Use a combination of the main kinds of details in your description, as shown in the following chart.

KINDS OF DETAILS	
Type	**Use**
sensory details—words and phrases that appeal to the five senses: sight, hearing, touch, smell, and taste	to describe the **sights, sounds,** and **smells** associated with your subject and the **actions, movements,** and **gestures** that make that person unique
factual details—names, dates, numbers, and quotations, as well as true statements	to provide details about your subject that you can't relate through the senses
figurative details—similes, metaphors, and examples of **personification**	to create imaginative comparisons between something unfamiliar and something familiar (For more on **similes, metaphors,** and **personification,** see pages 477–478.)
details of thoughts and feelings	to allow the audience to know what you think and how you feel about the subject

Determine a Controlling Impression

Mission Control Once you've gathered details, you must determine your **controlling impression**—the particular idea or feeling you are trying to communicate about your subject. Follow these steps to determine your controlling impression.

DO THIS

- Begin by looking at the details you've gathered.

- Next, write down a handful of nouns or adjectives that best sum up the majority of these details. Ignore details that seem out of place; they may not support your controlling impression.

- Finally, circle one or two of the best nouns or adjectives to use in a statement of the controlling impression.

   On the next page is an example that shows how a student writing about his uncle developed a statement of his controlling impression.

Writing Skills
Gather and organize information. Determine a controlling impression.

Subject: Uncle Samir

Details: proud of his unruly hair, smiling deep blue eyes, his dog smells, always looks you in the eye, smiles often, neatly groomed, graceful, stirring voice, physically fit, dresses nicely

Impression details give: kindness, (pride), (respect), cleanliness

Statement of controlling impression: From top to bottom, Uncle Samir is all pride and respect.

TIP Keep in mind that you can fine-tune your statement of the controlling impression as you progress through the stages of the writing process.

Once you've determined your controlling impression, discard any details that do not support it. For example, the description of Uncle Samir on page 543 is meant to impress readers, so the writer left out information about his uncle's dog smelling.

Organize Your Description

Making It All Make Sense Next, arrange your details in a clear and **logical order** that will make sense to your audience.

DO THIS

• **Spatial order** is the arrangement of details in space. You can describe your subject from near to far, from far to near, from top to bottom, from bottom to top, or from side to side. This order primarily uses sight details. For example, the Writer's Model describes Uncle Samir from his head to his feet. Give your readers transition clues as you shift attention from one detail to another. For example, write "**beneath** his nose," "**over** by his left ear," or "as you move **closer,** you notice. . . ."

• **Order of importance** presents details from most important to least important, or vice versa. For example, if Uncle Samir's shockingly blue eyes were his most outstanding characteristic, then the Writer's Model might have begun by focusing on those eyes and then giving less important details last, or vice versa. Begin with the most important detail if you want to capture your reader's attention right away. Finish with the most important detail if you want to create a strong final impression.

You can easily use a combination of spatial order and order of importance, too. Just begin your description by dividing your subject into rough areas—for example, head, body, and feet. Then, describe by order of importance the individual details of each area—for example, moving from the eyes to the ears to the nose, depending on each feature's importance.

PRACTICE & APPLY 1 Using the prewriting instructions on pages 540–542, select a subject, gather details, write a statement of your controlling impression, and logically organize your descriptive essay.

Writing

Describing a Person

Introduction

- Attract your readers' attention.
- Introduce the person you will describe.
- Make a clear statement of your controlling impression.

Body

- Use sensory, factual, and figurative details; include your thoughts and feelings.
- Use only details that support your controlling impression.
- Arrange your details spatially or by order of importance.

Conclusion

- Sum up the details you have related.
- Restate your controlling impression, expressing it in different words.
- Make a final comment about your subject.

A Writer's Model

Samir of the Kingdom of Jordan

Last summer, my father's brother, Samir, immigrated to the United States. Samir had lived his whole life in Amman, Jordan, and had spent his last eleven years there practicing dentistry. Because my father had immigrated to America before I was born, I had never met my uncle before. He is currently living in our house while he is looking for a place of his own. Getting to know him, I have found that from top to bottom, Uncle Samir is all pride and respect.

Uncle Samir is forty-five years old with a mass of tangled, dark brown hair (with some gray) that looks more like a bird's nest than a head of hair. He told me one morning, "This hair is impossible. The harder I try to tame it, the worse it fights back." I think he is proud that his hair has as much spirit as he does.

His eyes really seem to smile. They are shockingly blue—deeper than any eyes I have ever seen. They are certainly unique for our family, who all have brown eyes. When Uncle Samir speaks to you, he always looks you in the eye, which makes you feel that what you have to say is very important to him and draws your respect, too.

Since Uncle Samir came to stay, I've rarely seen him without a smile beneath his well-groomed mustache. He often emphasizes what he says with sweeping flourishes of his graceful hands. When he is in the shower or when he is cooking, you can hear Uncle Samir singing in Arabic with a voice like a great opera star—low, loud, and clear. I

(continued)

INTRODUCTION
Factual details

Controlling impression

BODY
Spatial order—top
Figurative detail
Thoughts

Sensory details—sight

Feelings

Sensory details—sight

Sensory details—hearing

(continued)

do not always know what he is singing about, but his voice is emotionally stirring.

Spatial order— middle

My uncle stands tall and walks with a confident stride. He is more physically fit than my father, who is actually the younger of the two brothers. He says that physical fitness is the fastest way to mental fitness. My father and he work out regularly at the community center, or as Uncle Samir says "I work out, your father tries to catch up!"

Factual details

It's hard for me to imagine my uncle at the community center because I have never seen Uncle Samir dressed in a T-shirt and shorts, or even blue jeans. Each morning when I wake up, he is already wearing freshly pressed clothing. His slacks always have a sharp crease, and he's never without his tie—even at the dinner table, which is unusual for my family. Though immaculate looking, his clothes do always smell like a dentist's office. I guess that's just one of the downsides to being a dentist.

Sensory detail— smell

Thoughts

Spatial order— bottom

When your eyes travel down Uncle Samir from head to toe, the journey ends with his shoes, shining with a clean, dark black radiance. He takes great care each day that these shoes are shiny enough he can see himself in them. Those shiny shoes are the ultimate contrast to his hurricane of hair.

Figurative detail

CONCLUSION

Restatement of controlling impression

Summary of details

Final comment

If I could describe my uncle in two words, they would be *proud* and *respectful*. I have only known him for a short time, but in that time I've come to truly admire him. You can sense that Uncle Samir is a quality person by the way he stands, walks, dresses, and talks. He has pride in who he is, where he's come from, and where he's going in life. I hope some of that will rub off on me as we get to know each other better in the future.

INTERNET

More Writer's Models

Keyword: LE5 10-7

PRACTICE & APPLY 2 Using the framework and Writer's Model on pages 543–544 as guides, write the first draft of your descriptive essay. Be sure to include a variety of details as you work to create a distinct controlling impression of your subject.

Revising

Evaluate and Revise Your Essay

The Finishing Touches Re-read your draft. First, evaluate and revise its content and organization by using the guidelines in the chart below. Then, focus on its style by using the chart on the next page. Think about your **audience,** your **purpose,** and the **formality** of the essay's context when revising.

▶ **First Reading: Content and Organization** Answer the questions in the left-hand column of the following chart. If you need help, use the tips in the middle column. To make any needed changes, use the revision techniques in the right-hand column.

PEER REVIEW

Exchange your essay with a peer before you revise. He or she may have ideas on how you can more clearly order the details in your description.

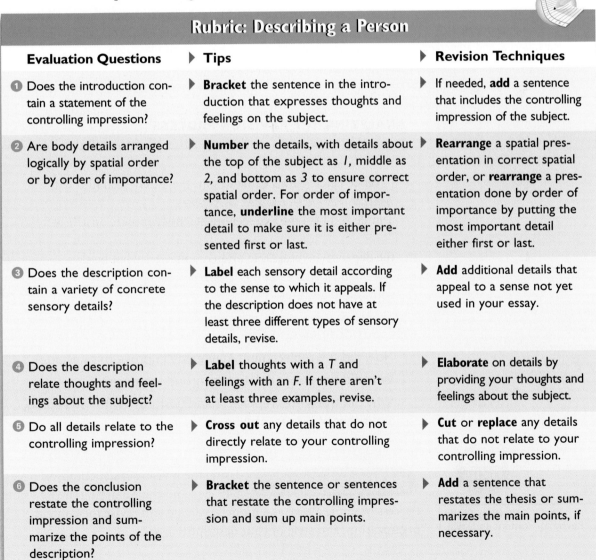

Rubric: Describing a Person

Evaluation Questions	▶ Tips	▶ Revision Techniques
❶ Does the introduction contain a statement of the controlling impression?	▶ **Bracket** the sentence in the introduction that expresses thoughts and feelings on the subject.	▶ If needed, **add** a sentence that includes the controlling impression of the subject.
❷ Are body details arranged logically by spatial order or by order of importance?	▶ **Number** the details, with details about the top of the subject as *1,* middle as *2,* and bottom as *3* to ensure correct spatial order. For order of importance, **underline** the most important detail to make sure it is either presented first or last.	▶ **Rearrange** a spatial presentation in correct spatial order, or **rearrange** a presentation done by order of importance by putting the most important detail either first or last.
❸ Does the description contain a variety of concrete sensory details?	▶ **Label** each sensory detail according to the sense to which it appeals. If the description does not have at least three different types of sensory details, revise.	▶ **Add** additional details that appeal to a sense not yet used in your essay.
❹ Does the description relate thoughts and feelings about the subject?	▶ **Label** thoughts with a *T* and feelings with an *F.* If there aren't at least three examples, revise.	▶ **Elaborate** on details by providing your thoughts and feelings about the subject.
❺ Do all details relate to the controlling impression?	▶ **Cross out** any details that do not directly relate to your controlling impression.	▶ **Cut** or **replace** any details that do not relate to your controlling impression.
❻ Does the conclusion restate the controlling impression and summarize the points of the description?	▶ **Bracket** the sentence or sentences that restate the controlling impression and sum up main points.	▶ **Add** a sentence that restates the thesis or summarizes the main points, if necessary.

Second Reading: Style During the second reading, you should focus on style—*how* you express your ideas. Just as your choice of clothing can be an expression of your style of dress, your choice of words can be an expression of your writing style. You can both dress up your essay and ensure that your readers get a crystal-clear image of the person you've described by replacing vague nouns, verbs, and adjectives with more **precise language.** For example, replace "ran" with "sprinted," "jogged," or "scampered." Replace "happy" with "exhilarated," "inspired," or "perky." Use the following style guidelines to find and fix any fuzzy language in your description.

Style Guidelines

Evaluation Question	▶ Tip	▶ Revision Technique
● Are the ideas in this essay made clear with precise nouns, verbs, and adjectives?	▶ **Circle** any vague nouns, verbs, and adjectives that do not give a crystal-clear picture of the subject.	▶ **Replace** vague nouns, verbs, and adjectives with more precise language.

ANALYZING THE REVISION PROCESS

Study these revisions, and answer the questions that follow.

replace, delete

Since Uncle Samir came to stay, I've rarely seen him without
beneath his well-groomed mustache.
a smile on his lips. ~~I've seen mustache trimmers on sale at~~

~~the department store.~~ He often emphasizes what he says
sweeping flourishes of his graceful hands.

replace

with ~~hand gestures.~~

Responding to the Revision Process

1. How did the replacement in line one improve this passage?

2. Why did the writer delete the second sentence?

3. Why did the writer replace "hand gestures" with "sweeping flourishes of his graceful hands"?

SKILLS FOCUS

Writing Skills
Revise for content and style.

PRACTICE & APPLY 3 Using the revising instructions on pages 545–546 and the Analyzing the Revision Process example above as a model, evaluate and revise the content, organization, and style of your descriptive essay.

Publishing

Proofread and Publish Your Essay

Get It Right Writers often hurry to get their ideas down on paper. Not surprisingly, first drafts usually contain many mistakes—and often these mistakes are carried over into later drafts. Consequently, it is vital that you re-read your description and exchange essays with a classmate for peer proofreading. Make sure the essay uses correct grammar, punctuation, and spelling.

Share and Share Alike Keep in mind that your descriptive essay is more than just a listing of the details you have gathered about a person. It also includes your perspective, or insights, on that person. Share this perspective with others by doing one of the following.

- With your classmates, create a collection of descriptive essays to use as a class reference source showing the different ways you've all described your subjects.

- If you described a person that you admire, such as a parent, teacher, or friend, enter your essay in a contest looking for "America's best."

- If your description is of a teacher or student at your school, ask if you may post it on your school's Web page. Browsers or future students may be interested to hear about the people at your school.

- Adapt your essay and deliver it as an oral descriptive presentation to your class, your family, or another interested audience. For more on **presenting a description,** see page 548.

Reflect on Your Essay

Seeking Closure After publishing your description, take some time to reflect on the processes you went through to create it. Answer the following questions on your own paper.

- What did writing about your subject teach you about yourself? What new insights did you gain about your relationship with your subject?

- How did you decide which sensory details to include about your subject and which to exclude?

- How did you decide the order in which you organized your details? How could you use this same organizational structure for other types of writing or for other classes?

PRACTICE & APPLY 4 Following the instructions on this page, proofread your description and correct any mistakes you find. Consider your publishing options; then, reflect on what you have learned in writing this essay.

TIP Proofreading will help ensure that your essay follows the **conventions** of standard American English. For example, you may find that your description compares your subject to someone or something else. Be sure that you use comparative and superlative forms correctly. For more on **comparative and superlative forms,** see Comparison of Modifiers, 5c and d, in the Language Handbook.

SKILLS FOCUS

Writing Skills
Proofread, especially for correct use of comparative and superlative modifiers.

Presenting a Description

Speaking Assignment
Adapt a descriptive essay for an oral presentation and deliver the presentation to your class.

You can add a whole new dimension to your description by presenting it orally. **Descriptive presentations** allow you to use your voice, gestures, and visuals to help your audience create a vivid mental image of your subject. Reading your essay aloud, however, would likely be dry and uninteresting to your audience. Instead, adapt your essay to make it more suited for oral delivery.

Adapt Your Description

A Reason for Everything Before you begin planning your presentation, consider your **purpose**—your reason for giving the presentation. As with your written essay, your purpose will be to describe a person and to convey your thoughts and feelings about him or her. However, in your descriptive presentation, you can also use your voice, body, and visuals to achieve your purpose.

Attitude Check Much of the audience's interest in your oral description will center on your relationship with the subject. Your subjective description will show your **personal involvement** with your subject to let your audience see why he or she is important to you. Be sure to provide a unique **point of view**—your thoughts and feelings about your subject.

Put It into Perspective Another way to adapt your description is to shift your **perspective,** or **vantage point**—the physical position from which you observe the subject. For example, the captain of the school's soccer team may appear small and ordinary from your seat in the bleachers, but your point of view could change drastically if you were to play next to her, or even meet her face to face after the game. Presenting details from more than one vantage point will allow your audience to form a more complete picture of your subject.

More, or Less, the Same? After you know how much time you'll have for your presentation, you may need to cut or add details. If you don't have time to include all of the **sensory, factual,** and **figurative details** from your written essay, be sure that you don't cut details that are essential to your **controlling impression.** The details you keep should not only provide **concrete imagery** to help your listeners picture the subject's appearance, but should also convey your thoughts and feelings about him or her. If you must add to your description, consider additional research, such as interviewing your subject or the people who know him or her.

SKILLS FOCUS

Listening and Speaking Skills
Give an oral presentation of a descriptive essay. Adapt a text for presentation.

Plan Your Presentation

Organize Your Ideas In a written essay, it's easy for readers to follow the flow of your ideas from paragraph to paragraph because they can go back and re-read if they get confused. However, in an oral presentation, listeners cannot go back and catch anything that they missed. Reexamine the **organizational pattern** of your written essay. Ask yourself whether the same pattern will be effective when presented aloud. Will the details you present first grab your audience's attention? Will the details you discuss in your conclusion leave a lasting impression? If your answer to either of these questions is no, then you may need to consider reorganizing your essay to suit your new audience.

Make Note Cards Next, put your ideas onto **note cards.** Make an introductory note card containing information to draw your audience into your presentation. Then, make one note card for the controlling impression, one for each supporting detail, and one for your concluding thoughts. Each card should include **summaries,** or brief notes about the key ideas you want to share, rather than word-for-word explanations. Number your cards to keep them in order.

Once your cards are complete, look for places to employ **visuals,** such as photos, props, or electronic media, in your presentation. For example, if you were describing your grandmother, you could bring in a picture of her or something else that's closely associated with her, such as her favorite book or a CD of the music that she listened to when she was your age.

Practice Your Presentation

Speak Easy While your note cards may be a convenient backup if you forget what to say, reading directly from them during the presentation may put your audience to sleep. Use verbal and nonverbal techniques to keep your listeners alert and to make your points clear.

- **Verbal techniques** include speaking clearly, loudly, and slowly so that everyone in the room can understand you.

- **Nonverbal techniques** include maintaining eye contact with audience members, making appropriate gestures, and occasionally changing your facial expressions to match your message. For example, you might raise your eyebrows to show surprise or scrunch your nose to indicate a feeling of disgust.

PRACTICE & APPLY 5 Adapt the descriptive essay you wrote in the Writing Workshop, and practice your verbal and nonverbal delivery techniques. Finally, present your description orally to your class.

Reference Note

For more on **spatial order** and **order of importance,** see page 542.

TIP When presenting your description, avoid using an overly formal tone or using gestures that might distract or offend your audience. Your vocabulary should suit your audience and purpose. For example, if your audience contains many children, do not use complex vocabulary.

SKILLS FOCUS

Listening and Speaking Skills
Plan your presentation. Practice your presentation using verbal and nonverbal techniques.

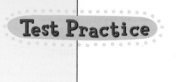

DIRECTIONS: Read the following poem. Then, read and respond to the questions that follow.

Fireworks

Amy Lowell

You hate me and I hate you,
And we are so polite, we two!

But whenever I see you, I burst apart
And scatter the sky with my blazing heart.
5   It spits and sparkles in stars and balls,
Buds into roses—and flares, and falls.

Scarlet buttons, and pale green disks,
Silver spirals and asterisks,
Shoot and tremble in a mist
10 Peppered with mauve and amethyst.

I shine in the windows and light up the trees,
And all because I hate you, if you please.

And when you meet me, you rend asunder
And go up in a flaming wonder
15 Of saffron cubes, and crimson moons,
And wheels all amaranths° and maroons.

Golden lozenges° and spades,
Arrows of malachites° and jades,
Patens° of copper, azure sheaves.
20 As you mount, you flash in the glossy leaves.

Such fireworks as we make, we two!
Because you hate me and I hate you.

---

16. **amaranths** (amʹə·ranthsʹ) *n.*: dark purplish reds similar to the color of the amaranth flower.
17. **lozenges** (läzʹ ənj·əz) *n.*: diamond shapes.
18. **malachites** (malʹə·kītsʹ) *n.*: gems made of a green mineral used in ornamental objects or as a source of copper ore.
19. **patens** (patʹʹns) *n.*: metal disks or plates.

SKILLS FOCUS

Literary Skills
Analyze imagery, figurative language, and the sounds of poetry.

1. "Fireworks" can be classified as —
   A a lyric poem
   B a narrative poem
   C an elegy
   D a ballad

2. From the poem, we can tell —
   F that the speaker is a man
   G that the speaker is a woman
   H that the speaker is a child
   J nothing about the speaker's sex or age

3. What has happened to cause the speaker's "blazing heart" (line 4)?
   A The speaker has been insulted.
   B The speaker has lost an argument.
   C The speaker has been jilted.
   D We never find out.

4. The **repetition** of the *s, b,* and *f* sounds in lines 5 and 6 is an example of —
   F onomatopoeia
   G alliteration
   H simile
   J free verse

5. How does Lowell use **meter** and **rhyme** in "Fireworks"?
   A She uses four stresses per line with a strict rhyme scheme.
   B She uses five stresses per line with no end rhyme.
   C She uses free verse with a strict rhyme scheme.
   D She uses free verse with no end rhyme.

6. The poem contains an **extended metaphor,** which begins in —
   F the first stanza
   G the second stanza
   H the third stanza
   J the fourth stanza

7. The fireworks in the poem describe —
   A a relationship between two people
   B a holiday celebration
   C a family get-together
   D a war scene

8. Most of the poem's **imagery** deals with —
   F natural landscapes
   G urban scenes
   H colors and smells
   J colors and shapes

9. The poem's first line, repeated twice (with variations), becomes a kind of —
   A stanza
   B refrain
   C simile
   D metaphor

10. The **rhymes** in the poem can be defined as —
    F free verse
    G internal only
    H exact
    J approximate

Constructed Response

11. If the story in the poem were written in prose, how would it change? Explain your answer.

DIRECTIONS: Read the following paragraph from a draft of a student's descriptive essay. Then, read the questions below it. Choose the best answer to each question, and mark your answers on your own paper.

(1) When I was young, I lived next door to a kind, elderly man named Mr. Osborne. (2) He was like the grandfather I never had. (3) Mr. Osborne was 76, had never married, and lived alone with his golden retriever. (4) His house was small and was within walking distance of the park. (5) He had gleaming white teeth and a smile that charmed all his neighbors. (6) Every day I would see him trimming the bushes outside his house, and if he saw me he would always pick the prettiest flower in his garden for me. (7) In school, I would paint pictures to give him in return, and later he would look at them with his deep blue eyes lined with melancholy creases, and tell me in his wavering voice that they were the best he'd ever seen. (8) When he died years later, he left in his house a brown portfolio containing all of the artwork I had ever given him.

1. Which sentence should be deleted to improve the controlling impression of the passage?

   A 1

   B 2

   C 4

   D 7

2. Which of the following phrases would be a more precise replacement for the phrase "trimming the bushes outside his house" in sentence 6?

   F trimming all of the plants in his big, beautiful yard

   G working on the landscape outside his house

   H cutting each one of the plants in his front yard

   J carefully pruning the rose bushes in front of his house

3. Which sentence would be most appropriate if the writer wanted to add sensory details to the passage?

   A His hands were always gnarled, scratched, and deeply tanned from working in his flower beds all day.

   B Mr. Osborne was a flower expert and knew of more than twenty different types of roses that grew in our area.

   C The first thing I did after school each day was hurry over to visit with Mr. Osborne and talk about our day.

   D Mr. Osborne's dog was named Rocky, and I often took him on long walks around the neighborhood.

4. Which of the following sentences, if added to the end of the paragraph, would reinforce its controlling impression?

   F Mr. Osborne was famous all over the community for his flower gardens and won several local contests.

   G I realized then that we had shared a common bond—I had been the granddaughter he had never had.

   H Mr. Osborne was the only person who thought that my artwork was worth anything.

   J Having close friendships with your neighbors is a good way to build community spirit.

5. If you were listening to an oral presentation of this description, what tone would you expect the speaker to use?

   A humorous

   B angry

   C sentimental

   D smug

Collection 8

LITERARY CRITICISM

Evaluating Style

INFORMATIONAL READING FOCUS

EVALUATING AN ARGUMENT

Proper words in proper places,
make the true definition of a style.

—Jonathan Swift

INTERNET

Collection
Resources

Keyword: LE5 10-8

Three Musicians (1921) by Pablo Picasso.
Oil on canvas (201 cm × 223 cm).

Museum of Modern Art, New York.
© Succession Picasso, 2000.

Elements of Literature

Evaluating Style *by* Mara Rockliff
HOW IT'S SAID

Style: Everybody's Got It

Suppose a friend sends you an e-mail from her dad's address. Chances are you wouldn't read too far before you realized who was really writing to you. *What* your friend said would clue you in, but *how* she said it—the words she picked and the way she put those words together—would also tell you a lot. That is, her **style** would be a giveaway.

Every piece of writing has a style—a special way of using words—though not all styles are equally distinct. If you pick up a city newspaper, all the front-page articles will sound alike, even though different reporters may have written them. Their style could be called straightforward news reporting—no frills, no fancy words. Flip to columns by Dave Barry or Miss Manners, and you'll find two different styles. Dave Barry is flip and funny. Miss Manners is, well, a little fussy.

Diction: The Power of a Word

Style starts with **diction**—the words a writer chooses. If you want a research paper to sound serious and scientific, will you use the expression *busted leg* or *fractured femur*? If you write a story for young children, will you call the hero *pertinacious, obdurate,* or simply *stubborn*?

Long words with Latin roots (like *pertinacious*) tend to come across as formal and intellectual. They might make the writer sound like a showoff. Shorter Anglo-Saxon words (like *stubborn*) sound plain and to the point. Even more casual are slang words (*pigheaded* or *die-hard*) and contractions (*He's stubborn, isn't he?* instead of *He is stubborn, is he not?*).

Formal diction is what makes many classic novels sound old-fashioned to contemporary readers. Take, for example, the first sentence of *Washington Square* by Henry James, published in 1880:

> During a portion of the first half of the present century, and more particularly during the latter part of it, there flourished and practiced in the city of New York a physician who enjoyed perhaps an exceptional share of the consideration which, in the United States, has always been bestowed upon distinguished members of the medical profession.

A writer today might say:

> Americans respect doctors, and in New York fifty years ago Dr. Sloper was respected even more than most.

Sentence Structure: Putting It All Together

Of course, the second version uses not just simpler words but fewer words. That's another aspect of style—**sentence structure,** or the way words are put together. A writer can use mostly long, elaborate sentences (as Henry James did) or simple, direct sentences, as the contemporary writer Gary Paulsen does:

> He had to fly it somehow. Had to fly the plane. He had to help himself.

SKILLS FOCUS

Literary Skills
Understand style, including diction, sentence structure, figures of speech, tone, and mood.

One Irish writer, James Joyce, wrote long run-on sentences that sound exactly like thoughts racing through a person's mind. One sentence in his novel *Ulysses* runs on for forty pages!

Ernest Hemingway wrote sentences so straightforward and plain that several generations of novelists have tried to copy his style; William Faulkner wrote sentences so elaborate and ornate that several generations of novelists have tried to copy *his* style.

Figures of Speech: Plain Style Versus Ornate Style

Figures of speech are expressions that are based on unusual comparisons and are not literally true.

Some writers prefer a plain style and so don't use many figures of speech. Those who favor a more ornate or poetic style use a great number of them. You might not realize it, but nonfiction writers often use figurative language. Here is a scientific writer, Lewis Thomas, using a simile to explain warts:

Warts are wonderful structures. They can appear overnight on any part of the skin, like mushrooms on a damp lawn.

Tone: An Attitude

Another aspect of a writer's style is tone. **Tone** is the attitude a writer takes toward the subject of a work, its characters, or the audience. Some writers, for example, convey a tone of pessimism: "I can't read another one of his books," someone might say. "They are so *depressing*." Other writers may use language that creates a tone of humor or joy. Some writers have a satiric tone (think of TV sitcoms). Some have tragic tones (think of a Shakespeare play like *Romeo and Juliet*).

Mood: An Atmosphere

Mood, which is the atmosphere a writer creates in a work, is also an aspect of style. Many writers become famous for the moods or atmospheres they create. Some readers buy every Stephen King novel that comes out because they love to enter his spooky settings.

Theme

A writer's style might not actually create his or her **theme,** the idea about life that a story is expressing. Style does have a powerful influence on theme, though. A story that presents a dark and sad worldview, for example, will almost certainly be written in a somber style.

Practice

Here is a simple sentence:

The boy walked through the woods.

1. Rewrite the sentence using **figurative language** to create an atmosphere of gloom.
2. Rewrite the sentence using an ornate style.
3. Rewrite the sentence to indicate a **tone** of affection for the boy.

Before You Read

Geraldo No Last Name

Make the Connection

Quickwrite ✏️

Sometimes our paths cross with other people's unexpectedly, and all too briefly. Have you ever wondered what might have happened if you had gotten to know one such person better? Complete a chart like the one below with notes about someone you met briefly whom you wish you could have known better.

What do you remember most about the person?		
How did you meet the person?	Where?	When?
Characteristics/Traits of the person:		

Literary Focus

Style: The Personal Stamp

Just as no two people in the world have the same fingerprints, so does everyone have a unique style. Your style is your own mode of expression. The way you dress is a style. So is the way you shape your sentences. Are they short and simple, or long and complicated? When you read your writing aloud, does it have the rhythm of poetry, or does it sound plain?

In literary works, **style** refers to the particular way writers use language to express their feelings and ideas. Style is largely created through sentence length and word choice. Some writers' styles are so famous that people can read a single sentence and know they are reading, for example, a short story by Ernest Hemingway. A Sandra Cisneros story has that kind of distinctive style. Listen for it.

Diction and Tone

Diction, or word choice, is one of the main ingredients of style. Writers carefully select particular words to express their thoughts and feelings and their attitude. For example, diction can be formal (*remove yourself*) or informal (*get a move on*). Diction can be plain (*clothing*) or fancy (*apparel*). Diction can also be colloquial, full of slang, poetic, and so on.

Diction has a powerful effect on creating tone in a piece of writing. **Tone,** which is not easy to define, can be described as the writer's attitude toward the subject or audience. The tone of a work can be, for example, serious, playful, sarcastic, or angry. Sometimes changing a single word can change the tone (*isn't/ain't, worker/brazer*). As you read, notice the diction Cisneros uses. What tone does she create?

Reading Skills 📖

Monitoring Your Reading: Questioning

Good readers **ask questions** as they read—perhaps about unfamiliar vocabulary, a confusing description, or a character's behavior. Good writers, like Cisneros, sometimes invite questions by purposely leaving some things unanswered. Jot down your questions as you read this story.

Geraldo No Last Name

Sandra Cisneros

An accident, don't you know. Hit and run.

She met him at a dance. Pretty too, and young. Said he worked in a restaurant, but she can't remember which one. Geraldo. That's all. Green pants and Saturday shirt. Geraldo. That's what he told her.

El Club (1990) by Nick Quijano. Gouache on paper (22″ × 30″).

nd how was she to know she'd be the last one to see him alive. An accident, don't you know. Hit and run. Marin, she goes to all those dances. Uptown. Logan. Embassy. Palmer. Aragon. Fontana. The manor. She likes to dance. She knows how to do cumbias and salsas and rancheras even. And he was just someone she danced with. Somebody she met that night. That's right.

That's the story. That's what she said again and again. Once to the hospital people and twice to the police. No address. No name. Nothing in his pockets. Ain't it a shame.

Only Marin can't explain why it mattered, the hours and hours, for somebody she didn't even know. The hospital emergency room. Nobody but an intern working all alone. And maybe if the surgeon would've come, maybe if he hadn't lost so much blood, if the surgeon had only come, they would know who to notify and where.

But what difference does it make? He wasn't anything to her. He wasn't her boyfriend or anything like that. Just another brazer[1] who didn't speak English. Just another wetback.[2] You know the kind. The ones who always look ashamed. And what was she doing out at 3:00 A.M. anyway? Marin who was sent home with her coat and some aspirin. How does she explain?

---

1. **brazer** (brā'zer) *n.:* Americanization of the Spanish word *bracero*, used in the United States to refer to a Mexican laborer allowed into the United States temporarily to work.
2. **wetback** *n.:* offensive term for a Mexican laborer who illegally enters the United States, often by swimming or wading the Rio Grande.

She met him at a dance. Geraldo in his shiny shirt and green pants. Geraldo going to a dance.

What does it matter?

They never saw the kitchenettes. They never knew about the two-room flats[3] and sleeping rooms he rented, the weekly money orders sent home, the currency exchange. How could they?

His name was Geraldo. And his home is in another country. The ones he left behind are far away, will wonder, shrug, remember. Geraldo—he went north . . . we never heard from him again. ■

---

3. **flats** *n.:* apartments.

Meet the Writer

Sandra Cisneros

"Unforgettable as a First Kiss"

Sandra Cisneros (1954–   ) spent her childhood moving back and forth between Chicago, where she was born, and Mexico, where her father was born. She currently lives in San Antonio, Texas.

Cisneros's first full-length work, *The House on Mango Street,* appeared in 1984. The narrator of this series of connected stories is a lively and thoughtful girl named Esperanza. (Her name means "hope" in Spanish.) Cisneros has also published collections of her poetry, including *My Wicked Wicked Ways* (1987), and another collection of stories, *Woman Hollering Creek* (1991). One critic has said that her stories "invite us into the souls of characters as unforgettable as a first kiss."

Cisneros did not find her unique voice as a writer until she attended the Writers' Workshop at the University of Iowa.

❝Everyone seemed to have some communal knowledge which I did not have. It was not until [the] moment when I separated myself, when I considered myself truly distinct, that my writing acquired a voice. I knew I was a Mexican woman, but I didn't think it had anything to do with why I felt so much imbalance in my life, whereas it had everything to do with it! My race, my gender, my class! That's when I decided I would write about something my classmates couldn't write about. ❞

For Independent Reading

"Geraldo No Last Name" is from Cisneros's first book, *The House on Mango Street,* a series of stories about Esperanza Cordero that range from Esperanza's first kiss to dreams of her own home. This coming-of-age classic is set in a Spanish-speaking area of Chicago.

Response and Analysis

Reading Check

1. Retell the **main events** of this story to a classmate as you imagine Marin told them to the police.

Thinking Critically

2. What questions do you still have about the story? Why do you think the writer has not provided this information?

3. Exactly what do you know about the **character** of Geraldo? What **inferences,** or guesses, can you make about the kind of person he was?

4. After Geraldo dies, Marin can't understand why their meeting mattered and why she spent so many hours in the hospital waiting room. Why do you think she keeps thinking about the meeting and wondering what it meant?

5. At the end of the story, Cisneros says "they" never saw certain aspects of Geraldo's life. Who are "they"? What is the story's **point of view**?

6. Do you think this is a story about love? Talk about your responses in class.

7. In just a few broad strokes, Cisneros sketches two characters and one tragic event. How would you express the **theme,** or central idea, of this very short story?

8. Look back at your Quickwrite notes. Are there any similarities between the "brief encounter" you described and the one in the story? Explain.

Literary Criticism

9. How would you describe Cisneros's **diction** in this story? How does it affect the story's **tone?** Try rewriting a few sentences, changing the diction (words, expressions) to create an altogether different tone.

10. Cisneros uses many short sentences and sentence fragments in her story. How does this aspect of her **style** contribute to the story's impact? Do you think it affects the **theme?** Explain your answer.

11. Cisneros consciously chose words to create touches of poetry. Find examples of **rhyme, rhythm,** or other **sound effects.** Do you think these aspects of her **style** add to the story or detract from its power? Explain.

WRITING

Whose Story Is It?

Who is the **protagonist,** the central **character** in this story—Geraldo or Marin? In a brief **essay,** cite details from the story to support your view.

LISTENING AND SPEAKING

Hearing a Style

Present an **oral interpretation** of the story. Decide how you should use your voice to emphasize Cisneros's unusual **style.** Think of when you should pause, read slowly, read quickly, and raise or lower your voice. Ask your audience for feedback.

Vocabulary Development

Words from Spanish

Peppering her stories with Spanish is part of Cisneros's unique **style.**

> "She knows how to do <u>cumbias</u> and <u>salsas</u> and <u>rancheras</u> even."

PRACTICE

Even if you don't understand Spanish, you probably use many common English words that came originally from Spanish. Fill in each blank with one of the words from Spanish listed in the box at the right. Before you begin, look up any unfamiliar words in a dictionary.

1. Maya prepared her special recipe for Texas _____.

2. The hikers enjoyed the view from the top of the steep _____.

3. Many buildings in the Southwest are constructed from _____.

4. When we visited the hundred-acre _____, we saw a black _____ running in the distance.

5. They decided to eat their dinner outdoors on the _____.

Words from Spanish
adobe
barbecue
bonanza
canyon
mustang
patio
poncho
ranch

Grammar Link

Revising Sentence Fragments

A **sentence** is a group of words that contains a subject and a verb and expresses a complete thought. A **sentence fragment** is a group of words that does not contain the basic parts of a complete sentence. If you answer no to any of the following questions, the word group is a fragment:

1. Does the group of words have a subject?

2. Does it have a verb?

3. Does it express a complete thought?

FRAGMENT Was her dancing partner. [subject missing]

SENTENCE <u>Geraldo</u> was her dancing partner.

FRAGMENT Marin at the hospital. [verb missing]

SENTENCE Marin <u>waited</u> at the hospital.

FRAGMENT When she was asked. [not a complete thought]

SENTENCE <u>She could not give his full name</u> when she was asked.

Why do you think Cisneros uses so many sentence fragments in this story? Writers often use fragments for emphasis or to make dialogue sound authentic. To revise a sentence fragment, add, subtract, or change words so that the group of words has all three essential sentence parts.

PRACTICE

Turn the following fragments into complete sentences. Exchange your sentences with a partner to be sure you've left no "frags."

Cisneros's *The House on Mango Street* (1984) a beautiful book. Consists of stories, sketches, and vignettes about family, friends, houses, and neighborhood. A young girl (Esperanza Cordero) the narrator. Deals with Chicano (Mexican American) culture in Chicago neighborhood. Although they are Americans. Many of the characters like outsiders in their own land.

SKILLS FOCUS

Vocabulary Skills
Use words from Spanish.

Grammar Skills
Revise sentence fragments.

Before You Read

Night Calls

Make the Connection

Quickwrite ✏️

When we love someone, we often perform very small acts of deception to make our loved one happy, or to keep bad news from him or her. Think of how children, in particular, can be affected by the loss of a parent and the grief of a survivor. What might a child do to help his or her parent feel happy again? Jot down your thoughts.

Literary Focus

Mood: A Feeling or Atmosphere

One of the important elements of fiction is mood. **Mood** is the feeling or atmosphere evoked by a piece of writing. Mood is created by language.

Some writers—Edgar Allan Poe is a good example—are famous for stories that evoke moods. (For a story by Poe, see page 419.) Poe's moods are created in part by his settings. His pits, blood-red rooms, and haunted houses create atmospheres of dread. Poe's stories have sent generations of readers to check their locks.

But suppose a writer wants to create a mood of joy. That writer might put us in sunlit gardens or flower-filled meadows, rather than in a prison or a pit. That writer's images would create a peaceful atmosphere—not the nightmare moods created by Poe's images of rat-filled pits.

Lisa Fugard, who wrote the next story, creates a powerful mood with her vivid descriptions and **sensory images** of a neglected South African wildlife sanctuary. Her **figures of speech,** or unusual comparisons, also help create the mood. (For more about figures of speech, see pages 477–478.)

The mood of her story is also affected by an event we learn about in a **flashback** near the start of the story. How does the neglected setting reflect the lives of Marlene and her grieving father?

Reading Skills

Monitor Your Reading

As you read this story, stop from time to time to think about what you have just read. Consider what is revealed about the characters. Think about the **mood** created by the setting. Notice the writer's use of language, especially her **figures of speech.** Be aware of **flashbacks,** and be sure you know why they are necessary to your understanding of the story. (The questions at the open-book signs will help you.)

Vocabulary Development

inevitably (in·ev′i·tə·blē) *adv.:* unavoidably.

avid (av′id) *adj.:* eager and enthusiastic.

indigenous (in·dij′ə·nəs) *adj.:* native; growing naturally in a region or country.

opulent (äp′yo͞o·lənt) *adj.:* rich; luxuriant.

adamant (ad′ə·mənt) *adj.:* unyielding; firm.

abutting (ə·but′iŋ) *v.* used as *adj.:* bordering upon; next to.

lauding (lôd′iŋ) *v.* used as *adj.:* praising.

tremulous (trem′yo͞o·ləs) *adj.:* trembling; quivering.

patina (pat′′n·ə) *n.:* color change resulting from age, as on old wood or silver.

go.hrw.com
INTERNET
Vocabulary Practice
Keyword: LE5 10-8

SKILLS FOCUS

Literary Skills
Understand mood.

Reading Skills
Monitor your reading.

564 Collection 8 Evaluating Style • Evaluating an Argument

Night Calls

Lisa Fugard

I saw that my father's eyes had gone dull like a dead animal's.

Landscape with Monkeys (c. 1910) by Henri Rousseau. Oil on canvas.

Barnes Foundation, Merion, Pennsylvania. © Barnes Foundation/SuperStock.

My father's hands were huge. Slablike. When he was idle, they seemed to hang off the ends of his arms like two chunks of meat. He sat on his hands during the months he courted my mother.

When I was thirteen, I watched my thin hand disappear into his. It was at the train station at Modder River. I'd come home for the September holidays. It was hot, and the only other car at the small station pulled away. The siding at Modder River, 150 miles north of Johannesburg, was never busy. I remember it all clearly, standing in the dust, watching him get out of the truck and walk toward me, noticing that there was no smile on his face but still feeling my body move toward him, my arms opening for an embrace, something rising in my throat. My father stopped and held out his right hand.

Once in the truck, I was filled with anxiety about how close to him I could sit. I settled in the middle of my half of the bench seat and watched his large, brown hand move from the steering wheel to the gearshift and back. I breathed deeply. Suddenly I was filled with the smell of him: Borkum Riff tobacco, sweat, the sweet odor of cheap Cape brandy. Filled with his secrets, I felt like a thief and moved a little closer to the window.

Then we were at the entrance to the Modder River Wildlife Sanctuary, and I jumped out of the car to open the gate. It swung easily, once I un-latched it, and banged against the wooden fence post, startling several guinea fowl that scampered into the veld.[1] "Krrdll . . . krrdll . . . krrdll," I called, and they slowed down. I mimicked their rattling cry again, and they stopped. Again, and a few of them stepped hesitantly toward me. Laughingly, I turned to find my father's smile,

but his face was gone, blotted out by the expanse of blue sky reflected in the wind-shield.

I have a gift for mimicking bird and animal calls. During my third year at boarding school I'd finally made myself popular and gained the respect of Wendy Venter, the bully of our dorm, by doing several calls late one night. It became a ritual, and every couple of weeks, around mid-night, I'd hear rustling and whis-pering from the eleven other girls in the dormitory; then a balled-up sock would land on my bed, usually right next to my head, and Wendy would call my name in a sly whisper, "Marlene." The dorm would fall silent. Lying back in the darkness I'd start with the deep moan of the spotted eagle owl; then the high-pitched yip of the black-backed jackal; the low snuffle and violent laugh of the hyena; and then a deadly combination: the rasp-ing, half-swallowed growl of the leopard, fol-lowed by the wild scream of the chacma baboon. Inevitably one of the younger girls would begin to cry, and I'd hear Wendy snickering in the darkness.

I'd told my father about this during my next trip home, about how much the other girls had enjoyed it, and I offered to do it for him one evening, offered to steal into his room at midnight, crouch at the foot of his bed, and make the calls for him. He'd shaken his head ever so slightly. "I've got the real thing right outside my window," he said.

---

1. **veld** *n.*: in South Africa, open grassy country with few bushes and almost no trees.

CHARACTER

1. What have you learned so far about the narrator and her father?

MAKING INFERENCES

2. What do you learn about the narrator from this **flashback** to her early years at boarding school?

Vocabulary
inevitably (in·ev′i·tə·blē) *adv.*: unavoidably.

As we drove up to our house now, I noticed the shabby state of the compound. The road was rutted and washed-out in many places by the spring rains. The visitors' kiosk was boarded up, and the map of the sanctuary had been knocked off its post and lay on the ground. Even the pond had been neglected. When my parents had first come to Modder River, five years before I was born, my father had had the pond dug out for my mother. An <u>avid</u> botanist,[2] she'd planted it with <u>indigenous</u> water lilies that she collected, along with bulrushes, seven-weeks ferns, and floating hearts. During the two years when the Modder River was reduced to a trickle by the drought, the local farmers had been astonished to hear that my father was actually pumping precious water from our borehole into the pond to prevent it from drying up. An <u>opulent</u> jewel in the dusty, cracked landscape, it became a haven for birds, being visited by pied kingfishers, mountain chats, spoonbills, bokmakieries, a pair of black-shouldered kites— all told, my mother counted 107 different species. Now a thick layer of brown scum covered the shallow, stagnant water. I remembered a letter that I'd received from my father several months before. The scrawled handwriting hadn't even looked like his. I'd read it once and then hidden it away, scared by the loneliness that the words hinted at.

IMAGES

3. Which **images** of the setting create a **mood** of sadness and a sense of decay?

None of this seemed to matter, however, when I stood among our dogs, being pelted with paws and tails and long pink tongues: King, with his tail plumed like an ostrich feather, and Blitz, a lean, black shadow. They clattered behind me as I went into my bedroom. The room was still and dark and smelled musty. Quickly I opened the wooden shutters. I moved to the chest of drawers and found the large framed photograph of my mother, frozen at age thirty-two. She was laughing, and her head was turned slightly as a lock of hair blew across her face. I traced her jaw line with my finger and moved to the mirror with the photograph, but the dogs were demanding, barking and pawing at my legs.

I ran outside with them and chased them up and down the cool stone lengths of the veranda, flying past the living room and the dining room, screeching past my father's study and back again with the dogs racing behind me. Back and forth I went, until the force of motion made me round the corner past my parents' old bedroom. I stopped, panting, trying to catch my breath. I stared at the large fenced-in area under the blue gum tree. It was where my father kept the red-crested night heron, one of the last of its kind.

The year that the park officials brought the bird to Modder River had been a difficult one. My mother was killed in a car accident just before my eighth birthday. Numbly, I watched my father make funeral arrangements with the help of his sister, Annette, who drove up from Johannesburg. She was <u>adamant</u>: There was no way I could stay at Modder River. It was too remote, and there was my schooling to consider; my mother had been my tutor. As for my father,

> I stopped, panting, trying to catch my breath.

---

2. **botanist** *n.:* scientist who studies plant life.

Vocabulary

avid (av′id) *adj.:* eager and enthusiastic.

indigenous (in·dij′ə·nəs) *adj.:* native; growing naturally in a region or country.

opulent (äp′yo͞o·lənt) *adj.:* rich; luxuriant.

adamant (ad′ə·mənt) *adj.:* unyielding; firm.

it made no sense for him to remain, grieving, in a place so closely associated with his wife. My father was on the verge of resigning as warden of the small sanctuary when park officials telephoned about the bird. The red-crested night heron had been captured at the vlei[3] on Nie Te Ver, the farm abutting the sanctuary's eastern border, and the National Parks Board wanted the heron kept at Modder River on the slim chance that they might find a mate for it.

A Mr. Vanjaarsveld arrived with the bird. "We had to tie the bugger's beak up, otherwise he'd have cut us to ribbons," he said, as he placed a large burlap bag in the pen that my father had hastily constructed. He opened the bag and then quickly stepped out and shut the gate. A few moments of silence—then a wild flurry of wings, the sound of the air being thumped, and the heron hit the wire at the top of the pen and came crashing down. Again and again, till the bird lay in the dust exhausted, its wings useless. Quietly my father opened the gate and stepped inside the pen. For several minutes he squatted on his haunches in the corner and then slowly he inched his way toward the bird. Kneeling alongside it, he checked the feathers for damage, spreading the wings on the ground in front of him, like a fan. Then, making soft noises in the back of his throat, he untied the strip of burlap around the heron's beak. My father stayed on at Modder River, and arrangements were made for me to go to boarding school.

During holidays I came home, and my father would share the latest news about the heron

PLOT

4. What two important events does this **flashback** reveal?

---

3. **vlei** *n.:* in South Africa, a temporary lake formed in a marshy area during the rainy season.

Vocabulary

abutting (ə·but′iŋ) *v.* used as *adj.:* bordering upon; next to.

Preening Heron by William H. Turner.

with me. He showed me articles from the local papers lauding the conservation efforts surrounding the bird, as well as articles from foreign countries in languages we couldn't understand. He showed me the stamp that the South African government issued—a thirty-seven-cent stamp with the heron's lean profile and brilliant crest. And once he gave me a feather, a long, steel-gray feather from the tip of the heron's wing, a flight feather, and it was smooth as I stroked it against my cheek during the overnight train ride back to boarding school. But after two or three years, interest in the heron faded. The articles died down, and in private the National Parks Board expressed their doubts to my father that they would ever find a mate for the bird. The sanctuary was small, and apart from a secretive leopard we didn't have any of the Big Five—animals like elephants and lions that attracted tourists. Modder River returned to the way it used to be, a trickle of visitors on the occasional weekend.

I stared at the pen for a long time now. I knew what was in there. A large gray bird, with ugly hooked feet, a long slithery neck that gave me nightmares, and a red crest that was raised during the courtship ritual. I had never seen the crest, but once I'd caught a glimpse of a small red feather that had escaped from the heron's crown. There was no need to walk through the dust to look at the bird under the swaying blue gum tree branches. I went anyway. Effortlessly, I climbed the blue gum tree, but now it was difficult for me to squeeze into the small fork halfway up. The heron pecked listlessly at a dried-out fish, and I noticed that the pen hadn't been cleaned in quite a while. I'd spent many school holidays in the tree watching my father as

he fed the bird, collected the feathers during the molt,[4] and proudly chatted with visitors. Maybe he'd known that I was up there all the time.

I shivered. The sun had set, taking all the warmth with it, and a thin veil of light pressed against our house and the Modder River as it crawled like a fat brown snake out of the mountains.

Walking back down the length of the veranda, I peered through the windows of the rooms we'd stopped using, the dining room with its yellow wood table, the living room where my mother's desk was still piled high with the field guides and books she'd used to identify unknown plants she'd come across. The outside light flickered on, and I found my father in the kitchen, heating up a tin of curry. We ate our dinner in silence, and then he read a book and I listened to the radio. I felt uncomfortable in the house and longed for the morning, when I could go racing through the veld with the dogs, go out looking for tracks and walk far into the sanctuary. At 10 P.M., as was custom, my father switched off the electricity generator and went to his study, where he slept.

The low hum now gone, I lay in bed and let the night overtake me, hungrily following the calls in the darkness. A jackal marking his territory, the rhythmic eruptions of spring bullfrogs, the steady breath of King at the foot of my bed. And then I heard another familiar sound, the

CHARACTER

5. What details seem to reveal the narrator's attitude toward the heron?

> I lay in bed and let the night overtake me . . .

---

4. **molt** *n.*: shedding of feathers at certain intervals, prior to replacement by new growth.

Vocabulary
lauding (lôd′iŋ) *v.* used as *adj.*: praising.

creaking of the gate on the heron's pen. Gently I felt my way down the hall and into my parents' old bedroom. I hid behind the soft lace curtains, and as my eyes grew accustomed to the night, I saw my father move slowly across the compound carrying the heron gently under his arm, its long legs dangling at his side. The heron's neck was liquid in the moonlight, curving and swaying, at times seeming to entwine my father. Its beak glinted like a dagger. One of my father's hands followed the bird's neck, lightly touching it at times, while the other was sunk deep into the heron's soft breast, pale gray feathers around his wrist. My father slipped by with the heron, and I went back to bed and stared into the darkness. Later on I heard a <u>tremulous</u> wail repeated several times. It came from the river. I knew it was the red-crested night heron, even though I'd never heard its call before, and I thought about my father in the darkness on the banks of the Modder River with the bird.

> ### IMAGES
> **6.** Which **images** and **figures of speech** in this passage help you hear and see the setting and the heron?

Detail of *Landscape with Monkeys* (c. 1910) by Henri Rousseau. Oil on canvas.

Barnes Foundation, Merion, Pennsylvania. © Barnes Foundation/SuperStock.

At breakfast the next morning, my father told me that a hyena had gotten the best of us, had finally broken into the heron's pen, because the bird had disappeared. Under the blue gum tree we examined a huge hole in the fence. "Yes, I think so, Dad," I said, and nodded in agreement as we watched King and Blitz sniff inside the pen. He seemed lighter and chatted with me about school as I helped him dismantle the fence. "Hyena," he had said with such authority. He told me that now he might even be able to come to the end-of-the-year recital at my school. That night I made fried bananas and ice cream for dessert, and we listened to a radio play together. At ten, just before he switched off the generator, I looked in the mirror and thought, I have his eyes.

> ### MAKING INFERENCES
> **7.** Why do you think the father releases the heron and lies about what he did?

In bed, in the blackness, I listened to the night again. The jackal that had been barking the previous night had moved on, and it seemed quiet out there. It wasn't long before I heard the heron calling. I knew my father heard it as well, and I tried to picture him in his bed. I wondered if his heart beat like mine, an urgent knocking in my chest. I rolled over and thought of the red-crested night heron, alone by the river, the last of its kind, and I imagined that its crest was raised and that it picked its way delicately through the muddy water, lifting its feet up like wet handkerchiefs.

The following night I heard the heron's call again, and I also heard footsteps leaving our house. I knew it was my father going down to the river. For ten nights the heron called and my father followed. During the days we worked on repairing things around the compound. We cleaned up the pond and made a day trip to the

Vocabulary
tremulous (trem′yo͞o·ləs) *adj.*: trembling; quivering.

western corner of the sanctuary, where the Modder River dropped abruptly into a densely forested ravine—gnarled trees hung with a thick gray moss that I called "old man's beard." We collected water lilies from the dappled pools, wrapping their roots in damp newspaper and placing them in our packs. Baboons barked from the rocky ledges. We saw the spoor of the leopard, two pugmarks[5] in the rich black mud. For the drive home I sat in the back of the truck. As my father shifted to low gear and negotiated the sandy part of the road that ran alongside the river, I scanned the banks, hoping to catch a glimpse of the heron roosting, waiting for nightfall. I spent a day repairing the signs along the Succulent Trail, a one-mile loop that wound through an area that my father had filled with rare plants—aloe albida, aloe monotropa, a lydenberg cycad. We put the map back on its post and touched it up with small pots of paint, the Modder River a blue vein in the brown landscape.

IMAGES

8. What **images** help you visualize the sanctuary?

Then, one long night, I didn't hear the heron's call. The bird had disappeared, and when I got out of bed the next morning, I saw that my father's eyes had gone dull like a dead animal's. I knew why but couldn't say anything. Then he started walking all the time, often coming home only for an hour or two in the early dawn. I'd hear the creak of the floorboards near the kitchen and the thud of Blitz's tail on the floor. I'd hear my father pacing, and then, eventually, stillness. He's lying on the sofa in his study, he's asleep now, I'd say to myself. Then the pacing again and the soft slam of the screen door. From the blue gum tree I'd see him crisscrossing the veld, like a rabid dog, always coming back to touch the river. Straining my eyes, I'd watch him

---

5. **spoor ... pugmarks:** *Spoor* is the track or trail of a wild animal. *Pugmarks* are the footprints or trail of an animal.

walk farther and farther away, until he vanished into the landscape.

FIGURES OF SPEECH

9. What **similes** describe the father in this paragraph?

Accidentally, I found the heron's remains. I was out late one afternoon, looking for a snakeskin for my next school biology project. I had chosen a rocky area, where I'd seen cobras and puff adders sunning themselves, and as I moved slowly through it, poking into crevices with a stick, I came across a broken fan of bloodied feathers. The steel-gray patina was unmistakable, and I knew it was part of the heron's wing. I scratched out a hole with my stick and buried the feathers, pushing a large rock over the small grave.

I made sandwiches for supper that night. I made extra ones for my father, but he didn't come home. I sat on the veranda with King and Blitz until ten o'clock, when I switched off the generator. Swiftly, silently, I followed the footpath down to the far bank of the river, pushing my way through the warm water that came up to my waist. I hid in the reeds and waited.

An hour later I saw my father on the opposite bank, looking, listening. He sat down on the dark sand and rolled a pebble in his large palms. I crouched even lower. Slowly I tilted my head back until my throat was wide open and a tremulous wail slid out. My father stood up and looked across the water to where I was crouched. Again I made the sound, again and again. He took three more small steps toward my side of the river and his hands fluttered like giant, tawny moths in the moonlight. ∎

FIGURES OF SPEECH

10. How did the narrator view her father's hands at the start of the story? How does she see them now?

Vocabulary

patina (pat′n·ə) *n.*: color change resulting from age, as on old wood or silver.

Meet the Writer

Lisa Fugard

Writing About Home

Lisa Fugard (1961–   ) grew up in South Africa, the daughter of the playwright, director, and actor Athol Fugard and Sheila Fugard, a novelist and poet. Fugard chose acting as her first career and performed in many stage productions, including a tour of black townships as the female lead in her father's play *My Children! My Africa!*

Eventually, Fugard says, she "let theater and acting go away." She turned instead to writing and discovered that her acting experience, especially its deep study of characters and motivations, helped her create believable fictional characters.

Fugard recalls how she came to write "Night Calls" and how the story changed as she revised it:

“ 'Night Calls' actually evolved from watching a program on public television about a pair of Japanese cranes. They were the last of their kind and they were being tended to by this Japanese man. I remember watching the program and being terribly moved by the idea of these two birds—that after they were gone, there was nothing left. ”

She set her story in Japan and recalls that she struggled to use unfamiliar Japanese names, plants, and animals. Halfway through her rewrite, she moved the story to South Africa—and felt completely at home. Through several drafts, "Night Calls" explored the relationship between a father and son, but in her final draft Fugard changed the main character to a daughter. The red-crested night heron, she says, is fictional too; no such bird has ever existed.

Fugard says that the source of writer's block is a desire to write down only perfect sentences and stories. She feels that writers need to learn how to

“ outfox the censor we all have, how to tap into the imagination, and how to take the risk to write from the heart. ”

Waiting for *E. gularis*

Linda Pastan

"An African heron was found on the northeast end of Nantucket Island. . . ."
—news release

"The sighting of the century . . ."
—Roger Tory Peterson

Exile
by accident
he came

against
5   all instinct
to this watery place,

mistaking it
perhaps
as the explorers did

10   for some
new
Orient.

This morning,
dreaming
15   of the inexplicable

I rise from sleep, smoothing
the sheets behind me
to match

the water smoothed sand
20   silk
under my bare feet.

I walk past morning joggers
who worship in pain
the crucible of breath,

25   past dune and marsh
stockaded with eel grass
to this pond,

just as a breeze comes up
like rumors
30   of his appearance.

Young people in bathing suits
lounge here, fans
waiting for their rock star

E. gularis—even his name
35   becomes
an incantation.

The pond
is all surface
this cloudy day,

40   the dark side of the mirror
where nothing shows
until you stare enough

as at those childhood puzzles—
how many faces can you find
45 concealed here?

And there moving towards us
is the turtle's miniature
face,

and there the mask
50 the wild duck wears, stitching
a ruffle

at the pond's far edge
where now
the Little Blue herons

55 curve their necks
to question marks
(why not me?)

where in a semi-circle
ornithologists
60 wait

to add another notch
to their life
lists,

binoculars
65 raised
like pistols.

Great Blue Heron by John James Audubon.

Response and Analysis

Reading Check

1. How does the narrator's life change just before her eighth birthday?

2. What is Marlene's special talent?

3. Why is the red-crested night heron sent to the Modder River sanctuary?

4. What happens to the plan to find a mate for the bird? What happens to the sanctuary as a result?

5. How does Marlene's father explain what happened to the heron when it disappeared from the sanctuary?

Thinking Critically

6. What details show that the father, narrator, and sanctuary are suffering from the loss of the narrator's mother?

7. To answer the following questions, you will have to **infer** the character's **motivation.** Give evidence from the story to support your inferences. Remember that a character's motivations may be purposely **ambiguous,** or open to several interpretations. (Check your Quickwrite notes also.)

   - What do you think the heron meant to the father?

   - Why does the father release it?

   - Why does the father lie to Marlene about how the heron escaped?

   - Why doesn't the narrator tell her father that the heron is dead?

   - Why does the narrator imitate the heron's call at the story's end?

Literary Criticism

8. When the narrator returns for the September holidays, she notices changes in the **setting.** How has the setting changed? What **mood** do these changes create?

9. One aspect of Fugard's **diction** and **style** is her use of words that help us hear the sounds made by various animals. Expain how each sound below helps you imagine the animal that makes it.

yip	wail	scream
growl	moan	snuffle

Comparing Literature

10. The poem by Linda Pastan (see the *Connection* on page 573) is also about a heron. How many similarities can you find between the poem and the story? In what important ways are the **moods** of the two pieces different?

WRITING

Analyzing Style

In a brief essay, analyze Fugard's **style.** Before you write, collect your details in a chart like the one below. Conclude your essay with a statement explaining your response to the story.

Elements of Style	Examples	My Comments
Imagery		
Figurative language		
Creation of mood		
Use of flashbacks		

Creating a Mood

A wildlife sanctuary and a lonely home are settings that create a strong mood in this story. Write a paragraph describing a setting that creates a **mood.** Word choice, or **diction,** will be important. Tell how the setting looks, smells, sounds, perhaps even tastes and feels.

SKILLS FOCUS

Literary Skills
Analyze mood.

Writing Skills
Write an essay analyzing a writer's style. Write a paragraph describing the mood of a setting.

Vocabulary Development

Verifying Meanings by Examples

PRACTICE 1

Word Bank

inevitably
avid
indigenous
opulent
adamant
abutting
lauding
tremulous
patina

You can own a new word (that is, add it to your working vocabulary) by using it, especially by giving examples of the word in action. Use complete sentences to write your answers to the questions that follow:

1. What inevitably follows lightning? Think of another example of something that inevitably follows something else.

2. If you are an avid reader, how do you feel about reading?

3. Name three things that are indigenous to your community.

4. You've been to an opulent wedding. Describe the wedding.

5. You are adamant about a proposed law banning the use of cell phones by drivers. Explain why.

6. Name two countries abutting the United States.

7. Write a sentence lauding a book you've read recently.

8. Describe two situations that might make a person feel tremulous.

9. Which of the following has a patina: tarnished silverware, a sunset, a hard-boiled egg, a copper statue that's turned green? Would you try to get rid of the patina? Explain.

PRACTICE 2

For each of the following words, make up a question like those in Practice 1 above: *idle* (page 566), *anxiety* (page 566), *scampered* (page 566), *mimicked* (page 566), *stagnant* (page 567), *listlessly* (page 569), and *authority* (page 570). Try out your questions on a classmate.

PRACTICE 3

Even when you've never seen a word before, the **context** may provide clues that help you accurately guess the word's meaning. What context clues would help you define the underlined words in these sentences?

1. "It was at the train station at Modder River. . . . It was hot, and the only other car at the small station pulled away. The siding at Modder River . . . was never busy." (page 566)

2. "The visitors' kiosk was boarded up, and the map of the sanctuary had been knocked off its post and lay on the ground." (page 567)

3. "During the two years when the Modder River was reduced to a trickle by the drought, the local farmers had been astonished to hear that my father was actually pumping precious water from our bore-hole into the pond to prevent it from drying up." (page 567)

SKILLS FOCUS

Vocabulary Skills
Demonstrate word knowledge. Use context clues.

Call of the Wild—Save Us!

Evaluating an Author's Argument

Persuasive writing tries to persuade you to believe an idea or take an action. You'll find persuasive writing in editorials, letters to the editor, speeches, position papers, advertisements, and magazine articles like the one you are about to read. To make up your mind about whether or not a writer's argument is **credible** and should persuade you, take these steps:

1. **Follow the author's argument.** An **argument** is a series of statements designed to persuade you. Usually it begins with a clear statement of the writer's **opinion** or **claim.** Then, to persuade you, the writer provides **reasons** as well as **evidence** to back up those reasons.

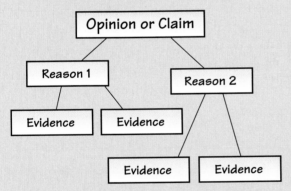

2. **Evaluate the support.** Don't believe anyone who tries to convince you by saying, "Because I say so." Make sure the author's opinions and generalizations are supported with enough **evidence** to be convincing. Evidence includes **logical appeals,** such as facts, statistics, examples, and expert opinions. Be on the lookout for **emotional appeals.** Emotional appeals can support an argument, but they are not evidence. (For more about logical and emotional appeals, see pages 284–285.) Be sure to distinguish **facts** (statements that can be proved true) from **opinions** (statements that can't be proved).

3. **Look at structure.** When you're analyzing a piece of persuasive writing, it's important to identify the writer's **main ideas** and the order in which they are presented. Are the main ideas convincing? Are they presented in a logical order?

   A good writer carefully orders an argument to be the most persuasive. Readers generally remember the beginning and the end of a piece the most. Therefore, a common way to structure an argument is from least important idea to most important idea—or the reverse. An effective variation on this is to start with the second most important idea and end with the most important one. (Other common ways in which writers structure their arguments are with comparison and contrast and with cause and effect.)

   Also look at **text organizers.** In a printed text, subheads help convey the writer's argument; so do important terms in boldface type. Photos and graphics may add new information—so be sure to read the captions.

4. **Identify the author's intent.** In a persuasive piece the author's **intent** is clearly to persuade you, but of what exactly? Sometimes the writer's goal is just to change your thinking, but often it is a **call to action,** asking you to go

INTERNET

Interactive Reading Model

Keyword: LE5 10-8

Reading Skills
Evaluate an author's argument.

out and *do* something. Are you being asked to buy a certain product, vote in a certain way, write a letter, send money? Look for a call to action; if you find one, it's an important part of the argument.

5. **Identify the author's tone.** An author's **intent** directly affects a work's **tone,** the writer's attitude toward the subject or audience. Identifying the tone may help you evaluate the credibility of an argument. If the intent is to persuade, the tone might be serious, sincere, concerned, or objective. If a writer uses a highly emotional tone for an argument that is meant to be objective—based on facts—then the argument is not credible. If you are not sure of the author's intent, the tone may clue you in.

6. **Evaluate the author's credentials.** You know by now not to believe everything you read. Before you decide how to respond to the persuasion, evaluate the writer's **credibility.** How knowledgeable is the writer about the subject being discussed? Is the writer an expert and currently working in the field? What are his or her qualifications? Sometimes this information is right there for you to read; sometimes you have to hunt for it.

▶ **For more about persuasive writing, see "Writing a Persuasive Essay," pages 294–301.**

Vocabulary Development

habitats (hab′i·tats′) *n.*: places where plants or animals normally grow or live.

extinct (ek·stiŋkt′) *adj.*: no longer in existence.

impoverishment (im·päv′ər·ish·mənt) *n.*: reducing to poverty or taking away of resources.

degradation (deg′rə·dā′shən) *n.*: decline.

ethical (eth′i·kəl) *adj.*: moral; having to do with goodness or rightness in conduct.

conservation (kän′sər·vā′shən) *n.* used as *adj.*: protection and preservation of natural resources.

bereft (bē·reft′) *adj.*: not having something needed or expected.

consumerism (kən·sōōm′ər·iz′əm) *n.*: buying and using of goods or services.

terminal (tʉr′mə·nəl) *adj.*: of or relating to an end, often an end to life.

veritable (ver′i·tə·bəl) *adj.*: actual; true.

Connecting to the Literature

In "Night Calls" the narrator's father, the warden of a small wildlife preserve, cares for the last of a species of heron. In the next article you'll read about how each of us can help save species from extinction. The danger of extinction is becoming all too common in our modern, industrialized world.

Call of the Wild—Save Us!

from *Good Housekeeping*, April 1991

Norman Myers

A garbage-filled swamp near Marseilles, France.

Each day we lose roughly fifty to one hundred wildlife species. They are crowded off the planet by human beings, who are deciding that there isn't enough room on the earth for them and us too.

We don't do it deliberately. We simply destroy their <u>habitats</u>. We chop down their forests, dig up their grasslands, drain their marshes, pollute their rivers and lakes, pave over their other habitats, and generally jump on whatever corners of the earth they have chosen to make their last stand. We certainly don't drive them <u>extinct</u> with malice aforethought.[1] Very few species are eliminated through over-hunting and other direct forms of assault. ❶

❶ **EVALUATING AN ARGUMENT**

According to the writer, why are we losing wildlife species?

1. **malice aforethought:** deliberate intention to do something unlawful.

Vocabulary

habitats (hab′i·tats′) *n.*: places where plants or animals normally grow or live.

extinct (ek·stiŋkt′) *adj.*: no longer in existence.

But effectively and increasingly, we are denying living space to thousands of fellow species, animals and plants, each year. By the time readers of this magazine climb into their rocking chairs, the total may well become millions, in fact a whopping half of *all* species. This is a holocaust[2]—a rending of the very fabric of life on earth—because mass extinction will impose a longer-lasting <u>impoverishment</u> on the planetary <u>ecosystem</u>[3] than any other environmental problem. All other kinds of environmental <u>degradation</u> are reversible. But when a species is gone, it is gone for good.

We Are All Losers

All too often we shall find that will be "for bad" in terms of our everyday welfare. When we visit our neighborhood drugstore, there is one chance in two that our purchase—an antibiotic, an antiviral, a diuretic, a laxative, an analgesic,[4] or a host of other items—would not be available for us without raw materials from wild plants and animals. The commercial value of all these products worldwide is more than $400 million a year. The rosy periwinkle of Madagascar provided one of the most significant breakthroughs against cancer in recent decades. It has led to the manufacture of two potent therapies against Hodgkin's disease, leukemia, and other blood cancers. Cancer specialists believe there could be at least another ten tropical forest plants with capacity to generate similar superstar drugs against other forms of cancer—provided the scientist can get to them before the chainsaw devastates their habitats. ❷

The economic argument in support of species carries weight with politicians and planners. If wildlife can pay its way in the marketplace, they will listen; if not, then they won't. But should we not consider a further

Rosy Periwinkle, a tropical dry-forest plant from Madagascar.

---

2. **holocaust** *n.*: great or total destruction of life.
3. **ecosystem** *n.*: community of living things and its physical environment.
4. **antibiotic, . . . analgesic:** types of medication. An antibiotic fights infection; an analgesic relieves pain.

Vocabulary

impoverishment (im·päv′ər·ish·mənt) *n.*: reducing to poverty or taking away of resources.

degradation (deg′rə·dā′shən) *n.*: decline.

argument as well—the ethical aspect? What right have we, a single species, to eliminate even a single other species, let alone to knock them off in vast numbers? Shouldn't our fellow passengers on planet Earth, many of them like us, the refined outcome of evolution, enjoy as much right to continued existence as we do?

Therein lies another irony. We are the sole species with the capacity to wantonly[5] snuff out the life of other species—yet we are also the sole species with the capacity to save other creatures. Fortunately, and at long glorious last, we are starting to realize this fundamental truth. The UN is putting together a global treaty to safeguard wildlife. This will mean an effort on the part of nations to preserve wildlife wherever it occurs; in practice it will entail a campaign on the part of the rich nations to finance conservation activities in developing, mainly tropical nations where species are most abundant—and where conservation resources are scarcest.

What Will It Cost?

Probably several billions of dollars a year. But it will be a sound investment. Suppose we save those anticancer plants: That alone would generate health benefits worth several billion annually.

Suppose, moreover, the entire bill were to be picked up by people in the world's rich nations. There are 1.2 billion of us. If the bill were, say, $2.5 billion a year, we would each pay just over $2 per year. For the cost of a beer or a hamburger, we could do it.

A rich-nation couple spends $175,000 to bring up a child from cradle through college. For the sake of a *tiny* additional investment, that child will grow up into a world deprived

of millions of wildlife species and bereft of much of what makes the world diverse and interesting, spectacular and special. The question is not "Can we afford to do it eventually?" It is "How can we possibly afford *not* to do it now?" ❸

❸ **EVALUATING AN ARGUMENT**

In the last three paragraphs, where does the writer appeal to **logic**? Where does he appeal to **emotion**?

What You Can Do

I am often asked what individuals can do while waiting for political leaders to get a move on. Lots of specific things. They can support their conservation group of choice, perhaps bearing in mind that the longest established is the World Wildlife Fund (1250 24th Street, N.W., Washington, D.C. 20037). After writing that check, they can write on another piece of paper, one that costs less yet seems to cost more, given the relatively small number of conservationists who do it! They can write to their senator and congressperson, urging support for the legislative initiative in behalf of global wildlife.

More importantly still, they can figure out ways to tread more lightly on the planet, notably by cutting back on excessive forms of consumerism and waste. This helps environments generally and habitats for wildlife specifically. There will ultimately be no healthy place for wildlife except on a planet

---

5. **wantonly** *adv.*: senselessly; in a deliberately cruel way.

Vocabulary

ethical (eth′i·kəl) *adj.*: moral; having to do with goodness or rightness in conduct.

conservation (kän′sər·vā′shən) *n.* used as *adj.*: protection and preservation of natural resources.

bereft (bē·reft′) *adj.*: not having something needed or expected.

consumerism (kən·soom′ər·iz′əm) *n.*: buying and using of goods or services.

The Bengal tiger is native to South Asia. It is an endangered species whose numbers decreased dramatically during the twentieth century.

that is healthy all 'round. So: more recycling, fewer gas-guzzling cars, and all the other "think globally, act locally" measures.

Above all, remember that not only our children will look back upon this time of gathering shadows for the wildlife world. Their children and thousands of generations into the future will wonder why more was not done to tackle the terminal threat to wildlife. Alternatively, if we get our conservation act together, our successors will marvel at how we measured up to the challenge and how we saved species in their veritable millions. We still have time, though only *just* time. Those species out there—they are waiting to hear from us. ❹

Norman Myers is a university lecturer, an author, and an environmental consultant to many organizations, including the United Nations.

Vocabulary

terminal (tʉr'mə·nəl) *adj.:* of or relating to an end, often an end to life.

veritable (ver'i·tə·bəl) *adj.:* actual; true.

Analyzing Informational Text

Reading Check

1. According to the author, how are we losing fifty to one hundred species of wildlife a day?

2. Why does the author mention the rosy periwinkle of Madagascar?

3. What three things does the author say that individuals can do to help solve the problem of endangered species?

Test Practice

1. The **opinion** or **claim** expressed in this article is that something must be done now to —
   A   bring back extinct species
   B   prevent more species from becoming extinct
   C   increase the number of species
   D   stop the destruction of rain forests

2. The *first* **reason** the writer gives to support his opinion is that —
   F   politicians and planners don't care
   G   tropical nations are already preserving wildlife
   H   rich nations have a moral duty to provide aid
   J   wild plants and animals are the source of medications

3. The *second* **reason** the writer gives to support his opinion is that —
   A   humans have an ethical obligation to preserve other species
   B   the United Nations has ignored the problem
   C   every nation is already doing its best
   D   the United States is funding the efforts of tropical nations

4. Next, the writer considers how to cope with the —
   F   politicians' objections
   G   public's lack of interest
   H   cost of conservation efforts
   J   worldwide economic problems

5. Under which heading is the **call-to-action** section found?
   A   "We Are All Losers"
   B   "What Will It Cost"
   C   "What You Can Do"
   D   "Call of the Wild—Save Us!"

6. Which of these sentences expresses an **opinion**?
   F   "Each day we lose roughly fifty to one hundred wildlife species."
   G   "What right have we, a single species, to eliminate even a single other species . . . ?"
   H   "The UN is putting together a global treaty to safeguard wildlife."
   J   "There are 1.2 billion of us."

(continued)

Reading Skills
Evaluate an author's argument.

7. Which of the following states a **fact**?

A "But should we not consider a further argument as well—the ethical aspect?"

B "Those species out there—they are waiting to hear from us."

C "Alternatively, if we get our conservation act together, our successors will marvel at how we measured up to the challenge. . . ."

D "The commercial value of all these products worldwide is more than $400 million a year."

8. The **tone** of this article is *best* described as —

F humorous

G ironic

H highly emotional

J concerned

9. How **credible** is the writer, according to the information given about him at the end of the article?

A Not very, because he is biased

B Not very, because he is an ordinary citizen

C Very, because he sincerely believes his opinions and is honest

D Very, because he is an expert on the topic

Constructed Response

Analyze *either* Myers's essay or another short piece of persuasive writing (an editorial, a letter to the editor, or a newspaper or magazine column) about a specific issue.

First, outline the writer's **argument** in a graphic like the one on the right. Then, evaluate how **credible,** or convincing, you find the argument. Do you find enough **evidence** and support for the writer's opinion or claim? How do the **structure** and **tone** of the text contribute to its effectiveness?

Writer's opinion or claim:
Reason 1:
Supporting evidence:
Supporting evidence:
Reason 2:
Supporting evidence:
Supporting evidence:
Structure:
Tone:

Vocabulary Development

Using Contexts

PRACTICE 1

Use **context clues** in the following sentences to help you choose the correct Word Bank word for each blank.

1. There are no dinosaurs today since they are _____.
2. He was concerned about the _____ of standards and values.
3. Her illness had grown severe and was now in a _____ stage.
4. Both law and religion deal with _____ questions and issues.
5. The charity was completely _____ of needed funds.
6. The _____ of many animals can be found in the rain forest.
7. Some critics feel too much _____ is highly wasteful.
8. The drought had turned the countryside into a _____ desert.
9. The careful _____ of resources is vital for our economy.
10. The economic decline has caused _____ of workers.

Word Bank

habitats
extinct
impoverishment
degradation
ethical
conservation
bereft
consumerism
terminal
veritable

Literal and Figurative Use of Words

When you use a word or phrase **literally,** you mean it to be understood in its literal sense, the way the word or words are defined in a dictionary. Sometimes, though, you use words **figuratively**—you don't *really* mean what you say. You expect that the reader or listener will understand that you are using some quality or aspect of the word or phrase to express an idea more colorfully or to create an original image.

"By the time readers of this magazine climb into their rocking chairs, the total may well become millions, in fact a whopping half of *all* species."

Does the writer mean that the readers of the magazine will literally climb into rocking chairs, or is he using this phrase figuratively, to mean "reach old age"?

PRACTICE 2

Rewrite each sentence from the selection, translating the underlined **figurative** expressions into **literal** ones.

1. "We chop down their forests, dig up their grasslands, . . . and generally jump on whatever corners of the earth they have chosen to make their last stand."
2. "This is a holocaust—a rending of the very fabric of life on earth. . . ."
3. "If wildlife can pay its way in the marketplace, they will listen. . . ."
4. "Above all, remember that not only our children will look back upon this time of gathering shadows for the wildlife world."

SKILLS FOCUS

Vocabulary Skills
Use context clues. Understand literal and figurative uses of words.

Before You Read

A Very Old Man with Enormous Wings

Make the Connection

Quickwrite ✏️

Brainstorm a list of characters from myth and legend who have wings. What happens to each of those characters? Then, brainstorm a list of modern stories or movies in which an alien visits the ordinary world on earth. What usually happens to those strangers visiting a strange land?

Literary Focus

Magic Realism

Like many contemporary South American writers, Gabriel García Márquez writes a kind of fiction called **magic realism.** This **style** of writing is characterized by elements of fantasy (often borrowed from mythology) that are casually inserted into earthy, realistic settings. The magic realists often suspend the laws of nature. In using this bizarre mixture of the commonplace and the outlandish, the magic realists can force us to think about our fixed notions of "reality" and "normality." This blurring of fantasy and reality is often an important part of the **themes,** or main ideas about life, that the magic realists want to convey.

Reading Skills 📖

Appreciating a Writer's Style

One of the great pleasures of reading is appreciating a writer's style—especially the writer's choice of words and images that help create a work's **tone, mood,** and theme. As you read this story by García Márquez, notice the way he tosses together the offbeat, the commonplace, and the sublime into that strange mix known as **magic realism.**

Notice, too, his unusual, even startling combinations of **images,** and be aware of the things they help you to see. Try to decide why some of his images seem funny, some sad, and some—appropriately enough—magical.

INTERNET

Vocabulary
Practice
•
More About Gabriel
García Márquez

Keyword: LE5 10-8

SKILLS FOCUS

Literary Skills
Understand characteristics of magic realism.

Reading Skills
Understand a writer's style.

Vocabulary Development

stench (stench) *n.*: offensive smell.

impeded (im·pēd'id) *v.* used as *adj.*: held back or blocked, as by an obstacle.

magnanimous (mag·nan'ə·məs) *adj.*: generous; noble.

reverence (rev'ə·rəns) *n.*: attitude or display of deep respect and awe.

frivolous (friv'ə·ləs) *adj.*: not properly serious; silly. *Frivolous* also means "trivial; of little value or importance."

impertinences (im·purt''n·ən·siz) *n.*: insults; disrespectful acts or remarks.

ingenuous (in·jen'yōō·əs) *adj.*: too trusting; tending to believe too readily.

prudence (prōō'dəns) *n.*: cautiousness; sound judgment.

cataclysm (kat'ə·kliz'əm) *n.*: disaster; sudden, violent event.

providential (präv'ə·den'shəl) *adj.*: fortunate; like something caused by a divine act.

affliction (ə·flik'shən) *n.*: suffering; distress.

lament (lə·ment') *v.*: feel very sorry.

A flesh-and-blood angel was held captive in Pelayo's house.

A Very Old Man with Enormous WINGS

A Tale for Children

Gabriel García Márquez
translated by Gregory Rabassa

On the third day of rain they had killed so many crabs inside the house that Pelayo had to cross his drenched courtyard and throw them into the sea, because the newborn child had a temperature all night and they thought it was due to the stench. The world had been sad since Tuesday. Sea and sky were a single ash-gray thing, and the sands of the beach, which on March nights glimmered like powdered light, had become a stew of mud and rotten shellfish. The light was so weak at noon that when Pelayo was coming back to the house after throwing away the crabs, it was hard for him to see what it was that was moving and groaning in the rear of the courtyard. He had to go very close to see that it was an old man, a very old man, lying face down in the mud, who, in spite of his tremendous efforts, couldn't get up, impeded by his enormous wings.

Frightened by that nightmare, Pelayo ran to get Elisenda, his wife, who was putting compresses on the sick child, and he took her to the rear of the courtyard. They both looked at the fallen body with mute stupor.[1] He was dressed like a ragpicker. There were only a few faded hairs left on his bald skull and very few teeth in his mouth, and his pitiful condition of a drenched great-grandfather had taken away any sense of grandeur he might have had. His huge buzzard wings, dirty and half plucked, were forever entangled in the mud. They looked at him so long and so closely that Pelayo and Elisenda very soon overcame their surprise and in the end found him familiar. Then they dared speak to him, and he answered in an incomprehensible dialect with a strong sailor's voice. That was how they skipped over the inconvenience of the wings and quite intelligently concluded that he was a lonely castaway from some foreign ship wrecked by the storm. And yet, they called in a neighbor woman who knew everything about life and death to see him, and all she needed was one look to show them their mistake.

"He's an angel," she told them. "He must have been coming for the child, but the poor fellow is so old that the rain knocked him down."

On the following day everyone knew that a flesh-and-blood angel was held captive in Pelayo's house. Against the judgment of the wise neighbor woman, for whom angels in those times were the fugitive survivors of a celestial conspiracy,[2] they did not have the heart to club him to death. Pelayo watched over him all afternoon from the kitchen, armed with his bailiff's[3] club, and before going to bed, he dragged him out of the mud and locked him up with the hens in the wire chicken coop. In the middle of the night, when the rain stopped, Pelayo and Elisenda were still killing crabs. A short time afterward the child woke up without a fever and with a desire to eat. Then they felt magnanimous and decided to put the angel on a raft with fresh water and provisions for three days and leave him to his fate on the high seas. But when they went out into the courtyard with the first light of dawn, they found the whole neighborhood in front of the chicken coop having fun with the angel, without the slightest reverence, tossing him things to eat through the openings in the wire as if he weren't a supernatural creature but a circus animal.

---

2. **celestial conspiracy:** According to the Book of Revelation in the Bible (12:7–9), Satan originally was an angel who led a rebellion in Heaven. As a result, he and his followers, called the fallen angels, were cast out of Heaven.
3. **bailiff's:** A bailiff is a minor local official.

Vocabulary

stench (stench) *n.*: offensive smell.

impeded (im·pēd′id) *v.* used as *adj.*: held back or blocked, as by an obstacle.

magnanimous (mag·nan′ə·məs) *adj.*: generous; noble.

reverence (rev′ə·rəns) *n.*: attitude or display of deep respect and awe.

---

1. **stupor** (stoo′pər) *n.*: dullness of the mind and senses.

Father Gonzaga arrived before seven o'clock, alarmed at the strange news. By that time on-lookers less <u>frivolous</u> than those at dawn had al-ready arrived and they were making all kinds of conjectures[4] concerning the captive's future. The simplest among them thought that he should be named mayor of the world. Others of sterner mind felt that he should be promoted to the rank of five-star general in order to win all wars. Some visionaries hoped that he could be put to stud in order to implant on earth a race of winged wise men who could take charge of the universe. But Father Gonzaga, before becoming a priest, had been a robust woodcutter. Standing by the wire, he reviewed his catechism[5] in an in-stant and asked them to open the door so that he could take a close look at that pitiful man who looked more like a huge decrepit hen among the fascinated chickens. He was lying in a corner drying his open wings in the sunlight among the fruit peels and breakfast leftovers that the early risers had thrown him. Alien to the <u>impertinences</u> of the world, he only lifted his an-tiquarian[6] eyes and murmured something in his dialect when Father Gonzaga went into the chicken coop and said good morning to him in Latin. The parish priest had his first suspicion of an impostor when he saw that he did not

---

4. **conjectures** (kən·jek**'**chərz) *n.:* guesses not com-pletely supported by evidence.
5. **catechism** (kat**'**ə·kiz'əm) *n.:* book of religious prin-ciples consisting of a series of questions and answers.

---

6. **antiquarian** (an'ti·kwer**'**ē·ən) *adj.:* ancient.

Vocabulary

frivolous (friv**'**ə·ləs) *adj.:* not properly serious; silly. *Frivolous* also means "trivial; of little value or importance."

impertinences (im·pʉrt**'**'n·ən·siz) *n.:* insults; disrespectful acts or remarks.

A Very Old Man with Enormous Wings 589

understand the language of God or know how to greet His ministers. Then he noticed that seen close up, he was much too human: He had an unbearable smell of the outdoors, the back side of his wings was strewn with parasites[7] and his main feathers had been mistreated by terrestrial[8] winds, and nothing about him measured up to the proud dignity of angels. Then he came out of the chicken coop and in a brief sermon warned the curious against the risks of being <u>ingenuous</u>. He reminded them that the devil had the bad habit of making use of carnival tricks in order to confuse the unwary. He argued that if wings were not the essential element in determining the difference between a hawk and an airplane, they were even less so in the recognition of angels. Nevertheless, he promised to write a letter to his bishop so that the latter would write to his primate[9] so that the latter would write to the Supreme Pontiff[10] in order to get the final verdict from the highest courts.

His <u>prudence</u> fell on sterile hearts. The news of the captive angel spread with such rapidity that after a few hours the courtyard had the bustle of a marketplace, and they had to call in troops with fixed bayonets to disperse the mob that was about to knock the house down. Elisenda, her spine all twisted from sweeping up so much marketplace trash, then got the idea of fencing in the yard and charging five cents admission to see the angel.

The curious came from far away. A traveling carnival arrived with a flying acrobat, who buzzed over the crowd several times, but no one paid any attention to him because his wings were not those of an angel but, rather, those of a sidereal[11] bat. The most unfortunate invalids on earth came in search of health: a poor woman who since childhood had been counting her heartbeats and had run out of numbers; a Portuguese man who couldn't sleep because the noise of the stars disturbed him; a sleepwalker who got up at night to undo the things he had done while awake; and many others with less serious ailments. In the midst of that shipwreck disorder that made the earth tremble, Pelayo and Elisenda were happy with fatigue, for in less than a week they had crammed their rooms with money and the line of pilgrims waiting their turn to enter still reached beyond the horizon.

The angel was the only one who took no part in his own act. He spent his time trying to get comfortable in his borrowed nest, befuddled by the hellish heat of the oil lamps and sacramental candles that had been placed along the wire. At first they tried to make him eat some mothballs, which, according to the wisdom of the wise neighbor woman, were the food prescribed for angels. But he turned them down, just as he turned down the papal[12] lunches that the penitents brought him, and they never found out whether it was because he was an angel or because he was an old man that in the end he ate nothing but eggplant mush. His only supernatural virtue seemed to be patience. Especially during the first days, when the hens pecked at him, searching for stellar parasites that proliferated[13] in his wings, and the cripples pulled out feathers to touch their defective parts

---

7. **parasites** *n.:* plants or animals that live on or in other living things, on which they feed.
8. **terrestrial** *adj.:* earthly.
9. **primate** (prī′mit) *n.:* archbishop or highest-ranking bishop in an area.
10. **Supreme Pontiff:** pope, head of the Roman Catholic Church.

11. **sidereal** (sī·dir′ē·əl) *adj.:* of the stars.
12. **papal** (pā′pəl) *adj.:* here, fit for the pope.
13. **proliferated** (prō·lif′ə·rāt′id) *v.:* quickly increased in number.

Vocabulary

ingenuous (in·jen′yo͞o·əs) *adj.:* too trusting; tending to believe too readily.

prudence (pro͞o′dəns) *n.:* cautiousness; sound judgment.

with, and even the most merciful threw stones at him, trying to get him to rise so they could see him standing. The only time they succeeded in arousing him was when they burned his side with an iron for branding steers, for he had been motionless for so many hours that they thought he was dead. He awoke with a start, ranting in his hermetic[14] language and with tears in his eyes, and he flapped his wings a couple of times, which brought on a whirlwind of chicken dung and lunar dust and a gale of panic that did not seem to be of this world. Although many thought that his reaction had been one not of rage but of pain, from then on they were careful not to annoy him, because the majority understood that his passivity was not that of a hero taking his ease but that of a cataclysm in repose.

Father Gonzaga held back the crowd's frivolity with formulas of maidservant inspiration while awaiting the arrival of a final judgment on the nature of the captive. But the mail from Rome showed no sense of urgency. They spent their time finding out if the prisoner had a navel, if his dialect had any connection with Aramaic,[15] how many times he could fit on the head of a pin, or whether he wasn't just a Norwegian with wings. Those meager letters might have come and gone until the end of time if a providential event had not put an end to the priest's tribulations.[16]

It so happened that during those days, among so many other carnival attractions, there arrived in town the traveling show of the woman who had been changed into a spider for having disobeyed her parents. The admission to see her was not only less than the admission to see the angel, but people were permitted to ask her all manner of questions about her absurd state and to examine her up and down so that no one would ever doubt the truth of her horror. She was a frightful tarantula the size of a ram and with the head of a sad maiden. What was most heart-rending, however, was not her outlandish shape but the sincere affliction with which she

---

14. **hermetic** *adj.:* difficult to understand; mysterious.
15. **Aramaic** (ar′ə·mā′ik) *n.:* ancient Middle Eastern language spoken by Jesus and his disciples.

---

16. **tribulations** (trib′yə·lā′shənz) *n.:* conditions of great unhappiness, such as oppression causes.

Vocabulary

cataclysm (kat′ə·kliz′əm) *n.:* disaster; sudden, violent event.

providential (präv′ə·den′shəl) *adj.:* fortunate; like something caused by a divine act.

affliction (ə·flik′shən) *n.:* suffering; distress.

recounted the details of her misfortune. While still practically a child, she had sneaked out of her parents' house to go to a dance, and while she was coming back through the woods after having danced all night without permission, a fearful thunderclap rent the sky in two and through the crack came the lightning bolt of brimstone[17] that changed her into a spider. Her only nourishment came from the meatballs that charitable souls chose to toss into her mouth. A spectacle like that, full of so much human truth and with such a fearful lesson, was bound to defeat without even trying that of a haughty angel who scarcely deigned to look at mortals. Besides, the few miracles attributed to the angel showed a certain mental disorder, like the blind man who didn't recover his sight but grew three new teeth, or the paralytic who didn't get to walk but almost won the lottery, or the leper whose sores sprouted sunflowers. Those consolation miracles, which were more like mocking fun,

---

17. **brimstone** *n.:* sulfur, a pale-yellow element that burns with a blue flame and a suffocating odor.

had already ruined the angel's reputation when the woman who had been changed into a spider finally crushed him completely. That was how Father Gonzaga was cured forever of his insomnia and Pelayo's courtyard went back to being as empty as during the time it had rained for three days and crabs walked through the bedrooms.

The owners of the house had no reason to lament. With the money they saved they built a two-story mansion with balconies and gardens and high netting so that crabs wouldn't get in during the winter, and with iron bars on the windows so that angels wouldn't get in. Pelayo also set up a rabbit warren close to town and gave up his job as bailiff for good, and Elisenda bought some satin pumps with high heels and many dresses of iridescent silk, the kind worn on Sunday by the most desirable women in those times. The chicken coop was the only thing that didn't receive any attention. If they washed it down with creolin and burned tears of myrrh[18] inside it every so often, it was not in homage[19] to the angel but to drive away the dung-heap stench that still hung everywhere like a ghost and was turning the new house into an old one. At first, when the child learned to walk, they were careful that he not get too close to the chicken coop. But then they began to lose their fears and got used to the smell, and before the child got his second teeth, he'd gone inside the chicken coop to play, where the wires were falling apart. The angel was no less standoffish with him than with other mortals, but he tolerated the most ingenious infamies[20] with the patience of a dog who had no illusions. They both came down with chickenpox at the same time. The doctor who took care of the child couldn't resist the temptation to listen to the angel's heart, and he found so much whistling in the heart and so many sounds in his kidneys that it seemed impossible for him to be alive. What surprised him most, however, was the logic of his wings. They seemed so natural on that completely human organism that he couldn't understand why other men didn't have them too.

When the child began school, it had been some time since the sun and rain had caused the collapse of the chicken coop. The angel went dragging himself about here and there like a stray dying man. They would drive him out of the bedroom with a broom and a moment later find him in the kitchen. He seemed to be in so many places at the same time that they grew to think that he'd been duplicated, that he was reproducing himself all through the house, and the exasperated and unhinged Elisenda shouted that it was awful living in that hell full of angels. He could scarcely eat and his antiquarian eyes had also become so foggy that he went about bumping into posts. All he had left were the bare cannulae[21] of his last feathers. Pelayo threw a blanket over him and extended him the charity of letting him sleep in the shed, and only then did they notice that he had a temperature at night and was delirious with the tongue twisters of an old Norwegian. That was one of the few times they became alarmed, for they thought he was going to die and not even the wise neighbor woman had been able to tell them what to do with dead angels.

And yet he not only survived his worst winter but seemed improved with the first sunny days. He remained motionless for several days in the farthest corner of the courtyard, where no one would see him, and at the beginning of December some large, stiff feathers began to grow on his wings, the feathers of a

---

18. **myrrh** (mʉr) *n.:* sweet-smelling substance used in making perfume.
19. **homage** (häm′ij) *n.:* any gift or action that shows reverence, honor, or respect.
20. **infamies** *n.:* here, disrespectful acts; insults.

---

21. **cannulae** (kan′yoō·lē′) *n.:* tubes.

Vocabulary
lament (lə·ment′) *v.:* feel very sorry.

scarecrow, which looked more like another misfortune of decrepitude.[22] But he must have known the reason for those changes, for he was quite careful that no one should notice them, that no one should hear the sea chanteys[23] that he sometimes sang under the stars. One morning Elisenda was cutting some bunches of onions for lunch when a wind that seemed to come from the high seas blew into the kitchen. Then she went to the window and caught the angel in his first attempts at flight. They were so clumsy that his fingernails opened a furrow in the vegetable patch and he was on the point of knocking the shed down with the ungainly flapping that slipped on the light and couldn't get a grip on the air. But he did manage to gain altitude. Elisenda let out a sigh of relief, for herself and for him, when she saw him pass over the last houses, holding himself up in some way with the risky flapping of a senile[24] vulture. She kept watching him even when she was through cutting the onions and she kept on watching until it was no longer possible for her to see him, because then he was no longer an annoyance in her life but an imaginary dot on the horizon of the sea. ∎

---

22. **decrepitude** *n.:* feebleness; weakness.
23. **chanteys** (shan'tēz) *n.:* songs sung by sailors to set a rhythm for their work.
24. **senile** (sē'nīl') *adj.:* showing confusion, loss of memory, and other signs of mental weakness or damage because of old age.

Meet the Writer

Gabriel García Márquez

Memory's Magician

Gabriel García Márquez (1928–   ) sets much of his fiction in the imaginary town of Macondo, which in many ways resembles the sleepy, decaying, backwater town of Aracataca, Colombia, where he was born. Because his parents were poor, young Gabriel was raised by his maternal grandparents, in a large old house crowded with relatives and relics of the family's past. His grandmother told him tales of ancestors, spirits, and ghosts; and his grandfather, a retired colonel (whom García Márquez has called "the most important figure of my life"), spoke continually of a past so vivid that it became as real to the young boy as the present.

After studying law and working abroad as a journalist for many years, García Márquez became an international celebrity with the publication of his novel *One Hundred Years of Solitude* (1967). This epic masterpiece tells the comic and tragic saga of seven generations of Macondo's founding family. The Chilean poet Pablo Neruda called the novel "the greatest revelation in the Spanish language since *Don Quixote*." García Márquez won the Nobel Prize for literature in 1982.

He says this about writing when you are young:

66 When you are young, you write almost—well, every writer is different, I'm talking about myself—almost like writing a poem. You write on impulses and inspiration. You have so much inspiration that you are not concerned with technique. You just see what comes out, without worrying much about what you are going to say and how. On the other hand, later, you know exactly what you are going to say and what you want to say. And you have a lot to tell. Even if all of your life you continue to tell about your childhood, later you are better able to interpret it, or at least interpret it in a different way. 99

For Independent Reading

García Márquez's many works of magic realism have delighted and intrigued readers around the world. You might enjoy his book of short stories, *Strange Pilgrims*.

Like Gabriel García Márquez, Jack Agüeros transforms ordinary realities with a touch of fantasy. In this poem he presents a startling vision of the homeless people who use the subways of New York City for shelter. Agüeros roots his images in the everyday through realistic details—references to Calcutta, a city in India where hundreds of thousands live on the streets, and the Gowanus Canal, a polluted body of water in Brooklyn, New York. But he also includes an **allusion** *(a reference) to Macondo, an imaginary village that is the setting for much of García Márquez's fiction.*

Sonnet for Heaven Below

Jack Agüeros

No, it wasn't Macondo, and it wasn't Calcutta in time past.
But subway magic turned the tunnels into Beautyrest mattresses
And plenty of God's children started sleeping there. Some
Were actually Angels fatigued from long hours and no pay.

5   This is an aside, but I have to alert you. Angels run
Around, don't shave or bathe; acid rain fractures their
Feathers, and french fries and coca cola corrupt
The color of their skin and make them sing hoarsely.
The gossamer shoes so perfect for kicking clouds
10 Stain and tear on the concrete and in the hard light
Of the city they start to look like abandoned barges
Foundering in the cancerous waters of the Gowanus Canal.

    Shabby gossamer shoes always arouse the derision of smart New Yorkers.
    Mercifully, Angels aren't tourists, so they are spared total disdain.

Response and Analysis

Reading Check

1. The townspeople have various ideas about what the winged old man is. What do Pelayo and Elisenda think he is? What does their neighbor think? and Father Gonzaga?

2. How does the winged old man change the lives of Pelayo and Elisenda?

3. What miracles are attributed to the old man?

4. What happens when another novelty, a spider-woman, comes to town?

Thinking Critically

5. Writing that ridicules human behaviors is called **satire.** What human shortcomings might García Márquez be satirizing in this story? Consider:

   - how Pelayo and Elisenda treat the old man

   - Father Gonzaga's reactions to him

   - how the townspeople react

6. Do you think the old man is a divine figure or an evil one, or neither? Explain your view. What other possibilities might explain his identity? (Check your Quickwrite notes.) ✎

7. Do you think this story is intended merely to amuse us, or does it have a deeper **theme?** Do you think the old man might **symbolize,** or represent, the miracles we wish for but cannot accept when they happen or the misunderstood artist whose imagination longs to soar?

8. How are the "angels" in "Sonnet for Heaven Below" (see the **Connection** on page 597) similar to the old man with enormous wings? Compare how "smart New Yorkers" treat the angels with the way the old man is treated.

Literary Criticism

9. What details in this story illustrate the **style** of **magic realism**—that is, elements of fantasy mixed in with the commonplace?

10. Which of García Márquez's **images** did you find most startling and memorable? How does the author use these images to create the story's **mood** and **tone?** 📖

11. García Márquez has said:

   > It always amuses me that the biggest praise for my work comes for the imagination while the truth is there is not a single line in all my work that does not have a basis in reality.

   Does the story seem based more on fantasy than on an underlying reality? Explain.

WRITING

Create Your Own Magic Realism

Write a **fantastic story** of your own about a character from folklore, mythology, or popular culture who falls into our world. Consider these possibilities:

   - Hercules, the strongest teenager in the world, enrolls at your school

   - a fairy godmother visits a poor girl in New York City

   - a dragon asks to be admitted to the local zoo

▶ **Use "Writing a Short Story," pages 602–609, for help with this assignment.**

SKILLS FOCUS

Literary Skills
Analyze magic realism.

Reading Skills
Analyze a writer's style.

Writing Skills
Write a fantasy story.

Vocabulary Development

Roots and Relations

Knowing a word's **root word** will help you to understand its related forms. For example, *antique, antiquated, antiquarian,* and *antiquity* come from the Latin root word *antiquus,* which means "ancient; old."

PRACTICE 1

Using a dictionary, trace the origin of each word in the Word Bank to find its **root word.** Also note its **part of speech.** Then, look for related forms and their parts of speech. (Some of the words have many related forms; one word has none.) Note that adding or changing a **suffix** often changes a word's part of speech. Summarize your findings for each word in a graphic like the one below for the word *impeded.*

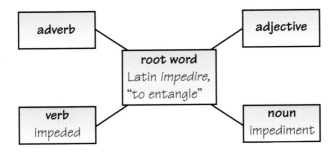

Literal and Figurative Language: Imagery

García Márquez's story is filled with **imagery,** language that appeals directly to our senses as well as to our imagination. When an image uses words in their **literal** (dictionary) sense, the words mean exactly what they say. But when an image uses **figurative language,** the words are not meant to be understood literally. That's because figurative language always involves an imaginative **comparison** of two basically unlike things.

LITERAL   "There were only a few faded hairs left on his bald skull and very few teeth in his mouth. . . ."

FIGURATIVE "And the sands of the beach, which on March nights glimmered like powdered light, had become a stew of mud and rotten shellfish."

PRACTICE 2

1. Look back at the story, and find at least three examples of unusual imagery. Do the images use **literal** or **figurative** language?

2. Write a description of a person or group of people in a specific setting. Use both literal and figurative language in your description and images that appeal to the senses.

SKILLS FOCUS

Vocabulary Skills
Understand word roots. Understand and use literal and figurative language.

Grammar Link

Varying Sentence Length and Structure

Experienced writers use a variety of sentence structures and sentence lengths so that their paragraphs don't have the singsong sound of beginning-readers' books. To vary your sentences, you'll first need to recall how to distinguish independent and subordinate clauses.

An **independent clause** expresses a complete thought and can stand by itself as a sentence.

"The curious came from far away."

A **subordinate clause** does not express a complete thought and cannot stand alone.

"when the rain stopped"
"that a flesh-and-blood angel was held captive in Pelayo's house"

Every English sentence can be placed in one of the four categories in the chart below:

Type of Sentence	Example
A **simple sentence** has one independent clause and no subordinate clauses. Its subject or verb or both may be compound.	"He was dressed like a ragpicker."
A **compound sentence** has two or more independent clauses but no subordinate clause.	"Then they dared speak to him, and he answered in an incomprehensible dialect with a strong sailor's voice."
A **complex sentence** has one independent clause and at least one subordinate clause.	"The simplest among them thought that he should be named mayor of the world."
A **compound-complex sentence** has two or more independent clauses and at least one subordinate clause.	"Sea and sky were a single ash-gray thing, and the sands of the beach, which on March nights glimmered like powdered light, had become a stew of mud and rotten shellfish."

PRACTICE

SKILLS FOCUS

Grammar Skills
Vary sentence length and structure.

Edit this choppy paragraph by combining some sentences into compound, complex, or compound-complex sentences. Then, check page 588 to see how García Márquez wrote this paragraph:

Pelayo was frightened by that nightmare. Pelayo ran to get Elisenda. She was his wife. She was putting compresses on the sick child. He took her to the rear of the courtyard. They both looked at the fallen body with mute stupor. He was dressed like a ragpicker. There were only a few faded hairs left on his bald skull. There were very few teeth in his mouth. His huge buzzard wings were dirty. They were also half plucked. They were forever tangled in the mud.

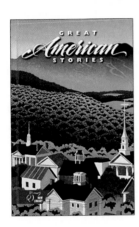

FICTION

Masters of Style

A man pursued by a headless horseman, two mothers sharing a dark secret in Rome, and an awkward waltz that never seems to end—these are just a few of the characters and situations you'll encounter in *Great American Stories.* This collection features the best of such admired authors as Nathaniel Hawthorne, Mark Twain, Edgar Allan Poe, and Willa Cather—all masters of style who helped change the shape of American literature.

This title is available in the HRW Library.

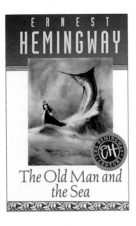

FICTION

High Seas Struggle

Ernest Hemingway earned his fame from his spare, powerful writing style and his ability to make words come alive on the page. In his novella *The Old Man and the Sea,* Hemingway's talents were in their finest form. This is the story of Santiago, an aging Cuban fisherman who glimpses an irresistible catch from his boat: a magnificent marlin that bobs to the surface of the Gulf Stream. Amazingly, the great fish takes the hook into its mouth—and then continues to swim for his life. A classic conflict of man versus nature ensues.

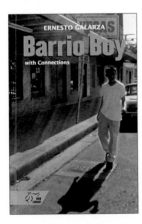

NONFICTION

Between Two Cultures

Ernesto Galarza, a teacher and political activist, is probably best known for his autobiography, *Barrio Boy.* Galarza first describes his early boyhood in western Mexico—a beautiful rural setting rich in song, folklore, and customs. Then the Mexican Revolution begins, and Galarza's family flees to a very different place: a barrio in Sacramento, California. *Barrio Boy* tells the story of a family caught between their heritage and their adopted land.

This title is available in the HRW Library.

NONFICTION

Life with Wolves

For most people, living near a den of wolves is a less than appealing prospect. Scientist Farley Mowat had no choice. The government's Wildlife Service sent him to northern Canada to investigate the wolves' killing of the endangered arctic caribou. Mowat found something he had never expected—sympathy for the noble wolf families—and a companionship with local Inuit people. Farley Mowat's *Never Cry Wolf* is the true story of his life-changing experience.

This title is available in the HRW Library.

Writing a Short Story

Writing Assignment
Use your creative talent to write an effective short story.

Have you ever admired the style of a short story like Sandra Cisneros's "Geraldo No Last Name"? Have you wished that you could put an event from your imagination into words that would captivate your audience as Gabriel García Márquez does in his short story, "A Very Old Man with Enormous Wings"? In this workshop you can create a **short story** with style and imagination.

Prewriting

Finding an Idea

Where to Start? A short story is a work of fiction that usually has a single idea as its starting point. That idea may arise from any source. From that point, the story evolves from the writer's imagination. If you are struggling for an idea for a story, brainstorm your personal experiences, dreams, ambitions, and interests.

Begin at the Beginning The main ingredients of any short story are **characters, plot, point of view, setting,** and **theme.** A writer can, of course, emphasize one or more elements more than others. As the writer, you decide which elements are most important in your story.

Characters Short stories usually fully develop only the main character. Supporting characters are developed as thoroughly as their roles in the story require; minor characters, for example, might be characterized in a single sentence. Examine the questions and one writer's responses to those questions about his main character in the chart below. Then, create a chart of your own to record details about your main and supporting characters.

| DO THIS →

Quick guide

SKILLS FOCUS

Writing Skills
Write a short story.

RECORDING CHARACTER DETAILS

Questions	Character
How does the character think, act, and feel?	Jesse—intensely moody 15-year-old; slouches and pouts; respectful and cooperative, at times grudgingly
What motivates the character?	Jesse is motivated by his desire to be a great basketball player. When he's not playing basketball, he's thinking about it.

(continued)

What does the character look like? What is his or her voice like?	Jesse—tall and lanky, not yet filled out. Black hair, dark complexion; voice changes from low to high when excited.
What distinct or unique mannerisms or habits does the character have?	Jesse—frequently interrupts whatever he's doing by going through the motions of a jump shot.

TIP An effective way to develop believable characters is to involve them in **dialogue,** conversation between characters. You can also reveal what a character is thinking or feeling through **interior monologue,** talk that goes on inside a character's head.

Plot **Plot** is what happens in a story—the actions or sequence of events. The events occur as the result of a **conflict,** or struggle between opposing forces. Conflicts are **external** when a character struggles against an outside force and **internal** when the struggle is within a character. Look at the types of conflicts in the chart below.

TYPES OF CONFLICT

Conflict	Definition	Example
Character vs. character (external)	The main character is in conflict with another character in the story.	Jesse struggles against the established star of the basketball team of his new team in Florida.
Character vs. the environment (external)	The main character is in conflict with an aspect of his or her environment.	Jesse struggles to keep up with his new teammates in the unfamiliar heat and humidity of Florida.
Character vs. a situation (external)	The main character is in conflict with a situation or circumstance outside him- or herself.	Jesse struggles against what he perceives as his new basketball coaches' prejudice against players new to the school.
Character vs. him- or herself (internal)	The main character struggles with conflicting desires, ideas, or feelings within him- or herself.	Jesse is torn between his resentment at being moved from his familiar life and his need to adjust to his new surroundings.

The plot of your story unfolds through a series of events, called the **rising action,** to the **climax,** or high point, of the story. Each plot event builds on the previous event until the climax. After the climax the **resolution,** or denouement, settles the conflict and ends the story. The resolution may also make clear the significance of the story's events. Here are some techniques you can use to construct your plot.

- Narrate the events of your plot in **chronological order,** the order in which the events occur. Consider using **flashbacks** to provide background information that is important to understanding your plot.

- **Pace** the action of your plot. For example, create a frantic mood by narrating events quickly, using short sentences. Create a leisurely mood by narrating events slowly, using longer sentences.

Writing Skills
Find and develop an idea.

- Provide abundant **sensory details** and **figurative language** (such as metaphor, simile, and personification) to create effective **images.** Help your readers imagine the sights, smells, and sounds of a scene or event and the actions, movements, gestures, and feelings of your characters.

- Locate scenes and incidents in **specific places.**

Point of View The **point of view** of a short story is the vantage point of the story's narrator. Each point of view has advantages and disadvantages. Once you decide on a point of view, stick to it. Shifting points of view can ruin your story's coherence and confuse your readers. Here are your choices.

POINTS OF VIEW

Points of View	Advantages	Disadvantages
First person: The main character or a supporting character tells the story using the pronoun *I*.	This point of view gives the reader a sense of hearing from the primary participant directly or from an eyewitness.	The narrator can't reveal everything. For example, he or she can't reveal the thoughts of other characters.
Third person omniscient: An outsider (rather than a character in the story) tells the story, using third-person pronouns—*he, she,* and *they*.	Omniscient narrators know all and can tell all. For example, they can use **shifting perspectives** to show the same event from the perspectives of several characters.	Stories with omniscient narrators often make readers feel far removed from the characters and action, as in a fairy tale.
Third person limited: An outsider tells the story through the eyes and mind of the main character, using third-person pronouns.	The third-person-limited narrator focuses attention on the thoughts and feelings of the main character, making it easy for the reader to identify with him or her.	Limited narrators may have trouble making minor characters seem real. The writer could slip into the omniscient point of view without being aware of it.

Setting The **setting** of your story is the time and location in which it takes place. Setting can be insignificant in a short story or vitally important. If, for example, you want to use the setting to help establish the mood or atmosphere of your story, or if the setting is important to the conflict of your story, describe it thoroughly.

Theme The **theme** of your story expresses an idea about what it means to be human. Themes usually have to do with basic human needs and emotions. You can directly state your story's theme, but most modern stories suggest, or imply, the theme. The reader pieces together the clues you provide and from them infers the story's theme.

SKILLS FOCUS

Writing Skills
Consider characters, plot, point of view, setting, and theme.

PRACTICE & APPLY 1 Using the guidelines provided on the preceding pages, choose an idea for your story. Then, select a point of view, and plan your story.

Writing

Writing a Short Story

A Writer's Model

Finding a Friend

Jesse, a tall and lanky fifteen-year-old, slouched on the edge of his bed, his expression sullen, pouting. He had been moping around his new house for the entire week he had been there. How could his father have moved the family away from sunny, warm, and beautiful California, home of the Hoopsters and Dunk Martin? They had moved to hot, rainy Florida, home of hurricanes and uh . . . who? Oh, yeah, the Sharks and the Keys were Florida's pro basketball teams. Big deal! He had to adjust, he knew, but he couldn't stop the movies of his California life from running in his head.

Jesse was upstairs unpacking his sizable collection of basketball souvenirs. He savored the feel of his miniature autographed basketball, which he had caught from a Hoopsters cheerleader who had tossed the autographed balls into the stands where he happened to be sitting. He could almost hear the roar of the crowd at that game as Dunk power-dunked over three helpless defenders. The last piece he unwrapped was a small gold medal, his greatest source of pride. He had received the medal when his team won first place in their division in last summer's basketball league—the same team now playing without him.

Jesse rose, put up a phantom jump shot, and slouched toward the window. Would he ever find anyone to shoot baskets with? Through

(continued)

BEGINNING

Main character

Point of view/ Interior monologue

Interior conflict

Metaphor

MIDDLE

Rising action

Flashback/Sensory details

Interior monologue

(continued)

Sensory details

Simile

Dialogue

Metaphor

Sensory details

Dialogue

Sensory details

END
Climax

Resolution

Theme (implied)

the window he saw an older man wearing ragged shorts and basketball shoes. Jesse watched as his next-door neighbor, limping noticeably on his left leg, pushed a lawn mower slowly across the wide green expanse in front of his house. He was surprised to see his mother scurrying toward the neighbor with a tall glass in her hand, like a waitress at a busy restaurant. The man drank the lemonade Mrs. Estrada had brought him, pausing between swallows to talk.

"Jesse, the man next door shouldn't have to mow his own lawn with that bad leg of his. You should mow his lawn when you mow ours," Jesse's mom said that night at dinner.

"Mom! His yard's bigger than ours!" Jesse whined.

"Jesse," she responded, "don't be so thoughtless."

Jesse, still irritated at his mom, remembered the man's limp and felt his anger slip quietly through him and away, a basketball swishing through the rim, hardly touching the net.

The next weekend, Jesse pulled on his favorite sneakers, so old and full of holes they could hardly be called shoes. He slowly headed out to mow his lawn—and his neighbor's. As he was finishing, the neighbor walked up to him. Jesse hadn't noticed before how tall the man was. "Hi, Jesse. I'm Dan. Thanks for a very nice job. Come on in and have a cold glass of tea." Jesse smiled and followed Dan into the house.

"Sit down while I get our drinks," Dan said. Jesse sat and began to look around the room. His eye caught sight of an ornate glass case in the far corner. Curious, he got up and crossed to the case for a closer look. On the top shelf was a large bronze trophy. It was surrounded by old photographs, framed newspaper articles, and smaller trophies. Jesse leaned in closer and read aloud the plaque attached to the trophy—"Dan Casey, Most Valuable Player, 1968 All-Star Game."

As Dan walked back into the room, Jesse wheeled around, sputtering, voice high, "Dan Casey! You're Dan Casey! I've got your 1968 All-Star card!"

"I saw your goal yesterday, Jesse. Mind if I come over and shoot a few baskets with you now and then? I was pretty good at it before I blew out this old knee," Dan said. Later that afternoon, Jesse put up a shot from the top of the key—nothin' but net—and thought how great Florida was.

INTERNET
More Writer's Models
Keyword: LE5 10-8

PRACTICE & APPLY **2** Refer to the framework on page 605 and the Writer's Model above as you write the first draft of the short story you planned earlier.

Revising

Evaluate and Revise Your Short Story

Fresh Eyes Writing a short story requires a significant expenditure of time, energy, and imagination, so you want it to be as good as it can be, which usually requires revision. If you have time, put the draft of your short story aside for a day or two to give your eyes and mind a break. Then, read it very carefully two more times, first to evaluate the content and organization and second to evaluate the style.

First Reading Use the following chart to help you evaluate and revise the content and organization of your short story. To use the chart, ask yourself the questions in the left-hand column. Use the tips in the middle column to help you answer the questions. Then, use the revision techniques in the right-hand column to make needed changes.

> **PEER REVIEW**
>
> Before you revise your work, exchange stories with a classmate. He or she will bring a fresh eye to the story, and may have ideas about how you can improve the dialogue.

Rubric: Writing a Short Story

Evaluation Questions	Tips	Revision Techniques
❶ Does the story open with an exciting event or intriguing introduction to the main character?	▶ **Underline** the event or introduction to the main character that seizes readers' attention.	▶ To draw readers in, **add** an exciting event or intriguing introduction to the main character.
❷ Is the point of view, or vantage point, from which the story is told consistent?	▶ **Circle** all the pronouns in the story that reveal the point of view.	▶ **Reword** any instances of inconsistent point of view.
❸ Is the conflict clear? Do the events in the story lead to a climax? Are all events relevant to the plot?	▶ **Double underline** the sentence(s) that makes the conflict clear. **Bracket** the sentence(s) containing the climax. **Draw a line** through irrelevant events.	▶ **Add** or **elaborate** on events to develop the plot. **Delete** events that do not contribute to the development of the plot.
❹ Does the story contain sensory details and figurative language that develop the events, characters, and setting?	▶ **Put a check mark** next to sensory details and figurative language that describe events, characters, and setting.	▶ **Add** sensory details and figurative language as necessary to describe vividly events, characters, and setting.
❺ Does the story contain dialogue?	▶ **Put a star** by conversations between characters.	▶ **Add** correctly punctuated dialogue.
❻ Is the conflict resolved logically? Is the theme directly stated or implied?	▶ **Highlight** the resolution of the conflict. **Put two stars** by the sentence(s) stating or implying the theme.	▶ **Elaborate** upon the resolution, the statement of theme, or the sentences that imply the theme.

Second Reading Sophisticated writers of fiction are always conscious of their use of language, including the verbs they use in their stories. They often choose vivid **action verbs** to express the physical or mental activity of their characters. Take a look at the difference between weak verbs and vivid ones in the examples below.

Weak Verbs Maria **walked** into her sister's room and **took** her new sweater.

Vivid Verbs Maria **tiptoed** into her sister's room and **snatched** her new sweater.

Now, take a look at the verbs you've used in your short story. Are they vivid, precise, and powerful? Use the chart below to evaluate and revise your style.

Style Guidelines

Evaluation Question	▶ Tip	▶ Revision Technique
● Does the story contain vivid action verbs?	▶ **Circle** all the action verbs in the story.	▶ **Replace** weak action verbs with vivid ones.

ANALYZING THE REVISION PROCESS

Study these revisions, and answer the questions that follow.

> "I saw your goal yesterday, Jesse. Mind if I come over and
>
> shoot a few baskets with you now and then? I was pretty good
>
> at it before I ~~hurt~~ ^blew out^ this old knee," Dan said. *Later that afternoon, Jesse put up a shot from the top of the key—nothin' but net—and thought how great Florida was.*

replace
elaborate

Responding to the Revision Process

1. Does the change the writer made to the third sentence improve the sentence? Why?

2. Why did the writer add a sentence?

PRACTICE & APPLY 3 Using the guidelines in this section, first evaluate and revise the content and organization of your story. Then, evaluate and revise the style of your story. Examine the Writer's Model and the revisions shown in the example paragraph above as models for your own revisions. If possible, work with a peer throughout the revision process.

SKILLS FOCUS

Writing Skills
Revise for content and style.

Publishing

Proofread and Publish Your Short Story

Be Conventional Writing a short story is a creative endeavor; nevertheless, you should follow the basic rules of grammar, usage, and mechanics when you write one. Minor errors in these areas can be annoying for readers. Major errors can cause them to deposit your story in the nearest recycling bin. The one exception is dialogue, where the rules of grammar and usage do not apply because dialogue should reflect the way people really talk. Proofread your short story to eliminate errors in grammar, usage, and mechanics.

Who Will Read My Story? Now that you've got your story in good form, it's time to let others read it. There are many ways that you can make your story available to a wider audience. Here are some ideas.

- Put your story together with your other writings to create a small collection of your work, and distribute it to family members and close friends.

- Submit your story to the school newspaper or any other publication that accepts work from young writers. Ask your teacher or your school librarian to help you find a list of publications that you can contact, or conduct an Internet search.

- Put your short story on the Internet, either on your own Web page, your school's Web site, or on one of the many sites that accept work from young writers.

Reflect on Your Short Story

Consider the Process Now think back about what you've done, and mull over what you've learned in the process of writing a short story. Here are some questions to consider.

- How did writing this short story help you understand and appreciate the process that professional authors go through?

- How do you think your story stacks up against some of the stories you've read during your study of literature? Compare your development of specific elements to the development of the same elements by authors whose stories you've read.

PRACTICE & APPLY 4 Using the guidelines on this page, first proofread your essay for errors in standard American grammar, usage, and mechanics. Then, publish your story for a wider audience. Finally, reflect on the process you went through in writing your story by answering the reflection questions above.

TIP Be sure that you observe the **conventions** of standard American English as you proofread. For example, check for errors in subject-verb agreement. Eliminate them unless you purposefully use them in dialogue. For more on **subject-verb agreement,** see Agreement of Subject and Verb, 2a–n, in the Language Handbook.

Writing Skills
Proofread, especially for agreement of subjects and verbs.

Test Practice

Literary Criticism: Evaluating Style

DIRECTIONS: Read the short-short story that follows. Then, read and respond to the questions that follow.

My Lucy Friend Who Smells Like Corn
Sandra Cisneros

Lucy Anguiano, Texas girl who smells like corn, like Frito Bandito chips, like tortillas, something like that warm smell of nixtamal[1] or bread the way her head smells when she's leaning close to you over a paper cut-out doll or on the porch when we are squatting over marbles trading this pretty crystal that leaves a blue star on your hand for that giant cat-eye with a grasshopper green spiral in the center like the juice of bugs on the windshield when you drive to the border, like the yellow blood of butterflies. *Have you ever eated dog food? I have.* After crunching like ice, she opens her big mouth to prove it, only a pink tongue rolling around in there like a blind worm, and Janey looking in because she said show me. But me I like that Lucy, corn smell hair and aqua flip flops just like mine which we bought at K-mart for only 79¢ same time. I'm going to sit in the sun, don't care if it's a million trillion degrees outside, so my skin can get so dark it's blue where it bends like Lucy's. Her whole family like that. Eyes like knife slits. Lucy and her sisters. Norma, Margarita, Ofelia, Herminia, Nancy, Olivia, Cheli, y la Amber Sue.

Screen door with no screen. BANG! Little black dog biting his fur. Fat couch on the porch. Some of the windows painted blue, some pink because her Daddy got tired that day or forgot. Mama in the kitchen feeding clothes into the wringer washer[2] and clothes rolling out all stiff and twisted and flat like paper. Lucy got her arm stuck once and had to yell Maaa! and her Mama had to put the machine in reverse and then her hand rolled back, the finger black and later, the nail fell off. *But did your arm get flat like the clothes? What happened to your arm? Did they have to pump it with air?* No, only the finger, and she didn't cry neither.

Lean across the porch rail and pin the pink sock of the baby Amber Sue on top of Cheli's flowered t-shirt, and the blue jeans of la Ofelia over the inside seam of Olivia's blouse, over the flannel nightgown of

---

1. **nixtamal** (niks·tä·mäl′) *n.*: partially cooked corn that has been boiled with lime in preparation for making corn tortillas.
2. **wringer washer:** old-fashioned washing machine in which clothing, after being washed, is rolled through a device (the wringer) that squeezes out the water.

Pages 610–612
cover
Literary Skills
Analyze a
writer's style.

Margarita so it don't stretch out, and then you take the workshirts of their Daddy and hang them upside down like this, and this way all the clothes don't get so wrinkled and take up less space and you don't waste pins. The girls all wear each other's clothes, except Olivia who is stingy, because there ain't no boys here. Only girls and one father who is never home hardly and one mother who says *Ay! I'm real tired* and so many sisters there's no time to count them.

I'm sitting in the sun even though it's the hottest part of the day, the part that makes the streets dizzy, when the heat makes a little hat on the top of your head and bakes the dust and weed grass and sweat up good, all steamy and smelling like sweet corn.

I want to rub heads and sleep in a bed with little sisters, some at the top and some at the feets. I think it would be fun to sleep with sisters you could yell at one at a time or all together, instead of alone on the fold-out chair in the living room.

When I get home Abuelita[3] will say *Didn't I tell you?* and I'll get it because I was supposed to wear this dress again tomorrow. But first I'm going to jump off an old pissy mattress in the Anguiano yard. I'm going to scratch your mosquito bites, Lucy, so they'll itch you, then put mercurochrome[4] smiley faces on them. We're going to trade shoes and wear them on our hands. We're going to walk over to Janey Ortiz's house and say *We're never ever going to be your friend again forever!* We're going to run home backwards and we're going to run home frontwards, look twice under the house where the rats hide and I'll stick one foot in there because you dared me, sky so blue and heaven inside those white clouds. I'm going to peel a scab from my knee and eat it, sneeze on the cat, give you three M&M's I've been saving for you since yesterday, comb your hair with my fingers and braid it into teeny-tiny braids real pretty. We're going to wave to a lady we don't know on the bus. Hello! I'm going to somersault on the rail of the front porch even though my chones[5] show. And cut paper dolls we draw ourselves, and color in their clothes with crayons, my arm around your neck. And when we look at each other, our arms gummy from an orange popsicle we split, we could be sisters right? We could be, you and me waiting for our teeths to fall and money. You laughing something into my ear that tickles, and me going Ha Ha Ha Ha. Her and me, my Lucy friend who smells like corn.

---

3. Abuelita (ä·bwel·ē′tä): affectionate Spanish word for "Grandma."
4. mercurochrome (mər·kyoʊrˈə·krōm′) *n.*: reddish solution painted on cuts and scrapes to prevent infection.
5. chones (chōˈnes) *n.*: Spanish slang for "pants."

Collection 8: Skills Review

1. Who is the **narrator** of this story?
   A   Lucy Anguiano
   B   One of Lucy's sisters
   C   Janey Ortiz
   D   An unnamed girl

2. Cisneros's description of a marble's center as being "like the juice of bugs on the windshield" is an example of which kind of **figurative language**?
   F   Extended metaphor
   G   Metaphor
   H   Simile
   J   Personification

3. The **images** and **figurative language** in the first paragraph help to create which of the following **moods**?
   A   Sad and somber
   B   Quiet and thoughtful
   C   Upbeat and lively
   D   Detached and cold

4. The writer's **tone,** or attitude, is best described as —
   F   affectionate
   G   critical
   H   fearful
   J   mocking

5.   All of the following contribute to the story's unique **style** *except* —
   A   the diction, or word choice
   B   the figurative language

C   the length of the sentences
D   the story's conflicts

6. What is the effect of the author's use of sentence fragments?
   F   They create a formal tone.
   G   They remind us of the importance of using good grammar.
   H   They create a friendly, informal tone.
   J   They show us that the narrator is unusual.

7. The author's **diction,** or word choice, suggests all of the following about the narrator *except* that she —
   A   is observant
   B   loves life
   C   is young
   D   is looking back on her childhood

8. Which statement *best* describes the story's **theme**?
   F   Friendship is important, especially to children.
   G   Friendships fade as you get older.
   H   True friendship lasts forever.
   J   Childhood friendships are not very deep.

Constructed Response

9. List five examples of the author's style from the story. Explain how they help create her unique style.

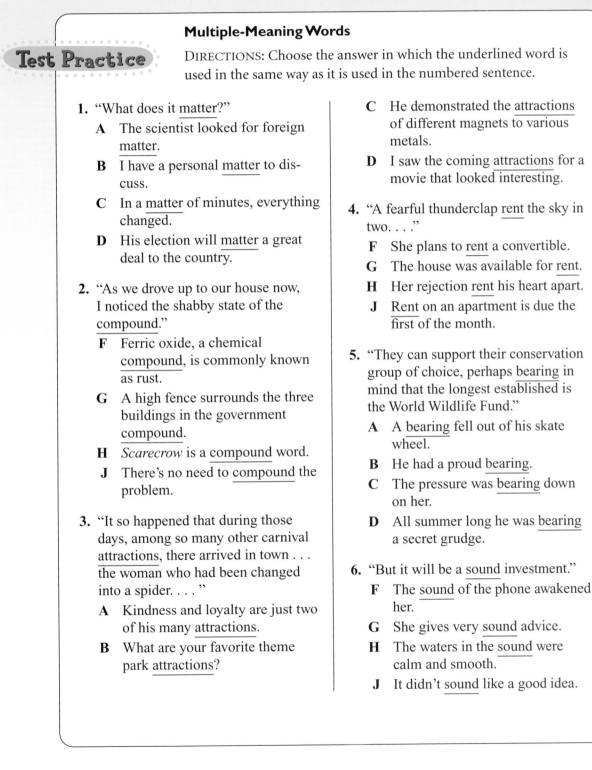

Test Practice

Multiple-Meaning Words

DIRECTIONS: Choose the answer in which the underlined word is used in the same way as it is used in the numbered sentence.

1. "What does it <u>matter</u>?"
   - **A** The scientist looked for foreign <u>matter</u>.
   - **B** I have a personal <u>matter</u> to discuss.
   - **C** In a <u>matter</u> of minutes, everything changed.
   - **D** His election will <u>matter</u> a great deal to the country.

2. "As we drove up to our house now, I noticed the shabby state of the <u>compound</u>."
   - **F** Ferric oxide, a chemical <u>compound</u>, is commonly known as rust.
   - **G** A high fence surrounds the three buildings in the government <u>compound</u>.
   - **H** *Scarecrow* is a <u>compound</u> word.
   - **J** There's no need to <u>compound</u> the problem.

3. "It so happened that during those days, among so many other carnival <u>attractions</u>, there arrived in town . . . the woman who had been changed into a spider. . . . "
   - **A** Kindness and loyalty are just two of his many <u>attractions</u>.
   - **B** What are your favorite theme park <u>attractions</u>?

   - **C** He demonstrated the <u>attractions</u> of different magnets to various metals.
   - **D** I saw the coming <u>attractions</u> for a movie that looked interesting.

4. "A fearful thunderclap <u>rent</u> the sky in two. . . ."
   - **F** She plans to <u>rent</u> a convertible.
   - **G** The house was available for <u>rent</u>.
   - **H** Her rejection <u>rent</u> his heart apart.
   - **J** <u>Rent</u> on an apartment is due the first of the month.

5. "They can support their conservation group of choice, perhaps <u>bearing</u> in mind that the longest established is the World Wildlife Fund."
   - **A** A <u>bearing</u> fell out of his skate wheel.
   - **B** He had a proud <u>bearing</u>.
   - **C** The pressure was <u>bearing</u> down on her.
   - **D** All summer long he was <u>bearing</u> a secret grudge.

6. "But it will be a <u>sound</u> investment."
   - **F** The <u>sound</u> of the phone awakened her.
   - **G** She gives very <u>sound</u> advice.
   - **H** The waters in the <u>sound</u> were calm and smooth.
   - **J** It didn't <u>sound</u> like a good idea.

SKILLS FOCUS

Vocabulary Skills
Use multiple-meaning words.

Collection 8: Skills Review

Writing Skills

DIRECTIONS: Read the following paragraph from a draft of a student's short story. Then, read the questions below it. Choose the best answer to each question, and mark your answers on your own paper.

(1) Julia's heart sank as she saw the red and blue squad car lights dance in her rearview mirror. (2) Why had she been driving so fast? (3) She'd been in a hurry to pick up her best friend, who had two expensive concert tickets for that evening, but now she was on the side of the road, stopped for speeding. (4) The officer, grim-faced, took her information very deliberately and walked slowly back to the squad car to check it. (5) Julia's palms were sweating as she clutched the hot steering wheel, fearful of doing anything the officer might think was disrespectful but wishing he would get on with it—give her the citation and let her go—before it was too late for the concert. (6) The officer returned and, frowning severely, returned her license and registration. (7) "Slow down, young lady," he growled, "because the next one won't be a warning."

1. To describe the setting with sensory details, which of the following sentences could the writer add?
   A The asphalt of the highway emitted a steamy heat that engulfed her car.
   B A wide, black belt cinched the officer's girth tightly.
   C She pictured herself in prison stripes.
   D She was painfully aware of passing cars slowing to see the criminal.

2. What sentence could the writer add to include effective details about the main character's physical appearance?
   F Her dirty car smudged the officer's uniform as he leaned on it.
   G She could just imagine her dad's face, contorted with anger, when he got the news.
   H Her face burned red with embarrassment as the officer walked toward her.
   J She had no idea that the stern police officer would think of taking pity on her.

3. To shift the perspective of the passage, which of the following sentences could the writer add?
   A She knew her mother would make her feel guilty for a month.
   B She wondered how her older brother had felt when he got his first ticket.
   C As Julia drove off, the officer smiled, remembering his first ticket.
   D She knew her mother would make her promise to be more careful.

SKILLS FOCUS

Writing Skills
Write a short story.

4. Which of the following sentences best describes the conflict of the passage?

F Students believed that the police in that area ticketed young drivers for any sort of minor traffic infraction.

G Julia was faced with a traffic ticket and a fine as well as potentially harsher consequences from her parents.

H Now Julia would have to give up a Saturday and take a defensive driving course to keep her insurance rates from going up.

J Julia was torn by her fear of appearing disrespectful of the officer and her desire to pick up her friend and get to the concert on time.

5. If the following sentence were added to the passage, how would it change the point of view of the passage? "As Julia drove away, the officer shook his head sadly, hoping the warning would be enough to slow the girl down."

A from third-person omniscient to third-person limited

B from first-person main character to first-person supporting character

C from third-person limited to third-person omniscient

D from first-person supporting character to first-person main character

Collection 9

LITERARY CRITICISM

Biographical and Historical Approach

INFORMATIONAL READING FOCUS

USING PRIMARY AND SECONDARY SOURCES

Literature is the memory of humanity.

—Isaac Bashevis Singer

"It hung upon a thorn and there he blew three deadly notes."
Illustration by N. C. Wyeth for *The Boy's King Arthur* (1917).
Oil on canvas.

Elements of Literature

Biography and History *by* Kylene Beers
HOW THE TWO AFFECT LITERARY CRITICISM

If you put on a pair of sunglasses whose lenses have a reddish tint, suddenly all the colors of the world are slightly different. Green leaves are greener. Yellow sunlight bouncing off the sidewalk is less harsh. Sunsets are more spectacular. Wearing those rose-colored lenses does indeed affect the way you see the world.

Writers, too, are looking at the world through "lenses." Writers live in particular times and places. Each writer brings to a work a family background, an educational background, a work background. All of these backgrounds of the writer—biographical and historical—affect his or her work.

Two Approaches to a Text: Biographical and Historical

Here we will talk about two ways of approaching a text: through biographical lenses and through historical lenses.

A **biographical approach** means that you use the writer's life experiences as you analyze and respond to a text. In other words, you look for ways in which the writer's personal experiences are revealed in the text. You might even find ways in which the writer's prejudices are reflected in the work.

In the story by Alice Walker on page 77, for example, you read about a simple woman in the rural South who is visited one day by a daughter who talks down to her. If you know that Walker herself grew up in the rural South and that, furthermore, she left home to attend a fine school in the North, you might decide that the story reflects some of Walker's per-

sonal history. In the same way, if you know that Saki grew up with two strict aunts, you will have an insight into the character of the disapproving aunt in "The Storyteller" (page 155).

A **historical approach** means that you use the time period in which a text was written as a help in analyzing and responding to the work. Ray Bradbury's "The Pedestrian" (page 47), for example, was written during the 1950s, a time when people thought that technology, and especially television, would limit their freedom. You see those concerns as you read that story. Furthermore, if you know that during the 1950s (a time marked by events known as the cold war), Americans feared the Soviet Union and the rise of totalitarianism, then you will read the story with even greater insight.

Try It Out: Biographical and Historical Criticism

Read the following poem as if you do not know anything about its author or the time when it was written:

I, Too

I, too, sing America.

I am the darker brother.
They send me to eat in the kitchen
When company comes,
But I laugh,
And eat well,
And grow strong.

SKILLS FOCUS

Literary Skills
Understand biographical and historical approaches to text.

Tomorrow,
I'll be at the table
When company comes.
Nobody'll dare
Say to me,
"Eat in the kitchen,"
Then.

Besides,
They'll see how beautiful I am
And be ashamed—

I, too, am America.

Think about what this poem means. Now, think about it again knowing that it was written by Langston Hughes, one of the most respected African American poets. How does having **biographical** knowledge about the writer shape your understanding of the poem? Suppose that you also know that Walt Whitman (1819–1892), a poet who strongly influenced Hughes, wrote a poem called "I Hear America Singing." What more can you now say about Hughes's poem?

Let's add another dimension—the **historical dimension.** Comments Hughes makes in "I, Too" are shaped by the historical period in which he lived. When Hughes wrote this poem, in 1924, segregation and discrimination were the norm in the United States. Laws kept African Americans attending separate schools, drinking from separate water fountains, riding at the backs of buses, eating in separate restaurants. Most professions were not open to African Americans, so many worked as "domestics" and as such were obliged to eat in the kitchen, not at the dining-room table. You quickly see that understanding history helps you understand a poem.

A historical lens is also helpful when you read myths and legends. **Myths** are

stories that are closely linked to a particular society, that are basically religious in nature, and that reflect the values of the society that tells them. **Legends** are stories based on real historical events. As they are told and retold, they tend to take on many fantastic, even supernatural elements.

In this chapter you will read myths and legends from three historical periods: late medieval Britain, ancient Greece, and medieval Scandinavia. The King Arthur stories were told in England by a people nostalgic for a glorious past, when knights roamed the land using might for right. The ancient Greek myths were told by a people who believed that the gods involved themselves in human affairs. The Scandinavian myths were told by a people with a pessimistic view of the world, seeing valor as the only certainty. Understanding that history will enrich your understanding of these works.

Practice

As you read the selections in this chapter, make a chart like the one below. Use it to see the selections in terms of biography and in terms of history.

| Selection: |
| Author: |
| Topic of selection: |
| What I know about the author's life: |
| What I know about the historical times in which the selection was told or written: |

Where Have You Gone, Charming Billy?

Make the Connection

Quickwrite ✏️

When you hear the word *war*, what do you think of? Why do people watch war movies? Why is war such a powerful subject? Jot down your thoughts about war.

Literary Focus

Understanding Historical Context

"Where Have You Gone, Charming Billy?" re-creates a young soldier's fears on his first night in the field during the Vietnam War. To appreciate the details in the story, you need to understand its **historical context.** There were no "front lines" in the war, and fighting took the form of unexpected guerrilla skirmishes. From moment to moment, the main character doesn't know what to expect—from his strange surroundings or from his own heart.

Seeing an Author in His Work

Tim O'Brien lived through the events he writes about. His experiences as a soldier in Vietnam have served as the focus of his fiction and nonfiction.

The Vietnam War divided the United States with particular bitterness. Although the war had a profound effect on our nation, for many years not many fiction writers dealt with it. O'Brien has written about it almost exclusively. Fact and fiction are interwoven in his work, and his attitudes about the war are reflected in the themes and issues that recur throughout his works—fear, courage, violence, and the constant threat of death. In the story that follows, he focuses on one soldier's feelings during his initiation into combat.

For more about O'Brien, see page 628.

INTERNET

Vocabulary
Practice
•
More About
Tim O'Brien

Keyword: LE5 10-9

SKILLS FOCUS

Literary Skills
Understand
historical
context.
Understand a
writer's back-
ground and
beliefs.

Background

After many centuries of independence from China, Vietnam became a colony of France in the nineteenth century. In 1954, Vietnam was divided in two after a bitter war for independence from France, with a Communist government set up in the north and a pro-Western one in the south.

Uneasy by the spread of communism in Asia, the U.S. began sending military advisors to South Vietnam in 1955 to help defend it against the north. U.S. troops began arriving in 1965. By 1969 more than half a million U.S. troops were fighting in South Vietnam. The government of North Vietnam eventually prevailed, however. In 1973, a peace agreement was signed, and U.S. troops withdrew from Vietnam.

Vocabulary Development

stealth (stelth) *n.*: secretiveness; sly behavior.

diffuse (di·fyoos′) *adj.*: spread out; unfocused.

skirted (skʉrt′id) *v.*: passed around rather than through. *Skirted* also means "missed narrowly; avoided."

agile (aj′əl) *adj.*: lively; moving easily and quickly.

inertia (in·ʉr′shə) *n.*: tendency to remain either at rest or in motion.

valiantly (val′yənt·lē) *adv.*: bravely.

consolation (kän′sə·lā′shən) *n.*: act of comforting.

Where Have You Gone, Charming Billy?

Tim O'Brien

He was pretending
he was not in the war . . .

The platoon of twenty-six soldiers moved slowly in the dark, single file, not talking. One by one, like sheep in a dream, they passed through the hedgerow, crossed quietly over a meadow, and came down to the rice paddy.[1] There they stopped. Their leader knelt down, motioning with his hand, and one by one the other soldiers squatted in the shadows, vanishing in the primitive stealth of warfare. For a long time they did not move. Except for the sounds of their breathing, the twenty-six men were very quiet: some of them excited by the adventure, some of them afraid, some of them exhausted from the long night march, some of them looking forward to reaching the sea, where they would be safe. At the rear of the column, Private First Class Paul Berlin lay quietly with his forehead resting on the black plastic stock of his rifle, his eyes closed. He was pretending he was not in the war, pretending he had not watched Billy Boy Watkins die of a heart attack that afternoon. He was pretending he was a boy again, camping with his father in the midnight summer along the Des Moines River.[2] In the dark, with his eyes pinched shut, he pretended. He pretended that when he opened his eyes, his father would be there by the campfire and they would talk softly about whatever came to mind and then roll into their sleeping bags, and that later they'd wake up and it would be morning and there would not be a war, and that Billy Boy Watkins had not died of a heart attack that afternoon. He pretended he was not a soldier.

In the morning, when they reached the sea, it would be better. The hot afternoon would be over, he would bathe in the sea, and he would

In the morning, when they reached the sea, it would be better.

forget how frightened he had been on his first day at the war. The second day would not be so bad. He would learn.

There was a sound beside him, a movement, and then a breathed "Hey!"

He opened his eyes, shivering as if emerging from a deep nightmare.

"Hey!" a shadow whispered. "We're *moving*. Get up."

"Okay."

"You sleepin', or something?"

"No." He could not make out the soldier's face. With clumsy, concrete hands he clawed for his rifle, found it, found his helmet.

The soldier shadow grunted. "You got a lot to learn, buddy. I'd shoot you if I thought you was sleepin'. Let's go."

Private First Class Paul Berlin blinked.

Ahead of him, silhouetted against the sky, he saw the string of soldiers wading into the flat paddy, the black outline of their shoulders and packs and weapons. He was comfortable. He did not want to move. But he was afraid, for it was his first night at the war, so he hurried to catch up, stumbling once, scraping his knee, groping as though blind; his boots sank into the thick paddy water, and he smelled it all around him. He would tell his mother how it smelled: mud and algae and cattle manure and chlorophyll;[3] decay, breeding mosquitoes and leeches as big as mice; the fecund[4] warmth of the paddy waters rising up to his cut knee. But he would not tell how frightened he had been.

---

1. **rice paddy:** flooded field for growing rice.
2. **Des Moines River:** river in Des Moines, Iowa.

---

3. **chlorophyll** (klôr′ə·fil′) *n.:* green substance found in plant cells.
4. **fecund** (fē′kənd) *adj.:* fertile; producing abundantly.

Vocabulary
stealth (stelth) *n.:* secretiveness; sly behavior.

Once they reached the sea, things would be better. They would have their rear guarded by three thousand miles of ocean, and they would swim and dive into the breakers and hunt crayfish and smell the salt, and they would be safe.

He followed the shadow of the man in front of him. It was a clear night. Already the Southern Cross[5] was out. And other stars he could not yet name—soon, he thought, he would learn their names. And puffy night clouds. There was not yet a moon. Wading through the paddy, his boots made sleepy, sloshing sounds, like a lullaby, and he tried not to think. Though he was afraid, he now knew that fear came in many degrees and types and peculiar categories, and he knew that his fear now was not so bad as it had been in the hot afternoon, when poor Billy Boy Watkins got killed by a heart attack. His fear now was <u>diffuse</u> and unformed: ghosts in the tree line, nighttime fears of a child, a boogeyman in the closet that his father would open to show empty, saying, "See? Nothing there, champ. Now you can sleep." In the afternoon it had been worse: The fear had been bundled and tight and he'd been on his hands and knees, crawling like an insect, an ant escaping a giant's footsteps, and thinking nothing, brain flopping like wet cement in a mixer, not thinking at all, watching while Billy Boy Watkins died.

Now, as he stepped out of the paddy onto a narrow dirt path, now the fear was mostly the fear of being so terribly afraid again.

He tried not to think.

There were tricks he'd learned to keep from thinking. Counting: He counted his steps, concentrating on the numbers, pretending that the steps were dollar bills and that each step through the night made him richer and richer, so that soon he would become a wealthy man, and he kept counting and considered the ways he might spend the money after the war and what he would do. He would look his father in the eye and shrug and say, "It was pretty bad at first, but I learned a lot and I got used to it." Then he would tell his father the story of Billy Boy Watkins. But he would never let on how frightened he had been. "Not so bad," he would say instead, making his father feel proud.

Songs, another trick to stop from thinking: *Where have you gone, Billy Boy, Billy Boy, oh, where have you gone, charming Billy? I have gone to seek a wife, she's the joy of my life, but she's a young thing and cannot leave her mother,* and other songs that he sang in his thoughts as he walked toward the sea. And when he reached the sea, he would dig a deep hole in the sand and he would sleep like the high clouds and he would not be afraid anymore.

The moon came out. Pale and shrunken to the size of a dime.

The helmet was heavy on his head. In the morning he would adjust the leather binding. He would clean his rifle, too. Even though he had been frightened to shoot it during the hot afternoon, he would carefully clean the breech and the muzzle and the ammunition so that next time he would be ready and not so afraid. In the morning, when they reached the sea, he would begin to make friends with some of the other soldiers. He would learn their names and laugh at their jokes. Then when the war was over, he would have war buddies, and he would write to them once in a while and exchange memories.

Walking, sleeping in his walking, he felt better. He watched the moon come higher.

Once they <u>skirted</u> a sleeping village. The smells again—straw, cattle, mildew. The men

---

5. **Southern Cross:** constellation, or group of stars, in the Southern Hemisphere.

Vocabulary

diffuse (di·fyōos′) *adj.*: spread out; unfocused.

skirted (skʉrt′id) *v.*: passed around rather than through. *Skirted* also means "missed narrowly; avoided."

were quiet. On the far side of the village, buried in the dark smells, a dog barked. The column stopped until the barking died away; then they marched fast away from the village, through a graveyard filled with conical-shaped[6] burial mounds and tiny altars made of clay and stone. The graveyard had a perfumy smell. A nice place to spend the night, he thought. The mounds would make fine battlements,[7] and the smell was nice and the place was quiet. But they went on, passing through a hedgerow and across another paddy and east toward the sea.

---

6. **conical-** (kän′i·kəl) **shaped** *adj.:* shaped like a cone.
7. **battlements** *n.:* fortifications from which to shoot.

He walked carefully. He remembered what he'd been taught: Stay off the center of the path, for that was where the land mines and booby traps were planted, where stupid and lazy soldiers like to walk. Stay alert, he'd been taught. Better alert than inert.[8] Ag-ile, mo-bile, hos-tile. He wished he'd paid better attention to the training. He could not remember what they'd said about how to stop being afraid; they hadn't given any lessons in courage—not that he could remember—and they hadn't mentioned how

---

8. **inert** (in·ʉrt′) *adj.:* without movement; here, dead.

Vocabulary
agile (aj′əl) *adj.:* lively; moving easily and quickly.

A Closer Look

Database: Vietnam

- Year first U.S. military advisors were sent to Vietnam: **1955**
- Year first U.S. combat troops were sent to Vietnam: **1965**
- Total number of U.S. soldiers who served in Vietnam during the war: **more than 2 million**
- Number of U.S. women who served in noncombat positions: **10,000**
- Number of people who rallied for peace in Washington, D.C., on April 17, 1965: **20,000;** on November 15, 1969: **300,000**
- Year cease-fire was declared: **1973**
- Money spent by the U.S. government for direct costs: **$150 billion**
- Vietnamese deaths: **2 million**
- U.S. deaths: **58,000**
- U.S. wounded: **300,000**
- U.S. soldiers missing and presumed dead: **2,300**
- Number of people who visit Vietnam Memorial in Washington, D.C., annually: **2.5 million**

All statistics are estimates.

Billy Boy Watkins would die of a heart attack, his face turning pale and the veins popping out.

Private First Class Paul Berlin walked carefully.

Stretching ahead of him like dark beads on an invisible chain, the string of shadow soldiers whose names he did not yet know moved with the silence and slow grace of smoke. Now and again moonlight was reflected off a machine gun or a wristwatch. But mostly the soldiers were quiet and hidden and faraway-seeming in a peaceful night, strangers on a long street, and he felt quite separate from them, as if trailing behind like the caboose on a night train, pulled along by inertia, sleep-walking, an afterthought to the war.

So he walked carefully, counting his steps. When he had counted to 3,485, the column stopped.

One by one the soldiers knelt or squatted down.

The grass along the path was wet. Private First Class Paul Berlin lay back and turned his head so that he could lick at the dew with his eyes closed, another trick to forget the war. He might have slept. "I *wasn't* afraid," he was screaming or dreaming, facing his father's stern eyes. "I wasn't afraid," he was saying. When he opened his eyes, a soldier was sitting beside him, quietly chewing a stick of Doublemint gum.

"You sleepin' again?" the soldier whispered.

"No," said Private First Class Paul Berlin. "Hell, no."

The soldier grunted, chewing his gum. Then he twisted the cap off his canteen, took a swallow, and handed it through the dark.

"Take some," he whispered.

"Thanks."

"You're the new guy?"

"Yes." He did not want to admit it, being new to the war.

The soldier grunted and handed him a stick of gum. "Chew it quiet—OK? Don't blow no bubbles or nothing."

"Thanks. I won't." He could not make out the man's face in the shadows.

They sat still and Private First Class Paul Berlin chewed the gum until all the sugars were gone; then the soldier said, "Bad day today, buddy."

Private First Class Paul Berlin nodded wisely, but he did not speak.

"Don't think it's always so bad," the soldier whispered. "I don't wanna scare you. You'll get used to it soon enough. . . . They been fighting wars a long time, and you get used to it."

"Yeah."

"You will."

They were quiet awhile. And the night was quiet, no crickets or birds, and it was hard to imagine it was truly a war. He searched for the soldier's face but could not find it. It did not matter much. Even if he saw the fellow's face, he would not know the name; and even if he knew the name, it would not matter much.

"Haven't got the time?" the soldier whispered.

"No."

"Rats. . . . Don't matter, really. Goes faster if you don't know the time, anyhow."

"Sure."

"What's your name, buddy?"

"Paul."

"Nice to meet ya," he said, and in the dark beside the path, they shook hands. "Mine's Toby. Everybody calls me Buffalo, though." The soldier's hand was strangely warm and soft. But it was a very big hand. "Sometimes they just call me Buff," he said.

Vocabulary

inertia (in·ur′shə) *n.*: tendency to remain either at rest or in motion.

> Better alert than inert.
> Ag-ile, mo-bile, hos-tile.

And again they were quiet. They lay in the grass and waited. The moon was very high now and very bright, and they were waiting for cloud cover. The soldier suddenly snorted.

"What is it?"

"Nothin'," he said, but then he snorted again. "A bloody *heart attack*!" the soldier said. "Can't get over it—old Billy Boy croaking from a lousy heart attack. . . . A heart attack—can you believe it?"

The idea of it made Private First Class Paul Berlin smile. He couldn't help it.

"Ever hear of such a thing?"

"Not till now," said Private First Class Paul Berlin, still smiling.

"Me neither," said the soldier in the dark. "Gawd, dying of a heart attack. Didn't know him, did you."

"No."

"Tough as nails."

"Yeah."

"And what happens? A heart attack. Can you imagine it?"

"Yes," said Private First Class Paul Berlin. He wanted to laugh. "I can imagine it." And he imagined it clearly. He giggled—he couldn't help it. He imagined Billy's father opening the telegram: SORRY TO INFORM YOU THAT YOUR SON BILLY BOY WAS YESTERDAY SCARED TO DEATH IN ACTION IN THE REPUBLIC OF VIET-NAM, VALIANTLY SUCCUMBING[9] TO A HEART ATTACK SUFFERED WHILE UNDER ENORMOUS STRESS, AND IT IS WITH GREATEST SYMPATHY THAT . . . He giggled again. He rolled onto his belly and pressed his face into his arms. His body was shaking with giggles.

The big soldier hissed at him to shut up, but he could not stop giggling and remembering the hot afternoon, and poor Billy Boy, and how they'd been drinking Coca-Cola from bright-red aluminum cans, and how they'd started on the day's march, and how a little while later poor Billy Boy stepped on the mine, and how it made a tiny little sound—*poof*—and how Billy Boy stood there with his mouth wide open, looking down at where his foot had been blown off, and how finally Billy Boy sat down very casually, not saying a word, with his foot lying behind him, most of it still in the boot.

He giggled louder—he could not stop. He bit his arm, trying to stifle it, but remembering:

---

9. succumbing *v.* used as *adj.* (used with *to*): here, dying from.

Vocabulary

valiantly (val'yənt·lē) *adv.:* bravely.

"War's over, Billy," the men had said in consolation, but Billy Boy got scared and started crying and said he was about to die. "Nonsense," the medic said, Doc Peret, but Billy Boy kept bawling, tightening up, his face going pale and transparent and his veins popping out. Scared stiff. Even when Doc Peret stuck him with morphine, Billy Boy kept crying.

"Shut up!" the big soldier hissed, but Private First Class Paul Berlin could not stop. Giggling and remembering, he covered his mouth. His eyes stung, remembering how it was when Billy Boy died of fright.

"Shut up!"

But he could not stop giggling, the same way Billy Boy could not stop bawling that afternoon.

Afterward Doc Peret had explained: "You see, Billy Boy really died of a heart attack. He was scared he was gonna die—so scared he had himself a heart attack—and that's what really killed him. I seen it before."

So they wrapped Billy in a plastic poncho, his eyes still wide open and scared stiff, and they carried him over the meadow to a rice paddy, and then when the medevac helicopter[10] arrived, they carried him through the paddy and put him aboard, and the mortar rounds were falling everywhere, and the helicopter pulled up, and Billy Boy came tumbling out, falling slowly and then faster, and the paddy water sprayed up as if Billy Boy had just executed a long and dangerous dive, as if trying to escape Graves Registration, where he would be tagged and sent home under a flag, dead of a heart attack.

"Shut up!" the soldier hissed, but Paul Berlin could not stop giggling, remembering: scared to death.

Later they waded in after him, probing for Billy Boy with their rifle butts, elegantly and delicately probing for Billy Boy in the stinking paddy, singing—some of them—*Where have you gone, Billy Boy, Billy Boy, oh, where have you gone, charming Billy?* Then they found him. Green and covered with algae, his eyes still wide open and scared stiff, dead of a heart attack suffered while—

"Shut up!" the soldier said loudly, shaking him.

But Private First Class Paul Berlin could not stop. The giggles were caught in his throat, drowning him in his own laughter: scared to death like Billy Boy.

Giggling, lying on his back, he saw the moon move, or the clouds moving across the moon. Wounded in action, dead of fright. A fine war story. He would tell it to his father, how Billy Boy had been scared to death, never letting on . . . He could not stop.

The soldier smothered him. He tried to fight back, but he was weak from the giggles.

The moon was under the clouds and the column was moving. The soldier helped him up. "You OK now, buddy?"

"Sure."

"What was so bloody funny?"

"Nothing."

"You can get killed, laughing that way."

"I know. I know that."

"You got to stay calm, buddy." The soldier handed him his rifle. "Half the battle, just staying calm. You'll get better at it," he said. "Come on, now."

He turned away and Private First Class Paul Berlin hurried after him. He was still shivering.

He would do better once he reached the sea, he thought, still smiling a little. A funny war story that he would tell to his father, how Billy Boy Watkins was scared to death. A good joke. But even when he smelled salt and heard the sea, he could not stop being afraid. ■

---

10. **medevac** (med′i·vak′) **helicopter:** helicopter used to evacuate wounded soldiers to hospitals and medical care.

Vocabulary
consolation (kän′sə·lā′shən) n.: act of comforting.

Meet the Writer

Tim O'Brien

The Power of the Heart

It was the Vietnam War that made Tim O'Brien (1946–   ) a writer. He was drafted immediately after graduating from Macalester College in St. Paul, Minnesota, in 1968. He then spent two years as an infantryman in Vietnam.

When he returned from Vietnam, O'Brien used his imagination to cope with memories of the war. Many of his stories are told from the point of view of a young soldier named Paul Berlin. These stories eventually grew into a novel, *Going After Cacciato,* which won the National Book Award in 1979. "Where Have You Gone, Charming Billy?" was used, with some changes, as Chapter 31 of that novel.

In 1990, O'Brien published *The Things They Carried,* referring to the burdens, both material and emotional, carried by the U.S. soldiers in Vietnam—the M-16 rifles, the comic books, the flak jackets, and the fear. In 1994, he published *In the Lake of the Woods,* another novel about his persistent theme—the lingering memory of Vietnam.

The following passage is from O'Brien's autobiographical account of his experiences in Vietnam, *If I Die in a Combat Zone, Box Me Up and Ship Me Home.* Mad Mark was the platoon leader.

“ One of the most persistent and appalling thoughts which lumbers through your mind as you walk through Vietnam at night is the fear of getting lost, of becoming detached from the others, of spending the night alone in that frightening and haunted countryside. It was dark. We walked in a single file, perhaps three yards apart. Mad Mark took us along a crazy, wavering course. We veered off the road, through clumps of trees, through tangles of bamboo and grass, zigzagging through graveyards of dead Vietnamese who lay there under conical mounds of dirt and clay. The man to the front and the man to the rear were the only holds on security and sanity. We followed the man in front like a blind man after his dog, like Dante following Virgil through the Inferno, and we prayed that the man had not lost his way, that he hadn't lost contact with the man to his front. We tensed the muscles around our eyeballs and peered straight ahead. We hurt ourselves staring at the man's back. We strained. We dared not look away for fear the man might fade and dissipate and turn into absent shadow. Sometimes, when the jungle closed in, we reached out to him, touched his shirt.

The man to the front is civilization. He is the United States of America and every friend you have ever known; he is Erik and blond girls and a mother and a father. He is your life, and he is your altar and God combined. And, for the man stumbling along behind you, you alone are his torch. ”

For centuries, women have gone to war, but their contributions have rarely been acknowledged. Lily Lee Adams was one of the thousands of women who cared for wounded and dying soldiers in Vietnam. She served with the Army Nurse Corps at the Twelfth Evacuation Hospital in Cu Chi from 1969 to 1970.

The Friendship Only Lasted a Few Seconds

Lily Lee Adams

He said "Mom,"
And I responded
And became her.
I never lied
5   to him.
And I couldn't
Explain that to others.
I got all and more back.
But the friendship
10 Only lasted a few seconds.

And he called me Mary.
I wished she could
Be there for him.
I felt I was in
15 Second place,
But I did the
Best I could
And the friendship
Only lasted a few seconds.

20 And he told me,
"I don't believe this,
I'm dying for nothing."
Then he died.
Again, the friendship
25 Only lasted a few seconds.

How can the World
Understand any of this?
How can I keep the
World from forgetting?
30 After all the friendship
Only lasted a few seconds.

Vietnam Women's Memorial in Washington, D.C.

Response and Analysis

Reading Check

1. Tell the story of Billy Boy's death to a partner as you imagine a TV news reporter based in Vietnam might have reported it on the day it happened. Tell **what** happened, **whom** it happened to, **where** it happened, **why** it happened, and **how** it happened.

Thinking Critically

2. There is a central irony in warfare, which has to do with the fact that soldiers kill people they do not even know. What is **ironic,** or contrary to what we would expect, about how Billy Boy dies? about how his body is removed?

3. Explain the significance of each of these story elements:

   • the song "Where Have You Gone, Billy Boy?"

   • the **flashbacks** to camping trips

   • Paul's fit of uncontrollable giggling

   • the **minor character** Toby

4. What do you think Paul has discovered about war and about himself on his first day of combat? What **theme,** or central idea, relating to war is O'Brien expressing in this story?

5. **Tone** is the writer's attitude toward the subject. How would you describe this story's tone? Analyze the way in which O'Brien creates that tone. Cite lines and incidents from the story.

6. In a sense this is a story about a hero's journey. Such journeys often take the form of a **quest,** a search for something of great value. What is it that Paul expects to find at the sea, the endpoint on his journey? Ironically, what does he find instead?

Literary Criticism

7. Think about the story's **historical context**—the 1960s and the period of U.S. involvement in the Vietnam War. (You will find some nonfiction accounts of the war on pages 634–641.) How does O'Brien's story reflect its historical period and the **themes** and **issues** of that time?

8. Having read this story and the biographical information about the author (see Meet the Writer on page 628), explain how the story likely reflects O'Brien's attitudes toward the Vietnam War. Give examples from the story to support your interpretation. Remember that the **tone** of a work is a good clue to the writer's attitude.

9. Look back at the poem written by a nurse in Vietnam (see the **Connection** on page 629). How does that poem affect your understanding of O'Brien's story and of the Vietnam War?

WRITING

Why War?

War is a recurring subject in literature and movies. Why do you think writers and moviemakers so often choose war as their subject? Write an **essay** proposing answers to this question. To support your **opinion,** give reasons why some people *write* about war and its violence and others *read* about it. At the end of your essay, explain how war stories like this one affect *you.* (Check your Quickwrite notes before you begin.) ✎

SKILLS FOCUS

Literary Skills
Analyze historical context. Analyze how a writer's background and beliefs are reflected in his or her writings.

Writing Skills
Write an essay supporting an opinion.

Vocabulary Development

Meaning Maps

On page 625, Tim O'Brien uses the word *inertia* to describe a feeling of being pulled as if by a train. Many people think of *inertia* only as laziness or inactivity, but the dictionary refers to it as the "tendency of an object in motion to keep moving in the same direction or of an object at rest to remain at rest, unless the object is affected by another force." Look at the meaning map one student made to understand this word:

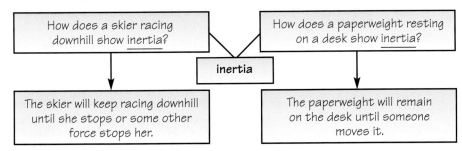

How does a skier racing downhill show inertia?	How does a paperweight resting on a desk show inertia?

inertia

| The skier will keep racing downhill until she stops or some other force stops her. | The paperweight will remain on the desk until someone moves it. |

PRACTICE 1

Make your own meaning maps for the remaining Word Bank words. You will have to think of your own questions and answers. Compare your maps with a classmate's when you're done.

Synonyms and Connotations

Most English words have several **synonyms,** words with the same or similar meanings. Synonyms usually have different **connotations,** or emotional associations. O'Brien carefully chooses words with connotations that create the effects he wants.

PRACTICE 2

Answer the questions below about connotations:

1. "With clumsy, concrete hands he clawed for his rifle. . . ."

   Try substituting *heavy* for *concrete* and *reached* for *clawed*. How does the image change?

2. "The moon came out. Pale and shrunken to the size of a dime."

   What are the connotations of *shrunken*? Why wouldn't *as big as a dime* have the same effect?

3. "But Billy Boy kept bawling, tightening up, his face going pale. . . ."

   What does *bawling* suggest that *crying* doesn't? Who might *bawl*?

4. " 'Shut up!' the big soldier hissed. . . ."

   Why do you think O'Brien uses *hissed* instead of *whispered* or *said*?

5. "Later they waded in after him, probing for Billy Boy with their rifle butts, elegantly and delicately probing for Billy Boy in the stinking paddy. . . ."

   Explain why the words *elegantly* and *delicately* in this context are ironic. What are their connotations?

SKILLS FOCUS

Vocabulary Skills
Make semantic maps.
Understand synonyms and connotations.

The War Escalates ◆ Dear Folks ◆ *from* Declaration of Independence from the War in Vietnam

Using Primary and Secondary Sources: Balancing Viewpoints

Research materials can be classified according to two main groups: primary sources and secondary sources. (The chart on this page shows examples of each.) Each type of source has advantages and limitations.

- A **primary source** is a firsthand account, original material that has not been interpreted or edited by any other writers. Good examples of primary sources are letters, speeches, oral histories, and interviews (you've already seen examples of the latter two on pages 89–92). Primary sources are valuable because they include details and feelings that only an eyewitness can provide. Their drawback is that they are usually highly subjective and limited to one person's viewpoint.

- A **secondary source** contains information (often researched in primary sources) that is retold, summarized, or interpreted by a writer. A secondary source is written by someone who did not participate in the events that are written about, and it is often written after the events occurred. The history textbooks you use in school are good examples of secondary sources. (You'll find an example on pages 634–636.) Other common secondary sources are encyclopedia articles and biographies.

  Most magazine and newspaper articles are secondary sources. It is important to note, though, that newspaper and magazine articles are primary sources if they are eyewitness reports,

editorials, or opinion pieces. (Also, a historian researching a past time would consider any newspaper article from that time a primary-source document of the era.)

Secondary sources are generally more objective and cover a broader range of information than primary sources.

Primary Sources	Secondary Sources
Letters	Encyclopedia articles
Speeches	Reference books
Oral histories	Biographies
Interviews	Textbooks
Diaries	Most newspaper articles
Autobiographies	Most magazine articles
Editorials	History books
Eyewitness news reports	Literary criticism
Literary works	
Public documents	

Using the Sources

Good researchers consult many sources and carefully balance the information found in them before drawing any conclusions. The following checklist can help you use both primary and secondary sources:

1. **Analyze.** Focus on what the text says and how the ideas are expressed.
   - Find the writer's **main idea,** and see how it's supported.
   - Determine the writer's **purpose.** For example, is the writer giving information, expressing feelings, describing an event or a person, or persuading you to do or to believe something? Texts may have several purposes, but one is usually dominant.

INTERNET

Interactive Reading Model

Keyword: LE5 10-9

SKILLS FOCUS

Reading Skills
Understand and use primary and secondary sources.

- Look for the text's **structure** or special features. For example, a textbook has subheads, key terms, quotations, photos, and illustrations that provide information and help guide you.
- Check for **facts** (which can be proved) and **opinions** (which can't). Both primary and secondary sources are likely to have a mixture of both.
- Determine the writer's **tone,** or attitude. A text may be totally **objective** (including only facts), or it may be **subjective** (expressing the writer's thoughts, feelings, and opinions). It may be written in formal or informal language. A personal letter, for example, usually uses informal language. A speech may use special techniques, such as **repetition** and **rhetorical questions** (questions that are not meant to be answered). Look for both of these techniques in the speech that follows.

2. **Evaluate.** Decide how much you should believe—and why.

- How **credible** is the source? How knowledgeable is the writer about the subject? This question is important for both primary and secondary sources. When using a secondary source, check the bibliography and other notes to evaluate the research the writer has done.
- Does the writer seem to have a **bias,** or prejudice toward the topic? Watch for words or phrases that present a one-sided view.
- When was the text written? A recent date may be better for a secondary source on a topic, but primary sources from the time of the event can be more valuable.

- What is the writer's **audience?** If the piece was written for a particular audience, it may affect the text's credibility.
- Is the source **accurate?** You should always try to check for accuracy.

3. **Elaborate.** Connect what you read in one source to information in other sources.

- Never make a generalization or draw conclusions based on reading a single source. Compare facts and details from several sources.
- When you finish researching, figure out your own thoughts, opinions, and feelings on the subject.

Vocabulary Development

facile (fas′il) *adj.:* easy.

rehabilitation (rē′hə·bil′ə·tā′shən) *n.:* bringing or restoring to a good condition.

manipulation (mə·nip′yoo·lā′shən) *n.:* skillful, often unfair management or control.

compassion (kəm·pash′ən) *n.:* deep sympathy; pity.

aghast (ə·gast′) *adj.:* horrified.

initiative (i·nish′ə·tiv) *n.:* action of taking the first step or movement.

Connecting to the Literature

You've just read Tim O'Brien's fictional picture of the Vietnam War. The non-fiction accounts that follow—a textbook excerpt, a soldier's letter, and a speech—will help you evaluate O'Brien's story and expand your knowledge of the war.

The War Escalates

EYEWITNESSES TO History

"*Renewed hostile actions against United States ships on the high seas in the Gulf of Tonkin have today required me to order the military forces of the United States to take action in reply. The initial attack on the destroyer Maddox, on August 2, was repeated today by a number of hostile vessels attacking two U.S. destroyers with torpedoes. . . . We believe at least two of the attacking boats were sunk. There were no U.S. losses. . . . But repeated acts of violence against the Armed Forces of the United States must be met not only with alert defense, but with positive reply. That reply is being given as I speak to you tonight. Air action is now in execution against gunboats and certain supporting facilities in North Vietnam which have been used in these hostile operations.*"

—Lyndon B. Johnson, nationally televised speech, August 4, 1964

The News American

U. S. BOMBERS BLAST N. VIET BASES, 2 PLANES SHOT DOWN

FBI Identifies Three Bodies as Rights Workers

Fliers Score On Oil Depot

The Gulf of Tonkin incident drew the United States deeper into the Vietnam War.

Near midnight on August 4, 1964, President Lyndon B. Johnson appeared on national television. His announcement to the American people that night marked a new stage in U.S. involvement in the war in Vietnam.

The Tonkin Gulf Resolution

In 1963 Secretary of Defense **Robert S. McNamara** had advised President Johnson that he would have to increase the U.S. military commitment to South Vietnam to prevent a Communist victory. Before increasing the U.S. commitment, Johnson needed to get congressional backing. The events in the Gulf of Tonkin gave him the opportunity. Johnson asked Congress to authorize the use of military force "to prevent further aggression." In response, both houses of Congress overwhelmingly passed the **Tonkin Gulf Resolution.** This gave the president authority to take "all necessary measures to repel any armed attack against forces of the United States."

Johnson claimed that the attacks in the Gulf of Tonkin were unprovoked. In reality, however, the U.S. destroyer *Maddox* had been spying in support of South Vietnamese raids against North Vietnam and had fired first. The second attack, moreover, probably never occurred. Some U.S. sailors apparently misinterpreted interference on their radar and sonar as enemy ships and torpedoes. Nonetheless, Johnson and his advisers got what they wanted: authority to expand the war.

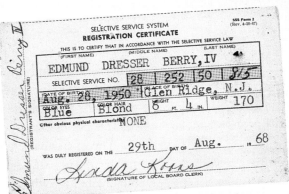

During the Vietnam War millions of American men received draft registration certificates like this one.

Wayne Morse of Oregon was one of just two senators who voted against the Tonkin Gulf Resolution. He warned, "I believe that history will record we have made a great mistake. . . . We are in effect giving the President war-making powers in the absence of a declaration of war." In other words, by passing the resolution, Congress had essentially given up its constitutional power to declare war.

READING CHECK: Analyzing Information How did President Johnson mislead the American public?

U.S. Forces in Vietnam

President Johnson soon called for an **escalation,** or buildup, of U.S. military forces in Vietnam. He ordered the Selective Service, the agency charged with carrying out the military draft, to begin calling up young men to serve in the armed forces. In April 1965 the Selective Service notified 13,700 draftees.

The troops. During the war more than 2 million Americans served in Vietnam. In the beginning most were professional soldiers who were already enlisted in the armed forces. As the demand for troops grew, however, more and more draftees were shipped to Vietnam. The average U.S. soldier in Vietnam was younger, poorer, and less educated than those who had served in World War II or in the Korean War.

One out of four young men who registered for the draft was excused from service for health reasons. Another 30 percent received non-health-related exemptions or deferments—postponements of service. Most of these were for college enrollment. Mainly because of college deferments, young men from higher-income families were the least likely to be drafted. As a result, poor Americans served in numbers far greater than their proportion in the general population.

ANALYZE

4. **Reading checks** are often provided to help you review or analyze the material.

What is the answer to the reading-check question on this page?

ANALYZE

5. Notice the levels of major **headings** and **subheadings** that help organize the material.

What is the main heading on this page?

EVALUATE

6. Textbooks should have an objective, unbiased **tone,** which is the writer's attitude.

What is the tone of the subsection "The troops"?

African Americans and Hispanics served in combat in very high numbers, particularly during the early years of the war. Many served in the most dangerous ground units. As a result, they experienced very high casualty rates. In 1965, for example, African Americans accounted for almost 24 percent of all battle deaths, even though they made up just 11 percent of the U.S. population.

The most vivid images of the war show soldiers facing the hardships and terrors of battle. Some confronted the enemy in well-defined battles in the highlands. Others cut their way through the jungle, where they heard but seldom saw the enemy. Still others waded through rice paddies and searched rural villages for guerrillas. Most Americans who went to Vietnam, however, served in support positions such as administration, communications, engineering, medical care, and supply and transportation. They were rarely safe. Enemy rockets and mortars could—and did—strike anywhere.

Some 10,000 servicewomen filled noncombat positions in Vietnam, mostly as nurses. Although they did not carry guns into battle, nurses faced the horrors of combat on a daily basis. Edie Meeks described the experience of working as a nurse at a field hospital.

History Makers Speak

"*We really saw the worst of it, because the nurses never saw any of the victories. If the Army took a hill, we saw what was left over. I remember one boy who was brought in missing two legs and an arm, and his eyes were bandaged. A general came in later and pinned a Purple Heart on the boy's hospital gown, and the horror of it all was so amazing that it just took my breath away. You thought, was this supposed to be an even trade?*"

—Edie Meeks, quoted in *Newsweek,* March 8, 1999

Another 20,000 to 45,000 women worked in civilian capacities, many as volunteers for humanitarian organizations such as the Red Cross.

ELABORATE

7. Compare Edie Meeks's quote with the poem on page 629. How are they alike, and how are they different?

ANALYZE

8. Captions that accompany photographs and illustrations provide further information and sometimes pose a question.

What is the answer to the question in the caption on this page?

INTERPRETING THE VISUAL RECORD

Nurses. First Lieutenant Elaine Niggemann served at the 24th EVAC Hospital. *What is the lieutenant doing?*

Dear Folks

Kenneth W. Bagby

The battle of the Ia Drang Valley, which took place in mid-November of 1965, was one of the hardest fought and most bloody of the entire war. The letter which follows is Sp4c[1] Kenneth W. Bagby's personal account of the action during that fierce encounter, written soon afterward to his parents in Winchester, Virginia.

Plei-Ku, Vietnam
Nov. 17, 1965

Dear Folks,

I met a boy on the ship coming over to Vietnam. He was a good guy from the State of Missouri. He was my friend. We lived in the same tent together, went into An Khe together, and spent most of our free time together. I got to know this boy well, and he was my best friend. His name was Dan Davis.

On Monday morning, the 15th of November, he died in my arms of two bullet wounds in the chest. He said, "Ken, I can't breathe." There was nothing I could do.

To the right of me another friend, whose last name was Balango, died of a wound in the throat. Up front Sergeant Brown, my squad leader, was hit in the chest and leg. To my left Sp4c A. Learn was hit in the ankle.

We were crossing a field and were pinned down by automatic weapons fire from the enemy. We were pinned down for about 45 minutes before the rest of the platoon could get to us, and save the rest of us.

So went the biggest and worst battle that any American force has had in Vietnam. We outdone the Marines and Airborne by a long shot. Estimated V.C.[2] killed, 2,000. Our casualties, I cannot give the information out. The battle took place on the Cambodian border. . . .

Our battalion, the 1st Bn. 7th Cav., is completely inactive due to the killed and wounded of its men. My squad which consists of nine men, three came out, myself, Sergeant Scott, and a boy named Stidell.

---

1. **Sp4c:** specialist, fourth class.
2. **V.C.:** abbreviation for "Viet Cong," a North Vietnamese guerrilla force that sought to overthrow the South Vietnamese government (1954–1975).

Folks, by all rights I should be dead. The good Lord evidently saw fit to spare me, for some reason. I prayed, and prayed and prayed some more, the three days we were in battle.

The many men that died, I will never forget. The odor of blood and decayed bodies, I will never forget. I am all right. I will never be the same though, never, never, never. If I have to go into battle again, if I am not killed, I will come out insane. I cannot see and go through it again. I know I can't. The friends I lost and the many bodies I carried back to the helicopters to be lifted out, I will never forget. ❶

The pen that I am writing this letter with belongs to Stash Arrows, the boy that rode up to Winchester with me, on my emergency leave. Pop, remember him. He was hit three times in the back. I don't know if he is still alive or not. I hope and pray he is. God, I hope so.

Folks, don't let these men die in vain. Appreciate what they are doing over here in Vietnam. They died protecting you all, and all the people in the United States. We just cannot have the enemy get to the folks back home. We have got to stop them here, before that happens. If it is God's will, we will do it. Tell the people back home to pray for us, as we need their prayers. . . . ❷

We raised the American flag on the grounds. We were fighting on Tuesday, the 16th of November. It waved proudly for the Armed Forces and the people of America, as it did in so many battles won in World War II and Korea. I sat beside a tree and looked at it, and hoped I would never see the day it would be torn down and destroyed.

Folks, I am glad Eddy is not here and my son Kenny is not here. I hope they never have to see or experience the horrors of war. I will give my life to see that they don't. . . . ❸

As always,

Your son,

Kenneth

❶ **ANALYZE**
What words would you use to describe the letter's **tone,** especially in this paragraph?

❷ **ANALYZE**
What are Bagby's reasons for fighting in Vietnam?

❸ **ELABORATE**
How does Bagby's view of the war compare with Paul Berlin's in "Where Have You Gone, Charming Billy?" (page 621)?

PRIMARY SOURCE

from Declaration of Independence from the War in Vietnam

Martin Luther King, Jr.

Martin Luther King, Jr., in Atlanta on April 30, 1967, speaking against U.S. involvement in Vietnam.

Since I am a preacher by trade, I suppose it is not surprising that I have . . . major reasons for bringing Vietnam into the field of my moral vision. There is at the outset a very obvious and almost <u>facile</u> connection between the war in Vietnam and the struggle I, and others, have been waging in America. A few years ago there was a shining moment in that struggle. It seemed as if there was a real promise of hope for the poor—both black and white—through the Poverty Program.[1] Then came the buildup in Vietnam, and I watched the program broken and eviscerated[2] as if it were some idle political plaything or a society gone mad on war, and I knew that America would never invest the necessary funds or energies in <u>rehabilitation</u> of its poor so long as Vietnam continued to draw men and skills and money like some demonic, destructive suction tube. So I was increasingly compelled to see the war as an enemy of the poor and to attack it as such. ❶

> ❶ **ANALYZE**
> What is the first reason King gives for opposing the Vietnam War?

1. **Poverty Program:** In May 1964, President Lyndon B. Johnson declared a nationwide war on poverty. He announced a number of federal programs to aid the nation's poor and to create what he called the Great Society.

2. **eviscerated** (ē·vis'ər·āt'id) *v.* used as *adj.*: gutted; having its force or significance taken away.

Vocabulary
facile (fas'il) *adj.*: easy.
rehabilitation (rē'hə·bil'ə·tā'shən) *n.*: bringing or restoring to a good condition.

A wounded U.S. soldier being helped by fellow soldiers during the Vietnam War.

watching Negro and white boys on TV screens as they kill and die together for a nation that has been unable to seat them together in the same schools. So we watch them in brutal solidarity[3] burning the huts of a poor village, but we realize that they would never live on the same block in Detroit. I could not be silent in the face of such cruel manipulation of the poor.

My third reason grows out of my experience in the ghettos of the North over the last three years—especially the last three summers. As I have walked among the desperate, rejected, and angry young men, I have told them that Molotov cocktails[4] and rifles would not solve their problems. I have tried to offer them my deepest compassion while maintaining my conviction that social change comes most meaningfully through nonviolent action. But, they asked, what about Vietnam? They asked if our own nation wasn't using massive doses of violence to solve its problems, to bring about the changes it wanted. Their questions hit home, and I knew that I

Perhaps the more tragic recognition of reality took place when it became clear to me that the war was doing far more than devastating the hopes of the poor at home. It was sending their sons and their brothers and their husbands to fight and to die in extraordinarily high proportions relative to the rest of the population. We were taking the young black men who had been crippled by our society and sending them eight thousand miles away to guarantee liberties in Southeast Asia which they had not found in southwest Georgia and East Harlem. So we have been repeatedly faced with the cruel irony of

---

3. **solidarity** *n.*: complete unity.
4. **Molotov cocktails:** makeshift explosives.

Vocabulary

manipulation (mə·nip′yo͞o·lā′shən) *n.*: skillful, often unfair management or control.

compassion (kəm·pash′ən) *n.*: deep sympathy; pity.

could never again raise my voice against the violence of the oppressed in the ghettos without having first spoken clearly to the greatest purveyor[5] of violence in the world today—my own government. . . .

Somehow this madness must cease. I speak as a child of God and a brother to the suffering poor of Vietnam and the poor of America who are paying the double price of smashed hopes at home and death and corruption in Vietnam. I speak as a citizen of the world, for the world as it stands aghast at the path we have taken. I speak as an American to the leaders of my own nation. The great initiative in this war is ours. The initiative to stop must be ours. . . .

We must move past indecision to action. We must find new ways to speak for peace in Vietnam and justice throughout the developing world—a world that borders on our doors. If we do not act, we shall surely be dragged down the long, dark, and shameful corridors of time reserved for those who possess power without compassion, might without morality, and strength without sight. ❷

Now let us begin. Now let us rededicate ourselves to the long and bitter—but beautiful—struggle for a new world. This is the calling of the sons of God, and our brothers wait eagerly for our response. Shall we say the odds are too great? Shall we tell them the struggle is too hard? Will our message be that the forces of American life militate[6] against their arrival as full men, and we send our deepest regrets? Or will there be another message, of longing, of hope, of solidarity with their yearnings, of commitment to their cause, whatever the cost? The choice is ours, and though we might prefer it otherwise, we *must* choose in this crucial moment of human history. ❸

—April 4, 1967

❷ **ANALYZE**
What does King want the listener to do or believe?

❸ **EVALUATE**
What effect do the **rhetorical questions** have in this paragraph? How convincing do you find King's speech? Why?

Vocabulary

aghast (ə·gast′) *adj.*: horrified.

initiative (i·nish′ə·tiv) *n.*: action of taking the first step or movement.

Children playing in the shadow of high-rise buildings in a North Carolina city in the mid-1960s.

---

5. **purveyor** (pər·vā′ər) *n.*: provider; supplier.
6. **militate** *v.* (used with *against*): work to prohibit.

Analyzing Informational Text

Reading Check

1. What power did the Tonkin Gulf Resolution give to the president?

2. How many American troops served in the Vietnam War? How many women served in the armed forces?

3. According to "Dear Folks," what happened to the men in Kenneth Bagby's squad?

4. According to King, why was the Vietnam War an enemy of poor Americans?

Test Practice

1. All three of the sources concern —
   A the history of Vietnam
   B the causes of the Vietnam War
   C the U.S. armed forces in Vietnam
   D the U.S. Congress and president

2. From what you've read in "The War Escalates," you can infer that the Tonkin Gulf Resolution —
   F was a turning point in U.S. involvement in the war
   G was an unimportant piece of legislation
   H gave unusual powers to Congress
   J confirmed the president's constitutional powers

3. Which is *not* a **purpose** of Kenneth Bagby's letter, "Dear Folks"?
   A To inform
   B To persuade
   C To express feelings
   D To entertain

4. The value of "Dear Folks" as a research source is that it —
   F is objective and factual
   G relates a firsthand experience of the war
   H is impassioned and sincere
   J is written by an expert

5. Which source seems to support King's claim that an extraordinarily high proportion of the poor were sent to fight in Vietnam?
   A "Dear Folks"
   B "The War Escalates"
   C "Where Have You Gone, Charming Billy?" (page 621)
   D "The Friendship Only Lasted a Few Seconds" (page 629)

6. The primary **purpose** of the excerpt from "Declaration of Independence from the War in Vietnam" is to —
   F give information about the war
   G give information about the Viet Cong
   H persuade listeners of King's point of view about the war
   J describe specific events in the war

7. Which source has the *most* credibility as a history of the Vietnam War?
   A "Dear Folks"
   B The excerpt from "Declaration of Independence from the War in Vietnam"
   C "The War Escalates"
   D "Where Have You Gone, Charming Billy?" (page 621)

SKILLS FOCUS

Reading Skills
Analyze primary and secondary sources.

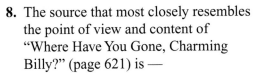

Test Practice

8. The source that most closely resembles the point of view and content of "Where Have You Gone, Charming Billy?" (page 621) is —

   F the section "U.S. Forces in Vietnam" from "The War Escalates"

   G Kenneth Bagby's letter, "Dear Folks"

   H the excerpt from King's speech, "Declaration of Independence from the War in Vietnam"

   J Lyndon Johnson's August 4, 1964, speech, which appears in "The War Escalates"

Constructed Response

In a brief essay, write your own analysis and evaluation of these primary and secondary sources about the Vietnam War. For each piece, first summarize its **main ideas.** Then, consider how **credible,** biased, or accurate each piece seems to be. Assess the value of each piece as a primary or secondary source. Finally, explain how these sources connect to what you already know about the Vietnam War, including the information about Tim O'Brien and his story "Where Have You Gone, Charming Billy?" (see page 621). Before you write, you can take notes in a chart like the one on the right:

> Primary ❑
> Secondary ❑
> Title:
> Analyze (main ideas):
> Evaluate (accuracy, reliability, bias):
> Elaborate (connections to other sources):

Vocabulary Development

Clarifying Word Meanings

PRACTICE

You reinforce your understanding of an unfamiliar word's meaning each time you use it in a sentence or think about how it should be used. Answer the following questions about each of the words from the Word Bank. Then, write an original sentence for each word. Check your original sentences with a partner or small group.

1. Identify several local, national, or world problems for which you think there is no <u>facile</u> solution.

2. What should be done for the <u>rehabilitation</u> of a person who has broken a leg?

3. How did Lyndon Johnson's actions demonstrate a <u>manipulation</u> of events during the Tonkin Gulf crisis?

4. How would you show your <u>compassion</u> for someone who has suffered a great loss?

5. What might someone do or say that would leave you <u>aghast</u>?

6. If you could take the <u>initiative</u> for a new project or organization at your school, what would you do?

> **Word Bank**
> facile
> rehabilitation
> manipulation
> compassion
> aghast
> initiative

SKILLS FOCUS

Vocabulary Skills
Clarify word meanings.

The Sword in the Stone

Make the Connection

Quickwrite ✏️

Jot down five or six qualities that you associate with the word *hero*.

Literary Focus

Arthurian Legend

A **legend** is a story about extraordinary deeds that has been told and retold for generations among a group of people. Legends, which are often about a particular person, are thought to have a historical basis but may also contain some elements of magic and myth. You can think of them as lying somewhere between historical fact and myth.

The King Arthur legends are probably based on a fifth- or sixth-century Celtic (kel′tik) chieftain, or warlord, who lived in Wales and led his people to victory against Saxon invaders from northern Germany. The chieftain was said to have been fatally wounded in battle and buried in the abbey of Glastonbury, where a gravestone can still be seen bearing his name.

Arthurian legend as we know it today emerged gradually over centuries as storytellers told and retold popular tales about a great chief who mysteriously disappeared but promised to return when his people needed him.

When Sir Thomas Malory wrote *Le Morte d'Arthur,* toward the end of the fifteenth century, the days of knights were over. Nonetheless, something in Malory's portrayal of those days seems to have answered a longing in his audience for the more orderly time of knights and lords and castles—a time when "might fought for right."

go.hrw.com

INTERNET

Vocabulary Practice
•
More About Sir Thomas Malory

Keyword: LE5 10-9

SKILLS FOCUS

Literary Skills
Understand characteristics of legends and Arthurian legends.

Background

Legendary heroes like King Arthur are born in dangerous times, when heroes are most needed. Here is the story of Arthur's birth: King Uther of England, who was unmarried, loved Igraine (ē′grān), another man's wife. In disguise the king deceived Igraine into thinking he was her husband. Arthur was the child born to Igraine as a result of that trick.

The wise man Merlin knew the baby was in danger because many men wanted Uther's throne, so he asked Sir Ector and his wife to raise the infant Arthur with their own son, Kay.

When King Uther died, no one except Merlin knew Arthur's true identity, which would be revealed when Arthur completed a task that only the rightful king could perform.

Vocabulary Development

confronted (kən·frunt′id) *v.*: faced.

inscription (in·skrip′shən) *n.*: something inscribed or engraved, as on a coin or monument.

oath (ōth) *n.*: solemn promise or declaration; vow.

ignoble (ig·nō′bəl) *adj.*: not noble in birth or position.

tumultuous (too·mul′choo·əs) *adj.*: wild; noisy.

realm (relm) *n.*: kingdom.

coronation (kôr′ə·nā′shən) *n.*: act or ceremony of crowning a sovereign.

THE SWORD IN THE STONE

from **Le Morte d'Arthur**
Sir Thomas Malory
retold by **Keith Baines**

...WERD OF THIS STONE AND ANVYLD IS RIGHT...

During the years that followed the death of King Uther, while Arthur was still a child, the ambitious barons fought one another for the throne, and the whole of Britain stood in jeopardy. Finally the day came when the Archbishop of Canterbury, on the advice of Merlin, summoned the nobility to London for Christmas morning. In his message the archbishop promised that the true succession to the British throne would be miraculously revealed. Many of the nobles purified themselves during their journey, in the hope that it would be to them that the succession would fall.

The archbishop held his service in the city's greatest church (St. Paul's), and when matins[1] were done, the congregation filed out to the yard. They were confronted by a marble block into which had been thrust a beautiful sword. The block was four feet square, and the sword passed through a steel anvil[2] which had been struck in the stone and which projected a foot from it. The anvil had been inscribed with letters of gold:

WHOSO PULLETH OUTE THIS SWERD OF THIS STONE AND ANVYLD IS RIGHTWYS KYNGE BORNE OF ALL BRYTAYGNE

The congregation was awed by this miraculous sight, but the archbishop forbade anyone to touch the sword before Mass had been heard. After Mass, many of the nobles tried to pull the sword out of the stone, but none was able to, so a watch of ten knights was set over the sword, and a tournament[3] proclaimed for New Year's Day, to provide men of noble blood with the opportunity of proving their right to the succession.

Sir Ector, who had been living on an estate near London, rode to the tournament with Arthur and his own son Sir Kay, who had been recently knighted. When they arrived at the tournament, Sir Kay found to his annoyance that his sword was missing from its sheath, so he begged Arthur to ride back and fetch it from their lodging.

Arthur found the door of the lodging locked and bolted, the landlord and his wife having left for the tournament. In order not to disappoint his brother, he rode on to St. Paul's, determined to get for him the sword which was lodged in the stone. The yard was empty, the guard also having slipped off to see the tournament, so Arthur strode up to the sword and, without troubling to read the inscription, tugged it free. He then rode straight back to Sir Kay and presented him with it.

Sir Kay recognized the sword and, taking it to Sir Ector, said, "Father, the succession falls to me, for I have here the sword that was lodged in the stone." But Sir Ector insisted that they should all ride to the churchyard, and once there, bound Sir Kay by oath to tell how he had come by the sword. Sir Kay then admitted that Arthur had given it to him. Sir Ector turned to Arthur and said, "Was the sword not guarded?"

"It was not," Arthur replied.

"Would you please thrust it into the stone again?" said Sir Ector. Arthur did so, and first Sir Ector and then Sir Kay tried to remove it, but both were unable to. Then Arthur, for the second time, pulled it out. Sir Ector and Sir Kay both knelt before him.

"Why," said Arthur, "do you both kneel before me?"

"My lord," Sir Ector replied, "there is only one man living who can draw the sword from the stone, and he is the true-born king of Britain." Sir Ector then told Arthur the story of his birth and upbringing.

"My dear father," said Arthur, "for so I shall always think of you—if, as you say, I am to be king, please know that any request you have to make is already granted."

Sir Ector asked that Sir Kay should be made royal seneschal,[4] and Arthur declared that while they both lived it should be so. Then the three of them visited the archbishop and told him what had taken place.

---

4. **royal seneschal** (sen′ə·shəl): person in charge of the king's household. This was a powerful and respected position.

---

1. **matins** (mat′nz) *n.*: morning prayers.
2. **anvil** *n.*: iron or steel block on which metal objects are hammered into shape.
3. **tournament** *n.*: sport in which two knights compete on horseback, trying to unseat each other with long polelike weapons called lances.

Vocabulary

confronted (kən·frunt′id) *v.*: faced.

inscription (in·skrip′shən) *n.*: something inscribed or engraved, as on a coin or monument.

oath (ōth) *n.*: solemn promise or declaration; vow.

All those dukes and barons with ambitions to rule were present at the tournament on New Year's Day. But when all of them had failed, and Arthur alone had succeeded in drawing the sword from the stone, they protested against one so young, and of ignoble blood, succeeding to the throne.

The secret of Arthur's birth was known to only a few of the nobles surviving from the days of King Uther. The archbishop urged them to make Arthur's cause their own; but their support proved ineffective. The tournament was repeated at Candlemas[5] and at Easter, with the same outcome as before.

Finally, at Pentecost,[6] when once more Arthur alone had been able to remove the sword, the commoners arose with a tumultuous cry and demanded that Arthur should at once be made king. The nobles, knowing in their hearts that the commoners were right, all knelt before Arthur and begged forgiveness for having delayed his succession for so long. Arthur forgave them and then, offering his sword at the high altar, was dubbed[7] first knight of the realm. The coronation took place a few days later, when Arthur swore to rule justly, and the nobles swore him their allegiance. ■

---

5. **Candlemas:** Christian festival that honors the purification of the Virgin Mary after the birth of Jesus. It falls on February 2.
6. **Pentecost:** Christian festival celebrated on the seventh Sunday after Easter, commemorating the descent of the Holy Spirit upon the Apostles.

7. **dubbed** *v.*: conferred knighthood on by tapping on the shoulder with a sword.

Vocabulary

ignoble (ig·nō′bəl) *adj.*: not noble in birth or position.

tumultuous (tōō·mul′chōō·əs) *adj.*: wild and noisy.

realm (relm) *n.*: kingdom.

coronation (kôr′ə·nā′shən) *n.*: act or ceremony of crowning a sovereign.

Meet the Writer

Sir Thomas Malory

A Master of Escape

We know only a little about the life of Sir Thomas Malory (1405?–1471). His title indicates that he was a knight, and we know that he was a soldier and a member of Parliament for a brief time. We also know that he spent most of the last twenty years of his life in prison, accused of some very unchivalrous crimes: assault, extortion, cattle rustling, poaching, jail breaking, plundering an abbey, and "waylaying the duke of Buckingham." Malory pleaded innocent to all charges, and it is likely that he was framed by political enemies. (It is also possible that Malory was something of a scoundrel.) During those miserable years in jail, Malory wrote his great romance.

The twelfth-century world of chivalrous knights in shining armor was almost as foreign to Malory as it is to us today. (For more about knights and chivalry, see page 651.) The invention of gunpowder and the rise of the middle class had already broken down the feudal order. While Malory scribbled heroic tales in a dark jail cell, English political and social life was in a state of turmoil that no amount of chivalry seemed likely to cure. Perhaps Malory yearned for a return to chivalry, to a simpler way of life with established codes of behavior. He might also have been trying to create a romantic escape from the grim realities of his personal life.

(For another knightly adventure from Malory's *Le Morte d'Arthur*, see page 652.)

The American novelist John Steinbeck (1902–1968), author of The Grapes of Wrath, Of Mice and Men, *and* The Pearl, *was nine years old when he first read an abridged version of Malory's King Arthur tales.*

"The Magic Happened"

John Steinbeck

Books were printed demons—the tongs and thumbscrews of outrageous persecution. And then, one day, an aunt gave me a book and fatuously ignored my resentment. I stared at the black print with hatred, and then, gradually, the pages opened and let me in. The magic happened. The Bible and Shakespeare and *Pilgrim's Progress*[1] belonged to everyone. But this was mine—it was a cut version of the Caxton *Morte d'Arthur* of Thomas Malory. I loved the old spelling of the words—and the words no longer used. Perhaps a passionate love for the English language opened to me from this one book. I was delighted to find out paradoxes[2]—that *cleave* means both "to stick together" and "to cut apart"; that *host* means both "an enemy" and "a welcoming friend"; that *king* and *gens* (people) stem from the same root. For a long time, I had a secret language—*yclept* and *hyght, wist*—and *accord* meaning "peace," and *entente* meaning "purpose," and *fyaunce* meaning "promise.". . . But beyond the glorious and secret words—"And when the chylde is borne lete it be delyvered to me at yonder privy posterne uncrystened"—oddly enough

King Arthur (detail), from tapestry of the "Nine Worthies" (c. 1490).

Historisches Museum, Basel, Switzerland.

I knew the words from whispering them to myself. The very strangeness of the language dyd me enchante, and vaulted me into an ancient scene.

And in that scene were all the vices that ever were—and courage and sadness and frustration, but particularly gallantry[3]—perhaps the only single quality of man that the West has invented. I think my sense of right and wrong, my feeling of noblesse oblige,[4] and any thought I may have against the oppressor and for the oppressed came from this secret book. It did not outrage my sensibilities as nearly all the children's books did. It did not seem strange to me that Uther Pendragon wanted the wife of his vassal[5] and took her by trickery. I was not frightened to find that there were evil knights, as well as noble ones. In my own town there were men who wore the clothes of virtue whom I knew to be bad. In pain or sorrow or confusion, I went back to my magic book. Children are violent and cruel—and good—and I was all of these— and all of these were in the secret book.

---

1. *Pilgrim's Progress n.:* famous allegory written by John Bunyan in 1678.
2. **paradoxes** *n.:* apparent contradictions that are actually true.
3. **gallantry** *n.:* act of great courtesy or bravery.
4. **noblesse oblige** (nō·bles′ ō·blēzh′) *n.:* obligation of people of high position to behave nobly.
5. **vassal** *n.:* medieval tenant or servant.

Response and Analysis

Reading Check

1. Make a **time line** showing the **main events** that take place in this part of Arthur's story. (You don't need to show the dates; just put the events in **chronological order.**) Start with the death of King Uther (before the story begins), and end with Arthur's coronation.

Thinking Critically

2. In what ways does Arthur, even as a young boy, show that he is a **hero**? How does Sir Kay, his foster brother, show signs that he is definitely *not* heroic material?

3. **Legends** often have both a historical basis and some element of exaggeration or fantasy. What elements of magic in this tale move it out of the realm of the ordinary and into that of legend?

4. What heroic values does this story teach? Which of these values are still important today? (Be sure to refer to your Quickwrite notes.) ✏️

Literary Criticism

5. During Arthur's time, England, like the rest of Europe, operated on a **feudal system** with three distinct social classes: the nobility, the commoners, and the clergy. What role does each class play in this story? Why would the tale have special appeal to the commoners?

6. "England's green and pleasant land" tempted invaders and conquerors— first the Celts, then Romans (first century), Saxons (beginning in the fifth century), Danes (eighth to eleventh centuries), and Normans (1066). Why would the question of succession to the throne have been of paramount importance to the people who first heard these tales recited?

7. In a typical **romance** (for more about romance, see page 651), the hero's origins are mysterious. He is frequently raised in obscurity before taking his rightful place as leader. How does the story of Arthur reflect this pattern?

Extending and Evaluating

8. Even today, Arthur lives. For example, T. H. White's novel based on the Arthurian legends, *The Once and Future King*, became a bestseller and the basis of the long-running Broadway musical *Camelot* (1960). There are even computer games retelling Arthur's story. Why do you suppose the story of King Arthur has had lasting appeal?

WRITING

Remembering "Magic"

"The magic happened" for John Steinbeck at the age of nine when he first read Malory's *Morte d'Arthur* (see the **Connection** on page 648). Think of a book, movie, or TV show that made a strong, almost "magical," impression on you at a young age. In a brief essay, explain how you felt about the work then, why it was important to you, and how you feel about the work now.

SKILLS FOCUS

Literary Skills
Analyze a legend.

Writing Skills
Write a reflective essay.

Vocabulary Development

Analogies: Matching Word Pairs

On pages 29–30 and 410, review the steps for completing analogy test questions and the different types of relationships that may appear in an analogy.

On pages 29–30 and 410

PRACTICE

Complete each analogy with a word from the Word Bank.

1. REPAIR : FIX :: _____ : faced

2. FOOTBALL : SPORT :: _____ : ceremony

3. BOLD : CAUTIOUS :: _____ : quiet

4. HARVESTED : CROP :: written : _____

5. JOKE : HUMOROUS :: _____ : solemn

6. WEAK : POWERFUL :: _____ : noble

7. CONCLUSION : ENDING :: _____ : kingdom

Word Bank

confronted
inscription
oath
ignoble
tumultuous
realm
coronation

Grammar Link

Misplaced Modifiers: Keep Them Close

A word, phrase, or clause that seems to modify the wrong word in a sentence is called a **misplaced modifier.** Place modifiers as close as possible to the words they modify. When they're separated, the meaning is unclear and often funny.

MISPLACED Miraculous, the congregation was awed by the appearance of the sword in the stone. [Was the congregation miraculous?]

CLEAR The congregation was awed by the miraculous appearance of the sword in the stone.

MISPLACED Stuck in the anvil, Arthur pulled out the sword. [Was Arthur stuck in the anvil?]

CLEAR Arthur pulled out the sword stuck in the anvil.

PRACTICE

Rewrite these sentences, correcting every misplaced modifier:

1. Arthur found the sword in the stone returning to St. Paul's.

2. Locked, Arthur could not get into the door of the lodging.

3. Sir Kay tried to become the king telling a lie.

4. Sir Kay finally told the true story of how he had gotten the sword bound by oath.

5. The commoners demanded that Arthur with a great cry be made king.

▶ **For more help, see Placement of Modifiers, 5i, in the Language Handbook.**

For more help, see Placement of Modifiers, 5i, in the Language Handbook.

SKILLS FOCUS

Vocabulary Skills
Complete word analogies.

Grammar Skills
Correct misplaced modifiers.

The Tale of Sir Launcelot du Lake

Make the Connection

Quickwrite 🖉

The days of knightly quests are long gone. How, then, can someone in today's world prove his or her heroism? Jot down your ideas, and save your notes.

Literary Focus

The Literature of Romance

During the Middle Ages a new form of literature, called the **romance,** developed in France and spread like a firestorm throughout Europe. Romances got their name because they were first told in Old French and Provençal, which are Romance languages (languages derived from Latin, the language of the Romans).

Romances began in the twelfth century as popular narratives describing the adventures of knights and other heroes. Wandering story singers collected these stories and recited them as they traveled from town to town. By the fourteenth century, romances had been taken over by the upper classes. As old oral storytellers gradually disappeared, the romances were passed on as written stories, polished and professional.

The primary purpose of romances was to celebrate the ideals of **chivalry,** the code of behavior the medieval knight was supposed to follow. He was to be brave, honorable, loyal, pious, and generous to foes, ready to help the weak and to protect women. The typical knight sought quests to prove his courage. The **knightly quest** (see page 657) typically involved saving maidens, slaying dragons, and battling less noble persons. Adventure was the call; heroism, the role.

Reading Skills 📖

**Summarizing:
Just What's Important**

A good **plot summary** contains only the main characters and events and omits all the delicious details. The summary states what the main character wants, what prevents him or her from getting it, and how the conflict is resolved.

As you read this story, stop at the open book signs to summarize what is happening.

Background

Of the 150 knights who serve King Arthur, Sir Launcelot is Arthur's favorite. Although Launcelot is devoted to Arthur, he falls in love with Arthur's wife, Queen Gwynevere, causing great suffering for the unfortunate trio. In this tale, as Launcelot goes searching for adventure, he runs into Morgan le Fay, Arthur's evil half sister. Famous for her enchantments, Morgan continually plots to destroy Arthur.

Vocabulary Development

diverted (də·vurt'id) *v.:* amused; entertained.

fidelity (fə·del'ə·tē) *n.:* loyalty; devotion.

oblige (ə·blīj') *v.:* compel by moral, legal, or physical force.

champion (cham'pē·ən) *v.:* fight for; defend; support.

adversary (ad'vər·ser'ē) *n.:* opponent; enemy.

sovereign (säv'rən) *n.:* king; ruler.

wrath (rath) *n.:* great anger.

INTERNET

Vocabulary
Practice
•
More About Sir
Thomas Malory

Keyword: LE5 10-9

**SKILLS
FOCUS**

Literary Skills
Understand
characteristics
of romantic
literature.

Reading Skills
Summarize a
text.

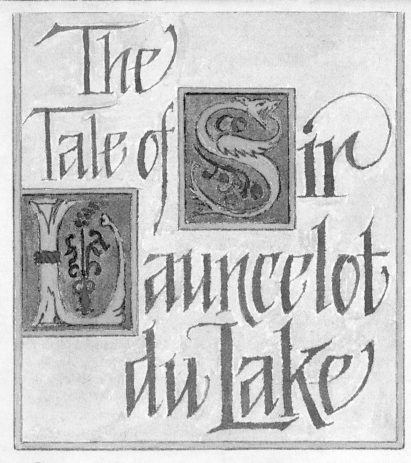

The Tale of Sir Launcelot du Lake

"Of all his knights one was supreme."

from Le Morte d'Arthur

Sir Thomas Malory
retold by Keith Baines

hen King Arthur returned from Rome he settled his court at Camelot, and there gathered about him his knights of the Round Table, who <u>diverted</u> themselves with jousting[1] and tournaments. Of all his knights one was supreme, both in prowess[2] at arms and in nobility of bearing, and this was Sir Launcelot, who was also the favorite of Queen Gwynevere, to whom he had sworn oaths of <u>fidelity</u>.

---

1. **jousting** (joust′iŋ) *v.* used as *n.:* form of combat between two knights on horseback. Each used a long lance to try to knock the other from his horse.
2. **prowess** (prou′is) *n.:* superior ability.

Vocabulary

diverted (də·vʉrt′id) *v.:* amused; entertained.
fidelity (fə·del′ə·tē) *n.:* loyalty; devotion.

One day Sir Launcelot, feeling weary of his life at the court, and of only playing at arms,[3] decided to set forth in search of adventure. He asked his nephew Sir Lyonel to accompany him, and when both were suitably armed and mounted, they rode off together through the forest.

At noon they started across a plain, but the intensity of the sun made Sir Launcelot feel sleepy, so Sir Lyonel suggested that they should rest beneath the shade of an apple tree that grew by a hedge not far from the road. They dismounted, tethered their horses, and settled down.

"Not for seven years have I felt so sleepy," said Sir Launcelot, and with that fell fast asleep, while Sir Lyonel watched over him.

While Sir Launcelot still slept beneath the apple tree, four queens started across the plain. They were riding white mules and accompanied by four knights who held above them, at the tips of their spears, a green silk canopy, to protect them from the sun. The party was startled by the neighing of Sir Launcelot's horse and, changing direction, rode up to the apple tree, where they discovered the sleeping knight. And as each of the queens gazed at the handsome Sir Launcelot, so each wanted him for her own.

"Let us not quarrel," said Morgan le Fay. "Instead, I will cast a spell over him so that he remains asleep while we take him to my castle and make him our prisoner. We can then oblige him to choose one of us for his paramour."[4]

Sir Launcelot was laid on his shield and borne by two of the knights to the Castle Charyot, which was Morgan le Fay's stronghold. He awoke to find himself in a cold cell, where a young noblewoman was serving him supper.

"What cheer?" she asked.

"My lady, I hardly know, except that I must have been brought here by means of an enchantment."

"Sir, if you are the knight you appear to be, you will learn your fate at dawn tomorrow." And with that the young noblewoman left him. Sir Launcelot spent an uncomfortable night but at dawn the four queens presented themselves and Morgan le Fay spoke to him:

"Sir Launcelot, I know that Queen Gwynevere loves you, and you her. But now you are my prisoner, and you will have to choose: either to take one of us for your paramour, or to die miserably in this cell—just as you please. Now I will tell you who we are: I am Morgan le Fay, Queen of Gore; my companions are the Queens of North Galys, of Estelonde, and of the Outer Isles. So make your choice."

"A hard choice! Understand that I choose none of you, lewd sorceresses that you are; rather will I die in this cell. But were I free, I would take pleasure in proving it against any who would <u>champion</u> you that Queen Gwynevere is the finest lady of this land."

"So, you refuse us?" asked Morgan le Fay.

"On my life, I do," Sir Launcelot said finally, and so the queens departed.

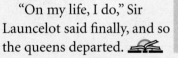

SUMMARIZING

1. **Summarize** Launcelot's adventure with the four queens.

Sometime later, the young noblewoman who had served Sir Launcelot's supper reappeared.

"What news?" she asked.

"It is the end," Sir Launcelot replied.

"Sir Launcelot, I know that you have refused

---

3. **playing at arms:** fighting with weapons as a sport only.
4. **paramour** (par′ə·moor′) *n.:* sweetheart; from Old French, meaning "with love." Today the term refers to an illicit lover.

Vocabulary

oblige (ə·blīj′) *v.:* compel by moral, legal, or physical force.

champion (cham′pē·ən) *v.:* fight for; defend; support.

the four queens, and that they wish to kill you out of spite. But if you will be ruled by me, I can save you. I ask that you will champion my father at a tournament next Tuesday, when he has to combat the King of North Galys, and three knights of the Round Table, who last Tuesday defeated him ignominiously."[5]

"My lady, pray tell me, what is your father's name?"

"King Bagdemagus."

"Excellent, my lady, I know him for a good king and a true knight, so I shall be happy to serve him."

"May God reward you! And tomorrow at dawn I will release you, and direct you to an abbey[6] which is ten miles from here, and where the good monks will care for you while I fetch my father."

"I am at your service, my lady."

As promised, the young noblewoman released Sir Launcelot at dawn. When she had led him through the twelve doors to the castle entrance, she gave him his horse and armor, and directions for finding the abbey.

"God bless you, my lady; and when the time comes I promise I shall not fail you."

Sir Launcelot rode through the forest in search of the abbey, but at dusk had still failed to find it, and coming upon a red silk pavilion,[7] apparently unoccupied, decided to rest there overnight, and continue his search in the morning.

He had not been asleep for more than an hour, however, when the knight who owned the pavilion returned, and got straight into bed with him. Having made an assignation[8] with his

paramour, the knight supposed at first that Sir Launcelot was she, and taking him into his arms, started kissing him. Sir Launcelot awoke with a start, and seizing his sword, leaped out of bed and out of the pavilion, pursued closely by the other knight. Once in the open they set to with their swords, and before long Sir Launcelot had wounded his unknown <u>adversary</u> so seriously that he was obliged to yield.

The knight, whose name was Sir Belleus, now asked Sir Launcelot how he came to be sleeping in his bed, and then explained how he had an assignation with his lover, adding:

"But now I am so sorely wounded that I shall consider myself fortunate to escape with my life."

"Sir, please forgive me for wounding you; but lately I escaped from an enchantment, and I was afraid that once more I had been betrayed. Let us go into the pavilion and I will staunch your wound."

Sir Launcelot had just finished binding the wound when the young noblewoman who was Sir Belleus' paramour arrived, and seeing the wound, at once rounded in fury on Sir Launcelot.

"Peace, my love," said Sir Belleus. "This is a noble knight, and as soon as I yielded to him he treated my wound with the greatest care." Sir Belleus then described the events which had led up to the duel.

"Sir, pray tell me your name, and whose knight you are," the young noblewoman asked Sir Launcelot.

"My lady, I am called Sir Launcelot du Lake."

"As I guessed, both from your appearance and from your speech; and indeed I know you better than you realize. But I ask you, in recompense

---

5. **ignominiously** (ig′nə·min′ē·əs·lē) *adv.:* dishonorably; disgracefully.
6. **abbey** (ab′ē) *n.:* place where monks or nuns live.
7. **pavilion** (pə·vil′yən) *n.:* large tent, often with a peaked top.
8. **assignation** (as′ig·nā′shən)*n.:* appointment, often made secretly.

Vocabulary
adversary (ad′vər·ser′ē) *n.:* opponent; enemy.

for[9] the injury you have done my lord, and out of the courtesy for which you are famous, to recommend Sir Belleus to King Arthur, and suggest that he be made one of the knights of the Round Table. I can assure you that my lord deserves it, being only less than yourself as a man-at-arms, and sovereign of many of the Outer Isles."

"My lady, let Sir Belleus come to Arthur's court at the next Pentecost.[10] Make sure that you come with him, and I promise I will do what I can for him; and if he is as good a man-at-arms as you say he is, I am sure Arthur will accept him."

Launcelot Enters a Tournament

As soon as it was daylight, Sir Launcelot armed, mounted, and rode away in search of the abbey, which he found in less than two hours. King Bagdemagus' daughter was waiting for him, and as soon as she heard his horse's footsteps in the yard, ran to the window, and, seeing that it was Sir Launcelot, herself ordered the servants to stable his horse. She then led him to her chamber, disarmed him, and gave him a long gown to wear, welcoming him warmly as she did so.

King Bagdemagus' castle was twelve miles away, and his daughter sent for him as soon as she had settled Sir Launcelot. The king arrived with his retinue[11] and embraced Sir Launcelot, who then described his recent enchantment, and the great obligation he was under to his daughter for releasing him.

"Sir, you will fight for me on Tuesday next?"

"Sire, I shall not fail you; but please tell me the names of the three Round Table knights whom I shall be fighting."

"Sir Modred, Sir Madore de la Porte, and Sir Gahalantyne. I must admit that last Tuesday they defeated me and my knights completely."

"Sire, I hear that the tournament is to be fought within three miles of the abbey. Could you send me three of your most trustworthy knights, clad in plain armor, and with no device,[12] and a fourth suit of armor which I myself shall wear? We will take up our position just outside the tournament field and watch while you and the King of North Galys enter into combat with your followers; and then, as soon as you are in difficulties, we will come to your rescue, and show your opponents what kind of knights you command."

This was arranged on Sunday, and on the following Tuesday Sir Launcelot and the three knights of King Bagdemagus waited in a copse,[13] not far from the pavilion which had been erected for the lords and ladies who were to judge the tournament and award the prizes.

> **SUMMARIZING**
> **2. Summarize** the way in which Launcelot ends up fighting in the tournament.

The King of North Galys was the first on the field, with a company of ninescore[14] knights; he was followed by King Bagdemagus with fourscore knights, and then by the three knights of the Round Table, who remained apart from both companies. At the first encounter King Bagdemagus lost twelve knights, all killed, and the King of North Galys six.

---

9. **in recompense** (rek′əm·pens′) **for:** in compensation for; make up for.
10. **Pentecost** (pen′tə·kôst′): Christian holiday that falls seven weeks after Easter.
11. **retinue** (ret′'n·o͞o′) *n.:* servants; attendants serving someone of importance.

12. **device** *n.:* design on a coat of arms. In a tournament, knights wore or carried a coat of arms to identify the noble for whom they were fighting.
13. **copse** (käps) *n.:* thicket of small trees or shrubs.
14. **ninescore** *n.:* 180. A *score* is 20.

Vocabulary
sovereign (säv′rən) *n.:* king; ruler.

With that, Sir Launcelot galloped on to the field, and with his first spear unhorsed five of the King of North Galys' knights, breaking the backs of four of them. With his next spear he charged the king, and wounded him deeply in the thigh.

"That was a shrewd blow," commented Sir Madore, and galloped onto the field to challenge Sir Launcelot. But he too was tumbled from his horse, and with such violence that his shoulder was broken.

Sir Modred was the next to challenge Sir Launcelot, and he was sent spinning over his horse's tail. He landed head first, his helmet became buried in the soil, and he nearly broke his neck, and for a long time lay stunned.

Finally, Sir Gahalantyne tried; at the first encounter both he and Sir Launcelot broke their spears, so both drew their swords and hacked vehemently at each other. But Sir Launcelot, with mounting <u>wrath</u>, soon struck his opponent a blow on the helmet which brought the blood streaming from eyes, ears, and mouth. Sir Gahalantyne slumped forward in the saddle, his horse panicked, and he was thrown to the ground, useless for further combat.

Sir Launcelot took another spear, and unhorsed sixteen more of the King of North Galys' knights, and with his next, unhorsed another twelve; and in each case with such violence that none of the knights ever fully recovered. The King of North Galys was forced to admit defeat, and the prize was awarded to King Bagdemagus.

That night Sir Launcelot was entertained as the guest of honor by King Bagdemagus and his daughter at their castle, and before leaving was loaded with gifts.

"He rode his way with the queen unto Joyous Gard." Illustration by N. C. Wyeth for *The Boy's King Arthur* (1917).

"My lady, please, if ever again you should need my services, remember that I shall not fail you." ■

Vocabulary
wrath (rath) *n.*: great anger.

Arthur's kingdom thrived while the Round Table existed, but "might for right" did not last. Several knights told King Arthur about the relationship between his wife and Launcelot. Gwynevere was judged guilty of adultery and sentenced to burn at the stake. At the last moment, Launcelot, charging through the guards, snatched Gwynevere from the flames and took her back to his castle. The resulting hostility between Arthur and Launcelot split the knights' allegiance. Thus, sexual immorality brought an end to the fellowship of the Round Table.

> **SUMMARIZING**
> 3. In two or three sentences, tell what happens at the tournament.

The world of romance was—and still is today—an ideal world of exaggeration and wish fulfillment, a world where the forces of good always triumph over the forces of evil.

The Romance: WHERE GOOD ALWAYS TRIUMPHS

David Adams Leeming

The hero's quest. A typical romance plot consists of a series of marvelous adventures with many magical events. The hero's adventures usually assume the form of a **quest,** a long, perilous journey in search of something of value: a kingdom, the rescue of a maiden, the destruction of a devouring beast, a treasure trove.

Joseph Campbell, author of *The Hero with a Thousand Faces,* writes that the hero's journey underlies the literature of all cultures. Typically the hero leaves the safety of home to cross into strange lands where he must prove that he has the wit, will, and strength to survive. During his quest the hero comes into conflict with a host of enemies—evil knights, monsters, and dragons—that he must fight or outsmart. He may be aided in his quest by a faithful companion or by a magic weapon. He often has a mysterious connection to the world of nature and is sometimes aided by animals. (In the modern quest trilogy *The Lord of the Rings* by J.R.R. Tolkien, the hero is aided by trees.) By the end of a typical romance, the hero has passed all the tests, suffered losses, gained what he had sought, and earned a measure of wisdom. In its purest form the hero's quest is a struggle between good and evil. Interpreted metaphorically, the quest is a journey into and out of the evil side of human nature.

Romances are still alive and well. Western novels and movies, science fiction and fantasy, adventure tales, mysteries, even some computer and video games—all use elements of the old romances. Good is still pitted against evil as the modern hero confronts new-age monsters. The hero still has incredible luck and strength, but his or her magical powers have disappeared.

Something new: The women step up. In medieval romances, women were usually betrayers, seducers, victims, or rewards. Today, especially in science fiction and fantasy, women pursue the hero's journey; they go on their own quests, take risks, and slay their own dragons. No matter who the questing hero is, modern romance stories continue to reveal our dreams of an ideal human community. Whether they were written yesterday or will be written tomorrow, romances show us the best that humans are capable of.

Response and Analysis

Reading Check

1. You are Sir Launcelot, reporting to King Arthur about your adventures. Using the first person, briefly **summarize** the **main events** that befell you on your journey.

Thinking Critically

2. Identify at least three of Launcelot's actions that are worthy of a chivalric **hero.** What, if anything, does he do that seems unheroic?

3. A **romance** usually includes these motifs: adventure, quests, wicked adversaries, even magic (see the **Connection** on page 657). Describe the typical elements of a romance that you find in this tale. Are any of these elements found in TV shows and movies today? Explain.

4. John Steinbeck, who was captivated by Malory's tales as a boy (see the **Connection** on page 648), once compared the Arthurian legends to the American western movie. Take notes in the form of a chart, **comparing and contrasting** these two kinds of stories. Then, tell which you prefer and why.

	Arthurian Legend	Westerns
Settings		
Characters		
Plots		
Themes		

Literary Criticism

5. Based on this tale, what can you say about the **character traits** medieval culture valued in its heroes?

6. **Compare and contrast** the medieval hero with your own ideas about heroes. (Where do your own ideas about heroes come from?) Be sure to refer to your Quickwrite notes.

7. The Arthurian stories are not dull; they are full of violence, betrayals, romantic intrigues, and even comedy. Which of these elements did you find in this tale and in "The Sword in the Stone" (page 645)? Cite details.

8. Knights really existed in twelfth-century England. Why do you think a romance such as this one would captivate a twelfth-century peasant, who struggled to survive, or a nobleperson?

WRITING

Stay Tuned for More About Arthur

What became of Gwynevere and Morgan le Fay? What special powers did Merlin have? What was medieval combat like? Make a list of Arthur-related questions. Do some research, and narrow your list to one topic about which you will write a **research paper.** Use both print and Internet sources for your report.

▶ **Use "Writing a Research Paper," pages 690–709, for help with this assignment.**

"Very good, Gary: 'A hero is a celebrity who did something real.'"

SKILLS FOCUS

Literary Skills
Analyze romantic literature.

Reading Skills
Summarize a text.

Writing Skills
Write a research paper.

Vocabulary Development

Demonstrating Word Knowledge

PRACTICE 1

Reinforce your understanding of the Word Bank words by writing an answer to each of the following questions.

1. When you've been very tense, what has <u>diverted</u> you?
2. Why is <u>fidelity</u> to a cause an admired quality?
3. What are some things that a dog owner is <u>obliged</u> to do to take good care of his or her pet?
4. What sports team do you <u>champion</u>?
5. How should a team member treat an <u>adversary</u> during a sporting event? afterward?
6. Why does a <u>sovereign</u> have power over his or her country?
7. What is something that could cause you to feel <u>wrath</u>?

Word Bank

diverted
fidelity
oblige
champion
adversary
sovereign
wrath

A Changing Language: English Word Origins

All languages change over time. English vocabulary, grammar, spelling, and pronunciation have changed a great deal since the fifteenth century, when Sir Thomas Malory wrote in the Midland dialect then spoken in London. For example, consider the **derivation** and the original **meaning** of *worship:* When Malory called a brave knight "a knight of much worship," he meant "a knight well-known for his worth." In Old English the word for this concept was *weorthscipe,* or *worthship,* that is, "worthy of honor, dignity, or rank." Gradually the word acquired religious connotations and lost its secular meaning, as well as its *th* sound. Today the meaning of *worship* is almost wholly religious.

PRACTICE 2

Translate this passage from *Le Morte d'Arthur* into the kind of English spoken in the United States today. First, read the passage aloud. Then, take a guess at the meanings of unfamiliar-looking words. Check your guesses in a dictionary's **etymologies,** or word origins. Do you find the Middle English spellings included in the word's **etymology**?

   "A, Launcelot!" he sayd, "thou were hede of al Crysten knyghtes! And now I dare say," sayd syr Ector, "thou sir Launcelot, there thou lyest, that thou were never matched of erthely knyghtes hande. And thou werre the curtest knyght that ever bare shelde!"

—Sir Thomas Malory

SKILLS FOCUS

Vocabulary Skills
Demonstrate word knowledge. Understand etymologies.

Before You Read

Theseus

Make the Connection

Quickwrite ✏️

Stories about heroes who embark on perilous journeys to fulfill a quest are still told today. Think about examples of perilous journeys in movies and video games as well as in books. Does the hero undertake the journey to use might for right or for some other purpose? Jot down some examples of modern heroes and quests.

Literary Focus

Myths and Society

In ancient Greece, as elsewhere, **myths**—traditional stories about gods and heroes—were much more than entertaining tales. Myths were part of the Greek religion, and like all myths they defined the culture of the people who believed in them. The myths—the word is from *mythos,* Greek for "story"—told the people who they were, where they came from, and what they should value in life.

By means of myths, people were also able to deal with the mysteries they encountered in life—mysteries they saw in the outside world and in their own inner worlds as well.

Though they often have supernatural powers, the heroes in the Greek myths are recognizably human. They are not divine, even though some of them were fathered by gods. They are not humanized animals, the way trickster heroes are in some mythologies (Coyote in North America and Spider in Africa).

In a typical hero myth, a young man is sent on a quest to find something of great value, including self-knowledge and self-control. These hero stories reveal the human qualities that the ancient Greeks valued and taught to their children. The Greek hero stories tell of people who are not always noble. Like most of us, the characters are sometimes selfish or stubborn or even cruel. They sometimes disobey the gods, with grave, even tragic, consequences. Some of them are pawns of the gods, and their worth is measured in how they respond to adversities.

Theseus, whose story you are about to read, was the hero particularly identified with the city of Athens. Theseus is an example of a hero who uses his might to do right—though even he sometimes fails.

SKILLS FOCUS

Literary Skills
Understand the relationship between myths and society.

Background

Ancient Greek Culture: The Context for the Myths

Ancient Greek civilization gave us the Olympic Games, drama, the concept of democracy—and much more.

From its earliest history, Greece was a land of small, independent city-states. Greece is mostly mountainous, with small valleys; off its coasts are numerous islands. Thus, the people lived in isolated mountain or island communities, each with its own government. The city of Athens, for instance, had its own king, who ruled the city and immediate surrounding countryside. There were many other separate kingdoms, including neighboring Salamis, Eleusis, and Sparta.

Though some Athenians today believe that the myths about Theseus are based on the life of an actual early king, scholars believe Theseus is totally mythic. According to legend,

---

when Theseus became king of Athens, he united the small independent kingdoms scattered across Attica (see the map) into a single federation—the great city-state of Athens. Theseus is thus credited with beginning the first people's democracy. Athens became the home of liberty, at least for free males, the first place in the world where people governed themselves.

How much of this myth is true? It is hard to answer that question, but certainly some episodes had a basis in reality. For example, if you go to the beautiful island of Crete today, you can see the ruins of King Minos's palace. You can even see a painting on the wall that shows a young man leaping over a great bull that is flanked by two women.

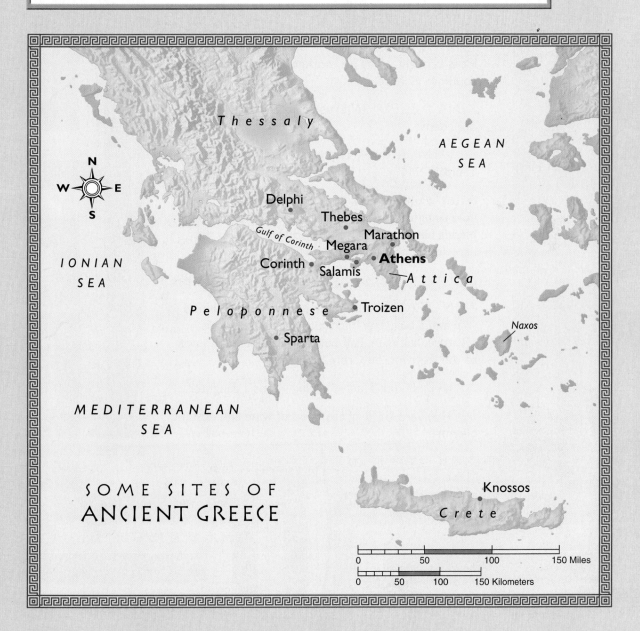

SOME SITES OF ANCIENT GREECE

CHARACTERS IN THE MYTH

THESEUS (thē′sē·əs): son of Aegeus and Aethra. He is brought up by his mother in Troizen, in southern Greece.

KING AEGEUS (ē′jē·əs): Theseus's father, king of Athens.

AETHRA (ē′thrə): Theseus's mother, princess of Troizen.

MEDEA (mē·dē′ə): enchantress from Corinth, now living with King Aegeus in Athens. Earlier Medea had used her magical powers to help the hero Jason steal the Golden Fleece.

MINOS (mī′näs′): king of Crete, enemy of Athens.

MINOTAUR (min′ə·tôr′): offspring of Minos's wife and a bull. The Minotaur was a monstrous creature, half-man, half-bull, and confined by Minos to the labyrinth on Crete.

ARIADNE (ar′ē·ad′nē): King Minos's daughter.

DIONYSUS (dī′ə·nī′səs): god of wine and ecstatic pleasure.

THESEUS

retold by Edith Hamilton

Head of Theseus. Detail of a mural from Herculaneum, Italy.

Theseus pictured on a Greek amphora, a type of jar (5th century B.C.).

The great Athenian hero was Theseus. He had so many adventures and took part in so many great enterprises that there grew up a saying in Athens, "Nothing without Theseus."

Painted figure of the Minotaur, on a Greek cup (c. 515 B.C.).

He was the son of the Athenian king, Aegeus. He spent his youth, however, in his mother's home, a city in southern Greece. Aegeus went back to Athens before the child was born, but first he placed in a hollow a sword and a pair of shoes and covered them with a great stone. He did this with the knowledge of his wife and told her that whenever the boy—if it was a boy— grew strong enough to roll away the stone and get the things beneath it, she could send him to Athens to claim him as his father. The child was a boy, and he grew up strong far beyond others, so that when his mother finally took him to the stone he lifted it with no trouble at all. She told him then that the time had come for him to seek his father, and a ship was placed at his disposal by his grandfather. But Theseus refused to go by water, because the voyage was safe and easy. His idea was to become a great hero as quickly as possible, and easy safety was certainly not the way to do that. Hercules, who was the most magnificent of all the heroes of Greece, was always in his mind, and the determination to be just as magnificent himself. This was quite natural, since the two were cousins.

He steadfastly refused, therefore, the ship his mother and grandfather urged on him, telling them that to sail on it would be a contemptible[1] flight from danger, and he set forth to go to Athens by land. The journey was long and very hazardous because of the bandits that beset the road. He killed them all, however; he left not one alive to trouble future travelers. His idea of dealing justice was simple but effective: What each had done to others, Theseus did to him. Sciron,[2] for instance, who had made those he captured kneel to wash his feet and then kicked them down into the sea, Theseus hurled over a precipice. Sinir, who killed people by fastening them to two pine trees bent down to the ground and letting the trees go, died in that way himself. Procrustes[3] was placed upon the iron bed which he used for his victims, tying them to it and then making them the right length for it by stretching those who were too short and

---

1. **contemptible** (kən·tempt′ə·bəl) *adj.*: hateful; worthy of contempt; disgraceful.
2. **Sciron** (sī′rōn′).
3. **Procrustes** (prō·krus′tēz).

cutting off as much as was necessary from those who were too long. The story does not say which of the two methods was used in his case, but there was not much to choose between them and in one way or the other Procrustes' career ended.

It can be imagined how Greece rang with the praises of the young man who had cleared the land of these banes[4] to travelers. When he reached Athens, he was an acknowledged hero, and he was invited to a banquet by the King, who of course was unaware that Theseus was his son. In fact, he was afraid of the young man's great popularity, thinking that he might win the people over to make him king, and he invited him with the idea of poisoning him. The plan was not his, but Medea's, the heroine of the Quest of the Golden Fleece, who knew through her sorcery who Theseus was. She had fled to Athens when she left Corinth in her winged car, and she had acquired great influence over Aegeus, which she did not want disturbed by the appearance of a son. But as she handed him the poisoned cup, Theseus, wishing to make himself known at once to his father, drew his sword. The King instantly recognized it and dashed the cup to the ground. Medea escaped, as she always did, and got safely away to Asia.

Aegeus then proclaimed to the country that Theseus was his son and heir. The new heir apparent soon had an opportunity to endear himself to the Athenians.

Years before his arrival in Athens, a terrible misfortune had happened to the city. Minos, the powerful ruler of Crete, had lost his only son, Androgenes,[5] while the young man was visiting the Athenian king. King Aegeus had done what no host should do: He had sent his guest on an expedition full of peril—to kill a dangerous bull. Instead, the bull had killed the youth. Minos invaded the country, captured Athens and declared that he would raze it to the ground unless every nine years the people sent him a tribute[6] of seven maidens and seven youths. A horrible fate awaited these young creatures. When they reached Crete they were given to the Minotaur to devour.

The Minotaur was a monster, half bull, half human, the offspring of Minos's wife Pasiphaë[7] and a wonderfully beautiful bull. Poseidon[8] had given this bull to Minos in order that he should sacrifice it to him, but Minos could not bear to slay it and kept it for himself. To punish him, Poseidon had made Pasiphaë fall madly in love with it.

When the Minotaur was born, Minos did not kill him. He had Daedalus,[9] a great architect and inventor, construct a place of confinement for him from which escape was impossible.

Daedalus built the Labyrinth, famous throughout the world. Once inside, one would go endlessly along its twisting paths without ever finding the exit. To this place the young Athenians were each time taken and left to the Minotaur. There was no possible way to escape. In whatever direction they ran, they might be running straight to the monster; if they stood still, he might at any moment emerge from the maze. Such was the doom which awaited fourteen youths and maidens a few days after Theseus reached Athens. The time had come for the next installment of the tribute.

> THE MINOTAUR WAS A MONSTER, HALF BULL, HALF HUMAN.

---

4. **banes** *n.*: causes of destruction or ruin.
5. **Androgenes** (an·drä′jə·nēz).
6. **tribute** *n.*: something paid by one nation or ruler to another as an acknowledgment of submission.
7. **Pasiphaë** (pə·sif′ā·ē′).
8. **Poseidon** (pō·sī′dən): god of horses and of the sea; brother of Zeus.
9. **Daedalus** (ded′′l·əs).

love with Theseus at first sight as he marched past her. She sent for Daedalus and told him he must show her a way to get out of the Labyrinth, and she sent for Theseus and told him she would bring about his escape if he would promise to take her back to Athens and marry her. As may be imagined, he made no difficulty about that, and she gave him the clue she had got from Daedalus, a ball of thread which he was to fasten at one end to the inside of the door and unwind as he went on. This he did and, certain that he could retrace his steps whenever he chose, he walked boldly into the maze, looking for the Minotaur. He came upon him asleep and fell upon him, pinning him to the ground; and with his fists—he had no other weapon—he battered the monster to death.

As an oak tree falls on the hillside
Crushing all that lies beneath,
    So Theseus. He presses out the life,
The brute's savage life, and now it lies
    dead.
Only the head sways slowly, but the horns
    are useless now.

When Theseus lifted himself up from that terrific struggle, the ball of thread lay where he had dropped it. With it in his hands, the way out was clear. The others followed, and taking Ariadne with them they fled to the ship and over the sea toward Athens.

Theseus and the Minotaur pictured on a black-figured cup from Athens (c. 550–540 B.C.).

At once Theseus came forward and offered to be one of the victims. All loved him for his goodness and admired him for his nobility, but they had no idea that he intended to try to kill the Minotaur. He told his father, however, and promised him that if he succeeded, he would have the black sail which the ship with its cargo of misery always carried changed to a white one, so that Aegeus could know long before it came to land that his son was safe.

When the young victims arrived in Crete, they were paraded before the inhabitants on their way to the Labyrinth. Minos' daughter Ariadne was among the spectators, and she fell in

On the way there they put in at the island of Naxos, and what happened then is differently reported. One story says that Theseus deserted Ariadne. She was asleep, and he sailed away without her, but Dionysus found her and comforted her. The other story is much more favorable to Theseus. She was extremely seasick, and he set her ashore to recover while he returned to the ship to do some necessary work. A violent wind carried him out to sea and kept him there a long time. On his return he found that Ariadne had died, and he was deeply afflicted.[10]

Both stories agree that when they drew near to Athens, he forgot to hoist the white sail. Either his joy at the success of his voyage put every other thought out of his head, or his grief for Ariadne. The black sail was seen by his father, King Aegeus, from the Acropolis,[11] where for days he had watched the sea with straining eyes. It was to him the sign of his son's death, and he threw himself down from a rocky height into the sea and was killed. The sea into which he fell was called the Aegean ever after.

So Theseus became King of Athens, a most wise and disinterested[12] king. He declared to the people that he did not wish to rule over them; he wanted a people's government where all would be equal. He resigned his royal power and organized a commonwealth, building a council hall where the citizens should gather and vote. The only office he kept for himself was that of commander in chief. Thus Athens became, of all earth's cities, the happiest and most prosperous, the only true home of liberty, the one place in the world where the people governed themselves. It was for this reason that in the great War of the Seven against Thebes,[13] when the victorious Thebans refused burial to those of the enemy who had died, the vanquished[14] turned to Theseus and Athens for help, believing that free men under such a leader would never consent to having the helpless dead wronged. They did not turn in vain. Theseus led his army against Thebes, conquered her, and forced her to allow the dead to be buried. But when he was victor, he did not return evil to the Thebans for the evil they had done. He showed himself the perfect knight. He refused to let his army enter and loot the city. He had come not to harm Thebes, but to bury the Argive[15] dead, and that duty done he led his soldiers back to Athens. ■

---

10. **afflicted** *adj.:* distressed; upset.
11. **Acropolis** (ə·kräp′ə·lis): fortified heights in Athens. A huge temple to Athena stands on top of the hill.
12. **disinterested** *adj.:* fair; impartial. (*Disinterested* should not be confused with *uninterested*, which means "not interested.")
13. **Thebes** (thēbz): chief city of Boeotia, a region in ancient Greece.
14. **vanquished** *v.* used as *n.:* conquered; defeated.
15. **Argive** (är′gīv): another word for "Greek." All of these people were Greek, but they gave allegiance to their separate small kingdoms.

Ariadne (15th century) by Antico (Pier Jacopo Alari Bonacolsi). Partially gilded bronze statue.

Meet the Writer

Edith Hamilton

A Passion for Ancient Greece

The retellings of the Greek myths that many people first encounter as children are probably those by Edith Hamilton (1867–1963). When Hamilton retired from teaching the classics at Bryn Mawr School in Baltimore, she decided she wanted to share her knowledge with a wider audience. Thus, she began writing *Mythology,* which soon became a bestseller. The miracle of Greek mythology, Hamilton said, is

> " a humanized world. . . . All the art and all the thought of Greece centered in human beings. "

The classics—the literature of ancient Greece and Rome—had been part of Hamilton's life from the time she was seven years old. She became so identified with Greece that in 1957 she was named an honorary citizen of Athens.

For Independent Reading

If you, like Hamilton, enjoy learning about the ancient world, try these Hamilton classics:

- *The Greek Way*
- *The Roman Way*

Theseus and the Minotaur pictured on a Greek amphora (c. 550–500 B.C.).

Joseph Campbell wrote many books on the importance of mythology in our everyday lives. Here is a portion of an interview with Campbell, done for a six-hour PBS series. The interviewer is the journalist Bill Moyers.

"All We Need Is That Piece of String"

Moyers. What's the significance of the trials, and tests, and ordeals of the hero?

Campbell. If you want to put it in terms of intentions, the trials are designed to see to it that the intending hero should be really a hero. Is he really a match for this task? Can he overcome the dangers? Does he have the courage, the knowledge, the capacity, to enable to serve? . . .

Moyers. I like what you say about the old myth of Theseus and Ariadne. Theseus says to Ariadne, "I'll love you forever if you can show me a way to come out of the labyrinth." So she gives him a ball of string, which he unwinds as he goes into the labyrinth, and then follows to find the way out. You say, "All he had was the string. That's all you need."

Campbell. That's all you need—an Ariadne thread.

Moyers. Sometimes we look for great wealth to save us, a great power to save us, or great ideas to save us, when all we need is that piece of string.

Campbell. That's not always easy to find. But it's nice to have someone who can give you a clue. That's the teacher's job, to help you find your Ariadne thread.

◉ ◉ ◉

Campbell. The big question is whether you are going to be able to say a hearty yes to your adventure.

Moyers. The adventure of the hero?

Campbell. Yes, the adventure of the hero—the adventure of being alive.

Hercules and the Centaur (16th century) after Giambologna.

Response and Analysis

Reading Check

1. This myth can be divided into eight episodes. **Summarize** in a few sentences the **main events** in each episode:

    a. Theseus's childhood

    b. his perilous journey to Athens

    c. recognition by his father

    d. trial in the labyrinth

    e. loss of Ariadne

    f. mistake with sails

    g. triumph in Athens

    h. war against Thebes

Thinking Critically

2. What is revealed about the **character** of Theseus when he insists on taking the land route to Athens?

3. In many **quest** stories the hero must descend into an underworld before the quest can be successfully completed. How could the labyrinth be seen as that underworld?

4. In Greek myths the hero is fully human. He is never part beast, part human. How is the Minotaur, then, the evil opposite of the ideal hero?

5. Explain the ways in which Theseus fits Joseph Campbell's definition of the hero (see the **Connection** on page 669).

6. What stories today are organized around a perilous journey? What are the goals of these modern questing heroes? How does the level of violence in these stories compare with the violence in the Theseus myth? (Check your Quickwrite notes.)

7. Explain what you think Joseph Campbell means by an "Ariadne thread." Have you had an Ariadne thread in your life? What was it?

Literary Criticism

8. What can you infer about the ancient Greek concept of justice by the way Theseus deals with the bandits he meets on his perilous journey?

9. What threatens Theseus at the moment of his reunion with his father? Since the ancient Greeks valued hospitality and courtesy to strangers, how would they have responded to this part of Theseus's story?

10. What other detail reveals the importance of kindness to strangers in ancient Greece?

11. From this myth, what can you infer about the relationship between Athens and Crete, two powerful Greek city-states? How does Theseus change the situation between the two cities?

12. An important Greek value is underscored in the Thebans' refusal to allow the burial of their slain enemies. One of the holiest laws of the Greeks demanded that certain rites be performed for the dead and that the body be buried. If the body was allowed to rot in the sun, the dead person would be condemned to eternal unrest. How did Theseus show respect for that religious principle?

13. What do Theseus's actions after the conquest of Thebes reveal about the Athenian code of honor in war? How does this code compare with the way wars are conducted today?

WRITING

Comparing Heroes

Both the Arthurian legend and the Theseus myths are about heroes who claim their rightful kingdom. In an essay, **compare and contrast** Theseus's story with Arthur's. Before you write, collect your details in a chart like the one below:

	Theseus	Arthur
Parentage		
Childhood		
Search for father		
Test to prove identity		
Quest		
Savior of a people		

Researching Heroes

According to Edith Hamilton, there were four great Greek heroes before the Trojan War. Theseus was one. Two others were men (Perseus and Herakles—also known as Hercules) and one was a woman (Atalanta). Choose one of these three other heroes, and research versions of his or her story. Consult at least two collections of Greek myths in your research. Use your findings as the basis of a **research paper.** Before you write, you will have to focus your research so that you have one main topic to present in your thesis statement.

▶ **Use "Writing a Research Paper," pages 690–709, for help with this assignment.**

Theseus in Panels

The Greek myths have provided rich subject matter for illustrators. Try your hand at reformulating the Theseus story into a series of cartoon panels. First, divide the story into discrete episodes, and assign one event to a panel. Put the characters' dialogue (you will have to make it up) in balloons, and provide a caption for each panel that explains what is happening. If you want to limit your story, you could focus on the adventure in the labyrinth.

Atalanta. Greek marble statue (3rd–2nd century B.C.).

Vocabulary Development

Words Derived from Greek and Roman Myths

Greek or Roman Word	English Word
Amazons	amazon
Atlas	atlas
Europa	Europe
Furies	fury
Hercules	herculean
Janus	January
Juno	June
Labyrinth	labyrinth
Mars	martial
Mercury	mercurial
Mount Olympus	olympic
Nemesis	nemesis
Oceanus	ocean
Odysseus	odyssey
Vulcan	volcano

PRACTICE

Read the information, and answer the questions that follow about words from the Greek and Roman myths. To answer the questions, you might need to look up the derivation of each underlined word in a college or unabridged dictionary.

1. A god called **Atlas** held up the whole earth and heavens on his shoulders.

   Why is a book of maps called an atlas?

2. The **Furies** were wild female spirits, with snakes for hair, who punished wrongdoers and avenged crimes.

   How is our word furious related to the Furies?

3. The Greek gods were said to live atop **Mount Olympus** in Greece.

   What northwestern U.S. mountain range is named for this home of the Greek gods?

4. **Nemesis** (nem'ə·sis) was the goddess who handed out justice or vengeance to wrongdoers.

   What do we mean when we make remarks like "That test was my nemesis"?

5. **Odysseus,** the hero of Homer's epic the *Odyssey,* took ten years to travel home from the Trojan War.

   How is the word odyssey related to Odysseus's journey?

6. **Vulcan** was the Roman god of fire, forges, and metalworking.

   How do you think the word volcano is related to this god's name?

7. **Mercury** was the messenger of the Roman gods. Mercury is identified with manual skill, eloquence, cleverness, travel, and thievery.

   What is meant when a person is described as mercurial?

8. The Greek hero Herakles is called **Hercules** by the Romans. He was renowned for his twelve labors, which required great strength and courage.

   Give an example of a herculean task someone today might be asked to perform.

9. Who were the Amazons, for whom the South American river was named?

10. You have read about the famous labyrinth on Crete.

    How is the word labyrinth used today?

Sigurd, the Dragon Slayer

Make the Connection

Quickwrite ✏️

What stories or movies feature a dragon or monster as the villain? What powers do these creatures usually have? What makes them a threat?

Literary Focus

Norse Myths and the Monster Slayer

A **myth** is a traditional story that is basically religious in nature. Myths usually explain a belief, a ritual, or a mysterious natural phenomenon. In almost all cultures, for example, you will find myths that explain why the seasons change, how humankind learned to make fire, and why we have to die.

Many myths have dragons and other monsters as characters. Traditionally the dragon guards a treasure hoard that was acquired through deceit or violence. "Sigurd, the Dragon Slayer," a Norse myth, features what might be the **archetypal** dragon slayer—the model of the hero who descends to the underworld to slay a monster.

Background

Norse mythology consists of stories that were told in Scandinavia and Germany for thousands of years. The oldest surviving written versions of these ancient tales, called *Eddas,* came from Iceland in the thirteenth century.

Norse mythology also includes great hero tales, called *sagas,* which are part of an oral storytelling tradition. The story of Sigurd is part of the Volsunga saga.

Unlike the Greek myths, the Norse myths foretell a day of doom when the entire world will be consumed by fire and all life ended. Not only will human life end on that day (called Ragnarok) but the gods will also perish. It is a tragic outlook—nothing will be able to change it. (The myths do contain a remote glimpse of hope, however—a prophecy of a new world to come after Ragnarok.)

In her introduction to *Legends of the North,* Olivia Coolidge writes this about the Norse myths:

"The violent history of the northern peoples and the harsh conditions of their lives have helped to form a body of legend which is highly individual. The gods of Asgard [home of the Norse gods and slain heroes], like the men who believed in them, were engaged in a constant struggle in which goodness warred against evil, light against darkness, warmth against cold. Boisterous humor was seen in contrast to shadowy forces at whose hands the earth was fated to perish at last on the Day of Doom.

Such being the religion of the Norsemen, it is not surprising to find that the human heroes of legend are people who have much to endure. Happy endings are rare. Life is short. The pathos is heightened by every man's intense love of life and interest in human affairs. Courage chiefly elevates these stories, since in them the hero accepts with a fine exultation every test of his power to endure."

SKILLS FOCUS

Literary Skills
Understand characteristics of Norse myths.

CHARACTERS IN THE MYTH

REGIN: a dwarf, brother of Fafnir. In Norse mythology, dwarfs are a race of ugly, deceitful creatures who live under the earth and work as master craftsmen. The word *dwarf* probably comes from an Indo-European base meaning "trick or injure."

SIGURD (sig′ərd): the most famous hero in Norse mythology, the last of the Volsung family.

SIGMUND (sig′mənd): Sigurd's father, who was killed in battle before Sigurd's birth.

HIORDIS (hē·ôr′dis): Sigurd's mother, who married King Alf after Sigmund's death.

FAFNIR (fäv′nir′): an evil dwarf who was turned into a dragon. Fafnir is Regin's brother.

REIDMAR (rēd′mär): the dwarf king, father of Regin, Otter, and Fafnir.

ODIN: the leader of the gods, and the god of war and wisdom.

Sigurd killing the dragon Fafnir. Carved portal from the Hylestad church, Norway (12th century).

SIGURD,
THE DRAGON SLAYER

retold by Olivia E. Coolidge

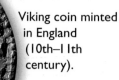

Viking coin minted in England (10th–11th century).

INTRODUCTION

Sigurd's story is part of a cycle of hero sagas. Before this particular story opens, Loki, the cunning god of fire, thoughtlessly kills an otter sunning itself—but the otter is actually the son of Reidmar, the king of the dwarfs.

That night, Reidmar captures Loki and Odin, king of the gods. Furious, the dwarf king threatens to kill both of them in revenge for his son's death. Odin suggests a ransom instead. So Loki is sent off to steal the famous gold hoard of the elf Andvari.

When Reidmar receives the gold, he frees his hostages—but the lust for gold can result in evil. That night the dwarf king's son, Fafnir, kills his own father and seizes the elfin treasure for himself. The third son of the dwarf king, Regin, flees, terrified for his own life.

Many years pass. Fafnir, the brother who stole his father's gold, has changed his shape into that of a dragon. Fafnir now lies coiled jealously around his golden treasure in his dead father's crumbling hall. Meanwhile Regin, the third son, has wandered the world looking for a hero who can slay Fafnir and seize the treasure for Regin.

One day a royal child is born in a peaceful kingdom. Regin recognizes the child as the one who will slay the dragon and get the gold. The baby, Sigurd, is the son of the great warrior Sigmund, who died in battle.

Now starts Sigurd's story.

THE DRAGON SLAYER

Regin saw the baby, Sigurd, and his heart was wonderfully stirred, for he knew the dragon slayer was born after ages of time. He said nothing to Hiordis, who had borne this son to Sigmund, the Volsung, after that great hero had died. He kept his own counsel while the child was an infant, but he burned with secret desire. Years passed more slowly than ever, but at last he saw Sigurd had become a tall, golden-haired lad. Then finally he went to King Alf, who had wedded the widowed Hiordis. "My long life draws to a close," he said. "Grant me a pupil before I die, that I may teach him the skill of my hands, the words of my songs, and my herbs of healing, lest my wisdom perish with me and be forgotten."

"It is a good request," answered Alf, "and I grant it. Whom will you have?"

"Give me Sigurd," answered Regin quickly.

"It is done," declared the king, marveling at the beautiful boy who seemed to have touched the heart of this dark, secretive old man.

After this time the aged Regin appeared to recover the fire of his earlier days. The hand of Sigurd became cunning with the harp strings. His strong, young voice delighted the feasters with the legends of ancient time. He worked also with Regin in the smithy,[1] but there he could never rival his master, though among men he was a notable smith. He learned much of strange herbs and of the ways of the woodlands. Of the evil workings of Regin's mind, he understood nothing at all. Yet though other people spoke of the old man's love for his pupil, Sigurd felt the cold craft behind it. Though he admired his wise master, he had no affection for him.

Sigurd was wielding the hammer in the smithy one day when Regin, studying his mighty form, judged the awaited time was near.

---

1. **smithy** *n.:* workplace of a smith, one who makes or repairs metal objects in a fiery forge. In former times, smiths used their hammers to shape the hot metal into armor, weapons, and shoes for horses.

"Sigurd," he said when the din[2] ceased and the iron was thrust back in the fire, "you are the last of the Volsungs, who were a great warrior race. Are you content in this tame little country where Alf's sons, your brothers, grow up to be kings?"

Sigurd turned from the fire toward him. "I would ride into the world tomorrow," he answered, "were it not for my mother, and for King Alf, who has treated me well."

"So well," replied Regin drily, "that you have neither horse nor sword."

"I ride what horse I please," retorted Sigurd, "as do the king's own sons."

"Your brothers are children. When they are men like you, they will have their own."

"I can have any horse for the asking," persisted Sigurd. This was true, for Alf was pleased by the youth's request.

"The horses are in the pasture at the head of the valley," said he. "Go up and choose which you will. It is time you had one of your own."

As Sigurd ran lightly toward the pasture, many a head turned after him. His bright hair shone in the sun, and in spite of his great size, he moved with the grace of a deer. "What will become of him," thought the elders. "Surely there was never before a young man so handsome and strong."

Odin himself stood in the way near the pasture, watching the young runner approach. The god seemed an old man in tattered garments of gray which stirred, as if in a breeze, though the air was perfectly still. "Greetings," said he, fixing the youth with his one bright eye of blue. "Greetings, Sigurd. Why do you run?"

"To choose me a horse," panted Sigurd. "Are you the herdsman?"

> "SURELY THERE WAS NEVER BEFORE A YOUNG MAN SO HANDSOME AND STRONG."

"Do I look like a herdsman?"

"No. Like a warrior."

"You say well," said the god. "I am indeed a warrior, and I knew your father, Sigmund, all his days. Come with me, and let us test the strength of these horses by driving them through the stream."

The river was running in flood, for the snows had melted. Here at the head of the valley it came foaming down from the mountains with a roar. Sigurd and Odin collected the horses and drove them at a gallop down to the riverbank. Some wheeled to right or left when they saw the boiling water, and fled splashing along the shallows, whinnying with alarm. Some plunged full into the torrent, which carried them away, tossing, kicking, rolling, now under and now up. A few swam steadily, though these too were carried down. Only one great gray horse leapt far out into the water and made for the opposite bank. They saw him reach the shallows, climb up, and stand in the flowering meadow to shake his silvery sides. Finally with a snort he plunged back into the water to return.

"I gave your father a sword," said Odin as they watched the great creature breasting the flood. "Now I give you this horse. Ride out and win fame. When you come to the shield-roofed hall of Odin where your father sits, the heroes shall rise to greet you as the greatest one of them all. Look now how Grayfell stands in the shallows. He is of the tireless strain of Sleipner, the horse that Odin rides."

Sigurd leapt down into the water and swung himself onto Grayfell's back. Air whistled past them as they raced down the meadow. Drops sprayed from the mane of Grayfell. Turf flew up behind his heels. The two came thundering down the valley like an avalanche from the hills, huge horse and huge rider gleaming in the light of the evening sun.

---

2. **din** *n*.: noise.

"Who gave you that horse?" asked Regin when the young man slid off at his door.

"An old man with the wind in his garments and a single, bright blue eye. He spoke to me of my father."

"I know that old man," said Regin sourly. "He knew my father too. Why must he meddle now? But tell me, where will you ride with your fine horse?"

"Into the world."

"But whither? Will you serve some other king?"

"Never that!" cried Sigurd hotly. "I will win my own wealth and fame."

"I have an adventure for you," said Regin. "No man could achieve it till now. It is the winning of a fabulous treasure, enough to make both of us kings."

"What is the deed?"

"Come into the smithy," said Regin. "Blow up the fire, for my tale is long. Sit down by the bench while I tell you who I am, whence came the treasure, and where lies the hideous dragon who was my brother once. Kill him, for he is utterly evil, and take what you will. All I ask is the wisdom which he has stored in his heart for ages on ages, while I squandered[3] mine on men. Roast me the heart of the dragon, that I may eat, and be wise. Then take your fill of the treasure, and leave me what little you please."

Sigurd listened long to the tale of Reidmar and of the curse on Andvari's gold.[4] The fire grew low. The moon came up, as the quiet voice of Regin poured forth his long-stored hate. Each to the other in the darkness seemed only a vague, black shape, but the eyes of Regin gloated[5]

on Sigurd, who peered back at his master with a half-formed feeling of doubt. At last silence fell. Sigurd burned for adventure, but Regin burned for the gold. "I will slay the dragon," said Sigurd slowly. "But first, you must make me a sword."

"Get up and light me the torches," answered Regin. "I have made you a sword against this day. Open my chest there, and take it. All my skill went into the work."

Sigurd opened the chest by the wall and took out a gold-hilted sword. Down the dark blade ran strange signs of magic, and the hilt was studded with gems. He turned it over in his hands and scanned it, but the great blade had never a flaw. "Let us prove your skill, master of smiths," said he. With that, he swung it high and brought it down on the anvil with all his force. The blade broke with a fearful crash, and the point quivered past Regin's ear. Sigurd laughed at his master's frightened face as he threw the hilt on the floor. "I see this adventure is not for us, since your skill is too poor," he mocked.

"I will make you another," cried Regin. "This time it will never break, though you drive the anvil into the floor."

"When it is done, I will come back," said the hero, "but from this time on nobody is master to me."

It was many days later before Regin was ready. His eyes were red from peering into the fire, as they had been in the workshop of Reidmar. "Come into the smithy," said he. "I have your sword."

The sword lay on the bench dully shining. From hilt to point it was of bare steel unadorned. "Try this on the anvil," said Regin. "I am the master smith, and I tell you that if you break this, no steel that is forged on earth will serve your turn."

Again Sigurd lifted the sword. Again he swung it. Again he brought it down. There was a crack, and the shattered pieces lay strewn at

---

3. **squandered** *v.*: used wastefully or extravagantly.

4. **curse . . . gold:** Loki, the Norse fire god and master of cunning, forced the elf Andvari to give him all of his golden treasure hoard. Andvari placed a curse on his gold, saying that it would bring sorrow to anyone who owned it.

5. **gloated** *v.*: looked at with spiteful pleasure.

The forging of the sword Gram, from the Sigurd myth. Carved portal from the Hylestad church, Norway (12th century).

Sigurd's feet. Regin stood astonished, for even he had never suspected the young man's giant strength. Sigurd laughed. "You say truly," he cried. "No sword will serve my turn but one which was not forged in an earthly fire." He cast the pieces from him and strode out.

Queen Hiordis was in the dairy, where the women were making cheese. "Mother," said Sigurd coming to her as she carried a pail of whey. "Mother, where is my father's sword?"

Hiordis started, and a great splash of whey fell from the pan onto the dairy floor. "What need do you have of a sword?" asked she, putting her burden down.

"I am a man," said Sigurd, "and a mighty hero's son. This land is too quiet for me. I will go out and win fame."

"Before you were even born," said Hiordis, "I knew that this day would come. Two months after I was wed, great Sigmund fell, and with him my father and all the men of my house. I alone hid in a thicket so that the plundering

Viking pendant from Sweden.

hosts of the enemy passed me by. Then I crept into the moonlight and found where my father lay, and mighty Sigmund with the dead heaped up before him like a wall. In his hand was the hilt of the sword that Odin gave, but the pieces of the shattered blade lay shining around him on the grass. Then I foresaw this day and gathered them up to be your inheritance."

Hiordis went to her room and opened the chest where her clothes were always stored. There, under stiff mantles and robes of silver and blue lay a long piece of gold tissue with something heavy within.

"Your father was old when I wedded him," said she. "His sons had grown up, and won fame, and were dead. Then he wooed me, and I chose him gladly, for I thought, 'What woman will bear a greater hero than the wife of the most famous warrior alive?'"

"My stepfather is no warrior, however," remarked Sigurd.

"Alf is a good man and kind. This is a peaceful land, and I am happy here, but it is not the place for which you were born."

"That is true," said her son, "and I will say farewell, for when I go, I shall never return."

"Your fame will come back," she answered. "It will ring in my ears till I die." She gave him the sword, and he went down the stair and out over the flowering meadow. His mother watched him out of her window till the path hid him from sight.

Regin still sat in the smithy when Sigurd strode in and laid the bundle before him. "There is my sword," he said.

Regin opened the bundle and looked at the pieces, which glowed with a strange, pale light. "This was forged in heavenly fires," he said slowly, "and I am of the dwarf people. There is death to me in the steel."

"There is death to the dragon," replied Sigurd.

"Be it so. Leave me the pieces. I will remake the blade."

When Sigurd came again to the smithy, the great sword lay on the bench, and a pale light ran down the center from the hilt to the end of the blade. The edges, however, were dark and sharpened fine as a hair. Sigurd looked at the magic symbols which were carved in the steel. He fitted his hand to the jeweled hilt, and the sword stirred in his grip. He lifted it high and swung it. Suddenly he brought it down. With a crash the anvil fell shattered, while the blade sprung back unharmed. Then he cried, "I name this sword 'the Wrath of Sigurd.' No man shall feel it and live."

Regin said, "The long day is done. It is now a month that I have toiled for you. Tonight let us sleep. Tomorrow we will ride out against Fafnir, and the treasure shall be your own."

FAFNIR'S END

The hall of the dwarf king, Reidmar, no longer blazed in the sun. The gilt[6] had washed off its beams, the wide door was fallen from its hinges, and grass grew on the roof. "Look!" said Regin, pointing where a great track ran from the threshold[7] down to the riverbank. It was

---

6. **gilt** *n.*: thin covering of gold.
7. **threshold** *n.*: entrance; doorway.

ground through the dirt of the hillside to the depth of a tall man.

"That path must be made by Fafnir," said Sigurd, "and he uses it often, for no grass grows in it."

"Men say," answered Regin, "that the treasure still lies where my father piled it on the ground before his seat. Around it coils Fafnir, the serpent, gloating over it all day long. But when the moon shines down on him through the rents[8] in the ruined hall, he dreams of his youth, and the spring in the woodlands, and of the great gods he saw when the world was young. The gray morning wakens him early, and at that hour he loathes what he has become. He leaves his treasure and goes out to drink of the river, yet by dawn desire overcomes him once more, so that he returns to the gold."

"When he goes down the path in the morning before it is yet quite light, I will meet him and smite[9] him," said Sigurd.

"His scales are as tough as steel, and it does no good to strike unless you can kill at a blow. Wound him, and he will crush you as you might step on an ant."

"I will dig a pit in the pathway and crouch there in the dark. When he comes, his eyes will be on the river and his mind still full of his dreams. Perhaps he will not see where I lie. Then as he rolls over me, I will thrust up through his belly where the scales are not so strong. This way I may reach his heart."

"But if he sees you?"

Sigurd laughed. "You will wait another thousand years for a dragon slayer. That is all."

The moon was full and rose early. It took little time to dig the pit. Sigurd wrapped himself in his cloak and went to sleep while Regin stood on guard. He never stirred until Regin, weary of

watching, touched his shoulder and whispered, "Hush! It is time."

Overhead at the edge of the mountains, the sky was pale gray by now, but a river mist hung in the valley and clung to the grassy slope, so that low in the depths of Fafnir's track, it was still dark as the grave.

Sigurd crouched, his sword under his cloak, for he feared lest its gleam should be seen. No wind stirred in the trees by the river. A fox barked. The little clouds overhead turned white with the approach of day.

Something moved in the house. There was a scraping sound as though a log were being pushed over the floor. The scales of the monster rattled. A stone rolled down the track. The sounds came closer, and with them a strong, damp, musty smell. Sigurd saw through the thinning mist that a dark shape was filling the sunken pathway from side to side. The dawn was very close. He could see the huge head now almost on the edge of his hole. It was flat and scaly like a snake's, but the weary eyes were human, though of monstrous size. They stared straight through the gloom at Sigurd, whose grip tightened on his sword. For a moment the two seemed to look at each other, eye to eye, yet the monster moved on, dull and unseeing, heavy with sleep.

Black darkness rolled over Sigurd. Stench stifled[10] him. Loose earth filled up the pit. Inch by inch the creature slid over him. Sigurd shut his eyes, set his teeth, and waited. He dared not strike too soon.

After what seemed minutes, he thought, I must risk it now. With that he straightened his knees and drove the sword upward with all his force. It tore up through the cloak, through the loose earth, and on with the force of his arm

THE SCALES OF THE MONSTER RATTLED.

---

8. **rents** *n.*: holes; gaps.
9. **smite** *v.*: kill.

10. **stifled** *v.*: smothered; suffocated.

Sigurd roasting the dragon Fafnir's heart. Carved portal from the Hylestad church, Norway (12th century).

until it buried itself to the hilt. A great cry came from the monster. The echoing hills threw back and forth to each another a long succession of cries. Fafnir writhed. His huge body arched like a bow. Sigurd leapt from the pit. The tail lashed wildly after its slayer. Blood rolled down the track to the stream.

The sun was up behind the mountains, but the valley was still cold and gray. When the long death struggles were over, Regin crept from the bushes to look at the endless monster, the color of weathered stone. He gave a great sigh. "You have killed him," he said to Sigurd. "He was my brother once."

Sigurd laughed shortly. "It is late to think of that."

"Yet he was my brother, and you killed him. The fire which burned within me is quenched now in his blood. The long years of my waiting are over, the days of work and the endless wakeful nights. Now let me sleep for an hour, since I watched all this night for you. Kindle me a fire while I rest, and roast me Fafnir's heart. I will eat it and be wise, and after that, we will look on the ancient treasure which has waited so long for us."

"I will gladly do that," replied Sigurd. "You are old, and our journey was long."

Regin lay on the bank by the river. Sigurd lighted a fire in the glade.[11] He spitted[12] the monster's heart on a stick and thrust it into the flame. It hissed and crackled as he turned it from side to side. The sun came over the hills. Two woodpeckers sat in the trees calling to each other over his head. The meat blackened a little at the edges, and Sigurd thought it was nearly done. He put out his hand to turn it. It sputtered, and the hot fat seared[13] his finger.

Sigurd put his hand to his mouth. As he tasted the fat with his tongue, all kinds of knowledge leapt suddenly into his head. The birds still chattered in the trees. Sigurd heard the first one say, "See how the hero, Sigurd, sits roasting Fafnir's heart."

"He roasts it for Regin," answered the other. "Does he not know that the wisdom and strength of the dragon go to him who eats?"

"Sigurd needs no strength from Fafnir, and he cares nothing for the wisdom of the dwarfs."

"Regin cares, but he covets[14] the wisdom, and he needs the strength to slay."

"To slay?"

"Fool! To slay Sigurd. Is not Sigurd his tool to kill Fafnir? Is not his use over? Regin planned this murder when he first saw the dragon slayer as a child in his mother's arms."

Sigurd turned from the fire to look at Regin. For the first time he understood the master of cunning who had reared him to this end. He saw how the love of gold burned in Regin, who must kill lest he have to divide. He understood the cold dwarfs who knew neither conscience nor pity, and who despised mankind for feeling these things.

Regin opened his eyes. The two stared a moment, and the truth was open to each. Regin snatched at his belt for a dagger and leapt at the young man, who sprang up and away, fumbling for his long sword. The dwarf struck too soon, and his dagger whistled savagely through the air. Again he jumped, like a wildcat, but this time the sword met him halfway. He gave a great cry as it pierced him, and he dropped twisting on the grass.

Sigurd looked soberly down on the two evil brothers, great serpent and scheming dwarf. He left them on the grass by the river and turned up to the hill to the crumbling house which hid the treasure he had won. ■

---

11. **glade** *n.:* open space in a forest.
12. **spitted** *v.:* roasted on a thin, pointed rod or bar that is turned over a fire.
13. **seared** *v.:* burned the surface of.

---

14. **covets** *v.:* envies.

A Closer Look
THE NORSE GODS

ODIN (or **Woden**) is the leader of the Norse gods. His job is to keep the world safe from destruction for as long as he can. Odin knows that eventually he and his race of gods and all the world will perish at the hands of the Giants. Two wolves crouch at Odin's feet. Two ravens perch on his shoulders and each day bring him news from earth. Odin once went to the Well of Wisdom to beg for wisdom; he was granted the gift, but he had to pay for it with one eye. He lives in **Asgard,** the golden home of the gods. **Wednesday** is named for him.

Odin. Hand-colored engraving.

Frigga escorted by Valkyries in the sky. Lithograph.
© Bettmann/CORBIS.

FRIGGA (or **Frigg**) is the wife of Odin and the goddess of the clouds. Frigga can see into the future. (**Friday** is generally believed to be named for Frigga.)

THOR is the god of thunder, the eldest son of Odin. Thor protects humans from the dangerous Giants in the underworld. His main weapon is his mighty hammer, which returns on its own to Thor's iron-gloved hand after it is thrown. **Thursday** is named for Thor.

Viking amber figurine, possibly representing Thor.

Thor swinging his mighty hammer. Illustration by Arthur Rackham (c. 1900).

FREY and **FREYA**, brother and sister, are beloved gods. Frey is the god of weather and the harvest. Freya is the goddess of love and beauty. **Friday** is sometimes considered to be named after Freya.

Freya, the most lovely of the gods. Illustration by J. Doyle Penrose.

A romantic portrayal of Balder by B. Fogelberg. Marble statue (1840).

BALDER (or **Baldur**) is the beloved son of Frigga and Odin. Frigga tried to save Balder from the curse of death. She extracted promises from all living things not to harm Balder—except that she ignored the humble mistletoe. The tricky Loki, jealous of Balder, discovered that Frigga had forgotten to extract a promise from mistletoe. Loki arranged for a branch of mistletoe to kill the god. After Balder's death, grief and sadness came to Asgard.

The god Tiu losing his hand to Fenris, from a manuscript page.

LOKI is one of the evil Giants. He is a trickster and a schemer. The **GIANTS** are the enemies of all that is good.

FENRIS is a wolf, another of Loki's unpleasant brood of children. Fenris was chained at last by the god **TIU** (or **Tyr**), who was left with only one hand after Fenris attacked him. **Tuesday** is named for Tiu.

Loki bound to a rock in punishment for the death of Balder. Illustration by J. Doyle Penrose (c. 1870).

Meet the Writer

Olivia Coolidge

Storyteller and Teacher

Olivia Coolidge (1908–   ) grew up in the English countryside midway between London and Oxford in a somewhat Spartan household, with no car, gas, electricity, central heating, or even hot water. From an early age, as she made up fairy stories with her sister that they would tell each other in bed, she knew that she was interested in writing.

Coolidge grew up to become a teacher. After she came to the United States for a long visit in the 1930s, she decided to stay on, eventually marrying and raising four children here. Finally she began writing the stories that had always interested her:

66 Because my own childhood was different from most people's here, I got in the habit of telling stories to groups of children around a fire, sometimes about things I had read. During World War II, I was teaching, and at the same time I was learning about what American children read, and what they don't like to read, and what they are missing. After the war, like all of us, I had time for myself. The very first thing I did with it was to write a children's book. 99

Coolidge has written more than two dozen books, most of them for young readers. They include biographies of Abraham Lincoln and the Indian leader Mohandas K. Gandhi. She is probably best known, however, for her collections of myths and legends, including *Legends of the North,* her book of Norse myths.

For Independent Reading

You'll find more myths and hero stories in Olivia Coolidge's *Greek Myths* and *The Trojan War.*

Response and Analysis

Reading Check

1. To review the **plot** structure of this myth, fill out a story map like the one that follows:

Characters:
Setting:
Problems or conflicts:
Main events:
Climax:
Resolution:

2. What is Regin's **motive,** or reason, for taking Sigurd on as a pupil?

3. Why does Regin want the dragon's heart?

Thinking Critically

4. In Sigurd's story, as in Arthur's (page 645) and Theseus's (page 663), a sword plays an important role. What similarities and differences do you find in the roles a sword plays in each story?

5. In hero stories there is often a prophecy of the hero's destiny. What does Odin say about Sigurd's future? What prophecy does Hiordis make?

6. What **images** help you imagine what Fafnir looks, smells, and feels like? How does Fafnir's appearance and character contrast with Sigurd's?

7. Describe Fafnir's **setting**—the hall in which he lives. What details in the setting suggest decay?

8. Describe Sigurd's plan to kill Fafnir. Heroes often must descend into a dark underworld to fulfill their quest. In what ways is Sigurd in a kind of underworld as he awaits the dragon?

9. What accident saves Sigurd's life?

Literary Criticism

10. What details in the story tell you that Sigurd is a hero who is favored by the gods? Based on your answer, explain the qualities that the Norse seem to value in their heroes.

11. The Norse hero sagas are full of magic. What examples of magic can you find in Sigurd's story?

12. Edith Hamilton writes,

> Like the early Christians, the Norsemen measured their life by heroic standards. The Christian, however, looked forward to a heaven of eternal joy. The Norseman did not. But it would appear that for unknown centuries, until the Christian missionaries came, heroism was enough.

How is this outlook on life mirrored in the Sigurd myth?

WRITING

A Modern Monster

This storyteller uses vivid **imagery** to help us see and even smell the monster. Write a **description** of your own monster that might appear in a modern hero story. Decide what your monster will look like, smell like, feel like, sound like. What treasure trove will your monster guard? (Check your Quickwrite notes.)

LISTENING AND SPEAKING

A Tale to Tell

Research another Norse myth, and retell it in your own words to a small group. Try one of these myths: the death of Balder, the apples of Idun, part of the story of Beowulf. How will you use your voice to capture your audience's attention?

SKILLS FOCUS

Literary Skills
Analyze Norse myths.

Writing Skills
Write a description using vivid imagery.

Listening and Speaking Skills
Present an oral retelling of a myth.

Vocabulary Development

Words from Old Norse and Anglo-Saxon

The Vikings were highly skilled sailors and warriors from Scandinavia who raided the coasts of Europe and the British Isles from the eighth to the tenth centuries. They even sailed as far as the New World. Many everyday words (such as *freckle, guess, sky, skirt,* and *ugly*) came into English from Old Norse, courtesy of the Vikings. A few of those words are directly tied to the Old Norse myths, as are our names for several of the days of the week (see ***A Closer Look,*** page 684).

PRACTICE 1

Read the information in each item, and answer the questions. Use a college or unabridged dictionary to look up the **derivation,** or **etymology,** of the English words.

1. What common English word comes from the name of *Hela,* the Norse goddess of death and the underworld?

2. The English word *saga* comes from an Old Norse word that means "thing said; story or tale." What are some examples of the way we use the word *saga* today?

3. *Berserkers* were Norse warriors (real warriors, not mythical ones) who wore bearskins and were known for their great ferocity in battle. What does our modern expression *to go berserk* mean? What might cause someone to go berserk?

PRACTICE 2

As the chart at the right shows, some of our most basic English words come from the Anglo-Saxon tribes that invaded England during the fifth and sixth centuries. They were Germanic peoples from various parts of northern Europe, and their language, which we call Old English, had a lasting impact on English. Old English was spoken in England from about A.D. 450 to about 1100.

Use a college or unabridged dictionary to look up and list the original forms (labeled *OE*) of the following words from "Sigurd, the Dragon Slayer." Which words have changed most?

1. bird
2. blood
3. brother
4. dwarf
5. gold
6. grass
7. hill
8. moon
9. morning
10. sword
11. truth

Modern English Word	Old English Word
go	*gan*
fight	*feohtan*
sleep	*slæp*
eat	*etan*
father	*fæder*
mother	*modor*
land	*land*
house	*hus*
home	*hām*
water	*wæter*

SKILLS FOCUS

Vocabulary Skills
Understand and analyze words derived from Old Norse and Anglo-Saxon.

FICTION

Before the Minotaur

Mary Renault's mythical novel ***The King Must Die*** takes us through the boyhood and early life of the Greek hero Theseus, who would one day be famous for slaying the Minotaur. Bored with his uneventful life and filled with dreams of glory, young Theseus sets out on a journey to find his fate. He encounters a series of challenges beyond his expectations and returns to Athens a great hero.

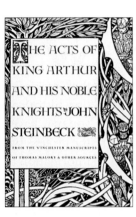

FICTION

Visiting Camelot

If you'd like to know more about the Arthurian legend, then John Steinbeck's ***The Acts of King Arthur and His Noble Knights*** is sure to please. Although this volume is focused on Arthur—older and more seasoned than he was when he first plucked the sword from the stone—it also features the adventures of such famous figures as Launcelot, Guinevere, and Gawain. John Steinbeck has converted their stories into clear, modern prose that opens the doors to the legendary city of Camelot.

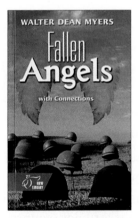

FICTION

Tour of Duty

Richie Parry wants nothing more than to attend college and become a great writer someday. When his hopes for college are dashed, he makes a choice that will define the rest of his life: He signs up to fight in the Vietnam War. Walter Dean Myers's novel ***Fallen Angels*** is the gritty story of an African American private who finds himself in an atmosphere of violence, prejudice, and fear—yet somehow manages to form lasting friendships through it all.

This title is available in the HRW Library.

NONFICTION

Vietnam Legacy

The Vietnam Veterans Memorial in Washington, D.C., is a place of remembrance for thousands of people who lost a loved one in the Vietnam War. Heartfelt letters, poems, and notes appear at the granite wall each year—some mourning a death, others celebrating a life. Journalist Laura Palmer tracked down the authors of these tributes and asked them to share more memories about the missing and the dead. The end product is ***Shrapnel in the Heart: Letters and Remembrances from the Vietnam Veterans Memorial,*** a moving book that gives faces and stories to the names engraved on the wall.

Writing a Research Paper

What is the historical background for Sigurd, the heroic character in Norse mythology? Why is Medea's nationality important in the Greek account of King Theseus? Is the figure of King Arthur based on a historical person? Finding the answers to these questions means you may have to dig for information—or do **research.** Doing research is the process by which you uncover treasures; that is, you unearth information that will help you answer complex questions like the ones above. Just as treasure hunters show off their finds, in this workshop you will also share your discoveries with others in a research paper.

Prewriting

Choose a Subject and Refine a Topic

When, What, or Who? The task—selecting a subject based on the historical or biographical background of a literary topic—at first may seem overwhelming, when you consider the amount of literature and history available. To help you find a direction for your investigation, consider the following areas for research.

- a historical event depicted in literature—for example, the Vietnam War used as background in a short story by Tim O'Brien

- a historical figure appearing in literature—such as Julius Caesar, dramatized in Shakespeare's *Julius Caesar*

- an author's interests as revealed through literature—for example, Emily Dickinson's interest in nature as shown in her poems

- the background of a piece of literature—such as a description of the Norse culture that created the myth of Sigurd

Scout It Out After you have selected an area for research, scout out possible subjects by browsing through your textbook, your school's library, or a bookstore. Skim newspapers and magazines for mention of connections between history and literature. Watch documentaries or films that explore biographical or historical connections between a piece of literature and the writer's world. Pick a search engine and search the Internet for key references to literature and history or biography. Then, choose a subject to research.

Survey the Landscape Once you've chosen a subject, get an overview of its possibilities by looking for the kinds of information available on it. Then, you can telescope in on a topic that you can manage. For example, one student who began with "King Arthur" as a possible subject narrowed her subject to the topic "the development of the legend of King Arthur." Here are some ideas for narrowing your broad subject to a more specific topic.

- **Read two or three general articles** about your subject in reference books such as encyclopedias. Notice headings and subheadings in the articles and consider using one of these as the topic of your paper.

- **Search the World Wide Web** for pages or sites containing key words related to your subject.

- **Look up your subject** in the *Readers' Guide to Periodical Literature* or in your library's card catalog or online catalog. Note the topics listed under subject headings.

- **Discuss your subject with someone** (a teacher or librarian, for example) who might have knowledge about it. See if your discussion gives you ideas for narrowing your subject.

Think About Purpose, Audience, and Tone

Setting Out on Your Mission . . . The basic **purpose** of a research paper is expository, or informational. As you research your topic, you'll uncover information and develop your own ideas about it. When you write your paper, you'll explain what you've learned.

As you plan your research, consider the needs and interests of your potential **audience**—your readers. To help your readers understand your topic, ask yourself, "What might my readers already know about the topic? How might I increase their understanding?" Make some notes about responses you could make to their questions. Keep in mind that your readers may already have some **expectations** about your topic, especially if you have chosen one as well known as King Arthur. If your research uncovers new ideas about the topic, you will want to address any **potential misunderstandings** that your readers may have.

Think also about your **tone**—your attitude toward your topic and readers. The typical research paper is formal in tone; that is, you'll use third-person pronouns, such as *he, she,* and *they,* to reflect your objective stance. You'll also avoid casual and informal language, such as slang, colloquial expressions, and contractions, to maintain a formal tone.

Develop Research Questions

Where Are You Going Next? Remember that a research paper should ask and answer good questions. Before you look for information on your topic, jot down some specific questions to explore. Working with a list of **research questions** will make it easier for you to sort through the information you find. Look at the following questions one student asked about her topic.

> • Who is the real King Arthur, and how did the stories about him develop?
> • Were the Knights of the Round Table real people? How did the Quest for the Holy Grail come to be a part of the story?
> • Have the stories about King Arthur always been the same, or have they changed?

Answer Research Questions

Looking for Answers The first step in finding information on your topic is knowing where to look. The following chart lists some library and community resources you can use to get started on your research investigation.

LIBRARY AND COMMUNITY RESOURCES	
Resource	**Source of Information**
Card catalog or online catalog	Books listed by title, author, and subject (most libraries also list audiovisual materials)
Readers' Guide to Periodical Literature or ***National Newspaper Index* (online and print versions)**	Subject and author index to magazine and journal articles; index to major newspapers
Microfilm or microfiche	Indexes to major newspapers such as *The LA Times*, back issues of newspapers and magazines
General reference books or CD-ROMs	Encyclopedias, encyclopedia yearbooks, dictionaries
Specialized reference books or CD-ROMs	Biographical reference sources, encyclopedias of special subjects, atlases, almanacs
Videotapes and audiotapes	Movies, documentaries, filmstrips, audiotapes of books
The librarian	Help in finding and using sources
World Wide Web and online services	Articles, interviews, bibliographies, pictures, videos, sound recordings
Museums and historical societies	Special exhibits, libraries and bookstores, experts on various subjects
Schools and colleges	Libraries, experts on various subjects

Finding Different Kinds of Answers The information you find in your resources may be either primary or secondary. A **primary source** is firsthand information, such as a historical document, a letter, a speech, or an oral history. A **secondary source** contains information derived from or about a primary source, such as an encyclopedia article, a documentary, or a history book. For example, the student researching King Arthur found primary source information in the various legends of King Arthur and secondary source information in books and articles about the legends.

Weighing Different Kinds of Answers Sometimes you'll have to judge the relative value and significance of information. To determine what information to include in your research, ask yourself, "Is the information from a *reliable* source? Is the information *relevant* to my limited topic? Is the information *recently* published?"

Record Information

Who Said What? Keeping track of all your sources is essential for giving credit within your paper as well as for preparing the *Works Cited* list that accompanies your final version. For each of the sources you find, record the author, title, publication information, and location on an index card (sometimes called a bibliography card) or sheet of paper or in a computer file. Then, assign each source a number. The following example shows how one student listed source information on an index card.

TIP The *Works Cited* list includes all the sources that you refer to in your paper; it allows readers a quick way to find out all the publication information about the specific sources.

③	source number
O'Neal, Michael. <u>King Arthur: Opposing Viewpoints.</u>	source
San Diego: Greenhaven Press, Inc., 1992.	
Public library	location
942.01/4	call number
One	first three letters of author's last name

The format for recording source information shown above and on the following pages is the one recommended by the **Modern Language Association of America (MLA)**. Your teacher may ask you to use a different format, such as that of the **American Psychological Association (APA)**. Be sure you know which format your teacher requires. Then, follow the style conventions of the required format for all your documentation.

SKILLS FOCUS

Writing Skills
Gather and record information.

Helpful Signs Along the Way Record information from your sources accurately—not only for yourself but also for your readers. If you have included complete information from your sources, then your readers will be able to do research into your topic themselves. The following guidelines tell you how to record information from different types of sources for a *Works Cited* list. Use this guide to help you complete your own *Works Cited* list.

GUIDELINES FOR RECORDING SOURCE INFORMATION

1. Source by One Author. Write the author's or editor's last name first (follow the names of editors with a comma and the abbreviation *ed.*); the title of the book; the place of publication; the publishing company's name; and the year of publication. (To make it easier to locate a book later, put its call number in the lower right-hand part of the index card, paper, or computer file.)

Day, David. <u>The Search for King Arthur</u>. New York: Facts on File, 1995.

2. Source by More Than One Author. For the first listed author, write the last name first. For all other authors, write the first name first. Then, follow the format for books with one author to complete the record.

Matthews, John, and Michael J. Stead. <u>King Arthur's Britain: A Photographic Odyssey</u>. New York: Sterling, 1995.

3. Magazine or Newspaper Article. Write the author's name (if given), last name first; the title of the article; the name of the magazine or newspaper; the day (if given), month, and year of publication; and page numbers on which the article begins and ends. For an article in a newspaper that has different editors or multiple sections, specify the editions (use *ed.*) or sections before the page number.

Menon, Shanti. "King Arthnou was here." <u>Discover</u>. Jan. 1999: 30.

4. Encyclopedia Article. Write the author's name (if given), last name first; the title of the article; the name of the encyclopedia; the edition (if given); and the year of publication. (Use the abbreviation *ed.* for *edition.*)

Reiss, Edmund. "Arthur, King." <u>The World Book Encyclopedia</u>. 2001 ed.

5. Radio or TV Program. Write the program title; the name of the network; the call letters and city of the local station (if any); and the broadcast date.

<u>ABC Nightly News</u>. ABC. KABC, Los Angeles. 14 June 2001.

6. Movie or Video Recording. Write the title of the work (and other pertinent information) and the director or producer's name (use *Dir.* for *Director* and *Prod.* for *Producer*); for movies, write the original distributor's name (for movies not available on video) and the year of release; for video recordings, write the word *Videocassette* or *Videodisc*, the distributor's name, and the year the video recording was released.

Le Morte D'Arthur: <u>The Legend of the King</u>. Great Books Ser. Dir. Dale Minor. Videocassette. Discovery Communications, 1993.

7. Interview. Write the interviewee's name, last name first; the type of interview (personal or telephone, for example); and the day, month, and year of the interview.

Morris, Sandy. Telephone interview. 22 June 2001.

8. CD-ROM. Write the author's name (if given), last name first; title (include print publisher, date, and page numbers if material was first in a print source); the term *CD-ROM;* city (if given); distributor; date of publication.

"Arthurian Legend." <u>Compton's Interactive Encyclopedia</u>. 1998 ed. CD-ROM. Compton's NewMedia, Inc. 1995.

9. Online Source. Write the author's name (if given), last name first; title of work; title of the site; volume number, issue number, or other identifying number; posting date; name of any institution or organization associated with the site; date of access; and Internet address.

Snell, Melissa. "The Truth of Arthur." <u>Medieval History</u>. 1999. About.com Inc. 21 June 2001 <http://historymedren.about.com/library/weekly/aa031099.htm>.

Words, Words, Words Begin gathering information by skimming a source. Look over the Table of Contents, or browse through the Index. Use self-adhesive notes or slips of paper to mark pages with answers to your research questions. Bookmark Web sites that look promising. Then, take notes using the following techniques.

DO THIS

- A **direct quotation** uses the author's exact words. Copy the material word for word, and put quotation marks around it.

- A **paraphrase** restates a passage from the source in your own words, with your own sentence structure. Your restatement is about the same length as the original.

- A **summary** is a highly condensed passage—usually one fourth to one third the length of the original—in which you record only the most important ideas from the source.

The following is an example of how one student practiced using the three techniques in taking notes from a passage in John Matthews and Michael J. Stead's book *King Arthur's Britain: A Photographic Odyssey.*

Direct quotation: "It is not possible to state, with any final certainty, whether or not such a person called Arthur ever lived. If he did, he most certainly was not a king, did not wear shining armour, and in all probability was not accompanied by a band of noble knights who sat together at a round table."

Paraphrase: Scholars don't know for sure whether Arthur was a real person, but they are almost positive that the real Arthur was not a king. He probably didn't even wear a suit of armor or go to battle with the Knights of the Round Table.

Summary: If a real Arthur did actually live, he probably was not the popular King Arthur most people think of today.

Card Collecting As you write down direct quotations, paraphrases, and summaries from your sources, you gather facts and details—the **evidence** that you will use as you begin to develop your ideas. To keep track of all the information you gather when you take notes, use a separate note card, sheet of paper, or computer file for each item of information. Make a heading at the top of the card by recording a key word or phrase about the information, and write down the source number. Write the direct quotation, paraphrase, or summary, and be sure to include the page number. The following shows a note card one student made about the Saxon invasions into Britain, events that led to Arthur's leadership.

source number	⑤
heading	Saxon invasions
text of note (paraphrase)	The Romans had been in control of Britain but left to fight in Europe. Once they left, Britain was an easy target for invaders called the Saxons. They came from what is now Germany.
page number	page 21

Analyze the Information

Weighing the Differences Now, analyze the information you've gathered. Begin by separating your note cards, using the headings to group all cards with similar information. As you sort through your research information, you may find that some sources disagree about issues or facts or that some of the information you've collected may be surprising to you and your readers. For example, the student writing about Arthur discovered that Arthur is not considered an exclusively English hero and that some scholars in fact disagree on whether Arthur was a real person.

To give an accurate picture of the complexity of your topic, follow these steps.

1. **Bring together—or** *synthesize***—all the information from the multiple sources you've consulted.** Look over your information, and compare the sources' interpretations of your topic. Look for ways that your sources agree on the facts and details of your research and for ways they disagree.

2. **Identify different interpretations about any significant points of your research.** Mentioning the differing points of view about your topic shows that you have been an objective investigator.

SKILLS FOCUS

Writing Skills
Take notes. Analyze information.

3. **Explain the importance of each interpretation.** In your explanation, you may offer your judgment about which interpretation seems most valuable or accurate to you. You should also explain why and how you arrived at that conclusion.

Write a Thesis Statement

What's It All About?   The thesis statement for a research paper states your main idea about your topic and lets your readers know what main points you plan to cover. You may first draft a preliminary thesis statement that acts as a guidepost, and then revise your thesis, perhaps more than once, as you continue shaping your paper. The writer who chose "the development of the legend of King Arthur" for a topic drafted this preliminary thesis statement based on her research findings.

> Legends about King Arthur developed because of history, story-tellers, and writers who changed the story.

Organize Your Ideas

In an Orderly Fashion   Review your notes, and divide them into different groups based on the headings of your note cards. Arrange the cards within each group according to your main idea and main points. Sorting your notes in this way helps you organize your main points and plan how you will support your thesis statement with your research and evidence. To show adequate development for each idea, use a coherent order by following one of the methods below or a combination of all three methods.

- **Chronological order** gives events in the order they happen.

- **Logical order** groups related ideas together.

- **Order of importance** begins with the most important detail and moves to the least important (or the reverse).

Sometimes you may need to include complicated material in your research paper. In order to maintain a coherent organization, consider using **visuals** such as charts, maps, and graphs in your paper to present information that is technical or complicated. Provide a key to explain any technical terms or notations on your visuals.

Where's the Map?   An outline is like a map for your research paper. It helps you see where your paper is headed and how you'll get there. A **formal outline** is divided into main points and subpoints, and is strictly balanced. Use the groups of cards that you have sorted as a basis for developing your outline. Look at the following example from an outline developed for a student's research paper on the legend of King Arthur.

SKILLS FOCUS

Writing Skills
Write a thesis statement.
Organize ideas.

TIP The outline shows that the third main point is "Key writers." That main point will include at least four paragraphs to cover the subpoints listed next to the capital letters.

III. Key writers
  A. Geoffrey of Monmouth
    1. Created <u>The History of the Kings of Britain</u>
    2. Established medieval time period for legend
  B. French writers
    1. Altered legend and translated into French (Robert Wace)
    2. Introduced chivalry and courtly love (Chrétien de Troyes)
  C. Cistercian monks
    1. Rearranged legend chronologically in <u>The Vulgate Cycle</u>
    2. Introduced Sir Galahad
  D. Sir Thomas Malory
    1. Changed legend again to focus on adventure
    2. Created epic masterpiece <u>Le Morte D'Arthur</u>

Credit Your Sources

Credit Where Credit Is Due   When you draft your essay, you need to give credit to any writer from whose work you have gathered specific information. The challenge is deciding when and how to do this. The following questions and answers should help you.

- **When?** Give credit for specific data (facts, dates, and so on), original ideas, opinions, insights, or any other information that you found in the work of another writer.

- **How?** Give credit within the body of your paper using MLA-style parenthetical citations, like those in the chart on the next page, unless your teacher gives you other directions.

Parenthetical citations are simply credits given within parentheses immediately following borrowed information. For example, the sentence below includes a parenthetical citation.

TIP Some teachers prefer **footnotes** (citations placed at the bottom of the same page on which they occur). Some prefer **endnotes** (citations identical to footnotes, but gathered at the end of the paper).

> The Saxon attacks, along with those of other invaders, devastated the civilization of Britain (Day 11–12).

You need to give only enough information in the parenthetical citation to enable the reader to find the full citation on the *Works Cited* page and to show exactly where in that source you found the information. (A *Works Cited* list that refers to books only is called a *Bibliography*.)

The chart on the next page provides specific guidelines for citing sources within your report, using MLA-style parenthetical citations.

SKILLS FOCUS

Writing Skills
Credit sources correctly.

GUIDELINES FOR GIVING CREDIT WITHIN A PAPER

Place the information in parentheses at the end of the sentence in which you used someone else's words or ideas.

1. **Source with one author.** Author's last name followed by page number(s). (Andronik 12)

2. **Sources by authors with the same last name.** First initial and last name of each author followed by page number(s). (J. Smith 38) and (L. Smith 72)

3. **Source with more than one author.** All authors' last names followed by page number(s). (Matthews and Stead 11)

4. **Source with no author given.** Title or a shortened form of it and page number(s). ("Arthur the King" 48)

5. **One-page source, unpaginated source, CD-ROM or online source, or article from an encyclopedia or other work arranged alphabetically.** Author's name only. If no author's name is given, title only. (Alexander)

6. **More than one source by the same author.** Author's last name and the title or shortened form of it followed by page number(s). (Ashe, "The Legend" 7; Ashe, "King Arthur" 23)

7. **Author's name given in paragraph.** Page number only. (144)

8. **Indirect source.** *Qtd. in* ("quoted in") before the source and page number. (qtd. in O'Neal 49)

Identifying Sources   You will list on a *Works Cited* page all those sources whose words or ideas you used in your paper. To prepare the *Works Cited* page, refer to the guidelines on pages 694–695 that you followed for preparing source cards. In addition, also use the following basic guidelines.

1. **Center the words *Works Cited*** one inch from the top. Use a separate sheet of paper for your *Works Cited* list.

2. **Follow the format** you used in listing the source on your source cards (page 693) for each entry on your *Works Cited* list.

3. **List your sources alphabetically** by authors' last names. If no author is given, alphabetize by the first important word in the title.

4. **Begin each listing at the left margin** and **indent all other lines** for the same listing one-half inch, or five spaces if you are using a computer. Remember to double-space each entry.

Writing Skills
Create a *Works Cited* list.

Integrate Direct Quotations into Your Paper

And I Quote . . . Using direct quotations in your research paper adds credibility to your writing. However, be sure to avoid using too many long quotations. If you overuse quotations, your paper will look like a cut-and-paste version of other authors' works. In the following example, one student experimented with various ways to weave quotations from Michael O'Neal's book *King Arthur: Opposing Viewpoints* into a paper.

- Use a phrase or a clause within the sentence and enclose it in quotation marks.

> O'Neal says the book was the "first organized version" of Arthur's life and victories (39).

- Include a short quotation (four lines or less) with your own words. Enclose the quotation within quotation marks.

> According to O'Neal, "Geoffrey devotes about one-fifth of his book to Arthur" (39).

- Set off a long quotation (more than four typed lines) by indenting each line ten spaces from the left margin, or one inch if you are using a computer. Introduce it in your own words, followed by a colon. Do not use quotation marks.

> The book <u>The History of the Kings of Britain</u> focuses extensively on Arthur:
>
>> Geoffrey devotes about one-fifth of his book to Arthur. In contrast to the piecemeal accounts of traveling storytellers, Geoffrey provides the first organized version of the story, giving it a beginning, middle, and end. Many of the elements found in later Arthurian legends, however, are missing (O'Neal 39).

SKILLS FOCUS

Writing Skills
Use conventions for citing direct quotations.

PRACTICE & APPLY 1   Use the information above to select a topic and research sources. Be sure to take notes and analyze the information. Then, write a thesis statement and develop an outline, organizing the information for a research paper.

Writing

Writing a Research Paper

A Writer's Framework		
Introduction	**Body**	**Conclusion**
• Create interest in your topic with an attention getter.	• Develop each main point from your outline with subpoints in separate body paragraphs.	• Summarize the main points of your research.
• Include a thesis statement that states your main idea about your topic and includes your main points.	• Support each main point and subpoint with facts and details in the form of direct quotations, paraphrases, and summaries.	• Restate your thesis in a new way.
• Indicate the order in which you will present your main points about the topic.	• Synthesize the different perspectives found in the research.	• Leave readers with an insight or a dramatic statement related to your topic.
• Include background information, if necessary.	• Integrate quotations and citations smoothly.	

A Writer's Model

A Legend Is Born

Stories of King Arthur and his glorious kingdom of Camelot have been enchanting listeners for over 1,000 years. Scholars still cannot agree, however, whether Arthur was a real person. Most scholars believe that if a real Arthur lived, "he most certainly was not a king, did not wear shining armour, and in all probability was not accompanied by a band of noble knights who sat together at a round table" (Matthews and Stead 11). Yet an elaborate and enduring legend developed around Arthur by the combination of a bit of history, a strong oral tradition, and writers who picked up and expanded the story.

The legend has many forms and variations, but the story that readers recognize tells of a young boy who pulls a sword from a stone, becomes king, forms a fellowship of knights known as the Round Table, and lives in a kingdom called Camelot with his queen Guinevere and his advisor, the wizard Merlin. Arthur's knights devote themselves to good deeds and to the quest of finding the Holy Grail. Trouble befalls the kingdom when one of Arthur's closest knights,

(continued)

INTRODUCTION
Attention getter

Direct quotation

Source with two authors

Thesis statement

Background information: Paraphrase

Summary

(continued)

Lancelot, falls in love with Guinevere and Arthur is betrayed by Mordred, his rebellious son. Betrayal of loyalty and trust destroy Camelot and its golden age in a great final battle between Arthur and Mordred (Alexander).

Online source
BODY
First main point: History

Source with one author

Summary

Discussion of different interpretations

Evaluating comment

Second main point: Oral tradition

Direct quotation

Author named in sentence

    The historical foundation for the Arthurian legend comes from the struggles of the people of Britain against first the Romans and then the Saxons. The Britons, as the people in Britain were known, came to appreciate the culture and protection that the Romans brought to their land during their long occupation (Andronik 5, 19). The Britons were from a race of Celtic people that had occupied the island of Britain for 1,000 years, but who in the first century A.D. thought of themselves as both Roman and Christian (Day 10). However, when the Roman soldiers began leaving Britain to fight for the Roman Empire in Europe, the Britons, or Celts as they were also called, were vulnerable to attack by Saxon invaders, who came from an area now called Germany (Andronik 21). The Saxon attacks, along with those of other invaders, devastated the civilization of Britain (Day 11–12).

    Desperate not to lose their way of life and their land, the Britons fought back, and in a decisive battle around 500 A.D. at Badon Hill, a military leader named Arthur—veteran of thirteen battles against the Saxons—led the Britons to victory. Their land and their culture had been saved, thanks to the military prowess of Arthur. The victory led to a period of peace (Alexander). Historians and writers disagree about how long the period of peace lasted. While writer David Day reports that this golden time lasted three decades (15), historian Michael O'Neal lists it as fifty years (32), and writer Caroline Alexander reports that it was forty. No matter how long it was, this time of peace meant the Britons were no longer under Roman rule nor under attack by invaders. For the Britons, "It was their heroic age and Arthur was their greatest hero" (Day 15).

    This tiny historical seed, which may or may not be accurate, was watered and nurtured by the oral tradition. Andronik points out that very few people could read or write during the time of the Dark Ages, roughly 400–800 A.D., but that "the oral tradition was very strong among the Celts" (5–6). When Britain finally succumbed to Anglo-Saxon rule, many Celts fled overland to Wales and overseas to Europe. There they told stories and sang songs for centuries about their great leader, Arthur (Alexander). O'Neal explains that as England and France came out of the Dark Ages, the aristocrats became hungry for learning and history (14). This hunger was satisfied by traveling storytellers, or minstrels, who told stories called "The Matter of Britain," which recapped Arthur's great victory and Britain's golden age (O'Neal 14–15). The oral tradition, however, is prone to exaggeration, so the stories about Arthur may have been changed by storytellers to please their listeners. New details, characters, and events no doubt crept into the story, and many versions of Arthur's deeds probably existed (O'Neal 16–17).

Despite his popularity, Arthur may have remained a minor hero of folklore if not for key writers who picked up and changed the legend. In 1135, the Welsh monk Geoffrey of Monmouth published <u>The History of the Kings of Britain</u>. He transformed Arthur into a king and included a full-length account of Arthur's life:

> Geoffrey devotes about one-fifth of his book to Arthur. In contrast to the piecemeal accounts of traveling storytellers, Geoffrey provides the first organized version of the story, giving it a beginning, middle, and end. Many of the elements found in later Arthurian legends, however, are missing (O'Neal 39).

Most scholars agree that Geoffrey's work is not real history, but "a bizarre combination of fact and fiction" (Day 39). The hand-lettered book, however, was a huge success similar to "an international best seller . . . that put Arthur on the map" (Alexander). O'Neal says the book also "established Arthur as a prominent historical figure," giving credibility to the portrayal of Arthur as a king (39).

Geoffrey's work also established an enduring framework by setting the time period for the Arthurian legend as medieval (Snell). Although the real Arthur would have lived and conquered in the Dark Ages—some 600 years before Geoffrey's history was written—Geoffrey portrays Arthur and his court using the monk's medieval culture of the twelfth century. Arthur is "usually imagined as living in the Middle Ages, and going around in castles with knights in armour and magnificently dressed ladies. But he certainly didn't," Arthurian expert Geoffrey Ashe explains ("A Conversation"). Geoffrey of Monmouth was simply following the practice of many medieval writers, who updated settings and customs in their works ("A Conversation"). Despite its inaccuracy, the medieval setting remained a central part of Arthurian legend.

French writers expanded the legend next, transforming Geoffrey's history into romances about knights in shining armor. Many of these changes were made to please an aristocratic female audience who dominated the courts of Europe (Day 113–114). The

Third main point: Key writers

Long quotation

Source with no author given

(continued)

(continued)

French poet Robert Wace translated Geoffrey's book into French and altered the original story (White xvii). According to O'Neal, Wace made his stories less violent and emphasized the pageantry of Arthur's court to appeal to the British queen Eleanor, who was French by birth (51). Even more significant, he introduced the Round Table, which immediately became a central part of Arthurian stories (White xvii; O'Neal 51).

The French poet Chrétien de Troyes made even more changes to the legend by writing romances that focused on chivalry and courtly love. Arthur became more interested in courtly pursuits than in fighting battles. In addition, the focus shifted to the Knights of the Round Table and their adventures, loves, and quests (White xviii). Chrétien's knight was "well-mannered, well-spoken, educated, generous, brave, gifted as an artist and musician, courteous and above all, without equal in battle" (Day 114). Chrétien's stories of courtly love and Arthur's knights with their "elaborate conventions of courtly love—the hidden messages, the midnight meetings, the violent emotions—provided a romantic escape" for Chrétien's patroness, Countess Marie, and her female companions (O'Neal 59–60). Chrétien's wildly popular romances produced three lasting additions to the legend: the love affair between Lancelot and Guinevere, Camelot, and the Quest for the Holy Grail (White xix, xx, 162). Although Chrétien introduced the Holy Grail, he did not say specifically what it was. That was left to another French writer, Robert De Boron, who described the Grail as the cup used by Christ during the Last Supper (O'Neal 76, 80).

The next evolution in the legend came when the French romances changed back into historical works, but this time with "a serious religious purpose" (Conlee). A group of Cistercian monks collected and arranged all the stories about Arthur and his knights into a chronological history, titled The Vulgate Cycle. The stories focus heavily on the Quest for the Holy Grail and "a great effort is made to bestow upon the events of the Arthur story a fundamentally religious purpose" (Conlee). The Vulgate Cycle introduced the knight Sir Galahad, reinforced the Christian symbolism of the Grail, and would serve as the basis for Sir Thomas Malory to create his masterpiece, Le Morte d'Arthur (Matthews and Stead 107).

Thomas Malory took the vast jumble of stories in The Vulgate Cycle and peeled away everything that made the stories hard to understand (Matthews and Stead 107). He rearranged the events,

Information found in two sources

Summary

Paraphrase

focused on the drama and action, added realistic dialogue, and cut religious commentary that took away from the adventure and characters of the story (Matthews, <u>Le Morte</u> xvii). The result was an epic masterpiece that would ensure Arthur's popularity for centuries and serve as the "basis for all the modern versions of the story" (Andronik 12). Good timing also played a part in the success of <u>Le Morte d'Arthur</u>. The printing press was a new invention, and the English printer William Caxton published it in 1485, making it "one of the first printed secular books in the English language" (Day 143).

Author of more than one source

Over five hundred years after <u>Le Morte d'Arthur</u> was published, King Arthur and his legends remain popular. Malory's work inspired other great works by literary giants in both England and the United States, including Alfred Lord Tennyson, Sir Walter Scott, William Wordsworth, Henry Wadsworth Longfellow, Mark Twain, and T. S. Eliot (Day 163). Just as writers have done through the centuries, filmmakers have also found find new ways to portray Arthur and his kingdom. He is spoofed in <u>Monty Python and the Holy Grail</u>, romanticized in the Broadway musical and film <u>Camelot</u>, and transformed into a space cowboy in the form of Luke Skywalker in <u>Star Wars</u> (<u>Le Morte</u>). Day points out that Luke's mentor Obi-wan Kenobe is a Merlin-inspired character (60).

Videocassette

CONCLUSION
Restatement of thesis

The enduring appeal of Arthurian legend highlights both the adaptability and timelessness of the legend. Tracing the evolution of the legend shows the way the story was easily adapted and changed to fit the time, interests, and ideals of the tellers and listeners. Despite the changes, however, the basic story maintained its universal appeal by portraying the timeless themes of love, loyalty, loss, commitment to lofty ideals, and the frailty of human nature. Richard Barber says that in many ways the Arthurian legend has replaced classical myths for modern writers and readers (3). The names Arthur, Guinevere, Lancelot, and Merlin are "as familiar in our literature as the gods of ancient Greece" (Barber 3). Whatever his form and however his story is cast, King Arthur has certainly proven that he "is truly a hero for all ages" (Day 157). Long live the King!

Summarizing statement

Final insight

TIP Research papers and their *Works Cited* lists are normally double-spaced. Because of limited space on these pages, A Writer's Model is single-spaced. To see a double-spaced version of a paper, go to go.hrw.com.

Works Cited

Alexander, Caroline. "A Pilgrim's Search for Relics of the Once and Future King." <u>Smithsonian</u> Feb. 1996: 32–41. <u>MasterFILE Elite</u>. EBSCOhost. Long Beach Public Library, Long Beach, CA. 28 May 2001.

Andronik, Catherine M. <u>Quest for a King: Searching for the Real King Arthur</u>. New York: Atheneum, 1989.

Barber, Richard. <u>The Arthurian Legends: An Illustrated Anthology</u>. New York: Dorset Press, 1985.

Conlee, John, ed. "Prose Merlin: Introduction." <u>Prose Merlin</u>. Kalamazoo, Michigan: Western Michigan University for TEAMS, 1998. <u>TEAMS Middle English Texts</u>. Ed. Russell Peck. The Medieval Institute at Western Michigan University. 20 June 2001 <http://www.lib.rochester.edu/camelot/teams/pmint.htm>.

"A Conversation with Geoffrey Ashe." <u>Britannia</u>. 23 May 2001 <http://www.britannia.com/history/arthur1html>.

Day, David. <u>The Search for King Arthur</u>. New York: Facts on File, 1995.

<u>*Le Morte D'Arthur:* The Legend of the King</u>. Great Books Ser. Dir. Dale Minor. Videocassette. Discovery Communications, 1993.

Matthews, John, ed. <u>Le Morte D'Arthur</u>. By Thomas Malory. New York: Sterling, 2000. xvi–xx.

Matthews, John, and Michael J. Stead. <u>King Arthur's Britain: A Photographic Odyssey</u>. New York: Sterling, 1995.

O'Neal, Michael. <u>King Arthur: Opposing Viewpoints</u>. San Diego: Greenhaven Press, Inc., 1992.

Snell, Melissa. "The Truth of Arthur." <u>Medieval History</u>. 1999. About.com Inc. 21 June 2001 <http://historymedren.about.com/library/weekly/aa031099.htm>.

White, Richard, ed. <u>King Arthur: In Legend and History</u>. New York: Routledge, 1998.

INTERNET

More Writer's Models

Keyword: LE5 10-9

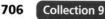

PRACTICE & APPLY 2 Use the Writer's Framework and the Writer's Model as guides to draft your research paper. Remember to include a thesis statement and develop each main idea with evidence from primary and secondary sources.

Revising

Evaluate and Revise Your Draft

Read and Read Again You might think at this point in the writing process that you've been shuffling information from pile to pile and from paragraph to paragraph. You probably need to step back and let your paper rest a day, if possible, so that you can look at it again with new insight. After all, you've made a great effort to be accurate in your research. Now check for accuracy in your writing. To make sure that your efforts show themselves in the best light, read your draft at least twice. The first time, focus on content and organization. The second time, concentrate on style.

PEER REVIEW

Exchange research papers with a classmate. Each of you should check to make sure that parenthetical citations document all direct quotations, paraphrases, and summaries.

▶ **First Reading: Content and Organization** Use the guidelines below to help you examine the content and organization of your research paper. If you need help in answering the questions in the left-hand column, use the tips in the middle column. Then, make revisions by following the revision techniques suggested in the right-hand column.

Rubric: Writing a Research Paper

Evaluation Questions	▶ Tips	▶ Revision Techniques
1 Does the introduction create interest in the topic? Does it include a clear thesis statement and the main points the paper covers?	▶ **Bracket** the sentence(s) that may interest the reader. **Underline** the thesis statement. **Double underline** the main points.	▶ **Add** an interesting opening sentence. **Add** a clear thesis statement. **Elaborate** by stating which main points the research paper covers.
2 Does the body of the paper develop each main point included in the thesis statement?	▶ **Number** in the margin of the paper each main point that develops the thesis.	▶ **Add** main points by using your own ideas or information from your sources.
3 Does the paper use direct quotations, paraphrases, or summaries to support each main point and subpoint?	▶ **Write** *DQ, P,* or *S* in the margin to identify the kinds of information used as supporting evidence.	▶ **Elaborate** on each point by adding direct quotations, paraphrases, or summaries from your sources.
4 Do parenthetical citations document source information within sentences or paragraphs?	▶ **Highlight** the information inside parentheses. **Draw an arrow** to the information it documents.	▶ **Add** parenthetical citations for any information requiring documentation.
5 Does the conclusion summarize the research, restate the paper's thesis, and include a final insight?	▶ **Draw a wavy line** under the summary of the research. **Circle** the restatement of the thesis. **Star** the final insight.	▶ **Add** a summary of the research, a restatement of thesis, or a final insight if any of these is missing.

Second Reading: Style Sometimes in writing a long research paper, you may find that your sentences begin to have the same short and choppy pattern. To make your ideas flow smoothly and increase sentence variety, look for short, choppy sentences that could be combined into **complex sentences.** For example, you may add words such as *after, as, because, that,* and *when* to the beginning of a short sentence and combine it with other short sentences to form a complex sentence.

Style Guidelines

Evaluation Question	▶ Tip	▶ Revision Technique
● Does the paper use several short, choppy sentences in a row?	▶ **Highlight** any short sentences. **Bracket** any two or three sentences that could be combined into a complex sentence.	▶ **Combine** short sentences into complex sentences to make sure that the ideas flow smoothly from one another.

ANALYZING THE REVISION PROCESS
Study these revisions, and answer the questions that follow.

add   *While*
         ∧Writer David Day reports that this golden time lasted

add, combine   *(15),*   *(32), and*
         three decades, Historian Michael O'Neal lists it as fifty years∧

add   *No matter how long*
         Writer Caroline Alexander reports that it was forty.∧
         it was, this time of peace meant the Britons were no longer
         under Roman rule nor under attack by invaders.

Responding to the Revision Process

1. Why did the writer combine the three sentences? What is the effect of this change?

2. What information did the writer add in parentheses? Why is the information important?

3. Why do you think the writer added information to the end of this passage?

SKILLS FOCUS

Writing Skills
Revise for content and style.

PRACTICE & APPLY 3 Revise the content and organization of your research paper, using the guidelines on page 707. Then, use the guidelines above to see whether you need to combine choppy sentences into longer, complex ones.

Publishing

Proofread and Publish Your Paper

Perfect It   When the Cistercian monks were hand copying the legends of King Arthur into *The Vulgate Cycle,* they probably made a mistake or two in the transcriptions. You, however, are doing more than rote copying, and your final paper should be worthy of all the time you have spent researching and writing. Before you submit your final copy, proofread your paper, checking for errors in grammar, spelling, and mechanics.

Spread the Word   After all your research, you probably are a local authority on your topic. Don't let all that work go to waste. Instead, share the results of your research with an audience, perhaps using one of the following suggestions.

- Present the results of your research to your classmates in an oral report.

- Ask a media specialist in your school if you can set up a multimedia display, showcasing the results of your research about literature.

- Find a Web site dedicated to information about literature, and ask permission to create a hyperlink to a Web publication of your research paper.

- Submit a portion of your paper to your school's literary magazine for possible publication.

- Dress as the subject of your research paper or in a costume appropriate to that time period for your literature class. In small groups, or on a panel, discuss the information you have learned.

Reflect on Your Paper

Learning from Experience   You are nearing the end of a complex project requiring persistence and skill. Reflect on your experience with the research paper by answering the following questions.

- How did researching and writing about your topic affect your understanding of the literature on which it was based?

- How did researching and writing about your topic affect your understanding of the time period you chose?

- What advice would you give a student a year or two younger than you about the process you used for this kind of research paper?

PRACTICE & APPLY 4   Using the guidelines on this page, proofread, publish, and reflect on your research paper. Make sure that your parenthetical citations and your *Works Cited* list adhere to the required format.

 TIP   Proofreading will help ensure that your paper follows the **conventions** of standard American English. Correct any dangling modifiers—modifiers that do not clearly and sensibly modify a group of words in a sentence. For more on **dangling modifiers,** see Placement of Modifiers, 5h, in the Language Handbook.

 SKILLS FOCUS

Writing Skills
Proofread, especially for correct use of modifiers.

Presenting Research

A research paper can be a complex, lengthy essay, filled with documentation. Reading a 1,500-word research paper aloud to your classmates would be a time-consuming activity, and the depth of your research might be lost on an audience with flagging interest. To adapt your research paper for an oral presentation, use the strategies in this workshop.

Adapt Your Research Paper

Your Listening Audience Generally, the **purpose** of both a written and an oral presentation of research is the same—expository, or informational. Unlike your reading audience, your listening **audience** may be your classmates, who probably have not read your research paper. Therefore, skim through your research paper and highlight any information that you think will be important to convey at the beginning of the oral presentation. Remember to catch your listening audience's attention early with an opening gambit—a clever anecdote, wise saying, or sage quote from your research.

TIP Remember to address briefly your audience's **expectations** or **misunderstandings** at the beginning of your oral presentation.

Simplify, Simplify, Simplify If you had world enough and time, presenting all the results of your research to your classmates could be sublime. However, you probably will find it necessary to limit your paper's range. Use the following suggestions about the elements of your research paper to help you make adjustments.

Thesis Statement Re-examine your thesis statement. Select the most important and most interesting main points from your thesis statement to guide you as you adapt the rest of your research paper.

Main Points Develop only one or two main points for your oral presentation, although you may briefly refer to other aspects of your topic. To supplement your presentation of your main points, to highlight the complexity of your additional research, or to convey additional information while you are speaking, consider using **visuals,** such as maps, pictures, photographs, or video clips; **graphics,** such as charts, outlines, or carefully drawn posters; or **electronic media,** such as a computer-generated presentation.

SKILLS FOCUS

Listening and Speaking Skills
Adapt a research paper for oral presentation.

Evidence For your oral presentation, include the most important supporting evidence for each of the main points you have selected. Review your written research to determine the **relative value and significance** of your evidence. Ask yourself, "What evidence is necessary to support this main point?"

Primary and Secondary Sources When you select evidence to support your main points, use information from both primary and secondary sources. Since your presentation will not include a *Works Cited* list, tell your audience your sources within the text of your speech. Be **accurate** by correctly citing the author and source, and be **coherent** by inserting the source information into your text either directly before or after your evidence as in the following example.

TIP Refer to your sources in your written research paper to double-check that any **technical terms** or **notations**—documented sources of information—that you use for your speech are accurate.

Written version	For the Britons, "It was their heroic age and Arthur was their greatest hero" (Day 15).
Spoken version	In <u>The Search for King Arthur</u>, writer David Day writes about the Britons, "It was their heroic age and Arthur was their greatest hero."

Finally, Then The last thing you say is probably what your audience will remember most. Review the conclusion in your written research paper. Plan to restate your thesis and end your oral presentation with a dramatic turn of phrase.

Off the Cuff You will deliver an **extemporaneous** speech—that is, a speech outlined and rehearsed, but not memorized. To help you sound natural, use note cards. Put one main point, possibly accompanied by a brief example or detail, on each card. Use colored cards for any special material you plan to read word for word, such as a quotation. Arrange your cards in a logical organizational pattern to help your audience follow your ideas.

Deliver Your Presentation

Sounds and Silence Use standard American English in your presentation. To enhance your delivery further, use a combination of the following **verbal** and **nonverbal techniques.** Speak slowly, clearly, distinctly, and loudly enough to be heard by the people in the back of the room. Emphasize important words or phrases by pausing after them. Finally, look directly at the audience, occasionally glancing at your notes to prompt your memory or to read a quotation.

Getting a Second Opinion Rehearse your oral presentation before a family member, friend, or teacher. Then, respectfully **interview** the person about your performance. Ask questions about your performance, such as "Was the source citation clear in my oral presentation?" Take notes on the responses. Compile the information and use it to adjust your oral presentation, according to the suggestions.

PRACTICE & APPLY 5 Use the instruction above to adapt your research paper for an oral presentation. Rehearse your presentation, using note cards. Deliver your polished presentation to an audience.

SKILLS FOCUS

Listening and Speaking Skills
Deliver your presentation using verbal and nonverbal techniques.

Using Primary and Secondary Sources

DIRECTIONS: Read the following excerpts from a variety of primary and secondary sources. Then, read and respond to the questions that follow.

The Media and the War

Paul Boyer

By the end of 1967 more than 16,000 Americans had been killed in Vietnam. Thousands more had been injured or disabled. Despite the government's optimistic forecasts, a U.S. victory seemed increasingly distant. American television news programs showed gruesome images of terrified Vietnamese civilians and dead or injured soldiers. Some Americans responded by demanding that the military be allowed to do whatever it took to win. Others wanted the United States to pull out of Vietnam.

The Vietnam War invaded American homes in a way that no previous conflict had. During previous wars the military had imposed tight press restrictions. In this war, reporters, photographers, and TV camera crews accompanied soldiers on patrol and interviewed people throughout South Vietnam. Television beamed footage and reports of the war into people's homes on a nightly basis. As a result, Americans saw images that seemed to contradict the government's reports.

Reporters such as David Halberstam of *The New York Times* and Neil Sheehan of United Press International criticized the government's optimism. As early as 1962 they argued that the war could not be won as long as the United States supported the unpopular and corrupt regime[1] of Ngo Dinh Diem. Journalists also reported on the ineffectiveness of South Vietnam's troops and accused the U.S. government of inflating[2] enemy body counts to give the appearance of progress.

As the gap between official government reports and media accounts grew wider, doubts at home increased. The administration found itself criticized by both **doves**—people who opposed the war—and **hawks**—people who supported the war's goals. Hawks criticized the way the war was being fought. They argued for more U.S. troops and heavier bombing. Air Force General Curtis LeMay expressed the frustration of many hawks. "Here we are at the height of our power. The most powerful nation in the world. And yet we're afraid to use that power."

---

1. **regime** (rə·zhēm′) *n.*: government; rule.
2. **inflating** *v.* used as *n.*: increasing beyond what is accurate.

Pages 712–715 cover
Reading Skills
Analyze primary and secondary sources.

Doves opposed the war for many reasons. Pacifists[3] such as Martin Luther King, Jr., believed that all war was wrong. Some doves, such as diplomat George Kennan, were convinced that Vietnam was not crucial to national security. Others feared that the United States might use nuclear weapons. Pediatrician and author Dr. Benjamin Spock and others argued that the United States was fighting against the wishes of a majority of Vietnamese.

—from *The American Nation*
(history textbook)

_____

3. **pacifists** (pas′ə·fists′) *n.:* people who oppose war for moral reasons.

from The Vietnam War: An Eyewitness History
edited by Sanford Wexler

JOHN M. G. BROWN

Thanks a lot for the Christmas presents. They were great. Yesterday I went up Thunder Road on a guarded truck convoy to see the Bob Hope USO Christmas show. It was really a good time and very moving. One of the girls started crying while she was singing "Silent Night" to us and got interrupted by a barrage of artillery going off nearby. If you see pictures of it, I'll be sitting just to the left of two tanks with "Merry Christmas" painted on them.

—Pfc. John M. G. Brown, U.S.A., First Aviation Battalion
from a **letter** to his family of December 25, 1967,
from *Rice Paddy Grunt* (1986)

DICKEY CHAPPELLE

As I fell into the hypnotic rhythm of the patrol—we were moving between trees and cane fields, stepping high so we would not trip and clatter on the uneven ground—I was obsessed by a question that had plagued me on other walks in other wars: Why?

Why was it that humans still got along so badly that conflicts were settled like this, by young men betting their lives at hide-and-seek? Did I truly think I could, with the camera around my neck, help end the need for the carbine[1] on my shoulder? Did I think I could make plain how warring really was, how quickly the cutting edge of fear excised[2] every human virtue, leaving only the need to live? Here, now, the supreme virtue was the ability to shoot fast. Or first.

> —Dickey Chappelle, journalist with a U.S. and Vietnamese River Assault Group in the Mekong Delta in 1965, **eyewitness account** in *National Geographic,* February 1966 [Chappelle, who died on November 4, 1965, was the first American correspondent to be killed in action in South Vietnam.]

DU LUC

For the third time my life turned to war again. For the liberation of our compatriots[3] in the south, a situation of boiling oil and burning fire is necessary! A situation in which husband is separated from wife, father from son, brother from brother is necessary. Now, my life is full of hardship. Not enough rice to eat, not enough salt to give taste to my tongue, not enough clothing to keep myself warm. But, in my heart, I keep loyal to the [Communist] Party and to the people.

> —Du Luc, Vietcong soldier **diary entry** of December 1960, from *Time,* December 15, 1961

RON KOVIC

In one big bang they have taken it all from me, in one clean sweep, and now I am in this place around all the others like me, and though I keep trying not to feel sorry for myself, I want to cry. There is no shortcut around this thing. It is too soon to die even for a man who has died once already.

I try to keep telling myself it is good to still be alive, to be back home. I remember thinking on the ambulance ride to the hospital that this was the Bronx, the place where Yankee Stadium was, where Mickey Mantle played. I think I realized then also that my feet would never touch the stadium grass; I would never play a game in that place.

> —Sgt. Ron Kovic, U.S.M.C., on being severely wounded in action in 1967, from his **autobiography,** *Born on the Fourth of July* (1976)

---

1. **carbine** (kär′bīn′) *n.*: light semiautomatic or automatic rifle.
2. **excised** (ek·sīzd′) *v.*: cut out, as if surgically removed.
3. **compatriots** (kəm·pā′trē·əts) *n.*: citizens of one's own country.

1. Which of these informational readings is a **secondary source**?
   - A   The textbook excerpt "The Media and the War"
   - B   Du Luc's diary entry
   - C   The excerpt from Ron Kovic's autobiography
   - D   John M. G. Brown's letter

2. The writer's **purpose** in the excerpts by Du Luc, Ron Kovic, and Dickey Chappelle is to —
   - F   express strong personal feelings
   - G   give detailed information about combat
   - H   persuade the reader to support the war
   - J   persuade the reader to oppose the war

3. "The Media and the War" presents information that helps us to understand —
   - A   the reasons for U.S. involvement in the war
   - B   the U.S. military strategy for the war
   - C   the reasons for Americans' antiwar feelings
   - D   the history of Vietnam before the war

4. Which writer's source would be *most* useful in researching the war as seen from the Vietnamese point of view?
   - F   Ron Kovic
   - G   Du Luc
   - H   Dickey Chappelle
   - J   The textbook writer, Paul Boyer

5. The sources by John M. G. Brown, Du Luc, and Ron Kovic are *alike* in that they —
   - A   are antiwar
   - B   strongly support the war

   - C   are based on other sources of information
   - D   provide an eyewitness point of view

6. What kind of source would you expect to provide the *most* objective reporting about the war?
   - F   An autobiography
   - G   A newspaper or magazine article
   - H   A diary entry
   - J   A letter home

7. The two texts that are private and personal (that the writers never intended to publish) are the ones by John M. G. Brown and —
   - A   the textbook writer, Paul Boyer
   - B   Du Luc
   - C   Ron Kovic
   - D   Dickey Chappelle

8. The writer who expresses despair over humankind's seeming dependence on war and the fate of humankind is —
   - F   Dickey Chappelle
   - G   Du Luc
   - H   Ron Kovic
   - J   the textbook writer, Paul Boyer

Constructed Response

9. Explain three major differences between primary and secondary sources.

Collection 9: Skills Review

Vocabulary Skills

Test Practice

Context Clues

DIRECTIONS: Use context clues to help you choose the answer that gives the best definition for the underlined word.

1. They <u>skirted</u> a sleeping village so that no one would be alerted to their presence.
   Skirted means —
   - **A** went directly through
   - **B** went around
   - **C** defended
   - **D** went in the opposite direction of

2. The telegram would say that he died <u>valiantly</u> while dutifully defending his country.
   Valiantly means —
   - **F** comically
   - **G** unexpectedly
   - **H** mistakenly
   - **J** bravely

3. To ease his fear, the men offered Billy words of <u>consolation</u>, but nothing could calm him.
   Consolation means —
   - **A** anger
   - **B** love
   - **C** comfort
   - **D** warning

4. The <u>realm</u> of Britain was in danger until a new king could be placed on the throne.
   Realm means —
   - **F** economy
   - **G** stability
   - **H** church
   - **J** kingdom

5. Sir Kay made an <u>oath</u> to tell the truth.
   Oath means —
   - **A** test
   - **B** promise
   - **C** curse
   - **D** opportunity

6. The commoners kept up their loud, <u>tumultuous</u> cry of protest when the nobles disputed Arthur's right to be king of Britain.
   Tumultuous means —
   - **F** sad and tearful
   - **G** extremely brief
   - **H** noisy and wild
   - **J** weak and uncertain

7. The knights challenging Launcelot at the tournament found him to be a powerful <u>adversary</u>.
   Adversary means —
   - **A** negotiator
   - **B** opponent
   - **C** personality
   - **D** friend

8. During the tournament, Sir Gahalantyne was no match for Launcelot's increasing <u>wrath</u>.
   Wrath means —
   - **F** anger
   - **G** fear
   - **H** attention
   - **J** pity

SKILLS FOCUS

Vocabulary Skills
Use context clues.

Test Practice

DIRECTIONS: Read the following paragraph from a draft of a student's research paper. Then, read the questions below it. Choose the best answer to each question, and mark your answers on your own paper.

(1) Senator at age thirty-two, Julius Caesar was a historical figure who accomplished many things. (2) Known as "one of Rome's greatest generals and statesmen," Caesar used his brilliant leadership and "helped make Rome the center of an empire that stretched across Europe." (3) After studying oratory—the art of making speeches—in Greece, Caesar worked his way up through various political positions. (4) He first became the quaestor of Spain, then the aedile of Rome, then the pontifex maximus under the Consul (McGill 51). (5) Caesar was assassinated on March 15, 44 B.C. (6) Caesar's sharp political instincts greatly advanced his economic and military power, allowing him to become the sole dictator of Rome in 44 B.C. (McGill 52).

1. Which of the following sentences based on a secondary source could the student add to support the thesis?
   A Caesar was captured by pirates on his way to study in Greece (McGill 51).
   B Caesar's marriage to Cornelia, against the wishes of his family, put his career at risk (Duggan 36).
   C Caesar had a secret alliance with the First Triumvirate (McGill 52).
   D Caesar won military prestige, losing only two battles in nine years (Gruen 12).

2. What should the student do to give credit for the quotations in sentence 2?
   F omit the quotation marks since they are unnecessary
   G use appropriate documentation in the text and in the *Works Cited* list
   H expand the quotation to include the entire sentence from the source
   J cite the source in the text but do not include it in the *Works Cited* list

3. To make sentence 4 more understandable for the reader, the student could
   A define the technical terms naming Caesar's political positions
   B include visuals by employing appropriate technology
   C relate whether the facts came from a primary or secondary source
   D cite more examples of Caesar's political aspirations

4. Which sentence should be deleted or moved to another paragraph?
   F 2   H 5
   G 4   J 6

5. To present the information in a research presentation, the student should
   A read aloud the *Works Cited* list to prove her research
   B answer listeners' potential questions by reading the entire paper aloud
   C include props and visuals, such as a representation of Caesar or a map
   D avoid citing primary or secondary sources altogether

SKILLS FOCUS

Writing Skills
Write a research paper.

Collection 10

DRAMA

INFORMATIONAL READING FOCUS

EVALUATING AN ARGUMENT

Drama began as the act of a whole community. Ideally, there would be no spectators. In practice, every member of the audience should feel like an understudy.

—W. H. Auden

INTERNET
Collection Resources
Keyword: LE5 10-10

David Hockney's stage set for the opera *Tristan and Isolde.*
Courtesy of the artist.

Elements of Literature

Drama *by* Diane Tasca
FORMS AND STAGECRAFT

A **drama** is a story that is enacted in real space and time by live actors for a live audience. The word *drama* is based on the Greek verb *dran,* which means "to do." It could be said, then, that a drama, or play, is something that involves people "doing things": Words are spoken, actions are taken, minds are changed.

The earliest plays that we have copies of were written in about the fifth century B.C. in ancient Greece. These plays were produced for festivals to honor Dionysus, the god of wine and fertility. Playwrights wrote new works each year to compete for top honors at this festival. The comedies and tragedies written for these competitions thousands of years ago established conventions in structure that are still followed by many playwrights today.

Dramatic Structure

Like stories, plays involve characters who take action to resolve a problem or **conflict** of some sort. The conflict in a play can take many forms. A conflict can develop between characters who want different things or the same thing. A conflict can develop between a character and his or her circumstances (perhaps he is imprisoned, or she is about to lose her job). A conflict can also exist *within* a character who is torn by competing desires (a son

> *Those tragedies written long ago in ancient Greece follow the fortunes of a protagonist known as the tragic hero.*

wants to know the truth about his father, but he is afraid to take the steps to find it). The important fact about any conflict is that it means a great deal to the person involved. No conflict is interesting for very long unless the playwright makes us *care about* that person.

As the character in a play takes steps to resolve a conflict—to get what he or she wants—**complications** keep arising. Eventually the events of the play build to a **climax,** an action that determines how the conflict will be resolved. The climax may be an argument, a love scene, a talk with a stranger. The **resolution** of the play follows, as the conflict is resolved and the action ends.

Tragedy: A Fatal Fall

A **tragedy** is a play that ends unhappily. Those tragedies written long ago in ancient Greece follow the fortunes of a protagonist known as the **tragic hero.** This hero is a noble figure who is admirable in many ways, but he or she has a **tragic flaw,** a personal failing, such as pride, rebelliousness, or jealousy. This flaw results in a choice that ultimately leads the hero to a tragic end, usually death.

Though the classic Greek tragedies deal with elevated figures, the problems they portray speak directly to their audiences: What is right and wrong, just and unjust?

What is the relationship between the individual and a high... ...e
...nd
...edy
...t the

...ding

...ly.
...nflicts
...on plot
...boy-
...s in
...e-

*...e conflict in comedy
...ly hinges on a problem
...the heart, such as a
...warted courtship or a
...ntic misunderstanding.*

...warted
...standing.
...a com-
...compli-
...e's
...ferent
...funny
...Like It, for
...ers, a
...and no-
...m their

...e It ends
...fact. Even
...ddings,

suggesting that life continues despite all of
our problems, that each wedding presents
the possibility of creating a whole new
society.

Modern Drama: Moving in Many Directions

Dramas today, both tragedies and comedies, usually focus on personal issues. The
psychological development of the characters often takes center stage, even when
the play deals with a larger social or ethical issue. Americans live in a democracy,
not a monarchy, so it's not surprising that
our contemporary protagonists are seldom kings and queens.
The people in plays
written today—whether
tragic or comic—are
usually ordinary people
much like the rest of us.
Contemporary dra-
mas also tend to be less
bound by conventional
structures than plays
from earlier times. Many
modern playwrights like to experiment
with structure. Modern plays might include long flashbacks to an earlier time.
They might include visual projections of a
character's fantasies. They might include
music. One experimental playwright had
his main characters act out the entire play
while buried up to their necks in sand.

Scene Design: Setting the Stage

Plays are meant to be performed. As you
read the text of a play, remember that the
playwright wrote those words to be acted

out on a stage. Theater artists—actors, directors, designers, lighting technicians, and stage crew—help the playwright's vision become an actuality on the stage.

Stages today vary greatly in dimension and layout. In Shakespeare's time the stage extended out into the viewing area, and the audience stood around (or sat in balconies) on three sides. Many modern theaters still use this type of "thrust" stage. Another type of stage is "in the round": The playing area is surrounded on all sides by the audience. In the most common type of modern stage, however, the playing area extends behind an opening called a *proscenium arch.* The audience sits on one side looking into the action, much as if they were looking into a window. The stage behind the arch has its own directions: *upstage* (away from the audience), *downstage* (toward the audience), *stage right* and *stage left* (to the actors' right and left when facing the audience).

Scene design—sets, lights, costumes, and props—can transform a bare stage into ancient Rome, a Russian drawing room, or a South African farm. The **set** for one play might be so realistic and detailed that the audience feels they are peering into someone's actual home. For another play the set might be abstract, consisting of a few platforms painted black.

Lighting also adds to the transformation of the stage. The mood and appearance of the set can be totally changed by a skilled lighting director.

The actors, of course, wear **costumes.** These are the responsibility of the costume designer, who works closely with the director of the play (and sometimes with the playwright). Like sets, costumes can be very specific to a particular historical period, or they can be abstract and minimal. In one famous production of *Hamlet,* for example, actor Richard Burton wore black leotards—no princely satins or crown.

Finally, **props** (short for *properties*) are portable items—handbags, phones, letters—that actors carry or handle onstage in order to perform the actions of the play. A person in charge of props must be certain the right props are available at the right moments in the play. If they are missing, the result can be unintentionally funny or can ruin a moment of high suspense.

Words and Action: Characters Onstage

The conversations of the characters onstage are called **dialogue.** Long speeches by individual characters are monologues or soliloquies. A **monologue** is spoken by one character to other characters onstage. A **soliloquy** is spoken by a character who is alone onstage, speaking to himself or herself or to the audience. Soliloquies often express a character's deepest feelings and may signal an important change in the character's thinking.

Sometimes characters, especially in Shakespeare's plays, comment on the action of the play, using asides. **Asides** are spoken to the audience or to one character; the other characters onstage do not hear an aside.

Written texts of plays also include **stage directions,** which describe the setting and the characters' actions. They often describe how a character should deliver a particular line (*angrily, stupidly,* *sweetly*). While modern playwrights often include detailed stage directions, Shakespeare and other early dramatists provided hardly any.

The Audience

Robert Anderson, the author of *Tea and Sympathy* and *I Never Sang for My Father,* writes about another "collaborator" who helps bring a play to life.

> **66** The playwright's final collaborator is the audience. The play exists somewhere between the stage and the spectator. In a sense, we get out of a play only what we bring to it. Out of some deep feeling of joy or sadness or excitement, a playwright writes a story, sounds a note, hoping to evoke a responsive chord from the audience. This response is what might be called the 'Oh, yes!' reaction. Playwrights write about particular experiences or observations. Enhancing these particulars with their imagination, they hope to reach something universal, something in everyone's experience. If they succeed, then members of the audience might ask, 'How did you know what my family is like?' The playwright, of course, did not know about the audience's families, but he knew his own, and in some ways all families are the same.

> One of the special qualities of the theater is that when we respond, we respond as a group. This mass response of laughter or tears or excitement gives us a reassuring feeling that we are not alone, that we are one with the people sitting around us, with everyone in the theater, and in a sense, with our community and the world. **99**

Practice

Choose a play or movie that you remember seeing, and discuss its dramatic elements. Start out by describing the **stage set** or sets. Next, indicate who the **characters** are and what their relationship is. Evaluate the characters' **dialogue.** Does it make clear what the characters want and why they are having trouble getting it? Finally, try your hand at writing a few of the **stage directions,** based on what you imagine them to have been.

Robert Anderson.

The Brute

Make the Connection

Quickwrite ✏️

Two people meet. One person is shy; the other is loud and aggressive. They hate each other on sight. They argue. Soon, however, they find themselves attracted to each other. Can you think of any movies, TV shows, or novels that are based on the idea that "opposites attract"? Do opposites attract in real life?

Literary Focus

Comedy: It Ends Happily

In both structure and characterization, a comedy is the opposite of a tragedy. A **comedy** is a story that ends happily—often with a marriage. Many comedies have a **plot** structured around boy-meets-girl (or, today, girl-meets-boy), in which the lovers must overcome obstacles so they can fall into each other's arms at the play's end. In the most typical example of a comedy, the plot is a celebration of the renewal of life and the power of love.

Farce: Exaggerated Comedy

A **farce** is a type of comedy in which exaggerated and often stereotyped characters are involved in ridiculous situations. The humor in farce is based on crude physical actions, or slapstick, and clowning. Characters may slip on banana peels, walk into doors, or disguise themselves in clothes of the opposite sex.

The word *farce* is from a French word meaning "stuffing." Years ago farces were used as "stuffing" during the interludes of a serious play. Even tragedies, however, may include farcical elements, for comic relief. Today farce is often the basic ingredient in TV sitcoms.

Reading Skills

Making Predictions

Chekhov's play spotlights two "battling lovers," Mrs. Popov and Smirnov. This basic dramatic situation—the meeting of two characters who are wildly antagonistic to each other at first—has been used in thousands of Hollywood comedies. The audience *knows* that the two are going to end up together eventually. The question that keeps us in suspense is: "*When* and *how* is that going to happen?"

Part of the fun of watching these stories is in seeing if we can predict when that moment of realization will take place. If the storyteller is clever, we find that our predictions are not always exactly right.

As you read the play, note the places where you make **predictions** about these characters and their future. How accurate are your predictions?

INTERNET

Vocabulary Practice
•
More About Anton Chekhov

Keyword: LE5 10-10

SKILLS FOCUS

Literary Skills
Understand characteristics of comedy and farce.

Reading Skills
Make predictions.

Vocabulary Development

indisposed (in′di·spōzd′) *adj.*: slightly ill.

emancipation (ē·man′sə·pā′shən) *n.*: liberation; the act of setting free from restraint or control or being set free.

malicious (mə·lish′əs) *adj.*: intentionally harmful.

insinuate (in·sin′yo͞o·āt′) *v.*: suggest.

incoherent (in′kō·hir′ənt) *adj.*: rambling; disjointed.

impudence (im′pyo͞o·dəns) *n.*: quality of being disrespectful.

impunity (im·pyo͞o′ni·tē) *n.*: freedom from punishment.

THE BRUTE
A Joke in One Act

Anton Chekhov
translated by Eric Bentley

CHARACTERS

Mrs. Popov, widow and landowner, small, with dimpled cheeks

Mr. Grigory S. Smirnov, gentleman farmer, middle-aged

Luka, Mrs. Popov's footman, an old man

Gardener

Coachman

Hired Men

The photographs throughout the play are from the 2002 production by the Expression Theater Ensemble.

The drawing room of a country house. MRS. POPOV, *in deep mourning, is staring hard at a photograph.* LUKA *is with her.*

Luka. It's not right, ma'am, you're killing yourself. The cook has gone off with the maid to pick berries. The cat's having a high old time in the yard catching birds. Every living thing is happy. But you stay moping here in the house like it was a convent,[1] taking no pleasure in nothing. I mean it, ma'am! It must be a full year since you set foot out of doors.

Mrs. Popov. I must never set foot out of doors again, Luka. Never! I have nothing to set foot out of doors *for.* My life is done. *He* is in his grave. I have buried myself alive in this house. We are *both* in our graves.

Luka. You're off again, ma'am. I just won't listen to you no more. Mr. Popov is dead, but what can we do about that? It's God's doing. God's will be done. You've cried over him, you've done your share of mourning, haven't you? There's a limit to everything. You can't go on weeping and wailing forever. My old lady died, for that matter, and I wept and wailed over her a whole month long. Well, that was it. I couldn't weep and wail all my life, she just wasn't worth it. (*He sighs.*) As for the neighbors, you've forgotten all about them, ma'am. You don't visit them and you don't let them visit you. You and I are like a pair of spiders—excuse the expression, ma'am—here we are in this house like a pair of spiders, we never see the light of day. And it isn't like there was no nice people around either. The whole county's swarming with 'em. There's a regiment quartered at Riblov, and the officers are so good-looking! The girls can't take their eyes off them.—There's a ball at the camp every Friday.—

> "Since Popov died, life has been an empty dream to me."

The military band plays most every day of the week.—What do you say, ma'am? You're young, you're pretty, you could enjoy yourself! Ten years from now you may want to strut and show your feathers to the officers, and it'll be too late.

Mrs. Popov (*firmly*). You must never bring this subject up again, Luka. Since Popov died, life has been an empty dream to me, you know that. *You* may think I am alive. Poor ignorant Luka! You are wrong. I am dead. I'm in my grave. Never more shall I see the light of day, never strip from my body this . . . raiment[2] of death! Are you listening, Luka? Let his ghost learn how I love him! Yes, *I* know, and *you* know, he was often unfair to me, he was cruel to me, and he was unfaithful to me. What of it? *I* shall be faithful to *him,* that's all. I will show him how *I* can love. Hereafter, in a better world than this, he will welcome me back, the same loyal girl I always was—

Luka. Instead of carrying on this way, ma'am, you should go out in the garden and take a bit of a walk, ma'am. Or why not harness Toby and take a drive? Call on a couple of the neighbors, ma'am?

Mrs. Popov (*breaking down*). Oh, Luka!

Luka. Yes, ma'am? What have I said, ma'am? Oh dear!

Mrs. Popov. Toby! You said Toby! He adored that horse. When he drove me out to the Korchagins and the Vlasovs, it was always with Toby! He was a wonderful driver, do you remember, Luka? So graceful! So strong! I can see him now, pulling at those reins with all his might and main! Toby! Luka, tell them to give Toby an extra portion of oats today.

Luka. Yes, ma'am.

---

1. **convent** *n.:* religious home for nuns.

2. **raiment** (rā′mənt) *n.:* clothing.

[*A bell rings.*]

Mrs. Popov. Who is that? Tell them I'm not home.

Luka. Very good, ma'am. (*Exit.*)

Mrs. Popov (*gazing again at the photograph*). You shall see, my Popov, how a wife can love and forgive. Till death do us part. Longer than that. Till death reunite us forever! (*Suddenly a titter breaks through her tears.*) Aren't you ashamed of yourself, Popov? Here's your little wife, being good, being faithful, so faithful she's locked up here waiting for her own funeral, while you—doesn't it make you ashamed, you naughty boy? You were terrible, you know. You were unfaithful, and you made those awful scenes about it, you stormed out and left me alone for weeks—

[*Enter* LUKA.]

Luka (*upset*). There's someone asking for you, ma'am. Says he must—

Mrs. Popov. I suppose you told him that since my husband's death I see no one?

Luka. Yes, ma'am. I did, ma'am. But he wouldn't listen, ma'am. He says it's urgent.

Mrs. Popov (*shrilly*). I see no one!!

Luka. He won't take no for an answer, ma'am. He just curses and swears and comes in anyway. He's a perfect monster, ma'am. He's in the dining room right now.

Mrs. Popov. In the dining room, is he? I'll give him his comeuppance. Bring him in here this minute. (*Exit* LUKA. *Suddenly sad again*) Why do they do this to me? Why? Insulting my grief,

intruding on my solitude? (*She sighs.*) I'm afraid I'll have to enter a convent. I will, I *must* enter a convent.

[*Enter* MR. SMIRNOV *and* LUKA.]

Smirnov (*to* LUKA). Dolt! Idiot! You talk too much! (*Seeing* MRS. POPOV. *With dignity*) May I have the honor of introducing myself, madam? Grigory S. Smirnov, landowner and lieutenant of artillery, retired. Forgive me, madam, if I disturb your peace and quiet, but my business is both urgent and weighty.

Mrs. Popov (*declining to offer him her hand*). What is it you wish, sir?

Smirnov. At the time of his death, your late husband—with whom I had the honor to be acquainted, ma'am—was in my debt to the tune of twelve hundred rubles. I have two notes to prove it. Tomorrow, ma'am, I must pay the interest on a bank loan. I have therefore no alternative, ma'am, but to ask you to pay me the money today.

Mrs. Popov. Twelve hundred rubles? But what did my husband owe it to you for?

Smirnov. He used to buy his oats from me, madam.

Mrs. Popov (*to* LUKA, *with a sigh*). Remember what I said, Luka: Tell them to give Toby an extra portion of oats today! (*Exit* LUKA.) My dear Mr.—what was that name again?

Smirnov. Smirnov, ma'am.

Mrs. Popov. My dear Mr. Smirnov, if Mr. Popov owed you money, you shall be paid—to the last ruble, to the last kopeck. But today—you must excuse me, Mr.—what was it?

Smirnov. Smirnov, ma'am.

Mrs. Popov. Today, Mr. Smirnov, I have no ready cash in the house. (SMIRNOV *starts to speak.*) Tomorrow, Mr. Smirnov, no, the day after tomorrow, all will be well. My steward[3] will be back from town. I shall see that he pays what is owing. Today, no. In any case, today is exactly seven months from Mr. Popov's death. On such a day you will understand that I am in no mood to think of money.

Smirnov. Madam, if you don't pay up now, you can carry me out feet foremost. They'll seize my estate.

Mrs. Popov. You can have your money. (*He starts to thank her.*) Tomorrow. (*He again starts to speak.*) That is: the day after tomorrow.

Smirnov. I don't need the money the day after tomorrow. I need it today.

Mrs. Popov. I'm sorry, Mr.—

Smirnov (*shouting*). Smirnov!

Mrs. Popov (*sweetly*). Yes, of course. But you can't have it today.

Smirnov. But I can't wait for it any longer!

Mrs. Popov. Be sensible, Mr. Smirnov. How can I pay you if I don't have it?

Smirnov. You don't have it?

Mrs. Popov. I don't have it.

Smirnov. Sure?

Mrs. Popov. Positive.

Smirnov. Very well. I'll make a note to that effect. (*Shrugging*) And then they want me to keep cool. I meet the tax commissioner on the street, and he says, "Why are you always in such a bad humor, Smirnov?" Bad humor! How can I help it, in God's name? I need money, I need it desperately. Take yesterday: I leave home at the

crack of dawn; I call on all my debtors. Not a one of them pays up. Footsore and weary, I creep at midnight into some little dive and try to snatch a few winks of sleep on the floor by the vodka barrel. Then today, I come here, fifty miles from home, saying to myself, "At last, at last, I can be sure of something," and you're not in the mood! You give me a mood! How the devil can I help getting all worked up?

Mrs. Popov. I thought I'd made it clear, Mr. Smirnov, that you'll get your money the minute my steward is back from town?

Smirnov. What the hell do I care about your steward? Pardon the expression, ma'am. But it was you I came to see.

Mrs. Popov. What language! What a tone to take to a lady! I refuse to hear another word. (*Quickly, exit.*)

Smirnov. Not in the mood, huh? "Exactly seven months since Popov's death," huh? How about me? (*Shouting after her*) Is there this interest to pay, or isn't there? I'm asking you a question: Is there this interest to pay, or isn't there? So your husband died, and you're not in the mood, and your steward's gone off someplace, and so forth and so on, but what can *I* do about all that, huh? What do *you* think I should do? Take a running jump and shove my head through the wall? Take off in a balloon? You don't know my *other* debtors. I call on Gruzdeff. Not at home. I look for Yaroshevitch. He's hiding out. I find Kooritsin. He kicks up a row, and I have to throw him through the window. I work my way right down the list. Not a kopeck. Then I come to you, and damn it, if you'll pardon the expression, you're not in the mood! (*Quietly, as he realizes he's talking to air*) I've spoiled them all, that's what; I've let them play me for a sucker. Well, I'll show them. I'll show this one. I'll stay right here

---

3. **steward** (sto͞o′ərd) *n.:* person in charge of running an estate.

> "I'm in a rage! I'm in a positively towering rage!"

till she pays up. Ugh! (*He shudders with rage.*) I'm in a rage! I'm in a positively towering rage! Every nerve in my body is trembling at forty to the dozen! I can't breathe, I feel ill, I think I'm going to faint, hey, you there!

[*Enter* LUKA.]

Luka. Yes, sir? Is there anything you wish, sir?
Smirnov. Water! Water!! No, make it vodka. (*Exit* LUKA.) Consider the logic of it. A fellow creature is desperately in need of cash, so desperately in need that he has to seriously contemplate hanging himself, and this woman, this mere chit of a girl, won't pay up, and why not? Because, forsooth, she isn't in the mood! Oh, the logic of women! Come to that, I never have liked them, I could do without the whole sex. Talk to a woman? I'd rather sit on a barrel of dynamite, the very thought gives me gooseflesh. Women! Creatures of poetry and romance! Just to see one in the distance gets me mad. My legs start twitching with rage. I feel like yelling for help.

[*Enter* LUKA, *handing* SMIRNOV *a glass of water.*]

Luka. Mrs. Popov is indisposed, sir. She is seeing no one.
Smirnov. Get out. (*Exit* LUKA.) Indisposed, is she? Seeing no one, huh? Well, she can see me or not, but I'll be here, I'll be right here till she pays up. If you're sick for a week, I'll be here for a week. If you're sick for a year, I'll be here for a year. You won't get around *me* with your widow's weeds[4] and your schoolgirl dimples. I know all about dimples. (*Shouting through the window*) Semyon, let the horses out of those shafts, we're not leaving, we're staying, and tell them to give the horses some oats, yes, oats, you

---

4. **widow's weeds:** black clothing worn by a widow to mourn a husband's death.

fool, what do you think? (*Walking away from the window*) What a mess, what an unholy mess! I didn't sleep last night, the heat is terrific today, not a one of 'em has paid up, and here's this—this skirt in mourning that's not in the mood! My head aches, where's that— (*He drinks from the glass.*) Water, ugh! You there!

[*Enter* LUKA.]

Luka. Yes, sir. You wish for something, sir?
Smirnov. Where's that confounded vodka I asked for? (*Exit* LUKA. SMIRNOV *sits and looks himself over.*) Oof! A fine figure of a man *I* am! Unwashed, uncombed, unshaven, straw on my vest, dust all over me. The little woman must've taken me for a highwayman. (*Yawns*) I suppose it wouldn't be considered polite to barge into a drawing room in this state, but who cares? I'm not a visitor, I'm a creditor—most unwelcome of guests, second only to Death.

[*Enter* LUKA.]

Luka (*handing him the vodka*). If I may say so, sir, you take too many liberties, sir.
Smirnov. What?!
Luka. Oh, nothing, sir, nothing.
Smirnov. Who do you think you're talking to? Shut your mouth!
Luka (*aside*). There's an evil spirit abroad. The devil must have sent him. Oh! (*Exit* LUKA.)
Smirnov. What a rage I'm in! I'll grind the whole world to powder. Oh, I feel ill again. You there!

Vocabulary
indisposed (in′di·spōzd′) *adj.*: slightly ill.

[*Enter* MRS. POPOV.]

Mrs. Popov (*looking at the floor*). In the solitude of my rural retreat, Mr. Smirnov, I've long since grown unaccustomed to the sound of the human voice. Above all, I cannot bear shouting. I must beg you not to break the silence.

Smirnov. Very well. Pay me my money and I'll go.

Mrs. Popov. I told you before, and I tell you again, Mr. Smirnov: I have no cash; you'll have to wait till the day after tomorrow. Can I express myself more plainly?

Smirnov. And *I* told *you* before, and *I* tell *you* again, that I need the money today, that the day after tomorrow is too late, and that if you don't pay, and pay now, I'll have to hang myself in the morning!

Mrs. Popov. But I have no cash. This is quite a puzzle.

Smirnov. You won't pay, huh?

Mrs. Popov. I *can't* pay, Mr. Smirnov.

Smirnov. In that case, I'm going to sit here and wait. (*Sits down*) You'll pay up the day after tomorrow? Very good. Till the day after tomorrow, here I sit. (*Pause. He jumps up.*) Now look, do I have to pay that interest tomorrow, or don't I? Or do you think I'm joking?

Mrs. Popov. I must ask you not to raise your voice, Mr. Smirnov. This is not a stable.

Smirnov. Who said it was? Do I have to pay the interest tomorrow or not?

Mrs. Popov. Mr. Smirnov, do you know how to behave in the presence of a lady?

Smirnov. No, madam, I do not know how to behave in the presence of a lady.

Mrs. Popov. Just what I thought. I look at you, and I say: ugh! I hear you talk, and I say to myself: "That man doesn't know how to talk to a lady."

Smirnov. You'd like me to come simpering[5] to you in French, I suppose. "*Enchanté, madame! Merci beaucoup* for not paying zee money, *madame! Pardonnez-moi* if I 'ave disturbed you, *madame!* How *charmante* you look in mourning, *madame!*"

Mrs. Popov. Now you're being silly, Mr. Smirnov.

Smirnov (*mimicking*). "Now you're being silly, Mr. Smirnov." "You don't know how to talk to a lady, Mr. Smirnov." Look here, Mrs. Popov, I've known more women than you've known kitty cats. I've fought three duels on their account. I've jilted twelve and been jilted by nine others. Oh, yes, Mrs. Popov, I've played the fool in my time, whispered sweet nothings, bowed and scraped and endeavored to please. Don't tell me I don't know what it is to love, to pine away with longing, to have the blues, to melt like butter, to be weak as water. I was full of tender emotion. I was carried away with passion. I squandered half my fortune on the sex. I chattered about women's emancipation. But there's an end to everything, dear madam. Burning eyes, dark eyelashes, ripe, red lips, dimpled cheeks, heaving bosoms, soft whisperings, the moon above, the lake below—I don't give a rap for that sort of nonsense any more, Mrs. Popov. I've found out about women. Present company excepted, they're liars. Their behavior is mere playacting; their conversation is sheer gossip. Yes, dear lady, women, young or old, are false, petty, vain, cruel, malicious, unreasonable. As for intelligence, any sparrow could give them points. Appearances, I admit, can be deceptive. In appearance, a woman may be all poetry and romance, goddess and angel, muslin[6] and fluff. To look at her exterior is to be transported to heaven. But I have looked at her interior, Mrs. Popov, and what did I find there—in her very soul? A crocodile. (*He has gripped the back of the chair so firmly that it snaps.*) And, what is more revolting, a crocodile with an illusion, a crocodile that imagines tender sentiments are its own special province, a crocodile that thinks itself queen of the realm of love! Whereas, in sober fact, dear madam, if a woman can love anything except a lap dog, you can hang me by the feet on that nail. For a man, love is suffering, love is sacrifice. A woman just swishes her train around and tightens her grip on your nose. Now, you're a woman, aren't you, Mrs. Popov? You must be an expert on some of this. Tell me, quite frankly, did you ever know a woman to be—faithful, for instance? Or even sincere? Only old hags, huh? Though some women are old hags from birth. But as for the others? You're right: A faithful woman is a freak of nature—like a cat with horns.

Mrs. Popov. Who *is* faithful, then? Who *have* you cast for the faithful lover? Not man?

Smirnov. Right first time, Mrs. Popov: man.

Mrs. Popov (*going off into a peal of bitter laughter*). Man! Man is faithful! That's a new one! (*Fiercely*) What right do you have to say this, Mr. Smirnov? Men faithful? Let me tell you something. Of all the men I have ever known, my late husband Popov was the best. I loved him, and

> "Mr. Smirnov, do you know how to behave in the presence of a lady?"

---

5. **simpering** *v.:* speaking in a silly, affected way.

6. **muslin** *n.:* a kind of cotton fabric.

Vocabulary

emancipation (ē·man'sə·pā'shən) *n.:* liberation; the act of setting free from restraint or control or being set free.

malicious (mə·lish'əs) *adj.:* intentionally harmful.

there are women who know how to love, Mr. Smirnov. I gave him my youth, my happiness, my life, my fortune. I worshipped the ground he trod on—and what happened? The best of men was unfaithful to me, Mr. Smirnov. Not once in a while. All the time. After he died, I found his desk drawer full of love letters. While he was alive, he was always going away for the weekend. He squandered my money. He flirted with other women before my very eyes. But, in spite of all, Mr. Smirnov, *I* was faithful. Unto death. And beyond. I am *still* faithful, Mr. Smirnov! Buried alive in this house, I shall wear mourning till the day I, too, am called to my eternal rest.

Smirnov (*laughing scornfully*). Expect me to believe that? As if I couldn't see through all this hocus-pocus. Buried alive! Till you're called to your eternal rest! Till when? Till some little poet—or some little subaltern[7] with his first moustache—comes riding by and asks: "Can that be the house of the mysterious Tamara, who for love of her late husband has buried herself alive, vowing to see no man?" Ha!

Mrs. Popov (*flaring up*). How dare you? How dare you insinuate—?

Smirnov. You may have buried yourself alive, Mrs. Popov, but you haven't forgotten to powder your nose.

Mrs. Popov (*incoherent*). How dare you? How—?

Smirnov. Who's raising his voice now? Just because I call a spade a spade. Because I shoot straight from the shoulder. Well, don't shout at me, I'm not your steward.

Mrs. Popov. I'm not shouting, you're shouting! Oh, leave me alone!

Smirnov. Pay me the money, and I will.

"I'm not shouting, you're shouting! Oh, leave me alone!"

Mrs. Popov. You'll get no money out of me!

Smirnov. Oh, so that's it!

Mrs. Popov. Not a ruble, not a kopeck. Get out! Leave me alone!

Smirnov. Not being your husband, I must ask you not to make scenes with me. (*He sits.*) I don't like scenes.

Mrs. Popov (*choking with rage*). You're sitting down?

Smirnov. Correct, I'm sitting down.

Mrs. Popov. I asked you to leave!

Smirnov. Then give me the money. (*Aside*) Oh, what a rage I'm in, what a rage!

Mrs. Popov. The impudence of the man! I won't talk to you a moment longer. Get out. (*Pause*) Are you going?

Smirnov. No.

Mrs. Popov. No?!

Smirnov. No.

Mrs. Popov. On your head be it. Luka! (*Enter* LUKA.) Show the gentleman out, Luka.

Luka (*approaching*). I'm afraid, sir, I'll have to ask you, um, to leave, sir, now, um—

Smirnov (*jumping up*). Shut your mouth, you old idiot! Who do you think you're talking to? I'll make mincemeat of you.

Luka (*clutching his heart*). Mercy on us! Holy saints above! (*He falls into an armchair.*) I'm taken sick! I can't breathe!

Mrs. Popov. Then where's Dasha? Dasha! Dasha! Come here at once! (*She rings.*)

Luka. They gone picking berries, ma'am, I'm alone here—Water, water, I'm taken sick!

Vocabulary

insinuate (in·sin′yŏŏ·āt′) *v.*: suggest.

incoherent (in′kō·hir′ənt) *adj.*: rambling; disjointed.

impudence (im′pyŏŏ·dəns) *n.*: quality of being disrespectful.

7. **subaltern** (səb·ôl′tərn) *n.*: a person of low rank.

Mrs. Popov (*to* SMIRNOV). Get out, you!

Smirnov. Can't you even be polite with me, Mrs. Popov?

Mrs. Popov (*clenching her fists and stamping her feet*). With you? You're a wild animal, you were never housebroken!

Smirnov. What? What did you say?

Mrs. Popov. I said you were a wild animal, you were never housebroken.

Smirnov (*advancing upon her*). And what right do you have to talk to me like that?

Mrs. Popov. Like what?

Smirnov. You have insulted me, madam.

Mrs. Popov. What of it? Do you think I'm scared of you?

> **"What of it? Do you think I'm scared of you?"**

Smirnov. So you think you can get away with it because you're a woman. A creature of poetry and romance, huh? Well, it doesn't go down with me. I hereby challenge you to a duel.

Luka. Mercy on us! Holy saints alive! Water!

Smirnov. I propose we shoot it out.

Mrs. Popov. Trying to scare me again? Just because you have big fists and a voice like a bull? You're a brute.

Smirnov. No one insults Grigory S. Smirnov with impunity! And I don't care if you *are* a female.

Mrs. Popov (*trying to out-shout him*). Brute, brute, brute!

Smirnov. The sexes are equal, are they? Fine: Then it's just prejudice to expect men alone to pay for insults. I hereby challenge—

Mrs. Popov (*screaming*). All right! You want to shoot it out? All right! Let's shoot it out!

Smirnov. And let it be here and now!

Mrs. Popov. Here and now! All right! I'll have Popov's pistols here in one minute! (*Walks away, then turns*) Putting one of Popov's bullets through your silly head will be a pleasure! *Au revoir.* (*Exit.*)

Smirnov. I'll bring her down like a duck, a sitting duck. I'm not one of your little poets, I'm no little subaltern with his first moustache. No, sir, there's no weaker sex where I'm concerned!

Luka. Sir! Master! (*He goes down on his knees.*) Take pity on a poor old man, and do me a favor: Go away. It was

Vocabulary
impunity (im·pyo͞o′ni·tē) *n.:* freedom from punishment.

The Brute   **733**

bad enough before, you nearly scared me to death. But a duel—!

Smirnov (*ignoring him*). A duel! That's equality of the sexes for you! That's women's emancipation! Just as a matter of principle I'll bring her down like a duck. But what a woman! "Putting one of Popov's bullets through your silly head . . ." Her cheeks were flushed, her eyes were gleaming! And, by Heaven, she's accepted the challenge! I never knew a woman like this before!

Luka. Sir! Master! Please go away! I'll always pray for you!

Smirnov (*again ignoring him*). What a woman! Phew!! *She's no sourpuss; she's no crybaby.* She's fire-and-brimstone.[8] She's a human cannonball. What a shame I have to kill her!

Luka (*weeping*). Please, kind sir, please, go away!

Smirnov (*as before*). I like her, isn't that funny? With those dimples and all? I like her. I'm even prepared to consider letting her off that debt. And where's my rage? It's gone. I never knew a woman like this before.

[*Enter* MRS. POPOV *with pistols.*]

Mrs. Popov (*boldly*). Pistols, Mr. Smirnov! (*Matter of fact*) But before we start, you'd better show me how it's done, I'm not too familiar with these things. In fact I never gave a pistol a second look.

Luka. Lord, have mercy on us, I must go hunt up the gardener and the coachman. Why has this catastrophe fallen upon us, O Lord? (*Exit.*)

Smirnov (*examining the pistols*). Well, it's like this. There are several makes: One is the Mortimer, with capsules, especially constructed for dueling. What you have here are Smith and Wesson triple-action revolvers, with extractor, first-rate job, worth ninety rubles at the very least.

You hold it this way. (*Aside*) My Lord, what eyes she has! They're setting me on fire.

Mrs. Popov. This way?

Smirnov. Yes, that's right. You cock the trigger, take aim like this, head up, arm out like this. Then you just press with this finger here, and it's all over. The main thing is, keep cool, take slow aim, and don't let your arm jump.

Mrs. Popov. I see. And if it's inconvenient to do the job here, we can go out in the garden.

Smirnov. Very good. Of course, I should warn you: I'll be firing in the air.

Mrs. Popov. What? This is the end. Why?

Smirnov. Oh, well—because—for private reasons.

Mrs. Popov. Scared, huh? (*She laughs heartily.*) Now don't you try to get out of it, Mr. Smirnov. My blood is up. I won't be happy till I've drilled a hole through that skull of yours. Follow me. What's the matter? Scared?

Smirnov. That's right. I'm scared.

Mrs. Popov. Oh, come on, what's the matter with you?

Smirnov. Well, um, Mrs. Popov, I um, I like you.

Mrs. Popov (*laughing bitterly*). Good Lord! He likes me, does he? The gall[9] of the man. (*Showing him the door*) You may leave, Mr. Smirnov.

Smirnov (*Quietly puts the gun down, takes his hat, and walks to the door. Then he stops, and the pair look at each other without a word. Then, approaching gingerly*). Listen, Mrs. Popov. Are you still mad at me? I'm in the devil of a temper myself, of course. But then, you see—what I mean is—it's this way—the fact is—(*roaring*) Well, is it my fault if I like you? (*Clutches the back of a chair. It breaks.*) What fragile furniture you have here! I like you. Know what I mean? I could fall in love with you.

Mrs. Popov. I hate you. Get out!

Smirnov. What a woman! I never saw anything

---

8. **fire-and-brimstone** *adj.*: often refers to eternal punishment in hell or describes fiery religious sermons; here, extremely lively.

9. **gall** (gôl) *n.*: nerve; rude boldness.

like it. Oh, I'm lost, I'm done for, I'm a mouse in a trap.

Mrs. Popov. Leave this house, or I shoot!

Smirnov. Shoot away! What bliss to die of a shot that was fired by that little velvet hand! To die gazing into those enchanting eyes. I'm out of my mind. I know: You must decide at once. Think for one second, then decide. Because if I leave now, I'll never be back. Decide! I'm a pretty decent chap. Landed gentleman, I should say. Ten thousand a year. Good stable. Throw a kopeck up in the air, and I'll put a bullet through it. Will you marry me?

Mrs. Popov (*indignant, brandishing[10] the gun*). We'll shoot it out! Get going! Take your pistol!

Smirnov. I'm out of my mind. I don't understand anything any more. (*Shouting*) You there! That vodka!

Mrs. Popov. No excuses! No delays! We'll shoot it out!

Smirnov. I'm out of my mind. I'm falling in love. I *have* fallen in love. (*He takes her hand vigorously; she squeals.*) I love you. (*He goes down on his knees.*) I love you as I've never loved before. I jilted twelve and was jilted by nine others. But I didn't love a one of them as I love you. I'm full of tender emotion. I'm melting like butter. I'm weak as water. I'm on my knees like a fool, and I offer you my hand. It's a shame; it's a disgrace. I haven't been in love in five years. I took a vow against it. And now, all of a sudden, to be swept off my feet, it's a scandal. I offer you my hand, dear lady. Will you or won't you? You won't? Then don't! (*He rises and walks toward the door.*)

Mrs. Popov. I didn't say anything.

Smirnov (*stopping*). What?

Mrs. Popov. Oh nothing, you can go. Well, no, just a minute. No, you can go. Go! I detest you! But, just a moment. Oh, if you knew how furious I feel! (*Throws the gun on the table*) My fingers have gone to sleep holding that horrid thing. (*She is tearing her handkerchief to shreds.*) And what are you standing around for? Get out of here!

Smirnov. Goodbye.

Mrs. Popov. Go, go, go! (*Shouting*) Where are you going? Wait a minute! No, no, it's all right, just go. I'm fighting mad. Don't come near me, don't come near me!

Smirnov (*who is coming near her*). I'm pretty disgusted with myself—falling in love like a kid, going down on my knees like some moon-gazing whippersnapper, the very thought gives me gooseflesh. (*Rudely*) I love you. But it doesn't make sense. Tomorrow, I have to pay that interest, and we've already started mowing. (*He puts his arm about her waist.*) I shall never forgive myself for this.

Mrs. Popov. Take your hands off me, I hate you! Let's shoot it out!

[*A long kiss. Enter* LUKA *with an axe, the* GARDENER *with a rake, the* COACHMAN *with a pitchfork,* HIRED MEN *with sticks.*]

Luka (*seeing the kiss*). Mercy on us! Holy saints above!

Mrs. Popov (*dropping her eyes*). Luka, tell them in the stable that Toby is *not* to have any oats today.

Curtain

> "I love you. But it doesn't make sense."

---

10. **brandishing** *v.:* waving about in a challenging way.

Meet the Writer

Anton Chekhov

"Slice-of-Life" Playwright

Anton Chekhov (1860–1904) is one of the two playwrights who have most influenced modern drama. The other is the Norwegian writer Henrik Ibsen (1828–1906), whose plays often deal with contemporary social problems and are called well-made plays because they have a well-crafted plot. Chekhov's major plays, on the other hand, are often called slices of life. Rather than focusing on plot, they are more concerned with psychological insights, with the slow ebb and flow of moods, and with subtly shifting relationships.

Chekhov was born in a small seaport in southern Russia, the son of an unsuccessful shopkeeper. His family was poor and totally dependent on young Anton's support. The money came in from short stories and sketches that Chekhov churned out for humor magazines. At the same time, he was studying medicine at the University of Moscow.

Chekhov became a doctor but did not practice long. Instead, he developed his skills in writing and produced hundreds of short stories and five major plays over the course of his tragically short life.

In one of his many letters, Chekhov gave this writing advice to Maxim Gorky, another famous Russian writer:

❝When you read proof, take out adjectives and adverbs wherever you can. You use so many of them that the reader finds it hard to concentrate and he gets tired. You understand what I mean when I say, 'The man sat on the grass.' You understand because the sentence is clear and there is nothing to distract your attention. Conversely, the brain has trouble understanding me if I say, 'A tall, narrow-chested man of medium height with a red beard sat on green grass trampled by passersby, sat mutely, looking about timidly and fearfully.' This doesn't get its meaning through to the brain immediately, which is what good writing must do, and fast. ❞

In his last years, ill with the tuberculosis that would soon kill him, Chekhov wrote five full-length serious plays, four of which are masterpieces that are still produced in theaters all over the world: *The Seagull, Uncle Vanya, The Three Sisters,* and *The Cherry Orchard.*

For Independent Reading

In *The Cherry Orchard,* as in his other full-length dramas, Chekhov lets "the things that happen on stage be as complex and yet as simple as they are in life. For instance, people are having a meal at the table, just having a meal, but at the same time their happiness is being created, or their lives are being smashed up."

Response and Analysis

Reading Check

1. Complete this **character web,** telling what each of the three characters wants at the beginning of the play:

Mrs. Popov — Smirnov — Luka

wants

2. By the end of the play, how have these wants changed?

Thinking Critically

3. Explain the play's **title.** Who or what is the brute? This title is sometimes translated as *The Bear*. Which title do you feel is more interesting?

4. What is the significance of Mrs. Popov's last line?

5. A **farce** is a kind of **comedy** that most of us are familiar with, since farces are standard fare in movies and on television. Here are some of the characteristics of a farce:

   - A farce is a knockabout comedy without complex characters.

   - A farce intends to make us laugh by using a lot of physical action.

   - Nothing tragic happens in a farce.

   - The characters in a farce make a lot of noise; the stage is busy with action.

   Which of these characteristics apply to *The Brute*? Be sure to cite specific situations in the play.

6. If the writer's **purpose** in a farce is to ridicule human behavior, when and how are the two **main characters** first shown to be ridiculous? As the

play develops, what new behaviors does Chekhov ridicule?

7. Why does Smirnov begin to change his mind about Mrs. Popov? At what **climactic** moment in the play do we know that she has changed her mind too? (Were you able to **predict** when this reversal would occur?)

8. **Repetition** is frequently used in comedies—people seem to find something funny in repeated patterns of speech or behavior. Find two examples of repetition in this play. Did you find the repetition funny? Explain your responses.

9. **Compare and contrast** Mrs. Popov and Smirnov. How are they alike, and how do they differ?

Extending and Evaluating

10. Do you find Chekhov's battling lovers to be **credible,** or believable? Do you think they would finally be attracted to each other? (Refer to your Quickwrite notes.)

WRITING

The Next Act

A **comedy** often ends with a marriage or with the promise of one, but comedies almost never follow the couple beyond their marriage. What do you think will happen to Smirnov and Mrs. Popov after they are married? Imagine a day in their lives ten years later, and write the **dialogue** for this next act. To get your dialogue going, have the characters face a decision—for example, how to spend some money; what to do about Luka, who still dislikes Smirnov; what to do about the photographs of Mrs. Popov's first husband, which are still around the house.

SKILLS FOCUS

Literary Skills
Analyze comedy, including farce.

Writing Skills
Write another act of a comedy.

Vocabulary Development

Word Analogies:
Word Pairs with the Same Relationship

In an **analogy** test item you have to choose the word that will give the second word pair the same relationship as the first word pair. The word pairs may be synonyms or antonyms, or they may have other relationships. (For more on analogies, see pages 29–30.)

PRACTICE 1

Write the word from the Word Bank that completes each analogy. Hint: Try reading the analogy item aloud: *Energetic* is to *vigorous* as *mean* is to which word in the Word Bank?

1. ENERGETIC : VIGOROUS :: mean : _____

2. ACCEPTANCE : REJECTION :: _____ : enslavement

3. JOYOUS : HAPPY :: ill : _____

4. CALM : DISQUIET :: _____ : respect

5. DEFY : RESIST :: assert : _____

6. OPTIMISM : HOPE :: protection : _____

7. ORDERLY : CHAOTIC :: clear : _____

Word Connotations: Powerful Associations

Every word has a **denotation,** or dictionary meaning, but many words also have **connotations,** powerful emotional overtones and associations. These passages from *The Brute* have words with rich connotations:

> "In appearance, a woman may be all poetry and romance, goddess and angel, muslin and fluff."

> "What a woman! Phew!! *She's* no sourpuss; *she's* no crybaby. She's fire-and-brimstone. She's a human cannonball."

PRACTICE 2

1. In each passage above, identify words that you think have strong connotations. Describe what the word or phrase suggests to you.

2. Rewrite each passage, substituting words with altogether different connotations. For example, *romance* might become *kindness*.

SKILLS FOCUS

Vocabulary Skills
Complete word analogies. Understand connotations.

Grammar Link

Using Transitions to Connect Related Ideas

Transitional words and **phrases,** such as those in the chart below, serve as signposts to help readers follow your thoughts. When you write, choose appropriate transitional words and phrases to connect related ideas. With these helpful transitions, you can combine short, choppy sentences that sound like a telegram to form smoother-sounding sentences that flow together and make more sense to the reader:

Transitional Words and Phrases	
Comparing	also, similarly, too, and, in addition
Contrasting	but, however, in contrast, even though, although
Cause and effect	for, since, so, as a result, so that, because
Example	for instance, for example, in fact, in other words
Chronological order	after, then, first, finally, next, when
Order of importance	first, last, mainly, then
Spatial order	next, into, there, behind, before, above, over, down

Notice how the underlined transitional words and phrases connect closely related ideas in the paragraph below:

> Anton Chekhov wrote hundreds of short stories and several hilarious one-act comedies, but he is best remembered for his serious full-length dramas. When *The Sea Gull* was first performed, in 1896 in St. Petersburg, it was very badly received. As a result, Chekhov left the theater after the performance and vowed never to write another play. However, the Moscow Art Theater's 1898 production of *The Sea Gull* was a tremendous success and established Chekhov as a leading playwright.

PRACTICE

SKILLS FOCUS

Grammar Skills
Use transitional words and phrases to connect ideas.

Revise the paragraph below using **transitional words** and **phrases** to connect closely related ideas. (You will be combining sentences.) In a small group, discuss your revised paragraphs.

Mrs. Popov remains faithful to her dead husband. He was a cad. He deceived her. He made terrible scenes. He left her alone for weeks at a time. One day, Smirnov enters. He demands payment for money he lent to Mr. Popov. Smirnov needs the cash. He owes the bank interest. He hasn't paid the interest. He will surely lose his land.

William Shakespeare's Life
A BIOGRAPHICAL SKETCH

by Robert Anderson

Compared with what we know about writers today, we know very little about William Shakespeare's life. In the early 1600s, nobody realized that this actor and writer would one day become known as the world's greatest playwright and poet. In the 1600s, there were no talk-show hosts to interview Shakespeare, no Sunday supplements to feature all the intimate details of his life. This neglect, however, has been corrected. By now more material has been written about Shakespeare and his works than about any other writer in the world.

What we do know about Shakespeare comes mainly from public records. We know that he was baptized on April 26, 1564, in Stratford-on-Avon, a market town about one hundred miles northwest of

William Shakespeare.
Popperfoto/Archive Photos.

London. It is assumed he was born a few days before his baptism, and so his birthday is celebrated on April 23, possibly only because he died on that date in 1616. He was one of eight children.

Shakespeare's birthplace on Henly Street in Stratford, England.

His father, John Shakespeare, was a merchant and a man of some importance in the town, serving at various times as alderman and high bailiff—the equivalent of a mayor today.

William went to the local grammar school, which was very different from grammar schools today. In those days it was rare for students to move on to a university; the Stratford grammar school provided Shakespeare and other boys of Stratford (no girls went to school) with all their formal education. What they learned in this school was Latin—Latin grammar and Latin literature, including the schoolboys' favorite: Ovid's amorous retelling of the Greek and Roman myths.

In 1582, Shakespeare married Anne Hathaway, who was eight years older than he was, and in 1583, their first child, Susanna, was born. In 1585, Anne gave birth to twins, Hamnet and Judith. Then, from 1585 until 1592, Shakespeare's history goes blank.

Many people believe that Shakespeare went to London to seek his fortune the year after the twins were born. We know that by 1592 he had become an actor and a playwright, because that year a rival playwright, Robert Greene, scathingly warned other playwrights against the actor who had become a writer:

There is an upstart crow, beautified with our feathers . . .
that supposes he is as well able to bombast out a blank verse
as the best of you. . . .

Greene refers to a fable in which a crow struts about in another bird's feathers—as an actor can only recite others' words. Greene was insulting an upstart, a mere actor who dared to *write*.

Actors were held in disrepute at the time. In fact, they were often lumped together with other unsavory groups: "rogues, vagabonds, sturdy beggars, and common players." Local officials frequently tried to close the theaters because they felt clerks and apprentices wasted time there (performances were in the daytime). They also felt that disease was too easily spread among the members of the audience. In fact, the London theaters were closed for long periods during the plague years of 1592–1594.

Thus, actors sought the protection and support of noblemen with the power to speak for their rights against critical town authorities. It appears that in 1594, Shakespeare became a charter member of a theatrical group called the Lord Chamberlain's Men, which became the King's Men in 1603. (The patron of the group was none other than King James himself.) Shakespeare acted and wrote for this company until he retired to Stratford in 1612. By that time he had written thirty-seven plays—**comedies, histories, tragedies,** and **romances**—including his tragic masterpieces *Hamlet, Othello, King Lear,* and *Macbeth*.

It is sometimes difficult to fix the dates of Shakespeare's works because plays were not routinely published after production,

Patrick Stewart and Anjanue Ellis in Shakespeare's *The Tempest* in a 1995 New York Shakespeare Festival production.

as they generally are now. In Shakespeare's day, plays became the property of the theaters, and the theaters were not eager to have copies made available for rival theaters to use. Some of Shakespeare's plays were published during his lifetime, but often in versions of dubious authenticity. It was not until 1623 that two men who had been with Shakespeare in the King's Men brought out what they called "True Original Copies" of all the plays. This volume is called the First Folio.

It is believed that *Julius Caesar* was written in 1599, because of what a Swiss traveler who was in England in September 1599 wrote about a visit to the Globe. The Swiss visitor was most impressed, for good reason, with the intricate and vigorous Elizabethan dancing:

> After dinner on the twenty-first of September, at about two o'clock, I went with my companions over the water, and in the strewn-roof house [the playhouse with a thatched roof] saw the tragedy of the first Emperor Julius with at least fifteen characters very well acted. At the end of the comedy they danced according to their custom with extreme elegance. Two men in men's clothes and two in women's gave this performance, in wonderful combination with each other.

Shakespeare died on April 23, 1616, at the age of fifty-two. He was buried in the Holy Trinity Church at Stratford, where his grave can still be seen today. A bequest he made in his will has attracted almost as much interest and curiosity as anything in his plays—he left his wife his "second-best bed."

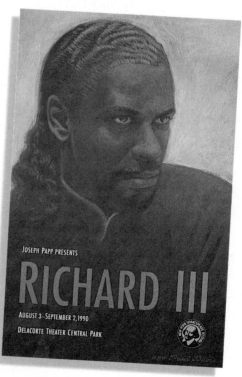

Poster featuring Denzel Washington in Shakespeare's *Richard III* in a 1990 New York Shakespeare Festival production.

The Elizabethan Stage

by Robert Anderson

The White Hart Inn, London. Engraving.

By permission of the Folger Shakespeare Library.

The Elizabethan stage would have seemed very strange to American theatergoers of fifty or sixty years ago, who were accustomed to elaborate and realistic settings placed on a stage separated from the audience by a huge velvet curtain. This is called a proscenium stage, and though it's still more or less standard today, the newer arena stages, thrust stages, and open stages have made us much more at home with Shakespeare's theater. The use of these simpler stages, which make the audience feel they're a part of the action, recalls the saying that all you need for a theater is "a platform and a passion or two."

As with Shakespeare's life, we have only sketchy information about the early English theaters. It appears that the wandering acting companies in England had originally set up their stages—mere platforms—wherever they could find space, often in the courtyards of inns. The audience stood around three sides of the stage, or if they paid more, they sat in chairs on the balconies surrounding the inn yard.

SKILLS FOCUS

Pages 745–749 cover
Literary Skills
Understand the history of the Elizabethan stage.

The Globe Theatre, a view of Shoreditch in 1590, by Cyril Walter Hodges. Watercolor with pen, ink, and body color (9″ × 6½″).

When James Burbage (the father of Richard Burbage, the actor who was to perform most of Shakespeare's great tragic parts) decided in 1576 to build the first permanent theater just outside the city of London, it was natural that he should duplicate the courtyard theaters in which his company had been performing. Burbage called his new playhouse simply "The Theatre."

The Globe—The "Wooden O"

In 1599, the owner of the land on which Burbage had built his theater apparently decided to raise the rent. Because the theater was somewhat behind in its rent payments, the landlord threatened to take it over. On

In *Henry V*, Shakespeare calls the theater "this wooden O."

the night of January 20, 1599, James Burbage's son Cuthbert and others in the company stealthily took their theater apart timber by timber and rowed the pieces across the river, where they later reconstructed the theater and called it the Globe. This was the theater where Shakespeare's greatest plays were performed.

In *Henry V,* Shakespeare calls the theater "this wooden O." It consisted of an open space, perhaps sixty-five feet in diameter, surrounded by a more or less circular building thirty feet high and consisting of three tiers of seats for spectators. As in the inn courtyards, the stage, which was forty feet by thirty feet and five feet off the ground, projected into the open space.

The interesting part of the stage was at the rear, where there was a small curtained inner stage flanked by two entrances, with an upper stage above it. Stout pillars held up a narrow roof over the rear part of the stage. This was called the Heavens. The front part of the stage was equipped with a trapdoor, which could be used for burial scenes, surprise entrances, and mysterious exits.

A replica of the Globe Theatre has been constructed very near its former location in London. The queen of England attended its opening in 1997, and Shakespeare's plays are still performed there today.

The Sets: Mostly Imagination

Shakespeare trusted his audience's imagination. He knew he did not need elaborate sets to re-create a battle scene or a bedroom or the Roman Forum. The audience members could do it for themselves. Moreover, without elaborate sets to move on and off the stage, Shakespeare could change scenes with the kind of fluidity we see in movies today.

Here is how Shakespeare prompted his audience to see hundreds of horsemen (and to costume his kings) in lines from the Prologue to *Henry V:*

> Let us . . .
> On your imaginary forces work. . . .
> Think, when we talk of horses, that you see them
> Printing their proud hoofs i' th' receiving earth;
> For 'tis your thoughts that now must deck our kings. . . .

Though Shakespeare made no attempt to use realistic settings, it appears that his kings and other characters were splendidly decked out. He also called for flags and banners and musicians, and the multilayered stage could produce special effects. Characters could be lowered from the Heavens by cranes, and there were sound effects as well. In fact, these special effects caused the destruction of the Globe. In 1613, during the battle scene of *Henry VIII,* a stagehand was lighting the fuse of a cannon. A spark flew up and started a fire in the thatched roof of the Heavens, and the theater burned down.

Because the plays were performed during the day in the open air, there was no need for stage illumination. Shakespeare had to convey the idea of night by having characters carry torches. (Today, to shoot a night scene in the daytime, movie directors darken the scene by using filters on their cameras.)

The Actors: All Males

In Shakespeare's time all actors were male. (It wasn't until 1660, when the exiled King Charles II was restored to the English throne and the repressive Puritan dominance ended, that women played in professional theaters.) Boys who had been recruited from the choir schools and trained professionally played the female roles. It was not too difficult to create the illusion that these boys were women. Shakespeare's plays were performed in contemporary Elizabethan costumes, and women's clothing of the day was very elaborate and concealing, with long, full skirts flowing from extremely narrow waists. Women of the time also wore elaborate wigs and powdered their faces heavily. So, all in all, the transformation of boys into women characters was not so unbelievable.

In yet another reversal of roles, the mezzo-soprano Tatiana Troyanos, a woman, portrays Caesar in Handel's opera *Julius Caesar.*
The Bettmann Archive.

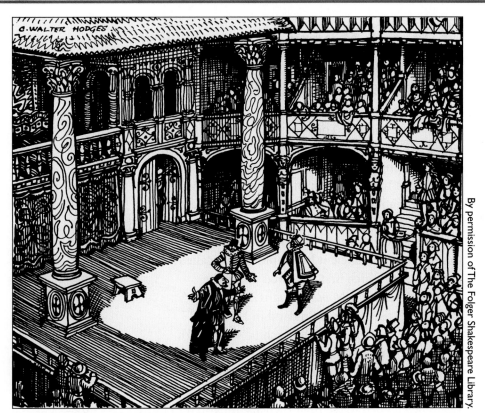

By permission of The Folger Shakespeare Library.

Drawing of a Globe Theatre performance.

Hooking the Audience's Attention

The Elizabethan theater was a convivial place where people arrived early, visited with friends, made new acquaintances, moved around freely, and ate and drank before and during the performance. (The occasion might have had something of the feeling of a Saturday matinee at a local shopping-mall movie theater.) Playwrights had to write scenes that would catch the attention of this audience, and many actors held their attention by vigorous and flamboyant acting. By comparison, today's movie cameras are so sensitive that sometimes all an actor has to do is think the right thoughts, and that is enough. Elizabethan actors had to do more than that since they were trying to hold the interest of three thousand restless people who were also busy eating, drinking, and talking. We get the impression that, like actors working on modern thrust or arena stages, the Elizabethan players had to keep on the move so that spectators on all three sides could catch their expressions and hear their voices.

> The occasion might have had something of the feeling of a Saturday matinee at a local shopping-mall movie theater.

The Play: The Results of Violence

Assassination. The murder of a public figure is an act that can take place in a split second yet change the course of history. We've seen a number of assassinations in recent history. This play is about the assassination of a Roman general and dictator who lived and died (an extremely violent death) more than two thousand years ago. Shakespeare drew his material from an ancient biographical text called *The Parallel Lives,* which first appeared under the title *The Lives of the Noble Grecians and Romans* in translation in England in 1579. This work was written by Plutarch (c. 46–c. 120), a Greek writer and biographer who lived close to the time of Julius Caesar. Greek and Roman history and culture had a great appeal for the English of the Elizabethan Age. They tended to see their own age mirrored in those great ancient civilizations.

Roman helmet from Judea.

Rome in Caesar's Day: Continuous War

We get the impression that the Roman world in Caesar's time was continuously at war. Today the generals of the U.S. Army are ultimately responsible to the president, who is their commander in chief. But two thousand years ago in Rome, the generals had enormous individual power. Powerful generals like Caesar moved with their plundering armies over the entire Mediterranean world. After these "private armies" subdued weaker countries, the territories were then ruled by Roman governors who exacted cruel taxes from the conquered people.

Sometimes the generals turned on one another, because they were strong men battling for power. This is what happened when the generals Caesar and Pompey clashed in the civil war that began in 49 B.C.

Caesar and Pompey: Jealousy and Murder

Caesar and Pompey were friends. Pompey married Caesar's daughter by his first wife. In 60 B.C., the two generals helped bring order to a weakened government, when they, along with Crassus, formed the First Triumvirate (three-man government).

Eager for still more power and realizing that he could achieve it only with conquests and money, Caesar departed for what has been called the Gallic Wars. For eight years he and his armies roamed Europe, subjugating France, Belgium, and parts of Holland, Germany, and Switzerland. Caesar amassed huge sums of money, which he sent back to Rome to gain favor among the people.

Caesar's daughter died in 54 B.C., and in 49 B.C. Pompey, jealous of Caesar's growing power and favor among the people, threw his weight to the Senate, which was also wary of Caesar's ambitions.

Caesar considered himself a defender of the people, but critics said that he gained the people's support with bribes and handouts. His enemies said he deprived the Romans of their liberty.

Caesar refused the Senate's order to give up his command and return to Rome as a private citizen. Instead, he marched his army on Rome, took control, and chased Pompey all the way to Egypt. There Pompey was murdered before Caesar could capture him. Caesar lingered in Egypt for nine months, bewitched by the twenty-two-year-old Cleopatra. Establishing her on the throne of Egypt under his protection, Caesar went to Spain, where he defeated an army led by Pompey's sons.

The Unconquerable God

When he returned to Rome, Caesar was invincible. He was declared dictator for ten years and saw to it that his supporters, including Brutus, became senators. As his desire for power grew obsessive, he had a statue of himself, bearing the inscription "To the Unconquerable God," erected in the temple of Quirinus. The common people loved him; later Caesar was declared dictator for life.

However, to a number of Romans, Caesar's ambition was deplorable. The last Roman king had been overthrown 450 years before, when the Romans set up a republican government. The idea of another king ruling the "free Romans" was unthinkable. As Caesar's arrogance and power became unbearable to certain senators, they made plans to assassinate him on March 15, 44 B.C. Shakespeare's play opens a month before the murder.

Bust of Julius Caesar (date unknown).
National Museum, Naples. The Bettmann Archive.

How to Read Shakespeare

Hear the Beat

As with all of Shakespeare's plays, *Julius Caesar* is written in blank verse. **Blank verse** duplicates the natural rhythms of English speech. Blank verse is unrhymed **iambic pentameter,** which means that each line of poetry in the play is built on five iambs. An **iamb** consists of an un-stressed syllable followed by a stressed syllable, as in the word prĕpáre. In this case, **pentameter** means that there are five iambs in a line. Read these lines aloud to feel the beat, or rhythm. Better yet, strike the strong and weak beats with your fingers (try it!):

The evil that men do lives after them,

The good is oft interrèd with their bones.

A whole play written in this pattern would have a singsong effect. To break the monotony and alter the emphasis, Shakespeare sometimes reverses the stressed and unstressed syllables.

Actors don't always read speeches with the same emphasis. You'll probably find variations in reading these lines in your own group. (Read this aloud.)

This was the noblest Roman of them all.
All the conspirators save only he
Did that they did in envy of great Caesar.

Shakespeare doesn't let all his charac-ters speak in blank verse. You'll notice that the commoners speak, as we all do, in ordinary prose. (So does Brutus in his funeral oration.)

Pauses and Stops for Breath

Follow the punctuation marks, and resist the temptation to stop at the end of each line. Thus, in the first passage on this page ("The evil . . ."), you pause at the end of the first line and come to a full stop at the end of the second. (Try it.) In the next passage, you make a full stop for breath at the end of the first line but not at the end of the second line. The second line has no end punctuation, and sense requires that you move on. (Try it.) Lines that end with a punctuation mark are called **end-stopped** lines. Lines that do not end with a punctuation mark are called **run-on** lines. (To determine the complete meaning, you must "run on" to the next line.)

Archaic Words

One character in the play is a sooth-sayer. In Shakespeare's day the word *sooth* meant "truth." Today we'd call such a person a fortuneteller. Here, from *Julius Caesar,* are some other words that are now archaic:

ague: fever.

alarum: call to arms, such as a trumpet blast.

an: if.

betimes: from time to time.

fleering: flattering.

hence, whence, thence: here, where, there.

hie: hurry.

knave: servant, or person of humble birth.

prithee: pray thee (beg thee).

smatch: small amount.

Words with Different Meanings

The most troublesome words in Shakespeare's plays are those that are still in use but now have different meanings. When Flavius calls the cobbler "thou naughty knave," he seems to be merely scolding the man. However, *naughty* here means "worthless," so the sense of Flavius's line is different from what you might have thought. Here are other familiar words from *Julius Caesar* that had different meanings in Shakespeare's day:

closet: small room, often a private study.

exhalations: meteors.

gentle: noble. *Gentleman* once referred to a man who had a title.

ghastly: ghostly.

humor: temper or disposition.

indifferently: impartially.

just: true.

merely: wholly; entirely.

repair: go.

sad: serious.

saucy: presumptuous.

soft: slowly; "wait a minute."

wit: intelligence.

Act It Out!

Don't forget that this play was created for an ordinary audience—people just like the ones who flock to movies or rock concerts today. To get a feel for the play as action, plan to perform as much of it as possible.

You might begin with the first scene—a brief street scene in which a group of working people encounter two military officers. Here are some suggestions for **oral interpretation:**

William Shakespeare.
Drawing by David Levine. Reprinted with permission from *The New York Review of Books.* Copyright ©1978 David Levine.

1. In small groups, assign a part to each group member.

2. For this first scene especially, you could do **choral readings.** Again, break into groups. Then, split your group into two smaller groups. Let one small group read the commoners' lines and the other small group read the speeches of the tribunes. Then, have the groups switch roles: The commoners become the tribunes, and the tribunes become the commoners.

As you read the scene, don't worry about the way the archaic words are pronounced. Don't worry about the poetry either: Read all the lines in the scene as if they were prose. Read for sense only: At this point, don't worry about acting out the scene.

After your reading, discuss with the members of your group what happens in the scene and how you feel about it. Who are these people? What is going on?

Now, give a **dramatic performance** of the scene. Some of you will be the **actors,** at least one will be the **director,** and some of you will be the **audience.** How will you set the scene? What are the characters doing as they speak? What props will you need, if any? How will you get audience feedback after your performance?

Beginnings and endings are important in Shakespeare. What did you learn from performing this opening scene?

The Tragedy of Julius Caesar

Make the Connection

In all of Shakespeare's plays the characters (no matter what historical period they live in) inhabit a world that is run by a just God who ultimately rewards good and punishes evil. In Shakespeare's day, people believed that the universe was essentially good and orderly. All order stemmed from the authority of God, the supreme ruler. The monarch's right to rule came from God too, and so opposition to the anointed ruler was considered opposition to God. When the chain of authority was snapped, the heavens would be offended, and a whole society could be plunged into disorder.

When Shakespeare wrote this play, Queen Elizabeth was old and in failing health. She had no children. When she died, what would become of the country she had ruled so peacefully for nearly forty years? Would there be a bloody struggle for the throne? Would the country slip back into the violence that had preceded Elizabeth's reign? These questions show that the story of Julius Caesar had immediate connections for the Elizabethans—it tapped into their own desire for stability in government, into their dread of civil war.

Quickwrite ✏️

Before you read *Julius Caesar*, think about the Elizabethan view of the universe. How is it different from our ideas about government? Write your responses to the following statements. Do you agree? disagree? Why? Are you unsure about some of them? Are any of them disturbing?

1. Chaos results when the lawful social order is broken.
2. The best intentions of good, noble people can lead to tragedy.
3. Language is a powerful weapon, and in the hands of a skilled person, it can be used to manipulate others.
4. Violence and bloodshed can never have morally good results.
5. Orderliness and stable rule, even rule by a dictator, are preferable to chaos.

(Save your notes.)

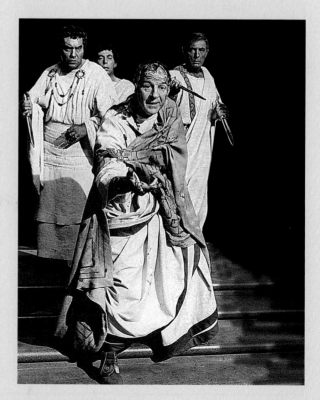

INTERNET

More About William Shakespeare

Keyword: LE5 10-10

SKILLS FOCUS

Literary Skills
Understand characteristics of tragedy.

Literary Focus

Tragedy: Alas, an Unhappy Ending

Lest we wonder, Shakespeare tells us in the title that *Julius Caesar* is a tragedy. A **tragedy** is a play, novel, or other narrative that depicts serious and important events and ends unhappily for the main character. Like the tragedies of the ancient Greeks, Shakespeare's tragedies share these characteristics:

- The main character is often high ranking and dignified, not an ordinary man or woman.

- The main character has a **tragic flaw** —a defect in character or judgment— that directly causes the character's downfall.

- The work ends unhappily, with the death of the main character.

All of Shakespeare's tragedies (for example, *Julius Caesar, Hamlet, King Lear, Macbeth,* and *Romeo and Juliet*) share a similar five-part structure.

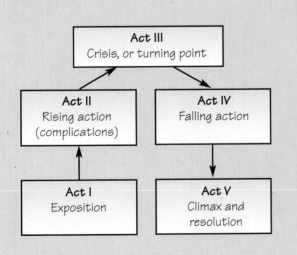

1. In **Act I,** the **exposition** introduces the main characters and their conflicts, establishes the setting, and provides background information.

2. In **Act II,** suspense builds as plot events create a **rising action,** a series of complications caused by the main characters when they try to resolve their conflicts.

3. In **Act III,** the **crisis,** or **turning point,** occurs. This is the dramatic and tense moment when the main character makes a choice that determines the rest of the play's action. (In a **comedy** the turning point lifts the play upward to a happy ending; in a **tragedy,** events spiral downward to an inevitable unhappy ending.)

4. **Act IV** presents the **falling action** —the consequences, or results, of actions taken during the **turning point.** This act propels the main character deeper and deeper into disaster; the tragic ending seems inevitable.

5. In **Act V,** near the end of the play, the **climax,** or moment of greatest tension, occurs. In a tragedy the climax is usually the death of the tragic hero. A brief **resolution** (or **denouement**) closely follows the climax, tying up any loose ends in the plot, and the play ends.

The **Staging the Play** sidenotes, which appear throughout the play, will help you visualize the performance of the play— including the way the stage is set, the way the actors move and interact onstage, and the way they say their lines.

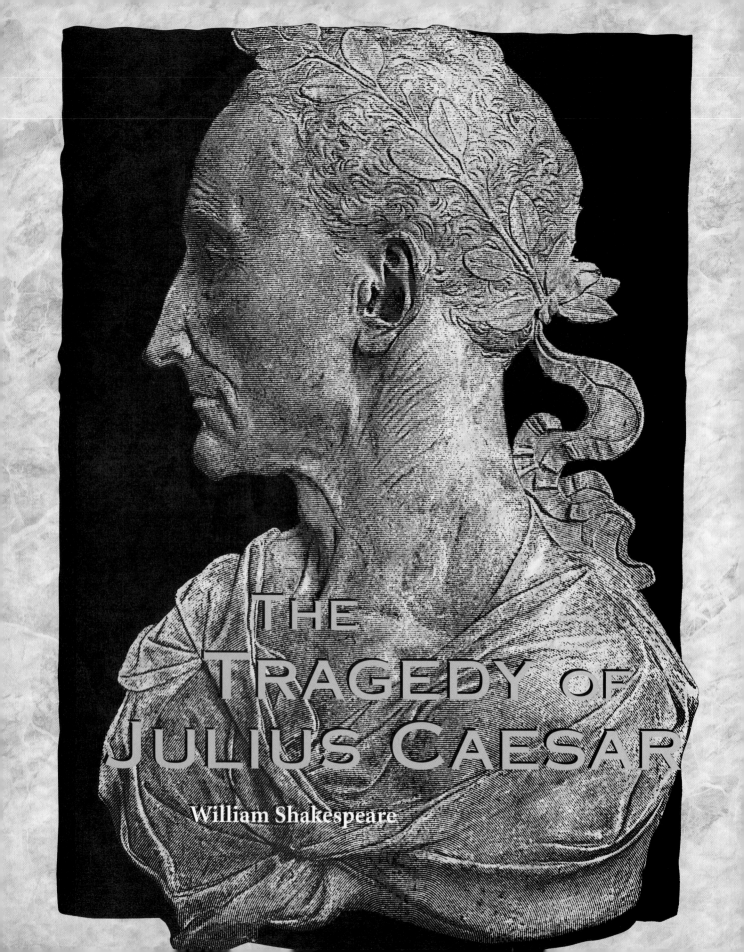

The Tragedy of Julius Caesar

William Shakespeare

CHARACTERS

Julius Caesar
Octavius Caesar ⎫
Marcus Antonius ⎬ triumvirs (three officials who share
M. Aemilius Lepidus ⎭ power) after the death of Julius Caesar

Cicero ⎫
Publius ⎬ senators
Popilius Lena ⎭

Marcus Brutus ⎫
Cassius ⎪
Casca ⎪
Trebonius ⎪ conspirators against
Ligarius ⎬ Julius Caesar
Decius Brutus ⎪
Metellus Cimber ⎪
Cinna ⎭

Flavius ⎫
Marullus ⎭ tribunes (officials appointed to administer the law)

Artemidorus of Cnidos, a teacher of rhetoric
A Soothsayer
Cinna, a poet
Another Poet

Lucilius ⎫
Titinius ⎪
Messala ⎬ friends of Brutus and Cassius
Young Cato ⎪
Volumnius ⎭

Varro ⎫
Clitus ⎪
Claudius ⎪
Strato ⎬ servants of Brutus
Lucius ⎪
Dardanius ⎭

Pindarus, servant of Cassius
Calphurnia, wife of Caesar
Portia, wife to Brutus
Senators, Citizens, Guards, Attendants, etc.

Scene: During most of the play, at Rome; later, near Sardis, and near Philippi.

Note: The text of this play is taken in entirety from the *Signet Classic Shakespeare*. The editors of the *Signet Classic Shakespeare* have refrained from making abundant changes in the text, but they have added line numbers and act and scene divisions, as well as indications of locale at the beginning of scenes.

(Background) The ruins of the Roman Forum.

ACT I

SCENE 1.
Rome. A street.

Enter FLAVIUS, MARULLUS, *and certain* COMMONERS *over the stage.*

Flavius.
Hence! Home, you idle creatures, get you home!
Is this a holiday? What, know you not,
Being mechanical,° you ought not walk
Upon a laboring day without the sign

5   Of your profession?° Speak, what trade art thou?
Carpenter. Why, sir, a carpenter.
Marullus.
Where is thy leather apron and thy rule?
What dost thou with thy best apparel on?
You, sir, what trade are you?

10 **Cobbler.** Truly, sir, in respect of a fine workman,° I am but,
as you would say, a cobbler.°
Marullus.
But what trade art thou? Answer me directly.
Cobbler. A trade, sir, that, I hope, I may use with a safe
conscience, which is indeed, sir, a mender of bad soles.
Flavius.

15 What trade, thou knave? Thou naughty° knave, what trade?
Cobbler. Nay, I beseech you, sir, be not out with me: yet, if
you be out, sir, I can mend you.
Marullus.
What mean'st thou by that? Mend me, thou saucy fellow?
Cobbler. Why, sir, cobble you.
Flavius.

20 Thou art a cobbler, art thou?
Cobbler. Truly, sir, all that I live by is with the awl:° I
meddle with no tradesman's matters, nor women's
matters; but withal,° I am indeed, sir, a surgeon to old
shoes: when they are in great danger, I recover them. As

25 proper men as ever trod upon neat's leather° have gone
upon my handiwork.
Flavius.
But wherefore art not in thy shop today?
Why dost thou lead these men about the streets?

Staging the Play
Stage direction. We are on a crowded street in Rome. It is lined with statues near what is today known as the Palatine Hill (which is where the palaces, or palatia, *were). A joyous, peaceful crowd is milling about. Two tribunes— military men—enter with the noisy mob of commoners. What tone does Flavius's first speech bring immediately to the play?*

3. mechanical: working class.

5. sign of your profession: your work clothes and tools.

10. In other words, in comparison with a skilled laborer.
11. cobbler: In Shakespeare's day the word meant both "shoemaker" and "bungler."

15. naughty: worthless.

Staging the Play
16. *It is important in this play to watch the moods of the crowd. Do you think these commoners are afraid of the military men, or are they acting comically and boldly?*

21. awl: sharp, pointed tool for making holes in wood or leather.

23. withal: nevertheless.

25. neat's leather: leather from cattle.

Cobbler. Truly, sir, to wear out their shoes, to get myself
30   into more work. But indeed, sir, we make holiday to see
      Caesar and to rejoice in his triumph.

Marullus.
      Wherefore rejoice? What conquest brings he home?
      What tributaries° follow him to Rome,
      To grace in captive bonds his chariot wheels?
35   You blocks, you stones, you worse than senseless things!
      O you hard hearts, you cruel men of Rome,
      Knew you not Pompey?° Many a time and oft
      Have you climbed up to walls and battlements,
      To tow'rs and windows, yea, to chimney tops,
40   Your infants in your arms, and there have sat
      The livelong day, with patient expectation,
      To see great Pompey pass the streets of Rome.
      And when you saw his chariot but appear,
      Have you not made an universal shout,
45   That Tiber trembled underneath her banks
      To hear the replication° of your sounds
      Made in her concave shores?°
      And do you now put on your best attire?
      And do you now cull out a holiday?
50   And do you now strew flowers in his way
      That comes in triumph over Pompey's blood?
      Be gone!
      Run to your houses, fall upon your knees,
      Pray to the gods to intermit° the plague
55   That needs must light on this ingratitude.

Flavius.
      Go, go, good countrymen, and, for this fault,
      Assemble all the poor men of your sort;
      Draw them to Tiber banks and weep your tears
      Into the channel, till the lowest stream
60   Do kiss the most exalted shores of all.

                       [*Exeunt all the* COMMONERS.]

      See, whe'r their basest mettle° be not moved;
      They vanish tongue-tied in their guiltiness.
      Go you down that way towards the Capitol;
      This way will I. Disrobe the images,°
65   If you do find them decked with ceremonies.

? 30. *Why might Shakespeare begin his tragedy on a comic note? What important facts does the cobbler reveal?*

33. tributaries: captives (captive enemies who have to pay tribute, or tax, to Rome).

? Staging the Play
*A **monologue** is a long speech that a character directs to other characters onstage. What might Marullus be doing as he speaks this monologue?*

37. Pompey: Roman politician and general who was defeated by Caesar in 48 B.C. and later murdered.

46. replication: echo; copy.
47. concave shores: carved-out banks of the river.

? Staging the Play
52. *How should this short line be spoken?*

54. intermit: hold back.

? 55. *What is the key word in the last line of this speech? Why is Marullus angry at the mob?*

? Staging the Play
Stage direction. Pay attention to the movements of the crowd. What mood has taken over these commoners as they leave the stage? Would you have them leave in a defiant mood, or are they ashamed?
61. basest mettle: basic substance; their "stuff."

64. images: statues.

Marullus.

    May we do so?

    You know it is the feast of Lupercal.°

Flavius.

    It is no matter; let no images

    Be hung with Caesar's trophies. I'll about

70   And drive away the vulgar° from the streets;

    So do you too, where you perceive them thick.

    These growing feathers plucked from Caesar's wing

    Will make him fly an ordinary pitch,°

    Who else would soar above the view of men

75   And keep us all in servile fearfulness.   [*Exeunt.*]

SCENE 2. *A public place.*

Enter CAESAR, ANTONY *(dressed for the race),*
CALPHURNIA, PORTIA, DECIUS, CICERO, BRUTUS,
CASSIUS, CASCA, *a* SOOTHSAYER; *after them,* MARULLUS
and FLAVIUS.

Caesar.

    Calphurnia!

Casca.   Peace, ho! Caesar speaks.

Caesar.   Calphurnia!

Calphurnia. Here, my lord.

Caesar.

    Stand you directly in Antonius' way

    When he doth run his course. Antonius!

5 **Antony.** Caesar, my lord?

Caesar.

    Forget not in your speed, Antonius,

    To touch Calphurnia; for our elders say

    The barren, touchèd in this holy chase,

    Shake off their sterile curse.

Antony.   I shall remember:

10   When Caesar says "Do this," it is performed.

Caesar.

    Set on, and leave no ceremony out.

Soothsayer. Caesar!

Caesar. Ha! Who calls?

Casca.

    Bid every noise be still; peace yet again!

67. Lupercal: old Roman fertility festival celebrated on February 15. In the ceremony young men raced around the Palatine Hill (at the base of which is the Lupercal cave) and whipped bystanders with strips of goatskin. Those who were whipped were assured of fertility. The Lupercal cave is believed to be where the twins Romulus and Remus, the founders of Rome, were suckled by a wolf.

70. vulgar: common people.

73. an ordinary pitch: at an ordinary height.

? **75.** *What does Flavius fear about Caesar?*

? **Staging the Play**
Stage direction. As Caesar and his retinue enter, the crowd makes way for them. Antony is dressed for the race held on the Feast of Lupercal, which this year also celebrates Caesar's latest victory. Caesar would be richly dressed—perhaps too richly. What mood would Marullus and Flavius be in?

? **10.** *This speech suggests something important about Antony. What is it?*

? **Staging the Play**
12. *A lot of ceremonial music and ritual have opened this scene, so our attention has been focused on Caesar and his followers. Now the soothsayer, or foreteller of the future, is suddenly visible. This is a dramatic moment, for it foreshadows what will happen. Where would you place the soothsayer? How should Caesar react to his call?*

"BEWARE THE IDES OF MARCH."

The performance photographs illustrating this play are of
the 1988 New York Shakespeare Festival production, starring
Al Pacino as Antony and Martin Sheen as Brutus.

© George E. Joseph.

Caesar.

15   Who is it in the press° that calls on me?
        I hear a tongue, shriller than all the music,
        Cry "Caesar." Speak; Caesar is turned to hear.

Soothsayer.

        Beware the ides of March.

Caesar.   What man is that?

Brutus.

        A soothsayer bids you beware the ides of March.

Caesar.

20   Set him before me; let me see his face.

Cassius.

        Fellow, come from the throng; look upon Caesar.

Caesar.

        What say'st thou to me now? Speak once again.

Soothsayer.

        Beware the ides of March.

Caesar.

        He is a dreamer, let us leave him. Pass.

        [*Sennet.° Exeunt all except* BRUTUS *and* CASSIUS.]

Cassius.

25   Will you go see the order of the course?

Brutus. Not I.

Cassius. I pray you do.

Brutus.

        I am not gamesome: I do lack some part
        Of that quick spirit that is in Antony.

30   Let me not hinder, Cassius, your desires;
        I'll leave you.

Cassius.

        Brutus, I do observe you now of late;
        I have not from your eyes that gentleness
        And show of love as I was wont to have;

35   You bear too stubborn and too strange a hand°
        Over your friend that loves you.

Brutus.   Cassius,
        Be not deceived: if I have veiled my look,
        I turn the trouble of my countenance
        Merely° upon myself. Vexèd I am

40   Of late with passions of some difference,°
        Conceptions only proper to myself,
        Which give some soil,° perhaps, to my behaviors;

---

15. **press:** crowd.

? **17.** *What physical disability might this line suggest?*

? **Staging the Play**
18. *The ides of March are March 15. In some productions this warning is heard as an ominous and disembodied cry. In what different ways could the line be spoken?*

Sennet: flourish, or fanfare of trumpets announcing a ceremonial entrance or exit.

? **Staging the Play**
Stage direction. Except for Brutus and Cassius, the stage is empty for a few moments as they stand looking at the departing Caesar. The action line of the play—the assassination—begins now with Cassius's rather casual question (line 25). How should Brutus speak his answer?

35. **You . . . hand:** Cassius is comparing Brutus's treatment of him with the way a trainer treats a horse.

39. **Merely:** wholly.

40. **passions of some difference:** conflicting feelings or emotions.

42. **give some soil:** stain or mar.

But let not therefore my good friends be grieved
(Among which number, Cassius, be you one)
45 Nor construe° any further my neglect
Than that poor Brutus, with himself at war,
Forgets the shows of love to other men.

Cassius.

Then, Brutus, I have much mistook your passion,°
By means whereof this breast of mine hath buried
50 Thoughts of great value, worthy cogitations.°
Tell me, good Brutus, can you see your face?

Brutus.

No, Cassius; for the eye sees not itself
But by reflection, by some other things.

Cassius.

'Tis just:°
55 And it is very much lamented, Brutus,
That you have no such mirrors as will turn
Your hidden worthiness into your eye,
That you might see your shadow.° I have heard
Where many of the best respect° in Rome
60 (Except immortal Caesar), speaking of Brutus,
And groaning underneath this age's yoke,
Have wished that noble Brutus had his eyes.

Brutus.

Into what dangers would you lead me, Cassius,
That you would have me seek into myself
65 For that which is not in me?

Cassius.

Therefore, good Brutus, be prepared to hear;
And since you know you cannot see yourself
So well as by reflection, I, your glass°
Will modestly discover to yourself
70 That of yourself which you yet know not of.
And be not jealous on° me, gentle Brutus:
Were I a common laughter,° or did use
To stale with ordinary oaths my love
To every new protester,° if you know
75 That I do fawn on men and hug them hard,
And after scandal them;° or if you know
That I profess myself in banqueting
To all the rout,° then hold me dangerous.

---

45. construe: interpret.

47. *How does Brutus explain his behavior?*

48. passion: feeling.

50. worthy cogitations: reflections of great value.

54. just: true.

58. shadow: reflection (of what others think of him).
59. respect: reputation.

Staging the Play
60. *How would Cassius say the parenthetical remark?*

68. glass: mirror.

71. jealous on: suspicious of.

72. common laughter: butt of a joke; object of mockery.

74. In other words, if he swore to love everyone who came along.

76. scandal them: ruin them by gossip.

78. rout (rout): common people; the mob.

78. *What, in sum, is Cassius telling Brutus here?*

[*Flourish° and shout.*]

Brutus.

What means this shouting? I do fear the people
Choose Caesar for their king.

80   **Cassius.**   Ay, do you fear it?
Then must I think you would not have it so.

Brutus.

I would not, Cassius, yet I love him well.
But wherefore do you hold me here so long?
What is it that you would impart to me?

85   If it be aught toward the general good,
Set honor in one eye and death i' th' other,
And I will look on both indifferently;°
For let the gods so speed me, as I love
The name of honor more than I fear death.

Cassius.

90   I know that virtue to be in you, Brutus,
As well as I do know your outward favor.°
Well, honor is the subject of my story.
I cannot tell what you and other men
Think of this life, but for my single self,

95   I had as lief° not be, as live to be
In awe of such a thing as I myself.
I was born free as Caesar; so were you:
We both have fed as well, and we can both
Endure the winter's cold as well as he:

100   For once, upon a raw and gusty day,
The troubled Tiber chafing with° her shores,
Caesar said to me "Dar'st thou, Cassius, now
Leap in with me into this angry flood,
And swim to yonder point?" Upon the word,

105   Accout'red as I was, I plungèd in
And bade him follow: so indeed he did.
The torrent roared, and we did buffet it
With lusty sinews, throwing it aside
And stemming it with hearts of controversy.°

110   But ere we could arrive the point proposed,
Caesar cried "Help me, Cassius, or I sink!"
I, as Aeneas,° our great ancestor,
Did from the flames of Troy upon his shoulder
The old Anchises bear, so from the waves of Tiber

115   Did I the tired Caesar. And this man
Is now become a god, and Cassius is

Flourish: brief, elaborate music played by trumpets.

? Staging the Play
Stage direction. The trumpets sound offstage, and the crowd's roar is heard again. How would Cassius and Brutus react?

? Staging the Play
80. *This is what Cassius has wanted to hear. How should he deliver this speech?*

87. indifferently: impartially; fairly.

? Staging the Play
89. *Brutus could sound noble here, or he could be played as foolishly idealistic, even priggish. How would you deliver this speech?*

91. outward favor: appearance.

95. as lief (lēf): just as soon.

? 97. *This is a long and important* **monologue.** *What is Cassius's chief complaint about Caesar?*

101. chafing with: raging against (the river was rough with waves and currents).

109. hearts of controversy: hearts full of aggressive feelings, or fighting spirit.

112. Aeneas (i·nē′əs): legendary forefather of the Roman people who, in Virgil's *Aeneid*, fled the burning city of Troy carrying his aged father on his back. (In many accounts of the legend, Romulus and Remus are descendants of Aeneas.)

A wretched creature, and must bend his body
If Caesar carelessly but nod on him.
He had a fever when he was in Spain,
120 And when the fit was on him, I did mark
How he did shake; 'tis true, this god did shake.
His coward lips did from their color fly,
And that same eye whose bend doth awe the world
Did lose his luster; I did hear him groan;
125 Ay, and that tongue of his, that bade the Romans
Mark him and write his speeches in their books,
Alas, it cried, "Give me some drink, Titinius,"
As a sick girl. Ye gods! It doth amaze me,
A man of such a feeble temper should
130 So get the start of the majestic world,
And bear the palm° alone.

[*Shout. Flourish.*]

Brutus.
Another general shout?
I do believe that these applauses are
For some new honors that are heaped on Caesar.
Cassius.
135 Why, man, he doth bestride the narrow world
Like a Colossus,° and we petty men
Walk under his huge legs and peep about
To find ourselves dishonorable graves.
Men at some time are masters of their fates:
140 The fault, dear Brutus, is not in our stars,°
But in ourselves, that we are underlings.
Brutus and Caesar: what should be in that "Caesar"?
Why should that name be sounded more than yours?
Write them together, yours is as fair a name;
145 Sound them, it doth become the mouth as well;
Weigh them, it is as heavy; conjure with 'em,
"Brutus" will start a spirit as soon as "Caesar."
Now, in the names of all the gods at once,
Upon what meat doth this our Caesar feed,
150 That he is grown so great? Age, thou art shamed!
Rome, thou hast lost the breed of noble bloods!
When went there by an age, since the great flood,°
But it was famed with more than with one man?
When could they say (till now) that talked of Rome,

Staging the Play
118. *How should Cassius say this last sentence?*

Staging the Play
121. *What word should be stressed here?*

131. bear the palm: hold the palm branch, an award given to a victorious general.

131. *Why has Cassius told Brutus these anecdotes about Caesar? What is his point?*

136. Colossus: huge statue of Helios that was said to straddle the entrance to the harbor at Rhodes, an island in the Aegean Sea. The statue, so huge that ships passed under its legs, was one of the Seven Wonders of the ancient world. It was destroyed by an earthquake in 224 B.C.
140. stars: Elizabethans believed that one's life was governed by the stars, or constellation, one was born under.

Staging the Play
142. *There is often a pause here, after the Colossus metaphor. How would Cassius say the names Brutus and Caesar?*

152. the great flood: in Greek mythology, flood sent by Zeus to drown all the wicked people on earth. Only the faithful couple Deucalion and Pyrrha were saved.

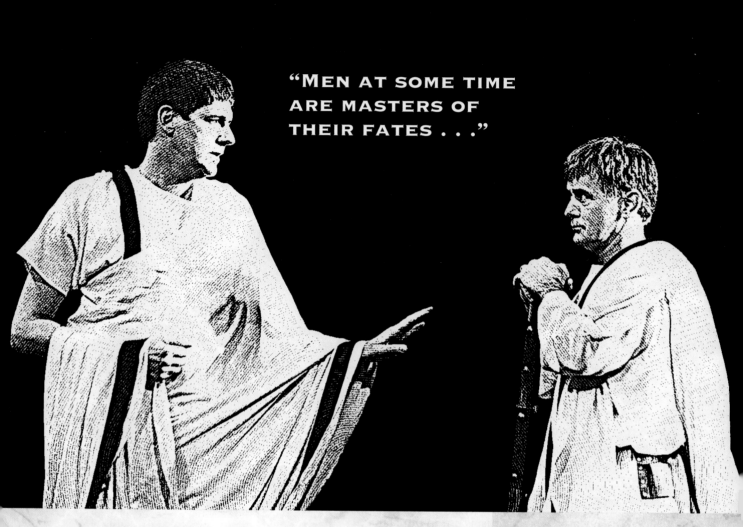

"MEN AT SOME TIME
ARE MASTERS OF
THEIR FATES . . ."

155   That her wide walks encompassed but one man?
      Now is it Rome indeed, and room° enough,
      When there is in it but one only man.
      O, you and I have heard our fathers say,
      There was a Brutus once that would have brooked°
160   Th' eternal devil to keep his state in Rome
      As easily as a king.°
   Brutus.
      That you do love me, I am nothing jealous;
      What you would work me to, I have some aim;°
      How I have thought of this, and of these times,

156. Rome . . . room: a pun; both
words were pronounced rōōm in
Shakespeare's day.

159. brooked: put up with.

161. This refers to an ancestor of
Brutus's who, in the sixth century
B.C., helped to expel the last king
from Rome and set up the republic.

? **161.** *Why does Cassius
mention Brutus's famous
ancestor?*

163. aim: idea.

165   I shall recount hereafter. For this present,
    I would not so (with love I might entreat you)
    Be any further moved. What you have said
    I will consider; what you have to say
    I will with patience hear, and find a time
170   Both meet° to hear and answer such high things.
    Till then, my noble friend, chew upon this:
    Brutus had rather be a villager
    Than to repute himself a son of Rome
    Under these hard conditions as this time
    Is like to lay upon us.

175   **Cassius.**   I am glad
    That my weak words have struck but thus much show
    Of fire from Brutus.

    [*Enter* CAESAR *and his* TRAIN.]

Brutus.
    The games are done, and Caesar is returning.
Cassius.
    As they pass by, pluck Casca by the sleeve,
180   And he will (after his sour fashion) tell you
    What hath proceeded worthy note today.
Brutus.
    I will do so. But look you, Cassius,
    The angry spot doth glow on Caesar's brow,
    And all the rest look like a chidden° train:
185   Calphurnia's cheek is pale, and Cicero
    Looks with such ferret° and such fiery eyes
    As we have seen him in the Capitol,
    Being crossed in conference by some senators.
Cassius.
    Casca will tell us what the matter is.
190 **Caesar.** Antonius.
Antony. Caesar?
Caesar.
    Let me have men about me that are fat,
    Sleek-headed men, and such as sleep a-nights.
    Yond Cassius has a lean and hungry look;
195   He thinks too much: such men are dangerous.
Antony.
    Fear him not, Caesar, he's not dangerous;
    He is a noble Roman, and well given.°

---

170. meet: appropriate.

[?] 175. *A **character foil** is a character who serves as a contrast to another character, so that each one stands out vividly. How is Cassius a foil to Brutus?*

[?] 177. *According to Cassius's speech, how has Brutus delivered his previous line? Has Cassius gotten what he wants?*

[?] Staging the Play
Stage direction. Cassius and Brutus move downstage left to allow the procession (Caesar's train) to pass across the width of the backstage area to an entrance downstage right. In this way the audience sees two acting areas at one time—one for the conspirators and their growing intimacy and one for the pompous world of public ceremony. Would the two actors next speak openly, or are they already acting secretively?

184. chidden (chid''n): rebuked; corrected.

186. ferret: weasel-like animal, usually considered crafty.

[?] 188. *Cicero at this time is sixty-two years old, famous as a great advocate of the republic. Though he had supported Pompey and opposed Caesar, Cicero liked Caesar personally and had nothing to do with the assassination. What does Brutus think of Cicero?*

[?] Staging the Play
190. *Cassius and Brutus move away, and we focus on Caesar, who casts a suspicious look at Cassius, now downstage left. What does Caesar's next speech tell you about Cassius's physical appearance?*

197. well given: well disposed to support Caesar.

Caesar.

　　Would he were fatter! But I fear him not.

　　Yet if my name were liable to fear,

200　I do not know the man I should avoid

　　So soon as that spare Cassius. He reads much,

　　He is a great observer, and he looks

　　Quite through the deeds of men.° He loves no plays,

　　As thou dost, Antony; he hears no music;

205　Seldom he smiles, and smiles in such a sort°

　　As if he mocked himself, and scorned his spirit

　　That could be moved to smile at anything.

　　Such men as he be never at heart's ease

　　Whiles they behold a greater than themselves,

210　And therefore are they very dangerous.

　　I rather tell thee what is to be feared

　　Than what I fear; for always I am Caesar.

　　Come on my right hand, for this ear is deaf,

　　And tell me truly what thou think'st of him.

　　　　　　[*Sennet. Exeunt* CAESAR *and his* TRAIN.]

Casca.

215　You pulled me by the cloak; would you speak with me?

Brutus.

　　Ay, Casca; tell us what hath chanced today,

　　That Caesar looks so sad.°

Casca.

　　Why, you were with him, were you not?

Brutus.

　　I should not then ask Casca what had chanced.

220　**Casca.** Why, there was a crown offered him; and being
　　offered him, he put it by° with the back of his hand, thus;
　　and then the people fell a-shouting.

Brutus. What was the second noise for?

Casca. Why, for that too.

Cassius.

225　They shouted thrice; what was the last cry for?

Casca. Why, for that too.

Brutus. Was the crown offered him thrice?

Casca. Ay, marry,° was't, and he put it by thrice, every time
　　gentler than other; and at every putting-by mine honest

230　neighbors shouted.

Cassius.

　　Who offered him the crown?

203. In other words, he looks through what men *do* to search out their feelings and motives.
205. sort: manner.

212. *Caesar's analysis of Cassius is accurate. Why does he fear Cassius? What does the speech tell us about Caesar himself?*

Staging the Play
Stage direction. As the procession leaves through an upstage portal at left, Brutus pulls on the toga of Casca as he passes. Casca is rough and sarcastic. How is his sarcasm suggested in the following lines?
217. sad: serious.

221. put it by: pushed it aside.

228. marry: mild oath meaning "by the Virgin Mary."

Casca. Why, Antony.

Brutus.

Tell us the manner of it, gentle Casca.

Casca. I can as well be hanged as tell the manner of it: it was
235   mere foolery; I did not mark it. I saw Mark Antony offer
him a crown—yet 'twas not a crown neither, 'twas one of
these coronets°—and, as I told you, he put it by once;
but for all that, to my thinking, he would fain° have had
it. Then he offered it to him again; then he put it by
240   again; but to my thinking, he was very loath to lay his
fingers off it. And then he offered it the third time. He
put it the third time by; and still as he refused it, the
rabblement hooted, and clapped their chopt° hands, and
threw up their sweaty nightcaps,° and uttered such a deal
245   of stinking breath because Caesar refused the crown,
that it had, almost, choked Caesar; for he swounded° and
fell down at it. And for mine own part, I durst not laugh,
for fear of opening my lips and receiving the bad air.

Cassius.

But, soft,° I pray you; what, did Caesar swound?

250 **Casca.** He fell down in the market place, and foamed at
mouth, and was speechless.

Brutus.

'Tis very like he hath the falling-sickness.°

Cassius.

No, Caesar hath it not; but you, and I,
And honest Casca, we have the falling-sickness.

255 **Casca.** I know not what you mean by that, but I am sure
Caesar fell down. If the tag-rag people° did not clap him and
hiss him, according as he pleased and displeased them, as
they use to do the players in the theater, I am no true man.

Brutus.

What said he when he came unto himself?

260 **Casca.** Marry, before he fell down, when he perceived the
common herd was glad he refused the crown, he plucked
me ope° his doublet° and offered them his throat to cut.
An° I had been a man of any occupation,° if I would not
have taken him at a word, I would I might go to hell
265   among the rogues. And so he fell. When he came to
himself again, he said, if he had done or said anything
amiss, he desired their worships to think it was his
infirmity. Three or four wenches,° where I stood, cried
"Alas, good soul!" and forgave him with all their hearts;

Staging the Play
233. *How would Brutus respond to this news about the crown?*

237. coronets: small crowns.
238. fain: happily.

243. chopt: chapped (raw and rough from hard work and the weather).
244. nightcaps: Casca is mockingly referring to the hats of the workingmen.
246. swounded: swooned; fainted.
248. *How does Casca feel about the Roman mob?*
249. soft: wait a minute.

252. falling-sickness: old term for the disease we now call epilepsy, which is marked by seizures and momentary loss of consciousness.
254. *What do you think Cassius means here?*
256. tag-rag people: contemptuous reference to the commoners in the crowd.

262. plucked me ope: plucked open. **doublet:** close-fitting jacket.
263. An: if. **man of any occupation:** working man.

268. wenches: girls or young women.

270 but there's no heed to be taken of them; if Caesar had
stabbed their mothers, they would have done no less.

Brutus.

And after that, he came thus sad away?

Casca. Ay.

Cassius.

Did Cicero say anything?

275 **Casca.** Ay, he spoke Greek.

Cassius. To what effect?

Casca. Nay, an I tell you that, I'll ne'er look you i' th' face
again. But those that understood him smiled at one
another and shook their heads; but for mine own part,
280 it was Greek to me. I could tell you more news too:
Marullus and Flavius, for pulling scarfs off Caesar's
images, are put to silence.° Fare you well. There was
more foolery yet, if I could remember it.

Cassius. Will you sup with me tonight, Casca?

285 **Casca.** No, I am promised forth.°

Cassius. Will you dine with me tomorrow?

Casca. Ay, if I be alive, and your mind hold, and your
dinner worth the eating.

Cassius. Good; I will expect you.

290 **Casca.** Do so. Farewell, both.   [*Exit.*]

Brutus.

What a blunt fellow is this grown to be!
He was quick mettle° when he went to school.

Cassius.

So is he now in execution
Of any bold or noble enterprise,
295 However he puts on this tardy form.°
This rudeness° is a sauce to his good wit,°
Which gives men stomach to disgest° his words
With better appetite.

---

271. *Casca gets very sarcastic here. What does he think of Caesar?*

282. put to silence: silenced, perhaps by dismissal from their positions as tribunes or by exile.

282. *Why are Marullus and Flavius silenced? What does this tell you about Caesar?*

285. forth: previously. (He has other plans.)

292. quick mettle: lively of disposition.

295. tardy form: sluggish appearance.
296. rudeness: rough manner.
wit: intelligence.
297. disgest: digest.

Brutus.

And so it is. For this time I will leave you.
300 Tomorrow, if you please to speak with me,
I will come home to you; or if you will,
Come home to me, and I will wait for you.

Cassius.

I will do so. Till then, think of the world.°

[*Exit* BRUTUS.]

Well, Brutus, thou art noble; yet I see
305 Thy honorable mettle may be wrought
From that it is disposed;° therefore it is meet
That noble minds keep ever with their likes;
For who so firm that cannot be seduced?
Caesar doth bear me hard,° but he loves Brutus.
310 If I were Brutus now and he were Cassius,
He should not humor° me. I will this night,
In several hands,° in at his windows throw,
As if they came from several citizens,
Writings, all tending to the great opinion
315 That Rome holds of his name; wherein obscurely
Caesar's ambition shall be glancèd at.°
And after this, let Caesar seat him sure;°
For we will shake him, or worse days endure.   [*Exit.*]

SCENE 3. *A street.*

Thunder and lightning. Enter from opposite sides CASCA *and*
CICERO.

Cicero.

Good even, Casca; brought you Caesar home?
Why are you breathless? And why stare you so?

Casca.

Are not you moved, when all the sway of earth°
Shakes like a thing unfirm? O Cicero,
5 I have seen tempests,° when the scolding winds
Have rived° the knotty oaks, and I have seen
Th' ambitious ocean swell and rage and foam,
To be exalted with° the threat'ning clouds;
But never till tonight, never till now,
10 Did I go through a tempest dropping fire.
Either there is a civil strife in heaven,

---

303. the world: the state of affairs in Rome.

? **304.** *Cassius delivers a* *soliloquy—a speech in which a character (who is usually alone onstage) expresses aloud thoughts and feelings that the audience overhears. How does Cassius feel about Brutus?*
306. In other words, he may be persuaded against his better nature to join the conspirators.
309. bear me hard: has a grudge (hard feelings) against me.
311. humor: influence by flattery.
312. hands: varieties of handwriting.

316. glancèd at: touched on.
317. seat him sure: make his position secure.
? **318.** *What is Cassius going to write in the letters to Brutus? What does he hope these letters will accomplish?*

? **Staging the Play** *Stage direction. In Shakespeare's day, other than a drum roll or "thunder sheet," there was no way to reproduce the drama of nature onstage. How might the actors themselves suggest the threatening weather?*

3. all the sway of earth: all the principles that govern earth.

5. tempests: storms.

6. rived (rīvd): split.

8. exalted with: elevated to.

Or else the world, too saucy° with the gods,
Incenses them to send destruction.

Cicero.

Why, saw you anything more wonderful?

Casca.

15 A common slave—you know him well by sight—
Held up his left hand, which did flame and burn
Like twenty torches joined, and yet his hand,
Not sensible of° fire, remained unscorched.
Besides—I ha' not since put up my sword—

20 Against° the Capitol I met a lion,
Who glazed° upon me and went surly by
Without annoying me. And there were drawn
Upon a heap a hundred ghastly° women,
Transformèd with their fear, who swore they saw

25 Men, all in fire, walk up and down the streets.
And yesterday the bird of night° did sit
Even at noonday upon the market place,
Hooting and shrieking. When these prodigies°
Do so conjointly meet, let not men say,

30 "These are their reasons, they are natural,"
For I believe they are portentous° things
Unto the climate° that they point upon.

Cicero.

Indeed, it is a strange-disposèd time:
But men may construe things after their fashion,

35 Clean from the purpose° of the things themselves.
Comes Caesar to the Capitol tomorrow?

Casca.

He doth; for he did bid Antonius
Send word to you he would be there tomorrow.

Cicero.

Good night then, Casca; this disturbèd sky
Is not to walk in.

40 **Casca.**   Farewell, Cicero.   [*Exit* CICERO.]

[*Enter* CASSIUS.]

Cassius.

Who's there?

Casca.   A Roman.

Cassius.   Casca, by your voice.

Casca.

Your ear is good. Cassius, what night is this?

---

12. saucy: disrespectful; presumptuous.

13. *How is Casca different here from the way he was depicted earlier?*

18. not sensible of: not sensitive to.

20. Against: opposite or near.

21. glazed: stared.

23. ghastly: ghostly; pale.

26. bird of night: owl (believed to be a bad omen).

28. prodigies (präd′ə·jēs): extraordinary happenings.

31. portentous (pôr·ten′təs): ominous.

32. climate: region or place.

32. *Shakespeare often uses disorder in nature to suggest a nation's disorder. What does Casca think?*

35. Clean from the purpose: contrary to the real meaning.

35. *How does the aged Cicero respond to Casca's report?*

Cassius.
  A very pleasing night to honest men.

Casca.
  Who ever knew the heavens menace so?

Cassius.
45 Those that have known the earth so full of faults.
  For my part, I have walked about the streets,
  Submitting me unto the perilous night,
  And thus unbracèd,° Casca, as you see,
  Have bared my bosom to the thunder-stone,
50 And when the cross° blue lightning seemed to open
  The breast of heaven, I did present myself
  Even in the aim and very flash of it.

Casca.
  But wherefore did you so much tempt the heavens?
  It is the part° of men to fear and tremble
55 When the most mighty gods by tokens° send
  Such dreadful heralds to astonish us.

Cassius.
  You are dull, Casca, and those sparks of life
  That should be in a Roman you do want,°
  Or else you use not. You look pale, and gaze,
60 And put on fear, and cast yourself in wonder,
  To see the strange impatience of the heavens;
  But if you would consider the true cause
  Why all these fires, why all these gliding ghosts,
  Why birds and beasts from quality and kind,°
65 Why old men, fools, and children calculate,°
  Why all these things change from their ordinance,°
  Their natures and preformèd faculties,°
  To monstrous quality,° why, you shall find
  That heaven hath infused them with these spirits°
70 To make them instruments of fear and warning
  Unto some monstrous state.
  Now could I, Casca, name to thee a man
  Most like this dreadful night,
  That thunders, lightens, opens graves, and roars
75 As doth the lion in the Capitol;
  A man no mightier than thyself, or me,
  In personal action, yet prodigious° grown
  And fearful, as these strange eruptions are.

Casca.
  'Tis Caesar that you mean, is it not, Cassius?

43. *Can you explain Cassius's response to the disordered night?*

48. unbracèd: with his jacket unfastened.

50. cross: jagged.

54. part: role.
55. tokens: signs.

58. want: lack.

64. from quality and kind: act against their natures.
65. calculate: prophesy; try to predict the future.
66. ordinance: natural behavior.
67. preformèd faculties: natural or normal qualities.
68. monstrous quality: unnatural condition.
69. spirits: supernatural powers.

Staging the Play
72. *How might Cassius's tone of voice change here?*

77. prodigious (prō·dij′əs): monstrous.

"THEREIN, YE GODS, YOU MAKE
THE WEAK MOST STRONG . . ."

Cassius.

80   Let it be who it is; for Romans now
      Have thews° and limbs like to their ancestors;
      But, woe the while!° Our fathers' minds are dead,
      And we are governed with our mothers' spirits;
      Our yoke and sufferance° show us womanish.

Casca.

85   Indeed, they say the senators tomorrow
      Mean to establish Caesar as a king;
      And he shall wear his crown by sea and land,
      In every place save here in Italy.

Cassius.

      I know where I will wear this dagger then;
90   Cassius from bondage will deliver Cassius.
      Therein,° ye gods, you make the weak most strong;
      Therein, ye gods, you tyrants do defeat.
      Nor stony tower, nor walls of beaten brass,
      Nor airless dungeon, nor strong links of iron,
95   Can be retentive to° the strength of spirit;
      But life, being weary of these worldly bars,
      Never lacks power to dismiss itself.
      If I know this, know all the world besides,
      That part of tyranny that I do bear
      I can shake off at pleasure.   [*Thunder still.°*]

100 **Casca.**   So can I;
      So every bondman in his own hand bears
      The power to cancel his captivity.

Cassius.

      And why should Caesar be a tyrant then?
      Poor man, I know he would not be a wolf
105   But that he sees the Romans are but sheep;
      He were no lion, were not Romans hinds.°
      Those that with haste will make a mighty fire
      Begin it with weak straws. What trash is Rome,
      What rubbish and what offal,° when it serves
110   For the base matter to illuminate
      So vile a thing as Caesar! But, O grief,
      Where hast thou led me? I, perhaps, speak this
      Before a willing bondman; then I know
      My answer must be made.° But I am armed,
115   And dangers are to me indifferent.

Casca.

      You speak to Casca, and to such a man

---

81. thews (th̄yo͞oz): sinews or muscles.

82. woe the while: too bad for our times.

84. Our yoke and sufferance: our burden and our timid acceptance of it.

Staging the Play
89. *Cassius's response to this news is usually played as one of anger. What is he probably holding in his hand?*
91. Therein: in other words, in the act of suicide.

95. be retentive to: restrain.

100. *What is Cassius threatening to do?*
100. still: continues.

106. hinds: female deer. (The word also means "peasants" and "servants.")

109. offal: garbage, especially the parts of a butchered animal that are considered inedible or rotten.

114. My answer must be made: I must later answer for my words.

115. *Does Cassius seriously mean that Casca is a willing slave of Caesar's? What reaction is he looking for?*

That is no fleering° tell-tale. Hold, my hand.
Be factious° for redress of all these griefs,
And I will set this foot of mine as far
As who goes farthest.   [*They clasp hands.*]

120 **Cassius.**   There's a bargain made.
Now know you, Casca, I have moved already
Some certain of the noblest-minded Romans
To undergo with me an enterprise
Of honorable dangerous consequence;
125 And I do know, by this° they stay for me
In Pompey's porch,° for now, this fearful night,
There is no stir or walking in the streets,
And the complexion of the element°
In favor's like° the work we have in hand,
130 Most bloody, fiery, and most terrible.

[*Enter* CINNA.]

Casca.
Stand close° awhile, for here comes one in haste.
Cassius.
'Tis Cinna; I do know him by his gait;
He is a friend. Cinna, where haste you so?
Cinna.
To find out you. Who's that? Metellus Cimber?
Cassius.
135 No, it is Casca, one incorporate
To° our attempts. Am I not stayed for,° Cinna?
Cinna.
I am glad on't. What a fearful night is this!
There's two or three of us have seen strange sights.
Cassius.
Am I not stayed for? Tell me.
Cinna.   Yes, you are.
140 O Cassius, if you could
But win the noble Brutus to our party—
Cassius.
Be you content. Good Cinna, take this paper,
And look you lay it in the praetor's chair,°
Where Brutus may but find it; and throw this
145 In at his window; set this up with wax
Upon old Brutus' statue.° All this done,
Repair° to Pompey's porch, where you shall find us.

117. fleering: flattering.
118. Be factious (fak′shəs): Go ahead and organize a faction, or group, opposed to Caesar.

125. by this: by this time.
126. Pompey's porch: the entrance to a theater built by Pompey.

128. complexion of the element: appearance of the sky.
129. In favor's like: in appearance is like.
? 130. *Cassius has begun his conversation with Casca by showing him his dagger and threatening suicide as a way to free himself from bondage. At what point does the conversation shift to an altogether different method of freeing himself?*
131. close: hidden.

136. incorporate to: bound up with. **stayed for:** waited for.

? 139. *What is Cassius's mood?*

143. praetor's (prē′tərz) **chair:** chief magistrate's chair; Brutus's chair.

146. old Brutus' statue: statue of Brutus's heroic ancestor.
147. Repair: go.

Is Decius° Brutus and Trebonius there?

Cinna.

All but Metellus Cimber, and he's gone
150   To seek you at your house. Well, I will hie,°
And so bestow these papers as you bade me.

Cassius.

That done, repair to Pompey's Theater.

                                            [*Exit* CINNA.]

Come, Casca, you and I will yet ere day
See Brutus at his house; three parts of him
155   Is ours already, and the man entire
Upon the next encounter yields him ours.

Casca.

O, he sits high in all the people's hearts;
And that which would appear offense in us,
His countenance,° like richest alchemy,°
160   Will change to virtue and to worthiness.

Cassius.

Him, and his worth, and our great need of him,
You have right well conceited.° Let us go,
For it is after midnight, and ere day
We will awake him and be sure of him.
      [*Exeunt.*]

148. Decius: Decimus, a relative of Brutus.

148. *What is Cassius asking Cinna to do?*

150. hie: hurry.

159. countenance: approval.
alchemy: "science" that was supposed to change ordinary metals into gold.

162. conceited: Cassius is punning here. The word means both "understood" and "described in an elaborate metaphor" (called a *conceit*).

"MEN AT SOME TIME ARE MASTERS OF THEIR FATES:
THE FAULT, DEAR BRUTUS, IS NOT IN OUR STARS,
BUT IN OURSELVES, THAT WE ARE UNDERLINGS."

—CASSIUS, ACT I, SCENE 2
(LINES 139–141)

A Closer Look

Roman Superstitions

At the time of Julius Caesar, just about everyone believed in magic, omens, and revelations.

The Romans examined everyday occurrences for warnings of good and evil. For example, they believed that the sound of a distant storm or a rooster crowing in the night could affect the outcome of a personal matter or even a political event. Politicians believed so strongly in signs that they created a site in Rome's Capitol where they could consult specialists.

Many people thought that animals were the spirits of their dead ancestors. Therefore, the physical characteristics and actions of certain animals were seen as signs of protection and warning. Ravens, owls, and crows supposedly revealed signs through their calls. Other meanings were taken from the flight of eagles, vultures, and buzzards.

Animals were killed and offered as sacrifices to the gods. Their entrails were examined by a haruspex (hə·rus′peks′), a soothsayer who specialized in foretelling events by studying internal organs. Abnormalities—imperfections and deformities in color, shape, or position—indicated the anger of a particular god.

The commanders of Roman military fleets counted on "sacred" chickens to predict success in battle. If the chickens ate vigorously and dropped food from their beaks on the morning of battle, all would go well in combat. If the chickens did not eat, the signs were unfavorable. One commander whose sacred chickens refused to eat at sea threw them overboard. "If they won't eat, let them drink!" he said. The commander lost the battle.

The owl was considered a bad omen. Once when an owl flew into Rome's Capitol, the Romans carefully scrubbed the building with water and sulfur to drive out the owl's supposed evil influences.

Solar eclipses were interpreted as supernatural and as omens of disaster. Speaking about an eclipse as a natural occurrence was against the law. Lightning was also seen as a bad omen. Even dreams were seen as messages from the gods.

As odd as all of this may seem to us today, during Julius Caesar's time these superstitions were held by everyone from the ruling classes to the common people.

Response and Analysis

Act I

Reading Check

1. Why are the workers celebrating in Scene 1? Why does Marullus scold them?

2. What does the soothsayer tell Caesar in Scene 2? How does Caesar respond?

3. What happens when Caesar is offered the crown?

4. At the end of Scene 2, what is Cassius planning to do to persuade Brutus to join the conspiracy against Caesar?

5. At the beginning of Scene 3, what do Cicero and Casca discuss? Why are they disturbed?

6. What happens at the end of Scene 3 to move the conspiracy plot forward?

Thinking Critically

7. Shakespeare uses nature to mirror the disorder in human lives. What details in Scene 3 do you think evoke a sense of danger and terror?

8. What is your impression of Cassius, the **protagonist,** or main character, who drives the action in Act I? By the act's end, what steps has he taken toward his goal?

9. The **exposition** of Act I introduces the characters and conflict. How would you describe the tragedy's **conflict** as it is established in Act I?

10. A healthy republic requires a reasonably intelligent and responsive citizenry. How do the nobles in the play speak of the citizens of Rome? What do you learn from this act about the moods and loyalties of the Roman people?

11. How would you evaluate the **character** of Brutus? Is he strong, weak, or something in between? (Do all readers agree?)

12. A **character foil** is a character who serves as a contrast to another character. Throughout the play, Cassius serves as a **character foil** to Brutus. In what ways is Cassius a foil to Brutus in this act?

13. Do you have conflicting feelings about Caesar during this act? Explain. Describe your impressions of his **character,** based on your responses to his speeches and actions and on what other characters say about him.

Extending and Evaluating

14. Does the play deal with issues that no longer concern us, or is it relevant to our lives today? Explain. Share with others some lines in this act that you think could be used to comment on current politics or politicians. (You might want to look back at your Quickwrite notes for page 754.)

WRITING

A Wily Persuader

Persuasion is the use of language to influence people to behave or think in certain ways. (For more on persuasion and its strategies, see pages 284–285.) You'll get a good idea of the power of persuasion if you examine Cassius's speeches in Act I, Scene 2, when he tries to persuade Brutus to turn against his friend and join the conspiracy to overthrow Caesar. Take notes on where the clever Cassius uses these **persuasive techniques:** specific **evidence** (facts, examples), **loaded words** (words with

SKILLS FOCUS

Literary Skills
Analyze tragedy.

Writing Skills
Write an essay analyzing a character's persuasive techniques.

Listening and Speaking Skills
Present an oral interpretation of dialogue.

emotional overtones), **repetition** for effect, **emotional appeals** to self-interest. Then, in a brief essay, analyze Cassius's persuasive techniques.

LISTENING AND SPEAKING

By Their Words You Will Know Them

Cassius and Brutus are clearly going to be important figures in the play. What kind of men are they? With a partner, choose a section of their **dialogue** (their conversation with other characters) that reveals the character of each man. Then, prepare an **oral interpretation** of the conversation. Present your dramatic reading to the class, and be sure to ask for feedback.

Bust of Julius Caesar.
© Art Resource, New York.

Vocabulary Development

Multiple Meanings: Recognizing Puns

Some people call puns juvenile humor, but Shakespeare's audiences enjoyed them. A **pun** is a word or phrase that means two different things at the same time. (Here's an old pun: What is black and white and read all over? Answer: a newspaper.)

In the first scene of *Julius Caesar*, when the cobbler says he is a cobbler, he plays on two meanings of the word. In Shakespeare's day the word could mean either "shoemaker" or "bungler." When he calls himself "a mender of bad soles," the cobbler also puns on the meaning of *soles*. *Soles* refers to parts of shoes but also sounds exactly like *souls*.

Some puns are based on two meanings of a word (*cobbler*). Others involve **homophones,** words that sound alike but have different spellings and meanings (*soles/souls*).

Here are two of Shakespeare's puns in Act I:

"All that I live by is with the <u>awl</u>. . . ." (Scene 1, line 21)

"I am . . . a surgeon to old shoes: when they are in great danger, I <u>recover</u> them." (Scene 1, lines 23–24)

PRACTICE

You could map the puns used by the cobbler and show the jokes like this:

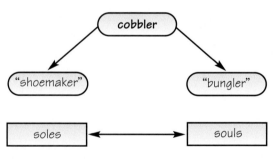

1. Make maps that explain the puns on *awl* and *recover* in the lines above.

2. Use two of the words below (or words of your choice) to create original puns. Do a pun map for each one.

   break   **flour**   **son**

SKILLS FOCUS

Vocabulary Skills
Recognize puns. Make semantic maps.

ACT II

SCENE 1.
Rome.

"HE WOULD BE CROWNED.
HOW THAT MIGHT CHANGE HIS NATURE,
THERE'S THE QUESTION."

Enter BRUTUS *in his orchard.*

Brutus.

What, Lucius, ho!
I cannot, by the progress of the stars,
Give guess how near to day. Lucius, I say!
I would it were my fault to sleep so soundly.
5   When, Lucius, when? Awake, I say! What, Lucius!

[*Enter* LUCIUS.]

Lucius. Called you, my lord?
Brutus.

Get me a taper° in my study, Lucius.
When it is lighted, come and call me here.
Lucius. I will, my lord.   [*Exit.*]
Brutus.

10   It must be by his death; and for my part,
I know no personal cause to spurn at° him,
But for the general.° He would be crowned.
How that might change his nature, there's the question.
It is the bright day that brings forth the adder,
15   And that craves° wary walking. Crown him that,
And then I grant we put a sting in him
That at his will he may do danger with.
Th' abuse of greatness is when it disjoins
Remorse° from power; and, to speak truth of Caesar,
20   I have not known when his affections swayed°
More than his reason. But 'tis a common proof°
That lowliness° is young ambition's ladder,
Whereto the climber upward turns his face;
But when he once attains the upmost round,
25   He then unto the ladder turns his back,
Looks in the clouds, scorning the base degrees°
By which he did ascend. So Caesar may;
Then lest he may, prevent.° And, since the quarrel°
Will bear no color° for the thing he is,
30   Fashion it thus:° that what he is, augmented,
Would run to these and these extremities;
And therefore think him as a serpent's egg
Which hatched, would as his kind grow mischievous,
And kill him in the shell.

Staging the Play
Stage direction. Brutus's garden often has a set of steps in the back, set in a half circle. Below the steps is a stone bench. On the right and left are the doorways of an impressive residence. The door to the left is the servants' entrance, where Brutus directs his call to Lucius. Why is Brutus so anxious about the time?

7. taper: candle.

10. *In this **soliloquy**, what is Brutus trying to convince himself of?*
11. spurn at: rebel against.
12. the general: the general good.

15. craves: demands.

19. Remorse: compassion.
20. affections swayed: emotions ruled.
21. common proof: matter of common experience.
22. lowliness: humility.

26. base degrees: low rungs of the ladder; also lower government offices and lower classes of people.
28. prevent: We must prevent it.
quarrel: argument.
29. bear no color: bear no weight.
30. Fashion it thus: state the case this way.

34. *According to Brutus, who is like a serpent's egg and why?*

[*Enter* LUCIUS.]

Lucius.

35   The taper burneth in your closet,° sir.
Searching the window for a flint, I found
This paper thus sealed up, and I am sure
It did not lie there when I went to bed.

[*Gives him the letter.*]

Brutus.

Get you to bed again; it is not day.
40   Is not tomorrow, boy, the ides of March?
Lucius. I know not, sir.
Brutus.

Look in the calendar and bring me word.
Lucius. I will, sir.   [*Exit.*]
Brutus.

The exhalations° whizzing in the air
45   Give so much light that I may read by them.

[*Opens the letter and reads.*]

"Brutus, thou sleep'st; awake, and see thyself.
Shall Rome, &c.° Speak, strike, redress.°
Brutus, thou sleep'st; awake."

Such instigations have been often dropped
50   Where I have took them up.
"Shall Rome, &c." Thus must I piece it out:
Shall Rome stand under one man's awe? What, Rome?
My ancestors did from the streets of Rome
The Tarquin° drive, when he was called a king.
55   "Speak, strike, redress." Am I entreated
To speak and strike? O Rome, I make thee promise,
If the redress will follow, thou receivest
Thy full petition at the hand of Brutus!

[*Enter* LUCIUS.]

Lucius.

Sir, March is wasted fifteen days.

[*Knock within.*]

Brutus.

60   'Tis good. Go to the gate; somebody knocks.

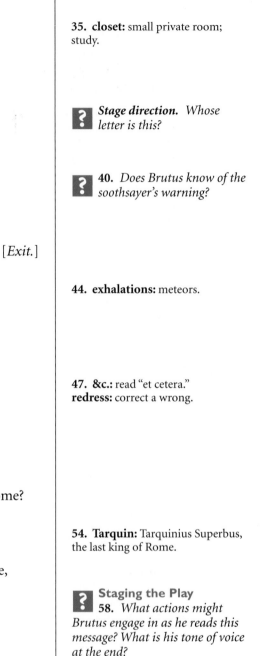

35. closet: small private room; study.

Stage direction. *Whose letter is this?*

40. *Does Brutus know of the soothsayer's warning?*

44. exhalations: meteors.

47. &c.: read "et cetera."
redress: correct a wrong.

54. Tarquin: Tarquinius Superbus, the last king of Rome.

Staging the Play
58. *What actions might Brutus engage in as he reads this message? What is his tone of voice at the end?*

[*Exit* LUCIUS.]

Since Cassius first did whet me against Caesar,
I have not slept.
Between the acting of a dreadful thing
And the first motion, all the interim is
65 Like a phantasma,° or a hideous dream.
The genius and the mortal instruments°
Are then in council, and the state of a man,
Like to a little kingdom, suffers then
The nature of an insurrection.

[*Enter* LUCIUS.]

Lucius.
70 Sir, 'tis your brother° Cassius at the door,
Who doth desire to see you.
Brutus.   Is he alone?
Lucius.
No, sir, there are moe° with him.
Brutus.   Do you know them?
Lucius.
No, sir; their hats are plucked about their ears,
And half their faces buried in their cloaks,
75 That by no means I may discover them
By any mark of favor.°
Brutus.   Let 'em enter.   [*Exit* LUCIUS.]
They are the faction. O conspiracy,
Sham'st thou to show thy dang'rous brow by night,
When evils are most free? O, then by day
80 Where wilt thou find a cavern dark enough
To mask thy monstrous visage? Seek none, conspiracy;
Hide it in smiles and affability:
For if thou path, thy native semblance on,°
Not Erebus° itself were dim enough
85 To hide thee from prevention.

65. **phantasma:** apparition; hallucination.
66. **The genius and the mortal instruments:** the mind (genius) and the emotions and physical powers of the body.

70. **brother:** brother-in-law; Cassius is married to Brutus's sister.

72. **moe:** more.

76. **favor:** appearance.

83. In other words, if you walk (path) in your true way.
84. **Erebus** (er′ə·bəs): in Greek mythology dark region of the underworld.

"BETWEEN THE ACTING OF A DREADFUL THING
AND THE FIRST MOTION, ALL THE INTERIM IS
LIKE A PHANTASMA, OR
A HIDEOUS DREAM."

[*Enter the conspirators,* CASSIUS, CASCA, DECIUS, CINNA, METELLUS CIMBER, *and* TREBONIUS.]

Cassius.
    I think we are too bold upon° your rest.
    Good morrow, Brutus; do we trouble you?
Brutus.
    I have been up this hour, awake all night.
    Know I these men that come along with you?
Cassius.
90   Yes, every man of them; and no man here
    But honors you; and every one doth wish
    You had but that opinion of yourself
    Which every noble Roman bears of you.
    This is Trebonius.
Brutus.   He is welcome hither.
Cassius.
    This, Decius Brutus.
95 **Brutus.**   He is welcome too.
Cassius.
    This, Casca; this, Cinna; and this, Metellus Cimber.
Brutus.
    They are all welcome.
    What watchful cares° do interpose themselves
    Betwixt your eyes and night?
100 **Cassius.** Shall I entreat a word?

[*They whisper.*]

Decius.
    Here lies the east; doth not the day break here?
Casca. No.
Cinna.
    O, pardon, sir, it doth; and yon gray lines
    That fret° the clouds are messengers of day.
Casca.
105   You shall confess that you are both deceived.
    Here, as I point my sword, the sun arises,
    Which is a great way growing on° the south,
    Weighing the youthful season of the year.
    Some two months hence, up higher toward the north
110   He first presents his fire; and the high east
    Stands as the Capitol, directly here.
Brutus.
    Give me your hands all over, one by one.

Staging the Play
Stage direction. Describe what the stage looks like right now. From what is said of the conspirators, how would you imagine they are dressed?
86. too bold upon: too bold in intruding on.

98. watchful cares: cares that keep you awake.
Staging the Play
100. *How would you have the actors placed onstage as Brutus and Cassius huddle and the others talk?*

104. fret: interlace.

107. growing on: tending toward.

Cassius.

    And let us swear our resolution.

Brutus.

    No, not an oath. If not the face of men,°

115   The sufferance° of our souls, the time's abuse°—

    If these be motives weak, break off betimes,°

    And every man hence to his idle bed.

    So let high-sighted tyranny range on

    Till each man drop by lottery. But if these

120   (As I am sure they do) bear fire enough

    To kindle cowards and to steel with valor

    The melting spirits of women, then, countrymen,

    What need we any spur but our own cause

    To prick° us to redress? What other bond

125   Than secret Romans that have spoke the word,

    And will not palter?° And what other oath

    Than honesty to honesty engaged

    That this shall be, or we will fall for it?

    Swear priests and cowards and men cautelous,°

130   Old feeble carrions° and such suffering souls

    That welcome wrongs; unto bad causes swear

    Such creatures as men doubt; but do not stain

    The even virtue of our enterprise,

    Nor th' insuppressive mettle of our spirits,

135   To think that or our cause or our performance

    Did need an oath; when every drop of blood

    That every Roman bears, and nobly bears,

    Is guilty of a several bastardy°

    If he do break the smallest particle

140   Of any promise that hath passed from him.

Cassius.

    But what of Cicero? Shall we sound him?

    I think he will stand very strong with us.

Casca.

    Let us not leave him out.

Cinna.   No, by no means.

Metellus.

    O, let us have him, for his silver hairs

145   Will purchase us a good opinion,

    And buy men's voices to commend our deeds.

    It shall be said his judgment ruled our hands;

    Our youths and wildness shall no whit appear,

    But all be buried in his gravity.°

---

114. If not the face of men: Our honest faces should be enough.
115. sufferance: endurance. **time's abuse:** abuses of the times.
116. betimes: at once.

124. prick: urge.

126. palter: deceive.

129. cautelous: deceitful.
130. carrions: people so old or sick they are almost dead and rotting.

138. of a several bastardy: of several acts that are not truly "Roman."

149. gravity: seriousness and stability.

Brutus.

150 O, name him not! Let us not break with him,°
     For he will never follow anything
     That other men begin.

Cassius.   Then leave him out.

Casca.
     Indeed, he is not fit.

Decius.
     Shall no man else be touched but only Caesar?

Cassius.

155 Decius, well urged. I think it is not meet
     Mark Antony, so well beloved of Caesar,
     Should outlive Caesar; we shall find of° him
     A shrewd contriver;° and you know, his means,
     If he improve° them, may well stretch so far

160 As to annoy° us all; which to prevent,
     Let Antony and Caesar fall together.

Brutus.
     Our course will seem too bloody, Caius Cassius,
     To cut the head off and then hack the limbs,
     Like wrath in death and envy° afterwards;

165 For Antony is but a limb of Caesar.
     Let's be sacrificers, but not butchers, Caius.
     We all stand up against the spirit of Caesar,
     And in the spirit of men there is no blood.
     O, that we then could come by Caesar's spirit,

170 And not dismember Caesar! But, alas,
     Caesar must bleed for it. And, gentle friends,
     Let's kill him boldly, but not wrathfully;
     Let's carve him as a dish fit for the gods,
     Not hew him as a carcass fit for hounds.

175 And let our hearts, as subtle masters do,
     Stir up their servants° to an act of rage,
     And after seem to chide 'em. This shall make
     Our purpose necessary, and not envious;
     Which so appearing to the common eyes,

180 We shall be called purgers,° not murderers.
     And for Mark Antony, think not of him;
     For he can do no more than Caesar's arm
     When Caesar's head is off.

Cassius.   Yet I fear him;
     For in the ingrafted° love he bears to Caesar——

---

150. **break with him:** break our news to him, reveal our plan.

152. *Why do they decide not to ask Cicero to join them?*

153. *What kind of person does Casca seem to be?*

157. **of:** in.
158. **shrewd contriver:** cunning and dangerous schemer.
159. **improve:** make good use of.
160. **annoy:** harm.

162. *This is the second time that Brutus contradicts Cassius. How does Cassius serve as a foil to Brutus?*
164. **envy:** malice.

Staging the Play
169–170. *How might the actor playing Brutus look when he speaks this sentence?*

176. **servants:** hands or emotions.

180. **purgers:** healers.
180. *What does Brutus want the public, or history, to think of him?*

184. **ingrafted:** firmly rooted.

Brutus.

185   Alas, good Cassius, do not think of him.
      If he love Caesar, all that he can do
      Is to himself—take thought° and die for Caesar.
      And that were much he should,° for he is given
      To sports, to wildness, and much company.

Trebonius.

190   There is no fear in him;° let him not die,
      For he will live and laugh at this hereafter.

[Clock strikes.]

Brutus.

      Peace! Count the clock.

Cassius.   The clock hath stricken three.

Trebonius.

      'Tis time to part.

Cassius.   But it is doubtful yet
      Whether Caesar will come forth today or no;

195   For he is superstitious grown of late,
      Quite from the main° opinion he held once
      Of fantasy, of dreams, and ceremonies.°
      It may be these apparent prodigies,°
      The unaccustomed terror of this night,

200   And the persuasion of his augurers°
      May hold him from the Capitol today.

Decius.

      Never fear that. If he be so resolved,
      I can o'ersway him; for he loves to hear
      That unicorns may be betrayed with trees,

205   And bears with glasses, elephants with holes,
      Lions with toils, and men with flatterers;
      But when I tell him he hates flatterers,
      He says he does, being then most flatterèd.

187. take thought: take to thinking too much and become depressed.
188. In other words, that is too much to expect of him.

190. no fear in him: nothing to fear in him.
191. *What do Brutus, Cassius, and Trebonius think of Antony?*

196. main: strong.
197. ceremonies: ceremonial rituals undertaken to determine the future, usually from the examination of signs in the entrails of slaughtered animals.
198. prodigies: disasters.
200. augurers (ô′gər·ərz): those who foretell the future.

"LET'S KILL HIM BOLDLY, BUT NOT WRATHFULLY;
LET'S CARVE HIM AS A DISH FIT FOR THE GODS,
NOT HEW HIM AS A CARCASS
FIT FOR HOUNDS."

Let me work;
210 For I can give his humor° the true bent,
And I will bring him to the Capitol.
Cassius.
Nay, we will all of us be there to fetch him.
Brutus.
By the eighth hour; is that the uttermost?°
Cinna.
Be that the uttermost, and fail not then.
Metellus.
215 Caius Ligarius doth bear Caesar hard,
Who rated° him for speaking well of Pompey.
I wonder none of you have thought of him.
Brutus.
Now, good Metellus, go along by him.°
He loves me well, and I have given him reasons;
220 Send him but hither, and I'll fashion him.
Cassius.
The morning comes upon 's; we'll leave you, Brutus.
And, friends, disperse yourselves; but all remember
What you have said, and show yourselves true Romans.
Brutus.
Good gentlemen, look fresh and merrily.
225 Let not our looks put on° our purposes,
But bear it as our Roman actors do,
With untired spirits and formal constancy.°
And so good morrow to you every one.

[*Exeunt all except* BRUTUS.]

Boy! Lucius! Fast asleep? It is no matter;
230 Enjoy the honey-heavy dew of slumber.
Thou hast no figures nor no fantasies°
Which busy care draws in the brains of men;
Therefore thou sleep'st so sound.

[*Enter* PORTIA.]

Portia.   Brutus, my lord.
Brutus.
Portia, what mean you? Wherefore rise you now?
235 It is not for your health thus to commit
Your weak condition to the raw cold morning.

210. humor: mood.

211. *According to Decius, what sort of man is Caesar? (What do you think of people like Decius?)*

213. uttermost: latest.

216. rated: berated; scolded.

218. him: his house.

Staging the Play
221. *How would you use lighting here to suggest the time?*

225. put on: display.

227. formal constancy: consistent good conduct.

231. figures ... fantasies: figments of the imagination.

Portia.

Nor for yours neither. Y'have ungently, Brutus,
Stole from my bed; and yesternight at supper
You suddenly arose and walked about,
240   Musing and sighing, with your arms across;°
And when I asked you what the matter was,
You stared upon me with ungentle looks.
I urged you further; then you scratched your head,
And too impatiently stamped with your foot.
245   Yet I insisted, yet you answered not,
But with an angry wafter° of your hand
Gave sign for me to leave you. So I did,
Fearing to strengthen that impatience
Which seemed too much enkindled, and withal°
250   Hoping it was but an effect of humor,°
Which sometime hath his hour with every man.
It will not let you eat, nor talk, nor sleep,
And could it work so much upon your shape
As it hath much prevailed on your condition,
255   I should not know you Brutus. Dear my lord,
Make me acquainted with your cause of grief.

Brutus.

I am not well in health, and that is all.

Portia.

Brutus is wise and, were he not in health,
He would embrace the means to come by it.

Brutus.

260   Why, so I do. Good Portia, go to bed.

Portia.

Is Brutus sick, and is it physical°
To walk unbracèd° and suck up the humors°
Of the dank morning? What, is Brutus sick,
And will he steal out of his wholesome bed,
265   To dare the vile contagion of the night,

240. arms across: crossed arms, a sign of melancholy or depression in Shakespeare's day.

246. wafter: wave.

249. withal: also.
250. humor: moodiness.

? Staging the Play
256. *Where would Portia be standing?*

? Staging the Play
260. *Some directors have Portia come too close to Brutus, physically and emotionally, and have him break away here. What would Portia's actions be?*
261. physical: healthy.
262. unbracèd: with his jacket opened. **humors:** Here the word means "dampness (of the air)."

"DWELL I BUT IN THE SUBURBS
OF YOUR GOOD PLEASURE? IF IT BE NO MORE,
PORTIA IS BRUTUS' HARLOT, NOT HIS WIFE."

And tempt the rheumy and unpurgèd air°
To add unto his sickness? No, my Brutus;
You have some sick offense within your mind,
Which by the right and virtue of my place
270 I ought to know of; and upon my knees
I charm° you, by my once commended beauty,
By all your vows of love, and that great vow
Which did incorporate and make us one,
That you unfold to me, your self, your half,
275 Why you are heavy,° and what men tonight
Have had resort to you; for here have been
Some six or seven, who did hide their faces
Even from darkness.

Brutus.   Kneel not, gentle Portia.

Portia.
I should not need, if you were gentle Brutus.
280 Within the bond of marriage, tell me, Brutus,
Is it excepted° I should know no secrets
That appertain to you? Am I your self
But, as it were, in sort or limitation,
To keep with you at meals, comfort your bed,
285 And talk to you sometimes? Dwell I but in the suburbs
Of your good pleasure? If it be no more,
Portia is Brutus' harlot, not his wife.

Brutus.
You are my true and honorable wife,
As dear to me as are the ruddy drops
290 That visit my sad heart.

Portia.
If this were true, then should I know this secret.
I grant I am a woman; but withal
A woman that Lord Brutus took to wife.
I grant I am a woman; but withal
295 A woman well reputed, Cato's° daughter.
Think you I am no stronger than my sex,
Being so fathered and so husbanded?
Tell me your counsels, I will not disclose 'em.
I have made strong proof of my constancy,
300 Giving myself a voluntary wound
Here in the thigh; can I bear that with patience,
And not my husband's secrets?

Brutus.   O ye gods,
Render me worthy of this noble wife!

266. unpurgèd air: The night was supposed to be unhealthy, since the air was not purified (purged) by the sun.

? Staging the Play
270. *What clue tells us what Portia does here? Is she becoming calmer or more agitated?*
271. charm: beg.

275. heavy: depressed (heavy-hearted).

? Staging the Play
278. *What is Brutus doing here?*

281. excepted: made an exception that.

295. Cato joined Pompey against Caesar and killed himself at the end to avoid living under the rule of a tyrant. He was a most respected man, famous for his integrity.

? Staging the Play
300. *What does Portia suddenly do to prove her loyalty and strength of character? How do you think Brutus should respond?*

"TELL ME YOUR COUNSELS, I WILL NOT DISCLOSE 'EM."

[*Knock.*]

    Hark, hark! One knocks. Portia, go in a while,
305   And by and by thy bosom shall partake
    The secrets of my heart.
    All my engagements I will construe to thee,
    All the charactery of my sad brows.°
    Leave me with haste.   [*Exit* PORTIA.]

[*Enter* LUCIUS *and* CAIUS LIGARIUS.]

                Lucius, who's that knocks?

Lucius.
310   Here is a sick man that would speak with you.

Brutus.
    Caius Ligarius, that Metellus spake of.
    Boy, stand aside. Caius Ligarius! How?

Ligarius.
    Vouchsafe° good morrow from a feeble tongue.

Brutus.
    O, what a time have you chose out, brave Caius,
315   To wear a kerchief!° Would you were not sick!

Ligarius.
    I am not sick, if Brutus have in hand
    Any exploit worthy the name of honor.

Brutus.
    Such an exploit have I in hand, Ligarius,
    Had you a healthful ear to hear of it.

Ligarius.
320   By all the gods that Romans bow before,
    I here discard my sickness! Soul of Rome,
    Brave son, derived from honorable loins,
    Thou, like an exorcist, hast conjured up
    My mortifièd° spirit. Now bid me run,
325   And I will strive with things impossible,
    Yea, get the better of them. What's to do?

Brutus.
    A piece of work that will make sick men whole.

Ligarius.
    But are not some whole that we must make sick?

Brutus.
    That must we also. What it is, my Caius,
330   I shall unfold to thee, as we are going
    To whom° it must be done.

308. In other words, the meaning of all the lines written in his forehead (from worry).

313. Vouchsafe: please accept.

315. kerchief: scarf. (It shows he is sick.)

Staging the Play
321. *What action might he make with this line?*

324. mortifièd: deadened.

331. To whom: to the house of whom.

Ligarius.   Set on° your foot,
     And with a heart new-fired I follow you,
     To do I know not what; but it sufficeth
     That Brutus leads me on.   [*Thunder.*]
Brutus.   Follow me, then.   [*Exeunt.*]

SCENE 2. *Caesar's house.*

Thunder and lightning. Enter JULIUS CAESAR *in his
nightgown.*

Caesar.
     Nor heaven nor earth have been at peace tonight:
     Thrice hath Calphurnia in her sleep cried out,
     "Help, ho! They murder Caesar!" Who's within?

[*Enter a* SERVANT.]

Servant. My lord?
Caesar.
5   Go bid the priests do present° sacrifice,
     And bring me their opinions of success.°
Servant. I will, my lord.   [*Exit.*]

[*Enter* CALPHURNIA.]

Calphurnia.
     What mean you, Caesar? Think you to walk forth?
     You shall not stir out of your house today.
Caesar.
10   Caesar shall forth. The things that threatened me
     Ne'er looked but on my back; when they shall see
     The face of Caesar, they are vanishèd.
Calphurnia.
     Caesar, I never stood on ceremonies,°
     Yet now they fright me. There is one within,
15   Besides the things that we have heard and seen,
     Recounts most horrid sights seen by the watch.°
     A lioness hath whelpèd° in the streets,
     And graves have yawned, and yielded up their dead;
     Fierce fiery warriors fought upon the clouds
20   In ranks and squadrons and right form of war,
     Which drizzled blood upon the Capitol;
     The noise of battle hurtled in the air,

331. **Set on:** set off on.

Staging the Play
Stage direction. Thunder is a kind of actor in Shakespeare's plays. What mood does it evoke? Would you have this thunder sound alone, or would you have it serve as background noise for these speeches?

5. **present** (prez′ənt): immediate.
6. **opinions of success:** opinions about the course of events.

13. **ceremonies:** again, a reference to the rituals of priests that were supposed to reveal omens.

16. **watch:** watchman.
17. **whelpèd:** given birth.

"WHEN BEGGARS DIE,
THERE ARE NO
COMETS SEEN . . ."

Horses did neigh and dying men did groan,
And ghosts did shriek and squeal about the streets.
25 O Caesar, these things are beyond all use,°
And I do fear them.

Caesar.   What can be avoided
Whose end is purposed by the mighty gods?
Yet Caesar shall go forth; for these predictions
Are to° the world in general as to Caesar.

Calphurnia.
30 When beggars die, there are no comets seen;
The heavens themselves blaze forth the death of princes.

Caesar.
Cowards die many times before their deaths;
The valiant never taste of death but once.
Of all the wonders that I yet have heard,
35 It seems to me most strange that men should fear,
Seeing that death, a necessary end,
Will come when it will come.

[*Enter a* SERVANT.]

                        What say the augurers?

Servant.
They would not have you to stir forth today.
Plucking the entrails of an offering forth,
40 They could not find a heart within the beast.

Caesar.
The gods do this in shame of cowardice:
Caesar should be a beast without a heart
If he should stay at home today for fear.
No, Caesar shall not. Danger knows full well
45 That Caesar is more dangerous than he.
We are two lions littered in one day,
And I the elder and more terrible.
And Caesar shall go forth.

Calphurnia.   Alas, my lord,
Your wisdom is consumed in confidence.
50 Do not go forth today. Call it my fear
That keeps you in the house and not your own.
We'll send Mark Antony to the Senate House,
And he shall say you are not well today.
Let me, upon my knee, prevail in this.

Caesar.
55 Mark Antony shall say I am not well,

---

25. beyond all use: beyond all we are used to in our normal experience.

? **Staging the Play**
26. *Calphurnia can be played here as hysterical and overly emotional or as truly frightened for her husband. Which way do you think the part should be played?*
29. Are to: apply to.
? **31.** *What does Calphurnia mean?*

? **37.** *How does Caesar feel about death? How does his tone change when he addresses the servant?*
? **37.** *The augurers were very important in ancient Rome. Their duty was to tell from certain signs whether some action was favored by the gods. Signs were read in the flights of birds, in thunder, in the way sacred chickens ate their food, and in the conditions of the organs of a sacrificial animal. What is Caesar's mood as he hears of the augury this morning?*

? **Staging the Play**
48. *Caesar could end this speech with pomposity, dignity, or even humor. How do you interpret his tone?*

? **Staging the Play**
54. *What is Calphurnia doing?*

And for thy humor,° I will stay at home.

[*Enter* DECIUS.]

Here's Decius Brutus, he shall tell them so.

Decius.
Caesar, all hail! Good morrow, worthy Caesar;
I come to fetch you to the Senate House.

Caesar.
60 And you are come in very happy° time
To bear my greeting to the senators,
And tell them that I will not come today.
Cannot, is false; and that I dare not, falser:
I will not come today. Tell them so, Decius.

Calphurnia.
Say he is sick.

65 **Caesar.**   Shall Caesar send a lie?
Have I in conquest stretched mine arm so far
To be afeard to tell graybeards the truth?
Decius, go tell them Caesar will not come.

Decius.
Most mighty Caesar, let me know some cause,
70 Lest I be laughed at when I tell them so.

Caesar.
The cause is in my will: I will not come.
That is enough to satisfy the Senate.
But for your private satisfaction,
Because I love you, I will let you know.
75 Calphurnia here, my wife, stays° me at home.
She dreamt tonight she saw my statue,°
Which, like a fountain with an hundred spouts,
Did run pure blood, and many lusty Romans
Came smiling and did bathe their hands in it.
80 And these does she apply for° warnings and portents

56. humor: mood.

? **Staging the Play**
56. *Here is a sudden change. Would a kiss between lines 54 and 55 explain it?*

60. happy: lucky.

? **Staging the Play**
65. *Is Caesar angry or gentle?*

75. stays: keeps.

76. statue: pronounced here in three syllables (stat·yo͞o·ə) for the meter.

80. apply for: explain as.

"COWARDS DIE MANY TIMES
BEFORE THEIR DEATHS;
THE VALIANT NEVER TASTE
OF DEATH BUT ONCE."

And evils imminent, and on her knee
Hath begged that I will stay at home today.

Decius.
This dream is all amiss interpreted;
It was a vision fair and fortunate:
85   Your statue spouting blood in many pipes,
In which so many smiling Romans bathed,
Signifies that from you great Rome shall suck
Reviving blood, and that great men shall press
For tinctures, stains, relics, and cognizance.°
90   This by Calphurnia's dream is signified.

Caesar.
And this way have you well expounded it.

Decius.
I have, when you have heard what I can say;
And know it now, the Senate have concluded
To give this day a crown to mighty Caesar.
95   If you shall send them word you will not come,
Their minds may change. Besides, it were a mock
Apt to be rendered, for someone to say
"Break up the Senate till another time,
When Caesar's wife shall meet with better dreams."
100   If Caesar hide himself, shall they not whisper
"Lo, Caesar is afraid"?
Pardon me, Caesar, for my dear dear love
To your proceeding° bids me tell you this,
And reason to my love is liable.°

Caesar.
105   How foolish do your fears seem now, Calphurnia!
I am ashamèd I did yield to them.
Give me my robe, for I will go.

[*Enter* BRUTUS, LIGARIUS, METELLUS CIMBER, CASCA,
TREBONIUS, CINNA, *and* PUBLIUS.]

And look where Publius is come to fetch me.

Publius.
Good morrow, Caesar.

Caesar.   Welcome, Publius.
110   What, Brutus, are you stirred so early too?
Good morrow, Casca. Caius Ligarius,
Caesar was ne'er so much your enemy°
As that same ague° which hath made you lean.
What is't o'clock?

Staging the Play
83. *Remember what Decius is here for. We should sense his hungry absorption of Caesar's dream. How should he explain the dream—is he confident, fawning, awed, nervous?*

89. cognizance: identifying emblems worn by a nobleman's followers.

Staging the Play
91. *There should be a pause here. Caesar's fate is about to be sealed. Does he seem relieved or amused?*

99. *What reaction from Caesar is Decius seeking when he refers to "Caesar's wife"? How is Decius playing on Caesar's fears?*
103. proceeding: advancement.
104. liable: subordinate.

107. *Suddenly Caesar changes his mind. Decius has succeeded. How would Calphurnia react now? Do you think Caesar concedes because he foolishly believes Decius, or because he heroically accepts his fate?*
Staging the Play
Stage direction. *What mood would the conspirators be in as they approach their victim?*
112. enemy: Ligarius had supported Pompey in the civil war and had recently been pardoned.
113. ague (ā′gyo͞o′): fever.
113. *Where else has Caesar mentioned that a character is lean?*

Brutus. Caesar, 'tis strucken eight.

Caesar.

115 I thank you for your pains and courtesy.

[*Enter* ANTONY.]

See! Antony, that revels long a-nights,
Is notwithstanding up. Good morrow, Antony.

Antony.

So to most noble Caesar.

Caesar. Bid them prepare within.

I am to blame to be thus waited for.

120 Now, Cinna; now, Metellus; what, Trebonius,
I have an hour's talk in store for you;
Remember that you call on me today;
Be near me, that I may remember you.

Trebonius.

Caesar, I will (*aside*) and so near will I be,

125 That your best friends shall wish I had been further.

Caesar.

Good friends, go in and taste some wine with me,
And we (like friends) will straightway go together.

Brutus (*aside*).

That every like is not the same,° O Caesar,
The heart of Brutus earns° to think upon.   [*Exeunt.*]

> **Staging the Play**
> **117.** *How can the actors playing Antony and Caesar establish the fact that a deep friendship exists between them?*

> **Staging the Play**
> **124.** *An* **aside** *is a speech addressed to one other character or to the audience, out of hearing of the other actors onstage. How would this aside be spoken?*
> **127.** *What* **irony** *do you feel here? (What do we know that Caesar is ignorant of?)*
> **128.** In other words, that those who appear to be friends are not really friends at all.
> **129. earns:** grieves.

SCENE 3. *A street near the Capitol, close to Brutus' house.*

Enter ARTEMIDORUS *reading a paper.*

Artemidorus. "Caesar, beware of Brutus; take heed of Cassius; come not near Casca; have an eye to Cinna; trust not Trebonius; mark well Metellus Cimber; Decius Brutus loves thee not; thou hast wronged Caius Ligarius. There is

5 but one mind in all these men, and it is bent against Caesar. If thou beest not immortal, look about you: security gives way to conspiracy.° The mighty gods defend thee!
                        Thy lover,° Artemidorus."
Here will I stand till Caesar pass along,

10 And as a suitor° will I give him this.
My heart laments that virtue cannot live
Out of the teeth of emulation.°
If thou read this, O Caesar, thou mayest live;
If not, the Fates with traitors do contrive.°   [*Exit.*]

7. In other words, a feeling of security gives the conspirators their opportunity.
8. lover: friend (one who loves you).
10. suitor: one who seeks a favor.

12. Out of the teeth of emulation: beyond the reach of envy.
14. contrive: plot or scheme.

Enter PORTIA *and* LUCIUS.

Portia.

    I prithee, boy, run to the Senate House;

    Stay not to answer me, but get thee gone.

    Why dost thou stay?

Lucius.   To know my errand, madam.

Portia.

    I would have had thee there and here again

5   Ere I can tell thee what thou shouldst do there.

    O constancy,° be strong upon my side;

    Set a huge mountain 'tween my heart and tongue!

    I have a man's mind, but a woman's might.

    How hard it is for women to keep counsel!°

    Art thou here yet?

10   **Lucius.**   Madam, what should I do?

    Run to the Capitol, and nothing else?

    And so return to you, and nothing else?

Portia.

    Yes, bring me word, boy, if thy lord look well,

    For he went sickly forth; and take good note

15   What Caesar doth, what suitors press to him.

    Hark, boy, what noise is that?

Lucius.

    I hear none, madam.

Portia.   Prithee, listen well.

    I hear a bustling rumor° like a fray,°

    And the wind brings it from the Capitol.

Lucius.

20   Sooth,° madam, I hear nothing.

[*Enter the* SOOTHSAYER.]

Portia.

    Come hither, fellow. Which way hast thou been?

Soothsayer.

    At mine own house, good lady.

Portia.

    What is't o'clock?

Soothsayer.   About the ninth hour, lady.

6. constancy: determination.

9. counsel: a secret.

9. *Is there a clue in this speech that Brutus has told Portia of the conspiracy to murder Caesar? Does the script provide an opportunity for him to tell her after their conversation in Scene 1? In "stage time" (the time at which the play's events take place), could he have told Portia of the plot?*

18. rumor: noise. **fray:** fight.

20. Sooth: in truth.

Portia.

　　Is Caesar yet gone to the Capitol?

Soothsayer.

25　　Madam, not yet; I go to take my stand,
　　To see him pass on to the Capitol.

Portia.

　　Thou hast some suit to Caesar, hast thou not?

Soothsayer.

　　That I have, lady; if it will please Caesar
　　To be so good to Caesar as to hear me,
30　　I shall beseech him to befriend himself.

Portia.

　　Why, know'st thou any harm's intended towards him?

Soothsayer.

　　None that I know will be, much that I fear may chance.
　　Good morrow to you. Here the street is narrow;
　　The throng that follows Caesar at the heels,
35　　Of senators, of praetors,° common suitors,
　　Will crowd a feeble man almost to death.
　　I'll get me to a place more void,° and there
　　Speak to great Caesar as he comes along.　　[*Exit.*]

Portia.

　　I must go in. Ay me, how weak a thing
40　　The heart of woman is! O Brutus,
　　The heavens speed thee in thine enterprise!
　　Sure, the boy heard me—Brutus hath a suit
　　That Caesar will not grant—O, I grow faint.
　　Run, Lucius, and commend me to my lord;
45　　Say I am merry; come to me again,
　　And bring me word what he doth say to thee.
　　　　　　　　　　　　　　　　[*Exeunt severally.*]

35. praetors (prē′tərz): magistrates; city officials.

37. void: empty.

? Staging the Play
46. *What does this **soliloquy** reveal about Portia's state of mind? Why might she deliver line 45 after a pause?*

Response and Analysis

Act II

Reading Check

1. A **soliloquy** is a speech given by a character alone onstage. Look at Brutus's soliloquy at the beginning of Act II. What reasons does he give for killing Caesar?

2. Who proposes the murder of Antony? Why does Brutus oppose it?

3. What does Portia demand in the **dialogue,** or conversation, with Brutus in Scene 1?

4. In Scene 2, what does Calphurnia try to persuade Caesar to do? Why?

5. How does Decius persuade Caesar to attend the Senate?

Thinking Critically

6. When you read rather than watch a play, you have to stage it in your imagination, to visualize the movements of characters and the sounds of voices. As you imagine Act II, tell how it compares with Act I—is the pace faster or slower? Are the characters calmer or more agitated? Which scenes make you think so?

7. Why won't Brutus swear an oath (Scene 1, lines 114–140)? What **character traits** does this speech reveal?

8. Describe the complexities of Caesar's **character.** How do you feel about him—is he a monstrous tyrant or a sympathetic man? Explain.

9. Where does Shakespeare use thunder and other storm sounds in the **setting** to suggest cosmic disorder? How does this weather make you feel?

10. In the **rising action** of Act II, describe how Shakespeare creates and builds **suspense** during Scenes 3 and 4. What questions are you left with as the second act of this **tragedy** ends?

Extending and Evaluating

11. In Scene 4, Portia appears to know that Brutus is involved in a plot to kill Caesar, although the play does not include a scene in which Brutus gives her this information. Is this omission a weakness in the play? If you were writing such a scene, how would you have Portia react to her husband's news?

WRITING

Women's Work

How do you feel about Portia's lament in her soliloquy in Scene 4, lines 39–40: "Ay me, how weak a thing / The heart of woman is!"? In a brief essay, **compare and contrast** the characters of Portia and Calphurnia, and analyze their function in this act.

LISTENING AND SPEAKING

A Play Within a Play

Caesar's scene with Calphurnia and later with Decius (Scene 2) is a perfect play-within-a-play. Prepare the scene for **dramatic performance.** Before you rehearse, be sure you understand the characters' **motivations.**

SKILLS FOCUS

Literary Skills
Analyze tragedy.

Writing Skills
Write an essay comparing and contrasting two characters.

Listening and Speaking Skills
Perform a dramatic scene.

Vocabulary Development

Understanding Elizabethan English

The English language classifies words as nouns, verbs, and so on. When someone mixes up the parts of speech, purists are outraged. (Today, for example, purists deplore the use of the noun *network* as a verb.) Shakespeare freely used the same words as different parts of speech.

1. Here he makes a verb out of the noun *conceit*:

   "You have right well conceited."
   —Act I, Scene 3, line 162

2. Here he uses an adjective (*vulgar*) as a noun (we'd say *vulgar people*):

   ". . . drive away the vulgar from the streets. . . ."
   —Act I, Scene 1, line 70

3. In some passages he omits words:

   "So Caesar may;
   Then lest he may, prevent."
   —Act II, Scene 1,
   lines 27–28

   What's understood here is "prevent him from doing it."

PRACTICE

Use the notes alongside the text of Act II for help with these questions:

1. In Scene 1, line 3 (page 783), Brutus says he cannot "Give guess how near to day." How would you expand this phrase?

2. What word does Brutus omit after the word *general* in line 12 of Scene 1 (page 783)?

3. What do you think Lucius means in Scene 1, line 73 (page 785), when he says the conspirators' "hats are plucked about their ears"?

4. In Scene 1, line 83 (page 785), what noun does Shakespeare use as a verb?

SKILLS FOCUS

Vocabulary Skills
Understand Elizabethan language.

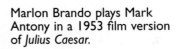

Marlon Brando plays Mark Antony in a 1953 film version of *Julius Caesar*.

ACT III

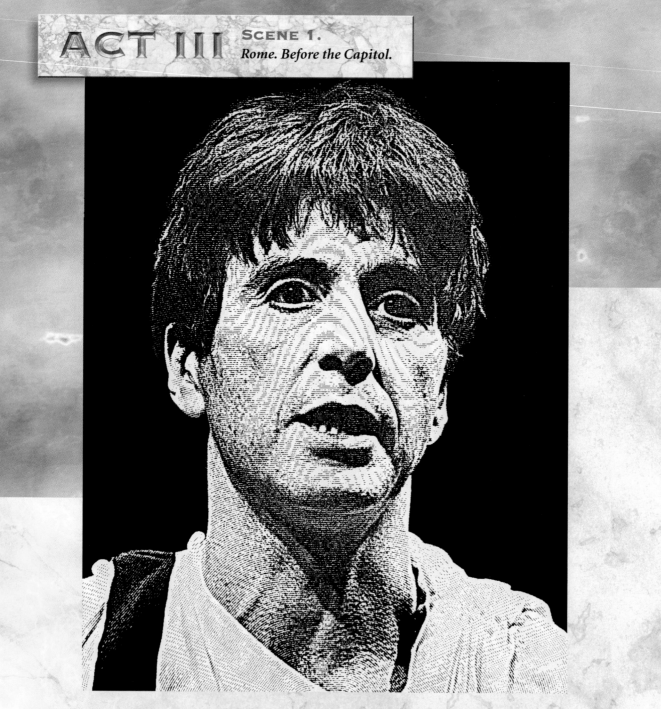

"FRIENDS, ROMANS, COUNTRYMEN,
LEND ME YOUR EARS . . ."
—ANTONY, ACT III, SCENE 2
(LINE 73)

Flourish. Enter CAESAR, BRUTUS, CASSIUS, CASCA, DECIUS,
   METELLUS CIMBER, TREBONIUS, CINNA, ANTONY,
   LEPIDUS, ARTEMIDORUS, PUBLIUS, POPILIUS, *and the*
   SOOTHSAYER.

Caesar.
   The ides of March are come.
Soothsayer.
   Ay, Caesar, but not gone.
Artemidorus.
   Hail, Caesar! Read this schedule.°
Decius.
   Trebonius doth desire you to o'er-read,
5   At your best leisure, this his humble suit.
Artemidorus.
   O Caesar, read mine first; for mine's a suit
   That touches° Caesar nearer. Read it, great Caesar.
Caesar.
   What touches us ourself shall be last served.
Artemidorus.
   Delay not, Caesar; read it instantly.
Caesar.
   What, is the fellow mad?
10 **Publius.**   Sirrah,° give place.
Cassius.
   What, urge you your petitions in the street?
   Come to the Capitol.

[CAESAR *goes to the Capitol, the rest following.*]

Popilius.
   I wish your enterprise today may thrive.
Cassius.
   What enterprise, Popilius?
Popilius.   Fare you well.

[*Advances to* CAESAR.]

Brutus.
15   What said Popilius Lena?

Staging the Play
Stage direction. *This scene
takes place on the Capitol Hill,
where the temple of Jupiter is
located. A half circle of steps is
seen at the back of the stage, with
a throne on top. A statue of
Pompey—the enemy Caesar
defeated in the recent civil war—
is seen to the side. Caesar walks to
center stage, and the others flank
him. How should Caesar regard
the soothsayer and Artemidorus?
Should he address his first remark
to the soothsayer or to the crowd
in general?*
  3. schedule: scroll of paper.

  7. touches: concerns.

8. *Is this sincerity or false
humility?*

10. Sirrah (sir′ə): like *sir,* but used
to address an inferior, often
intending disrespect or anger.
Staging the Play
10. *Publius speaks to
Artemidorus, and the conspirators
rush the petitioner away from
Caesar. Whom is Cassius
addressing in the next speech?*

13. *Popilius speaks to
Cassius. Do you think he
knows about the conspiracy?*

Cassius.

He wished today our enterprise might thrive.

I fear our purpose is discoverèd.

Brutus.

Look how he makes to° Caesar; mark him.

Cassius.

Casca, be sudden, for we fear prevention.°

20 Brutus, what shall be done? If this be known,

Cassius or Caesar never shall turn back,°

For I will slay myself.

Brutus.   Cassius, be constant.°

Popilius Lena speaks not of our purposes;

For look, he smiles, and Caesar doth not change.

Cassius.

25 Trebonius knows his time; for look you, Brutus,

He draws Mark Antony out of the way.

[*Exeunt* ANTONY *and* TREBONIUS.]

Decius.

Where is Metellus Cimber? Let him go

And presently prefer his suit to Caesar.

Brutus.

He is addressed.° Press near and second him.

Cinna.

30 Casca, you are the first that rears your hand.

Caesar.

Are we all ready? What is now amiss

That Caesar and his Senate must redress?

Metellus.

Most high, most mighty, and most puissant° Caesar,

Metellus Cimber throws before thy seat

An humble heart.   [*Kneeling.*]

35 **Caesar.**   I must prevent thee, Cimber.

These couchings° and these lowly courtesies

Might fire the blood of ordinary men,

And turn preordinance and first decree°

Into the law of children. Be not fond°

40 To think that Caesar bears such rebel blood

That will be thawed from the true quality°

With that which melteth fools—I mean sweet words,

Low-crookèd curtsies, and base spaniel fawning.

Thy brother by decree is banishèd.

45 If thou dost bend and pray and fawn for him,

18. makes to: makes his way toward.

19. prevention: being prevented from carrying out their deed.

21. turn back: come out alive.

22. constant: calm.

? 26. *Why is Trebonius getting Antony out of the way?*

29. addressed: ready.

? Staging the Play
29. *What is happening near Caesar now?*

33. puissant (py$\overline{oo}$'i·sənt): powerful.

36. couchings: very low bows.

38. These were old Roman laws. Caesar warns that the laws might be changed at whim if they are not vigilant (just as the laws of children can be changed).
39. fond: so foolish as.
41. true quality: that is, firmness.

I spurn thee like a cur out of my way.
Know, Caesar doth not wrong, nor without cause
Will he be satisfied.

Metellus.

Is there no voice more worthy than my own,
50   To sound more sweetly in great Caesar's ear
For the repealing of my banished brother?

Brutus.

I kiss thy hand, but not in flattery, Caesar,
Desiring thee that Publius Cimber may
Have an immediate freedom of repeal.°

Caesar.

What, Brutus?

55 **Cassius.**   Pardon, Caesar; Caesar, pardon!
As low as to thy foot doth Cassius fall
To beg enfranchisement° for Publius Cimber.

Caesar.

I could be well moved, if I were as you;
If I could pray to move,° prayers would move me;
60   But I am constant as the Northern Star,
Of whose true-fixed and resting° quality
There is no fellow° in the firmament.
The skies are painted with unnumb'red sparks,
They are all fire and every one doth shine;
65   But there's but one in all doth hold his place.
So in the world; 'tis furnished well with men,
And men are flesh and blood, and apprehensive;
Yet in the number I do know but one
That unassailable holds on his rank,°
70   Unshaked of motion; and that I am he,
Let me a little show it, even in this—
That I was constant° Cimber should be banished,
And constant do remain to keep him so.

Cinna.

O Caesar——

Caesar.   Hence! Wilt thou lift up Olympus?°

Decius.

Great Caesar——

75 **Caesar.**   Doth not Brutus bootless° kneel?

Casca.

Speak hands for me!

[*They stab* CAESAR.]

Staging the Play
48. *What is Caesar doing during this speech? What is Metellus doing in response to Caesar's words?*

51. *Whom is Metellus addressing here?*
Staging the Play
52. *Brutus steps forward; notice that he uses the pronoun* thy *in an insulting way, since Caesar is not his social inferior, nor is the situation intimate. How might Caesar react to Brutus's surprising words?*
54. freedom of repeal: permission to return from exile.
57. enfranchisement: restoration of the rights of citizenship.

59. pray to move: beg others to change their minds.

61. resting: changeless.

62. fellow: equal.

69. rank: position.
Staging the Play
70. *At what point in this speech would Caesar rise from his throne? The senators now rush in around Caesar and, in most productions, kneel before him. Casca has worked his way in back of Caesar.*
72. constant: firmly determined.
74. Olympus: in Greek mythology, the mountain where the gods lived.
75. bootless: in vain.
Staging the Play
75. *This line is often spoken to show Caesar's great fondness for Brutus. How else might it be spoken?*
Staging the Play
76. *What does this line mean? What is Casca doing?*

"LIBERTY, FREEDOM, AND ENFRANCHISEMENT!"

Caesar.

  Et tu, Brutè?° Then fall Caesar.   [*Dies.*]

Cinna.

  Liberty! Freedom! Tyranny is dead!

  Run hence, proclaim, cry it about the streets.

Cassius.

80   Some to the common pulpits, and cry out

  "Liberty, freedom, and enfranchisement!"

Brutus.

  People, and senators, be not affrighted.

  Fly not; stand still; ambition's debt is paid.

Casca.

  Go to the pulpit, Brutus.

Decius.   And Cassius too.

77. Et tu, Brutè?: Latin for "And you also, Brutus?"

？ Staging the Play
  77. *The murder of Caesar has been staged in many ways. Low-budget productions have to worry about laundry bills for stained togas, but most productions show blood. In some productions each dagger has attached to it a plastic capsule, which the actors break with their fingernails. In other productions, Caesar has a "blood" bag concealed under his toga. To stage the murder, directors often have the conspirators standing at different places onstage—all points to which Caesar runs in his attempt to escape. The last point is Brutus's. What does Caesar see as he utters his last words? Why does he say, "Then fall Caesar"?*

Brutus.

85 　　Where's Publius?°

Cinna.

　　Here, quite confounded with this mutiny.

Metellus.

　　Stand fast together, lest some friend of Caesar's
　　Should chance——

Brutus.

　　Talk not of standing. Publius, good cheer;
90 　　There is no harm intended to your person,
　　Nor to no Roman else. So tell them, Publius.

Cassius.

　　And leave us, Publius, lest that the people
　　Rushing on us should do your age some mischief.

Brutus.

　　Do so; and let no man abide° this deed
95 　　But we the doers.

[*Enter* TREBONIUS.]

Cassius.

　　Where is Antony?

Trebonius.　　　　　Fled to his house amazed.
　　Men, wives, and children stare, cry out and run,
　　As it were doomsday.

Brutus.　　　　　　　Fates, we will know your pleasures.
　　That we shall die, we know; 'tis but the time,
100 　　And drawing days out, that men stand upon.°

Casca.

　　Why, he that cuts off twenty years of life
　　Cuts off so many years of fearing death.

Brutus.

　　Grant that, and then is death a benefit.
　　So are we Caesar's friends, that have abridged
105 　　His time of fearing death. Stoop, Romans, stoop,
　　And let us bathe our hands in Caesar's blood
　　Up to the elbows, and besmear our swords.
　　Then walk we forth, even to the market place,°
　　And waving our red weapons o'er our heads,
110 　　Let's all cry "Peace, freedom, and liberty!"

85. Publius is a very old senator, too old to flee.

94. abide: take the consequences of.

100. stand upon: wait for.

? **Staging the Play**
107. *What are the conspirators doing now?*
108. market place: Forum, center of public and commercial life in Rome.

Cassius.

    Stoop then, and wash. How many ages hence

    Shall this our lofty scene be acted over

    In states unborn and accents yet unknown!

Brutus.

    How many times shall Caesar bleed in sport,

115   That now on Pompey's basis° lies along°

    No worthier than the dust!

Cassius.   So oft as that shall be,

    So often shall the knot of us be called

    The men that gave their country liberty.

Decius.

    What, shall we forth?

Cassius.   Ay, every man away.

120   Brutus shall lead, and we will grace his heels

    With the most boldest and best hearts of Rome.

[Enter a SERVANT.*]*

Brutus.

    Soft, who comes here? A friend of Antony's.

Servant.

    Thus, Brutus, did my master bid me kneel;

    Thus did Mark Antony bid me fall down;

125   And, being prostrate, thus he bade me say:

    Brutus is noble, wise, valiant, and honest;

    Caesar was mighty, bold, royal, and loving.

    Say I love Brutus, and I honor him;

    Say I feared Caesar, honored him, and loved him.

130   If Brutus will vouchsafe that Antony

    May safely come to him and be resolved°

    How Caesar hath deserved to lie in death,

    Mark Antony shall not love Caesar dead

    So well as Brutus living; but will follow

135   The fortunes and affairs of noble Brutus

    Thorough° the hazards of this untrod state

    With all true faith. So says my master Antony.

Brutus.

    Thy master is a wise and valiant Roman;

    I never thought him worse.

140   Tell him, so please him come unto this place,

    He shall be satisfied and, by my honor,

    Depart untouched.

Servant.   I'll fetch him presently.°

[Exit SERVANT.*]*

115. basis: base (of Pompey's statue). **lies along:** stretches out.

? **Staging the Play**
118. *These speeches can be delivered in various ways. Would you emphasize the self-righteousness of the conspirators or their idealism?*

131. resolved: satisfied.

136. Thorough: through.
? **137.** *What does Antony ask of Brutus?*

142. presently: immediately.

**"HOW MANY AGES HENCE
SHALL THIS OUR LOFTY SCENE
BE ACTED OVER
IN STATES UNBORN AND
ACCENTS YET UNKNOWN!"**

Brutus.
    I know that we shall have him well to friend.

Cassius.
    I wish we may. But yet have I a mind
145   That fears him much; and my misgiving still
    Falls shrewdly to the purpose.°

[*Enter* ANTONY.]

Brutus.
    But here comes Antony. Welcome, Mark Antony.

Antony.
    O mighty Caesar! Dost thou lie so low?
    Are all thy conquests, glories, triumphs, spoils,
150   Shrunk to this little measure? Fare thee well.
    I know not, gentlemen, what you intend,
    Who else must be let blood,° who else is rank.°
    If I myself, there is no hour so fit
    As Caesar's death's hour, nor no instrument
155   Of half that worth as those your swords, made rich
    With the most noble blood of all this world.
    I do beseech ye, if you bear me hard,°
    Now, whilst your purpled hands do reek and smoke,
    Fulfill your pleasure. Live a thousand years,
160   I shall not find myself so apt to die;
    No place will please me so, no mean of death,
    As here by Caesar, and by you cut off,
    The choice and master spirits of this age.

Brutus.
    O Antony, beg not your death of us!
165   Though now we must appear bloody and cruel,
    As by our hands and this our present act
    You see we do, yet see you but our hands
    And this the bleeding business they have done.

146. In other words, my misgivings, or doubts, are usually justified.

? Staging the Play
146. *How does Cassius say this line? Notice that at this moment the play takes a turn and that the hunters now become the hunted.*

? Staging the Play
148. *Where should Antony position himself? In this speech, where would you have the actor playing Antony pause? What movements or gestures would he make?*

152. Antony is punning here: "Let blood" can mean "bleed a sick person in order to cure the illness," or it can mean "shed blood (kill)." **rank:** another pun—swollen with disease (and thus in need of bleeding) or swollen with power.

157. bear me hard: bear a grudge against me.

? 163–253. *We've had a glimpse of Antony earlier in the play, but this scene is the first time he speaks at length. What is the purpose of this **dialogue,** or conversation, between Brutus, Antony, and Cassius?*

Our hearts you see not; they are pitiful;°
170 And pity to the general wrong of Rome—
As fire drives out fire, so pity pity—
Hath done this deed on Caesar. For your part,
To you our swords have leaden° points, Mark Antony:
Our arms in strength of malice, and our hearts
175 Of brothers' temper, do receive you in
With all kind love, good thoughts, and reverence.

Cassius.
Your voice shall be as strong as any man's
In the disposing of new dignities.°

Brutus.
Only be patient till we have appeased
180 The multitude, beside themselves with fear,
And then we will deliver you the cause
Why I, that did love Caesar when I struck him,
Have thus proceeded.

Antony.   I doubt not of your wisdom.
Let each man render me his bloody hand.
185 First, Marcus Brutus, will I shake with you;
Next, Caius Cassius, do I take your hand;
Now, Decius Brutus, yours; now yours, Metellus;
Yours, Cinna; and, my valiant Casca, yours;
Though last, not least in love, yours, good Trebonius.
190 Gentlemen all—alas, what shall I say?
My credit° now stands on such slippery ground
That one of two bad ways you must conceit° me,
Either a coward or a flatterer.
That I did love thee, Caesar, O, 'tis true!
195 If then thy spirit look upon us now,
Shall it not grieve thee dearer than thy death
To see thy Antony making his peace,
Shaking the bloody fingers of thy foes,
Most noble, in the presence of thy corse?°
200 Had I as many eyes as thou hast wounds,

169. pitiful: full of pity.

173. leaden: blunt (not made of steel).

178. dignities: titles.
[?] 178. *Again, Cassius serves as* **foil** *to Brutus. What differences in character do Brutus and Cassius reveal here in replying to Antony?*

[?] Staging the Play
185. *This is a rather bold step on Antony's part. What is he doing? What is his motive?*

191. credit: reputation.
192. conceit: judge.

[?] Staging the Play
194. *What is Antony's position on stage now—is he standing or kneeling? Is he near the corpse or far away from it?*

199. corse (kôrs): corpse.

"THAT I DID LOVE THEE, CAESAR, O, 'TIS TRUE!"

Weeping as fast as they stream forth thy blood,
It would become me better than to close
In terms of friendship with thine enemies.
Pardon me, Julius! Here wast thou bayed, brave hart;°
205   Here didst thou fall, and here thy hunters stand,
Signed in thy spoil and crimsoned in thy lethe.°
O world, thou wast the forest to this hart;
And this indeed, O world, the heart of thee.
How like a deer, stroken by many princes,
210   Dost thou here lie!

Cassius.
Mark Antony—

Antony.   Pardon me, Caius Cassius.
The enemies of Caesar shall say this;
Then, in a friend, it is cold modesty.°

Cassius.
I blame you not for praising Caesar so;
215   But what compact mean you to have with us?
Will you be pricked in number of° our friends,
Or shall we on, and not depend on you?

Antony.
Therefore I took your hands, but was indeed
Swayed from the point by looking down on Caesar.
220   Friends am I with you all, and love you all,
Upon this hope, that you shall give me reasons
Why, and wherein, Caesar was dangerous.

Brutus.
Or else were this a savage spectacle.
Our reasons are so full of good regard
225   That were you, Antony, the son of Caesar,
You should be satisfied.

Antony.   That's all I seek;
And am moreover suitor that I may
Produce° his body to the market place,
And in the pulpit, as becomes a friend,
230   Speak in the order of his funeral.

Brutus.
You shall, Mark Antony.

Cassius.   Brutus, a word with you.
(*Aside to* BRUTUS.) You know not what you do; do not
    consent
That Antony speak in his funeral.
Know you how much the people may be moved

204. Antony compares Caesar to a deer (hart) hunted down by barking (baying) hounds. "Brave hart" is also a pun on "brave heart."
206. In other words, marked with the wounds of your slaughter and reddened by your blood (compared to the river Lethe in the underworld).

? **210.** *Why is the imagery of the hunted deer (hart) so appropriate here? How does it make you feel about Caesar?*

213. modesty: moderation.

216. pricked in number of: counted with. In counting off a list of people, the Romans would prick a hole in a wax-covered tablet.

228. Produce: take.

? **232.** *An **aside** is words spoken by one character to another character, or to the audience, that others onstage are not supposed to hear. What is the function of Cassius's aside to Brutus?*

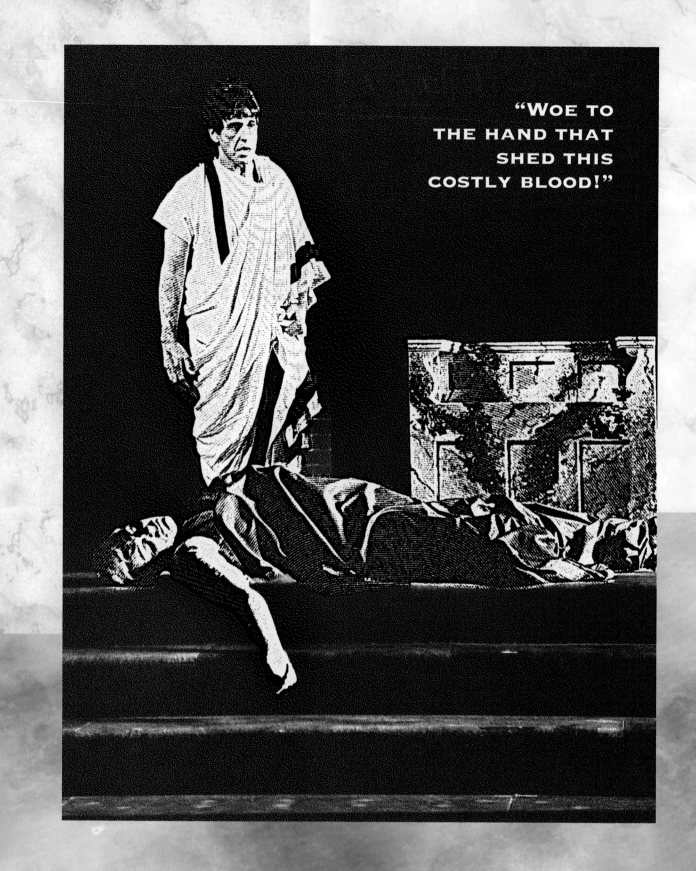

"WOE TO
THE HAND THAT
SHED THIS
COSTLY BLOOD!"

By that which he will utter?

235 **Brutus.**   By your pardon:
    I will myself into the pulpit first,
    And show the reason of our Caesar's death.
    What Antony shall speak, I will protest
    He speaks by leave and by permission,
240 And that we are contented Caesar shall
    Have all true rites and lawful ceremonies.
    It shall advantage more than do us wrong.

Cassius.
    I know not what may fall;° I like it not.

Brutus.
    Mark Antony, here, take you Caesar's body.
245 You shall not in your funeral speech blame us,
    But speak all good you can devise of Caesar,
    And say you do't by our permission;
    Else shall you not have any hand at all
    About his funeral. And you shall speak
250 In the same pulpit whereto I am going,
    After my speech is ended.

Antony.   Be it so;
    I do desire no more.

Brutus.
    Prepare the body then, and follow us.

                    [*Exeunt all except* ANTONY.]

Antony.
    O pardon me, thou bleeding piece of earth,
255 That I am meek and gentle with these butchers!
    Thou art the ruins of the noblest man
    That ever livèd in the tide of times.
    Woe to the hand that shed this costly blood!
    Over thy wounds now do I prophesy
260 (Which like dumb mouths do ope their ruby lips
    To beg the voice and utterance of my tongue),
    A curse shall light upon the limbs of men;
    Domestic fury and fierce civil strife
    Shall cumber° all the parts of Italy;
265 Blood and destruction shall be so in use,
    And dreadful objects so familiar,
    That mothers shall but smile when they behold
    Their infants quartered° with the hands of war,

243. **fall:** befall; happen.

Staging the Play
254. *How should Antony immediately change his tone? Whom is he talking to?*

Staging the Play
263. *During this speech some directors let us hear the offstage noise of the crowd. At what moments in this speech would the offstage cries of the mob and even other street noises be appropriate?*
264. **cumber:** burden.
268. **quartered:** butchered (cut in four parts).

All pity choked with custom of fell° deeds,

270 And Caesar's spirit, ranging for revenge,
With Atè° by his side come hot from hell,
Shall in these confines with a monarch's voice
Cry "Havoc,"° and let slip the dogs of war,
That this foul deed shall smell above the earth
275 With carrion° men, groaning for burial.

[*Enter Octavius's* SERVANT.]

You serve Octavius Caesar, do you not?

Servant.
I do, Mark Antony.

Antony.
Caesar did write for him to come to Rome.

Servant.
He did receive his letters and is coming,
280 And bid me say to you by word of mouth—
O Caesar! [*Seeing the body.*]

Antony.
Thy heart is big;° get thee apart and weep.
Passion, I see, is catching, for mine eyes,
Seeing those beads of sorrow stand in thine,
285 Began to water. Is thy master coming?

Servant.
He lies tonight within seven leagues° of Rome.

Antony.
Post° back with speed, and tell him what hath chanced.
Here is a mourning Rome, a dangerous Rome,
No Rome of safety for Octavius yet.
290 Hie° hence and tell him so. Yet stay awhile;
Thou shalt not back till I have borne this corse
Into the market place; there shall I try°
In my oration how the people take
The cruel issue° of these bloody men;
295 According to the which, thou shalt discourse
To young Octavius of the state of things.
Lend me your hand. [*Exeunt.*]

269. fell: evil.

271. Atè (ā′tē): Greek goddess of revenge.

273. Cry "Havoc": give the signal for the devastation and disorder to begin.
275. carrion: dead and rotting.

282. big: full of grief.

? **Staging the Play**
284. *What might Antony do to the servant to make us feel his compassion?*

286. seven leagues: about twenty-one miles.

287. Post: ride on horseback (changing horses along the way).

290. Hie: hurry.

292. try: test.

294. cruel issue: cruel deed; also, the outcome, or result, of cruelty.

? **Staging the Play**
297. *Would you end this scene with Antony raising the body in his arms, or would you have him stand over it? Would the noise of the crowd be heard from offstage?*

Enter BRUTUS *and goes into the pulpit, and* CASSIUS, *with the* PLEBEIANS.°

Plebeians.
>   We will be satisfied! Let us be satisfied!

Brutus.
>   Then follow me, and give me audience, friends.
>   Cassius, go you into the other street
>   And part the numbers.

5
>   Those that will hear me speak, let 'em stay here;
>   Those that will follow Cassius, go with him;
>   And public reasons shall be renderèd
>   Of Caesar's death.

First Plebeian.   I will hear Brutus speak.

Second Plebeian.
>   I will hear Cassius, and compare their reasons,

10
>   When severally we hear them renderèd.

[*Exit* CASSIUS, *with some of the* PLEBEIANS.]

Third Plebeian.
>   The noble Brutus is ascended. Silence!

Brutus. Be patient till the last.
>   Romans, countrymen, and lovers, hear me for my cause,
>   and be silent, that you may hear. Believe me for mine

15
>   honor, and have respect to mine honor, that you may
>   believe. Censure° me in your wisdom, and awake your
>   senses,° that you may the better judge. If there be any in
>   this assembly, any dear friend of Caesar's, to him I say
>   that Brutus' love to Caesar was no less than his. If then

20
>   that friend demand why Brutus rose against Caesar, this

Plebeians: the common people.

? **Staging the Play**
Stage direction. The Roman Forum was a busy, crowded, open area. At one end of the Forum was the Rostrum, a "pulpit" from which Rome's great public figures spoke. In stage sets the pulpit is usually set on a semicircular platform with steps leading up to it. This scene is wild and noisy. What is Brutus's mood as he fights free of the mob and goes up to the pulpit?

16. **Censure:** judge.
17. **senses:** reasoning powers.

"ROMANS, COUNTRYMEN, AND LOVERS, HEAR ME FOR MY CAUSE . . ."

is my answer: Not that I loved Caesar less, but that I loved Rome more. Had you rather Caesar were living, and die all slaves, than that Caesar were dead, to live all free men? As Caesar loved me, I weep for him; as he was
25 fortunate, I rejoice at it; as he was valiant, I honor him; but, as he was ambitious, I slew him. There is tears, for his love; joy, for his fortune; honor, for his valor; and death, for his ambition. Who is here so base, that would be a bondman?° If any, speak; for him have I offended.
30 Who is here so rude,° that would not be a Roman? If any, speak; for him have I offended. Who is here so vile, that will not love his country? If any, speak; for him have I offended. I pause for a reply.

All. None, Brutus, none!

35 **Brutus.** Then none have I offended. I have done no more to Caesar than you shall do to Brutus. The question of his death is enrolled° in the Capitol; his glory not extenuated,° wherein he was worthy, nor his offenses enforced,° for which he suffered death.

[*Enter* MARK ANTONY, *with Caesar's body.*]

40 Here comes his body, mourned by Mark Antony, who, though he had no hand in his death, shall receive the benefit of his dying, a place in the commonwealth, as which of you shall not? With this I depart, that, as I slew my best lover for the good of Rome, I have the same
45 dagger for myself, when it shall please my country to need my death.

All. Live, Brutus! Live, live!

First Plebeian.
Bring him with triumph home unto his house.

Second Plebeian.
Give him a statue with his ancestors.

Third Plebeian.
Let him be Caesar.

50 **Fourth Plebeian.**   Caesar's better parts°
Shall be crowned in Brutus.

First Plebeian.
We'll bring him to his house with shouts and clamors.

Brutus. My countrymen—

Second Plebeian.   Peace! Silence! Brutus speaks.

First Plebeian. Peace, ho!

---

22. *In this important **monologue,** what reasons does Brutus give for killing Caesar?*

29. bondman: slave.
30. rude: rough and uncivilized.

33. *Notice that Brutus's speech is in prose, not poetry. What value does Brutus presume the people cherish—as he cherishes it?*

37. In other words, there is a record of the reasons he was killed.
extenuated: lessened.
38. enforced: exaggerated.

50. better parts: better qualities.
50. *Why is this cry from the mob, in lines 50–51, ironic? Has the crowd understood Brutus's motives at all?*

Staging the Play
52. *What would you have Antony doing while the mob is talking? (Remember: He has brought Caesar's body to the Forum.)*

Brutus.

55 Good countrymen, let me depart alone,
And, for my sake, stay here with Antony.
Do grace to Caesar's corpse, and grace his speech°
Tending to Caesar's glories, which Mark Antony
By our permission, is allowed to make.
60 I do entreat you, not a man depart,
Save I alone, till Antony have spoke.   [*Exit.*]

First Plebeian.

Stay, ho! And let us hear Mark Antony.

Third Plebeian.

Let him go up into the public chair;°
We'll hear him. Noble Antony, go up.

Antony.

65 For Brutus' sake, I am beholding to you.

57. grace his speech: listen respectfully to Antony's funeral oration.

63. public chair: pulpit or rostrum.

"NOT THAT I LOVED CAESAR LESS, BUT THAT I LOVED ROME MORE."

Fourth Plebeian.
　　What does he say of Brutus?
Third Plebeian.　　　　　　He says, for Brutus' sake,
　　He finds himself beholding to us all.
Fourth Plebeian.
　　'Twere best he speak no harm of Brutus here!
First Plebeian.
　　This Caesar was a tyrant.
Third Plebeian.　　　　　Nay, that's certain.
70　　We are blest that Rome is rid of him.
Second Plebeian.
　　Peace! Let us hear what Antony can say.
Antony.
　　You gentle Romans—
All.　　　　　　Peace, ho! Let us hear him.
Antony.
　　Friends, Romans, countrymen, lend me your ears;
　　I come to bury Caesar, not to praise him.
75　　The evil that men do lives after them,
　　The good is oft interrèd with their bones;
　　So let it be with Caesar. The noble Brutus
　　Hath told you Caesar was ambitious.
　　If it were so, it was a grievous fault,
80　　And grievously hath Caesar answered° it.
　　Here, under leave of Brutus and the rest
　　(For Brutus is an honorable man,
　　So are they all, all honorable men),
　　Come I to speak in Caesar's funeral.
85　　He was my friend, faithful and just to me;
　　But Brutus says he was ambitious,
　　And Brutus is an honorable man.
　　He hath brought many captives home to Rome,
　　Whose ransoms did the general coffers° fill;
90　　Did this in Caesar seem ambitious?
　　When that the poor have cried, Caesar hath wept;
　　Ambition should be made of sterner stuff.
　　Yet Brutus says he was ambitious;
　　And Brutus is an honorable man.
95　　You all did see that on the Lupercal

? **Staging the Play**
73. *An important question: Where would you place Caesar's body so that Antony can use it most effectively? Be sure to perform this famous funeral oration. What different tones do you hear in Antony's* **monologue**?

80. answered: paid the penalty for.

89. general coffers: public funds.

? **Staging the Play**
93. *Remember that the crowd is pressing in on Antony. What movements or sounds would they make as Antony says things that are meant to sway their feelings?*

I thrice presented him a kingly crown,
Which he did thrice refuse. Was this ambition?
Yet Brutus says he was ambitious;
And sure he is an honorable man.
100   I speak not to disprove what Brutus spoke,
But here I am to speak what I do know.
You all did love him once, not without cause;
What cause withholds you then to mourn for him?
O judgment, thou art fled to brutish beasts,
105   And men have lost their reason! Bear with me;
My heart is in the coffin there with Caesar,
And I must pause till it come back to me.

First Plebeian.
Methinks there is much reason in his sayings.

Second Plebeian.
If thou consider rightly of the matter,
Caesar has had great wrong.

110   **Third Plebeian.**   Has he, masters?
I fear there will a worse come in his place.

Fourth Plebeian.
Marked ye his words? He would not take the crown,
Therefore 'tis certain he was not ambitious.

First Plebeian.
If it be found so, some will dear abide it.°

Second Plebeian.
115   Poor soul, his eyes are red as fire with weeping.

Third Plebeian.
There's not a nobler man in Rome than Antony.

Fourth Plebeian.
Now mark him, he begins again to speak.

Antony.
But yesterday the word of Caesar might
Have stood against the world; now lies he there,
120   And none so poor to° do him reverence.
O masters! If I were disposed to stir
Your hearts and minds to mutiny and rage,
I should do Brutus wrong and Cassius wrong,
Who, you all know, are honorable men.

Staging the Play
107. *What do lines 106–107 mean? What could Antony be doing at this point, as our attention is drawn again to the crowd?*

114. dear abide it: pay dearly for it.

120. so poor to: so low in rank as to.

125   I will not do them wrong; I rather choose
       To wrong the dead, to wrong myself and you,
       Than I will wrong such honorable men.
       But here's a parchment with the seal of Caesar;
       I found it in his closet; 'tis his will.
130   Let but the commons hear this testament,
       Which, pardon me, I do not mean to read,
       And they would go and kiss dead Caesar's wounds,
       And dip their napkins° in his sacred blood;
       Yea, beg a hair of him for memory,
135   And dying, mention it within their wills,
       Bequeathing it as a rich legacy
       Unto their issue.°
       Fourth Plebeian.
           We'll hear the will; read it, Mark Antony.
       All. The will, the will! We will hear Caesar's will!
       Antony.
140   Have patience, gentle friends, I must not read it.
           It is not meet you know how Caesar loved you.
           You are not wood, you are not stones, but men;
           And being men, hearing the will of Caesar,
           It will inflame you, it will make you mad.
145   'Tis good you know not that you are his heirs;
           For if you should, O, what would come of it?
       Fourth Plebeian.
           Read the will! We'll hear it, Antony!
           You shall read us the will, Caesar's will!
       Antony.
           Will you be patient? Will you stay awhile?
150   I have o'ershot myself° to tell you of it.
           I fear I wrong the honorable men
           Whose daggers have stabbed Caesar; I do fear it.
       Fourth Plebeian.
           They were traitors. Honorable men!
       All. The will! The testament!
155   **Second Plebeian.** They were villains, murderers! The will!
           Read the will!
       Antony.
           You will compel me then to read the will?
           Then make a ring about the corpse of Caesar,
           And let me show you him that made the will.
160   Shall I descend? And will you give me leave?
       All. Come down.

133. napkins: handkerchiefs.

137. issue: children; heirs.

? **137.** *Antony says he is not going to read the will, but what has he already implied about its contents?*

? **Staging the Play**
146. *Again, how has Antony scored his point indirectly? How could an actor play Antony in this scene to make him seem manipulative?*

150. o'ershot myself: gone farther than I intended.

? **Staging the Play**
152. *The irony here is so obvious that an actor playing Antony must make a choice about how to say these lines: Will he continue his pretense of honoring Caesar's assassins, or will he finally drop this pose and speak with obviously scathing sarcasm?*

"BUT HERE'S A PARCHMENT WITH THE SEAL OF CAESAR . . . 'TIS HIS WILL."

Second Plebeian. Descend.

[ANTONY *comes down.*]

Third Plebeian. You shall have leave.
Fourth Plebeian. A ring! Stand round.
First Plebeian.

165   Stand from the hearse, stand from the body!
Second Plebeian.

    Room for Antony, most noble Antony!
Antony.

    Nay, press not so upon me; stand far off.
All. Stand back! Room! Bear back.
Antony.

    If you have tears, prepare to shed them now.
170   You all do know this mantle; I remember
    The first time ever Caesar put it on:
    'Twas on a summer's evening, in his tent,
    That day he overcame the Nervii.°
    Look, in this place ran Cassius' dagger through;
175   See what a rent the envious° Casca made;

? Staging the Play
168. *How do you visualize the placement of the actors at this point? Where is Caesar's body?*

? Staging the Play
169. *Watch for clues that tell what Antony is doing for effect as he delivers this speech. What is he holding in line 170?*

173. Nervii: one of the tribes conquered by Caesar, in 57 B.C.

175. envious: spiteful.

Through this the well-belovèd Brutus stabbed,
And as he plucked his cursèd steel away,
Mark how the blood of Caesar followed it,
As rushing out of doors, to be resolved
180   If Brutus so unkindly knocked, or no;
For Brutus, as you know, was Caesar's angel.
Judge, O you gods, how dearly Caesar loved him!
This was the most unkindest cut of all;
For when the noble Caesar saw him stab,
185   Ingratitude, more strong than traitors' arms,
Quite vanquished him. Then burst his mighty heart;
And, in his mantle muffling up his face,
Even at the base of Pompey's statue°
(Which all the while ran blood) great Caesar fell.
190   O, what a fall was there, my countrymen!
Then I, and you, and all of us fell down,
Whilst bloody treason flourished over us.
O, now you weep, and I perceive you feel
The dint° of pity; these are gracious drops.
195   Kind souls, what weep you when you but behold
Our Caesar's vesture° wounded? Look you here,
Here is himself, marred as you see with traitors.

First Plebeian. O piteous spectacle!

Second Plebeian. O noble Caesar!

200   **Third Plebeian.** O woeful day!

Fourth Plebeian. O traitors, villains!

First Plebeian. O most bloody sight!

Second Plebeian. We will be revenged.

All. Revenge! About! Seek! Burn! Fire! Kill! Slay! Let not a
205   traitor live!

Antony. Stay, countrymen.

First Plebeian. Peace there! Hear the noble Antony.

Second Plebeian. We'll hear him, we'll follow him, we'll die
with him!

Antony.
210   Good friends, sweet friends, let me not stir you up
To such a sudden flood of mutiny.
They that have done this deed are honorable.
What private griefs° they have, alas, I know not,
That made them do it. They are wise and honorable,
215   And will, no doubt, with reasons answer you.
I come not, friends, to steal away your hearts;
I am no orator, as Brutus is;

188. statue: pronounced in three syllables.

? Staging the Play
193. *What is the crowd doing as Antony speaks?*
194. dint: stroke.

196. vesture: clothing.
? Staging the Play
197. *What has Antony done with the body now?*

213. griefs: grievances.

? 215. *Notice that Antony implies that reasons have not already been given. Have they?*

"HERE IS HIMSELF,
MARRED AS YOU
SEE WITH
TRAITORS."

But (as you know me all) a plain blunt man
That love my friend, and that they know full well
220 That gave me public leave to speak of him.
For I have neither writ, nor words, nor worth,
Action, nor utterance, nor the power of speech
To stir men's blood; I only speak right on.
I tell you that which you yourselves do know,
225 Show you sweet Caesar's wounds, poor poor dumb mouths,
And bid them speak for me. But were I Brutus,
And Brutus Antony, there were an Antony
Would ruffle up your spirits, and put a tongue
In every wound of Caesar that would move
230 The stones of Rome to rise and mutiny.

All.
We'll mutiny.

First Plebeian. We'll burn the house of Brutus.

Third Plebeian.
Away, then! Come, seek the conspirators.

Antony.
Yet hear me, countrymen. Yet hear me speak.

All.
Peace, ho! Hear Antony, most noble Antony!

Antony.
235 Why, friends, you go to do you know not what:
Wherein hath Caesar thus deserved your loves?
Alas, you know not; I must tell you then:
You have forgot the will I told you of.

All.
Most true, the will! Let's stay and hear the will.

Antony.
240 Here is the will, and under Caesar's seal.
To every Roman citizen he gives,
To every several° man, seventy-five drachmas.°

Second Plebeian.
Most noble Caesar! We'll revenge his death!

Third Plebeian. O royal Caesar!

245 **Antony.** Hear me with patience.

All. Peace, ho!

Antony.
Moreover, he hath left you all his walks,
His private arbors, and new-planted orchards,
On this side Tiber; he hath left them you,
250 And to your heirs forever: common pleasures,°

223. *How does Antony characterize himself, as compared with Brutus? What is his motive?*

230. *Again, the irony is obvious here. What is the key word in Antony's* **monologue***?*

238. *Notice how many times the mob goes to run off and how Antony pulls it back again. How do you think Antony feels about this herd of people he has so cleverly manipulated?*

242. **several:** individual.
drachmas (drak′məs): silver coins (Greek currency).

250. **common pleasures:** public recreation areas.

To walk abroad and recreate yourselves.
Here was a Caesar! When comes such another?

First Plebeian.
Never, never! Come, away, away!
We'll burn his body in the holy place,
255 And with the brands fire the traitors' houses.
Take up the body.

Second Plebeian. Go fetch fire.

Third Plebeian. Pluck down benches.

Fourth Plebeian. Pluck down forms, windows,° anything!

[Exeunt PLEBEIANS *with the body.]*

Antony.
260 Now let it work: Mischief, thou art afoot,
Take thou what course thou wilt.

[Enter SERVANT.]

How now, fellow?

Servant.
Sir, Octavius is already come to Rome.

Antony. Where is he?

Servant.
He and Lepidus are at Caesar's house.

Antony.
265 And thither will I straight to visit him;
He comes upon a wish. Fortune is merry,
And in this mood will give us anything.

Servant.
I heard him say, Brutus and Cassius
Are rid° like madmen through the gates of Rome.

Antony.
270 Belike° they had some notice of the people,
How I had moved them. Bring me to Octavius.

[Exeunt.]

SCENE 3. *A street.*

Enter CINNA *the poet, and after him the* PLEBEIANS.

Cinna.
I dreamt tonight that I did feast with Caesar,
And things unluckily charge my fantasy.°

259. forms, windows: long benches and shutters.

Staging the Play
260. *Antony is alone onstage. The noise of the mob dies off in the distance. We might in some productions see the reflection of flames and hear the sounds of rioting. How should Antony speak these lines?*

269. Are rid: have ridden.
269. *What have Brutus and Cassius done?*
270. Belike: probably.

2. That is, events unluckily fill his imagination (with ominous ideas).

I have no will to wander forth of doors,
Yet something leads me forth.

5 **First Plebeian.** What is your name?

Second Plebeian. Whither are you going?

Third Plebeian. Where do you dwell?

Fourth Plebeian. Are you a married man or a bachelor?

Second Plebeian. Answer every man directly.

10 **First Plebeian.** Ay, and briefly.

Fourth Plebeian. Ay, and wisely.

Third Plebeian. Ay, and truly, you were best.

Cinna. What is my name? Whither am I going? Where do I
dwell? Am I a married man or a bachelor? Then, to

15 answer every man directly and briefly, wisely and truly:
wisely I say, I am a bachelor.

Second Plebeian. That's as much as to say, they are fools
that marry; you'll bear me a bang° for that, I fear.
Proceed directly.

20 **Cinna.** Directly, I am going to Caesar's funeral.

First Plebeian. As a friend or an enemy?

Cinna. As a friend.

Second Plebeian. That matter is answered directly.

Fourth Plebeian. For your dwelling, briefly.

25 **Cinna.** Briefly, I dwell by the Capitol.

Third Plebeian. Your name, sir, truly.

Cinna. Truly, my name is Cinna.

First Plebeian. Tear him to pieces! He's a conspirator.

Cinna. I am Cinna the poet! I am Cinna the poet!

30 **Fourth Plebeian.** Tear him for his bad verses! Tear him for
his bad verses!

Cinna. I am not Cinna the conspirator.

Fourth Plebeian. It is no matter, his name's Cinna; pluck
but his name out of his heart, and turn him going.°

35 **Third Plebeian.** Tear him, tear him!

[*They attack him.*]

Come, brands, ho! Firebrands! To Brutus', to Cassius'!
Burn all! Some to Decius' house, and some to Casca's;
some to Ligarius'! Away, go!

[*Exeunt all the* PLEBEIANS *with* CINNA.]

18. bear me a bang: get a blow
from me.

? **31.** *What is the function of
this scene, with its bit of
comedy at this point in the play?*

34. turn him going: send him
packing.

? **Staging the Play**
38. *What has the mob done
to the innocent poet Cinna? Try
performing this chilling mob
scene, perhaps using a chorus for
the plebeians' lines.*

Roman Government: Rule by the Rich

Roman politics often resembled a theatrical production, complete with performers and an audience. The Forum was the stage, the politicians were the actors, and citizens from all social classes came to watch the show. Assemblies, elections, and trials were held outdoors. Noisy crowds often booed and heckled the politicians.

With the abolition of the monarchy in 509 B.C., the Roman republic was established. (A *republic* is a state in which power is vested in the citizens, who are entitled to vote; they elect representatives, who govern on behalf of the citizens.) Yet a huge gap continued to exist between rich and poor, and for centuries only the rich were allowed to hold public office. Some of the wealthiest members of society were members of the Senate, which controlled Rome's domestic and foreign affairs. Not until more than two hundred years after the Roman republic was established were a select few from the lower classes allowed to enter politics.

According to Marcus Cicero (106–43 B.C.), orator, philosopher, and senator, "the difficulty of devising policy has caused the transfer of power from a king to a group, and the ignorance and rashness of the masses have caused its transfer from the many to the few." His words affirm his belief in the ignorance of the "lower classes," a prejudice common among members of the privileged classes at the time.

The United States is a representative democracy, or a republic, in which citizens elect others to make public-policy decisions for them in assemblies instead of attending the assemblies and making their own decisions, as Roman citizens did. The Roman republic, however, was a direct democracy, not an indirect or representative one. In Rome eligible voters could attend assemblies, vote on legislation, and elect government officials. However, Rome was the only place where voting was authorized, so many citizens could not exercise their voting rights because they had neither the time nor the money to travel from their homes to Rome.

In Rome, legislation was proposed, formulated, and discussed by the Senate and then presented to the assemblies for approval. Because the upper classes controlled the Senate, they controlled all legislation. Even though each citizen had the right to vote on every issue, the Roman republic wasn't an ideal democracy. Lacking the guiding principle of government of the people, for the people, and by the people, it amounted to rule by the aristocracy, which served the interests of the elite while pretending to give voice to the populace.

(Background) Ruins of the Roman Forum.
R. G. Everts/Photo Researchers.

Response and Analysis

Act III

Reading Check

1. In Scene 1, a chance still exists that the conspiracy might be foiled. Why does Artemidorus fail to get Caesar to read his warning?

2. In Scene 1, why does Cassius argue against allowing Antony to speak at Caesar's funeral? What reasons does Brutus give for overruling him?

3. After the assassination the **protagonist** appears—the main character, who drives the rest of the play. Who is this person, and what does he want? How have we been prepared for his appearance?

4. What information concerning Caesar's will does Antony disclose to the crowd in Scene 2? How does the crowd react?

5. What do the plebeians do in Scene 3?

Thinking Critically

6. Explain how Brutus and Cassius act as **character foils** (contrasting characters) in their responses to Antony in Scene 1.

7. How does Antony's **soliloquy** at the end of Scene 1 (lines 254–275) indicate his intentions regarding the assassins? What could this speech **foreshadow,** or hint at?

8. An **aside** is a speech or remark spoken by a character to the audience or to another character onstage that others onstage are not supposed to hear. Why is the aside that Cassius makes to Brutus in Scene 1 before Antony's speech important?

9. One of the great examples of **persuasive oratory** is found in Act III, Scene

2, lines 73–107, in which Antony changes the mood of the mob. What specific **emotional appeals** does Antony use? Find, for example, uses of **loaded words** (words with strong emotional overtones) and **repetition.**

10. Until Act III, Antony has barely figured in the play. How have others **characterized** him? Do you agree? Why?

11. The third act of a Shakespearean **tragedy** usually contains the **turning point,** the moment when all the action of the play begins to spiral toward the **tragic ending.** Which of the following events do you think is the turning point in this **tragedy?** Why?

    • the assassination of Caesar

    • Brutus's decision to allow Antony to address the crowd

12. Lines 111–118 of Scene 1 suggest that the conspirators' deed will be "acted over," or repeated, "many ages hence." What meaning do you think Shakespeare intended in these lines?

Extending and Evaluating

13. Whose funeral speech—Brutus's or Antony's—comes closer to expressing your own thoughts about Caesar's death? Whose speech is more powerfully persuasive? Support your view.

WRITING

Behind the Scenes

We never again see the cobbler from Act I. Suppose the shoemaker is in the crowd that listens to Brutus and Antony, carries away Caesar's body, and then attacks the poet Cinna. Write a **new scene** in which the shoemaker and another character talk about the events of the ides of March. Perform your **dialogue.**

Literary Skills
Analyze tragedy.

Reading Skills
Paraphrase a text.

Writing Skills
Write a new scene for a play.

Reading Skills

Paraphrasing: Your Own Words

When you **paraphrase** a passage, you express all of its ideas in your own words. (A paraphrase is different from a **summary,** which expresses only the main ideas.) Look at Caesar's speech and its paraphrase:

SPEECH

Caesar.
Thy brother by decree is banishèd.
If thou dost bend and pray and fawn for him,
I spurn thee like a cur out of my way.
                    —Act III, Scene 1, lines 44–46

PARAPHRASE
Your brother is banished by law. If you lower yourself to grovel and beg for him, I'll treat you like a dog and kick you out of my way.

PRACTICE

Read the following passages in their contexts in the play. Then, **paraphrase** every idea in each passage below:

1. **Antony.**
    That I did love thee, Caesar, O, 'tis true!
    If then thy spirit look upon us now,
    Shall it not grieve thee dearer than thy death
    To see thy Antony making his peace,
    Shaking the bloody fingers of thy foes,
    Most noble, in the presence of thy corse?
                    —Act III, Scene 1, lines 194–199

2. **Antony.**
    Friends, Romans, countrymen, lend me your ears;
    I come to bury Caesar, not to praise him.
    The evil that men do lives after them,
    The good is oft interrèd with their bones . . .
                    —Act III, Scene 2, lines 73–76

Mark Antony.
Roman sculpture.
Museum of the Vatican, Rome, Italy.

ACT IV

SCENE 1.
A house in Rome.

Enter ANTONY, OCTAVIUS, *and* LEPIDUS.

Antony.
These many then shall die; their names are pricked.
Octavius.
Your brother too must die; consent you, Lepidus?
Lepidus.
I do consent—
Octavius.   Prick him down, Antony.
Lepidus.
Upon condition Publius shall not live,
5   Who is your sister's son, Mark Antony.
Antony.
He shall not live; look, with a spot I damn him.
But, Lepidus, go you to Caesar's house;
Fetch the will hither, and we shall determine
How to cut off some charge in legacies.°
Lepidus.
10   What, shall I find you here?
Octavius.
Or here or at the Capitol.   [*Exit* LEPIDUS.]
Antony.
This is a slight unmeritable man,
Meet to be sent on errands; is it fit,
The threefold world° divided, he should stand
One of the three to share it?°
15   **Octavius.**   So you thought him,

9. In other words, cut down on some of the expenses by changing the legacies.

14. threefold world: three parts of the Roman Empire: Europe, Asia, and Africa.
15. Antony, Octavius, and Lepidus now govern the Roman Empire as a triumvirate, or three-member ruling body.

"... WE ARE AT THE STAKE, AND BAYED ABOUT WITH MANY ENEMIES ..."

And took his voice° who should be pricked to die
In our black sentence and proscription.°

Antony.
Octavius, I have seen more days than you;
And though we lay these honors on this man,
20 To ease ourselves of divers sland'rous loads,°
He shall but bear them as the ass bears gold,
To groan and sweat under the business,
Either led or driven, as we point the way;
And having brought our treasure where we will,
25 Then take we down his load, and turn him off,
(Like to the empty ass) to shake his ears
And graze in commons.°

Octavius.   You may do your will;
But he's a tried and valiant soldier.

Antony.
So is my horse, Octavius, and for that
30 I do appoint him store of provender.°
It is a creature that I teach to fight,
To wind, to stop, to run directly on,
His corporal motion governed by my spirit.
And, in some taste,° is Lepidus but so.
35 He must be taught, and trained, and bid go forth.
A barren-spirited fellow; one that feeds
On objects, arts, and imitations,
Which, out of use and staled by other men,
Begin his fashion.° Do not talk of him
40 But as a property.° And now, Octavius,
Listen great things. Brutus and Cassius
Are levying powers;° we must straight make head.°
Therefore let our alliance be combined,
Our best friends made, our means stretched;
45 And let us presently go sit in council
How covert matters may be best disclosed,
And open perils surest answerèd.

Octavius.
Let us do so; for we are at the stake,
And bayed about with many enemies;°
50 And some that smile have in their hearts, I fear,
Millions of mischiefs.   [*Exeunt.*]

SCENE 2. *Camp near Sardis.*

Drum. Enter BRUTUS, LUCILIUS, LUCIUS, *and the* ARMY.
TITINIUS *and* PINDARUS *meet them.*

Brutus. Stand ho!
Lucilius. Give the word, ho! and stand.
Brutus.
　What now, Lucilius, is Cassius near?
Lucilius.
　He is at hand, and Pindarus is come
5　To do you salutation from his master.
Brutus.
　He greets me well.° Your master, Pindarus,
　In his own change, or by ill officers,°
　Hath given me some worthy cause to wish
　Things done undone; but if he be at hand,
　I shall be satisfied.°
10　**Pindarus.**　　　　I do not doubt
　But that my noble master will appear
　Such as he is, full of regard and honor.
Brutus.
　He is not doubted. A word, Lucilius,
　How he received you; let me be resolved.°
Lucilius.
15　With courtesy and with respect enough,
　But not with such familiar instances,°
　Nor with such free and friendly conference
　As he hath used of old.
Brutus.　　　　　　Thou hast described
　A hot friend cooling. Ever note, Lucilius,
20　When love begins to sicken and decay
　It useth an enforcèd ceremony.
　There are no tricks in plain and simple faith;
　But hollow men, like horses hot at hand,°
　Make gallant show and promise of their mettle;

[*Low march within.*]

25　But when they should endure the bloody spur,
　They fall their crests, and like deceitful jades°
　Sink in the trial. Comes his army on?

Stage direction. *Several months have passed since the assassination. Brutus and Cassius are in Sardis, the capital of ancient Lydia, a kingdom in Asia Minor. Why did Brutus and Cassius flee from Rome with their armies?*

6. He greets me well: He sends greetings with a good man.
7. In other words, either from a change of feelings or because of the bad advice or the bad deeds of subordinates.
10. be satisfied: get a satisfactory explanation.

14. resolved: informed.

16. familiar instances: friendly behavior.

18. *What details show that a split might be taking place in the conspirators' ranks?*

23. hot at hand: very energetic at the start of the race.

26. jades: old horses.

"JUDGE ME, YOU GODS!
WRONG I MINE ENEMIES?
AND IF NOT SO, HOW SHOULD
I WRONG A BROTHER?"

Lucilius.
    They mean this night in Sardis to be quartered;
    The greater part, the horse in general,°
    Are come with Cassius.

[*Enter* CASSIUS *and his* POWERS.]

30   **Brutus.**   Hark! He is arrived.
    March gently on to meet him.
    Cassius. Stand, ho!
    Brutus. Stand, ho! Speak the word along.
    First Soldier. Stand!
35   **Second Soldier.** Stand!
    Third Soldier. Stand!
    Cassius.
    Most noble brother, you have done me wrong.
    Brutus.
    Judge me, you gods! Wrong I mine enemies?
    And if not so, how should I wrong a brother?
    Cassius.
40   Brutus, this sober form of yours hides wrongs;
    And when you do them—
    Brutus.   Cassius, be content.°
    Speak your griefs softly; I do know you well.
    Before the eyes of both our armies here
    (Which should perceive nothing but love from us)
45   Let us not wrangle. Bid them move away;
    Then in my tent, Cassius, enlarge° your griefs,
    And I will give you audience.
    Cassius.   Pindarus,
    Bid our commanders lead their charges off
    A little from this ground.

29. the horse in general: all the cavalry.

? Staging the Play
36. *What do you picture happening on stage here?*

41. content: calm.

46. enlarge: express in greater detail.

Brutus.

50   Lucilius, do you the like, and let no man
    Come to our tent till we have done our conference.
    Let Lucius and Titinius guard our door.

[*Exeunt all except* BRUTUS *and* CASSIUS.]

SCENE 3. *Brutus' tent.*

Cassius.

    That you have wronged me doth appear in this:
    You have condemned and noted° Lucius Pella
    For taking bribes here of the Sardians;
    Wherein my letters, praying on his side,
5   Because I knew the man, was slighted off.

Brutus.

    You wronged yourself to write in such a case.

Cassius.

    In such a time as this it is not meet
    That every nice offense should bear his comment.°

Brutus.

    Let me tell you, Cassius, you yourself
10   Are much condemned to have an itching palm,
    To sell and mart° your offices for gold
    To undeservers.

Cassius.   I an itching palm?
    You know that you are Brutus that speaks this,
    Or, by the gods, this speech were else your last.

Brutus.

15   The name of Cassius honors° this corruption,
    And chastisement doth therefore hide his head.

Cassius. Chastisement!

Brutus.

    Remember March, the ides of March remember.
    Did not great Julius bleed for justice' sake?
20   What villain touched his body, that did stab,
    And not for justice? What, shall one of us,
    That struck the foremost man of all this world
    But for supporting robbers,° shall we now
    Contaminate our fingers with base bribes,
25   And sell the mighty space of our large honors°
    For so much trash as may be graspèd thus?
    I had rather be a dog, and bay the moon,
    Than such a Roman.

2. noted: publicly disgraced.

8. That . . . comment: that every trivial offense should be criticized.

11. mart: trade; traffic in.

12. *What has Brutus accused Cassius of?*

15. honors: gives an air of respectability to.

23. supporting robbers: supporting or protecting dishonest public officials.
25. our large honors: capacity to be honorable and generous.

Cassius.   Brutus, bait not me;
I'll not endure it. You forget yourself
30   To hedge me in. I am a soldier, I,
Older in practice, abler than yourself
To make conditions.
Brutus.   Go to! You are not, Cassius.
Cassius. I am.
Brutus. I say you are not.
Cassius.
35   Urge° me no more, I shall forget myself;
Have mind upon your health, tempt me no farther.
Brutus. Away, slight man!
Cassius.
Is't possible?
Brutus.   Hear me, for I will speak.
Must I give way and room to your rash choler?°
40   Shall I be frighted when a madman stares?
Cassius.
O ye gods, ye gods! Must I endure all this?
Brutus.
All this? Ay, more: fret till your proud heart break.
Go show your slaves how choleric you are,
And make your bondmen tremble. Must I budge?°
45   Must I observe° you? Must I stand and crouch
Under your testy humor? By the gods,
You shall digest the venom of your spleen,°
Though it do split you; for, from this day forth,
I'll use you for my mirth, yea, for my laughter,
When you are waspish.
50   **Cassius.**   Is it come to this?
Brutus.
You say you are a better soldier:
Let it appear so; make your vaunting° true,
And it shall please me well. For mine own part,
I shall be glad to learn of noble men.
Cassius.
55   You wrong me every way; you wrong me, Brutus;
I said, an elder soldier, not a better.
Did I say, better?
Brutus.   If you did, I care not.
Cassius.
When Caesar lived, he durst° not thus have moved° me.

35. Urge: goad; bully.

36. *What threat is Cassius making to Brutus?*

39. choler: anger.

44. budge: defer.

45. observe: wait on.

47. spleen: fiery temper. (The spleen was believed to be the seat of the emotions.)

52. vaunting: boasting.

57. *What did Cassius say?*

58. durst: dared. **moved:** exasperated.

Brutus.

Peace, peace, you durst not so have tempted him.

60 **Cassius.** I durst not?

Brutus. No.

Cassius.

What? Durst not tempt him?

Brutus.   For your life you durst not.

Cassius.

Do not presume too much upon my love;

I may do that I shall be sorry for.

Brutus.

65 You have done that you should be sorry for.

There is no terror, Cassius, in your threats;

For I am armed so strong in honesty

That they pass by me as the idle wind,

Which I respect not. I did send to you

70 For certain sums of gold, which you denied me;

For I can raise no money by vile means.

By heaven, I had rather coin my heart

And drop my blood for drachmas than to wring

From the hard hands of peasants their vile trash

75 By any indirection.° I did send

To you for gold to pay my legions,

Which you denied me. Was that done like Cassius?

Should I have answered Caius Cassius so?

When Marcus Brutus grows so covetous

80 To lock such rascal counters° from his friends,

Be ready, gods, with all your thunderbolts,

Dash him to pieces!

Cassius.   I denied you not.

Brutus.

You did.

Cassius.   I did not. He was but a fool

That brought my answer back. Brutus hath rived° my
    heart.

85 A friend should bear his friend's infirmities;

But Brutus makes mine greater than they are.

Brutus.

I do not, till you practice them on me.

Cassius.

You love me not.

Brutus.   I do not like your faults.

75. indirection: illegal methods.

? 75. *What do you think of Brutus's moral position here? Does it seem honorable or hypocritical?*

80. counters: coins.

84. rived: broken.

Cassius.

A friendly eye could never see such faults.

Brutus.

90   A flatterer's would not, though they do appear

As huge as high Olympus.

Cassius.

Come, Antony, and young Octavius, come,

Revenge yourselves alone on Cassius,

For Cassius is aweary of the world:

95   Hated by one he loves; braved° by his brother;

Checked like a bondman; all his faults observed,

Set in a notebook, learned and conned by rote°

To cast into my teeth. O, I could weep

My spirit from mine eyes! There is my dagger,

100   And here my naked breast; within, a heart

Dearer than Pluto's mine,° richer than gold;

If that thou be'st a Roman, take it forth.

I, that denied thee gold,° will give my heart.

Strike as thou didst at Caesar; for I know,

When thou didst hate him worst, thou lovedst him

105   better

Than ever thou lovedst Cassius.

Brutus.   Sheathe your dagger.

Be angry when you will, it shall have scope.

Do what you will, dishonor shall be humor.°

O Cassius, you are yokèd with a lamb

110   That carries anger as the flint bears fire,

Who, much enforcèd, shows a hasty spark,

And straight is cold again.

Cassius.   Hath Cassius lived

To be but mirth and laughter to his Brutus

When grief and blood ill-tempered vexeth him?

Brutus.

115   When I spoke that, I was ill-tempered too.

Cassius.

Do you confess so much? Give me your hand.

Brutus.

And my heart too.

Cassius.   O Brutus!

Brutus.   What's the matter?

91. *We haven't seen Brutus and Cassius alone together since the assassination. What does this* **dialogue** *reveal about their characters? their feelings?*

95. braved: defied.

97. conned by rote: learned by heart.

Staging the Play
99. *What is Cassius doing, and why?*

101. Pluto's mine: the riches under the earth. Pluto was the Roman god of the underworld (akin to the Greek god Hades); Shakespeare confuses him with Plutus, god of riches.

103. that ... gold: that *you say* denied you gold.

108. In other words, dishonor or insults will be seen merely as the result of eccentric personality traits.

112. *Have Brutus's feelings changed? Why or why not?*

Staging the Play
117. *What actions could mark the change in feelings now?*

Cassius.

    Have not you love enough to bear with me

    When that rash humor which my mother gave me

    Makes me forgetful?

120 **Brutus.**   Yes, Cassius, and from henceforth,

    When you are over-earnest with your Brutus,

    He'll think your mother chides, and leave you so.

[*Enter a* POET, *followed by* LUCILIUS, TITINIUS, *and*
LUCIUS.]

Poet.

    Let me go in to see the generals;

    There is some grudge between 'em; 'tis not meet

    They be alone.

125 **Lucilius.**   You shall not come to them.

Poet. Nothing but death shall stay me.

Cassius. How now. What's the matter?

Poet.

    For shame, you generals! What do you mean?

    Love, and be friends, as two such men should be;

130   For I have seen more years, I'm sure, than ye.

Cassius.

    Ha, ha! How vilely doth this cynic° rhyme!

Brutus.

    Get you hence, sirrah! Saucy fellow, hence!

Cassius.

    Bear with him, Brutus, 'tis his fashion.

Brutus.

    I'll know his humor when he knows his time.°

135   What should the wars do with these jigging° fools?

    Companion,° hence!

Cassius.   Away, away, be gone!

[*Exit* POET.]

Brutus.

    Lucilius and Titinius, bid the commanders

    Prepare to lodge their companies tonight.

Cassius.

    And come yourselves, and bring Messala with you

    Immediately to us.   [*Exeunt* LUCILIUS *and* TITINIUS.]

140 **Brutus.**   Lucius, a bowl of wine.

[*Exit* LUCIUS.]

? Staging the Play
122. *How could a humorous note be sounded here?*

131. cynic: rude person.

134. his time: the right time to speak.
135. jigging: rhyming.
136. Companion: lower-class fellow.

? 136. *Remember that Shakespeare himself was a "jigging fool." What is the point of this scene with the poet?*

Cassius.

    I did not think you could have been so angry.

Brutus.

    O Cassius, I am sick of many griefs.

Cassius.

    Of your philosophy you make no use,
    If you give place to accidental evils.

Brutus.

145   No man bears sorrow better. Portia is dead.

Cassius. Ha? Portia?

Brutus. She is dead.

Cassius.

    How scaped I killing when I crossed you so?
    O insupportable and touching loss!
    Upon what sickness?

150 **Brutus.**   Impatient of my absence,
    And grief that young Octavius with Mark Antony
    Have made themselves so strong—for with her death
    That tidings came—with this she fell distract,°
    And (her attendants absent) swallowed fire.°

Cassius.

    And died so?

Brutus.   Even so.

155 **Cassius.**   O ye immortal gods!

[*Enter* LUCIUS, *with wine and tapers.*]

Brutus.

    Speak no more of her. Give me a bowl of wine.
    In this I bury all unkindness, Cassius.

[*Drinks.*]

Cassius.

    My heart is thirsty for that noble pledge.
    Fill, Lucius, till the wine o'erswell the cup;

160   I cannot drink too much of Brutus' love.

[*Drinks. Exit* LUCIUS.]

[*Enter* TITINIUS *and* MESSALA.]

Brutus.

    Come in, Titinius! Welcome, good Messala.
    Now sit we close about this taper here,
    And call in question° our necessities.

Staging the Play
144. *This reference is to Brutus's philosophy of Stoicism, which taught that we should master our emotions, lead lives dictated by reason and duty, and submit to fate. How might Brutus deliver his next shocking line?*

Staging the Play
145–160. *Who is probably more emotional in this scene— Brutus or Cassius? (Many fine actors have shown no emotion as they played Brutus in this scene.)*

153. fell distract: became distraught.
154. According to Plutarch, Portia killed herself by putting hot coals in her mouth.

163. call in question: consider.

Cassius.

Portia, art thou gone?

Brutus.   No more, I pray you.

165   Messala, I have here receivèd letters

That young Octavius and Mark Antony

Come down upon us with a mighty power,

Bending their expedition toward Philippi.°

Messala.

Myself have letters of the selfsame tenure.°

Brutus.

170   With what addition?

Messala.

That by proscription and bills of outlawry°

Octavius, Antony, and Lepidus

Have put to death an hundred senators.

Brutus.

Therein our letters do not well agree.

175   Mine speak of seventy senators that died

By their proscriptions, Cicero being one.

Cassius.

Cicero one?

Messala.   Cicero is dead,

And by that order of proscription.

Had you your letters from your wife, my lord?

180   **Brutus.** No, Messala.

Messala.

Nor nothing in your letters writ of her?

Brutus.

Nothing, Messala.

Messala.   That methinks is strange.

Brutus.

Why ask you? Hear you aught of her in yours?

Messala. No, my lord.

Brutus.

185   Now as you are a Roman, tell me true.

Messala.

Then like a Roman bear the truth I tell,

For certain she is dead, and by strange manner.

Brutus.

Why, farewell, Portia. We must die, Messala.

With meditating that she must die once,°

190   I have the patience to endure it now.

168. Philippi: ancient city in northern Greece.

169. tenure: tenor; meaning.

171. bills of outlawry: lists of proscribed people.

Staging the Play
179. *A peculiar scene now takes place, in which Brutus seems again to hear for the first time the news of his wife's death. Some scholars believe that the original account of Portia's death was told in lines 179–193 and that Shakespeare later rewrote the scene, which is now lines 141–155. A production might not use both scenes. Which would you use, and why? (If a director did decide to use both scenes, how should Brutus act in the second one?)*

189. once: at some time.

Staging the Play
190. *The actor playing Brutus must be careful not to make him seem cold and unfeeling. How could this scene be played to suggest Brutus's humanity, as well as his Stoicism?*

Messala.

    Even so great men great losses should endure.

Cassius.

    I have as much of this in art° as you,

    But yet my nature could not bear it so.

Brutus.

    Well, to our work alive. What do you think

195   Of marching to Philippi presently?

Cassius.

    I do not think it good.

Brutus.   Your reason?

Cassius.   This it is:

    'Tis better that the enemy seek us;

    So shall he waste his means, weary his soldiers,

    Doing himself offense, whilst we, lying still,

200   Are full of rest, defense, and nimbleness.

Brutus.

    Good reasons must of force° give place to better.

    The people 'twixt Philippi and this ground

    Do stand but in a forced affection;°

    For they have grudged us contribution.

205   The enemy, marching along by them,

    By them shall make a fuller number up,

    Come on refreshed, new-added and encouraged;

    From which advantage shall we cut him off

    If at Philippi we do face him there,

    These people at our back.

210 **Cassius.**   Hear me, good brother.

Brutus.

    Under your pardon. You must note beside

    That we have tried the utmost of our friends,

    Our legions are brimful, our cause is ripe.

    The enemy increaseth every day;

192. in art: the art of being a Stoic.

? 200. *What plan does Cassius propose regarding Antony's forces at Philippi?*
201. of force: of necessity.

203. That is, they support us only grudgingly.

"THERE IS A TIDE IN THE AFFAIRS OF MEN
WHICH, TAKEN AT THE FLOOD, LEADS ON
TO FORTUNE;
OMITTED, ALL THE VOYAGE OF THEIR LIFE
IS BOUND IN SHALLOWS AND IN
MISERIES."

215   We, at the height, are ready to decline.
      There is a tide in the affairs of men
      Which, taken at the flood, leads on to fortune;
      Omitted,° all the voyage of their life
      Is bound in shallows and in miseries.
220   On such a full sea are we now afloat,
      And we must take the current when it serves,
      Or lose our ventures.

Cassius.   Then, with your will,° go on;
      We'll along ourselves and meet them at Philippi.

Brutus.
      The deep of night is crept upon our talk,
225   And nature must obey necessity,
      Which we will niggard with a little rest.°
      There is no more to say?

Cassius.   No more. Good night.
      Early tomorrow will we rise and hence.

[*Enter* LUCIUS.]

Brutus.
      Lucius, my gown.   [*Exit* LUCIUS.]
                    Farewell, good Messala.
230   Good night, Titinius. Noble, noble Cassius,
      Good night, and good repose.

Cassius.   O my dear brother,
      This was an ill beginning of the night.
      Never come such division 'tween our souls!
      Let it not, Brutus.

[*Enter* LUCIUS, *with the gown.*]

Brutus.   Everything is well.
Cassius.
      Good night, my lord.
235 **Brutus.**   Good night, good brother.
Titinius, Messala.
      Good night, Lord Brutus.
Brutus.   Farewell, every one.

                                        [*Exeunt.*]

      Give me the gown. Where is thy instrument?°
Lucius.
      Here in the tent.

218. Omitted: neglected.

222. *Where does Brutus want to fight Antony, and why?*
222. with your will: as you wish.
223. *Which man seems to dominate the action now?*

226. niggard with a little rest: cheat with a short period of sleep.

Staging the Play
231. *In some productions at this point in the scene, Brutus takes a letter out of his pocket and burns it. What letter are we to assume he is destroying, and what does his action demonstrate?*

237. instrument: probably a lute.

"HA! WHO COMES HERE?
I THINK IT IS THE WEAKNESS OF
MINE EYES
THAT SHAPES THIS MONSTROUS
APPARITION."

Brutus.   What, thou speak'st drowsily?
Poor knave, I blame thee not; thou art o'erwatched.°

240   Call Claudius and some other of my men;
I'll have them sleep on cushions in my tent.

Lucius. Varro and Claudius!

[*Enter* VARRO *and* CLAUDIUS.]

Varro. Calls my lord?

Brutus.
I pray you, sirs, lie in my tent and sleep.

245   It may be I shall raise you by and by
On business to my brother Cassius.

Varro.
So please you, we will stand and watch your pleasure.°

Brutus.
I will not have it so; lie down, good sirs;
It may be I shall otherwise bethink me.

[VARRO *and* CLAUDIUS *lie down.*]

250   Look, Lucius, here's the book I sought for so;
I put it in the pocket of my gown.

Lucius.
I was sure your lordship did not give it me.

Brutus.
Bear with me, good boy, I am much forgetful.
Canst thou hold up thy heavy eyes awhile,

255   And touch thy instrument a strain or two?

Lucius.
Ay, my lord, an't please you.

239. o'erwatched: exhausted.

247. watch your pleasure: wait for your orders.

Brutus.   It does, my boy.
  I trouble thee too much, but thou art willing.
Lucius. It is my duty, sir.
Brutus.
  I should not urge thy duty past thy might;
260 I know young bloods look for a time of rest.
Lucius. I have slept, my lord, already.
Brutus.
  It was well done, and thou shalt sleep again;
  I will not hold thee long. If I do live,
  I will be good to thee.

[*Music, and a song.*]

265 This is a sleepy tune. O murd'rous° slumber!
  Layest thou thy leaden mace° upon my boy,
  That plays thee music? Gentle knave, good night;
  I will not do thee so much wrong to wake thee.
  If thou dost nod, thou break'st thy instrument;
270 I'll take it from thee; and, good boy, good night.
  Let me see, let me see; is not the leaf turned down
  Where I left reading? Here it is, I think.

[*Enter the* GHOST *of Caesar.*]

  How ill this taper burns. Ha! Who comes here?
  I think it is the weakness of mine eyes
275 That shapes this monstrous apparition.
  It comes upon° me. Art thou anything?
  Art thou some god, some angel, or some devil,
  That mak'st my blood cold, and my hair to stare?°
  Speak to me what thou art.
Ghost.
  Thy evil spirit, Brutus.
280 **Brutus.**   Why com'st thou?
Ghost.
  To tell thee thou shalt see me at Philippi.
Brutus. Well; then I shall see thee again?
Ghost. Ay, at Philippi.
Brutus.
  Why, I will see thee at Philippi then.

[*Exit* GHOST.]

Staging the Play
? Stage direction. *How could lighting be used to suggest an intimate, drowsy, and nonmilitaristic scene?*
265. murd'rous: deathlike.

266. mace: heavy club carried by public officials.

276. upon: toward.

278. stare: stand on end.

Staging the Play
? 279. *How would you "stage" the Ghost? Would you have him in military dress? in his bloodied toga? Would you not show the Ghost at all, but merely project his voice onstage?*
? 281. *What does the Ghost's appearance foreshadow, or hint at?*

285 Now I have taken heart thou vanishest.
Ill spirit, I would hold more talk with thee.
Boy! Lucius! Varro! Claudius! Sirs, awake!
Claudius!

Lucius. The strings, my lord, are false.°

Brutus.

290 He thinks he still is at his instrument.
Lucius awake!

Lucius. My lord?

Brutus.

Didst thou dream, Lucius, that thou so criedst out?

Lucius.

My lord, I do not know that I did cry.

Brutus.

295 Yes, that thou didst. Didst thou see anything?

Lucius. Nothing, my lord.

Brutus.

Sleep again, Lucius. Sirrah Claudius!
(*To* VARRO.) Fellow thou, awake!

Varro. My lord?

300 **Claudius.** My lord?

Brutus.

Why did you so cry out, sirs, in your sleep?

Both.

Did we, my lord?

Brutus.   Ay. Saw you anything?

Varro.

No, my lord, I saw nothing.

Claudius.   Nor I, my lord.

Brutus.

Go and commend me to my brother Cassius;
305 Bid him set on his pow'rs betimes before,°
And we will follow.

Both.   It shall be done, my lord.

[*Exeunt.*]

289. Lucius sleepily supposes that his instrument is out of tune.

? **Staging the Play**
293. *In one production the Ghost scene was staged so that the Ghost's words seemed to come from the mouth of the sleeping Lucius. How would this explain Brutus's question to Lucius about "crying out"?*

305. That is, lead his forces out early in the morning, ahead of Brutus and his troops.

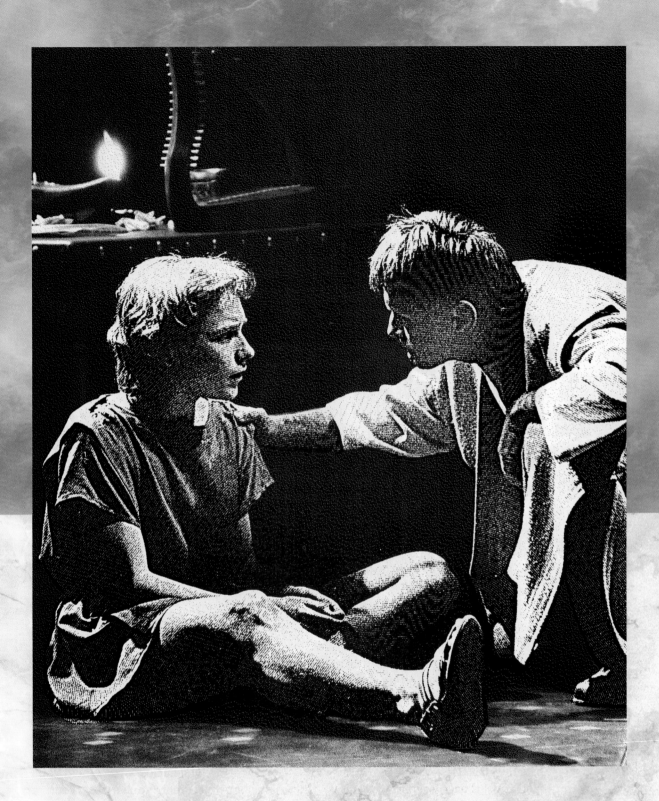

"DIDST THOU DREAM, LUCIUS,
THAT THOU SO CRIEDST OUT?"

Response and Analysis

Act IV

Reading Check

1. Describe the military situation presented in Act IV. What is going on between the conspirators and the triumvirate?

2. As Scene 1 opens, what are Antony, Octavius, and Lepidus doing? What breach has opened among them?

3. Why is Brutus uneasy at the beginning of Scene 2?

4. Throughout the play, Brutus and Cassius have been **foils,** or contrasting characters. What are the issues that cause them to quarrel in their **dialogue,** or conversation, in Scene 3?

5. According to Brutus, what were the reasons for Portia's death? How does he respond to her death?

6. What vision does Brutus see at the end of Act IV?

Thinking Critically

7. How is Antony **characterized** by his words and actions in Scene 1? In your opinion, is the Antony we see in this scene consistent with the Antony we saw earlier? Explain.

8. If you were **staging** the play, how would you let your audience know that in Scene 2 the **setting,** or **scene design,** has changed—instead of a house in Rome, the setting is now a battlefield?

9. In **drama,** relationships burst open under pressure and reveal certain truths. After the burst the relationship is either renewed or ended. Brutus and Cassius have been friends throughout the play, with Cassius clearly the subordinate. In Scene 3, they quarrel. How is their **conflict** resolved? What has become of their relationship by the end of the scene?

10. **Compare and contrast** the meeting of the conspirators in Scene 3 with the meeting of the triumvirate in Scene 1. In what ways are the scenes parallel? In what ways do they differ?

11. The scene with Cassius shows a harsh Brutus. What kind of Brutus appears with Lucius and the guards?

12. As the director of the play, you would have to decide how to **stage** the Ghost. You could have an actor play the Ghost, or you could use just a voice. What would each choice suggest about whether the Ghost is real? What might the Ghost represent to Brutus?

13. In lines 141–160 of Scene 3, Brutus and Cassius display different reactions to Portia's death. Why are their reactions different? How do you feel about these men now?

14. Which **character** do you sympathize with most by the end of Act IV? Why?

15. In Act IV of this **tragedy,** what consequences of the turning point in Act III do we see? How does Brutus's situation worsen?

Extending and Evaluating

16. Think about the two groups preparing for war here. Which side would you want to be on? Why?

WRITING

A Boy's View

If you were young Lucius, what would you think about the events you've observed? How would you feel about Brutus? Write Lucius's thoughts and fears in a **journal entry.** Read your entry aloud to the class.

Reading Skills

Recognizing Anachronisms

An **anachronism** (from *ana–*, "against," and *chronos,* "time") is an event or a detail that is inappropriate for the time period. For example, a car in a story about the Civil War would be an anachronism; cars had not yet been invented. In a play set in the 1920s, the word *nerd* would be an anachronism. *Nerd* wasn't used as slang until much later in the twentieth century.

Remember that *Julius Caesar* is set in 44–42 B.C. in ancient Rome. Do you see anachronisms in these passages?

1. ". . . he plucked me ope his doublet and offered them his throat to cut."

   —Act I, Scene 2, lines 261–262

2. "Peace! Count the clock."
   "The clock hath stricken three."

   —Act II, Scene 1, line 192

3. "Look, Lucius, here's the book I sought for so;
   I put it in the pocket of my gown."

   —Act IV, Scene 3, lines 250–251

PRACTICE

1. Find the one word in each passage at the left that is out of its time. Suppose Shakespeare wanted to correct his errors. How could he eliminate the anachronisms? Rewrite each passage, and then compare the changes you made with your classmates' versions.

2. Make a class list of other situations that would be anachronistic. An example might be the conspirators' use of guns instead of daggers to kill Caesar or Brutus's receipt of a telegram telling him of Portia's death.

Roman Forum, Rome, Italy.

ACT V

SCENE 1.
The plains of Philippi.

Enter OCTAVIUS, ANTONY, *and their* ARMY.

Octavius.
Now, Antony, our hopes are answerèd;
You said the enemy would not come down,
But keep the hills and upper regions.
It proves not so; their battles° are at hand;
5   They mean to warn us at Philippi here,
Answering before we do demand of them.

Antony.
Tut, I am in their bosoms,° and I know
Wherefore they do it. They could be content
To visit other places, and come down
10   With fearful bravery, thinking by this face
To fasten in our thoughts that they have courage;
But 'tis not so.

[*Enter a* MESSENGER.]

Messenger.   Prepare you, generals,
The enemy comes on in gallant show;
Their bloody sign° of battle is hung out,
15   And something to be done immediately.

Antony.
Octavius, lead your battle softly on
Upon the left hand of the even° field.

Octavius.
Upon the right hand I; keep thou the left.

Antony.
Why do you cross me in this exigent?°

Octavius.
20   I do not cross you; but I will do so.

[*March. Drum. Enter* BRUTUS, CASSIUS, *and their* ARMY;
   LUCILIUS, TITINIUS, MESSALA, *and others.*]

Brutus.
They stand, and would have parley.

Cassius.
Stand fast, Titinius, we must out and talk.

Staging the Play
Stage direction. *This act is crammed with action and could be confusing to follow. As you read, you might take notes about the movements of the armies. What props might be used to indicate that we are now on the plains of Philippi with Antony's and Octavius's army?*

4. battles: armies.

7. am in their bosoms: know their secret thoughts.

14. sign: flag.

17. even: level.

19. exigent (ek′sə·jənt): critical moment.
20. *What does this **dialogue** reveal about the relationship between Antony and Octavius?*
Staging the Play
Stage direction. *The armies should be placed at opposite sides of the stage, with a kind of no man's land between them. In the next lines, notice which man in which army speaks. They are taunting one another across the short distance that separates them.*

Octavius.

Mark Antony, shall we give sign of battle?

Antony.

No, Caesar, we will answer on their charge.

25 Make forth, the generals would have some words.

Octavius.

Stir not until the signal.

Brutus.

Words before blows; is it so, countrymen?

Octavius.

Not that we love words better, as you do.

Brutus.

Good words are better than bad strokes, Octavius.

Antony.

30 In your bad strokes, Brutus, you give good words;

Witness the hole you made in Caesar's heart,

Crying "Long live! Hail, Caesar!"

Cassius.   Antony,

The posture of your blows are yet unknown;

But for your words, they rob the Hybla° bees,

And leave them honeyless.

35 **Antony.**   Not stingless too.

Brutus.

O, yes, and soundless too;

For you have stol'n their buzzing, Antony,

And very wisely threat before you sting.

Antony.

Villains! You did not so, when your vile daggers

40 Hacked one another in the sides of Caesar.

You showed your teeth like apes, and fawned like
     hounds,

And bowed like bondmen, kissing Caesar's feet;

Whilst damnèd Casca, like a cur, behind

Struck Caesar on the neck. O you flatterers!

Cassius.

45 Flatterers! Now, Brutus, thank yourself;

This tongue had not offended so today,

If Cassius might have ruled.°

Octavius.

Come, come, the cause. If arguing make us sweat,

The proof of it will turn to redder drops.

34. Hybla: town in Sicily famous for its honey.

47. ruled: gotten his way.

? **47.** *What is Cassius referring to?*

50   Look,
        I draw a sword against conspirators.
        When think you that the sword goes up again?
        Never, till Caesar's three and thirty wounds
        Be well avenged; or till another Caesar°

55   Have added slaughter to the sword of traitors.
        Brutus.
        Caesar, thou canst not die by traitors' hands,
        Unless thou bring'st them with thee.

54. **another Caesar:** meaning Octavius himself.

"... I DRAW A SWORD AGAINST CONSPIRATORS."

Octavius.   So I hope.
     I was not born to die on Brutus' sword.
Brutus.
     O, if thou wert the noblest of thy strain,
60   Young man, thou couldst not die more honorable.
Cassius.
     A peevish schoolboy, worthless° of such honor,
     Joined with a masker and a reveler.
Antony.
     Old Cassius still!

61. worthless: unworthy.

62. *Whom is Cassius taunting here? What does he think of this "new Caesar"?*

Octavius.   Come, Antony; away!
   Defiance, traitors, hurl we in your teeth.
65   If you dare fight today, come to the field;
   If not, when you have stomachs.

                    [*Exeunt* OCTAVIUS, ANTONY, *and* ARMY.]

Cassius.
   Why, now blow wind, swell billow, and swim bark!
   The storm is up, and all is on the hazard.°

Brutus.
   Ho, Lucilius, hark, a word with you.

[LUCILIUS *and* MESSALA *stand forth.*]

Lucilius.   My lord?

[BRUTUS *and* LUCILIUS *converse apart.*]

Cassius.
   Messala.

Messala.   What says my general?

70   **Cassius.**   Messala,
   This is my birthday; as this very day
   Was Cassius born. Give me thy hand, Messala:
   Be thou my witness that against my will
   (As Pompey was) am I compelled to set
75   Upon one battle all our liberties.
   You know that I held Epicurus strong,°
   And his opinion; now I change my mind,
   And partly credit things that do presage.°
   Coming from Sardis, on our former ensign°
80   Two mighty eagles fell, and there they perched,
   Gorging and feeding from our soldiers' hands,
   Who to Philippi here consorted° us.
   This morning are they fled away and gone,
   And in their steads do ravens, crows, and kites
85   Fly o'er our heads and downward look on us
   As we were sickly prey; their shadows seem
   A canopy most fatal, under which
   Our army lies, ready to give up the ghost.

Messala.
   Believe not so.

Cassius.   I but believe it partly,
90   For I am fresh of spirit and resolved
   To meet all perils very constantly.

68. **on the hazard:** at risk.

76. **held Epicurus strong:** believed in the philosophy of Epicurus, a philosopher of the third century B.C. who held that omens were worthless.
78. **presage** (prē·sāj′): foretell.
79. **former ensign:** foremost flag.

82. **consorted:** accompanied.

88. *What images in this* **monologue** *suggest death and decay?*

Brutus.

    Even so, Lucilius.

Cassius.   Now, most noble Brutus,

    The gods today stand friendly, that we may,

    Lovers in peace, lead on our days to age!

95   But since the affairs of men rests still incertain,

    Let's reason with the worst that may befall.

    If we do lose this battle, then is this

    The very last time we shall speak together.

    What are you then determinèd to do?

Brutus.

100   Even by the rule of that philosophy

    By which I did blame Cato for the death

    Which he did give himself; I know not how,

    But I do find it cowardly and vile,

    For fear of what might fall, so to prevent

105   The time° of life, arming myself with patience

    To stay the providence of some high powers

    That govern us below.

Cassius.   Then, if we lose this battle,

    You are contented to be led in triumph°

    Thorough the streets of Rome?

Brutus.

110   No, Cassius, no; think not, thou noble Roman,

    That ever Brutus will go bound to Rome;

    He bears too great a mind. But this same day

    Must end that work the ides of March begun;

    And whether we shall meet again I know not.

115   Therefore our everlasting farewell take.

    Forever, and forever, farewell, Cassius!

    If we do meet again, why, we shall smile;

    If not, why then this parting was well made.

Cassius.

    Forever, and forever, farewell, Brutus!

120   If we do meet again, we'll smile indeed;

    If not, 'tis true this parting was well made.

Brutus.

    Why then, lead on. O, that a man might know

    The end of this day's business ere it come!

    But it sufficeth that the day will end,

125   And then the end is known. Come, ho! Away!

                           [Exeunt.]

Staging the Play

92. *Remember that the two pairs of men have been talking separately. What action should now take place onstage?*

105. time: term, or natural span.

107. *Brutus refers again to his Stoic philosophy, which taught that he should be ruled by reason, not by emotion. What is Brutus saying about suicide?*

108. in triumph: as a captive in the victor's procession.

109. *According to this speech, what will happen to the losing armies?*

SCENE 2. *The field of battle.*

Alarum.° Enter BRUTUS *and* MESSALA.

Brutus.
> Ride, ride, Messala, ride, and give these bills°
> Unto the legions on the other side.

[*Loud alarum.*]

> Let them set on at once; for I perceive
> But cold demeanor° in Octavius' wing,
5   And sudden push° gives them the overthrow.
> Ride, ride, Messala! Let them all come down.

[*Exeunt.*]

SCENE 3. *The field of battle.*

Alarums. Enter CASSIUS *and* TITINIUS.

Cassius.
> O, look, Titinius, look, the villains fly!
> Myself have to mine own turned enemy.
> This ensign° here of mine was turning back;
> I slew the coward, and did take it° from him.

Titinius.
5   O Cassius, Brutus gave the word too early,
> Who, having some advantage on Octavius,
> Took it too eagerly; his soldiers fell to spoil,°
> Whilst we by Antony are all enclosed.

[*Enter* PINDARUS.]

Pindarus.
> Fly further off, my lord, fly further off!
10   Mark Antony is in your tents, my lord.
> Fly, therefore, noble Cassius, fly far off!

Cassius.
> This hill is far enough. Look, look, Titinius!
> Are those my tents where I perceive the fire?

Titinius.
> They are, my lord.

Cassius.   Titinius, if thou lovest me,
15   Mount thou my horse and hide thy spurs in him°
> Till he have brought thee up to yonder troops

Alarum: call to arms by drum or trumpet.

1. bills: orders.

4. cold demeanor: lack of fighting spirit.
5. push: attack.
 6. *What orders has Brutus given his army?*

3. ensign: standard-bearer.
4. it: the flag (standard).

7. spoil: loot.
 8. *What have Brutus's and Cassius's armies done?*

15. In other words, dig your spurs into him to make him go at top speed.

And here again, that I may rest assured
Whether yond troops are friend or enemy.

Titinius.

I will be here again even with a thought.°   [*Exit.*]

Cassius.

20   Go, Pindarus, get higher on that hill;
My sight was ever thick. Regard Titinius,
And tell me what thou not'st about the field.

[*Exit* PINDARUS.]

This day I breathèd first. Time is come round,
And where I did begin, there shall I end.
25   My life is run his compass.° Sirrah, what news?

Pindarus (*above*). O my lord!

Cassius. What news?

Pindarus (*above*).

Titinius is enclosèd round about
With horsemen that make to him on the spur;°
30   Yet he spurs on. Now they are almost on him.
Now, Titinius! Now some light. O, he lights too!
He's ta'en! (*Shout.*) And, hark! They shout for joy.

Cassius.

Come down; behold no more.
O, coward that I am, to live so long,
35   To see my best friend ta'en before my face!

[*Enter* PINDARUS.]

Come hither, sirrah.

19. even with a thought: immediately.

24. *What is Cassius referring to here?*

25. is run his compass: has completed its appointed span.

Staging the Play

26. *Pindarus stands on the upper stage, suggesting that he is on the hilltop, looking over the field of battle. What does he report to Cassius, who stands below?*

29. on the spur: at top speed.

"O, COWARD THAT I AM,
TO LIVE SO LONG,
TO SEE MY BEST FRIEND
TA'EN BEFORE MY FACE!"

In Parthia° did I take thee prisoner;
And then I swore thee, saving of° thy life,
That whatsoever I did bid thee do,
40   Thou shouldst attempt it. Come now, keep thine oath.
Now be a freeman, and with this good sword,
That ran through Caesar's bowels, search this bosom.
Stand not to answer. Here, take thou the hilts,
And when my face is covered, as 'tis now,
45   Guide thou the sword—Caesar, thou art revenged,
Even with the sword that killed thee.   [*Dies.*]

Pindarus.

So, I am free; yet would not so have been,
Durst I have done my will. O Cassius!
Far from this country Pindarus shall run,
50   Where never Roman shall take note of him.   [*Exit.*]

[*Enter* TITINIUS *and* MESSALA.]

Messala.

It is but change,° Titinius; for Octavius
Is overthrown by noble Brutus' power,
As Cassius' legions are by Antony.

Titinius.

These tidings will well comfort Cassius.

Messala.

Where did you leave him?

55   **Titinius.**   All disconsolate,
With Pindarus his bondman, on this hill.

Messala.

Is not that he that lies upon the ground?

Titinius.

He lies not like the living. O my heart!

Messala.

Is not that he?

Titinius.   No, this was he, Messala,
60   But Cassius is no more. O setting sun,
As in thy red rays thou dost sink to night,
So in his red blood Cassius' day is set.
The sun of Rome is set. Our day is gone;
Clouds, dews, and dangers come; our deeds are done!
65   Mistrust of° my success hath done this deed.

Messala.

Mistrust of good success hath done this deed.
O hateful Error, Melancholy's child,

37. Parthia: ancient country (corresponding to part of modern Iran) that was the site of many Roman military campaigns.
38. saving of: sparing.

? Staging the Play
46. *What does Cassius have Pindarus do for him? What does he believe has happened?*

51. change: exchange of fortune.

? Staging the Play
54. *Titinius and Messala enter from the wings and do not see Cassius's body at first. What irony do we in the audience feel when we hear their conversation?*

65. Mistrust of: disbelief in.
? 65. *What does Titinius think caused Cassius to kill himself?*

"THE SUN OF ROME IS SET."

Why dost thou show to the apt° thoughts of men
The things that are not? O Error, soon conceived,
70 Thou never com'st unto a happy birth,
But kill'st the mother° that engend'red thee!

Titinius.
What, Pindarus! Where art thou, Pindarus?

Messala.
Seek him, Titinius, whilst I go to meet
The noble Brutus, thrusting this report
75 Into his ears. I may say "thrusting" it;
For piercing steel and darts envenomèd
Shall be as welcome to the ears of Brutus
As tidings of this sight.

Titinius.   Hie you, Messala,
And I will seek for Pindarus the while.

[*Exit* MESSALA.]

80 Why didst thou send me forth, brave Cassius?
Did I not meet thy friends, and did not they
Put on my brows this wreath of victory,
And bid me give it thee? Didst thou not hear their shouts?
Alas, thou hast misconstrued everything!
85 But hold thee, take this garland on thy brow;
Thy Brutus bid me give it thee, and I
Will do his bidding. Brutus, come apace,°
And see how I regarded Caius Cassius.
By your leave, gods.° This is a Roman's part:°
90 Come, Cassius' sword, and find Titinius' heart.

[*Dies.*]

[*Alarum. Enter* BRUTUS, MESSALA, YOUNG CATO, STRATO,
VOLUMNIUS, *and* LUCILIUS.]

Brutus.
Where, where, Messala, doth his body lie?

Messala.
Lo, yonder, and Titinius mourning it.

Brutus.
Titinius' face is upward.

Cato.   He is slain.

Brutus.
O Julius Caesar, thou art mighty yet!
95 Thy spirit walks abroad, and turns our swords
In our own proper entrails.   [*Low alarums.*]

68. apt: credulous; easily impressed.

71. the mother: that is, Cassius, who conceived the error.

87. apace: quickly.

89. He asks the gods' permission to end his life before the time they have allotted to him. **part:** role; duty.

96. *Why does Brutus invoke Caesar's name?*

Cato.   Brave Titinius!

    Look, whe'r° he have not crowned dead Cassius.

Brutus.

    Are yet two Romans living such as these?

    The last of all the Romans, fare thee well!

100   It is impossible that ever Rome

    Should breed thy fellow.° Friends, I owe moe tears

    To this dead man than you shall see me pay.

    I shall find time, Cassius; I shall find time.

    Come, therefore, and to Thasos° send his body;

105   His funerals shall not be in our camp,

    Lest it discomfort° us. Lucilius, come,

    And come, young Cato; let us to the field.

    Labeo and Flavius set our battles on.

    'Tis three o'clock; and, Romans, yet ere night

110   We shall try fortune in a second fight.   *[Exeunt.]*

97. whe'r: whether.

101. fellow: equal.

104. Thasos: island in the Aegean Sea, near Philippi.

106. discomfort: discourage.

SCENE 4. *The field of battle.*

Alarum. Enter BRUTUS, MESSALA, YOUNG CATO, LUCILIUS, *and* FLAVIUS.

Brutus.

    Yet, countrymen, O, yet hold up your heads!

               [Exit, with followers.]

Cato.

    What bastard° doth not? Who will go with me?

    I will proclaim my name about the field.

    I am the son of Marcus Cato,° ho!

5   A foe to tyrants, and my country's friend.

    I am the son of Marcus Cato, ho!

    [Enter SOLDIERS *and fight.]*

2. bastard: low fellow.

4. Thus he is Portia's brother.

"O, JULIUS CAESAR, THOU ART MIGHTY YET!
THY SPIRIT WALKS ABROAD, AND TURNS OUR SWORDS
IN OUR OWN PROPER ENTRAILS."

Lucilius.

    And I am Brutus, Marcus Brutus, I;
    Brutus, my country's friend, know me for Brutus!

[YOUNG CATO *falls.*]

    O young and noble Cato, art thou down?
10   Why, now thou diest as bravely as Titinius,
    And mayst be honored, being Cato's son.

First Soldier.

    Yield, or thou diest.

Lucilius.   Only I yield to die.
    There is so much that thou wilt kill me straight;°
    Kill Brutus, and be honored in his death.

First Soldier.

15   We must not. A noble prisoner!

[*Enter* ANTONY.]

Second Soldier.

    Room, ho! Tell Antony, Brutus is ta'en.

First Soldier.

    I'll tell the news. Here comes the general.
    Brutus is ta'en, Brutus is ta'en, my lord.

Antony.

    Where is he?

Lucilius.

20   Safe, Antony; Brutus is safe enough.
    I dare assure thee that no enemy
    Shall ever take alive the noble Brutus.
    The gods defend him from so great a shame!
    When you do find him, or alive or dead,
25   He will be found like Brutus, like himself.°

Antony.

    This is not Brutus, friend, but, I assure you,
    A prize no less in worth. Keep this man safe;
    Give him all kindness. I had rather have
    Such men my friends than enemies. Go on,
30   And see whe'r Brutus be alive or dead,
    And bring us word unto Octavius' tent
    How everything is chanced.°   [*Exeunt.*]

Staging the Play

7. *Lucilius is impersonating Brutus. What are these young men doing, and why?*

13. That is, there is so much inducement to kill me that you will surely do so right away. (Some editors have interpreted this line to mean that Lucilius is offering his captors money to kill him rather than take him prisoner.)

25. like himself: true to his own noble nature.

32. chanced: turned out.

32. *Not long ago Antony was compiling a list of the enemies he was to have murdered. How does he seem to have changed?*

Enter BRUTUS, DARDANIUS, CLITUS, STRATO, *and*
VOLUMNIUS.

Brutus.
Come, poor remains of friends, rest on this rock.
Clitus.
Statilius showed the torchlight, but, my lord,
He came not back; he is or ta'en or slain.°
Brutus.
Sit thee down, Clitus. Slaying is the word;
5   It is a deed in fashion. Hark thee, Clitus.

[*Whispers.*]

Clitus.
What, I, my lord? No, not for all the world!
Brutus.
Peace then, no words.
Clitus.   I'll rather kill myself.
Brutus.
Hark thee, Dardanius.   [*Whispers.*]
Dardanius.   Shall I do such a deed?
Clitus. O Dardanius!
10   **Dardanius.** O Clitus!
Clitus.
What ill request did Brutus make to thee?
Dardanius.
To kill him, Clitus. Look, he meditates.
Clitus.
Now is that noble vessel° full of grief,
That it runs over even at his eyes.
Brutus.
15   Come hither, good Volumnius; list° a word.
Volumnius.
What says my lord?
Brutus.   Why, this, Volumnius:
The ghost of Caesar hath appeared to me
Two several° times by night; at Sardis once,
And this last night here in Philippi fields.
I know my hour is come.
20   **Volumnius.**   Not so, my lord.

3. According to Plutarch, Statilius volunteered to see what was happening at Cassius's camp. If all was well, he was to signal with his torchlight. He did signal but then was killed while returning to Brutus's camp.

5. *What is Brutus's mood?*

13. vessel: figure of speech meaning "human being."

15. list: listen to.

18. several: separate.

Brutus.

Nay, I am sure it is, Volumnius.
Thou seest the world, Volumnius, how it goes;
Our enemies have beat us to the pit.°

[*Low alarums.*]

It is more worthy to leap in ourselves
25   Than tarry till they push us. Good Volumnius,
Thou know'st that we two went to school together;
Even for that our love of old, I prithee
Hold thou my sword-hilts whilst I run on it.

Volumnius.

That's not an office for a friend, my lord.

[*Alarum still.*]

Clitus.

30   Fly, fly, my lord, there is no tarrying here.

Brutus.

Farewell to you; and you; and you, Volumnius.
Strato, thou hast been all this while asleep;
Farewell to thee too, Strato. Countrymen,
My heart doth joy that yet in all my life
35   I found no man but he was true to me.
I shall have glory by this losing day
More than Octavius and Mark Antony
By this vile conquest shall attain unto.
So fare you well at once, for Brutus' tongue
40   Hath almost ended his life's history.
Night hangs upon mine eyes; my bones would rest,
That have but labored to attain this hour.

[*Alarum. Cry within,* "Fly, fly, fly!"]

Clitus.

Fly, my lord, fly!

Brutus.   Hence! I will follow.

            [*Exeunt* CLITUS, DARDANIUS, *and* VOLUMNIUS.]

I prithee, Strato, stay thou by thy lord,
45   Thou art a fellow of a good respect.°
Thy life hath had some smatch° of honor in it;
Hold then my sword, and turn away thy face,
While I do run upon it. Wilt thou, Strato?

23. pit: trap for capturing wild animals; also, a grave.

41. *What does he mean by saying that "night hangs upon" his eyes?*

45. respect: reputation.
46. smatch: trace; taste.

Strato.

> Give me your hand first. Fare you well, my lord.

Brutus.

50
> Farewell, good Strato—Caesar, now be still;
> I killed not thee with half so good a will.   [*Dies.*]

> [*Alarum. Retreat. Enter* ANTONY, OCTAVIUS, MESSALA,
> LUCILIUS, *and the* ARMY.]

Octavius. What man is that?

Messala.

> My master's man. Strato, where is thy master?

Staging the Play

51. *How many bodies now lie on the stage? It is important for a director of a Shakespearean tragedy to remember how many bodies are onstage. Getting rid of them is often a challenge.*

"HOLD THEN MY SWORD, AND TURN AWAY THY FACE, WHILE I DO RUN UPON IT."

"THIS WAS THE NOBLEST ROMAN OF THEM ALL. . . .
HIS LIFE WAS GENTLE, AND THE ELEMENTS
SO MIXED IN HIM THAT NATURE
MIGHT STAND UP
AND SAY TO ALL THE WORLD,
'THIS WAS A MAN!'"

Strato.

　　Free from the bondage you are in, Messala;
55　The conquerors can but make a fire of him.
　　For Brutus only overcame himself,
　　And no man else hath honor by his death.

Lucilius.

　　So Brutus should be found. I thank thee, Brutus,
　　That thou hast proved Lucilius' saying true.

Octavius.

60　All that served Brutus, I will entertain them.
　　Fellow, wilt thou bestow° thy time with me?

Strato.

　　Ay, if Messala will prefer° me to you.

Octavius. Do so, good Messala.

Messala. How died my master, Strato?

Strato.

65　I held the sword, and he did run on it.

Messala.

　　Octavius, then take him to follow thee,
　　That did the latest service to my master.

Antony.

　　This was the noblest Roman of them all.
　　All the conspirators save only he
70　Did that they did in envy of great Caesar;
　　He, only in a general honest thought
　　And common good to all, made one of them.°
　　His life was gentle, and the elements
　　So mixed in him that Nature might stand up
75　And say to all the world, "This was a man!"

61. bestow: spend.

? 61. *How does Octavius indicate by his words to his former enemies that the strife is finally over?*

62. prefer: recommend.

72. made one of them: joined their group.

Octavius.

According to his virtue, let us use° him
With all respect and rites of burial.
Within my tent his bones tonight shall lie,
Most like a soldier ordered honorably.
80 So call the field to rest, and let's away
To part° the glories of this happy day.

[*Exeunt omnes.*]

76. **use:** treat.

81. **part:** divide.

Staging the Play
81. *Order has been restored; healing will begin. Which actor would you have exit last?*

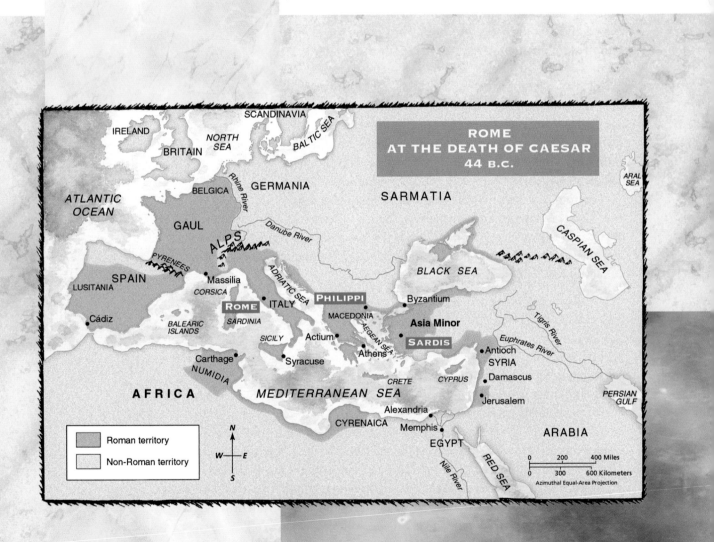

ROME
AT THE DEATH OF CAESAR
44 B.C.

IRELAND
BRITAIN
SCANDINAVIA
NORTH SEA
BALTIC SEA
GERMANIA
SARMATIA
ARAL SEA
ATLANTIC OCEAN
BELGICA
Rhine River
GAUL
ALPS
Danube River
CASPIAN SEA
PYRENEES
SPAIN
LUSITANIA
Massilia
CORSICA
ADRIATIC SEA
BLACK SEA
Byzantium
Cádiz
ROME
ITALY
PHILIPPI
MACEDONIA
Asia Minor
BALEARIC ISLANDS
SARDINIA
Tigris River
Euphrates River
SICILY
Actium
AEGEAN SEA
SARDIS
Antioch
SYRIA
Carthage
Syracuse
Athens
Damascus
NUMIDIA
CRETE
CYPRUS
Jerusalem
PERSIAN GULF
AFRICA
MEDITERRANEAN SEA
Alexandria
ARABIA
CYRENAICA
Memphis
EGYPT
Nile River
RED SEA

Roman territory
Non-Roman territory

N
W—E
S

0   200   400 Miles
0   300   600 Kilometers
Azimuthal Equal-Area Projection

Tragedy was first defined by the Greek philosopher Aristotle (384–322 B.C.), and critics have been arguing about it ever since. Aristotle's definition is not a rule for what tragedy should be; it is a description of what he believed tragedy was, based on his observations of Greek drama, particularly the works of Sophocles.

Aristotle. Hellenic sculpture. (32 cm high).
Louvre, Paris.

What Is a Tragic Hero?

According to Aristotle, the function of **tragedy** is to arouse pity and fear in the audience so that we may be purged, or cleansed, of these unsettling emotions. Aristotle's term for this emotional purging is the Greek word *catharsis*. Although no one is exactly sure what Aristotle meant by *cartharsis,* it seems clear that he was referring to that strangely pleasurable sense of emotional release we experience after watching a great tragedy. For some reason, we usually feel exhilarated, not depressed, at the end.

According to Aristotle, a tragedy can arouse these twin emotions of pity and fear only if it presents a certain type of hero, who is neither completely good nor completely bad.

Aristotle also says that the **tragic hero** should be someone "highly renowned and prosperous," which in Aristotle's day meant a member of the royalty. Why not an ordinary working person? we might ask. The answer is simply that the hero must fall from tremendous good fortune. Otherwise, we wouldn't feel such pity and fear.

> . . . the change of fortune presented must not be the spectacle of a virtuous man brought from prosperity to adversity: For this moves neither pity nor fear; it merely shocks us. Nor again, that of a bad man passing from adversity to prosperity: For nothing can be more alien to the spirit of tragedy; . . . it neither satisfies the moral sense nor calls forth pity or fear. Nor, again, should the downfall of the utter villain be exhibited. A plot of this kind would, doubtless, satisfy the moral sense, but it would inspire neither pity nor fear; for pity is aroused by unmerited misfortune, fear by the misfortune of a man like ourselves. . . . There remains, then, the character between these two extremes—that of a man who is not eminently good and just, yet whose misfortune is brought about not by vice or depravity, but by some error or frailty. . . .
>
> —Aristotle, from the *Poetics,* translated by S. H. Butcher

Critics have argued over what Aristotle meant by the tragic hero's "error or frailty." Is the hero defeated because of a single error of judgment, or is the cause of the hero's downfall a **tragic flaw**—a fundamental character weakness, such as destructive pride, ruthless ambition, or obsessive jealousy? In either interpretation the key point is that the hero is on some level responsible for his or her own downfall. The hero is not the mere plaything of the gods—the helpless victim of fate or of someone else's villainy. By the end of the play, the tragic hero comes to recognize his or her own error and to accept its tragic consequences. The real hero does not curse fate or the gods. The real hero is humbled—and enlightened—by the tragedy.

Yet we, the audience, feel that the hero's punishment exceeds the crime, that the hero gets more than he or she deserves. We feel pity because the hero is a suffering human being who is flawed like us. We also feel fear because the hero is *better* than we are, and *still* he failed. What hope can there be for us?

Melpomene, muse of tragedy. Detail from the Mosaic of the Nine Muses, Rome.
© Gilles Mermet/Art Resource, New York.

THE FEAR AND THE FLAMES

Jimmy Breslin

The 1960s was a time of great unrest and change in this country. Two situations contributed to the social and political upheavals: The United States was involved in an increasingly unpopular and bloody war in Vietnam, and African Americans were organizing a powerful movement to demand their civil rights, which had been denied them for decades. At the head of the nonviolent civil rights movement was Martin Luther King, Jr. A popular and respected leader, King had helped organize the Montgomery, Alabama, bus boycott in 1955 and later spoke out against U.S. involvement in Vietnam. In 1963, more than 250,000 Americans gathered to hear King deliver his now famous "I Have a Dream" speech at the Lincoln Memorial.

On April 4, 1968, this preacher of nonviolent resistance was assassinated by a sniper in Memphis, Tennessee. As news of King's murder took hold, the cities of the United States erupted in violence. Rioters attacked others, set fires, and stole goods from stores.

Here is journalist Jimmy Breslin's powerful feature article describing the scene in Washington, D.C., following King's assassination.

WASHINGTON, April 6—In the end, in the fear and the smoke there seems to be no society at all. A Nobel Peace Prize–winner is dead in an assassination, and the cities that make up the country are dotted with flames. Last night, America became a place where you could understand the meaning of the word *anarchy*.[1]

When the traffic light on the corner of Thirteenth and V turned red, the body on the sidewalk could be seen. It was a man in his thirties, lying on his back. One leg was drawn up under him. People walked through the smoke from the fires and went past the man without bothering to look at him.

Two dogs that had been rooting at spoiled garbage came up and were sniffing at the man. Two Army trucks, staying close to the curb, came rushing past. The dogs jumped back and went away.

The man was in a brown suit and had on a shirt and tie. Blood ran from his nose and mouth. In the dark you couldn't tell whether there was dirt or blood from a chest wound on his shirt. "He's dead," somebody said.

"No, I think he's just about breathing," somebody else said.

---

1. ***anarchy*** (an'ər·kē) *n.*: absence of government; lawlessness; chaos.

A hospital was in the middle of the block. The man probably had been dumped on the corner with the idea that the hospital would come out and get him. The hospital has a circular driveway in front of it. It is five stories high. The sign says "Children's Hospital, Founded in 1870." Glass entrance doors were locked. A guard opened them, but only grumpily.

"You've got a man dying up on the corner," he was told.

The guard turned and walked into the dimly lit lobby. A short man in a business suit came out from an office behind the reception counter. "I'm the administrator,"[2] he said.

"There's a man dying on the corner," he was told.

"What do you want us to do?" the administrator said.

"Help him."

The man shook his head. "I'm not sending anybody from this place outside tonight for any reason," he said. "Let somebody else come and do it. We're not taking any chances."

Outside, people kept walking past the body on the street. The police finally came and took the man away to a hospital emergency ward. Washington, D.C., the capital of the nation, was like this last night.

---

2. **administrator** *n.:* manager or director.

Martin Luther King, Jr., speaking in Memphis, Tennessee, on April 3, 1968, the day before he was assassinated.

AP photo/Charles Kelly.

On Fourteenth Street, firetrucks were parked in the middle of the street for blocks. Firemen and soldiers from the Sixth Cavalry, who had fixed bayonets,[3] walked through the broken glass that covered the streets of all Washington last night. The firemen threw water high into the air at buildings that were burning out of control. The water streams caught the light of the fire, and the water cascaded off the tops of the burning buildings and went high into the air in an orange spray. Smoke covered the street and the sky over the street. The Capitol of the United States was gray and dim behind a shroud of smoke from fires set by people who are black and who no longer will live in this country as white people want them to.

✗

Jimmy Flood stood on the corner of Fourteenth and Gerard and watched the water run under the broken furniture piled in the gutter. Jimmy Flood

---

3. fixed bayonets *n.:* guns with blades attached to the barrels.

Smoke obscures the traffic of city streets in Washington, D.C., after the rioting that followed the assassination of Martin Luther King, Jr., in April 1968.

stared at the fire, which was turning a six-story corner apartment house into a shell. His eyes brightened and his teeth showed in a smile. The smile of Detroit and Newark and Watts and Chicago[4] and all the other places that should have shown us how bad it would be.

"It's hard to believe this is Washington," somebody said.

"Washington's just another town to me," Jimmy Flood said. "I live in Atlantic City. I live in Washington. It makes no difference. I get sixty dollars a week whether I'm here or some other place."

Smoke blew with the wind and billowed low along Fourteenth Street, and he had to duck into the doorway of a smashed shoe store to breathe. Smoke was everywhere in the city. It was hanging in front of the brilliant television lights they had set up in front of the West Wing of the White House.

The living part of the White House was dark, except for light showing through drapes on the second floor.

At Fourteenth and F in the city's main business district, a business district that has been looted,[5] shattered, and set afire, troops walked eight and ten abreast with both hands on their weapons. They wore helmets and gas masks and their voices were muffled while they talked to each other through the gas masks.

A captain with the name Rhodes sewed to his fatigues stood alongside a parked jeep and listened to a radio.

"The gas masks?" he was saying. "Oh, that's because we're going to use a chemical deployment if anything happens. It's better to do that than a straight show of force."

"I see. What do you use, Mace?"

"No. We'll just use gas," he said.

This was Washington, D.C., the place the world looks at, on Friday night, April 6, 1968. And this was for all of the past and for Martin Luther King, who now is all of the present. . . .

A building destroyed by fire during riots in Washington, D.C., following the assassination of Martin Luther King, Jr.

---

4. **Detroit . . . Chicago:** cities that experienced civil rights problems in the 1960s.
5. **looted** *v.*: robbed.

Response and Analysis

Act V

Reading Check

1. Which four characters finally confront one another in Scene 1 of Act V?

2. What are the results of the first round of battle at Philippi? In the end, who triumphs over whom?

3. What mistaken assumptions lead to Cassius's death?

4. Why does Brutus think he must commit suicide?

5. How do Antony and Octavius react to Brutus's death?

Thinking Critically

6. In this **tragedy** the plot's rising action peaks at the **climax,** the moment of greatest tension, when we find out how the **conflict** will be resolved. Identify the play's climax.

7. In the **resolution,** the last scene, why is it significant that Octavius delivers the play's final speech?

8. In Scene 3, Cassius's death scene, identify at least three examples of **irony,** a turn of events that is contrary to our expectations. How do these ironies make you feel?

9. Look at Scenes 3 and 5 and the dying words of Cassius and Brutus. How does each man view Caesar's murder? Do you think each man had a choice other than suicide? Explain.

10. Brutus makes two mistakes—one in Act II and one in Act III—that stem from his idealized vision of the assassination and his self-image as an "honorable man." What are these errors, and how do they lead to Brutus's **tragic** downfall?

11. Describe your final view of Brutus and the choices he made. Did he misread the evidence that Caesar might become king? Should he have betrayed a friend for the public good? Was he wrong to kill the only man who could bring order out of chaos? Support your responses with evidence from the play.

12. Critics argue that Julius Caesar dominates the play (Cassius says in Act I that he "doth bestride the narrow world / Like a Colossus."). How would you defend this view? How is Caesar "present" in the second half of the play?

13. In Aristotle's essay the *Poetics* (see the **Connection** on page 872), he describes the **tragic hero** as a person more noble than evil, whose fortunes go from good to bad, someone with a character flaw that leads to his downfall. Does Brutus fit this description, or is the tragic hero someone else—perhaps Caesar? Do you think, instead, that the play lacks a tragic hero? Defend your answer.

Extending and Evaluating

14. Few words inspired such anxiety in the ancient Romans as the word *king.* Consider these questions about kingship: Were the anxieties of Brutus and others about Caesar's potential "kingship" justified? How do you think Shakespeare's audience, living under the strong and stable monarchy of the aging Queen Elizabeth I, might have felt about choosing between dictatorship and anarchy? How do you think American audiences of today feel about this issue? (Look back at your Quickwrite notes for page 754.)

WRITING

Choose from among the following assignments to respond to the play:

1. Comparing a Play and a Movie

In a video store or a library, look for a movie version of *Julius Caesar*. You might find the 1953 version, starring James Mason as Brutus, or the 1970 version, starring Charlton Heston as Antony. After you watch the movie, compare it with Shakespeare's play. How closely does the movie stick to the original? Which of Shakespeare's scenes are dropped? Which ones are "opened up"— moved offstage into different settings? Write a brief essay **comparing and contrasting** the movie and the play. Consider what a movie has that a play does not—realistic settings, closeups, fadeouts, additional stage movements, and a musical score.

▶ **Use "Comparing a Play and a Film," pages 890–897, for help with this assignment.**

2. Comparing Caesar and King

In a brief **essay, compare** Jimmy Breslin's account of events in Washington, D.C., following the assassination of Martin Luther King, Jr. (see the **Connection** on page 874), with Shakespeare's depiction of events following Julius Caesar's assassination (see Act III, Scenes 2 and 3). What similarities can you find in these two accounts? What, if anything, do they reveal about human nature?

3. You Be the Critic

Using what you've learned in this chapter about the purposes and characteristics of drama, write a **critical review** of a movie or TV drama you've watched recently. Begin by identifying the work's genre (tragedy, comedy, drama), and think about the criteria you will use to evaluate the work. Are the characters and plot believable? Is the action suspenseful, the ending satisfying? How effective are the dialogue, scene designs, and costumes? Cite details to support any general statements you make about the work. (Before you begin, you might want to read the review on page 882 of a production of *Julius Caesar*.)

4. Analyzing a Character

In a brief essay, write a **character analysis** of Brutus. First, read the following critical comments. Then, become a critic yourself. Evaluate the comments, and use them as you form your own **thesis statement,** a clear statement of your main idea or argument. Be sure to include details from the play to elaborate on and support your statements about Brutus.

> Brutus is humorlessly good. If his duty is to know himself, his performance fails. Nobility has numbed him until he cannot see himself for his principles. . . . He is not mad or haunted or inspired or perplexed in the extreme. He is simply confused.
>
> —Mark Van Doren

> Brutus is an intellectual who can do things, who is not . . . hampered by doubts. . . . He cannot realize that men seek their own interests, for he has never sought his own, he has lived nobly among noble thoughts, wedded to a noble wife.
>
> —E. M. Forster

Reading Skills 📖

Memorizing Famous Passages: Making Them Yours

If you memorize some of Shakespeare's famous speeches now, you'll find yourself remembering them years later. One way to memorize speeches easily is to use the "bricklayer" method. Like a bricklayer who lays down row upon row of bricks, an actor memorizes lines by building one line upon another. Read the first line of a speech until you can say it without looking at it. Then, read that line and the next line until you can say the first two lines without looking at them. Continue until you can say the whole speech without looking at it. Then, you can work on your **interpretation** and **dramatic presentation.**

1. Why, man, he doth bestride the narrow world
   Like a Colossus, and we petty men
   Walk under his huge legs and peep about
   To find ourselves dishonorable graves.
   Men at some time are masters of their fates:
   The fault, dear Brutus, is not in our stars,
   But in ourselves, that we are underlings.
                              —Act I, Scene 2, lines 135–141

2. Cowards die many times before their deaths;
   The valiant never taste of death but once.
   Of all the wonders that I yet have heard,
   It seems to me most strange that men should fear,
   Seeing that death, a necessary end,
   Will come when it will come.
                              —Act II, Scene 2, lines 32–37

3. The evil that men do lives after them,
   The good is oft interrèd with their bones. . . .
                              —Act III, Scene 2, lines 75–76

4. There is a tide in the affairs of men
   Which, taken at the flood, leads on to fortune;
   Omitted, all the voyage of their life
   Is bound in shallows and in miseries.
   On such a full sea are we now afloat,
   And we must take the current when it serves,
   Or lose our ventures.
                              —Act IV, Scene 3, lines 216–222

PRACTICE

Choose at least two of the speeches above. Using the bricklayer technique, memorize the speeches. Then, in a small group, **evaluate** one another's dramatic presentations. How did they differ? Does your group have a favorite one?

Julius Caesar in an Absorbing Production

Evaluating an Author's Argument: A Critical Review

How do you choose which new movie or TV show to watch? You might listen to friends' recommendations. You might also turn to a professional review.

What to Look for in a Review

1. **What is the intent, or purpose?** In a review the author's **purpose** is **persuasive.** The writer's argument includes an **opinion statement** (usually worded as a **generalization**) followed by support to convince you that the opinion is right. Ask yourself: "What is the writer trying to get me to *believe*? How does the writer's purpose affect the **structure** of the argument and the **tone**? Does the tone seem appropriate for the **audience**?"

2. **What are the criteria?** Whenever you make a judgment about how good or bad something is (from fajitas to TV comedies), you base your evaluation on **criteria,** or standards of excellence. For example, what are the qualities that make a screenplay or an actor's performance outstanding?

3. **What's the evidence?** A critical review of a play would probably include the following types of **evidence:** critical judgments, examples, and facts. The reviewer would discuss the **elements of drama** (plot, characters, conflict, theme) as well as the **staging** (acting, sets, costumes, lighting).

4. **Is the evidence comprehensive?** Remember that you can't *prove* an opinion (as you can a fact). You can only support it—and the more support you give, the more convincing you are. Is the reviewer's evidence comprehensive, or has something important been omitted?

5. **Who is the writer?** To decide how **credible** and convincing a review is, you need to know whose opinion you are reading. Is the writer experienced and qualified to write about this topic? Is the author biased in some way? How can you tell?

Vocabulary Development

gaunt (gônt) *adj.:* here, grim and forbidding.

vitality (vī · tal′ə · tē) *n.:* energy; vigor.

surly (sʉr′lē) *adj.:* bad-tempered; rude.

unorthodox (un · ôr′thə · däks′) *adj.:* unusual; not conforming to usual norms.

sinister (sin′is · tər) *adj.:* evil.

reticent (ret′ə·sənt) *adj.:* silent; reserved.

perplexed (pər · plekst′) *adj.:* uncertain.

idealist (ī · dē′əl · ist) *n.:* someone who is guided by ideals, or standards of perfection.

Connecting to the Literature

In 1937, with dictators such as Adolf Hitler in power, the American director Orson Welles staged a modern-dress production of *Julius Caesar* at the Mercury Theater in New York City. In this version, Brutus was viewed as a hero for killing the tyrant Caesar. One critic's review of the production follows.

INTERNET
Interactive Reading Model
Keyword: LE5 10-10

Reading Skills
Evaluate an author's argument.

Julius Caesar in an Absorbing Production

from the *New York Post*, November 12, 1937

John Mason Brown

This is no funeral oration such as Miss Bankhead and Mr. Tearle forced me to deliver yesterday when they interred *Antony and Cleopatra*.[1] I come to praise *Caesar* at the Mercury, not to bury it. Of all the many new plays and productions the season has so far revealed, this modern-dress version of the mob mischief and demagoguery[2] which can follow the assassination of a dictator is by all odds the most exciting, the most imaginative, the most topical, the most awesome, and the most absorbing. **❶**

> **❶ EVALUATING AN ARGUMENT**
>
> **Paraphrase** Brown's **opinion,** or **claim,** about the production.

The astonishing, all-impressive virtue of Mr. Welles's *Julius Caesar* is that, magnificent as it is as theater, it is far larger than its medium. Something deathless and dangerous in the world sweeps past you down the darkened aisles at the Mercury and takes possession of the proud, <u>gaunt</u> stage. . . . It is an ageless warning, made in such arresting terms that it not only gives a new <u>vitality</u> to an ancient story but unrolls in your mind's eye a map of the world which is increasingly splotched with sickening colors.

Mr. Welles does not dress his conspirators and his Storm Troopers in Black Shirts or in Brown.[3] He does not have to. The antique Rome, which we had thought was securely Roman in Shakespeare's tragedy, he shows us to be a dateless state of mind. . . . To an extent no other director in our day and country has equaled, Mr. Welles proves in his production that Shakespeare was indeed not of an age but for all time. After this <u>surly</u> modern Caesar, dressed in a green uniform and scowling behind the mask-like face of a contemporary dictator, has fallen at the Mercury and new mischief is afoot, we cannot but shudder before the prophet's wisdom of those lines which read:

"How many ages hence
Shall this our lofty scene be acted over
In states unborn and accents yet unknown!"[4] **❷**

> **❷ EVALUATING EVIDENCE**
>
> In the second paragraph, Brown cites his *first* main point about the production—"it is an ageless warning." What **evidence** does he then give to support this view?

---

1. The movie actress Tallulah Bankhead opened in *Antony and Cleopatra* on November 10, 1937. Mr. Brown gave the production an unfavorable review.
2. **demagoguery** (dem′ə · gäg′ər · ē) *n.:* appealing to the emotions and prejudices of people in order to stir up discontent and gain power.
3. **Storm . . . Brown:** Storm troopers, members of Hitler's Nazi-party militia, wore brown shirts. In Italy, Mussolini's Fascist party members wore uniforms with black shirts.
4. Lines 111–113, spoken by Cassius in Act III, Scene 1.

Vocabulary

gaunt (gônt) *adj.:* here, grim and forbidding.
vitality (vī · tal′ə · tē) *n.:* energy; vigor.
surly (sʉr′lē) *adj.:* bad-tempered; rude.

The Orson Welles production of *Julius Caesar* (Mercury Theater, New York, 1937).

To fit the play into modern dress and give it its fullest implication,[5] Mr. Welles has not hesitated to take his liberties with the script. Unlike Professor Strunk, however, who attempted to improve upon *Antony and Cleopatra,* he has not stabbed it through the heart. He has only chopped away at its body. You may miss a few fingers, even an arm and leg in the *Julius Caesar* you thought you knew. But the heart of the drama beats more vigorously in this production than it has in years. If the play ceases to be Shakespeare's tragedy, it does manage to become ours.

That is the whole point and glory of Mr. Welles's unorthodox, but welcome, restatement of it. ③

He places it upon a bare stage, the brick walls of which are crimson[6] and naked. A few steps and a platform and an abyss[7] beyond are the setting. A few steps—and the miracle of enveloping shadows, knifelike rays, and superbly changing lights. . . .

③ **EVALUATING AN ARGUMENT**

What is Brown's **opinion** of what Welles has done to Shakespeare's text?

---

6. **crimson** *adj.:* deep red.
7. **abyss** (ə · bis′) *n.:* deep gulf or pit.

Vocabulary

unorthodox (un · ôr′thə · däks′) *adj.:* unusual; not conforming to usual norms.

---

5. **implication** *n.:* suggested meaning.

His direction, which is constantly creative, is never more so than in its first revelation of Caesar hearing the warning of the soothsayer, or in the fine scene in which Cinna, the poet, is engulfed by a sinister crowd of ruffians.[8] Even when one misses Shakespeare's lines, Mr. Welles keeps drumming the meaning of his play into our minds by the scuffling of his mobs when they prowl in the shadows, or the herd-like thunder of their feet when they run as one threatening body. It is a memorable device. Like the setting in which it is used, it is pure theater: vibrant, unashamed, and enormously effective. ❹

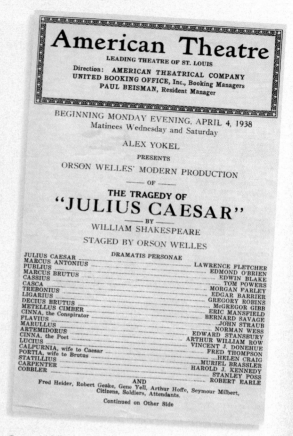

Orson Welles's popular production of *Julius Caesar* toured the country. This playbill is for a performance in St. Louis.

Bettmann/CORBIS.

> ❹ **ANALYZING STRUCTURE**
>
> In the previous two paragraphs, what aspects of the play does Brown discuss?

The theatrical virtues of this modern-dress *Julius Caesar* do not stop with its excitements as a stunt in showmanship. They extend to the performances. As Brutus Mr. Welles shows once again how uncommon is his gift for speaking great words simply. His tones are conversational. His manner is quiet. The deliberation of his speech is the mark of the honesty which flames within him. His reticent Brutus is at once a foil to the staginess of the production as a whole and to the oratory[9] of Caesar and Antony. He is a perplexed liberal, this Brutus; an idealist who is swept by bad events into actions which have no less dangerous consequences for the state. His simple reading of the funeral oration is in happy contrast to what is usually done with the speech.

George Coulouris is an admirable Antony. So fresh is his characterization, so intelligent his performance that even "Friends, Romans, countrymen" sounds on his tongue as if it

---

8. **ruffians** *n.*: toughs; hoodlums.
9. **oratory** *n.*: skilled public speaking.

Vocabulary

sinister (sin′is · tər) *adj.*: evil.

reticent (ret′ə · sənt) *adj.*: silent; reserved.

perplexed (pər · plekst′) *adj.*: uncertain.

idealist (ī · dē′əl · ist) *n.*: someone who is guided by ideals, or standards of perfection.

Cast members of *Julius Caesar* gather for a toast on January 4, 1938. Orson Welles is toward the center, holding a pipe.

Bettmann/CORBIS.

were a rabble-rousing harangue[10] which he is uttering for the first time. Joseph Holland's Caesar is an imperious[11] dictator who could be found frowning at you in this week's newsreels. He is excellently conceived and excellently projected. Some mention, however inadequate, must be made of Martin Gabel's capable Cassius, of John Hoysradt's Decius Brutus, of the conspirators whose black hats are pluck'd about their ears, and Norman Lloyd's humorous yet deeply affecting Cinna. ⑤

> **⑤ EVALUATING EVIDENCE**
>
> List several examples Brown gives as **evidence** to support his opinion of the acting.

It would be easy to find faults here and there: to wonder about the wisdom of some of the textual changes even in terms of the present production's aims; to complain that the whole tragedy does not fit with equal ease into its modern treatment; and to wish this or that scene had been played a little differently. But such faultfindings strike me in the case of this *Julius Caesar* as being as picayune[12] as they are ungrateful. What Mr. Welles and his associates at the Mercury have achieved is a triumph that is exceptional from almost every point of view. ⑥

> **⑥ EVALUATING AN ARGUMENT**
>
> How does the last paragraph affect the **credibility** of Brown's argument?

---

10. **rabble-rousing harangue:** scolding speech designed to arouse people to anger.
11. **imperious** (im · pir′ē · əs) *adj.:* arrogant; domineering.

---

12. **picayune** *adj.:* trivial; unimportant.

Analyzing Informational Text

Reading Check

1. What type of costumes does Welles use in his production of *Julius Caesar*?

2. Name four aspects of the play that Brown discusses in his review.

Test Practice

1. The writer's **opinion statement** about the play is best stated in —
   - **A** the first sentence of paragraph 1
   - **B** the last sentence of paragraph 1
   - **C** the last sentence of paragraph 2
   - **D** the first sentence of the last paragraph

2. To support his **opinion,** Brown discusses —
   - **F** the staging of the production
   - **G** the history of the play
   - **H** Shakespeare's biography
   - **J** Welles's previous successes as a director

3. One aspect of the production that Brown does *not* discuss in this review is the —
   - **A** actors' performances
   - **B** set
   - **C** costumes
   - **D** audience's reaction

4. How does Brown **structure** his review?
   - **F** He uses a cause-and-effect structure.
   - **G** He uses a comparison-contrast structure.
   - **H** He discusses different aspects of the production, one at a time.
   - **J** He opens by anticipating readers' objections.

5. Which of the following statements about the writer of this review is accurate?
   - **A** He is biased against the play.
   - **B** He is biased against modern-dress productions of Shakespeare.
   - **C** He presents a great deal of evidence to support his opinion.
   - **D** He does not give enough evidence to be convincing.

6. Which of these statements is *not* an **opinion**?
   - **F** "It is a memorable device."
   - **G** "But the heart of the drama beats more vigorously in this production than it has in years."
   - **H** "George Coulouris is an admirable Antony."
   - **J** "He places it upon a bare stage, the brick walls of which are crimson and naked."

SKILLS FOCUS

Reading Skills
Evaluate an author's argument.

7. The **tone** of this article is best described as —

A humorous

B sarcastic

C informal

D admiring

8. Brown tailors his argument to fit his **audience,** who are —

F high school students

G professional actors and directors

H readers of a New York newspaper

J listeners of a radio program

9. Before you decide whether you find Brown's critical review **credible,** you'd want to know more about —

A Orson Welles's movies

B William Shakespeare's comedies

C Julius Caesar's life and death

D Brown's qualifications as a reviewer

Constructed Response

Brown clearly gives a thumbs-up to Orson Welles's production of *Julius Caesar*. Do you give a thumbs-up to Brown's review? In a brief essay, evaluate Brown's review. First, summarize Brown's **opinion statement.** Then, discuss the **structure** and **tone** Brown uses for his review. Next, evaluate the types of **evidence** he uses and decide whether the evidence is sufficiently convincing. Finally, discuss how **credible** you find his argument—in other words, if you were able to see Welles's production, would you want to? (A chart like the one below will help you gather your notes.)

Evaluating a Review
Opinion statement:
Structure:
Tone:
Evidence:
Credibility:

Vocabulary Development

Clarifying Meanings: Words in Context

PRACTICE

Word Bank

gaunt
vitality
surly
unorthodox
sinister
reticent
perplexed
idealist

Answer the following questions for help clarifying the meanings of the Word Bank words.

1. *Gaunt* can mean "harsh; forbidding; grim"—or, when describing a person, "very thin; worn out." Why would Brown describe the stage setting as gaunt and proud? How do you imagine such a setting?

2. *Vitality, vital, revitalize,* even *vitamin*—all share a common Latin root word, *vita,* meaning "life." Describe a person or a situation that is full of vitality. What do you think is meant by a *vital organ,* such as the heart?

3. Is surly high on your list of favorite character traits? Think of someone you know or have observed who is frequently surly. What don't you like about his or her behavior?

4. What is it about Orson Welles's production of *Julius Caesar* that's unorthodox? What connotations does the word *unorthodox* have that *unusual* does not have?

5. Would you be comfortable in a situation that seemed sinister? Why? Can you think of a sinister character in literature?

6. Is an extremely reticent person likely to gossip or run for political office? Explain why or why not.

7. Some people find themselves perplexed when faced with a difficult situation or a confusing issue. What kind of problem might make you perplexed? Why?

8. In the play review, the character of Brutus is described as an idealist. What kind of person is an idealist? What kinds of activities might he or she get involved with?

The director and actor Orson Welles in 1951.
©Hulton-Deutsch/CORBIS.

SKILLS FOCUS

Vocabulary Skills
Use words in context. Demonstrate word knowledge.

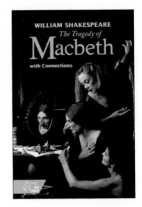

PLAY

Scottish Tragedy

Julius Caesar is not the only assassinated leader featured in a Shakespearean tragedy. In 1040, a Scottish chieftain named Macbeth killed King Duncan I and seized the throne of Scotland. Shakespeare dramatized this story in his tragedy *Macbeth*—a play whose characters grapple with family loyalties, greed, and the price of ambition. You may find that this tale of medieval intrigue provides shocking contrasts to *The Tragedy of Julius Caesar*. **This title is available in the HRW Library.**

PLAY

Chasing the Dream

Lorraine Hansberry's stirring drama *A Raisin in the Sun* takes us inside the home of the Younger family— five larger-than-life personalities cramped but not crushed by their small, shabby living space. Each of the Youngers has big dreams— and no one's dreams are bigger than those of Walter, who thinks that money will solve his family's problems. You'll be moved by this story of an African American family's fortunes, losses, and hopes. **This title is available in the HRW Library.**

PLAY

Uninvited Guest

Major General Tom Powers is a man who commands respect. As a dyed-in-the-wool army man and a proud husband and father, he enjoys all the comforts of suburban life. Then the impossible happens: A flying saucer lands in his backyard, and from it emerges a visitor named Kreton—a distinguished alien in an 1860s costume who is looking for Robert E. Lee. Gore Vidal's comedy *Visit to a Small Planet* is a wildly funny study of what happens when worlds collide—and unite.

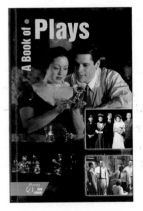

PLAYS

All the World's a Stage

Some of the greatest plays ever to hit the stage are compiled in *A Book of Plays.* Here you'll have a front-row seat to drama that is astonishing in scope—featuring everything from a heartbreaking family story (Tennessee Williams's *The Glass Menagerie)* to a witty dialogue (Dorothy Parker's *Here We Are)* to a page-turning whodunit (Susan Glaspell's *Trifles)*. The Russian playwright Anton Chekhov and the Irish playwright John Millington Synge add a distinguished international flavor to the collection. **This title is available in the HRW Library.**

Comparing a Play and a Film

Writing Assignment
Write an essay in which you compare a scene from a film to the play from which it was adapted, and analyze the film techniques the director uses.

Imagine that you're watching a film adaptation of *The Tragedy of Julius Caesar,* the play you read earlier in this chapter. Early in the movie, you notice that Cassius is missing and lines that he speaks in the play are instead showing up in Brutus's dialogue. Filmmakers often alter plays in order to convey personal visions, appeal to specific audiences, or create certain reactions in viewers. It's little wonder that adaptations can look and feel radically different from the plays that inspired them. In this workshop you will compare a scene from a film adaptation of a play with the same scene in the written play, and then you will analyze and evaluate some of the techniques used in the film.

Prewriting

Choose a Film and Focus on One Scene

On with the Show To begin, find a video of a film adaptation of a play you've read or one you'll read before watching the film. If you have trouble finding an adaptation, try one of the following suggestions.

- Browse a video store, looking for movies with familiar play titles.
- Read film reviews online and in newspapers and magazines.
- Ask a friend, teacher, or family member for a recommendation.
- Borrow a couple of videos from your school or public library. The librarian should be able to direct you toward film adaptations of plays.

Tunnel Vision Limit the scope of your evaluation by focusing on one important scene in the film. To find that scene, first sit down and **watch the video actively.** Pay close attention to each scene, and take notes on your reactions. Does a scene bring out a strong emotional response in you? Do you see a connection between the themes or issues in a scene and in your life? After watching the video, review your notes and select the scene to which you had the strongest reaction.

Compare the Film to the Play

What's New? Once you've chosen a scene from the film, re-read the same scene from the play and take notes on any differences. Specifically, write down ways in which the film scene's **narrative techniques** differ from the written scenes. Narrative techniques in the film will involve changes to the story itself, such as changes in

SKILLS FOCUS

Writing Skills
Write an essay comparing a play and a film. Choose subjects for comparison.

characters, setting, plot, dialogue, or theme. Ask yourself the following
questions to analyze the film's narrative techniques.

ANALYZING NARRATIVE TECHNIQUES

Characters, setting, and plot	Has the filmmaker eliminated, added, combined, or otherwise changed characters? Has the filmmaker changed the setting or plot? If so, how do the changes affect the story?
Dialogue	Are there differences in dialogue between the play and the film? For example, are lines added or cut in the film? Does a character in the film deliver lines that were spoken by another in the play?
Theme	Did the filmmaker alter the theme, or message, of the original story? How does the change affect the viewer's reaction to the story?

TIP Keep in mind that you'll probably need to view the film scene and read the play version several times as you make your comparisons. You should add new observations to your notes each time you view the film or read the play.

Pictures Speak? In addition to narrative techniques, filmmakers use film techniques to make a film from a play. **Film techniques** include using lighting, camera shots and angles, sound and music, and special effects to bring out a reaction in the viewer. For example, a filmmaker might combine ominous music, dramatic lighting, and a tilted camera angle to create suspense and make an audience worry that something bad is about to happen. Answer the following questions to analyze the filmmaker's use of film techniques.

ANALYZING FILM TECHNIQUES

Lighting	How is lighting used in the scene? Does it affect the mood of the scene?
Camera shots and angles	What types of camera shots are used—long shots, medium shots, close-ups? Why might the filmmaker use different shots? From what angles does the camera shoot the scene's characters and actions? How do the angles affect your reactions to the scene?
Sound and music	What music and sound effects are included? What effect do they create?
Special effects	Are there special effects that you wouldn't expect to see in a stage presentation of the play? If so, do they enhance your appreciation of the story or distract you from it?

One student took the notes on the following page while viewing Franco Zeffirelli's 1990 production of *Hamlet*. She will later look back at these notes to find specific **references** to the play and the film to support her thesis statement.

Plot: Act 1, scene 1, is cut. The audience doesn't learn the significance of the ghost's armor.

Setting: Film viewers see and hear the banquet, which is only described in the play.

Sound: Footsteps, soft music, and a moaning wind add to the suspenseful atmosphere.

Lighting: The battlements are moonlit with areas that are very dark. The lighting allows us to see the cold temperature through the icy breath coming from the characters.

Camera shots and angles: Camera angles show the characters on the battlements looking down on the celebration. Close-ups of Hamlet's face show that he's sweating and troubled.

Write Your Thesis Statement

What's It All About? Narrative and film techniques result from specific choices made by the filmmaker to create certain **aesthetic effects,** or emotional and intellectual responses, in the viewer. Look back at your viewing notes to see how you responded to the scene. Then, look at the notes you took on narrative and film techniques to see what the filmmaker did to create those responses. Write a **thesis statement** that identifies your reponses, as shown in this student example.

| DO THIS |

> In reworking Shakespeare's ghost scenes, director Franco Zeffirelli uses narrative and film techniques to create a suspenseful atmosphere and to generate feelings of empathy for Hamlet.

TIP Because you want to convey a serious and knowledgeable **tone,** choose your words carefully when writing your thesis statement.

Gather Evidence and Organize

Picking Up the Pieces Once you've written your thesis statement, look at the text of the original play and your notes on the film to find **evidence**—quotations or examples—to support it. For example, the Writer's Model on page 893 gives specific examples of how lighting and sound create the film's suspenseful atmosphere.

Putting It All Together Your essay combines a comparison of the narrative techniques with an analysis and evaluation of the film techniques. Because of this, you will use two organizational patterns.

- First, arrange your comparison of narrative techniques in **point-by-point order,** comparing points until you've covered them all.

- Next, arrange the film techniques by **order of importance,** discussing the most important technique either first or last.

SKILLS
FOCUS

Writing Skills
Write a thesis statement.
Gather and organize
information.

PRACTICE & APPLY 1 Compare a play to its film adaptation by analyzing the narrative and film techniques the filmmaker used. Then, write your thesis statement, gather evidence, and organize your essay.

Writing

Comparing a Play and a Film

A Writer's Framework

Introduction

- Provide an interesting opener.
- Introduce the original play and playwright, and the film adaptation and filmmaker.
- Clearly state your thesis.

Body

- Compare narrative techniques in point-by-point order.
- Analyze film techniques by order of importance.
- Use evidence to support your ideas.

Conclusion

- Remind readers of your thesis by restating it in different words.
- End with a closing thought or question that readers can ponder after they've finished reading.

A Writer's Model

Zeffirelli's *Hamlet*: A Ghost of the Original?

Are you the kind of person who thinks nothing can surpass the genius of Shakespeare, or do you wish someone would update the language and add effects to make his plays more interesting to a twenty-first-century audience? Sometimes you can get the best of both worlds. William Shakespeare's *Hamlet* and Franco Zeffirelli's film version of the play share the same characters and the same basic story. However, in reworking Shakespeare's ghost scenes, Zeffirelli uses narrative and film techniques to create a suspenseful atmosphere and to generate feelings of empathy for Hamlet.

Zeffirelli changes the plot of *Hamlet* to get straight to the main action and characters. In the play, the audience first encounters the ghost in Act 1, Scene 1. Audience members learn that the king, Hamlet's father, is dead and that a ghost in his armor is walking the castle's battlements at night. The characters in the scene think that the ghost's appearance may be an omen that hints at Denmark's troubled political situation, which includes a possible Norwegian invasion.

In the film, however, this scene is replaced by one of the king's funeral—a scene that is not in the play. By making this replacement, Zeffirelli has chosen to focus his film on the personal, rather than political, side of the story. As in the play, when Horatio and Hamlet first meet, Horatio tells Hamlet about the ghost on the battlements. Zeffirelli moves this exchange from Act 1, Scene 2 of the play to the beginning of his suspense-filled ghost scene.

(continued)

INTRODUCTION

Interesting opener

Play and playwright, film and filmmaker

Thesis statement

Comparison of narrative techniques:

1. Plot—play

Plot—film

(continued)

2. Setting—play

Quotation

Setting—film

Evaluation of film techniques:

1. Sound effects

2. Lighting

3. Camera angles

4. Camera shots

CONCLUSION

Restatement of thesis
Closing thought

Zeffirelli also adds to his story's setting. In the play, while Horatio, Hamlet, and friends await the ghost on the battlements, stage directions indicate "A flourish of trumpets, and ordinance shot off, within" (I.iv.7). Hamlet indicates that this is a part of the new king's custom of staying up late and carousing. The play's audience doesn't see the celebration; however, Zeffirelli's film does show it—full of warmth, color, music, and laughter. The celebration acts as a sharp contrast to the cold, dark, suspenseful atmosphere on the battlements where Hamlet encounters the ghost.

The film techniques Zeffirelli uses are as important as his narrative techniques. His ghost scene incorporates subtle yet important sound effects. Footsteps on the battlements, quiet notes of soft music, and the moaning wind add to the suspenseful atmosphere. They differ greatly from the lively music and laughter of the celebration.

Visually, the battlements are bathed in fog, harsh moonlight, and shadows. Icy clouds of breath float through the shot, chilling the viewer. The empty sky creates a sense of being up very high in a stony, isolated place. To create the visual contrast with the celebration, the camera angle shows Hamlet and the others standing on the battlements, looking down into the banquet hall through an opening in the roof.

When Hamlet and the ghost go off on their own, the camera follows Hamlet as he climbs a steep circular stairway to a higher portion of the battlements. Once Hamlet is there, the camera cuts back and forth from close-ups of the ghost as it tells its tale of horror to close-ups of Hamlet's face reacting. The audience sees every detail of Hamlet's sweating, pain-wracked face as he listens. This creates empathy for Hamlet, since we can vividly see his emotions and understand what is going on inside him.

Franco Zeffirelli's film version of *Hamlet* is interesting, dramatic, and entertaining. Although the play shares these qualities, viewers also benefit from Zeffirelli's gifted use of film techniques. The filmmaker has created a charged, suspenseful atmosphere in which the viewer feels empathy for Hamlet. While movie audiences miss out on the complexity of the original play, they may still enjoy sitting back and taking in the thrill of this suspenseful, fast-moving adaptation.

go.
hrw
.com

INTERNET
More Writer's Models
Keyword: LE5 10-10

PRACTICE & APPLY 2 Refer to the framework on page 893 and the Writer's Model above as you write the first draft of your essay. Include citations whenever you quote sources. For more on **crediting your sources,** see page 698.

Revising

Revise Your Essay

The Big Picture Writing that hasn't gone through the revision process is much like a piece of unfinished furniture. It will serve its purpose just fine in its rough state, but it's not until the final touches are done that the piece becomes truly beautiful. When you revise, you shape your ideas and their expression so that they can best achieve their desired effect. Read through your draft at least twice to evaluate and revise it, first for content and organization and then for style.

PEER REVIEW

Exchange your essay with a peer before you revise. He or she can help ensure that you discuss the narrative techniques in point-by-point order and the film techniques by order of importance.

➤ **First Reading: Content and Organization** Evaluate the content and organization of your essay, using the guidelines below as a **think sheet.** First, answer the questions in the left-hand column. If you need help answering them, refer to the tips in the middle column. Then, make the changes suggested in the right-hand column.

editor in charge

Rubric: Comparing a Play and a Film

▶ Evaluation Questions	▶ Tips	▶ Revision Techniques
❶ Is the opening engaging? Does the first paragraph introduce the play and its film adaptation? Does it include their creators?	▶ **Underline** the engaging opening. **Bracket** the introduction of the play, the film adaptation, and their creators.	▶ **Add** an intriguing question or an interesting quotation from the play or movie. **Add** a sentence that introduces the play, the film, and their creators.
❷ Does the thesis statement identify the responses of the viewer?	▶ **Highlight** the thesis statement.	▶ **Add** a thesis that identifies your responses to the film's narrative and film techniques.
❸ Is the essay well organized?	▶ **Label** the narrative and film techniques discussed in the essay.	▶ **Rearrange** the techniques so that all the narrative techniques are discussed first in point-by-point order, followed by all the film techniques organized by order of importance.
❹ Is the discussion of each technique supported with evidence?	▶ **Put a check mark** by each quotation and example from the play or film.	▶ **Add** evidence or **elaborate** on existing evidence.
❺ Does the conclusion restate the thesis? Does it leave the audience with a closing thought or question?	▶ **Underline** the sentence restating the thesis. **Double-underline** the closing thought or question.	▶ **Add** a restatement of the thesis. If necessary, **add** a sentence or two that gives the essay's readers something to consider after they finish reading.

Second Reading: Style Once you've revised the content and organization of your essay, you can then concentrate on your **style**—the unique way that you use language to express yourself and your ideas. One way to improve your style is to use vivid **sensory details** that appeal to the senses of sight, hearing, smell, taste, and touch. Try to add a variety of these details to your discussions of narrative and film techniques so that your readers can picture the scenes you're describing.

Style Guidelines

Evaluation Question	▶ **Tip**	▶ **Revision Technique**
● Does the essay include vivid details that appeal to the five senses in its discussions of narrative and film techniques?	▶ **Put a check mark** next to sensory details that describe the techniques, which you have already labeled.	▶ If necessary, **add** sensory details to the descriptions that lack them, or **reword** existing details to make them more vivid.

ANALYZING THE REVISION PROCESS
Study these revisions, and answer the questions that follow.

reword

> *bathed in fog, harsh moonlight, and shadows. Icy clouds of*
> Visually, the battlements are ~~dark and cold~~. The empty sky
> *breath float through the shot, chilling the viewer.*
> creates a sense of being up very high in a stony, isolated place.

rearrange

> The play's audience doesn't see the celebration; however,
> Zeffirelli's film does show it—full of warmth, color, music,
> and laughter. ⟨ *move up* ⟩

Responding to the Revision Process

1. How does rewording the first sentence improve the description of the film technique?

2. Why do you think the writer moved the last sentence to an earlier part of the paper?

SKILLS FOCUS

PRACTICE & APPLY ③ Revise the content and organization of your draft by following the guidelines on page 895. Then, use the guidelines on this page to evaluate and revise the style of your essay.

Writing Skills
Revise for content and style.

Publishing

Proofread and Publish Your Essay

Make It Shine! After you've revised your essay, be sure to proofread it. Check for and correct any errors in grammar, usage, and mechanics. Have someone else—a classmate, parent, or friend—proofread your paper, too. Two sets of eyes are better than one when it comes to proofreading.

Tell It to the World Now that you have written, revised, and proofread your essay, it's time for others to read it. Here are some suggestions for publication.

- Post your essay to an online bookstore or video outlet that invites people to submit comments on various videos.

- With a group of classmates, compile your essays into a classroom reference book. Future classes doing similar projects can then read your essays to get ideas for their own.

- Using **publishing software** and **graphic programs,** jazz up your essay to create a Web site dedicated to the play or film you have chosen. Ask for feedback from visitors to your site.

Reflect on Your Essay

The Final Take Finally, take a look back on what you have learned in the process of writing this essay. Closely examining your progress through each step of the process can help you recognize your strengths and weaknesses as a writer as well as your understanding of media presentations. Use these questions to focus your thoughts.

- Which stage of the writing process—prewriting, writing, revising, or publishing—was the most difficult for you? Why? Which skills do you need to sharpen to make that stage easier the next time you write?

- How did writing this essay help you understand the choices made by filmmakers?

- How will your knowledge of narrative and film techniques influence the way you view other films that are based on plays? other films in general?

- How has viewing the film influenced your reading of the play?

 **PRACTICE & APPLY** Take time to proofread your paper carefully. Then, look over the publishing options given above and select one to get your essay in front of an audience. Finally, answer the reflection questions.

 TIP Proofreading will help ensure that your essay follows English **conventions.** As you proofread, check that you have correctly punctuated items in a series, such as a list of narrative techniques. For more on **serial commas,** see Commas, 12f, in the Language Handbook.

COMPUTER TIP

To create a well-designed Web site, see *Designing Your Writing* in the Writer's Handbook.

SKILLS FOCUS

Writing Skills
Proofread, especially for correct use of commas.

Analyzing and Evaluating Speeches

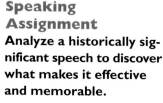

Earlier in this chapter you read Mark Antony's powerful eulogy presented at the funeral of Julius Caesar. Although his speech was full of sound reasoning, Antony turned the crowd into an angry mob through his passion and eloquent speaking style. Rhetoric—the art of speaking well—has played an important role in history as well as literature. Throughout history, speakers have used rhetoric to change people's minds, to sway their hearts, and to spur them to action. In this workshop you will have the opportunity to evaluate the impact of rhetoric in a **historically significant speech.**

Select a Speech

Lend Me Your Ears Your school and public libraries, history textbook, and the Internet are all good places to begin your search for a speech to analyze. Look for written texts, audio recordings, and videotapes of historically significant speeches. Think about topics that interest you, such as environmental protection, freedom of speech, or civil rights, and do a little research for speeches that have been made on those topics. You might also want to consider historical events, such as the fall of the Berlin Wall (1989), and find important speeches that were given during that time period. If possible, find a speech that you can watch on video. While the words and ideas expressed in a great speech are important, the speaker's voice, gestures, and body posture also add to the speech's effectiveness.

Analyze Content

Tricks of the Trade Most speeches—unless they are purely informational, like research presentations—contain elements of persuasion. That is, the speaker is trying to convince his or her listeners to believe an idea, support a cause, or take an action. Therefore, any analysis of a speech must include a look at the types of **arguments** and **rhetorical devices** a speaker can use to be persuasive. Examine the speech you've chosen for examples of each.

Arguments In order to persuade an audience, a speaker must provide **arguments**—reasons and evidence (facts, statistics, examples, and expert testimony) that show why listeners should change their minds or take action on an issue. Some common types of arguments used in persuasive speaking are listed on the next page.

- **argument by causation:** demonstrates how a cause-and-effect relationship supports the speaker's point

- **analogy:** explains or illustrates a point by making a literal comparison between two unlike things

- **appeal to authority:** cites an expert on a subject to support a point

- **appeal to emotion:** uses examples or language that appeals to the audience's emotional needs and values

- **appeal to logic:** gives facts, statistics, and examples that appeal to the listeners' minds

Rhetorical Devices Good speakers use **rhetorical devices**—certain ways of using language to persuade listeners or get their attention. Look for these common rhetorical devices in the speech you analyze.

> **TIP** Some speakers misuse rhetoric to cover up a lack of meaning or to mislead listeners. Be sure the speaker's arguments are sound and logical before making up your mind about any issue.

- **allusion:** referring to literature or to an actual event, person, or place

- **diction:** choosing words to create a certain **tone** (the attitude the speaker expresses toward the subject) or **mood** (the speech's overall impression on the audience)

- **metaphor:** imaginatively comparing unlike things

- **repetition:** repeating important words or phrases

- **rhetorical question:** posing a question without expecting an answer

- **parallelism:** using the same **syntax,** or sentence structure, to point out a similarity in ideas

Analyze Organization

Taking Orders You should also look at how a speech is organized. Good speeches are **coherent**—logically organized and showing a clear connection between ideas. Which of the following organizational patterns can you find in the speech you're analyzing?

- **deductive pattern:** The speaker states the thesis at the beginning of the speech, then gives arguments and reasons to support the thesis. Speakers organize their material **deductively** to move their audiences from general ideas to more specific ones.

- **inductive pattern:** The speaker first presents arguments and reasons, then states the thesis later in the speech. Speakers organize their material **inductively** to move their audiences from specific ideas to more general ones.

Analyze This! Read the excerpt on the next page from a speech given in Washington, D.C., by Chief Joseph of the Nez Perce. In 1879, Chief Joseph traveled to the nation's capital to speak with the country's

SKILLS FOCUS

Listening and Speaking Skills
Analyze content, organization, and delivery.

leaders. Although he was given assurances that his people would have justice, Chief Joseph didn't believe in words not supported by actions. The annotations on the left side illustrate the arguments and rhetorical devices Chief Joseph used in his speech.

Parallelism and Repetition

Appeal to emotions

Appeal to logic

Analogy

Metaphor and rhetorical question

Appeal to authority

Thesis
Appeal to emotions

. . . Good words do not last long unless they amount to something. Words do not pay for my dead people. They do not pay for my country now overrun by white men. They do not protect my father's grave. They do not pay for my horses and cattle. Good words do not give me back my children. Good words will not make good the promise of your war chief, General Miles. Good words will not give my people a home where they can live in peace and take care of themselves. I am tired of talk that comes to nothing. It makes my heart sick when I remember all the good words and all the broken promises. . . . If the white man wants to live in peace with the Indian he can live in peace. There need be no trouble. Treat all men alike. Give them the same laws. Give them all an even chance to live and grow. All men were made by the same Great Spirit Chief. They are all brothers. The earth is the mother of all people, and all people should have equal rights upon it. You might as well expect rivers to run backward as that any man who was born a free man should be contented penned up and denied liberty to go where he pleases. If you tie a horse to a stake, do you expect he will grow fat? If you pen an Indian up on a small spot of earth and compel him to stay there, he will not be contented nor will he grow and prosper. I have asked some of the Great White Chiefs where they get their authority to say to the Indian that he shall stay in one place, while he sees white men going where they please. They cannot tell me.

I only ask of the Government to be treated as all other men are treated. If I cannot go to my own home, let me have a home in a country where my people will not die so fast. . . .

Analyze Delivery

Not What but How Often, *how* a speaker delivers his or her message is as important as the message itself. When you view or listen to a speech, pay close attention to the speaker's **delivery**—how he or she uses voice and body. Delivery reinforces the speaker's tone and the speech's mood. For example, speakers who stand tall, speak clearly, use natural gestures, and make direct eye contact with audience members show that they care about their subject and audience. When listeners can feel the speaker's respect, they are more receptive to the speaker's message, which creates a positive mood.

Speakers who slouch, mumble, use no gestures, and stare directly at their papers show audience members that either they're uninterested in the subject or care little about what the audience thinks. This indifference from the speaker makes for an uninterested, unfriendly mood.

Evaluate a Speech

What's It Worth? The most important test of a good persuasive speech is your own reaction. As you evaluate a speech, use the questions in the following chart to form your own **judgments** and to support them with evidence.

EVALUATING SPEECHES

CONTENT

- **Arguments:** What kinds of arguments did the speaker use? Which were most effective? Why?
- **Evidence:** What kinds of evidence did the speaker provide (facts, statistics, examples, expert testimony)? What evidence did you find most effective? Why?
- **Rhetorical Devices:** What rhetorical devices did the speaker use? Which had the greatest effect?
- **Tone and Mood:** How did the speaker's language affect the tone and mood of the speech?

ORGANIZATION

- **Coherence and Clarity:** How was the speech organized (deductively or inductively)? Did the speaker make and support one point at a time? How clearly were the speaker's points connected to each other and to the speech's main idea?

DELIVERY

- **Voice:** Did the speaker speak clearly? Could you understand him or her without straining?
- **Gestures:** What kinds of gestures did the speaker use? Were they appropriate and effective? What important points did they reinforce?
- **Tone and Mood:** How did the speaker's voice and gestures express his or her attitude toward the audience and the speech's subject? How did the speaker's delivery affect the mood of the speech?

GENERAL

- **Effectiveness:** Did the speech broaden your view of the issue? Did it change your mind? Explain.

PRACTICE & APPLY 5 Depending on your access to audiovisual resources, choose one of these options to analyze a historically significant speech.

- If the speech is available on video and you have access to a player, answer all the questions in the above chart.
- If the speech is not available on video or you do not have access to a player, use the written text to answer only the questions about its content, organization, and general effectiveness.

Use your responses to the questions in the chart to write a one-paragraph evaluation of the speech.

SKILLS FOCUS

Listening and Speaking Skills
Evaluate a speech.

Test Practice

Evaluating an Author's Argument

DIRECTIONS: Read the following essay. Then, read and respond to the questions that follow.

The following essay discusses Brutus's speech to the Romans in Act III, Scene 2, of Julius Caesar.

Brutus's Funeral Speech
Phyllis Goldenberg

When Brutus speaks to the Romans, he has two purposes. His first (and surely more important) purpose is to convince his listeners that Caesar's murder was justified.[1] His second purpose is to introduce Mark Antony. Brutus gets a D– on his speech, while Antony walks away with an A+. Brutus's speech is practically a failure.

The most serious flaw in Brutus's speech is that his evidence is too vague. This is the essence of Brutus's argument: You know that I am an honorable man. (Is it honorable to assassinate a leader for the reasons Brutus offers?) I loved Caesar as much as you did, but Caesar was a threat to Rome because he was ambitious. Brutus is vague about Caesar's "crimes"; he never tells exactly how Caesar was ambitious or why his ambition was bad. In fact, the word *ambitious* is a poor choice because it has favorable connotations as well as negative ones. For example, we admire someone for being ambitious and striving to achieve a high goal. Yet Brutus assumes that all ambition is bad. He doesn't give any convincing evidence to prove that Caesar deserved to die.

Brutus's logic is faulty also. As part of his justification of Caesar's murder, he

says, "Had you rather Caesar were living, and die all slaves, than that Caesar were dead, to live all free men?" (Act III, Scene 2, lines 22–24). This is an example of the either-or fallacy,[2] one kind of faulty reasoning. Brutus says that only two positions are possible: Either Caesar is allowed to live and all Rome is in slavery, or Caesar is killed and all Rome is free. In reality there are many other possibilities between these two extremes. Why should we believe Brutus anyway? He doesn't substantiate[3] either of the claims he makes: Why does Caesar alive mean slavery? Why does Caesar dead mean freedom?

Brutus uses a powerful emotional appeal when he appeals to his listeners' patriotism, but it's not enough to justify Caesar's murder. He says, "Who is here so rude,[4] that would not be a Roman? . . . Who is here so vile,[5] that will not love his country?" (Act III, Scene 2, lines 30–32). He pauses for effect, knowing full well that no one will publicly admit to being unpatriotic. *Vile,* of course, is a loaded word, and it's "vile" not to love one's country.

---

2. **either-or fallacy:** type of faulty reasoning in which a situation is described as if there were only two choices when there may be several.
3. **substantiate** *v.*: confirm; show to be true.
4. **rude** *adj.*: rough; uncivilized.
5. **vile** *adj.*: evil.

---

1. **justified** *v.*: shown to be just, or right.

SKILLS FOCUS

Reading Skills
Evaluate an author's argument.

If we had only Brutus's speech in this act, we'd probably think it wasn't bad. He is very sincere. Yet Brutus is far less passionate and thus far less convincing to the mob than Antony is. Brutus doesn't use any of the persuasive devices that Antony uses. He also ignores rule 1 of persuasive speaking: Nobody believes anybody without proof. Brutus is vague and illogical, and his appeal to patriotism isn't enough to save his speech. Brutus may or may not be an honorable man, but he is certainly a terrible orator.[6]

---

6. **orator** (ôr′ət·ər) *n.*: public speaker.

1. The writer's **opinion statement,** or **claim,** appears in —
   A the first sentence of the first paragraph
   B the last sentence of the first paragraph
   C the first sentence of the second paragraph
   D the last sentence of the second paragraph

2. The author's **intent,** or **purpose,** is to —
   F prove that Brutus is honorable
   G persuade us that Brutus is a hero
   H evaluate Brutus's character
   J persuade us that Brutus's funeral speech is a failure

3. The writer's **purpose** controls the essay's **structure,** since the second through the fifth paragraphs deal with flaws in —
   A Shakespeare's logic
   B Brutus's character
   C Brutus's funeral speech
   D the play's plot

4. The essay's **evidence** consists of —
   F quotations from the play and references to specific events in the play
   G quotations from literary critics about the play
   H quotations from Shakespeare about the play
   J facts about the historical Brutus

5. The writer discusses Brutus's either-or fallacy as **evidence** to support which statement?
   A Brutus's evidence is too vague.
   B Brutus uses an emotional appeal.
   C Brutus's logic is faulty.
   D Brutus is insincere.

6. Which word *best* describes the essay's overall **tone?**
   F sympathetic
   G angry
   H persuasive
   J passionate

7. From the first sentence of the second paragraph, we can infer that the writer has **structured** her argument with —
   A the least important reason first
   B the most important reason first
   C the most important reason last
   D no apparent order

Constructed Response

8. Explain three ways to improve a speech. Use material from the text to support your answer.

Collection 10: Skills Review

Vocabulary Skills

Test Practice

Synonyms

DIRECTIONS: Choose the best synonym for the underlined word in each sentence.

1. Luka says that Mrs. Popov is indisposed.
   A busy
   B ill
   C away
   D forgetful

2. Smirnov seems to sneer at the idea of the emancipation of women.
   F kindness
   G restriction
   H respectability
   J liberation

3. Smirnov's harsh remarks about women sound malicious.
   A lighthearted
   B logical
   C spiteful
   D confused

4. Mrs. Popov is offended by Smirnov's impudence.
   F disrespect
   G stupidity
   H evilness
   J unattractiveness

5. Mrs. Popov's incoherent response to Smirnov's remark shows how upset she is.
   A humorous
   B insincere
   C rapid
   D rambling

6. John Mason Brown says that Orson Welles's production of *Julius Caesar* brings new vitality to the story.
   F energy
   G color
   H hope
   J insight

7. Orson Welles plays Brutus as a reticent character.
   A bold
   B fearful
   C reserved
   D serious

8. Brown considers this version of *Julius Caesar* to be new and unorthodox.
   F unusual
   G unremarkable
   H unclear
   J unsuccessful

9. In Welles's production, Brutus is depicted as a perplexed individual.
   A political
   B complex
   C uncertain
   D selfish

SKILLS FOCUS

Vocabulary Skills
Identify synonyms.

Test Practice

DIRECTIONS: Read the following paragraph from a draft of a student's comparison of a scene from the film and play versions of *The Crucible.* Then, answer the questions below it.

(1) The action in the film version of Arthur Miller's play *The Crucible* continues long after the play's curtain falls. (2) The final scene is shot with the camera behind three nooses, ominously observing the arrival of the prisoner cart. (3) The background music is sad and slow, and no other sound can be heard until the prisoners begin praying in unison as the ropes are placed around their necks. (4) Fortunately, this form of punishment is no longer commonly used in this country. (5) After a noise, the camera cuts to a shot showing only the top of the rope against the sky. (6) The viewer is left stunned by this sharp final image.

1. Which sentence could the writer add after sentence 1 to provide a clear thesis?
   A The film version is much shorter than the written play.
   B The movie uses sound and visual effects to show the exciting landscape.
   C The movie uses visual and sound effects to create a sense of tragedy.
   D In the film version, conversation is more important than action.

2. Which of the following should be added to sentence 1?
   F the name of the film's lead actor
   G the name of the filmmaker
   H the setting of the film
   J the film's distributor

3. Which sentence could be added to elaborate on sentence 3?
   A The soft music contrasts with the growing volume of the prayers to create a tense atmosphere.
   B The sound techniques make the viewer feel happy that John Proc-

tor is getting the punishment he deserves.
   C The sounds in the film scene are no more effective than the stage directions found in the play's original text.
   D This use of gentle sound makes the viewer feel relieved that the witch hunt is finally over.

4. Which sentence should replace sentence 5 in order to add sensory details?
   F After a scary noise, the camera cuts to a shot showing only the rope.
   G The camera cuts to a shot showing only a rope against a blue sky.
   H After a thump, the camera cuts to a shot showing only a taut rope against a blue sky.
   J After a terrible noise, the camera cuts to a shot showing only the hangman's rope.

5. Which sentence should be deleted to improve the organization?
   A 1   C 4
   B 3   D 6

SKILLS FOCUS

Writing Skills
Write an essay comparing a play and a film.

Collection 11

CONSUMER AND WORKPLACE DOCUMENTS

Music on the E-frontier

by Flo Ota De Lange
and Sheri Henderson

Introduction	908
Evaluating the Logic of Functional Documents	909
Following Technical Directions	913
Analyzing Functional Workplace Documents	916
Citing Internet Sources	921
Reading Consumer Documents	927
Writing Technical Documents	932
Writing Business Letters	934

Introduction

Music on the E-frontier

Music is your own experience, your own thoughts, your wisdom. If you don't live it, it won't come out of your horn.

—Charlie Parker

Joining the E-music Revolution

In this collection you'll step into the e-music revolution as you imagine you're part of a garage band composing and recording its songs.

Not so many years ago portable music was a person shoeing the sidewalk, shouldering a boombox some four cinderblocks large and just about as heavy. Flash forward in time, and the portable music scene has been radically transformed. It's almost as if someone had taken that old boombox, sent it down a rabbit hole, and pulled it out the other side as an MP3 player.

With the arrival of MP3 music files, almost any kind of music has become little more than a mouse click away. You need to be careful about what is legal on the music e-frontier, though. It is **legal** to rip tracks from a CD you own to a computer or to the Internet as long as they are for your own use and not for the use of other people. You may download free promotional tracks from the Internet; they are clearly marked, usually under the heading "Free Music." You may buy a track for your own use. It is **not legal** to download music that someone other than the copyright holder has put on the Internet.

Using Informational Materials

In this chapter you'll be relating **informational materials** to different aspects of the e-music revolution. You'll work with various kinds of documents—**workplace, consumer, public,** and **technical documents,** as well as **business letters.**

For example, you'll critique a magazine article on audio-speaker information, learn how to install a sound card, and review the consumer documents that come with a digital multitrack recorder. You'll also learn how to write conflict-resolution rules to settle conflicts that might arise in a garage band, and you'll learn how to write a business letter to promote that band.

In this section, you'll learn a great deal about reading consumer, public, workplace, and technical documents. You'll also become a more informed participant in the e-music revolution.

Some Types of Informational Materials

Consumer documents
- contracts
- instruction manuals
- product information
- warranties

Public documents
- government regulations
- schedules of events and services

Workplace documents
- business letters
- contracts
- instruction manuals
- memorandums

Technical documents
- how-to instructions
- installation instructions
- scientific procedures

Evaluating the Logic of Functional Documents

Computer Sounds

Think about how excited people must have been to hear a computer make its first beep and chirp. Back then few people thought of combining computers and music. Why would anyone do that? What kind of song could be made out of chirps and beeps?

Since then computer sound engineers have gotten so good at deciphering the tricks of 3-D sound that they can convince us a meteorite is hurtling at us from behind and cause us to duck!

In its broadest sense, *e-music* refers to any sound a computer can produce. It includes not only the latest CDs but also the sound of that meteorite, streaming audio, sound bites, and so on. So how does one get the best out of the e-music revolution? A good place to start is with your sound equipment.

Criteria for Functional Documents

In this lesson you'll have a chance to critique a magazine article that reviews computer speakers and sound cards. Such a **product review** is one type of **functional document.** Other types include **instructions, contracts,** and **warranties.** All functional documents share a basic goal: to help get things done. To be successful, they must meet two criteria:

- They must be **clearly organized** and **easily understood.**
- They must present information, procedures, or both in a **logical sequence.**

Failure to meet either of these criteria can cause serious misunderstandings. When documents confuse rather than inform a reader, a product is likely to get sent back. No matter how good a product may be, what good is it to you if you can't figure out how to make it work?

Logical Sequence

Here are three types of **logical sequences** and the kinds of functional documents that use them:

- **step by step**—recipes and other instructions (such as the directions for installing a sound card on page 914)
- **point by point**—legal documents (such as the Collaboration Agreement on page 918) and articles (such as "First Things First" on page 910)
- **highest to lowest (or lowest to highest),** which may be based on price or quality—product reviews (such as those on page 911)

Evaluating a Functional Document

As you read the following document, ask yourself these questions:

- Is each section clear and easy to understand?
- Is the sequence of information logical?

Read carefully. Can you spot any errors in logical sequence?

In the first part of the article, the marginal notes suggest the kinds of questions you might ask yourself. After that you're on your own.

SKILLS FOCUS

Pages 909–912 cover **Reading Skills** Evaluate the logic of functional documents.

AUDIO ASSERTIONS the expert audio magazine

Multimedia Sound Card and Speakers: Buying Guide and Reviews

First Things First

Before you plunk down your hard-earned cash on a new sound card and speakers, know what you already own:

1. If your computer has expansion slots, check to see if one slot is free. If all your slots are in use, check to see if one of them is housing your current sound card. You can probably use that slot for a new card.

> I'd better check my slots.

2. Your computer's user's manual will tell you its specific requirements, but here are some tips:

   A. Most of the newer sound cards use a PCI (peripheral component interface) bus, but some use an ISA (industry standard architecture) bus. Be sure that the card you choose fits the slot you have free. Also be sure that the new card can run at the speed required by your computer's free slot. PCI can run at clock speed of 33 or 66 MHz (megahertz). If the card you install will run at only 66 MHz and your computer requires 33MHz, your computer can be damaged. Most cards run at both speeds, but check it out to be sure.

   B. Power consumption is important. Your computer has a maximum that all slots combined may use—for example, 45 watts. You risk damaging your computer if you exceed this limit by plugging power-hungry cards into all of your slots.

> Whew! PCI or ISA? 33 or 66 MHz? Watts? I'll need my user's manual.

3. Regarding sound-card quality, keep the following points in mind:

   - **sampling rates:** Higher rates produce better quality sound.
   - **signal-to-noise ratio:** Higher ratios (decibels, or dBs) produce clearer sound.
   - **voices:** More voices produce richer sound.
   - **wave-table synthesis:** This method produces sound that is far superior to the older FM synthesis.
   - **MIDI** (musical-instrument digital interface) **input/output jacks:** These are necessary if you want to write or perform music and record your work.

> Signal-to-noise ratios, dBs, MIDI—I'd better look these technical terms up before I buy anything.

4. Does your computer have expansion slots? Some computers of the all-in-one variety come with fixed sound capabilities pre-installed. If you own such a model, your best option for improved sound is to upgrade your speakers.

> Wait a minute. This item is out of order. If I don't have any slots, I could have skipped items 1–3!

5. Finally, it's important to remember that your sound card and your speakers must work together. It will be useless to purchase top-of-the-line speakers if you do not have a sound card that can deliver the sound the speakers were built to accommodate, and the same goes the other way around. In general, the more you spend on speakers and sound cards, the more powerful your system will be. On the other hand, how much power do you *really* need?

> Need? Well, I guess I *want* more than I really *need*. I'll have to think hard about that one.

Buying Guide and Reviews

Multimedia Speakers	Price	Date*	Review
Scornucopia	$299	9/01	Best sub + satellite system to be heard, with an ultra-clean sound that's a bit cerebral and bass light. A thinking-person's choice.
Infinite-space	$180	10/00	Worthwhile midprice system with clean, if hygienic sound. A can't-go-wrong choice.
Aurllogic	$142	12/99	Great value with a tight, punchy sound. Knockout bass.
Airtight	$80	8/99	Nicely built and nice musical sound. Nice choice.

Sound Cards	Price	Date*	Review
SonicBombardier	$249.95	8/01	Excellent package, including almost everything you'll need to record your own music: SonicBoltblaster sound card (see below); full GS-compliant instrument set; great software bundle with award-winning MIDI sequencing software; cables.
SonicBoltblaster	$189.99	8/01	One of the best consumer-oriented cards on the market today, with MIDI input/output; headphone jack; 5.1-channel output; 1,024 wave-table voices, 64 of them hardware accelerated; > 96-dB signal-to-noise ratio; sample at 2, 4, and 8 megabytes; wave-table or FM synthesis; minimal software bundle.
SonicBonanza	$99.95	6/00	Surprisingly affordable for its features: card supporting 2, 4, or 6 speakers; wave-table synthesizer with capacity to support 64 hardware-accelerated voices and 1,240 software voices; > 96-dB signal-to-noise ratio; sample at 2, 4, and 8 megabytes. Good software bundle for MP3, MIDI, and WAV file conversion, playback, and rip to CD.
TD3S200	$24.95	2/98	Bargain-basement 3-D sound. Card supporting 2 speakers; samples up to 48 kHz; > 96-dB signal-to-noise ratio; 320 voices; wave-table or FM synthesis, software limited to drivers. Look for a used model at auction for an even better price.

*The date indicates the month and year in which a full review of the product appeared in *Audio Assertions*.

Understanding the Document

You may not understand all of the **technical language** in this article, but you can probably follow the writer's main ideas. Using the information in the article and the product reviews, you can pick out speakers and a sound card that meet your needs and your wallet.

Analyzing Informational Text

Reading Check

1. According to "First Things First," where in your computer do you put a new sound card?
2. What does the article say about matching sound cards to speakers?
3. Under what conditions can a sound card damage your computer?
4. Why should a sound card have high sampling-rate capability?

Test Practice

1. To correct the error in **logical sequence** in the article "First Things First," where should step 4 be moved?
   - **A** Directly before step 1
   - **B** Between steps 1 and 2
   - **C** Between steps 2 and 3
   - **D** After step 5

2. "First Things First" item 2A covers all of the following topics *except* —
   - **F** PCI and ISA buses
   - **G** 33 and 66 MHz
   - **H** finding your slot
   - **J** matching sound-card and slot capabilities

3. The product reviews in "Buying Guide and Reviews" are written in language that is —
   - **A** informal yet informative
   - **B** vague and imprecise
   - **C** too simplistic
   - **D** understandable only by an expert sound engineer

4. In "Buying Guide and Reviews," the speakers are arranged in which **logical sequence**?
   - **F** Step by step
   - **G** Point by point
   - **H** Highest to lowest
   - **J** Lowest to highest

5. Before buying one of the sound cards that are reviewed, readers will need to investigate all of the following aspects of their computer *except* its —
   - **A** MHz
   - **B** expansion slots
   - **C** wattage
   - **D** signal-to-noise ratio

6. The general relationship of price to quality shown in the "Buying Guide and Reviews" can *best* be expressed by which of the following statements?
   - **F** You get what you pay for.
   - **G** What you see is what you get.
   - **H** Cheaper products are better.
   - **J** Products are cheaper by the dozen.

SKILLS FOCUS

Reading Skills
Evaluate the logic of functional documents.

Application

Is it a **logical sequence** to place "First Things First" before "Buying Guide and Reviews"? Explain why or why not. What possible **reader misunderstandings** are created or avoided by the order of these two sections?

Following Technical Directions

How to Install a Sound Card

Early personal computers only beeped and chirped because they had no sound cards. Now, however, advances in computer-sound capabilities are so rapid that there is a practical value in knowing how to install a sound-card upgrade. Let's take a look at the directions for doing that.

Reading Technical Directions

The directions for using electronic, mechanical, and scientific products and procedures are called **technical directions.** You follow technical directions whenever you

- program your friends' numbers in your cell phone
- install a TV satellite dish on your roof
- do an experiment in biology lab

When you first look at them, technical directions may seem hard to understand. How will you ever be able to sort through all that information? All you have to do is **pay attention** and **follow each step carefully in the sequence presented.** Technical directions will teach you how to do whatever you want to do—for instance, install that sound-card upgrade. When you're finished, you can sit back, relax, and listen to awesome new sounds.

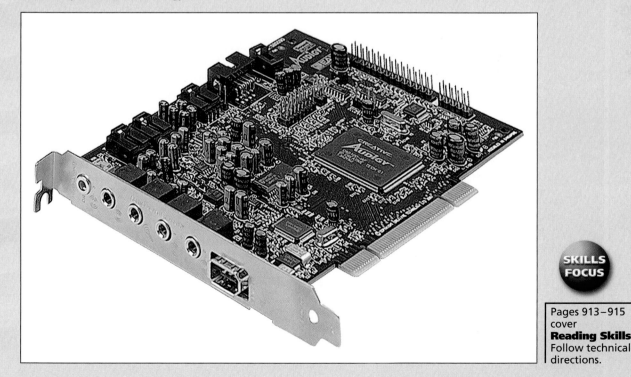

SKILLS FOCUS

Pages 913–915 cover
Reading Skills
Follow technical directions.

Installing a Computer Sound Card*

1. Be sure the computer is switched off.

2. To avoid damaging your computer, touch something metal on the outside of your computer with your fingers to discharge static electricity. Then, unplug your computer.

3. Open the computer case.

4. Locate the slot you want on the motherboard. See the user's manual for specific instructions on the location and types of slots on the computer.

5a. If the slot is empty, remove the screw that holds the metal slot cover in place, slide the cover out, and set both the screw and the cover aside for later.

5b. If the slot currently contains the old sound card, remove the screw that holds the card in place, and gently pull the card from the slot. It may need a firm yet careful tug. CAUTION: If rocked against the sides of the slot, the card might snap off in the slot or pry the slot from the motherboard. You will see an audio cable attached at one end to the sound card and at the other end to the CD- or DVD-ROM drive. Disconnect this cable from the drive by pulling gently.

6. Plug the new sound card into the prepared slot by pressing down firmly until the connector is fully inserted. It should be a tight fit, but do not use undue force. If you encounter resistance, take the card out, check for alignment and possible obstructions, and try again.

7. To be sure the card is in place, give it a gentle tug. It should resist and stay in place. The connector strip's metal conductors should also be just barely visible when viewed at eye level.

8. Find the screw and the slot cover that were removed in step 5a. Both may need to be replaced. If the card is built with an integrated slot cover, only the screw that will hold the new card in place will need to be replaced. Be sure the slot is covered. Then, tighten the screw to hold the new sound card in place.

9. Connect the audio cable to the sound card and to the CD- or DVD-ROM drive. Find connector pins on the sound card and on the back of the disk drive that correspond to the plugs on each end of the audio cable. Be sure to line these pins up carefully and press gently. As in step 6, if you encounter resistance, check to see that all pins are straight and that there are no other obstructions. Then, try again.

10. Close the computer case.

11. Connect the external speakers to their appropriate jacks.

12. Plug in the power cord, and turn on the computer and monitor. Once the computer is up and running, insert the CD that accompanies the sound card, and complete the software driver installation by following the on-screen instructions.

---

* Instructions for PC users.

Analyzing Informational Text

Reading Check

1. Why should you touch something metal before opening the computer case?

2. Describe the dangers involved in removing a sound card, according to step 5b. What precautions must be taken with the card, and what could go wrong?

3. How will you know when the sound card is properly in place?

4. How does the sound card connect to the CD- or DVD-ROM drive?

5. What information will you need to look up in the user's manual? At what point in the project should you get this information?

Test Practice

1. Which of the following steps should be broken into several steps for improved clarity?

   A Step 3

   B Step 4

   C Step 5a

   D Step 5b

2. How can you find out where to install the new sound card?

   F Look in the user's manual that came with your computer.

   G Find the location of the old sound card, if there is one.

   H Follow the audio cable from the CD- or DVD-ROM.

   J Do all of the above.

3. Users whose computers already have an old sound card installed will complete which step *first*?

   A Turn the computer on.

   B Remove the old card.

   C Install the new card.

   D Install the new software driver.

4. Where will you find the instructions for installing the software driver for the sound card?

   F Elsewhere in the instruction manual

   G In step 12

   H In step 9

   J On the CD that accompanies the sound card

Application

Challenge yourself by learning how to do something that requires following **technical directions.** Browse through the user's manual of a computer or software program until you find a skill you'd like to master. Before you start, carefully read *all* the directions to get the big picture. Then, follow each instruction step by step. When you finish, try it out— to check that you've accomplished what you set out to do.

SKILLS FOCUS

Reading Skills
Analyze technical directions.

Analyzing Functional Workplace Documents

A Workplace Document for Musicians

A time of great change is usually also a time of great opportunity. For example, the unparalleled growth of the Internet has contributed to the e-music revolution, and the e-music revolution combined with the advent of the World Wide Web has given songwriters and musicians new ways of reaching their audience. What does all this mean to you?

Let's say you've written a song. Since the process by which a songwriter develops the germ of an idea into a full-blown song varies with the individual, we'll pick up on the life of your song at the point when your band is playing it for the very first time. You enter the rehearsal studio. Your fellow musicians are tuning up their instruments. What happens then?

You pull out a functional workplace document. A what? A **functional workplace** document can be defined as any document that helps people get things done effectively. One of the workplace documents that help a songwriter and a band get things done is a **music lead sheet.** Let's take a look at one.

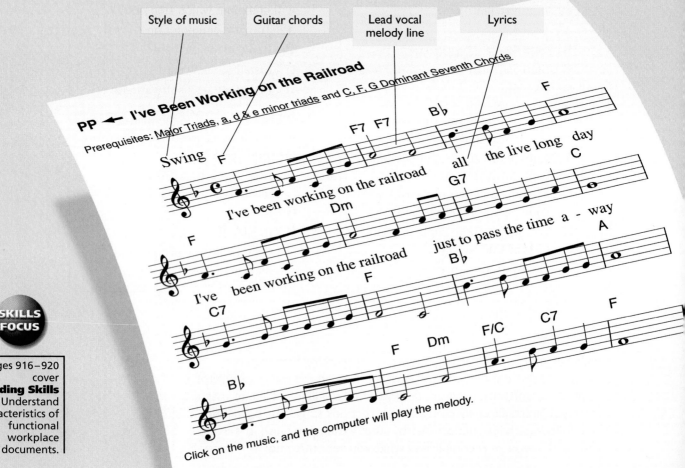

Style of music   Guitar chords   Lead vocal melody line   Lyrics

SKILLS FOCUS

Pages 916–920 cover **Reading Skills** Understand characteristics of functional workplace documents.

916

Analyzing a Lead Sheet

As you can see, a lead sheet includes several types of information about a musical piece:

- style of music
- guitar chords
- lead vocal melody line
- lyrics

The lead sheet provides this information clearly and concisely. It enables band members to learn a song quickly and efficiently, thus cutting down on rehearsal time and on recording time and costs.

Emphasizing Important Points

Most workplace documents rely on elements such as **font style, headers,** and **graphics** to emphasize important points and present information clearly. Lead sheets, in contrast, rely on the traditions of music notation. Music is formatted on a five-line staff begun with a clef. Even people who are not musicians often know what treble and bass clefs look like because those symbols have come to stand for music, as in the cartoon below.

Analyzing a Collaboration Agreement

Another type of workplace document in the field of music is one that specifies who owns a work and how royalties will be divided. Say you and your fellow band members have written a song that you want to publish yourselves. You have created something of potential value. How will you divide up the royalties that you are sure will come rolling in? You can prepare for this eventuality by signing a **collaboration agreement,** a kind of **contract.**

Let's look at how two musicians handled this problem. Sara Songster wrote the lyrics and Mike Melodic wrote the music to "All Day," a song they published themselves. They agreed to split any royalties fifty-fifty, and they signed the collaboration agreement that appears on the next page.

COLLABORATION AGREEMENT
Self-published Musical Composition

Date: _2/8/02_

In a Collaboration Agreement dated _February 8, 2002_, Sara Songster and Mike Melodic have agreed that they are equal co-authors of both the words and the music of the song titled "All Day," hereinafter called the Composition.

I.   The worldwide copyrights for the Composition, and any and all extensions and renewals thereof, are owned as follows:

> Sara Songster: undivided 50 percent
> Mike Melodic: undivided 50 percent

II. Sara Songster and Mike Melodic are entitled to administer their respective copyright shares in the Composition.

III. The Composition is to be registered with the U.S. Copyright Office, ASCAP, BMI, and/or SESAC, and other U.S. and foreign music agencies, in accordance with the provisions of this Agreement.

IV. The Authors' share of all royalties and other earnings derived from the Composition are to be apportioned and paid as follows:

> Sara Songster: undivided 50 percent
> Mike Melodic: undivided 50 percent

V.   The Publishers' share of all royalties and other earnings derived from the Composition are to be apportioned and paid as follows:

> Sara Songster: undivided 50 percent
> Mike Melodic: undivided 50 percent

Signed:

Sara Songster _Sara Songster_ Date _2-8-02_

Mike Melodic _Mike Melodic_ Date _2/8/02_

Analyzing the Document

This collaboration agreement is based on a straight-down-the-middle, fifty-fifty split. There are, of course, other ways to split proceeds from a self-published song. For example, if Sara Songster had written not only the lyrics but also parts of the melody, her share might be 60 percent and Mike Melodic's, 40 percent. Royalty income can be split in a variety of ways, depending on the number of people involved and each person's contribution. A collaboration agreement is important because it is a **legally binding document** (assuming the parties are old enough to enter a binding contract). It eliminates surprises by settling the matter of shares before there is any royalty income to pay out.

The collaboration agreement on page 918 makes effective use of **structure** and **format** to achieve its purpose. Some of its features are

- a centered **title,** or **header,** clearly stating the purpose of the document
- a **new section** for each major point
- **numerical headers** for each major section
- **spacing** between each major section
- **indentation**

The information in the collaboration agreement also follows a **logical sequence:**

1. It first lists copyright shares (I).
2. In the next two steps (II, III), it defines issues related to copyright.
3. It defines royalty shares of each signer as author (IV) and publisher (V).

Analyzing the Elements of Workplace Documents

Let's take a closer look at common elements of many effective workplace documents.

Structure

Written text is often daunting to the human eye when black type stretches on with nary a white space in sight. By the time a reader gets to the end, the beginning might be long forgotten. To remedy this problem, writers break text into sections. The **sections** in a functional document might be a short paragraph or maybe only a sentence.

In a legal document like the one on page 918, each **main idea** is given its own **section,** separated by a line of **space.** This format makes it simple to locate a particular point among many. Separating points in this way also increases the likelihood that the entire text will be both read and understood.

Sections are often introduced by **headers,** such as **titles** and **subtitles.** In this document the section headers are **roman numerals.** The numbers help readers locate information easily. A person who wants to talk about a particular point can simply cite the number of the section and begin the discussion.

Sequence

The **sequence,** or order, in which ideas are presented makes a big difference to a reader's understanding. Sequence governs the flow of a document and facilitates comprehension. Some common types of sequencing are

- chronological
- alphabetical
- spatial
- logical

Most functional documents follow a **logical sequence,** such as the **point-by-point** (numbered) sequence used in the collaboration agreement (page 918) or the **step-by-step sequence** used in technical directions, as in "Installing a Computer Sound Card" (page 914).

Format

The **format,** or design, of a document highlights important information and focuses the reader's attention on key words, sections, and ideas. To format a document, a designer draws on

- **formatting elements**—bold or italic type, margin width, indentation, line spacing
- **graphic elements**—drawings, photographs, and other artwork
- **design elements**—placement of the text and graphics on the page, use of white space, choice of color

Analyzing Informational Text

Reading Check

1. What does the music lead sheet help musicians do?
2. What are some of the most common **structural elements** of functional workplace documents?
3. What type of **sequence** does the collaboration agreement use?
4. How have Sara Songster and Mike Melodic divided their royalties?

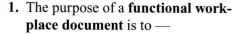 Test Practice

1. The purpose of a **functional workplace document** is to —
   A increase paperwork
   B have something to download
   C help people get things done
   D reduce work

2. A music lead sheet is formatted —
   F in paragraphs
   G on a five-line staff
   H with colored headers
   J by indentations

3. The **main points** in the collaboration agreement are indicated by —
   A roman numerals
   B italic type and a line of space

   C boldface key words
   D titles that summarize each main idea

4. The collaboration agreement uses all of the following **elements** *except* —
   F indentations
   G sections
   H graphics
   J spaces

5. The collaboration agreement follows which type of **sequence**?
   A Point by point
   B Step by step
   C Alphabetical
   D Spatial

Application

A Web site can be considered a functional document. Log on to the Internet, and go to the home page of a Web site you visit regularly. Analyze the structure and format of that page. Then, see if you can identify a sequence used to present information to the viewer. How effectively has the page designer used graphic, design, and formatting elements? How could the page be improved? If you don't have access to the Internet, use the Web site shown on page 207.

SKILLS FOCUS

Reading Skills
Analyze functional workplace documents.

Citing Internet Sources

Following Your Research Trail

The Internet is what made the e-music revolution possible, and any information on the e-music world you might want to research is only a mouse click away—whether it is how to use your computer as a composing device or how to understand 3-D sound.

When you prepare a report on e-music (or any other topic) using information you find on the Internet, you must include an orderly list of the sources you used. This list, which appears at the end of the report, is called a *Works Cited* list. Its purpose is to allow your readers to follow your research trail.

Documenting Internet Sources

When you cite a printed book, you can usually assume your reader will be able to find the book in a library. But online information is frequently updated, daily in some cases. Therefore, Internet sources require more documentation than print sources do.

You cannot, of course, be expected to document changes made in a Web site between the time you make your notation and the time your reader goes to the site to find the work. You should, though, give your reader as much information as you have. In particular, it is crucial to reproduce exactly the **URL** (uniform resource locator), or Internet address.

How do you cite sources you find on the Internet? Do you do it as if you were citing a book, or do you do something else? In the sections that follow, you'll learn how to cite works from the World Wide Web.

The box below shows the general format for an online source. The chart on page 922 lists in greater detail the **order** in which items should appear in your citations. It is a long list, and your *Works Cited* list will not likely include every item on the list.

The conventional punctuation marks that you should use appear in boldface within brackets. For example, a period will be noted as "[.]." Where no punctuation appears in brackets (as in item 14), simply insert a space and go on.

GENERAL FORMAT FOR AN ONLINE SOURCE

Author's Last Name, Author's First Name (if known). "Title of Work."
  Title of Web Site or Database. Date of electronic publication. Name
  of Sponsoring Institution. Date information was accessed <URL>.

Note: Enclose an electronic address, or URL, in angled brackets. If the URL must continue on a new line, divide the address immediately after one of the slash marks within it. Do not use a hyphen or any other mark of punctuation to divide the address.

Pages 921–926 cover **Reading Skills** Understand how to cite Internet sources in a *Works Cited* list.

Order in Which Information Is Presented in an Internet Citation

1. Author's Last Name [,] Author's First Name and Middle Initial (if given) [,] abbreviation such as Ed. (if appropriate) [.]

2. ["] Title of Work Found in Online Scholarly Project, on Database, or in Periodical ["] *or* ["] Title of Posting to Discussion List or Forum (taken from the subject line) [.] ["] followed by the description Online posting [.]

3. Title of Book (underlined) [.]

4. The abbreviation Ed. followed by Name of Editor (if relevant and not cited earlier, as in Ed. Susan Smith) [.]

5. Publication information for any print version of the source: City of Publication [:] Name of Publisher [,] year of publication [.]

6. Title of Scholarly Project, Database, Magazine, Professional Site, or Personal Site (underlined) [.]

7. Name of Editor of Scholarly Project or Database (if available) [.]

8. Volume number, issue number, or other identifying number of the source (if available) [.]

9. Date of electronic publication, posting, or latest update (often found at the bottom of the site's home page) [.]

10. Name of Subscription Service [,] and, if a library, Name of Library [,] Name of City [,] and Abbreviation of State in which library is located [.]

11. For a posting to a discussion list or forum, Name of List or Forum [.]

12. If sections are numbered, number range or total number of pages, paragraphs, or other sections (if information is available) [.]

13. Name of Institution or Organization Sponsoring or Associated with the Web Site [.]

14. Date on which source was accessed

15. [<] Electronic address (URL) of source [>] *or,* if a subscription service, [<] URL of service's main page (if known) [>] and [[] Keyword: Keyword Assigned by Service []] *or* [[] Path: sequence of topics followed to reach the page cited, as in first topic [;] second topic [;] third topic [;] and so on, ending with the page you are citing []] [.]

Sample Citations

Let's look now at some citations for **consumer, public, and workplace sites**—sources you might find when surfing the Internet for information about e-music. (Some of these are made-up sources.)

All of the sample citations in this collection follow the style of the Modern Language Association (MLA). You can look at the MLA's stylebook in the library for more information on how to prepare citations. Other styles for documenting sources are also available and acceptable. The style you use is less important than choosing one and sticking to it. Be sure to ask your teacher whether he or she wants you to follow a particular style.

Sample Works Cited
Citations for Consumer, Public, and Workplace Documents

Product Information from a Commercial Site

"About the Latest Sound Cards." Sound Cards Update Page. 10 Aug. 2001.
New Sounds 4 Sept. 2001 <http://www.NewSoundstoday.com/
article/index.asp>.

Article from an Online Nonprofit Magazine Dedicated to Protecting Consumers

Sleuthing, I. B. "Sound Cards and Speakers: Buying Guide and Reviews."
Audio Assertions 8 Aug. 2001. 7 Sept. 2001 <http://
www.audioassertions.org/main/article/soundcard/1.html>.

Article from a Reference Database (Encyclopedia)

"Musical Notation." Electric Library Presents: Encyclopedia.Com. The
Columbia Electronic Encyclopedia, Sixth Ed. 2000. Columbia UP.
15 July 2001 <http://www.encyclopedia.com/articles/08892.html>.

Online Information from a University Library Site

The Hoagy Carmichael Collection. 1 Nov. 1999. Digital Library Program
and The Archives of Traditional Music at Indiana U. 4 Sept. 2001
<http://www.dlib.indiana.edu/collections/hoagy/index.html>.

Copyright Forms from the Library of Congress (Government Office)

United States. Library of Congress. US Copyright Office. Form PA—For a
Work of the Performing Arts. Washington: GPO, 1999. 30 Sept.
2001 <http://www.loc.gov/copyright/forms/formpa.pdf>.

Information from a Company's FAQ Page

"Supermusicnotation Software." The Music's Muse, Inc. 3 Jan. 2001
<http://www.themusicsmuse.com/corp/faqs/faqslist.html>.

Posting to a Discussion List (Message Board)

Chart Climbers. "Why Surfers Pause and Pass." Online posting. 3 June
2001. Way Kool Net. 19 Sept. 2001 <http://www.waykoolnet.com/
mboards/boards.cgi?board=prgm&read=9218>.

Quotation from an E-mail Communication

Nguyen, W. "Re: 3-D sound, how to do it cheaply." E-mail to the author.
21 Aug. 2001.

Using Note Cards

As you find sources on the Internet, it is a good idea to record the information you will need for your *Works Cited* list on three-by-five inch note cards. You can also include other important information about your sources on these cards. Here are some examples. (Some of these are made-up sources.)

Source type: Public document
What it is: Online interview
Author(s): none listed
Title: EMP Interviews: Nick Hornby
Other Information: Experience Music Project is a museum in Seattle, Washington, devoted completely to music. The site had last been updated on Sept. 4, 2001. That was the day I visited. A lot of what the site has is digital, so it's very useful for doing research. You could spend days on this site.
URL: http://www.emplive.com — I went to the home page, then to archives, then EMP Interviews, then Nick Hornby.

Source type: Consumer document
What it is: Online consumer newsletter
Author(s): Stewart Cheifet
Title: Hardware Damage from Incorrect Clock Speed in PCI Cards
Other information: from Inside the Internet newsletter, June 1999 [vol. 6, issue 8], page 3. Published by Superior Technical Data, Inc. A really clear explanation of the problem and how to avoid it. Accessed on Sept. 3, 2001.
URL: http://www.suptechdata.com/text/press/letter.html

Source type: Workplace document
What it is: Reference source
Author(s): none listed; published by Mpeg.TV and edited by
Tristan Savatier
Title: MPEG Audio Resources and Software
Other Information: A good overview of MPEG audio and a
place to start getting other resources. The page had been last
updated May 31, 2000. I accessed it on August 31, 2001.
URL: http://www.mpeg.org/MPEG/audio.html

Formatting a *Works Cited* List

The final step in writing your report is compiling all the sources you have used in a *Works Cited* list. Follow these formatting steps:

- Begin a new page. At the top of the page, center the title Works Cited.

- Alphabetize your sources by the last name of each entry's author (or first author listed if there are more than one). If no author is cited, alphabetize the source by the first two words in the title, ignoring *A, An,* and *The.*

- If you used two or more sources by the same author, use the author's full name in the first entry only. For the other entries, type three dashes in place of the name, followed by a period and the rest of the citation.

- Double-space the list, and begin each entry at the left margin. If an entry runs longer than one line, indent the succeeding lines five spaces.

Analyzing Informational Text

Reading Check

1. How does a *Works Cited* list help others?
2. How do Internet citations differ from citations for printed materials?
3. What style is followed in the sample citations on page 923?
4. What style should you follow in preparing your *Works Cited* list?

Test Practice

1. According to MLA style, when you cite an Internet source, what is the *last* item mentioned?
   - **A** The author's first name
   - **B** The date you accessed the source
   - **C** The publisher
   - **D** The URL

2. According to MLA style, when you cite an Internet source, where should you put the date that you accessed the site?
   - **F** At the very end of the citation
   - **G** At the very beginning of the citation
   - **H** Just before the URL
   - **J** Just after the URL

3. According to MLA style, which is the correct way to cite a URL ?
   - **A** www.hrw.com
   - **B** http://www.hrw.com
   - **C** //www.hrw.com
   - **D** <http://www.hrw.com>.

4. How would a work with no author be alphabetized in a *Works Cited* list?
   - **F** Use Anonymous as the author.
   - **G** Alphabetize by the first two words in the title, excluding *A, An,* or *The.*
   - **H** Place two dashes and a period; then, alphabetize by the title, as above.
   - **J** Alphabetize by the first word in the URL.

5. In preparing your *Works Cited* list, you should —
   - **A** use cursive handwriting
   - **B** always follow MLA style
   - **C** not be concerned about the style you use
   - **D** follow the style your teacher requests

Application

SKILLS FOCUS

Reading Skills
Analyze Internet citations on a *Works Cited* list.

Prepare a *Works Cited* list using the sources listed on the note cards shown on pages 924–925. Follow the MLA style used in the examples listed on pages 921–923. Then, if you have access to a computer, find three other *credible* Internet sources dealing with e-music, and add them to the *Works Cited* list.

Reading Consumer Documents

Messages from the Manufacturer

The band has learned your song, and now you are ready to record it. You are standing in a working studio, surrounded by the latest in digital recording equipment. When a recording studio makes an investment in digital electronic equipment, it pays attention to the **consumer documents** that come with the equipment. Why? Because the studio's owners know from experience that the **contract, warranty, product information,** and **instruction manual** contain information vital to the smooth operation of the equipment.

Elements Versus Features

They have learned the difference between the elements and the features of a warranty, for example. What is the difference between elements and features, you ask?

For a moment, think of cars. You know that all cars have engines, transmissions, accelerators, and brakes. These are **elements**—the basic parts—of all cars. But not all cars have leather upholstery. Leather seats are a feature of some makes and models. **Features** are what make a model distinct from other models out there.

Similarly, all **warranties** contain certain **elements:** They all exist to assure the buyer (you) that the product will live up to the claims of the manufacturer. They also specify what the manufacturer will do if the product fails to deliver as promised. These elements are basic to all warranties.

The **features** of a warranty, on the other hand, are what make some warranties better than others. For example,

say you are looking at two MP3 players that appear identical except for their names. How do you decide which one to buy? Try looking at the warranties. Which warranty offers you a better deal if you need to have the item repaired? Which provides longer coverage? In other words, which warranty has better features?

Elements of Consumer Documents

Here are some different types of consumer documents and the **elements** each type of document contains:

- **product information**—descriptions of the product and what it will do for you
- **contract**—a legal agreement spelling out the rights and obligations of the purchaser and the manufacturer, seller, or service agency
- **warranty**—a legal document stating what the manufacturer will do if the product fails to live up to the manufacturer's claims and what the buyer must do to obtain service
- **instruction manual**—instructions on how to use the product and how to troubleshoot problems
- **technical directions**—directions for installation and use

The next three pages show examples of consumer documents. For the contract on page 928, boxed notes help you identify key elements and some features. As you read the documents, look for other elements and features.

Pages 927–931 cover
Reading Skills
Understand elements of consumer documents.

Aulsound Extended Service Contract

CONTRACT

Element: offers repair when warranty expires.

ADMINISTRATOR

Aulsound Warranty Service Corporation
P.O. Box 840001
Century City, CA 90067
SERVICE CONTRACT AGREEMENT
Digital Multitrack Recorder DMR88

TERMS AND CONDITIONS

Element: details of coverage. **Feature:** two years parts *and* labor.

Details of coverage. This Service Contract provides coverage of any operating parts or labor required for the product listed above, for two years from date of original purchase. There will be no cost to the Purchaser for any authorized covered repair that is performed by one of our highly skilled service associates.

Element: limitations.

Limitations. This Service Contract covers product failures occurring during normal use. It does not cover misuse or abuse of the product during delivery, installation, or setup adjustments. It does not cover damage that occurs while adjusting consumer controls, loss of data or programming support, unauthorized repair, customer-sponsored specification changes, cosmetic damage, or simple maintenance as recommended in the product owner's guide. It also does not cover repairs that are necessary because of improper installation or improper electrical connections. Consequential or incidental damages are not covered. Damage due to acts of God are not covered.

Element: maintenance requirement.

Maintenance requirement. The Purchaser must maintain the product in accordance with the requirements or recommendations set forth by the manufacturer to keep this Service Contract in force. Evidence of proper maintenance and/or service, when required by Administrator, must be submitted to validate a claim.

Element: unauthorized-repair clause.

Unauthorized-repair clause. IMPORTANT: Unauthorized repairs may void this Service Contract. The cost of unauthorized repairs will be the responsibility of the Purchaser.

Element: transfer of ownership. **Features:** twenty-five-dollar fee and registration within fifteen days.

Transfer of ownership. This Service Contract is transferable with ownership of the product. Transfer may be accomplished only if the Purchaser mails or delivers to the Administrator a twenty-five dollar [$25.00] transfer fee and registers the name and address of the new owner within fifteen [15] days of change of ownership.

Element: cancellation clause. **Features:** cancel any time for pro-rated refund; 100 percent if within thirty days.

Cancellation clause. This Service Contract may be canceled by the Purchaser at any time, for any reason. In event of cancellation, we will provide a pro-rated refund minus reasonable handling costs and any claims that may have been paid. Any cancellation requested by the Purchaser within thirty [30] days of the Service Contract application date will be 100 percent canceled by the Administrator.

Element: contract insurance.

Contract insurance. Your Service Contract is fully insured by Aulquiet Insurance Company, 80 Sampler Way, Los Angeles, CA 90017. Purchasers who do not receive payment within sixty [60] days of submitting a pre-authorized covered claim may submit the claim directly to Aulquiet Insurance Company, Contractual Liability Claims Department, at the above address.

Element: renewal clause.

Renewal clause. This Service Contract may be renewed at the discretion of the Administrator. The renewal premium will be based on the age of the covered product, current service costs, the covered product's repair history, and actuarial data.

Troubleshooting Guide

If you encounter problems operating your Aulsound
DMR88 or if the product does not work as expected, look
up the problem in this table, and follow the advice provided.

PROBLEM	ADVICE
The DMR88 does not turn on.	• Make sure that the power cord is plugged into an AC wall outlet. • Check the AC IN connector at the rear of DMR88. • Make sure that the DMR88 power switch is in the ON position. • If there is still no power, contact your Aulsound dealer.
No sound is coming from a connected music source.	• Make sure that the MONITOR LEVEL control is raised. • Make sure that the FLIP and MONITOR SELECT switches are set correctly.
The DMR88 does not record.	• Make sure that the disc's write-protect tab is set to UNPROTECT. • Make sure that the PLAY function is not on. • Press a REC SELECT button, and make sure that the track is ready to record. • Make sure that the signal you wish to record has been selected at the recording source for the appropriate track. Use the CUE LEVEL control to determine whether the signal is being sent to the track.
Lever meters do not indicate signal levels.	• Make sure that the track you wish to record has been selected. • Press the REC button, and make sure that the DMR88 is in RECORD-PAUSE mode.
Recordings play back at the wrong pitch.	• Make sure that the PITCH function is not set at VARIABLE. • Make sure that the 1/2 PLAY function is turned off.

FCC* Information (USA)

1. **IMPORTANT NOTICE: DO NOT MODIFY THIS UNIT!**
   This unit, when installed as indicated in the instructions contained in this manual, meets FCC requirements. Modifications not expressly approved by Aulsound may void your authority, granted by the FCC, to use this product.

2. **IMPORTANT:** When connecting this product to accessories and/or another product, the high-quality shielded cables supplied with this product MUST be used. Follow all installation instructions. Failure to follow instructions could void your FCC authorization to use this product in the United States.

3. **NOTE:** This product has been tested and found to comply with the requirements listed in FCC Regulations, Part 15 for Class "B" digital devices. Compliance with these requirements provides a reasonable level of assurance that your use of this product in a residential environment will not result in harmful interference with other electronic devices. This equipment generates and uses radio frequencies and, if not installed and used according to the instructions found in the user's manual, may cause interference harmful to the operation of other electronic devices. Compliance with

FCC regulations does not guarantee that interference will not occur in all installations. If this product is found to be the source of interference, which can be determined by turning the unit OFF and ON, try to eliminate the problem by using one of the following measures:

- Relocate either this product or the device that is being affected by the interference.
- Utilize other outlets that are on different branch (circuit breaker or fuse) circuits, or install AC line filter(s). In the case of radio or TV interference, relocate or reorient the antenna.
- If the antenna lead-in is a 300-ohm ribbon lead, change the lead-in to a coaxial type cable.

If these corrective measures do not produce satisfactory results, contact the local retailer authorized to distribute this type of product. If you cannot locate the appropriate retailer, contact Aulsound Corporation of America, Electronic Service Division, 1000 Wilshire Blvd., Los Angeles, CA 90017.

---

*FCC: Federal Communications Commission, U.S. agency that regulates communication by telegraph, telephone, radio, TV, cable TV, and satellite.

Purpose of Consumer Documents

By now you probably have a pretty good understanding of what consumer documents are meant to do—serve you. They are a source of information that makes it easier for you to operate and enjoy the products you use.

Since you are using a good digital-recording system, your new CD is sure to sound great when your friends—and strangers all over the world—listen to it on the Internet. Congratulations!

Analyzing Informational Text

Reading Check

1. List three **elements** of an extended service contract.

2. What are some **features** of the limitations clause of Aulsound's extended-service contract (on page 928)?

3. What are the common **elements** of a troubleshooting guide?

4. Why does the FCC have jurisdiction over a digital multisound recorder?

Test Practice

1. An element common to all **consumer documents** is —
   A a product warranty
   B legal information
   C instructions
   D useful information

2. The **features** of a particular consumer document —
   F are what the document shares with all other consumer documents
   G distinguish it from other documents of the same type
   H make the product extremely desirable to the consumer
   J describe the limitations of the document

3. To make sure repairs to a digital multitrack recorder are covered beyond the period specified in the warranty, you would obtain a(n) —
   A extensive instruction manual
   B FCC information sheet
   C installation guide
   D extended-service contract

4. A **troubleshooting guide** is designed to help you —
   F install a product
   G solve problems operating the product
   H customize the product
   J change the product's specifications

5. The FCC-information document (page 930) and the troubleshooting guide (page 929) *both* provide information on —
   A what to do when something doesn't work right
   B the legal responsibilities of the purchaser and the manufacturer
   C product specifications
   D warranty coverage when the product breaks down

Application

Examine some consumer documents (production information, instruction manuals, warranties, and so on). Find the documents for at least one product in your home (anything from a TV to a toaster), and identify their features and elements. Then, bring the documents to class. In a small group, compare and contrast the documents you and the other members of your group have found. How many elements can you find in common? What types of features do you find?

SKILLS FOCUS

Reading Skills
Analyze elements of consumer documents.

Writing Technical Documents

Anyone can become angry. That is easy. But to be angry with the right person, in the right degree, at the right time, for the right reason, and in the right way—that is not easy.

—Aristotle

Writing Rules for Conflict Resolution

When you're just getting started in music and hoping to make a splash in the world, how do you and your bandmates arrive at decisions that will further the group's efforts? How do you turn your inevitable conflicts into productive discussions?

It is better to deal with conflict before it reaches a crisis than to let it get so far out of hand that you cannot control it. This means that you deal with a problem as soon as you sense there is a problem. It is easier to do this if you have worked out beforehand some rules for **conflict resolution** that the group can refer to and use when problems arise. See, for example, the rules below.

Six Rules for Conflict Resolution

The word *candor* refers to the quality of being fair and unprejudiced. It also refers to expressing yourself honestly and frankly. Here are six rules for conflict resolution based on the word *candor:*

Cease what you're doing. Count to ten. Take a walk. Do whatever you do to cool down.

Ask yourself what is going on. Try to figure out what the conflict is all about.

Name the problem as you see it. Describe it to the other persons involved without blaming anyone, without adding fuel to the fire.

Discover a problem-solving plan by talking things out with those involved. Often this involves some sort of **compromise,** in which each person gives in a little in order to reach an agreement.

Operate that plan. Put it into effect by cooperating with the others involved.

Reevaluate the plan. Quite often people do not complete the process of putting a plan of action in place because they feel better after talking things over or they get distracted. When the problem reoccurs, they think their problem-solving efforts have been wasted. Instead, resolve to use the plan.

SKILLS FOCUS

Writing Skills
Write technical documents.

Some Useful Technical Documents

Conflict-resolution rules constitute a type of **technical document,** as do **procedures for conducting a meeting** and **minutes of a meeting.** You will probably find the ability to write such documents useful at some time or other in your life.

Minutes are usually taken at every official meeting in order to keep track of what has been decided, and you probably go to lots of meetings. Your band is not likely to be the only organization you belong to. You might also be a member of your school government or on the committee to decorate the gym for the class prom, for instance. If any of the organizations you belong to do not already have written rules for conflict resolution and procedures for conducting a meeting, you might want to form a committee to write them.

Tips for Writing Technical Documents

Here are some tips for writing a successful technical document:

- Convey all information **clearly, concisely,** and **correctly.**
- Arrange information in a **logical order.**
- Be **specific.**
- Include **definitions** and **examples** to aid comprehension.
- Anticipate possible reader misunderstandings.

When people in a group are trying to work together toward a common goal, many problems can arise. Pick one of the situations described below, and write some **conflict-resolution rules** to help solve the group's problems. Be clear and specific, and include **definitions, examples,** and **scenarios** (specific situations) if they will help make the rules clear.

1. Julie thinks that John isn't doing his fair share of the work. John was supposed to have the band fliers printed before their next gig, but he hasn't done it, and now time is running out. Julie has stepped in for John before when he has slacked off, but now she is angry. She thinks John should do what he said he would do. Write some conflict-resolution rules that would help Julie and John resolve this problem.

2. Gary is the band's treasurer. There isn't enough money for everything the band would like to do, so Gary wants to set budget priorities. Write some budget rules that would help prevent conflicts about money in the band.

3. Ted believes the band's drummer is taking up too much rehearsal time tuning her drums. He says Sari should get her drums in shape before rehearsals begin. Sari argues that her drumheads go out of tune because other people are fooling around with her equipment when she isn't there. Write some rules that would help resolve this conflict.

Writing Business Letters

A Request Letter

You and your band are giving a performance in the public-library auditorium to help raise money for the children's bookmobile. You are in charge of publicizing the event. You've noticed that your local newspaper runs a public-announcement column. To submit your listing, you'll write a business letter.

Business letters require a **style** of writing that is different from the one you use to write your song lyrics. ("Don't be cruel" is a great lyric, but in a business letter . . . Well, you get the point.) Often the purpose of a business letter is to **request** that someone do something for you: hire you, donate money to your cause, provide you with information, fix your problem, or as in this case, promote your band. Therefore, you want to make the best possible impression. One way to make a good impression is to pay attention to the elements of a proper business letter.

Elements of a Business Letter

The style, tone, and vocabulary of a business letter should be appropriate to the subject matter and audience. A **personal letter** to your uncle Pete asking for a loan to buy a new amp for your band will have a very different style from a business letter making the same request of a bank. The **style** and **tone** of a business letter are **formal.** Focus on these elements whenever you write a business letter:

- **Clarity**—clarity and conciseness are extremely important in business letters. The recipient should not have to sift through irrelevant details or poor organization to find your main points.
- **Courtesy**—all business letters should be polite. Even if you are writing a **complaint letter,** there is little to be gained

from discourtesy. Remember: You want to gain the reader's cooperation.

- **Tone**—the **tone** of a business letter, although friendly, is usually **formal**—as if you were talking to your principal or to the interview committee at the college you hope to attend.
- **Style**—the **style** of a business letter is **formal.** That means it contains no slang, no contractions, and no sentence fragments.
- **Vocabulary**—your vocabulary should take into account the knowledge and interest of the reader. You may wish to try on some of those not-so-everyday vocabulary words you are constantly studying in books like this one. However, don't overdo it. Your letter should reflect your own personality.

Format of a Business Letter

Business letters are expected to follow a conventional **format,** or style, as shown in the example on the next page. Note that every business letter has these six parts:

- heading
- inside address
- salutation
- body
- closing
- signature

The example letters on pages 935 and 936 use a **block-style format.** Notice that all six parts of the business letter (heading, inside address, salutation, body, closing, and signature) align at the left margin.

In a **modified-block-style format** the heading, closing, and signature are indented, as is every paragraph in the body of the letter. See the letter on page 937 for an example of the modified block style.

SKILLS FOCUS

Pages 934–937 cover **Writing Skills** Write a business letter.

Business Letter Format

Heading.

Your Street Address
Your City, State, and ZIP code
Date on which letter is written

Inside
address.

Recipient's Title [Mr., Miss, Dr., Professor, Rev., etc.]
   and First and Last Name
Recipient's business title
Company Name
Street Address
City, State, and ZIP code

Salutation, followed by
a colon.

Dear [Title and Last Name of Recipient]:

Body:
paragraph 1.

In this paragraph, tell the recipient why you are writing, stating what you are requesting in clear and concise language.

Body:
paragraph 2.

In this paragraph, include information relevant to your goal, such as relevant facts about your background or questions you have for the recipient.

Body:
paragraph 3.

Here you thank the recipient in advance for whatever actions he or she may take in regard to your request in the first paragraph.

Closing, followed by
a comma.

Sincerely,

Four blank lines for
signature—followed by
your typed name.

Your Signature

Your Full Name

Two Sample Business Letters

You've learned the format. Now, see what some business letters look like.

440 Melody Lane
Rockville, CA 91112
June 2, 2002

Ms. Bettina Johnson
Editor, "Doings in Town"
The Rockville Observer
1 Main Street
Rockville, CA 91111

Dear Ms. Johnson:

I am writing to submit a news item for inclusion in your column,
"Doings in Town," for the June 17 edition of *The Rockville Observer.*
I understand that you list town events that are open to the public.

Our band, The DumpStar Gang, is giving a benefit performance to raise
funds for the public library's children's bookmobile. The performance
will take place in the public-library auditorium on June 21 at 7:30 P.M.
Admission is free, but a ten-dollar donation is requested. Refreshments
will be served after the performance.

Thank you in advance for including our performance in your column.
The publicity should make it possible for us to raise additional funds for
the children's bookmobile.

Sincerely yours,

Mike Musicano

Mike Musicano
The DumpStar Gang

THE ROCKVILLE OBSERVER
1 MAIN STREET, ROCKVILLE, CA 91111

June 4, 2002

Mr. Mike Musicano
440 Melody Lane
Rockville, CA 91112

Dear Mr. Musicano:

We received your letter and will be happy to list your benefit performance in the "Doings in Town" column in our June 17 edition. In addition, in order to further support the library's children's bookmobile, we would like to help publicize your event with a feature article on your band.

Our reporter Ritsa Lott will call you this Friday to arrange an interview. Since time is short, I am requesting now that you send us some photographs and information about The DumpStar Gang. Please address these materials to Ritsa Lott, Staff Reporter.

Thank you for your prompt attention to our request and for your good work in support of the library.

Sincerely,

Bettina Johnson

Bettina Johnson
Editor, "Doings in Town"

PRACTICE

What a great reply! The extra publicity should give both the library and the band a big boost. Your assignment is to write Mike Musicano's reply to Bettina Johnson's letter. To do so, it might help you to know that when you enclose materials such as photographs and press releases in an envelope along with a business letter, it is customary to leave a space below your name and then type "enc." (short for *enclosure*).

Collection 11: Skills Review

Informational Reading Skills

Test Practice

Consumer and Workplace Documents

DIRECTIONS: Read and respond to the questions about consumer and workplace documents that follow.

1. What is the *most* important thing to do when following **technical directions**?
   - **A** Read all the directions quickly to get the big picture.
   - **B** Complete the project in one uninterrupted session.
   - **C** Follow each step carefully and in the correct sequence.
   - **D** Decide ahead of time how much time to allow for the project.

2. Which type of **sequence** do *most* **functional documents** follow?
   - **F** Alphabetical
   - **G** Logical
   - **H** Spatial
   - **J** Chronological

3. Which type of **functional document** is *most* suited to a **logical sequence** that progresses from highest to lowest?
   - **A** A contract
   - **B** A recipe
   - **C** A product review
   - **D** A set of directions

4. The *most* **logical order** for presenting a set of **instructions** is —
   - **F** chronological order
   - **G** step-by-step order
   - **H** order of importance
   - **J** spatial order

5. A set of **technical directions** is badly flawed if it —
   - **A** omits a step
   - **B** puts a step in the wrong order
   - **C** does either of the above
   - **D** does none of the above

6. The **purpose** of a **functional workplace document** is to —
   - **F** eliminate some jobs
   - **G** increase paperwork
   - **H** help people get things done
   - **J** lessen people's dependence on computers

7. Which type of document is a **collaboration agreement**?
   - **A** A warranty
   - **B** A contract
   - **C** Technical directions
   - **D** U.S. Copyright Office registration

8. In an **Internet citation** the *most* crucial piece of information to reproduce accurately is the —
   - **F** author's name
   - **G** title of the site
   - **H** URL
   - **J** date the site was accessed

Pages 938–939 cover
Reading Skills
Understand elements of consumer and workplace documents.

9. According to MLA style, where in an **Internet citation** do you place the date a site was accessed?

   A Right after the URL

   B Just before the URL

   C At the beginning of the entry

   D At the end of the entry

10. According to MLA style, which of the following citations of a URL is correct?

    F <http.www.yourschool.edu

    G www.yourschool.edu

    H <http://www.yourschool.edu>.

    J http://www.yourschool.edu

11. In a *Works Cited* list, in what order are the entries listed?

    A Alphabetically by the title of the work

    B Alphabetically by the author's last name (when known)

    C Alphabetically by the URL

    D Chronologically by the date the source was accessed

12. Which **consumer document** is *most* likely to help you if you encounter problems operating a product?

    F A contract

    G A troubleshooting guide

    H A warranty

    J Product information

13. What is the **purpose** of an **extended-service contract**?

    A To provide a basic warranty for a product

    B To give advice on how to repair a product

    C To provide coverage for repairs to a product after the warranty expires

    D To provide a money-back guarantee of a product

14. FCC (Federal Communications Commission) information is included with some products to —

    F provide a U.S. government warranty for the product

    G teach consumers how to use the product

    H warn consumers against tampering with the product

    J offer government advice for repairing the product

15. In which of these **consumer documents** are you *most* likely to find out how powerful a new computer is?

    A A warranty

    B Product information

    C Safety guide

    D Instruction manual

Constructed Response

16. Write a business letter complaining about a product you purchased recently. Use all six elements, or parts, of a business letter.

Resource Center

Reading Matters
by Kylene Beers **941**

Writer's Handbook **955**

Test Smarts **967**

Handbook of Literary Terms . . . **979**

Handbook of Reading and
Informational Terms **993**

Language Handbook **1009**

Glossary **1053**

Spanish Glossary **1059**

The Parisian Novels (The Yellow Books), Vincent van Gogh, 1888.

Why Reading Matters

I read good enough. I mean, most of the time I don't know the answers to the questions that are at the end of the chapter like in my science book or even at the end of stories we read in English, but that's okay, because those questions are hard. Right? Anyway, how are those questions going to help me in real life, you know, when I'm out of school and working?

—Collin, grade 10

Collin takes driver's ed, plays basketball, works at a bagel shop on weekends, and struggles in school. He'd like to make better grades, but because he doesn't read well, he has problems doing his homework and studying for tests. But when you ask (as I did) how he reads, he says, "Good enough." It's good enough for him because he doesn't see the connection between being able to read well and doing well in school and in the job he'll someday have as an adult.

He asks how answering the questions in his social studies, science, and literature books is going to help him in "real life." Well, being able to answer questions in school helps in two ways. First, answering questions is a quick way to show yourself and your teachers what you understand about content. Second, since most of the questions you answer either force you to recall specific information or push you to figure out more complex problems, answering questions can help you become a better thinker. Being a better thinker is helpful in any job.

It all starts with reading. If you can't read the stories and essays in your textbooks or the questions or the tests, then all sorts of negative things begin to happen. That's because no matter where you live, no matter what you do, you are surrounded by print—from textbooks, e-mail messages, and Web pages to how-to instruction manuals and magazines. In a literate society, reading is critical.

The following section is designed to help you with reading. In it you'll find strategies that will help you better comprehend the texts you read. Take some time right now to flip through the pages of this section. You'll see that each lesson is brief—so you can learn a lot in a little bit of time. You can return to this section as often as you need to. Use the strategies suggested here with the selections in this book. Then, try them as you read other texts. The more you think about the topics covered in this section and practice what's suggested here, the better you'll be at reading.

That's important because, after all, *reading matters.*

—Kylene Beers

When the Text Is Tough

Remember the reading you did back in first, second, and third grades? Big print. Short texts. Easy words. Now in high school, however, the texts you read are often filled with small print, long chapters, and complicated plots or topics. Also, you now find yourself reading a variety of material—from your driver's-ed handbook to college applications, from job applications to income-tax forms, from e-mail to e-zines, from classics to comics, from textbooks to checkbooks.

Doing something every day that you find difficult and tedious isn't much fun—and that includes reading. So, this section of this book is designed for you, to show you what to do when the text gets tough. Let's begin by looking at some *reading* matters.

READING UP CLOSE

▶ How to Use This Section

- **This section is for you.** Turn to it whenever you need to remind yourself about what to do when the text gets tough. Don't wait for your teacher to assign this section for you to read. It's your handbook. Use it.

- **Read the sections that you need.** You don't have to read every word. Skim the headings, and find the information you need.

- **Use this information for help with reading for other classes,** not just for the reading you do in this book.

- **Don't be afraid to re-read the information you find in Reading Matters.** The best readers constantly re-read information.

- **If you need more help, then check the index.** The index will direct you to other pages in this book with information on reading skills and strategies.

Improving Your Comprehension

Have you seen the reruns of an old weekly television show called *Lost in Space*? Perhaps you saw the more recent movie version of it? If so, you probably remember the robot that constantly tried to warn the young boy, Will Robinson, when danger was near by waving his robot arms and announcing loudly, "Danger approaching, Will Robinson!" Then Will would look up from whatever he was doing, notice whatever evil was moments away, and take action. But until the robot warned him, Will would ignore all warning signs that danger was at hand.

Wouldn't it be nice if something would warn us as we were about to enter a dangerous area when we were reading—a part of the text that we might not understand? Perhaps our own little robots could pop up in books, saying, "Danger, reader! Misunderstandings approaching!" Then we'd know to slow down, pay attention, and carefully study the text we were reading.

Actually those signs do appear, but not as arm-waving robots in the margins of books. Instead, the signs appear in our minds as we are reading. However, unless we are paying attention, we often read on past them, not noticing the warnings they offer. What we need to do is learn to recognize the danger signs so that like Will Robinson, we will know when to look up and take action.

READING UP CLOSE

▶ Looking for the Danger Signs

Study each of the signs to the right, and decide what type of danger each could signify when you read. You might want to copy these signs onto stick-on notes to put on your texts as you read.

► Danger Sign 1

You can't remember what you read.

This happens to all readers occasionally. You read something, and your attention wanders for a moment, but your eyes don't quit moving from word to word. In a few minutes you realize you are several pages beyond the last point where you can remember thinking about what you were reading. Then you know you need to back up and start over.

Forgetting what you've read is a danger sign only if it happens to you frequently. If you constantly complete a reading assignment but don't remember anything that you've been reading, then you probably are in the habit of letting your mind focus on something else while your eyes are focusing on the words. That's a habit you need to break.

READING UP CLOSE

▶ Measure Your Attention Quotient

Take the following survey to see what your attention quotient is. The lower the score, the less attention you pay to what you are reading.

When I read, I . . .

1. let my mind wander
   a. most of the time
   b. sometimes
   c. almost never

2. forget what I'm reading
   a. most of the time
   b. sometimes
   c. almost never

3. get confused and stay confused
   a. most of the time
   b. sometimes
   c. almost never

4. discover I've turned lots of pages and don't have a clue as to what I've read
   a. most of the time
   b. sometimes
   c. almost never

5. rarely finish whatever I'm supposed to be reading
   a. most of the time
   b. sometimes
   c. almost never

Tips for Staying Focused

1. Don't read from the beginning of the assignment to the end without pausing. Set up checkpoints for yourself, either every few pages or every five minutes. At those checkpoints, stop reading and ask yourself some basic questions—"What's happening now? What do I not understand?"

2. As you read, keep paper and pen close by. Take notes as you read, in particular jotting down questions you have about what confuses you, interests you, or perhaps even surprises you.

Danger Sign 2

You don't "see" what you are reading.

The ability to visualize—or see in your mind—what you are reading is important for comprehension. To understand how visualizing makes a difference, try this quick test. When you get home, turn on a television to a program you enjoy. Then, turn your back to the television set. How long will you keep "watching" the program that way? Probably not long. Why not? Because it would be boring if you couldn't see what was happening. The same is true of reading: If you can't see in your mind what is happening on the page, then you probably will tune out quickly. You can improve your ability to visualize a text by practicing the following strategies:

1. **Read a few sentences; then, pause, and describe what is happening on the page.** Forcing yourself to describe the scene will take some time at first, but it will help in the long run.

2. **On a sheet of paper or a stick-on note, make a graphic representation of what is happening as you are reading.** For instance, if two characters are talking, draw two stick figures with arrows pointing between them to show yourself that they are talking.

3. **Discuss a scene or a part of a chapter with a buddy.** Talk about what you "saw" as you were reading.

4. **Read aloud.** If you are having trouble visualizing the text, it might be because you aren't really "hearing" it. Try reading a portion of your text aloud, using good expression and phrasing. As you hear the words, you may find it easier to see the scenes.

READING UP CLOSE

▸ **Visualizing What You Read**

Read this scene from "Where Have You Gone, Charming Billy?" (p. 622), and discuss what you see:

"The platoon of twenty-six soldiers moved slowly in the dark, single file, not talking. One by one, like sheep in a dream, they passed through the hedgerow, crossed quietly over a meadow, and came down to the rice paddy. There they stopped. Their leader knelt down, motioning with his hand, and one by one the other soldiers squatted in the shadows, vanishing in the primitive stealth of warfare. For a long time they did not move. Except for the sounds of their breathing, the twenty-six men were very quiet. . . ."

▶ Danger Sign 3

You constantly answer "I don't know" to questions at the end of reading selections.

If you consistently don't know the answers to questions about what you've been reading, then you probably would benefit from the following strategies:

Think-Aloud. Comprehension problems don't appear only after you *finish* reading. Confusion occurs *as* you read. Therefore, don't wait until you complete your reading assignment to try to understand the text; instead, work on comprehending while reading by becoming an active reader.

Active readers **predict, connect, clarify, question,** and **visualize** as they read. If you don't do those things, then you need to pause while you read to

- make predictions
- make connections
- clarify in your own thoughts what you are reading
- question what you don't understand
- visualize the text and observe key details

Use the Think-Aloud strategy to practice your active-reading skills. Read a selection of text aloud to a partner. As you read, pause to make comments and ask questions. Your partner's job is to tally your comments and classify each according to the list above.

READING UP CLOSE

▶ One Student's Think-Aloud

Here's Jarred's Think-Aloud for "Everyday Use," by Alice Walker (p. 77):

Page 77, first sentence: "What in the world is this talking about when it says they made the yard so wavy? How do you make a yard wavy?" **(Question)**

Page 77, fifth sentence: "Okay, I get it. It's not a grass yard, but like clay and sand." **(Clarification)**

Page 79, top of second column: "Maggie and Dee remind me of my two sisters. My older sister thinks she is so much better than the other one." **(Connection)**

Page 79 bottom and top 80: "I can just imagine what Dee and her boyfriend look like with their bright clothes and long hair." **(Visualization)**

Retelling. While the Think-Aloud strategy keeps you focused as you read, the Retelling strategy helps you after reading. Read the tips for retelling on this page, and then practice retelling small portions of your reading assignments. You might ask a friend to listen to you retell what you have read, or you might record yourself as you retell a selection.

READING UP CLOSE

▶ **Evaluate Your Retelling**

Listen to your retelling, and ask yourself:

1. Does my retelling make sense?
2. Does it have enough information?
3. Is the information in the correct order?
4. Could a drawing or a diagram help my retelling?
5. If someone listening to my retelling hadn't read the text, what would that person visualize?
6. To improve my next retelling, should I focus on characters, sequence of events, amount of detail, or general conclusions?

Retelling Prompts for Fiction

1. State what text you are retelling.
2. Give characters' names, and explain who they are.
3. Sequence the events using words like *first, second, third, then, later, next,* and *last.*
4. Identify the conflict in the story.
5. Explain the resolution of the conflict.
6. Tell what you enjoyed or did not enjoy about the text.

Retelling Prompts for Informational Texts

State what text you are retelling, and identify the structure of the text.

- If the structure is a **sequence** (the water cycle), use words like *first, second, third, then, later, afterwards, following that, before,* and *last.*

- If the structure is **comparison and contrast** (the differences between World War I and World War II), use words or phrases such as *by comparison, by contrast, on the other hand, yet, but, however, nevertheless, conversely, then again,* or *in opposition.*

- If showing **cause-and-effect relationships,** use words like *reason, motive, basis,* and *grounds* to discuss **causes,** and use words like *outcome, consequence, result,* and *product* to discuss **effects.**

Re-reading and Rewording. The best way to improve your comprehension is simply to **re-read.** The first time you read something, you get the basic idea of the text. The next time you read it, you revise your understanding. Try thinking of your first reading as a draft—just like the first draft of an essay. As you revise your essay, you are improving your writing. As you revise your reading, you are improving your comprehension.

Sometimes, as you re-read, you find some specific sentences or even passages that you just don't understand. When that's the case, you need to spend some time closely studying those sentences. One effective way to tackle tough text is to **reword** it:

1. On a sheet of paper, write the sentences that are confusing you.

2. Leave a few blank lines between each line you write.

3. Then, choose the difficult words, and replace them in the space above.

4. While you wouldn't want to reword every line of a text, this is a powerful way to help you understand key sentences.

READING UP CLOSE

▶ One Student's Rewording

After tenth-grader Katie read "The Masque of the Red Death" (p. 419), she copied a few sentences she didn't understand. After re-reading them, she reworded them, using a thesaurus and a dictionary. Later she explained that "rewording helps me understand what the author is trying to say."

 decided   *ways*   *entrance or exit*
1. They ~~resolved~~ to leave ~~means~~ neither of ~~ingress or egress~~ to the

 urges   *desperation or unrest*
sudden ~~impulses~~ of ~~despair or of frenzy~~ from within. (page 420)

 thin   *covered*
2. The figure was tall and ~~gaunt,~~ and ~~shrouded~~ from head to foot

 clothing
in the ~~habiliments~~ of the grave. (pages 424–425)

Summarizing Narrative Text. Understanding a long piece of text is easier if you can summarize chunks of it. If you are reading a **narrative,** or story, then use a strategy called **Somebody Wanted But So (SWBS)** to help you write a summary of what you are reading. SWBS is a powerful way to think about the characters in a story and note what each did, what conflict each faced, and what the resolution was. As you write an SWBS statement for different characters in the same story, you are forcing yourself to rethink the story from different **points of view.** By analyzing point of view in this way, you get a better understanding of the impact of the author's choice of narrator.

Here are the steps for writing SWBS statements:

1. Write the words *Somebody, Wanted, But,* and *So* at the top of four columns.
2. In the "Somebody" column, write a character's name.
3. Then, in the "Wanted" column, write what that character wanted to do.
4. Next, in the "But" column, explain what happened that kept the character from doing what he or she wanted.
5. Finally, in the "So" column, explain the eventual outcome.
6. If you're making an SWBS chart for a long story or novel, you'll need to write several statements at different points in the story.

READING UP CLOSE

▶ **One Student's SWBS Chart**

Here's Josh's SWBS chart for "Through the Tunnel" (p. 401). He's written an SWBS statement for Jerry up to where he gets swimming goggles (page 404). Write another for the same character from page 404 to the end. Then, write an SWBS statement for his mother.

Somebody	Wanted	But	So
Jerry	wanted to swim through the rock,	but he couldn't hold his breath long enough,	so he has to practice holding his breath.

Summarizing Expository Text. If summarizing the information in **expository,** or informational, texts is difficult, try a strategy called GIST.

Steps for GIST

1. Divide the text you want to summarize into three or four sections.
2. Read the first section.
3. Draw twenty blank lines on a sheet of paper.
4. Write a summary of the first section of text using exactly twenty words—one word for each blank.

5. Read the next section of text. In your next set of twenty blanks, write a new summary statement that combines your first summary with whatever you want to add from this second section of text. It's important to note that even though you've now got two sections of text to cover, you still have only twenty blanks to fill, not forty.

6. Repeat this one or two more times, depending on how much more text you have. When you are finished, you'll have a twenty-word statement that gives you the gist, or overall idea, of what the entire text is about.

READING UP CLOSE

▸ **One Student's GIST**

After reading "Vision Quest" (p. 413), Tony wrote the following GIST statements:

GIST 1 (first paragraph)
To reach adulthood, boys in some American Indian tribes underwent a vision quest—a solitary vigil of prayer and fasting.

GIST 2 (for paragraphs 1 and 2)
During their vision quest initiation rites, American Indian boys prayed and fasted until they received a significant sign or vision.

GIST 3 (complete article)
Vision quests of prayer and fasting are important to American Indian adults as well as to boys undergoing initiation rites.

Key Words. Sometimes you don't want to write a summary or outline of what you've been reading. Sometimes you just want to jot down some key words to remind yourself about a specific topic. To keep your key words organized, don't forget your ABCs. Just make yourself a copy of a page filled with boxes, as in the following example. You can use your computer to make this page or just grab a pencil and notebook paper. Once your boxes are drawn, all you have to do is decide what information to include.

For instance, Amy uses her Key Word chart while reading "Two Kinds" (page 99). She puts "Mother" in blue at the top of the page and "*Ni kan*" in red. As she reads the story and thinks of words to describe each character, she puts those key character-description words in the correct box in the correct color. So, she writes "demanding" in blue (because she thinks that word describes Mother) in the C–D box. She writes "angry" in red (because this word is for *Ni kan*) in the A–B box. Amy's completed Key Word chart can serve as a starting point for writing a comparison-contrast essay.

READING UP CLOSE

▶ Using a Key Word Chart

Here is Amy's partially filled-out Key Word chart for "Two Kinds." Read the story, and find more key words to describe the two main characters.

Mother			Ni Kan		
A–B	C–D	E–F	G–H	I–J	K–L
angry	demanding				
M–N	O–P	Q–R	S–T	U–V–W	X–Y–Z

Kwan used his Key Word chart in history class as he was reading the chapter on World War II. He used it to keep up with countries (*Allies* written in red, *Axis* in blue), military leaders, and major battles.

Improving Your Reading Rate

If your reading concerns are more about getting through the words than figuring out the meaning, then this part of Reading Matters is for you.

If you think you are a slow reader, then reading can seem overwhelming. But you can change your reading rate—the pace at which you read. All you have to do is practice. The point isn't to read so fast that you just rush over words—the I'mgoingtoreadsofastthatallthewordsruntogether approach. Instead, the goal is to find a pace that keeps you moving comfortably through the pages. Why is it important to establish a good reading rate? Let's do a little math to see why your silent reading rate counts.

> **MATH PROBLEM!**
> If you read 40 words per minute (WPM) and there are 400 words on a page, then how long will it take you to read 1 page? 5 pages? 10 pages? How long will it take if you read 80 WPM? 100 WPM? 200 WPM?

As you figure out the problem, you see that it takes 100 minutes to read 10 pages at the slowest pace and only 20 minutes at the fastest pace. See the chart for all the times:

	1 page @400 words/page	5 pages @400 words/page	10 pages @400 words/page
40 WPM	10 minutes	50 minutes	100 minutes
80 WPM	5 minutes	25 minutes	50 minutes
100 WPM	4 minutes	20 minutes	40 minutes
200 WPM	2 minutes	10 minutes	20 minutes

Reading Rate and Homework

Now, assume that with literature homework, science homework, and social studies homework, in one night you have 40 pages to read. If you are reading at 40 WPM, you are spending over 6 *hours* just reading the information; but at 100 WPM, you would spend only about 2 hours and 45 minutes. And at 200 WPM, you'd finish in 1 hour and 20 minutes.

READING UP CLOSE

▶ **Tips on Varying Your Reading Rate**

- Increasing your rate doesn't help if your comprehension goes down.

- Remember that your rate will vary as your purpose for reading varies. You'll read more slowly when you are studying for a test than when you are skimming a text.

Figuring Out Your Reading Rate

To determine your silent-reading rate, you'll need three things: a watch or clock with a second hand, a book, and someone who will watch the time for you. Then, follow these steps:

1. Have your friend time you as you begin reading to yourself.

2. Read at your normal rate. Don't speed just because you're being timed.

> **Example**
> 1st minute   180 words
> 2nd minute   215 words
> 3rd minute   190 words
> 585 words ÷ 3 = 195 WPM

3. Stop when your friend tells you one minute is up.

4. Count the number of words you read.

5. Repeat this process several more times using different passages.

6. Then, add the number of words together, and divide by the number of times you timed yourself. That's your average rate.

Reading Rate Reminders

You can improve your reading rate by using the following strategies:

1. **Make sure you aren't reading just one word at a time, with a pause between each word.** Practice phrasing words in your mind as you read. For instance, look at the sample sentence, and pause only where you see the slash marks. One slash (/) means pause a bit. Two slashes (//) mean pause a bit longer.

   > Jack and Jill/ went up the hill/ to fetch a pail of water.// Jack fell down/ and broke his crown/ and Jill came tumbling after.//

   Now, read it again, pausing after each word:

   > Jack/ and/ Jill/ went/ up/ the/ hill/ to/ fetch/ a/ pail/ of/ water.// Jack/ fell/ down/ and/ broke/ his/ crown/ and/ Jill/ came/ tumbling/ after.//

   Hear the difference? Word-at-a-time reading is much slower than phrase reading. You can hear good phrasing by listening to a book on tape.

2. **Make sure you aren't sounding out each word.** At this point in school, you need to be able to recognize whole words and save the sounding-out strategy for words you haven't seen before. In other words, you ought to be able to read *material* as "material" and not as "ma-ter-i-al," but you might need to move more slowly through *metacognition* so that you read that word as "met-a-cog-ni-tion."

3. **Make sure when you are reading silently that you really are reading silently.** Don't move your lips or read aloud very softly when reading. These habits slow you down. Remember, if you need to slow down (for instance, when the information you are reading is confusing you), then reading aloud to yourself is a smart thing to do. But generally, silent reading means reading silently!

4. **Don't use your finger to point to words as you read.** If you find that you always use your finger to point to words as you read (instead of just occasionally, when you are really concentrating), then you are probably reading one word at a time. Instead, use a bookmark to help yourself stay on the right line, and practice your phrase reading.

5. **As you practice your fluency, remember that the single best way to improve your reading rate is simply to read more!** You won't get better at what you never do. So start reading more, and remember these tips. Soon you'll find that reading too slowly isn't a problem anymore.

Writer's Handbook

The Writing Process

There may be as many ways to write as there are kinds of texts. While individual writers' techniques may vary, successful writers do have one thing in common: the writing process. The writing process is made up of four stages, and each stage involves certain activities. The chart below summarizes what happens during each stage of the writing process.

STAGES OF THE WRITING PROCESS	
Prewriting	• Choose your topic.
	• Identify your purpose and audience, and select a form.
	• Generate ideas and gather information about the topic.
	• Begin to organize the information.
	• Decide the main point you want to express.
Writing	• Grab your readers' attention in the introduction.
	• Provide background information.
	• State your main points, support, and elaboration.
	• Follow a plan of organization.
	• Wrap up with a conclusion.
Revising	• Evaluate your draft.
	• Revise the draft's content, organization, and style.
Publishing	• Proofread, or edit, your final draft.
	• Publish, or share your finished writing with readers.
	• Reflect on your writing experience.

TIP The writing process is **recursive,** meaning that writers go back and forth between the stages as necessary. For example, as you revise an essay you may realize that one paragraph contains no details to support your main idea. You can go back to the prewriting and drafting stages, gathering and adding more information to the paragraph.

At every stage of the writing process, you'll need to stay focused on your goal for the piece of writing and on your specific audience. Use the following suggestions to keep your writing on track.

- **Keep your ideas focused.** Every idea in a piece must clearly support your thesis or the controlling impression you want to create. Those ideas must also be **coherent,** or strongly connected to one another. Keep your thesis and purpose in mind every step of the way, eliminating any ideas that might take the reader's attention away from your distinct perspective or from a tightly reasoned argument.

- **Use a consistent tone.** Using the same tone throughout a piece will help to unify the ideas you present. Consider what tone—from slangy and joking to serious and formal—will best fit your audience and your topic, and stick with that tone.

- **Plan to publish.** Make publishing a piece—sharing it with an audience—easier by carefully revising and proofreading. Enlist the help of classmates to catch errors you might miss because you know the piece too well, and use the following proofreading guidelines. The numbers in parentheses indicate the sections in the Language Handbook in which instruction on each skill begins.

GUIDELINES FOR PROOFREADING

1. Is every sentence complete, not a fragment or run-on? (9a, b)

2. Are punctuation marks used correctly? (12a–s, 13a–l, 14a–n)

3. Are the first letters of sentences and proper nouns and adjectives capitalized? (11d)

4. Does each verb agree in number with its subject? (2a) Are verb forms and tenses used correctly? (3a–f)

5. Are subject and object forms of personal pronouns used correctly? (4a–c) Do pronouns agree with clear antecedents in number and in gender? (4i)

As you proofread, mark corrections using the symbols below.

SYMBOLS FOR REVISING AND PROOFREADING

Symbol	Example	Meaning of Symbol
≡	Maple High school	Capitalize a lowercase letter.
/	the First person	Lowercase a capital letter.
∧	on the fourth ^of May	Insert a missing word, letter, or punctuation mark.
⌐	in the East West	Replace a word.
℮	tell me the the plan	Delete a word, letter, or punctuation mark.
∽	recieve	Change the order of letters.
¶	¶"Help!" someone cried.	Begin a new paragraph.

Paragraphs

A **paragraph** is made up of sentences grouped together for a reason—
usually to present and support a single main idea, or central focus.
In the same way, a composition is made up of a group of paragraphs
working together to develop and support a thesis or controlling idea
that makes the composition work as a whole.

Parts of a Body Paragraph

While paragraphs in narrative writing don't always have a central
focus, paragraphs in most other types of compositions do usually
emphasize a main idea. These **body paragraphs** usually include
a **topic sentence, supporting sentences,** and, sometimes, a
clincher sentence.

PARTS OF PARAGRAPHS

Topic Sentence	• directly states the paragraph's main idea
	• often is the first sentence in the paragraph, but may occur at the end for emphasis or variety
Supporting Sentences	• support the main idea of a paragraph
	• use the following kinds of details
	sensory details: information collected using sight, hearing, smell, touch, or taste
	facts: information that can be proved
	statistics: information in number form
	examples: specific instances or illustrations of a general idea
	anecdotes: extended examples or brief personal stories
	scenarios: general descriptions of potential events or common situations
	commonly held beliefs: ideas on which most people agree
	hypotheses: unproven theories that serve as the basis for investigation
	definitions: explanations of a concept
Clincher Sentence	• sometimes (but not always) found at the end of longer paragraphs
	• emphasizes or summarizes the main idea

 TIP You can provide many other types of information as supporting evidence, including descriptions, expert opinions, reasons, and personal experience. Use a combination of types of support to give your writing variety.

Putting the Parts Together A typical paragraph that includes the parts listed in the chart on page 957 uses the following structure. Be aware, though, that you can use a different structure for effect—for example, you might occasionally leave out the clincher sentence and place your topic sentence at the end of the paragraph to drive home your point.

Typical Body Paragraph Structure

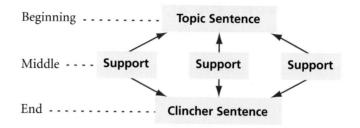

The following passage from an online magazine article shows how the parts of a paragraph work together to support a main idea—in this case, the idea that electric "bug zappers" do a poor job of protecting humans from insect bites.

Topic sentence

Supporting sentences

(Facts and statistics)

Clincher sentence

Electric insect traps, or "bug zappers," are effective killing machines, but they kill the wrong kind of insects, claims University of Delaware entomologist Doug Tallamy. Over the course of a summer, Tallamy and a high school student, Tim Frick, analyzed the victims of the electric traps installed in six yards in Newark, Delaware. Of the 13,789 insects killed, just 31—less than one-quarter of one percent—were biting insects. Tallamy and Frick estimate that the millions of traps employed in the U.S. needlessly kill 71 billion to 350 billion "nontarget insects" each year, causing untold damage to ecosystems. Bug zappers, they conclude, are "worthless" as well as "counterproductive."

Steve Nadis, "Bug Zappers Miss Their Mark," *Omni Online*

Notice that the topic sentence immediately calls the reader's attention to the paragraph's main idea: These traps kill the wrong insects. The rest of the paragraph maintains a consistent focus on this idea. Each supporting sentence contains evidence that supports this main idea, including facts and statistics. The final sentence, a clincher sentence, emphasizes the main idea by presenting a judgment based on the facts and statistics in the supporting sentences.

Qualities of Paragraphs

Having the parts of a paragraph in place is just the beginning of developing a good paragraph. The next step is to consider the **unity** and **coherence** of the ideas within the paragraph. Think of these qualities as the strong glue that holds the parts of a well-written paragraph together.

Unity Unity is the quality achieved when all of the sentences in a paragraph work together as a unit to express or support one main idea and to maintain a consistent focus. Unrelated ideas spoil unity and distract the reader. Unity is present in a paragraph when all sentences relate to an implied or stated main idea or to a sequence of events. In a narrative paragraph, unity is achieved when all the sentences work together to narrate the event.

Coherence Along with unity, good paragraphs have coherence. Coherence is achieved when all of the details and ideas in a paragraph are both logically arranged and clearly connected.

To ensure that the ideas in a paragraph are arranged in a way that makes sense, pay attention to the structure or organizational pattern of the ideas. You will usually use one of the orders described in the chart below; in some cases, though, you may use a combination of two or even more of these orders.

TYPES OF ORDER

Order	When To Use	How It Works
Chronological	• to tell a story • to explain a process	presents actions and events according to the order in which they occur
Spatial	• to describe a place or object	arranges details or ideas according to their location in space
Logical	• to explain or classify (by defining, dividing a subject into parts, or comparing and contrasting)	groups related details or ideas together to show their relationship
Order of Importance	• to inform or to persuade	arranges details or ideas from the most important to the least important, or vice versa

In addition to presenting details in an order that makes sense, a paragraph that has coherence should also show readers how those details are connected. You can show connections between ideas by using direct references or transitional expressions. **Direct references** refer to an idea presented earlier. **Transitional expressions** are words or phrases that take readers from one idea to the next, signaling the relationship between the ideas. The following chart explains how to use these two strategies for connecting ideas.

CONNECTING IDEAS

Connecting Strategy	How To Use It
Direct References	• Use a noun or pronoun that refers to a noun or pronoun used earlier. • Repeat a word used earlier. • Use a word or phrase that means the same thing as a noun or pronoun used earlier.
Transitional Expressions	• Compare ideas (*also, and, besides, in addition, similarly, too*). • Contrast ideas (*although, but, however, instead, nevertheless, otherwise, yet*). • Show cause and effect (*as a result, because, consequently, so, therefore, thus*). • Show time (*after, before, eventually, finally, first, meanwhile, then, when*). • Show place (*above, across, around, beyond, from, here, in, on, over, there, to, under*). • Show importance (*first, last, mainly, then, to begin with*).

PRACTICE & APPLY Develop a paragraph on the topic of your choice. After identifying the main idea you will present, take the following steps to draft your paragraph.

• Plan your topic sentence, supporting sentences with a variety of types of support, and clincher sentence.

• Create unity and coherence to maintain a consistent focus in your paragraph. Use an appropriate order, and connect your ideas using direct references and transitional expressions.

The Writer's Language

As part of revising a draft, fine-tune its **style** so that it will grab readers. To improve your paper's style, consider your **word choice** and use the **active voice.** Also, analyze the **tone** of your writing to make your style not only engaging but also appropriate.

Give It Flair! Consider what is missing from the following passage.

> As I hiked around a bend, I saw a snake smack in the middle of the path. Its skin was being shed. It moved against the rocks. Eventually it got out of its old skin. Now it looked real different. It was smooth. There was a lot of sun. My forehead was covered with sweat. I couldn't hear nothing. I looked at the snake's eyes. They were black.

The passage poorly shares the writer's experience. The writer must improve word choice, using **precise language, sensory details, action verbs,** and **appropriate modifiers,** and use the **active voice** when possible.

Precise Language The passage above describes the snake in a vague way. Changing *moved* to *wriggled* or *slithered* would vividly show the snake's movement. Also, what kind of snake is it? What does the snake look like before, during, and after shedding its skin? Revise your own writing to show your subject vividly through precise language.

Sensory Details The statement "It was smooth" doesn't give readers much information about the snake. The description "smooth as silk" or "smooth as a stone" would explain how it feels to touch the snake. Words like *stone* and *silk* are the building blocks of sensory details, details that tell how things look, feel, taste, sound, or smell.

Action Verbs Which is more interesting—"They were black" or "They glittered like black stones"? Generally, *be* verbs (such as *were*) and other dull verbs such as *go, have,* and *do* don't tell readers much. Action verbs such as *glittered* and *sparkled* bring a subject to life.

Appropriate Modifiers An appropriate modifier clearly relates to the correct word or phrase. For example, the word *real* in the passage is an adjective used incorrectly to modify the adjective *different.* The writer should use the adverb *really* or, even better, eliminate the tired word *really* altogether. Check that each modifier you use is both necessary and correct.

Active Voice In the **passive** voice, the action happens to the subject. For example, "Its skin was being shed" uses the passive voice. In the

active voice, the subject does the action. The more forceful sentence "The snake was shedding its skin" uses the active voice.

Toning Up Your **tone** expresses your attitude toward your audience and topic and comes through in the formality of your language, including your word choice. Consider these points.

TIP Word choice directly affects tone and level of formality. For example, consider the difference between "A veggie burrito packs a nutritious punch" and "A vegetarian burrito provides many nutrients."

- **Who is my audience?** When you speak, you adjust your tone based on listener reactions. For example, if listeners frown at a joke, you probably turn more serious. In writing, imagine your readers' attitude toward your topic and adopt a tone reflecting that attitude.

- **Why am I writing?** Your tone must fit your **purpose.** For example, if your purpose is to inform, avoid a sarcastic tone—even if your readers enjoy sarcasm—because irony could interfere with your goal.

- **For what context, or occasion, am I writing?** Are you writing for a school assignment or to share a story with a friend? The occasion that prompts your writing determines its formality. For a formal occasion, use standard English, avoiding contractions and slang.

Read the following revision of the passage on page 961. Notice how revisions in word choice, voice, and tone bring the passage to life.

A Writer's Model

Precise language
Active voice
Action verbs
Appropriate modifiers
Sensory details
Precise language

Sensory detail

> As I hiked around a bend, I saw a gopher snake right in the middle of the path. The snake was shedding its skin. It wriggled and rubbed itself against the rough rocks. Eventually it slithered out of the flaky, dead layer of skin. Now it was as smooth as a polished apple, black and brown like shiny shoes. The morning sun was hot, and beads of sweat ran down my forehead. The world was silent—even the birds had stopped chirping. I looked right into the snake's eyes. They glittered like tiny chips of black stone.

PRACTICE & APPLY Revise the following paragraph for style, and use your imagination to add details.

Roosevelt Park is nice. People play softball there. Kids play on the playground, sliding down the slides and swinging on the swings. There's a petting zoo, too, with different kinds of animals that can be touched. There's a merry-go-round that first goes around slow and then fast. If you are hungry, there are places to eat. Or you can do nothing. I'm glad there's a place to go with my friends on weekends.

Designing Your Writing

If you've ever tried to read a messy, confusing flier or a scientific report filled with statistics, you know how important design and visuals are in making documents readable. A document's design should help to communicate its information clearly and effectively. Visuals, such as a photograph or chart, should be used when needed to help readers grasp a point.

Page Design

Eye Appeal Your page design, or **layout,** can influence your audience's desire and ability to read your document. When you design a document, make it as appealing and easy to read as possible, whether you create it by hand or using word-processing or publishing software. Use the following design elements to improve readability.

- **Columns** arrange text in separate sections printed side by side. Text in reference books and newspapers usually appears in columns. A **block** is a rectangle of text shorter than a page, such as a single newspaper story. Blocks are separated by white space.

- A **bullet** (•) is a dot or symbol used to make information stand out. Bullets often separate information into lists like this one. They attract attention and help readers remember the ideas listed.

- A **callout** is an important sentence from the text printed in a large font. Many magazine articles catch readers' attention with callouts.

- A **heading** tells what a section of text, such as a chapter, will be about. Headings appear at the beginning of a section of text. A **subheading** indicates a new idea or section within a heading. Several subheadings may appear under one heading. Headings and subheadings are often set in large letters, boldface type, or a different font.

- **White space** is any area on a page where there is little or no text or visuals. Usually, white space is limited to the margins and the spaces between words, lines, and columns. Advertisements have more white space than books or articles in newspapers or magazines.

- **Contrast** refers to the balance of light and dark areas on a page. Dark areas are those that contain blocks of text or graphics. Light areas have little type and few graphics. A page with high contrast, or balanced light and dark areas, is easier to read than a page with low contrast, such as one that is mostly light or one that is filled with text and images.

● **Emphasis** is how a page designer indicates to a reader which information on a page is most important. For example, the front page of a newspaper uses photographs and bold or large headlines to place emphasis on a particular story.

Type

Bold and Beautiful To enhance the readability of your documents, choose type carefully, considering especially the **case** and **font** of letters.

Case Most texts you read use mostly lowercase letters with capital letters at the beginnings of sentences. However, you can use all capital letters and small capitals for specific purposes within a document.

● **Uppercase letters** All uppercase, or capital, letters may be used in headings or titles. Because words in all capitals can be difficult to read, use all caps only for emphasis, not for large bodies of text.

● **Small caps** Small capitals are uppercase letters that are reduced in size. They appear in abbreviations of time, such as 9:00 A.M. and A.D. 1500.

Font A **font** is one complete set of characters (such as letters, numbers, and punctuation marks) of a given size and design.

● **Types of fonts** All fonts belong to one of three categories:

FONT CATEGORIES

Category	Explanation	How It Is Used
decorative, or **script,** fonts	elaborately designed characters that convey a distinct mood or feeling	Decorative fonts are difficult to read and should be used in small amounts for an artistic effect.
serif fonts	characters with small strokes (serifs) attached at each end	Because the strokes on serif characters help guide the reader's eyes from letter to letter, serif type is often used for large bodies of text.
sans serif fonts	characters formed of neat straight lines, with no serifs at the ends of letters	Sans serif fonts are easy to read and are used for headings, subheadings, callouts, and captions.

● **Font size** The size of type is called the font size or point size. Most newspapers and textbooks use type measured at 12 points, with larger type for headings and headlines and smaller type for captions.

● **Font styles** Most text is set in roman type (not slanted). *Italic,* or slanted, type has special uses, as for captions or book titles. Underscored or boldface type can be used for emphasis.

Visuals

Get the Picture? Some information can be communicated much more effectively visually than in writing. Your visuals must meet the same standards of accuracy as your text, and their design must also be uncluttered. Use only one or two colors for emphasis to keep your visuals clear. Here are some visuals you might find useful.

Charts Charts show relationships among ideas or data. A **flowchart** uses geometric shapes linked by arrows to show the sequence of events in a process. A **pie chart** is a circle divided into wedges, with each wedge representing a certain percentage of the total. As in the example below, a legend usually notes the concept each wedge color represents.

EXAMPLE

Where Old Tires Go

What happens to the 242 million scrap tires that are disposed of each year?

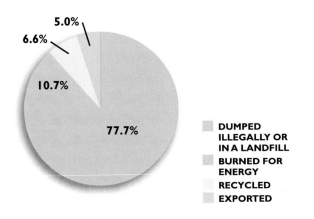

5.0%
6.6%
10.7%
77.7%

- DUMPED ILLEGALLY OR IN A LANDFILL
- BURNED FOR ENERGY
- RECYCLED
- EXPORTED

Diagrams Diagrams are simple drawings that show what something looks like, how something works, or how to do something. This diagram shows how water moves to create an ocean swell.

EXAMPLE

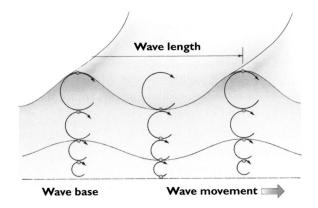

Wave length

Wave base   Wave movement

Graphs Graphs present numeric information visually and can show how one thing changes in relation to another. A **line graph** can show changes or trends over time, compare trends, or show how two or more variables interact. A **bar graph,** such as the one below, can compare quantities at a glance, show trends or changes over time, or indicate the parts of a whole.

EXAMPLE

Top Five Longest North American Rivers

Other Visuals Other visuals you might use in your documents include illustrations, time lines, and maps.

- **Illustrations** include drawings, photographs, and other artwork.

- **Time lines** identify events that have taken place over a given period of time. Usually, events are identified or described above the time line, and the time demarcations are indicated below it.

- **Maps** represent part of the earth or space. Maps of the earth may show geographical features, roads, cities, and other important locations.

PRACTICE & APPLY Choose a visual to effectively communicate the following information. Then, use the guidelines in this section to create the visual.

One hundred students at Chavez High School are involved in team sports. Thirty-five students play soccer, twenty-three students play softball, twenty-seven play football, and fifteen play volleyball.

Test Smarts

by Flo Ota De Lange *and* Sheri Henderson

Strategies for Taking Multiple-Choice Tests

Whatever you choose to do in the future, a high school diploma can open doors for you. It is a basic requirement for many, many jobs as well as for getting into college. But to get that diploma, you'll have to pass a lot of tests—pop quizzes in class, midterm exams, finals, your state's standardized tests required for graduation, and the SAT or ACT if you are thinking about college.

Taking tests doesn't have to be the scary nightmare many students make it out to be. With some preparation you'll do just fine. The first thing you have to do, of course, is study. Yes, study, study, study! Read all your assignments at least once, and make sure you have mastered the skills being taught.

Even when you know all the material, however, you might not do well on a test if you get nervous or are not familiar with the kinds of questions being asked. This section will give you some strategies that will help you approach your tests with confidence—and let your abilities shine through.

Stay Calm

It's test time. You have studied the material, and you know your stuff, but you're still nervous. That's OK. A little nervousness will help you focus, but so will a calm body. Take a few deep breaths—five slow counts in, five slow counts out. Now you're ready to begin the test.

Track Your Time

First, take a few minutes to estimate how much time you have for each question. Then, set checkpoints for yourself—the number of questions that should be completed at a quarter of the time, half of the time, and so on. That way you can **pace yourself** throughout the test. If you're behind, you can speed up. If you're ahead, you can—and should—slow down.

Master the Directions

Read the directions carefully to be sure you know exactly what to do and how to do it. If you are supposed to fill in an oval, fill it in cleanly and carefully. Don't make a checkmark in it or scribble outside the lines. Be careful also to match the number of the question to the number on the answer sheet. Do just what the directions say to do.

Study the Questions

Read each question once, twice, three times—until you are certain you know what the question is asking. Watch for words like *not* and *except;* they tell you to look for choices that are false, different, or opposite in some way.

Anticipate Answers

Once you are sure you understand the question, **anticipate the answer.** Then, read the choices. If the answer you gave is there, it is probably correct. To be sure, though, check out each choice. If you don't know the answer, eliminate any choices you think are wrong. Then, make an educated—not a wild—guess about the choices that remain. Be careful to **avoid distracters,** answers that are true but don't fit the question.

Don't Give Up

If you are having a hard time with a test, take a deep breath and **keep on going.** On most tests the questions do not get more difficult as you go, and an easier question is probably coming up soon. Remember: The last question on a test is worth just as many points as the first, so give it your all—all the way to the end.

Types of Test Questions

You will feel a lot more confident taking a test if you are familiar with the kinds of questions given. The following pages describe and give examples of the different types of multiple-choice questions you'll find on many of your tests. Tips on how to approach the questions are also included.

Reading Comprehension Questions

Reading comprehension questions seek to determine not only whether you have gotten the facts straight but also how well you can think critically about what you have read. You have to make accurate **inferences** and **predictions** as well as determine the author's attitude, purpose, and meaning.

The readings and the questions may be long and complicated or short and easy. Pay attention to the purpose of the question, and you will have a good chance of selecting the correct answer.

Following the informational reading below, you will find examples of some of the most common types of reading comprehension questions.

DIRECTIONS: Read the following selection. Then, choose the best answer for each question that follows.

E-Music Appreciation

There you are, back in the time when the usual way of packaging music albums was on long-playing vinyl records. Sharing a song discovery with a friend meant either having that friend over to your house or schlepping your new album over to the friend's house. And as for moving your album collection—it meant getting specially constructed packing boxes from a local moving-van company and preparing yourself to do a lot of hefting. Then the advent of audio on compact discs cut the size and weight of one's music collection by some 75 percent and relieved a lot of aching backs. But what's that your friend just tossed you? Her music collection on

a one-ounce hard drive? Well, well, well. Talk about downsizing.

How did a person's music collection make the trip from pounds-heavy long-playing vinyl records to a one-ounce hard drive? Before 1987, compact-disc-quality sound files were so big and cumbersome and computer modems and processors were so slo-o—o—ow that the idea of downloading and uploading music files on a PC seemed an impossibility, something outside the realm of the practical. Then, in 1987, a German engineering firm devised a compression standard known as mpeg-1 Audio Layer 3—a standard that in the vernacular would be known as MP3.

What the MP3 standard accomplished was the compression of a digital audio file from, say, the size of a one-hundred-page book to the size of a ten-page book. So compressed, an audio file could now be cost effectively stored and carried on computers, and just as important, it could be played without significant loss in sound quality. How to play an MP3 music file?

MP3 audio files had significant software problems when it came to playability. The few players available were not user friendly and lacked several of the features of home stereo hardware.

What now? Enter one Justin Frankel, a teenager who wanted a better player. For months, Justin Frankel wrote code twelve hours a day. When his mother suggested he spend some time outdoors, he observed that outdoors was "overrated." And when he had completed his code-writing marathon, Justin Frankel had fulfilled his longtime dream of having compact-disc-quality music on his personal computer.

(continued)

Did the software he wrote have the features people wanted? Frankel uploaded his freeware onto his Web site. He had forty thousand visitors a day during his first month. In the following seventeen months his MP3-player software had been downloaded fifteen million times. Talk about building a better mousetrap.

FACTUAL-RECALL QUESTIONS ask you to do a close reading to find **details** or **facts** straight from the selection. Search carefully. The words may not be identical, but the answer will be there.

1. The article provides the *most* information on —
   A e-mail
   B technology
   C personal computers
   D e-music

Answer: **The correct answer is D.** Although choices **A, B,** and **C** are all mentioned, the *most* information is about e-music.

2. Which of the following is *not* discussed in this article?
   A Vinyl records
   B Audiocassettes
   C Justin Frankel
   D MP3

Answer: Did you spot the word *not*? **The correct answer is B.** This is a detail, or close-reading, question. Audiocassettes are not mentioned in this selection; choices **A, B,** and **C** are all discussed in the selection.

INFERENCE QUESTIONS ask you to connect **clues.** You read between the lines to make an **educated guess.** An inference

question sometimes requires you to apply what you already know.

3. Based on this selection, which of the following is the most important characteristic of a successful software programmer?
   A Self-motivation
   B Love of music
   C Scattered interests
   D Desire to keep things as they are

Answer: This question requires a careful reading. **The correct answer is A.** Frankel had to be highly self-motivated to sit in his room writing code for month after month with no guarantee of success. Choice **B** is consistent with Frankel's interest in music, but it is not a characteristic that is essential for a computer programmer. **C** is incorrect because it suggests an inability to focus on one thing—not true of Frankel. **D** is incorrect because this is certainly not one of Frankel's goals or a goal of anyone creating new computer software.

MAIN-IDEA QUESTIONS ask you to state the selection's **main idea** or **draw a conclusion.** Sometimes a main-idea question asks you to choose the **best title** for a selection.

4. The main idea of this article is —
   A clever inventions can make life more fun
   B music is big business
   C the popularity of personal computers has grown as they have become smaller, faster, and less expensive
   D big sound and small size have fueled the explosion of MP3 onto the music scene

Answer: **D is the correct answer** because it makes a statement that reflects the entire selection. **A** and **B** are way too broad and reflect only part of the selection—if at all. **C** is a true statement but doesn't have anything to do with this article.

EVALUATION QUESTIONS ask you to use your own knowledge and life experience to give an **opinion** about the selection. Sometimes an evaluation question asks about the writer's purpose or style of writing.

5. The factual information in this article seems to be —

   A reliable because it mentions facts and dates that can be checked in other sources

   B reliable because the writer is a well-known expert on e-music

   C unreliable because the writer is clearly biased against e-music

   D unreliable because the tone is informal and somewhat humorous

Answer: **A is the correct answer** to this tough question. **B** is incorrect but could trick you because we don't know who wrote this selection; the writer isn't identified. **C** is incorrect because the article contains no evidence of the writer's bias against e-music. **D** has a **distracter** designed to make you think. The tone of the article *is* informal and somewhat humorous, but that wouldn't necessarily make the information unreliable.

Vocabulary Questions

Vocabulary questions test your understanding of word meanings—both in and out of context. Some are simple and some are tricky. Read each question carefully.

   After the excerpt from a novel below, you will find examples of some of the most common types of vocabulary questions:

DIRECTIONS: Read the following novel excerpt about a cat named Stripey that lives on a small ship anchored offshore. Then, choose the best answer for each question.

Through years of attempting to lick herself clean, for she had never quite lost her self-respect, Stripey had become as thickly coated with mud inside as out. She was in a perpetual process of readjustment, not only to tides and seasons, but to the rats she encountered on the wharf. Up to a certain size, that is to say the size attained by rats at a few weeks old, she caught and ate them, and, with a sure instinct for authority, brought in their tails to lay them at the feet of Martha. Any rats in excess of this size chased Stripey. The resulting uncertainty as to whether she was coming or going had made her, to some extent, mentally unstable.

—from *Offshore* by Penelope Fitzgerald

DEFINITION OR SYNONYM QUESTIONS are the simplest type of vocabulary question. They ask for a definition or synonym of a word. There are no clues to help you. You are expected to know the word's meaning.

6. Instinct means —

   A respect

   B hatred

   C relating to cats

   D inborn tendency

Answer: **D is the correct answer.** You just plain have to know the word's meaning.

CONTEXT-CLUE QUESTIONS ask you to define an unfamiliar word. You will find clues to the word's meaning in the sentence in which the word appears or in the sentences immediately before or after it. You choose the answer that best defines the underlined word.

7. "She was in a perpetual process of re-adjustment, not only to tides and seasons, but to the rats she encountered on the wharf."

Perpetual means —

A important

B humorous

C continual

D immediate

Answer: **C is the correct answer.** The context clues ("tides and seasons" that are continually changing and "rats" that are always around) indicate that Stripey is continually having to re-adjust. **A** is incorrect but may at first seem like a possible answer. It does not fit the full context of change over time. **B** is incorrect. Mention of rats in the sentence is clearly not humorous. **D** is incorrect. The mention of tides and seasons indicates something that happens over time and not just immediately.

MULTIPLE-MEANING QUESTIONS ask

you to recognize which meaning of a familiar word is the one being used in a sentence. You choose the sentence that uses the underlined word in the same way it is used in the original sentence.

8. Stripey moved in a kind of crawl.

A Fia moved that the meeting be adjourned.

B Sean's family moved to Los Angeles from Chicago.

C Carla moved quickly to send the fly ball to the infield.

D The movie's ending moved her to tears.

Answer: **The correct answer is C.** Stripey isn't (**A**) putting an idea up for a vote, (**B**) changing where she lives, or (**D**) tugging at people's heartstrings. You need a sentence using *moved* in a way that involves motion or changing position, which is choice **C.**

SENTENCE-COMPLETION OR FILL-IN-THE-BLANK QUESTIONS ask you to

use the appropriate vocabulary word to complete a sentence. Sometimes questions have two blanks, but these aren't any harder than one-blank questions. The trick is to find the choice that fits both blanks correctly. As a short-cut, determine which choices contain a word that fits the first blank. Then, consider only those choices when filling in the second blank. Be sure to notice words that indicate similarity (*and, because*) or difference (*but, although, though*).

9. The paragraph about Stripey is _____, but it is also _____.

A funny, comic

B sad, somber

C autobiographical, funny

D comic, ironic

Answer: First, eliminate choices that will not work in the first blank. Answer **C** will not work in the first blank: The passage is not autobiographical. Then, review the possibilities for the second blank in the remaining choices—**A, B,** and **D.** The question includes *but,* a word that indicates a difference, so you know that the choices must be different in some way. Since the two words in choices **A** and **B** are synonyms, **the correct answer is D:** comic, ironic.

ANALOGY QUESTIONS ask you to recog-

nize the relationship between a pair of words and to identify a second pair of words that has the same relationship. An analogy question is written in this form: A : B :: C : D, which can be read as "A is to B as C is to D."

The tricky part of these questions is figuring out the relationship. There are many types of relationships, including the following ones:

- **degree** (*pink : red :: beige : brown*)
- **size** (*hummingbird : ostrich :: house cat : tiger*)
- **part to whole** (*leg : lion :: fin : fish*)
- **cause and effect** (*cold : shiver :: hot : sweat*)

- **synonyms** (*happy : cheery :: sad : glum*)
- **antonyms** (*happy : sad :: nice : mean*)

Once you figure out the relationship between the first pair of words, try expressing it as a sentence—for example, *A leg is a part of a lion.* Then, pick from the choices the pair of words that has the same relationship—for example, *A fin is a part of a fish.* (For more about analogies, see pages 29–30.)

> **10.** Stripey : cat ::
>
> **A** rats : wharf
>
> **B** Martha : character
>
> **C** mud : season
>
> **D** Martha : rat

Answer: **The correct answer is B.** Try turning the incomplete analogy into a sentence, as in, *Stripey is the name of a cat.* Now, try out each answer in the same sentence: *Rats are the name of a wharf? Martha is the name of a character? Mud is the name of a season? Martha is the name of a rat?* Only one answer, **B,** fits this sentence.

Multiple-Choice Writing Questions

Multiple-choice writing questions are designed to test your knowledge of **standard written English.** To answer them, you will need to know the rules of punctuation, such as when and how to use commas, quotation marks, end marks, italics, and so on. You will also need to know some basic rules of grammar: active versus passive voice, subject-verb agreement, correct verb tense, correct sentence structure, correct diction, parallel construction in sentences and paragraphs, to name a few. Here are the three most common types of multiple-choice writing questions:

IDENTIFYING-SENTENCE-ERRORS QUESTIONS ask you to look at underlined sections of a sentence and choose the section that includes an error. You are not expected to correct the error.

> **11.** A widely distributed memo from a tele-
> graph company in 1876 reportedly stated,
>   A
> "This 'telephone' has too many short-
>   B
> comings to be seriously considered as a
> means of communication. The device is
>   C
> inherently of no value to us." No error.
>   D   E

Answer: **The correct answer is E.** Sentences with no error may be the hardest to figure out because you keep looking for an error. But this answer is sometimes used, so look carefully, and then trust yourself when you find nothing wrong.

IMPROVING-SENTENCES QUESTIONS may ask you to choose the correct version of an underlined section:

> **12.** A big record company is said to have
> rejected the Beatles in 1962, stating as a
> reason "we don't like their sound, and
> guitar music is on the way out."
>
> **A** stating as a reason, "we
>
> **B** stating as a reason, "We
>
> **C** stating as a reason, We
>
> **D** stating as a reason "We

Answer: **B is the correct answer.** A direct quotation that's a sentence begins with a capital letter and is enclosed in quotation marks. A comma follows the introductory part of the sentence—right before the quotation begins.

13. The head of a major movie studio, he said in 1927, "Who wants to hear actors talk?"

A The head of a major movie studio, said in 1927, "Who

B The head of a major movie studio said in 1927, Who

C The head of a major movie studio said in 1927, "Who

D The Head of a major movie studio said in 1927, "Who

Answer: **C is the correct answer.** You have to read the choices very carefully to see that **A** is wrong because of the comma before *said*. **B** is incorrect because there's no quotation mark before *Who*, and **D** is incorrect because the word *head* should not be capitalized.

IMPROVING-THE-PARAGRAPH QUESTIONS are preceded by a paragraph. You may be asked to pick a choice that combines or rewrites portions of sentences. You may be asked to decide which sentences could be added or removed from the paragraph. You may be asked which sentence could be used to strengthen the writer's argument, or you could be asked to pick a thesis statement for the paragraph.

> **DIRECTIONS:** Re-read the last paragraph of the informational reading "E-Music Appreciation" on pages 968–969. Then, choose the best answer for each question based on that paragraph.

14. Which is the *best* way to combine the second and third sentences in the last paragraph of "E-Music Appreciation" without omitting important information?

A In the first month of having uploaded his freeware for distribution from his Web site, Frankel was getting forty thousand visitors a day.

B Frankel had more than thirty thousand visitors a day when his software was distributed on the Internet.

C In the first month, Frankel was swamped with visitors.

D Frankel's Web site had more than forty thousand visitors a day, and he distributed his software, which was free, from his Web site.

Answer: **A is the best answer.** All of the choices are punctuated correctly. You are looking for the sentence that contains all of the important information and says it smoothly without repetition. **B** leaves out important information (in the first month) and gets the number of visitors wrong. **C** uses the vague word *swamped* without giving any idea of how many visitors the Web site had. **D** contains the appropriate information, but it's awkwardly worded.

Strategies for Taking Writing Tests

Writing a Response to Literature

On a test, you may be asked to respond in writing to an autobiographical narrative. To do so effectively, you must draw conclusions that show your understanding of the ideas in the text as well as the author's purpose and style. Follow the steps below. The sample responses provided are based on the prompt to the right. ("By Any Other Name" begins on page 113.)

Prompt

In the autobiographical narrative "By Any Other Name," Indian students are given English names. In an essay, analyze the effect the English had on Indian students' identities, and note the author's point about this episode in her life.

THINKING IT THROUGH • Writing a Response to Literature

STEP 1 First, read the prompt carefully; then, read the selection. Decide what tasks the prompt calls for, and get an overview of the selection.

The essay relates experiences the author had while attending an English school in India. I have to explain what effect the English doing things like changing students' names had on the Indian students' identities and what the author's point is.

STEP 2 Choose a topic, and identify your main points. Skim the selection to identify and support the main points you will make.

My topic is assigned in this case. My main points will be that the writer felt that "Cynthia" (her English name) was not herself but a separate person, that there was pressure on the Indian students to change their culture as well as their names, and that despite those changes, the English people were still prejudiced against the Indian students.

STEP 3 Develop a thesis for your essay. Your thesis will sum up your main points and draw a conclusion about your topic.

My thesis will be: The teachers tried to make the Indian students more "English" by changing their names and their culture, but nothing could change the teachers' prejudice against the Indian students.

STEP 4 Gather support for your thesis. Choose details and examples that will provide strong support, and elaborate on those details and examples by drawing on your own knowledge and experience.

Along with other support, I'll explain that the girl with the braids became like the English students, but she clearly missed her own identity and culture.

STEP 5 Write your essay. Arrange your ideas to show how they relate to each other and to your thesis. As you draft your essay, maintain a serious, objective tone, vary your sentence types, and use precise language. Revise your essay to grab readers' interest from the very beginning. Finally, proofread carefully.

Writing a Response to Expository Text

Sometimes, you read an informative selection and immediately forget the important ideas. However, when you are asked to *respond* to expository text, you not only remember the ideas but draw conclusions based on them, developing a deeper understanding of the selection. To write a response to expository text, follow the steps below. ("An Ancient Enemy Gets Tougher" begins on page 207.)

Prompt

In the informative Web site article, "An Ancient Enemy Gets Tougher," the writer uses an informal tone, including contractions and slang. Write an essay in which you analyze this tone and the content of the article to determine the writer's intended audience. Support your points with relevant examples.

THINKING IT THROUGH

Writing a Response to Expository Text

STEP 1 **First, read the prompt carefully; then, read the selection.** Decide what tasks the prompt calls for, and get an overview of the selection.

I need to read looking for clues about the audience for this article.

STEP 2 **Decide on your general answer, and identify your main supporting points.** Skim the selection to identify the main points you will make to support your answer to the prompt.

This article seems to be written for kids, based on the word choice and over-all sentence style. The content is fairly simple, too—it doesn't get into scientific detail but just explains the big concept.

STEP 3 **Develop a thesis statement for your essay.** Your thesis statement will sum up your main points and draw a conclusion about your topic.

My thesis statement will be: The article's sentence style, tone, and content make it clear that it was written for an audience of younger readers.

STEP 4 **Gather support for your thesis.** Choose details and examples that will provide strong support, and elaborate on those details and examples by drawing on your own knowledge and experience.

Word choices like "the little guy that packs a TB wallop," the use of simple sentences and lots of questions, and not explaining things like exactly how TB affects the body's functions are all evidence supporting my thesis. My experience in reading about diseases in my biology textbook tells me there's more to explain and a more adult way to explain it than what is shown here.

STEP 5 **Write your essay.** Begin with an introduction that grabs attention and clearly states your thesis. Using examples from the text, explain your conclusions about the piece. End by restating your thesis. Finally, proofread and correct any errors in grammar, usage, and mechanics.

Writing a Biographical Narrative

A **biographical narrative** shares true events experienced by a person, describing not only *what* happened, but also *how* and *why* these events occurred. If you are asked to write a biographical narrative for a test, follow the steps below. The sample responses provided are based on the prompt to the right.

Prompt

Choose an older person who has been a positive influence on your life. Relate an incident from that person's life that involved you, and explain why you think this event was important.

THINKING IT THROUGH · **Writing a Biographical Narrative**

▶ **STEP 1** **Carefully read the prompt, and choose a subject.** You must address all parts of the prompt in your narrative.

I'll write about my grandfather because he's important to me and we do lots of things together.

▶ **STEP 2** **Choose an incident to relate, and identify its parts.** Outline in sequence the smaller events that make up your chosen experience.

I'll describe the time my grandfather came to talk to my middle school social studies class about growing up in Laos.

1. He was looking forward to speaking to the class.
2. I had to tell him the English words for a couple of things, and he mispronounced some words.
3. One kid laughed at him, but the rest of the class was more respectful.
4. After class he went and talked to the boy who laughed, and they became friends.

▶ **STEP 3** **Identify important details about the people, events, and setting.** Details should be relevant and specific to bring the incident to life.

I'll describe my grandfather's appearance and the way he talked, the classroom, and the sound of the boy's laughter. I'll also explain how the boy's tone and facial expressions changed as he and my grandfather talked.

▶ **STEP 4** **Draw a conclusion based on the events.** Decide why the incident is significant; this conclusion will be the basis for your narrative's thesis.

This incident is important because I got to see my grandfather confront and eliminate prejudice in a kind and courageous way.

▶ **STEP 5** **Write a draft of your biographical narrative.** Include an introduction to provide context for readers. Revise your draft to use a consistent tone and point of view and appropriate pacing. Then, proofread and correct any errors in grammar, usage, and mechanics.

Writing an Expository Composition

The purpose of an **expository composition** is to inform readers. You must clearly explain ideas new to your audience, anticipating their questions, misunderstandings, and biases about the topic. Follow these steps to write an expository composition for a test. The sample responses provided below are based on the prompt to the right.

Prompt

Consider a hobby or extra-curricular activity in which you participate. Explain the essential information—for example, rules, definitions, or techniques—to help a reader unfamiliar with this activity to understand it.

THINKING IT THROUGH ○○ Writing an Expository Composition

▶ **STEP 1 Carefully read the prompt, and choose a topic.** Make sure you address all parts of the prompt and choose a topic you know well.

I need to explain the important information about an activity. I'll write about the video productions we do in the school media club.

▶ **STEP 2 Divide the topic into parts.** Outline the main categories of information you will provide about your topic.

The essential information is about the equipment we use, the techniques we use in creating a production, and the planning process. My body paragraphs will cover those three parts.

▶ **STEP 3 Brainstorm details about each part of the topic you have identified.** Details should keep readers interested and answer the *5W-How?* questions *(Who? What? Where? When? Why? How?).*

I'll focus on the details that most people don't know, such as how certain effects are achieved and everything that goes into planning and creating our daily school newscast.

▶ **STEP 4 Synthesize your ideas to plan a thesis and conclusion.** Decide what point the information about your topic makes. Draft a thesis sentence based on this point, and plan to drive that point home in your conclusion.

I want to emphasize that a lot more goes into creating a video production than most people realize. That will be my thesis. I'll restate that idea in my conclusion while pointing out that despite all the work, video production is really fun and rewarding.

▶ **STEP 5 Write a draft of your expository composition.** Grab readers' attention from the beginning, and keep them interested by doing more than stringing together obvious information about your topic. Instead, point out more intriguing ideas and explain how they support your thesis. Revise your draft to use an authoritative voice and to make clear connections between ideas. Then, proofread to correct any errors in grammar, usage, and mechanics.

Writing a Persuasive Composition

Often on tests you will be asked to write a **persuasive composition** on an assigned topic. Although you might think you have little to say about an issue you didn't choose, you can explore your ideas to develop a convincing argument using the strategy below. The sample responses provided are based on the prompt to the right.

Prompt

Imagine that your school district is debating whether to hold athletics practices only during the school day or only after school. Choose a position on this issue, and write a letter to the school board in which you support that position.

THINKING IT THROUGH — Writing a Persuasive Composition

STEP 1 Carefully read the prompt, and identify your point of view.

The options are to hold practices only during the school day or only after school. If practices are held only after school, students who ride the bus and students who have jobs or other responsibilities won't be able to participate. I think practices should be during the school day so everyone has a chance to participate.

STEP 2 Identify reasons and evidence in favor of your position. Brainstorm a variety of reasons and evidence based on your knowledge and experience. Choose only the strongest support to use in your essay.

1. After-school practices might exclude good athletes. My friend Paloma is a great runner but has to take care of her little brother after school.
2. It might keep students from developing their skills. I tried volleyball just for fun and wound up getting good at it and learning teamwork.
3. It might discourage students from exercising. Studies show that people who don't exercise have more health problems than people who do.

STEP 3 Draft a thesis statement, and arrange ideas in order of importance.

My thesis statement will preview the order of my reasons: After-school practices would deny some students the opportunity to participate in athletics, preventing them from discovering their skills, shortchanging our teams, and most important, endangering the health of our student body.

STEP 4 Consider and address a possible counterargument. Decide why a reader might oppose your position on the issue, and plan a response to that reason.

Some people might say that practicing after school will allow more time for developing skills, but if athletics is a class, athletes can have "homework" to practice those skills.

STEP 5 Draft your essay. Use a respectful and serious tone to show readers you mean business. Develop your reasons in the order you have chosen, and conclude by addressing a counterargument and restating your opinion. Finally, check that your spelling, punctuation, grammar, and usage are correct.

Handbook of Literary Terms

For more information about a topic, turn to the page(s) in this book indicated on a separate line at the end of most entries. For example, to learn more about *Alliteration,* turn to pages 505 and 531.

On another line are cross-references to entries in this handbook that provide closely related information. For instance, at the end of *Alliteration* are cross-references to *Assonance* and *Rhythm.*

ALLEGORY Narrative in which characters and settings stand for abstract ideas or moral qualities. In addition to the literal meaning of the story, an allegory contains a symbolic, or **allegorical,** meaning. Characters and places in allegories often have names that indicate the abstract ideas they stand for: Justice, Deceit, Vanity. Many of Edgar Allan Poe's stories are allegories, including "The Masque of the Red Death" (page 419).

See pages 399, 418.

ALLITERATION Repetition of the same or similar consonant sounds in words that are close together. Although alliteration most often consists of sounds that begin words, it may also involve sounds that occur within words:

> Where the quail is whistling betwixt the woods
>   and the wheat-lot.
>
> —Walt Whitman, from "Song of Myself"

See pages 505, 531.
See also *Assonance, Rhythm.*

ALLUSION Reference to a statement, a person, a place, an event, or a thing that is known from literature, history, religion, myth, politics, sports, science, or the arts. Can you identify the literary allusion in the cartoon at the top of the next column? If not, turn to page 810.

See pages 140, 316, 597.

"Et tu, Baxter?"

AMBIGUITY Element of uncertainty in a text, in which something can be interpreted in a number of different ways. Ambiguity adds a layer of complexity to a story, for it presents us with a variety of possible interpretations, all of which are valid. The ending of "Night Calls" by Lisa Fugard (page 565) is a good example of ambiguity. That ending is open to several interpretations. **Subtleties,** or fine distinctions, help create ambiguity.

See pages 315, 374.

ANALOGY Comparison made between two things to show how they are alike. In "The Man in the Water" (page 273), the writer draws an analogy between a man's struggle to stay alive in freezing water and a battle against "an implacable, impersonal enemy."

See also *Metaphor, Simile.*

ANECDOTE Very brief account of a particular incident. Like **parables,** anecdotes are often used by philosophers and teachers of religion to point out truths about life.

See also *Fable, Folk Tale, Parable.*

ASIDE In a play, words spoken by a character directly to the audience or to another character but not overheard by others onstage. In Act II, Scene 2 (page 801) of *Julius Caesar,* Trebonius and Brutus speak ominous asides that Caesar cannot hear.

See page 815.

ASSONANCE Repetition of similar vowel sounds followed by different consonant sounds in words that are close together. Like alliteration, assonance creates musical and rhythmic effects:

> And so all the night-tide, I lie down by the side,
> Of my darling, my darling, my life and my bride
>
> —Edgar Allan Poe, from "Annabel Lee"

See also *Alliteration, Rhythm.*

ATMOSPHERE See Mood.

AUTOBIOGRAPHY Account by a writer of his or her own life. "Typhoid Fever" (page 194) is a selection from a famous autobiography by Frank McCourt. "By Any Other Name" (page 113) by Santha Rama Rau is an example of a short autobiographical essay.

See also *Biography.*

BALLAD Song or songlike poem that tells a story. Ballads often tell stories that have tragic endings. Most ballads have a regular pattern of **rhythm** and **rhyme** and use simple language and repetition. Generally they have a **refrain**—lines or words repeated at regular intervals. **Folk ballads** (such as "Bonny Barbara Allan," page 510) were composed by unknown singers and passed on orally for generations before being written down. **Literary ballads** and some country-and-western songs imitate folk ballads.

See page 509.

BIOGRAPHY Account of a person's life written or told by another person. A classic American biography is Carl Sandburg's multivolume work about Abraham Lincoln. Today biographies of writers, actors, sports stars, and TV personalities are often bestsellers.

See also *Autobiography.*

BLANK VERSE Poetry written in unrhymed iambic pentameter. *Blank verse* means that the poetry is unrhymed. *Iambic pentameter* means that each line contains five iambs; an **iamb** is a type of **metrical foot** that consists of an unstressed syllable followed by a stressed syllable (˘ ′). Blank verse is the most important metrical form in English dramatic and epic poetry and the major verse line in Shakespeare's plays. One reason blank verse has been popular, even with some modern poets, is that it combines the naturalness of unrhymed verse and the structure of metrical verse.

> When I see birches bend to left and right
> Across the line of straighter darker trees,
> I like to think some boy's been swinging them.
>
> —Robert Frost, from "Birches"

See page 752.
See also *Iambic Pentameter, Meter.*

CHARACTER Individual in a story, poem, or play. A character always has human traits, even if the character is an animal, as in Aesop's fables. In myths the characters are divinities or heroes with superhuman powers, such as the hero Theseus in "Theseus" (page 662) or Sigurd in "Sigurd, the Dragon Slayer" (page 674). Most characters are ordinary human beings, however.

A writer can reveal a character's personality by

1. telling us directly what the character is like (generous, deceitful, timid, and so on)
2. describing how the character looks and dresses
3. letting us hear the character speak
4. letting us listen to the character's inner thoughts and feelings
5. revealing what other people think or say about the character
6. showing the character's actions

The first method listed above is called **direct characterization:** The writer tells us directly what the character is like. The other five methods are **indirect characterization.** We have to put clues together to figure out what a character is like, just as we do in real life when we are getting to know someone.

Static and flat characters often function as **subordinate characters** in a story. This means that they may play important roles in a story, but they are not the main actors in the plot.

A **static character** does not change much in the course of a story. A **dynamic character,** on the other hand, changes in some important ways as a result of the story's action. **Flat characters** have only one or two personality traits and can be summed up in a single phrase. In contrast, **round characters** are complex and have many different traits. The needs or conflicts that drive a character are called **motivation.**

> See pages 45, 74–75, 76, 96–97, 112.
> See also *Protagonist.*

COMEDY In general, a story that ends happily. The hero of a comedy is usually an ordinary character who overcomes a series of obstacles that block what he or she wants. Many comedies have a boy-meets-girl (or girl-meets-boy) plot, in which young lovers must face figures from the older generation who do not want them to marry. At the end of such comedies, the lovers marry, and everyone celebrates the renewal of life and love, as in Shakespeare's play *A Midsummer Night's Dream.* In structure and characterization a comedy is the opposite of a **tragedy.**

In a serious literary work a humorous scene is said to provide **comic relief.**

> See pages 721, 724.
> See also *Drama, Tragedy.*

CONFLICT Struggle or clash between opposing characters, forces, or emotions. In an **external conflict** a character struggles against an outside force, which may be another character, society as a whole, or something in nature. In "The Cold Equations" (page 164), Barton and Cross find themselves in a fight with the harsh laws of nature.

An **internal conflict** is a struggle between opposing needs, desires, or emotions within a single character. The main character in W. D. Wetherell's "The Bass, the River, and Sheila Mant" (page 244) is torn between his desire to land a fish and his desire to impress a girl. Many works, especially longer ones, contain both internal and external conflicts, and an external conflict often leads to internal problems.

> See pages 2–3, 45, 96, 98, 243.

CONNOTATIONS All the meanings, associations, or emotions that a word suggests. For example, an expensive restaurant might advertise its delicious "cuisine" rather than its delicious "cooking." *Cuisine* and *cooking* have the same **denotation** (literal meaning): "prepared food." However, *cuisine,* a word from French, has connotations of elegance and sophistication; *cooking,* a plain English word, suggests the plainness of everyday food. Connotations play an important role in creating **diction, mood,** and **tone.**

> See pages 54, 282, 631.
> See also *Diction, Mood, Tone.*

COUPLET Two consecutive lines of poetry that form a unit, often emphasized by rhythm or rhyme. Since the Middle Ages the couplet has been used to express a completed thought or to provide a sense of closure, as in this final speech from Shakespeare's play *Julius Caesar:*

> So call the field to rest, and let's away
> To part the glories of this happy day.

> See page 493.

DESCRIPTION Type of writing intended to create a mood or an emotion or to re-create a person, a place, a thing, an event, or an experience. Description uses **images** that appeal to the senses, helping us imagine how a subject looks, sounds, smells, tastes, or feels. Description is used in fiction, nonfiction, drama, and poetry.

> See also *Imagery.*

DIALECT Way of speaking that is characteristic of a particular region or group of people. A dialect may have a distinct vocabulary, pronunciation system, and grammar. In the United States the dialect used in formal writing and spoken by most TV and radio announcers is known as standard English. This is the dialect taught in schools. To bring characters to life, writers often use dialects.

> See page 95.

DIALOGUE Conversation between two or more characters. Dramas are made up of dialogue, which is also important in novels and stories and in some poems and nonfiction.

> See pages 74, 76, 722.

DICTION **Writer's or speaker's choice of words.** Diction is an essential element of a writer's **style.** A writer can choose words that are simple or flowery *(clothing/apparel)*, modern or old-fashioned *(dress/frock)*, general or specific *(pants/designer jeans)*. Writers choose words for their connotations (emotional associations) as well as their literal meanings, or denotations.

> See pages 139, 556, 558.
> See also *Connotations, Tone.*

DRAMA **Story that is written to be acted for an audience.** The action of a drama is driven by a character who wants something and who takes steps to get it. The major elements of a dramatic plot are **exposition, complications, climax,** and **resolution.** The term *drama* is also used to refer to a serious play that is neither a **comedy** nor a **tragedy.**

> See pages 720–723, 745–749, 754.

DRAMATIC MONOLOGUE **A poem in which a speaker addresses one or more silent listeners, often reflecting on a specific problem or situation.** Though the person addressed in a dramatic monologue does not speak, we often can discover something about the listener or listeners by paying close attention to the speaker's words. The most famous dramatic monologues in English literature are those written by Robert Browning. Here are the opening lines of "My Last Duchess," spoken by a duke to his agent. The agent remains silent. As the monologue continues, we learn the duke's dark secret:

> That's my last Duchess painted on the wall,
> Looking as if she were alive. I call
> That piece a wonder, now: Frà Pandolf's hands
> Worked busily a day, and there she stands.
> Will 't please you sit and look at her?
>
> —Robert Browning, from
> "My Last Duchess"

> See pages 75, 85.

EPIC **Long narrative poem that relates the great deeds of a larger-than-life hero who embodies the values of a particular society.** Most epics include elements of myth, legend, folklore, and history; their tone is serious and their language grand.

Epic heroes undertake quests to achieve something of tremendous value to themselves or their society. Homer's *Odyssey* and *Iliad* and Virgil's *Aeneid* are the best-known epics in the Western tradition. The great epic of India is the *Mahabharata;* Japan's is *The Tale of the Heike;* and Mali's is *Sundiata.*

ESSAY **Short piece of nonfiction that examines a single subject from a limited point of view.** Most essays can be classified as personal or formal. A **personal essay** (sometimes called **informal**) is generally subjective, revealing a great deal about the writer's personality and feelings. Its tone is conversational, sometimes even humorous.

A **formal essay** is usually serious, objective, and impersonal in tone. Because formal essays are often written to inform or persuade, they are expected to be factual, logical, and tightly organized.

> See pages 254, 272.

EXPOSITION **Type of writing that explains, gives information, or clarifies an idea.** Exposition is generally objective and formal in tone (as in a magazine article on nutrition).

Exposition is also the term for the first part of a plot (also called the **basic situation**), which presents the main characters and their conflicts.

> See page 2.
> See also *Plot.*

FABLE **Brief story in prose or verse that teaches a moral, or a practical lesson about life.** The characters of most fables are animals that behave and speak like humans. Some of the most popular fables are those attributed to Aesop, who scholars believe was a slave in ancient Greece. Other widely read fables are those in the *Panchatantra*, ancient Indian tales about the art of ruling wisely.

> See page 399.
> See also *Folk Tale, Parable.*

FIGURE OF SPEECH **Word or phrase that describes one thing in terms of another and that is not meant to be understood on a literal level.** Figures of speech, or **figurative language,** always involve some sort of imaginative comparison between seemingly unlike things. The most common are the **simile** ("My heart is like a singing bird"), the **metaphor** ("Life's but a walking shadow"), and **personification** ("Death has reared himself a throne").

> See pages 242, 557, 564, 585, 599.
> See also *Metaphor, Personification, Simile, Symbol.*

FLASHBACK **Scene in a movie, play, short story, novel, or narrative poem that interrupts the present action of the plot to show events that happened at an earlier time.** In "Everyday Use" (page 77), the narrator uses a flashback to a house fire to explain family conflicts. Flashbacks are commonly used in movies.

> See pages 3, 31, 564.

FLASH-FORWARD **Scene in a movie, play, short story, novel, or narrative poem that interrupts the present action of the plot to shift into the future.** Writers may use a flash-forward to create dramatic irony. By means of the flash-forward, we know the future, but the story characters do not.

> See page 3.

FOIL **Character who serves as a contrast to another character.** Writers use a foil to emphasize differences between two characters. In *Julius Caesar,* the solemn, self-controlled Octavius is a foil for the excitable, impetuous Antony.

> See pages 767, 779, 788.

FOLK TALE **Anonymous traditional story originally passed down orally from generation to generation.** Folk tales are told in every culture, and similar tales are told throughout the world. Many of these stories have been written down. Scholars draw a sharp distinction between folk tales and myths. **Myths,** unlike folk tales, are stories about humans and gods and are basically religious in nature. Examples of folk tales are fairy tales, fables, legends, ghost stories, tall tales, anecdotes, and even jokes. Folk tales tend to travel, so the same plot often appears in several cultures. For example, there are said to be nine hundred versions of the folk tale about Cinderella.

> See also *Fable, Myth, Tall Tale.*

FORESHADOWING **The use of clues to hint at events that will occur later in the plot.** Foreshadowing arouses the reader's curiosity and increases **suspense.** In Act I, Scene 3, of *Julius Caesar* (page 771), references to violent disturbances in the heavens foreshadow the turbulence and violence that will soon occur in the human world.

> See pages 3, 31.
> See also *Plot, Suspense.*

FREE VERSE **Poetry that does not have a regular meter or rhyme scheme.** Poets writing in free verse try to capture the natural rhythms of ordinary speech. To create musical effects, they may use **alliteration, assonance, internal rhyme,** and **onomatopoeia.** They also often repeat words or grammatical structures.

> Women sit or move to and fro, some old,
>   some young,
> The young are beautiful—but the old are more
>   beautiful than the young.
>
> —Walt Whitman, from "Beautiful Women"

> See pages 504, 513.
> See also *Alliteration, Assonance, Meter, Onomatopoeia, Rhythm.*

GENRE (zhän′rə) **The category that a work of literature is classified under. Five major genres in literature are nonfiction, fiction, poetry, drama, and myth.** Collections 7 and 10 of this book are organized by genre: by poetry and by drama.

> See pages 255, 256.

HAIKU **Japanese verse form consisting of three lines and usually seventeen syllables (five in the first line, seven in the second, and five in the third).** The writer of a haiku uses association and suggestion to describe a particular moment of discovery or enlightenment. A haiku often presents an image of daily life that relates to a particular season. Many modern American poets (such as William Carlos Williams, Amy Lowell, Ezra Pound, Richard Wright, and Gary Snyder) have tried to capture the spirit of haiku, though they have not always followed the form strictly.

HYPERBOLE **Figure of speech that uses exaggeration to express strong emotion or create a comic effect.** Writers often use hyperbole (hī·pɚr′bə·lē), also called **overstatement,** to intensify a description or to emphasize the essential nature of something. If you say that a limousine is as long as an ocean liner, you are using hyperbole.

IAMBIC PENTAMETER **Line of poetry made up of five iambs.** An **iamb** is a metrical foot consisting of an unstressed syllable followed by a stressed syllable, as in dĕný and ĕxpéct. Iambic pentameter is by far the most common meter in English poetry.

See pages 518, 752.
See also *Blank Verse, Meter.*

IDIOM **Expression peculiar to a particular language that means something different from the literal meaning of the words.** "It's raining cats and dogs" and "We heard it straight from the horse's mouth" are idioms of American English. One of the difficulties of translating a work from another language is translating idioms.

See page 521.

IMAGERY **Language that appeals to the senses.** Imagery is used in all types of writing but is especially important in poetry. Most images are visual—that is, they create in the reader's mind pictures that appeal to the sense of sight. Imagery may also appeal to the senses of sound, smell, touch, and taste, as in the following lines about winter. (*Saw* in line 2 is a wise saying; *crabs* in line 5 are crab apples; and to *keel* is to cool by stirring.)

> When all aloud the wind doth blow,
>   And coughing drowns the parson's saw,
> And birds sit brooding in the snow,
>   And Marian's nose looks red and raw,
> When roasted crabs hiss in the bowl,
> Then nightly sings the staring owl—Tu whit,
> Tu-who, a merry note,
> While greasy Joan doth keel the pot.
>
> —William Shakespeare
> from *Love's Labor's Lost*

See pages 456–457, 564, 599.

INCONGRUITY (in′kän·grōō′i·tē) **A lack of fitness or appropriateness.** When someone goes to a formal dinner party dressed in a bathing suit, the situation is incongruous. Incongruity is often used to create situational irony in literature.

See page 349.
See also *Irony.*

INVERSION **Reversal of normal word order in a sentence.** The normal word order in an English sentence is subject-verb-complement (if there is a complement). Modifiers are usually placed immediately before or after the word they modify. Poets use inversion to give emphasis and variety and to create rhymes or accommodate a meter.

> Open here I flung the shutter, when, with
>   many a flirt and flutter,
> In there stepped a stately Raven of the
>   saintly days of yore;
> Not the least obeisance made he; not a
>   minute stopped or stayed he. . . .
>
> —Edgar Allan Poe, from "The Raven"

See page 162.

IRONY **Contrast or discrepancy between expectation and reality.** In **verbal irony** a speaker says one thing but means the opposite. In Shakespeare's *Julius Caesar,* Antony uses **verbal irony** during his funeral oration for Caesar. When he insists that "Brutus is an honorable man," he means precisely the opposite.

In **situational irony** what actually happens is the opposite of what is expected or appropriate. In Tim O'Brien's story "Where Have You Gone, Charming Billy?" (page 621), we feel a strong sense of irony when Paul Berlin is overcome with laughter upon being told of the death of his fellow soldier, Billy Boy Watkins.

Dramatic irony occurs when the reader or the audience knows something important that a character does not know. In "The Cold Equations" by Tom Godwin (page 164), when Marilyn mischievously asks what her punishment will be, she expects simply to be fined; we know that her fate will be much graver.

See pages 314–315, 316, 328, 349.
See also *Tone.*

LYRIC POETRY **Poetry that expresses a speaker's emotions or thoughts and does not tell a story.** The term **lyric** comes from ancient Greece, where such poems were recited to the accompaniment of a stringed instrument called a lyre. Most lyric poems are short, and they imply, rather than state directly, a single strong emotion. Li-Young Lee's "Eating Together" (page 466) and John Masefield's "Sea Fever" (page 507) are lyric poems.

See page 482.
See also *Sonnet.*

MAGIC REALISM **Style of fiction, commonly associated with contemporary Latin American writers, in which fantasy and reality are casually combined, producing humorous and thought-provoking results.** "A Very Old Man with Enormous Wings" (page 587), in which an old, winged, humanlike creature lands in a poor family's backyard, is an example of magic realism.

See page 586.

METAPHOR **Figure of speech that makes a comparison between two unlike things without using a connective word such as *like, as, than,* or *resembles.*** Some metaphors, such as Gerard Manley Hopkins's comparison "I am soft sift / In an hourglass," are **direct.** (If he had written, "I am *like* soft sift . . . ," he would have been using a **simile.**) Other metaphors are **implied,** such as the one in Walt Whitman's lines "O Captain! my Captain! our fearful trip is done, / The ship has weather'd every rack, the prize we sought is won." The images imply a comparison between a captain commanding his ship and a president leading his country (in this case, the president was Lincoln).

An **extended metaphor** is developed over several lines or throughout an entire poem. In the poem "Fireworks" (page 550), Amy Lowell uses an extended metaphor when, over many lines of poetry, she compares strong feelings to fireworks.

A **mixed metaphor** is the inconsistent combination of two or more metaphors. Mixed metaphors are usually unintentional and often humorous: "It's no use closing the barn door after the milk has been spilled."

See pages 478, 484.
See also *Analogy, Figure of Speech, Personification, Simile, Symbol.*

METER **A generally regular pattern of stressed and unstressed syllables in poetry.** To indicate the metrical pattern of a poem, we mark the stressed syllables with the symbol (′) and the unstressed syllables with the symbol (˘). Analyzing the metrical pattern of a poem in this way is called **scanning** the poem, or **scansion** (skan′shən).

Meter is measured in units called feet. A **foot** usually consists of one stressed syllable and one or more unstressed syllables. Here are examples of the standard feet in English poetry:

1. **iamb** (iambic): an unstressed syllable followed by a stressed syllable, as in *forget, deceive.* This line from "The Eagle" by Alfred, Lord Tennyson, has four iambic feet:

   The wrinkled sea beneath him crawls

2. **trochee** (trochaic): a stressed syllable followed by an unstressed syllable, as in *listen, lonely.* This line from William Shakespeare's *Macbeth* is in trochees:

   Double, double, toil and trouble

3. **anapest** (anapestic): two unstressed syllables followed by one stressed syllable, as in *understand, luncheonette.* This line from "The Destruction of Sennacherib" by George Gordon, Lord Byron, is in anapests:

   The Assyrian came down like the wolf on the fold

4. **dactyl** (dactylic): one stressed syllable followed by two unstressed syllables, as in *excellent, temperate.* This extract from Shakespeare's *Macbeth* contains dactyls:

   . . . you murdering ministers . . .

5. **spondee** (spondaic): two stressed syllables, as in *heartbeat* and *football.* This foot is used for emphasis, as in these lines from *Leaves of Grass* by Walt Whitman:

   Come up here, bard, bard,
   Come up here, soul, soul. . . .

A metrical line is named for the type of foot and the number of feet in the line. (*Dimeter* is two feet, *trimeter* three feet, *tetrameter* four feet, and *pentameter* five feet.) Thus a line of five iambs is called *iambic pentameter;* a line of four trochees is *trochaic tetrameter.*

See pages 503, 506.
See also *Blank Verse, Iambic Pentameter.*

MOOD A story's atmosphere or the feeling it evokes. Mood is often created by the story's setting. A story set on a dreary moor where cold water seeps into the hero's boots will probably convey a mood of suspense and uneasiness. A story set in a garden full of sunlight and the chirps of birds will probably create a mood of peace. Edgar Allan Poe's bizarre setting of "The Masque of the Red Death" (page 419) creates a dizzying atmosphere of horror.

See pages 44–45, 46, 140.
See also *Setting.*

MYTH Traditional story that is rooted in a particular culture, is basically religious, and usually serves to explain a belief, a ritual, or a mysterious natural phenomenon. Most myths grew out of religious rituals; almost all of them involve the influence of gods on human affairs. Every culture has its own mythology. For centuries the myths of ancient Greece and Rome were influential in the Western world.

See pages 619, 660–661, 673.

NARRATION Type of writing that tells about a series of related events. Narration can be long (an entire book) or short (a brief anecdote). Narration is most often found in fiction, drama, and narrative poetry (such as epics and ballads), but it also is used in nonfiction works (such as biographies and essays).

NARRATOR The voice telling a story. The choice of a narrator is very important in storytelling. For example, in "By the Waters of Babylon" (page 141), we know only what the narrator knows, and like him, we must figure out the mysteries of the Place of the Gods.

See also *Point of View.*

NONFICTION Prose writing that deals with real people, things, events, and places. The most popular forms are biography and autobiography. Essays, newspaper stories, magazine articles, historical accounts, scientific reports, and even personal diaries and letters are also nonfiction.

See page 255.

NOVEL Long fictional prose narrative, usually of more than fifty thousand words. In general, the novel uses the same basic literary elements as the short story **(plot, character, setting, theme,** and point of view), but these elements are usually more fully developed in the novel. Many novels have several subplots, for instance. Some modern novels are basically character studies, with only the barest plot. Others concentrate on setting, tone, or even language itself.

ONOMATOPOEIA (än′ō·mat′ō·pē′ə) **Use of a word whose sound imitates or suggests its meaning.** *Buzz, splash,* and *bark* are examples of onomatopoeia. In poetry, onomatopoeia reinforces meaning and creates evocative and musical sound effects.

See pages 505, 535.

PARABLE Brief story that teaches a lesson about life. A parable has human characters, and its events are drawn from the stuff of everyday life. Parables usually illustrate moral or religious lessons. A fable, in contrast, usually has animal characters and teaches a practical lesson about how to succeed in life. The most famous parables in Western literature are found in the Bible.

See pages 278, 399.
See also *Fable, Folk Tale.*

PARADOX A statement or a situation that seems to be a contradiction but that reveals a truth. Paradoxes are designed to make readers stop and think. They often express aspects of life that are mysterious, surprising, or difficult to describe. When the ancient Mariner in Samuel Taylor Coleridge's poem cries, "Water, water everywhere, / Nor any drop to drink," he is expressing a paradox. He is dying of thirst adrift in the ocean, the water from which he cannot drink.

PARALLELISM Repetition of words, phrases, or sentences that have the same grammatical structure or that state a similar idea. Parallelism, or parallel structure, helps make lines rhythmic and memorable and heightens their emotional effect:

Bring me my bow of burning gold!
Bring me my arrows of desire!
Bring me my spear! O clouds, unfold!
Bring me my chariot of fire!

—William Blake, from "Jerusalem"

PERSONA **Mask or voice assumed by a writer.** Authors often take on other identities in their works. In a short story a writer may assume a persona by using a first-person narrator. When a poet is not the speaker of a poem, the poet is creating a persona.

> See pages 138, 140.
> See also *Point of View, Speaker.*

PERSONIFICATION **Type of metaphor in which a nonhuman thing or quality is talked about as if it were human.** In the example below, trees are personified as women throwing off their robes.

> The trees are undressing, and fling in many places—
> On the gray road, the roof, the window sill—
> Their radiant robes and ribbons and yellow laces.
>
> —Thomas Hardy
> from "Last Week in October"

> See pages 478, 487.
> See also *Figure of Speech, Metaphor.*

PERSUASION **Type of writing designed to change the way a reader or listener thinks or acts.** Persuasive writing can be found in speeches, newspaper editorials, essays, and advertisements.

> See pages 284–285.

PLOT **Series of related events that make up a story or drama.** Plot is "what happens" in a story, novel, or play. A story map shows the parts of a plot.

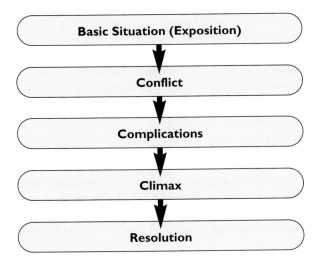

Basic Situation (Exposition)

↓

Conflict

↓

Complications

↓

Climax

↓

Resolution

The **climax** is the most intense moment in the plot, the moment at which something happens that reveals how the conflict will turn out. In the **resolution,** or denouement (dā′nōō·män′), all the problems in the story are resolved, and the story is brought to a close.

> See pages 2–3, 4.

POETRY **Type of rhythmic, compressed language that uses figures of speech and imagery to appeal to the reader's emotions and imagination.** The major forms of poetry are **lyric** and **narrative.** A popular type of lyric is the **sonnet.** Two major types of narrative are the **epic** and the **ballad.** Though poetry is one of the oldest forms of human expression, it is extremely difficult to define.

> See pages 456–457, 477–478, 503–505.
> See also *Ballad, Epic, Lyric Poetry, Sonnet.*

POINT OF VIEW **Vantage point from which a writer narrates, or tells, a story.** The three main points of view are omniscient, third-person-limited, and first-person.

In the **omniscient** (or "all-knowing") **point of view,** the narrator plays no part in the story but can tell us what all the characters are thinking and feeling as well as what is happening in other places. For example, in "Through the Tunnel" (page 401), the storyteller can tell us what both Jerry and his mother are thinking and feeling.

In the **third-person-limited point of view,** the narrator, who plays no part in the story, zooms in on the thoughts and feelings of one character. In "Catch the Moon" by Judith Ortiz Cofer (page 234), we know Luis's thoughts and feelings but the emotions of his father and of Naomi are revealed only through their words and Luis's observations.

In the **first-person point of view,** the narrator (using the first-person pronoun *I*) is a character in the story. When we read a story told in the first person, we hear and see only what the narrator hears and sees. We must ask ourselves if the narrator is **credible,** or **reliable.** An **unreliable narrator** does not always know what is happening in the story, or he or she might be lying or telling us only part of the story. For example, in "By the Waters of Babylon" (see page 141), we cannot rely on the narrator to tell us the mystery of the Place of the Gods because he does not know it.

> See pages 138–139, 140, 154, 163.
> See also *Narrator.*

PROTAGONIST Main character in fiction or drama. The protagonist is the character we focus our attention on, the person who sets the plot in motion. The character or force that blocks the protagonist is called the **antagonist.** Most protagonists are rounded, dynamic characters who change in some important way by the end of the story, novel, or play. The antagonist is often, but not always, the villain in a story. Similarly, the protagonist is often, but not always, the hero.

See page 96.
See also *Character*.

PUN Play on the multiple meanings of a word or on two words that sound alike but have different meanings. Many jokes and riddles are based on puns. ("When is a doctor most annoyed?" Answer: "When he runs out of patients.") Shakespeare was one of the greatest punsters of all time. In Antony's speech to the conspirators after Caesar's murder in Act III (page 813), Antony puns on the expression "to let blood." Doctors used to draw, or let, blood from sick people to cure them; murderers also "let blood."

See page 781.

REFRAIN Repeated word, phrase, line, or group of lines. Though refrains are usually associated with poetry and songs, they are sometimes used in prose, especially in speeches. Refrains create rhythm and may also build suspense or emphasize important words or ideas.

See page 527.

RHYME Repetition of accented vowel sounds and all sounds following them in words that are close together in a poem. *Heart* and *start* rhyme, as do *plaster* and *faster*. The most common type of rhyme, **end rhyme,** occurs at the ends of lines.

When she I loved looked every day
Fresh as a rose in June,
I to her cottage bent my way,
Beneath the evening moon.

—William Wordsworth
from "Strange Fits of Passion
Have I Known"

The pattern of rhymed lines in a poem is called its **rhyme scheme.** You indicate a rhyme scheme by giving each new end rhyme a new letter of the alphabet. For example, the rhyme scheme in Wordsworth's stanza is *abab*.

Internal rhymes occur within lines.

The warm sun is failing, the bleak wind is
wailing,
The bare boughs are sighing, the pale flowers
are dying . . .

—Percy Bysshe Shelley
from "Autumn: A Dirge"

Words that sound similar but do not rhyme exactly are called **approximate rhymes** (or **half rhymes, slant rhymes,** or **imperfect rhymes**). The approximate rhymes at the ends of lines in this stanza from a poem about war keep the reader off balance and even uneasy, in keeping with the poem's subject:

Let the boy try along this bayonet blade
How cold steel is, and keen with hunger of
blood;
Blue with all malice, like a madman's flash;
And thinly drawn with famishing for flesh.

—Wilfred Owen, from "Arms and the Boy"

See pages 504–505, 506.

RHYTHM Musical quality in language, produced by repetition. Rhythm occurs naturally in all forms of spoken and written language. Poems written in **meter** create rhythm by a strict pattern of stressed and unstressed syllables. Writers can also create rhythm by repeating grammatical structures, by using pauses, by varying line lengths, and by balancing long and short words or phrases.

See page 503.
See also *Meter*.

ROMANCE Centuries ago, in France and England, a romance was a verse narrative about the adventures of a hero who undertakes a quest for a high ideal. The tales of King Arthur are typical romances. The term *romance* later came to mean any story set in a world of wish fulfillment, with larger-than-life characters having superhuman powers. Romances usually involve a series of adventures that end with good triumphing over evil. Fairy tales and western movies are often built on the old romance plots and use the characters typical of romance literature.

See pages 651, 657.

SATIRE Type of writing that ridicules human weakness, vice, or folly in order to reveal a weakness or to bring about social reform. Satires often try to persuade the reader to do or believe something by showing the opposite view as absurd—or even as vicious and inhumane. One of the favorite techniques of the satirist is **exaggeration**—overstating something to make it look worse than it is.

See page 154.
See also *Hyperbole, Irony.*

SCENE DESIGN Sets, lights, costumes, and props, which bring a play to life onstage. Sets are the furnishings and scenery that suggest the time and place of the action. **Props** (short for *properties*) are all the objects that the actors use onstage, such as books, telephones, suitcases.

See pages 721–722.

SETTING Time and place of a story or play. Setting can function in several ways in a story. It can provide atmosphere, as the ice-coated world does in Jim Heynen's "What Happened During the Ice Storm" (page 306). Setting may provide conflict in a story, as it does in Tim O'Brien's "Where Have You Gone, Charming Billy?" (page 621). One of the most important functions of setting is to reveal character. In Alice Walker's "Everyday Use" (page 77), the narrator's home helps show us who she is and what her life is like.

See pages 44–45, 46, 140.
See also *Mood.*

SHORT STORY Short piece of narrative fiction. Edgar Allan Poe (see page 428), who lived and wrote during the first half of the nineteenth century, is often credited with writing the first short stories. He defined the short story (which he called the "prose tale") as a narrative that can be read in a single sitting and that creates a "single effect."

SIMILE Figure of speech that makes a comparison between two seemingly unlike things by using a connective word such as *like, as, than, or resembles.* Here is a simile that creates a dramatic visual image; like any good figure of speech, Hardy's simile is original and vivid:

> The Roman Road runs straight and bare
> As the pale parting-line in hair
>
> —Thomas Hardy
> from "The Roman Road"

See pages 477, 479.
See also *Analogy, Figure of Speech, Metaphor.*

SOLILOQUY Long speech in which a character who is alone onstage expresses private thoughts or feelings. The soliloquy (sə·lil′ə·kwē), especially popular in Shakespeare's day, is an old dramatic convention. Near the beginning of Act II in *Julius Caesar* (page 783), Brutus's speech in which he decides to join the conspiracy against Caesar is a soliloquy.

See pages 75, 722.

SONNET Fourteen-line lyric poem, usually written in iambic pentameter. There are two major types of sonnets. The **Italian sonnet,** also called the **Petrarchan sonnet,** is named after the fourteenth-century Italian poet Francesco Petrarch, who popularized the form. The Petrarchan sonnet has two parts: an eight-line **octave** with the rhyme scheme *abbaabba,* and a six-line **sestet** with the rhyme scheme *cdecde.* The octave usually presents a problem, poses a question, or expresses an idea, which the sestet then resolves, answers, or drives home. A modern variation on the Italian sonnet, by E. E. Cummings, can be found on page 485. Like many sonnets, Cummings's poem is about love.

The other major sonnet form is called the **Shakespearean sonnet,** or the **English sonnet.** It has three **quatrains** (four-line units) followed by a concluding **couplet** (two-line unit). The three quatrains often express related ideas or examples; the couplet sums up the poet's conclusion or message. The most common rhyme scheme for the Shakespearean sonnet is *abab cdcd efef gg.* A Shakespearean sonnet—also about love—can be found on page 494.

See page 493.
See also *Lyric Poetry.*

SPEAKER **The voice that is talking to us in a poem.** Sometimes the speaker is the same as the poet, but the poet may also create a different voice, speaking as a child, a woman, a man, a nation, an animal, or even an object.

See page 465.

See also *Dramatic Monologue, Persona.*

STANZA **Group of consecutive lines that form a single unit in a poem.** A stanza in a poem is something like a paragraph in prose: It often expresses a unit of thought. A stanza may consist of only one line or of any number of lines beyond that. John Updike's "Ex–Basketball Player" (page 519) consists of five six-line stanzas, each expressing a unit of thought.

See also *Sonnet.*

STYLE **The particular way in which a writer uses language.** Style is created mainly through **diction** (word choice), use of **figurative language,** and sentence patterns. Style can be described as plain, ornate, formal, ironic, conversational, sentimental, and so on.

See pages 556–557, 558, 586.

SUSPENSE **The uncertainty or anxiety we feel about what is going to happen next in a story.** Writers often create suspense by dropping hints or clues foreshadowing something—especially something bad—that is going to happen later. Writers also create suspense by setting up time limits, as in "R.M.S. Titanic" (page 330), where our suspense builds as we are shown the minutes ticking away.

See page 3.

See also *Foreshadowing, Plot.*

SYMBOL **Person, place, thing, or event that stands both for itself and for something beyond itself.** Many symbols have become so widely recognized that they are **public symbols:** In Western cultures, for example, most people recognize the heart as a symbol of love and the snake as a symbol of evil. Writers often invent new, personal symbols. For example, in this mysterious poem, "The Sick Rose," what might the rose and the worm symbolize?

O Rose, thou art sick!
The invisible worm,
That flies in the night,
In the howling storm,
Has found out thy bed
Of crimson joy:
And his dark secret love
Does thy life destroy.

—William Blake

See pages 398–399, 400, 433.

See also *Figure of Speech.*

TALL TALE **An outrageously exaggerated and obviously unbelievable humorous story.** In pre-TV days, the tall tale was a kind of oral entertainment. In the Southwest, cowboys sat around their campfires telling stories about Pecos Bill, who invented the lariat, rode a bucking Kansas tornado, and dug the Rio Grande river. Other tall tale heroes include the Northwest logger Paul Bunyan (and Babe, his gigantic blue ox), the Pennsylvania steel man Joe Magarac, and the New England fisherman Captain Stormalong. Tall tales were told about real-life figures, too, such as Tennessee frontiersman Davy Crockett and sharp-shooter Annie Oakley.

A modern **urban tall tale**—perennially rumored to be true—tells of a baby pet alligator someone flushed down a toilet in New York City. The result, according to this tale, is that monster alligators populate the sewers beneath the city.

See *Folk Tale.*

THEME **The central idea or insight about human life revealed by a work of literature.** A theme is not the same as a work's subject, which can usually be expressed in a word or two: old age, ambition, love. The theme is the revelation the writer wishes us to discover about that subject. There is no single correct way to express a theme, and sometimes a work has several themes. Many works have **ambiguous themes;** that is, they have no clear single meaning but are open to a variety of interpretations, even opposing ones. Some themes are so commonly found in the literature of all cultures and all ages that they are called **universal themes.** Here are some universal themes found in stories throughout the ages: "Heroes must undergo trials and endure losses before they can claim their rightful kingdom." "Arrogance and pride can bring destruction." "When the rule of law is broken, chaos and anarchy will result." "Love will endure and triumph over evil."

Although a few stories, poems, and plays have themes that are stated directly, most themes are implied. The reader must piece together all the clues the writer has provided to arrive at a discovery of the work's total meaning. Two of the most important clues to consider are the way the main character has changed and the way the conflict has been resolved.

See pages 230–231, 232, 233, 243, 255, 256.

TONE **The attitude a writer takes toward a subject, a character, or the reader.** Tone is conveyed through the writer's choice of words and details. For example, Tim O'Brien's story "Where Have You Gone, Charming Billy?" (page 621) is ironic in tone. John Masefield's "Sea Fever" (page 507) has a nostalgic tone for a life that is now past.

See pages 44, 139, 193, 557, 558.
See also *Connotations, Diction, Irony.*

TRAGEDY **Play, novel, or other narrative, depicting serious and important events, in which the main character comes to an unhappy end.** In a tragedy, the main character is usually dignified and courageous and often high ranking. This character's downfall may be caused by a **tragic flaw** (a serious character weakness) or by forces beyond the hero's control. The tragic hero usually wins self-knowledge and wisdom, even though he or she suffers defeat, possibly even death. Shakespeare's *The Tragedy of Julius Caesar* (page 756) is a tragedy. Tragedy is distinct from **comedy,** in which an ordinary character overcomes obstacles to get what he or she wants. At the end of most comedies, the characters are all happily integrated into society (comedies often end with weddings). Tragedies often end with death or separation or alienation.

See pages 720, 754.
See also *Comedy, Drama.*

VOICE **The writer's or speaker's distinctive use of language in a text.** Voice is created by a writer's **tone** and **diction,** or choice of words. Some writers have such a distinctive voice that you can identify their works on the basis of voice alone. Frank McCourt creates a distinctive voice in his memoir about growing up in Ireland, "Typhoid Fever" (see page 194).

See pages 139, 193, 205, 465.

Handbook of Literary Terms

Handbook of Reading and Informational Terms

For more information about a topic, turn to the page(s) in this book indicated on a separate line at the end of most entries. To learn more about *Inference,* for example, turn to page 76.

The words in **boldface** are other key terms, with definitions provided in context. On another line there are cross-references to entries in this Handbook that provide closely related information. For instance, *Logic* contains a cross-reference to *Logical Order.*

ARGUMENT **A series of statements in a text designed to convince us of something.** What the writer or speaker wants to prove is called the **claim** (or the **opinion**). An argument might appeal to both our reason and our emotions. An argument in a scientific or historical journal, for instance, would probably present only **logical appeals,** which include sound reasons and factual evidence. An argument in a political text would probably also include emotional appeals, which are directed more to our "hearts" than to our minds. Some arguments use **loaded words** (words loaded with emotional connotations) and **anecdotes** (brief, personal stories) that also appeal to our feelings. It is important to be able to recognize emotional appeals used in arguments—and to be aware of how they can trick an audience.

Arguments may be found in editorials, magazine articles, political speeches, professional journals, and primary source material.

See pages 284–285, 577–578, 881.

CAUSE AND EFFECT **A text structure that shows how or why one thing leads to another.** The **cause** is the reason that an action takes place. The **effect** is the result or consequence of the cause. A cause can have more than one effect, and an effect may have several causes. Writers may explain causes only or effects only.

A text may be organized in a cause-effect chain. One cause leads to an effect, which causes another effect, and so on. Notice the cause-effect chain in the following paragraph from "An Ancient Enemy Gets Tougher" (page 207):

> But if there's a glitch in the body's defense system, and it doesn't work quite right, these once tiny balls can grow, some to the size of a baseball, as the bacteria inside them reproduce. These balls can erupt, spreading bacteria to other parts of the body through the blood. More balls, or "tubercles," grow, eventually clogging up the way the body does its daily business.

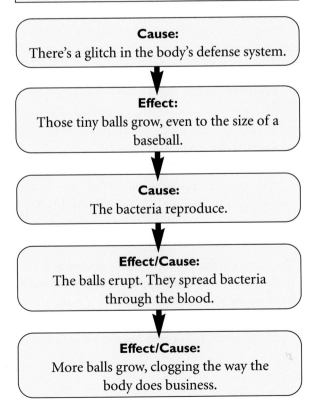

Cause:
There's a glitch in the body's defense system.

Effect:
Those tiny balls grow, even to the size of a baseball.

Cause:
The bacteria reproduce.

Effect/Cause:
The balls erupt. They spread bacteria through the blood.

Effect/Cause:
More balls grow, clogging the way the body does business.

Writers use the cause-and-effect pattern in both narrative and informational texts. In most short stories, events in the plot are connected in a cause-effect chain. Some words and phrases that signal the cause-effect pattern are *because, depended on, inspired, produced, resulting in, led to,* and *outcome.* Never assume, either in your reading or in real life, that one event causes another just because it happened before it.

> See pages 4, 349.
> See also *Text Structures.*

CHRONOLOGICAL ORDER **The arrangement of details in time order, that is, in the order in which they occurred.** Chronological order is used in a narrative, which describes a series of events, and in texts that explain the steps in a process.

> See page 4.
> See also *Text Structures.*

CLAIM **The idea or opinion that a writer tries to prove or defend in an argument.** The claim is stated as a **generalization,** a broad statement or conclusion that covers many situations (or follows from the evidence). The following statements are examples of claims stated as generalizations.

> Everyone should feel a moral responsibility to come to the aid of others in need. ("If Decency Doesn't, Law Should Make Us Samaritans," page 286)
>
> Nations must preserve wildlife species wherever they occur. ("Call of the Wild— Save Us!" page 579)

The author of the argument then supports the "claim with either logical appeals (reasons backed by factual evidence), emotional appeals, or both.

> See pages 284, 577.
> See also *Argument, Generalization.*

COHERENT **Logically integrated, consistent, and understandable.** A text is **coherent** (kō·hir′ənt) when its ideas are arranged in an order that makes sense to the reader. To aid in coherence, writers help readers follow a text by using **transitions,** words and phrases that show how ideas are connected.

Common Transitional Words and Phrases	
Comparing Ideas also, and, too, moreover, similarly, another	**Contrasting Ideas** although, still, yet, but, on the other hand, instead
Showing Cause-Effect for, since, as a result, therefore, so that, because	**Showing Importance** first, last, to begin with, mainly, more important
Showing Location above, across, over, there, inside, behind, next to, through, near	**Showing Time** before, at last, now, when, eventually, at once, finally

> See page 740.

COMPARISON AND CONTRAST **A method of organizing information by showing similarities and differences among various groups of details.**

> See pages 112, 254, 283.
> See also *Text Structures.*

CONSUMER DOCUMENTS **Informative texts directed to consumers, such as warranties, contracts, or instruction manuals.** Here are some points to keep in mind when you read consumer documents:

1. Try to read the consumer document before you buy the product. Then you can ask the clerk to explain anything you don't understand.

2. Read all of the pages in whatever language comes most easily to you. (Many documents are printed in two or three languages.) You will often find important information where you least expect it, such as at the end of the document.

3. Read the fine print. *Fine* here means "tiny and barely readable." Some fine-print statements in documents are required by law. They are designed to protect you, the consumer, so the company may not be interested in emphasizing these points.

4. Don't expect the document to be interesting or easy to read. If you don't understand a statement, and you can't ask someone at the store that sold you the product, call or write to the company that made it. You should complain to the company if you find its consumer document confusing.

5. Before you sign anything, read everything on the page, and be sure you understand what you're agreeing to. Ask to take the document home, and have your parent or guardian read it. If you are not of legal age, an adult may be responsible for whatever you've signed. Make a copy of any document that you've signed—and keep the copy in a place where you can find it.

See pages 927–930.

CONTEXT CLUES **The words and sentences surrounding a word.** Context clues can sometimes help you guess at the meaning of an unfamiliar word. You will find examples below of three types of context clues. In the examples, the unfamiliar word appears in **boldface**. The context clue is underlined.

Definition: Look for words that define the unfamiliar word, often by giving a synonym or a definition for it.

> He was an EDS pilot, **inured** to the sight of death, long since accustomed to it.

Example: Look for examples that reveal the meaning of the unfamiliar word.

> . . . I performed **listlessly,** my head propped on one arm. I pretended to be bored. And I was.

Contrast: Find words that contrast the unfamiliar word with a word or phrase you already know.

> But when they went out into the courtyard with the first light of dawn, they found the whole neighborhood in front of the chicken coop having fun with the angel, without the slightest **reverence,** tossing him things to eat through the openings in the wire as if he weren't a supernatural creature but a circus animal.

See pages 87, 432.

CREDIBILITY **The believability of a writer's argument.** To evaluate credibility, you first need to determine the author's claim, or opinion. Then you need to look at the **reasons** (statements that explain *why* the author holds the opinion) and the **evidence** (information that supports each reason). To be credible, evidence must be **relevant,** that is, directly related to the argument; **comprehensive,** that is, sufficient to be convincing; and **accurate,** that is, from a source that can be trusted as factually correct or otherwise reliable.

The writer's **intent** should also be considered. If you're reading an opinion essay, for instance, be sure to note any credentials or background information about the writer. Does the writer work for an institution that represents a particular point of view? Has the writer published a book on the same topic? Do emotional appeals and fallacious reasoning reveal a bias even though the writer pretends to be fair to both sides of the argument?

Notice the **tone** of the text. An argument that is based on logical appeals will usually have a serious, sincere tone. An angry or self-righteous tone might make you question the credibility of the argument.

See pages 284–285, 577–578, 881.

See also *Argument.*

DICTIONARY You use a dictionary to find the precise meaning and usage of words. The elements of a typical entry are explained below.

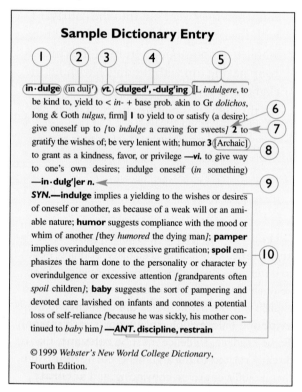

Sample Dictionary Entry

© 1999 *Webster's New World College Dictionary,* Fourth Edition.

1. Entry word. The entry word shows how the word is spelled and divided into syllables. It may also show capitalization and other spellings.

2. Pronunciation. Phonetic symbols (such as the *schwa,* ə) and **diacritical marks** (such as the *dieresis,* ä) show how to pronounce the entry word. A key to these symbols and marks usually appears at the bottom of every other page of a dictionary. In this book a pronunciation guide appears at the bottom of every other page of the Glossary (pages 1053–1058).

3. Part-of-speech label. This label tells how the entry word is used. When a word can be used as more than one part of speech, definitions are grouped by part of speech. The sample entry shows three definitions of *indulge* as a transitive verb *(vt.)* and one as an intransitive verb *(vi.).*

4. Other forms. Sometimes the spellings of plural forms of nouns, principal parts of verbs, and comparative and superlative forms of adjectives and adverbs are shown.

5. Word origin. A word's origin, or **etymology** (et′ə·mäl′ə·jē), shows where the word comes from. *Indulge* comes from the Latin *indulgere,* which probably comes from the prefix *in–,* meaning "not," added to the Greek *dolichos,* "long," and the Gothic *tulgus,* "firm."

6. Examples. Phrases or sentences show how the entry word is used.

7. Definitions. If a word has more than one meaning, the meanings are numbered or lettered.

8. Special-usage labels. These labels identify special meanings or special uses of the word. Here, *Archaic* indicates an outdated meaning.

9. Related word forms. Other forms of the entry word are listed. Usually these are created by the addition of suffixes.

10. Synonyms and antonyms. Synonyms (words similar in meaning) and **antonyms** (words opposite in meaning) may appear at the end of the entry.

Handbook of Reading and Informational Terms *(side margin)*

A dictionary is available as a book or a CD-ROM or as part of a word-processing program or Web site.

EVIDENCE **Specific information or proof that backs up the reasons in an argument.** **Factual evidence** includes statements that can be proved by direct observation or by checking reliable reference sources. **Statistics** (facts in the form of numbers) and **expert testimony,** statements from people who are recognized as experts or authorities on an issue, may all be considered factual evidence.

In fields where discoveries are constantly being made, such as in astronomy and genetics, facts need to be checked in a recently published source. Remember that a Web site on the Internet may be current, but it may not be reliable because anybody can post a statement on the Internet. If you suspect that a statement presented as a fact is not true, try to find the same fact in another source.

See pages 206, 284.

FALLACIOUS (fə·lā′shəs) **REASONING** **Faulty reasoning, or mistakes in logical thinking.** (The word *fallacious* comes from a Latin word meaning "deceptive; tricky." The word *false* comes from the same root word as does the word *fallacy*.) Fallacious reasoning leads to false or incorrect conclusions. Here are some types of fallacious reasoning:

1. **Begging the question,** also called **circular reasoning,** assumes the truth of a statement before it has been proved. You appear to be giving a reason to support your opinion, but all you're doing is restating your opinion in different words.

> College graduates are financially successful because they can get high-paying jobs.

2. **Name-calling** uses labels to attack a person who holds an opposing view, instead of giving reasons or evidence to attack the opposing view itself. This fallacy includes criticizing the person's character, situation, or background.

> Computer geeks are out of touch with the real world.

3. **Stereotyping** gives all members of a group the same (usually undesirable) characteristics. It assumes that everyone (or everything) in that group is alike. (The word *stereotype* comes from the word for a metal plate that was used to print the same image over and over.) Stereotypes are often based on misconceptions about racial, social, religious, gender, or ethnic groups.

> Teenagers are too self-centered to participate in service programs.

4. **Hasty generalization** is a broad, general statement or conclusion that is made without sufficient evidence to back it up. A hasty generalization is often made on the basis of only one or two experiences or observations.

> **Insufficient evidence:** Jenna's cat has fleas, and she spends a lot of money on cat food.
>
> **Hasty generalization:** Cats don't make good pets.

If any exceptions to the conclusion can be found, the generalization is *not* true.

5. **Either-or fallacy** assumes that there are only two possible choices or solutions (usually extremes), even though there may be many.

> I have to get a driver's license, or I'll lose all my friends.

6. False cause and effect occurs when one event is said to be the cause of another event just because the two events happened in sequence. You cannot assume that an event caused whatever happened afterward.

> As soon as I started jogging, my grades improved.

GENERALIZATION **A broad statement that applies to or covers many individuals, experiences, situations, observations, or texts.** A **valid generalization** is a type of conclusion that is drawn after considering as many of the facts as possible. Here are some specific facts from "Ill-Equipped Rescuers Dig Out Volcano Victims" (page 267) and a generalization based on them. Notice that each fact is one piece of evidence. The generalization then states what the evidence adds up to, drawing a conclusion that applies to all members of the group.

> **Specific facts:** Thousands of people were trapped alive in the ruins. There was no organization or plan to search for the living and help the survivors. There were few helicopters available to carry the victims to a nearby town. Emergency vehicles could not be brought in because the roads were not passable.
>
> **Generalization:** More victims of the volcanic eruption could have been saved if the relief effort had been better organized.

A generalization jumps from your own specific experiences and observations to a larger, general understanding.

See page 233.

GRAPHS **Graphic depiction of information.** **Line graphs** generally show changes in quantity over time. **Bar graphs** usually compare quantities within categories. **Pie graphs,** or **circle graphs,** show proportions by dividing a circle into different-sized sections, like slices of a pie.

How to Read a Graph

1. **Read the title.** The title will tell you the subject and purpose of the graph.

2. **Read the headings and labels.** These will help you determine the types of information presented.

3. **Analyze the details.** Read numbers carefully. Note increases or decreases. Look for the direction or order of events and trends and for relationships.

INFERENCE **A guess based on observation and prior experience.** When you make inferences about a literary work, you use evidence from the text, from other texts you have read, and from your own prior experience. One way to analyze a character, for instance, is to consider what the person says and how he or she interacts with other characters. In the short story "The Leap" (page 36), the narrator says:

> Since my father's recent death, there is no one to read to her, which is why I returned, in fact, from my failed life where the land is flat. I came home to read to my mother, to read out loud, to read long into the dark if I must, to read all night.

Here are some clues to look for when making inferences:

Character. In a work of literature, look at a character's speech, actions, thoughts, and appearance. What do others think and say about the character?

Tone (the writer's attitude). In both literary and informational texts, look at the writer's choice of words and details.

Theme or **main idea.** Look for the writer's most important point, opinion, or message. What idea can you take from the text that extends beyond it to the world at large?

You infer, or predict, what will happen next in the plot of a story based on what the writer has already told you. You change your inferences as the writer gives you more information. Sometimes a writer will deliberately drop a clue that leads you, for a short time, to an incorrect inference. That's part of the fun of reading. Until you get to the end of a suspenseful story, you can never be sure how the plot will turn out.

When you're writing about a story or an informational text, you must be sure your inferences are supported by details in the text.

Supported inferences are based directly on evidence in a text that you can point to and on reasonable prior knowledge. Some interpretation of the evidence is possible, but you cannot ignore or contradict facts that the writer gives you.

Unsupported inferences are conclusions that are not logical. They ignore the facts in the text or misinterpret them. Whenever you're asked to write an essay about a text, it's a good idea to re-read the text before and after you write your essay. Check each inference you make against the text to make sure you can find evidence for it. For example, if you write an analysis of a character and you say that the character never answers a question directly, you should cite details from the text to support your inference.

See pages 76, 98, 374.

INFORMATIVE TEXTS Texts that communicate information and data. When you're reading informative texts, you need to read slowly, looking for main ideas and important details. Slow and careful reading is especially important when you're trying to get meaning from consumer, workplace, and public documents. These documents are often not written by professional writers, so they may be difficult to read.

See also *Consumer Documents, Public Documents, Workplace Documents.*

LOGIC Correct reasoning. A logical text presents reasons supported by evidence (facts and examples). A text is illogical when it does not provide reasons backed by evidence. Notice how each sentence in this paragraph from "Explorers Say There's Still Lots to Look For" (page 368) gives evidence that supports the writer's main idea that there are still many places to explore.

Explorers still scale peaks that have never been climbed, crawl through caves to the insides of earth, hurtle into space to walk among the stars. They find ancient tribes and ancient cities. They dig up dinosaurs. They journey to places where no one has reported being before: the jungles of central Congo, the Amazon and Peru, the deserts of Tibet and China, vast underwater caves in Mexico and Belize. They are only beginning to probe the oceans; 5 percent has been explored, though water covers 71 percent of the planet.

See pages 284–285.
See also *Logical Order.*

LOGICAL ORDER A method of organizing information by putting details into related groupings. Writers use logical order most often when they want to classify information, that is, to examine a subject and its relationship to other subjects. For example, when you classify, you can divide a subject into its parts (considering men's responsibilities at work and at home, "Double Daddy," page 22). You can also use the comparison-contrast pattern to show similarities and differences among various groups (comparing laws that protect good Samaritans in various states, "Good Samaritans U.S.A. Are Afraid to Act," page 288).

See pages 254, 283, 542, 959.
See also *Text Structures.*

MAIN IDEA **The writer's most important point, opinion, or message.** The main idea may be stated directly, or it may be only suggested or implied. If the idea is not stated directly, it's up to you to look at the details and decide on the idea that they all seem to support. Try to restate the writer's main idea in your own words.

In an argument the main idea (the generalization that the writer is trying to prove) is called the **claim,** or **opinion.**

Main idea of an essay: A book can change a child's life ("The Magic Happened," page 648).

Claim of an argument: The Vietnam War must be stopped ("Declaration of Independence from the War in Vietnam," page 639).

See page 272.

MAP **A drawing showing all or part of the earth's surface or of bodies in the sky.** **Physical maps** illustrate the natural landscape of an area, using shading, lines, and color to show landforms and elevation. **Political maps** show political units, such as states and nations. They usually also show borders and capitals and other major cities. **Special-purpose maps** present specific information, such as the locations of Annapurna and Everest in the Himalayas ("Into Thin Air," page 351), and the Roman Empire at the death of Caesar (*Julius Caesar,* page 871).

How to Read a Map

1. **Determine the focus of the map.** The map's title and labels tell you its focus—its subject and the geographical area it covers.

2. **Study the legend.** The **legend,** or **key,** explains the symbols, lines, colors, and shadings used in the map.

3. **Check directions and distances.** Maps often include a **compass rose,** a diagram that shows north, south, east, and west. If there isn't one, assume that north is at the top, west to the left, and so on. Many maps also include a scale that relates distances on the map to actual distances.

4. **Look at the larger context.** The **absolute location** of any place on earth is given by its **latitude** (the number of degrees north or south of the equator) and its **longitude** (the number of degrees east or west of the **prime meridian,** or 0 degrees longitude). Some maps also include **locator maps,** which show the area depicted in relation to a larger area.

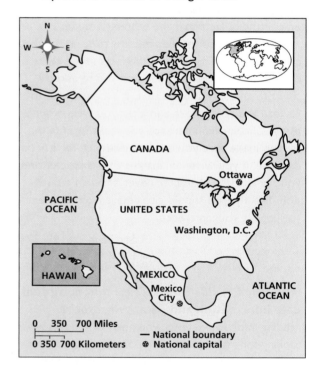

OPINION **A statement of a person's belief, idea, or attitude.** A **fact** is something that can be verified or proved by direct observation or by checking a reliable reference source. An **opinion** cannot be proved to be either true or false—even when it is supported by facts. The following statement is an unsupported opinion.

> *Julius Caesar* is an outstanding play.

A **valid opinion** is an opinion that is supported by verifiable facts. In the following example, the verifiable facts are underlined.

> *Julius Caesar* is an outstanding play because it <u>contains moral conflicts as well as ideas about power and politics that are still important today.</u>

When you read a persuasive text, remember that statements of opinion can't be proved, but they can and should be supported by facts and logical reasoning.

See pages 284, 577.

ORDER OF IMPORTANCE **A means of organizing information by ranking details in the order of their importance.** Writers of persuasive texts have to decide whether to give the strongest reason first or to present the weakest reason first and end with the strongest point. Informational texts such as news articles always begin with the most important details because they want to grab the reader's attention immediately. The structure of a news article looks like an upside-down triangle, with the least important details at the bottom.

See pages 296, 542.
See also *Text Structures.*

OUTLINING **A way of organizing information to show relationships among key details in a text.** You can use outlining as a writer and as a reader.

Outlining puts main ideas and details in a form that you can review quickly. An **informal outline,** sometimes called a working outline, should have at least three main ideas. You put supporting details under each main idea, like this:

> **Informal Outline**
> I. First main idea
>   A. Detail supporting first main idea
>   B. Another detail supporting first main idea
>   C. Third detail supporting first main idea
> II. Second main idea
>   [etc.]

A **formal outline** is especially useful if you're writing a research paper. You might start with a working outline and then revise it into a formal one. Your teacher may ask you to submit a formal outline with your completed research paper.

Formal outlines use Roman numerals (I, II, III), capital letters (A, B, C), and Arabic numerals (1, 2, 3) to show order, relationship, and relative importance of ideas. The headings in a formal outline should have the same grammatical structure, and you must be consistent in your use of either phrases or sentences. (You can't switch back and forth between them.) There should always be at least two divisions under each heading or none at all.

Here is the beginning of a formal outline of a textbook chapter on the Vietnam War (page 634):

> **Formal Outline**
> I. TV speech by Lyndon B. Johnson, 8/4/64
>   A. Destroyer *Maddox* attacked on 8/2 in Gulf of Tonkin
>   B. U.S. military forces ordered to take action against gunboats
> II. The Tonkin Gulf Resolution
>   A. In 1963, Johnson advised by McNamara to increase U.S. commitment to South Vietnam

(continued)

B. Johnson's need for congressional support
   1. The Gulf of Tonkin events an opportunity
   2. Request for authorization of military force overwhelmingly passed

See pages 697–698.

PARAPHRASING **Restating each sentence of a text in your own words.** Paraphrasing is usually used only for difficult texts. Paraphrasing a text helps you to be certain you understand it. When you paraphrase, you follow the author's sequence of ideas. You carefully reword each line (if it's a poem) or sentence (if it's prose) without changing the author's ideas or leaving anything out. You restate each figure of speech to be sure you understand the basis of the comparison. If sentences are missing words or if the words are wrenched out of the usual order, you rephrase the sentence.

A paraphrase is longer than a **summary,** which is a brief statement of the main ideas in a text. Here are a paraphrase and a summary of a paragraph from the Parable of the Good Samaritan (page 278):

Paraphrase: A man traveling from Jerusalem to Jericho was attacked by robbers who tore off his clothes, injured him, and left him half dead. When a priest passed that way and saw the wounded man, he crossed to the other side of the road. A Levite did the same thing; he looked at the victim and ignored his need for help. But when a Samaritan encountered the wounded man, he pitied him. He treated the man's wounds with oil and wine. Then he put him on the animal

he had been riding and took him to an inn, where he continued to treat his wounds. The next day, before he left, he gave the innkeeper money and told him to take care of the wounded man. "If you spend more money taking care of him," he said, "I'll pay you back when I return."

Which of the three travelers acted as a neighbor to the man attacked by robbers?

Summary: On the road from Jerusalem to Jericho, robbers attacked a traveler and left him half dead. A priest and a Levite passed the victim and ignored him, but a Samaritan gave him the help he needed. Which of the three behaved as if he were the victim's neighbor?

See pages 411, 833.

PRIMARY SOURCE **An original, firsthand account.** Primary sources may include an autobiography; an eyewitness testimony; a letter, speech, or literary work; a historical document; and information gathered from firsthand surveys or interviews. "A Fireman's Story" (page 345) is an example of a primary source. It's important to use primary sources whenever they are available on a topic, but you need to research widely to make sure that a primary source is not biased.

Be sure to keep track of your primary sources by numbering each source and recording the necessary publishing information. If you quote directly from the primary source, be sure to use quotation marks and to give credit to your source.

See pages 88, 632–633.
See also *Secondary Source*.

PUBLIC DOCUMENTS **Informative texts put out by the government or public agencies. Public documents include political**

platforms, public policy statements, speeches, and debates. These documents inform the public about government policy, laws, municipal codes, records, schedules, and the like.

See pages 639, 908.

RESEARCH QUESTIONS **Questions that are focused on a specific subject, which the researcher searches to answer.** Questions are essential tools for focusing your research.

One way to generate research questions is to use a KWL chart as a research guide. This kind of chart is an easy way to organize questions and answers, especially if you know how to set up columns and rows on your computer. In the K column, you note what you already know about the subject. In the W column, you note what you'd like to find out. As you do your research, complete the L column by answering the questions you've asked in the W column.

Research questions can also be generated by brainstorming or by using the *5W-How* questions: *Who? What? When? Where? Why?* and *How?* As you seek primary and secondary source information at libraries and museums, in various electronic media (Internet, films, tapes), and from personal interviews, you will come up with more research questions. Always remember to keep your questions focused on the specific subject you have chosen.

See page 187.

ROOTS, PREFIXES, SUFFIXES
English words are often made up of two or more word parts. These words parts include

- **roots, which carry a word's core meaning**
- **prefixes, added onto the beginning of a word or in front of a word root to form a new word**
- **suffixes, added onto the end of a word or after a word root to form a new word**

Most word roots come from Greek and Latin. Prefixes and suffixes come from Greek, Latin, and Anglo-Saxon.

Greek Roots	Meaning	Examples
−astro−, −aster−	star	**astro**nomy, **aster**isk
−cosmo−	world; order	**cosmo**logy, **cosmo**politan
−eu−	good; well	**eu**phoria, **eu**phemism
−gno−, −kno−	know	**kno**wledge, a**gno**stic
−hypno−	sleep	**hypno**tize, **hypno**tic
−mis−	hatred of	**mis**anthrope, **mis**ology
−ortho−	straight	**ortho**pedics, **ortho**dontics
−pseudo−	false	**pseudo**nym, **pseudo**morph
−the−, −them−, −thet−	place; put	epi**thet**, anti**thes**is
−theo−	god	**theo**logy, **theo**cracy

Latin Roots	Meaning	Examples
–anima–, –anim–	life; mind	**anima**l, **anima**te
–aqua–	water	**aqua**rium, **aqua**naut
–cid–, –cis–	cut off; kill	homi**cide**, con**cise**
–cor–, –card–	heart	**cor**onary, **card**iac
–fum–	smoke; scent	**fum**igate, per**fume**
–gen–	race; family	**gen**ealogy, pro**gen**itor
–leg–	law	**leg**al, **leg**islate
–noc–, –nox–	night	equi**nox**, **noc**turne
–tract–	pull; draw	at**tract**, sub**tract**ion
–voc–, –vok–	voice; call	**voc**al, re**voke**

Greek Prefixes	Meaning	Examples
anti–	against	**anti**body, **anti**social
dia–	through; across	**dia**gram, **dia**lectic
hypo–	under; below	**hypo**dermic, **hypo**allergenic
para–	beside; beyond	**para**legal, **para**llel
peri–	around	**peri**scope, **peri**phery

Latin Prefixes	Meaning	Examples
bene–	good	**bene**fit, **bene**diction
contra–	against	**contra**dict, **contra**st
extra–	outside	**extra**curricular, **extra**ordinary
intra–	within	**intra**venous, **intra**mural
trans–	across; over	**trans**atlantic, **trans**cend

Anglo-Saxon/Old English Prefixes	Meaning	Examples
be–	around	**be**dew, **be**get
for–	away; off; from	**for**get, **for**go
mis–	badly; not	**mis**hap, **mis**take
over–	above	**over**look, **over**coat
un–	not; reverse of	**un**sound, **un**kempt

Greek Suffixes	Meaning	Examples
—ess	female	poet**ess**, lion**ess**
—ic	having; showing	parapleg**ic**, ton**ic**
—ize	resemble; cause to be	American**ize**, ostrac**ize**
—meter	measure	thermo**meter**, baro**meter**
—oid	like; resembling	fact**oid**, andr**oid**

Latin Suffixes	Meaning	Examples
—age	act; result of	marri**age**, voy**age**
—fic	making; creating	horri**fic**, scienti**fic**
—ive	relating to; belonging to	inquisit**ive**, sport**ive**
—let	small	pig**let**, rivu**let**
—ure	act; state of being	leis**ure**, compos**ure**

Anglo-Saxon/Old English Suffixes	Meaning	Examples
—en	become	bright**en**, sull**en**
—ful	full of; marked by	cheer**ful**, fear**ful**
—ness	quality; state	kind**ness**, crazi**ness**
—ship	quality of	kin**ship**, relation**ship**
—ward	in the direction	for**ward**, sky**ward**

SECONDARY SOURCE **A secondhand account written by a writer who did not participate directly in the events he or she interprets, relates, or analyzes.** Secondary sources may include encyclopedias, magazine articles, textbooks, biographies, and technical journals. The historical article "The Day the Clowns Cried" (page 40) is an example of a secondary source that was found on a Web site. A research paper may include both primary and secondary sources.

See pages 88, 632–633.

SPATIAL (spā′shəl) **ORDER** **A means of organizing information by showing where things are located.** (The word *spatial* is related to the word *space*. Spatial order shows where things are located in space.) Spatial order is often used in descriptive writing. Here is an example from the beginning of "Through the Tunnel" (page 401). Phrases showing spatial order are underlined.

> Going <u>to the shore</u> on the first morning of the vacation, the young English boy stopped <u>at a turning of the path</u> and looked <u>down at a wild and rocky bay</u> and then <u>over to the crowded beach</u> he knew so well from other years.

See page 542.
See also *Text Structures*.

SYNTHESIZING **Putting all the different sources of information together in a process that gives you a better understanding of the whole subject.** In order to synthesize information, you first gather information about a topic from several sources. Then, you find each writer's main ideas. Paraphrasing ideas, restating them in your own words, can help you understand difficult texts. Next, you examine the ideas in each source. You

compare and contrast the ideas you've found. To synthesize what you have learned, you draw conclusions about the information you have gathered.

See pages 21, 411.
See also *Generalization*.

TEXT STRUCTURES **Any organizational patterns that writers use to make their meaning clear.** In imaginative literature text structures range from the plot structures in stories and dramas to the sonnet structure in poetry.

In nonfiction and informational texts, the writer's **intent** or **purpose** in creating the text determines how the text will be organized. Don't expect writers of informational texts and nonfiction to use the same structure throughout an entire text. Most writers switch from one type of structure to another and may even combine structures. Four basic ways of arranging ideas or details in nonfiction and informational texts are

1. **Chronological order, time order,** or **sequence**—putting events or steps in the order in which they occur. For an example of chronological order, see "Diary of a Mad Blender" (page 24). Most narrative and historical texts are written in chronological order. Chronological order is also found in writing that explains a process, such as in technical directions and in recipes. This type of chronological order is called **step-by-step order.**

2. **Spatial order**—the order that shows where things are located. This pattern is used in descriptive writing. It is especially useful in helping readers visualize setting. See the first paragraph of "From a Lifeboat" (page 346).

3. **Order of importance**—ranking details from most important to least important, or from least important to most important. Writers of persuasive texts in particular have to decide which order makes the strongest impact: putting the strongest reason first, and the weaker ones later, or saving the strongest reason for

last. For an example of a text that uses order of importance, see the concluding section of "R.M.S. Titanic" (pages 342–343). News articles always begin with the most important details because they want to grab the reader's attention immediately.

4. **Logical order**—classifying details into related groups. One type of logical order is the **comparison and contrast** text structure, which shows similarities and differences among various groups. See "Crossing a Threshold to Adulthood" (page 414), in which growing up in Uzbekistan is contrasted with growing up in America.

Other methods used to organize texts include

- **enumeration** (ē·nōō′mər·ā·shen)—also called **listing**—citing a list of details: first, second, and so on. See the alphabetical list of noted explorers in "Explorers Say There's Still Lots to Look for" (page 367).
- **cause-and-effect**—showing how events happen as a result of other events. See " 'Thinkin' on Marryin' ' " (page 91).
- **problem-solution**—explaining how a problem may be solved. See "Taste—the Final Frontier" (page 188).
- **question-answer**—asking questions, then giving the answers. See "The Child's View of Working Parents" (page 26).

Recognizing these structures will help you understand the ideas in a text. The following guidelines can help you recognize text structures:

1. Search the text for the main idea. Look for clue words (**transitions**) that signal a specific pattern of organization. Also note colors, special type, headers, numbered lists, and icons that may be used to highlight terms or indicate text structure.

2. Analyze the text for other important ideas. Think about how the ideas connect, and look for an obvious pattern.

3. Remember that a writer might use one organizational pattern throughout a text or combine two or more patterns.

4. Draw a graphic organizer that maps how the text is structured. Some common graphic organizers are a **causal chain** (for the cause-effect text structure), a **flowchart** (showing chronological sequence), and a **Venn diagram** (showing similarities and differences).

See pages 296, 542, 577, 919.
See also *Chronological Order, Logical Order, Order of Importance, Spatial Order.*

WORKPLACE DOCUMENTS Job-related texts, such as job applications, memos, instructional manuals, and employee handbooks. When you read workplace documents, keep these points in mind (in addition to the points about reading consumer documents, cited on pages 994–995):

1. Take all the time you need to read and understand the document. Don't let anyone rush you or tell you that a document is unimportant or just a formality.

2. Read technical directions carefully, even if they're just posted on the side of a device you're supposed to operate. Read all of the directions before you start. Ask questions if you're not sure how to proceed. Don't try anything out before you know what will happen next.

3. The employee handbook contains the "rules of the game" at that particular business. It tells you about holidays, work hours, break times, and vacations as well as other important company policies. Read the employee handbook from cover to cover.

See page 919.
See also *Consumer Documents.*

Language Handbook

1 THE PARTS OF SPEECH

PART OF SPEECH	DEFINITION	EXAMPLES
NOUN	Names person, place, thing, or idea	father, singers, U2, crew, valley, poem, "With All Flags Flying," age, wisdom
PRONOUN	Takes place of one or more nouns or pronouns	
Personal	Refers to one(s) speaking (first person), spoken to (second person), spoken about (third person)	I, me, my, mine, we, us, our, ours you, your, yours he, him, his, she, her, hers, it, its, they, them, their, theirs
Reflexive	Refers to subject and directs action of verb back to subject	myself, ourselves, yourself, yourselves, himself, herself, itself, themselves
Intensive	Refers to and emphasizes noun or another pronoun	(See Reflexive.)
Demonstrative	Refers to specific one(s) of group	this, that, these, those
Interrogative	Introduces question	what, which, who, whom, whose
Relative	Introduces subordinate clause and refers to noun or pronoun outside clause	that, which, who, whom, whose
Indefinite	Refers to one(s) not specifically named	all, any, anyone, both, each, either, everybody, many, none, nothing
ADJECTIVE	Modifies noun or pronoun by telling *what kind, which one, how many,* or *how much*	**a young, self-assured** officer; **a Mexican** tradition; **a suspenseful horror** story; **many** passengers
VERB	Shows action or state of being	
Action	Expresses physical or mental activity	read, dance, fly, care, pretend, argue
Linking	Connects subject with word identifying or describing it	appear, be, seem, become, feel, look, smell, sound, taste
Helping (Auxiliary)	Helps another verb express time	be, have, may, can, shall, will, would
ADVERB	Modifies verb, adjective, or adverb by telling *how, when, where,* or *to what extent*	drives **carefully,** spoke **loudly, very** old, **almost** ready, coming **here tomorrow**
PREPOSITION	Relates noun or pronoun to another word	across, between, into, near, of, on, with, aside from, instead of, next to
CONJUNCTION	Joins words or word groups	
Coordinating	Joins words or word groups used in same way	and, but, for, nor, or, so, yet

(continued)

PART OF SPEECH	DEFINITION	EXAMPLES
Correlative	A pair of conjunctions that joins parallel words or word groups	both . . . and, either . . . or, neither . . . nor, not only . . . but (also)
Subordinating	Begins subordinate clause and connects it to independent clause	as though, because, if, since, so that, than, when, where, while
INTERJECTION	Expresses emotion	hooray, yikes, ouch, wow

Determining Parts of Speech

The way a word is used in a sentence determines the word's part of speech. Many words can be used as different parts of speech.

EXAMPLES

The wolf came **near**. [adverb]
All their **near** relations were with them. [adjective]
At least all of them would be **near** each other.
   [preposition]
Finally, the bus would **near** the camp. [verb]

The room was filled with **light**. [noun]
Let's **light** some candles. [verb]
A **light** snowfall covered the trees. [adjective]

What did you say? [pronoun]
I don't know **what** time it is. [adjective]
What! I won the contest! [interjection]

Have you ever been there **before**? [adverb]
Before they all died out, dinosaurs ruled the earth
   for millions of years. [conjunction]
The moon rose **before** sunset. [preposition]

Avoiding Overused Words

The adverbs *really, too, so,* and *very* are often overused. To keep your writing lively and interesting, replace those inexact, overused words with adverbs such as these: *completely, definitely, especially, entirely, extremely, generally, largely, mainly, mostly, particularly, rather,* and *unusually.*

Try It Out

For each of the following sentences, replace the words *really, too, so,* and *very* with more lively adverbs. Use a different adverb in each sentence.

1. This is a very intriguing poem.
2. E. E. Cummings really can be a commentator on writing.
3. Some critics feel that he is too clever.
4. Punctuation can be so expressive.
5. Isn't this fact really overlooked?

2 AGREEMENT

AGREEMENT OF SUBJECT AND VERB

2a. A verb should always agree with its subject in number. Singular subjects take singular verbs. Plural subjects take plural verbs.

SINGULAR Her **father has** an accident while working.
PLURAL **They have moved** to Florida.

SINGULAR **She was staying** home from school.
PLURAL Her **brothers were** back at school the next day.

COMPUTER NOTE Some word-processing programs can identify problems in subject-verb agreement. If you have access to such a program, use it to help you search for errors when you are proofreading your writing. If you are not sure whether a problem found by the program is truly an error, check rules 2a–2n in this section of the Language Handbook.

2b. The number of the subject is not changed by a phrase following the subject.

SINGULAR **Friends** of the girl **are** sympathetic.
PLURAL **Tears,** absent in the day, **fall** at night.

SINGULAR The **aim** of her stories **is** to express truth.
PLURAL The **words** of their mother **reassure** them.

 For more about kinds of phrases, see Part 6: Phrases.

The number of the subject is not changed by a negative construction following the subject.

EXAMPLE
Miami, not the Florida Keys, **is** their home.

The number of the subject is also not affected when it is followed by a phrase beginning with *as well as, along with, in addition to,* or a similar expression.

EXAMPLE
The **teacher,** as well as her students, **looks** forward to spring break.

2c. The following indefinite pronouns are singular: *anybody, anyone, anything, each, either, everybody, everyone, everything, neither, nobody, no one, nothing, one, somebody, someone, something.*

EXAMPLES
One of her mother's friends **asks** about him.
Somebody in the class **does** not **use** commas.

2d. The following indefinite pronouns are plural: *both, few, many, several.*

EXAMPLES
Both of the boys **want** to stay.
Several of the students **offer** explanations.

2e. The indefinite pronouns *all, any, most, none,* and *some* are singular when they refer to singular words and are plural when they refer to plural words.

SINGULAR **Most** of the garden still **needs** to be weeded.
PLURAL **Most** of the plants also **need** to be watered.

SINGULAR **All** of the kitchen **was** clean.
PLURAL **All** of them **begin** to cry.

2f. A *compound subject,* which is two or more subjects that have the same verb, may be singular, plural, or either.

(1) Subjects joined by *and* usually take a plural verb.

EXAMPLES
Eddie and **Lee sleep.**
Jean and her **mother talk** in the car.

A compound subject that names only one person or thing takes a singular verb. Also, a compound noun used as a subject usually takes a singular verb.

EXAMPLES
Jean's **friend** and **classmate was** Nancy Dryer.
Has law and order been restored yet?

(2) Singular subjects joined by *or* or *nor* take a singular verb.

EXAMPLES
Eddie or **Jean washes** dishes.
Neither **Mother** nor **Eddie wants** to return to Indiana.

(3) When a singular subject and a plural subject are joined by *or* or *nor,* the verb agrees with the subject nearer the verb.

EXAMPLES
Neither the plot nor the **characters were** too complex.
Neither the characters nor the **plot was** too complex.

 NOTE If such a construction sounds awkward, revise the sentence to give each part of the subject its own verb.

EXAMPLE
The **plot wasn't** too complex, and neither **were** the **characters.**

2g. *Don't* and *doesn't* must agree with their subjects.

With the subjects *I* and *you* and with plural subjects, use *don't* (do not).

EXAMPLES
I **don't** agree.
You **don't** sound well.
Some people **don't** listen.

With other subjects, use *doesn't* (does not).

EXAMPLES
She **doesn't** bring a lunch.
It **doesn't** matter.
Jean **doesn't** sleep well.

2h. A *collective noun* (such as *club*, *family*, or *swarm*) is singular in form but names a group of persons or things. A collective noun takes a singular verb when the noun refers to the group as a unit. However, a collective noun takes a plural verb when the noun refers to the parts or members of the group.

SINGULAR The family **is** going home. [family = a unit]

PLURAL The family **are** getting into the van. [family = individual family members]

Collective Nouns

army	club	flock	public
assembly	committee	group	squad
audience	crew	herd	staff
band	crowd	jury	swarm
choir	faculty	majority	team
chorus	family	number	troop
class	fleet	pair	wildlife

2i. A verb agrees with its subject, not with its predicate nominative.

SINGULAR The best **part** of her lunch **is** the **cheese and crackers.**

PLURAL The **cheese and crackers are** the best **part** of her lunch.

2j. A verb agrees with its subject even when the verb precedes the subject, as in sentences beginning with *here* or *there* and in questions. Contractions such as *here's* and *there's* are used only with subjects that are singular in meaning.

SINGULAR Here **is** [*or* here's] my **locker.**

PLURAL Here **are** the **lockers.**

SINGULAR Where **is** [*or* where's] the school **bus?**

PLURAL Where **are** your gym **clothes?**

2k. An expression of an amount (a length of time, a statistic, or a fraction, for example) is singular when the amount is thought of as a unit or when it refers to a singular word. However, such an expression is plural when the amount is thought of as many parts

or when it refers to a plural word or more than one word.

SINGULAR **Twenty-five cents is** the amount Dad gave my brother.

PLURAL **Twenty-five cents were** jingling in his pocket.

SINGULAR **One half** of the class **has** finished.

PLURAL **One half** of the students **are** still working.

NOTE Use a singular verb when the expression *the number* comes before a prepositional phrase. Use a plural verb when the expression *a number* comes before a prepositional phrase.

SINGULAR **The number** of students **has** increased.

PLURAL **A number** of students **have** transferred.

2l. The title of a creative work (such as a book, song, film, or painting) or the name of an organization, a country, or a city (even if it is plural in form) takes a singular verb.

EXAMPLES
"**Boys and Girls**" **was written** by Alice Munro.
The **United States is voting** in favor of the measure.
Wichita Falls is in Texas, not Kansas.

2m. Some nouns that are plural in form are singular in meaning.

Nouns that always take singular verbs include

civics	gymnastics	measles	news
electronics	mathematics	molasses	physics

EXAMPLE
Mathematics is my favorite course.

Some nouns that end in *–s*, such as the following ones, take a plural verb even though they refer to single items.

binoculars	pants	shears	Olympics
eyeglasses	pliers	shorts	scissors

EXAMPLE
The **scissors are** in the sewing basket.

2n. Subjects preceded by *every* or *many a* take singular verbs.

EXAMPLES
Many a child **wants** a dog.
Every student **has** a dream.

AGREEMENT OF PRONOUN AND ANTECEDENT

A pronoun usually refers to a noun or another pronoun, which is called the pronoun's *antecedent.*

 2o. A pronoun agrees with its antecedent in number and gender. Singular pronouns refer to singular antecedents. Plural pronouns refer to plural antecedents.

A few singular pronouns indicate gender:
Feminine—*she, her, hers, herself*
Masculine—*he, him, his, himself*
Neuter—*it, its, itself*

EXAMPLES
The **man** had made the choice **himself.** [singular, masculine]

His **daughter** wanted **her** father to stay with **her.** [singular, feminine]

2p. A singular pronoun is used to refer to *anybody, anyone, anything, each, either, everybody, everyone, everything, neither, nobody, no one, nothing, one, somebody, someone,* or *something.* The gender of any of these pronouns is determined by the gender of the pronoun's antecedent.

EXAMPLE
Each of the boys brought **his** uniform.

When the antecedent could be either masculine or feminine, use both the masculine and the feminine pronoun forms connected by *or.*

EXAMPLE
Not **everyone** gets a chance to know **his or her** grandparents.

2q. A singular pronoun is used to refer to two or more singular antecedents joined by *or* or *nor.*

EXAMPLES
Tim or **Jason** will read **his** poem next.
Did **Heidi** or **Lynn** read **hers** yet?

If a sentence sounds awkward when antecedents are of different genders, revise it.

AWKWARD Neither **Eric nor Sue** finished **his or her** part.
REVISED **Eric** didn't finish **his** part, and **Sue** didn't finish **hers** either.

Avoiding the *His or Her* Construction

When the antecedent of a pronoun could be either masculine or feminine, you can avoid using the awkward *his or her* construction by revising the sentence.

AWKWARD Bill or Eva will bring his or her recorder.
REVISED Bill will bring his recorder, or Eva will bring hers.
REVISED Bill or Eva will bring a recorder.

Try It Out

Revise each of the following sentences to eliminate the *his or her* construction.

1. Ask Joseph or Victoria to loan us his or her copy.
2. Anyone who is late must take his or her test later.
3. Does everyone have a theme for his or her paper?
4. Mark or Ellen can explain his or her own drawing.
5. Will Otis or Dee read his or her essay in assembly?

2r. A plural pronoun is used to refer to two or more antecedents joined by *and.*

EXAMPLES
The **man** and his **granddaughter** have a good relationship despite the difference in **their** ages.
My **father** and my **brother** have **their** fishing licenses with **them.**

2s. The number of a relative pronoun (such as *who, whom, whose, which,* or *that*) depends on the number of its antecedent.

EXAMPLES
He is one **man who** insists on deciding **his** own fate. [*Who* refers to the singular noun *man.* Therefore, the singular form *his* is used to agree with *who.*]

Many who are growing old make **their** homes there. [*Who* refers to the plural pronoun *many.* Therefore, the plural form *their* is used to agree with *who.*]

 For more about relative pronouns in adjective clauses, see 7d.

3 USING VERBS

THE PRINCIPAL PARTS OF VERBS

3a. The four *principal parts* of a verb are the *base form,* the *present participle,* the *past,* and the *past participle.*

BASE FORM	use	sing
PRESENT PARTICIPLE	using	singing
PAST	used	sang
PAST PARTICIPLE	used	sung

All verbs form the present participle by adding *–ing* to the base form. All verbs, however, do not form the past and past participle in the same way.

3b. A *regular verb* forms its past and past participle by adding *–d* or *–ed* to the base form.

3c. An *irregular verb* forms its past and past participle in some other way than by adding *–d* or *–ed* to the base form.

COMMON REGULAR VERBS

BASE FORM	PRESENT PARTICIPLE	PAST	PAST PARTICIPLE
ask	(is) asking	asked	(have) asked
happen	(is) happening	happened	(have) happened
plan	(is) planning	planned	(have) planned
try	(is) trying	tried	(have) tried
use	(is) using	used	(have) used

COMMON IRREGULAR VERBS

BASE FORM	PRESENT PARTICIPLE	PAST	PAST PARTICIPLE
be	(is) being	was, were	(have) been
begin	(is) beginning	began	(have) begun
bring	(is) bringing	brought	(have) brought
catch	(is) catching	caught	(have) caught
drink	(is) drinking	drank	(have) drunk
drive	(is) driving	drove	(have) driven
eat	(is) eating	ate	(have) eaten
fall	(is) falling	fell	(have) fallen
find	(is) finding	found	(have) found
freeze	(is) freezing	froze	(have) frozen
go	(is) going	went	(have) gone
have	(is) having	had	(have) had
keep	(is) keeping	kept	(have) kept
lead	(is) leading	led	(have) led
pay	(is) paying	paid	(have) paid
ride	(is) riding	rode	(have) ridden
shake	(is) shaking	shook	(have) shaken
sing	(is) singing	sang	(have) sung
steal	(is) stealing	stole	(have) stolen
swim	(is) swimming	swam	(have) swum
swing	(is) swinging	swung	(have) swung
tear	(is) tearing	tore	(have) torn

NOTE The examples in the chart include *is* and *have* in parentheses to show that helping verbs (forms of *be* and *have*) are used with the present participle and past participle forms.

TIPS FOR SPELLING Drop the final silent e after a consonant in the base form of a verb before adding *–ing* to form the present participle and *–ed* to form the past participle.

PRESENT PARTICIPLE
spare + ing = spar**ing**
outline + ing = outlin**ing**

PAST PARTICIPLE
spare + ed = spar**ed**
outline + ed = outlin**ed**

☞ For more about correct spelling when adding suffixes to words, see 15e–j.

NOTE If you are not sure about the principal parts of a verb, look in a dictionary. Entries for irregular verbs give the principal parts. If no principal parts are listed, the verb is a regular verb.

TENSE

3d. **The *tense* of a verb indicates the time of the action or state of being that is expressed by the verb.**

Every English verb has six tenses: *present, past, future, present perfect, past perfect,* and *future perfect.* The tenses are formed from the verb's principal parts.

Past	*Present*	*Future*
existing or happening in the past	existing or happening now	existing or happening in the future

Past Perfect	*Present Perfect*	*Future Perfect*
existing or happening before a specific time in the past	existing or happening sometime before now	existing or happening before a specific time in the future

Each of the six tenses has an additional form called the **progressive form.** The progressive form expresses a continuing action or state of being. It consists of the appropriate tense of *be* followed by the verb's present participle. For the perfect tenses, the progressive form also includes one or more helping verbs.

Present Progressive	am, are, is singing
Past Progressive	was, were singing
Future Progressive	will (shall) be singing
Present Perfect Progressive	has, have been singing
Past Perfect Progressive	had been singing
Future Perfect Progressive	will (shall) have been singing

3e. **Each of the six tenses has its own special uses.**

(1) The **present tense** is used mainly to express an action or a state of being that is occurring now.

EXAMPLES
Tara **knows** the answer.
Can you **hear** the music?

The present tense is also used
- to show a customary or habitual action or state of being
- to express a general truth—something that is always true
- to make historical events seem current (such use is called the **historical present**)
- to discuss a literary work (such use is called the **literary present**)
- to express future time

EXAMPLES
He **works** here. [customary action]
Basketball **entertains** millions. [general truth]
The Roman Empire **falls.** [historical present]
The poem **describes** Flick. [literary present]
We **leave** on vacation next week. [future time]

(2) The **past tense** is used to express an action or a state of being that occurred in the past but is not occurring now.

EXAMPLES
Flick once **scored** almost four hundred points.
We **remembered** his kindness.

A past action or state of being can also be shown with the verb *used to* followed by the base form.

EXAMPLE
My brother **used to ride** his bike to school.

(3) The **future tense** (formed with *will* or *shall* and the verb's base form) is used to express an action or a state of being that will occur.

EXAMPLES
Probably, he **will stay** in town.
We **will read** Maya Angelou's poem next.

(4) The **present perfect tense** (formed with *have* or *has* and the verb's past participle) is used to express an action or a state of being that occurred at some indefinite time in the past.

EXAMPLES
Her poems **have commented** on many situations.
She **has published** widely.

The present perfect tense is also used to express an action or a state of being that began in the past and continues into the present.

EXAMPLE
We **have lived** in the same house for nearly nine years.

(5) The **past perfect tense** (formed with *had* and the verb's past participle) is used to express an action or a state of being that was completed in the past before some other past action or event.

EXAMPLES
Other people remembered what he **had accomplished.** [The accomplishing occurred before the remembering.]
I **had driven** for hours, and I arrived on time. [The driving occurred before the arriving.]

(6) The *future perfect tense* (formed with *will have* or *shall have* and the verb's past participle) is used to express an action or a state of being that will be completed in the future before some other future occurrence.

EXAMPLES

After tonight, I **will have seen** the film twice.
Next Tuesday, we **will have lived** here two years.

3f. Do not change needlessly from one tense to another.

INCONSISTENT	Her family packed up and moves.
CONSISTENT	Her family **packed** up and **moved.**
CONSISTENT	Her family **packs** up and **moves.**

INCONSISTENT	They marry and finally bought a house.
CONSISTENT	They **married** and finally **bought** a house.
CONSISTENT	They **marry** and finally **buy** a house.

Using Appropriate Verb Tenses

Using different verb tenses is often necessary to show the order of events that occur at different times.

NONSTANDARD

I wished that I wrote that poem.

STANDARD

I **wished** that I **had written** that poem. [Since the action of writing was completed before the action of wishing, the verb should be *had written,* not *wrote*.]

Try It Out ✎

For each of the following sentences, correct the verb tenses to show the order of events.

1. After the clock had struck eight, Mr. Leonard Mead had gone for a walk.
2. For years, he had enjoyed the cool air and only occasionally has had trouble from roaming dogs.
3. Nothing had moved on the street for an hour, and now he has heard no sounds.
4. While he was walking, a police car has approached him.
5. A voice had told him to stop, and he does so.

ACTIVE AND PASSIVE VOICE

3g. A verb in the *active voice* expresses an action done by its subject. A verb in the *passive voice* expresses an action received by its subject.

| ACTIVE VOICE | Dick Fool Bull **told** his story. |
| PASSIVE VOICE | The story **was told** by Dick Fool Bull. |

| ACTIVE VOICE | The holy man **instructed** them. |
| PASSIVE VOICE | They **were instructed** by the holy man. |

3h. Use the passive voice sparingly.

The passive voice is not any less correct than the active voice, but it is less direct, less forceful, and less concise. As a result, a sentence in the passive voice can be wordy and sound awkward or weak.

| AWKWARD PASSIVE | Instructions were given to them by the holy man. |
| ACTIVE | The holy man gave them instructions. |

The passive voice is useful, however, in certain situations:

1. when you do not know the performer of the action

   EXAMPLE
   The First National Bank **was robbed** last night.

2. when you do not want to reveal the performer of the action

   EXAMPLE
   Police **were notified.**

3. when you want to emphasize the receiver of the action

   EXAMPLE
   Already, seven suspects **have been questioned.**

COMPUTER NOTE Some software programs can identify verbs in the passive voice. If you use such a program, keep in mind that it can't tell why you have used the passive voice. If you did so for a good reason, you may want to leave the verb in the passive voice.

4 USING PRONOUNS

CASE

Case is the form that a noun or pronoun takes to indicate its use in a sentence. In English, there are three cases: *nominative, objective,* and *possessive.*

The form of a noun is the same for both the nominative case and the objective case. For the possessive case, however, a noun changes its form, usually by adding an apostrophe and an *s* to most singular nouns and only an apostrophe to most plural nouns.

NOMINATIVE	**Dick Fool Bull** told his story.
OBJECTIVE	The events at Wounded Knee greatly affected **Dick Fool Bull.**
POSSESSIVE	**Dick Fool Bull's** story made me think.

Most personal pronouns, however, have a different form for each case.

The Nominative Case

4a. A subject of a verb is in the nominative case.

EXAMPLES
They knew that **he** was sincere. [*They* is the subject of *knew; he* is the subject of *was.*]
Has **he** or **she** visited Wounded Knee? [*He* and *she* are the subjects of *has visited.*]

4b. A predicate nominative is in the nominative case.

A *predicate nominative* follows a linking verb and explains or identifies the subject of the verb.

EXAMPLES
One of the witnesses was my **uncle.** [*Uncle* follows *was* and identifies the subject *one.*]
The narrators will be **Larry** and **I.** [*Larry* and *I* follow *will be* and identify the subject *narrators.*]

 NOTE Expressions such as *It's me, That's him,* and *Could it have been her?* are examples of informal usage. Avoid using such expressions in formal speaking and writing.

The Objective Case

4c. A direct object of a verb is in the objective case.

A *direct object* follows an action verb and tells *whom* or *what.*

EXAMPLES
I haven't met **her** yet. [*Her* tells *whom* I haven't met yet.]
They made **shirts** and painted **them.** [*Shirts* tells *what* they made, and *them* tells *what* they painted.]

PERSONAL PRONOUNS			
SINGULAR			
	NOMINATIVE	**OBJECTIVE**	**POSSESSIVE**
FIRST PERSON	I	me	my, mine
SECOND PERSON	you	you	your, yours
THIRD PERSON	he, she, it	him, her, it	his, her, hers, its
PLURAL			
	NOMINATIVE	**OBJECTIVE**	**POSSESSIVE**
FIRST PERSON	we	us	our, ours
SECOND PERSON	you	you	your, yours
THIRD PERSON	they	them	their, theirs

 NOTE Notice in the chart that *you* and *it* are the only personal pronouns that have the same forms for the nominative and the objective cases. Notice also that only third-person singular pronouns indicate gender.

☞ For more information about possessive pronouns, see page 1052.

4d. An indirect object of a verb is in the objective case.

An **indirect object** comes before a direct object and tells *to whom* or *to what* or *for whom* or *for what*.

EXAMPLES
The vision had given **them** hope. [*Them* tells *to whom* hope was given.]
Tell **me** another story. [*Me* tells *for whom* the story is told.]

4e. An object of a preposition is in the objective case.

An **object of a preposition** comes at the end of a phrase that begins with a preposition.

EXAMPLES
The sight of the baby and **her** haunts the narrator.
For **us**, such a sight is difficult to imagine.

SPECIAL PRONOUN PROBLEMS

4f. The pronoun *who* (*whoever*) is in the nominative case. The pronoun *whom* (*whomever*) is in the objective case.

NOMINATIVE **Who** was Sitting Bull? [*Who* is the subject of *was.*]
OBJECTIVE With **whom** was he traveling? [*Whom* is the object of *with.*]

When choosing between *who* and *whom* in a subordinate clause, do not be misled by a word outside the clause. Be sure to base your choice on how the pronoun functions in its own subordinate clause.

NOMINATIVE Do you know **who** the bean eaters are? [*Who* is the predicate nominative identifying the subject of the subordinate clause *who the bean eaters are.* The entire subordinate clause serves as the direct object of *do know.*]
OBJECTIVE Perhaps Gwendolyn Brooks was acquainted with the people **whom** she wrote about. [*Whom* is the object of *about.* The entire subordinate clause *whom she wrote about* serves as an adjective modifying *people.*]

NOTE In spoken English, the use of *whom* is becoming less common. In written English, however, you should distinguish between *who* and *whom.*

INFORMAL **Who** did you see at the dance?
FORMAL **Whom** did you see at the dance?

Using *Whom*
Frequently, *whom* is left out of a subordinate clause.

EXAMPLE
The poet [**whom**] I like best is Emily Dickinson. [*Whom* is the unstated direct object of *like.*]

Leaving out *whom* in such cases tends to make writing sound more informal. In formal situations, it is generally better to include *whom.*

Try It Out ✎

Revise each of the following sentences to include *whom.*

1. Has anyone identified the person Dickinson was writing about in that poem?
2. In this poem, she presents herself as a woman conflict has divided into heart and mind.
3. Did she, in fact, forget the man she loved?
4. The Dickinson we know from literary legend seems both shy and eloquent.
5. Was there someone she might have told of her feelings?

4g. An appositive is in the same case as the noun or pronoun to which it refers.

An **appositive** is a noun or pronoun placed next to another noun or pronoun to identify or explain it.

NOMINATIVE They, **Lacy and she,** played the sisters. [The appositive, *Lacy and she,* is in the nominative case because it identifies the subject, *they.*]
OBJECTIVE The sisters were played by them, **Lacy and her.** [The appositive, *Lacy and her,* is in the objective case because it identifies *them,* the object of a preposition.]

Sometimes the pronouns *we* and *us* are used with noun appositives.

EXAMPLES
We actors like to pretend. [The pronoun is in the nominative case because it is the subject of *like.*]
Pretending is fun for **us** actors. [The pronoun is in the objective case because it is the object of the preposition *for.*]

☞ For more information about appositives, see 6g.

4h. **A pronoun following *than* or *as* in an incomplete construction is in the same case as it would be if the construction were completed.**

Notice how the meaning of each of the following sentences depends on the pronoun form in the incomplete construction.

| NOMINATIVE | I liked Kim more than **he** [did]. |
| OBJECTIVE | I liked Kim more than [I liked] **him.** |

| NOMINATIVE | You called me more than **he** [called me]. |
| OBJECTIVE | You called me more than [you called] **him.** |

Clear Pronoun Reference

4i. **A pronoun should refer clearly to its antecedent.**

(1) Avoid an *ambiguous reference,* which occurs when a pronoun can refer to any one of two or more antecedents.

| AMBIGUOUS | Dee talked to Mama while she was eating. [*She* can refer to either Mama or Dee.] |
| CLEAR | While **Mama** was eating, Dee talked to **her.** |

(2) Avoid a *general reference,* which occurs when a pronoun refers to a general idea rather than to a specific antecedent.

GENERAL	Dee insisted on having the quilt. This did not surprise Maggie. [*This* has no specific antecedent.]
CLEAR	That Dee insisted on having the quilt did not surprise Maggie.
CLEAR	Maggie was not surprised that Dee insisted on having the quilt.

(3) Avoid a *weak reference,* which occurs when a pronoun refers to an implied antecedent.

| WEAK | She made quilts, but it was more than a hobby. [No antecedent is given for *it.*] |
| CLEAR | Making quilts was more than a hobby for her. |

(4) Avoid an *indefinite reference,* which occurs when a pronoun (such as *you, it,* or *they*) refers to no particular person, place, thing, or idea.

| INDEFINITE | In that museum, they display fine quilts. [*They* has no antecedent in the sentence.] |
| CLEAR | That museum displays fine quilts. |

 NOTE The indefinite use of *it* is acceptable in familiar expressions such as *It is snowing, It seems as though . . . ,* and *It's late.*

5 USING MODIFIERS

A *modifier* is a word or group of words that limits the meaning of another word or group of words. The two kinds of modifiers are adjectives and adverbs, both of which may consist of a word, a phrase, or a clause.

ONE-WORD MODIFIERS

Adjectives

5a. **Use an *adjective* to limit the meaning of a noun or pronoun.**

EXAMPLES
Maggie was also a **skilled** quilter. [*Skilled* limits the meaning of the noun *quilter.*]
Arrogant and **grasping,** she forfeited the quilts. [*Arrogant* and *grasping* limit the meaning of the pronoun *she.*]

Adverbs

5b. **Use an *adverb* to limit the meaning of a verb, an adjective, or another adverb.**

EXAMPLES
Suddenly, Mama made her decision. [*Suddenly* limits the meaning of the verb *made.*]
Mama was **not** talkative. [*Not* limits the meaning of the adjective *talkative.*]
She **quite** abruptly gave the quilts to Maggie. [*Quite* limits the meaning of the adverb *abruptly.*]

 NOTE Some modifiers can function as adjectives or as adverbs, depending on the word or words they modify.

| ADJECTIVE | That's a **hard** job. |
| ADVERB | We worked **hard.** |

Using Adjectives and Adverbs

Adjectives often follow linking verbs. Adverbs often follow action verbs. You can tell whether a verb is a linking or an action verb by replacing it with a form of *seem*. If the substitution makes sense, the original verb is a linking verb and should be followed by an adjective. If the substitution does not make sense, the original verb is an action verb and should be followed by an adverb.

ADJECTIVE	Behind the mist, the sun appeared dim. [*The sun seemed dim* makes sense. In this case, *appeared* is a linking verb.]
ADVERB	From behind the mist, the sun appeared suddenly. [*The sun seemed suddenly* doesn't make sense. In this case, *appeared* is an action verb.]

Try It Out ✎

For each of the following sentences, choose the correct modifier in parentheses.

1. The collard greens tasted (*delicious, deliciously*).
2. He looked (*suspicious, suspiciously*) at the dish.
3. That car is (*noisy, noisily*).
4. She looked around (*quick, quickly*) and took photos.
5. Maggie's hands were (*cold, coldly*).

COMPARISON OF MODIFIERS

5c. The forms of modifiers change to show comparison.

The three degrees of comparison are *positive, comparative,* and *superlative.*

(1) Most one-syllable modifiers form the comparative and superlative degrees by adding *–er* and *–est.*

(2) Some two-syllable modifiers form their comparative and superlative degrees by adding *–er* and *–est.* Other two-syllable modifiers form the comparative and superlative degrees by using *more* and *most.*

(3) Modifiers of more than two syllables form the comparative and superlative degrees by using *more* and *most.*

(4) To show decreasing comparisons, all modifiers form their comparative and superlative degrees with *less* and *least.*

(5) Some modifiers form the comparative and superlative degrees in other ways.

POSITIVE	COMPARATIVE	SUPERLATIVE
rude	ruder	rudest
happy	happier	happiest
skillful	more skillful	most skillful
quickly	more quickly	most quickly
artistic	more artistic	most artistic
carefully	more carefully	most carefully
ripe	less ripe	least ripe
safely	less safely	least safely

TIPS FOR SPELLING

Drop the final silent e before adding *–er* or *–est.*

EXAMPLES
safe + er = saf**er**
ripe + est = rip**est**

☞ For more information about correct spelling when adding suffixes to words, see 15e–j.

☞ The following pairs of modifiers are frequently confused: *bad, badly* and *good, well.* For discussions of the correct uses of these modifiers, see page 1050.

POSITIVE	COMPARATIVE	SUPERLATIVE
bad	worse	worst
good/well	better	best
little	less	least
many/much	more	most

5d. Use the comparative degree when comparing two things. Use the superlative degree when comparing more than two.

COMPARATIVE   Maggie was **more respectful** than Dee.
I liked this story **better** than that one.

SUPERLATIVE   Is this the **best** story of the ones you've read?
Which of the three poems was the **least complex?**

5e. Include the word *other* or *else* when comparing one thing with others in the same group.

ILLOGICAL   This image is more vivid than any in the poem. [This image is in the poem. Logically, this image cannot be more vivid than itself.]

LOGICAL   This image is more vivid than any **other** in the poem.

ILLOGICAL   Rita understands plot better than everyone does. [*Everyone* includes Rita. Logically, she cannot understand better than she herself does.]

LOGICAL   Rita understands plot better than everyone **else** does.

5f. Avoid a *double comparison*—the use of both *–er* and *more* (or *less*) or both *–est* and *most* (or *least*) to modify the same word.

EXAMPLES
Alice Walker, **better** [*not* more better] known as the author of *The Color Purple,* wrote this story.
The test was **easier** [*not* more easier] than I thought it would be.

5g. Be sure your comparisons are clear.

UNCLEAR   The traffic here is faster than Detroit. [This sentence incorrectly compares traffic with a city.]

CLEAR   The traffic here is faster than **traffic in** Detroit.

State both parts of an incomplete comparison if there is any chance of misunderstanding.

UNCLEAR   I see her more than Mark.
CLEAR   I see her more than Mark **sees her.**
CLEAR   I see her more than **I see** Mark.

PLACEMENT OF MODIFIERS

5h. Avoid using a *dangling modifier*—a modifying word or word group that does not sensibly modify any word or word group in the same sentence.

You may correct a dangling modifier
- by adding a word or words that the dangling modifier can sensibly modify
- by adding a word or words to the dangling modifier
- by rewording the sentence

DANGLING   To understand Shakespeare's plays, some knowledge of his vocabulary is necessary.

CLEAR   To understand Shakespeare's plays, **readers** need some knowledge of his vocabulary.

DANGLING   While studying for the math test, my phone rang incessantly.

CLEAR   While **I was** studying for the math test, my phone rang incessantly.

DANGLING   After giving an example of a simile, our next task was to create one.

CLEAR   **Our tasks were to give an example of a simile and then to create one.**

5i. Avoid using a *misplaced modifier*—a modifying word or word group that sounds awkward or unclear because it seems to modify the wrong word or word group.

To correct a misplaced modifier, place the modifying word or word group as near as possible to the word you intend it to modify.

MISPLACED   Sunglasses hid her face on her nose.
CLEAR   Sunglasses **on her nose** hid her face.

MISPLACED   A scrap from a uniform was part of the quilt that had been worn during the Civil War.

CLEAR   A scrap from a uniform **that had been worn during the Civil War** was part of the quilt.

MISPLACED   Made from pieces of old clothing, Dee held the quilts.

CLEAR   Dee held the quilts **made from pieces of old clothing.**

6 PHRASES

6a. A *phrase* is a group of related words that is used as a single part of speech and does not contain both a verb and its subject.

VERB PHRASE have been writing
PREPOSITIONAL PHRASE with you and me

 For information about placement of modifying phrases, see 5h–i.

PREPOSITIONAL PHRASES

6b. A *prepositional phrase* begins with a preposition and ends with the *object of the preposition,* a word or word group that functions as a noun.

EXAMPLES
They were covered **with golden fur.** [The noun *fur* is the object of the preposition *with.*]
According to John Steinbeck, coyotes can be pests. [The noun *John Steinbeck* is the object of the preposition *according to.*]

(1) A prepositional phrase that modifies a noun or pronoun is called an *adjective phrase.*

An adjective phrase tells *what kind* or *which one.*

EXAMPLES
The stories **of American Indians** sometimes feature coyotes. [*Of American Indians* modifies *stories,* telling *what kind.*]
Stories **about coyotes** depict them as tricksters. [*About coyotes* modifies *stories,* telling *which ones.*]

An adjective phrase generally follows the word it modifies. That word may be the object of another preposition.

EXAMPLE
Did you see the film **about the coyotes of the desert?** [*Of the desert* modifies *coyotes,* the object of the preposition *about.*]

More than one adjective phrase may modify the same noun or pronoun.

EXAMPLE
The sight **of them through the scope** made Steinbeck think. [*Of them* and *through the scope* modify the noun *sight.*]

(2) A prepositional phrase that modifies a verb, an adjective, or an adverb is called an *adverb phrase.* An adverb phrase tells *when, where, how, why,* or *to what extent.*

EXAMPLES
In a moment, he reached for his rifle. [*In a moment* modifies *reached,* telling *when.*]
The coyotes were not far **from him.** [*From him* modifies *far,* telling *where.*]
They were not dangerous **to him.** [*To him* modifies *dangerous,* telling *how* they were dangerous.]

An adverb phrase may come before or after the word it modifies.

EXAMPLES
To me, this was a wonderful story.
This was a wonderful story **to me.**

More than one adverb phrase may modify the same word.

EXAMPLE
In 1962, John Steinbeck received the Nobel Prize **at age sixty.** [Both *in 1962* and *at age sixty* modify *received.*]

VERBALS AND VERBAL PHRASES

A *verbal* is a form of a verb used as a noun, an adjective, or an adverb. A *verbal phrase* consists of a verbal and its modifiers and complements. Three kinds of verbals are *participles, gerunds,* and *infinitives.*

Participles and Participial Phrases

6c. A *participle* is a verb form that can be used as an adjective. A *participial phrase* consists of a participle and all the words related to the participle.

(1) *Present participles* end in *–ing.*

EXAMPLES
It was certainly an **embarrassing** moment. [The present participle *embarrassing* modifies the noun *moment.*]
Hammering loudly, Sobel took out his frustration in hard work. [The participial phrase *hammering loudly* modifies *Sobel.* The adverb *loudly* modifies the present participle *hammering.*]

(2) Most *past participles* end in *–d* or *–ed*. Others are irregularly formed.

EXAMPLES

The **injured** player did not return. [The past participle *injured* modifies the noun *player*.]

Feld, **dazzled by Max's college education,** thinks that the boy is a good match for Miriam. [The participial phrase modifies the noun *Feld*. The adverb phrase *by Max's college education* modifies the past participle *dazzled*.]

Read aloud, the story entertained the kindergarten class. [The participial phrase modifies the noun *story*. The adverb *aloud* modifies the past participle *read*.]

 NOTE Do not confuse a participle used as an adjective with a participle used as part of a verb phrase.

ADJECTIVE	What are **fighting** fish?
VERB PHRASE	They **are fighting.**

Gerunds and Gerund Phrases

6d. A *gerund* is a verb form ending in *–ing* that is used as a noun. A *gerund phrase* consists of a gerund and all the words related to the gerund.

SUBJECT	**Reading** was Sobel's pastime. [The gerund *reading* is the subject of *was*.]
DIRECT OBJECT	She didn't like **speaking in class.** [The gerund phrase *speaking in class* is the direct object of the verb *did like*. The prepositional phrase *in class* modifies the gerund *speaking*.]
PREDICATE NOMINATIVE	The best part was **winning the match.** [The gerund phrase *winning the match* is the predicate nominative identifying the subject *part. Match* is the direct object of *winning*.]
OBJECT OF A PREPOSITION	After **waiting for two years,** Sobel can propose to Miriam. [The gerund phrase *waiting for two years* is the object of the preposition *after*. The prepositional phrase *for two years* modifies *waiting*.]

A noun or pronoun should be in the possessive form when preceding a gerund.

EXAMPLES

Sobel's pounding bothered Feld because it interfered with **his** daydreaming.

 NOTE Do not confuse a gerund with a present participle used as an adjective or as a part of a verb phrase.

EXAMPLE

Meddling, Feld was **arranging** for Max and Miriam to go out. [*Meddling* is a present participle modifying *Feld. Arranging* is part of the verb phrase *was arranging*.]

Infinitives and Infinitive Phrases

6e. An *infinitive* is a verb form, usually preceded by *to*, that can be used as a noun, an adjective, or an adverb. An *infinitive phrase* consists of an infinitive and all the words related to the infinitive.

NOUN	**To have friends** is important. [The infinitive phrase *to have friends* is the subject of *is. Friends* is the direct object of the infinitive *to have*.]
	Maggie did not want **to argue with Dee.** [The infinitive phrase *to argue with Dee* is the object of the verb *did want*. The prepositional phrase *with Dee* modifies the infinitive *to argue*.]
	Dee's plan was **to take the quilts.** [The infinitive phrase *to take the quilts* is the predicate nominative identifying the subject *plan. Quilts* is the direct object of the infinitive *to take*.]
ADJECTIVE	Her refusal **to answer questions** puzzled him. [The infinitive phrase *to answer questions* modifies the noun *refusal. Questions* is the direct object of the infinitive *to answer*.]
ADVERB	We were ready **to go to the game.** [The infinitive phrase *to go to the game* modifies the adjective *ready*. The prepositional phrase *to the game* modifies the infinitive *to go*.]

NOTE Do not confuse an infinitive with a prepositional phrase that begins with *to*.

EXAMPLE

Eric went **to the gym** [prepositional phrase] **to meet Clint** [infinitive phrase].

Sometimes the *to* of the infinitive is omitted.

EXAMPLES

Would you help me [to] proofread this?
You need not [to] make the corrections.

6f. An infinitive may have a subject, in which case it forms an *infinitive clause.*

EXAMPLE

He asked **the teacher to excuse him.** [The infinitive clause *the teacher to excuse him* is the direct object of the verb *asked. The teacher* is the subject of the infinitive *to excuse. Him* is the direct object of the infinitive.]

☞ For more about clauses, see Part 7: Clauses.

Avoiding Split Infinitives

A *split infinitive* occurs when a word is placed between the *to* and the verb in an infinitive. Although split infinitives are commonly used in informal speaking and writing, you should avoid using them in formal situations.

SPLIT It was better to just mind his own business.
REVISED It was better just **to mind** his own business.

Try It Out ✏️

Revise each of the following sentences to eliminate the split infinitive.

1. Mrs. Johnson liked to sometimes tell jokes that nobody understood.
2. Ken pretended to not know the answers.
3. She began to suddenly smile at him.
4. Clint wanted to right away escape.
5. To simply take the next train was the boys' advice.

Appositives and Appositive Phrases

6g. An *appositive* is a noun or pronoun placed beside another noun or pronoun to identify or explain it. An *appositive phrase* consists of an appositive and its modifiers.

EXAMPLES

Janet Frame, **a resident of New Zealand,** wrote the essay. [The appositive phrase *a resident of New Zealand* identifies the subject *Janet Frame.*]

Have you seen *The Maltese Falcon,* **one of Humphrey Bogart's most famous films**? [The appositive phrase *one of Humphrey Bogart's most famous films* explains the direct object *The Maltese Falcon.*]

Who wrote the poem **"Mother to Son"**? [The appositive *"Mother to Son"* identifies the direct object *poem.*]

An appositive phrase usually follows the noun or pronoun it refers to. For emphasis, however, it may come at the beginning of a sentence.

EXAMPLE

A big brother all my life, I rushed to help the little girl who reminded me of my sister.

Appositives and appositive phrases are usually set off by commas. However, some appositives are necessary to identify or explain a noun or pronoun and therefore should not be set off by commas.

EXAMPLES

My cousin **Jim** lives in Alaska. [The appositive is not set off by commas because it is necessary to tell which of the writer's cousins lives in Alaska.]

My cousin**,** **Jim,** lives in Alaska. [The appositive is set off by commas because the writer has only one cousin, and the appositive is not necessary.]

7 CLAUSES

7a. A *clause* is a group of words that contains a verb and its subject and is used as part of a sentence.

SENTENCE Lichens are small, rootless plants that are composed of both fungi and algae.
CLAUSE Lichens are small, rootless plants. [complete thought]
CLAUSE that are composed of both fungi and algae [incomplete thought]

KINDS OF CLAUSES

7b. An *independent* (or *main*) *clause* expresses a complete thought and can stand by itself as a sentence.

EXAMPLES

His cousin had an apartment, and Shorty roomed there.

When his hair was long enough, he got it conked.

7c. A *subordinate* (or *dependent*) *clause* does not express a complete thought and cannot stand alone.

EXAMPLE
When his hair was long enough, he got it conked.

Subordinate clauses can be used as adjectives, adverbs, or nouns.

7d. An *adjective clause* is a subordinate clause that modifies a noun or a pronoun.

An adjective clause, which usually follows the word it modifies, usually begins with a **relative pronoun**—*who, whom, whose, which,* or *that.* Besides introducing an adjective clause, a relative pronoun has its own function within the clause.

EXAMPLES
Alex Haley, **who helped write this story,** wrote *Roots.* [The adjective clause modifies *Alex Haley. Who* serves as the subject of *helped.*]
Malcolm X, **whose life touched many,** was an extraordinary man. [The adjective clause modifies the noun *Malcolm X. Whose* serves as an adjective modifying *life.*]

A relative pronoun may sometimes be left out of an adjective clause.

EXAMPLE
Was lye one of the ingredients [**that**] **he used**?

Occasionally an adjective clause begins with the relative adverb *where* or *when.*

EXAMPLES
That was the time **when it started to burn.**
Sores formed in the places **where the congolene remained.**

Depending on how it is used, an adjective clause is either essential or nonessential. An **essential clause** provides information that is necessary to the meaning of a sentence. A **nonessential clause** provides additional information that can be omitted without changing the meaning of a sentence. A nonessential clause is always set off by commas.

ESSENTIAL	Students **who are going to the track meet** can take the bus at 7:45 A.M.
NONESSENTIAL	Austin Stevens, **whose mother is a pediatrician,** plans to study medicine.

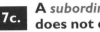 For more information about punctuating essential and nonessential clauses, see 12i.

7e. An *adverb clause* is a subordinate clause that modifies a verb, an adjective, or an adverb.

An adverb clause, which may come before or after the word it modifies, tells *how, when, where, why, to what extent* (*how much*), or *under what condition.* An adverb clause begins with a **subordinating conjunction,** such as *although, because, if, so that,* or *when.*

EXAMPLES
Because he wanted to transform himself, he submitted to the pain. [The adverb clause modifies *submitted,* telling *why.*]
If he touched the jar, it felt hot. [The adverb clause modifies *felt,* telling *under what condition.*]
He was amazed **when he saw himself in the mirror.** [The adverb phrase modifies the verb *was amazed,* telling *when.*]
Malcolm X may be more famous today **than he was during his lifetime.** [The adverb clause modifies *famous,* telling *to what extent.*]

7f. A *noun clause* is a subordinate clause used as a subject, a predicate nominative, a direct object, an indirect object, or an object of a preposition.

The words commonly used to begin noun clauses include *that, what, whether, who,* and *why.*

SUBJECT	**What he had** was especially strong determination.
PREDICATE NOMINATIVE	Potatoes and other ingredients were **what they used** in making the stew.
DIRECT OBJECT	Who could have guessed **where his desire for transformation would take him**?
INDIRECT OBJECT	His story gives **whoever listens** the benefit of his experience.

The word that introduces a noun clause may or may not have a function within the noun clause.

EXAMPLES
Later, he regretted **what he had done.** [*What* is the direct object of *had done.*]
He believed **that the practice of conking was demeaning.** [*That* has no function in the clause.]

Sometimes the word that introduces a noun clause is not stated, but its meaning is understood.

EXAMPLE
He is a **man** [**whom**] **you should respect.**

Revising Short, Choppy Sentences

Although short sentences can be effective, it's usually a good idea to alternate between shorter sentences and longer ones. Often, you can combine short sentences by changing some of them into subordinate clauses and inserting them in other sentences.

CHOPPY   Malcolm X had a troubled youth. He landed in jail. There, he changed his life completely.

REVISED   Malcolm X, who had a troubled youth, landed in jail, where he changed his life completely.

Try It Out ✎

The following paragraph consists mostly of short sentences. Revise the paragraph by changing some of these sentences into subordinate clauses and then combining them with other sentences and clauses to create longer, smoother sentences.

[1] Many people are slaves to fashion. [2] They worry about their hair. [3] Some people have straight hair. [4] They want curly hair. [5] Some people have curly hair. [6] They want straight hair. [7] They spend millions of dollars. [8] That money might be put to better use. [9] These people discover something. [10] Their appearance can't change who they really are.

8 SENTENCE STRUCTURE

SENTENCE OR SENTENCE FRAGMENT?

8a. A *sentence* is a group of words that contains a subject and a verb and that expresses a complete thought.

A sentence should begin with a capital letter and end with a period, a question mark, or an exclamation point. A group of words that either does not have a subject and a verb or does not express a complete thought is called a *sentence fragment.*

FRAGMENT   While his father was getting the wagon.

SENTENCE   While his father was getting the wagon, the boys got ready.

FRAGMENT   Their father up early on Saturday morning.

SENTENCE   Why was their father up early on Saturday morning?

FRAGMENT   What fun!
SENTENCE   What fun that was!

FRAGMENT   Meeting on Friday to make plans.
SENTENCE   We are meeting on Friday to make plans.

☞ For information on how to correct fragments, see 9a. For more information about capitalizing and punctuating sentences, see 11a and 12a–e.

SUBJECT AND PREDICATE

8b. A sentence consists of two parts: the subject and the predicate. The *subject* tells *whom* or *what* the sentence is about. The *predicate* tells something about the subject.

In the following examples, all the words labeled *subject* make up the **complete subject,** and all the words labeled *predicate* make up the **complete predicate.**

SUBJECT | PREDICATE
They | rode in the wagon.

SUBJECT | PREDICATE
A maze of streets and alleys | led to the dump.

PREDICATE | SUBJECT | PREDICATE
Doesn't | Brian's car | have a tape deck?

The Simple Subject

8c. The *simple subject* is the main word or group of words that tells *whom* or *what* the sentence is about.

EXAMPLES
The railroad **crossing** south of 86th Street was noisy. [The complete subject is *the railroad crossing south of 86th Street.*]
The gifted **Hugo Martinez-Serros** wrote "Distillation." [The complete subject is *the gifted Hugo Martinez-Serros.*]

The Simple Predicate

 8d. The *simple predicate, or verb,* is the main word or group of words that tells something about the subject.

EXAMPLES
He **ran** faster and faster up the hill. [The complete predicate is *ran faster and faster up the hill.*]
Have you ever **had** such a wild ride on a sled before? [The complete predicate is *have ever had such a wild ride on a sled before.*]

 NOTE In this book, the term *subject* refers to the simple subject and the term *verb* refers to the simple predicate unless otherwise noted.

The Compound Subject and the Compound Verb

8e. A *compound subject* consists of two or more subjects that are joined by a conjunction and have the same verb.

EXAMPLES
He and his **brothers** were frightened.
Were the **boys or** their **father** hurt?

8f. A *compound verb* consists of two or more verbs that are joined by a conjunction and have the same subject.

EXAMPLES
They **ran** to the shack **and hid** inside.
Pa **protected** them **but was pelted** with hail himself.

A sentence may have a compound subject and a compound verb.

EXAMPLE
Both my **aunt** and my **uncle have** nice cars but rarely **drive** anywhere.

Finding the Subject of a Sentence

 8g. To find the subject of a sentence, ask "Who?" or "What?" before the verb.

(1) The subject of a sentence is never in a prepositional phrase.

EXAMPLES
Piles of rotten garbage stood before them. [What stood? *Piles* stood, not *garbage,* which is the object of the preposition *of.*]
In the trash hid **rats.** [What hid? *Rats* hid. *Trash* is the object of the preposition *in.*]

(2) The subject of a sentence expressing a question usually follows the verb or part of the verb phrase. Questions often begin with a verb, a helping verb, or a word such as *what, when, where, how,* or *why.*

Turning the question into a statement may help you find the subject.

QUESTION Is hail dangerous to people?
STATEMENT **Hail** is dangerous to people.

(3) The word *there* or *here* is never the subject of a sentence.

EXAMPLES
There is the **tarp.** [What is there? A *tarp* is.]
Here is your **water.** [What is here? *Water* is.]

(4) The subject of a sentence expressing a command or request is always understood to be *you* although *you* may not appear in the sentence.

EXAMPLE
[You] Pay attention to his metaphors. [Who is to pay attention? *You* are.]

The subject of a command or request is *you* even when the sentence contains a **noun of direct address,** a word naming the one or ones spoken to.

EXAMPLE
Ed, [you] please explain this story's ending.

COMPLEMENTS

8h. A *complement* is a word or group of words that completes the meaning of a verb.

Three kinds of complements are *subject complements* (*predicate nominative* and *predicate adjective*), *direct objects,* and *indirect objects.*

The Subject Complement

 8i. A *subject complement* is a word or a word group that completes the meaning of a linking verb and that identifies or modifies the subject.

(1) A *predicate nominative* is a noun or pronoun that follows a linking verb and identifies the subject of the verb.

EXAMPLES
Their father was a powerful **man.** [*Man* identifies the subject *father.*]
Was the author the youngest **son?** [*Son* renames the subject *author.*]

(2) A *predicate adjective* is an adjective that follows a linking verb and modifies the subject of the verb.

EXAMPLES
Was their father **strong**? [The adjective *strong* modifies the subject *father*.]
The wagon was **sturdy** and **large**. [The adjectives *sturdy* and *large* modify the subject *wagon*.]

NOTE A subject complement may precede the subject and the verb.

PREDICATE ADJECTIVE How **glad** they were to have the tarp!

☞ For more information about the different kinds of verbs, see Part 1: The Parts of Speech.

The Direct Object and the Indirect Object

8j. A *direct object* is a noun or pronoun that receives the action of a verb or that shows the result of the action. The direct object tells *whom* or *what* after a transitive verb.

EXAMPLES
Ice covered the **ground**. [covered what? *ground*]
How he admires his **father** and **mother**! [admires whom? *father* and *mother*]

8k. An *indirect object* is a noun or pronoun that precedes the direct object and usually tells *to whom* or *for whom* (or *to what* or *for what*) the action of the verb is done.

EXAMPLES
They brought their **mother** sacks of food. [brought sacks for whom? *mother*]
He had given the **wheels** and **gears** some grease. [had given grease to what? *wheels* and *gears*]

CLASSIFYING SENTENCES BY PURPOSE

8l. Sentences may be classified as *declarative, imperative, interrogative, or exclamatory*.

(1) A *declarative sentence* makes a statement. It is followed by a period.

EXAMPLE
They gazed out over the city.

(2) An *imperative sentence* makes a request or gives a command. It is usually followed by a period. A very strong command, however, is followed by an exclamation point.

EXAMPLES
Let me know when you are free. [request]
Be careful not to fall. [mild command]
Hurry! [strong command]

(3) An *interrogative sentence* asks a question. It is followed by a question mark.

EXAMPLE
What is the high point of the action?

(4) An *exclamatory sentence* expresses strong feeling. It is always followed by an exclamation point.

EXAMPLE
Watch out!

☞ For more information about end punctuation for sentences, see 12a–e.

CLASSIFYING SENTENCES BY STRUCTURE

8m. Sentences may be classified as *simple, compound, complex,* or *compound-complex*.

(1) A *simple sentence* has one independent clause and no subordinate clauses.

EXAMPLES
Warehouses and markets sent all of their refuse to the dump.
Look at this!

(2) A *compound sentence* has two or more independent clauses but no subordinate clauses.

EXAMPLES
A shack had sheltered them, but then the wind tore its roof off.
The lightning diminished; the storm was over.
The children were afraid; however, Pa calmed them.

NOTE Do not confuse a compound sentence with a simple sentence that has a compound subject or a compound predicate.

	S V V
COMPOUND PREDICATE	He **rose** and **stretched** his arms.

	S V S V
COMPOUND SENTENCE	Pa **rose**, and he **stretched** his arms.

(3) A *complex sentence* has one independent clause and at least one subordinate clause.

EXAMPLES
After they got home, they unloaded the wagon. [The subordinate clause is *after they got home;* the independent clause is *they unloaded the wagon.*]

As he ran, sweat darkened the shirt that he was wearing. [The subordinate clauses are *as he ran* and *that he was wearing.*]

☞ For information about independent clauses and subordinate clauses, see Part 7: Clauses.

(4) A *compound-complex sentence* contains two or more independent clauses and at least one subordinate clause.

EXAMPLE
When the boys were ready, they piled in the wagon, and Pa slipped into the harness. [The independent clauses are *they piled in the wagon* and *Pa slipped into the harness.* The subordinate clause is *when the boys were ready.*]

☞ For information about using varied sentence structure and improving sentence style, see Part 10: Writing Effective Sentences.

Varying Sentence Structure

To keep readers interested in your ideas, evaluate your writing to see whether you have used a variety of sentence structures. Then, use revising techniques to vary the structure of your sentences.

Try It Out ✎

The following paragraph contains only simple sentences. Revise the paragraph to create a variety of sentence structures.

[1] Many people immigrate to the United States. [2] Some bring children along. [3] These children often face enormous difficulties. [4] Many do not have the same cultural background as the other students at their new schools. [5] The young immigrants may not speak English. [6] They do not know the customs of their new home. [7] Yet, their parents have high hopes for them. [8] The children try to fulfill those hopes. [9] Millions of immigrants have done so. [10] Somehow these children adapt to life in the United States.

WRITING COMPLETE SENTENCES

9

SENTENCE FRAGMENTS

9a. **Avoid using sentence fragments.**

A *sentence* is a word group that has a subject and a verb and expresses a complete thought. A *sentence fragment* is a word group that does not have the basic parts of a complete sentence.

To find out whether a word group is a complete sentence or a sentence fragment, use this simple three-part test. If you answer no to any of these questions, the word group is a fragment.

1. Does the group of words have a subject?
2. Does it have a verb?
3. Does it express a complete thought?

SUBJECT MISSING	Was her dancing partner. [*Who was her dancing partner?*]
SENTENCE	**Geraldo** was her dancing partner.
VERB MISSING	Marin at the hospital. [*What did she do at the hospital?*]
SENTENCE	Marin **waited** at the hospital.
NOT A COMPLETE THOUGHT	When she was asked. [*What happened* when she was asked?*]
SENTENCE	**She could not give his full name** when she was asked.

Phrase Fragments

A *phrase* is a group of words that does not have a subject and a verb.

FRAGMENT	Attending many dances.
SENTENCE	She enjoyed **attending many dances.**
FRAGMENT	To wonder about him.
SENTENCE	His family began **to wonder about him.**

FRAGMENT	Living far away from him.
SENTENCE	**Living far away from him,** they will never know his fate.
FRAGMENT	A writer of Mexican heritage.
SENTENCE	Sandra Cisneros, **a writer of Mexican heritage,** wrote this story.
FRAGMENT	In green pants and a fancy shirt.
SENTENCE	Marin danced with the boy **in green pants and a fancy shirt.**

Subordinate Clause Fragments

A *clause* is a group of words that has a subject and a verb. An *independent clause* expresses a complete thought and can stand on its own as a sentence.

INDEPENDENT CLAUSE   She found her voice.

However, a *subordinate clause* does not express a complete thought and can't stand by itself as a sentence.

FRAGMENT	When Sandra Cisneros found her point of view.
SENTENCE	**When Sandra Cisneros found her point of view,** she found her voice.

RUN-ON SENTENCES

9b.   Avoid run-on sentences.

A *run-on sentence* is two or more complete sentences that are run together as one. Because a reader cannot tell where one idea ends and another begins, run-on sentences can be confusing.

There are two kinds of run-ons. In the first kind, called a *fused sentence,* the sentences have no punctuation at all between them.

RUN-ON   He had no papers on him no one knew his identity.

In the other kind of run-on, called a **comma splice,** only a comma separates the sentences from one another.

RUN-ON   He had no papers on him, no one knew his identity.

Revising Run-on Sentences

There are several ways that you can revise run-on sentences. Usually, the easiest way is to make two separate sentences. However, if the two thoughts are closely related and equally important, you may want to make a compound sentence. Here are three ways to make a compound sentence out of a run-on.

1. You can use a comma and a coordinating conjunction—*and, but, or, yet, for, so,* or *nor.*

    REVISED   He had no papers on him**, and** no one knew his identity.

2. You can use a semicolon.

    REVISED   He had no papers on him**;** no one knew his identity.

3. You can use a semicolon and a *conjunctive adverb*—a word such as *therefore, instead, also, meanwhile, still, nevertheless,* or *however.* Follow a conjunctive adverb with a comma.

    REVISED   He had no papers on him**; consequently,** no one knew his identity.

10 WRITING EFFECTIVE SENTENCES

SENTENCE COMBINING

Inserting Words

10a.   Combine short sentences by inserting a key word from one sentence into another sentence.

Sometimes you can simply insert a key word without changing its form. In many cases, however, you will need to change the form of the key word in some way before you can insert it smoothly into another sentence.

ORIGINAL	Abioseh Nicol is a writer. He is from Africa.
COMBINED	Abioseh Nicol is an **African** writer.
ORIGINAL	You will read one of his stories. It involves a mystery.
COMBINED	You will read one of his **mystery** stories.

When you change the form of a key word, you often need to add an ending that makes the word an adjective or an adverb. Usually the ending is *–ed, –ing,* or *–ly.* For information about the correct spelling of words when adding suffixes, see pages 1047–1048.

Inserting Phrases

10b. Combine closely related sentences by taking a phrase from one sentence and inserting it in another sentence.

Prepositional Phrases

A *prepositional phrase,* a preposition with its object, can usually be inserted into another sentence without changing the phrase. All you have to do is leave out some of the words in one of the sentences.

ORIGINAL	Nicol studied in Africa and abroad. He studied at Cambridge.
COMBINED	Nicol studied in Africa and abroad **at Cambridge.**

Participial Phrases

A *participial phrase* contains a participle and words related to the participle. The entire phrase acts as an adjective, modifying a noun or a pronoun. Sometimes, you can insert a participial phrase just as it is. At other times, you can change the verb from one sentence into a participle and insert it in the other sentence.

ORIGINAL	Bola's son came to visit. He was wearing a scarf around his neck.
COMBINED	Bola's son came to visit, **wearing a scarf around his neck.**
ORIGINAL	He showed Asi a necklace. The necklace bore a gold locket.
COMBINED	He showed Asi a necklace **bearing a gold locket.**

Appositive Phrases

An *appositive phrase* is placed next to a noun or pronoun to identify or explain it. Sometimes you can combine sentences by changing one of the sentences to an appositive phrase.

ORIGINAL	Meji was Bola's only son. He was Asi's father.
COMBINED	Meji, **Bola's only son,** was Asi's father.

Using Compound Subjects and Compound Verbs

 10c. Combine sentences by making compound subjects and compound verbs.

Look for sentences that have the same subject or the same verb. Then, make the subject, verb, or both compound by using a coordinating conjunction.

ORIGINAL	Meji went for a walk. Asi went with him. [same verb with different subjects]
COMBINED	**Meji and Asi** went for a walk. [compound subject]
ORIGINAL	He came for a visit. He could not stay long. [same subject with different verbs]
COMBINED	He **came** for a visit **but could** not **stay** long. [compound verb]
ORIGINAL	Bola slept. So did Asi. The next day, they learned of Meji's death. [same verb (*slept*) with different subjects and plural subject (*they*) that refers to the same two subjects with a different verb]
COMBINED	**Bola and Asi slept and learned** the next day of Meji's death. [compound subject and compound verb]

Creating a Compound Sentence

 10d. Combine sentences by creating a compound sentence.

A *compound sentence* is two or more simple sentences linked by

- a comma and a coordinating conjunction
  or
- a semicolon
  or
- a semicolon and a conjunctive adverb

ORIGINAL	Asi was Meji's daughter. She lived with Bola.
COMBINED	Asi was Meji's daughter**, but** she lived with Bola. [comma and coordinating conjunction]
	Asi was Meji's daughter**;** she lived with Bola. [semicolon]
	Asi was Meji's daughter**; however,** she lived with Bola. [semicolon and conjunctive adverb]

☞ For more information about compound sentences, see 8m and 12h.

Using Compound Sentences

Before linking two thoughts in a compound sentence, make sure that the thoughts are closely related to one another and equally important. Otherwise, you may confuse your readers.

UNRELATED IDEAS The spirit of Africa is noble. This story takes place in a village.

CLOSELY RELATED IDEAS The spirit of Africa is noble, and this story depicts that nobility.

Try It Out

Most of the following pairs of sentences can be combined into a compound sentence. Combine each pair of sentences that have closely related ideas. If a pair of sentences contains unrelated ideas, write *unrelated*.

1. Some people love ghost stories. Other people do not.
2. Spirits can help people. Spirits can harm people.
3. Meji is a friendly ghost. He is kind to his family.
4. He helps his mother. She is grateful for his visit.
5. Did you like the story? When did you know about Meji?

Creating a Complex Sentence

10e. Combine sentences by creating a complex sentence.

A **complex sentence** includes one independent clause and one or more subordinate clauses.

☞ See 7a–f and 9a for more about independent and subordinate clauses.

Adjective Clauses

You can change a sentence into an adjective clause by inserting *who, whom, which,* or *that* in place of the subject. Then you can use the adjective clause to give information about a noun or a pronoun in another sentence.

ORIGINAL Musa attended the service. Musa was the village's magician.

COMBINED Musa, **who was the village's magician,** attended the service.

Adverb Clauses

You can turn a sentence into an adverb clause by placing a subordinating conjunction (such as *after, if, although, because, when,* or *where*) at the beginning of the sentence. Then you can use the clause to modify a verb, an adjective, or an adverb in another sentence.

ORIGINAL Bola had suffered greatly. She did not regret her choice.

COMBINED **Although Bola had suffered greatly,** she did not regret her choice.

Noun Clauses

You can make a sentence into a noun clause and insert it into another sentence, using it just as you would use a noun. You can create a noun clause by inserting a word such as *that, how, what,* or *who* at the beginning of a sentence. When you place the noun clause in the other sentence, you may have to change or remove some words or revise the sentence in other ways.

ORIGINAL Asi knew about the locket. Did the mourners believe how?

COMBINED Did the mourners believe **how Asi knew about the locket**? [The word *how* introduces the noun clause, which becomes the object of the verb *believe*.]

IMPROVING SENTENCE STYLE

Using Parallel Structure

10f. Use the same form to express equal ideas.

Using the same form for equal ideas creates balance in a sentence. For example, you balance a noun with a noun, a phrase with the same type of phrase, and a clause with a clause. This balance is called **parallel structure**.

NOT PARALLEL I like reading, writing, and to draw. [two gerunds and an infinitive]

PARALLEL I like **reading, writing,** and **drawing.** [three gerunds]

NOT PARALLEL Some of these stories are funny, entertaining, and teach me a lot. [two adjectives and a complete predicate]

PARALLEL Some of these stories are **funny, entertaining,** and **educational.** [three adjectives]

NOT PARALLEL	I knew that an airplane had crashed but not about the passenger's heroic rescue. [a clause and a phrase]
PARALLEL	I knew **that an airplane had crashed** but not **that a passenger had made a heroic rescue.** [two clauses]

Revising Stringy Sentences

 Avoid using stringy sentences.

A *stringy sentence* usually has too many independent clauses strung together with coordinating conjunctions like *and* or *but*. Since all the ideas are treated equally, the reader has trouble seeing how they are related. To fix a stringy sentence, you can break the sentence into two or more sentences or turn some of the independent clauses into subordinate clauses or phrases.

STRINGY	The water was freezing cold, and a few survivors clung to some wreckage, and a helicopter came, but it could only take one person at a time, and one man let the others go first.
REVISED	Although the water was freezing cold, a few survivors clung to some wreckage. A helicopter came, but it could only take one person at a time. One man let the others go first.

Revising Wordy Sentences

 Avoid using wordy sentences.

Extra words and unnecessarily difficult words clutter your writing and make it hard to follow. Compare the following sentences.

WORDY	I wonder if you would be so kind as to take the time to enlighten me as to the current weather conditions in the immediate vicinity.
IMPROVED	What's the weather?

Avoiding Wordy Sentences

Here are three tips for avoiding wordy sentences.

- Don't use complicated words where simple ones will do.

- Don't repeat yourself unless repetition is absolutely necessary.
- Don't use more words than you need to.

WORDY	The rescuers were brave men who bravely risked death to rescue the injured.
REVISED	The rescuers bravely risked death to save the injured.

Try It Out

Using the techniques you have learned, revise the following wordy paragraph to make it clear and direct.

[1] Roger Rosenblatt attests to the fact that he wrote "The Man in the Water" in less time than it takes for an hour to pass. [2] However, any piece composed in this manner may be—and often, as practical experience indicates, is—flawed. [3] This possible eventuality Rosenblatt admits. [4] Writers, consequently, who are not far along in years should eschew procrastination, remembering one thing. [5] Rosenblatt has spent many, many years, decades even, editing, revising, and learning to perfect his skills.

Varying Sentence Structures

10i. **Vary the structure of your sentences.**

Using a variety of sentence structures makes your writing livelier. Instead of using all simple sentences, you can use a mix of simple, compound, complex, and compound-complex sentences.

ALL SIMPLE SENTENCES

I visited a friend on her grandparents' farm. I was about ten years old at the time. There wasn't much room in the farmhouse. My friend and I begged hard. We got to sleep in the hayloft in the barn. It was wonderful. We lay awake at night. We counted shooting stars. We told each other our dreams and our hopes for the future.

VARIED SENTENCE STRUCTURE

When I was about ten years old, I visited a friend on her grandparents' farm. Because there wasn't much room in the farmhouse and because we begged hard, my friend and I got to sleep in the hayloft in the barn. It was wonderful. We counted shooting stars as we lay awake at night, and we told each other our dreams and our hopes for the future.

Varying Sentence Beginnings

10j. **Vary the beginnings of your sentences.**

The basic structure of an English sentence is a subject followed by a verb. But following this pattern all the time can make your writing dull. Compare the following paragraphs.

SUBJECT-VERB PATTERN

The young girl's mother dies. Her father remarries. His new wife is beautiful but cruel. The girl grows up and becomes more beautiful. The new wife becomes jealous. She tells a woodsman to take the girl into the woods and kill her. The woodsman cannot bring himself to do so. He lets her go. The girl discovers a house in the forest. The house is inhabited by seven tiny men.

VARIED SENTENCE BEGINNINGS

After the young girl's mother dies, her father remarries. Although beautiful, his new wife is cruel. As the girl grows up and becomes more beautiful, the new wife becomes jealous. "Take the girl into the woods and kill her," she tells a woodsman. Unable to bring himself to do so, the woodsman lets the girl go. In the forest, the girl discovers a house inhabited by seven tiny men.

You can use the methods given in the chart to vary sentence beginnings.

VARYING SENTENCE BEGINNINGS
SINGLE-WORD MODIFIERS
Courageously, the man remained behind. [adverb] **Cautious,** the copilot doubted an instrument reading. [adjective] **Iced,** the plane's wings were dangerous. [participle] **Laughing,** they dismissed their fear. [participle]
PHRASES
With haste, the rescue team rushed to the river. [prepositional phrase] **Writing of the incident,** Roger Rosenblatt says that people must fight back against nature. [participial phrase] **To operate safely,** wings must be clear of ice. [infinitive phrase]
SUBORDINATE CLAUSES
Because no one knew the hero's name, all people could identify with him. [adverb clause] **When Lenny Skutnik saw the injured woman,** he dragged her to shore. [adverb clause]

11 CAPITALIZATION

11a. **Capitalize the first word in every sentence.**

EXAMPLES
This poem has no title.
Does the author say why?

(1) Capitalize the first word of a direct quotation.

EXAMPLE
Roger answered, "**Y**es, I believe she does."

(2) Traditionally, the first word of a line of poetry is capitalized.

EXAMPLES
He turned his face to the wall;
She turned her back upon him;
—Anonymous, "Bonny Barbara Allan"

11b. **Capitalize the first word both in the salutation and in the closing of a letter.**

EXAMPLES
Dear Ann,   **D**ear Sir: **S**incerely,   **Y**ours truly,

11c. **Capitalize the pronoun *I* and the interjection *O*.**

The interjection *O* is always capitalized. The common interjection *oh* is not capitalized unless it is the first word in a sentence.

EXAMPLES
"'**O** Father, **O** Father, go dig my grave'" is a line from "Bonny Barbara Allan."
The play was a hit, but, **oh,** how nervous **I** was.

11d. **Capitalize proper nouns and proper adjectives.**

A *common noun* is a general name for a person, place, thing, or idea. A *proper noun* names a particular person, place, thing, or idea. *Proper adjectives* are formed from proper nouns. Common nouns are not capitalized unless they begin a sentence, begin a direct quotation, or are included in a title.

COMMON NOUNS	poet
	nation
PROPER NOUNS	Shakespeare
	Sioux
PROPER ADJECTIVES	Shakespearean sonnet
	Sioux art

In proper nouns with more than one word, do *not* capitalize

- articles (*a, an, the*)
- short prepositions (those with fewer than five letters, such as *at* and *with*)
- coordinating conjunctions (*and, but, for, nor, or, yet*)
- the sign of the infinitive (*to*)

EXAMPLES
Attila **t**he Hun
"The Tale **o**f **t**he Sands"

Notice in the second example above that these words are capitalized if they are the first word in a proper noun.

(1) Capitalize the names of persons and animals.

GIVEN NAMES	Oliver	Gwendolyn	Tomás
SURNAMES	Brown	Furuya	Muñoz
ANIMALS	Big Red	Bambi	Wildfire

Descriptive names and nicknames also should be capitalized.

EXAMPLES
Ivan the **T**errible   **O**ld **G**lory

Abbreviations such as *Ms., Mr., Dr.,* and *Gen.* should always be capitalized. Capitalize the abbreviations *Jr.* (*junior*) and *Sr.* (*senior*) after a name, and set them off with commas.

EXAMPLES
Is **G**en. Daniel James**,** **J**r.**,** still on active duty?

Capitalization is part of the spelling for names with more than one word. Always check the spelling of such a name with the person whose name it is, or look in a reference source.

EXAMPLES
La **C**roix   **D**u **P**ont   **M**c**E**wen   **O**'**C**onnor

(2) Capitalize geographical names.

TYPE OF NAME	EXAMPLES	
Towns and Cities	Rio de Janeiro	St. Louis
Counties, Townships, and Parishes	Osceola County Hayes Township	East Baton Rouge Parish Brooklyn Borough
States	North Dakota	Hawaii
Countries	Mexico	United States of America
Continents	North America	Asia
Islands	Cayman Islands	Isle of Man
Mountains	Mesabi Range	Camelback Mountain
Other Land Forms and Features	Cape Horn Angel Falls	Death Valley Dismal Swamp
Bodies of Water	Dead Sea	Lake of the Woods
Parks	Williams Park	Cedar Point Primitive Area
Regions	New England the South	Bermuda Triangle the Corn Belt
Roads, Streets, and Highways	Interstate 4 Route 66	West First Street North Tenth Street

 The abbreviations of names of states are always capitalized. For more about using and punctuating such abbreviations, see page 1038.

NOTE Words such as *north, western,* and *southeast* are not capitalized when they indicate direction.

EXAMPLES
western Iowa
driving south

NOTE In a hyphenated number, the second word begins with a lowercase letter.

EXAMPLE
Forty-second Street

(3) Capitalize the names of organizations, teams, business firms, institutions, buildings and other structures, and government bodies.

TYPE OF NAME	EXAMPLES	
Organizations	B'nai B'rith	Chess Club
Teams	Los Angeles Lakers	New England Patriots
Business Firms	Apple Computer, Inc.	Walgreen Company
Institutions	Lakes High School	Cedars Hospital
Buildings and Other Structures	Empire State Building the Alamo	Oak Mall London Bridge
Government Bodies	Congress	House of Commons

 NOTE Capitalize words such as *democratic* and *republican* only when they refer to a specific political party.
EXAMPLES
The new leaders promised to establish democratic elections.
Was Abraham Lincoln a Republican?

(4) Capitalize the names of historical events and periods, special events, holidays and other calendar items, and time zones.

TYPE OF NAME	EXAMPLES	
Historical Events and Periods	Industrial Revolution War on Poverty	Battle of Camlan Paleozoic Era
Special Events	Interscholastic Debate Tournament Spring Fling	
Holidays and Other Calendar Items	Sunday Election Day	Memorial Day Yom Kippur
Time Zones	Central Daylight Time (**CDT**) Eastern Standard Time (**EST**)	

NOTE Do not capitalize the name of a season unless the season is personified or is used as part of a proper noun.
EXAMPLES
Soon, summer will be here.
Striding across the fields, Summer scorched the crops.
Are you going to the Summer Spectacular at the lake?

(5) Capitalize the names of nationalities, races, and peoples.
EXAMPLES
Greek, Caucasian, African Americans, Asian, Cherokee, Hispanic, Viking, Roman

NOTE The words *black* and *white* may or may not be capitalized when they refer to races.

(6) Capitalize the brand names of business products.
EXAMPLES
Cadillac, Teflon, Kleenex, Lee

NOTE Do not capitalize a common noun that follows a brand name.
EXAMPLES
Cadillac convertible, Teflon pan

(7) Capitalize the names of ships, trains, aircraft, spacecraft, monuments, awards, and planets, stars, and other heavenly bodies.

TYPE OF NAME	EXAMPLES	
Ships and Trains	*Californian* *City of New Orleans*	
Aircraft and Spacecraft	*Air Force One* *Vanguard II*	
Monuments and Memorials	Statue of Liberty Tomb of the Unknowns	
Awards	Distinguished Flying Cross Academy Award	
Planets, Stars, and Other Heavenly Bodies	Saturn Orion 51 Pegasi	Betelgeuse Little Dipper Milky Way

 NOTE Do not capitalize the words *sun* and *moon.* Do not capitalize the word *earth* unless it is used along with the capitalized names of other heavenly bodies.

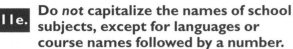

11e. Do *not* capitalize the names of school subjects, except for languages or course names followed by a number.

EXAMPLES
You need not take **art** or a **foreign language**, but you must take **English**, **civics**, and **Mathematics II**.

11f. Capitalize titles.

(1) Capitalize the title of a person when it comes before the person's name.

EXAMPLES
President Taft   **Professor** Hayakawa

Do not capitalize a title that is used alone or following a person's name, especially if the title is preceded by *a* or *the*.

EXAMPLES
Was the **reverend** at the concert?
When did Cleopatra become **queen** of Egypt?

When a title is used alone in direct address, it is usually capitalized.

EXAMPLES
Hurry, **Doctor**!   Pardon me, **Sir** [*or* sir]?

(2) Capitalize words showing family relationship when used with a person's name but *not* when preceded by a possessive.

EXAMPLES
my **mother**   **Auntie** Em   **Dad**   your **father**

(3) Capitalize the first and last words and all important words in titles of books, periodicals, poems, stories, essays, speeches, plays, historical documents, movies, radio and television programs, works of art, musical compositions, and cartoons. Unimportant words in a title are

- articles: *a, an, the*
- short prepositions (fewer than five letters): *of, to, for, from, in, over,* and so on.
- coordinating conjunctions: *and, but, so, nor, or, yet, for*

TYPE OF TITLE	EXAMPLES	
Books	*Spoon River Anthology*	*Travels with Charley*
Periodicals	*Family Computing*	*Horse and Pony*
Poems	"The Power of a Poem"	"What the Mirror Said"
Stories	"Life Is Sweet at Kumansenu"	"The Bet"
Essays and Speeches	"Where I Find My Heroes"	Gettysburg Address
Plays	*Antigone*	*I Never Sang for My Father*
Historical Documents	Declaration of Independence	Emancipation Proclamation
Movies	*Dances with Wolves*	*The Bear*
Radio and Television Programs	*Dinosaurs!*	*Home Improvement*
Works of Art	*View of Toledo*	*David*
Musical Compositions	"Greensleeves"	*La Mer*
Cartoons	*Calvin and Hobbes*	*The Neighborhood*

(4) Capitalize the names of religions and their followers, holy days and celebrations, holy writings, and specific deities.

TYPE OF NAME	EXAMPLES		
Religions and Followers	Judaism	Baptist	Taoist
Holy Days and Celebrations	Passover	Ramadan	Lent
Holy Writings	Bible	Upanishads	Koran
Specific Deities	Brahma	God	Allah

 NOTE The word *god* is not capitalized when it refers to the gods of mythology. The names of such gods are capitalized, however.

EXAMPLE
The Egyptian **god** of the sun was **Ra**.

Revising Capitalization

You may notice that various publications differ in the way they use capital letters. Nevertheless, making sure your own capitalization agrees with the rules and guidelines presented in this part of the Language Handbook will help you communicate clearly with nearly any audience.

Try It Out ✎

Revise the capitalization in the following sentences.

1. Have you read the story "What happened during the ice storm"?
2. I asked, "isn't this a Prince Tennis Racket?"
3. That is professor John Luís nickol Bell, jr.
4. Most of the Senators were already present.
5. I'm taking Shop II and Home Economics.

12 PUNCTUATION

END MARKS

End marks—periods, question marks, and exclamation points—are used to indicate the purpose of a sentence.

12a. **A statement (or declarative sentence) is followed by a period.**

EXAMPLE
Butterflies can symbolize rebirth.

12b. **A question (or interrogative sentence) is followed by a question mark.**

EXAMPLES
Who drew this picture of a butterfly? Did you?

12c. **An exclamation (or exclamatory sentence) is followed by an exclamation point.**

EXAMPLE
What a great idea!

12d. **A command or request (or imperative sentence) is followed by either a period or an exclamation point.**

When an imperative sentence makes a request, it is followed by a period. When an imperative sentence makes a command or shows strong feeling, an exclamation point is used.

EXAMPLES
Let me see it.
Be quiet!

12e. **An abbreviation is usually followed by a period.**

If a statement ends with an abbreviation, do not use an additional period as an end mark. However, do use a question mark or an exclamation point if one is needed.

EXAMPLES
Abraham lived around the nineteenth century B.C.
Was the story written in the eighth century B.C.?

TYPE OF ABBREVIATION	EXAMPLES				
Personal Names	A. E. Housman		Hanson W. Baldwin		
Organizations and Companies	Assn. Corp.	Co. Ltd.	Inc.		
Titles Used with Names	Mr.	Ms.	Mrs.	Jr.	Dr.
Times of Day	A.M.	P.M.			
Years	B.C. (written after the date) A.D. (written before the date)				
Addresses	Ave.	St.	Blvd.	Hwy.	
States	Calif.	Mass.	Tex.	N. Dak.	

NOTE Two-letter state abbreviations without periods are used only when the ZIP Code is included.

EXAMPLE
Cincinnati, OH 45233

NOTE Usually, abbreviations are capitalized only if the words they stand for are capitalized. If you are unsure about capitalizing an abbreviation or using periods with it, look in a dictionary.

Abbreviations for government agencies and official organizations and some other frequently used abbreviations are written without periods. Abbreviations for most units of measure are usually written without periods, especially in science books.

EXAMPLES
CPR, FM, IQ, TV, USAF, cm, km, lb, ml, rpm
EXCEPTION
To avoid confusion with the word *in*, use *in.* for *inch*.

COMMAS

 12f. Use commas to separate words, phrases, or clauses in a series.

EXAMPLE
Three major forms of poetry are the lyric, the epic, and the ballad.

(1) If all items in a series are joined by *and* or *or,* do not use commas to separate them.

EXAMPLE
They need firestone **and** some sticks **or** twigs.

 NOTE Some words—such as *bread and butter, rod and reel,* and *table and chairs*—are used in pairs and may be considered one item in a series.

EXAMPLE
My waders, tackle box, **rod and reel,** and bait are already in the boat.

(2) As a rule, independent clauses in a series are separated by semicolons. Short independent clauses, however, may be separated by commas.

EXAMPLE
God called, Abraham answered, and Isaac obeyed.

12g. Use commas to separate two or more adjectives preceding a noun.

EXAMPLE
What a strange, awesome, dramatic story this is!

When the last adjective in a series is thought of as part of the noun (as in a compound noun), the comma before the adjective is omitted.

EXAMPLE
These are great short stories.

 NOTE The comma may be omitted before a coordinating conjunction that joins the last two items in a series if the meaning is clear without the comma. However, using the comma is never wrong, and many writers prefer always to do so. Follow your teacher's instructions on this point.

 12h. Use commas before *and, but, or, nor, for, so,* and *yet* when they join independent clauses.

EXAMPLE
Abraham raised his hand, **but** an angel called to him.
You may omit the comma before *and, but, or,* or *nor* if the clauses are very short and there is no chance of misunderstanding.

 For more information about using coordinating conjunctions to join independent clauses, see 8m and 10d.

 12i. Use commas to set off nonessential clauses and nonessential phrases.

A **nonessential** (or **nonrestrictive**) clause or phrase adds information that is not needed to understand the main idea in the sentence.

NONESSENTIAL CLAUSE   Isaac, **who was Abraham's son,** was spared. [Omitting the clause would not change the main idea of the sentence.]

When a clause or phrase is necessary to the meaning of a sentence, the clause or phrase is **essential** (or **restrictive**), and commas are *not* used.

ESSENTIAL PHRASE   The blessings **given to Abraham** were numerous. [Omitting the clause would change the meaning of the sentence.]

 For more information about phrases and clauses, see Part 6: Phrases and Part 7: Clauses.

 12j. Use commas after certain introductory elements.

(1) Use commas after words such as *next* and *no* and after introductory interjections such as *why* and *well.*

EXAMPLE
Yes, Wilfred Owen wrote that poem.

(2) Use a comma after an introductory participial phrase.

EXAMPLE
Drawing from the Bible, Owen updated its message.

(3) Use a comma after one long introductory prepositional phrase or two or more short introductory prepositional phrases.

EXAMPLE
At the end of Owen's poem, the son is slain.

(4) Use a comma after an introductory adverb clause.

EXAMPLE
When the angel speaks, the father ignores it.

12k. **Use commas to set off elements that interrupt a sentence.**

EXAMPLE
The thief, **in fact,** later became a disciple.

(1) Appositives and appositive phrases are usually set off by commas.

EXAMPLE
Shichiri, **a man of his word,** denied any theft.

(2) Words used in direct address are set off by commas.

EXAMPLE
What, **David,** is the meaning of this parable?

(3) Parenthetical expressions are set off by commas.
Parenthetical expressions are side remarks that add minor information or that relate ideas to each other.

EXAMPLE
It is, **I believe,** about generosity.

 12l. **Use commas in certain conventional situations.**

(1) Use a comma to separate items in dates and addresses.

EXAMPLES
My sister was born in Akron, Ohio, on May 7, 1991.
Leon's new address is 945 Oak Drive, Covington, KY 41011.

(2) Use a comma after the salutation of a friendly letter and after the closing of any letter.

EXAMPLES
Dear Aunt Hazel,   Sincerely yours,

(3) Use a comma after a name followed by an abbreviation such as *Jr., Sr.,* or *M.D.* Follow such an abbreviation with a comma unless it ends the sentence.

EXAMPLE
My report is about Martin Luther King, Jr.

 12m. **Do not use unnecessary commas.**

Too much punctuation is just as confusing as not enough punctuation, especially in the case of commas.

CONFUSING A man thought that a boy, who was a neighbor, was a thief, but, then, the man found, to his surprise, that he was wrong.

CLEAR A man thought that a boy who was a neighbor was a thief, but then the man found to his surprise that he was wrong.

SEMICOLONS

 12n. **Use a semicolon between independent clauses in a sentence if they are not joined by** *and, but, or, nor, for, so,* **or** *yet.*

EXAMPLE
The tiger was in a cage; a Brahman let him out.

Similarly, a semicolon can take the place of a period to join two sentences that are closely related.

TWO SIMPLE The man opened the door.
SENTENCES Then the tiger jumped out.

ONE COMPOUND The man opened the door;
SENTENCE then the tiger jumped out.

 12o. **Use a semicolon between independent clauses joined by a conjunctive adverb or a transitional expression.**

EXAMPLES
The tiger thought the jackal was stupid; **however,** it was the jackal who outsmarted the tiger.
The tiger was angry; **in fact,** he yelled at the jackal.

Notice in the two examples above that a comma is placed after the conjunctive adverb and the transitional expression.

Commonly Used Conjunctive Adverbs

besides	indeed	nevertheless	then
consequently	instead	next	therefore

Commonly Used Transitional Expressions

as a result	for instance	in fact
for example	in addition	in other words

 12p. **Use a semicolon (rather than a comma) before a coordinating conjunction to join independent clauses that contain commas.**

EXAMPLE
The tree, buffalo, and road were no help; but the jackal was.

12q. **Use a semicolon between items in a series if the items contain commas.**

EXAMPLE
We visited Lima, Peru; Rome, Italy; and Oslo, Norway.

COLONS

 12r. Use a colon to mean "note what follows."

(1) In some cases, a colon is used before a list of items, especially after the expressions *the following* and *as follows.*

EXAMPLE
Discuss the following elements of the story**:** theme, plot, and conflict.

NOTE Do not use a colon before a list that follows a verb or a preposition.

> **INCORRECT** Additional figures of speech are: image, symbol, and metaphor.
>
> **CORRECT** Additional figures of speech are image, symbol, and metaphor.

(2) Use a colon before a long, formal statement or a long quotation.

EXAMPLE
An angel spoke this message to Abraham**:** "Because you have done this and have not withheld your son, your favored one, I will bestow My blessing upon you and make your descendants as numerous as the stars."

12s. Use a colon in certain conventional situations.

(1) Use a colon between the hour and the minute.

EXAMPLES
7**:**30 A.M.   3**:**10 P.M.

(2) Use a colon between chapter and verse when referring to passages from the Bible.

EXAMPLES
Genesis 1**:**1   John 3**:**10–16

(3) Use a colon between a title and a subtitle.

EXAMPLE
"Nisei Daughter**:** The Second Generation"

(4) Use a colon after the salutation of a business letter.

EXAMPLES
Dear Ms. Ash**:**   Dear Sir**:**
To Whom It May Concern**:**

 **Using Punctuation**

In speaking, your tone and pitch, your pauses in your speech, and your gestures and expressions all help make your meaning clear. In writing, marks of punctuation signal these verbal and nonverbal cues.

Try It Out ✎

Correct any errors in punctuation in each of the following sentences.

1. Do you know about: Camelot, Arthur, and the sword Excalibur?
2. The sword the mighty Excalibur was in a stone.
3. Did anyone, in the region, pull the sword out.
4. No no one could; until Arthur did.
5. Aren't knights, and ladies, and magic in the tales?

13 PUNCTUATION

ITALICS

When writing or typing, indicate italics by underlining. If your composition were to be printed, the typesetter would set the underlined words in italics, *like this.*

 13a. Use underlining (italics) for titles of books, plays, long poems, films, periodicals, works of art, recordings, long musical works, television series, trains, ships, aircraft, and spacecraft.

TYPE OF TITLE	EXAMPLES
Books	*Tales of King Arthur* *Silent Dancing*
Plays	*Macbeth* *A Raisin in the Sun*
Long Poems	*Odyssey* *Evangeline*
Films	*Pocahontas* *Free Willy*
Periodicals	*Life* *The New York Times*

NOTE The words *a, an,* and *the* written before a title are italicized only when they are part of the official title. The official title of a book appears on the title page. The official title of a newspaper or periodical appears on the masthead, which is usually found on the editorial page.

EXAMPLES
The Wall Street Journal
the Miami Herald

TYPE OF TITLE	EXAMPLES
Works of Art	*Christina's World* *Discobolos*
Recordings	*Into the Light* *The Bridge*
Long Musical Works	*Treemonisha* *Swan Lake*
Television Series	*Ancient Mysteries* *Avonlea*
Trains and Ships	*Orange Blossom Special* *Titanic*
Aircraft and Spacecraft	*Hindenburg* *Voyager 2*

For examples of titles that should be placed in quotation marks rather than being italicized, see 13k. For information about capitalizing titles, see 11f.

COMPUTER NOTE If you use a personal computer, you can probably set words in italics yourself.

13b. Use underlining (italics) for words, letters, and figures referred to as such and for foreign words not yet part of English vocabulary.

EXAMPLES
There is only one *r* in *Kari.*
Put six *0*'s after that *5.*
Hawaiians say *aloha oe* as both a greeting and a farewell.

If you are not sure whether or not to italicize a foreign word or phrase, look it up in a current dictionary.

QUOTATION MARKS

13c. Use quotation marks to enclose a *direct quotation*—a person's exact words.

EXAMPLES
I asked, "Where does Gabriel García Márquez get his ideas?"
"Apparently, from everywhere," answered Eric.

Do not use quotation marks for **indirect quotations,** which are rewordings of direct quotations.

DIRECT   She said, "I'll call them later."
INDIRECT   She said she will call them later.

An interrupting expression is not a part of a quotation and therefore should never be inside quotation marks.

EXAMPLE
"Let's go," Larry whispered, "right now."

When two or more sentences by the same speaker are quoted together, use only one set of quotation marks.

EXAMPLE
Al said, "Cassius was right. The fault is not in the stars."

13d. A direct quotation begins with a capital letter.

EXAMPLE
Ms. Wells asked, "**Who** is Cassius?"

NOTE If a direct quotation is obviously a fragment of the original quotation, it should begin with a lowercase letter.

EXAMPLE
Cassius is described as having "**a** lean and hungry look."

13e. When a quoted sentence is divided into two parts by an interrupting expression, the second part begins with a lowercase letter.

EXAMPLE
"The film version," he said, "**w**as great."

If the second part of a quotation is a new sentence, the second part begins with a capital letter.

EXAMPLE
"I enjoy seeing a stage play," Paul commented. "It's more interesting."

13f. A direct quotation is set off from the rest of the sentence by commas or by a question mark or an exclamation point.

EXAMPLES

"I have to leave now," Alison said, "so that I will be on time."

"Wow!" he cried. "Wasn't that a great speech?"

13g. When used with quotation marks, other marks of punctuation are placed according to the following rules.

(1) Commas and periods are always placed inside the closing quotation marks.

EXAMPLES

After "Secrets," we will read "Candles."

(2) Semicolons and colons are always placed outside the closing quotation marks.

EXAMPLES

I've finally decided to title my paper "Caesar's March"; it's done now.

Study the following in "First Lesson": rhyme, meter, and image.

(3) Question marks and exclamation points are placed inside closing quotation marks if the quotation is a question or an exclamation; otherwise, they are placed outside.

EXAMPLES

"Jennifer," Mr. Finn asked, "can you give us an example?"

Is the good in people really "oft interrèd with their bones"?

After lunch, the principal said, "All classes for the rest of the day are canceled"!

I shouted, "Hooray!"

13h. When you write dialogue (a conversation), begin a new paragraph every time the speaker changes.

EXAMPLE

"Hey, I've got a great idea! Why don't we do our own modern version of *Julius Caesar*?" suggested Matt.

"What do you mean?" Ben replied. "We'd wear business suits and stuff?"

Matt seemed surprised and said, "Well, no, but that's a good idea."

"It sure is," Paula commented. "What were *you* thinking, Matt?"

"Well, let me explain."

13i. When a quoted passage consists of more than one paragraph, put quotation marks at the beginning of each paragraph and at the end of the entire passage. Do not put quotation marks after any paragraph but the last.

EXAMPLE

"On Saturday, March 24," read the press release, "Hills High School will present *The Tragedy of Julius Caesar*.

"Tickets will be available at the box office. Advance tickets can be purchased by contacting the school at 555-0915.

"The performance will begin at 7 P.M. The box office will open at 6 P.M."

13j. Use single quotation marks to enclose a quotation within a quotation.

EXAMPLE

He asked, "What is the main theme in the story 'The Man to Send Rain Clouds'?"

13k. Use quotation marks to enclose titles of articles, short stories, essays, poems, songs, individual episodes of TV shows, chapter titles, and other parts of books and periodicals.

TYPE OF TITLE	EXAMPLES
Short Stories	"The Cold Equations" "Secrets"
Poems	"We Real Cool" "Those Winter Sundays"
Essays	"A 'Piercing' Issue" "The Lowest Animal"
Articles	"What About Diets?" "Saving the Whales"
Songs	"Ave Maria" "If I Had a Hammer"
TV Episodes	"The Sure Thing" "Monarch in Waiting"
Chapters and Parts of Books and Periodicals	"Medieval Life" "Guide to the Dictionary" "All in a Day's Work"

 For information about titles of works that are italicized, see 13a.

13i. Use quotation marks to enclose slang words, technical terms, and other special uses of words.

EXAMPLES

I'm fresh out of "long green."

She "birdied" (shot one under par on) the sixth hole.

Using Quotations from Interviews

Whenever you conduct an interview, always ask permission to quote the person, and use the person's *exact* words. When quoting someone's exact words, be sure to enclose them in quotation marks.

Try It Out ✎

You are a reporter for your school paper and have just conducted an interview with a local actor, Mr. Thespian, who is playing the role of Mark Antony in *The Tragedy of Julius Caesar*. Use the following quotations from Mr. Thespian to write a paragraph or two for your article. Be sure to use at least four direct quotations.

1. "Acting is more than playing dress-up."
2. "To learn to act is to learn to live."
3. "The plot of *Julius Caesar* is enacted all over the world every day."
4. "The main thing is to be able to see—no, to feel—events from anyone's point of view."
5. "Antony loved Rome and Caesar, as the people did."

14 PUNCTUATION

APOSTROPHES

Possessive Case

14a. The *possessive case* of a noun or pronoun shows ownership or relationship. To form the possessive case of a singular noun, add an apostrophe and an *s*.

EXAMPLES

Malamud's story   a shoemaker's problem

Add only an apostrophe if the added *s* will make the noun hard to pronounce.

EXAMPLES

Sophocles' play   Ms. Fuentes' class

14b. To form the possessive case of a plural noun ending in *s*, add only the apostrophe.

EXAMPLES

shoes' soles   fathers' hopes

To form the possessive case of a plural noun that does not end in *s*, add an apostrophe and an *s*.

EXAMPLES

children's dreams   mice's tails

14c. Possessive pronouns do not require an apostrophe.

EXAMPLES

Whose book is that?

That opinion is **yours.**

The dog chased **its** own tail.

 For more information about possessive pronouns, see Part 4: Using Pronouns.

14d. Indefinite pronouns in the possessive case require an apostrophe and an *s*.

EXAMPLES

nobody's fault   another's help

14e. In compound words, names of organizations and businesses, and word groups showing joint possession, only the last word is possessive in form.

EXAMPLES

father-in-**law's** shop   Cattle **Company's** corrals

Mom and **Dad's** car   United **Way's** volunteers

14f. When two or more persons possess something individually, each name is possessive in form.

EXAMPLES

Pat **Mora's** and Audre **Lorde's** poems

Contractions

 14g. Use an apostrophe to show where letters, words, or numerals have been omitted in a contraction.

EXAMPLES

she will . . . she'll	I am . . . I'm
who is . . . who's	Bill has . . . Bill's
is not . . . isn't	were not . . . weren't
1992 . . . '92	of the clock . . . o'clock

EXCEPTION
will not . . . won't

HYPHENS

 14h. Use a hyphen to divide a word at the end of a line.

EXAMPLE
At first, Feld did not consider the assistant shoe-maker suitable for his daughter.

When you divide a word at the end of a line, keep in mind the following rules.

1. Do not divide one-syllable words.
   gasped [*not* gas-ped]

2. Divide a word only between syllables.
   frag-ment [*not* fra-gment]

3. Words with double consonants may usually be divided between those two consonants.
   drum-mer

4. Usually, a word with a prefix or a suffix may be divided between the prefix or suffix and the base word (or root).
   pre-judge, fall-ing

5. Divide a hyphenated word only at a hyphen.
   mother-in-law [*not* moth-er-in-law]

6. Do not divide a word so that one letter stands alone.
   elec-tricity [*not* e-lectricity]

14i. Use a hyphen with compound numbers from twenty-one to ninety-nine and with fractions used as adjectives.

EXAMPLES
thirty-five years
one-half pound [*One-half* is an adjective modifying *pound*.]
one half of the flour [*Half* is a noun modified by the adjective *one*.]

14j. Use a hyphen with the prefixes *ex–*, *self–*, and *all–*; with the suffix *–elect*; and with all prefixes before a proper noun or proper adjective.

EXAMPLES

ex-wife	all-star	self-employed
governor-elect	pro-American	

14k. Hyphenate a compound adjective when it precedes the noun it modifies.

EXAMPLES
a **well-designed** engine
an engine that is **well designed**

a **world-famous** skier
a skier who is **world famous**

Do not use a hyphen if one of the modifiers is an adverb ending in *–ly*.

EXAMPLE
a **partly finished** research paper

 NOTE Some compound adjectives are always hyphenated, whether they precede or follow the words they modify.

EXAMPLES
an **up-to-date** dictionary
a dictionary that is **up-to-date**

a **self-reliant** person
a person who is **self-reliant**

If you are unsure about whether a compound adjective should always be hyphenated, look up the word in a current dictionary.

DASHES

 14l. Use a dash to indicate an abrupt break in thought or speech or an unfinished statement or question.

EXAMPLES
Jim—Tim, I mean—will show us his video.
"But, I'm—" Tim began and then stopped.

14m. Use a dash to mean *namely, that is, in other words,* and similar expressions that introduce an explanation.

EXAMPLES
I know who wrote that story—Ray Bradbury.
No, Arthur C. Clarke—he wrote *2001: A Space Odyssey*—was the author.

Using Dashes Sparingly

In general, avoid using dashes in formal writing, and don't overuse them in any case. When you evaluate your writing, make sure you haven't used dashes unnecessarily or in place of commas, semicolons, colons, or end marks. Using dashes only for special emphasis will make them more effective.

Try It Out ✎

Revise the following sentences to eliminate the dashes.

1. Mark Twain—by the way—is widely recognized as a master of humor.
2. His essay—"The Lowest Animal"—is quite amusing.

3. Will you—Michael—comment on Twain's theme in this story?
4. Twain—whose real name was Samuel Clemens—preferred to write under a pen name.
5. What or who—as he sees it—is the lowest animal?

PARENTHESES

14n. Use parentheses to enclose explanatory or additional information.

EXAMPLES
Richard Burton (as Mark Antony) appears in *Cleopatra*.
Emily Dickinson (1830–1886) was a unique person.
Fill in the application carefully. (Use a pen.)
After reading the story (it was great), I ate.

15 SPELLING

UNDERSTANDING WORD STRUCTURE

Many English words are made up of word parts from other languages or earlier forms of English.

Roots

The **root** is the part of the word that carries the word's core meaning. Other word parts can be added to a root to create many different words.

ROOTS	MEANINGS	EXAMPLES
–aud–, –audit–	hear	audible, auditorium
–anthrop–	human	anthropology, misanthrope
–biblio–	book	bibliography, bibliophile
–chron–	time	chronological, synchronize
–vid–, –vis–	see	evident, television

NOTE Some word parts have alternate spellings. The spelling used in a particular word is influenced by how the word sounds. If you try pronouncing "televidion," for example, you'll see why –vis–, not –vid–, is the form used in *television*.

Prefixes

A **prefix** is a word part that is added before a root. When a prefix is added to a root, the new word combines the meanings of the prefix and the root.

PREFIXES	MEANINGS	EXAMPLES
bi–	two	bimonthly, bisect
mis–	badly, not, wrongly	misfire, misspell
re–	back, again, backward	revoke, reflect
tra–, trans–	across, beyond	traffic, transport
un–	reverse of, not	untrue, unfold

Suffixes

A *suffix* is a word part that is added after a root. Often, adding a suffix to a word changes the word's part of speech as well as its meaning.

SUFFIXES	MEANINGS	EXAMPLES
–dom	state, rank, condition	freedom, wisdom
–en	cause to be, become	deepen, darken
–ful	full of, marked by	thankful, hopeful
–ly	characteristic of, like	friendly, cowardly
–ness	quality, state	softness, shortness

SPELLING RULES

ie and *ei*

 15a. **Write *ie* when the sound is long e, except after c.**

EXAMPLES
belief   achieve   thief   grief
deceive   receive   ceiling   conceit

EXCEPTIONS
leisure   protein   either   seize

15b. **Write *ei* when the sound is not long e.**

EXAMPLES
heifer   rein   beige   weight

EXCEPTIONS
view   ancient   patient   friend

–cede, –ceed, and –sede

15c. **Only one English word ends in –sede: supersede. Only three words end in –ceed: exceed, proceed, and succeed. Most other words with this sound end in –cede.**

EXAMPLES
accede   intercede   recede
concede   precede   secede

Adding Prefixes

 15d. **When a prefix is added to a word, the spelling of the original word remains the same.**

EXAMPLES
bi + monthly = **bi**monthly
un + natural = **un**natural
re + edit = **re**edit

Adding Suffixes

 15e. **When the suffix –ness or –ly is added to a word, the spelling of the original word remains the same.**

EXAMPLES
careful + ly = careful**ly**
kind + ness = kind**ness**

EXCEPTIONS
Words ending in y usually change the y to i before –ness and –ly:
shady + ness = shad**iness**   busy + ly = bus**ily**

 NOTE Most one-syllable adjectives ending in y follow rule 15e.

EXAMPLES
coy + ness = coy**ness**   shy + ly = shy**ly**

 15f. **Drop the final silent e before adding a suffix that begins with a vowel.**

EXAMPLES
tape + ing = tap**ing**
eliminate + ed = eliminat**ed**

EXCEPTIONS
Keep the final silent e

- in words ending in *ce* or *ge* before a suffix that begins with *a* or *o*:
peac**eable**, knowledg**eable**, courag**eous**, outrag**eous**
- in *dye* and *singe* before –ing:
dy**eing**, sing**eing**
- in *mile* before –age:
mil**eage**

 15g. **Keep the final silent e before adding a suffix that begins with a consonant.**

EXAMPLES
care + less = care**less**   ease + ment = eas**ement**

EXCEPTIONS
argue + ment = argu**ment**   nine + th = nin**th**
true + ly = tru**ly**   whole + ly = whol**ly**

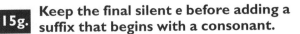

15h. When a word ends in y preceded by a consonant, change the y to i before any suffix except one beginning with i.

EXAMPLES
hurry + ed = hur**ried**
hardy + ness = hard**iness**

EXCEPTIONS
1. some one-syllable words:
  shy + ness = shy**ness**   sky + ward = sky**ward**
2. *lady* and *baby* with suffixes:
  lady**like**   lady**ship**   baby**hood**

15i. When a word ends in y preceded by a vowel, simply add the suffix.

EXAMPLES
survey + ed = survey**ed**
gray + est = gray**est**

EXCEPTIONS
day + ly = da**ily**   say + ed = sa**id**

15j. When a word ends in a consonant, double the final consonant before a suffix that begins with a vowel only if the word

- has only one syllable or is accented on the last syllable
  and
- ends in a *single* consonant preceded by a *single* vowel.

EXAMPLES
wrap + ing = wra**pping**
occur + ence = occu**rrence**

Forming Plurals of Nouns

15k. To form the plurals of most English nouns, simply add –s.

SINGULAR ship pan horse piano
blacksmith Johnson
PLURAL ships pans horses pianos
blacksmiths Johnsons

15l. To form the plurals of other nouns, follow these rules.

(1) If the noun ends in s, x, z, ch, or sh, add –es.

SINGULAR guess fox buzz
peach wish Hernandez
PLURAL guesses foxes buzzes
peaches wishes Hernandezes

NOTE Proper nouns also usually follow rule 15l.

EXAMPLES
the Joneses   the Sánchezes

(2) If the noun ends in y preceded by a consonant, change the y to i and add –es.

SINGULAR fly city quality puppy
PLURAL flies cities qualities puppies
EXCEPTIONS
The plurals of proper nouns: the Darcys, the Lacys

(3) If the noun ends in y preceded by a vowel, add –s.

SINGULAR key boy journey Momaday
PLURAL keys boys journeys Momadays

(4) For some nouns ending in f or fe, add –s. For other such nouns, change the f or fe to v and add –es.

EXAMPLES
thief hoof belief roof
thieves hooves beliefs roofs

(5) If the noun ends in o preceded by a vowel, add –s.

SINGULAR curio rodeo kangaroo Julio
PLURAL curios rodeos kangaroos Julios

(6) If the noun ends in o preceded by a consonant, add –es.

SINGULAR potato echo torpedo
hero veto tomato
PLURAL potatoes echoes torpedoes
heroes vetoes tomatoes
EXCEPTIONS
Some common nouns ending in o preceded by a consonant, especially musical terms, and some proper nouns form the plural by adding only –s.

SINGULAR taco hairdo alto piano
photo Latino Sakamoto
PLURAL tacos hairdos altos pianos
photos Latinos Sakamotos

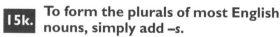
NOTE Some nouns that end in o preceded by a consonant have two plural forms.

SINGULAR **PLURAL**
zero zeros *or* zeroes

(7) The plurals of some nouns are formed irregularly.

SINGULAR foot man tooth child
PLURAL feet men teeth children

(8) Some nouns have the same form in both the singular and the plural.

SINGULAR deer Chinese species
AND PLURAL Sioux series aircraft

(9) If a compound noun is written as one word, form the plural by adding –*s* or –*es* to the end of the compound.

SINGULAR	ballgame	background	housefly
PLURAL	ballgame**s**	background**s**	housef**lies**

(10) If a compound noun is hyphenated or written as two words, make the main noun plural. The *main noun* is the noun that is modified.

SINGULAR	mother-in-law	runner-up
PLURAL	mother**s**-in-law	runner**s**-up

A few compound nouns form the plural in irregular ways.

SINGULAR	go-between	mix-up
	sixteen-year-old	
PLURAL	go-between**s**	mix-up**s**
	sixteen-year-old**s**	

NOTE Whenever you're not sure about the plural form of a compound noun, check a recent dictionary.

(11) Some nouns borrowed from Latin and Greek form the plural as they do in the original language.

SINGULAR	PLURAL
analysis	analys**es**
crisis	cris**es**
datum	dat**a**
phenomenon	phenomen**a**

Some nouns borrowed from other languages have two plural forms.

SINGULAR	PLURAL
cactus	cactus**es** *or* cact**i**
index	index**es** *or* indic**es**
antenna	antenna**s** *or* antenna**e**

(12) To form the plurals of numerals, most capital letters, symbols, and words used as words, add either an –*s* or an apostrophe and an –*s*.

EXAMPLES
These *R*'**s** [*or* *R*s] look like *K*'**s** [*or* *K*s].
Erase these *&*s [*or* *&*'s] and write *and***s** [*or* *and*'s].
These *1*'**s** [*or* *1*s] look like *7*'**s** [*or* *7*s].

NOTE Using both an apostrophe and an *s* is never wrong. Therefore, if you have any doubt about whether or not to use the apostrophe, use it.

Using Apostrophes in Spelling

To prevent confusion, it is a good idea to get in the habit of using both an apostrophe and an –*s* to form the plurals of lowercase letters, certain capital letters, and some words used as words.

EXAMPLES
These *i*'**s** should be *e*'**s**. [Without an apostrophe, the plural of *i* would look like *is*.]
My sister always gets all A'**s**. [Without an apostrophe, the plural of *A* would look like *As*.]

Try It Out ✎

For each of the following sentences, insert apostrophes where appropriate.

1. These #s are known as "pound signs."
2. People sometimes mistake *to*s for *too*s.
3. The *3*s in this column should be omitted.
4. I've spelled these *toe*s with *w*s instead of es.
5. These *I*s mean "incomplete."

16 GLOSSARY OF USAGE

The Glossary of Usage is an alphabetical list of words, expressions, and special terms with definitions, explanations, and examples. Some of the examples have specific labels. *Standard* or *formal* usages are appropriate in serious writing and speaking, such as compositions and speeches. *Informal* words and expressions are standard English usages generally appropriate in conversation and in everyday writing such as personal letters. *Nonstandard* usages do not follow the guidelines of standard English.

a lot Always write the expression *a lot* as two words. *A lot* may be used as a noun meaning "a large number or amount" or as an adverb meaning "a great deal; very much." Avoid using *a lot* in formal writing.

EXAMPLES
Ray Bradbury writes **a lot** of science fiction. [noun]
Your last draft is **a lot** more interesting. [adverb]

among See **between, among.**

and etc. The abbreviation *etc.* (*et cetera*) means "and other things." Do not use *and* with *etc.*

EXAMPLE
They sell CDs, videos, **etc.** [*not* and etc.]

anyways, anywheres Use these words (and others like them, such as *everywheres, nowheres,* and *somewheres*) without the final *s*.

EXAMPLES
She didn't like the piano **anyway** [*not* anyways].
They couldn't find the Grail **anywhere** [*not* anywheres].

as See **like, as.**

as if See **like, as if.**

at Do not use *at* after *where*.

NONSTANDARD Where was the pendulum at?
STANDARD **Where** was the pendulum?

bad, badly *Bad* is an adjective. *Badly* is an adverb. In standard English, only the adjective form, *bad,* should follow a linking verb, such as *feel, see, hear, taste,* or *smell,* or forms of the verb *be.*

EXAMPLE
Does that conk solution smell **bad** [*not* badly]?

 NOTE The expression *feel badly* has become acceptable in informal situations, but use *feel bad* in formal speaking and writing.

being as, being that Use *since* or *because* instead of these expressions.

EXAMPLE
Because [*not* being as] they were Japanese, they were sent to Manzanar.

beside, besides *Beside* is a preposition that means "by the side of" or "next to." As a preposition, *besides* means "in addition to" or "other than." As an adverb, *besides* means "moreover."

EXAMPLES
People stood **beside** the coop.
Who **besides** Brutus was in this group? [preposition]
His wings were dirty; **besides,** he was almost toothless. [adverb]

between, among Use *between* when you are referring to two things at a time, even though they may be part of a group consisting of more than two.

EXAMPLES
She walked **between** her mother and father.
I couldn't decide which of the ten poems to study because there were so many differences **between**

them. [Although there are more than two poems, each one is being compared separately with each of the others.]

Use *among* when you are thinking of a group rather than of separate individuals.

EXAMPLE
There were conflicts **among** the passengers on the raft. [The passengers are thought of as a group.]

bust, busted Avoid using these words as verbs. Use a form of either *burst* or *break,* depending on the meaning.

EXAMPLES
The airtight compartments **burst** [*not* busted].
A torrent of water **broke** [*not* busted] the doors.

could of See **of.**

done *Done* is the past participle of *do.* Avoid using *done* for *did,* which is the past form of *do* and which does not require a helping verb.

NONSTANDARD The captain done all that he could do.
STANDARD The captain **did** all that he could do.
STANDARD The captain **had done** all that he could do.

etc. See **and etc.**

everywheres See **anyways, anywheres.**

fewer, less *Fewer* tells "how many"; it is used with plural nouns. *Less* tells "how much"; it is used with singular nouns.

EXAMPLES
We have **fewer** students in class this year.
There is **less** emphasis on symbolism in this poem than in that one.

good, well *Good* is an adjective. *Well* may be used as an adjective or an adverb. Never use *good* to modify a verb; instead, use *well* as an adverb meaning "capably" or "satisfactorily."

EXAMPLE
Leslie Marmon Silko writes **well** [*not* good].

 NOTE *Feel good* and *feel well* mean different things. *Feel good* means "feel happy or pleased." *Feel well* simply means "feel healthy."

EXAMPLES
I didn't feel **well** that day.
Helping others always makes me feel **good** about myself.

had of See **of.**

had ought, hadn't ought Unlike other verbs, *ought* is not used with *had.*

NONSTANDARD	Her mother had ought to come out of her room; she hadn't ought to stay in there so long.
STANDARD	Her mother **ought** to come out of her room; she **ought not** to stay in there so long.

he, she, it, they Do not use an unnecessary pronoun after the subject of a clause or a sentence. This error is called the **double subject.**

NONSTANDARD	Gary Soto he writes stories and poems.
STANDARD	Gary Soto writes stories and poems.

hisself, theirselves Avoid using these words for *himself* and *themselves.*

EXAMPLES
Phillip said that he would put up his tent **himself** [*not* hisself] and that they could put up their tents **themselves** [*not* theirselves].

imply, infer *Imply* means "suggest indirectly." *Infer* means "interpret" or "draw a conclusion [from a remark or an action]."

EXAMPLES
This language **implies** a symbolic meaning.
From this metaphor, we may **infer** his deep fear.

it See **he, she, it, they.**

kind of, sort of Avoid using these terms in formal situations. Instead, use *somewhat* or *rather.*

INFORMAL	Edgar Allan Poe's stories can be kind of scary.
FORMAL	Edgar Allan Poe's stories can be **somewhat** [*or* **rather**] scary.

kind of a, sort of a In formal situations, omit the *a.*

INFORMAL	What kind of a rhyme scheme does it have?
FORMAL	What **kind of** rhyme scheme does it have?

kind(s), sort(s), type(s) Use *this* or *that* with the singular form of each of these nouns. Use *these* or *those* with the plural form.

EXAMPLES
This kind of guitar is less expensive than **those kinds.**

learn, teach *Learn* means "acquire knowledge." *Teach* means "instruct" or "show how."

EXAMPLE
If you will **teach** me, I will **learn.**

leave, let *Leave* means "go away" or "depart from." *Let* means "allow" or "permit." Avoid using *leave* for *let.*

EXAMPLES
Let [*not* leave] her stay if she wants.
They **let** [*not* left] the children go first.

less See **fewer, less.**

like, as In informal English, the preposition *like* is often used as a conjunction meaning "as." In formal English, use *like* to introduce a prepositional phrase, and use *as* to introduce a subordinate clause.

EXAMPLES
This song sounds **like** the other one.
She should do **as** her mother says.

like, as if In formal situations, *like* should not be used for the compound conjunction *as if* or *as though.*

EXAMPLE
It looked **as if** [*not* like] the crew would see them.

might of, must of See **of.**

nowheres See **anyways, anywheres.**

of *Of* is a preposition. Do not use *of* in place of *have* after verbs such as *could, should, would, might, must,* and *ought* [*to*]. Also, do not use *had of* for *had.*

NONSTANDARD	They should of signaled.
STANDARD	They **should have** [*or* **should've**] signaled.

Do not use *of* after other prepositions such as *inside, off,* or *outside.*

EXAMPLES
Hundreds jumped **off** [*not* off of] the ship.
What's **inside** [*not* inside of] survival kits?

off of See **of.**

ought See **had ought, hadn't ought.**

ought to of See **of.**

she See **he, she, it, they.**

some, somewhat In formal situations, do not use *some* to mean "to some extent." Instead, use *somewhat.*

INFORMAL	Your advice helped some.
FORMAL	Your advice helped **somewhat.**

somewheres   See **anyways, anywheres.**

sort(s)   See **kind(s), sort(s), type(s)** and **kind of a, sort of a.**

sort of   See **kind of, sort of.**

teach   See **learn, teach.**

than, then   *Than* is a conjunction used in comparisons. *Then* is an adverb meaning "at that time" or "next."

EXAMPLES

I liked "Everyday Use" better **than** that story.
Had you heard of Langston Hughes **then**?
I wrote a thesis statement; **then** I made an outline.

them   *Them* should not be used as an adjective. Use *those*.

EXAMPLE

I like **those** [*not* them] Stephen King novels.

then   See **than, then.**

this, that, these, those   See **kind(s), sort(s), type(s).**

try and   Use *try to*, not *try and*.

EXAMPLE

He would **try to** [*not* try and] send a message.

type(s)   See **kind(s), sort(s), type(s).**

way, ways   Use *way*, not *ways*, in referring to a distance.

INFORMAL   The sisters walked a long ways to school.
   FORMAL   The sisters walked a long **way** to school.

well   See **good, well.**

what   Use *that*, not *what*, to introduce an adjective clause.

EXAMPLE

The poem **that** [*not* what] I studied was "George Gray."

when, where   Do not use *when* or *where* to begin a definition.

NONSTANDARD   A "stanza" in poetry is when lines are grouped to form a unit.
   STANDARD   A "stanza" in poetry is a group of lines that form a unit.

where   Do not use *where* for *that*.

EXAMPLES

I read **that** [*not* where] Alice Walker is speaking here.
Roger saw on TV **that** [*not* where] the mayor has been reelected.

where . . . at   See **at.**

who, which, that   The relative pronoun *who* refers to persons only; *which* refers to things only; *that* may refer to either persons or things.

EXAMPLES

Isn't Louis L'Amour the man **who** [*or* that] writes westerns? [person]
Arthur's sword, **which** is called Excalibur, is legendary. [thing]
The psalm **that** I memorized is beautiful. [thing]

would of   See **of.**

Using Contractions and Possessive Pronouns

Do not confuse contractions with possessive pronouns.

POSSESSIVE PRONOUNS	CONTRACTIONS
This one is **theirs.**	**There's** [There is] Lana.
Their bus is here.	**They're** [They are] on the bus.
Your turn is next.	**You're** [You are] next.
Whose book is this?	**Who's** [Who is] your partner?
What is **its** title?	**It's** [It is] time to eat.

Try It Out ✎

Proofread the following sentences, and correct each error in the use of contractions and possessive pronouns.

1. Whose it's author?
2. Are you done with you're report on they're lives?
3. Their here to see who's name was chosen.
4. Paul, your late, and theirs your ride.
5. They're team won, and its about time, too.

Glossary

The glossary that follows is an alphabetical list of words found in the selections in this book. Use this glossary just as you would use a dictionary—to find out the meanings of unfamiliar words. (Some technical, foreign, and more obscure words in this book are not listed here but instead are defined for you in the footnotes that accompany many of the selections.)

Many words in the English language have more than one meaning. This glossary gives the meanings that apply to the words as they are used in the selections in this book. Words closely related in form and meaning are usually listed together in one entry (for instance, *compassion* and *compassionate*), and the definition is given for the first form.

The following abbreviations are used:

adj.	adjective
adv.	adverb
n.	noun
v.	verb

Each word's pronunciation is given in parentheses. A guide to the pronunciation symbols appears at the bottom of this page. For more information about the words in this glossary or for information about words not listed here, consult a dictionary.

A

abiding (ə·bīd′iŋ) *adj.*: continuing; lasting.
abut (ə·but′) *adj.*: border upon; lie next to. —**abutting** *v.* used as *adj.*
adamant (ad′ə·mənt) *adj.*: unyielding; firm.
administer (ad·min′is·tər) *v.*: give; apply. —**administered** *v.* used as *adj.*
adversary (ad′vər·ser′ē) *n.*: opponent; enemy.
affliction (ə·flik′shən) *n.*: suffering; distress.
aghast (ə·gast′) *adj.*: horrified.

agile (aj′əl) *adj.*: lively; moving easily and quickly.
allegation (al′ə·gā′shən) *n.*: in law, assertion, or positive statement, made without proof.
annihilate (ə·nī′ə·lāt′) *v.*: destroy; demolish.
antipathy (an·tip′ə·thē) *n.*: feeling of hatred; powerful and deep dislike.
antiseptic (an′tə·sep′tik) *n.*: substance used to sterilize or to prevent infection.
anxiety (aŋ·zī′ə·tē) *n.*: state of being worried or uneasy.
apex (ā′peks′) *n.*: highest point; top.
apprehension (ap′rē·hen′shən) *n.*: dread; fear of a future event.
arresting (ə·rest′iŋ) *adj.*: interesting; striking.
ascertain (as′ər·tān′) *v.*: find out with certainty; determine.
assail (ə·sāl′) *v.*: attack.
autonomy (ô·tän′ə·mē) *n.*: independence.
avid (av′id) *adj.*: eager and enthusiastic.

B

benign (bi·nīn′) *adj.*: here, favorable or harmless.
bereft (bē·reft′) *adj.*: not having something needed or expected.
betrayal (bē·trā′əl) *n.*: **1.** failure to fulfill another's hopes. **2.** act of disloyalty; deception.
breach (brēch) *v.*: break through.

C

callous (kal′əs) *adj.*: unfeeling.
cataclysm (kat′ə·kliz′əm) *n.*: disaster; sudden, violent event.

---

at, āte, cär; ten, ēve; is, īce; gō, hôrn, look, tōol; oil, out; up, fur; ə *for unstressed vowels, as* a *in* ago, u *in* focus; ′ *as in* Latin (lat′'n); chin; she; thin; *the*; zh *as in* azure (azh′ər); ŋ *as in* ring (riŋ)

cessation (se·sā'shən) *n.:* ceasing or stopping.

champion (cham'pē·ən) *v.:* fight for; defend; support.

chronic (krän'ik) *adj.:* constant; habitual.

clamor (klam'ər) *v.:* cry out; ask. —**clamoring** *v.* used as *adj.*

colleague (käl'ēg') *n.:* fellow worker.

commemorate (kə·mem'ə·rāt') *v.:* serve as a reminder of.

commiserate (kə·miz'ər·āt') *v.:* show or express sympathy.

compassion (kəm·pash'ən) *n.:* deep sympathy; pity.

concussion (kən·kush'ən) *n.:* powerful shock or impact.

confirmation (kän'fər·mā'shən) *n.:* proof.

confront (kən·frunt') *v.:* face.

conservation (kän'sər·vā'shən) *n.:* protection and preservation of natural resources. —**conservation** *n.* used as *adj.*

consolation (kän'sə·lā'shən) *n.:* act of comforting.

console (kən·sōl') *v.:* comfort. —**consoling** *v.* used as *adj.*

conspicuous (kən·spik'yōō·əs) *adj.:* obvious or easy to see.

constrict (kən·strikt') *v.:* limit; confine. —**constricting** *v.* used as *adj.*

construe (kən·strōō') *v.:* interpret.

consumerism (kən·sōōm'ər·iz'əm) *n.:* buying and using of goods or services.

contagion (kən·tā'jən) *n.:* spreading of disease.

contrition (kən·trish'ən) *n.:* regret or sense of guilt at having done wrong.

conviction (kən·vik'shən) *n.:* strong belief; certainty.

coronation (kôr'ə·nā'shən) *n.:* act or ceremony of crowning a sovereign.

corroborate (kə·räb'ə·rāt') *v.:* support; uphold the truth of.

cower (kou'ər) *v.:* draw back or huddle in fear. —**cowering** *v.* used as *adj.*

crucial (krōō'shəl) *adj.:* extremely important; decisive.

D

dawdle (dôd''l) *v.:* waste time; linger.

defiant (dē·fī'ənt) *adj.:* challenging authority.

degradation (deg'rə·dā'shən) *n.:* decline.

denizen (den'ə·zen) *n.:* inhabitant or occupant.

deplorable (dē·plôr'ə·bəl) *adj.:* very bad. —**deplorably** *adv.*

depraved (dē·prāvd') *adj.:* immoral.

deteriorate (dē·tir'ē·ə·rāt') *v.:* worsen.

diffuse (di·fyōōs') *adj.:* spread out; unfocused.

discard (dis·kärd') *v.:* abandon; get rid of. —**discarding** *v.* used as *adj.*

discordant (dis·kôrd''nt) *adj.:* clashing; not in harmony.

dismantle (dis·mant''l) *v.:* take apart.

diversion (də·vur'zhən) *n.:* something that distracts the attention.

divert (də·vurt') *v.:* amuse; entertain.

doctrine (däk'trin) *n.:* principle; teaching; belief.

dubious (dōō'bē·əs) *adj.:* doubtful; not sure.

E

ebb (eb) *v.:* lessen or weaken. The ebb is the flow of water away from the land as the tide falls.

ebony (eb'ə·nē) *adj.:* dark or black.

emanate (em'ə·nāt') *v.:* come forth; emerge, as from a source.

emancipation (ē·man'sə·pā'shən) *n.:* liberation; the act of setting free from restraint or control or being set free.

encroach (en·krōch') *v.:* advance. —**encroaching** *v.* used as *adj.*

equanimity (ek'wə·nim'ə·tē) *n.:* calmness; composure.

ethical (eth'i·kəl) *adj.:* moral; having to do with goodness or rightness in conduct.

exhalation (eks'hə·lā'shən) *n.:* something breathed out; breath.

extinct (ek·stiŋkt') *adj.:* no longer in existence.

extravagant (ek·strav'ə·gənt) *adj.:* excessive; showy.

extricate (eks'tri·kāt') *v.:* release; disentangle. —**extricating** *v.* used as *n.*

F

facile (fas'il) *adj.:* easy.

feign (fān) *v.:* pretend.

fiasco (fē·as'kō) *n.:* total failure.

fidelity (fə·del'·ə·tē) *n.:* loyalty; devotion.

filial (fil'ē·əl) *adj.:* pertaining to or due from a son or a daughter.

flail (flāl) *v.:* wave wildly. —**flailing** *v.* used as *adj.*

formidable (fôr′mə·də·bəl) *adj.*: remarkable; impressive.

fortitude (fôrt′ə·tōōd′) *n.*: firm courage; strength to endure pain or danger.

frivolous (friv′ə·ləs) *adj.*: **1.** not properly serious; silly. **2.** trivial; of little value or importance.

furtive (fur′tiv) *adj.*: **1.** acting as if trying not to be seen. **2.** done secretly.

G

garble (gär′bəl) *v.*: confuse; mix up. —**garbled** *v.* used as *adj.*

gaunt (gônt) *adj.*: here, grim and forbidding.

generate (jen′ər·āt′) *v.*: arise; come into being.

H

habitat (hab′i·tat′) *n.*: person's environment or living space; place where plants or animals normally grow or live.

harass (har′əs) *v.*: bother; trouble. —**harassing** *v.* used as *n.*

hospitality (häs′pi·tal′ə·tē) *n.*: friendly, caring treatment of guests.

I

idealist (ī·dē′əl·ist) *n.*: someone who is guided by ideals, or standards of perfection.

ignoble (ig·nō′bəl) *adj.*: not noble in birth or position.

illiterate (i·lit′ər·it) *adj.*: uneducated; unable to read or write.

illusion (i·lōō′zhən) *n.*: misleading or inaccurate idea.

immunity (i·myōōn′ə·tē) *n.*: freedom from a legal obligation.

immutable (i·myōōt′ə·bəl) *adj.*: unchangeable; never changing or varying.

impede (im·pēd′) *v.*: hold back or block, as by an obstacle. —**impeded** *v.* used as *adj.*

imperceptible (im′pər·sep′tə·bəl) *adj.*: so slight as to be almost unnoticeable. —**imperceptibly** *adv.*

imperial (im·pir′ē·əl) *adj.*: majestic; of great size or superior quality.

impertinence (im·purt′'n·əns) *n.*: insult; disrespectful act or remark.

implacable (im·plak′ə·bəl) *adj.*: relentless; not affected by attempts at change.

impoverish (im·päv′ər·ish) *v.*: make poor. —**impoverished** *v.* used as *adj.*

impoverishment (im·päv′ər·ish·mənt) *n.*: reducing to poverty or taking away of resources.

impudence (im′pyōō·dəns) *n.*: quality of being disrespectful.

impunity (im·pyōō′ni·tē) *n.*: freedom from punishment.

incoherent (in′kō·hir′ənt) *adj.*: rambling; disjointed.

incomprehensible (in·käm′prē·hen′sə·bəl) *adj.*: not understandable.

incredulous (in·krej′oo·ləs) *adj.*: disbelieving; skeptical.

increment (in′krə·mənt) *n.*: small increase.

indemnify (in·dem′ni·fi′) *v.*: in a legal sense, protect.

indigenous (in·dij′ə·nəs) *adj.*: native; growing naturally in a region or country.

indisposed (in′di·spōzd′) *adj.*: slightly ill.

induce (in·dōōs′) *v.*: persuade; lead on.

ineffable (in·ef′ə·bəl) *adj.*: indescribable; inexpressible. —**ineffably** *adv.*

inertia (in·ur′shə) *n.*: tendency to remain either at rest or in motion.

inevitable (in·ev′i·tə·bəl) *adj.*: unavoidable; certain to happen. —**inevitably** *adv.*

ingenuity (in′jə·nōō′ə·tē) *n.*: cleverness; originality; skill.

ingenuous (in·jen′yōō·əs) *adj.*: too trusting; tending to believe too readily.

initiative (i·nish′ə·tiv) *n.*: action of taking the first step or movement.

innocuous (i·näk′yōō·əs) *adj.*: harmless.

inquisitive (in·kwiz′ə·tiv) *adj.*: questioning; curious.

inscription (in·skrip′shən) *n.*: something inscribed or engraved, as on a coin or monument.

insinuate (in·sin′yōō·āt′) *v.*: suggest.

---

at, āte, cär; ten, ēve; is, īce; gō, hôrn, look, tōōl; oil, out; up, fur; ə *for unstressed vowels, as* a *in* ago, u *in* focus; ′ *as in* Latin (lat′'n); chin; she; thin; *the*; zh *as in* azure (azh′ər); ŋ *as in* ring (riŋ)

insular (in'sə·lər) *adj.*: isolated from one's surroundings; narrow-minded.

integrate (in'tə·grāt) *v.*: combine; unify.

interminable (in·tur'mi·nə·bəl) *adj.*: endless.

intermittent (in'tər·mit''nt) *adj.*: appearing or occurring from time to time.

intimidate (in·tim'ə·dāt') *v.*: make afraid.

inure (in·yoor') *v.*: make accustomed to something difficult or painful. —**inured** *v.* used as *adj.*

irrelevant (i·rel'ə·vənt) *adj.*: not relating to the point or situation. —**irrelevantly** *adv.*

irrevocable (i·rev'ə·kə·bəl) *adj.*: irreversible; incapable of being canceled or undone.

J

jeopardize (jep'ər·dīz') *v.*: endanger.

jeopardy (jep'ər·dē) *n.*: great danger; peril.

judicious (joo·dish'əs) *adj.*: wise and careful.

L

lament (lə·ment') *v.*: **1.** say with regret or sorrow. **2.** feel very sorry.

laud (lôd) *v.*: praise. —**lauding** *v.* used as *adj.*

liability (lī'ə·bil'ə·tē) *n.*: legal obligation or responsibility to make good a damage or loss.

listless (list'lis) *adj.*: without energy or interest. —**listlessly** *adv.*

luminous (loo'mə·nəs) *adj.*: glowing; giving off light.

luxuriate (lug·zhoor'ē·āt') *v.* (used with *in*): take great pleasure.

M

magnanimous (mag·nan'ə·məs) *adj.*: generous; noble.

magnitude (mag'nə·tood') *n.*: greatness or size.

malicious (mə·lish'əs) *adj.*: intentionally harmful.

manifest (man'ə·fest') *v.*: **1.** appear; become evident. **2.** show; reveal.

manipulation (mə·nip'yoo·lā'shən) *n.*: skillful, often unfair management or control.

maroon (mə·roon') *v.*: leave stranded, helpless, or isolated. —**marooned** *v.* used as *adj.*

maximize (mak'sə·mīz') *v.*: increase as much as possible.

mesmerize (mez'mər·īz') *v.*: spellbind; fascinate. —**mesmerizing** *v.* used as *adj.*

metabolism (mə·tab'ə·liz'əm) *n.*: process by which living organisms turn food into energy and living tissue.

minute (mī·noot') *adj.*: small; tiny.

mutiny (myoot''n·ē) *n.*: rebellion or revolt against authority.

N

navigator (nav'ə·gāt'ər) *n.*: person who plots the course of a vehicle, usually a ship or plane.

nonchalant (nän'shə·länt') *adj.*: without interest or concern; indifferent. —**nonchalantly** *adv.*

notorious (nō·tôr'ē·əs) *adj.*: famous, usually in an unfavorable sense.

nudge (nuj) *v.*: push lightly; bump.

O

oath (ōth) *n.*: solemn promise or declaration; vow.

oblige (ə·blīj') *v.*: compel by moral, legal, or physical force.

oppress (ə·pres') *v.*: persecute; keep down by unjust use of power.

opulent (äp'yoo·lənt) *adj.*: rich; luxuriant.

P

palatable (pal'it·ə·bəl) *adj.*: tasty; fit to be eaten or drunk.

palpitate (pal'pə·tāt') *v.*: throb; quiver. —**palpitating** *v.* used as *adj.*

pandemonium (pan'də·mō'nē·əm) *n.*: wildly noisy, chaotic scene.

paramount (par′ə·mount′) *adj.*: supreme; dominant.

patina (pat″n·ə) *n.*: color change resulting from age, as on old wood or silver.

peevishness (pē′vish·nis) *n.*: irritability.

pensive (pen′siv) *adj.*: dreamily thoughtful.

perfunctory (pər·fuŋk′tə·rē) *adj.*: not exerting much effort; unconcerned.

perplexed (pər·plekst′) *adj.*: uncertain.

persistent (pər·sist′ənt) *adj.*: continuing.

pertinent (pʉrt″n·ənt) *adj.*: having some connection with the subject.

pervade (pər·vād′) *v.*: spread throughout.

petulant (pech′ə·lənt) *adj.*: impatient; irritable; peevish.

phenomenon (fə·näm′ə·nən) *n.*: observable event, fact, or circumstance.

pit (pit) *v.*: place in competition.

placid (plas′id) *adj.*: calm; tranquil.

poignant (poin′yənt) *adj.*: emotionally moving; touching.

poise (poiz) *v.*: balance; keep steady. —**poised** *v.* used as *adj.*

ponderous (pän′dər·əs) *adj.*: heavy and slow moving.

portable (pôr′tə·bəl) *adj.*: able to be carried.

potent (pōt″nt) *adj.*: powerful; convincing.

precarious (pri·ker′ē·əs) *adj.*: in danger of falling down; unstable.

predominant (prē·däm′ə·nənt) *adj.*: most frequent or noticeable.

premises (prem′is·iz) *n.*: house or building and its surrounding property.

presentiment (prē·zent′ə·mənt) *n.*: foreboding; feeling that something bad is about to happen.

presumable (prē·zōōm′ə·bəl) *adj.*: probable. —**presumably** *adv.*

prodigy (präd′ə·jē) *n.*: child of highly unusual talent or genius.

profuse (prō·fyōōs′) *adj.*: given or poured forth freely and abundantly; plentiful.

projection (prō·jek′shən) *n.*: something that juts out from a surface.

propriety (prə·prī′ə·tē) *n.*: quality of being proper, fitting, or suitable.

providential (präv′ə·den′shəl) *adj.*: fortunate; like something caused by a divine act.

provincial (prə·vin′shəl) *adj.*: belonging to a province, especially a rural one; also, unsophisticated.

prudence (prōō′dəns) *n.*: cautiousness; sound judgment.

Q

quell (kwel) *v.*: quiet; subdue.

quizzical (kwiz′i·kəl) *adj.*: puzzled; questioning.

R

radiance (rā′dē·əns) *n.*: brightness; light.

rancid (ran′sid) *adj.*: stale or spoiled.

rationalization (rash′ən·ə·lə·zā′shən) *n.*: seemingly reasonable excuse or explanation for one's behavior—but not the real reason.

realm (relm) *n.*: kingdom.

rebound (ri·bound′) *v.*: bounce back.

recede (ri·sēd′) *v.*: move back or away.

recoil (ri·koil′) *v.*: draw back in fear, surprise, or disgust.

recrimination (ri·krim′ə·nā′shən) *n.*: accusation against an accuser; countercharge.

regressive (ri·gres′iv) *adj.*: moving backward or returning to an earlier or less advanced condition.

rehabilitation (rē′hə·bil′ə·tā′shən) *n.*: bringing or restoring to a good condition.

relic (rel′ik) *n.*: object or thing from the past that may have a special meaning or association, sometimes a religious one.

resignation (rez′ig·nā′shən) *n.*: passive acceptance; submission.

resolute (rez′ə·lōōt′) *adj.*: determined.

reticent (ret′ə·sənt) *adj.*: silent; reserved.

retort (ri·tôrt′) *n.*: sharp reply.

reverence (rev′ə·rəns) *n.*: attitude or display of deep respect and awe.

rifle (rī′fəl) *v.*: search thoroughly or in a rough manner. —**rifling** *v.* used as *n.*

---

at, āte, cär; ten, ēve; is, īce; gō, hôrn, look, tōol; oil, out; up, fur; ə *for unstressed vowels, as* a *in* ago, u *in* focus; ′ *as in* Latin (lat″n); chin; she; thin; *the*; zh *as in* azure (azh′ər); ŋ *as in* ring (riŋ)

S

sagacious (sə·gā′shəs) *adj.*: wise; showing sound judgment.

sarcastic (sär·kas′tik) *adj.*: mocking; taunting; in a manner that makes fun of something or someone.

sedate (si·dāt′) *adj.*: calm and dignified; quiet. —**sedately** *adv.*

sidle (sīd′′l) *v.*: move sideways, especially in a shy or sneaky manner.

sinister (sin′is·tər) *adj.*: evil.

skirt (skurt) *v.*: **1.** pass around rather than through. **2.** miss narrowly; avoid.

solidarity (säl′ə·dar′ə·tē) *n.*: complete unity in a group or organization.

solitary (säl′ə·ter′ē) *adj.*: without others.

sovereign (säv′rən) *n.*: king; ruler.

speculate (spek′yə·lāt′) *v.*: think; guess.

speculation (spek′yə·lā′shən) *n.*: thought; guesswork.

splice (splīs) *v.*: join by inserting and binding together. —**splicing** *v.* used as *n.*

stealth (stelth) *n.*: secretiveness; sly behavior.

stench (stench) *n.*: offensive smell.

stricken (strik′ən) *adj.*: heartbroken; affected by or suffering from something painful or distressing.

submerge (səb·murj′) *v.*: cover with water.

subterranean (sub′tə·rā′nē·ən) *adj.*: underground.

sultry (sul′trē) *adj.*: hot and humid; sweltering.

superlative (sə·pur′lə·tiv) *adj.*: supreme; better than all others.

supplication (sup′lə·kā′shən) *n.*: humble appeal or request.

surly (sur′lē) *adj.*: bad-tempered; rude.

surreptitious (sur′əp·tish′əs) *adj.*: stealthy; sneaky. —**surreptitiously** *adv.*

T

tangible (tan′jə·bəl) *adj.*: that can be touched.

tenacity (tə·nas′ə·tē) *n.*: stubborn persistence and determination.

tentative (ten′tə·tiv) *adj.*: timid; hesitant.

tenuous (ten′yoo·əs) *adj.*: weak; slight.

tepid (tep′id) *adj.*: neither hot nor cold; lukewarm.

terminal (tur′mə·nəl) *adj.*: of or relating to an end, often an end to life.

torrent (tôr′ənt) *n.*: violent, forceful rush.

traverse (trə·vurs′) *v.*: cross.

trek (trek) *v.*: journey.

tremulous (trem′yoo·ləs) *adj.*: trembling; quivering.

tumultuous (too·mul′choo·əs) *adj.*: wild; noisy.

U

unimpeded (un′im·pēd′id) *adj.*: not blocked; unobstructed.

unorthodox (un·ôr′thə·däks′) *adj.*: unusual; not conforming to usual norms.

V

vain (vān) *adj.*: without success; fruitless. —**vainly** *adv.*

valiant (val′yənt) *adj.*: brave. —**valiantly** *adv.*

valid (val′id) *adj.*: meeting the requirements of established standards.

veritable (ver′i·tə·bəl) *adj.*: actual; true.

vigil (vij′əl) *n.*: watchful staying awake during the usual hours of sleep.

vintage (vin′tij) *adj.*: dating from a time long past.

vitality (vī·tal′ə·tē) *n.*: energy; vigor.

W

whimsy (hwim′zē) *n.*: quaint or odd humor.

wizened (wiz′ənd) *adj.*: wrinkled and dried up.

wrath (rath) *n.*: great anger.

Glossary

Spanish Glossary

A

abiding/duradero *adj.* perpetuo; perdurable; respetuoso de las leyes.

abutting/lindante *adj.* limítrofe; adyacente; vecino.

adamant/inflexible *adj.* inexorable; firme.

administer/administrar *v.* aplicar un castigo; formular o hacer preguntas; tomar juramento; entregar.

adversary/adversario *s.* enemigo, contrincante; antagonista.

affliction/aflicción *s.* pesar; angustia; consternación.

aghast/espantada *adj.* horrorizado; pasmado.

agile/ágil *adj.* ligero; alerta; veloz; que se desplaza con agilidad o ágilmente.

allegation/alegato *s.* alegación; aserción; afirmación realizada sin comprobación.

annihilate/aniquilar *v.* destruir; exterminar.

antipathy/antipatía *s.* hostilidad; repugnancia; aversión.

antiseptic/antiséptico *s.* sustancia que se utiliza para esterilizar o para evitar una infección; desinfectante.

anxiety/ansiedad *s.* angustia; estado de preocupación; incertidumbre; inquietud.

apex/cima *s.* punto más elevado; cumbre.

apprehension/aprensión *s.* recelo; temor del futuro.

arresting/llamativo *adj.* interesante; provocador.

ascertain/comprobar *v.* averiguar; determinar con seguridad.

assail/asaltar *v.* atacar; acometer un ataque; abrumar con preguntas.

autonomy/autonomía *s.* independencia; emancipación; soberanía.

avid/ávido *adj.* deseoso; apasionado; entusiasta.

B

benign/benigno *adj.* favorable; sano; propicio; clemente; bondadoso.

bereft/privado *adj.* despojado; desconsolado; necesitado.

betrayal/traición *s.* ingratitud; acto desleal; decepción.

breach/infringir *v.* abrir una brecha.

C

callous/insensible *adj.* duro; despiadado.

cataclysm/cataclismo *s.* desastre; suceso imprevisto y violento.

cessation/cese *s.* fin; conclusión; interrupción.

champion/defender *v.* hacerse el campeón de; luchar por.

chronic/crónico *adj.* constante; rutinario; empedernido; inexorable; frecuente; asiduo.

clamor/clamar *v.* reclamar a voces; vociferar; pedir a gritos.

colleague/colega *s.* asociado; condiscípulo; compañero; camarada.

commemorate/conmemorar *v.* recordar; rememorar.

commiserate/compadecer *adj.* expresar simpatía; apiadarse; conmoverse.

compassion/compasión *s.* clemencia; caridad.

concussion/conmoción *s.* fuerte choque, golpe o impacto; conmoción cerebral.

confirmation/confirmación *s.* comprobante; prueba; certificación.

confront/enfrentar *v.* oponer; encarar; afrontar.

conservation/conservación *s.* protección y preservación de los recursos naturales.

consolation/consuelo *s.* alivio; desahogo; remedio.

console/consolar *v.* tranquilizar; calmar; dar sosiego.

conspicuous/visible *adj.* obvio; llamativo; notable; patente; que llama la atención.

constrict/limitar *v.* estrechar; oprimir; estrangular.

construe/interpretar *v.* descifrar; analizar una frase.

consumerism/consumerismo *s.* compra y uso de bienes o servicios.

contagion/contagio *s.* propagación de una enfermedad; contaminación; infección.

contrition/contrición *s.* sentimiento de culpabilidad por una mala acción; arrepentimiento; remordimiento.

conviction/convicción *s.* certidumbre; también condena; sentencia.

coronation/coronación *s.* ceremonia; investidura de un soberano.

corroborate/corroborar *v.* confirmar; ratificar.

cower/acobardarse *v.* amedrentarse; intimidarse; esconderse por temor.

crucial/crucial *adj.* decisivo; de gran importancia; crítico.

D

dawdle/vaguear *v.* perder el tiempo; no aprovechar el tiempo; ir despacio.

defiant/provocativo *adj.* desafiante; tono de voz retador.

degradation/degradación *s.* declinación; ocaso; descenso.

denizen/habitante *s.* residente; gente de un lugar.

deplorable/deplorable *adj.* lamentable; triste; insuficiente.

depraved/depravado *adj.* corrompido; disoluto; inmoral.

deteriorate/deteriorar *v.* estropear; perjudicar; empeorarse.

diffuse/difuso *adj.* dilatado; desvanecido; disipado.

discard/descartar *v.* separar; apartar; desechar; abandonar.

discordant/discordante *adj.* opuesto; contrario; disonante; desafinado.

dismantle/desmantelar *v.* desarmar; desmontar.

diversion/diversión *s.* distracción; desviación.

divert/distraer *v.* entretener; divertir.

doctrine/doctrina *s.* principio; dogma; credo.

dubious/dudoso *adj.* poco seguro; ambiguo; equívoco.

E

ebb/menguar *v.* disminuir; decaer. La marea menguante es la bajamar.

ebony/ébano *adj.* color oscuro o negro.

emanate/emanar *v.* proceder; derivar; emerger; brotar de una fuente.

emancipation/emancipación *s.* autonomía; independencia; liberación.

encroach/inmiscuirse *v.* mezclarse; avanzar; entremeterse.

equanimity/ecuanimidad *s.* paciencia; imparcialidad; serenidad.

ethical/ético *adj.* moral; asociado con un comportamiento noble; digno.

exhalation/exhalación *s.* respiración.

extinct/extinto *adj.* extinguido; que ha cesado de existir.

extravagant/extravagante *adj.* estrafalario; excéntrico; excesivo.

extricate/librar *v.* liberar; soltar; largar; desenredar.

F

facile/fácil *adj.* sencillo; simple.

feign/fingir *v.* aparentar; simular.

fiasco/fiasco *adj.* fracaso; malogro.

fidelity/fidelidad *s.* lealtad; sinceridad; constancia; devoción.

filial/filial *adj.* que se trata de, o se debe a, un hijo o una hija.

flail/agitarse *v.* moverse; menearse; sacudirse.

formidable/formidable *adj.* tremendo; terrible; impresionante; que inspira la admiración de otros; que causa pavor.

fortitude/fortaleza *s.* fuerza para tolerar el dolor o el peligro; entereza; aguante.

frivoulous/frívolo *adj.* **1.** de poco peso; mundano. **2.**trivial; de poca importancia.

furtive/furtivo *adj.* **1.** que actúa a escondidas. **2.** que se hace en secreto.

G

garble/confundir *v.* embrollar; enredar.

gaunt/lúgubre *adj.* sombrío; taciturno.

generate/generar *v.* forjar; engendrar.

H

habitat/hábitat *s.* entorno o ambiente de una persona; ecosistema en el que suelen vivir o crecer las plantas o los animales.

harass/acosar *v.* hostigar; molestar.

hospitality/hospitalidad *s.* albergue; trato generoso de los invitados.

I

idealist/idealista *s.* persona guiada por sus ideales o sus principios de perfección.

ignoble/innoble *adj.* **1.** que no es de nacimiento o posición noble. **2.** vil; villano; infame.

illiterate/analfabeto *adj.* iletrado; inculto; que no puede ni leer ni escribir.

illusion/ilusión *s.* sueño; espejismo; concepto falso.

immunity/inmunidad *s.* exención de una obligación legal; dispensa.

immutable/inmutable *adj.* inalterable; invariable.

impede/impedir *v.* frenar; paralizar; imposibilitar.

imperceptible/imperceptible *adj.* gradual; paulatino, inapreciable.

impertinence/impertinencia *s.* descaro; arrogancia; comentario insolente.

imperial/imperial *adj.* soberano; soberbio; majestuoso; de gran tamaño o calidad.

implacable/implacable *adj.* inclemente; severo; inflexible; que no cambia.

impoverish/empobrecer *v.* agotar; arruinar; extenuar.

impoverishment/empobrecimiento *s.* ruina; destrucción; agotamiento.

impudence/impudencia *s.* descaro; insolencia; petulancia; falta de respeto.

impunity/impunidad *s.* exención; perdón.

incoherent/incoherente *adj.* confuso; indescifrable.

incomprehensible/incomprensible *adj.* enigmático; denso; que no se comprende.

incredulous/incrédulo *adj.* descreído; desconfiado; receloso.

increment/incremento *s.* pequeño aumento.

indemnify/indemnizar *v.* proteger en el sentido legal.

indigenous/indígena *s.* nativo; oriundo; que crece naturalmente en una región o en un país.

indisposed/indispuesto *adj.* enfermo; fatigado; doliente.

induce/inducir *v.* persuadir; convencer; incitar.

ineffable/inefable *adj.* indecible; indescriptible.

inertia/inercia *s.* apatía; tendencia a permanecer en estado inmóvil o móvil.

inevitable/inevitable *adj.* ineludible; que no se puede evitar; forzoso.

ingenuity/ingenio *s.* chispa; inspiración; originalidad.

ingenous/ingenuo *adj.* cándido; inocente; sencillo; demasiado confiado.

initiative/iniciativa *s.* decisión; acción de tomar un primer paso.

innocous/inocuo *adj.* inofensivo; anodino; que no puede hacer daño.

inquisitive/curioso *adj.* preguntón; mirada inquisitiva; inquieto.

inscription/inscripción *s.* leyenda inscrita o cincelada, en un monumento o en una moneda, por ejemplo.

insinuate/insinuar *v.* sugerir; indicar.

insular/insular *adj.* aislado; inflexible.

integrate/integrar *v.* completar; componer; reunir.

interminable/interminable *adj.* sin fin; imperecedero; eterno; perpetuo.

intermittent/intermitente *adj.* esporádico; ocasional; que ocurre o aparece alternamente.

intimidate/intimidar *v.* acobardar; amedrentar; atemorizar.

inure/habituar *v.* acostumbrar; endurecer; aclimatar.

irrelevant/irrelevante *adj.* fuera de lugar; no pertinente; improcedente; ajeno al tema discutido.

irrecovable/irrevocable *adj.* inevitable; inapelable, que no se puede anular o deshacer.

J

jeopardize/arriesgar *v.* poner en peligro; comprometer.

jeopardy/peligro *s.* riesgo; amenaza inminente.

judicious/juicioso *adj.* sensato; razonable.

L

lament/lamentar *v.* **1.** lamentarse de un suceso; arrepentirse. **2.** afligirse; llorar la muerte de alguien.

laud/alabar *v.* levantar hasta las nubes; ensalzar.

liability/responsabilidad *s.* obligación legal hacia daños o pérdidas.

listless/decaído *adj.* indiferente; sin energía ni interés, abúlica; aburrida.

luminous/luminoso *adj.* radiante; resplandeciente; brillante.

luxuriate/disfrutar *v.* deleitarse.

M

magnanimous/magnánimo *adj.* generoso; noble; altruista.

magnitude/magnitud *s.* dimensión; importancia; alcance.

malicious/malicioso *adj.* pícaro; pérfido; deseoso de hacer el mal.

manifest/manifestar *v.* **1.** aparecer; exponerse. **2.** mostrar; indicar; revelar.

manipulation/manipulación *s.* procedimiento; maniobra; falseamiento.

maroon/desertar *v.* abandonar en una isla desierta; aislar.

maximize/maximizar *v.* extender lo máximo posible.

mesmerize/hipnotizar *v.* hechizar; magnetizar.

metabolism/metabolismo *s.* la conversión de alimentos en energía y tejido por organismos vivos; asimilación.

minute/minúsculo *adj.* microscópico; pequeñísimo.

mutiny/motín *s.* rebeldía; sedición; levantamiento en contra de la autoridad.

N

navigator/navegante *s.* persona que traza el curso de un vehículo, de una nave o un avión; marino.

nonchalant/imperturbable *adj.* indiferente; sin interés ni preocupación; impávido.

notorious/célebre *adj.* famoso; popular; conocido; renombrado; un criminal notorio.

nudge/codear *v.* empujar levemente; dar un codazo.

O

oath/juramento *s.* promesa; acción de jurar bandera; palabra de honor.

oblige/obligar *v.* exigir; imponer moral, legal o físicamente.

oppress/oprimir *v.* dominar; abusar; subyugar.

opulent/opulento *adj.* cuantioso; lujoso; rico.

P

palatable/sabroso *adj.* suculento; gustoso; apetitoso; digno de comerse o beberse.

palpitate/palpitar *v.* latir; pulsar; estremecerse.

paramount/supremo *adj.* dominante; sumo; primordial.

patina/pátina *s.* cambio en el color a transcurrir el tiempo, en la madera o la plata, por ejemplo.

peevishness/malhumor *s.* terquedad; irritabilidad.

pensive/pensativo *adj.* meditabundo; ensimismado; absorto.

perfunctory/negligente *adj.* descuidado; superficial; somero.

perplex/complicar *v.* dejar perplejo; aturdir; quedar indeciso o apurado.

persistent/persistente *adj.* continuo; constante.

pertinent/pertinente *adj.* oportuno; acertado; apto; una observación referente al tema.

pervade/extenderse *v.* difundirse; propagarse; esparcirse.

petulant/irritable *adj.* susceptible; quisquilloso.

phenomenon/fenómeno *s.* entidad o evento extraordinario; prodigio.

pit/oponer *v.* enfrentar en una competición; enfrentarse a alguien.

placid/plácido *adj.* apacible; tranquilo; sosegado.

poignant/conmovedor *adj.* patético; triste; melancólico; dolor agudo; mordaz.

poise/equilibrar *v.* balancear.

ponderous/laborioso *adj.* pesado; que se mueve con lentitud.

portable/portátil *adj.* movible; que se puede desplazar fácilmente.

potent/potente *adj.* poderoso; eficaz; fuerte.

precarious/precario *adj.* inestable; inseguro.

predominant/predominante *adj.* preponderante; superior; que prevalece.

premises/local *s.* casa o edificio y la propiedad alrededor.

presentiment/presentimiento *s.* corazonada; instinto, predicción.

presumable/probable *adj.* posible; presumible. - **presumably/probablemente** *adv.*

prodigy/prodigio *s.* fenómeno; niño dotado de un talento extraordinario.

profuse/profuso *adj.* abundante; pródigo; copioso.

projection/proyección *s.* saliente; reborde; protuberancia.

propriety/decoro *s.* decencia; comportamiento correcto, recato.

providential/providencial *adj.* propicio, como un acto divino; predestinado.

provincial/provincial *adj.* pueblerino; oriundo de la provincia.

prudence/prudencia *s.* sensatez; moderación; cautela.

Q

quell/mitigar *v.* calmar; atenuar; disipar.

quizzical/curioso *adj.* interrogativo; perplejo; desconcertado.

R

radiance/resplandor s. halo; luminosidad; nimbo.

rancid/rancio adj. podrido; pasado.

rationalization/razonamiento s. excusa o motivo aparentemente razonable de un comportamiento; justificación.

realm/reino s. terreno; esfera.

rebound/rebotar v. repercutir; botar.

recede/retroceder v. retirarse; volverse atrás.

recoil/rechazar v. echarse atrás; alejarse; sentir repugnancia por; tener horror.

recrimination/recriminación s. reprimenda; sermón; regaño; acusación contra un acusador.

regressive/regresivo adj. retrógrado; contraproducente; que hace marcha atrás o que regresa a una condición previa.

rehabilitation/rehabilitación s. restauración, reconstrucción; restablecimiento; recuperación.

relic/reliquia s. vestigio; objeto o cosa del pasado que puede tener un significado especial, o religioso; relicario.

resignation/resignación s. mansedumbre; docilidad, pasividad.

resolute/resuelto adj. determinado; decidido; audaz; temerario.

reticent/reticente adj. reservado; silencioso; circunspecto; evasivo.

retort/réplica s. argumento; objeción.

reverence/reverencia s. veneración; respeto; consideración.

rifle/saquear v. vaciar; registrar sin recato.

sidle/avanzar v. mover furtivamente o clandestinamente.

sinister/siniestro adj. funesto; nefasto.

skirt/rodear v. **1.** circundar; contornear; bordear. **2.** evadir; prevenir; eludir.

solidarity/solidaridad s. apoyo; adhesión; unión.

solitary/solitario adj. solo; aislado; lejano.

sovereign/soberano s. rey; monarca; gobernante.

speculate/especular v. reflexionar; teorizar; suponer.

splice/empalmar v. acoplar; ensamblar; enchufar; unir.

stealth/cautela s. sigilo; secreto; disimulo.

stench/peste s. hedor; fetidez; pestilencia; olor insoportable.

stricken/afectado adj. conmovido; afligido; herido; apesadumbrado.

submerge/sumergir v. cubrir con agua; bañar; empapar.

subterranean/subterráneo adj. debajo de la tierra; profundo; hondo.

sultry/bochornoso adj. sofocante; clima caluroso y húmedo.

superlative/superlativo adj. superior; supremo; extraordinario; mejor que todo lo demás.

supplication/súplica s. ruego; demanda humilde; solicitud.

surly/malhumorado adj. hosco; irritable, maleducado.

surreptitious/subrepticio adj. clandestino; disimulado. - **surreptitiously/secretamente** adv.

S

sagacious/sagaz adj. perspicaz; prudente; sensato.

sarcastic/sarcástico adj. punzante; que se burla de algo o de alguien; satírico.

sedate/sosegado adj. tranquilo; sereno; juicioso; moderado.

T

tangible/tangible adj. que se puede tocar; palpable; asequible.

tenacity/tenacidad s. constancia; firmeza; tesón.

tentative/indeciso adj. vacilante; irresoluto; tímido.

tenous/tenue *adj.* sutil; frágil; delicado.

tepid/tibio *adj.* templado; ni caliente ni frío.

terminal/terminal *adj.* posterior; último; que trata del fin o de la muerte.

torrent/torrente *s.* arroyo; cascada; llover a cántaros; tumulto.

traverse/cruzar *v.* atravesar o recorrer un espacio determinado; traspasar.

trek/viaje *s.* marcha; itinerario.

tremulous/trémulo *adj.* tembloroso; estremecido; palpitante.

tumultous/tumultuoso *adj.* disturbado; alborotado; turbulento; revuelto.

U

unimpeded/continuo *adj.* que no se bloquea; perpetuo, imperecedero.

unorthodox/inconforme *adj.* heterodoxo; disidente; que no se conforma.

V

vain/vano *adj.* sin éxito; infructuoso; inútil.

valiant/valiente *adj.* valeroso, bravo; indomable.

valid/válido *adj.* lícito, que cumple con normas establecidas.

veritable/verdadero *adj.* exacto; vigente; que es verdad.

vigil/vela *s.* vigilia; vigilancia durante las horas de sueño.

vintage/antiguo *adj.* añejo; vetusto; remoto.

vitality/vitalidad *s.* fuerza; vigor; energía.

W

whimsy/capricho *s.* antojo; rareza; humor insólito.

wizened/marchito *adj.* arrugado; envejecido; seco.

wrath/ira *s.* cólera; furia.

For permission to reprint copyrighted material, grateful acknowledgment is made to the following sources:

Lily Lee Adams: "The Friendship Only Lasted a Few Seconds" by Lily Lee Adams from *Connections,* newsletter of the William Joiner Center at University of Massachusetts, Boston, Spring 1990. Copyright © 1990 by Lily Lee Adams.

Bill Adler Books Inc.: From "Dear Folks" by Kenneth W. Bagby from *Letters from Vietnam,* edited by Bill Adler. Copyright © 1967 by Bill Adler.

Norma Bradley Allen: From *The Quilters: Women and Domestic Art* by Norma Bradley Allen and Patricia Cooper. Copyright © 1977 by Patricia Cooper Baker and Norma Allen.

Gloria Allred and Lisa Bloom: From "If Decency Doesn't, Law Should Make Us Samaritans" by Gloria Allred and Lisa Bloom from *Houston Chronicle,* September 18, 1997. Copyright © 1997 by Gloria Allred and Lisa Bloom.

Applause Theatre & Cinema Books: The Brute by Anton Chekhov, English version by Eric Bentley. Copyright © 1956 and renewed © 1984 by Eric Bentley. Published by Samuel French, Inc.

Arte Público Press: "Same Song" from *Borders* by Pat Mora. Copyright © 1986 by Pat Mora. Published by Arte Público Press–University of Houston, Houston, TX, 1986.

The Associated Press: From "Explorers Say There's Still Lots to Look For" by Helen O'Neill from *The Seattle Times,* May 21, 2000. Copyright © 2000 by The Associated Press. From "Jack Finney, 84; his novel became cult classic 'Body Snatchers'" from *Boston Globe,* November 17, 1995. Copyright © 1995 by The Associated Press.

Jessica Barnes: "Crossing a Threshold into Adulthood" by Jessica Barnes from *Times Union,* September 24, 2000. Copyright © 2000 by Jessica Barnes.

Belles Lettres: From "Lucille Clifton," an interview by Naomi Thiers, from *Belles Lettres,* Summer 1994. Copyright © 1994 by Belles Lettres.

Susan Bergholz Literary Services, New York: "Geraldo No Last Name" from *The House on Mango Street* by Sandra Cisneros. Copyright © 1984 by Sandra Cisneros. Published by Vintage Books, a division of Random House, Inc., and in hardcover by Alfred A. Knopf in 1994. All rights reserved. "My Lucy Friend Who Smells Like Corn" from *Woman Hollering Creek* by Sandra Cisneros. Copyright © 1991 by Sandra Cisneros. Published by Vintage Books, a division of Random House, Inc., New York, and originally in hardcover by Random House, Inc. All rights reserved.

Robert Bly: From "Ode to My Socks" by Pablo Neruda from *Neruda and Vallejo: Selected Poems,* edited and translated by Robert Bly. Copyright © 1971 by Robert Bly. Published by Beacon Press.

BOA Editions, Ltd.: "miss rosie" from *Good Woman: Poems and a Memoir 1969–1980* by Lucille Clifton. Copyright © 1987 by Lucille Clifton. "Eating Together" from *Rose: Poems* by Li-Young Lee. Copyright © 1986 by Li-Young Lee.

The Book Report, Inc.: From "Exclusive TBR Interview with Frank McCourt" by Jesse Kornbluth from *Author Transcripts* Web site, accessed September 11, 1998, at http://www.bookwire.com/TBR/transcripts.article$3259.

The Boston Globe: From "Coming of Age, Latino Style: Special Rite Ushers Girls into Adulthood" by Cindy Rodriguez from *The Boston Globe,* January 5, 1997. Copyright © 1997 by The Boston Globe.

Brandt & Hochman Literary Agents, Inc.: "By the Waters of Babylon" from *The Selected Works of Stephen Vincent Benét.* Copyright © 1937 by Stephen Vincent Benét; copyright renewed © 1964 by Thomas C. Benét, Stephanie P. Mahin, and Rachel Benét Lewis.

Jimmy Breslin: "The Fear and the Flames" by Jimmy Breslin from *New York Post,* April 6, 1968. Copyright © 1968 by Jimmy Breslin.

Broadside Press: From *Report from Part One* by Gwendolyn Brooks. Copyright © 1972 by Gwendolyn Brooks. Published by Broadside Press, Detroit.

Brooks Permissions: "We Real Cool" from *Blacks* by Gwendolyn Brooks. Copyright © 1991 by Gwendolyn Brooks. Published by Third World Press, Chicago, 1991.

Curtis Brown, Ltd.: "R.M.S. Titanic" by Hanson W. Baldwin from *Harper's Magazine,* January 1934. Copyright © 1934 by Hanson W. Baldwin.

Rick J. Brown: From "The Day the Clowns Cried" by Rick Brown from *History Buff* Web site, accessed October 31, 2000, at http://www.discovery.com/guides/history/historybuff/library/reffire.html.

The Christian Science Monitor: "Deprived of Parent Time? Not Most Kids" by Kim Campbell from *The Christian Science Monitor,* April 5, 2000. Copyright © 2000 by The Christian Science Monitor. All rights reserved. Online at csmonitor.com. "A State Championship vs. Runner's Conscience" by John Christian Hoyle from *The Christian Science Monitor,* February 5, 1999. Copyright © 1999 by The Christian Science Monitor. Online at csmonitor.com.

Judith Ortiz Cofer: Quotes by Judith Ortiz Cofer from *The Global Education Project,* accessed January 10, 2001, at http://ultrix.ramapo.edu/global/cofer.html, January 10, 2001.

Don Congdon Associates, Inc.: "The Pedestrian" by Ray Bradbury from *The Reporter,* August 7, 1951. Copyright © 1951 by the Fortnightly Publishing Co.; copyright renewed © 1979 by Ray Bradbury. From "Drunk and in Charge of a Bicycle" from *The Stories of Ray Bradbury.* Copyright © 1980 by Ray Bradbury. "Contents of the Dead Man's Pockets" by Jack Finney. Copyright © 1956 by Crowell-Collier Co.; copyright renewed © 1984 by Jack Finney.

Estate of Roald Dahl and David Higham Associates: "Lamb to the Slaughter" from *Someone Like You* by Roald Dahl. Copyright © 1961 by Roald Dahl.

The Dallas Morning News: From "Alice in Wonderland" by Toni Y. Joseph from *The Dallas Morning News,* May 27, 1992. Copyright © 1992 by The Dallas Morning News.

Dell Publishing, a division of Random House, Inc.: "Where Have You Gone, Charming Billy?" slightly adapted from *Going After Cacciato* by Tim O'Brien. Copyright © 1975, 1976, 1977, 1978 by Tim O'Brien. From *If I Die in a Combat Zone, Box Me Up and Ship Me Home* by Tim O'Brien. Copyright © 1973 by Tim O'Brien.

The Denver Post: From "Double Daddy" by Penny Parker from *The Denver Post,* September 5, 1999. Copyright © 1999 by The Denver Post.

Barbara Sande Dimmitt: From "The Education of Frank McCourt" by Barbara Sande Dimmitt from *Reader's Digest,* November 1997. Copyright © 1997 by Barbara Sande Dimmitt.

Discovery Communications, Inc.: "Epidemic! On the Trail of Killer Diseases" by Karen Watson from *Discovery Channel* Web site, accessed March 9, 2001, at http://www.discovery.com/exp/epidemic/tb/tb.html. Copyright © by Discovery Communications, Inc.

Doubleday, a division of Random House, Inc.: From *The Power of Myth* by Joseph Campbell with Bill Moyers. Copyright © 1988 by Apostrophe S Productions, Inc. and Alfred van der Marck Editions. From *The Language of Life: A Festival of Poets* by Bill Moyers. Copyright © 1995 by Public Affairs Television, Inc. and David Grubin Productions, Inc.

Rita Dove: "Grape Sherbet" from *Museum* by Rita Dove. Copyright © 1983 by Rita Dove. Published by Carnegie-Mellon University Press.

Dutton Signet, a division of Penguin Putnam Inc.: "The Sword in the Stone" and "The Tale of Sir Launcelot du Lake" from *Le Morte D'Arthur* by Sir Thomas Malory, translated by Keith Baines. Translation copyright © 1962 by Keith Baines; copyright renewed © 1990 by Francesca Evans.

Encyclopaedia Britannica, Inc.: Entry for "vision quest" from *The New Encyclopaedia Britannica, 15th Edition,* vol. 12. Copyright © 1995 by Encyclopaedia Britannica, Inc.

Farrar, Straus & Giroux, LLC: From "For the Union Dead" from *For the Union Dead* by Robert Lowell. Copyright © 1959 by Robert Lowell; copyright renewed © 1987 by Harriet Lowell, Caroline Lowell, and Sheridan Lowell. From "The Country Boy" and "Lost in the City" from *Memoirs* by Pablo Neruda, translated by Hardie St. Martin. Translation copyright © 1976, 1977 by Farrar, Straus & Giroux, LLC. "A Storm in the Mountains" from *Stories and Prose Poems* by Alexander Solzhenitsyn, translated by Michael Glenny. Translation copyright © 1971 by Michael Glenny. From Introduction from *The Acts of King Arthur and His Noble Knights* by John Steinbeck, edited by Chase Horton. Copyright © 1976 by Elaine Steinbeck.

Fortune Magazine: From "The Child's View of Working Parents" (retitled "Kids' View of Parenting") by Cora Daniels from *Fortune,* vol. 140, no. 9, November 8, 1999. Copyright © 1999 by Time, Inc.

Lisa Fugard: "Night Calls" by Lisa Fugard from *Outside,* vol. XX, no. 5, May 1995. Copyright © 1995 by Lisa Fugard. Quotes by Lisa Fugard from *Selected Shorts* radio interview. Copyright © by Lisa Fugard.

Tom Godwin and Scott Meredith Literary Agency, 845 Third Avenue, New York, NY 10022: From *The Cold Equations* by Tom Godwin. Copyright 1954 by Tom Godwin.

Greenhaven Press, Inc.: From *Great Mysteries: King Arthur, Opposing Viewpoints®* by Michael O'Neal. Copyright © 1992 by Greenhaven Press, Inc.

Guardian Newspapers Limited: From "Taste—The Final Frontier" by Esther Addley from *The Guardian,* April 21, 2000. Copyright © by Guardian Newspapers Limited.

Hanging Loose Press: "Sonnet for Heaven Below" from *Correspondence Between the Stonehaulers* by Jack Agüeros. Copyright © 1991 by Jack Agüeros.

Harcourt, Inc.: From "Tentative (First Model) Definitions of Poetry" from *Good Morning, America* by Carl Sandburg. Copyright 1928 and renewed © 1956 by Carl Sandburg. "Everyday Use" from *In Love & Trouble: Stories of Black Women* by Alice Walker. Copyright © 1973 by Alice Walker.

HarperCollins Publishers, Inc.: From *Paula* by Isabel Allende, translated by Margaret Sayers Peden. Copyright © 1994 by Isabel Allende; translation copyright © 1995 by HarperCollins Publishers. "The Black Death" from *When Plague Strikes: The Black Death, Smallpox, AIDS* by James Cross Giblin. Copyright © 1995 by James Cross Giblin. From "Hands: For Mother's Day" from *The Selected Poems of Nikki Giovanni.* Compilation copyright © 1996 by Nikki Giovanni. "A Very Old Man with Enormous Wings" from *Leaf Storm and Other Stories* by Gabriel García Márquez. Copyright © 1971 by Gabriel García Márquez. "By Any Other Name" from *Gifts of Passage* by Santha Rama Rau. Copyright 1951 and renewed © 1979 by Santha Rama Rau. Originally appeared in *The New Yorker.*

Harper's Magazine: "The Leap" by Louise Erdrich from *Harper's Magazine,* March 1990. Copyright © 1990 by Harper's Magazine. All rights reserved.

Harvard University Press and the Trustees of Amherst College: "Heart! We will forget him!," "The Moon was but a Chin of Gold," from "This is my letter to the World," and "This is the land the Sunset washes" from *The Poems of Emily Dickinson,* edited by Thomas H. Johnson. Copyright © 1951, 1955, 1979 by the President and Fellows of Harvard College. Published by The Belknap Press of Harvard University Press, Cambridge, MA.

Henry Holt and Company, LLC: "Stopping by Woods on a Snowy Evening" from *The Poetry of Robert Frost,* edited by Edward Connery Lathem. Copyright 1923, © 1969 by Henry Holt and Company, LLC; copyright 1951 by Robert Frost.

Garrett Hongo: Comment on "The Legend" by Garrett Hongo. Copyright © 1997 by Garrett Hongo.

Houghton Mifflin Company: "All Watched Over by Machines of Loving Grace" and "It's Raining in Love" from *The Pill Versus the Springhill Mine Disaster* by Richard Brautigan. Copyright © 1965 by Richard Brautigan. All rights reserved. From *Offshore* by Penelope Fitzgerald. Copyright © 1979 by Penelope Fitzgerald. From Introduction, "The Dragon Slayer," and "Fafnir's End" from *Legends of the North* by Olivia E. Coolidge. Copyright © 1951 by Olivia E. Coolidge. All rights reserved.

The Estate of Martin Luther King, Jr., c/o Writers House as agent for the proprietor: From "Declaration of Independence from the War in Vietnam" by Martin Luther King, Jr. Copyright © 1963 by Martin Luther King; copyright renewed © 1991 by Coretta Scott King. From "Martin Luther King Explains Nonviolent Resistance" from *The Negro in American History,* edited by William Loren Katz. Copyright © 1960 by Martin Luther King, Jr.; copyright renewed © 1988 by Coretta Scott King.

Alfred A. Knopf, a division of Random House, Inc.: "What Happened During the Ice Storm" from *The One Room Schoolhouse* by Jim Heynen. Copyright © 1993 by Jim Heynen. "The Legend" from *The River of Heaven* by Garrett Hongo. Copyright © 1988 by Garrett Hongo. "I, Too" from *The Collected Poems of Langston Hughes* by Langston Hughes. Copyright © 1994 by The Estate of Langston Hughes. "Through the Tunnel" from *Stories* by Doris Lessing. Copyright © 1978 by Doris Lessing. "Gracious Goodness" from *Circles on the Water* by Marge Piercy. Copyright © 1982 by Marge Piercy. "Ex-Basketball Player" from *The Carpentered Hen and Other Tame Creatures* by John Updike. Copyright © 1982 by John Updike. "Powder" from *The Night in Question: Stories* by Tobias Wolff. Copyright © 1996 by Tobias Wolff.

Sheila Mant" from *The Man Who Loved Levittown* by W. D. Wetherell. Copyright © 1985 by W. D. Wetherell.

Villard Books, a division of Random House, Inc.: From *Into Thin Air* by Jon Krakauer. Copyright © 1997 by Jon Krakauer.

Vintage Books, a division of Random House, Inc.: "How sad that I hope . . . ," "Should the world of love . . . ," and "Since my heart placed me . . ." from *The Ink Dark Moon: Love Poems* by Ono No Komachi and Izumi Shikibu, translated by Jane Hirshfield and Mariko Aratani. Copyright © 1990 by Jane Hirshfield and Mariko Aratani.

The Virginian-Pilot: "Good Samaritans U.S.A. Are Afraid to Act" by Ann Sjoerdsma from *The Virginian-Pilot,* September 15, 1997. Copyright © 1997 by The Virginian-Pilot.

The Wall Street Journal: From "Diary of a Mad Blender: A Week of Managing Every Spare Minute" by Sue Shellenbarger from *The Wall Street Journal,* March 22, 2000. Copyright © 2000 by Dow Jones & Company, Inc.

The Washington Post Writers Group: From "Ill-Equipped Rescuers Dig Out Volcano Victims: Aid Slow to Reach Colombian Town" by Bradley Graham from *The Washington Post,* November 16, 1985. Copyright © 1985 by The Washington Post Writers Group.

Wesleyan University Press: "Moons" from *The Stone Harp* by John Haines. Copyright © 1971 by John Haines.

W. D. Wetherell: From "A Trout for Celeste" from *Vermont River* by W. D. Wetherell. Copyright © 1984 by W. D. Wetherell.

Wiley Publishing, Inc.: Entry for *indulge* and pronunciation key from *Webster's New World™ College Dictionary,* Fourth Edition. Copyright © 1999, 2000 by Wiley Publishing, Inc. All rights reserved.

The H. W. Wilson Company: Quote from "Olivia Coolidge" from *More Junior Authors* Web site, accessed November 19, 2001, at http://vweb.hwwilsonweb.com/cgi-bin/webspirs.cgi. Copyright © 2001 by The H. W. Wilson Company.

Sources Cited:
From letter to Maxim Gorki from *The Selected Letters of Anton Chekhov,* edited by Lillian Hellman, translated by Sidonie Lederer. Published by Farrar, Straus & Company, New York, 1955.

From "James Stevenson" from *Contemporary Authors,* January 10, 2001. Published by The Gale Group, Farmington Hills, MI, 2001.

Quote by Frank McCourt from "From 'Ashes' to Stardom" by Malcolm Jones, Jr., from *Newsweek,* August 25, 1997. Published by Newsweek, Inc., New York, 1997.

Quote by Roald Dahl from *The New York Times Book Review.* Published by The New York Times Company.

Picture Credits

The illustrations and/or photographs on the Contents pages are picked up from pages in the textbook. Credits for those can be found either on the textbook page on which they appear or in the listing below.

Page 2: © cartoonbank.com; 5: © Pete Seaward/Getty Images; 9: © Nat Norman/Getty Images; 10: © Pete Seaward/Getty Images; 13: © Lawrence Thornton/Getty Images; 14: © Euan Myles/Getty Images; 17: Kim Komenich/TimePix; 18: © Amos Morgan/Getty Images; 27: © Bruce Ayres/Getty Images; 32: © Sarto/Lund/Getty Images; 34: © Dewitt Jones/CORBIS; 36–37: © Frank Herholdt/Getty Images; 39: Keri Pickett/TimePix; 40: AP/Associated Press; 47: © Getty Images; 52: © Syndicated Features Limited/The Image Works; 55: (top left) Cover photo: Lambert Studios/Archive Photos; (top right) Cover from *Nectar in a Sieve* by Kamala Markandaya, copyright © 1954 by The John Day Company. Used by permission of Signet, a division of Penguin Putnam Inc.; (bottom left) From *Fahrenheit 451* by Ray Bradbury. Used with permission of Ballantine Books, a division of Random House, Inc.; (bottom right) From *The Hot Zone* (jacket cover) by Richard Preston, copyright. Used by permission of Doubleday, a division of Random House, Inc.; 78–82 (borders): Detail of *His Grandmother's Quilt.* Courtesy of the artist; 83: © Anthony Barboza/Buddha Studio; 84: Romare Howard Bearden Foundation. Licensed by VAGA, New York; 85: © Baron/Getty Images; 89: © 2001 Roland L. Freeman, Washington, D.C.; 97: © cartoonbank.com; 99: © Stephanie Dalton Cowan/Getty Images; 101: © Lake County Museum/CORBIS; 105: © David Perry/Getty Images; 108: © Reuters/CORBIS; 113: Copyright © 1977 by Santha Rama Rau. Reprinted by permission of William Morris Agency, Inc., on behalf of the author; 117: © Lindsay Hebberd/CORBIS; 118: © Elliot Erwitt/Magnum Photos; 121: (top left) Cover from *Washington Square* by Henry James. Courtesy of the Oxford University Press/National Gallery of London; (top right) Cover from *Fences* by August Wilson, copyright © 1986 by August Wilson. Used by permission of Dutton Signet, a division of Penguin Putnam Inc.; (bottom left) Cover used by permission of University Press of New England; (bottom right) Cover from *Fifth Chinese Daughter* by Jade Snow Wong, courtesy University of Washington Press; 139: Reprinted courtesy of The Saturday Evening Post; 141: © Getty Images; 149: Fisk University Galleries, Nashville, Tenn.; 151: Culver Pictures, Inc.; 160: E. O. Hoppé/TimePix; 164: (top right) © WY/Getty Images; (center) John Lei, Omni–Photo Communications, Inc.; (bottom left) © Joe Sohm/The Stock Market/CORBIS; 166: (background) © NASA/Getty Images; (inset) John Lei, Omni–Photo Communications, Inc.; 168: (top) © Stephen Simpson/Getty Images; (bottom) Jon Davison/The Image Bank; 171: © Aram Gesar/Getty Images; 177: (background) Chris Butler/Science Photo Library/Photo Researchers, Inc.; (inset) John Lei, Omni–Photo Communi-

cations, Inc.; 180–181: © Stephen Simpson/Getty Images; 184: Morgan-Cain & Associates; 188, 189, 190: NASA; 194–195 (background): © Bettmann/CORBIS; 195 (inset): From *Angela's Ashes* by Frank McCourt. © 1996 by Frank McCourt. Reproduced by permission of Scribner's, a division of Simon & Schuster. All rights reserved; 196–199 (background): © CORBIS; 196 (inset): © Bettmann/CORBIS; 200: AP/Wide World Photos; 201, 202–203: Morgan-Cain & Associates; 207: (top left) Kwangshin Kim/Photo Researchers, Inc.; (top right) S. Camazine/Photo Researchers, Inc.; (bottom right) © S. Lowry/University of Ulster/Getty Images; 208: (top) © Barts Hospital/Getty Images; (bottom) Richard Falco/Black Star Publishing/PictureQuest; 209: © Hulton-Deutsch Collection/CORBIS; 211: (top left) Cover photo: A. P. Allenson, E. O. Hoppé. Courtesy of Royal Photographic Society; (top right) From *Dune* by Frank Herbert. Used by permission of G. P. Putnam's Sons, a division of Penguin Putnam Inc.; (bottom left) Cover from *Platero and I* by Juan Ramón Jiménez. Jacket illustration copyright © 1994 by Antonio Frasconi. Reprinted by permission of Clarion Books/Houghton Mifflin Company. All rights reserved; (bottom right) Cover from *Hiroshima* by John Hersey. Illustrated by Wendell Minor. Used by permission of Vintage Books, a division of Random House, Inc.; 222: University of California at Irvine/NASA; 223: NASA Marshall Space Flight Center, photo by Dennis Olive; 233: © Getty Images; (background) Timothy Fuller/PhotoSpin; 234: (left, right, middle center, background) © Getty Images; (top center) PhotoSpin; (bottom center) Timothy Fuller; 236: Timothy Fuller; 239: © Getty Images; (background) Timothy Fuller/PhotoSpin; 240: Photo of Judith Ortiz Cofer is reprinted with permission from the publisher, Arte Público Press; 243: © Burton McNeely/Getty Images; 244: (top) © Burton McNeeley/Getty Images; (bottom) © Gerald Brimacombe; 244–245: Kirchoff/Wohlberg; 246: © Gerald Brimacombe; 249: © Burton McNeeley/Getty Images; 250: Francois Camoin; 257: © Getty Images; 259: J. N. Marso/USGS; 265: © Getty Images; 266: © Ed Kashi/CORBIS; 267: Frank Fournier/Contact Press Images; 273, 274, 276: © Terry Ashe/Getty Images; 277: Bernard Gotfryd/Woodfin Camp & Associates; 278: © Todd Gipstein/CORBIS; 279: © Dennis O'Clair/Getty Images; 287: Ellis Herwig/Stock Boston Inc./PictureQuest; 293: (top left) From *A Tale of Two Cities* by Charles Dickens. Cover art © HRW, cover design Chris Smith, background © CORBIS/Owen Franken/Jeremy Homer; (top right) Cover from *The Sound of Waves* by Yukio Mishima. Used by permission of Vintage Books, a division of Random House, Inc.; (bottom left) Cover from *Laughing Boy* by Oliver La Farge, copyright © 1929 by Oliver La Farge. Used by permission of Dutton Signet, a division of Penguin Putnam Inc.; (bottom right) Cover from *The Perfect Storm* by Sebastian Junger. Cover photo by Th. D.A. DeLange/FPG. Copyright © 1997 by Sebastian Junger. Used by permission of W. W. Norton & Company; 306: Walter

Geiersperger/Index Stock Photography; **307:** Stephen John Krasemann/Photo Researchers, Inc.; **325:** Nancy Crampton; **328:** © CORBIS/Sygma; **329:** (left) Titanic Historical Society, Don Lynch Collection, Indian Orchard (MA); (right) The Illustrated London News Picture Library; **330–331:** Illustrations by Ken Marschall © 1992 from *Titanic: An Illustrated History*, a Hyperion/Madison Press Book; **333:** (background) Color Box/FPG International; (left) Reproduced by courtesy of White Star Publications; (right) The Illustrated London News Picture Library; **334:** (background) Color Box/FPG International; (top) Hulton-Deutsch Collection, London; (bottom) Titanic Historical Society, Indian Orchard (MA); **337:** (background) Color Box/FPG International; (top) Titanic Historical Society, Indian Orchard (MA); (bottom) © Bettmann/CORBIS; **338–339:** Illustrations by Ken Marschall © 1992 from *Titanic: An Illustrated History*, a Hyperion/Madison Press Book; **344:** (top) AP/Wide World Photos; (bottom) Detail of an illustration by Ken Marschall © 1992 from *Titanic: An Illustrated History,* a Hyperion/Madison Press Book; **345:** (left) © Bettmann/CORBIS; (top right) The Illustrated London News Picture Library; (bottom right) AP/Wide World Photos; **346:** (top) Titanic Historical Society, Don Lynch Collection, Indian Orchard (MA); (bottom) Titanic Historical Society, Indian Orchard (MA); **349–351** (background): © Gordon Wiltsie/Alpenimage Ltd.; **351:** (top) © Ed Viesturs/Ethereal, Inc.; (bottom) Caroline Mackenzie/Woodfin Camp & Associates; **352–353:** © Neil Beidleman/Woodfin Camp & Associates; **354–363** (background): © Gordon Wiltsie; **356:** © Neil Beidleman/Woodfin Camp & Associates; **359:** Scott Fischer/Woodfin Camp & Associates; **362:** © Chris Noble/Getty Images; **363:** © Andrew Eccles/CORBIS Outline; **368:** Royal Geographical Society, London; **369:** NASA; **370:** © Bettmann/CORBIS; **378:** Courtesy of HarperCollins; **381:** (top left) *Tales of the Unexpected;* (top right) *Alice's Adventures in Wonderland & Through the Looking-Glass;* (bottom left) *A Night to Remember;* (bottom right) *The Endurance: Shackleton's Legendary Antarctic Expedition;* **396–397:** AKG Berlin/SuperStock; **400–401:** M. Rubio/West Stock; **401:** Jerry Jones/Photo Researchers, Inc.; **403:** (top) John Neubauer/PhotoEdit; (bottom) M. Rubio/West Stock; **407:** © Andy Sacks/Getty Images; **408:** © Bettmann/CORBIS; **415:** Shamil Zhumatov/Reuters/TimePix; **422–423:** © Erich Lessing/Art Resource, NY; **425:** © Erich Lessing/Art Resource, NY; **426:** Julian Hartnoll, London/Private collection/Bridgeman Art Library; **428:** Mansell/TimePix; **429–430** (background): Planet Art; **430:** © Historical Picture Archive/CORBIS; **434:** © David Muench/CORBIS; **435:** © Burstein Collection/CORBIS; **436:** © Christie's Images/CORBIS; **437:** Eric Schaal/TimePix; **439:** (top left) *Watership Down;* (top right) *A Separate Peace* by John Knowles. Cover © HRW; (bottom left) *The Tale of the Unknown Island* (book jacket) by José Saramago. Jacket illustration by Peter Sis. Used by permission of Harcourt; (bottom right) *Black Ice;* **454–455:** © Christie's Images, Inc.; **458:** AGE/FotoStock/SuperStock; **459:** © Craig Aurness/CORBIS; **460:** AP/Wide World Photos; **461:** (left) John Henley/The Stock Market; (right) Paul Simcock/The Image Bank; **462:** Stockbyte/PictureQuest; **463:** Arte Público Press/University of Houston; **464:** (top) © EyeWire/Getty Images; (bottom) © CORBIS; **465:** Réunion des Musées Nationaux/Art Resource, NY; **466:** (background) Honeychurch Antiques, Ltd./CORBIS; (inset) © Getty Images; **467:** Arthur Furst; **468–469:** Private collection/Jessie Coates/

SuperStock; **469:** © Tim Wright/CORBIS; **470:** © The Barnes Foundation, Merion Station, Penn./CORBIS; **471:** © John Johnson/Getty Images; **472:** © Scala/Art Resource, NY; **475:** Charles Wright; **476:** © Jayme Thornton/Getty Images; **479:** Manfred Danegger/Photo Researchers, Inc.; **480:** Nancy Crampton; **481:** Pictor International, Ltd./PictureQuest; **483:** Alexandria King/Albuquerque Journal; **485:** Joe Travers/Liaison International; **487:** © Francis G. Mayer/CORBIS; **489:** Morgan-Cain & Associates; **494:** Kaoru Mikami/Photonica; **497:** © Kim Sayer/CORBIS; **500:** © Archivo Iconografico, S.A./CORBIS; **501:** 2002 Banco de México, Diego Rivera and Frida Kahlo Museums Trust, Av. Cinco de Mayo No. 2, Col. Centro, Del Cuauhtémoc 06059, México, D. F. Schalkwijk/Art Resource, NY; **506:** M. P. Kahl/Photo Researchers, Inc.; **507:** (background) © Harold Sund/Getty Images; (inset) © Bettmann/CORBIS; **508:** Picture Images; **509:** © Victoria and Albert Museum, London/Art Resource, NY; **513:** Renee Purse/Photo Researchers, Inc.; **514–515:** © G. K. & Vikki Hart/Getty Images; **515:** James H. Evans; **516:** Lynn Saville; **517:** © Getty Images; **518:** © Alan Thornton/Getty Images; **519:** © Pascal Rondeau/Getty Images; **520:** Rick Friedman/Black Star Publishing/PictureQuest; **522:** © Sean Ellis/Getty Images; **523:** Nancy Crampton; **526:** © Getty Images; © Paul Abdoo; **530:** Werner Forman/Art Resource, NY; **531:** © janet Century; **532:** Artwork © 2002 Gwendolyn Knight Lawrence, courtesy of The Jacob and Gwendolyn Lawrence Foundation; **533:** (top) © Getty Images; (bottom) © Bettmann/CORBIS; **535:** Private collection/Gil Mayers/SuperStock; **537:** Archive Photos/PictureQuest; **539:** (top left) From *Poetry Out Loud,* edited by Robert A. Rubin. Copyright © 1993 by Algonquin Books of Chapel Hill. Reprinted by permission of Algonquin Books of Chapel Hill, a division of Workman Publishing; (top right) *This Same Sky: A Collection of Poems from Around the World.* Cover illustration © 1992 by Deborah Maverick Kelley; (bottom left) Cover from *Emily Dickinson: Collected Poems.* Jacket design by Leah Lococo. Courtesy of Barnes & Noble, Inc.; (bottom right) Cover from *Neruda: Selected Poems* (Boston: Houghton Mifflin, 1990). Reprinted by permission of Houghton Mifflin Company. All rights reserved; **552:** © Getty Images; **559:** © Donald Johnson/Getty Images; **561:** © 1994 Rubén Guzmán; **565** (background): Morgan-Cain & Associates, Inc.; **568:** Turner Sculpture; **572:** © John Scranton; **573:** © Getty Images; **574:** © Francis G. Mayer/CORBIS; (feather) © Getty Images; **579:** © Getty Images; **580:** Richard Shiell/Earth Scenes; **582:** © Alan and Sandy Carey/Getty Images; **587, 589, 590, 592, 593, 595:** Art by Sergio Bustamante/photographs © Clint Clemens. All rights reserved; **596:** © Ulf Andersen/Gamma Press, Inc.; **597:** Sepp Seitz/Woodfin Camp & Associates; **601:** (top left) *Great American Stories,* cover © HRW, art by Sabra Field © 1991; (top right) Cover from *The Old Man and the Sea* by Ernest Hemingway, Hemingway Century Edition (New York: Scribner, a division of Simon & Schuster, Inc., 1999). Cover illustration © 1999 Production Pascal Blais, Inc., Imagica Corp., Panorama Film Studio of Yaroslav; (bottom right) *Barrio Boy* by Ernesto Galarza. Cover © HRW, photo by Rick Williams; (bottom right) *Never Cry Wolf* by Farley Mowat. Cover art by Bob Ziering. Used by permission of HRW; **621:** Philip Jones Griffiths/Magnum Photos, Inc.; (background) © Dirck Halstead/Getty Images; **624:** © B. Hemphill/Photo Researchers, Inc.; **626:** © Dirck Halstead/Getty Images; **628:** AP/Wide World Photos; **629:** © Paul S. Conklin/UNIPHOTO;

634: The News Archive/PRC Archive; 635: PRC Archive; 636: The National Archives; 639: AP/Wide World Photos; 640: Charles Bonnay/Black Star Publishing/PictureQuest; 641: © CORBIS; 645: © Chapman & Perry/The Image Works; 648: Art Resource, NY; 656: Reprinted with the permission of Atheneum Books for Young Readers, an imprint of Simon and Schuster Children's Publishing Division, from *The Boy's King Arthur* by Sydney Lanier, illustrated by N. C. Wyeth. Copyright 1917, 1924 Charles Scribner's Sons, copyright renewed 1945 N. C. Wyeth and 1952 John Lanier, David Lanier, and Sterling Lanier; 661: Morgan-Cain & Associates; 662: © Mimmo Jodice/CORBIS; 667: © Erich Lessing/Art Resource, NY; 668: (top) James Whitmore/TimePix; (bottom) © Gianni Dagli Orti/CORBIS; 669: © Arte & Immagini SRL/CORBIS; 671: Louvre, Paris/Bridgeman Art Library; 674: Ronald Sheridan, Ancient Art & Architecture Collection; 676: Werner Forman/Art Resource, NY; 676–685 (border): Morgan-Cain & Associates; 679, 680, 682: © Werner Forman/CORBIS; 684: (top) Ny Carlsberg Glyptotek, Copenhagen/North Wind Picture Archives; (center) © Bettmann/CORBIS; (bottom right) Arthur Rackham/Wood River Gallery/PictureQuest; (bottom left) Werner Forman/Art Resource, NY; 685: (top left) Mary Evans Picture Library; (top right) Fogelberg, BE NM 394 Balder. Photo: The National Museum of Fine Arts, Stockholm; (bottom left) Royal Library, Copenhagen/Bridgeman Art Library; (bottom right) Mary Evans Picture Library; 686: Houghton Mifflin Company, Boston; 689: (top left) From *The King Must Die* (book cover) by Mary Renault, copyright © 1958 by Mary Renault. Used by permission of Vintage Books, a division of Random House, Inc.; (top right) Jacket design by Louise Fili from *The Acts of King Arthur and His Noble Knights* by John Steinbeck. Jacket design copyright © 1993 by Louise Fili. Reprinted by permission of Farrar, Straus and Giroux LLC;

(bottom left) *Fallen Angels* by Walter Dean Myers. Cover art © HRW, cover photo by Steve Harris, cover design by Scott Stricker; (bottom right) *Shrapnel in the Heart: Letters and Remembrances from the Vietnam Veterans Memorial;* 718: 1997 Production of *Tristan and Isolde* performed at the Los Angeles Opera. Production conceived and directed by David Hockney. Photo by Robert Millard; 723: © Nancy Crampton; 725, 727, 730, 733, 735: 2002 production of *The Brute* performed by The Expression Theatre Ensemble. Photos by Rade Vranesh; 737: © Bettmann/CORBIS; 741: Popperfoto Ltd.; 742: © The Photo Works/Photo Researchers, Inc.; 743: © Michal Daniel/New York Shakespeare Festival; 744: © Paul Davis. Courtesy of the artist; 748: © Bettmann/CORBIS; 749: The Shakespeare Centre Library, Stratford-on-Avon, England; 750: © Erich Lessing/Art Resource, NY; 751: © Bettmann/CORBIS; 755: Photofest; 756: © Giraudon/Art Resource, NY; 757: © Ray Manley/SuperStock, Florida; 761, 766, 774: © George E. Joseph; 778: Rod Planck/Photo Researchers, Inc.; 780: Art Resource, NY; 782: © Martha Swope/TimePix; 792, 794, 797: © George E. Joseph; 805: Courtesy MGM/Ronald Grant Archive; 806, 810, 816, 821, 825, 827: © George E. Joseph; 831: © R. G. Everts/Photo Researchers, Inc.; 833: © Bettmann/CORBIS; 842, 851, 856–857, 863, 869: © George E. Joseph; 872: Réunion des Musées Nationaux/Art Resource, NY; 873: Gilles Mermet/Art Resource, NY; 875: AP/Wide World Photos; 876, 877: Dennis Brack/Black Star Publishing/PictureQuest; 883, 884, 885: © Bettmann/CORBIS; 888: © Hulton-Deutsch Collection/CORBIS; 889: (top left) *Macbeth;* (top right) *A Raisin in the Sun;* (bottom left) *Visit to a Small Planet;* (bottom right) *A Book of Plays;* 906–907: Mark Richards/PhotoEdit; 913: Creative Labs; 916: Morgan-Cain & Associates; 917: PEANUTS © United Features Syndicate. Reprinted by Permission; 924–925, 936: © Getty Images.

Illustrations

Dykes, John, 23, 25
Forkan, Joe, 66, 68
Hargreaves, Greg, 375
High, Richard, 652–657

Lopez, Rafael, 43, 498–499
Newbold, Greg, 154–155, 156–157, 158–159
Reagan, Mike, 871
Steinberg, James, 317, 319, 320, 321, 323, 324

Maps

Nepal, Tibet, and India, 351
Some Sites of Ancient Greece, 661

Rome at the Death of Caesar, 871
North America, 1000

Index of Skills

The boldface page numbers indicate an extensive treatment of the topic.

LITERARY SKILLS

Actions, of characters, 74–75
Allegorical meaning, 431
Allegory, **399, 418,** 431, 450, 451, **979**
Alliteration, **504,** 505, 508, 518, 524, **531,** 534, 979, 983
Allusion, 140, 152, 316, 379, 460, 461, 464, 597, **979**
Ambiguity, **315,** 326, **374,** 379, 575, **979**
Ambiguous theme, 990
Anachronism, **853**
Analysis questions (Interpretations), 19, 41, 53, 86, 109, 119, 152, 161, 185, 204, 241, 252, 270, 281, 326, 347, 364, 379, 409, 431, 438, 460, 464, 470, 476, 481, 486, 492, 495, 502, 508, 512, 517, 524, 530, 534, 538, 562, 575, 598, 630, 649, 658, 670, 687, 738, 779, 804, 832, 852, 878
Anapest, 503, **985**
Antagonist, 96, **988**
Appearance, **74**
Approximate rhyme, **504**
Archaic words, **752**
Archetype, 673
Arthurian legend, **644,** 658
Aside, **722,** 801, 815, 832, **980**
Assonance, **980,** 983
Atmosphere, **44,** 46
Audience, **723**
Author's purpose. *See* Purpose.
Autobiography, 112, 193, 204, 714, **980**
Ballad, **509,** 512, **980**
Basic situation, **2,** 3, 161, 165, **982**
Believability, 185
Believable character, 97
Bible parable, 278
Biographical approach, **618–619**
Biography, **618–619,** 741, **980**
Blank verse, **752, 980**
Character, 41, 45, **74–75,** 112, 130–133, 180, 185, 232, 562, 660, 670, 723, 738, 779, 804, 852, **980,** 986
  believable, 97
  dynamic, **96–97,** 981
  flat, **75,** 981
  inference about, **76,** 86
  main, 109, 119, 233, 738, 754
  minor, 379, 630
  round, **75,** 981
  static, **96,** 981

stock, **75**
  subordinate, **96,** 119, 980
  traits, 74, 75, 76, 86, 109, 133, 241, 658, 804
Character foil, 767, 779, 788, 814, 832, 852
Character interactions, **96–97**
Characterization, 119, 252, 264, 832, 852
  direct, **74**
  indirect, **74,** 112
Chivalry, 651
Chronological order, **3, 4,** 19, 41, 347, 649, **994**
Climax, **3,** 252, 431, 720, 738, **754,** 878, 982, 987
Comedy, **721, 724,** 738, 754, 830, **981,** 982, 991
Comic relief, 204, **981**
Compare and contrast themes, **232**
  across genres, **255,** 270, **283,** 306
Comparing
  literature, 575
  similes, 481
  universal themes, **232**
Comparison, 460, 477, 492, 495, 524
Complications, 2, 3, 720, 982
Conflict, 45, 86, 109, 119, 133, 231, 243, 281, 309, 438, 451, 651, **720, 721,** 779, 852, 878, **981**
  external, 2, 19, **96,** 98, 243, 252, 981
  internal, 2, 19, **96,** 98, 243, 252, 981
  motivation and, **98**
Connotation, 534, **981**
Contradiction, 349, 358, 364
Costumes, **722**
Couplet, 493, 495, **981,** 989
Credibility, 41, **193,** 204, 326, 379, 738
Credible first-person narrator, **138**
Crisis, **754**
Dactyl, **503,** 985
Denotation, 981
Denouement, **3, 754**
Dialect, **95**
Dialogue, 74, 76, 86, 133, **722,** 723, 804, 813, 835, 841, 852, 854
Diction, **139,** 193, 471, **556, 558,** 562, 575, 612, 981, **982, 990,** 991
Direct characterization, **74, 980**
Direct metaphor, **478**
Drama, **720–723,** 852, **982,** 983
  aside, **722,** 801, 815, 832
  audience, **723**
  climax, **3,** 252, 431, 720, 738, **754,** 878
  comedy, **721, 724,** 738, 743, 754, 830

complications, 2, 3, 720
  dialogue, **74,** 76, 86, 133, **722,** 723, 804, 813, 835, 841, 852, 854
  modern, **721**
  monologue, **722,** 759, 764, 820, 828, 858
  resolution, **3,** 19, 651, 720, 754, 878
  scene design, **721–722,** 852
  soliloquy, **75, 722,** 771, 783, 803, 804, 832
  stage directions, **722–723**
  tragedy, **720–721,** 743, **754,** 804, 832, 852, 872, 878
  See also Conflict.
Dramatic irony, **314–315,** 316, 326, 328, 347, 984
Dramatic monologue, **75, 982**
Dramatic presentation, 880
Dynamic character, **96–97**
Emotional appeals, 832
End rhyme, **504**
End-stopped lines, **752**
English sonnet, 493
Epic, **982**
Essay, **272, 982**
Evaluating style, **556–557, 610–612**
Evaluation questions, 19, 41, 53, 86, 109, 119, 152, 185, 204, 241, 252, 270, 281, 326, 347, 364, 379, 409, 431, 502, 517, 534, 649, 738, 779, 804, 832, 852, 878
Exact rhyme, **504**
Exaggeration, 989
Exposition, 2, 347, **754,** 779, **982**
Extended metaphor, **478,** 497, 502, 551
Extended simile, 479, 481, 497, 502
External conflict, 2, 19, **96,** 98, 243, 252, 981
Fable, 399, **982**
Facts, 328, 347
Falling action, **754**
Fantasia, **535**
Farce, **724,** 738
Feudal system, 649
Fiction, 256, **983**
Figurative language, 399, **477–478,** 557, 612, 982, **990**
Figures of speech, 477, 478, 479, 486, 492, 524, **557,** 564, 570, 571, **982**
  personification, **478, 487,** 492, 495, 524, 530, 538
  See also Metaphor, Simile.
First-person point of view, **138,** 140, 152, 161, 185
Flashback, **3, 31,** 41, 564, 630, 721, **983**
Flash-forward, **3, 983**

Flat character, **75**
Foil, **983**. *See also* Character foil.
Folk ballad, **509**, 980
Folk tale, 983
Foot, poetic, **503**, 980
Foreshadowing, **3, 31**, 41, 53, 326, 832, 849, **983**
Formal essay, 982
Frame story, 161
Free verse, **503, 504, 513**, 517, **983**
Generalization, 231, **233**, 241
Genres, 230, 255, 256, 270, 283, 309, **983**
    comparing and contrasting theme across, **255, 283**, 306
Graphic organizers
    analysis data bank, 97
    cause-and-effect diagram, 364
    character chart, 75
    character web, 738
    comparison-and-contrast chart, 232, 255, 658
    extended simile and metaphor chart, 502
    genres chart, 255, 283
    irony chart, 315
    plot diagram, 3
    prediction table, 185
    selection chart, 619
    setting chart, 45
    story map, 687
    summary chart, 379
    theme charts, 231, 232, 255
    time line, 649
    tragedy structure, 754
Haiku, **983**
Hero, 649, 658, 660, 670, 671, 687
Historical approach, **618–619**
Historical context, **620**, 630
History, **618–619**, 743
Hyperbole, 984
Iamb, **503, 752**, 980, 984, 985
Iambic pentameter, **518, 524, 752, 984**
Idiom, **521**, 524, **984**
Imagery, **456–457**, 461, 551, 815, **984**
Images, 185, 456, 458, 461, 464, 476, 492, 495, 508, 509, 538, 567, 570, 571, 586, 598, 612, 687, 981
Implied metaphor, **478**
Incongruity, 349, 364, **984**
Indirect characterization, **74**, 112, 980
Inference, 35, 109, 243, 326, 347, **374**, 379, 562, 575, 670, **998–999**
    about characters, **76**, 86, 243, 562
    about motivation, **98**, 109, 243, 575
Informal essay, **272**
Internal conflict, 2, 19, **96**, 98, 243, 252, 981
Internal rhyme, **504**, 518, 524, 983
Interpretation, 880
Inversion, **984**
Irony, **314–315**, 316, 326, 347, 349, 362, 630, 801, 824, 862, 878, **984**

Key passages, 46, 161
Knightly quest, 651
Legend, **619, 644**, 649, 658
Lighting, 722, 790
Literal reading, 438
Literary criticism, 161, 241, 326, 562, 598, 610–612, 630, 649, 658, 670, 687
Loaded words, 46, 161, 832
Lyric poem, 486
Lyric poetry, **482, 985**
Magic realism, **586**, 598, **985**
Main character, 109, 119, 233, 738, 754. *See also* Protagonist.
Main events, 152, 364, 409, 562, 649, 658, 670
Main idea, 255, **272**, 281
Memorizing, 880
Metaphor, 438, 470, **478, 484**, 486, 495, 502, 508, 524, 530, 538, 983, **985**
    direct, **478**, 985
    extended, **478**, 497, 502, 551, 985
    implied, **478**, 985
    mixed, 985
Meter, **503, 506**, 508, 509, 534, 551, **985**, 988
Metrical poetry, **503**
Minor character, 379, 630
Modern drama, **721**
Monologue, **722**, 759, 764, 820, 828, 858
    dramatic, **75**
Mood, **44, 46**, 53, **140**, 152, 315, 347, 379, 457, 492, **557, 564**, 575, 586, 598, 758, 760, 776, 779, 798, 867, 981, **986**
Moral, 231
Motivation, character's, **97, 98**, 109, 133, **243**, 252, 575, 651, 687, 981
Myth, 364, **619, 660, 673**, 983, **986**
Narration, **986**
Narrative, 347
Narrative poem, 512
Narrator, 76, 133, 260, 309, 612
    omniscient, **138**, 409, **986**
    reliable first-person, **138**
    third-person-limited, **138–139, 163**, 169, 185
    unreliable, 987
    See also Point of view.
Nonfiction, 256, 983, **986**
Novel, **986**
Objective writing, **328**, 347
Objectivity, 364
Octave, 989
Ode, **497**, 502
Omniscient narrator, 409
Omniscient point of view, **138, 154**, 161
Onomatopoeia, **505, 535**, 538, 983, **986**
Overstatement, 984
Parable, 278, **399**, 979, **986**

Paradox, **986**
Parallelism, 517, **986**
Parody, **502**
Pentameter, **752**
Persona, **138**, 140, 152, **987**
Personal essay, **272**, 982
Personification, **478, 487**, 492, 495, 524, 530, 538, 983, **987**
Persuading, 256
Persuasive oratory, 832
Plot, **2–3**, 4, 133, 232, 687, 724, 986, **987**
    basic situation, **2**, 3, 161, 165
    chronological order, **3, 4**, 19, 41, 347, 649
    climax, **3**, 252, 431, **720**, 738, **754**, 878
    complications, 2, 3, 720
    denouement, **3, 754**
    exposition, 2, 347, **754**, 779
    resolution, **3**, 19, 651, 720, **754**, 878
    suspense, 3, 19, 185, 347, 409, 804
    See also Conflict, Time and sequence.
Plot diagram, 3
Plot summary, 651
Poem, narrative, 512
Poetry, **503–505**, 983, **987**
    alliteration, **505**, 508, 518, 524, **531**, 534
    ballad, 987
    epic, 987
    figurative language, **477–478**
    foot, 503
    free verse, **503, 504, 513**, 517
    imagery, **456**
    lyric, **482**, 987
    meter, **503, 506**, 508, 509, 534, 551
    metrical, **503**
    narrative, 987
    onomatopoeia, **505, 535**, 538
    rhythm, **503**, 505, 538, 562
    scanning, 503
    structure of, **518**
    See also Rhyme.
Point of view, **138–139**, 174, 379, 562, 986, **987**
    first person, **138**, 140, 152, 161, 185, 987
    omniscient, **138, 154**, 161, 409, 987
    third person limited, **138–139, 163**, 169, 185, 987
    tone, **44, 139**, 152, 161, 185, 309, 465, 470, **471**, 476, 495, 502, 530, 534, **557, 558**, 562, 586, 598, 612, 630, 758, 798, 822
    voice, **139, 193**, 204, 465
    See also Narrator.
Prologue, 822
Props, **722**, 854, 989
Prose poem, 458, 460
Protagonist, **96**, 562, 779, 832, **987**
Public symbol, 398
Pun, **988**

Purpose, **46,** 53, **154,** 161, 255, **256,** 258, 262, 265, 270, 347, 379, 738
Quatrain, 493, 495, 989
Quest, 630, 651, 670
Reading Comprehension (Reading Check), 19, 41, 53, 86, 109, 119, 152, 161, 185, 204, 241, 252, 270, 281, 326, 347, 364, 379, 409, 431, 438, 460, 464, 470, 476, 486, 492, 495, 502, 508, 512, 517, 524, 530, 534, 538, 562, 575, 598, 630, 649, 658, 670, 687, 738, 779, 804, 832, 852, 878
Reading Comprehension (Test Practice), 130–133, 306–309, 450–451, 550–551, 610–612
Refrain, 486, **509,** 512, **527,** 530, 980, **988**
Reliable first-person narrator, **138**
Repetition, 347, 512, **527,** 551, 738, 832
Resolution, **3,** 19, 651, 720, **754,** 878, 982
Rhyme, **504,** 505, **506,** 508, 534, 551, 562, 980, **988**
approximate, **504,** 988
end, **504,** 988
exact, **504**
internal, **504,** 518, 524, 988
Rhyme scheme, **506,** 508, 988
Rhythm, **503,** 505, 538, 562, 980, **988**
Rising action, **754,** 804
Romance, 649, **651,** 658, 743, **988**
Round character, **75**
Run-on lines, **752**
Satire, **154,** 161, 598, **989**
Scanning poetry, **503,** 524, 534
Scene design, **721–722,** 852, **989**
Sensory images, 564
Sentence structure, **556–557**
Sestet, 989
Sets, 722, 723, 747–748, 989
Setting, 19, **44–45, 46,** 53, **140,** 152, 165, 185, 476, 575, 687, 747–748, 804, 852, 986, **989**
Shakespearean sonnet, 493
Short story, **989**
Simile, 470, **477,** 478, **479,** 502, 538, 571, 983
comparing, 481, **989**
extended, 479, 481, 497, 502
Situational irony, **314,** 315, 316, 326, 328, 347, 349, 364, 984
Soliloquy, **75, 722,** 771, 783, 803, 804, 832, **989**
Sonnet, 493, 495, 987, **989**
Italian (Petrarchan), 989
See also Shakespearean sonnet.
Sound effects, 505, 524, 538, 562
Speaker, **465,** 470, 476, 481, 486, 492, 495, 502, 508, 517, 530, 534, 538, **990**
Spondee, **503,** 985
Stage, **722**

Stage directions, **722–723,** 758, 759, 760, 762, 764, 767, 768, 771, 783, 784, 786, 796, 800, 807, 819, 836, 849, 854
Staging the Play, 755, 758, 759, 760, 762, 763, 764, 765, 767, 768, 769, 771, 773, 775, 783, 784, 786, 788, 790, 791, 793, 795, 796, 798, 799, 800, 801, 803, 807, 808, 809, 810, 811, 812, 813, 814, 817, 818, 819, 820, 822, 823, 824, 825, 826, 829, 830, 837, 841, 843, 844, 845, 846, 847, 849, 850, 852, 854, 859, 861, 862, 866, 869, 871
Stanza, **990**
Static character, **96**
Stock character, **75**
Story map, 687
Structure of poetry, **518**
Style, **556–557, 558,** 562, 563, 575, 586, 598, 612, **982, 990**
evaluating, **556–557, 610–612**
Subjective writing, **328,** 347
Subjectivity, 364
Subordinate character, **96,** 119, 980
Subtitle, 379
Subtlety, **374,** 379, 979
Summarizing, 19, 41, 152, 185, **272,** 281, 379, **651,** 653, 655, 656, 658, 670, 833
Supporting details, 272
Suspense, 3, 19, 185, 347, 409, 804, 983, **990**
Symbol, **398, 400,** 433, 451, 524, 598, **990**
public symbols, 990
Symbolic meaning, 400, 409, **433,** 438, 451
Symbolism, **398–399,** 409, 438, 450–451
Tall tale, 990. *See also* Folk tale.
Tanka, **489,** 492
Text structure, **328,** 347
Theme, 19, 119, 161, **230–231,** 232, 233, 241, 243, 252, 255, 256, 265, 270, 281, 309, 315, 399, 409, 438, 464, 534, **557,** 562, 586, 598, 612, 630, 986, **990**
compare and contrast, **232,** 252, 254
compare and contrast, across genres, **255, 283,** 306–309
generalization, 231, **233,** 241
genres, 230, 255, 256, 270, 283, 309
See also Ambiguous theme, Universal theme.
Third-person-limited point of view, **138–139, 163,** 169, 185
Time and sequence
chronological order, 3, 4, 19, 41, 347, 649
flashback, **3, 31,** 41, 564, 630, 721
flash-forward, **3**
foreshadowing, **3, 31,** 41, 53, 326, 832, 849

Time frame, 44
Time line, 649
Title, 41, 86, 109, 152, 185, 231, 241, 252, 270, 316, 326, 379, 508, 738
Tone, **44, 139,** 152, 161, 185, 309, 465, 470, **471,** 476, 495, 502, 530, 534, **557, 558,** 562, 586, 598, 612, 630, 758, 798, 822, 981, **991**
Tragedy, **720–721,** 743, **754,** 804, 832, 852, 872, 878, 981, 982, **991**
five-part structure, **754**
Tragedy structure, 754
Tragic ending, 832
Tragic flaw, **720,** 754, 873, 991
Tragic hero, **720,** 872, 878
Trochee, **503,** 985
Turning point, **754,** 832
Universal theme, 231, 241, **991**
comparing, **232**
Verbal irony, **314,** 315, 984
Verse, free, **513,** 517
Visualizing, 804
Vivid verbs, 538
Voice, **139, 193,** 204, 465, **991**

INFORMATIONAL READING SKILLS

Accuracy, 633, 995
checking for, 366
Analyzing, 28–29, 66–69, **88,** 92, 94–95, 191, 210, 222–225, 290–291, 372, 390–393, 416, 583–584, **632–633,** 634, 635, 636, 638, 639, 641, 642–643, 712–715, 886–887, 902–903, 912, 915, 920, 926, 931, 938–939
collaboration agreement, 917, 918
functional workplace documents, 916–919
music lead sheet, 917
Anecdote, 21, 284, **979,** 993
Annotated photograph, 351
Argument, 291, 577, 584, **993**
evaluating, **284, 577–578,** 579, 581, 881, 882, 885, 902–903
graphic, 285, 584
Attitude, 69
Audience, 411, 633, 881, 887
Author's intent, **577–578**
Autobiography, **980**
Bias, 366, 633
Bibliography, 88
Biography, **980**
Block method of organization, **254,** 283
chart, 254
Body of essay, 254, 283
Business letter, 939
writing, 934–937
Call to action, **577–578,** 583
Citation, Internet, 921, 926, 938, 939
Claim, 284, 290, 291, 577, 583, 882, 903, 993, **994,** 1000

Clear organization, 909
Collaboration agreement, 917, 918, 938
   analyzing, 917, 918
Compare and contrast, 21, **254,** 411, 416, 636, 638, 931, **994**
Comparing, 283
   themes across genres, **255, 283,** 306
   universal themes, 254
Comparison-contrast essay, **254, 283**
Computer database, 206
Conclusion of essay, 254, 283
Connecting to sources, 411
Connecting to the Literature, 21, 88, 187, 206, 285, 366, 411, 578, 633, 881
Consumer documents, 908, 931, 939, **994**
   purpose of, 930
   reading, 927–931
Consumer Web sites, 922–923
Contract, 909, 917, 927
   example, 928
Contrast, compare and. See Compare and contrast.
Credentials of sources, checking, 366
Credibility, 284, 291, 411, 577, 578, 584, 633, 881, 885, 887, **995**
Design elements, of workplace documents, 919
Dictionary, **996**
   definitions, 996
   entry word, 996
   examples, 996
   other forms, 996
   part-of-speech label, 996
   pronunciation, 996
   related word forms, 996
   special-usage labels, 996
   synonyms and antonyms, 996
   word origin, 996
Elaborating, **88,** 254, 283, 633, 636, 638
Elements
   of consumer documents, 927, 928, 929, 931
   of drama, 881
Emotional appeal, **284,** 286, **577,** 581
Essay, **982**
   comparison-contrast, **254, 283**
Evaluating, **88,** 90, 91, 93, 94, 191, 633, 635, 641
   arguments, **284, 577–578,** 579, 581, **881,** 882, 885, 902–903
   evidence, **284–285,** 287, 288, 289, 291, 577, 580, 584, 881, 885
   logic of functional documents, 909
   sources, **88,** 206, 411, 633
Evidence, **284–285,** 287, 288, 289, 291, 577, 584, 881, 883, 885, 903, 995
   evaluating, 287, 288, 289, 580, 881, 885, **996**
   supporting, 21, 28, 69, 881
   expert testimony, 997
   statistics, 997

Extended-service contract, 928, 939
Facts, 88, 366, 577, 578, 580, 584, 633
Fallacious reasoning, 997
   begging the question, 997
   either-or fallacy, 997
   false cause and effect, 998
   hasty generalization, 997
   name-calling, 997
   stereotyping, 997
FCC (Federal Communications Commission) Information, 930, 939
Features of consumer documents, 927, 928, 931
5W-How? questions, 187
Functional documents, 909, 938
   evaluating logic of, 909
Functional workplace documents, 916, 920, 938
   analyzing, 916–919
   format, 919
   graphic elements of, 919
   sequence, 919
   structure, 919
Generalization, 284, 287, 288, 289, 881, **994, 998**
   valid generalization, 998
Genres, comparing themes across, **255, 283**
Graphic organizers
   annotated photograph, 351
   block-method chart, 254
   evaluating chart, 285
   informational materials chart, 908
   opinion/claim chart, 577
   point-by-point-method chart, 283
   source chart, 632
   synthesis chart, 411
   theme chart, 255
Graphs, **998**
   bar graph, 998
   line graph, 998
   pie graph, 998
Informational materials, using, 908
Informative texts, **999**
Instruction manual, 927
   example, 914, 929
Instructions. See Functional documents.
Intent, **285, 881,** 903
   author's, **577–578,** 995
Internet, 920, 921, 926, 930
   citations, 921–925, 926, 938, 939
   search engine, 206, 210
   search term, 206, 210
   using, **206,** 210, 366
Legally binding document, 919
Letter, business. See Business letter.
Library, **206,** 210
Loaded words, 284, 286, 290, 993
Logic, **999**
Logical appeal, 284, **577,** 581, 993
Logical sequence, 909, 912, 913, 919, 920, 938, **999**

highest-to-lowest, 909
lowest-to-highest, 909
point-by-point, 909, 919
step-by-step, 909, 919
See also Methods of organization.
Main idea, 21, 28, 69, 88, 94, 187, 191, 255, 393, 411, 577, 632, 919, **1000**
Methods of organization of comparison-contrast essay
   block, **254,** 283
   point-by-point, 254, **283**
   See also Logical sequence.
Minutes of a meeting, 933
Modern Language Association (MLA), 922, 926, 939
Music lead sheet, 916
   analyzing, 917
Nonfiction book, 206
Note cards, using, 924
Numerical header of workplace documents, 919
Objective sources, 411
Objective text, 633
Opinion, 88, 90, 284, 366, 577, 583, 633, 881, 882, 884, 885, 886, 993
   chart, 577
Opinion statement, 881, 886, 903
Oral history, 89, 94
Organizational patterns. See Logical sequence, Methods of organization.
Paraphrasing, 21, 29, 288, 411, 416, 882, **1002**
   summary, 1002
Periodicals, 206
Persuasion, **987**
Persuasive purpose, 881
Persuasive writing, **577–578**
Point-by-point logical sequence, 909, 919
Point-by-point method of organization, 254, **283**
   chart, 283
Primary source, **88,** 89, 91, **632–633,** 634, 637, 639, 712–715, **1002**
Procedures for conducting a meeting, 933
Product information, 927
   example, 930
Product review, 909
Public documents, 908, **1002**
Public Web sites, 922
Purpose, 411, 416, 632, 642, 715, 881, 903, 938, 939
Reader misunderstanding, 912
Readers' Guide to Periodical Literature, 206
Reading
   consumer documents, 927–931
   technical directions, 913
Reading Comprehension (Reading Check), 28, 94, 191, 210, 290, 372, 416, 583, 642, 886, 912, 915, 920, 926, 931

Reading Comprehension (Test Practice), 28–29, 66–69, 94–95, 191, 210, 222–225, 290–291, 372, 390–393, 416, 583–584, 642–643, 712–715, 886–887, 902–903, 912, 915, 920, 926, 931, 938–939
Reasons, 284, 288, 377, 583, 995
Reference materials, 206
Relevance, checking, 366, 995
Repetition, 633
Researching information, **206**
Research questions, generating, **187,** 222–225, **366,** 390–393, **1003**
Rhetorical question, 633, 641
Roman numerals, 919
Secondary source, **88,** 89, 93, 94, **632–633,** 634, 712–715, **1006**
Sources, 210, 632
  connecting to, 411
  credentials of, checking, 366
  evaluating, 206, 390–393, 411
  relevance of, 366
  synthesizing, 66–69, **411,** 416
  timeliness of, checking for, 366
Spatial order, **1003**
Staging, 881
Step-by-step logical sequence, 909, 919
Structure
  of document, 919
  of essay, 903
  of review, 881, 886
  of text, 584, 633
Subheading, 635
Subheads, checking, 187
Subjective sources, 411, 416
Subjective text, 633
Supporting details, 411
Supporting evidence, 21, 28, 69, 881
Synthesis chart, 411
Synthesizing, **21,** 29, 416, **1006**
  sources, 66, **411**
Technical directions, 913, 915, 927, 938
  reading, 913
Technical documents,
  writing, 932–934
Text organizers, **577**
Text structures, **1007**
  causal chain, 1007
  chronological order, 1007
  flowchart, 1007
  logical order, 1007
  order of importance, 1007
  spatial order, 1007
  Venn diagram, 1007
Theme, 255
  comparing, across genres, **255, 283,** 306
  universal, comparing, **254**
Theme chart, 255
Thesis statement, 254
Timeliness of sources, checking for, 366
Tone, 28, 285, 287, **578,** 582, 584, 633, 635, 638, 881, 887, 903, 996

Troubleshooting guide, 929, 931
Universal theme, comparing, **254**
Warranty, 909, 927
Web site, **206,** 366, 920
  external links, 206, 209
  interactive features, 206
  internal links, 206, 207
  links, 206, 207, 209, 210
  multimedia features, 206, 207
  table of contents, 206, 207
Workplace documents, 908, **1007.** See also Functional workplace documents.
Workplace Web sites, 922
Works Cited list, 88, 921, 924, 926, 939
  formatting, 925
  order in, 921, 922
  sample, 923
Writing
  business letters, 934–937
  technical documents, 932–933

VOCABULARY SKILLS

Analogy, **29–30, 365, 410,** 650, **739, 979**
  multiple-choice tests, 971–972
Anglo-Saxon words, 556, **688**
Antonym, 29, 110, **205, 253,** 432, 739
Archaic words, **496,** 752
Comparison, **110,** 599
Connotation, **54,** 186, **282, 631, 739**
Context, **87, 120, 373, 417, 432,** 576, **585, 888**
Context clues, 87, 134, 192, 292, 365, 373, 394, **432,** 576, 585, 716, 888, 995
  definition, 87, 432
  example, 87, 576
  multiple-choice tests, 970–971
  restatement, 87, 432
  using, **162, 327**
Contrast, **110**
Denotation, 54, 739
Derivation, 42, 659, 688. See also Etymologies.
Elizabethan English, 805
Etymologies, 20, **42, 271, 659, 688**
Figurative language, **242, 599**
Graphic organizers
  analogy chart, 30
  antonym map, 253
  cluster diagrams, 120
  context diagram, 87
  meaning map, 192, 631
  prefix chart, 20
  prefix diagram, 20
  pun map, 781
  root-word chart, 599
  semantic map, 192, 417
  suffix chart, 153
  synonym chart, 186

  synonym map, 253
  technical vocabulary chart, 526
  word derivation chart, 672, 688
  word map, 110, 271, 348, 417, 526
  word-root chart, 271, 373, 380, 599
Greek myths, words derived from, **672**
Greek roots, 271, 373
Homophone, 781
Idiom, **242,** 525, **984**
Imagery, **599**
Jargon, **292,** 365, **526**
Latin roots, 271, 373, 380, 556, 599
Legalese, **292**
Literal language, **599**
Meaning map, 192, 631
Metaphor, **242**
Middle English spellings, 659
Multiple-choice tests
  analogy questions, 971–972
  context-clue questions, 970–971
  definition or synonym questions, 970
  multiple-meaning questions, 971
  sentence-completion or fill-in-the-blank questions, 971
Multiple-choice writing questions
  identifying-sentence-errors questions, 972
  improving-sentences questions, 972
  improving-the-paragraph questions, 972
Multiple meanings, 70, 310, 613, 781
  multiple-choice tests, 971
Mythology, words from, **348**
Old English words, 659, 688
Old Norse words, **688**
Prefixes, **20,** 42, **1003**
Pun, **781**
Roman myths, words derived from, **672**
Root word. See Word root.
Semantic map, 192, 417
Signal words, **110**
Simile, **242**
Spanish words, **563**
Suffixes, **153,** 599, **1003**
Synonym, 29, 110, 186, 205, 226, **253, 282,** 365, 432, 452, **631,** 739, 904
  multiple-choice tests, 970
Technical vocabulary, **365,** 526
Test practice, 70, 134, 226, 310, 394, 452, 613, 716, 904
Thesaurus, 110, **186**
Vocabulary development, 20, 29–30, 42, 54, 70, 87, 110, 120, 134, 153, 162, 186, 192, 205, 226, 242, 253, 271, 282, 292, 310, 327, 348, 365, 373, 380, 394, 410, 417, 432, 452, 496, 525–526, 563, 576, 585, 599, 613, 631, 643, 650, 659, 672, 688, 716, 739, 781, 805, 888, 904
Vocabulary for business letter, 934
Vocabulary resource file, **54**
Word analogies. See Analogy.

Word map, 110, **192**, 271, **348, 417,** 526
Word meanings
  changing, **753**
  clarifying, **87, 110, 643**
  verifying, **576**
Word origins, **271, 659**
  See also Etymologies.
Word root, 42, 153, **271, 373, 380,** **599, 1003**

READING SKILLS

Anachronism, 853
Author's purpose. *See* Purpose.
Cause and effect, **4,** 19, 349, 355, 357, 358, 359, 360, 362, 364, **993**
Clarifying the text, 946
Comparing and contrasting, 86, **112,** 119, 270, 438, 658, 738, 852
  theme, across genres, **255**
  themes, **232**
Connections, making, 946
Contrasting, comparing and. *See* Comparing and contrasting.
Credibility, evaluating, **193,** 204
Details, reading for, **400,** 409
Dramatic presentation, 880
Drawing conclusions, **140,** 152
Entertaining, as author's purpose, 256
Fact, multiple-choice tests, 969
Generalization, **233,** 241
Genres, comparing and contrasting theme across, **255**
Gist strategy, 949–950
Graphic organizers
  cause-and-effect diagram, 364
  comparison-and-contrast chart, 232, 255
  key word chart, 951
  re-reading chart, 433
Heading as text structure, 328, 347
Independent Reading (Read On). *See* **Independent Reading.**
Inference, 35, **76, 98,** 109, **243, 374,** 379, 566, 570, **998–999**
  multiple-choice tests, 969
Informing, as author's purpose, 256
Key passages, 46, 161
Literal reading, 438
Loaded words, 46, 161
Main ideas or events, multiple-choice tests for, 969. *See also* Summarizing.
Making predictions. *See* Prediction.
Memorizing, **880**
Monitoring reading, **163, 418,** 420, 421, 422, 424, 425, 427, **564**
Multiple-choice tests
  evaluation questions, 970
  factual-recall questions, 969
  inference questions, 969
  main-idea questions, 969
  strategies, for taking, 967
Notes, taking, 944

Opinion, multiple-choice tests, 970
Paraphrasing, 833, **1002**
Persuading, as author's purpose, 256
Predictions, **31,** 33, 38, 41, 165, 170, **316,** 326, 425, **724,** 738, 946
Purpose, **46,** 53, **154,** 161, **256,** 258, 262, 265, 270
Questioning, **163,** 165, 167, 169, 170, 173, 174, 176, 180, 183, 185, **418,** **558,** 562
Questioning the text, 946
Reading checkpoints, 944
Reading for details, **400,** 409
Reading rate, 951–953
  determining strategies for improving, 953
  varying, 952
Re-reading, **400, 433,** 438, 948
Result, 355, 358. *See also* Cause and effect.
Retelling, 947
Rewording, 948
Setting a purpose for reading (Before You Read), 4, 31, 46, 76, 98, 112, 140, 154, 163, 193, 233, 243, 256, 272, 316, 328–329, 349, 374, 400, 418, 433, 458, 461, 465, 471, 479, 482, 484, 487, 489, 493, 497, 506, 509, 513, 518, 521, 527, 531, 535, 558, 564, 586, 620, 644, 651, 724, 754–755
Setting a purpose for reading (Reading Informational Materials), 21, 88, 187, 206, 284–285, 366, 411, 577–578, 632–633, 881, 909, 913, 916–919, 921–922, 927
Style, appreciating a writer's, **586**
Summarizing, **272,** 281, 347, 438, **651,** 653, 655, 658, 833, 949–950
Supporting details, 272, 281
Text structures, **328,** 347. *See also* Heading.
Think-Aloud strategy, 946
Visualizing, 421, 945, 946

WRITING SKILLS

Accuracy, 643, 707
Action, 57
Action verbs, 57, 71, 608, 961
Active voice, 300, 961
Adjective clauses, 446
Adverbs, 128
Aesthetic effects, 892
Alliteration, 534
Ambiguity, 379, 442
American Psychological Association (APA), 693
Anachronism, 853
Analogy, 214, 295
Analysis log, 383
Analysis of problems and solutions, **212–219**

building an argument for, 214
considering purpose and audience for, 212
evaluating and revising, 217–218
finding a problem to analyze for, 212
investigating the problem and solutions for, 213
peer review of, 217
prewriting, 212–214
proofreading, 219
publishing, 219
reflecting on writing of, 219
writer's framework, 215
writer's model, 215–216
writing first draft of, 215–216
writing your thesis statement for, 214
Analysis of a short story, **440–447**
  analyzing the story and developing a thesis for, 440–441
  choosing a story for, 440
  evaluating and revising, 445–446
  gathering and organizing support for, 441–442
  peer review of, 445
  prewriting, 440–442
  proofreading, 447
  publishing, 447
  reflecting on writing of, 447
  writer's framework, 443
  writer's model, 443–444
  writing first draft of, 443–444
Analyzing, 212
  film techniques, 891
  the information for research paper, 696–697
  narrative techniques, 890–891
  the story and developing a thesis for analysis of a short story, 440–441
  style, 575
Anecdote, 122, 123, 214, 295
Answering research questions for research paper, 692–693
Appearance, 541
  specific, 57
Appropriate modifiers, 961
Argument, 295
  outline, 584
Article, 29, 210
Association, 433
Audience, 56, 127, 212, 219, 294–295, 299, 387, 447, 540, 691, 709
  considering your, for persuasive essay, 294–295
Audiotapes, 692
Autobiographical incident, 204
Autobiographical narrative, **56–63**
  choosing an experience for, 56
  considering purpose and audience for, 56
  evaluating and revising, 61–62
  gathering details for, 56–57
  organizing details for, 58

peer review of, 61
prewriting, 56–58
proofreading, 63
publishing, 63
reflecting on writing of, 63
reflecting on your experience for, 58
writer's framework, 59
writer's model, 59–60
writing first draft of, 59–60
Bar graph, 966
Beginning
    of biographical narrative, 125
    of short story, 605
Bias, 212, 295, 643
Bibliography, 698
Biographical narrative, 119, **122–129,** 976
    choosing a subject for, 122–123
    creating a controlling impression for, 123
    defined, 122
    evaluating and revising, 127–128
    peer review of, 127
    planning organization and pacing for, 124
    prewriting, 122–124
    proofreading, 129
    publishing, 129
    reflecting on writing of, 129
    writer's framework, 125
    writer's model, 125–126
    writing first draft, 125–126
Biographical sketch, 281
Block, 963
Block method of organization, 254, 283, 384
    modified, 384
Body
    of analysis of problems and solutions, 215
    of analysis of a short story, 443
    of autobiographical narrative, 59
    of comparison-contrast essay, 254, 283
    of comparison of media genres, 385
    of comparison of a play and a film, 893
    of description of a person, 543
    of persuasive essay, 297
    of research paper, 701
Brainstorming, 56, 120, 212, 538, 586
Brief report, 347, 364
Browsing, 890
Building an argument for analysis of problems and solutions, 214
Bullet, 963
Business letter
    format of, 934, 935
    sample, 936, 937
    writing, 934–937
Callout, 963
Camera shots and angles, 891, 892
Captions, 671
Card catalog, 692
Cartoon panels, 671

Case
    small caps, 964
    uppercase, 964
Case study, 214, 295
CD-ROMs, 692, 695
Ceremony essay, 416
Character, 441, 602–603, 804, 891
Character analysis, 326, 879
Character sketch, 109, 119
Charts, 965
Choosing
    an experience for autobiographical narrative, 56
    a film and focusing on one scene for comparison of a play and a film, 890
    an issue for persuasive essay, 294
    a news event for comparison of media genres, 382
    a story for analysis of a short story, 440
    a subject
        for biographical narrative, 122–123
        for description of a person, 540
        and refining a topic for research paper, 690–691
Chronological order, 58, 71, 124, 214, 442, 603, 697, 959
Clarity, 933, 934
Clear and distinctive perspective, 540
Clear thesis statement, 384
Cliché, 218
Climax, 440, 603
Clincher sentence, 957
Coherence, 959, 994
Coherent thesis statement, 384
Colleges, 692
Columns, 963
Commonly accepted beliefs, 214
Comparing, 254, 283
    coverage for comparison of media genres, 382–383
    the film to the play for comparison of a play and a film, 890–892
    themes, 252, 281
    universal themes, 254
Comparison-contrast chart, 438, 470, 486, 512, 525
Comparison-contrast essay, **254, 283,** 438, 470, 486, 512, 525, 671, 804, 879
    revising, 283
Comparison of media genres, **382–389**
    choosing a news event for, 382
    comparing coverage for, 382–383
    developing a thesis for, 384
    evaluating and revising, 387–388
    peer review of, 387, 388
    prewriting, 382–384
    proofreading, 389
    publishing, 389
    reflecting on writing of, 389
    writer's framework, 385
    writer's model, 385–386
    writing first draft of, 385–386

Comparison of a play and a film, **890–897**
    choosing a film and focusing on one scene for, 890
    comparing the film to the play for, 890–892
    evaluating and revising, 895–896
    gathering evidence and organizing for, 892
    peer review of, 895
    prewriting, 890–892
    proofreading, 897
    publishing, 897
    reflecting on writing of, 897
    writer's framework, 893
    writer's model, 893–894
    writing first draft of, 893–894
    writing your thesis statement for, 892
Complexity, 442
Concern, 212
Conciseness, 933
Conclusion
    of analysis of problems and solutions, 215
    of analysis of a short story, 443
    of autobiographical narrative, 59
    of comparison-contrast essay, 254, 283
    of comparison of media genres, 385
    of comparison of a play and a film, 893
    of description of a person, 543
    of persuasive essay, 297
    of research paper, 701
Concrete details, 541
Concrete sensory details. See Sensory details
Conflict, 440, **603**
    external, 603
    internal, 603
Conflict-comparison paragraph, 252
Conflict-resolution rules, 932, 933
Connotation, 433
Considering your purpose and audience
    for analysis of problems and solutions, 212
    for autobiographical narrative, 56
    for description of a person, 540
    for persuasive essay, 294–295
Contrast, 963
Contrasting, 254, 283
Controlling impression, 58, 123, 541
Correctness, 933
Counterargument, 295
Counterclaim, 212, 295
Creating a controlling impression for biographical narrative, 123
Creative nonfiction, 241
Credibility, 643, 700
Crediting your sources for research paper, 698–699
Critical review, 879
Definitions, 933
Description, 540, 687, **981**
    of an object, 492

of a person, 524, **540–547**
of a point of view, 517
in a setting, 599
Description of a person, 524, **540–547**
   choosing a subject for, 540
   considering purpose and audience
      for, 540
   determining a controlling impression
      for, 541–542
   evaluating and revising, 545–546
   gathering your details for, 541
   organizing your description for, 542
   peer review of, 545
   prewriting, 540–542
   proofreading, 547
   publishing, 547
   reflecting on writing, 547
   writer's framework, 543
   writer's model, 543–544
   writing first draft for, 543–544
Descriptive paragraph, 161
Designing Your Writing, 963–966
Detail list, 57
Details, 123, 441, 521, 541, 542, 696,
      879, 896
   chart, 458, 460, 671
Determining a controlling impression
      for description of a person,
      541–542
Developing
   research questions for research
      paper, 691–692
   a thesis for comparison of media
      genres, 384
Diagrams, 965
Dialogue, 57, 123, 603, 609, 738, 891
Diction, 441, 575
Dictionary, 432
   of idioms, 525
Direct quotation, 442, 695, 700
Direct reference, 960
Editorial, 21, 29
Editor in Charge: Content and
      Organization
   analysis of problems and solutions, 217
   analysis of a short story, 445
   autobiographical narrative, 61
   biographical narrative, 127
   comparison of media genres, 387
   comparison of a play and a film, 895
   description of a person, 545
   persuasive essay, 299
   research paper, 707
   short story, 607
Editor in Charge: Style Guidelines
   analysis of problems and solutions, 218
   analysis of a short story, 446
   autobiographical narrative, 62
   biographical narrative, 128
   comparison of media genres, 388
   comparison of a play and a film, 896
   description of a person, 546
   persuasive essay, 300
   research paper, 708

short story, 608
Elaborating, 441, 442
   for comparison-contrast essay, 254,
      283
   on newspaper article, 270
Elements of fiction, 440
   chart, 440–441
Emotional appeal, 214, 295, 780
Emphasis, 964
Encyclopedia, 691, 692
Encyclopedia article, 694
Encyclopedia yearbooks, 692
End
   of biographical narrative, 125
   of short story, 605
Endnote, 698
Essay, 409, 495, 562, 575, 630, 643,
      649, 671, 780
   of comparison and contrast, 470,
      486, 512, 525
   of opinion, 464
Ethical appeal, 214, 295
Etymologies, 42
Evaluating writing. See Revising
Evaluation of speech, 901
Event outline, 57
Events, 57
Evidence, 213, 214, 295, 696, 779,
      892
   chart, 295
   relevant, 296
   reliable, 296
   representative, 296
   trusting, for persuasive essay,
      295–296
Example, 214, 295, 495, 933
Example words, 271
Expectation, 212, 691
Expert opinion, 214, 295
Exposition, 212
   analysis of problems and solutions,
      212–219
   analysis of a short story, **440–447**
   comparison of media genres,
      382–389
   comparison of a play and a film,
      890–897
   research paper, 671, **690–709**
Expository composition, 977
External conflict, 603
Facts, 214, 295, 696
Factual details, 57, 541
Fantastic story, 598
Fiction, elements of, 440
Figurative details, 541
Figurative language, 57, 441, 538, 604
Figures of speech, 478
   metaphor, 57, 478, 541
   personification, 57, 478, 541
   pun, 781
   simile, 57, 478, 541
Film techniques, analyzing, 891
Finding
   an idea for short story, 602–604

a problem to analyze for analysis of
      problems and solutions, 212
First-person point of view, 604
5W-How? questions, 213, 512
Flashback, 58, 603
Flowchart, 965
Focus, 57, 61, 384
Font, 964
   decorative, 964
   sans serif, 964
   script, 964
   serif, 964
   size, 964
   styles, 964
   types of, 964
Footnote, 698
Formality, 387
   less, 127
Formal outline, 697–698
Formal style, 934
Format of business letter, 934, 935
Free-verse poem, 517, 538
Freewriting, 400
Gathering
   and organizing for comparison of a
      play and a film, 892
   and organizing support for analysis of
      a short story, 441–442
   your details for autobiographical nar-
      rative, 56–57
   your details for description of a per-
      son, 541
   See also Evidence.
General reference books, 692
Gestures, 57
Graphic organizers
   analysis log, 383
   argument outline, 584
   bar graphs, 966
   body paragraph structure, 958
   comparison-contrast chart, 438, 470,
      486, 512, 525
   detail chart, 458, 460, 671
   detail list, 57
   diagram, 965
   elements of fiction chart, 440–441
   event outline, 57
   evidence chart, 295
   image chart, 433
   key-points chart, 442
   news-story chart, 476
   person chart, 558
   pie chart, 965
   problem chart, 213
   significance/anecdotes chart, 122
   sonnet chart, 495
   source chart, 643
   story map, 431
   style-element chart, 575
   support chart, 296
   symbol chart, 409
   think sheet, 387
   time line, 347
Graphic programs, 897

Graphics, incorporating, 301
Graphs, 966, **998**
Heading, 963
Headline for news story, 512
Historical societies, 692
Hyperlink, 709
Illustrations, 966
Imagery, 123, 433, 441, 508, 604, 687
    chart, 433
Incorporating graphics, 301
Indirect source, 699
Instructions, 530
Integrating direct quotations into your
    research paper, 700
Interior monologue, 57, 123, 603
Internal conflict, 603
Internet, 347, 609, 658, 690
Internet bulletin board, 301
Interview, 270, 694
Introduction
    of analysis of problems and solutions,
        215
    of analysis of a short story, 443
    of autobiographical narrative, 59
    of comparison-contrast essay, 254, 283
    of comparison of media genres, 385
    of comparison of a play and a film, 893
    of description of a person, 543
    of persuasive essay, 297
    of research paper, 701
Investigating the problem and solutions
    for analysis of problems and solu-
    tions, 213
"I remember" sentences, 530
Issue, 294
Journal entry, 152, 270, 492, 852
Key points, 441
    chart, 442
Layout, 963
Letter, 21, 476, 492
    of complaint, 934
Library, 690, 692, 890
Lighting, 891, 892
Line graphs, 966
List of questions, 658
Literary analysis, 440
Literary present tense, 442
Loaded words, 779–780
Logical appeal, 214, 295
Logical order, 542, 697, 933, 959
Logical reasoning, 214
Magazine article, 694
Main ideas, 643
Maps, 966
Metaphor, 57, 478, 541
Meter, 508
Method of organization
    block, 254, 283, 384
    point-by-point, 254, 283, 384, 892
Microfilm or microfiche, 692
Middle
    of biographical narrative, 125
    of short story, 605
Minutes of a meeting, 933

Misunderstanding, 212
Models. See Writer's Models
Modern Language Association of
    America (MLA), 693
Modified-block style of organization,
    384, 934
Mood, 53, 575
Movie recording, 694
Multiple-choice writing questions, 972
    identifying-sentence-error questions,
        972
    improving-sentences questions, 972
    improving-the-paragraph questions,
        973
Museums, 692
Narration, **986**
    autobiographical narrative, 56–63
    biographical narrative, 119, **122–129**
    short story, 270, **602–609**
Narrative, 19
Narrative poem, 63
Narrative techniques, analyzing,
    890–891
National Newspaper Index, 692
New scene, 832
Newspaper article, 270, 694
News story, 512
    chart, 476
Nonfiction, creative, 241
Notes, taking, 122, 409, 433, 438
Nuance, 442
Ode, 502
Online catalog, 692
Online services, 692
Online source, 695
Onomatopoeia, 538
Opening paragraph, 139
Opinion, 41, 630, **1000**
    supporting your, for persuasive essay,
        295–296
    valid opinion, 1000
Opinion essay, 464
Opinion statement, 294
Order of importance, 214, 296, 442,
    542, 697, 892, 959, **1000**
    chronological, 58, 71, 124, 214, 442,
        603, 697
    logical, 542, 697, 933
    spatial, 542
Organizational pattern, 442
Organizational strategies, 124
Organizing
    persuasive essay, 296
    your description for description of a
        person, 542
    your ideas for research paper, 697–698
Outlining, 347, **1000**
    formal outline, 1000
    informal outline, 1000
Pace, 58, 124, 603
Page design, 963
Pamphlet, 301
Paragraph, 957
    comparing conflicts, 252

comparing poems, 481
creating a mood, 575
discussing sound effects in poetry, 505
parts of a body, 957
qualities of, 959
Paraphrasing, 29, 295, 442, 695, **1000**
    summary, 1000
Parenthetical citation, 698
Peer review
    of analysis of problems and solutions,
        217
    of analysis of a short story, 445
    of autobiographical narrative, 61
    of biographical narrative, 127
    of comparison of media genres, 387,
        388
    of comparison of a play and a film, 895
    of description of a person, 545
    of persuasive essay, 299
    of research paper, 707
    of short story, 607
Periodicals, 129
Personal letter, 934
Person chart, 558
Personification, 57, 478, 541
Perspectives, shifting, 57
Persuading, 212
Persuasion
    persuasive essay, 281, **294–301**
Persuasive composition, 978
Persuasive essay, 281, **294–301**
    choosing an issue for, 294
    considering your purpose and audi-
        ence for, 294–295
    evaluating and revising, 299–300
    organizing, 296
    peer review of, 299
    prewriting, 294–296
    proofreading, 301
    publishing, 301
    reflecting on writing of, 301
    stating your position for, 294
    supporting your opinion for, 295–296
    trusting evidence for, 295–296
    writer's framework, 297
    writer's model, 297–298
    writing first draft of, 297–298
Persuasive techniques, 779–780
Pie chart, 965
Plagiarism, 696
Planning organization and pacing for
    biographical narrative, 124
Plot, 440, 602, 603, 891, 892
Poem, 270, 476, 481, 492, 508, 525, 534
Point-by-point method of organization,
    254, 283, 384, 892
Point of view, 602, 604, 696
    first person, 604
    third person limited, 604
    third person omniscient, 604
Points of comparison, 382
Potential misunderstandings, 691
Precise language, 541, 546, 961
Prequel, 152, 379

Prewriting
  analysis of problems and solutions, 212–214
  analysis of a short story, 440–442
  autobiographical narrative, 56–58
  biographical narrative, 122–124
  comparison of media genres, 382–384
  comparison of a play and a film, 890–892
  description of a person, 540–542
  persuasive essay, 294–296
  research paper, 690–700
  short story, 602–604
Primary source, 693
Problem chart, 213
Problem-solution essay, 185
Procedures for conducting a meeting, 933
Proofreading
  analysis of problems and solutions, 219
  analysis of a short story, 447
  autobiographical narrative, 63
  biographical narrative, 129
  comparison of media genres, 389
  comparison of a play and a film, 897
  description of a person, 547
  persuasive essay, 301
  research paper, 709
  short story, 609
Prose poem, 460
Pruning prose, 282
Publishing
  analysis of problems and solutions, 219
  analysis of a short story, 447
  autobiographical narrative, 63
  biographical narrative, 129
  comparison of media genres, 389
  comparison of a play and a film, 897
  description of a person, 547
  persuasive essay, 301
  research paper, 709
  short story, 609
Publishing software, 897
Purpose, 56, 127, 212, 299, 387, 540, 691, 962
  considering your, for persuasive essay, 294–295
Questions, 210
Quick guide!
  analyzing elements of fiction, 440–441
  analyzing film techniques, 891
  analyzing narrative techniques, 891
  connecting ideas, 960
  font categories, 964
  guidelines for giving credit within a paper, 699
  guidelines for proofreading, 956
  guidelines for recording source information, 694–695
  kinds of evidence, 214
  library and community resources, 692
  parts of paragraphs, 957
  points of comparison, 383

points of view, 604
recording character details, 602–603
stages of the writing process, 955
symbols for revising and proofreading, 956
types of order, 959
Quickwrite, 4, 19, 31, 41, 46, 53, 76, 86, 98, 109, 112, 119, 140, 152, 154, 161, 163, 185, 193, 204, 233, 241, 243, 252, 256, 270, 272, 281, 316, 326, 329, 347, 349, 364, 374, 379, 400, 409, 418, 431, 433, 438, 458, 460, 461, 464, 465, 470, 471, 476, 479, 481, 482, 486, 489, 492, 493, 495, 497, 502, 513, 517, 527, 530, 531, 534, 535, 536, 558, 562, 564, 575, 586, 598, 620, 630, 644, 649, 651, 658, 660, 670, 673, 687, 724, 738, 755, 779, 878
Quotations, 295
Radio program, 694
Readers' Guide to Periodical Literature, 691, 692
Reasons, 214
Recording information for research paper, 693–696
References, 891
  to the text, 442
Reflecting on writing
  analysis of problems and solutions, 219
  analysis of a short story, 447
  autobiographical narrative, 63
  biographical narrative, 129
  comparison of media genres, 389
  comparison of a play and a film, 897
  description of a person, 547
  persuasive essay, 301
  research paper, 709
  short story, 609
Reflecting on your experience for autobiographical narrative, 58
Relationship analysis, 109
Relevant evidence, 296
Reliable evidence, 296
Repetition, 780
Reply to letter, 937
Representative evidence, 296
Research, 658, 671, 690
Research paper, 671, **690–709**
  analyzing the information for, 696–697
  answering research questions for, 692–693
  choosing a subject and refining a topic for, 690–691
  crediting your sources for, 698–699
  developing research questions for, 691–692
  evaluating and revising, 707–708
  integrating direct quotations into your paper for, 700
  organizing your ideas for, 697–698
  peer review of, 707

prewriting, 690–700
proofreading, 709
publishing, 709
recording information for, 693–696
reflecting on writing, 709
thinking about purpose, audience, and tone for, 691
writer's framework, 701
writer's model, 701–706
writing a first draft of, 701–706
writing a thesis statement for, 697
Research questions, 191, 372, 692
Research report, 21
Resolution, 440, 603
Response to expository text, 975
Response to literature, 974
Response to poem, 495
Retelling events, 270
Revising, 961–962
  analysis of problems and solutions, 217–218
  analysis of a short story, 445–446
  autobiographical narrative, 61–62
  biographical narrative, 127–128
  comparison-contrast essay, 283
  comparison of media genres, 387–388
  comparison of a play and a film, 895–896
  persuasive essay, 299–300
  research paper, 707–708
  short story, 607–608
Rewriting
  as first-person narrator, 185
  paragraphs, 43, 95, 111, 253, 327
  sentences, 557
  thesis, 220
Rhetorical devices, 214, 295
Rising action, 603
Scenarios, 933
Schools, 692
Script, 534
Secondary source, 693
Sensory details, 19, 57, 71, 123, 538, 541, 547, 575, 604, 896, 961
Sensory images, 524
Sentence length, varying, 388
Sequel, 379
Sequence of events, 57, 124
Setting, 53, 123, 409, 440, 575, 602, 604, 891, 892
Shifting perspectives, 57
Short essay, 291
Short story, 270, **602–609**
  evaluating and revising, 607–608
  finding an idea for, 602–604
  peer review of, 607
  prewriting, 602–604
  proofreading, 609
  publishing, 609
  reflecting on writing of, 609
  writer's framework, 605
  writer's model, 605–606
  writing first draft, 605–606

Significance, 58, 122
    chart, 122
Significant ideas, 442
Simile, 57, 478, 541
Song, 270
Sonnet chart, 495
Sound and music, 891, 892
Sound effects, 538
Sources
    chart, 643
    recording, 694
Spatial order of importance, 542
Spatial organization, 124, 959
Special effects, 891
Specialized reference books, 692
Specific appearances, 57
Specificity, 933
Specific places, 57, 123, 604
Speech, 21
Stage directions, 723
Standard-English equivalents, 95
Stating your position for persuasive
    essay, 294
Statistics, 214, 295
Story, 431
    map, 431
Story-symbol essay, 409
Style, 896, 934
    analyzing, 575
Style-element chart, 575
Stylistic devices, 441
Subheading, 963
Subtlety, 379
Summarizing, 643
Summary, 347, 442, 695
Support chart, 296
Supporting details, 442
Supporting sentence, 957
Supporting your opinion for persuasive
    essay, 295–296
Symbolic meaning, 409
Symbolism, 409
    chart, 409
Synthesizing, 29, 696
Technical documents, writing, 932–934
Technical terms, 365
Test practice, 71, 135, 227, 311, 395,
    453, 542–543, 614–615, 717, 905
Test Smarts
    biographical narrative, 976
    expository composition, 977
    persuasive composition, 978
    response to expository text, 975
    response to literature, 974
Theme, 441, 602, 604, 891
    comparing, 252, 281
        across genres, 283
        universal, 254
Thesis, 384, 441
Thesis statement, 214, 254, 283, 441,
    697, 879, 892
Thinking about purpose, audience, and
    tone for research paper, 691
Think sheet, 299, 387, 445, 895

Third-person-limited point of view,
    604
Third-person-omniscient point of view,
    604
Time line, 347, 966
Title
    of poem, 508
    of popular song, 509
Tone, 71, 299, 441, 502, 691, 892, 934,
    961
Topic, 671
Topic sentence, 957
Transitional expressions, 58, 960
Trusting evidence for persuasive essay,
    295–296
TV program, 694
Type, 966
Unity, 959
Universal theme, comparing, **254**
Vague modifier, 62
Video recording, 694
Videotapes, 692
Visuals, 697, 965
Vivid verbs, 608
Vocabulary, 934
Web site, 447
    creating, 897
White space, 963
Word choice, 961
Word processing and desktop publish-
    ing. See Designing Your Writing
    incorporating visuals, 301
Works Cited list, 693, 694, 698, 699, 709
World Wide Web, 692
Writer's Models
    analysis of problems and solutions,
        215–216
    analysis of a short story, 443–444
    autobiographical narrative, 59–60
    biographical narrative, 125–126
    comparison of media genres, 385–386
    comparison of a play and a film,
        893–894
    description of a person, 543–544
    persuasive essay, 297–298
    research paper, 701–706
    short story, 605–606
Writing
    business letters, 934–937
    technical documents, 932–934
    your thesis statement
        for analysis of problems and solu-
            tions, 214
        for comparison of a play and a film,
            892
        for research paper, 697
Writing first draft
    of analysis of problems and solutions,
        215–216
    of analysis of a short story, 443–444
    of autobiographical narrative, 59–60
    of biographical narrative, 125–126
    of comparison of media genres,
        385–386

    of comparison of a play and a film,
        893–894
    of description of a person, 543–544
    of persuasive essay, 297–298
    of research paper, 701–706
    of short story, 605–606
Writing rules for conflict resolution, 932
Writing tests, strategies for taking
    writing a response to literature, 974
    writing a response to expository
        text, 975
    writing a biographical narrative, 976
    writing an expository composition,
        977
    writing a persuasive composition, 978
Writing Workshops
    analysis of problems and solutions,
        212–219
    analysis of a short story, **440–447**
    autobiographical narrative, **56–63**
    biographical narrative, **122–129**
    comparison of media genres, **382–389**
    comparison of a play and a film,
        890–897
    description of a person, **540–547**
    persuasive essay, **294–301**
    research paper, **690–709**
    short story, **602–609**

LANGUAGE (GRAMMAR, USAGE, AND MECHANICS) SKILLS

Abbreviations, 1035, 1038–1039
Active voice, **327,** 1016
Adjective clauses, 1025, 1032
Adjective phrases, 1022
Adjectives, 1009, 1019–1020
    compound, 1045
    defined, 1009
    predicate, 1028
    proper, 1035
Adverb clauses, 1032
Adverb phrases, 1022
Adverbs, 128, 1009, 1019–1020
    avoiding overused, 1010
    conjunctive, 1030, 1040
    defined, 1009, 1019
    relative, 1025
Agreement
    with amounts, 1012
    of pronouns and antecedents, 1013
    of subjects and verbs, **186,**
        1010–1012
A lot, 1049
Ambiguous pronoun references, **120**
Among, between, 1050
Amounts, agreement with, 1012
And etc., 1050
Antecedents, 1013, 1019
    clear pronoun reference to, 120,
        1019
    pronoun agreement with, 120, 1013
Anyways, anywheres, 1050

Apostrophes, 1044–1045, 1049
Appositives and appositive phrases, 1018, 1024, 1031, 1040
As if, like, 1051
As, like, 1051
At, 1050
Bad, badly, 1050
Being as, being that, 1050
Beside, besides, 1050
Between, among, 1050
Bust, busted, 1050
Capitalization, 1034–1038
  of abbreviations, 1035
  of calendar items, 1036
  of directions, 1035
  of direct quotations, 1034
  of first word
    in lines of poetry, 1034
    in salutations and closings of letters, 1034
    in sentences, 1034
  of *I,* 1034
  of names
    of brands, 1036
    of buildings, 1036
    of geographical names, 1035
    of historical events and periods, 1036
    of monuments and awards, 1036
    of more than one word, 1035
    of nationalities, races, and peoples, 1036
    of organizations and teams, 1036
    of people and animals, 1035
    of planets and stars, 1036
    of religions, holy days, holy writings, and deities, 1037
    of ships, trains, aircraft, and spacecraft, 1036
  of *O,* 1034
  of proper nouns and proper adjectives, 1035
  of school subjects, 1037
  of titles of works, 1037
  of words showing family relationships, 1037
Cases of personal pronouns, 43
Clauses, 111, 1024–1026
  adjective, 1025, 1032
  adverb, 1025, 1032
  defined, 1024
  essential (restrictive), 1025, 1039
  independent (main), 1024, 1030, 1039, 1040
  infinitive, 1024
  nonessential (nonrestrictive), 1025, 1039
  noun, 1025, 1032
  as sentence fragments, 1030
  subordinate (dependent), 1025–1026, 1030
Collective nouns, 1012
Colloquialisms, 95
Colons, 1041

Commas, 1039–1040
  with adjectives, 1039
  with appositives and appositive phrases, 1024
  in conventional situations, 1040
  with independent clauses, 1039
  with interrupters, 1040
  with introductory elements, 1039
  with items in a series, 1039
  with nonessential items, 1039
  unnecessary, 1040
Comma splices, 1030
Comparative and superlative degrees, of modifiers, 1020–1021
  double comparisons, avoiding, 1021
  forming, 1020
Comparative form, 380, 547, 1020–1021
Comparison of modifiers, **380**
Complements, 1027–1028
  defined, 1027
  direct objects as, 1017, 1028
  indirect objects as, 1018, 1028
  subject complements as, 1027–1028
    predicate adjectives, 1028
    predicate nominatives, 1012, 1017, 1027
Complex sentences, 600, 1029, 1032
Compound adjectives, 1045
Compound-complex sentences, 600, 1029
Compound nouns, 1049
Compound numbers, 1045
Compound sentences, 600, 1028, 1030, 1031–1032
Compound subjects, 1011, 1027, 1031
Compound verbs, 1027, 1031
Computers, using
  to check grammar, 1010, 1016
  to detect problems in subject-verb agreement, 1010
  to identify passive-voice verbs, 1016
  to print italic type, 1042
Conjunctions, 1009–1010
  coordinating, 1009, 1039, 1040
  correlative, 1010
  subordinating, 1010, 1025
Conjunctive adverbs, 1030, 1040
Contractions, 1045, 1052
Coordinating conjunctions, 253, 1009, 1039, 1040
Correlative conjunctions, 1010
Could of, 1050
Dangling modifiers, 709, 1021
Dashes, 1045–1046
Declarative sentences, 1028, 1038
Degrees of comparison, 380, 1020–1021
Demonstrative pronouns, 1009
Dependent (subordinate) clauses, 1025–1026, 1030
Dialect, **95**, 205
Dialogue, punctuating, 129, 1043
Direct address, nouns of, 1027, 1040
Direct objects, 1017, 1028

Direct quotations, 1042–1043
Done, 1050
Don't, doesn't, 1011
Double comparisons, avoiding, 380, 1021
Double subjects, 1051
Else, other, 1021
End marks, 1038
English language, history of, 659
Etc., 1050
Every, preceding a subject, 1012
Everywheres, 1050
Exclamation points, 1038
Exclamatory sentences, 1028, 1038
Fewer, less, 1050
Fractions, 1045
Fragments, and sentences, 1026, 1029–1030
Fused sentences, 1030
Gerund phrases, 1023
Gerunds, 1023
Glossary of usage, 1049–1052
Good, well, 1050
Grammar checker, 1010, 1016
Graphic organizers
  sentence chart, 600
  transitional words and phrases chart, 740
Had of, 1051
Had ought, hadn't ought, 1051
His-or-her construction, avoiding, 1013
Hisself, 1051
Hyphens, 1045
Imperative sentences, 1028, 1038
Imply, infer, 1051
Incomplete constructions, 1019
Indefinite pronouns, 1009, 1011, 1013, 1044
Independent (main) clauses, 111, **600,** 1024, 1030, 1039, 1040
Indirect objects, 1018, 1028
Infer, imply, 1051
Infinitive clauses, 1024
Infinitive phrases, 1023
Infinitives, 1023–1024
  avoiding split, 1024
Intensive pronouns, 1009
Interjections, 1010
Interrogative pronouns, 1009
Interrogative sentences, 1027, 1028, 1038
Inverted order in sentences, **162, 496**
Irregular verbs, 1014
Italics (underlining), 1041–1042
Its, it's, 1052
Kind of, sort of, 1051
Kind(s), sort(s), type(s), 1051
Learn, teach, 1051
Leave, let, 1051
Less, fewer, 1050
Let, leave, 1051
Like, as, 1051
Like, as if, 1051
Main (independent) clauses, **111,** 1024, 1030, 1039, 1040

Many a, preceding a subject, 1012
Might of, 1051
Misplaced modifiers, **650,** 1021
Modifiers, 1019–1021
   adjective phrases as, 1022
   adjectives as, 1009, 1019–1020
   adverb phrases as, 1022
   adverbs as, 1019–1021
   clauses as, 1025
   comparison of, **380,** 1020–1021
   dangling, 1021
   defined, 1019
   misplaced, **650,** 1021
   participial phrases as, 1022–1023, 1031
   participles as, 1014, 1022–1023
   prepositional phrases as, 1022, 1031
   using, 1019–1021
Must of, 1051
Nominative case, 43, 1017–1019
Nonstandard grammar, **95,** 1049
Noun clauses, 1025, 1032
Nouns
   capitalization of, 1035–1038
   clauses, 1025, 1032
   collective, 1012
   common and proper, 1035–1048
   compound, 1049
   defined, 1009
   of direct address, 1027, 1040
   as objects of prepositions, 1018,
     1022
   plural in form but singular in meaning,
     1012
   plurals of, 1048–1049
   possessive, 1044
Nowheres, 1050, 1051
Number, a, 1012
Number, the, 1012
Number of subjects, 186
Objective case, 43, 1017–1019
Objects, 1017–1018, 1028
   direct, 1017, 1028
   indirect, 1018, 1028
   of prepositions, 1018, 1022
Of, 1051
Off of, 1051
Other, else, 1021
Ought, ought to of, 1051
Parallel structure, 389, 1032–1033
Parentheses, 1046
Parenthetical expressions, 1040
Participial phrases, **410,** 1022–1023,
   1031, 1039
Participles, **410,** 1014, 1022–1023
Parts of speech, 1009–1010
   determining, 1010
Passive voice, **327,** 1016
Periods, 1038–1039
Personal pronouns, **43,** 1009, 1017
Phrases, 1022–1024
   adjective, 1022
   adverb, 1022
   appositive, 1024
   defined, 1022

essential, 1039
   as fragments, 1029–1030
   gerund, 1023
   infinitive, 1023–1024
   participial, 1022–1023, 1031, 1039
   prepositional, 1022, 1031, 1039
   verbal, 1022–1024
Plural subjects and verbs, 186,
   1010–1012
Possessive case, 1017, 1044, 1052
Possessive pronouns, 1017, 1044, 1052
Predicate adjectives, 1028
Predicate nominatives, 1012, 1017,
   1027
Predicates, 1026–1028
   complete, 1026
   simple, 1027
Prefixes, 1045, 1046, 1047
Prepositional phrases, 1022, 1031, 1039
Prepositions
   defined, 1009
   objects of, 1018, 1022
Present participles, 410
Principal parts, of verbs, 1014
Pronouns
   agreement of, with antecedents, 1013
   case of, 1017–1019
     nominative, 1017
     objective, 1017–1018
     possessive, 1017, 1044, 1052
     possessive and contractions, 1052
   clear references for, **120**
   defined, 1009
   demonstrative, 1009
   gender of, 1017
   and *his-or-her* construction, avoiding,
     1013
   I, capitalizing, 1034
   indefinite, 1009, 1011, 1013, 1044
   intensive, 1009
   interrogative, 1009
   personal, 1009, 1017
   plural, 1013
   possessive, and contractions, 1052
   problems with, 1018–1019
   and reference to antecedents, 1019
   reflexive, 1009
   relative, 1009, 1013, 1025
   singular, 1013
   unnecessary (double subjects), 1051
   who, whom, 1018
   whoever, whomever, 1018
Proper adjectives, 1035–1038
Proper nouns, 1035–1038, 1048
Punctuation marks, 1038–1046
   apostrophes, 1044–1045, 1049
   colons, 1041
   commas, 1024, 1030, 1039–1040
   dashes, 1045–1046
   in dialogue, 1043
   as end marks, 1038
   exclamation points, 1038
   hyphens, 1045
   italics (underlining), 1041–1042

parentheses, 1046
   periods, 1038–1039
   question marks, 1038
   quotation marks, 447, 1042–1044
   semicolons, 1040
   in a series of items, 1039, 1040
   underlining (italics), 1041–1042
Question marks, 1038
Questions. *See Interrogative sentences.*
Quotation marks, 129, 301, 1042–1044
Quotations, 447, 1042–1043
Reflexive pronouns, 1009
Relative pronouns, 1009, 1013, 1025
Roots, 1046
Run-on sentences, **253,** 1030
Semicolons, 253, 1040
Sentence combining, 1026, 1030–1032
   with complex sentences, 1032
   with compound sentences, 1031
   with compound subjects and verbs,
     1031
   by inserting phrases, 1031
   by inserting words, 1030
Sentence fragment, 111, 219, **563**
Sentence length and structure, varying,
   600
Sentences, 563, 1026–1034
   chart, 600
   classified by purpose, 1028
   classified by structure, 1028–1029
   combining, 740, 1026, 1030–1032
   and commas splices, 1030
   complements in, 1027–1028
   complex, 1029, 1032
   compound, 1028, 1030, 1031–1032
   compound-complex, 1029
   declarative, 1028, 1038
   defined, 1026, 1029
   exclamatory, 1028, 1038
   finding the subject of, 1027
   and fragments, 1026, 1029–1030
   fused, 1030
   imperative, 1028, 1038
   interrogative, 1028, 1038
   inverted order in, **162, 496**
   parallel structure in, 1032
   run-on, **253,** 1030
   short, choppy, 1026
   simple, 1028
   stringy, 1033
   structure of, 1028–1029
   style of, improving, 1032–1034
   subject and predicate in, 1026–1027
   varying beginnings of, 1034
   varying structure of, 1029, 1033
   word order in, 1027, 1028, 1034
   wordy, 282
   writing complete, 1029–1030
   writing effective, 1026, 1030–1034
Serial commas, 897, 1039
Should of, 1051
Simple sentences, 600, 1028
Singular subjects and verbs, 186,
   1010–1012

Some, somewhat, 1051
Somewheres, 1050
Sort of, kind of, 1051
Sort(s), type(s), kind(s), 1051
Split infinitives, avoiding, 1024
Standard English, 95, 1049
Standard usage, 205
Stringy sentences, 1033
Style, **205**
Subjects, 1026–1027
   agreement with verbs, **186,**
     1010–1012
   complete, 1026
   compound, 1011, 1027, 1031
   double, 1051
   finding, 1027
   nominative case for, 1017
   simple, 1026
   verbs before, in sentences, **162**
   you understood, 1027
Subject-verb agreement, 186,
   1010–1012
Subordinate (dependent) clauses, **111,**
   600, 1025–1026, 1030
Subordinating conjunctions, 1010, 1025
Suffixes, 1014, 1020, 1031, 1047–1048
Superlative form, 380, 547, 1020–1021
Syntax, 496
Teach, learn, 1052
Tenses of verbs, 1015–1016
   changing the, 1016
   using appropriate, 1016
Than, then, 1052
Theirselves, 1051
Theirs, there's, 1052
Their, they're, 1052
Them, 1052
Then, than, 1052
There, here, 1027
They're, their, 1052
This, that, these, those, 1051
Titles of works
   agreement with, 1012
   capitalizing, 1037
   punctuating, 1041–1042, 1043
Transitional words and phrases, **740,**
   994, 1040
   chart, 740
Try and, 1052
Type(s), kind(s), sort(s), 1051
Underlining (italics), 1041–1042
Usage, glossary of, 1049–1052
Verbs, 1014–1016
   action, 1009
   active or passive, **327,** 1016
   agreement with subjects, **186,**
     1010–1012
   base forms of, 1014
   before subjects in sentences, **162**
   compound, 1027, 1031
   defined, 1009
   helping (auxiliary), 1009
   irregular, 1014
   linking, 1009

   past participles of, 1014
   preceding subjects, 1012
   present participles of, 1014, 1022
   principal parts of, 1014
   progressive forms of, 1015
   regular, 1014
   subjects and, 1010–1012
   tenses of, 1015–1016
     changing, 1016
     consistency of, 1016
     future, 1015
     future perfect, 1016
     historical present, 1015
     literary present, 1015
     past, 1015
     past perfect, 1015
     present, 1015
     present perfect, 1015
     using appropriate, 1016
Verb tense, 63, 1015–1016
Verbal and verbal phrases, 1022–1024
   gerund phrases, 1023
   gerunds, 1023
   infinitive phrases, 1023–1024
   infinitives, 1023–1024
   participial phrases, 1022–1023
   participles, 1022–1023
Voice, active and passive, 1016
Voice, creating, **205**
Way, ways, 1052
Well, good, 1050
What, 1052
When, where, 1052
Where . . . at, 1052
Whoever, whomever, 1018
Who's, whose, 1052
Who, which, that, 1052
Who, whom, 1018
Word parts, 1046–1049
Word roots. *See* Roots.
Word structure, understanding,
   1046–1047
Wordiness, eliminating, **282,** 1033
Would of, 1051
You, understood as subject, 1027

LISTENING AND SPEAKING SKILLS

Accuracy, 711
Actors, 753
Adapting
   presentation for descriptive presenta-
     tion, 548
   your research paper for research
     presentation, 710–711
   your written analysis
     for literary response presentation,
      448–449
     for persuasive speech, 220–221
Affirmative team, 302, 304
Allusion, 899
Ambiguity, 449
Analogy, 899

Analysis and evaluation of speeches,
   898–901
   analyzing content for, 898–899
   analyzing delivery for, 900–901
   analyzing organization for, 899–900
   evaluating a speech for, 901
   selecting a speech for, 898
Analyzing
   content for analysis and evaluation of
     speeches, 898–899
   delivery for analysis and evaluation of
     speeches, 900–901
   organization for analysis and evalua-
     tion of speeches, 899–900
   short story, 97
Appeal to authority, 899
Appeal to emotion, 899
Appeal to logic, 899
Argument, 898–899, 901
   by causation, 899
Assertion, 220
Audience, 220, 438, 562, 687, 710–711,
   753, 780, 899
Audiotape recording, 512
Background music, 534
Body of oral presentation, 449
Body posture, 898, 900–901
Burden of proof, 302
Chairperson, 302
Character-trait diagram, 86
Choral reading, 511, 753
Chronological order, 64
Clarity, 901
Coherence, 711, 899, 901
Compare and contrast, 86
Complexity, 449
Concern, 220
Conclusion, 711
   of narrative presentation, 65
   of oral presentation, 449
Concrete imagery, 548
Conducting
   debate, 304–305
   interview, 220–221
Constructive argument, 304
Constructive speech, 304
Controlling impression, 548
Counterarguments, 220
Creating quilt squares, 95
Credibility, 887
   of evidence, 303
Debate, 219, 301, **302–305**
   conducting, 304–305
   judging chart, 305
   preparing for, 302–303
   schedule chart, 305
Debate etiquette, 304
Debate information, organizing, 304
Deductive pattern, 899
Delivering
   literary response presentation, 449
   speech, 221
   your presentation for research pre-
     sentation, 711

Delivery, 900, 901
  extemporaneous, 65, 449
Descriptive presentation, **548–549**
  adapting your presentation for, 548
  planning your presentation for, 549
  practicing your presentation for,
  549
Descriptive strategies
  descriptive presentation, **548–549**
Dialogue, 780, 832
Diction, 899
Director, 753
Discussing, 129, 486, 709, 723, 740,
  753
Discussion session, 389
Dramatic monologue, 85, 86
Dramatic performance, 753, 780, 804,
  832
Dramatic presentation, 880
  evaluating, 880
Effectiveness, 901
Elaboration, extra, 449
Electronic media, 710
Essay, 887
Etiquette, debate, 304
Evaluating, 53
  dramatic presentation, 880
  evidence, 887
  a speech for analysis and evaluation
  of speeches, 901
Evidence, 220, 710, 711, 901
  chart, 303
  evaluating, 887
Expository strategies
  literary response presentation,
  448–449
  research presentation, **710–711**
Extemporaneous delivery, 65, 449
Extemporaneous speech, 711
Extra elaboration, 449
Eye contact, 65, 449, 549, 900–901
Facial expressions, 65, 449, 549
Facts, 303
Factual details, 548
Feedback, 221, 780
Figurative details, 548
Formal presentation, 221
Gestures, 65, 449, 511, 549, 898,
  900–901, 901
Graphic organizers
  character-trait diagram, 86
  debate-judging chart, 305
  debate-schedule chart, 305
  evidence chart, 303
  review-evaluating chart, 887
Graphics, 710
Group reading, 129
Group work, 20, 95, 129, 153, 191,
  204, 221, 231, 271, 389, 417, 437,
  447, 515, 517, 525, 534, 538, 547,
  643, 687, 709, 740, 753, 779, 853,
  880, 897, 931
Historically significant speech, 898
Inductive pattern, 899

Interactive features of Web sites, 206
Internet, 898
Interpretation, 880
Interview, 711
  conducting, 29, 213, 220–221
Introduction
  of narrative presentation, 65
  of oral presentation, 448–449
Judgment, 449, 901
Library, 898
Listening & Speaking Workshops
  analysis and evaluation of speeches,
  898–901
  debate, **302–305**
  descriptive presentation, **548–549**
  literary response presentation,
  448–449
  narrative presentation, **64–65**
  persuasive speech, **220–221**
  research presentation, **710–711**
Literary response presentation, **448–449**
  adapting your written analysis for,
  448–449
  delivering, 449
Memorizing, 221, 880
Metaphor, 899
Mood, 900–901, 901
Motivation, 804
Multimedia display, 709
Multimedia features of Web sites, 206
Multimedia presentation, 389
Music, background, 534
Narrative presentation, **64–65**
  adapting, 64–65
  delivering, 65
Narrative strategies
  narrative presentation, **64–65**
Negative team, 302, 304
News media, 389
Nonverbal techniques, 549, 711
Note cards, 549, 711
Nuance, 449
Opinion statement, 887
Oral descriptive presentation, 547
Oral interpretation, 438, 534, 538, 562,
  753, 780
Oral presentation, 517, 710–711
Oral reading, 204
Oral report, 709
Oral response, 438
  to literature, 448
  to poem, 495
Order of importance, 221
Organization, 901
Organizational pattern, 549, 899
Organizing debate information, 304
Panel discussion, 53
Parallelism, 899
Partner work, 20, 45, 61, 97, 120, 127,
  129, 153, 192, 217, 271, 282, 299,
  301, 365, 387, 388, 389, 410, 417,
  432, 445, 495, 505, 538, 545, 563,
  576, 607, 608, 630, 631, 643, 691,
  707, 709, 711, 780, 895, 897

Personal involvement, 548
Perspective, 548
Persuasive speech, **220–221**
  adapting your written analysis for,
  220–221
  rehearsing and delivering, 221
Persuasive strategies
  analysis and evaluation of speeches,
  898–901
  debate, 219, 301, **302–305**
  persuasive speech, **220–221**
Pitch of voice, 511
Planning your presentation for descrip-
  tive presentation, 549
Point of view, 548
Practicing your presentation for
  descriptive presentation, 549
Preparing for debate, 302–303
Presenting
  your ideas, 305
  yourself, 304
Primary source, 711
Problem bank, 219
Proof, 303
Proposition, researching, 302–303
Props, 753
Prose poem, 84
Purpose, 220, 548, 710
Quality of evidence, 304
Quantity of evidence, 304
Quick guide!
  conducting interviews, 220–221
  developing introductions, 448
  evaluating speeches, 901
  questions for judging a debate, 305
  traditional debate schedule, 305
Reading aloud, 205, 264, 458, 484, 496,
  505, 508, 513, 534, 535, 538, 548,
  659, 752, 852
Reasoning, 304
Reasons, 220, 303
Rebuttal, 304
Rebuttal speech, 304
Recording a story, 512
References to the text, 449
Refutation, 304
Rehearsing, 65, 711, 804
  poem, 517
  speech, 221
Relative value, 710
Relevance of evidence, 303
Repetition, 899
Re-reading, 87, 432, 476, 530, 547, 707,
  890, 891, 895
Research, 687, 898
Researching proposition, 302–303
Research presentation, **710–711**
  adapting your research paper for,
  710–711
  delivering your presentation for, 711
Resolution, 302
Retelling story, 687
Review-evaluating chart, 887
Rhetoric, 898

Rhetorical devices, 220, 898, 899, 901
Rhetorical question, 899
Secondary source, 711
Selecting a speech for analysis and evaluation of speeches, 898
Sensory details, 64, 548
Sentence structure, simplifying, 64
Significance, 710
Skimming, 710
Speaking in turn in debates, 305
Specific instances, 303
Speech
    analysis and evaluation of. See Analysis and evaluation of speeches
    constructive, 304
    delivering, 221
    extemporaneous, 711
    historically significant, 898
    persuasive. See Persuasive speech
    rebuttal, 304
Statement of theme, 231
Statistics, 303
Status quo, 302
Strategies
    descriptive: descriptive presentation, **548–549**
    expository. See Expository strategies
    narrative: narrative presentation, **64–65**
    persuasive. See Persuasive strategies
Structure of review, 887
Style, 562
Summarizing, 53, 549, 887
Survey, 525
Syntax, 899
Tape recorder, 221
Task force, 219
Testimony, 303
Thesis statement, 710
Tone, 887, 900, 901
    of voice, 511
Transitional words and phrases, 449
Validity of evidence, 303
Vantage point, 548
Verbal techniques, 549, 711
Video, actively watching, 890
Video recorder, 221

Videotape recording, 512
Visuals, 549, 710
Vocabulary, simplifying, 64
Voice, 438, 449, 511, 517, 534, 549, 562, 687, 711, 898, 900–901
Volume of voice, 65, 511, 534, 538
Watching video actively, 890

INDEPENDENT READING

About Time, 55
"Acquainted with the Night," 437
Acts of King Arthur and His Noble Knights, The, 689
Alice's Adventures in Wonderland, 381
Angela's Ashes, 200
Annotated Alice, The, 381
Barrio Boy, 601
"Birches," 437
Black Ice, 439
Book of Plays, A, 889
Boy: Tales of Childhood, 325
"Cask of Amontillado, The," 428
Cherry Orchard, The, 737
Complete Saki, The, 211
Dandelion Wine, 52
"Desert Places," 437
"Design," 437
"Devil and Daniel Webster, The," 151
Dune, 211
Emily Dickinson: The Collected Poems, 539
Endurance: Shackleton's Legendary Antarctic Expedition, The, 381
Fahrenheit 451, 55
Fallen Angels, 689
Fences, 121
Fifth Chinese Daughter, 121
From Time to Time, 17
"Gift Outright, The," 437
Great American Stories, 601
Greek Myths, 686
Greek Way, The, 668
Habibi, 515
Hiroshima, 211
"Hop-Frog," 428
Hot Zone, The, 55
House Made of Dawn, 480
House on Mango Street, The, 561

In Search of Our Mothers' Gardens, 83
Into the Wild, 363
Into Thin Air, 363
Island Like You: Stories of the Barrio, An, 240
Joy Luck Club, The, 108
King Must Die, 689
Laughing Boy, 293
Macbeth, 889
Maud Martha, 533
Nectar in a Sieve, 55
Never Cry Wolf, 601
Night to Remember, A, 381
Old Man and the Sea, The, 601
"Open Window, The," 160
Pablo Neruda: Selected Poems, 539
Perfect Storm, The, 293
"Pit and the Pendulum, The," 428
Platero and I, 211
Poetry Out Loud, 539
Raisin in the Sun, A, 889
"Road Not Taken, The," 437
Roald Dahl's Tales of the Unexpected, 381
Roman Way, The, 668
"Schartz-Metterklume Method, The," 160
Separate Peace, A, 439
Shrapnel in the Heart: Letters and Remembrances from the Vietnam Veterans Memorial, 689
Sound of Waves, The, 293
"Sredni Vashtar," 160
Strange Pilgrims, 596
Summer Life, A, 121
Tale of the Unknown Island, The, 439
Tale of Two Cities, A, 293
"Tell-Tale Heart, The," 428
This Same Sky: A Collection of Poems from Around the World, 539
Through the Looking-Glass, 381
'Tis, 200
Trojan War, The, 686
Visit to a Small Planet, 889
Washington Square, 121
Watership Down, 439
Way to Rainy Mountain, The, 480

Index of Art

Addams, Chas.
 Edgar Allan Poe, 504
Antico (Pier Jacopo Alari Bonacolsi)
 Ariadne, 667
Aristotle (sculpture), 872
Atalanta (statue), 671
Audubon, John James
 Great Blue Heron, 574
Bearden, Romare
 Quilting Time, 84
 Jazz Series: Tenor Sermon, 536
Beasley, Phoebe
 His Grandmother's Quilt, 77
Booth, George
 "Remorse sits in my stomach . . . ,"
 477
Cezanne, Paul
 Plate with Grapes and Peach, 470
Chagall, Marc
 The Couple at the Eiffel Tower, 229
 Lovers, 484
Chast, Roz
 Story Template, 2
Coates, Jessie
 Spending Time, 468–469
Dali, Salvador
 The Persistence of Memory, 396–397
Dine, Jim
 The Heart in Bliss, 251
Doolin, James
 Highway Patrol, 50
Dove, Arthur G.
 Sun, 528
Emily Dickinson (colored photograph),
 488
Ensor, James
 Masks and Death, 425
Fogelberg, B.
 Romantic portrayal of Balder, 685
Forging of the sword Gram, from the
 Sigurd myth (church portal), 679
Frigga escorted by Valkyries in the sky
 (lithograph), 684
Gandarias, Sofia
 Pablo Neruda, 500
Gauguin, Paul
 The Meal or The Bananas, 465
Giambologna (after)
 Hercules and the Centaur, 669
Globe Theatre performance (drawing),
 749
God Tiu losing his hand to Fenris
 (manuscript page), 685
Gogh, Vincent van,
 Portrait of Dr. Gachet, 73
 The Good Samaritan, 278

The Parisian Novels
 (The Yellow Books), 940
Guardi, Francesco
 The Redoute, 422–423
Hamilton, William
 "Very good, Gary . . . ," 658
Head of Theseus (detail) (mural), 663
Hilliard, Nicholas
 Alice Hilliard, 493
Hockney, David
 Stage set for Tristan and Isolde, 718–719
Hodges, Cyril Walter
 The Globe Theatre (watercolor), 746
Hokkei
 The Poetess Ono Komachi, 491
Howe, Catherine
 Mirage, 521
Hunting party (carving), 509
Hurley, Frank
 Ship from the Shackleton expedition,
 the Endurance, 368
Huxley, Hannah
 Star of Bethlehem or Lone Star, 92
Ishiyamagire: Poems of Ki no Tsurayuki
 (manuscript page), 490–491
Johnston, Lynn
 For Better or for Worse, 615
Julius Caesar (busts), 751, 780
King Arthur, from tapestry of the
 "Nine Worthies" (detail), 648
Lawrence, Jacob
 Men exist for the sake of one
 another . . . , A42
 Pool, 532
Levine, David
 William Shakespeare (caricatures),
 495, 753
Longhi, Pietro
 Masked Ball in the Card Room, 419
Lovers in a garden (illuminated manu-
 script), 510
Magritte, René
 The Human Condition, 312
Mankoff, Robert
 "Et tu, Baxter?," 979
Mark Antony (sculpture), 833
Maslin, Michael
 "O.K., so I dig a hole . . . ," 97
Mayers, Gil
 Bass, 535
Melpomene, from the Mosaic of the
 Nine Muses (detail), 873
Modigliani, Amedeo
 Elvira Sitting at a Table, 487
Moses, Anna Mary Robertson
 ("Grandma")

Let Me Help, 136–137
News American, The (newspaper page),
 634
Noel
 Mirrors on Sale, 139
Odin (engraving), 684
O'Keeffe, Georgia
 Lake George with Crows, 143
 Radiator Building—Night, New York, 149
Painted figure of the Minotaur, on a
 Greek cup, 664
Penrose, J. Doyle
 Freya, the most lovely of the gods
 (illustration), 685
 Loki bound to a rock in punishment
 for the death of Balder (illustra-
 tion), 685
Picasso, Pablo
 Three Musicians, 554–555
Playbill for Orson Welles's production
 of Julius Caesar, 884
Poster featuring Denzel Washington in
 Richard III, 744
Prentice, Levi Wells
 Apple Harvest, 436
Quijano, Nick
 El Club, 560
Rackham, Arthur
 Thor swinging his mighty hammer
 (illustration), 684
Raimondi, Marcantonio
 The Plague, 430
Rancillac, Bernard
 Cherry Rouge, 538
Rembrandt
 Portrait of an Old Man, 472
Rivera, Diego
 Fruit of the Earth (Los Frutos) (detail),
 501
Roerich, Nikolai
 Celestial Combat, 458
Roman helmet, 750
Rousseau, Henri
 Landscape with Monkeys, 565, 570
 (detail)
Schulz, Charles
 Peanuts, 917
Selective Service System Registration
 Certificate, 635
Shaw, John Byam Liston
 "And Darkness and Decay and the Red
 Death . . ." (illustration for "The
 Masque of the Red Death"), 426
Shell disc inscribed with a spider and
 sacred-cross-of-fire design
 (Mississippi culture), 530

Sigurd killing the dragon Fafnir (church portal), 674–675

Sigurd roasting the dragon Fafnir's heart (church portal), 682

Sun Dance (Plains Indian painting), 527

Theseus and the Minotaur pictured on a black-figured cup, 666

Theseus and the Minotaur pictured on a Greek amphora, 668

Theseus pictured on a Greek amphora, 663

Thiebaud, Wayne
Freeway Interchange, 48

Turner, William H.
Preening Heron, 568

Vietnam Women's Memorial, Washington, D.C., 629

Viking coin, 676

Viking figurine, possibly representing Thor, 684

Viking pendant, 680

Watterson, Bill
Calvin and Hobbes, 457

White Hart Inn, London (engraving), 745

Whittredge, Worthington
Apples, 435

William Shakespeare (portrait), 741

Wyeth, N. C.
"It hung upon a thorn . . ." (illustration for *The Boy's King Arthur*), 616
"He rode his way with the queen . . ." (illustration for *The Boy's King Arthur*), 656

Yashima Gakutei
Bridge Across the Moon, 492

Yun Shouping
Poppies, 455

Index of Authors and Titles

Page numbers in italic type refer to the pages on which author biographies appear.

Adams, Lily Lee, 629
Addley, Esther, 188
After Apple-Picking, 435–436
Agüeros, Jack, 597
Allen, Norma Bradley, 91
Allende, Isabel, 257, *266,* 270
Allred, Gloria, 286
All Watched Over by Machines of Loving Grace, 184
"All We Need Is That Piece of String," 669
American Nation, The, from, 634, 713
Ancient Enemy Gets Tougher, An, 207–209
Anderson, Robert, 723, 741, *745*
And of Clay Are We Created, 257–265
Angela's Ashes, from, 194
Aratani, Mariko, 490
Aristotle, 872, 932
Auden, W. H., 719

Baby's Quilt to Sew Up the Generations, A, 93
Baca, Jimmy Santiago, 483, *483*
Bagby, Kenneth W., 637
Baines, Keith, 645, 652
Baldwin, Hanson W., 330, *344*
Barnes, Jessica, 414
Bass, the River, and Sheila Mant, The, 244–250
Benét, Stephen Vincent, 141, *151*
Bentley, Eric, 725
Bishop, Mrs. D. H., 346
Black Death, The, 429–430
Bloom, Lisa, 286
Blue Stones, The, 450
Bly, Robert, 498
Bonny Barbara Allan, 510–511
Born on the Fourth of July, from, 714
Bowen, Elizabeth, 73
Boyer, Paul, 634, 712
Bradbury, Ray, 47, *52*
Brautigan, Richard, 184, 251
Breslin, Jimmy, 874
Brooks, Gwendolyn, 532, *533,* 534
Brown, John M. G., 713
Brown, John Mason, 882
Brown, R. J., 40
Brute, The, 725–736
Brutus's Funeral Speech, 902–903
Butcher, S. H., 872
By Any Other Name, 113–118
By the Waters of Babylon, 141–150
Call of the Wild—Save Us!, 579–582

Campbell, Joseph, 669
Campbell, Kim, 67
Capote, Truman, 137
Catch the Moon, 234–240
Cather, Willa, 229
Chappelle, Dickey, 713
Chekhov, Anton, 725, *737*
Chief Joseph, 900
Child's View of Working Parents, The, 26–27
Cisneros, Sandra, 559, *561,* 610
Clifton, Lucille, 522, *523,* 525
Cofer, Judith Ortiz, 234, *240,* 241
Cold Equations, The, 164–183
Coming of Age, Latino Style, 412–413
Communion of the Spirits: African American Quilters, Preservers, and Their Stories, A, from, 89, 91
Contents of the Dead Man's Pocket, 5–16
Coolidge, Olivia, 673, *675, 686*
Cooper, Patricia, 91
Crossing a Threshold to Adulthood, 414–415
Cummings, E. E., 485, *485*

Dahl, Roald, 317, *325,* 326
Daniels, Cora, 26
Davies, Robertson, 1
Day the Clowns Cried, The, 40
Dear Folks, 637–638
Declaration of Independence from the War in Vietnam, from, 639–641
Deprived of Parent Time?, 67–68
Diary of a Mad Blender, 24–25
Dickinson, Emily, 457, 487, *488,* 505
Dimmitt, Barbara Sande, 201
Dinesen, Isak, 450
Double Daddy, 22–23
Dove, Rita, 468, *469*

Eating Together, 466
Education of Frank McCourt, The, 201–203
Elizabethan Stage, The, 745–749
Emerson, Ralph Waldo, 397
Encyclopaedia Britannica, from, 413
Erdrich, Louise, 32, *39,* 41
Everyday Use, 77–83
Ex–Basketball Player, 519
Explorers Say There's Still Lots to Look For, 367–371

Fear and the Flames, The, 874–877
Finney, Jack, 5, *17*
Fireman's Story, A, 345
Fireworks, 550
Flying Cat, The, 514
Forster, E. M., 879

Freeman, Roland L., 89, 91
Friendship Only Lasted a Few Seconds, The, 629
From a Lifeboat, 346
Frost, Robert, 434, 435, *437*
Fugard, Lisa, 565, *572*

García Márquez, Gabriel, 587, *596,* 598
Geraldo No Last Name, 559–561
Giblin, James Cross, 429
Giovanni, Nikki, 84
Glenny, Michael, 459
Godwin, Tom, 164, *183*
Goldenberg, Phyllis, 902
Good Samaritans U.S.A. Are Afraid to Act, 288–289
Gracious Goodness, 308
Graham, Bradley, 267
Grape Sherbet, 468

H. D., 313
Haines, John, 456
Hamilton, Edith, 663, *668,* 687
Hands: For Mother's Day, from, 84
Harjo, Joy, 528, *529*
Heart! We will forget him!, 487
Heynen, Jim, 306
Hirshfeld, Jane, 490
Hongo, Garrett, 472, 474, *475*
Hongo Reflects on "The Legend," 474–475
Hoyle, John Christian, 279
Hughes, Langston, 618

I Am Offering This Poem, 483
If Decency Doesn't, Law Should Make Us Samaritans, 286–287
Ill-Equipped Rescuers Dig Out Volcano Victims; Aid Slow to Reach Colombian Town, 267–269
Interview with Alice Walker, 89–90
Interview with Naomi Shihab Nye, 516
Interview with Nikki Giovanni, 91
Into Thin Air, from, 352–362
I, Too, 618–619
It's Raining in Love, 251

Jazz Fantasia, 536
Johnson, Lyndon B., 634
Julius Caesar in an Absorbing Production, 882–885
King, Martin Luther, Jr., 639
King James Bible, from the, 278
Koch, Kenneth, 18
Komachi, Ono, 490, *491*
Kovic, Ron, 714
Krakauer, Jon, 353, *363*

Lamb to the Slaughter, 317–324
Langguth, A. J., 161
Last Frontier, The, 390–392
Leap, The, 32–38
Lee, Felicia R., 93
Lee, Li-Young, 466, 467
Leeming, David Adams, 657
Legend, The, 472–473
Lemonick, Michael D., 390
Le Morte d'Arthur, from, 645–647, 652–656
Lessing, Doris, 401, 408
Lewis, Len, 66
Local Hands on a New Space Project, 222–224
Lowell, Amy, 481, 550
Lowell, Robert, 478
Luc, Du, 714
Lucinda Matlock, 85

"Magic Happened, The," 648
Malory, Sir Thomas, 645, 647, 652
Man in the Water, The, 273–277
Masefield, John, 507, 507
Masque of the Red Death, The, 419–427
Masters, Edgar Lee, 85
McCourt, Frank, 194, 200
Media and the War, The, 712–713
Meeks, Edie, 636
Mehta, Seema, 222
miss rosie, 522
Momaday, N. Scott, 479, 480
Moons, 456
Moon was but a Chin of Gold, The, 457
Mora, Pat, 462, 463
Moyers, Bill, 516, 669
Munro, Hector Hugh. See Saki.
Myers, Norman, 579
My Lucy Friend Who Smells Like Corn, 610–611

Neruda, Pablo, 498, 500, 501
Night Calls, 565–571
Notes from a Bottle, 375–377
Nye, Naomi Shihab, 514, 515, 516

O'Brien, Tim, 621, 628
Ode to My Socks, 498–499
O'Neill, Helen, 367

Parable of the Good Samaritan, The, 278
Parker, Charlie, 908
Parker, Penny, 22
Pastan, Linda, 573
Peden, Margaret Sayers, 257
Pedestrian, The, 47–51
Piercy, Marge, 308
Poe, Edgar Allan, 419, 428
Poetics, from the, 872
Powder, 130–132

Quilters: Women and Domestic Art, The, from, 91

Rabassa, Gregory, 587
Rama Rau, Santha, 113, 118
Remember, 528–529
R.M.S. Titanic, 330–343
Rodriguez, Cindy, 412
Romance, The, 657
Rosenblatt, Roger, 273, 277

Saki, 155, 160
Same Song, 462
Sandburg, Carl, 536, 537
Sea Fever, 507
Senior, Harry, 345
Shakespeare, William, 494, 756
Shall I Compare Thee to a Summer's Day?, 494
Shellenbarger, Sue, 24
Sigurd, the Dragon Slayer, 675–683
Simile, 479
since feeling is first, 485
Singer, Isaac Bashevis, 617
Sjoerdsma, Ann, 288
Solzhenitsyn, Aleksandr, 459, 460
Sonnet for Heaven Below, 597
State Championship Versus Runner's Conscience, A, 279–280
Steinbeck, John, 648
Stevenson, James, 375, 378
Stopping by Woods on a Snowy Evening, 434
Storm in the Mountains, A, 459
Storyteller, The, 155–159
Strand, Mark, 455
Swift, Jonathan, 555
Sword in the Stone, The, 645–647

Tale of Sir Launcelot du Lake, The, 652–656
Tan, Amy, 99, 108
Taste—The Final Frontier, 188–190
Taxi, The, 481
Theseus, 662–667
"Thinkin' on Marryin'," 91–92
This is the land the Sunset washes, 505
Three Japanese Tankas, 490
Through the Tunnel, 401–408
Tragedy of Julius Caesar, The, 756–777, 782–803, 806–830, 834–851, 854–871
Two Kinds, 99–107
Typhoid Fever, 194–199

Updike, John, 519, 520

Van Doren, Mark, 879
Very Old Man with Enormous Wings, A, 587–595
Vietnam War: An Eyewitness History, The, from, 713–714
Vision Quest, 413

Waiting for E. gularis, 573–574
Walker, Alice, 77, 83, 89
War Escalates, The, 634–636
Watson, Karen, 207
We Real Cool, 532
Web site, 207–209
Wetherell, W. D., 244, 250
Wexler, Sanford, 713
What Happened During the Ice Storm, 306–307
What Is a Tragic Hero?, 872–873
What Price Glory?, 66–67
When Plague Strikes, from, 429
Where Have You Gone, Charming Billy?, 621–627
William Shakespeare's Life, 741–744
Wolff, Tobias, 130
Word, The, 501

You want a social life, with friends, 18